EUI – Series C – 6.4

Flora (Ed.), Growth to Limits

European University Institute
Institut Universitaire Européen
Europäisches Hochschulinstitut
Istituto Universitario Europeo

Series C

Political and Social Sciences
Sciences Politiques et Sociales
Politik- und Sozialwissenschaften
Scienze Politiche e Sociali

6.4

Badia Fiesolana – Firenze

Growth to Limits

The Western European Welfare States
Since World War II

Volume 4

Appendix
(Synopses, Bibliographies, Tables)

Edited by

Peter Flora

1987

Walter de Gruyter · Berlin · New York

Library of Congress Cataloging-in-Publication Data
(Revised for volume 4)

Growth to limits.
(Series C--Political and social sciences = Sciences politiques et sociales ; 6)
Includes bibliographies.
Contents: Sweden, Norway, Finland, Denmark -- v. 2. Germany, United Kingdom, Ireland, Italy.--v. 4. Appendix (synopses, bibliographies, tables)
1. Europe--Social conditions--20th century. 2. Welfare state.
3. Europe--Politics and government--1945- .
4. Europe--Economic and conditions--1945- .
I. Flora, Peter, 1944- . II. Series: Series C--Political and social sciences ; 6.
HN377.G76 1986 361.6'5'094 86-19938
ISBN 0-89925-266-4 (U.S. : v. 1)

CIP-Kurztitelaufnahme der Deutschen Bibliothek

Growth to limits : the Western European welfare states since World War II / ed. by Peter Flora. - Berlin ; New York : de Gruyter
(European University Institute : Ser. C, Political and social sciences ; 6)
NE: Flora, Peter [Hrsg.]; Istituto Universitario Europeo (Fiesole): European University Institute / C
Vol. 4. Appendix : (synopses, bibliogr., tab.). - 1987.
ISBN 3-10-011133-0

Dust Cover Design: Rudolf Hübler, Berlin. – Setting: Satz-Rechen-Zentrum, Berlin.
Printing: H. Heenemann GmbH & Co., Berlin.
Binding: Verlagsbuchbinderei Dieter Mikolai, Berlin.
Printed in Germany.

Preface

The five volumes *Growth to Limits - The Western European Welfare States Since World War II* represent only one stretch of a longer road. To understand the destination, it may be useful to get a picture of the whole distance. At the beginning stood an encounter with one of the leading social scientists of the postwar period, the late Stein Rokkan. I first met him in 1971 at the Lausanne 'Workshop on Indicators of National Development' which he had organized under the auspices of the International Social Science Council. The conference was one of his manifold efforts to advance comparative research in the social sciences. This as well as later encounters have had a great impact on my work, in giving my own predilections a more specific meaning and above all providing continuing encouragement in times of uncertainty.

Rokkan's message was simple:

- Most of the 'big old questions' referring to the evolution and future of the industrial society and the modern state, of capitalism and mass democracy, of war and peace, are still essential for the social sciences.
- The progress already made in the development of new techniques and organizations of social research must be further advanced and made productive for an analysis of the development of global societies.
- Comparison, over time and across countries, is the essential method in this kind of analysis, linking theory and empirical research at a conceptual level which is not too remote from everyday language and experience.
- Europe is the ideal place for this comparative research, as the laboratory of the modern world with basic concepts and models deriving from its experiences, as well as because of its persisting diversity.
- Europe, however, is more than a testing ground for scientific hypotheses, its study more than an academic concern. Its development will be relevant not only for the Europeans, but for the future of the entire world.
- Comparative research, the study of Europe, must be a collective endeavour, an enterprise of the scientific community, requiring large-scale organization as well as networks of friendship among social scientists across national borders.

More than any other social scientist I have known, the Norwegian Stein Rokkan has embodied this philosophy: a classical scholar and promoter of new research methods, an ingenious inventer of complex models and scrupulous student of national experiences, a true European from the Northern periphery, an eminent organizer and father-figure for younger social scientists. Sometimes personality is more important than arguments, even in science, or should it be said that personality *is* the argument?

Apart from this general view, Rokkan provided me with two more concrete stimuli which have had an impact on my life. First, I made the crazy decision to produce a huge historical data handbook on Western Europe since the early nineteenth century in order to - as Rokkan expressed it - 'pin down numbers on the European variations'. Second, I decided that his studies on the long-term development of the European mass democracies and nation states should be supplemented by analyses of the development of the European welfare states. Both purposes were served through the HIWED Project (Historical Indicators of the Western European Democracies), which I began with Wolfgang Zapf in 1973 in Mannheim and took with me to Cologne in 1977. Through its entire duration from 1973 to 1979, this project received generous financial support from the Volkswagenwerk Foundation.

We began the work on the data handbook with much enthusiasm - which everyone knows is only another word for naïveté. First, the sources for European statistics had to be determined. In this connection I published in 1977 a bibliography along with an institutional history of official statistics (*Quantitative Historical Sociology. Current Sociology 23.2.* Paris, Mouton). Later a bibliography of all census publications was added. Throughout the good ten-year period in which we worked on the completion of the handbook, our naïveté gradually faded and with it our enthusiasm. Finally in 1983 we published the first volume (subtitle: *The Growth of Mass Democracies and Welfare States*) of our data handbook entitled *State, Economy and Society in Western Europe 1815-1975* (Frankfurt, Campus; London, Macmillan, 1983). The second and concluding volume followed in 1986 (subtitle: *The Growth of Industrial Societies and Capitalist Economies*). As a by-product of our work on the data handbook, the West-European-Data-Archive (WEDA) was formed, consisting of a combination of an old-fashioned collection of data sources and a new-fashioned collection of computer tapes. Winfried Pfenning was responsible for the set-up of this archive from 1979 to 1984, and since then Franz Kraus has taken charge. Today WEDA is a part of the Institute of the Social Sciences at the University of Mannheim and should serve as an important instrument for this Institute's future research on Western Europe.

Concurrent with our work on the data handbook, we began with the analysis of certain aspects of the long-term development of the West European welfare states since the end of the nineteenth century. First results were published in a book which I edited together with Arnold J. Heidenheimer (*The Development of Welfare States in Europe and America.* New Brunswick and London, Transaction Books, 1981). The most important in the series of comparative studies were the works of Jens Alber on the development of social insurance (*Vom Armenhaus zum Wohlfahrtsstaat.* Frankfurt, Campus, 1982) which won him the Stein Rokkan Prize of the International Social Science Council, Jürgen Kohl on the development of public expenditure (*Staatsausgaben in Westeuropa.* Frankfurt, Campus, 1985), and finally Franz Kraus on the development of income inequality (*Income Distribution in Western Europe 1900-1980.* Forthcoming).

When I moved from Cologne to the European University Institute in Florence in Autumn 1979, it was also swith the intention of deepening our studies of the long-term development of the European welfare states (today I think perhaps I should have devoted myself more to the study of Renaissance art and Italian cooking). In Spring 1980, with the financial support of the European Community, I launched a comparative project on the growth of the European welfare states (Austria, Belgium, Denmark, Finland, France, Germany, Great Britain, Ireland, Italy, Netherlands, Norway, Sweden, Switzerland) since World War II, along with a group of social scientists from these countries.

I would like to thank at this point Hans Daalder most warmly. He had the courage to recruit me, then a rather young and unknown sociologist, for the European University Institute. And he encouraged the kind of comparative research which I then started in Florence. Having grown up myself in a slightly cynical Catholic culture, I have always admired his Protestant *Prinzipientreue*.

By the first project meeting in 1980 I had been successful (with Austria, Switzerland, and Belgium as exceptions) in recruiting social scientists from these countries who were prepared to collaborate on this extensive project. The majority were younger scientists, some old friends, and some only known to me through the literature. As in real life, so in scientific projects: you lose some people and win others. Competent contributors were found for the three remaining countries. On the other hand, new teams had to be formed subsequently for Austria and the Netherlands, and it was unfortunately impossible to replace our French colleagues who left the project after two years.

Thus 12 countries remained and were researched by the following persons or teams:

Austria	Anton Amann/ Wolfgang Weigel	University of Vienna
Belgium	Jos Berghman/ Jan Vranken	Univ. of Antwerp/Univ. of Tilburg University of Antwerp
Denmark	Lars N. Johansen	University of Odense
Finland	Matti Alestalo/ Hannu Uusitalo	University of Helsinki Helsinki School of Economics
Germany	Jens Alber	European Univ. Institute, Florence/ Univ. of Cologne
Ireland	Maria Maguire	European Univ. Institute, Florence/ OECD Paris
Italy	Maurizio Ferrera	European Univ. Institute, Florence/ Univ. of Pavia
Netherlands	Theo Berben/ Joop Roebroek/ Goran Therborn	University of Nijmegen
Norway	Stein Kuhnle	University of Bergen
Sweden	Sven Olson	University of Stockholm
Switzerland	Peter Gross	University of Bamberg (FRG)
United Kingdom	Richard Parry	University of Edinburgh

In Spring 1980 my old friend and colleague Jens Alber joined the project as additional support for the project coordination. At the same time I had the good fortune of acquiring a Swiss secretary, Ursula Nocentini, who proved to me that the old saying that the Swiss even 'sweep the fields clean' is no myth. In the true style of the Swiss, she was able to put some order into our multi-national chaos.

In respect to the goal setting of the project, my ideas were simple. It was not my intention to examine a specific hypothesis or study a particular limited area. Much more than that, I wanted to initiate broadly based studies on the postwar development of the welfare states in a number of European countries. These studies were to be based on the same questions, work with comparable data, and utilize the same methods. I thought that it would then be possible to draw a picture of the major variations between the European welfare states, thus laying the groundwork for further research.

Naturally I knew that the way to hell is paved with good intentions. In order to get started on the right track, I employed two means: first, sections of the entire studies were written step-by-step for one or two countries and, after discussion in subsequent meetings, served as models for the other countries. Secondly, I met with the project members on a regular basis in order to work on the text and data 'on location' and to attain a greater cohesion and comparability (in a sometimes viscious battle sentence by sentence). Some years of my life were spent on this, and therefore I keep telling myself that the work *must* have been somehow meaningful.

As is well-known, several languages are spoken in Western Europe. Thus, a common language had to be found, and this was pidgin English. And as I am only familiar with the Austrian version of pidgin English, it was necessary to recruit the services of native English speakers. Often up to five different versions of a text (which grew to a country average of almost 150 pages) were being worked on. The reader may thus understand that even the old myth of Sisyphos was of little consolation. I am sure that my periodic despair was shared by Clare Gardiner, who worked in Florence on the numerous versions of the various chapters, as well as by Margaret Herden, who took on this work in Mannheim with refreshing American optimism.

Scientific work is certainly not unimportant in the production of such books, and editorial work may also be useful. *Conditio sine qua non*, however, is the actual typing of the manuscripts, not to mention the patience and creativity necessary for the production of the hundreds of tables and graphs which embellish these volumes. Computer readable texts and tables were done with passionate devotion by the two Ursulas (Ursula Nocentini in Florence and Ursula Rossi in Mannheim) and the graphs were produced reluctantly but meticulously by our artist in residence, Siegbert Sussek.

The completed manuscripts would never have gone to print without the Publication Officer of the European University Institute, Brigitte Schwab. Our common Bavarian-Tyrolian view of the world has certainly facilitated our collaboration. I would also wish to thank President Maihofer, who not only followed the endless progress with fatherly understanding, but also offered his energetic support.

The monumental product of our multi-phase cross-national chaos consists of five volumes which, following the tradition of the publishing house de Gruyter, are at least aesthetically pleasing and thus convey a respectable impression: three volumes (I-III) with four country studies each, one Appendix volume (IV) containing for each country an institutional synopsis, an annotated bibliography and a collection of documented time-series data, and finally a comparative study (V) by the editor. The first three volumes contain the following country studies: Sweden, Norway, Finland, Denmark (I); Germany, United Kingdom, Ireland, Italy (II); Austria, Switzerland, Netherlands, Belgium (III). Volumes I and II were published in December 1986. Now, volume IV is being published. It will be followed by volume III in Summer 1987, and volume V is scheduled for early 1988.

I both fear and hope that with the completion of these volumes only a 'stop-over' point is reached. On the occasion of the twentieth anniversary of the Mannheim Institute of Social Sciences, a symposium on 'Western Europe in Transition' was organized in Autumn 1985, the contributions of which will be published in German (Peter Flora (ed.), *Westeuropa im Wandel*. Frankfurt, Campus) and in English (*Europe in Transition*. London, Macmillan) in 1987. With this symposium the Mannheim Faculty of Social Sciences has documented its intention to develop a new research centre on Western Europe in order to expand and systematize its previous research, and to assure a greater continuity of research in this important field.

Mannheim, March 1987 Peter Flora

Table of Contents

Introduction

Peter Flora

This Appendix volume does not need a lengthy introduction, but only a short explanation of its purpose and structure. The purpose is threefold: The volume has an empirical, psychological and 'philosophical' raison d'être.

The empirical purpose is obvious: the Appendix comprises quantitative and qualitative information which forms the basis for the analyses in the country studies. The psychological purpose may be less obvious, but it was crucial for the project: the production of this volume was an exercise in self-discipline. Through it we tried to force ourselves to ensure a lasting empirical basis, not only for our own analyses, but also as a point of departure for future studies.

This leads to the 'philosophical' purpose of the Appendix which may be more controversial. It concerns the role of data bases in comparative research. To be sure, the age of inductivism is long passed, and no one still believes that knowledge accumulates from the mere stockpiling of data. We've learned that research must begin with questions, and that its goal must be the systematic formulation and testing of hypotheses. In this process, variables must be precisely defined and operationalized, and they must be measured for carefully selected cases.

The realities of research can be quite different however. Normally we have very few cases (countries) upon which to base generalizations. As we all know, their selection is - more often than not - arbitrary rather than random. Most comparativists know the simple rule: 'Include Switzerland in your "sample" and your results will be completely different'. Not only is the number of cases usually limited, but also the investigation period, making its definition just as arbitrary as the selection of cases. This indeed relativizes the emphasis placed on the testing of general hypotheses. Usually such hypotheses are meaningful only in relation to specific contexts as defined by types of society or levels of development.

But even if we were successful in defining such contexts, the testing of hypotheses remains problematic due to the weakness of our data basis. The availability of data more often determines the way in which variables are operationalized than vice versa. As a result, we do not really measure what we want to measure; and we measure it in ways differing from case to case, often without knowing it. Thus we find examples in comparative research, where variations are explained which do not exist. They are simply statistical artefacts. For all these reasons we should invest a little more in establishing better data bases. Their role in comparative research is certainly greater than a textbook philosophy of science would suggest.

We do not profess to have solved the above-mentioned problems or to have created the ultimate data basis for the comparative study of the European welfare states, but we have at least tried to make a contribution to this goal.

The Appendix volume is sub-divided according to the twelve countries of Volumes I to III and follows the same order. It consists of three parts per country: an institutional synopsis with a detailed description of each programme, an annotated bibliography and a documented set of tables. A great effort has been made to standardize these parts; variations reflect differences in institutional structures as well as in the state of research in the individual countries which is evident in the volume of available literature and data.

Institutional synopsis

With only small variations, the institutional synopsis is divided into eight sections:

I Pensions
II Sickness insurance/Health services
III Industrial accidents/Occupational injuries
IV Unemployment benefits/Employment policy
V Families and children
VI Social assistance
VII Education
VIII Housing

Each of these sections begins with a quantitative overview of various benefits and services in terms of public expenditure. It concludes with a list of the most important laws since 1945. The selection of these laws has followed a principle of 'informed arbitrariness', taking into consideration the more essential changes in coverage, the types and levels of benefits and the financing and administration of programmes. Each of the laws is described briefly and is categorized by its publication number. This allows for easy identification of the laws for any further in-depth study.

The central part of each section consists of a detailed account of the institutional provisions at the beginning of the 1980s. This account is standardized to the greatest extent for the individual programmes in social security: A differentiation is made throughout between 'services' and 'income maintenance', which is further broken down into: coverage of population groups; types and levels of benefits; financing and administration.

Bibliography

The purpose of the bibliography is to offer to the foreign reader a well-balanced selection of the literature available and not to provide a comprehensive survey of the literature, which would have been impossible for some countries. The bibliography thus includes only an average of 100 items. It is divided into three sections: general studies and sources for the study of social policy; more specific studies of single programmes; and a limited number of studies on the impact of social programmes. A translation of the title and a brief account of the contents is given for each item in order to facilitate further study.

Tables

The appendix tables with the most important time-series form the basis for the descriptive and explanatory Sections II and IV of the country chapters. Emphasis is placed on public expenditure statistics. The sequence is straightforward: the time-series begin with the most highly aggregated expenditures. These are compiled from the subsequent tables which provide a more in-depth breakdown of expenditure categories. The first table always includes the figures for the gross national product, the various deflators and total public expenditure. The second table normally provides a breakdown of public expenditure by economic category, level of government, and major purpose. These sub-categories do not always refer to the same aggregates because the first is based on the system of national accounts while the others refer to budget statistics.

The two following tables contain the crucial figures of social expenditure by major component, at current and constant prices, as share of GDP and of total expenditure and as percent distribution. The three major expenditure categories: income maintenance, health, and education are relatively easy to compare. This is much less the case for housing and the category 'other' which consists of a conglomeration of miscellaneous items, making any comparison difficult.

A major effort was made to differentiate between cash benefits and benefits in kind and services (and administrative costs) in order to arrive at a total figure for 'income maintenance'. This succeeded in most cases; however, for some countries it was only possible to provide for some social security schemes tables in which cash benefits are combined with other expenditures.

In addition to the basic tables on the development of social expenditure, the appendix volume contains three other types of tables: time-series on the financing of public expenditure and social security; time-series on the development of the various clienteles of the welfare states; and tables with various demographic, economic and political data (elections), which are referred to mainly in the analyses in Section IV of the country chapters.

The tables are documented in detail, the objective being the ability to replicate the data. It thus includes not only relevant sources, but also additional comments and notes on the definition of the categories.

Sweden

Sven Olsson

Institutional Synopsis

Contents

Glossary of abbreviations

AMS	*Arbetsmarknadsstyrelsen* (National Labour Market Board)
ATP	*Allmän tilläggspension* (Earnings-related Supplementary Pension)
CSN	*Centrala studiestödsnämnden* (State Authority for Student Grants and Loans)
ITP	*Industrins tilläggspension* (Pension Scheme for Private Sector Salaried Employees)
KPA	*Kommunernas pensionsanstalt* (Pension Scheme for Local and Regional Authority Employees)
SCB	*Statistiska centralbyrån* (National Bureau of Statistics, now called 'Statistics Sweden')
SÖ	*Skolöverstyrelsen* (National Board of Education)
SOS	*Sveriges Officiella Statistik* (Official Statistics of Sweden)
SPV	*Statens personalpensionsverk* (Pension Scheme for State Employees)
STP	*Särskild tilläggspension* (Pension Scheme for Wage-earners in Private Industry)
UHA	*Universitets- och högskoleäbetet* (National Board of Universities and Colleges)

I Pensions

In 1981 the bulk of social expenditure for pensioners consisted of transfer payments: almost 59 billion Swedish Kronors (SKR) were spent as cash benefits and more than 10 billion on related services. Together, this amounted to 12% of GDP and 38% of social security expenditure.

Expenditure on pensions and related services 1981, in mill. SKR

		%	%
Income Maintenance	58 978	85.0	
Basic pension scheme:	35 709	51.4	100.0
of which: old age pension	23 613		66.1
invalidity pension	5 558		15.6
widows' pension	1 199		3.4
orphans' pension	185		0.5
wife's supplement	729		2.0
handicap allowances	264		0.7
child handicap allowances	306		0.9
child's supplement	50		0.1
municipal housing allowances	3 805		10.7
Supplementary pension scheme:	21 723	31.3	100.0
of which: old age pension	14 130		
invalidity pension	5 277		
widows' pension	2 030		
orphans' pension	286		
Part-time pension	1 546	2.2	
Services for elderly and invalid pensioners:	10 457	15.1	100.0
- homes for the elderly	3 376		32.3
- home help, transport services etc.	4 208		40.2
- care of the disabled	2 873		27.5
Total	69 435	100.0	

Source: National Insurance Board, *Allmän försäkring 1981*, and Statistics Sweden (*Socialvården 1981*), and *Bostads- och byggnadsstatistisk årsbok 1982*. All SOS's.

Income maintenance

Coverage

The 1962 National Insurance Act established coverage for all persons resident in Sweden over 16 years of age, including most foreigners, under the National Pension System. This system includes three schemes: (1) basic pension (*folkpension*), which consists of a universal minimum flat-rate pension, together with various partially income-tested supplements; (2) earnings-related supplementary pension (*allmän tilläggspension*, ATP), introduced in 1959, and (3) partial pension (*delpension*) consisting of part-time early retirement pension, introduced in 1976. Both the basic and the supplementary pension schemes provide old-age pensions (*ålderspension*), invalidity pensions (*förtidspension*), and family pensions (*familjepension*), i.e. survivors' pensions.

In 1980, a total of 1,984,000 persons received at least one type of pension, i.e. ca. 24% of total population.

Number of pensions and pensioners in 1980 by type of pension and pension scheme (in thousands)

Pension scheme	Type of pension				Total
	Old age	Invalidity[b]	Widows	Orphans	
Basic pension[a]	1 363	293	84	43	1 783
Supplementary pens.	757	209	217	44	1 227
Part-time pens.	67				67
Total number of pensioners	1 430	293	217	44	1 984

Source: Statistical Yearbook 1981, p. 267.

[a] The numbers of persons receiving supplements (see below) are not shown separately. In 1980 a total of 970,000 persons were in receipt of the special supplement (*pensionstillskott*), of which 801,000 were old age pensioners; 56,532 were in receipt of wives' supplements (*hustrutillägg*), 9,087 handicap allowances (*handikappersättning*), 13,699 invalidity allowances for children (*vårdbidrag*) and 812,536 municipal housing allowances (*kommunalt bostadstillägg*).

[b] Includes invalidity pensions (*förtidspension*) and temporary invalidity pensions (*sjukbidrag*, see below) for both the basic and the supplementary pension schemes.

All pension benefits are indexed using a 'base amount'. Initially, this base amount was linked to the consumer price index and adjusted monthly. When the concept was introduced (September 1957), the base amount was set at 4,000 SKR, and in January

1984 it had reached 20,300 SKR. From July 1981, the indexation was changed; the base amount is now adjusted annually (in January) and is linked to a special 'base amount index' which omits changes in sales taxes, and government price subsidies.

All pensions are calculable from the base amount, which may be seen as a subsistence minimum index. Since 1983, a single pensioner is entitled to a guaranteed 'minimum pension' which amounts to 144% of the base amount (consisting of a basic pension which equals 96% of base amount, and a pension supplement which equals 48% of base amount).

In principle, all pension benefits (except the housing supplement, see below) constitute taxable income. However, pensioners whose only source of income is the 'minimum pension', do not pay tax because of a special tax deduction. With any additional income, this tax deduction is reduced accordingly.

Occupational and voluntary pension schemes

In addition to the major public pension schemes there are four important occupational pension schemes, referred to here as 'private pension schemes' as they are established by collective agreement and not by law. They cover: (1) state employees (*Statens personalpensionsverk*, SPV), (2) those employed by local and regional authorities (*Kommunernas pensionsanstalt*, KPA), (3) salaried employees in the private sector (*Industrins tilläggspension*, ITP), and (4) wage-earners in private industry (*Särskild tilläggspension*, STP).

All of them provide a secondary supplementary pension in addition to the public pension. All public employees are entitled to this secondary supplementary pension as are most salaried employees in the private sector. The majority of wage-earners in private industry are included, however, the system does not normally cover those born before 1911, consequently the majority of retired workers are without this secondary supplement.

There are also some minor pension schemes: (1) the banks, the cooperative movement and a few individual firms operate their own pension schemes; (2) private and voluntary insurance with commercial insurance companies; (3) voluntary pension insurance (in accordance with the National Insurance Act) financed by contributions from the insured. The number of those voluntary insured with this scheme, - some 56,000 in 1979, has been declining since 1960. Throughout the 1970s, approximately 20,000 persons have received pensions from this scheme each year.

1. Basic pensions

A universal, means-tested, pension system was introduced as early as 1913. The present system dates from 1948 and provides old age, invalidity and survivors' pensions in addition to a variety of supplements.

Old age pension is normally payable from the age of 65. However, it may also be drawn from the age of 60, in which case the pension is reduced by 0.5% for every month under the age of 65 (which means 70% of the normal pension at the age of 60). The lower amount is paid until the death of the insured (see special early retirement regulations under 'invalidity pension' below). Retirement can also be deferred until the age of 70. For every month over the age of 65 the pension increases by 0.6%, and can thus reach up to 136% of a normal pension.

Old age pension is a universal flat-rate benefit consisting of a basic pension (*folkpension*) and a special pension supplement (*pensionstillägg*). In January 1982, the basic pension for a single person was 95% (96% from 1983) of the 'base amount', i.e. 16,910 SKR or 32% of average disposable income for a single industrial worker (OECD, *The 1982 Tax/Benefit Position of a Typical Worker in the OECD Member Countries*, Paris, 1984). For a married couple where both were pensioners, the basic pension for each of them was 77.5% (78.5% from 1984) of the base amount or together 155%. In January 1982, this pension amounted to 27,590 SKR or 45% of the disposable income for a married working couple with two children.

Since 1969 a special pension supplement has been payable in addition to the basic pension, where a pensioner has no or only a low supplementary pension (see below). Since 1983, the special pension supplement has been 48% of the base amount, but is reduced in proportion to any supplementary pension received by the beneficiary. In January 1982, the old age pension including the pension supplement, amounted to 25,276 SKR (29,232 SKR in 1984) for a single person (i.e. 48% of average disposable income for a single industrial worker in 1982), and to 44,322 SKR (51,359 SKR in 1984) for a couple of two pensioners (i.e. 73% of the disposable income for married working couples).

Invalidity pension (*förtidspension*) is paid to persons over 16 years of age whose working capacity is reduced by at least 50% due to illness, physical disability or mental handicap. If the person can be expected to recover wholly or partially, he may receive a temporary invalidity pension (*sjukbidrag*). Persons with physically or mentally strenuous work with which they are unable to cope, can retire at the age of 60 (in exceptional circumstances at 55). An unemployed person who has used all his rights to unemployment benefit can retire at the age of 60 even if his working capacity is not reduced.

Invalidity pension is payable at full, two-thirds or 50% rates, depending on the degree of working incapacity. The full (permanent or temporary) invalidity pension equals the old age pension but with the difference that a double pension supplement is paid if the disabled has either no or only a low supplementary pension. At the age of 65 invalidity pension is replaced by old age pension and the pension supplement is reduced correspondingly.

Family (*familjepension*) or survivors' pensions include benefits for widows and orphans. A widows' pension (*änkepension*) is payable to a widow from the time of her husband's death until the age of 65, if she is responsible for a child under 16 (living permanently in her household) or if she is at least 36 years old and has been married for a minimum of five years. In the latter case, a full pension (identical with an old age pension for a single person) is paid, if the widow has reached the age of 50. The widows' pension ceases on remarriage.

Children's (*barnpension*) or orphans' pensions are payable to children under 19, where either one or both parents are dead. They receive at least 25% of the base amount, and more (up to 40%) if they have either no or only small benefits from the supplementary pension scheme. For public expenditure, children's pensions are also dealt with under the heading of Families and Children (see section V).

In addition to the special supplement, the basic pension can be combined with the following supplements: income-tested wife's supplement (introduced in 1948), universal child supplement (1948), child care disability allowance (1976), handicap allowance (1976), and means-tested municipal housing supplements (1954).

A wife's supplement (*hustrutillägg*) is an income-tested benefit payable to a wife between the ages of 60 and 65 if married to a man receiving a basic old age pension (but not if the pension is drawn before the age of 65) or invalidity pension. The wife must not be a recipient of a basic pension. The supplement amounts to the difference between a single person's pension and the pension for a married couple who are both pensioners.

A child's supplement (*barntillägg*) is payable to any pensioner with a child under 16 years of age living at home. It amounts to 25% of the base amount. If only one parent is still living and the child receives an orphans' pension, the child supplement amounts to 10% of the base amount. This supplement is not income-tested, but is reduced successively when the supplementary pension exceeds 50% of the base amount.

A child care disability allowance (*vårdbidrag*) is payable to parents taking care of a child under 16 years of age and living at home, who is mentally retarded, physically handicapped or suffering from a long-term illness or injury. The allowance is equal to a full invalidity pension.

A handicap allowance (*handikappersättning*) is payable to insured persons between the ages of 16 and 65 who are blind or otherwise disabled and in need of constant care, but still able to maintain themselves economically. The allowance may be paid as a supplement to the invalidity or old age pension if the handicapped person is unable to look after himself and is in need of daily help from another person. The disablement must have occured before the age of 65.

Municipal housing supplement (*kommunalt bostadstillägg*) is payable to those in receipt of basic pensions. They are subject to a means-test in accordance with rules fixed by central government. The amount, however, is determined by the municipality councils and may vary from one municipality to another. Pensioners with an income not exceeding the basic pension including the various supplements, are exempted from taxation.

Financing

The basic pension scheme is financed by contributions from employers (62% in 1981), central government (31% in 1981) and local government (for municipal housing allowances). The contributions from the employer are not earmarked for the pension but are in fact a payroll tax.

2. General supplementary pensions

The general supplementary pension scheme (*allmän tilläggspension*, ATP) was introduced in 1959 and the first pensions were paid in 1963. The scheme is compulsory and covers all economically active persons over 16 years of age (employed and self-employed). Self-employed persons have the right to contract-out of supplementary pension insurance, but only with respect to that part of their income derived from self-employment. The supplementary pension is earnings-related, and is payable to persons who have earned more than the 'base amount' for at least three years.

The amount of a supplementary pension depends on the 'average pensionable income' earned in previous years and on the number of years of gainful activity. For each year, a ratio is calculated by dividing the individual income by the general base amount for the respective year ('pension points'). However, only income up to a ceiling of 7.5 times the base amount is taken into account. The average number of pension points for all years of gainful activity (for a period of more than 15 years, the average is calculated for the 15 best years) is then multiplied by the base amount for the month/year in which a person retires. This gives the average pensionable income.

A full supplementary old age pension amounts to 60% of the average pensionable income and requires a 30 years' record of accumulated pension points. For each missing year the pension is reduced by 1/30 or 2 percentage points. Certain interim rules exist for persons born between 1896 and 1923, i.e. a smaller number of years is required (at least 20) to qualify for a full pension. For the supplementary old age pension the normal age of retirement is 65, with the same possibilities of early or deferred retirement as in the case of the basic pension scheme.

To qualify for a supplementary invalidity pension, a person must have accumulated pension points for at least one year of gainful activity. The rules are in principle the same as for the supplementary old age pension, with the difference that pension points (above one year) are calculated on the basis of present, former, and future assumed income (particularly in cases of total disablement) up to the age of 65, in relation to the reduction of working capacity.

Supplementary family or survivors' pensions are payable to children under the age of 19 on the death of one or both parents (if both parents were entitled to a pension, the higher one is taken as a basis) and to widows (but not widowers), under the following conditions: the husband must have been entitled to a supplementary pension; the marriage must have taken place on or prior to the husband's sixtieth birthday; the couple must have had children together or must have been married for at least five years. Survivors' pensions are calculated on the basis of the invalidity pension to which the deceased would have been entitled at the moment of his death. A widow without children or a full orphan receives 40% of this pension. An additional 10% is payable for each child.

Financing

The general supplementary pension scheme is financed by contributions from employers and, to a lesser extent, from the self-employed. Contributions are a certain percentage of wages, determined by central government (9.8% in 1984). Self-employed persons pay the same percentage of their income (or that part of income derived from self-employment respectively).

3. Part-time early retirement pensions

Since 1976 employees between the age of 60 and 65 may combine part-time work with a partial pension (*delpension*). Persons who voluntarily reduce their working time by at least five hours a week or have an average working week of seventeen hours, are entitled to partial compensation for loss of income. This compensation amounts to 50% of the difference between their former full income (up to a ceiling of 7.5 times the base amount) and their new, reduced income. To be eligible for a partial pension, one must have gained pension points for at least 10 years after the age of 45, and have worked for a minimum of five of the twelve months prior to partial retirement. The partial pension is optional for self-employed persons.

Financing

The scheme is financed by employers' contributions (0.5% of payroll).

Services

The municipalities are responsible for the provisional services for the elderly and disabled. These include different types of housing, various forms of home help, housing grants and a special transportation system (*färdtjänst*).

There are four types of housing: apartments in service buildings (*servicehus*, ca 27,000 persons in 1982), homes for pensioners (*pensionärslägenheter*, ca. 60,000 dwellings in 1982), old people's homes (*ålderdomshem*, ca. 56,000 persons in 1982), and wards for chronic invalids (*hem for längvarigt sjuka*, ca. 1,300 persons in 1982). Service buildings are for pensioners in quite good health as are homes for pensioners consisting of special dwelling units in which some necessary services are offered. Old people's homes cater for pensioners needing more care and supervision. Nursing homes offer medical care for chronically ill pensioners.

Local authorities also organize social home help (*hemtjänst*) which is provided either free or at a very low charge, and includes services such as cleaning, cooking, shopping and laundering. In 1981 some 62,000 municipal home helpers (*hemsamariter*) were employed in this programme and about 350,000 persons received this kind of help.

Pensioners living at home are entitled to a means-tested non-repayable grant for housing improvements.

There is a special municipal transport service (*färdtjänst*) for elderly or handicapped persons who have difficulties using the public transportation system. The fare paid for this service is equal to the normal fare charged by the public transportation system. This service is used by more than 300,000 persons.

Core laws

Bracketed figures refer to the chronological number of laws passed in the respective year.

1913
First law; effective from 1914; universal basic pension; greatest part consisting of an income-tested pension supplement; financed by contributions; pensionable age of 67.

1946 (no. 431)
Effective from 1948; introduction of tax-financed flat-rate universal basic pension (different for couples and singles); income-test abolished.

1951 (no. 157)
Effective from 1951; indexation of basic pension (consumer price index).

1952 (no. 396)
Effective from 1954; introduced municipal housing allowances.

1956 (no. 264)
Effective from 1958; ten-year programme to raise basic pension and link it to general standard of living; income-test for widows' pension abolished.

1959 (no. 291)
Effective from 1960; decision on implementation of compulsory earnings-related supplementary pensions for employees; financed by contributions from employers; first pensions paid in 1963 and first 'full' supplementary pension paid in 1979.

1960 (no. 102)
Effective from 1960; income-test for children's pension abolished.

1969 (no. 205)
Effective from 1969; introduction of special pension supplement related to the basic amount, to complement pensions with no or low supplementary pension.

1970 (no. 186)
Effective from 1971; eligibility for invalidity pensions extended with greater opportunities for employees over the age of 60.

1974 (no. 784)
Effective from 1976; lowered pension age from 67 to 65 and made retirement flexible between 60 and 70.

1975 (no. 380)
Effective from 1976; introduction of a part-time pension programme from the age of 60.

1980 (no. 1041)
Effective from 1981; introduction of a special 'base amount index', excluding changes in energy prices (included again in 1983), sales taxes and food subsidies.

II Sickness insurance/Health services

In 1981, expenditure on sickness cash benefits, medical and dental benefits, and the various public health services was in excess of 64 billion SKR, i.e. 36% of social security expenditure and 11% of GDP.

Expenditure on sickness insurance and health services in 1981 in million SKR

	Total	%
Sickness Insurance:	25 791	39.8
- sickness cash benefits	12 830	19.8
- medical benefits	8 115	12.5
- dental benefits	2 446	3.8
- administration	2 400	3.7
Health Services:	38 965	60.2
- national health service, hospitals, midwifery service	35 026	54.1
- national dental service	1 075	1.7
- care for mentally handicapped	2 864	4.4
Total	64 756	100.0

Source: National Insurance Board, *Allmän försäkring 1981* and Statistics Sweden, *Socialvården 1981*.

Sickness insurance and the supply of medical care are two largely separate activities with separate sources of finance. Whereas hospitals and other local public health services are run and mainly financed by the county councils (with some contributions from sickness insurance), sickness insurance is financed by employers' contributions with some support from central tax revenues.

Coverage

State subsidies had been given to voluntary sickness insurance societies since 1891, but a compulsory sickness insurance scheme was only introduced in 1955. It provided sickness cash benefits and medical benefits (excluding dental care). Since 1963 it has been an integral part of the national insurance system which also includes pensions and work injuries. Dental insurance dates from 1974.

All resident persons (Swedish citizens and most foreigners), are entitled to health care (hospital treatment, out-patient care, medicines, dental care). All residents above the age of 16 are entitled to draw sickness cash benefits, provided that their annual income from gainful activity is estimated to be at least 6,000 SKR in 1983 (for exceptions from this rule, see below).

Benefits

Sickness cash benefits

Since 1974 sickness cash benefits amount to 90% of last gross earnings up to an income ceiling of 7.5 times the 'base amount' (see under Pensions). Sickness cash benefit is taxable income and is counted for the supplementary pension scheme. To qualify for benefit, a person must have been reported as sick to the local insurance office; after one week of sickness a doctor's certificate is necessary. Sickness cash benefit is paid from the second day of illness and its duration is in principle unlimited (with exceptions for pensioners with earned income).

A flat-rate sickness cash benefit is paid to married persons under 65 and in permanent cohabitation, even if the annual income is less than 6,000 SKR. The same rule applies to unmarried persons living together permanently with children under the age of 16. These persons receive a daily allowance of 8 SKR (1984), which is not taxable. This allowance may be increased up to a maximum of 20 SKR through a voluntary insurance scheme (also available for students).

Self-employed persons can choose a waiting period for sickness cash benefit of 3, 33, or 93 days.

Medical benefits

The National Health Insurance Law, amended in 1962 and renewed in 1982, gave all residents the legal right to a refund of expenses for medical care. Patients receive out-patient medical care and drugs for which a certain charge is payable, and virtually free public ward in-patient treatment for an unlimited period of time.

The great bulk of out-patient care is provided by the county councils at their hospitals, polyclinics or medical centres. The patient is free to consult a private practitioner but at slightly greater expense (if the doctor is not registered the patient must pay the full fees). A uniform tariff applies to the public out-patient services. In 1984, patients paid 40 SKR for a visit to a health service doctor, while the local insurance office paid 127 SKR for the visit to the county council providing the medical service. Visits to private practitioners come under a separate reimbursement rate decided by government. For each visit the patient paid 50 SKR while the doctor received up to 540 SKR from the local insurance office. These charges cover x-rays and other examinations, any treatment prescribed by the doctor, and a specialist consultation if necessary. Other benefits include treatment such as physiotherapy, occupational therapy and speech therapy. Contraceptive advice, abortion and sterilization are provided free of charge. Assistance is also available for any travel expenses above a certain amount for patients receiving any of these types of care.

Drugs are provided at heavily subsidized costs and certain life-saving drugs are available free of charge. In 1984 the patient paid a maximum charge of 50 SKR for each prescription. If 15 payments are made within 12 months, the following 12 months are free of charge. The pricing, advertising and prescription of drugs is severely controlled by the government.

Dental care

Children are entitled to free dental care up to the age of 19 under the provisions of the school health service. The dental insurance scheme includes all persons over 19 years of age. Treatment by the national dental service or by private practitioners (who still provide the greater part of dental care), is covered by insurance. Private dentist's charges must not exceed rates set by an established tariff. In general the patient pays 60% of the costs up to a maximum amount of 2,500 SKR, and 25% above this sum. The remainder is covered by the local social insurance offices.

Financing and administration

The Health Insurance Scheme is mainly financed by employers' contributions (86% in 1981), contributions from self-employed and some state subsidies (13.5% in 1981). Employees' contributions were abolished in 1974 and the cost transferred to the employers. In 1981, employers' contributions amounted to 10.5% of the reported payroll, and self-employed persons were charged 10.5% of their taxable income (or that part of income deriving from self-employment respectively). The state also subsidizes voluntary insurance (mainly sickness cash benefits for students and housewives).

The health insurance programme is administered by 26 semi-autonomous regional social insurance offices which replaced the voluntary sickness benefit societies in 1955. The societies handle claims for sickness cash benefits, collect charges payable by patients and pay hospitals, doctors, dentists and others the sums due to them. They are supervised by the National Insurance Board.

Health services

A 1955 law (revised in 1962) made the counties responsible for the provision of hospital care, out-patient medical care and certain preventive health services, particularly in respect of the health of mothers and young children. Thus, the counties, under the supervision of the National Board of Health and Welfare (*Socialstyrelsen*) play a dominant part in the actual supply of medical care which is mainly hospital-based. They are responsible for approximately 95% of all hospital beds (including hospitals for the mentally sick) and the bulk of out-patient care is provided by them through out-patient departments of hospitals, local medical centres (*distriktsläkarmot-*

tagning) and public health officers. The preventive maternity care and the child guidance centres (*mödra- och barnavårdscentral*) are linked to this out-patient health service.

The county councils provide health services for all persons living within their boundaries (and to all persons in the case of acute emergency). Hospital treatment is free of charge, but there can be a small reduction in the patient's sickness cash benefit. A part of the costs of hospital treatment is directly payable out of sickness insurance to the county councils. Patients pay a small fee for out-patient health services (see above, medical benefits).

The county councils are also responsible for public dental care. Under this scheme, children and young people up to the age of 19 are given dental care free of charge in close cooperation with the schools.

The health services are mainly financed by local taxes (only a minor part being covered by health insurance or by fees), i.e. the county councils raise an income-tax on all private incomes earned in their areas.

Core laws

1864
County councils made responsible for hospital treatment throughout the country (with tax-raising power).

1891
Introduced state subsidies to voluntary sickness insurance benefit societies.

1947 (no. 1)
Principle decision taken on flat-rate sickness insurance; postponed twice and never put into practice.

1953 (no. 569)
Effective from 1955; extended earnings-related compulsory sickness insurance covering hospital treatment to the whole population; rebates on purchases of pharmaceutical preparations; maternity insurance coordinated with sickness insurance.

1962 (no. 242)
Effective from 1963; county councils assumed responsibility for out-patient care.

1962 (no. 381)
Effective from 1963; law on general insurance coordinating sickness insurance, basic pension and national supplementary pension under supervision of National Board of Social Insurance, also administrating occupational injury insurance and child allowances.

1966 (nos. 585-7)
Effective from 1967; county councils assumed responsibility for psychiatric care, whole health system now administered on a regional level.

1967 (no. 921)
Effective from 1968; waiting days for sickness cash benefits abolished and level of compensation raised to 80% of net earnings.

1969 (nos. 650-9)
Effective from 1970; introduced uniform tariff applying to all out-patient care in public health.

1973 (no. 456)
Effective from 1974; introduced universal dental insurance.

1973 (no. 465)
Effective from 1974; level of compensation from sickness insurance raised to 90% of gross earnings; cash benefits taxable.

1982 (no. 763)
General Health and Sickness Law: effective from 1983; replaced the 1962 Law (no. 242); defined the responsibilities of the county councils for preventative health care, out-patient medical care, hospital treatment, etc.

III Occupational injuries/Industrial safety

In 1981, expenditure on occupational injury insurance and industrial safety amounted to over one and a half billion SKR, or almost 1% of social security expenditure and 0.3% of GDP.

Expenditure on occupational injuries and industrial safety in 1981, in million SKR

	Total	%
Occupational injury insurance:	1 570	93.0
Industrial safety	119	7.0
Total	1 689	100.0

Source: Statistics Sweden, *Socialvården 1981*.

Coverage

This insurance scheme dates back to the beginning of the twentieth century when employers were obliged by law to provide compensation for work accidents. In 1916 industrial accident insurance was made compulsory and in the 1920s it was extended to cover various occupational diseases. Today, the insurance scheme covers all gainfully employed persons (self-employed as well as full-time and part-time employees) and certain students. It provides benefits in cash and kind for: accidents occuring in connection with a person's employment or work accidents on the way to or from work, and occupational diseases.

Benefits

The treatment and compensation of industrial accidents and occupational diseases is closely linked to the National Health Insurance Scheme. It provides both medical and cash benefits for an injured/sick workman until the occupational/industrial origin of the injury/sickness is established, or until 90 days have elapsed, after which time the industrial insurance scheme takes over responsibility. Four types of benefits are provided: sickness cash benefits, pensions, medical care, and funeral allowances.

Sickness cash benefits are paid for the first 90 days through the health insurance scheme at a rate of 90% of gross earnings. After this coordination period they are raised to 100% (up to an income ceiling of 7.5 times the 'base amount', see under Pensions) and paid by the occupational injury insurance.

In the case of a lasting impairment of working capacity, insured persons are entitled to a life-annuity (*livränta*), i.e. a kind of complementary pension which is related, not to the degree of disablement but to relative income loss. This pension covers 100% of the difference between income before and after work injury (up to an income ceiling of 7.5 times the 'base amount').

Victims of work injuries are accorded special treatment as regards the receipt of medical benefits. They are exempt from paying fees and are entitled to a wider range of benefits, including free dental treatment. During the coordination period medical expenses are paid in principle by the health insurance scheme, and after the 90 days, by the occupational injury insurance.

In the case of death, survivors' pensions are paid according to the same rules as for the general pension system. In addition, funeral allowances are provided by the occupational injury insurance scheme.

Financing and administration

The occupational injury insurance is mainly financed by employers' contributions. All employers are obliged to insure themselves against liability for industrial accidents or occupational diseases with the National Insurance Board which administers the insurance scheme.

Industrial safety

Since 1889, when a law on factory inspection was passed, industrial safety forms part of welfare policies. Today, the National Board for Industrial Safety (*Arbetarskyddsstyrelsen*) is responsible for work environment policies and the regional agencies of the Board, the Labour Inspectorate (*yrkesinspektionen*) carries out investigations in plants and offices. It is supported by a special institute (*arbetsmedicinska institutet*) which offers education and training in the field of industrial safety.

Core laws

1889
First law; safety inspectorate established together with the first industrial safety law.

1901
Established liability for employers in mining and other dangerous industrial activities in the event of work accident; compulsory industrial injury insurance (1916).

1949 (no. 1)
New extended industrial safety law and National Board of Industrial Safety established.

1954 (no. 243)
Effective from 1955; occupational injury insurance extended to new diseases, and coordinated with the introduction of compulsory sickness insurance.

1976 (no. 380)
Effective from 1977; work injury law replaced employment injury law.

1977 (no. 1160)
Effective from 1978; work environment law replaced industrial safety law.

IV Unemployment benefits/Employment policy

In 1981, expenditure on unemployment benefits and employment related measures amounted to approximately 11.4 billion SKR or 6% of social security expenditure and 2% of GDP.

Expenditure on employment/unemployment in 1981, in mill. SKR

		%
Unemployment insurance benefits	2 703	23.7
Unemployment assistance benefits	409	3.6
Employment exchange services	1 078	9.4
Retraining of unemployed a.o.	2 375	20.8
Public works	4 850	42.5
Total	11 415	100.0

Source: Statistics Sweden, *Socialvården 1981* and National Labour Market Board, *Arbetsmarknadsverket 1981/82.*

Income maintenance

Coverage

There is still no compulsory universal unemployment insurance scheme in Sweden. Since 1934 the state has subsidized voluntary unemployment insurance funds organized by trade unions, and in 1974 a cash labour market support (*kontant arbetsmarknadsstöd*, here referred to as unemployment assistance), was introduced for persons not covered by unemployment insurance schemes.

1. Unemployment insurance

Most full-time employees (ca. two-thirds of the labour force) belong to an approved voluntary insurance society operating in close connection with the trade unions and under the supervision of the National Labour Market Board (*Arbetsmarknadsstyrelsen*, AMS). To be eligible for unemployment benefit, a person must have been a member of a fund for at least 52 weeks, including 20 weeks during the 12 months preceding unemployment; he must be registered at the local employment office and be capable of work; unemployment must be involuntary and the unemployed must not decline any offer of a suitable job.

Unemployment insurance benefit is an earnings-related daily allowance, payable for not more than five days a week. Payments start after a waiting period of five days for a maximum duration of 300 days, and up to 450 days for members between 55 and 65 years of age. Every insured person is placed by the unemployment insurance society into one of 10 daily allowance groups, but most full-time employees are in the 'top group' in which the daily allowance in 1984 amounted to 280 SKR. In principle (as a political goal) the daily allowance should replace 90% of gross earnings. In practice it may vary between a maximum of 11/12 and 45% of previous earnings, but only a few (part-time) employees belong to the 'bottom group'. Benefit levels are decided by the government on the basis of proposals put forward by the AMS. Unemployment benefit is taxable and thus makes the recipient eligible for the supplementary pension schemes.

Financing

Unemployment insurance (there are about 40 funds) is partly financed by state subsidies and to a smaller part by employees' contributions and, since 1974, by employers' contributions. The state subsidies vary considerably between funds, mainly due to different unemployment risks in the various economic branches. In the late 1970s, the subsidies on average accounted for 70% of the revenues of unemployment insurance funds.

2. Unemployment assistance

Unemployment assistance is granted to persons not covered by unemployment insurance, who do not have twelve months prior membership of an insurance fund, or who have fallen out of unemployment insurance after a period of 300 or 450 days.

In principle an applicant must have worked for five of the last 12 months and have applied for a job via the Employment Service, without having found suitable work, before unemployment assistance is payable. People who have been unemployed since finishing their studies (basic education, upper secondary school, other vocational training, adult education or labour market training) are also entitled to unemployment assistance. However, these unemployed must have applied for a job through the Employment Service for at least three months after having finished their education or training.

Unemployment assistance consists of a flat-rate daily allowance which amounted to 100 SKR in 1984. The duration of the benefit varies with age: 150 days up to the age of 55, 300 days from the age of 55 to 60, and without limitation from 60 to 65. Employees who have reached the age of 60 (in exceptional cases 55) and have fallen out of unemployment insurance, may choose between unemployment assistance and old age or invalidity pension.

Financing and administration

About two-thirds of the costs of unemployment assistance are covered by employers' contributions and the remaining one-third by general state revenues. Applications for unemployment assistance are considered by the county employment board (*länsarbetsnämnden*) and payments are made by the local social insurance office.

Services

The bulk of unemployment expenditure is spent on labour market policies to create jobs directly through retraining, rather than on income maintenance. The AMS organizes various programmes on the basis of parliamentary decisions.

The local Employment Service (*arbetsförmedlingen*) acts as an employment exchange and provides labour market information, and vocational guidance. It is supervised by the AMS and works in close contact with local trade unions, employers' associations and municipalities. The employment service offers travel allowances and starting grants for employees moving from one part of the country to another. In 1984, the travel allowance amounted to a maximum of 4,000 SKR for single persons, and to 9,000 SKR for family households.

Labour market training programmes are organized by the National School Board (*Skolöverstyrelsen*) in cooperation with the AMS. (From January 1986 the Labour Market Education Board (*Arbetsmarknadsutbildning*, AMU) will be an independent state authority). Persons enroled in labour market training programmes receive an educational allowance. For insured persons this allowance is equal to their unemployment insurance benefit, for the non-insured it equals unemployment assistance benefit, with a higher allowance for persons with children. The AMS may also pay temporary training grants to companies willing to retrain their personnel rather than create redundancies.

Public work projects are used as a complement to other measures against unemployment resulting from structural changes in certain branches of the economy or employment of a seasonal or cyclical character. In areas with high unemployment the government offers regional development grants to companies or may subsidize wages directly.

Core laws

1906
State subsidies to municipal employment offices introduced.

1934
State subsidies to voluntary unemployment benefit societies.

1948 (nos. 439-40)
Effective from 1949; nationalization of local employment offices; National Labour Market Board (AMS) set up as central authority covering local employment offices and control of voluntary unemployment benefit societies.

1953 (nos. 323)
Increased state subsidies due to regulation of minimum benefit level; minimum of 50% of net earnings.

1956 (no. 629)
Extended duration of unemployment benefit; payable after fewer waiting days.

1958 (no. 329)
Initiation of 'active' manpower policy under supervision of AMS.

1965 (no.101)
Introduced regional subsidies to employers/industries.

1968 (no.140)
Extended duration and special allowances for elderly unemployed in the labour force (over 60, in some cases also age group 55-59).

1973 (nos. 370-1)
Effective from 1974; extended duration from 150 to 300 days (450 for members over 55); cash benefits taxable; unemployment cash benefits for non-members, or those not covered by voluntary benefit societies (maximum 150 days).

V Families and children

In 1981, expenditure on transfer payments and services related to family policy amounted to over 29 billion SKR, or 16% of social security expenditure and 5% of GDP.

Expenditure on families and children in 1981, in million SKR

		%
Income Maintenance:	13 815	47.0
- general child allowances	5 171	17.5
- advance payments	1 004	3.4
- parents' allowances	4 135	14.1
- housing allowances to families	1 651	5.6
- orphans' pensions	415	1.4
- educational allowances	1 439	4.9
Services:	15 605	53.0
- child day care institutions	7 189	24.4
- home help service	282	1.0
- other child care services	2 728	9.3
- school meals	1 767	6.0
- individual and family assistance[a]	3 411	11.6
- other public assistance[a]	228	0.8
Total	29 420	100.0

Source: Statistics Sweden, *Socialvården 1981.*

Income maintenance

Coverage

Income maintenance programmes and public services for families and children date back to the 1930s when maternity benefits in cash and kind were introduced. Today, the main part of public expenditure on services goes to day-care institutions, while income maintenance consists of a variety of cash benefits: (1) general child allowance,

(2) advance payments, (3) parents' allowances, (4) rent allowances for families with children, (5) orphans' pensions, and (6) education (child) allowances for young people between 16 and 19 years of age.

1. General child allowances

Since 1948 a general child allowance has been payable to all persons resident in Sweden with at least one child under the age of 16. It is .a flat-rate and tax-free benefit payable four times a year. It is not indexed, but regularly adjusted by parliamentary decision. In 1983, the annual benefit amounted to 3,300 SKR per child with supplements to families with three (one-quarter allowance) or more children (one-half allowance for every child over the limit of four). The child allowance will be augmented to 4,800 SKR from January 1985. The scheme is financed out of general state revenues.

2. Advance payments

If only one parent is actually providing for a child, she/he is either entitled to a maintenance allowance (*underhållsbidrag*) from the other parent, or to an advance maintenance payment (*bidragsförskott*), if the other parent does not, or cannot pay. This advance payment is a way of guaranteeing a minimum subsistence for the child (in addition to the general child allowance). It is granted on application to the local social insurance office which administers the payment. The scheme is financed by the central government (75%), and by the municipalities (25%). Maintenance advances are normally payable at a rate equaling 41% of the base amount. They can be paid up to and including the month of the child's eighteenth birthday. The payment is tax-free.

3. Parental insurance

In 1974 former maternity benefits were replaced by a parental allowance (*föräldrapenning*) which is claimable by every family for a period of 180 days in connection with childbirth. This allowance is paid at the same rate as sickness cash benefit, i.e. 90% of taxable income. Economically non-active persons (housewives etc.) are entitled to a minimum daily allowance which amounted to 37 SKR in 1984. Parents can choose who will stay at home with the child, but both are entitled to cash benefits for 10 days in connection with delivery. The mother is entitled to draw parental allowance for a period of up to 60 days prior to delivery.

In addition, a special parental allowance (*särskild föräldrapenning*) is payable for another 180 days, if the mother/father abstains from work to take care of the child. One parent, however, can draw only half of this special benefit, and parents are thus obliged to share in the care of their child. For the first 90 days the benefit is payable at the same rate as sickness cash benefit (see above) and for the remaining period as flat-rate benefit (37 SKR in 1984). The special parental benefit may be drawn at any time between the birth of a child and the end of his first year at school.

Parental benefit for temporary child care (*föräldrapenning vid tillfällig vård av barn*), which is equal to the parent's sickness cash benefit, is payable for a period of up days per year, if a parent has to stay away from work in order to look after a sick child under the age of 12.

Parental insurance (*föräldraförsäkring*) also covers adoptive or foster parents. They are entitled to parental allowances for a maximum of 180 days when they adopt a child under the age of 10, and they are also entitled to draw parental benefits for temporary child care.

Parental benefits constitute taxable income and thus qualify for the supplementary pension scheme. The financing and administration of parental insurance forms part of the health insurance scheme (see above).

4. Housing allowances for families

In the Swedish account of social expenditure, rent allowances are included under the heading of Families and Children. For the institutional regulations, however, see under Housing (Section VIII).

5. Orphans' pensions

See under Pensions above.

6. Educational allowances

Between the ages of 16 and 19, pupils in lower and upper secondary schools are entitled to educational allowances (*förlängt barnbidrag/studiebidrag*) for nine months per year (or less if the duration of the courses is shorter). The study allowance consists of a general allowance equal to the general child allowance and payable to all pupils, and a special income-tested educational allowance which equals the housing allowance. There are also travel and accommodation allowances for pupils studying away from home, in addition to special means-tested study grants and repayable loans. At the age of 20 pupils become entitled to study loans (see under Education).

Services

Institutional child care is generally organized as a municipal social service. The first state support for day-care centres was approved by parliament in 1944. The child minding sector has grown immensely (especially since the mid-1960s). In 1982 there were more than 120,000 places in day-care centres for about 17% of all children under school age. The fees are relatively low: in 1980, ca. 5,000 SKR per year out of a ca. 40,000 SKR total costs per place. Another form of child minding is family day care. The municipalities hire child minders who take one or more children into their own homes for day care. About 90,000 children are in family day care. Temporary home help is provided by the municipalities for families in the event of illness, childbirth or other conditions in which assistance is required.

In addition, a variety of public child and family welfare services are offered, such as a family counselling service, a mental welfare service for children and young people, school welfare officers and psychologists, juvenile homes, etc. Children with unacceptable home conditions can be placed in private foster homes or in public children homes.

Most municipalities provide free school meals for pupils in comprehensive schools. School books and the school health service (see Section II, Health services) are also provided free of charge.

Core laws

1937
Maternity allowances through voluntary sickness insurance, special assistance to non-insured mothers; advance maintenance payments; income-tested child allowances for widows and invalidity pensioners.

1947 (no. 529)
Effective from 1948; introduced general child allowances without means-test up to the age of 16; municipal housing allowances for families with children (income-tested).

1954 (no. 266)
Effective from 1955; compulsory maternity insurance coordinated with sickness insurance.

1964 (nos. 143, 400-2)
New and extended law covering allowances payable in advance; study loans and assistance for children between 16 and 20 in full-time education.

1968 (nos. 425-6)
Extended rights to housing allowances for families with children, low-income families and single persons.

1972 (no. 47)
Considerably raised housing allowances.

1973 (no. 915)
Effective from 1974; replaced maternity insurance with parental insurance.

VI Social assistance

Income maintenance

Prior to 1982, means-tested public assistance providing cash benefits was regulated by a separate law. Nowadays, social assistance forms a part of 'individual and family assistance' (see Section V). In 1981, expenditure on social assistance amounted to slightly more than one billion SKR or less than 1% of public social expenditure and was negligible in relation to GDP.

During 1981 social assistance was given to 351,780 relief recipients (this concept refers to all persons in a family in receipt of social assistance, irrespective of whether the whole family or only one of its members has been assisted), 125,970 of whom were children under the age of 16. In that year social assistance costs amounted to 1,180 million SKR equivalent to 3,354 SKR per relief recipient.

Social assistance is the last instance for securing income maintenance. According to the Social Assistance Act municipalities are responsible for providing maintenance for those who, due to illness, childhood or old age are unable to maintain themselves. This assistance corresponds to need and is thus means-tested.

There are two statutory forms of social assistance: mandatory assistance and voluntary assistance, the latter being given on grounds decided by the local municipal council, or in accordance with what the local social welfare committee deems necessary.

Core laws

1918
Municipalities obliged to provide poor relief; they had been obliged to provide poor relief previously by a law of 1847, but this obligation was withdrawn again in 1871.

1956 (no. 2)
Social Assistance Act: effective from 1957; replaced 1918 Poor Relief Act; two forms of assistance introduced: mandatory assistance due to illness, childhood, old age or work incapacity, and voluntary assistance according to decisions made by local councils or social welfare committees.

1980 (no. 620)
Social Service Act: effective from 1982; replaced Social Assistance Act, Child Care Act and Temperance Act.

VII Education

In 1981, public expenditure on education amounted to approximately 42 billion SKR or 7% of GDP.

Expenditure on education in 1981, in million SKR

		%
Compulsory school system	13 538	32.1
Integrated upper secondary school system	4 538	10.7
Other expenditure[a]	9 437	22.3
Administration	1 354	3.2
Adult education	2 221	5.3
County council education[b]	1 692	4.0
Higher education	5 054	12.0
Student support[c]	4 396	10.4
Total	42 230	100.0

Source: Statistics Sweden, *Kommunernas finanser 1981*, (SOS), and Ministry of Finance, *The Swedish Budget 1981/82*.

[a] Mainly building costs but also school transport and, to a much lesser extent, extra mural activities, e.g. music school, etc.

[b] Mainly nursing courses formally in the upper secondary school system (but not included in that expenditure figure) and some support to folk high schools, otherwise counted under adult education in the table.

[c] The main part of student support consists of interest-subsidized long-term study loans. According to the state budget more than half a billion SKR were repaid in 1981.

The Swedish education system consists of a compulsory pre-school, comprehensive school, upper secondary school, higher tertiary education system (universities, vocational colleges etc.), folk high school system, municipal adult education, and voluntary adult educational associations.

As from 1975 the municipalities will be obliged to offer pre-school for all six-year olds and five-year olds with special needs. It may be run on a half-day basis for children from the age of five, but is otherwise fulltime. At both the national and local levels, pre-schools come under the jurisdiction of the health and welfare authorities, i.e. they do not form a part of the regular school system (see child minding Section V, services). The nine-year comprehensive school is compulsory for pupils aged 7-16. It includes a lower primary level (grades 1-3), an upper primary level (grades 4-6) and a lower secondary level (grades 7-9). The comprehensive system covers approximately one million pupils.

For students aged 16-20 there is an integrated upper secondary school. It is non-compulsory but 85-90% of all young people continue from the comprehensive school to the upper secondary school. It consists of three sectors (arts and social studies, science and technical studies, and commercial and economic studies) divided into 22 'study lines' requiring two, three of four years of study. The upper secondary school system covers approximately 250,000 students.

The higher education system - universities and colleges - covers approximately 150,000 students. Study programmes are of different lengths, from one semester (single courses which may be parts of a full study programme) up to six years. Of the total student population, approximately 10,000 are post-graduate students studying for a doctorate.

The folk high schools are mainly residential and for students aged 18 and above. They take 15,000 students each year in courses lasting more than 30 weeks. An average of 100,000 persons take part in shorter courses.

Municipal adult education provides instruction according to the standard school curriculum (mainly the lower secondary level at the comprehensive school and the upper secondary school). Nearly 300,000 students over the age of 20 take part in this kind of education.

The voluntary adult educational associations operate study circles (particularly in the evenings) in cooperation with companies, trade unions, political parties and other voluntary associations, and caters for approximately two million participants each year.

In addition to the above, there are a few private schools, but their role is negligible. Nearly 100,000 persons take part in labour market training (job retraining for adults) (see section IV, services).

Benefits in kind include free schooling, school health and dental care programmes, free school meals, transportation and teaching materials. Cash benefits include study grants (see Section V, educational allowances), and interest-subsidized study loans. University students and students over 18 are entitled to study loans from a separate state authority (*Centrala Studiestöds*, CSN). The combined study loan and grant amounted to 142% of the base amount or 28, 826 SKR in 1984.

Financing

The main part of the school system is financed by the state through general taxation. A smaller proportion is financed by the municipalities through municipal taxation.

The folk high schools, voluntary adult education associations and private schools are heavily subsidized by the state and receive contributions from participants, various organizations and other sources.

Administration

The compulsory comprehensive school, upper secondary school and municipal adult education are the responsibility of the local authorities. At the national level this part of the school system comes under the jurisdiction of the National Board of Education (*Skolöverstyrelsen*, SÖ), with supervisory regional bodies (*länsskolnämnd*).

Higher education is administered by the state and operated by the National Board of Universities and Colleges (*Universitets- och högskoleämbetet*, UHÄ).

Core laws

1842
Introduced compulsory schooling.

1950 (no. 549)
Ten-year experimental period established to build up a nine-year compulsory comprehensive school to replace the old parallel system.

1955 (nos. 503-4)
State subsidies to municipally organized vocational schools.

1958 (nos. 478-80)
State subsidies to folk high schools.

1962 (no. 319)
Final decision on nine-year compulsory comprehensive school; implemented over a ten-year period.

1964 (no. 899)
Effective from 1966; revised upper secondary school; introduced special preparatory vocational school (*fackskola*) to complement the high school (*gymnasium*).

1964 (nos. 461-2)
Expanded higher education; new decentralized universities and colleges.

1967
Municipal adult education (*vuxenutbildning*) instituted.

1969 (nos. 326-33)
Reformed universities; new study lines and 'open' admission for persons with a five-year work record and certain formal qualifications.

1970 (no. 290)
Effective from 1971; in upper secondary school system '*gymnasium*', '*fackskola*' and vocational '*yrkesskola*' integrated to form one school with three sectors (arts and social science, technical and natural sciences, economic and commercial).

1975 (no. 389)
Established free admission to universities.

1977 (no. 218)
Effective from July 1977; various professional colleges and some secondary school

study programmes integrated with traditional universities to form a unified higher educational system.

1977 (no. 551)
Reformed folk high school.

VIII Housing

In 1981, public expenditure and tax credits for housing amounted to more than 30 billion SKR or 5% of GDP.

Housing expenditure in 1981, in million SKR

		%
Housing allowances, of which:	5 456	18.3
for pensioners (see Section I)	3 805	12.8
for families, etc. (see Section V)	1 651	5.5
Interest subsidies	7 100	23.9
Housing loans[a]	5 700	19.2
Tax deductions	11 500	38.6
Total	29 756	100.0

[a] Long-term loans which are not a proper expenditure item; repayments amounted to over one billion SKR in 1981, according to the State Revenue Report.

Source: Ministry of Finance, *The Swedish Budget 1981/82.*

Public involvement in housing increased heavily during the Second World War: housing construction and the housing market came almost entirely under public control. Through interest-free state loans and interest subsidies, housing construction was maintained throughout the war and rents were protected from general increases in living costs by means of general rent controls. Despite this, there was a serious housing shortage after the war, thus both state housing loans and rent control became part of the national housing policy outlined in the immediate postwar period. The regulation of rents was gradually phased-out from 1968 to 1974 when rent control was abolished and replaced by a principle of 'use-value' for rents in municipally owned houses.

In addition to different forms of physical planning, controls and regulations at all levels of public authority, housing policy entails the following measures of economic support: subsidies for housing construction, tax deductions for interest paid on housing loans, and housing allowances to subsidize rents for low-income earners.

The policy of promoting housing construction by granting low-interest loans has continued since the Second World War. Over 90% of all newly constructed housing is subsidized by the state through loans and interest allowances. State loans cover at least 70% of the costs of new houses and dwellings, and up to 100% of municipal rented appartments. The role played by private loans and savings is extremely limited.

In 1981, over six billion SKR in the state budget were reserved for loans, and interest subsidy to state loans amounted to over eight billion SKR.

The state also supports the construction of owner-occupied one-family houses, not only through loans and interest allowances, but also by tax deductions for parts of the remaining interest expenses. Consequently house-owners receive an annual extra subsidy for their housing expenses via their tax returns.

As mentioned earlier, persons living on pensions, families (mainly with children) living in rented or owner-occupied dwellings and other low-income earners are entitled to income-tested housing allowances. In 1980, over 300,000 families with children, almost 800,000 pensioners and more than 60,000 other households received housing allowances. In 1981 the total cost for housing allowances amounted to over five billion SKR.

Public housing policy is financed by the state (loans, interest subsidies and part of housing allowances), and by the municipalities (housing allowances primarily), out of general taxation. Non-taxation or tax deduction are also used as an instrument.

The central authority for the supply of housing and housing loans is the National Housing Board (*bostadsstyrelsen*). On a municipal level the executive committee (*kommunstyrelsen*) is responsible for planning in general, and the social welfare committee (*socialnämnden*) is in charge of housing allowances.

Core laws

1935
First Law; state subsidies for construction of appartment houses for families with three or more children, combined with housing allowances for families with more than two children living in these houses.

1946 (nos. 551, 523)
Effective from 1947; state loans for construction of dwellings and owner-occupied one-family houses combined with subsidized interests.

1947 (no. 529)
Effective from 1948; housing allowances for families with children.

1952 (no. 396)
Effective from 1954; housing allowances for pensioners.

1967 (no. 552)
Effective from 1968; new type of state loan for housing construction replaced 1947 system; partly loans with a different, future-oriented, subsidization.

1968 (nos. 425-6)
Effective from 1969; transformed housing allowances for families with children.

1973 (no. 379)
Effective from 1974; raised housing allowances for families with children and extended them to other low-income groups.

1974 (nos. 946-7)
Effective from 1975; parity loans replaced by new type of subsidized construction loan.

1975 (no. 1080)
Rent control abolished.

Bibliography

Contents

I General contributions

1.1 General treatises on social policy

BAGGE, Gösta: Socialpolitik (Social Policy). Stockholm, Socialinstitutet, 1931. Collected lectures and seminar papers by the first professor of social policy (and political economy), later chairman of the Conservative Party.

HOLGERSSON, Leif: Socialvård (Social Services). Jönköping, Tiden, 1981. Traces the historical development of the Poor Law.

HOLGERSSON, Leif, LINDBLOM, Paul: Utvecklingstendenser och problem i socialpolitiken (Development Tendencies and Problems in Social Policy). Lund, Studentlitteratur, 1974. A general exposition of the main features of present-day Swedish social policy.

HOLMBERG, Per: Socialpolitikens teori och praktik (Theory and Practice in Social Policy). Stockholm, Prisma, 1978. A discussion of various theoretical approaches to welfare state development combined with an evaluation of the main welfare programmes.

KORPI, Walter, OLSSON, Sven E., STENBERG, Sten-Åke: Svensk socialpolitik (Swedish Social Policy). *In* SÖNDERSTEN, Bo (ed.): Svensk ekonomi (The Swedish Economy). Borås, Raben and Sjögren, 1982, 39 p. A theoretical and empirical discussion of the development of social policy in Sweden with special reference to the goal of equality.

LINDBLOM, Paul: Socialpolitiken och den problematiska välfärden (Social Policy and Welfare Problems). Stockholm, AWE-Gebers, 1982. A description of the framework of welfare programmes and a discussion of current problems in social policy in Sweden.

MYRDAL, Gunnar: Socialpolitikens dilemma (The Dilemma of Social Policy). Stockholm, Spektrum, 1932. First outline of Myrdal's perspectives on population policy and social reforms.

NASENIUS, Jan, RITTER, Kerstin: Delad välfärd (Shared Welfare). Stockholm, Esselte, 1974. A description of the historical development of social policy from the 1870s to the mid-1970s.

OTTOSSON, Bertil et al.: Den svenska sociallagstiftningen (The Swedish Social Laws). Malmö, Wahlström and Widstrand, 1974. Outline of the historical development of the Poor Laws from the Middle Ages to the present from a critical leftist position.

SJÖSTRÖM, Kurt: Socialpolitiken i det kapitalistiska samhället (Social Policy in Capitalist Society). Stockholm, Arbetarkultur, 1974. A critical discussion of the historical role of social policy with a final chapter on the 1974 State Commission on Social Services.

STEFFEN, Gustaf: 'Socialpolitikens förutsättningar och uppgifter' (Conditions and goals of social policy). *Sociala studier*, III, 1906, Stockholm. An early sociological contribution to the theory of social policy and social problems.

SÖDERSTEN, Bo: Socialpolitik och ekonomisk politik (Social Policy and Economic Policy). Karlkrona, Raben and Sjögren, 1973.

1.2 General histories of social policy

ELMER, Åke: Från fattigsverige till välfärdsstaten (From 'Poor Sweden' to the Welfare State). Stockholm, Aldus, 1965. A popular description of the historical development from the 1870s to the present.

HÖIJER, Karl J.: Svensk socialpolitisk historia (A History of Social Policy in Sweden). Malmö, Norstedts, 1952. A detailed account of law-making on social policy from the eighteenth century to the first half of the twentieth century.

SAMUELSSON, Kurt: Från stormakt till välfärdsstat (From Great Power to Welfare State). Stockholm, Raben and Sjögren, 1968. A general account of the historical transformation of Sweden from the seventeenth century to the present date with special reference to welfare state developments.

1.3 Accounts of specific periods

BAUDE, Annika (ed.): Från fattigdom till välfärd - en studie i svensk jämlikshetspolitik (From Poverty to Welfare - a Study in Politics of Equality in Sweden). Stockholm, Publica/Liber, 1978. Covers some of the main areas of social policy and tries to evaluate the contribution of 44 years of Social Democratic government (1932-1976).

BERGGREN, H., NILSSON, G.: Liberal socialpolitik (Liberal Social Policy). Uppsala, Almquist and Wicksell, 1965. Study of the parliamentary and legislative development of the Poor Laws during the period 1853-1884.

BOALT, G., BERGRYD, U.: Centralförbundet för socialt arbete (The Central Association of Social Work). Karlskrona, CSA, 1974. A sociological analysis of the first nationwide civil organization propagating and administering both public and private social work.

BOALT, G. et al.: De socialpolitiska centralförbunden (Central Associations of Social Policy). Karlskrona, CSA, 1975. A sociological analysis of the organizational efforts of the Central Organization of Social Work during the first two decades of the twentieth century.

BOALT, G. et al.: Ett genombrott - festskrift till Gustav Möllers 60-årsdag (A Breakthrough - In commemoration of the 60th birthday of Gustav Möller). Stockholm, Tiden, 1944. A collection of articles describing the development of the first twelve years of social policy under Social Democratic government with Gustav Möller as responsible minister (1932-1944).

JÄGERSKIÖLD, S.: 'Från fattigvård till socialhjälp' (From poor relief to social help), *Juridisk Tidskrift*, 1955. Stockholm. A study of in the development of social laws between the eighteenth century and the first part of the twentieth century.

JÄGERSKIÖLD, S.: Allmosa eller socialförsäkring (Charity or Social Insurance). Uppsala, Acta Universitatis Upsaliensis Studie Juridica, 1977. A comparison and discussion of the principles behind social insurance and public assistance.

MARKLUND, S.: Klass, stat och socialpolitik (Class, State, and Social Policy). Lund, Arkiv, 1982. A historical and empirical analysis of the development of social insurance in Sweden during the Social Democratic era, and a comparative study of this development in nine Western countries 1930-1975.

MONTGOMERY, A.: Svensk socialpolitik under 1800-talet (Swedish Social Policy during the Nineteenth Century). Stockholm, Kooperative förbundets förlag, 1934. An economic history contribution to the understanding of wealth, poverty and legislative development during the agrarian and first part of the industrial revolution.

ONLIN, B. et al.: Social Problems and Policies in Sweden. *The Annals of the American Academy of Political and Social Science* Philadelphia, 1938. The preface states: "The attention of the world is more and more focused on the intelligent manner in which Sweden is earnestly and successfully striving to achieve social justice and to make democracy work in an age when the democratic ideal is being boldly challenged by totalitarian ideologies. It is the aim of this volume of the Annals to review the legislation and to describe the policies, agencies, and institutions which have been created to deal with social problems in Sweden".

STÅHL, R.: De fattige (The Poor). Unpublished dissertation. Uppsala, Institute of Sociology, 1974. A sociological analysis of the development of poor relief, particularly during the first part of the nineteenth century, but also taking into account later observations of the number of recipients.

THERBORN, G. et al.: 'Sweden before and after social Democracy'. *Acta Sociologica*, 1978 supplement. A discussion of the impact of social democracy on social policy in the twentieth century.

1.4 Introductions into the system of social policies

ELMŒR, Å.: Svensk socialpolitik (Swedish Social Policy). Lund, Gleerups, 1981. A description of the current schemes and the scope and goals of legislation in social policy with an international perspective.

FOLKSAM: Vår trygghet 1983 (Our Security 1983). Folksams sociala råd. Published annually, Stockholm, 1982. Description of the social security schemes and related programmes in Sweden.

1.5 Reports by investigating committees or experts

ARBETSMARKNADSDEPARTEMENTET (Ministry of Labour): En allmän arbetslöshetsförsäkring (A General Unemployment Insurance), SOU 1978. Stockholm, 1978. Parliamentary committee discussion on the possibilites of integrating trade union unemployment insurance with national insurance.

BOSTADSDEPARTEMENTET (Ministry of Housing): Bostadsbidragen (Housing allowances), SOU 1982:58. Stockholm, 1982. An investigation made by a state commission on housing costs and social welfare.

INRIKESDEPARTEMENTET (Ministry of Domestic Affairs): Dew svenska köpkraftsfördelningen (The Distribution of Purchasing Power in Sweden), SOU 1971: 39. Stockholm, 1971. A report from the State Commission on Low Incomes analysing the distribution of income and wealth, particularly among low-income earners.

SOCIALDEPARTEMENTET (Ministry of Health and Social Affairs): En allmän socialförsäkring (A General Social Insurance), SOU 1979:94. Stockholm, 1979. Report prepared by the social policy coordination committee on the further integration of various social insurance schemes.

SOCIALDEPARTEMENTET: Socialvården - mål och medel (Social Services - Goals and Means), SOU 1974:39, 40. Stockholm, 1974. Evaluation of the social services provided by local government and the central state.

SOCIALDEPARTEMENTET: Socialtjänst och Socialförsäkringstillägg (Social Services and Supplementary Social Insurance Benefit), SOU 1977:40. Stockholm, 1977. Reform proposals by the State Commission on Social Policy.

SOCIALDEPARTEMENTET: SOFT (Supplementary Social Insurance Benefit), Ds S 1980:1. Stockholm, 1980. A report from a consultative group within the Swedish Ministry of Health and Social Affairs suggesting a new, complementary benefit in the Swedish social security system.

1.6 Social science interpretations, evaluations, analyses

JOHANSSON, S.: Om levnadsnivåundersökningen (On the Standard of Living Investigation). Stockholm, Allmänna förlaget, 1970. A presentation of the background and goals of the standard of living investigation sponsored by the Ministry of the Interior.

JOHANSSON, S.: Mot en teori för social rapportering (Towards a Theory of Social Reports). Stockholm, Swedish Institute of Social Research, 1979. An elaboration of the standard of living approach and social indicators.

1.7 Policy proposals and debates

BÖÖK, I.: 'Staten och socialpolitik' (State and social policy). *Zenit*, 62, 1979, Lund. A contribution to the debate between Persson and Sjöström discussing the role of social policy in everyday life as an aspect of state expansionism during the postwar era.

Ekonomisk debatt, 7, 1979: Following a translation of an article by Victor R. Fuchs originally published in *The Public Interest* four Swedish experts made comments and suggestions regarding Swedish health policy: BIÖRCK, G.: 'Sjukvården - ett ekonomiskt eller humanitärt problem?' (Sick care - An economic or humanitarian problem?). BORGENHAMMAR, E.: 'För en offensiv hälsopolitik' (For an active health policy). JÖNSSON, B.: 'Sjukvärdsutgifter i en internationell jämförelse' (Costs of sick care in a comparative perspective). STÅHL, I.: 'Sijukvården - problem och lösningar' (Sick care - problems and solutions).

FÖRSÄKRINGSKASSEFÖRBUNDET: För en allmän och aktiv socialförsäkring (For a General and Active Social Insurance). Stockholm, Försäkringskasseförbundet and Försäkringsanställdas förbund, 1982. A reform proposal from a trade union and the organization of the independent social insurance authorities.

HOLLANDER, A.: 'Kvinnoperspektiv på socialpolitiken' (A female perspective of social policies). *Sociologisk Forskning*, 1977: 3. An analysis of the relation between changes in the role of women in production and in the home with changes in the social security system.

JOHANSSON, S.: 'Förslag till revision av familjepolitiken' (A proposal for a revision of family policy). *Tiden*, Nos. 9-10, 1980. A critique of the present family policy adopted by the Social Democratic party in the mid-1970s, followed by several critical comments in *Tiden* during 1981.

LANDSORGANISATIONEN: Fackföreningsrörelsen och välfärdsstaten (The Trade Union Movement and the Welfare State). Stockholm, LO, 1986. A discussion of the current welfare system and possible reforms written by the central trade union organization.

MYRDAL, A., MYRDAL, G.: Kris i befolkningsfrågan (Crisis in the Population Question). Stockholm, Tiden Bonniers folkbibliotek, 1934. A discussion of population trends and possible social reforms inspiring public debates and reform proposals in the 1930s and 1940s.

PERSSON, G.: 'Skall sjukvården privatiseras?' (Should sick care be privatized?). *Ekonomisk debatt*, 4, 1980. A critique of the perspectives outlined in the above-mentioned issue of *Ekonomisk debatt*

PERSSON, G.: 'Socialpolitiken, marknaden och marxismen' (Social Policy, market, and marxism)'. *Zenit*, 58, 1978, Lund. A critique of the general Marxist approach to social policy under capitalism and in particular of the contributions by Kurt Sjöström (see 1.1).

PERSSON, G.: 'Till socialpolitikens försvar' (In defence of Social Policy)'. *Zenit*, 65, 1980, Lund. A reply to Sjöström in particular and also to Böök.

SAP-LO ARBETSGRUPP FÖR JÄMSTÄLLDHETSFRÅGOR: Jämlikhet (Equality). Borås, Tiden, 1969. The general reform programme for the 1970s by the Joint Committee of the Trade Union Confederation and the Social Democratic Party.

SJÖSTRÖM, K.: 'Socialpolitiken och socialismen' (Social policy and socialism). *Zenit*, 60, 1969, Lund. A reply to Persson's critique from a Leninist position emphasizing limited possibilities of working class influence in the bourgeois state including social policy under capitalism.

STÅHL, I.: 'Trygghetssverige - ett genomgripande reformforslag' (Security/Sweden - A proposal of complete reform). *In* WESTHOLM, C. J.: Skapande eller bevakande Sverige, Vol. 2. Stockholm, Svenska arbetsgivareföreningen, 1979. A reform proposal presented by an independent expert and published by the central employers organization.

TJÄNSTEMÄNNENS CENTRALORGANISATION: Socialpolitiskt program (Social Policy Programme). Stockholm, TCO, 1982. Suggestions concerning social security and services presented by the central white-collar trade union confederation.

1.8 Opinion polls

ZETTERBERG, Hans L.: 'En socialpolitik för åttiotalet' (A social policy for the 1980s). *In* WESTHOLM, C. J. (ed.): Skapande eller bevande Sverige, Vol. 2. Stockholm, Svenska Arbetsgivareföreningen, 1979. A presentation of survey data on attitudes towards social policy and a discussion of the history and future of the Swedish welfare state.

1.9 Sources of statistics or institutional regulations

NORDISK STATISTISK SKRIFTSERIE: Social trygghet i de nordiska länderna (Social Security in the Nordic Countries). Published every four years since 1948, Stockholm, Nordiska socialstatistikkommitten. A comparative outline of social security, welfare regulations and relevant statistics on expenditure and financing in the five Nordic countries (Denmark, Finland, Iceland, Norway and Sweden).

RIKSFÖRSÄKRINGSVERKET: Allmän försäkring (General Insurance). Published annually since 1963, Stockholm. Provides statistics particularly on pensions and sickness insurance (expenditure, financing, benefits and beneficiaries), and information on the rules governing the system.

STATISTISKA CENTRALBYRÅN: Socialvården (Social Services). Published annually, Stockholm. Statistics related to the social services (child care, disablement, family welfare, drug abuse, criminality, services for the elderly etc.), particularly municipal welfare but also including an overview of total public welfare expenditure.

1.10 Major periodicals

Acta sociologica: Published quarterly, Oslo, Nordic Sociological Association. A general journal for social science research which frequently publishes articles on welfare state topics.

Ekonomisk debatt (Economic Debate): Published eight times a year, Stockholm. A general journal on economic matters which regularly takes welfare state problems into account.

Social försäkring (Social Insurance), Stockholm, 12 issues per year. Published by Försäkringskasseförbundet. Primarily a forum for information and new developments in the field of social insurance.

Socialnytt (Social News): Published ten times a year, Stockholm. Published by the National Board of Health and Welfare covering areas of responsibility of the Board.

Socialt arbete (Social Work): Published ten times a year, Stockholm. Independent journal supported by trade unions and cooperatives in the field of social policy concentrating on social conditions and welfare policies.

Sociologisk forskning (Sociological Research): Quarterly journal published by the Swedish Sociological Association, frequently with articles on social and political issues.

Statsvetenskaplig tidskrift (Journal of Political Science): Published quarterly, Lund. General journal for policy research and political science.

Svensk tidskrift (Swedish Review): Published eight times a year, Stockholm. Published by the Conservative Party covering politics in general including debates on welfare state issues.

Tiden (The Time): Published ten times a year, Stockholm. The main intellectual journal in the Social Democratic press regularly discussing welfare policies.

Zenit: Published five times a year, Lund. Independent left journal which often publishes analyses of social problems and state intervention.

II Single programmes or aspects

2.1 Pensions

BERGLIND, H.: Pensionering i ett internationellt perspektiv (Old Age in an International Perspective). Stockholm, Arbetsgruppen för studiet av de äldres problem, 1980. A Swedish report to an international investigation on old age.

ELMER, Å.: Folkpensioneringen i Sverige (The People's Pension in Sweden). Lund, Gleerups, 1960. An historical and sociological analysis of the introduction of the universal pension scheme 1884-1948.

HEDSTROM, P.: Förtidspension - välfärd eller ofärd? (The Disablement Pension - Welfare or Mischief). Stockholm, Institutet for social forskning, 1980. An analysis of the causes and effects of disablement pension since 1968.

MOHLIN, B.: Tjänstepensionsfrågan (The Superannuation Pension Question). Göteborg, Akademiförlaget, 1965. An analysis by a political scientist of the debate and decision on the introduction of a superannuation pension in Sweden in the 1950s.

2.2 Health

BORGENHAMMAR, E.: Hälsans pris (The Price of Health). Stockholm, SNS, 1981. An examination of sick care and health policy costs arguing for more preventative care.

BROBERG, R.: Så formades trygghet (The Formation of Social Security). Stockholm, Försäkringskasseförbundet, 1973. A description of the introduction and development of general sickness insurance 1946-1972.

FÜRTH, T.: Folkrörelse- eller myndighetstradition (Social Movement or Government Tradition). Stockholm, Arbetslivscentrum, 1980. An historical analysis of the organizational principles governing social insurance in Sweden.

HEIDENHEIMER, A.J., ELVANDER, N.: The Shaping of the Swedish Health System. London, Croom Helm, 1980. A discussion of the development of medical care and health insurance in the Scandinavian context and comments on the policy reforms of the 1970s.

2.3 Unemployment

EDEBALK, P.G.: Arbetslöshetsförsäkringsdebatten (The Unemployment Insurance Debate). Lund, The Economic History Association, 1975. Deals with the debates concerning unemployment insurance in Sweden from 1892 up to the introduction of state support and control of trade union unemployment relief funds.

ERICI, B., ROTH, N.: Arbetslöshetsförsäkringen i Sverige 1935-1980 (The Unemployment Insurance in Sweden 1930-1980). Stockholm, Arbetslöshetskassornas samorganisation, 1981. A documentation of the development of unemployment insurance after the introduction of state subsidies published by the coordinating committee of the trade union unemployment insurance societies.

FURÅKER, B.: Stat och arbetsmarknad (State and Labour Market). Lund, Arkiv, 1976. A Marxist analysis of state intervention in labour market mobility during the postwar era.

ROTHSTEIN, B.: 'AMS som socialdemokratisk reformbyråkrati' (The National Labour Market Board as a Social Democratic reform bureaucracy), *Arkiv*, 18, Lund. An analysis of the establishment of trade union influence on recruitment for the National Labour Market Board.

ROTHSTEIN, B.: 'Från det svenska systemet till den svenska modellen' (From the Swedish system to the Swedish model). *Arkiv* 23-24, 1982, Lund. An analysis of the relationship between post-war active labour market policy in Sweden and the pre-war system of relief work.

STEIGER, O.: 'Bakgrunden till socialdemokratins krispolitik' (The background to the Social Democratic crisis policy). *Arkiv* 1, 1972, Stockholm. A discussion of the intellectual formation of the 'new economic policy' in Sweden during the 1930s.

UNGA, N.: Socialdemokratin och arbetslöshetsfrågan 1912-1934 (Social Democracy and the Unemployment Question 1912-1934). *Arkiv*, 1976, Lund. An analysis of trade union influence on the formation of a 'new economic policy' in Sweden.

ÖHMAN, B.: Svensk arbetsmarknadspolitik 1900-1947 (Swedish Labour Market Policy 1900-1947). Halmstad, Prisma, 1970.

2.4 Accidents

KELLMAN, S.: Regulating America, Regulating Sweden. Cambridge, MIT Press, 1981. A comparative analysis of present day occupational safety and health policies in the United States and Sweden from an evaluation research approach.

MOBERG, K., et al.: Från yrkesfarelag till arbetsmiljölag (From Occupational Safety Law to Work Environment Law). Lund, Studentlitteratur, 1982. An historical analysis of state intervention in the work environment since the beginning of industrialization in Sweden to the present.

NORDFORS, L.: Makten, hälsan och vinsten (Power, Profit and Health). Lund Studentlitteratur, 1985. An analysis of the development from occupational safety to occupation health focussing on the introduction of the 1978 Work Environment Act.

SELLBERG, H.: Staten och arbetarskyddet (State and Workers' Protection). Uppsala, 1950. A political science analysis of social policy and state intervention in the factory system between 1850 and 1919.

2.5 Social assistance

GUSTAVSSON, B.: Socialhjälpens bestämningsfaktorer (Determinants of Poor Relief). Stockholm, Delegationen för social forskning, DSF-projekt 1983:1, 1983. A statistical analysis of the variations in municipal social assistance and the role of unemployment, pension levels etc.

KORPI, W.: Fattigdom i välfärden (Poverty in Welfare). Stockholm, Tiden, 1971. A description of social assistance in Sweden and analysis of the causes of poverty.

KORPI, W.: 'Social policy and poverty in postwar Sweden'. *Acta Sociologica*, 18: 2-3, 1975. A further discussion of trends in social assistance in Sweden and changes resulting from introduction of social policy reforms.

LUNDEQVIST, K.: 'Socialhjälpstagande - utveckling och orsaker 1945-1956' (Social relief recipients - development and causes 1945-1956). *Studies in Economic History*, 13, 1976, Uppsala. An analysis of the development of social assistance during the last ten years of the Poor Law before the introduction of the Social Assistance Law in 1956.

SZULKIN, R.: Socialhjälpsfrekvensen och dess bestämningfaktorer (The frequency of social assistance and its determinants). *Sociologisk forskning*, 18: 4, 1981. An analysis of the development of the social background of recipients and the causes of social assistance in the 1970s.

2.6 Family programmes

ABUKHANFUSA, K.: Beredskapsfamiljernas försörjning (The Provision for Draftees' Families). Stockholm, Liber, 1975. A discussion of the wartime family allowances and the living standard particularly among families who temporarily lost their principal income earner during the Second World War.

CERVIN, U.: 'Makarna Myrdal och befolkningsfrågan' (The Myrdals and the population question). *Meddelande från Historiska institutionen*, 10, 1976, Lund. A presentation of the discussion after the publication of the Myrdals 'Crisis in the Population Question'.

HATJE, A. K.: Befolkningsfrågan och välfärden (The Population Question and Social Welfare). Stockholm, Allmana forlaget, 1974. Traces the development of family welfare policy from the publication of Myrdal's book in the early 1930s to the introduction of general child allowances in the late 1940s.

2.7 Housing

FRANZEN, M., SANDSTEDT, E.: Grannskap och stadsplanering - om stat och byggande i efterkrigstidens Sverige (Neighbourhood and Townplaning - the State and Construction in Postwar Sweden). Uppsala, Acta Universitates Upsaliensis, 1981. A theoretical and historical analysis of public intervention in housing and local communities.

SANDELIN, B., SÖDERSTEN, B.: 'Bostadekonomi och bostadsförsörjning under efterkrigstiden' (Housing economy and housing supply in the postwar period). *In* SÖDERSTEN, B. (ed.), Svensk ekonomi. Borås, 1982. A study of the development of the housing market and housing subsidies in Sweden.

2.8 Education

ISLING, Å.: Kampen för och emot en demokratisk skola (The Struggle For and Against a Democratic School). Stockholm, Sober, 1980. A discussion of the historical development of general education in Sweden.

JOHANSSON, L.: Utbildning - empirisk del (Education - Empirical Part). Stockholm, Allmana forlaget, 1971. A report from the Low Income Commission on the distribution of educational resources among the Swedish population.

MARKLUND, S.: Från reform till reform (From Reform to Reform). Stockholm, Liber, 1980. An examination of the educational policy discussion in Sweden between 1950 and 1975, particularly covering the development of the comprehensive school system.

2.9 The public household

FORSMAN, A.: En teori om staten och de offentliga utgifterna (A Theory of the State and Public Expenditure). Uppsala, Almqvist and Wiksell, 1980. A short description of the expansion of the public sector during the postwar era, followed by an examination of various theories accounting for the development of government expenditure.

GUSTAFSSON, B. (ed): Den offentliga sektorns expansion - teori- och metodproblem (The Expansion of the Public Sector - Problems of Theory and Methods). Uppsala, Almqvist and Wiksell, 1976. A collection of essays from a seminar dealing with different aspects of the development of the public sector.

HÖÖK, E.: Den offentliga sektorns expansion (The Expansion of the Public Sector). Stockholm, Industrins utredningsinstitut, 1962. A detailed examination of the development of central and local government expenditure in Sweden between 1913 and 1958.

RODRIGUEZ, E.: Offentlig inkomstexpansion (Public Income Expansion). Uppsala, Gleerups, 1980. An analysis of the causes behind the development of public revenues in Sweden during the twentieth century.

TARSCHYS, D.: Den offentliga revolutionen (The Public Revolution). Falköping, Publica, 1978. A description and discussion of the development of the public sector in Sweden from the absolutist period up to the present era.

TARSCHYS, D.: Offentlig sektor i tillväxt (Growth in the Public Sector). Stockholm, SNS, 1975. A collection of essays dealing with various aspects of public sector development.

2.10 Public employment

INDUSTRIDEPARTEMENTET (Ministry of Industry): Offentlig verksamhet och regional välfärd (Public Activity and Regional Welfare), SOU 1980:6. Stockholm, Liber, 1980. An investigation of public employment in Sweden mainly during the last two decades.

III The impact of social programmes

3.1 Poverty

INGHE, G.: Fattiga i folkhemmet (Poor in the People's Home). Stockholm, Monografier utgivna av Stockholms kommunalforvaltning, 1960. An investigation of the standard of living among poor relief recipients.

INGHE, G., INGHE, M. B.: Den ofärdiga välfärden (Unachieved Welfare). Stockholm, Tiden, 1970. A critical examination of poverty in the Swedish welfare state.

JOHANSSON, S.: 'The level of living survey - a presentation'. *Acta Sociologica*, 1973:3. A presentation of the first level of living survey made by the Low Income Commission.

JOHANSSON, S: Välfärdsförändringar vid sidan av inkomster 1968-1974-1981 (Changes in Welfare Besides Income 1968-1974-1981). Stockholm, Institutet för socialforskning, 1981. A presentation of preliminary results from the third level of living survey in the light of the first and second surveys.

SUNDBOM, L.: De extremt lågavlönade (Extremely Low-Paid Employees). Stockholm, Allmänna förlaget, 1971. A report from the Low Income Commission.

3.2 Inequality and income distribution

SPÅNT, R.: Den svenska inkomstfördelningens utveckling (The Development of Income Distribution in Sweden). Uppsala, Alqvist and Wiksell, 1976. A picture of income distribution in Sweden, an identification of the factors underlying it and the elements of change.

SPÅNT, R.: Förmögenhetsfördelningen i Sverige (The Distribution of Wealth in Sweden). Falköping, Prisma, 1975. An investigation of tax statistics indicating the assets held by different financial institutions.

3.3 Economic effects of social programmes

BJÖRKLUND, A., HOLMLUND, B.: Arbetslöshetsersättningen i Sverige - motiv, regler och effekter (Unemployment Insurance Compensation in Sweden - Motives, Rules and Effects). Stockholm, Expertgruppen för studier i offentlig ekonomi, 1983. An investigation of the effects on labour market behaviour of persons being unemployed and receiving cash benefits from the unemployment insurance.

STAHLBERG, A. C.: Ålderspensionen i ATP (Old Age Pension in the Superannuation Pension System). Stockholm, Expertgruppen för studier i offentlig ekonomi, 1983. A critical discussion of the present distribution effects of the Swedish superannuation pension.

Appendix Tables

Contents

Table 1 Gross Domestic Product and Total Public Expenditure

Year	GDP (at market prices, in million SKR) at current prices	at constant (1975) prices	annual real growth rate	Deflators gross domestic product A	public expend. B	consumer price index C	Total public expenditure (in million SKR) at current prices	as % of GDP	at constant (1975) prices A	B	annual real growth rate	Year
1950	32 066	119 765		26.8		29.1	7 729	24.1	28 840			1950
1951	39 593	123 302	3.0	32.1		33.7					4.4	1951
1952	43 159	125 424	1.7	34.4		36.3	10 813	25.1	31 433			1952
1953	44 437	129 478	3.2	34.3		36.9					6.7	1953
1954	47 279	137 216	6.0	34.8		37.2	12 452	26.3	35 782			1954
1955	50 827	141 340	3.0	36.0		38.3					5.4	1955
1956	55 241	146 038	3.3	37.8		40.1	15 031	27.2	39 765			1956
1957	58 963	149 492	2.4	39.4		41.8					6.4	1957
1958	62 269	153 018	2.4	40.7		43.8	18 311	29.4	44 990			1958
1959	66 275	160 997	5.2	41.1		44.1					5.6	1959
1960	72 160	167 133	3.8	43.2		45.8	21 654	30.0	50 125			1960
1961	78 522	176 682	5.7	44.4	39.2	47.0					9.1	1961
1962	85 196	184 260	4.3	46.2	41.5	49.0	27 565	32.4	59 664	66 422		1962
1963	91 359	193 862	5.2	47.1	42.7	50.4					9.7	1963
1964	101 893	207 072	6.8	49.2	45.5	52.2	35 322	34.3	71 793	77 631		1964
1965	112 112	214 988	3.8	52.1	48.7	54.5					7.1	1965
1966	121 957	219 484	2.1	55.6	52.6	58.2	45 764	37.1	82 309	87 004		1966
1967	132 376	226 878	3.4	58.3	55.6	60.8					10.8	1967
1968	140 472	235 140	3.6	59.7	57.6	62.0	60 371	42.6	101 124	104 811		1968
1969	152 555	246 913	5.0	61.8	59.5	63.7					7.3	1969
1970	170 836	262 897	6.5	65.0	63.5	68.0	75 716	44.6	116 486	119 238		1970
1971	185 408	264 946	0.8	70.0	69.5	73.2					5.8	1971
1972	202 928	270 669	2.2	75.0	74.5	77.5	97 799	48.4	130 398	131 274		1972
1973	225 919	281 194	3.9	80.3	80.0	82.7					6.3	1973
1974	255 432	293 361	4.3	87.0	88.9	91.1	128 104	50.5	147 246	144 099		1974
1975	299 821	299 821	2.2	100.0	100.0	100.0					5.1	1975
1976	338 593	303 343	1.2	111.6	112.1	110.1	181 375	53.5	162 522	161 797		1976
1977	367 278	297 345	- 2.0	123.5	127.9	122.8					6.9	1977
1978	409 246	301 306	1.3	135.8	140.7	135.2	252 389	61.7	185 853	179 381		1978
1979	458 165	313 775	4.1	146.0	151.6	144.7					3.0	1979
1980	519 187	318 244	1.4	163.1		164.6	321 582	61.9	197 169			1980

Table 2 Public Expenditure by

Year	Purpose						Economic Function					Level of Government					Year
	Total exp. at curr. pr. in mill. SKR	Percent distribution					Total exp. at curr. pr. in mill. SKR	Percent distribution				Total exp. at curr. pr. in mill. SKR	Percent distribution				
		publ. adm.	de-fence	welfare	econ. serv.	other		subs./ transf.	final cons.	inter. on debt	capit. form.		central gov.	reg. gov.	local gov.	social insur.	
1950	7 729	9.4	17.0	47.2	16.6	9.8						7 729	29	6	41	23	1950
1951																	1951
1952	10 813	8.1	18.6	46.4	18.2	8.5											1952
1953																	1953
1954	12 452	8.3	18.4	49.0	15.6	8.8											1954
1955																	1955
1956	15 031	8.3	16.9	49.2	16.6	9.0											1956
1957																	1957
1958	18 311	8.5	15.2	50.6	16.6	9.1											1958
1959																	1959
1960	21 654	9.3	13.5	50.2	17.5	9.5						21 654	29	7	40	24	1960
1961							24 544	30.2	50.7	5.0	14.4						1961
1962	27 565	9.1	13.3	49.8	17.0	10.8	27 746	30.3	51.4	4.4	14.5						1962
1963							31 756	30.0	50.1	3.8	16.0						1963
1964	35 322	10.1	12.2	50.5	16.0	11.2	35 661	29.6	49.5	3.8	17.2						1964
1965							40 521	30.4	49.4	3.8	16.4						1965
1966	45 764	10.9	10.9	50.6	15.4	12.2	46 573	30.3	49.9	3.7	16.1						1966
1967							52 946	30.5	49.3	3.7	16.5						1967
1968	60 371	10.3	8.7	54.2	15.2	11.5	59 880	31.6	48.4	3.9	16.1						1968
1969							65 485	32.1	48.5	4.2	15.2						1969
1970	75 716	11.0	8.5	56.5	16.0	8.0	75 226	31.6	48.9	4.4	15.1	75 716	23	12	42	23	1970
1971							84 419	32.7	49.3	4.5	13.4						1971
1972	97 799	12.2	7.8	57.0	15.3	7.6	93 880	34.0	49.1	4.3	12.7						1972
1973							102 555	33.7	49.9	4.3	12.0						1973
1974	128 104	13.1	7.3	56.3	15.9	7.4	123 118	37.6	48.0	4.5	9.9						1974
1975							146 977	38.4	48.4	4.5	8.7						1975
1976	181 375	(13.6)	(6.4)	(56.1)	(16.2)	(7.8)	175 740	40.0	47.9	4.2	8.0	181 375	17	14	41	28	1976
1977							212 186	40.0	47.7	4.5	7.8						1977
1978	252 389	(14.3)	(5.9)	(55.1)	(16.4)	(8.2)	243 510	40.6	47.1	4.6	7.6	252 389	16	15	41	28	1978
1979							280 101	41.0	46.7	5.2	7.2						1979
1980	321 582	(13.2)	(4.5)	(61.1)	(12.8)	(8.4)	321 582	39.0	47.2	6.8	6.9						1980

Table 3

Social Expenditure

Year	At current prices (in million SKR)					As % of gross domestic product					As % of public expenditure					As % of social expenditure				Year
	Total	Income Maint.	Educa-tion	Health	Soc. serv.	Total	Income Maint.	Educa-tion	Health	Soc. serv.	Total	Income Maint.	Educa-tion	Health	Soc. serv.	Income Maint.	Educa-tion	Health	Soc. serv.	
1950	3 617	1 803	1 006	561	247	11.3	5.6	3.1	1.7	0.8	46.9	23.4	13.0	7.3	3.2	49.8	27.8	15.5	6.8	1950
1951		1 961		687	287		5.0		1.7	0.7										1951
1952	4 931	2 216	1 505	861	332	11.4	5.2	3.5	2.0	0.8	45.7	20.7	13.9	8.0	3.1	45.3	30.5	17.5	6.7	1952
1953		2 515		864	344		5.7		1.9	0.8										1953
1954	5 972	2 836	1 785	954	397	12.6	6.0	3.8	2.0	0.8	48.0	22.8	14.3	7.7	3.2	47.5	29.9	16.0	6.6	1954
1955		3 049		1 346	427		6.0		2.6	0.8										1955
1956	7 489	3 318	2 160	1 469	548	13.6	6.0	3.9	2.7	1.0	49.6	22.1	14.3	9.8	3.6	44.2	28.8	19.6	7.3	1956
1957		3 620		1 727	633		6.1		2.9	1.1										1957
1958	9 323	4 035	2 731	1 882	675	15.0	6.5	4.4	3.0	1.1	50.9	22.0	14.9	10.3	3.7	43.3	29.3	20.2	7.2	1958
1959		4 270		2 005	821		6.4		3.0	1.2										1959
1960	10 976	4 623	3 282	2 206	865	15.2	6.4	4.5	3.1	1.2	50.7	21.3	15.2	10.2	4.0	42.1	29.9	20.1	7.9	1960
1961		4 927		2 463	932		6.3		3.1	1.2										1961
1962	13 684	5 490	4 268	2 854	1 072	16.1	6.4	5.0	3.3	1.3	49.7	19.9	15.5	10.4	3.9	40.1	31.2	20.9	7.8	1962
1963		6 534		3 360	1 339		7.2		3.7	1.5										1963
1964	17 993	7 252	5 263	3 825	1 653	17.7	7.1	5.2	3.8	1.6	50.9	20.5	14.9	10.8	4.7	40.3	29.3	21.3	9.2	1964
1965		8 376		4 476	1 840		7.5		4.0	1.6										1965
1966	24 275	9 508	7 135	5 432	2 200	19.9	7.8	5.9	4.5	1.8	52.3	20.8	15.6	11.9	4.8	39.2	29.4	22.4	9.1	1966
1967		11 255		6 559	2 718		8.5		5.0	2.0										1967
1968	34 273	12 535	10 538	7 717	3 483	24.4	8.9	7.5	5.5	2.5	56.9	20.8	17.5	12.8	5.8	36.6	30.7	22.5	10.2	1968
1969		13 862		8 850	4 053		9.0		5.8	2.7										1969
1970	44 306	15 562	12 773	11 122	4 849	25.9	9.1	7.5	6.5	2.8	58.5	20.6	16.8	14.7	6.4	35.1	28.8	25.1	10.9	1970
1971		19 495		11 707	5 773		10.5		6.3	3.1										1971
1972	55 908	21 190	15 053	12 943	6 722	27.6	10.4	7.4	6.1	3.3	56.7	21.7	15.4	13.2	6.9	37.9	26.9	23.2	12.0	1972
1973		23 966		15 048	7 387		10.6		6.7	3.3										1973
1974	76 436	32 646	18 124	17 641	8 025	29.9	12.8	7.1	6.9	3.1	59.7	25.5	14.1	13.8	6.3	42.7	23.7	23.1	10.5	1974
1975		38 018		21 756	11 011		12.7		7.3	3.7										1975
1976	113 361	45 648	25 134	27 506	15 073	33.5	13.5	7.4	8.1	4.5	62.6	25.2	13.9	15.2	8.3	40.3	22.2	24.3	13.3	1976
1977		54 617		31 324	19 021		14.9		8.5	5.2										1977
1978	156 163	63 422	34 521	35 943	22 277	38.2	15.5	8.4	8.9	5.4	61.6	25.1	13.7	14.2	8.8	40.6	22.1	23.0	14.3	1978
1979		71 313		39 901	23 438		15.5		8.7	5.1										1979
1980	196 529	82 742	37 408	46 406	29 940	37.9	15.9	7.2	8.9	5.8	61.0	25.7	11.6	14.4	9.3	42.1	19.0	23.6	15.2	1980

Table 4

S o c i a l   E x p e n d i t u r e

in million SKR at constant (1975) prices

Year	Total		Education		Health	Social services		Income maintenance	Year
	GDP deflator	Publ. expend. deflator	GDP deflator	Publ. expend. deflator	(a)	GDP deflator	Publ. expend. deflator	(b)	
1950	12 974		3 754		2 093	931		6 196	1950
1951					2 140	894		5 819	1951
1952	13 947		4 375		2 503	965		6 105	1952
1953					2 519	1 003		6 816	1953
1954	16 635		5 129		2 741	1 141		7 624	1954
1955					3 655	1 186		7 879	1955
1956	19 138		5 714		3 826	1 450		8 148	1956
1957					4 322	1 607		8 536	1957
1958	22 019		6 710		4 545	1 668		9 096	1958
1959					4 795	1 998		9 544	1959
1960	24 604		7 597		5 035	2 002		9 958	1960
1961					5 848	2 099	2 378	10 483	1961
1962	28 713	30 563	9 238	10 284	6 099	2 320	2 583	11 056	1962
1963					7 019	2 843	3 136	12 621	1963
1964	35 219	36 842	10 697	11 567	7 066	3 360	3 633	13 496	1964
1965					8 497	3 532	3 778	14 925	1965
1966	42 392	43 790	12 833	13 565	9 677	3 957	4 183	15 925	1966
1967					11 156	4 662	4 888	17 995	1967
1968	56 004	57 230	17 652	18 295	12 822	5 834	6 047	19 696	1968
1969					14 235	6 558	6 812	21 245	1969
1970	66 423	67 385	19 651	20 115	16 966	7 460	7 632	22 346	1970
1971					16 601	8 247	8 306	27 024	1971
1972	73 769	74 059	20 071	20 205	17 161	8 963	9 023	27 574	1972
1973					18 636	9 199	9 234	28 979	1973
1974	86 001	85 005	20 832	20 387	20 109	9 224	9 027	35 836	1974
1975					21 756	11 011	11 011	38 018	1975
1976	102 200	101 950	22 522	22 421	24 711	13 506	13 446	41 461	1976
1977					25 392	15 402	14 872	44 475	1977
1978	115 225	113 039	25 420	24 535	26 492	16 404	15 833	46 909	1978
1979					27 379	16 420	15 460	49 283	1979
1980	120 496		22 936		28 372	18 357		50 269	1980

Table 5

Expenditure on Income maintenance programmes

in million SKR at current prices

Year	Basic pens.	Supplem. pens.	old age pens. (of which:)	surviv. pens. (of which:)	invalid. pens. (of which:)	old age hous.all.	Sickness cash benefits	Occup. inj. benef.	Unempl. benefits	Child allow.	Matern. Parents benef.	Family housing allow.	Social ass.	Other	Total income maint.	Flat-rate benef.	Earn.-related benef.	Income-tested benef.	Year
1950	861					103	165	102	28	455	19	32	125	16	1 803	1 213	295	295	1950
1951	991					111	175	107	21	462	17	44	127	17	1 961	1 342	303	316	1951
1952	1 116		753	12	165	135	189	112	31	523	17	50	160	18	2 216	1 504	332	380	1952
1953	1 315		799	13	168	151	211	116	51	520	20	61	187	34	2 515	1 684	378	453	1953
1954	1 541		1 059	18	218	209	242	121	79	525	20	77	188	43	2 836	1 857	442	537	1954
1955	1 617		1 116	20	231	239	380	71	72	528	58	92	188	43	3 049	1 906	566	577	1955
1956	1 809		1 175	29	230	272	465	82	98	532	69	102	115	45	3 318	2 069	696	553	1956
1957	1 999		1 360	35	260	301	519	85	120	536	73	106	136	45	3 620	2 235	776	609	1957
1958	2 196		1 450	38	272	304	525	87	118	740	80	103	143	43	4 035	2 632	787	616	1958
1959	2 351		1 650	43	305	335	546	89	151	735	83	112	150	53	4 270	2 751	847	672	1959
1960	2 590		1 684	44	312	367	600	91	121	815	83	116	154	53	4 623	3 038	871	714	1960
1961	2 900		1 920	156	356	408	609	100	99	804	90	121	149	55	4 927	3 296	868	763	1961
1962	3 227		2 036	184	370	480	644	100	114	968	98	118	161	60	5 490	3 715	915	860	1962
1963	3 698	72	2 441	267	497	474	1 004	114	119	957	194	155	162	59	6 534	4 181	1 482	871	1963
1964	4 100	141	2 563	297	495	628	1 060	118	106	1 081	228	207	151	60	7 252	4 553	1 632	1 067	1964
1965	4 662	206	2 989	377	587	702	1 138	122	134	1 386	256	210	180	82	8 376	5 346	1 829	1 201	1965
1966	5 329	355	3 425	458	713	588	1 226	125	164	1 567	271	178	200	93	9 508	6 308	2 110	1 090	1966
1967	5 918	533	3 906	540	845	693	1 927	136	299	1 579	339	183	244	97	11 255	6 804	3 209	1 242	1967
1968	6 429	704	4 304	606	946	757	2 237	167	368	1 587	355	307	276	105	12 535	7 259	3 800	1 476	1968
1969	6 976	935	4 747	693	1 079	868	2 476	177	349	1 591	366	518	335	139	13 862	7 699	4 266	1 897	1969
1970	7 917	1 285	5 309	776	1 267	974	2 662	123	462	1 600	407	555	401	150	15 562	8 543	4 899	2 120	1970
1971	9 178	1 747	6 082	897	1 669	1 147	2 861	201	668	2 144	438	857	479	922	19 495	10 295	5 915	3 285	1971
1972	10 130	2 221	7 237	1 067	2 210	1 292	2 980	256	669	2 148	479	788	534	985	21 190	11 122	6 605	3 463	1972
1973	11 335	2 936	7 964	1 171	2 674	1 413	3 157	251	638	2 369	510	1 148	563	1 059	23 966	12 458	7 492	4 016	1973
1974	13 758	3 887	9 452	1 398	3 354	1 511	6 660	357	807	3 046	946	1 487	565	1 133	32 646	15 503	12 657	4 486	1974
1975	15 821	5 005	11 765	1 689	4 197	1 986	8 005	458	780	2 828	1 352	1 900	644	1 225	38 018	16 910	15 600	5 508	1975
1976	18 693	6 943	13 482	1 907	4 869	2 261	9 828	545	925	3 233	1 564	1 790	738	1 389	45 648	19 920	19 805	5 923	1976
1977	22 342	9 719	19 277	2 004	5 245	2 524	10 740	661	1 253	3 503	1 812	2 190	860	1 537	54 617	23 626	24 185	6 806	1977
1978	25 565	12 371	22 994	2 338	6 462	2 873	11 748	769	1 866	3 968	2 283	2 080	899	1 873	63 422	27 000	29 037	7 385	1978
1979	28 368	15 096	27 336	2 730	7 814	3 166	12 426	1 049	2 060	4 431	2 737	2 215	863	2 068	71 313	30 006	33 367	7 936	1979
1980	33 119	19 042	30 916	3 050	8 861	3 240	12 631	1 313	2 145	4 995	3 539	2 534	945	2 483	82 742	35 978	38 666	8 098	1980

Table 6

Expenditure on Income maintenance programmes

in million SKR at constant (1975) prices

Year	Basic pens.	Supplem. pens.	of which: old age pens.	surviv. pens.	invalid. pens.	old age hous. all.	Sickness cash benefits	Occup. inj. benef.	Unempl. benefits	Child allow.	Matern.- Parents benef.	Family housing allow.	Social ass.	Other	Total income maint.	Flat-rate benef.	Earn.-related benef.	Income-tested benef.	Year
1950	2 959					354	567	351	96	1 564	65	110	430	56	6 198	4 168	1 014	1 014	1950
1951	2 941					329	519	318	62	1 371	50	131	377	50	5 819	3 982	899	938	1951
1952	3 074		2 074	33	455	372	521	309	86	1 441	47	138	441	50	6 105	4 143	915	1 047	1952
1953	3 564		2 165	35	455	409	572	314	138	1 409	54	165	507	92	6 816	4 564	1 024	1 228	1953
1954	4 142		2 847	48	586	562	651	325	212	1 411	54	207	505	116	7 624	4 992	1 188	1 444	1954
1955	4 222		2 921	52	603	624	1 022	185	188	1 379	151	240	491	112	7 879	4 977	1 395	1 507	1955
1956	4 511		2 930	72	574	678	1 160	204	244	1 327	172	254	287	112	8 148	5 160	1 609	1 379	1956
1957	4 782		3 254	84	622	720	1 242	203	287	1 282	175	254	325	108	8 536	5 347	1 732	1 457	1957
1958	5 014		3 318	87	621	694	1 199	199	269	1 689	189	235	326	98	9 096	6 009	1 662	1 425	1958
1959	5 331		3 741	98	692	760	1 238	202	342	1 667	188	254	340	98	9 544	6 238	1 782	1 524	1959
1960	5 590		3 677	96	681	801	1 310	199	264	1 779	181	253	336	94	9 958	6 633	1 773	1 552	1960
1961	6 170		4 085	332	757	868	1 296	213	211	1 711	191	257	317	117	10 483	7 013	1 719	1 604	1961
1962	6 586		4 155	376	755	980	1 314	204	233	1 976	200	241	329	122	11 056	7 582	1 750	1 724	1962
1963	7 337	143	4 845	530	986	940	1 992	226	236	1 899	385	308	321	117	12 621	8 296	2 597	1 728	1963
1964	7 854	270	4 910	569	948	1 203	2 031	226	203	2 071	437	397	289	115	13 496	8 722	2 730	2 044	1964
1965	8 538	377	5 474	690	1 075	1 288	2 088	223	245	2 538	470	385	330	150	14 925	9 791	2 934	2 200	1965
1966	9 156	610	5 885	787	1 225	1 010	2 107	215	282	2 692	466	306	344	160	15 925	10 838	3 214	1 873	1966
1967	9 734	877	6 424	888	1 390	1 140	3 169	224	499	2 597	558	301	401	160	17 995	11 191	4 761	2 043	1967
1968	10 369	1 135	6 942	977	1 526	1 221	3 608	269	594	2 560	573	495	445	169	19 696	11 708	5 607	2 381	1968
1969	10 951	1 468	7 452	1 088	1 694	1 362	3 887	278	548	2 498	575	813	526	218	21 245	12 086	6 181	2 978	1969
1970	11 643	1 890	7 807	1 141	1 863	1 432	3 915	260	679	2 353	599	816	590	221	22 346	12 563	6 665	3 116	1970
1971	12 538	2 387	8 309	1 225	2 280	1 567	3 908	275	913	2 929	598	1 171	654	1 260	27 024	14 456	8 080	4 488	1971
1972	13 071	2 866	9 338	1 377	2 852	1 667	3 845	330	863	2 772	618	1 017	689	1 271	27 574	14 583	8 523	4 468	1972
1973	13 706	3 550	9 630	1 416	3 233	1 709	3 817	304	771	2 865	617	1 388	681	1 281	28 979	15 064	9 059	4 856	1973
1974	15 102	4 267	10 375	1 535	3 682	1 659	7 311	392	886	3 344	1 038	1 632	620	1 244	35 836	17 018	13 894	4 924	1974
1975	15 821	5 005	11 765	1 689	4 197	1 986	8 005	458	780	2 828	1 352	1 900	644	1 225	38 018	16 910	15 600	5 508	1975
1976	16 978	6 306	12 245	1 732	4 422	2 054	8 926	495	840	2 936	1 421	1 626	670	1 262	41 461	18 093	17 988	5 380	1976
1977	18 194	7 914	15 698	1 632	4 271	2 055	8 746	538	1 020	2 853	1 476	1 783	700	1 252	44 475	19 239	19 694	5 542	1977
1978	18 909	9 150	17 007	1 729	4 780	2 125	8 689	569	1 380	2 935	1 689	1 538	665	1 385	46 909	19 970	21 477	5 462	1978
1979	19 605	10 433	18 891	1 887	5 400	2 188	8 587	725	1 424	3 062	1 891	1 531	596	1 429	49 283	20 737	23 059	5 487	1979
1980	20 121	11 569	18 783	1 853	5 383	1 968	7 674	798	1 303	3 035	2 150	1 539	574	1 509	50 269	21 858	23 491	4 920	1980

Table 7

Expenditure on Social Services

(at current prices, in million SKR)

Year	Old age/invalidity			Families/children		Unemployment			Industrial safety	Adminis-tration	Total	Year
	handicap services	homes for the aged	home help	general	day care	employment guidance	retraining	public work etc.				
1950	27	7		146		19	2	11	2	33	247	1950
1951	31	6		172		22	2	7	2	45	287	1951
1952	35	8		208		24	2	8	3	45	332	1952
1953	37	9		213		24	-	13	3	45	344	1953
1954	37	10		258		25	-	14	3	50	397	1954
1955	29	9		291		26	-	16	3	52	427	1955
1956	24	95		320		28	1	20	4	56	548	1956
1957	27	113		370		31	1	27	4	60	633	1957
1958	35	111		386		33	2	44	4	64	678	1958
1959	40	117		428		36	16	109	4	71	821	1959
1960	38	126		464		40	29	90	5	73	865	1960
1961	43	148		511		45	33	73	5	73	932	1961
1962	41	163		574		58	56	91	5	84	1 072	1962
1963	76	179		665		67	83	175	6	88	1 339	1963
1964	52	256		858		76	109	177	6	119	1 653	1964
1965	61	278		981		83	125	183	7	122	1 840	1965
1966	75	382		1 120		102	148	218	8	148	2 200	1966
1967	91	464		1 250		121	257	370	9	156	2 718	1967
1968	108	759		1 522		130	344	445	10	164	3 483	1968
1969	148	906		1 834		168	369	453	13	162	4 053	1969
1970	189	1 219		2 085		174	453	538	15	176	4 849	1970
1971	363	913	558	1 131	870	211	548	956	18	205	5 773	1971
1972	416	1 063	660	1 340	1 165	220	550	1 027	21	260	6 722	1972
1973	367	1 145	835	1 472	1 305	264	630	1 038	25	306	7 387	1973
1974	398	1 369	911	1 498	1 645	312	564	945	39	344	8 025	1974
1975	674	1 855	1 377	1 738	2 454	402	694	1 349	46	422	11 011	1975
1976	627	1 927	1 777	2 039	3 443	462	1 437	2 409	53	899	15 073	1976
1977	733	2 246	2 262	2 363	4 511	686	2 372	2 702	65	1 080	19 021	1977
1978	790	2 415	2 697	2 422	5 790	813	2 576	3 452	75	1 247	22 277	1978
1979	888	2 715	3 011	1 865	7 039	962	2 821	2 647	89	1 401	23 438	1979
1980	2 599	3 064	3 706	3 368	8 910	1 025	2 153	3 449	103	1 563	29 940	1980

Table 8

Expenditure on Social Services

(at constant prices, in million SKR)

Year	Old age/invalidity: handicap services	Old age/invalidity: homes for the aged	Old age/invalidity: home help(a)	Families/children: general	Families/children: day care	Unemployment: employment guidance	Unemployment: retraining	Unemployment: public work et.	Industrial safety	Adminis- tration	Total	Year
1950	101	26		545		71	7	41	7	123	931	1950
1951	97	19		536		69	3	22	6	140	894	1951
1952	102	23		605		70	6	23	9	131	965	1952
1953	108	26		621		70	-	38	9	131	1 003	1953
1954	106	29		741		72	-	40	9	144	1 141	1954
1955	81	25		808		72	-	44	8	144	1 186	1955
1956	63	251		847		74	3	53	11	148	1 450	1956
1957	69	287		939		79	3	69	10	152	1 607	1957
1958	86	273		948		81	5	108	10	157	1 668	1958
1959	97	287		1 041		88	39	265	10	173	1 998	1959
1960	88	292		1 074		93	67	208	12	169	2 002	1960
1961	97	333		1 304		115	84	186	11	164	2 099	1961
1962	89	353		1 344		140	135	219	11	182	2 320	1962
1963	161	380		1 557		157	194	410	13	187	2 843	1963
1964	106	520		1 886		167	240	389	12	242	3 360	1964
1965	117	534		2 014		170	257	376	13	234	3 532	1965
1966	135	687		2 129		194	281	414	14	266	3 957	1966
1967	156	796		2 248		218	462	665	15	268	4 662	1967
1968	181	1 271		2 642		226	597	773	17	275	5 834	1968
1969	239	1 466		3 082		282	620	761	21	262	6 558	1969
1970	291	1 875		3 283		270	713	847	23	271	7 460	1970
1971	519	1 304	797	1 615	1 243	304	788	1 376	26	293	8 247	1971
1972	555	1 417	880	1 786	1 553	295	738	1 379	28	347	8 963	1972
1973	457	1 426	1 040	1 833	1 631	330	788	1 298	31	381	9 199	1973
1974	457	1 574	1 047	1 722	1 891	351	634	1 063	45	395	9 224	1974
1975	674	1 855	1 377	1 738	2 454	402	694	1 349	46	422	11 011	1975
1976	562	1 727	1 592	1 827	3 085	412	1 282	2 149	47	806	13 506	1976
1977	594	1 819	1 832	1 913	3 653	536	1 855	2 113	53	874	15 402	1977
1978	582	1 778	1 986	1 784	3 550	578	1 831	2 453	55	918	16 404	1978
1979	608	1 860	2 062	1 277	4 821	635	1 861	2 275	61	960	16 420	1979
1980	1 594	1 879	2 272	2 046	5 466	628	1 320	2 115	63	958	18 357	1980

Table 9

Expenditure on Cash Benefits and Services

(at current prices, in million SKR)

Year	Old age/invalidity			Occupational injuries/ industrial safety			Families/ children			Unemployment/ employment			Year
	cash	services	total	cash	services	total	cash	services	total	cash	services	total	
1950	861	34	895	102	2	104	490	146	636	28	32	60	1950
1951	991	37	1 028	107	2	109	496	172	668	21	31	51	1951
1952	1 116	43	1 159	112	3	115	558	208	766	31	33	65	1952
1953	1 315	46	1 361	116	3	119	574	213	787	51	37	88	1953
1954	1 541	47	1 588	121	3	124	588	258	846	79	39	118	1954
1955	1 617	38	1 655	71	3	74	629	291	920	72	43	114	1955
1956	1 809	119	1 928	82	4	86	646	320	966	98	49	147	1956
1957	1 999	140	2 139	85	4	89	654	370	1 024	120	59	179	1957
1958	2 196	146	2 342	87	4	91	863	386	1 249	118	79	197	1958
1959	2 351	157	2 508	89	4	93	871	428	1 299	151	161	312	1959
1960	2 590	164	2 754	91	5	96	951	464	1 415	121	164	280	1960
1961	2 900	191	3 091	100	5	105	949	511	1 460	99	152	250	1961
1962	3 227	204	3 431	100	5	105	1 126	574	1 700	114	205	319	1962
1963	3 770	255	4 025	114	6	120	1 210	665	1 875	119	325	444	1963
1964	4 210	308	4 549	118	6	124	1 369	858	2 227	106	362	468	1964
1965	4 868	339	5 206	122	7	129	1 724	981	2 705	134	391	525	1965
1966	5 684	457	6 141	125	8	133	1 931	1 120	3 051	164	467	630	1966
1967	6 451	555	7 006	136	9	145	2 015	1 250	3 265	299	748	1 047	1967
1968	7 133	867	8 000	167	10	177	2 047	1 522	3 569	368	920	1 287	1968
1969	7 911	1 054	8 965	177	13	190	2 096	1 834	3 930	349	990	1 339	1969
1970	9 202	1 403	10 610	123	15	138	2 157	2 085	4 242	462	1 165	1 627	1970
1971	10 925	1 834	12 759	201	18	219	3 504	2 001	5 505	668	1 715	2 333	1971
1972	12 351	2 139	14 490	256	21	277	3 612	2 505	6 117	669	1 797	2 466	1972
1973	14 271	2 347	16 618	251	25	276	3 938	2 777	6 715	638	1 932	2 570	1973
1974	17 645	2 678	20 323	357	39	396	5 125	3 143	8 268	807	1 821	2 628	1974
1975	20 826	3 906	24 532	458	46	504	5 405	4 192	9 597	780	2 445	3 225	1975
1976	25 636	4 331	29 967	545	53	598	6 186	5 482	11 668	925	4 308	5 233	1976
1977	32 061	5 242	37 303	661	65	726	6 852	6 874	13 726	1 253	5 760	7 013	1977
1978	37 936	5 902	43 838	769	75	844	8 124	8 212	16 336	1 866	6 841	8 707	1978
1979	43 464	6 614	50 078	1 049	89	1 138	9 236	8 904	18 140	2 060	5 430	8 490	1979
1980	52 161	9 369	61 530	1 313	103	1 416	11 017	12 278	23 295	2 145	6 627	8 773	1980

Table 10

Expenditure on Cash Benefits and Services

(at constant prices, in million SKR)

Year	Old age/invalidity			Occupational injuries/ industrial safety			Families/ children			Unemployment/ employment			Year
	cash	services	total	cash	services	total	cash	services	total	cash	services	total	
1950	2 959	127	3 086	351	7	358	1 684	538	2 186	96	119	215	1950
1951	2 941	115	3 056	318	6	324	1 472	536	2 008	62	97	159	1951
1952	3 074	125	3 199	309	9	318	1 537	605	2 142	86	96	182	1952
1953	3 564	134	3 698	314	9	323	1 556	621	2 177	138	108	246	1953
1954	4 142	135	4 277	325	9	334	1 581	741	2 322	212	112	324	1954
1955	4 222	106	4 328	185	8	193	1 642	808	2 450	188	119	307	1955
1956	4 511	315	4 826	204	11	215	1 611	847	2 458	244	130	374	1956
1957	4 782	355	5 137	203	10	213	1 565	939	2 504	287	150	437	1957
1958	5 014	359	5 373	199	10	209	1 970	948	2 918	269	194	463	1958
1959	5 331	382	5 713	202	10	212	1 975	1 041	3 016	342	391	734	1959
1960	5 590	380	5 970	199	12	211	2 076	1 074	3 150	264	380	644	1960
1961	6 170	430	6 600	213	11	224	2 019	1 151	3 170	211	342	553	1961
1962	6 586	442	7 028	204	11	215	2 298	1 242	3 540	233	444	677	1962
1963	7 840	541	8 381	226	13	239	2 401	1 412	3 818	236	690	926	1963
1964	8 124	626	8 750	226	12	238	2 623	1 744	4 367	203	736	935	1964
1965	8 915	651	9 566	223	13	236	3 163	1 883	5 046	245	750	995	1965
1966	9 766	822	10 588	215	14	229	3 318	2 014	5 332	282	840	1 122	1966
1967	10 611	952	11 563	224	15	239	3 314	2 144	5 458	499	1 283	1 775	1967
1968	11 504	1 452	12 956	269	17	286	3 302	2 549	5 851	594	1 541	2 135	1968
1969	12 419	1 706	14 125	278	21	299	3 290	2 968	6 258	548	1 602	2 150	1969
1970	13 533	2 166	15 699	260	23	283	3 172	3 208	6 380	679	1 792	2 441	1970
1971	14 925	2 620	17 545	275	26	301	4 787	2 859	7 646	913	2 450	3 363	1971
1972	15 937	2 852	18 789	330	28	358	4 661	3 340	8 001	863	2 396	3 259	1972
1973	17 256	2 923	20 179	304	31	335	4 762	3 458	8 220	771	2 406	3 177	1973
1974	19 369	3 078	22 447	392	45	437	5 626	3 613	9 239	886	2 093	2 879	1974
1975	20 826	3 906	24 732	458	46	504	5 405	4 192	9 597	780	2 445	3 225	1975
1976	23 284	3 881	27 165	495	47	542	5 619	4 912	10 531	840	3 860	4 700	1976
1977	26 108	4 245	30 353	538	53	591	5 580	5 566	11 146	1 020	4 664	5 684	1977
1978	28 059	4 346	32 405	569	55	624	6 009	6 047	12 056	1 380	5 038	6 418	1978
1979	30 038	4 530	34 568	725	61	786	6 383	6 099	12 482	1 424	3 719	5 143	1979
1980	31 690	5 744	37 434	798	63	861	6 693	7 528	14 221	1 303	4 063	5 366	1980

Table 11

Expenditure on Sickness and Health

Year	at current prices (in million SKR)					at constant prices (in million SKR)					Year
	Cash benefits	Medical benefits	Sickness insurance	Public health	Total	Cash benefits	Medical benefits	Sickness insurance	Public health	Total	
1950	165		165	561	726	567		567	2 093	2 660	1950
1951	175		175	687	862	519		519	2 140	2 659	1951
1952	189		189	861	1 050	521		521	2 503	3 024	1952
1953	211		211	864	1 075	572		572	2 519	3 091	1953
1954	242		242	954	1 196	651		651	2 741	3 392	1954
1955	380	325	705	1 021	1 726	1 022	849	1 871	2 836	4 707	1955
1956	465	392	857	1 077	1 934	1 160	977	2 137	2 849	4 986	1956
1957	519	423	942	1 304	2 246	1 242	1 012	2 254	3 310	5 564	1957
1958	525	450	975	1 432	2 407	1 199	1 027	2 226	3 518	5 744	1958
1959	546	505	1 051	1 500	2 551	1 238	1 145	2 383	3 650	6 033	1959
1960	600	540	1 140	1 666	2 806	1 310	1 179	2 489	3 856	6 345	1960
1961	609	588	1 197	1 875	3 072	1 296	1 251	2 547	4 597	7 144	1961
1962	644	644	1 288	2 210	3 498	1 314	1 314	2 629	4 784	7 413	1962
1963	1 004	828	1 832	2 532	4 364	1 992	1 643	3 635	5 376	9 011	1963
1964	1 060	924	1 984	2 901	4 885	2 031	1 770	3 801	5 896	9 697	1964
1965	1 138	1 034	2 172	3 442	5 614	2 088	1 890	3 978	6 607	10 585	1965
1966	1 226	1 144	2 370	4 288	6 658	2 107	1 965	4 072	7 712	11 784	1966
1967	1 927	1 346	3 273	5 213	8 486	3 169	2 214	5 383	8 942	14 325	1967
1968	2 237	1 668	3 905	6 049	9 954	3 608	2 690	6 298	10 132	16 430	1968
1969	2 476	1 768	4 244	7 082	11 326	3 887	2 775	6 662	11 460	18 122	1969
1970	2 662	2 132	4 794	8 990	13 784	3 915	3 135	7 050	13 831	20 881	1970
1971	2 861	1 987	4 848	9 720	14 568	3 908	2 715	6 623	13 886	20 509	1971
1972	2 980	2 226	5 206	10 717	15 923	3 845	2 872	6 717	14 289	21 006	1972
1973	3 157	2 875	6 032	12 173	18 205	3 817	3 477	7 294	15 159	22 453	1973
1974	6 660	3 241	9 901	14 400	24 301	7 311	3 557	10 868	16 552	27 420	1974
1975	8 005	3 868	11 873	17 888	29 761	8 005	3 868	11 873	17 888	29 761	1975
1976	9 828	5 248	15 071	22 263	37 334	8 926	4 762	13 688	19 949	33 637	1976
1977	10 740	6 125	16 865	25 199	42 064	8 746	4 988	13 734	20 404	34 138	1977
1978	11 748	7 476	19 224	28 467	47 691	8 689	5 530	14 219	20 962	35 181	1978
1979	12 426	8 045	20 471	31 856	52 327	8 587	5 560	14 147	21 819	35 966	1979
1980	12 631	10 029	22 660	36 337	58 997	7 677	6 090	13 767	22 279	36 046	1980

Table 12

Expenditure on Housing

Year	at current prices (in million SKR)						at constant prices (in million SKR)						Year
	Housing allowances	Interest subventions on state loans	Sub-total	Expenditure on public housing loans	Tax credits for private housing loans	Total housing	Housing allowances	Interest subventions on state loans	Sub-total	Expenditure on public housing loans	Tax credits for private housing loans	Total housing	
1950	135	1	136	392	124	652	464	3	467	1 347	426	2 240	1950
1951	155	10	165	451	134	750	460	30	490	1 338	398	2 226	1951
1952	185	7	192	860	173	1 225	510	19	529	2 369	477	3 375	1952
1953	212	11	223	804	182	1 209	574	30	604	2 178	493	3 275	1953
1954	286	15	301	982	221	1 504	769	40	809	2 640	594	4 043	1954
1955	331	25	356	966	155	1 477	864	65	929	2 522	405	3 856	1955
1956	374	60	434	1 009	199	1 642	932	150	1 082	2 516	496	4 094	1956
1957	407	86	493	947	231	1 671	974	206	1 180	2 266	553	3 999	1957
1958	407	139	546	1 044	326	1 916	929	317	1 246	2 384	744	4 374	1958
1959	447	160	607	924	378	1 909	1 014	363	1 377	2 095	857	4 329	1959
1960	483	199	682	1 021	432	2 135	1 054	434	1 488	2 229	943	4 660	1960
1961	529	242	771	1 143	480	2 394	1 125	515	1 640	2 432	1 021	5 093	1961
1962	598	273	871	1 460	542	2 873	1 221	557	1 778	2 980	1 106	5 864	1962
1963	629	220	849	1 202	559	2 610	1 248	437	1 685	2 385	1 109	5 152	1963
1964	835	211	1 046	1 567	613	3 226	1 600	404	2 004	3 002	1 174	6 180	1964
1965	912	250	1 162	1 596	788	3 296	1 673	459	2 132	2 928	1 449	6 509	1965
1966	766	382	1 148	2 136	1 029	4 313	1 316	656	1 972	3 670	1 768	7 410	1966
1967	876	334	1 210	1 727	1 313	4 250	1 441	549	1 990	2 840	2 160	6 990	1967
1968	1 064	168	1 232	2 166	1 450	4 848	1 716	271	1 987	3 494	2 339	7 820	1968
1969	1 386	15	1 401	1 970	1 851	5 222	2 175	24	2 199	3 093	2 906	8 198	1969
1970	1 529	3	1 532	1 997	2 448	5 977	2 248	4	2 252	2 937	3 600	8 785	1970
1971	2 004	1	2 005	2 125	3 039	7 169	2 738	1	2 739	2 903	4 152	9 794	1971
1972	2 080	2	2 082	2 004	3 300	7 386	2 684	3	2 687	2 586	4 258	9 531	1972
1973	2 561	0	2 561	1 885	4 300	8 746	3 097	0	3 097	2 279	5 200	10 576	1973
1974	2 998	5	3 003	2 215	5 400	10 618	3 291	5	3 296	2 431	5 928	11 655	1974
1975	3 886	1 837	5 723	2 644	6 300	14 667	3 886	1 837	5 723	2 644	6 300	14 667	1975
1976	4 051	2 255	6 306	3 601	6 800	16 707	3 680	2 048	5 728	3 271	6 176	17 126	1976
1977	4 714	2 851	7 565	4 497	9 500	21 562	3 838	2 322	6 160	3 662	7 736	17 558	1977
1978	4 953	3 126	8 079	5 890	10 200	24 169	3 663	2 312	5 975	4 357	7 544	17 876	1978
1979	5 381	3 666	9 047	5 934	11 500	26 481	3 719	2 534	6 253	4 101	7 947	18 301	1979
1980	5 774	5 027	10 801	6 874	15 400	33 075	3 507	3 054	6 561	4 176	9 356	20 093	1980

Table 13

Public Revenues

Year	Total current receipts at current prices (in million SKR)	Total current receipts at constant (1975) prices (in million SKR)	Total current receipts annual growth rate	Total current receipts as % of GDP	Savings/Net lending as % of GDP	Savings/Net lending as % of GDP	Percent distribution of receipts: Total direct taxes	Central direct taxes	Local direct	Indirect taxes	Social security contrib.	Other receipts	Year
1950	7 756	28 940		24.2			48.2			30.0	5.5	15.5	1950
1951	9 731	30 314	4.7	24.6			52.9			27.7	4.9	14.5	1951
1952	11 442	33 261	10.1	26.5			58.3			26.0	4.6	11.1	1952
1953	11 778	34 338	3.2	26.5			55.7			27.0	4.8	12.5	1953
1954	12 919	37 123	8.1	27.3			56.1			26.5	5.6	11.8	1954
1955	14 773	41 036	10.5	29.1			53.5			27.3	7.3	11.9	1955
1956	16 405	43 399	5.8	29.7			54.2			27.5	7.5	10.7	1956
1957	17 914	45 467	4.8	30.4			53.5			26.9	8.3	11.3	1957
1958	19 163	47 084	3.6	30.8			51.6			28.3	8.1	12.0	1958
1959	20 119	48 951	4.0	30.4			49.1			28.8	9.9	12.2	1959
1960	23 214	53 736	9.8	32.2			46.4			31.0	11.3	11.3	1960
1961	26 391	59 439	10.6	33.6			47.6			30.6	11.0	10.8	1961
1962	30 230	65 433	10.1	35.5	7.6	4.0	44.9	25.7	19.1	31.7	12.5	10.9	1962
1963	33 437	70 992	8.5	36.6	7.4	2.4	43.6	23.2	20.4	31.2	14.5	10.9	1963
1964	37 579	76 380	7.6	36.9	7.8	2.7	44.2	23.2	21.0	30.8	14.8	10.6	1964
1965	44 444	85 305	11.7	39.6	9.5	4.4	45.7	25.4	20.2	29.7	14.1	10.5	1965
1966	50 402	90 651	6.3	41.3	9.4	3.9	45.2	22.3	22.3	29.9	14.3	10.6	1966
1967	56 517	96 942	6.9	42.7	9.9	3.7	44.3	20.7	23.5	29.0	15.7	11.0	1967
1968	64 141	107 439	10.8	45.7	9.8	3.7	41.7	18.6	23.1	29.6	16.9	11.8	1968
1969	71 248	115 288	7.3	46.7	10.1	4.4	42.3	19.6	22.7	28.3	16.8	12.6	1969
1970	80 340	123 600	7.2	47.0	9.9	4.4	43.6	21.8	21.7	27.1	16.3	13.1	1970
1971	91 997	131 396	6.3	49.6	10.2	5.2	40.6	18.6	22.0	30.0	16.5	12.9	1971
1972	100 779	134 372	2.3	49.7	9.2	4.4	40.5	16.0	24.5	28.7	17.3	13.5	1972
1973	108 105	134 626	0.2	47.9	7.9	4.1	38.7	14.8	23.8	30.3	17.3	13.7	1973
1974	125 014	143 694	6.7	48.9	5.5	2.0	42.2	19.2	23.0	27.3	17.1	13.4	1974
1975	151 945	151 945	5.7	50.7	5.8	2.8	42.1	20.6	21.5	27.4	17.0	13.5	1975
1976	187 408	167 928	10.5	55.3	7.6	4.5	41.1	20.2	20.9	26.3	20.5	12.1	1976
1977	214 400	173 603	3.4	58.4	5.4	1.7	39.3	15.7	23.6	26.3	22.3	12.1	1977
1978	237 088	174 586	0.6	57.9	3.5	- 0.5	39.8	13.2	26.6	24.3	23.8	12.1	1978
1979	260 826	178 648	2.3	56.9	1.5	- 3.0	40.0	13.6	26.4	23.7	24.0	12.3	1979
1980	296 368	181 709	1.7	56.4	- 0.6	- 4.2	38.0	12.4	25.6	24.1	25.2	12.7	1980

Table 14 Financing of Social Security

Year	Receipts of social insurance programmes (in mill. SKR, at curr. pr.)				Total receipts by source (percent distribution)					Year
	Basic pension	Sick- ness	Unemploy- ment	Total incl. other	central gvt.	local gvt.	employ- ers	insured	funds	
1950	861	171	46	2 709	55.3	28.2	4.5	10.2	1.7	1950
1951	991	185	43	3 059	55.9	28.4	4.5	9.7	1.5	1951
1952	1 117	208	49	3 498	55.3	29.1	4.4	9.9	1.3	1952
1953	1 315	234	68	3 810	56.1	28.3	4.1	10.4	1.1	1953
1954	1 542	232	102	4 229	56.8	29.2	3.2	9.6	1.2	1954
1955	1 616	825	96	4 964	48.8	27.1	5.5	17.5	1.1	1955
1956	1 809	913	118	5 424	48.8	26.7	6.3	17.1	1.1	1956
1957	1 999	1 018	132	6 080	48.1	28.4	6.9	15.7	1.0	1957
1958	2 197	1 067	116	6 694	47.4	27.8	6.3	17.4	1.1	1958
1959	2 351	1 104	160	7 141	48.0	27.5	5.8	17.3	1.4	1959
1960	2 591	1 179	145	7 749	43.6	27.8	5.8	21.2	1.6	1960
1961	2 900	1 234	127	8 362	43.5	28.5	5.6	20.8	1.5	1961
1962	3 227	1 363	152	9 506	43.8	29.5	5.1	20.1	1.5	1962
1963	3 698	1 873	151	13 185	38.0	23.3	19.7	16.4	2.7	1963
1964	4 100	2 028	145	15 294	37.2	23.6	20.0	16.0	3.3	1964
1965	4 662	2 184	169	17 793	37.5	23.8	20.0	14.7	3.9	1965
1966	5 321	2 388	200	20 884	39.3	22.8	19.9	13.6	4.4	1966
1967	5 918	3 288	293	25 028	37.6	22.2	22.2	12.7	5.4	1967
1968	6 429	3 873	348	29 268	34.1	24.3	23.6	12.7	5.3	1968
1969	6 977	4 261	362	33 047	32.6	25.7	22.7	12.9	6.1	1969
1970	7 917	4 888	459	40 469	27.2	28.5	26.9	11.2	6.2	1970
1971	9 178	4 842	638	45 424	32.7	28.0	21.7	10.6	7.0	1971
1972	10 129	5 407	639	51 175	31.7	27.6	22.1	11.3	7.3	1972
1973	11 335	6 128	646	57 314	31.5	28.3	21.4	10.9	7.8	1973
1974	13 758	10 084	914	69 775	35.7	25.4	20.5	11.0	7.4	1974
1975	15 821	11 882	892	82 938	33.2	26.7	31.9	0.8	7.5	1975
1976	18 693	15 115	1 055	101 958	27.9	26.0	37.7	1.2	7.3	1976
1977	22 342	16 917	1 407	120 844	25.8	26.3	39.4	1.2	7.3	1977
1978	25 564	19 760	1 991	138 421	26.2	25.7	39.5	1.2	7.4	1978
1979	28 368	22 524	2 168	154 261	25.7	26.3	39.0	1.2	7.8	1979
1980	33 119	25 587	2 285	180 506	26.3	25.5	39.3	1.1	7.9	1980

Table 15

Financing of Single Insurance Programmes
(percent distributions)

Year	Basic pension				Sickness insurance			Unemployment insurance				Year
	Central gvt.	Local gvt.	Employers	Insured	Central gvt.	Employers	Insured	Central gvt.	Insured	Employers	Funds	
1950	68.8	12.0		16.0	33.9		64.3	28.3	65.2		6.5	1950
1951	71.4	11.2		14.5	33.5		65.4	18.6	69.8		11.6	1951
1952	69.7	12.1		15.7	30.8		67.8	24.5	65.3		10.2	1952
1953	71.5	11.5		15.1	29.1		69.2	33.8	52.9		11.8	1953
1954	71.8	13.6		12.9	31.0		67.7	40.2	48.0		10.8	1954
1955	60.0	14.8		23.5	26.5	20.2	54.3	37.5	55.2		7.3	1955
1956	60.6	15.0		22.8	25.5	23.5	50.7	46.6	45.8		7.6	1956
1957	62.2	15.1		21.4	24.6	28.5	46.5	50.0	40.9		7.6	1957
1958	56.1	13.8		28.4	23.6	28.3	47.1	58.6	31.0		6.9	1958
1959	56.1	14.2		27.3	23.3	27.4	48.3	54.4	36.9		6.3	1959
1960	43.7	14.2		39.9	23.4	28.9	46.2	44.1	42.8		12.4	1960
1961	46.0	14.1		38.0	22.3	29.1	46.8	38.6	51.2		10.2	1961
1962	47.3	14.9		36.1	21.1	27.5	49.4	38.5	44.7		15.1	1962
1963	52.9	12.8		32.7	20.4	30.9	47.1	41.7	45.7		12.6	1963
1964	52.3	15.3		30.9	19.6	31.3	47.5	33.8	49.0		17.2	1964
1965	54.7	15.1		29.0	19.4	32.3	46.5	43.8	43.2		13.0	1965
1966	64.2	8.3		26.4	18.7	32.4	46.9	50.5	36.5		12.5	1966
1967	63.7	8.9		26.4	13.0	46.8	38.6	63.8	25.3		9.6	1967
1968	61.1	9.3		28.7	12.8	48.0	38.3	67.5	23.3		8.0	1968
1969	51.5	10.7		30.8	12.3	47.0	39.7	62.4	26.5		10.2	1969
1970	59.4	10.7		29.0	11.6	49.8	37.1	67.8	22.4		8.9	1970
1971	59.6	10.8		28.8	16.1	53.1	29.3	70.4	19.6		6.6	1971
1972	56.9	10.6		31.8	14.9	49.4	34.4	69.4	19.2		7.2	1972
1973	58.5	10.2		30.7	15.7	50.6	32.7	65.0	27.6		7.4	1973
1974	63.1	9.7		26.7	34.1	33.7	30.9	42.7	24.7	26.0	6.6	1974
1975	59.6	9.6	30.4	-	25.8	72.7		39.8	27.3	27.8	5.2	1975
1976	39.0	9.1	49.5	1.9	14.8	83.6		40.4	24.9	28.6	5.2	1976
1977	26.7	8.7	61.9	2.4	14.8	83.6		26.7	18.0	50.5	4.8	1977
1978	25.0	8.6	63.0	3.1	14.4	83.7		51.4	12.6	32.4	3.6	1978
1979	27.5	8.5	60.8	2.9	13.5	84.9		50.9	11.1	34.0	3.9	1979
1980	29.3	6.4	61.3	2.7	13.2	86.8		49.4	10.7	34.4	5.5	1980

Table 16

Coverage of Social Insurance Programmes
(members in thousands)

Year	Total pop.	Pop. aged 15–64	Labour force	Employ-ees	Sickness cash benefits insurance: All members	As % of pop. 15–64	Earnings-related benefits	As % of pop. 15–64	Flat-rate benefits (house-w.)	As % of female p. 15–64	Unemployment insurance: Members	As % of labour force	As % of employ-ees	Year
1950	6 986	4 651	3 093		3 088	66.4					1 063	34.4		1950
1951	7 044	4 680									1 085			1951
1952	7 099	4 697			3 306	70.4					1 122			1952
1953	7 150	4 708			3 372	71.6					1 143			1953
1954	7 192	4 722			3 168	67.1					1 148			1954
1955	7 235	4 745	3 154		4 367	92.0	3 221	67.9	1 146	48.2	1 212	38.4		1955
1956	7 290	4 770			4 461	93.5	3 294	69.1	1 167	48.9	1 243			1956
1957	7 339	4 800			4 506	93.9	3 343	69.6	1 163	48.5	1 258			1957
1958	7 389	4 842			4 527	93.5	3 366	69.5	1 161	48.0	1 273			1958
1959	7 430	4 884			4 546	93.1	3 393	69.5	1 153	47.3	1 285			1959
1960	7 463	4 926	3 586		4 579	93.0	3 444	69.9	1 135	46.2	1 317	36.7		1960
1961	7 498	4 972	3 683	3 052	4 623	93.0	3 501	70.4	1 122	45.3	1 340	36.4	43.9	1961
1962	7 542	5 015	3 676	3 072	4 649	92.7	3 539	70.6	1 110	44.4	1 367	37.2	44.5	1962
1963	7 581	5 054	3 749	3 142	4 651	92.0	3 593	71.1	1 058	42.1	1 396	37.2	44.4	1963
1964	7 628	5 093	3 710	3 155	4 694	92.3	3 654	71.7	1 040	41.1	1 431	38.6	45.4	1964
1965	7 695	5 133	3 738	3 210	4 726	92.1	3 710	72.3	1 016	39.9	1 563	41.8	48.7	1965
1966	7 773	5 168	3 792	3 273	4 748	92.2	3 751	72.6	997	38.9	1 571	41.4	48.0	1966
1967	7 843	5 189	3 774	3 211	4 758	91.7	3 782	72.9	976	38.9	1 633	43.3	50.9	1967
1968	7 893	5 203	3 822	3 246	4 764	91.6	3 814	73.3	950	36.9	1 660	43.4	51.1	1968
1969	7 932	5 230	3 840	3 298	4 801	91.8	3 901	74.6	900	34.8	1 682	43.8	51.0	1969
1970	8 004	5 267	3 913	3 433	4 838	91.9	4 005	76.0	833	32.0	1 766	45.1	51.4	1970
1971	8 081	5 287	3 961	3 467	4 840	91.5	4 049	76.6	791	30.3	2 166	54.7	62.5	1971
1972	8 115	5 290	3 970	3 493	4 861	91.9	4 123	77.9	738	28.3	2 280	57.4	65.3	1972
1973	8 129	5 267	3 977	3 521	4 806	91.2	4 092	77.7	714	27.4	2 373	59.7	67.4	1973
1974	8 144	5 260	4 043	3 609	4 787	91.0	4 083	77.6	704	27.1	2 510	62.0	69.5	1974
1975	8 177	5 259	4 129	3 715	4 783	90.9	4 124	78.4	659	25.4	2 618	63.4	70.5	1975
1976	8 208	5 264	4 155	3 752	4 712	89.5	4 163	79.0	549	21.1	2 748	66.1	73.2	1976
1977	8 236	5 272	4 174	3 770	4 721	89.5	4 239	80.4	482	18.5	2 800	67.1	74.3	1977
1978	8 267	5 286	4 209	3 783	4 715	89.2	4 278	80.9	437	16.7	2 907	69.1	76.9	1978
1979	8 284	5 305	4 268	3 843	4 727	89.1	4 338	81.8	289	14.8	3 000	70.3	78.1	1979
1980	8 303	5 328	4 318	3 895	4 713	88.5	4 363	81.9	350	13.3	3 061	70.9	78.6	1980

Table 17

Pensioners (in thousands)

Year	Basic pensioners: Old age	Basic: Inva-lidity	Basic: Survivors widows	Basic: Survivors orphans	Basic: Wives suppl.	Basic: Total	Supplementary pensioners: Old age	Suppl.: Inva-lidity	Suppl.: Survivors widows	Suppl.: Survivors orphans	Suppl.: Total	Part time pens.	Population 60+	Population 65+	Population 67+	Year
1950	603	134	15	32	17	801							1 034	708	594	1950
1951	605	150	14	37	18	824							1 051	721	603	1951
1952	619	147	17	34	18	835							1 071	736	616	1952
1953	633	145	18	31	18	845							1 090	753	630	1953
1954	648	142	19	30	21	860							1 111	770	645	1954
1955	664	144	20	31	23	882							1 133	784	661	1955
1956	681	140	22	31	24	898							1 159	801	677	1956
1957	694	138	24	30	27	913							1 183	819	691	1957
1958	707	139	25	29	29	929							1 205	833	704	1958
1959	723	140	25	28	31	947							1 232	851	720	1959
1960	739	143	26	27	34	969							1 259	870	736	1960
1961	754	145	59	40	36	1 034							1 283	886	749	1961
1962	771	145	61	40	37	1 054							1 313	908	766	1962
1963	789	151	73	38	41	1 092	2	4	6	4	16		1 340	926	782	1963
1964	807	147	79	36	40	1 109	26	9	12	8	55		1 368	947	800	1964
1965	827	151	84	36	42	1 140	51	18	20	13	102		1 398	968	819	1965
1966	852	161	89	36	45	1 183	81	28	28	17	154		1 428	992	839	1966
1967	874	167	93	35	47	1 216	113	38	37	20	208		1 461	1 018	858	1967
1968	898	172	96	35	49	1 248	148	46	47	24	265		1 492	1 042	879	1968
1969	921	178	98	35	50	1 282	186	57	57	27	327		1 523	1 062	899	1969
1970	947	188	101	34	54	1 324	225	70	68	30	393		1 557	1 086	921	1970
1971	969	212	104	34	60	1 379	262	93	80	32	467		1 592	1 114	945	1971
1972	992	236	106	33	65	1 432	300	116	93	34	543		1 625	1 140	969	1972
1973	1 014	260	106	33	66	1 483	340	140	107	36	623		1 654	1 166	990	1973
1974	1 038	278	106	42	65	1 541	380	160	122	38	700		1 684	1 196	1 016	1974
1975	1 062	289	106	45	68	1 595	420	174	136	40	770		1 711	1 225	1 041	1975
1976	1 084	297	105	44	70	1 659	459	186	152	41	838	15	1 732	1 250	1 066	1976
1977	1 284	258	87	44	56	1 839	623	164	168	42	997	31	1 751	1 274	1 090	1977
1978	1 315	273	86	43	57	1 913	670	181	184	43	1 078	41	1 772	1 300	1 115	1978
1979	1 340	284	85	43	57	1 974	714	196	200	44	1 154	49	1 790	1 324	1 139	1979
1980	1 363	293	84	43	56	2 040	757	209	217	44	1 227	68	1 806	1 346	1 162	1980

Table 18

Other Welfare Clienteles
(in thousands)

Year	Sickness cash ben.	Maternity/ Parents all.	(% men)	Child allowances children	families	Mainte- nance advances	Unemployment insur. benef.	assist. benef.	Social assist.	Educ. allow.	Study loans	Housing allowances (households)	Year
1950				1 700		38	22		293				1950
1951				1 733		39	19		293				1951
1952				1 759		40	23		298				1952
1953				1 782		44	28		313				1953
1954				1 801		48	26		307				1954
1955		106		1 812		52	25		275				1955
1956		111		1 825		56	19		287				1956
1957		113		1 837		62	23		315			119	1957
1958		111		1 847		66	32		329			118	1958
1959		110		1 838		69	27		327			128	1959
1960		105		1 816		74	19		302			132	1960
1961		107		1 794		78	17		283			119	1961
1962		108		1 741		78	19		282			115	1962
1963	1 725	122		1 727		79	20		270			135	1963
1964	1 601	132		1 727		90	17		267			183	1964
1965	1 744	134		1 734		104	17		276	209	67	174	1965
1966	1 738	147		1 748		107	22		298	219	76	153	1966
1967	2 189	145		1 760		110	29		322	237	88	156	1967
1968	2 368	137		1 745		111	33		358	237	97	-	1968
1969	2 516	131		1 776		120	30		388	226	103	422	1969
1970	2 487	136		1 790		127	30		445	223	107	452	1970
1971	2 507	140		1 791		167	45		515	227	104	464	1971
1972	2 440	138		1 795		185	48		521	234	94	519	1972
1973	2 600	137		1 796		191	46		480	224	86	521	1973
1974	2 705	160	(2.8)	1 797	1 049	200	39	57	436	218	75	570	1974
1975	2 788	158	(4.0)	1 791	1 056	211	37	41	417	219	78	660	1975
1976	2 860	153	(5.2)	1 790	1 061	212	33	48	392	219	77	596	1976
1977	2 870	152	(7.0)	1 788	1 064	208	33	80	373	229	78	591	1977
1978	2 933	141	(6.6)	1 777	1 062	216	46	102	377	238	87	565	1978
1979	2 926	143	(6.8)	1 760	1 057	224	45	102	354	261	89	513	1979
1980	2 861	146	(6.2)	1 739	1 047	231	44	101	343	277	92	472	1980

Table 19

Distribution of Seats in Riksdag, 1945–88 (a)

	1945		1949		1953		1957		1959		1961		1965(b)		1969		1971	1974	1976	1979	1982	1985(c)
	LC	UC	LC	UC	LC	UC	LC	UC	LC	UC	LC	UC	LC	UC	LC	UC						
Conservatives																						
number	39	30	23	24	31	20	42	13	45	16	39	19	33	26	32	25	41	51	55	73	86	76
percentage	18.2		12.4		13.4		14.4		16.0		15.1		15.4		14.6		11.7	14.6	15.8	20.9	24.6	21.8
Liberals																						
number	24	14	57	18	58	22	58	30	38	32	40	33	43	26	34	26	58	34	39	38	21	51
percentage	10.5		19.7		21.1		23.1		20.2		19.1		18.0		15.6		16.6	9.7	11.2	10.9	6.0	14.6
Centre																						
number	35	21	30	21	26	25	19	25	32	22	34	20	36	19	39	20	71	90	86	64	56	44
percentage	14.7		13.4		13.4		12.1		14.7		14.1		14.3		15.6		20.3	25.7	24.6	18.3	16.0	12.6
Social Democrats																						
number	115	83	112	84	110	79	106	79	111	79	114	77	113	78	125	79	163	156	152	154	166	159
percentage	52.1		51.6		49.7		48.6		49.7		49.7		49.7		53.1		46.6	44.6	43.6	44.1	47.6	45.6
Communists																						
number	15	2	8	3	5	4	6	3	5	2	5	2	8	2	3	1	17	19	17	20	20	19
percentage	4.5		2.9		2.4		2.4		2.1		1.8		2.6		1.0		4.9	5.4	4.9	5.7	5.7	5.4
	230	150	230	150	230	150	231	150	231	151	232	151	233	151	233	151	350	350	349	349	349	349

(a) Up to 1969, the periodization follows the directly-elected Lower Chamber (LC = Lower Chamber, UC = Upper Chamber), then the uni-cameral Parliament elections.
(b) The three representatives for the Citizen Rally in the Lower Chamber in 1965 have been assigned to the Conservatives, Liberals and Centre Party respectively. The latter representative, however, was not accepted by the Centre Party parliamentary group. The Citizens Rally representative in the Upper Chamber in 1965 has been assigned to the Conservatives since he was elected on a Conservative slate.
(c) The tiny Christian Democratic Party, participating in all national elections since 1964 and achieving some 1.5 – 2.0 percent, obtained one seat on the Centre ticket.

Table 20 Membership in Central Interest Organizations (a)

Year	LO	TCO	SACO		SR	LRF (b)	Year
1950	1 278	272	16		21	196	1950
1951	1 313	292			22	200	1951
1952	1 339	308	28		22	201	1952
1953	1 351	313			15	199	1953
1954	1 355	323	30		16	201	1954
1955	1 384	338			15	198	1955
1956	1 404	345			15	199	1956
1957	1 423	353	36		15	198	1957
1958	1 447	365			16	197	1958
1959	1 467	375	39		16	195	1959
1960	1 486	394	42		16	192	1960
1961	1 501	421	45		17	189	1961
1962	1 523	447	48		17	186	1962
1963	1 547	465	51		17	182	1963
1964	1 563	489	53		18	176	1964
1965	1 565	510	63		17	171	1965
1966	1 588	543	67		18	164	1966
1967	1 607	565	70		18	157	1967
1968	1 625	592	73		16	147	1968
1969	1 660	620	78		19	140	1969
1970	1 680	658	81		19	133	1970
1971	1 733	709	85		19	131	1971
1972	1 772	742	87		20	133	1972
1973	1 808	774	94		20	134	1973
1974	1 863	816		113		137	1974
1975	1 918	881		122		141	1975
1976	1 961	922		134		145	1976
1977	2 018	968		145		148	1977
1978	2 057	991		155		150	1978
1979	2 089	1 009		164		152	1979
1980	2 127	1 033		174		151	1980
1981	2 141	1 041		182		150	1981
1982	2 161	1 080		191		150	1982
1983	2 196					154	1983

(a) LO – Confederation of Trade Unions (blue collar); TCO – Central Organization of Salaried Employees (white collar); SACO/SR – confederation of Professional Associations (white collar); LRF – Federation of Swedish Farmers.

(b) Unpublished figures from the organization. For earlier Years (1974 and back) they show membership figures in the RLF (Riksförbundet Landsbygdens Folk).

Notes to and sources for appendix tables

Table 1

The series of GDP at current and constant prices are based on the three series (1950-1962; 1963-1969; and 1970-1980) reported in source (1). Public expenditure data are based on two national studies (2), (3) for the period up to 1974 and thereafter on the OECD-series (1). Both GDP and total public expenditure figures have been deflated by the GDP-deflator in (1). The public expenditure deflator is from (1) and is based on the cost of consumption per fixed consumption unit, while consumer price index follows national statistics (4).

Table 2

The distribution of public expenditure by purpose is based on the national studies (2) and (3) for the period up to 1974, and thereafter on national statistics (4) which are not completely comparable. The distribution by economic function is based on the OECD-series (1), while the distribution by level of government is based on a combination of some figures reported by a State Commission (5) and our own calculation of income maintenance expenditure (as no figures on social insurance expenditure are reported in (1)).

Table 3

Expenditure figures on income maintenance, health and social services are taken from the appendix tables 5, 7, and 11, expenditure figures on education directly from sources (2) and (3), which only contain data on a two-year basis.

Table 4

Total social expenditure (GDP deflator) = Education (GDP deflator) + Health (for deflation see notes to Table 11) + Social services (GDP deflator) + Income maintenance (deflated by consumer price index).
Total social expenditure (public expenditure deflator) = Education (publ. expend. deflator) + Health (see notes to Table 11) + Social services (publ. expend. deflator) + Income maintenance (consumer prices index).
For deflators see Table 1.

Table 5

Basic pension: sum of basic old age pensions, basic invalidity pensions, basic survivors' (orphans' and widows') pensions, old age housing allowances and some other small items (wife's supplement, etc. - see Institutional Synopsis).
Sources: (4), (6), (7), (8).

Supplementary pension: sum of supplementary old age, invalidity and survivors' pensions.
Sources: (4), (6), (7).

From 1963 expenditure on old age, invalidity, and survivors pensions consists of both basic and supplementary pension expenditure, prior to 1963 only of basic pension expenditure; old age housing allowances are a sub-item of basic pension expenditure.

Sickness cash benefits: between 1950 and 1954 all outlays by the sickness insurance funds are attributed to 'cash benefits' (see Table 11); from 1955 this item consists only of daily cash allowances.
Sources: (4), (6).

Occupational injuries benefits:
Sources: (4), (7).

Unemployment benefits mainly include insurance cash benefits but from 1974 also the minor sub-item 'assistance cash benefits'.
Sources: (4), (7), (9), (10).

Child allowances:
Sources: (4), (6), (7).

Maternity/parents' benefits: up to 1970 only maternity care; thereafter maternity benefits and from 1974 parents' benefits.
Sources: (4), (6), (7).

Family housing allowances:
Sources: (4), (7), (11).

Social assistance: prior to 1956 poor relief, incl. old age assistance.
Sources: (4), (7), (12).

Other: includes maintenance advances (including special child allowances), educational allowances, and child pensions.
Sources: (4), (7).

The main part of table 5 refers to official Swedish statistical classifications, but the decomposition of income maintenance programs into 'flat-rate', 'earnings-related' and 'income- and means-tested' benefits is our own classification (for a similar decomposition see SOU (Statens offentlig utredningar) 1979:94; see also footnote 40 of the Swedish chapter in Volume I).
Flat-rate benefits consist of 'basic pensions' (excluding 'old age housing allowances') and child allowances and from 1971 also child pensions (included under 'other').
Earnings-related benefits include sickness cash benefits, occupational injuries benefits, and unemployment benefits, from 1963 supplementary pensions, and from 1971 parents' benefits. Income- and means-tested benefits consist of old age housing allowances, family housing allowances and social assistance. Maternity benefits are included up to 1970, but parents' benefits excluded thereafter; the category 'other' is completely included up to 1970, but only partially thereafter, excluding child pensions.

Table 6

Deflator: consumer price index (see Table 1).

Table 7

Old-age/invalidity: up to 1970 home help included under homes for the aged.
Families/children: up to 1970 day care a sub-item of 'general'. Administration only refers to the cost of central government departments concerned with social welfare; regional and local administrative costs are included under the various items of social security.

Sources: (4), (7).

Table 8

Deflated using the GDP-deflator (see Table 1).

Table 9

Old age/invalidity: cash benefits are a sum of basic and supplementary pensions (see Table 5), services a sum of the items in Table 7.
Occupational injuries/industrial safety: see Tables 5 and 7. Families/children: cash benefits are a sum of child allowances, maternity/parents' benefits and 'other' in Table 5; for services see Table 7.
Unemployment/employment: for cash benefits see unemployment insurance in Table 5 and for employment services the sub-items in Table 7.

Table 10

Deflators: consumer price index for cash benefits and GDP-deflator for services (see Table 1).

Table 11

Sickness cash benefits:
Sources: (4), (6).

Medical benefits include reimbursements from the insurance funds to hospitals and other medical centres (county councils, etc.), to private phycisians, to public and private dentists, to pharmacies, repayments to the insured for travel expences, and some administrative costs for the sickness insurance funds.
Source: (6).

Total sickness insurance: sum of cash and medical benefits.

Public health refers to country council administred hospitals and medical centres, a few hospitals financed by the central government (up to 1967 also psychiatric hospitals), public dental service, and outlays on temperance welfare (drug addicts, etc.).
Sources: (4), (7).

Deflators: Cash and medical benefits deflated by consumer price index, public health by GDP-deflator (see Table 1).

Table 12

In contrast to Tables 5-11, Table 12 does not correspond to the official Swedish statistical classification of social expenditure as 'tax expenditure/credits' and 'public housing loans' are added to 'total housing expenditure'.

Housing allowances: sum of old age housing allowances and family housing allowances (see Table 5).
Sources: (4), (8).

Interest subventions on state loans: up to 1960 figures are taken from the State budget (13) and refer to yearly estimated costs; for actual costs no figures are available except for a few years in the 1950s; in 1968 interest subventions were abolished but reintroduced in 1975.
Sources: (4), (11), (13).

Expenditure on public housing loans: refers to total state guarantees and over-estimates public outlays as no re-payments on state-guaranteed loans are included; figures on the net expenditure on public housing loans are not available.
Sources: (4), (6).

Tax credits for private housing loans: prior to 1972 figures refer to net loss on source of income for assessment for state income tax; from 1972 estimates by the Ministry of Housing.
Sources: (4), (13), (14).

Deflator: consumer price index (see Table 1).

Table 13

Source: (1).

Table 14

Social security is defined according to the Swedish official statistical classification and includes both benefits in cash and in kind; apart from basic pension, sickness (insurance) and unemployment (insurance), the main items are health services and family programs (see footnote 38 of the Swedish chapter in Volume I).

Source: (4).

Table 15

Basic pension: from 1976 figures under 'insured' refer to contributions by the self-employed only.

Source: (4).

Table 16

Total population and population aged 15-64:
Source: (4).

Labour force and employees:
Source: (15).

Sickness cash benefit insurance:
Sources: (4), (6).

Unemployment insurance:
Source: (9).

Table 17

Pensioners: figures refer to the end of the year.
Sources: (4), (6), (8).

Population aged 60+, 65+, and 67+: figures as of January 1st.
Source: (4).

Table 18

Sickness cash beneficiaries: persons receiving at least one daily allowance during a year.
Source: (6).

Maternity/parents' allowances: prior to 1974 maternity allowance, from 1974 parents' allowance and special parents' allowance (see 'Institutional Synopsis').
Source: (6).

Child allowances:
Source: (6).

Maintenance advances: number of children receiving an advance payment through the social insurance fund.
Sources: (4), (6), (7).

Unemployment insurance benefits: average number of recipients during a month.
Source: (16).

Unemployment assistance benefits:
Source: (10).

Social assistance: prior to 1956 poor relief recipients.
Sources: (4), (7), (12).

Educational allowances: pupils in upper secondary schools, etc. aged 16-19 and students aged 20+.
Source: (17).

Study loans: only students aged 20+ entitled.
Sources: (18), (19).

Housing allowances: family housing allowances (to households) not including pensioners' households; from 1969 new system (see Institutional Synopsis); no figures published for 1968; from 1974 also low-income households without children entitled to this benefit (some 50-100,000 households from 1974 to 1980).
Sources: (4), (11).

Table 19

Figures for 1985 are preliminary.
Source: (20).

Table 20

LO = Trade Union Confederation (blue-collar); TCO = Central Organization of Salaried Employees; SACO/SR = Confederation of Professional Associations.
Sources: (4), (21).

LRF = Federation of Swedish Farmers; prior to 1974, National Association of the People on the Countryside (RLF).
Source: Unpublished figures kindly provided by the organization.

Enumerated sources to appendix tables

(1) OECD, *National Accounts*, Vols I and II. Paris, various years.

(2) E. Höök, *Den offentliga sektorns expansion* (The Expansion of the Public Sector). Uppsala. Almqvist and Wiksell, 1962.

(3) A. Forsman, *En teori om staten och de offentliga utgifterna* (A Theory of the State and Public Expenditure). Uppsala, Acta Universitatis Uppsaliensis, 1980.

(4) *Statistical Yearbook* (of Sweden). Stockholm, various years.

(5) SOU 1980:6, 'Offentlig verksamhet och regional välfärd'.

(6) Riksförsäkringsverket, *Allmän försäkring* (National Insurance). Stockholm, 1963ff.

(7) Statistiska centralbyrån, *Socialvården* (Social Service). Stockholm 1960ff.

(8) SOS, *Folkpensioneringen om åren 1951-1962 och Sjukkasse- väsendet åren 1951-1953*, Riksförsäkringsverket, Stockholm, 1964.

(9) B. Erici and N. Roth, *Arbetslöshetsförsäkringen i Sverige 1935-1980* (Unemployment Insurance in Sweden 1935-80). Stockholm, Arbetslöshetskassornas samorganisation, 1981.

(10) Arbetsmarknadsstyrelsen, *Verksamhetsberättelse* (Activity Report). Stockholm, various years.

(11) Statistiska centralbyrån, *Bostads- och byggnadsstatistsk årsbok* (Yearbook of Housing and Construction Statistics). Stockholm, 1977ff.

(12) Socialdepartementet, *Socialhjälpsundersökningen 1968* (Social Assistance Survey 1968). (DS S 1969:9).

(13) Government Bill 100 (each year; the State Budget), Stockholm, various years.

(14) *Regeringens budgetförslag - sammandrag*. Stockholm, various years. (The official summary of the central government budget proposals published by the Ministry of Finance each year.)

(15) OECD, *Labour Force Statistics*. Paris, various years.

(16) Statistiska centralbyrån, *Arbetsmarknadsstatistisk årsbok* (Yearbook of Job Market Statistics). Stockholm, 1978.

(17) Statistiska centralbyrån, *Utbildningsstatistisk årsbok* (Yearbook of Educational Statistics). Stockholm, 1978.

(18) Centrala studiestödsnämnden: Rapport 1978:3.

(19) Centrala studiestödsnämnden: Rapport 1983:3.

(20) SOS, *Riksdagsmannavalen*, Stockholm, various years.

(21) A. Kjellberg, *Facklig organisering i tolv länder*. Arkiv, Lund, 1983.

Norway

Stein Kuhnle

Institutional Synopsis

Contents

General introduction

During the 1960s, efforts were made to coordinate the various insurance and pension schemes into one comprehensive scheme. The efforts resulted in a law on a National Insurance Scheme (*Folketrygden*) passed unanimously by parliament in 1966 and put into effect in 1967. The National Insurance Scheme replaced the previous old age pensions, invalidity pensions, widows' and unmarried mothers' pensions, survivors' benefit for children and rehabilitation assistance to cover expenses for retraining for gainful employment.

In 1971, health insurance, unemployment insurance, and occupational injuries insurance were incorporated into the National Insurance Scheme. The purpose of National Insurance is to provide benefit in cases of sickness, infirmity, pregnancy and childbirth, unemployment, old age, invalidity, death and loss of breadwinner. The scheme also provides support for single-parent families (unmarried, separated or divorced mothers or fathers who are bringing up a child or children alone). The National Insurance covers, with few exceptions, the entire resident population, irrespective of citizenship, and is compulsory. One is normally entitled to cash benefits after a minimum period of insurance which is set at three years. The 'insurance period' is the number of years a person has been a member of the National Insurance Scheme after the age of 16.

The scheme is financed by means of premiums paid by the insured (i.e. all gainfully employed persons), premiums paid by employers for each person employed, and contributions from central government. A regular system of contributions from municipalities was abolished in 1977. In 1984, the insured (gainfully employed persons) are estimated to have contributed 31.5%, employers 45.8%, central government 22.0%, and unspecified sources 0.7% of the financing of the National Insurance Scheme.

The premium paid by the insured is calculated partly on the basis of assessed taxable income in cases of sickness benefits, and partly on the basis of gross earnings ('pensionable income' or *pensjonsgivende inntekt*) in cases of all other benefits unless gross earnings amount to less than NKR 15,000 in 1984, in which case one is exempted from paying premiums. In 1984, premiums for employers were 4.4% of assessed taxable income plus 5.9% of gross earnings, and for self-employed 4.4% plus 10.8%. Premiums based on gross earnings are paid by all gainfully employed persons from the age of 17 until the age of 66 (or 69 for those who become pensioners when 70).

Premium is not calculated for earnings which exceed 12 times 'basic amount' (*grunnbeløpet*). The entire National Insurance Scheme is built on the technical concept of a 'basic amount' which is regulated annually by parliament according to the price index and consideration of the general economic development. Almost all National Insurance cash benefits are related to the basic amount. From May 1983 the basic amount was NKR 22,600.

The employers' premium is based on wages and other cash payments paid to their employees, and is geographically differentiated (for reasons of regional policy) dependent upon the place of residence of the employees. In 1984, the premium varied between 6.0, 11.0, 13.6, and 16.8% of gross earnings of every employee. Contributions from the central government are determined by the *Storting* each year in connection with the budget proceedings.

The National Insurance Scheme is administered by the National Insurance Institution (*Rikstrygdeverket*) which supervises local insurance offices. In general each municipality (now 454 altogether) has an insurance office which administers the insurance programmes locally. The local offices are managed by elected boards. The central administration is supervised by the Ministry of Social Affairs.

I Pension system

In 1980 total pension expenditure amounted to 23,881 million NKR (Source 25), and expenditure on old age and invalidity services amounted to 1,396 million NKR. Together, this expenditure totalled 8.9% of GDP and 43.1% of social security expenditure.

In 1983 the number of old age pensioners was 566,000, which constituted 13.7% of the total population, and the total number of pension recipients was 838,000, which constituted 20.3% of the total population.

Number of pensioners in January 1981 by type of pension and pension scheme (in thousands)[a].

Type of Pension	Pension scheme: National Insurance Scheme[b]	War Pensions	Early Retirement Pensions[h]	Total	%
Old age	520		23[i]	543	63.9
Invalidity	192[c]	11[f]		203	23.9
Survivors	45[d]	6[g]	15[j]	66	7.8
Unmarried mothers	15[e]			15	1.8
Orphans	22	0.3		22.3	2.6
Total	794	17.3	38	849.3	100.0
%	93.5	2.0	4.5	100.0	

[a] (Source 2).

[b] The numbers of pensioners include those whose state (94,000), local government (20,500), or other public occupational pension is coordinated with the pensions of the National Insurance Scheme.

[c] Includes 32,000 receiving 'basic support' or 'assistance support' only, i.e. recipients who do not qualify for pensions.

[d] Includes 700 receiving 'assistance support' only, and 1,800 'family care survivors'.

[e] Of which 12,000 with transitory benefit and 3,000 with 'assistance support' only. Transitory benefit equals the 'basic amount' of the National Insurance Scheme. 'Assistance support' is a smaller amount for those who do not qualify for the full basic amount.

[f] Of which 3,000 military personnel.

[g] Of which 1,300 military personnel.

[h] Pension schemes for seamen, forestry workers, and fishermen.

[i] Of which 19,600 retired seamen.

[j] Including orphans. The actual figure is 14,944, of which 14,900 are covered by the pension scheme for seamen.

Pension expenditure by type of pension and pension scheme in mill. NKR in 1980[a]

Type of pension	Pension scheme							
	N.I. scheme [b]	War pens. [b]	Early retire-ment pens. [g]	State pens. [i]	Local govt. pens. [j]	Other occup. pens. [k]	Total	%
Old age pensions	12.261		384[h]	1.473	94	53[l]	14.265	63.5
Invalidity pensions[c]	5.144	418[e]	1	193	39	2	5.797	25.8
Survivors' pensions[c]	1.093	156[f]	60	354	20	5	1.688	7.5
Unmarried mothers' pensions[c]	295						295	1.3
Orphans' pensions	147	1	1	19			168	0.8
Other	216[d]				29		245	1.1
Total	19.156	575	446	2.039	182	60	22.458	100.0
%	85.3	2.5	2.0	9.1	0.8	0.3	100.0	

[a] In 1981 private life insurance companies paid a total of 1,794 million NKR in pensions. Expenses for the Local Government Pension Fund are included in this figure and these expenses (182 million NKR) are the only ones singled out for inclusion in the table. Of the total of 1,794 million, 50% covered old age pensions, 18% survivors' benefit, and 11% invalidity pensions (Source 6).

[b] (Source 1).

[c] Expenditure for regular pensions and transitory and other cash benefits.

[d] Lump sum payments.

[e] Of which 298 million to civilian victims and 120 to military personnel.

[f] Of which 122 million to survivors of civilian victims and 34 to survivors of military personnel.

[g] Pension schemes for seamen, forestry workers, and fishermen. (Sources 2 and 3).

[h] Pension expenditure for forestry workers (6 million) and fishermen (33 million). (Source 2).

[i] (Source 4). Net pension expenditure (after coordination with National Insurance Scheme); see paragraph I, 8.

[j] (Source 5). Expenses for individual municipal pension schemes of communes not members of the Local Government Pension Fund are not included.

[k] Pension schemes for nurses and pharmacists (net pension expenditure).

[l] Pension expenditure for nurses (37 million) includes benefits other than old age pensions (Source 5). Source 4 gives a breakdown by type of pension for the pharmacists' pension scheme.

Income maintenance

Coverage

The pension system consists of: the National Insurance Scheme (*Folketrygden*), which provides minimum old age pensions for all citizens, together with earnings-related supplementary pensions, invalidity pensions, survivors' (widows' and widowers') pensions, orphans' pensions, transitional allowances for unmarried mothers, separated and divorced supporters, and various other transitory or lump sum payments; the State Pension Fund (*Statens pensjonskasse*) which covers all government employees; local government pension schemes; occupational pension schemes for forestry workers, fishermen, and Lapps, which are administered by the National Insurance Institution; war pension schemes for military and civilian victims administered by the National Insurance Institution (*Rikstrygdeverket*, RTV); occupational schemes for seamen, with their own administration; occupational schemes for pharmacists and government ministers administered by the State Pension Fund; an occupational scheme for nurses administered by the Local Government Pension Fund (*Kommunal Landespensjonskasse*); and private occupational and individual pension schemes.

1. National Insurance

Coverage

The National Insurance Scheme provides old age, invalidity, survivors' (widows' and widowers'), orphans', pensions and transitional allowances for single-parent families, together with various other transitory or lump sum payments. A national old age pension scheme (*alderstrygd*), covering all resident citizens, was introduced in 1936. It was mainly financed by a 1% income tax. Pensions were means-tested and payable from the age of 70. In 1957 the means test was abolished and everyone over the age of 70 became entitled to a pension. In 1967 the scheme was incorporated into the National Insurance Scheme, and in 1973 eligibility for an old age pension was reduced to 67, but with an option to postpone drawing the pension until the age of 70.

Invalidity pension (*uførhetstrygd*) was not introduced until 1960, but special groups (the blind and crippled) had received help since 1936. In 1967 the scheme was incorporated into the National Insurance Scheme, and invalidity pensions have since been payable to persons between 16 and 66 years of age whose working capacity is permanently reduced by at least 50%.

Orphans' pensions (*forsørgertrygden for barn*) were introduced in 1957, and are payable to all fatherless and/or motherless children under the age of 18. Widows' and mothers' pensions (*enke- og morstrygd*) came into force in 1965 and cover certain categories of women under 70 not entitled to an old age pension: widows who had been married for at least five years or fulfilled some other conditions; unmarried mothers; unmarried women who have remained at home for a long period of time in order to nurse and care for parents or other close relatives; and divorced women under certain conditions. In 1967, a general survivors' pension scheme and a separate scheme for unmarried mothers was set up and incorporated into the National Insurance Scheme. From 1981, the unmarried mothers' scheme was reformed to include separated and divorced supporters of both sexes, as well as unmarried fathers taking care of their own children (Source 20).

Benefits

Old age pensions consist of the following benefits:
- a basic pension (*grunnpensjon*) and a compensation benefit (*kompensasjonstillegg*) paid to everybody;
- an earnings-related supplementary pension (*tilleggspensjon*) depending on previous contributions;
- other supplements depending on various conditions.

Entitlement to a basic pension is dependent upon a minimum residence record of three years. A full basic pension is paid if the pensioner has lived in Norway for at least 40 years since the age of 16, and is reduced by 2.5% per year for shorter insurance periods, or where the pensioner's spouse also receives a pension. A full basic pension is equivalent to the 'basic amount' (*grunnbeløpet*), which is adjusted annually by parliament in accordance with changes in the cost of living and general levels of income, but it is not indexed automatically. In May 1983 the basic amount was 22,600 NKR, i.e. 25% of average annual gross earnings for male industrial workers in 1982 (Source 21). In addition to the basic pension, everyone is entitled to a compensation benefit, which was introduced in 1970 to compensate for the effects of the value-added tax system. In 1984 it amounted to 500 NKR per year for single pensioners, and the supplement is increased by 250 NKR a year if the recipient also receives an additional amount for a supported spouse.

In order to receive an earnings-related supplementary pension, a pensioner must have earned an income above the basic amount for a minimum period of three years since 1966. The supplementary pension is calculated by multiplying three factors: basic amount x pension points x 0.45.
- the basic amount, annually defined by parliament, depends on the number of contribution years (full basic amount = 40 years);
- pension points (*pensjonspoeng*) are calculated on the basis of the best 20 years; for each year the basic amount as defined for that year, is subtracted from the respective earnings and the result is divided again by the basic amount; earnings in excess of 12 times the basic amount are not taken into account and earnings between eight and twelve times the basic amount are counted as a third; in the formula the average of the 20 years is used;
- the factor 0.45 reflects the aim that a full supplementary pension should amount to 45% of average earnings above the basic amount.

In cases where a person has been insured for a period of less than 40 years, the pension is reduced correspondingly.

Those too old to have earnt the right to an earnings-related supplement (introduced in 1966), are paid a special supplement benefit (*særtillegg*) which amounted to 51.5% of the basic amount for single pensioners and for pensioners supporting a spouse, and 47.5% for a pensioner married to another pensioner (total 95% for a married couple) in May 1984 (Source 22). In May 1983, a age pension (consisting of full basic pension, compensation supplement, special supplement), i.e. a pension for a person who has lived in Norway for 40 years and is not entitled to an earnings-related supplementary pension, amounted to 34,739 NKR or 38.5% of average annual gross earnings for male industrial workers in 1980 (Sources 20,21). In addition, a provider's supplement benefit is paid if a pensioner has a spouse without income or a child under the age of 18. In this case the pension amounted to 46,289 NKR. If a pensioner's spouse is also entitled to a pension, they both received a minimum pension of 28,060 NKR. In 1983 the minimum pension for a married couple (both pensioners) amounted to

62.3% of the average annual gross earnings for male industrial workers in 1982 (Sources 20,21). Old age and invalidity pensioners qualify for special deductions on their income tax declaration, such that pensioners with a minimum pension in practice do not pay income tax.

Invalidity pensions are paid to persons between the age of 16 and 67, if their working capacity is reduced by at least 50% - due to illness, injury or disability - and if they have been insured for at least three years. Old age is equated with sickness if the insured reaches the age of 64 (Source 22). A full invalidity pension (basic plus supplementary pension) is paid if the person is 100% disabled. The pension is reduced according to level of disablement (minimum 50% disablement). The pension corresponds to the old age pension to which the claimant would have been entitled had they continued in employment until the age of 67. A providers' supplement is payable for a spouse over 60 years of age without income and/or with a child or children below the age of 18. In addition to, or instead of invalidity pensions, insured persons may receive a basic benefit (*grunnstønad*) or assistance benefit (*hjelpestønad*) where disablement entails severe problems. In May 1984 the basic support varied between 3,348 NKR and 16,695 NKR, and the assistance support amounted to 5,588 NKR per year (i.e. 15%, 74%, and 25% of the basic amount).

Survivors' pension is dependent upon the pension rights of the deceased. A full basic pension, equal to the basic amount, is paid to widows/widowers if the deceased spouse lived in Norway for a minimum of 40 years. A special supplement and compensation benefits are also paid. A full supplementary survivors' pension amounts to 55% of the (expected) supplementary pension of the deceased. Surviving children under the age of 18 receive 40% (first and second child, the latter where both parents are dead) or 25% (all other children) of the basic amount.

Supporters in single-parent families are entitled to a transitional allowance (maximum 100% of basic amount in 1984) (Source 22); unmarried mothers are entitled to a childbirth benefit (31% of basic amount in 1984) (Source 22); education benefits; assistance support; child care support and after giving birth a woman who has not been in employment will be entitled to a lump sum maternity grant of 3,480 NKR. This is paid in addition to the childbirth benefit she receives as the supporter in a single-parent family.

Financing and administration

See general introduction.

2. War pensions

War pensions for military personnel and civilians were introduced in 1941. In 1946 two new pension schemes were instituted: one for military personnel (all Norwegians or foreign citizens who had served in Norwegian military organizations), the other for civilians and members of the resistance movement. The laws only cover injuries resulting from the Second World War. The schemes provide invalidity, survivors' and orphans' pensions. Pensions for persons with a disability of less than 20% are payable as lump sums. In 1983 maximum invalidity pension amounted to 94,356 NKR, and minimum invalidity pension to 54,696 NKR (i.e. 105% and 61% respectively of average annual gross earnings for male industrial workers in 1982 (Sources 21,22). A survivors' pension amounts to a full widow's pension if the pensioner at the time of death was drawing a 100% invalidity pension. If the degree of disability was less, the widow's pension will be correspondingly reduced, but never to below two-thirds of the full widow's pension. Orphans' pensions are paid on the same basis as in the National Insurance Scheme.

Financing and administration

War pensions for military personnel are covered by general government revenues, while the expenses of the other schemes are covered by premiums paid for the National Insurance Scheme. Both schemes are administered by the National Insurance Institution.

3. Early retirement occupational pensions

A special pension insurance for seamen was introduced in 1948, for forestry workers in 1951, and for fishermen in 1957. They were introduced primarily as supplementary schemes to the National Pension Scheme to cover occupational groups with a lower eligibility age. The pensionable ages are 60, 63, and 62 respectively and the schemes provide old age pensions up to the age of 67 at which point the National Insurance Scheme replaces the special schemes. The seamen's scheme also provides pensions for disablement incurred prior to 1967 when the National Insurance Scheme was introduced. All three schemes provide survivors' pensions to a certain extent.

Financing and administration

Expenses for the seamen's scheme are covered by premiums from seamen and shipowners, and contributions from sea-related duties and the scheme's fund, plus allocations from the state. The scheme has its own administration.

The fishermen's scheme is financed by premiums from the insured and revenues from various duties and a turn over tax on fish. It is administered by the National Insurance Institution.

The forestry workers scheme is financed by premiums from the insured and contributions from employers. It is administered by the National Insurance Institution.

4. Public sector occupational pensions

The State Pension Fund (*Statens pensjonskasse*) was established in 1917 and membership was made compulsory for all central government employees. The fund also covers a number of mixed government and municipal agencies. In 1983 the number of persons insured totalled 304,000 and the number of pensioners totalled 106,500 (Source 20). Public sector occupational pensions are coordinated with the national pensions (see paragraph I, 8).

Benefits

Pensions are calculated on the basis of the insured person's 'pension basis' (*pensjonsgrunnlag*) and years of service. The pension basis is the gross regular wage (*bruttoregulativlønn*) together with approved supplements in the last year before retirement (or disablement). Wages amounting to over 'wage level 26' (162,917 NKR in 1983), are counted as one-third, and wages above 'wage level 35' (233,885 NKR) are not counted at all. Full pension is paid if the number of years of service is 30 or more at retirement age.

The scheme offers old age, invalidity, survivors', and orphans' pensions. Full old age pension constitutes a minimum of 66% of the pension basis in the last year of employment, plus a quarter of the basic amount, and the compensation benefit (after coordination with the national pension). A children's supplement is offered for every child below the age of 18, and equals 10% of the pension. Invalidity pensions are paid to members who are forced to retire completely or partly due to sickness or injury. No minimum level of disablement is required. The pension is calculated as for old age pensions and years of service as if the person had remained a member until retirement. Survivors' pensions amount to a maximum of 60% of the pension to which the deceased would have been entitled. No pension is payable if the survivor remarries. Orphans receive pensions until the age of 18. The amount is dependent upon the number of children, and is equal to 20% of the old age pension for one child, increasing to 60% for five or more children. Where no survivors' pensions are paid, orphans' pensions are increased, varying from 50% to 100%. All pensions from the State Pension Fund are coordinated according to the 1957 law on the coordination of pension benefits (see below).

Financing and administration

The State Pension Fund is financed by members who pay a premium of 2% of the pension basis, which amounts to 2% of wages for most members; some government agencies who pay an employers' contribution of 8% of gross wage; and by interest on property. Expenditure not covered by these sources is financed out of general revenues. The State Pension Fund has its own administration, and also incorporates the following schemes: the Norwegian Widows' Fund (*Den norske enkekasse*); the pension scheme for government workers; the railway pension fund; the pension scheme for pharmacists and the pension scheme for government ministers.

5. Local government pensions

Local government pension schemes cover almost all employees of local government or the municipalities (*kommuner*), counties (*fylkeskommuner*) and municipal enterprises (*kommunale foretak*). The earliest schemes were established at the turn of the century, but most are of post-World War II origin. Of the 454 municipalities, only five do not have pension schemes. In 1976 about 50 municipalities had their own pension schemes with 151,000 members and 13,000 pensioners, while the Local Government Pension Fund had 104,000 members and 7,500 pensioners (Sources 8 and 9).

Benefits

Benefits normally include old age, invalidity, survivors' and orphans' pensions. Pensions are generally calculated using the same criteria as for the State Pension Fund schemes. Some municipalities offer means-tested supplementary pensions.

Financing and administration

Schemes are generally financed through premiums from the insured (2% of wages), and contributions from employers. Schemes are established partly through membership in the Local Government Pension Fund, and partly through collective pension insurance in an insurance company. The Local Government Pension Fund administers the great majority of schemes.

6. Private sector occupational pensions

There are a number of occupational pension schemes for employees in the private sector. Circa 400,000 employees (ca. 21% of the labour force) participated in such schemes in 1981 (Source 20). These schemes constitute collective pension insurance in an insurance company; a pension fund for employees in a firm; pension schemes based on an agreement between organizations for employers and employees approved by the Ministry for Social Affairs as a 'tariff-fixed pension scheme according to the tax law'. Pension schemes must satisfy certain requirements in order that employers and employees are able to deduct premiums and contributions from their pre-tax income. Current rules were established by a 1968 Royal Resolution.

Benefits

Most private occupational pension schemes offer old age, invalidity, survivors' or divorced spouses' and orphans' pensions.

7. Private pension insurance

Individuals may take out their own pension insurance according to the tax law. Current rules were established in a 1968 Royal Resolution. This opportunity to draw an individual pension insurance is particularly important for the self-employed, persons in the professions, and for employees in firms with no supplementary pension scheme for employees. Premiums may be deducted on income prior to taxation, but cannot exceed 15% of average income in the year for which deductions are claimed and in the two years prior to that. Individual pension insurance has increased in importance in recent years. In 1981, 130,000 citizens had taken out their own pension insurance, i.e. ca. 6.7% of the total labour force (Source 20).

Benefits

Most insurance schemes include old age pensions (starting at 67), survivors', invalidity, and orphans' pensions.

8. Pension coordination

A law on the coordination of pension benefits was passed in 1957, in order to limit the possibility of drawing full benefits from several pension schemes simultaneously. Thus, the law aims at reducing pensions to a 'reasonable' level. Today, a civil servant's pension (disposable income) is equal to 70-95% of last earnings, i.e. the last year prior to retirement. The law maintains that in principle a person who moves from one place to another should not receive a larger pension than they would have been entitled to if they had remained in the same employment. The law, amended several times, most recently in 1979, covers the coordination of benefits from two or more of the following schemes:

- public sector occupational pension schemes;
- occupational injury insurance (for injuries incurred before 1971) and war pension schemes;
- National Insurance Scheme.

The law does not cover private occupational pension schemes, but the coordination of pensions from schemes provided under occupational injury insurance, with pensions from the National Insurance Scheme may be affected by the existence of a private pension. The coordination of benefits from the several different schemes is covered by specific rules.

Services

In 1980 there were 655 old people's homes with a total of 14,042 beds. In 1980 there were 630 nursing institutions, of which many were combined old people's homes and nursing institutions, with a total of 27,404 beds (Source 23). Various kinds of educational, rehabilitation, and employment services for the partially disabled are provided, in addition to communal home help services for the old and disabled. In 1980 the number of people employed in home help services amounted to 44,694.

Old age and invalidity pensioners and the blind, are entitled to a 50% rebate on all government subsidized means of collective transport. Spouses or those entitled to travelling rebates are also covered by this rule. Pensioners are entitled to allowances to cover acquisition of telephones, on the basis of a means-test.

Expenditure on old age and invalidity services in 1980, in mill. NKR[a]

	Total	%
Training and employment of partially disabled	406	29.1
Homes for the old and for pensioners	936	67.0
Communal home-help services for the old and handicapped	54	3.9
Total	1 396	100.0
% of all social security expenditure		2.4%

[a] (Source 25).

Core laws

The dates of the laws refer to the day when they were passed by parliament.

16.7.1936 (no. 10)
Lov om alderstrygd (Old Age Insurance Law): introduced national pension insurance; compulsory for all income earners aged 18-70; 1% income tax; pensions based on income test and varied by municipality.

6.7.1957 (no. 16)
Lov om alderstrygd (Old Age Insurance Law): effective from 1959; income test abol-

ished; pension qualifying age of 70, lower for special groups; flat-rate pensions for all citizens; spouses entitled to pensions (50% of basic pension).

26.4.1957 (no. 3)
Lov om forsørgertrygd for barn (Law on Providers' Pension for Orphans): scheme introduced.

6.7.1957 (no. 26)
Lov om samordning av pensjons- og trygdeytelser (Coordination of Pension and Insurance Benefits Law): effective from 1959; coordinated pension entitlements from two or more schemes.

22.1.1960 (no. 1)
Lov om uførthetstrygd (Invalidity Insurance Law): effective from 1961; introduced invalidity pension scheme; a two-third loss working capacity entitled claimant to pension; pension the same as for old age pensioners according to 1957 law.

20.6.1964 (no. 1)
Lov om enke- og morstrygd (Widows' and Mothers' Insurance Law): effective from 1965; covered widows, unmarried mothers, and unmarried women who nurse a close relative.

17.6.1966 (no. 12)
Lov om folketrygd (National Insurance Law): effective from 1967; introduced National Insurance Scheme; replaced earlier laws on old age pensions, invalidity pensions, widows' and unmarried mothers' pensions; introduced supplementary earnings-related pensions; self-employed covered; basic amount subject to annual adjustment by the *Storting*.

28.6.1968
Royal Resolution on the regulation of private occupational schemes: employer and employee contributions deducted from income before taxation.

19.6.1969 (no. 61)
Lov om særtillegg til ytelser fra folketrygden (Special Supplement to National Insurance Benefits Law): introduced special supplement for those not entitled to supplementary pension.

19.12.1969 (no. 80)
Lov om kompensasjonstillegg til ytelser fra folketrygden (Law on Compensation Supplement to National Insurance Benefits): supplement introduced to compensate for the introduction of a value-added tax system.

17.12.1971 (no. 119)
Lov om stønad til fraskilte og separerte forsørgere (Law on Allowances for Divorced and Separated Supporters): temporary law (extended to 1981) on benefits for divorced and separated supporters.

16.6.1972 (no. 60)
Lov om endringer i lov av 17. juni 1966 nr. 12 om folketrygd og andre lover (Amendments to National Insurance Law of 17.6.1966 and other laws): pension age reduced to 67.

25.4.1980 and 31.10.1980 (nos. 9, 50)
Lov om endringer i lov av 17. juni 1966 nr 12 om folketrygd og lov av 19. juni 1969 nr 1 om særtillegg til ytelser fra folketrygden (Amendments to National Insurance Law of 17.6.1966 and the law of 19.6.1969 on special supplements to National Insur-

ance benefits): the National Insurance Scheme extended to cover benefits to unmarried, divorced and separated supporters (men and women); replaced the law of 17.12.1971 (no. 119).

II Sickness insurance/Health services

In 1980 expenditure for sickness and health insurance amounted to 25,450 million NKR. This sum constituted 41.3% of total social security expenditure and 9.3% of GDP. The major components were:

Sickness and health expenditure in 1978 in mill. NKR[a]

	Total	%
Sickness cash benefits and wage continuation	7 308	29.0
General health/hospital care	16 513	65.6
Mentally handicapped	874	3.5
Dental care	476	1.9
Total	25 171	100.0

[a] (Source 25). Wage continuation paid by employers for the first 10 days of sickness included. Sickness cash benefits do not include maternity benefits. These and other allowances to mothers and young children are included in Section V on Families and Children.

National sickness insurance

Compulsory sickness and health insurance was introduced in 1909. The first law only covered workers and employees with small means, but with the possibility of voluntary insurance for certain other groups. In 1953 compulsory sickness insurance was extended to include all employees and from 1956 it covered all residents in Norway. In 1971 sickness and health insurance was incorporated into the National Insurance Scheme.

Income maintenance

Benefits

The National Insurance Scheme offers three major kinds of cash benefits: sickness cash benefits, maternity benefits and coverage of extra outlays.

1. Wage continuation and sickness cash benefits

Sickness cash benefits are payable to persons whose annual earned income exceeds 10,000 NKR in 1983 and who have had a work contract for a minimum of 14 days prior to sickness.

Since 1978 employees receive 100% compensation of gross wage from the first day of sickness. The employer pays the first 14 days of sickness benefit, and the National Insurance Scheme thereafter. No sickness allowance is payable for any part of the income which exceeds eight times the National Insurance basic amount. Employers with few employees may take out an insurance against liability for paying sickness cash benefits. The self-employed receive 65% of estimated gross annual earnings from the fifteenth day of sickness, with an option to join a voluntary supplementary insurance scheme which can provide up to 100% wage compensation from the first day of sickness.

Benefits are taxed and 'pension points' for the earnings-related old age pension scheme are accumulated as for ordinary income. Since January 1983 benefits are paid for five days of the week and for a period of 260 days for the same sickness. An insured person who is drawing a full old age pension is not entitled to sickness allowance.

2. Maternity benefits

The National Insurance Scheme offers maternity benefits for a period of 90 days to women who have been gainfully employed for a minimum of six of the last 10 months prior to giving birth. Benefits amount to 100% wage compensation. Fathers are entitled to up to 60 days of the maternity benefits, if they stay at home and care for their children, but benefits are not offered for more than a total of 90 days for both parents together. Economically non-active women receive a lump sum which amounted to 3,480 NKR from May 1981 (15% of the 'basic amount' on an annual basis in 1983). An unmarried mother receives a childbirth support of NKR 7,020 (May 1983), which equals 31% of 'basic amount' on an annual basis, together with maternity benefits (100% wage compensation) for 90 days if economically active or a lump sum of 3,480 NKR if not. Unmarried mothers are entitled to allowances for child supervision and education. Widows giving birth after the death of the child's father are entitled to a lump sum payment of 7,020 NKR.

3. Coverage of extra outlays

The National Insurance Scheme covers extra outlays incurred as a result of sickness or treatment of sickness, such as: transport and travel, food, telephones, laundry, assistance in the house, special care and nursing. Chronically ill persons who need assistance in the house are entitled to 'assistance support' (*hjelpestønad*) which equals 25% of the basic amount per year, and/or 'basic support' (*grunnstønad*) to cover extra outlays for the purposes listed above.

Financing and administration

See general introduction.

Services

Medical treatment and care in hospitals and recognized health institutions are free of charge. Consultations and treatment at municipal health care centres (*helsestasjoner*) are free of charge for children and mothers, in addition to the family advisory centres (*familievernkontor*). Home nursing (*hjemmesykepleie*) is also a free service. Medical assistance at birth, together with the assistance of a midwife, are free of charge, as is ante-natal care. Treatment by a psychologist in connection with an illness is free. Doctors' fees are shared between the patient and the National Insurance Scheme. Persons in need of medical assistance or other health services (medicines or 'blue prescriptions', travelling expenses, technical aids) must as a general rule pay part of the cost themselves up to a certain annual sum (the cost ceiling) which equalled 600 NKR in 1984 (for the period 1.4-31.12). Physiotherapeutic, chiropractic, and some kinds of dental treatment are partly refunded.

The National Insurance Scheme also offers various kinds of rehabilitation services and benefits. Rehabilitation services and benefits serve the primary function of enabling handicapped people to provide for themselves through gainful employment. The scheme contributes to rehabilitation efforts.

In December 1978 there were 107 general hospitals. Of these 65% were owned by the counties (province-level government) which provided 77% of all beds, 28% of hospitals were privately owned (16% of all beds), while the state owned 6.5% of hospitals (7% of the beds). In addition, there are more than 600 nursing institutions (*pleiehjem*) and/or homes for the sick (*sykehjem*) mostly run by the municipalities together with 19 psychiatric institutions, 15 of which are owned by the counties. Expenses for hospital care are shared between the National Insurance Scheme and the owners (counties and municipalities). The running costs of private hospitals may also be paid by the county if they follow the general health care plan of the country. There are approximately 1,350 health care centres for mothers and children run by the municipalities which have most of the responsibility for preventive services. All children are 'supervised' by such centres from birth and are to undergo regular health checks and vaccinations. The National Insurance Scheme, via the counties, covers part of the running costs of institutions for alcoholics, psychiatric patients, the mentally retarded, physically handicapped, and others. The National Insurance Scheme offers assistance (for example cash benefits) for rehabilitation.

Core laws

18.9.1909
Lov om sykeforsikring (Sickness Insurance Law): effective from 1911; first sickness insurance law; provided compulsory coverage for workers and employees below certain income limit (approximately 45% of all wage earners); free medical assistance, cash benefits equalling 60% of average gross daily income in the income class of the insured, cash benefits for six weeks plus free medical assistance for female members in case of childbirth and funeral benefits; free hospital treatment, during which time the member's family dependents would receive cash benefits equalling 20% of daily income for one dependent, 35% for two, and 50% for three or more dependents; free medical assistance for spouse and children of the insured, and maternity benefit for the wife of the insured; income limit for inclusion in the insurance scheme has gradually been raised and the scope of voluntary insurance extended.

15.7.1953 (no. 15)
Lov om endringer i lov om syketrygd av 6. juni 1930 (Amendments to the 1930 Sickness Insurance Law): introduced compulsory insurance for all wage-earners; premiums and cash benefits graded by income.

2.3.1956 (no. 2)
Lov om syketrygd (Sickness Insurance Law): compulsory insurance for all residents.

19.6.1969 (no. 57)
Lov om sykehus (Hospitals' Law): responsibility for construction and running of hospitals placed with the counties.

19.6.1970 (no. 67)
Lov om endringer i lov om folketrygd av 17. juni 1966 (Amendments to the 1966 National Insurance Law): sickness and health insurance incorporated into the National Insurance Scheme.

16.6.1972 (no. 64)
Lov om helsestasjoner og helsetiltak blant barn, m.v. (Law on Health Centres and Services for Children etc): municipalities made responsible for preventive health care centres for mothers and children.

9.6.1978 (no. 54)
Lov om endringer i lov av 17. juni 1966 nr. 12 om folketrygd, m.v. (Amendments to 1966 Law): sickness benefits to equal 100% of gross wage from first day of sickness for up to 312 days for same sickness.

19.11.1982 (no. 66)
Lov om helsetjenesten i kommunene (Municipal Health Services Law): a number of other laws repealed (e.g. 16.6.1972, no. 64), and revised (e.g. 19.6.1969, no. 57, and 17.6.1966, no. 12); municipalities made responsible for the existence of necessary health services for all permanent and temporary residents; municipalities to be responsible for all medical treatment, nursing and care which takes place outside health institutions.

17.12.1982 (no. 95)
Lov om endringer i lov av 17. juni 1966 nr. 12 om folketrygd (Amendments to the 1966 Law): new rules on the payment of sickness benefits and allowances - no benefits on Saturdays and reduction of maximum duration to 260 days for sickness benefits and 90 days for maternity benefits.

III Occupational injuries

Income maintenance

Expenditure for occupational injuries, incurred after occupational injuries' insurance, was incorporated in the National Insurance Scheme in 1971. In the accounts of the National Insurance Institution such expenditure is included in the general categories of sickness benefits, invalidity benefits and pensions, and rehabilitation benefits. Occupational injuries incurred before the 1971 law are still covered on the basis of the old law on occupational injuries' insurance. Expenditure for coverage according to the old law totalled 121 million NKR in 1980 (Source 25). This amounted to 0.2% of total social security expenditure and 0.04% of GDP.

Coverage

Various accident insurance laws were substituted by a common, universal, occupational injuries scheme in 1958 (effective from 1960). This scheme was incorporated into the National Insurance Scheme in 1971. The National Insurance Scheme offers support in cases of physical injury caused by work accidents, certain occupational diseases and climatic and epidemic diseases. The injury must have been incurred at work, during working hours and at the workplace. No minimum duration of work prior to occupational injury is required. All workers and employees are covered by the law as well as military personnel, students and pupils. Voluntary insurance is optional for the self-employed.

Benefits

Benefits are awarded on the same basis as for sickness and health insurance, except that doctors' fees, medicines and the cost of other aids and treatment are 100% covered. Cash benefits for sickness are calculated according to the general rules of the National Insurance Scheme and there are no conditions on length of work contract prior to the injury. Invalidity benefits are generally paid on the same basis as for disablement not caused by occupational injury, i.e. pensions, 'basic benefit', and 'assistance benefit'. Pensions are paid regardless of the length of the insurance period (as if the insured was entitled to a full basic pension), and supplementary pension is offered in full (no reduction for lack of accumulated pension points). Pensions are offered provided that the ability to work has been reduced by at least 15%. 'Assistance support' may be increased by 40% of the 'basic amount' (see Section I for an explanation of the various terms) compared to the ordinary level of disablement if caused by an occupational injury. Rehabilitation aid is offered as in cases of disablement not caused by occupational injury.

If the degree of disablement is estimated to be less than 30% the pension is paid as a lump sum, which varies by degree of disablement. The maximum (25-29% disablement) amounted to nine times the annual pension. If the occupational injury entails permanent serious medical consequences, the injured person is entitled to an annual compensation of up to 75% of the 'basic amount'. Pension rights of surviving dependents are subject to the usual conditions of the National Insurance Scheme, though subject to certain modifications (no requirement of a minimum insurance period, minimum number of point-accummulating years, duration of stay in Norway, or duration of marriage to the deceased). Children's pensions are also awarded on general terms, but can be extended to the age of 21.

Financing and administration

Occupational injuries expenditure is financed by the National Insurance Scheme. Expenses are covered by contributions from employers to the National Insurance Scheme. The self-employed may insure themselves voluntarily and pay their own premiums, while central government covers the premiums of students and military personnel. For administration see general introduction.

Services

Hospital care and rehabilitation aid are provided according to general rules of the National Insurance Scheme; see the paragraph on Sickness and Health Insurance.

Core laws

1894
Lov om ulykkesforsikring for arbeidere i fabrikker (Accident Insurance for Factory Workers Law): first law providing compulsory accident insurance for industrial workers; premiums paid by employers; organized by the new government created National Insurance Institution (*riksforsikringsanstalten*), now referred to as (*Rikstrygdeverket*).

1894
Lov om ulykkesforsikring for fiskerer (Fishermen's Accident Insurance Law): premiums paid by fisherman and state.

1911
Lov om ulykkesforsikring for sjømenn (Seamen's Accident Insurance Law): premiums paid by employers.

12.12.1958 (no. 10)
Lov om yrkesskadetrygd (Occupational Injuries Insurance Law): effective from 1960; scheme covered all groups of workers and employees (paid by employers), students and pupils (paid by state); the self-employed may take out voluntary insurance; certain occupational diseases covered.

9.6.1961 (no. 19)
Lov om endringer i lov om yrkesskadetrygd av 12. des. 1958 (Amendment to 1958 Law): extended coverage to military personnel and conscripts; premiums paid by state.

19.6.1970 (no. 67)
Lov om endring i lov om folketrygd av 17. juni 1966 (Amendment to the 1966 National Insurance Law): incorporated the occupational injuries scheme into the National Insurance Scheme; expenses covered by employers' contribution; old law still pertains to injuries sustained prior to 1971.

IV Unemployment insurance/Employment policy

In 1980 unemployment expenditure amounted to 1,501 million NKR, which made up 2.6% of total social security expenditure and 0.5% of GDP.

Expenditure for unemployment in 1978, in million NKR[a]

	Total	%
Unemployment insurance	1 037	69.1
Labour exchange and services	199	13.3
Education/retraining of unemployed	264	17.6
Total	1 501	100.0

[a] (Source 25).

Income maintenance

Coverage

Governmental support for unemployment insurance was first introduced in 1906, when voluntary insurance organized by trade unions was subsidized. Unemployment insurance was made compulsory for all employed persons outside the primary sector in 1938, and extended to agricultural workers and certain other groups in 1949. Unemployment insurance was incorporated into the National Insurance Scheme in 1971. It covers all occupational groups together with the self-employed over the age of 64.

Benefits

The National Insurance Scheme offers cash benefits in the form of daily allowances during unemployment. To qualify for cash benefits, the insured must have been at work with an income of at least 75% of the 'basic amount' during the last year or as an average during the last three years. Daily allowances are paid for a maximum of 40 weeks in the year for persons under 64 years, and for 52 weeks for persons between 64 and 67 years of age, thus in practice functioning as unemployment pensions. Saturdays and Sundays are excluded. The amount is determined on a basis of the work income in the year prior to application for benefits, or of the average of the last three years if this average is higher. In 1984 allowances amounted to 2 per mille of annual gross wage per day. The amount of the wages which make up between 8 and 12 times the 'basic amount' is only calculated as one-third, and wage beyond 12 times the basic amount is not considered. Unemployed persons providing for children receive an additional 6 NKR per day for each dependent child, and an additional 6 NKR per day to cover the cost of domestic help, if they are 'spouseless'. Daily allowances are taxed, and pension points are accumulated.

Travel support is offered to persons who take on a new job provided through the labour exchange and family support may be offered on certain conditions. Unemployed persons above normal school leaving age may receive cash support during periods of retraining for suitable work.

Persons who refuse to accept offers of suitable work or occupational training/ retraining are denied unemployment benefit for a period of eight weeks from the day of registration as unemployed.

Financing and administration

Unemployment insurance is part of the National Insurance Scheme and as such expenses are part of the accounts of the National Insurance Institution. The scheme is administered centrally by the Directorate of Labour (*Arbeidsdirektoratet*) and subject to the Ministry of Municipal and Labour Affairs. Administration is carried out by the county (provincial) labour force offices and committees at local level, and and by local insurance offices at municipal level.

Employment services

The right to work has been embodied in the Norwegian constitution since 1954 which states that it is the duty of the central state authorities to enable every person fit to work to obtain gainful employment.

Two types of government policy are directed towards this commitment. One of these focuses on groups who, for various reasons, have problems obtaining work. Efforts in this field, labelled protected work (*vernet sysselsetting*), include governmental subsidies to firms for protected employment, and contributions to protected employment in the public sector. In 1979, there were 117 firms with 4,700 protected jobs, and 3,000 persons were employed in protected jobs in the public sector.

The other type of policy concerns efforts to influence the labour market, partly through general economic policies and partly through specific efforts (cf. 'public work' in the table above) to help groups of wage earners who have become unemployed due to lay-offs in industry, young people without suitable training for work, housewives who would like to enter the labour market, elderly wage earners who require alternative employment and others.

In every county (19 in all) there is a labour exchange whose major task is to establish contacts between employers and job-seekers. Every week, national overviews of vacancies and job-seekers willing to take jobs outside their home town are published and in addition local overviews in each county. (Private labour exchanges are not allowed in Norway). The Directorate of Labour and the local exchange offices organize courses and publish information on occupational training and retraining. Participants receive cash support for travel, board, accommodation and dependents. A scheme to encourage private employers to hire young people has recently been established. It offers a maximum support of 3,000 NKR per person under 18 employed. Special series of meetings to encourage women to seek gainful employment are also organized. Since the rate of unemployment began to rise in 1982, the government has initiated a number of efforts to create more jobs through subsidies to local government for apprenticeships, vocational training, etc. Efforts are especially directed towards the young unemployed.

Core laws

1906
Lov om stats- og kommunebidrag til arbeidsledighetskasser (Law on Central and Local Government Contributions to Unemployment Funds): introduced subsidized voluntary insurance.

24.6.1938 (no. 8)
Lov om trygd mot arbeidsløshet (Unemployment Insurance Law): effective from 1939; compulsory unemployment insurance for all workers and employees outside primary sector who were compulsorily insured under the sickness insurance scheme; means-tested benefits; those with incomes above or below certain levels not entitled to benefits.

28.7.1949 (no. 20)
Lov om endringer i lov om trygd mot arbeidsløshet (Amendments to the Unemployment Insurance Law): coverage extended to agricultural workers and certain other groups.

19.6.1970 (no. 67)
Lov om endringer i lov om folketrygd av 17. juni 1966 (Amendments to the 1966 National Insurance Law): insurance incorporated into National Insurance Scheme.

V Families and children

In 1980 expenditure on family transfers and services amounted to 5,937 million NKR. This corresponded to 10.1% of total social security expenditure and 2.1% of GDP. In January 1983, 557,400 families received family allowances. Benefits were paid for altogether 993,600 children.

Expenditure on family transfers and services in 1980, in mill. NKR[a]

	Total	%
Child allowances	2 819	47.5
Pre-payment of maintenance	127	2.1
Kindergartens and day care	677	11.4
Home help for families with children	464	7.8
Public child welfare	883	14.9
Help to parents with children	866	14.6
Rent subsidies to families with children	100	1.7
Total	5 936	100.0

[a] (Source 25). Orphans' pensions and pensions for unmarried mothers are included in Section I on Pensions. For maternity benefits see Section II on Sickness and Health Insurance. For housing allowances to families with many children see Section VIII on Housing.

Income maintenance

Coverage

Child allowances were introduced in 1946. The scheme covers all those providing for children under the age of 16 residing in Norway. Until 1970 allowances were only available for the second and any successive children, but are now also available for the first child.

Benefits

From January 1984, cash benefits paid per year amounted to 4,164 NKR for the first child, 5,028 NKR for the second child, 6,228 NKR for the third child, 6,684 NKR for the fourth, and 7,020 NKR for the fifth child and any subsequent children (Source 22). Child allowances are flat-rate benefits, i.e. independent of the size of family income, and are tax-free. They are not indexed annually, but fixed by parliament. A single parent receives an extra child allowance which amounts to 5,028 NKR per year for the first child, 1,200 NKR for the second, 456 NKR for the third and 336 NKR for the fourth child. No additional allowance is given for the fifth child and any additional children.
Maternity benefits are dealt with under Sickness and Health, and orphans' pensions are dealt with under Pensions.

Financing and administration

Child allowances are financed by the central government through general revenues and administered by the National Insurance Institution.

Services

Municipalities organize services of day care institutions and kindergartens, and private institutions receive public subsidies. These services are subsidized by both central and local authorities. Children are accepted on the basis of a number of criteria, for example a means-test, but the law also requires that day care institution/kindergartens be made up of children of all kinds of social background. Municipalities organize holiday camps for children, which are financed jointly by the central government and municipalities. Maladjusted children or children with unacceptable home conditions are taken care of in public children's or young people's homes. These are financed jointly by central and local authorities. Home help services are covered under the National Insurance Scheme. Health care centres are dealt with under Health Services.

Core laws

24.10.1946 (no. 2)
Lov om barnetrygd (Child Allowances Law): provided allowances for second and subsequent children under the age of 16; not means-tested; single-parent families also received allowance for first child; financed by central (7/8) and local (1/8) government.

29.6.1962 (no. 8)
Lov om endringer i lov om barnetrygd av 24. oktober 1946 (Amendment to 1946 Law): central government pays 100% of expenses.

14.2.1969 (no. 11)
Lov om endringer i lov om barnetrygd av 24. oktober 1946 (Amendments to 1946 Law): allowance extended to first child under age of 16; single-parent families receive one extra allowance in addition to the number of children.

VI Social assistance

In 1978 social assistance expenditure amounted to 442 million NKR. This corresponded to 0.9% of total social security expenditure and 0.2% of GDP.

Income maintenance

Coverage

A 1964 law on social care replaced the Poor Law of 1900. It was designed to supplement the various programmes in the National Insurance Scheme. Social assistance represents the last resort of income maintenance. The law is administered, and largely financed, by the municipalities.

Benefits

Benefits are offered by municipalities on the basis of a means-test, and may vary from one municipality to another. In general, levels are below the minimum benefit levels of the National Insurance Scheme. In 1978 the national average for cash benefits per social care case (the period for which benefits are paid varies) amounted to 2,948 NKR, or 4.4% of average annual gross earnings for male industrial workers in 1978 (Source 1).

Financing and administration

Social care is financed by central government (the major part) and the municipalities according to the law on social care, and is administered by municipal 'social offices'.

Services

The law also provides for benefits in kind, and offers various home-help services. Among these are special home-help programmes for the elderly and sick. In 1980 a total of 98,390 households were in receipt of home-help services for the elderly and sick (Source 23).

Core laws

5.6.1964 (no. 2)
Lov om sosial omsorg (Social Care Law): effective from 1965; replaced last Poor Law and replaced or modified 30 other laws; each municipality to have a 'social board' (*sosialstyre*) responsible for coordination of social care; normally, each municipality to have a 'social office' (*sosialkontor*), which must offer certain kinds of social service or economic assistance.

VII Education

In 1979 expenditure for education amounted to 16,871 million NKR, or 7.1% of GDP.

Expenditure for education in 1979, in million NKR

	Total	%
Education services[a]:		
- Central government	8 843	52.4
- Local government	7 291	43.2
Study allowances[b]	563	3.3
Interest subsidies[b] for study loans	174	1.0
Total	16 871	99.9

[a] (Source 11). Includes expenditure for research at universities and other higher institutions. Not included are 1,301 million NKR spent on research outside these institutions.
[b] (Source 12).

Number of pupils/students on 1 October 1979, in 1 000s (Source 1)

		% of all pupils and students	% of total population
Elementary/comprehensive schools (*grunnskoleutdanning*)	574.4	70.0	14.6
Secondary/continuation schools (*videregaende utdanning*)	179.3	21.0	4.4
Higher education (universities, etc.)	71.4	8.4	1.7
Students abroad	4.5	0.5	0.1
Total	829.6	99.9	20.8

1. Education system

By 1935-36 the parallel school system had been replaced by a compulsory seven-year elementary school for all pupils. The most important law during the post-1945 period is the 1969 law which introduced nine-year compulsory schooling. All children attend comprehensive school from the age of seven (six) until the age of 16 (15). Thereafter, they may choose between a three-year secondary school (*den videregående skole*), previously known as *gymnasium*; an additional year at a comprehensive school; vocational school; a 'Folk High School'; or seek employment (for which options are limited until the age of 18). Secondary education is the normal route to higher education such as universities, regional colleges, technical colleges, teachers' training colleges, etc., but entrance to these institutions is no longer conditional upon secondary education examinations.

In 1980/1981 a total of 852,736 pupils and students were registered at all levels, of which 27,000 or 3% of total student/pupil population attended private schools (Sources 11,23). Almost all education is provided by public institutions and expenditure is shared between the central government, counties and municipalities. The major proportion of current expenses for comprehensive education are normally covered by municipalities, while the counties and central government have financial responsibility for secondary and post-secondary education.

Comprehensive schools provide most services free of charge for pupils: instruction, educational materials and health services. Transport is subsidized. There are no fees charged in secondary schools, but pupils may have to pay for books in the curriculum. Higher education institutions charge no tuition fees, but students have to provide themselves with all necessary educational materials.

Adult education was legislated in 1976 and is provided primarily by about 30 nationwide popular education associations, which receive financial support from the central government. There are continuous efforts to integrate adult education with the educational system, and to commit, for example, universities to offer courses. In 1980/81 a total of 1,052,872 participants took part in 97,020 courses (Source 23).

2. Study allowances and loans

Study allowances (*stipends*) and loans are granted by the State Fund for Education (*Statens lånekasse for utdanning*) to students in secondary, vocational and higher education. Allowances are of several types. The general and most important allowances are:

- universal basic study allowance (*borgebørstipend*) covering all secondary school pupils and students not living at home (i.e. with their parents) and irrespective of parental income; in 1982 the study allowance amounted to 5,500 NKR per year, which was designed to cover 19% of a student's expected total expenditure;
- means-tested graduated allowance (*behovsprovd stipend*) for pupils and students below 20 years of age; the allowance is dependent upon parental income, and the income of the applicant and spouse (where applicable);
- means-tested graduated allowance (*behovsprovd stipend*) for pupils and students below 20 years of age; the allowance is dependent upon parental income, and the income of the applicant and spouse (where applicable);
- basic allowance (*grunnstipend*), which amounted to 500 NKR per year from 1982 onwards, dependent upon the income and property of the applicant and spouse (where applicable). Male students aged 20-30, and female students, irrespective of age, are eligible for this allowance; the allowance was reduced by 50% from 1981 to 1982.
- travel and tuition allowance (*reise- og gebyrstipend*) for students studying at recognized schools and universities abroad.

Loans are granted on the basis of the income and property of the applicant (over 20 years), or on parental income (under 20 years of age). The interest on loans is regulated by parliament. In 1982 the interest was fixed at 10.5%, but no interest is calculated for the period of education. Loans must now be repaid within a maximum of 20 years after education has finished. Students must take examinations within the average period of education for various studies in order to maintain allowances and grants. In 1981, 108,450 out of a total of 260,000 pupils/students received loans (Source 11).

Core laws

The following overview is based on Sources 13 and 14.

10.5.1935
Lov om hoiere almenskoler (Secondary Education Law): secondary education, consisting of two years *realskole* and three years *gymnas* to follow seven-year compulsory elementary schooling.

16.7.1936 (no. 8 and 9)
Lov om folkeskolen på landet; Lov om folkeskolen i kjopstedene (Law on Elementary Schools in Rural Areas; Law on Elementary Schools in Towns): established qualifying criteria for entry to secondary schools; laws of 1935 and 1936 organized and structured the coordination of hitherto uncoordinated primary and secondary education.

6.6.1947 (no. 2)
Lov om Statens lanekasse for studerende ungdom (State Fund for Student Loans Law): offered loans (primarily) to university students; now called *statens lane kasse for utdanning* (State Fund for Education).

8.7.1954 (no. 3)
Lov om folkeskolen (Comprehensive Schooling Law): established nine-year comprehensive schooling on a trial basis.

10.4.1959 (no. 1)
Lov om folkeskolen (Elementary Schools Law): first law common to rural areas and towns; changes in organization of schools and centralization and changes in curricula; option for local education authorities to introduce compulsory nine-year comprehensive schooling on a trial basis.

12.6.1964 (no. 2)
Lov om realskoler og gymnas (Secondary and Upper Secondary Education Law): effective until 1976; for this period *realskoler* existed as an alternative to comprehensive schooling for eighth and ninth school years; administrative responsibility placed with counties.

13.6.1969 (no. 24)
Lov om grunnskolen (Basic Schooling Law): effective from 1.7.1971; nine-year compulsory comprehensive schooling (already introduced by most municipalities).

19.6.1969 (no. 49)
Lov om stonad til ungdom i videregående utdanning (Financial Support for Upper Secondary and Higher Education Students Law): outlined the various types of grants or loans to pupils in secondary and vocational education and to students.

20.6.1969
Parliament decided to establish Regional Colleges on trial basis.

6.3.1970 (no. 4)
Lov om tilskudd til privatskoler (Private Schools Contributions Law): defined conditions under which private, especially religious schools may obtain public subsidies.

8.6.1973 (no. 49)
Lov om lærerutdanning (Teachers' Training Law): first move to raise teacher training to university status.

21.6.1974 (no. 55)
Lov om videregående opplæring (Continuation Education Law): coordination of general secondary and vocational education; most types of secondary education integrated into new continuation school (*videregående skole*); eight types of specialized studies (*studieretninger*) offered.

28.5.1976 (no. 35)
Lov om voksenopplæring (Adult Education Law): effective from 1977; government grants to adult education courses organized by private firms (e.g. labour market training as part of employment policy), associations of various kinds, state schools, and private schools; first-time education for adults in principle to be provided within state school system.

VIII Housing

In 1980 housing expenditure amounted to 2,257 NKR or 0.8% of GDP.

Expenditure for housing purposes in 1980, in million NKR

	Total	%
Interest subsidies:	899	39.8
- Norwegian State Housing Bank[a]	867	38.4
- State Agricultural Bank[b]	32	1.4
Housing allowances:	521	23.1
- Families with children[c]	187	8.4
- Old people, survivors and disabled[d]	263	11.7
- Other needy groups[e]	71	3.1
Contributions to social building[f]	837	37.1
Total	2 257	100.0

[a] (Source 15).
[b] (Source 16). The figure is for 1981 and covers residential buildings.
[c] (Source 15).
[d] (Source 17).
[e] (Source 15). Also covers expenditure for the improvement of houses and residential environments.
[f] (Source 15). Covers the area subsidy scheme (*arealtilskotts ordning*) which offers contributions to all new buildings, except privately financed houses larger than 100 sq.m.

1. Government supported loans

In 1946 the Norwegian State Housing Bank (*Den Norske Stats Husbank*) was established which is supervised by the Ministry of Municipal and Labour Affairs. The Bank offers loans and administers governmental support for the construction of dwellings and apartments, homes for the elderly, and other buildings, together with improvement of old houses, homes for the elderly, kindergartens, health and welfare centres. It also administers the housing allowance scheme and the area subsidy scheme. The Housing Bank concentrates on loans for urban housing, while the activities of the Smallholding Bank, reorganized in 1948, have been confined mainly to rural districts. Since 1966 a new State Agricultural Bank has taken over the functions of the Smallholding Bank. The amount of total housing investments by the State Housing Banks has been determined by parliament. During recent years, the Housing Bank and Agricultural Bank have financed approximately 80-85% of all new dwellings per year (Source 18).

There is no income or property means-test on application for Housing Bank loans, but an applicant must accept the Bank's regulations regarding housing standard and size. Construction and building costs must not exceed certain limits, and since 1969 the maximum accepted size of a dwelling on one floor has been 95 sq.m. and 100 sq.m. for houses on two floors. Large families (five or more members) may build bigger dwellings. Applicants must be able to raise 20-30% of the capital needed. The purpose of this housing policy is to enable people with an average standard of living and income to invest in and make use of new houses of high standard.

The Housing Bank also offers special loans and subsidies for the improvement of dwellings which benefit specific groups of the population, such as the elderly, physically handicapped, students, children and mothers, and employers who build dwellings to be rented by employees. Selective, rather than general schemes of loans and support have become much more important in the 1980s. The interest on normal Housing Bank loans was 11.5% in 1983 (Source 24). Loans for the improvement of old dwellings have been offered since 1969. The interest on these loans amounted to 5.5% in 1978. Interest on all private loans is deductible on income before tax. There is no maximum limit on deductions. Due to the progressive taxation of incomes, the benefit of deduction increases with income level.

The Housing Bank also administers a scheme of grants for the improvement of old dwellings if these are owned by elderly people, the disabled, or families with small means. In 1980 a total of 8,400 persons received an average support of 5,000 NKR for improvement of old dwellings. All types of allowances are tax-free.

2. Housing allowances

Housing allowances have been offered since 1947, but both the scheme and its title have been changed several times. Today it covers: households with children under the age of 18; persons over 65; recipients of invalidity pension or occupational injury compensation; those over the age of 55 who have received rehabilitation benefits or who receive survivors' pension; recipients of occupational injury pension or war pension; recipients of benefits according to the law on social care. The dwelling must fulfill at least one of the following criteria: either it must have been built after 1963, whatever the means of financing or, if older, it must have been mortgaged in the State Housing Bank or State Agricultural (or earlier: Smallholding) Bank. Allowances will in most cases depend on the size of the total net income of the household and on the amount of housing expenses. Benefits amount to 70% of the difference between housing expenses and estimated 'reasonable' (defined by local authorities) housing expenses for the household concerned. For pensioners, the benefits amount to 80%.

In 1982 a total of 99,858 households or 6.6% of all households received housing allowances (Source 24). Average allowance per month amounted to 320 NKR, or 3,840 NKR per year, which corresponded to 5% of the average annual gross earnings for male industrial workers.

The schemes for housing allowances are financed by the central government. All schemes are administered centrally by the State Housing Bank, with the exception of that covering old people etc., which is administered centrally by the Ministry for Social Affairs. All housing allowance schemes are administered locally by municipal housing allowance offices, which are often part of municipal social offices. Applications for allowances are processed and decided on at the municipal level.

Core laws

1894

Government Housing Loan Fund (*Huslanefondet*) established, offering credit for housing on a social basis.

9.6.1903

Lov om arbeiderbrug- og boliglån (Workers' Agricultural Property and Housing Loans Law): bank established.

23.7.1915
Lov om småbruk og boliglån m.v. (Smallholding and Housing Loans Law): new bank replaces bank of 1903.

1.3.1946
Lov om Den Norske Stats Husbank (Norwegian State Housing Bank Law): introduced relatively cheap loans for individual private builders and cooperative housing societies.

1947
Introduction of housing allowances for families with two or more children below 16, who live in dwellings financed through Housing Bank and in municipalities which pay one-third of the allowance.

1954
Parliament to decide the scope of loans available from Housing Bank.

1957
Housing allowances also for single-parent families with children; income and property means test introduced; Housing Allowances Law made compulsory for all municipalities.

1965
Allowances for families with children below 18, the elderly, disabled people living in certain types of dwelling and below a certain income level.

19.6.1969 (no. 55)
Lov om endringer i lov av 1. mars 1946 om Den Norske Stats Husbank (Amendment to the 1946 Law): Housing Bank offers loans for improvement of old dwellings.

1970
Allowances extended to families with children under 18, persons 65 and over, and persons receiving invalidity pension; rehabilitation benefits according to the National Insurance Scheme; eligibility depends on net income of household and amount of housing expenses.

Sources

(1) Rikstrygdeverket. Årsmelding og regnskap 1980, Oslo, 1981.

(2) Sosialtrygdene i Norge, Rikstrygdeverket, Oslo, 1981.

(3) Pensjonstrygden for sjomenn. Årsmelding og regnskap 1980, Oslo, 1981.

(4) Arsberetning for 1980. Statens Pensjonskasse, m.m., Bergen, 1981.

(5) Kommunal Landspensjonskasse. Beretning og regnskap for 1980.

(6) Forsikringstidende, no. 2, 1982 February-March.

(7) Stonad fra folketrygden til ugifte, skilte og separerte forsorgere, Rikstrygdeverket, July 1981.

(8) Kort om trygd, Rikstrygdeverket, August 1981.

(9) NOU 1978: 12 Pensjonsutredningen.

(10) Social Security in the Nordic Countries 1978, Statistical Reports of the Nordic Countries, No. 37, Stockholm, 1980.

(11) St.prp. nr. 1 (1981-82), Kirke- og undervisningsdepartementet (Proposition no. 1 to the *Storting*, 1981-82, Ministry for Church Affairs and Education.

(12) St.prp. nr. 1 (1979-80), Kirke- og undervisningsdepartementet.

(13) Reidar Myhre, *Den norske skoles utvikling*, Oslo, Fabritius, 1976.

(14) Anna-Lisa Sysiharju, 'Primary education and secondary schools', in Erik Allardt *et al.* (eds.), *Nordic Democracy*, Copenhagen, Det Danske Selskab, 1981.

(15) St.prp.nr. 1 (1981-82), Kommunal- og Arbeiderdepartmentet, Proposition no. 1 to the *Storting*, 1981-82, Ministry for Municipal and Labour Affairs.

(16) St.prp. nr. 1 (1981-82), Landbruksdepartementet, Proposition no. 1 to the *Storting*, 1981-82, Ministry of Agriculture.

(17) St.prp. nr. 1 (1981-82) Sosialdepartementet, Proposition no. 1 to the *Storting*, 1981-82, Ministry for Social Affairs.

(18) *Sosial trygghet i Norge*, Sosialdepartementet, Oslo, Universitetsforlaget, 1981.

(19) *Den Norske Stats Husbank, Husbanken etter 25 ar*, Oslo, 1971.

(20) Aksel Hatland, *Folketrygdens framtid*, Oslo, Universitetsforlaget, 1984.

(21) Rikstrygdeverket, Årsmelding og regnskap, 1982, Oslo, 1983.

(22) Social Insurance in Norway, The National Insurance Administration, March 1984.

(23) Statistical Yearbook 1982.

(24) St.prp.nr.1 (1982-83), Kommunnal- og Arbeidsdepartementet, Proposition No. 1 to the *Storting*, 1982-83, Ministry for Municipal and Labour Affairs.

(25) Nordic Statistical Yearbook, 1982.

Bibliography

Contents

I General Contributions

1.1 General histories of social policy

KLUGE, Liv: Sosialhjelp før og nå (Social Assistance in Earlier Times and at Present). Oslo, Fabritius, 1979. An historical account of social assistance in Norway from the middle ages to the present.

KUHNLE, Stein: Velferdsstatens utvikling: Norge i komparativt perspektiv (The Development of the Welfare State: Norway in a Comparative Perspective). Bergen, Universitetsforlaget, 1983, 196 p. Traces the historical development of poor relief and social insurance legislation in Norway; offers models of explanations and comparisons with developments in other countries

ORMESTAD, M.: De sosiale trygder (The Laws on Social Insurance). Oslo, Sem & Stenersen, 1948, 97 p. A description of the development of social insurance legislation in Norway since the 1880s.

SALVESEN, Kaare: Norsk sosial politikk - i går, i dag og i morgen (Norwegian Social Policy - Yesterday, Today, Tomorrow). Stockholm, reprint of Sociale meddelanden 1965, No. 7-8, 1966, 63 p.

SEIP, Anne-Lise: Om velferdsstatens framvekst (On the Development of the Welfare State). Oslo, Universitetsforlaget, 1981, 101 p. A collection of essays on various aspects of the growth of the welfare state and a historical description and interpretation of developments since the 1870s until the present.

WARMEDAHL, Johan, ELDEN, John: Sosialpolitikken i Norge (Social Policy in Norway). Oslo, Høyres opplysningsorganisasjon, 1965, 303 p. The development of social policies as interpreted and described by representatives of the Conservative Party.

1.2 Accounts of specific historical periods

JOHANNSON, T.: Fra sosialpolitikk til krisepolitikk? Arbeiderpartiets syn på krisepolitikk, nødsarbeid og bureising under arbeidsløshetskrisa 1920-1939 (From Social Policies to Crisis Policies? The Labour Party View on the Unemployment Crisis during 1920-1939). Oslo, unpublished dissertation, 1979.

KUHNLE, Stein: 'The growth of social insurance programs in Scandinavia: Outside influences and internal forces'. *In* FLORA, P., HEIDENHEIMER, A.J. (eds): The Development of Welfare States in Europe and America. New Brunswick and London, Transaction Books and Holt Saunders, 1981. Describes and analyses the first initiatives towards, and earlier legislation on social insurance in Scandinavia, covering mainly the period 1880-1914.

MJÅNES, Willy: Sjukeforsikringsspørsmålet i det politiske ordskiftet 1885-1909 (The Sickness Insurance Issue in the Political Debate 1885-1909). Bergen, unpublished dissertation, 1975. Gives an historical-analytical account and interpretations of partisan positions on sickness insurance legislation.

NORSTRAND, Leiv: Mellom to fattiglover: norsk fattigvesen 1863-1900 (Between Two Poor Laws: Norwegian Poor Relief 1863-1900). Bergen, unpublished dissertation, 1976.

PETTERSEN, Per Arnt: Linjer i norks sosialpolitikk (Trends in Norwegian Social Policy). Oslo, Universitetsforlaget, 1982, 240 p. Analysis of various aspects of social policy development in Norway, with a special focus on the 1918-1940 period.

1.3 Histories of social policy in Norway (see 1.1 and 1.2)

1.4 Introductions to the Norwegian system of social policies

LUND, Ottar, LANGHOLM, Magne: Folketrygden (National Insurance). Oslo, 1967. Description of and comments on all legislation relating to the National Insurance in 1966.

OHLDIECK, F.W., LITLERE, I., RYGH, H.: Lov om folketrygd med utfyllende forskrifter og kommentarer til bestemmelsene om omfang, sykestønad, m.v. (National Insurance Law). Oslo,

Sem & Stenersen, 1973, 685 p. Description of and comments on the goals and scope of National Insurance legislation.

RIKSTRYGDEVERKET (National Insurance Institution): Sosialtrygdene i Norge (Social Insurance Schemes in Norway). Oslo, 1981, 72 p. Description of current schemes.

SALVESEN, Kaare: Social Legislation in Norway. Oslo, 1967, 70 p. Description of social security schemes in Norway.

SKÅRDAL, Dorothy B.: Social Insurance in Norway. Oslo, 1960, 261 p. Description of the system of social insurance in Norway as of 1960.

SOSIALDEPARTEMENTET (Ministry for Social Affairs): Sosial trygghet i Norge (Social Security in Norway). Oslo, Universitetsforlaget, 1981, 360 p. A comprehensive guide to the development and current status of the Norwegian social and health care system.

1.5 Reports by investigating committees or experts

DEPARTEMENTET FOR FAMILIE- OG FORBRUKERSAKER (Department for Family and Consumer Affairs): Innstilling om barnefamiliens økonomi (Report on the Economy of Families with Children). Oslo, 1971, 248 p. An investigatory report prepared by the Ministry for Family and Consumer Affairs on the economic situation of families with children.

SOSIALDEPARTEMENTET: Innstilling fra pensjonsalderkomitéen (Report from the Pension Age Committee). Oslo, 1971, 237 p. Study carried out by the Ministry for Social Affairs on pensionable age.

SOSIALDEPARTEMENTET: Sosiale tjenester (Social Services). NOU-series, No. 30, 1972, Oslo, Universitetsforlaget, 171 p. Study and evaluation of the social services at the municipal and provincial levels. Reform proposals.

SOSIALDEPARTEMENTET: Sosiale og helsemesige konsekvenser av petroleumsvirksomheten (Social and Health-related Consequences of the Oil Industry). NOU-series, No. 38, 1975, Oslo, Universitetsforlaget, 25 p. Report by the Ministry for Social Affairs into the possible negative social effects of the development of the oil sector in Norway.

SOSIALDEPARTEMENTET: Den sosiale utvikling i Norge 1975-1977 (Social Development in Norway 1975-1977). Oslo, 1977, 63 p. One of a number of reports made after World War II, evaluating social development in Norway.

SOSIALDEPARTEMENTET: Folketrygdens uførebegrep (The Concept of Invalidity in the National Insurance scheme). NOU-series, No. 14, 1977, Oslo, Universitetsforlaget, 207 p. Report dealing with the concept of invalidity in the context of current legislation.

SOSIALDEPARTEMENTET: Helse- og sosialtjenesten i lokalsamfunnet (Health and Social Services in the Local Community). NOU-series, No. 28, 1979, Oslo, Universitetsforlaget, 262 p. Report on, and evaluation of the distribution of tasks and responsibilities and methods of financing health and social services in Norway. Reform proposals.

1.6 Social science interpretations, evaluations or analyses

FORBRUKER- OG ADMINISTRASJONSDEPARTEMENTET (Ministry for Consumer Affairs): Levekårsundersøkelsen: Sluttrapport (Levels of Living Study: Final Report). NOU-series, No. 28, 1976, Oslo, Universitetsforlaget, 172 p. Summary of findings by the Ministry for Consumer Affairs and Administration, on the various aspects of standards of living based primarily on a nationwide survey.

HANOA, Rolf: EEC og sosialpolitikken (The European Community and Social Policies). Oslo, Pax, 1972, 99 p. Critical discussion of the social policies of the European Community.

HATLAND, Aksel: Folketrygdens framtid (The Future of the National Insurance Scheme). Oslo, Universitetsforlaget, 1984, 248 p. Gives a description and evaluation of the National Insurance Scheme 1967-1982; includes a historical chapter and discusses future policy options.

KOLBERG, Jon Eivind, KILDAL, Nanna, VIKEN, Arvid: Uførepensjon og samfunnsstruktur (Invalidity Pensions and Social Structure). NOU-series, No. 2, 1977, Oslo, Universitetsforlaget,

116 p. Analysis of survey data and ecological (municipal) data on the relationship between social structures and the scope and character of invalidity pensions in different parts of Norway.

KOLBERG, J.E. WÆRNESS, Kari: Trygd og samfunn (Pensions and Society). Oslo, Universitetsforlaget, 1979. Presents a new perspective on the growth of social security schemes and social development.

KOLBERG, J.E.: Farvel til velferdsstaten? (Goodbye to the Welfare State?). Oslo, Cappelen, 1985, 192 p. Gives an overview of social policy models, a history of the welfare state and an analysis of cuts in the Norwegian welfare state.

LINGÅS, Lars Gunnar (ed.): Myten om velferdsstaten (The Myth of the Welfare State). Oslo, Pax, 1973, 227 p. A collection of critical, analytical essays on aspects of the development of the welfare state.

NORDBØ, Eldrid: Kommunenes ytelser i sosialsektoren (The Social Expenditure of Municipalities). Oslo, unpublished dissertation, 1968, p. 109. Analysis of economic and political determinants of social expenditure in Norwegian municipalities.

ØYEN, Else: Velferd (Welfare).*In* ØYEN, E (ed.):, Sosiologi og ulikhet (Sociology and Inequality). Bergen, Universitetsforlaget, 1976 (new edition, 1983). Analysis of the welfare concept and themes of conflict in the welfare debate.

RINGEN, Anders (ed.): Velferdsforskning og sosialpolitikk (Welfare Research and Social Policy). Oslo, Institute of Applied Social Research, 1975, 456 p. Collection of conference papers by sociologists, economists, and political scientists.

RINGEN, Stein: Hvor går velferdsstaten? (Quo vadis the Welfare State?). Oslo, Gyldendal, 1981, 108 p. Analysis and evaluation of the origin and future of (re)distribution policies.

SOSIALDEPARTEMENTET: Sosialpolitikken og samfunnsforskningen (Social Policies and the Social Sciences). Oslo, Universitetsforlaget, 1970, 157 p. Based on papers presented at a conference sponsored by the Ministry for Social Affairs and the Norwegian Research Council.

SOSIALDEPARTEMENTET: Sosialpolitikken og oljen (Social Policy and Oil). Oslo, Universitetsforlaget, 1976.

STJERNØ, Steinar (ed.): Velferd eller nød? Helse- og sosialpolitikk i 80-åra (Welfare or Distress? Health and Social Policy in the 80s). Oslo, Pax, 1982, 206 p. Collection of essays evaluating developments in the Norwegian welfare state from a 'leftist' or 'socialist' viewpoint.

1.7 Policy proposals and debates (See also 1.5 and 1.6)

ARBEIDERPARTIETS SOSIALREFORMKOMITÉ (Labour Party Committee for Social Reform): Social reform i 70 åra (Social Reform in the 1970s). Oslo, Tiden, 1971. Reform proposals of the Labour party.

KOLBERG, J.E.: 'Trygdesystem, samfunnssystem og samfunnsendring (Social insurance system, social system, and social change)'. *Kontrast*, No. 8, 1971. Discussion of the ways in which the characteristics of society and the processes of change affect the emergence and maintenance of social problems. Suggests alternative ways of distributing resources.

RINGEN, Stein, WÆRNESS, Kari (eds): Sosialpolitikk i 1980-åra (Social Policies in the 1980s). Oslo, Gyldendal, 1982, 111 p. Collection of essays on current and future problems of the welfare state.

SOSIALDEPARTEMENTET: Pensjonsutredningen (The Study of Pensions). NOU-series, No. 12, 1978, Oslo, Universitetsforlaget, 240 p. A comprehensive analysis by a committee appointed by the Ministry for Social Affairs, of ways to improve minimum pensions and other benefits in the National Insurance scheme.

WÆRNESS, Kari: Kvinneperspektiv på sosialpolitikken (A Woman's View of Social Policies). Oslo, Universitetsforlaget, 1982.

1.8 Opinion polls

KOLBERG, Jon Eivind, VIKEN, Arvid: 'Trygdehetsens struktur (The structure of opinions on welfare abuse)'. *Tidsskrift for samfunnsforskning*, Vol. 19, 1978. Analysis of public opinion data on conceptions regarding abuses of pension and welfare benefits.

KOLBERG, J.E., PETTERSEN, P.A.: 'Om velferdsstatens politiske basis (On the political basis of the welfare state)'. *Tidsskrift for samfunnsforskning*, Vol. 22, Nos. 2-3, 1981. Analysis of survey data on attitudes to social security or welfare measures.

MARTINUSSEN, Willy: 'Høyrebølgens understrømmer (The undercurrents of the conservative wave)'. *Tidsskrift for samfunsforskning*, Vol. 22, Nos. 2-3, 1981 Analysis of survey data on attitudes to social policies.

1.9 Sources of statistics or institutional regulations

1.9.1 Official sources

RIKSTRYGDEVERKET (National Insurance Institution): Årsmelding og regnskap (Annual Report and Account). Oslo. Annual series. The annual report of the National Insurance Institution, giving a comprehensive overview of the social insurance system and changes in laws or regulations, together with statistics on financing, benefits and beneficiaries of the various schemes.

SOSIAL TRYGGHET I DE NORDISKE LAND (Social Security in the Nordic Countries): Place of publication varies, Nordisk Statistisk Skriftserie since 1954. First publication on social security in 1955 (Copenhagen), No. 2 in the series. Published every three years. Gives a comparative outline of social security and welfare institutions and statistics on financing and expenditure in Denmark, Finland, Iceland, Norway and Sweden.

STATISTISK SENTRALBYRÅ (Central Bureau of Statistics): Sosialstatistikk (Social Statistics). Oslo. Annual series. A wide coverage of statistics related to social conditions and social welfare.

STATISTIK SENTRALBYRÅ: Socialt utsyn (Social Survey). Oslo, 1974. Published every three years, latest edition in 1983.Offers a comprehensive statistical overview of living conditions, covering areas such as work, health, education, income, private consumption, housing, leisure, demography, criminality, cultural, social and political participation.

STATISTISK SENTRALBYRÅ: Historisk statistikk 1978 (Historical Statistics 1978). Oslo, 1978.Presents historical statistical overviews on expenditure, beneficiaries, and members of social insurance schemes.

1.9.2 Private Sources

FØRSUND, Hildegunn Marie, ØYEN, Else: Stevnemøte med sosialomsorgen (Rendez-vous with the Social Care Programme). Bergen, Universitetsforlaget, 1983,228 p. Annotated bibliography of sources on, and studies of social assistance and social care programmes.

GUNDERSEN, Håkon, ØYEN, Else: Trygd i Norge (Social Security in Norway). Bergen, Universitetsforlaget, 1980, 157 p. Annotated bibliography of sources on and studies of social insurance institutions, social insurance clients, and the overall social insurance system in Norway.

KUHNLE, Stein: Fakta om Norge. Velferdsstaten (Facts about Norway. The Welfare State). Oslo, Tiden, 1983. Offers statistics from the postwar period on subjects such as international comparisons, personnel, financing, expenditure, beneficiaries, levels of welfare, public opinion data, all relating to social insurance, social welfare, and health policies and institutions.

1.9.3 Major periodicals

SOSIAL TRYGD (Social Security): Oslo, Trygdekontorenes landsforening (The National Association of Social Insurance Offices). Monthly. Primarily a forum for information on new developments in the field of social insurance.

TIDSSKRIFT FOR SAMFUNNSFORSKNING (Journal of Social Science Research): Oslo. Published every two months. A general journal for social science which frequently publishes results from analyses relating to welfare state topics.

II Single programmes or aspects

2.1 Pensions (see also 1.6 and 1.7)

HANOA, Rolf: Stilling: trygdet (Occupation: Pensioner). Oslo, Pax, 1972, 117 p. Description of the situation of pensioners together with comments on laws and regulations, rights, benefits, and comments on factors which account for the growth in the number of pensioners.

KOLBERG, Jon E.: Trygde-Norge (Pension-Norway). Oslo, Gyldendal, 1974. Analysis of the 'consumption' of pensions in different parts of Norway.

ORVIN, Harald W.: Statens pensjonskasse 1917-1967 (The State Pension Fund 1917-1976). Oslo, Statens pensjonskasse, 1969, 58 p. An overview of the activity of the Fund during its first 50 years of operation.

PALSTRØM, Henrik: Pensjon og samfunn (Pension and Society). Oslo, 1961, 305 p. Analysis of the problems of being a pensioner.

2.2 Health

BERG, Ole: Medisinen som samfunnsinstitusjon (Medicine as a Social Institution). Oslo, Institute for Social Research and Institute of Political Science, 1973, mimeo, 159 p. Essays on the social and political functions of the medical profession.

BERG, Ole: Helsetjenestens logikk (The Logic of the Health Delivery System). Institute of Political Science, Oslo, 1982, 352 p. Six studies of various aspects and dimensions of the historical and current state of the health service.

EDØY, Jan: Fra offentlig forsorg til sosial forsikring (From Public Relief to Social Insurance). Institute of Comparative Politics, Bergen, unpublished dissertation, 1984, 211 p. A historical and qualitative analysis of the role of political parties at the time of the introduction of sickness insurance laws in Norway and Denmark.

ERICSSON, Kjersti: Den tvetydige omsorgen (The Ambiguous Care). Oslo, 1974, 205 p. Analysis of the development of psychiatric services.

EVANG, Karl: Health Services in Norway. Oslo, The Norwegian Joint Committee on International Social Policy, 1970, 205 p. An overview and evaluation of the Norwegian health service.

HANOA, Rolf: Folkehelse og sosialpolitikk (The Health of People and Social Policy). Oslo, Pax, 119 p. Analysis of work conditions, health and social problems in a class society.

HANSEN, Finn Henry: Vekstprosesser i helsesektoren (Growth Processes in the Health Sector). Bergen, unpublished dissertation, 1975.

KOMMUNAL- OG ARBEIDSDEPARTEMENTET: Helsepolitikken (Health Policy). NOU-series, No. 10, 1979, Oslo, Universitetsforlaget. Overview and evaluation of health policies.

ROMØREN, Tor Inge: Helse i Norge (Health in Norway). Oslo, Pax, 1973, 125 p.

STATISTISK SENTRALBYRÅ (Central Bureau of Statistics).: Helsestatistikk (Health Statistics). Annual series.

STOKKE, Steinar: Fra sykeforsikring til folketrygd (From Sickness Insurance to National Insurance). Oslo, unpublished dissertation, 1981. Historical analysis of the development of sickness insurance in Norway.

URDAL, Nils: Syketrygden i femti år (Fifty Years of Sickness Insurance). Oslo, Norges trygdekasselag, 1961, 370 p. Historical-political outline of the development of sickness insurance.

2.3 Unemployment

BRUNSTAD, Rolf, COLBJØRNSEN, Tom, RØDSETH, Tor: Sysselsettingen i søkelyset (Employment under a Cloud). Bergen, Universitetsforlaget, 1981, 202 p. Collection of essays on employment and labour market problems written by sociologists and economists.

HAAGENSEN, E.: Frivillige arbeidsløshetskasser eller obligatorisk statlig arbeidsløshetstrygd?

(Voluntary or State-organized Compulsory Unemployment Insurance?). Oslo, unpublished dissertation, 1972. Historical analysis of the voluntary versus compulsory insurance issue.

HALVORSEN, Knut: Arbeid eller trygd? (Work or Pension?). Oslo, Pax, 1977. Analysis of processes which may lead to more persons being made unemployed.

STATISTISK SENTRALBYRÅ (Central Bureau of Statistics): Arbeidsmarkedsstatistikk (Labour Market Statistics).

WADEL, Cato: Trygdeliv og arbeidsliv (Pension Life and Working Life). Tromsø, Universitetsforlaget, 1978.

2.4 Accidents

KJØNSTAD, Asbjørn: Yrkesskadetrygden (Occupational Injuries Insurance). Oslo, 1979. Overview of and comments on the law and its regulations.

2.5 Social assistance (see also 1.1, 1.2, and 1.5)

HOVEN, Finn Holmer: Klienten og likebehandling i lokalforvaltningen (The Client and Equal Treatment in Local Administration). Agder distriktshøgskole, Forskningsserie 1/77, Kristiansand, 1977. Analysis of demand and supply of public benefits in two Norwegian municipalities.

ØYEN, Else: Sosialomsorgen og dens forvaltere (Social Assistance and its Custodians). Oslo, Universitetsforlaget, 1974. Analysis of the ways in which the Social Assistance Law (social care), which replaced the Poor Law in 1964, is being interpreted and applied in various areas.

SEIP, Anne-Lise: Sosiallhjelpstaten blir til (The Emergence of the Social Assistance State: Norwegian Social Policies 1740-1920). Oslo, Gyldendal, 1984, 360 p. A comprehensive historical analysis of the poor relief systems and the development towards social insurance policies.

2.6 Family programmes

CHRISTIANSEN, Vidar: A Theoretical and Empirical Analysis of Child Allowances. Oslo, Institute of Economics, 1978, mimeo, 34 p.

LANGHOLM, Magne: Family and Child Welfare in Norway. Oslo, 146 p.

SOSIALDEPARTEMENTET (Ministry for Social Affairs): (Main Principles of Child Protection and Family Policy in Norway). Oslo, 1964, mimeo, 16 p.

SOSIALDEPARTEMENTET (Ministry for Social Affairs): (Child and Youth Welfare in Norway). Oslo, 1973, mimeo, 35 p.

2.7 Housing

AÅS, DAGFINN (ed.): Boforhold i Norge i 70-årene (Housing Conditions in Norway in the 1970s). Oslo, Norske Byggforskningsinstitutt, NBI (Norwegian Institute for Housing Research), 1979. Oslo, 1979. Summary of results from the study of housing conditions in 1973, carried out by the Central Bureau of Statistics.

DEN NORSKE STATS HUSBANK (The Norwegian State Housing Bank): Årsstatistikk (Annual Statistics).

DEN NORSKE STATS HUSBANK (The Norwegian State Housing Bank): Husbanken etter 25 år. (The Housing Bank after 25 Years). Oslo, 1971.

ERIKSEN, John R.: De eldre og deres boligforhold (Housing Conditions of Elderly People). Oslo, Institute of Applied Social Research, 1969, 46 p.

GULBRANDSEN, Lars: Boligmarked og boligpolitikk (Housing Market and Housing Policies). Oslo, Gyldendal, 1983. A major study of housing policies in the 20th century, with a focus on the capital of Oslo.

GULBRANDSEN, Lars, TORGERSEN, Ulf: Unge familier og boligproblemer i Oslo (Young Families and Housing Problems in Oslo). Oslo, Institute of Political Science, 1975.

2.8 Education

HERNES, Gudmund, KNUDSEN, Knud: Utdanning og ulikhet (Education and Inequality). NOU-series, No. 46, 1976, Oslo, Universitetsforlaget, p. 108. Part of a study of living standards based on survey data. Empirical analysis of the social inequalities of educational opportunities and achievements.

KIRKE- OG UNDERVISNINGSDEPARTEMENTET (Ministry for Church and Educational Affairs): Velferd for elever og studenter (Welfare for Pupils and Students). NOU-series, No. 33, 1976, Oslo, Universitetsforlaget, 110 p. Committee report on policy efforts improving the economic and social welfare of pupils and students.

KNUDSEN, Knud: Ulikhet i grunnskolen (Inequality in the Elementary School). Bergen, Universitetsforlaget, 1980, 423 p. Major study (doctoral dissertation) of educational inequalities in Norway.

LINDBEKK, Torre: Skolesosiologi (The Sociology of Education). Trondheim, Tapir, 1973. The most comprehensive summary of research on education and schooling by Norwegian sociologists.

MYHRE, Reidar: Den norske skoles utvikling (The Development of the Norwegian School System). Oslo, Fabritius, 1967. Description of the institutional development of the school system since the eighteenth century.

STATISTISK SENTRALBYRÅ (Central Bureau of Statistics): Utdanningsstatistikk (Educational Statistics). Annual series.

2.9 Public household

AUKRUST, Odd: Tjue års økonomisk politikk i Norge: suksesser og mistak (Twenty Years of Economic Policies in Norway: Successes and Failures). Oslo, Central Bureau of Statistics, 1965, 38 p. An economist's evaluation of postwar economic policies.

AUKRUST, Odd, BORGENVINK, Hallvard: Inntektsfordelingsvirkninger av skattereformen av 1969 (Effects on Income Distribution of the 1969 Tax Reform). Oslo, Central Bureau of Statistics, Art. 33, 1969, 29 p.

NORGES ØKONOMI ETTER KRIGEN (Norway's Economy after the War): Oslo, Central Bureau of Statistics, Samfunnsøkonomiske skrifter, No. 12, 1965. Description and evaluation of postwar economic development.

SEIERSTAD, Staåle: Norsk økonomi (The Norwegian Economy). *In* RAMSØY, N; VAA, M (eds): Det Norske Samfunn. Vol. 1, Oslo, Gyldendal, 1975, pp. 95-145. Description of the economic structure, power relationships, distribution processes, and trends of development.

STATISTISK SENTRALBYRÅ (Central Bureau of Statistics): Produces the following relevant publications: Public Sector Finances 1962-67. Oslo, 1972. Public Sector Finances. Oslo, 1973. Public Sector Finances 1971-73. Oslo, 1976. Public Sector Finances 1973-76. Oslo, 1979. Tax statistics, last Vol. 1979, Oslo 1981. Annual series.

2.10 Public employment

STATISTISK SENTRALBYRÅ (Central Bureau of Statistics): Lønns- og sysselsettingsstatistikk for statens embets- og tjenestemenn 1. October 1980 (Wage and Employment Statistics for Central Government Employees October 1, 1980). Oslo, 1981, 97 p.

III Impact of social programmes

3.1 Poverty

AUBERT, Vilhelm: 'Fattigdommen i Norge (Poverty in Norway)'. *Kontrast*, No. 1, 1967, pp. 10-20.

CHRISTIE, Vigdis: 'Sosialklasse, fattigdom og kontakt (Social class, poverty and communication)'. *Tidsskrift for samfunnsforskning*, Vol. 17, 1976, pp. 113-134.

GUTTORMSEN, Gro, HØIGÅRD, Cecile: Fattigdom i en velstandskommunel (Poverty in a Prosperous Municipality). Oslo, Universitetsforlaget, 1977, 245 p. Study of the social assistance programme in Bærum.

3.2 Inequality and income distribution

BJØRN, E.: The Distributive Effects of Indirect Taxation: an Econometric Model and Empirical Results based on Norwegian Data. The Swedish Journal of Economics, No. 1, 1975.

FLØYSTAD, G.: Allocation and Distribution. Bergen, Norwegian School of Business Administration, 1965.

RØDSETH, Tor: Utredning om lavtlønnsproblemer i Norge (Study of Low-wage Problems in Norway). Oslo, Lønns- og prisdepartementet, 1969.

RØDSETH, Tor: Inntektsfordeling i Norge (Income Distribution in Norway). NOU-series, No. 44, 1977, Oslo, Universitetsforlaget, p. 187. Analysis of income and tax statistics as part of the study of living standards in Norway.

STATISTISK SENTRALBYRÅ (Central Bureau of Statistics): Innteksstatistikk 1970 (Income Statistics 1970). Oslo, 1973.

STATISTISK SENTRALBYRÅ (Central Bureau of Statistics): Den personlige inntektsfordeling 1958, 1962 or 1967 (The Distribution of Personal Incomes in 1958, 1962 and 1967). Oslo, 1972.

3.3 Economic effects

NORD, Erik: Velferdsteori og økonomisk politikk (Welfare Theory and Economic Policy). Oslo, Fondet for marketds- og distribusjonsforskning, Arbeidsrapport No. 16, 1978.

PEDERSEN, Rolf: Nasjonaløkonomiske konsekvenser av en gjennomføring av folkepensjonen (National Economic Consequences of the Implementation of the National Insurance Scheme). Oslo, 1967, mimeo, 80 p.

Appendix Tables

Contents

Table

Table 1 Gross Domestic Product and Total Public Expenditure

Year	GDP (at market prices, in million crowns)			Deflators			Total public expenditure (in million crowns)				Year
	At current prices	At constant (1975) prices	Annual real growth rate	GDP (base 1975)	Consumer price index (base 1975)	Consumer price index (base 1978)	At current prices	As % of GDP	At constant (1975) prices	Annual real growth rate	
1950	15 073	55 133		27.3	27.7	21.5	3 962	26.3	14 512		1950
1951	18 765	57 679	4.6	32.5	32.2	25.0	4 451	23.7	13 695	-5.6	1951
1952	20 732	59 753	3.6	34.7	35.0	27.2	5 312	25.6	15 308	11.8	1952
1953	21 013	62 735	5.0	33.5	36.2	28.1	5 783	27.5	17 262	12.8	1953
1954	22 799	65 148	3.8	35.0	37.3	29.0	6 250	27.4	17 857	3.4	1954
1955	24 278	66 540	2.1	36.5	37.7	29.3	6 528	26.9	17 884	0.2	1955
1956	27 642	69 942	5.1	39.2	39.0	30.3	7 254	26.4	18 505	3.5	1956
1957	29 248	71 551	2.3	40.9	40.5	31.5	8 171	27.9	19 977	8.0	1957
1958	29 207	72 492	1.3	40.3	42.0	32.6	8 559	29.3	21 238	6.3	1958
1959	30 958	74 593	2.9	41.5	43.1	33.5	9 298	30.0	22 404	5.5	1959
1960	33 058	78 109	4.7	42.3	43.6	33.9	9 876	29.9	23 347	4.2	1960
1961	36 062	82 071	5.1	43.9	44.1	34.3	10 701	29.7	24 375	4.4	1961
1962	38 843	85 921	4.7	45.2	46.7	36.3	12 236	31.5	27 070	11.1	1962
1963	41 682	89 178	3.8	46.7	48.8	37.9	13 789	33.1	29 526	9.1	1963
1964	45 837	93 644	5.0	48.9	50.5	39.2	15 160	33.1	31 002	5.0	1964
1965	50 563	98 592	5.3	51.3	52.6	40.9	17 302	34.2	33 727	8.8	1965
1966	54 568	102 326	3.8	53.3	54.2	42.1	18 982	34.8	35 613	5.6	1966
1967	59 700	108 729	6.3	54.9	56.8	44.1	21 719	36.4	39 561	11.1	1967
1968	63 749	111 183	2.3	57.3	58.6	45.5	24 148	37.9	42 143	6.5	1968
1969	69 418	116 193	4.5	59.7	60.0	47.1	27 703	39.9	46 403	10.1	1969
1970	79 877	118 514	2.0	67.3	66.9	52.0	32 742	41.0	48 650	4.8	1970
1971	89 107	123 940	4.6	71.9	70.9	55.1	38 350	43.0	53 337	9.6	1971
1972	98 403	130 346	5.2	75.5	76.2	59.2	43 935	44.6	58 192	9.1	1972
1973	111 854	135 705	4.1	82.4	81.9	63.0	49 909	44.6	60 569	4.1	1973
1974	129 729	140 884	3.8	92.1	89.7	69.7	57 890	44.6	62 855	3.8	1974
1975	148 701	148 701	5.5	100.0	100.0	77.7	69 272	46.6	62 272	10.2	1975
1976	170 709	158 830	6.8	107.5	109.1	84.8	82 848	48.5	77 067	11.3	1976
1977	191 534	164 516	3.6	116.4	118.9	92.4	96 022	50.1	82 493	7.0	1977
1978	213 079	171 986	4.5	123.9	128.7	100.0	111 415	52.3	89 923	9.0	1978
1979	238 668	179 758	4.5	132.7	135.0	104.9	121 725	51.0	91 729	2.0	1979
1980	283 512	186 549	3.8	152.0	149.7	116.3	139 721	49.3	91 921	0.2	1980

Table 2

Public Expenditure by

Year	Purpose: Total expend. (mill. N.kr.)	Welfare	Per cent distribution: Defence	Gen. adm. and publ. order	Econ. growth	Other	Economic Function: Total expend. (mill. N.kr.)	Per cent distribution: Governm. final consump.	Subsid. and transf.	Gross fixed capital formation	Interest on publ. debt.	Level of Government: Estim. total (mill. N.kr.)	Per cent distribution: Centr. gov.	Local gov.	Nation. insur.	Year
1950	3 962	34.9	12.2	7.1	14.9	30.9	3 962	38.1	47.6	9.1	5.2	3 687	65.5	32.9	1.4	1950
1951	4 451	39.3	15.7	7.1	14.9	23.0	4 451	42.7	43.7	9.1	4.5	4 171	66.3	32.4	1.3	1951
1952	5 312	35.6	19.4	6.7	16.1	22.2	5 312	44.0	41.8	10.0	4.2	5 249	67.9	30.8	1.3	1952
1953	5 783	37.8	16.3	8.4	30.9	6.6	5 783	46.1	39.6	10.6	3.7	5 869	70.0	28.7	1.3	1953
1954	6 250	37.7	14.4	8.2	27.3	12.4	6 250	45.5	39.5	11.1	3.8	5 986	67.5	31.2	1.4	1954
1955	6 528	40.0	12.7	8.9	28.6	9.8	6 528	43.2	40.4	11.8	4.6	6 469	66.5	32.1	1.4	1955
1956	7 254	40.9	13.9	9.1	27.3	8.8	7 254	44.1	39.2	11.7	5.0	7 227	66.9	31.6	1.4	1956
1957	8 171	39.7	12.1	8.7	28.1	11.4	8 171	43.3	41.3	10.7	4.7	7 958	68.1	30.4	1.5	1957
1958	8 559	40.2	12.7	9.2	25.7	12.2	8 559	43.7	40.0	11.6	4.7	8 468	65.9	32.4	1.7	1958
1959	9 298	45.0	10.5	8.8	26.5	9.2	9 298	44.0	39.5	11.6	4.8	9 351	59.7	30.3	10.0	1959
1960	9 876	45.7	10.8	8.6	28.3	6.6	9 876	43.0	40.5	11.7	4.8	10 011	60.3	29.9	9.7	1960
1961	10 701	44.4	10.7	8.0	26.4	10.5	10 701	43.3	40.8	11.0	4.9	11 694	56.6	24.8	18.6	1961
1962	12 236	45.3	10.9	8.2	24.7	10.9	12 236	44.4	39.8	11.2	4.6	12 962	55.2	24.6	20.2	1962
1963	13 789	45.8	10.3	8.0	24.6	11.3	13 789	43.3	40.1	11.9	4.6	14 450	54.0	25.7	20.3	1963
1964	15 160	47.4	10.1	8.3	24.0	10.2	15 160	43.8	39.0	12.5	4.8	15 918	53.7	25.4	20.8	1964
1965	17 302	45.9	10.8	7.9	23.1	12.3	17 302	44.0	39.8	11.5	4.6	17 633	54.2	24.6	21.2	1965
1966	18 982	47.3	10.1	7.7	21.9	13.0	18 982	44.4	39.5	11.5	4.6	18 847	51.8	26.0	22.2	1966
1967	21 719	48.2	9.6	7.9	21.0	13.3	21 719	44.3	39.4	12.0	4.4	21 600	50.5	26.0	23.5	1967
1968	24 148	47.2	9.5	7.8	20.8	14.7	24 148	43.7	40.4	11.3	4.5	24 233	50.6	25.4	24.0	1968
1969	27 703	49.3	9.1	7.6	20.2	13.8	27 703	42.1	41.7	11.7	4.4	27 897	51.2	24.5	24.3	1969
1970	32 742	51.5	8.5	7.2	17.1	15.7	32 742	41.3	43.4	10.9	4.4	33 273	48.0	22.5	29.5	1970
1971	38 350	53.5	7.8	7.3	18.3	13.1	38 350	41.7	43.1	11.0	4.2	39 382	46.9	23.0	30.2	1971
1972	43 935	54.9	7.3	6.2	31.6		43 935	40.6	43.6	11.4	4.4	43 935			31.6	1972
1973	49 909	54.6	7.0	6.3	32.1		49 909	40.9	44.0	10.6	4.5	49 909			31.8	1973
1974	57 890	53.3	6.8	6.6	33.3		57 890	41.0	43.9	10.4	4.6	57 890			30.8	1974
1975	69 272	52.9	6.9	6.5	33.7		69 272	41.4	43.7	10.3	4.6	69 272			30.4	1975
1976	82 848	52.1	6.4	6.7	34.8		82 848	41.1	43.9	9.8	5.1	82 848			30.1	1976
1977	96 022	51.8	6.3	6.6	35.3		96 022	40.2	44.4	9.7	5.7	96 022			27.7	1977
1978	111 415	51.6	6.2	6.5	35.7		111 415	39.1	45.0	9.6	6.3	111 415			27.8	1978
1979	121 725	53.4	6.5	6.3	33.8		121 725	38.4	45.7	8.5	7.4					1979
1980	139 721	52.9	6.1	6.0	34.9		139 721	38.3	45.5	8.0	8.2					1980

Table 3

Social Expenditure

Year	At current prices (in million crowns)					At constant (1978) prices (in million crowns)					Year
	Total	Income maint.	Education	Health	Housing	Total	Income maint.	Education	Health	Housing	
1950	1 381	495	442	338	106	6 423	2 302	2 056	1 572	493	1950
1951	1 749	737	498	397	117	6 996	2 948	1 992	1 588	468	1951
1952	1 892	766	543	431	152	6 955	2 816	1 996	1 584	559	1952
1953	2 185	853	654	497	181	7 755	3 035	2 327	1 768	644	1953
1954	2 356	956	667	548	185	8 124	3 296	2 300	2 013	638	1954
1955	2 613	1 041	776	597	199	8 918	3 552	2 648	2 037	679	1955
1956	2 966	1 175	912	687	192	9 788	3 877	3 010	2 267	634	1956
1957	3 247	1 281	988	805	173	10 307	4 066	3 137	2 555	549	1957
1958	3 442	1 254	1 114	893	181	10 558	3 846	3 417	2 739	555	1958
1959	4 180	1 790	1 229	991	170	12 477	5 343	3 669	2 958	507	1959
1960	4 517	1 893	1 384	1 056	184	13 324	5 584	4 083	3 115	543	1960
1961	4 752	1 952	1 455	1 159	186	13 854	5 690	4 242	3 379	542	1961
1962	5 543	2 332	1 740	1 282	189	15 144	6 424	4 793	3 531	521	1962
1963	6 316	2 597	2 041	1 470	208	16 664	6 852	5 385	3 878	549	1963
1964	7 182	2 927	2 349	1 688	218	18 321	7 466	5 992	4 306	556	1964
1965	7 940	3 241	2 604	1 856	239	19 413	7 924	6 367	4 537	584	1965
1966	8 979	3 654	3 011	2 082	232	21 327	8 679	7 152	4 945	551	1966
1967	10 461	4 383	3 499	2 361	218	23 721	9 938	7 934	5 353	494	1967
1968	11 406	5 001	3 870	2 675	231	25 068	10 991	8 505	5 879	508	1968
1969	13 662	5 937	4 275	3 009	441	29 006	12 605	9 076	6 388	936	1969
1970	16 867	7 639	4 687	3 729	812	32 436	14 690	9 013	7 171	1 562	1970
1971	20 504	8 915	5 644	4 710	1 245	37 212	16 179	10 243	8 548	2 260	1971
1972	24 102	11 165	6 333	5 503	1 101	40 712	18 859	10 698	9 295	1 860	1972
1973	27 240	12 537	6 971	6 571	1 161	42 830	19 900	10 961	10 430	1 825	1973
1974	30 857	13 816	7 952	7 831	1 258	44 271	19 822	11 409	11 235	1 805	1974
1975	36 641	16 122	9 475	9 858	1 186	47 157	20 749	12 194	12 687	1 526	1975
1976	43 143	18 568	11 043	12 182	1 350	50 876	21 896	13 022	14 365	1 592	1976
1977	49 736	22 005	12 540	13 936	1 255	53 826	23 814	13 571	15 082	1 358	1977
1978	57 507	25 756	14 124	15 914	1 713	57 507	25 756	14 124	15 914	1 713	1978
1979	65 056	31 043	14 833	17 535	1 645	62 014	29 593	14 140	16 718	1 563	1979
1980	73 951	35 187	16 378	20 284	2 102	63 586	30 255	14 083	17 441	1 807	1980

Table 4

Social Expenditure

Year	as % of gross domestic product					as % of public expenditure					as % of social expenditure				Year
	Total	Income maint.	Educa-tion	Health	Hous-ing	Total	Income maint.	Educa-tion	Health	Hous-ing	Income maint.	Educa-tion	Health	Hous-ing	
1950	9.2	3.3	2.9	2.2	0.7	34.9	12.5	11.2	8.5	2.7	35.8	32.0	24.5	7.7	1950
1951	9.3	3.9	2.7	2.1	0.6	39.3	16.5	11.2	8.9	2.6	42.1	28.5	22.7	6.7	1951
1952	9.1	3.7	2.6	2.1	0.7	35.6	14.4	10.2	8.1	2.9	40.5	28.7	22.8	8.0	1952
1953	10.4	4.1	3.1	2.4	0.9	37.8	14.8	11.3	8.6	3.1	39.0	29.9	22.7	8.3	1953
1954	10.3	4.2	2.9	2.4	0.8	37.7	15.3	10.7	8.8	3.0	40.6	28.3	23.3	7.9	1954
1955	10.8	4.3	3.2	2.5	0.8	40.0	15.9	11.9	9.1	3.0	39.8	29.7	22.8	7.6	1955
1956	10.8	4.3	3.3	2.5	0.7	40.9	16.2	12.6	9.5	2.6	39.6	30.7	23.2	6.5	1956
1957	11.1	4.4	3.4	2.8	0.6	39.7	15.7	12.1	9.9	2.1	39.5	30.4	24.8	5.3	1957
1958	11.8	4.3	3.8	3.1	0.6	40.2	14.7	13.0	10.4	2.1	36.4	32.4	25.9	5.3	1958
1959	13.5	5.8	4.0	3.2	0.5	45.0	19.3	13.2	10.7	1.8	42.8	29.4	23.7	4.0	1959
1960	13.7	5.7	4.2	3.2	0.6	45.7	19.2	14.0	10.7	1.9	41.9	30.6	23.4	4.1	1960
1961	13.2	5.4	4.0	3.2	0.5	44.4	18.2	13.6	10.8	1.7	41.1	30.6	24.4	3.9	1961
1962	14.3	6.0	4.5	3.3	0.5	45.3	19.1	14.2	10.5	1.5	42.1	31.4	23.1	3.4	1962
1963	15.2	6.2	4.9	3.5	0.5	45.8	18.8	14.8	10.7	1.5	41.1	32.3	23.3	3.3	1963
1964	15.7	6.4	5.1	3.7	0.5	47.4	19.3	15.5	11.1	1.4	40.8	32.7	23.5	3.0	1964
1965	15.7	6.4	5.2	3.7	0.5	45.9	18.7	15.1	10.7	1.4	40.8	32.8	23.4	3.0	1965
1966	16.5	6.7	5.5	3.8	0.4	47.3	19.2	15.8	11.0	1.2	40.7	33.5	23.2	2.6	1966
1967	17.5	7.3	5.9	4.0	0.4	48.2	20.2	16.1	10.9	1.0	41.9	33.4	22.6	2.1	1967
1968	17.9	7.8	6.1	4.2	0.4	47.2	20.7	16.0	11.1	1.0	43.8	33.9	23.5	2.0	1968
1969	19.7	8.6	6.2	4.3	0.6	49.3	21.4	15.4	10.9	1.6	43.5	31.3	22.0	3.2	1969
1970	21.1	9.6	5.9	4.7	1.0	51.5	23.3	14.3	11.4	2.5	45.3	27.8	22.1	4.8	1970
1971	23.0	10.0	6.3	5.3	1.4	53.5	23.2	14.7	12.3	3.2	43.5	27.5	23.0	6.1	1971
1972	24.4	11.3	6.4	5.6	1.1	54.8	25.4	14.4	12.5	2.5	46.3	26.3	22.8	4.0	1972
1973	24.3	11.2	6.2	5.9	1.0	54.6	25.1	14.0	13.2	2.3	46.0	25.6	24.1	3.7	1973
1974	23.8	10.6	6.1	6.0	1.0	53.3	23.9	13.7	13.5	2.2	44.8	25.8	25.4	3.5	1974
1975	24.6	10.8	6.4	6.6	0.8	52.9	23.3	13.7	14.2	1.7	44.0	25.9	26.9	2.7	1975
1976	25.3	10.9	6.5	7.1	0.8	52.0	22.4	13.3	14.7	1.6	43.0	25.6	28.2	2.6	1976
1977	26.0	11.5	6.5	7.3	0.7	51.8	22.9	13.1	14.5	1.3	44.2	25.2	28.0	2.2	1977
1978	27.0	12.1	6.6	7.5	0.8	51.6	23.1	12.7	14.3	1.5	44.8	24.6	27.7	2.6	1978
1979	27.3	13.0	6.2	7.3	0.7	51.0	25.5	12.2	14.4	1.4	47.7	22.8	27.0	2.5	1979
1980	26.1	12.4	5.7	7.2	0.7	49.3	25.2	11.7	14.5	1.5	47.6	22.1	27.4	2.8	1980

Table 5 Expenditure on Income Maintenance

Year	at current prices (in million NKR) Total	Pensions	Occup. injur.	Sickness, maternity	Child allow.	Unempl. benefits	Public assist.	percent distribution Pensions	Occup. injur.	Sickness, maternity	Child allow.	Unempl. benefits	Public assist.	Year
1950	328	136	19	49	77	10	37	41.5	5.8	14.9	23.5	3.0	11.3	1950
1951	402	163	29	50	106	15	39	40.5	7.2	12.4	26.4	3.7	9.7	1951
1952	473	204	38	60	96	31	44	43.1	8.0	12.7	20.3	6.6	9.3	1952
1953	518	224	44	70	97	38	45	43.2	8.5	13.5	18.7	7.3	8.7	1953
1954	597	267	49	102	100	37	42	44.7	8.2	17.1	16.8	6.2	7.0	1954
1955	727	380	51	107	102	41	46	52.3	7.0	14.7	14.0	5.6	6.3	1955
1956	775	390	51	111	129	47	47	50.3	6.6	14.3	16.6	6.1	6.1	1956
1957	895	477	49	139	132	48	50	53.3	5.5	15.5	14.7	5.4	5.6	1957
1958	1 090	581	52	165	157	78	57	53.3	4.8	15.1	14.4	7.2	5.2	1958
1959	1 304	726	69	174	184	93	58	55.7	5.3	13.3	14.1	7.1	4.4	1959
1960	1 358	740	96	185	184	95	58	54.5	7.1	13.6	13.5	7.0	4.3	1960
1961	1 560	950	103	191	183	80	53	60.9	6.6	12.2	11.7	5.1	3.4	1961
1962	1 924	1 281	110	201	182	99	51	66.6	5.7	10.4	9.5	5.1	2.7	1962
1963	2 178	1 435	122	214	229	122	56	65.9	5.6	9.8	10.5	5.6	2.6	1963
1964	2 393	1 632	134	222	230	111	64	68.2	5.6	9.3	9.6	4.6	2.7	1964
1965	2 731	1 973	137	223	231	111	56	72.2	5.0	8.2	8.5	4.1	2.1	1965
1966	2 968	2 199	139	236	233	114	47	74.1	4.7	8.0	7.9	3.8	1.6	1966
1967	3 613	2 704	154	304	283	122	46	74.8	4.3	8.4	7.8	3.4	1.3	1967
1968	4 164	3 149	150	333	322	160	50	75.6	3.6	8.0	7.7	3.8	1.2	1968
1969	4 878	3 800	161	346	338	174	59	77.9	3.3	7.1	6.9	3.6	1.2	1969
1970	6 817	4 735	179	450	1 202	186	65	69.5	2.6	6.6	17.6	2.7	1.0	1970
1971	7 975	5 673	81	803	1 209	138	71	71.1	1.0	10.1	15.2	1.7	0.9	1971
1972	8 890	6 437	73	882	1 243	168	87	72.4	0.8	9.9	14.0	1.9	1.0	1972
1973	10 185	7 603	87	902	1 332	161	100	74.6	0.9	8.9	13.1	1.6	1.0	1973
1974	11 413	8 764	80	959	1 365	145	100	76.9	0.7	8.4	12.0	1.3	0.9	1974
1975	13 207	10 149	98	1 168	1 383	293	116	76.8	0.7	8.8	10.5	2.2	0.9	1975
1976	15 501	11 886	100	1 328	1 581	473	133	76.7	0.6	8.6	10.2	3.1	0.9	1976
1977	17 713	13 931	104	1 499	1 608	432	139	78.6	0.6	8.5	9.1	2.4	0.8	1977
1978	21 261	16 153	105	2 632	1 585	624	162	76.0	0.5	12.4	7.5	2.9	0.8	1978
1979	24 989	17 482	105	4 716	1 666	834	186	70.0	0.4	18.9	6.7	3.3	0.7	1979
1980	29 237	19 900	105	5 132	2 841	1 037	222	68.1	0.4	17.6	9.7	3.5	0.8	1980

Table 6

Expenditure on Pensions

Year	at current prices (in million NKR)						at constant (1978) prices (in million NKR)						Year
	Total	Old age pensions	Invalidity pensions	Survivors' pensions	War pensions	Unmarried mothers' p.	Total	Old age pensions	Invalidity pensions	Survivors' pensions	War pensions	Unmarried mothers' p.	
1950	136	114	4		18		633	530	19		84		1950
1951	163	138	5		20		652	552	20		80		1951
1952	204	178	5		21		738	654	18		66		1952
1953	224	201	6		17		796	715	21		60		1953
1954	267	237	8		22		920	817	27		76		1954
1955	380	345	9		26		1 297	1 177	31		89		1955
1956	390	353	10		27		1 287	1 165	33		89		1956
1957	477	434	13		30		1 513	1 377	41		95		1957
1958	581	530	14	10	27		1 782	1 626	43	30	83		1958
1959	726	657	19	16	34		2 167	1 961	57	48	101		1959
1960	740	667	18	23	32		2 183	1 968	53	68	94		1960
1961	950	748	147	23	32		2 769	2 180	429	67	93		1961
1962	1 281	934	292	23	32		3 500	2 552	798	63	87		1962
1963	1 435	1 042	329	27	37		3 786	2 749	868	71	98		1963
1964	1 632	1 182	385	28	37		4 162	3 015	982	71	94		1964
1965	1 973	1 336	450	134	53		4 825	3 267	1 100	328	130		1965
1966	2 199	1 457	507	179	56		5 223	3 461	1 204	425	133		1966
1967	2 704	1 761	629	220	64	31	6 133	3 993	1 426	499	145	70	1967
1968	3 149	1 949	755	284	119	42	6 921	4 284	1 659	624	262	92	1968
1969	3 800	2 219	971	351	203	56	8 068	4 711	2 062	745	431	119	1969
1970	4 735	2 634	1 307	454	268	72	9 104	5 065	2 513	873	515	138	1970
1971	5 673	3 046	1 684	548	293	102	10 295	5 528	3 056	995	531	185	1971
1972	6 437	3 356	2 082	620	286	93	10 873	5 669	3 517	1 047	483	157	1972
1973	7 603	4 547	2 045	589	308	114	11 953	7 149	3 215	926	484	179	1973
1974	8 764	5 239	2 387	675	334	129	12 572	7 516	3 424	968	479	185	1974
1975	10 149	6 143	2 696	742	419	149	13 061	7 906	3 469	955	539	192	1975
1976	11 886	7 268	3 147	843	452	176	14 016	8 570	3 711	994	533	208	1976
1977	13 931	8 602	3 703	951	471	204	15 077	9 309	4 008	921	510	221	1977
1978	16 153	10 006	4 314	1 083	515	235	16 153	10 006	4 314	1 083	515	235	1978
1979	17 482	11 037	4 575	1 133	482	255	16 664	10 521	4 361	1 080	459	243	1979
1980	19 900	12 646	5 144	1 240	575	295	17 111	10 874	4 423	1 066	494	254	1980

Table 7

Expenditure on Sickness and Health

Year	at current prices (in million NKR)				at constant (1978) prices (in million NKR)					Year
	Sickness cash benefits	Refunds of medical costs	Health/ hospital services	Total sickness/ health	Sickness cash benefits	Refunds of medical costs	Health/ hospital services	Total sickness/ health	Occup. injury benefits	
1950	49	46	292	387	228	214	1 358	1 800	88	1950
1951	50	51	346	447	200	204	1 384	1 788	116	1951
1952	60	61	370	491	221	224	1 360	1 805	140	1952
1953	70	73	424	567	249	259	1 509	2 017	157	1953
1954	102	79	469	650	352	396	1 617	2 365	169	1954
1955	107	83	514	704	365	283	1 754	2 402	174	1955
1956	111	96	591	798	366	317	1 950	2 633	168	1956
1957	139	120	685	944	441	380	2 175	2 996	156	1957
1958	165	124	769	1 058	506	380	2 359	3 245	160	1958
1959	174	138	853	1 165	519	341	2 617	3 477	206	1959
1960	185	153	903	1 241	546	451	2 664	3 661	283	1960
1961	191	163	996	1 350	557	475	2 904	3 918	300	1961
1962	201	176	1 106	1 483	554	484	3 047	4 085	301	1962
1963	214	201	1 269	1 684	565	530	3 348	4 443	322	1963
1964	222	234	1 454	1 910	566	597	3 709	4 872	342	1964
1965	223	252	1 604	2 079	545	615	3 922	5 082	335	1965
1966	236	273	1 809	2 318	561	648	4 297	5 506	330	1966
1967	304	322	2 039	2 665	689	729	4 624	6 042	349	1967
1968	333	367	2 308	3 008	732	806	5 073	6 611	330	1968
1969	346	421	2 588	3 355	735	893	5 495	7 123	342	1969
1970	450	397	3 332	4 179	865	763	6 408	8 036	344	1970
1971	803	609	4 101	5 513	1 457	1 105	7 443	10 005	147	1971
1972	882	659	4 844	6 385	1 490	1 113	8 182	10 785	123	1972
1973	902	789	5 782	7 473	1 432	1 339	9 091	11 862	137	1973
1974	959	892	6 939	8 790	1 376	1 279	9 956	12 611	115	1974
1975	1 168	1 018	8 840	11 026	1 503	1 310	11 377	14 190	126	1975
1976	1 328	1 327	10 855	13 510	1 566	1 565	12 800	15 931	118	1976
1977	1 499	1 295	12 641	15 435	1 622	1 401	13 681	16 704	113	1977
1978	2 632	1 459	14 455	18 546	2 632	1 459	14 455	18 546	105	1978
1979	4 716	1 827	15 708	22 251	4 496	1 741	14 974	21 211	100	1979
1980	5 132	1 960	18 324	25 416	4 413	1 685	15 756	21 854	90	1980

Table 8

Expenditure on Children and Families

Year	at current prices (in million NKR)				at constant (1978) prices (in million NKR)				Year
	Child allowances	Child day care	Other services	Total	Child allowances	Child day care	Other services	Total	
1950	77				358				1950
1951	106				424				1951
1952	96	14	14	124	353	51	51	455	1952
1953	97				345				1953
1954	100	22	17	139	345	76	59	480	1954
1955	102				348				1955
1956	129	28	20	177	426	92	66	584	1956
1957	132				419				1957
1958	157	34	24	215	482	104	74	660	1958
1959	184				549				1959
1960	184	36	28	248	543	106	83	732	1960
1961	183				534				1961
1962	182	45	33	260	497	124	91	712	1962
1963	229				604				1963
1964	230	54	41	325	587	138	105	830	1964
1965	231				565				1965
1966	233	79	53	365	553	188	126	867	1966
1967	283				642				1967
1968	322	115	64	501	708	253	141	1 102	1968
1969	338				718				1969
1970	1 202	141	93	1 436	2 312	271	179	2 762	1970
1971	1 209				2 194				1971
1972	1 243	198	63	1 504	2 100	334	206	2 640	1972
1973	1 332				2 094				1973
1974	1 365	301	158	1 824	1 958	432	227	2 617	1974
1975	1 383				1 780				1975
1976	1 581		186		1 864		219		1976
1977	1 608				1 740				1977
1978	1 585	863	464	2 912	1 585	863	464	2 912	1978
1979	1 666				1 602				1979
1980	2 841				2 443				1980

Table 9

Expenditure on Unemployment

Year	at current prices (in million NKR)				at constant (1978) prices (in million NKR)				Year
	Unemployment cash benefits	Employment services	Publik work for unempl.	Total	Unemployment cash benefits	Employment services	Public work for unempl.	Total	
1950	10	5	5	20	47	23	23	93	1950
1951	15				60				1951
1952	31	7	12	50	114	26	44	184	1952
1953	38				135				1953
1954	37	8	14	59	128	28	48	204	1954
1955	41				140				1955
1956	47	12	16	75	155	40	53	248	1956
1957	48				152				1957
1958	78	14	13	105	245	43	40	328	1958
1959	93				278				1959
1960	95	14	17	126	280	41	50	371	1960
1961	80				233				1961
1962	99	21	21	141	270	58	58	386	1962
1963	122				322				1963
1964	111	29	34	174	283	74	87	444	1964
1965	111	31	32	174	271	76	78	425	1965
1966	114	34	34	182	271	81	81	433	1966
1967	122	38	54	214	277	86	122	485	1967
1968	160	41	47	248	352	90	103	545	1968
1969	174	47	59	280	369	100	125	594	1969
1970	186	57	50	293	358	110	96	564	1970
1971	138	69	56	263	250	125	102	477	1971
1972	168	69	41	278	284	117	69	470	1972
1973	161	69	45	275	253	110	71	434	1973
1974	145	65	60	270	208	93	86	387	1974
1975	293	79	63	435	377	102	81	560	1975
1976	473	125	145	743	558	147	171	876	1976
1977	432	136	150	718	468	147	162	777	1977
1978	624	152	102	878	624	152	102	878	1978
1979	834				795				1979
1980	1 037				892				1980

Table 10

Financing of Public Expenditure

at current prices, in million NKR

Year	Total receipts	as % of GDP	Savings	as % of GDP	Net lending	as % of GDP	Total receipts by major source: soc.sec. contrib.	direct taxes	indirect taxes	inter-ests	other	Percent distribution: soc.sec. contrib.	direct taxes	indirect taxes	inter-ests	other	Year
1950	5 923	39.3	2 322	15.4				2 630	1 953	108	1 232		44.4	33.0	1.8	20.8	1950
1951	5 921	31.6	1 874	10.0				2 905	2 622	87	307		49.1	44.3	1.5	5.2	1951
1952	6 423	31.0	1 643	7.9				3 289	2 962	80	92		51.2	46.1	1.2	1.4	1952
1953	6 517	31.0	1 347	6.4				3 505	2 861	64	87		53.8	43.9	1.0	1.3	1953
1954	6 906	30.3	1 351	5.9				3 680	3 006	149	71		53.3	43.5	2.2	1.0	1954
1955	7 260	29.9	1 505	6.2				3 898	3 194	160	8		53.7	44.0	2.2	0.1	1955
1956	8 201	29.9	1 795	6.5				4 352	3 657	184	8		53.1	44.6	2.2	0.1	1956
1957	9 524	32.6	2 224	7.6				5 294	4 024	203	3		55.6	42.3	2.1	0.0	1957
1958	9 784	33.5	2 322	8.0				5 484	4 082	217	1		56.1	41.7	2.2	0.0	1958
1959	10 400	33.6	2 184	7.1				5 817	4 315	268	-		55.9	41.5	2.6	-	1959
1960	10 936	33.1	2 212	6.7				5 966	4 612	358	-		54.6	42.2	3.3	-	1960
1961	12 337	34.2	2 813	7.8				6 637	5 075	624	1		53.8	41.1	5.1	0.0	1961
1962	13 795	35.5	2 933	7.6	1 780	4.6	2 449	5 186	5 493	659	8	17.8	37.5	39.8	4.8	0.1	1962
1963	14 788	35.5	2 637	6.3	1 241	3.0	2 654	5 507	5 822	797	8	17.9	37.3	39.4	5.4	0.1	1963
1964	16 513	36.0	3 242	7.1	1 621	3.5	2 963	6 232	6 507	801	10	17.9	37.8	39.4	4.8	0.1	1964
1965	18 605	36.8	3 299	6.5	1 609	3.2	3 386	6 884	7 379	945	11	18.2	37.0	39.7	5.1	0.1	1965
1966	20 889	38.3	4 092	7.5	2 248	4.1	3 966	7 714	8 190	1 007	12	19.0	36.9	39.2	4.8	0.1	1966
1967	24 198	40.5	5 076	8.5	2 869	4.8	5 480	8 560	9 047	1 096	15	22.6	35.4	37.4	4.5	0.1	1967
1968	26 208	41.1	4 796	7.5	2 469	3.9	6 073	9 427	9 433	1 260	15	23.2	35.9	36.0	4.8	0.1	1968
1969	30 082	43.3	5 633	8.1	2 842	4.1	6 704	10 654	11 174	1 533	17	22.3	35.4	37.1	5.1	0.1	1969
1970	34 755	43.5	5 591	7.0	2 590	3.2	7 730	10 591	14 568	1 846	20	22.2	30.5	41.9	5.3	0.1	1970
1971	41 485	46.6	7 342	8.2	3 801	4.3	10 386	12 800	16 597	1 679	23	25.0	30.9	40.0	4.0	0.1	1971
1972	47 646	48.4	8 725	8.9	4 462	4.5	12 455	14 897	18 193	2 070	31	26.1	31.3	38.2	4.3	0.1	1972
1973	55 473	49.6	10 853	9.7	6 420	5.7	15 330	17 372	20 331	2 402	38	27.6	31.4	36.7	4.3	0.1	1973
1974	62 934	48.5	11 053	8.5	6 055	4.7	17 023	19 979	22 741	3 150	41	27.0	31.8	36.1	5.0	0.1	1974
1975	73 798	49.6	11 647	7.8	5 681	3.8	19 863	23 790	26 455	3 646	44	26.9	32.3	35.8	4.9	0.1	1975
1976	86 818	50.9	12 124	7.1	5 348	3.1	21 866	29 464	31 011	4 421	56	25.2	33.9	35.7	5.1	0.1	1976
1977	97 610	51.0	10 910	5.7	3 204	1.7	24 733	31 583	36 327	4 907	60	25.3	32.4	37.2	5.0	0.1	1977
1978	110 888	52.0	10 210	4.8	1 341	0.6	27 757	37 900	37 946	7 219	66	25.0	34.2	34.2	6.5	0.1	1978
1979	121 259	50.8	12 613	5.3	4 296	1.8	29 914	44 201	41 106	5 940	98	24.7	36.5	33.9	4.9	0.1	1979
1980	150 344	53.1	26 842	9.5	17 715	6.2	34 176	61 191	48 105	6 966	108	22.7	40.6	32.0	4.6	0.1	1980

Table 11

Social Security Receipts by Major Source

Year	At current prices, in million NKR					Percent distribution				Year
	Employ-ers	Insured	Central govt.	Local govt.	Total	Employ-ers	In-sured	Central govt.	Local govt.	
1950										1950
1951										1951
1952										1952
1953										1953
1954										1954
1955										1955
1956										1956
1957										1957
1958										1958
1959	438	723	322	192	1 691	25.9	42.8	19.0	11.4	1959
1960	522	803	341	196	1 888	27.6	42.5	18.1	10.4	1960
1961	607	949	347	240	2 175	27.9	43.6	16.0	11.0	1961
1962	837	1 101	382	289	2 642	31.7	41.7	14.5	10.9	1962
1963	930	1 157	467	284	2 872	32.4	40.3	16.3	9.9	1963
1964	1 052	1 264	499	312	3 169	33.2	39.9	15.7	9.8	1964
1965	1 291	1 419	542	352	3 656	35.3	38.8	14.8	9.6	1965
1966	1 607	1 603	580	399	4 247	37.8	37.7	13.7	9.4	1966
1967	2 388	2 120	708	465	5 750	41.5	36.9	12.3	8.1	1967
1968	2 814	2 294	788	491	6 469	43.5	35.5	12.2	7.6	1968
1969	3 243	2 495	858	531	7 215	44.9	34.6	11.9	7.4	1969
1970	3 752	2 841	2 391	811	9 881	38.0	28.8	24.2	8.2	1970
1971	5 236	3 575	2 388	903	12 168	43.0	29.4	19.6	7.4	1971
1972	6 655	4 311	2 543	1 030	14 613	45.5	29.5	17.4	7.0	1972
1973	8 183	5 498	2 708	1 316	17 816	45.9	30.9	15.2	7.4	1973
1974	9 580	6 026	2 970	1 531	20 107	47.6	30.0	14.8	7.6	1974
1975	11 308	6 644	3 380	1 742	23 074	49.0	28.8	14.6	7.5	1975
1976	13 142	7 113	3 769	1 921	25 945	50.7	27.4	14.5	7.4	1976
1977	14 611	8 164	4 709	96	27 580	53.0	29.6	17.1	0.3	1977
1978	16 597	8 485	6 048	375	31 505	52.7	26.9	19.2	1.2	1978
1979	17 372	10 462	6 781	182	34 798	49.9	30.7	19.5	0.5	1979
1980	19 024	11 399	10 854	85	41 362	46.0	27.6	26.2	0.2	1980

Table 12

Social Insurance Contributions and Expenditure

at current prices, in million NKR; contributions as percentage of expenditure (ratio)

Year	Pension insurance			Occup. injuries ins.			Sickness insurance			Unemployment insur.			National Insurance			Year
	contrib. (C)	expend. (E)	C/E ratio	contrib. (C)	expend. (E)	C/E ratio	contrib. (C)	expend. (E)	C/E ratio	contrib. (C)	expend. (E)	C/E ratio	contrib. (C)	expend. (E)	C/E ratio	
1950																1950
1951																1951
1952																1952
1953																1953
1954																1954
1955																1955
1956																1956
1957																1957
1958																1958
1959	570	585	97	83	69	120	757	718	105	109	93	117				1959
1960	580	597	97	127	95	134	780	770	101	111	92	121				1960
1961	951	866	110	133	103	129	828	792	105	120	80	150				1961
1962	1 308	1 191	110	135	110	123	936	883	106	128	99	129				1962
1963	1 417	1 305	109	146	122	120	987	984	100	131	122	107				1963
1964	1 552	1 501	103	140	134	104	1 103	1 125	98	139	111	125				1964
1965	1 779	1 732	103	145	137	106	1 213	1 215	100	147	111	132				1965
1966	2 067	1 919	108	145	139	104	1 476	1 365	108	151	114	132				1966
1967	3 496	2 707	129	145	154	94	1 732	1 590	109	151	122	124				1967
1968	3 989	3 161	126	150	159	94	1 866	1 763	106	172	160	108				1968
1969	4 543	3 774	120	148	161	92	1 946	1 961	99	176	174	101				1969
1970	5 389	4 837	111	152	179	85	2 818	2 911	97	185	186	99				1970
1971													10 850	10 033	108	1971
1972													13 236	11 701	113	1972
1973													16 318	13 789	118	1973
1974													18 639	15 751	118	1974
1975													21 491	18 842	114	1975
1976													24 074	22 136	109	1976
1977													25 588	23 563	109	1977
1978													29 790	27 973	106	1978
1979													32 998	32 870	100	1979
1980													38 523	37 147	104	1980

Table 13 Population, Beneficiaries, Earnings

Year	Total population	Population aged 0–16	Population aged 65+	No. of child allowances	No. of old age pensioners	Average gross annual earnings of male ind. workers at curr. pr.	at 1978 pr.	Year
1950	3 263 988	830 889	316 779	417 500	162 714	7 335	34 116	1950
1951	3 295 559	850 471	318 430	430 000	170 816	8 393	33 572	1951
1952	3 326 788	869 594	325 608	442 592	183 601	9 338	34 330	1952
1953	3 359 313	889 097	332 871	453 000	192 592	9 743	34 672	1953
1954	3 392 016	907 457	339 620	463 500	202 217	10 238	35 303	1954
1955	3 428 832	924 062	347 755	474 000	190 073	10 755	36 706	1955
1956	3 461 730	941 074	355 986	484 500	202 598	11 610	38 316	1956
1957	3 493 992	959 390	346 143	495 919	214 707	12 397	39 355	1957
1958	3 525 365	974 591	327 736	500 000	231 930	12 984	39 828	1958
1959	3 555 543	984 652	381 768	504 250	299 187	13 684	40 848	1959
1960	3 585 223	989 127	391 351	510 600	308 726	14 142	41 716	1960
1961	3 614 512	989 112	401 472	504 815	314 759	15 034	43 830	1961
1962	3 638 919	985 162	415 943	501 598	325 082	16 394	45 162	1962
1963	3 666 539	980 258	425 522	502 110	333 784	17 418	45 958	1963
1964	3 694 339	979 368	435 127	503 923	337 891	18 443	47 048	1964
1965	3 723 153	981 932	445 715	506 818	352 495	20 069	49 068	1965
1966	3 752 749	986 486	456 649	511 912	362 152	21 278	50 541	1966
1967	3 784 262	992 478	467 549	514 019	340 051	22 834	51 778	1967
1968	3 818 983	999 228	481 224	518 286	337 865	24 188	53 160	1968
1969	3 850 977	1 005 511	491 469	525 345	347 598	25 614	54 382	1969
1970	3 877 386	1 010 223	499 743	1 059 525	352 735	28 357	54 332	1970
1971	3 903 039	1 013 805	507 832	1 064 594	358 000	31 470	57 114	1971
1972	3 933 004	1 017 025	517 107	1 068 205	364 678	33 969	57 380	1972
1973	3 960 613	1 018 340	526 752	1 066 936	459 915	37 345	58 718	1973
1974	3 985 258	1 017 679	537 438	1 065 191	472 471	43 321	62 154	1974
1975	4 007 313	1 014 638	548 495	1 061 882	484 127	51 743	66 593	1975
1976	4 026 152	1 009 189	559 336	1 055 230	497 490	58 406	68 875	1976
1977	4 043 205	1 001 472	570 938	1 046 442	509 210	62 644	67 796	1977
1978	4 058 671	992 415	582 426	1 037 378	518 843	67 209	67 209	1978
1979	4 072 517	987 188	592 972	1 029 267	531 459			1979
1980	4 085 620	975 422	603 422	1 017 651	542 432			1980

Notes to and sources for appendix tables

Table 1

GDP data at current prices are from sources (1), (2), (3) and (6). Figures at 1975-prices for the period 1950-1974 are from the OECD-source (4). For the period 1950-1961, the OECD-figures at current prices are slightly higher, while being identical to figures from national sources for the 1962-1974 period. Public expenditure data are taken from sources (1)-(3). The consumer price indices with bases 1978=100 and 1975=100 have been recalculated from base 1980=100 which is published in source (5). The figures for 1953, 1957, 1960 and 1963 have been estimated by linear interpolation.

Table 2

Data on public expenditure by purpose are from sources (1)-(3). For the years 1972-1980, the categories 'economic growth' and 'other' have been merged, calculated by subtracting expenditure for 'welfare', 'defence' and 'general administration and public order' from 'total expenditure'. 'Welfare' includes expenditure on health, pensions and social insurance, education, housing. 'Defence' includes local government expenditure on civil defence. 'General administration and public order' include general administration, tax authorities, foreign office and foreign representation, justice and police.

Data on public expenditure by economic function are from sources (1)-(3).

Figures on central and local government net expenditure 1950-65 are taken from source (7), figures for 1965-1971 from source (8). Figures for the period 1972-80 are not included since local government figures comparable with earlier years have not been published. Transfers to social insurance which have been paid out by the National Insurance Institution, have been substracted from the central and local government figures for the central and local government figures for the years 1961-71. Expenditure figures of the National Insurance Institution are from source (9) for the years 1950-1960, and from source (8) for the years 1961-1978. Surplus has been subtracted. Figures on total public expenditure differ somewhat negligible from those in Table 1 and in the other tables for the years 1950-1971, due to different sources.

Table 3

Income maintenance expenditure cover expenditure by central government, local government and the National Insurance Institution on income maintenance. Transfers between the various levels/institutions have been taken into account. Expenditure on hospitalization, medical treatment, medicines are excluded, as well as surplus of the National Insurance Institution. Local government expenditure cover expenditure for benefits in kind to some extent. Statistics on 'social measures for foreigners' have been excluded since they cover developmental aid. Sources (3), (7), (8), (10) plus unpublished figures on local government expenditure on *stønader* (transfers to households) for the period 1972-1980 provided by the Central Bureau of Statistics.

Figures on education cover expenditure by central and local government.
Sources: (7) (for the period 1950-1971); (3) (for the period 1979-1980).

Figures on health include expenditure by central and local government, plus expenditure on hospitalization covered by the National Health Insurance and other approved health insurance institutions for the years 1950-1971 (7). Figures for 1972-1978 are from source (3) and cover expenditure for all public consumption expenditure on health and social security and welfare services, plus public gross fixed capital formation for the same purposes. Figures for the two periods may not be directly comparable.

Figures on housing cover housing, parks, sport ground in the case of central government and local government expenditure until 1971. Since 1972, local government expenditure covers housing only. Source: (7).

Deflators: consumer price index (see Table 1).

Table 4

Percentages based on absolute figures given in Tables 1-3. Sources: see notes to Tables 1-3.

Table 5

These data differ from those in Table 3, because they were generated in a different way, and partly from different sources. Figures in Table 3 include some benefits in kind.

Pensions: see notes and sources for Table 6.

Occupational injuries: data include schemes for industrial workers, seamen, and fishermen. Sources: 1950-58: (7), 1959-66: (11), 1967-1980: (5) and (10). Figures for post-1971 period cover expenses according to the old law. Since 1971, other occupational injuries expenses are part of expenses covered by the sickness insurance or invalidity insurance of the National Insurance Scheme: it is not possible to differentiate total expenses for occupational injuries after 1971.

Sickness and maternity: the data from source (7) cover cash benefits; physicians' fees, medicines and hospitalization expenditure are included under 'health' (see Table 3).

Child allowances:
Source (7) for 1950-60 and source (10) for 1961-1980.

Unemployment benefits: source (8) for 1950-51, (11) for 1952-1970, and (7) for 1971-1980. Administrative expenses (negligible figures) are included in the 1952-1970 figures.

Public assistance: source (7) for 1950-1959, and 1976-1980 and (8) for 1960-1975. The law was changed in 1964, effective from 1965. The figure for 1965 is not available, and has been estimated as the average of the 1964 and 1966 figures. The data cover only cash benefits.

Table 6

Old age pension expenditure include pension schemes for seamen; for forestry workers (since 1951); for fishermen (since 1957); national old age pension scheme (until 1966); old age pension scheme of the National Insurance Scheme (since 1967). Expenditure for seamen's pensions is estimated by interpolation for the years 1951, 1953, 1955, 1957, 1959 on the basis of figures for the years 1950, 1952, etc. Also expenditure figures for seamen's pensions for the years 1975-1978 are estimated on the basis of known figures for 1974 and 1980 (217 and 345 million NKR respectively).

An invalidity pension law was introduced in 1961. Expenditure before this data cover assistance to blind and crippled. Figures for 1951 and 1953 are estimates based on interpolation.

Survivors' pension include expenditure on orphans' pensions (since 1957); widows' pensions (since 1965); widowers' pensions (since 1967).

Source (8) covers all data for 1950, 1952, 1954, 1956, 1958, 1960-1974. War pension data for 1951, 1953, 1955, 1957, 1959 from source (10). Other pension data for 1951, 1953, 1955, 1957, 1959 from source (7). All data for 1975-1980 are from source (10).

Deflator: consumer price index (see Table 1).

Table 7

See notes and sources on health and sickness cash benefits expenditure for Tables 3 and 5.
Deflator: consumer price index (see Table 1).

Table 8

Figures on child allowances are from sources (7) for 1950-1960 and (10) for 1961-1980. Figures on child day care cover kindergartens, day care institutions, children's homes, etc. and are from source (12). Figures on other services cover consultation agencies for mothers and children, ambulant nurses, etc. and are from sources (12) and (13).
Deflator: consumer price index (see Table 1).

Table 9

Data on unemployment cash benefits are from sources (8) for 1950-1951, (11) for 1952-1970 and (7) for 1971-1980. Figures on employment services and public work for unemployed are from sources (12) and (13).
Deflator: consumer price index (see Table 1).

Table 10

Figures on total receipts and the breakdown by major source are from sources (1)-(3). Separate figures on social security contributions exist only from 1962. The category 'other' covers transfers from abroad (1950-1961), and transfers from households (since 1962). Figures on savings are from sources (4) for 1950-1978 and (14) for 1979-1980. Figures on net lending are available only since 1962. Source (4) covers 1962-76, source (14) covers 1977-1980.

Table 11

Sources (11) for 1959-1973, (8) for 1974-1975 and (7) for 1976-1980. The figures cover social security schemes administered by the National Insurance Institution. Pre-1959 figures are not available. Figures on interest and other income not included.

Table 12

Sources (11) for 1959-1970, (19) for 1971-1980. Since 1971, all schemes have been incorporated in the National Insurance Scheme, and figures are not easily disaggregated by type of purpose. Hospital benefits are included in the sickness insurance expenditure data.

Table 13

Data on total population, population aged 0-16 and population aged 65+ are from sources (7) and (8), data on number of child allowances are from sources (7) and (10). Figures on number of old age pensioners are calculated on the basis of data given in sources (7), (8), (10) and (15). Figures on average gross annual earnings of male industrial workers are taken from source (10).

Enumerated sources for appendix tables

(1) NOS B 239, *National Accounts 1949-1962*, revised edition, Oslo, Central Bureau of Statistics, 1981.

(2) NOS B 48, *National Accounts 1962-1978*, Oslo, CBS, 1979.

(3) NOS B 222, *National Accounts 1969-1980*, Oslo, CBS, 1980.

(4) OECD, *National Accounts Statistics, 1950-1979*, Vol. I Aggregates, Paris, 1981.

(5) Rikstrygdeverket. *Årsberetning og regnskap 1980*, Oslo 1981. (National Insurance Institution. Annual report and accounts, 1980.)

(6) *Statistical Yearbook 1982*

(7) *Statistical Yearbook*, various years.

(8) *Historical Statistics 1978*

(9) NOS A 143, *Central Government and Social Security Funds Finances 1946-1960*, Oslo, CBS.

(10) Rikstrygdeverket. *Årsberetning og regnskap*, (National Insurance Institution, Annual report and accounts), various years.

(11) Rikstrygdeverket. *Oversikt over utgifter og inntekter, m.v. i sosiale trygder m.v. 1959-1973* (Overview of expenditures and revenues of social insurance schemes), Oslo, 1975.

(12) *Statistical Reports on the Nordic Countries*, various years.

(13) *Nordic Statistical Yearbook*, various years.

(14) OECD, *Economic Surveys 1982-83. Norway*, Paris, 1983.

(15) *Pensjonstrygden for sjømenn. Årsmelding og regnskap, 1979, 1980.* (The Pension Insurance for Seamen. Annual reports and accounts, 1979, 1980.)

Finland

Matti Alestalo and Hannu Uusitalo

Institutional Synopsis

Contents

Glossary of abbreviations

KVTEL	*Kunnallisten viranhaltijain ja työntekijäin eläkelaki 1964* (1964 Local Government Employees' Pension Act)
LEL	*Lyhytaikaisissa työsuhteissa olevien työntekijäin eläkelaki 1962* (1962 Temporary Employees' Pension Act)
MYEL	*Maatalousyrittäjien eläkelaki 1969* (1969 Farmers' Pension Act)
TEL	*Työntekijäin eläkelaki 1961* (1961 Employees' Pension Act)
VEL	*Valtion eläkelaki 1966* (1966 State Pension Act)
NSI	*Sairausvakuutus* (National Sickness Insurance)
YEL	*Yrittäjien eläkelaki 1969* (1969 Self-Employed Persons' Pension Act)

Introduction

In the following description the schemes have been arranged into seven groups, most of which are then subdivided into income maintenance, services and core laws. Data normally refer to 1982. They do not correspond exactly with those presented in the country chapter in Volume I, where it was more important to construct time series of data with a maximum comparability over time. Income maintenance benefits are typically taxable, if not, this is stated. Expenditure on services is expressed in net terms, i.e. user fees charged are deducted [1].

I Pensions/Services for the old

The pension system consists mainly of transfer payments. In 1982, cash benefit expenditure amounted to around 24,000 million Finnish Marks (FM) and expenditure on related services amounted to 2,000 million FM. Taken together, this amounted to 11% of GDP or 46% of total social security expenditure [2].

Income maintenance

Coverage

The pension system consists of the National Pension Scheme (*Kansaneläke*) which provides basic pension security for all citizens, and different earnings-related pension schemes, the most important being the Occupational Pension Schemes (*Työeläke*), the State Pension Scheme (VEL), and the Local Government Employees' Pension Scheme (KVTEL). The occupational pension system incorporates separate schemes for full-time employees (TEL), those in seasonal employment (LEL), the self-employed (YEL), and farmers (MYEL). Both the national pension scheme and the earnings-related pension schemes provide old age, survivors', invalidity and unemployment pensions.

Taken together, the national pension and the earnings-related pension should not exceed 60-66% of the highest index-adjusted pension-carrying wage/salary. National pensions, with the exception of basic and assistance amounts, are tax-free, whereas occupational pensions are taxable. Benefits are closely linked to changes in wages and prices, the indexation varies, however, between the major schemes.

Table 1: Number of pensions in 1982 by type of pension and pension scheme (in thousands)[a]

Pension scheme	Old age pensions	Inval. pensions	Unempl. pensions	Surv. pensions	Total no. pensions
National pensions[b]	598	236	23	56	913
Occupat. pensions[c]	322	171	23	112	628
State[d]		112		39	151
Local govt. (1964)	35	14	2	8	59
Local govt. (old)	15			5	20

Table 2: Pension expenditure in 1982 (in million FM)[a]

Pension scheme	Old age	Surviv-ors'	Invalid-ity	Unem-ploy-ment	Other	Total mill. FM	%
-National pensions[b]	5637.8	229.3	2194.1	158.9	-	8220.1	34.5
-Employees/ temporary employees	2450.5	758.2	1801.7	218.9	-	5229.3	21.9
-Self-employed	820.4	160.3	403.5	25.4	140.1[c]	1549.7	6.5
-Seamen	65.7	14.7	28.7	1.2	-	110.3	0.5
-State employees	2118.0	626.5	402.9	13.9	806.3[d]	3967.6	16.6
-Pension rules[e]	-	108.0	-	-	520.0	628.0	2.6
-Local govt. employees	731.4	142.8	450.3	5.0	7.0[f]	1336.5	5.6
-Church employees		23.5			94.3	117.8	0.5
-War disabled/ dependents	-	-	-	-	1579.6	1579.6	6.6
-Additional pension protection	-	171.3	-	-	838.9	1010.2	4.2
-Invalidity assistance	-	-	-	-	86.1	86.1	0.4
Total	11823.8	2234.6	5281.2	423.3	4072.3	23835.2	99.9

Notes to Tables 1 and 2, see page 128.

1. National pensions

The first general pension scheme was introduced in 1937 and became effective in 1939. It was based on the accumulation of premiums paid by the insured (employees 18-55 years) and employers, excluding invalids and persons over 55 years of age. The first invalidity pensions were paid in 1942 and the first old age pensions in 1949. However, this insurance-based system was destroyed by inflation during and after the war.

The present national pension scheme dates from the 1956 National Pension Act which became effective in 1957. It was successively extended to include various kinds of supplements granted to those with low incomes (1966) and those in receipt of survivors' pensions (1969), supplements for housing allowances (1970), unemployment benefits (1971) and supplements and pensions for war veterans (1971). It also includes a national burial grant, a widows' training allowance and certain rehabilitation services.

Since 1980, the national pension scheme has been under reform, which should be completed in the latter half of the 1980s. The major goals of this reform are to improve the lowest pensions, to make pensions independent of pensioners' earnings, to create individual pensions (i.e. not reducible by spouse's income), and to make national pensions taxable. In the first phase of the reform (effective from 1980/1981) the assistance supplement was increased, the effect of income on the supplement was reduced, and the effect of spouse's income on national pensions was also reduced. In the second phase (effective from 1983/1984), the assistance supplement was integrated with assistance amount, which was improved. National pensions were no longer earnings-related and the basic and assistance amounts became taxable, while changes in taxation were made in order to avoid the taxation of those only in receipt of national pensions. In the third phase (planned to be effective from 1985), property, property income and entrepreneurial income will no longer affect the size of national pensions. In the final phase, spouses' assistance amounts will be equal to those of single pensioners, i.e. the effect of spouse's income on own pension will be totally removed.

Notes to Table 1:

[a] (Source 1, p. 52); (Source 4, p. 24); (Source 2, p. 5); (Source 10, pp. 12, 27).

[b] Does not include those in receipt of old age assistance (3,200), child care allowances (12,000), and war veterans' pensions (23,000).

[c] Do not include additional private occupational pensions.

[d] Includes the 'old' and the new 1967 scheme.

Notes to Table 2:

[a] Source (3), pp. 62-64, and additional unpublished data by the author of source (3).

[b] Not including war veterans' pensions, national pension child supplements, and child care allowances (see Section IV).

[c] Includes farm closure schemes for those who stopped farming and sold their farms in the period 1974-1982.

[d] Includes pensions under the old Government Employees' Pension Act, and extra pensions.

[e] Includes pensions granted by the member bodies of the Local Government Pension Authority.

[f] Includes appointed representatives' pensions.

Table 3 Qualifying conditions and components of pensions by type of pension

Pension type	Qualifying conditions	Components						
		Basic amount	Assistance amount	Housing allowance	Spouse in-crease	Child in-crease	Helplessness supplement	War veteran's supplement
Old age	All citizens over 65	yes	yes, if low income	yes, if low income, dependent upon housing exp.	yes, if spouse unable to work	yes, if child under 16	yes, in case of helplessness or advanced age	yes, for war veteran's badge holders
Invalidity	People aged 16 to 64 not capable of working, taking into account age, occupation and other relevant factors	,,	,,	,,	,,	,,	yes, in case of helplessness; no, if pension granted for a specified period only	,,
Unemployment	People aged 55 to 64 who have been unemployed for an extended period	,,	,,	,,	,,	,,	no	,,
Widows	Widow's under 65 years of age without national pension in own right; who were married at least three years and whose husband were under 65 at the time of marriage							
	Pension initially payable for 6 months	,,	,,	,,	no	no	no	no
	Pension thereafter (if children)	,,	,,	,,	,,	,,	,,	,,
	Pension thereafter (no children)	no	,,	,,	,,	,,	,,	,,
Orphans	Half and full orphan's under 16; those aged 16 to 21 in education and unable to maintain themselves	Benefit 20 % of the basic amount and full assistance amount for half orphans, double for full orphans						
War veteran's	Needy holders of the war veteran's badge aged 55 to 65; under 60 only on condition of reduced working capacity	Pension dependent on income; may include housing allowance						
Child care allowance	Children under 16 who are financially or otherwise a burden to their families due to sickness or handicap	The size of the allowance dependent on the burden						

Benefits

The national pension scheme includes old age pensions, invalidity pensions, unemployment pensions, survivors' pensions, war veterans' pensions and supplements, child care allowances, and old age assistance, which have not been granted since 1980. These pensions include various kinds of components, which are given in Table 3 above.
As seen from the table, old age, invalidity and unemployment pensions may consist of quite the same components, whereas survivors' pensions, war veterans' pensions and child care allowances are determined differently. In 1984, the basic amount totalled 288 FM per month, or 5.9% of the average gross wage/salary [3]. The size of the assistance amount depends on income, and its full amount was 1,274 - 1,344 FM in 1984, or 26.2 - 27.6% of the average gross wage/salary, depending on the place of residence. Housing allowances are paid to low-income pensioners, and their size depends on income and housing expenses. Spouse increase is a flat-rate benefit amounting to 262 FM in 1984, as is child increase, amounting to 169 FM in 1984. Smaller helplessness supplements amount to 262 FM and larger to 386 FM, the former being paid to all people over the age of 80, and the latter to all those over 85.

Financing and administration

The National Pension System is financed mainly by contributions from employers (amounting to 4.1-5.6% of payroll and 59% of costs in 1982), and taxpayers (1.82% of income and 23% of costs in 1982). Other contributions are made by: the state and local government authorities (17% in 1982), and the national pension fund (1%) (Source 1, 1982, p. 99; Source 3, p. 62). The national pension system is financed on a pay-as-you-go basis and administered by the Social Insurance Institution under the direct supervision of parliament. For administrative purposes, the country is divided into five insurance regions and 202 insurance districts, each of which has at least one office.

2. State pensions

The pension system for central government civil servants is the oldest form of old age security. It dates from the eighteenth and nineteenth centuries. The first general scheme for central government civil servants was introduced in 1926. The retirement age was 65, but was subsequently raised to 67 in 1930. The present system dates from the State Pension Act (*Valtion eläkelaki*, VEL), effective from 1967. The majority of state pensions are granted in accordance with this 'New Pension Act', but there are still persons who receive a pension according to the old system.

Benefits

VEL provides for old age, invalidity, unemployment, and survivors' pensions, for both civil servants and other public employees. The old age pension is paid to those who have reached the age of 63 and who are no longer working. A state employee is, however, permitted to retain his post until he reaches the age of 67. In some occupations, earlier retirement is possible, the lowest pensionable age being 55. The size of the pension is dependent on the length of service and the wage or salary earned. A full pension, amounting to 66% of salary/wage (see occupational pensions below) is payable after 30 years of service. For those covered by the new VEL, the average old age pension amounted to 2,784 FM per month in December 1982 or 61% of average gross wage/salary and 3,503 FM under the old Pension Act (Source 2, p. 3).

Invalidity pensions are granted where loss of working capacity (i.e. ability to hold a post) is due to illness or injury. The amount of invalidity pension depends on the length of service and the salary/wage earned. In December 1982, average invalidity pension amounted to 1,551 FM per month or 34% of average gross wage/salary (Source 2, p. 3).

Unemployment pension is paid to those aged 58 or over who are unemployed, and for whom the employment service is unable to find suitable work. The beneficiary must have received unemployment assistance for at least 200 days during the past 60 weeks. At the end of 1982, average unemployment pension amounted to 308 FM per month or 7% of average gross wage/salary (Source 2, p. 3).

Survivors' pension is paid after the death of an employee with the right to a state pension. Contrary to other major schemes a widower is also entitled to survivors' pension after the death of a female state employee. The widow or widower is entitled to survivors' pension: if the marriage was contracted before the employee reached 65 years of age; if the beneficiary has a child below 18 years of age, or if the widow has reached the age of 40 at the time of the employee's death; or if the couple had been married for at least three years. In the case of remarriage, the beneficiary receives a lump sum corresponding to the pension for a period of two years. Survivors' pension for a child is normally paid until the age of 18. Survivors' pension amounts to 30%-66% of the deceased's salary. In the case of four or more survivors the pension reaches the 66% level. In December 1982, average survivors' pension amounted to 1,235 FM or 27% of average gross wage/salary (Source 2, p. 3).

Financing and administration

All state pensions are financed out of general revenues and administered by the State Treasury.

3. Local government pensions

The present system for employees of: town councils, rural communities, federations of municipalities, etc. is based on the 1964 Local Government Employees' Pension Act (*Kunnallisten viranhaltijain ja työntekijäin eläkelaki*, KVTEL). It is modelled in accordance with the state pension scheme.

Benefits

In general, benefits granted under KVTEL are very similar to those granted under VEL. There are, however, exceptions for some occupational groups especially as regards old age pensions. Local government old age pension is paid to all those who have reached the age of 63. The pension varies according to whether or not the beneficiary is employed by the local authority at the time of retirement. A beneficiary who is otherwise employed at the time of retirement is only entitled to the so-called basic pension. At the end of 1982, monthly average pensions were as follows: old age pension amounted to 2,178 FM or 47% of average gross wage/salary; invalidity pension amounted to 1,848 FM or 40% of average gross wage/salary; unemployment pension amounted to 291 FM or 6% of average gross wage/salary; and survivors' pension amounted to 1,414 FM or 31% of average gross wage/salary (Source 10, p. 13).

Financing and administration

The system is financed by local taxation through the member-bodies of the Local Government Pension Authority which also administers the system.

4. Occupational pensions

Compared with the long history of earnings-related state pensions, the private occupational pension system is of relatively recent origin. During the 1950s, trade unions and employers' associations began to develop plans for an adequate occupational pension system for private sector employees. The current system is based mainly on four acts: the 1961 Employees' Pension Act (*Työntekijäin eläkelaki*, TEL) covering private employees who have been working for at least one month without interruption and whose monthly wage/salary exceeds a certain limit; the 1962 Temporary Employees' Pension Act (*Lyhytaikaisissa työsuhteissa olevien työntekijäin eläkelaki*, LEL), covering those in seasonal employment; the 1969 Farmers' Pension Act (*Maatalousyrittäjien eläkelaki*, MYEL), also covering farmers' wives and other unpaid family members; and the 1969 Self-Employed Persons' Pension Act (*Yrittäjien eläkelaki*, YEL).

In 1983, approximately 1,130,000 persons were insured under TEL. The number of temporary employees covered was 240,000 (average for the year). The number of self-employed and farmers insured was 125,000 and 225,000 respectively (the total number of insured persons was 1,720,000, covering all private sector employees, or 67% of labour force. (Unpublished data from Central Pension Security Institute).

Benefits

Initially, the Occupational Pension System only provided benefits for old age and invalidity. A survivors' pension was introduced in 1967, an unemployment pension in 1971, and a pension for the partially disabled in 1973. The age requirement for an old age pension is 65, but it is possible to defer retirement. The self-employed, farmers, and seasonal workers receive a pension irrespective of whether or not they continue to work. Old age, invalidity, and unemployment pensions may include a child supplement provided that the beneficiary is not in receipt of a full pension.

The general formula for old age pensions is 1.5% of the average index-adjusted salary for the last four years of each period of employment multiplied by the years in employment, reaching a maximum of 60% of the salary or wage.

The average occupational old age pension at the end of 1982 amounted to 885 FM per month (19% of average gross wage/salary). The average pension resulting from the Employees' Pension Act amounted to 1,215 FM (26% of average gross wage/salary), and the corresponding figures were 633 FM for temporary employees (14%), 369 FM for farmers (8%), and 1,494 for other self-employed persons (33%) (Source 4, p. 28).

Any employee or self-employed person who has lost three-fifths of his working capacity for a year is entitled to a full invalidity pension (155,000 in 1982). A loss of two-fifths entitles him/her to a partial invalidity pension (17,000 in 1982). In assessing the pension, training, previous employment work, age, housing conditions, and other relevant factors are taken into account. The full invalidity pension is equal to the old age pension. The amount for partial invalidity pension is normally one-half of a full pension. For the older age group it is, however, higher.

At the end of 1982, average full invalidity pension amounted to 1,122 FM or 24% of average gross wage/salary, and average partial invalidity pension amounted to 546 FM or 12% of average gross wage/salary. In the same year full invalidity pension amounted to 1,462 FM or 32% of average gross wage/salary under the Employees' Pension Act (TEL), 900 FM or 20% under the Temporary Employees' Pension Act (LEL), 449 FM or 10% under the Farmers' Pension Act (MYEL) and 1,401 FM or 31% under the Self-Employed Persons' Pension Act (YEL), (Source 4, p. 28).

An occupational unemployment pension is paid to unemployed persons aged 58-64 who have received unemployment assistance for at least 200 days during the past 60 weeks, and who are unable to find suitable work according to a certificate granted by the employment service. Unemployment pension is determined in the same way as the invalidity pension, but the average pension is somewhat lower. Occupational survivors' pensions are payable using criteria similar to those used in the calculation of state survivors' pensions.

Financing

Occupational pensions for employees are financed entirely by employers who insure their permanent employees through one of the authorized pension insurance companies, through their own enterprise pension funds or through sectoral pension funds. In 1982, the employers' premium amounted to an average 12.4% of the payroll (Source 11, p. 118). Occupational employees' pensions are partly financed on a pay-as-you-go basis and partly by accumulating funds which are usually invested as loans to the enterprises belonging to the scheme.

Pensions for farmers and the self-employed are financed jointly by the insured and the state. In 1982, contributions from insured persons amounted to between 5.04 -12.6% of income, depending on the amount of income. The state pays two-thirds of the costs of the Farmers' Pension Institution and one-half of the pensions paid under the YEL.

Administration

In May 1980, there were eight pension insurance companies, thirteen sectoral pension funds, and about 100 enterprise pension funds established by the employers. These pension institutions are coordinated and advised by the Central Pension Security Institute (*Eläketurvakeskus*), which is in turn supervised by the Ministry of Social Affairs and Health. It is directed by representatives from trade unions, employers' associations, organizations of the self-employed, and the pension institutions.

5. Matching pensions

People may be entitled to pensions from several schemes, and the pensions are adjusted so that the total does not exceed 60-66% of the index-adjusted pension-carrying wage or salary. The following table gives the number of pensioners having different combinations of pensions as well as their average total pension.

Table 4
Pensioners by major scheme and average total pension at end of 1982[a]

	Number of pensioners (in 1,000s)	%	Average (FM per month)	Total pension as % of average gross earnings
Pensioners with:				
-National (old age, invalidity or unemployment) pensions only[b]	292	33.3	1 147	25
-National (old age, invalidity or unemployment) pensions and private sector occupational pensions	423	48.2	1 846	40
-National (old age, invalidity, or unemployment) pensions and private and public sector occupational pensions	64	7.3	2 550	56
-National (old age, invalidity or unemployment) pensions and public sector occupational pensions	77	8.8	3 835	84
-National widows' pensions	4	0.5	862	19
-National widows' pensions and occupational widows' pensions	17	1.9	1 374	30

[a] (Source 1, pp. 33-34)
[b] National pensions were tax-free in 1982.

As seen from the table, only one-third of old age, invalidity or unemployment pensioners are dependent on national pensions (which give the lowest income maintenance levels) for their main source of income. Pension level is highest among public sector pensioners. Private sector occupational pensions are, on average, much lower as they were established much later.

In relation to the average wage/salary, public sector pensioners have a very high income level, whereas those dependent upon national pensions have very low incomes, indicating that there are large income inequalities between pensioners (see Section V of the country chapter).

Services

The earliest services for the old and handicapped incapable of fully maintaining themselves were the poor-relief homes established in the nineteenth century. In 1982, there were about 420 communal homes and about 120 private old people's homes in Finland. Over 30,000 persons were cared for in these institutions (Source 5). In addition, there are various kinds of rehabilitation and employment services for the partially disabled. In 1981, the number of permanent employees in the home help services for the old and disabled had reached 4,500 (Source 3, p. 88).

Table 5
Expenditure on old age and invalidity services in 1982, mill. FM[a]

	Mill. FM	%
Rehabilitation and employment for partially disabled	444.5	22.8
Communal and old people's homes	1 125.0	57.8
Home help services for old and handicapped	343.7	17.6
Grants to organizations providing services	34.1	1.8
Total	1 947.3	100.0
% of social security expenditure		3.5

[a] (Source 3, pp. 58-67)

Core laws

1937 (no. 248)
Kansaneläkelaki (National Pension Act): first general old age and invalidity pension act providing old age and disability insurance for all persons between 18-55, excluding invalids.

1956 (no. 347)
Kansaneläkelaki (National Pension Act): old age and invalidity pensions for all citizens over the age of 16; flat-rate old age pension (basic amount) to all citizens over 65; assistance amount for low income groups; invalidity pensions for those unable to maintain themselves due to illness or injury; old age supplement for single women aged 63-64. Major extensions: assistance supplements in 1966, housing allowances in 1971.

1961 (no. 395)
Työntekijäin eläkelaki (Employees' Pension Act): old age and invalidity pensions for private sector full-time employees over the age of 18; invalidity pension in the case of illness or injury; pensions from different sources should not exceed 60% of the highest pension-carrying salary/wage.

1962 (no. 134)
Lyhytaikaisissa työsuhteissa olevien työntekijäin eläkelaki (Temporary Employees' Pension Act): old age and invalidity pensions for those in seasonal employment.

1964 (no. 202)
Kunnallisten viranhaltijain ja työntekijäin eläkelaki (Local Government Employees' Pension Act): old age and invalidity pensions for employees in local government and municipality federations similar to those granted under the Employees' Pension Act; survivors' pensions for widows and orphans.

1966 (no. 280)
Valtion eläkelaki (State Pension Act): provided old age and invalidity pensions for all state employees; full pensions amounting to 66% of pension-carrying salary, and survivors' pensions for widows, widowers and orphans.

1966 (nos. 639-640)
Acts covering private sector survivors' pensions for employees.

1969 (no. 38)
Yleinen perhe-eläkelaki (National Survivors' Pension Act): provided survivors' pension for children under 16, those between 16 and 20 in full-time education, widows with a child under 16, and widows between 40 and 59 who have been married for at least three years.

1969 (no. 467)
Maatalousyrittäjäin eläkelaki (Farmers' Pension Act): old age, invalidity, and survivors' pensions for farmers and their wives.

1969 (no. 468)
Yrittäjien eläkelaki (Self-Employed Persons' Pension Act): old age, invalidity and survivors' pensions for the self-employed.

1971 (no. 294)
Laki rintamasotilaseläkkeestä (War Veterans' Pension Act): provided national pensions for war veterans with low incomes, aged 55-64; extended in 1977.

1971 (nos. 499-503)
Acts on unemployment pensions under the occupational pension schemes and National Unemployment Pension Act: established unemployment pension for those over 60 (over 55 in 1978) who have received unemployment assistance for at least 200 days during the last 52 weeks (60 weeks in 1977) and who are unable to find suitable work.

1974 (no. 16)
Luopumiseläkelaki (Farm Closure Pension Act): provided pensions for those of at least 55 years of age who stop farming and sell their farm between 1974-1976; extended for the period 1976-1986.

1974 (no. 749-752)
Acts covering private sector occupational pensions: full pensions raised from 40% to 60% of the index-adjusted pension-carrying wage or salary; changes in levels of minimum pension benefits.

1978 (nos. 588-598)
First phase of the national pension reform; extended assistance supplement to low-income national pension recipients and housing allowances for low-income national pension recipients, effective from 1980; the effect of spouse's earnings on national pension reduced, effective from 1981.

1982 (nos. 103-112)
Second and third phase of the national pension reform; assistance amount and supplement combined and improved, income from employment no longer affects national pension, basic and assistance amounts became taxable, taxation of pensions and deductions due to pensions, effective from 1983; assistance amount increased, the effect of spouse's income on pensions stopped, effective from 1984; property, property income and entrepreneurial income no longer affect the size of pensions (from 1985).

1982 (no. 13)
Rintamaveteraanien varhaiseläkelaki (War Veterans' Early Retirement Pension Act): introduced early retirement for war veterans as part of the occupational pension schemes, on fulfillment of certain qualifying conditions.

II Sickness insurance/Health services

In 1982 sickness and health expenditure amounted to 15,000 million FM, i.e. 7% of GDP, or 28% of total social expenditure.

Table 6
Sickness and health expenditure in 1982, in million FM[a]

	Mill. FM	%
National sickness insurance:	2 966.5	19.3
- daily allowances	(1 334.5)	(8.7)
- curative care compensations	(1 367.3)	(8.9)
- employee health services	(210.7)	(1.4)
- other[b]	(54.0)	(0.4)
Employer wage contribution payments	1 548.0	10.1
Occupational injury insurance	673.2	4.4
Hospital care	5 526.7	36.0
Health centres	3 706.0	24.2
Other[c]	915.7	6.0
Total	15 336.1	100.0

[a] (Source 3, pp. 58-59).
[b] Includes prevention of diseases and rehabilitation, and other compensation and expenditure.
[c] Includes temperance activities and care of alcoholics and drug addicts, welfare for the mentally subnormal, and other health care expenditure.

Income maintenance

1. National sickness insurance

National Sickness Insurance (*Sairausvakuutus*, NSI), was instituted relatively late in Finland. Prior to its establishment in 1963, cover was provided by voluntary sickness assistance funds. However, the present role of these funds is small; there were 208 such funds in 1983 covering 215,000 members (Source 12).

Coverage

The NSI covers all Finnish residents and provides compensation for loss of earnings due to sickness and maternity, and reimburses outpatient care expenses.

A daily allowance is paid to persons, aged 16 to 64, who are incapable of working due to illness, including students and housewives. Payment is not made for the first seven working days, during which time the employer is responsible for paying the wage/salary (see wage continuation). Sickness benefit is limited to a period of 300 days. Daily allowance is payable for working days only. The minimum daily allowance amounted to 30.10 FM in 1983 for those not working, and was dependent upon income for those in the labour force, being in most cases 80% of daily wage or salary. Daily allowance includes supplements for a spouse and any children under 16.

Married beneficiaries only qualify for these supplements if their earnings exceed those of their spouse. Daily allowance is not payable to persons receiving hospital care.

Maternity allowance is awarded under the NSI, and is payable to every expectant and nursing mother for a period of 258 working days. The amount of maternity allowance is determined according to the same criteria as for daily allowance for the first 100 days, after which time the earnings-replacement ratio is 70%. Part of the allowance is transferable to the father for a period of up to 100 days.

The NSI refunds outpatient care expenses: expenses for medicines, examinations and treatment prescribed by a doctor, also travel and overnight accommodation necessary for diagnosis and treatment are all reclaimable. Some medicines are reimbursed in part, some fully. NSI refunding on examinations, treatment and doctors' services is assessed on the basis of tariff charges. When NSI-covered services are provided by municipal health care centres, the NSI pays the fee. When NSI-covered services are provided by the private sector, the NSI pays from 50% to 75% of expenditure exceeding a certain amount. In 1982, refunds covered about 62% of those expenses for which NSI pays refunds, varying from 42-100% (Source 1, p. 88).

The cost of private dental care is not covered. The cost of medical treatment, dental care and medicine not covered by insurance is, up to a given amount, deductible from taxable income. In 1978, the value of these tax credits was estimated at around 295.5 million FM (own estimate based on Source 7, pp.23,42).

Financing

In principle, NSI contributions are paid by employers, employees and the state, although in most years the state contribution has not been needed. In 1982, social security tax amounted to 1% of wage/salary for employees, and 1.9% and 2.35% of payroll for private and public sector employers respectively. The NSI was 57% financed by employer contributions, whilst employees contributed about one-third (Source 1, pp. 98, 102).

Administration

The NSI is administered by the Social Insurance Institution (see Pensions, Administration).

2. Wage continuation

In 1970, a law on employment contracts obliged employers to pay the full wage/salary to employees for the first seven days after notification of illness. In many employment contracts this period is considerably longer, in most cases at least three weeks. Sick leave exceeding three working days must be certified by a doctor.

3. Occupational injury insurance

Employers must insure their employees against loss of income due to occupational injury. Private employees are insured by private insurance companies. Public employees are covered by a specific public institution, which also provides compensation in the case of military injury. Occupational injury insurance refunds health care expenses, pays daily allowances, covers medical and occupational rehabilitation expenditure, and pays invalidity and survivors' pensions, in addition to certain other benefits.

Services

Hospital care is almost exclusively provided by public institutions and is financed mainly by the state and municipalities. Less than 8% of costs were paid by patients in 1982. Public out-patient medical services are provided by health care centres, organized by municipality federations. They are financed mainly by the municipalities and the state. In 1982, about 6% of the costs were covered by patients (Source 3, p. 58). Due to the shortage of these services, however, the role of private practitioners and private health care centres is still significant in urban areas.

Preventive and rehabilitative services are provided by the Social Insurance Institution. The state and municipalities finance services for alcoholics, drug addicts and the mentally handicapped. The state also pays about 75% of labour protection services, the remainder being shared between employers and municipalities (Source 3, p. 60). The organization of maternity and child care guidance centres is linked to that of health care centres.

Core laws

1943 (no. 413)
Keskussairaalalaki (Central Hospital Act): municipalities made responsible for the acquisition of hospital places; renewed in 1948; first act in long series which re-organized hospital health care in Finland - 1950 Central Hospital Building Act, 1956 Hospital Act, 1964 General Municipal Hospital Act, 1965 Health Care Act.

1948 (no. 608)
Tapaturmavakuutuslaki (Occupational Injury Insurance): employers made responsible for insuring their employees against occupational injury; refunds health care expenses, pays daily allowances, covers medical and occupational rehabilitation expenditure and pays invalidity and survivors' pensions; revisions made in 1958, 1968, and 1971.

1948 (no. 404)
Sotavammalaki (Military Injury Act): state made responsible for the payment of compensation for military injury in the form of health care, daily allowances, survivors' pensions and funeral grants; revised in 1956.

1958 (no. 299)
Työturvallisuuslaki (Occupational Safety Act): provided framework and organization for occupational safety revisions.

1963 (no. 364)
Sairausvakuutuslaki (Sickness Insurance Act): first phase of sickness insurance came into force in 1964; introduced daily and maternity allowances, refunding of laboratory and x-ray examinations and travel due to sickness and maternity.

1967
Second phase of Sickness Insurance Act came into force; refunds for doctors' fees; annual revisions of benefit size, list of reimbursable medicines, and number of days for which allowances are payable.

1967 (no. 638)
Ammattitautilaki (Occupational Disease Act): defined criteria for occupational diseases.

1970 (no. 320)
Työsopimuslaki (Labour Contract Act): employers obliged to pay the wage/salary in the case of illness, for a period of seven days.

1972 (no. 66)
Kansanterveyslaki (Public Health Act): health care centres made compulsory for municipality federations; important framework act which gave strong impetus to the development of out-patient and preventive health care services.

1978 (no. 743)
Työterveyshuoltolaki (Occupational Health Act): prescribed private sector employers to organize health services for employees.

1981 (no. 471)
Changes in Sickness Insurance Act: daily and maternity allowances dependent upon income and with a minimum for those not working; allowances made taxable; effective from 1982, with changes from 1983.

1981 (no. 1026)
Maatalousyrittäjien tapaturmavakuutuslaki (Farmers' Occupational Injury Insurance Act): compulsory injury insurance for farmers and their assisting family members; effective from 1982.

III Unemployment insurance/Employment policy

In 1982 unemployment expenditure amounted to approximately 3,600 million FM, i.e. 1.5% of GDP or 6.5% of total social security expenditure.

Table 7
Expenditure for unemployment in 1982, in million FM[a]

	Mill. FM	%
Unemployment insurance	638.1	17.7
Unemployment assistance	619.1	17.1
Retraining for the unemployed	1 036.8	28.7
Public work for the unemployed	1 175.5	32.5
Other[b]	144.3	4.0
Total	3 613.8	100.0

[a] (Source 3, p. 61)
[b] Including employment service and labour force mobility.

Income maintenance

Unemployment insurance benefits are provided by unemployment funds organized by trade unions. When unemployed, members of trade unions are entitled to compensation which is payable after five days of registered unemployment and consists of a sum not exceeding three-quarters of the person's daily wage or a given upper limit. Dependents entitle the applicant to higher benefits. Unemployment insurance benefits are paid for a maximum of 200 unemployment days per year for a maximum of 500 unemployment days during three consecutive calendar years. This is tax-free income. Unemployment insurance is financed by: the state (10/15), the central employment fund financed by employers (4/15), and the membership fees of the trade unions

(1/15). In 1982, 1.6 million employees, i.e. 74% of all employees, were members of the unemployment funds, and these provided benefits for 62,000 unemployed (yearly average) (Source 13, p. 65).

Unemployment assistance is paid only if the applicant is not in receipt of unemployment insurance benefits. This may be due to the fact that he is not a member of a trade union or has been unemployed for so long that he is no longer entitled to unemployment insurance. The payment of unemployment assistance is secondary to retraining the unemployed or placing them in some form of public work. Furthermore, payment is only made if the employee did not resign voluntarily or refuse an offer of suitable employment. Assistance is paid after five days of unemployment. The amount is graduated according to family size, and is tax-free. If the spouse's income exceeds a certain limit, unemployment assistance is not paid. This assistance is granted on application, administered by municipal boards, and financed by central government.

Services

The employment service and occupational guidance are organized by labour force offices maintained by the central government. In 1984 there were 166 labour force offices in the country. In addition to conveying jobs, the employment service provides assistance for travel and removal costs for any unemployed person finding employment elsewhere in the country.

Retraining for the unemployed is organized and maintained by central government. Persons in retraining receive a tax-free assistance amount. In 1982 about 17,000 unemployed (yearly average), i.e. approximately 11% of all the unemployed, participated in retraining programmes (Source 13, p. 65).

Central government also finances full-time and part-time public sector employment for the unemployed. In 1982 about 3,700 unemployed persons (i.e. 2.5% of the total unemployed population) were employed in this way (Source 3, p. 80).

Core laws

1959 (no. 246)
Työnvälityslaki (Employment Service Act): central government took over employment services from the municipalities.

1960 (no. 43)
Laki ammatinvalinnan ohjauksesta (Occupational Guidance Act): provided framework and organization for occupational guidance activities.

1960 (no. 328)
Laki työttömyyskassoista (Unemployment Funds Act): improved state aid for unemployment insurance funds and established a central unemployment fund.

1971 (no. 946)
Työllisyyslaki (Employment Act): regulated unemployment assistance first introduced in 1963.

1971 (no. 949)
Laki työvoiman liikkuvuuden edistämisestä (Promotion of Geographical Mobility of Labour Force Act): provided payment of travel and removal costs for the unemployed.

1976 (no. 31)
Laki työllisyyskoulutuksesta (Employment Training Act): provided framework for retraining of unemployed.

IV Families and children

In 1982 expenditure on family transfers and services amounted to nearly 7,500 million FM, i.e. 3.1% of GDP and 13.4% of total social security expenditure.

Table 8
Expenditure on family transfers and services in 1982, mill. FM[a]

	Mill. FM	%
Child allowances	1 817.1	24.4
Maternity allowances and grants	1 284.0	17.2
Child deductions in taxation	1 005.0	13.5
Prepayments of maintenance	183.0	2.4
Child care allowances/child increase under national pension scheme	153.4	2.1
Child day-care	1 795.7	24.1
School meals	727.9	9.8
Public child welfare	342.2	4.6
Other[b]	143.0	1.9
Total	7 451.3	100.0

[a] (Source 3, pp. 89-94).
[b] Including home help assistance, and holidays for housewives and children.

Income maintenance

As from 1948 all residents with one or more children are entitled to child allowance *(lapsilisä)*. In 1962 allowances were staggered according to the number of children and in 1973, when special child allowances and family allowances were abolished, an additional allowance was introduced for children under three years of age. In 1983, child allowance amounted to 1,876 FM per year for the first child, and 5,402 FM for the fifth child and any subsequent children under three years of age (Source 6, p. 81). The allowance is paid, usually to the mother, for children under age 16, and is tax-free. It is funded by the employers' social security tax and general revenues, and administered by municipal welfare boards. In addition to child allowance, taxpayers are entitled to a certain flat-rate deduction from their taxable income for each dependent child.

The 1937 Maternity Grant Act provided benefits in cash or kind for poor mothers. Means-testing was gradually removed and since 1949 all mothers are entitled to receive a maternity grant. It is provided on the condition that the mother consults a doctor or midwife, or attends the maternity guidance centre during the first four months of pregnancy. In 1983 it amounted to 440 FM, but it may also be given in the form of baby care supplies. Maternity allowances come under the NSI (see Health).

When maternity allowance days end, it is possible (since 1983) to obtain an allowance for the care of a child at home (*Lasten kotihoidon tuki*) if there are at least two young children in the family. The benefit is tax-free and in 1983 amounted to 700 FM per month.

Under the Children's Maintenance Act, both parents are obliged to make provision for their children, even in the case of divorce or illegitimacy. If one of the parents neglects this duty, the other parent may receive advance payments. These payments are granted on application and administered by municipal welfare boards. State aid covers 80% of costs, the remainder being paid by the municipalities.

Services

Municipalities organize public nursery schools and day-care institutions. Corresponding private institutions are entitled to receive state aid. Child day-care in private households is also partly organized by the municipalities and supported by the state. State-subsidized services charge fees that are considerably below market prices. To a large extent children are accepted on the basis of a means-test.

All pupils in comprehensive schools are provided with free school meals. Most municipalities provide free school meals for upper secondary, and vocational schools, although there is no legal obligation for them to do so.

Maladjusted children or children with unacceptable home conditions are taken into the care of public children's homes. These are maintained by municipalities with the financial help of central government, which also subsidizes private children's homes. Other public child welfare services are provided by child guidance clinics.

Home help assistance is provided mainly for families where the mother or children's guardian is unable to take care of the children and home due to illness, birth or other circumstances. The service is provided by special municipal employees. In 1982, the state covered 51%, municipalities 44%, and users 5% of costs (Source 3, p. 66). Below a certain income level, home help assistance is free of charge. Above this level a fee is charged depending on family income. Municipalities, parishes and associations may receive state aid in order to organize holidays for poor mothers with children.

Core laws

1937 (no. 322)
Äitiysavustuslaki (Maternity Grant Act): introduced maternity grants in cash or kind for poor mothers; means-testing reduced in 1941 and 1945, and abolished in 1949.

1943 (no. 637)
Laki kansakoululaitoksen kustannuksista annetun lain muuttamisesta (Elementary Public Schools' Expenditure Act): provided free school meals for all pupils.

1944 (no. 224)
Laki kunnallisista äitiys- ja lastenneuvoloista (Municipal Maternity and Child Care Guidance Centre Act): established municipal maternity and child care guidance centres to provide advice and services for various health-related issues.

1945 (no. 1177)
Kodinperustamislaki (Home-Making Loans for Young Married Couples Act): entitled young couple to low-interest loans in order to start families; number of new loans gradually decreased during the 1950s.

1948 (no. 541)
Lapsilisälaki (Child Allowance Act): entitled parents to child allowance for every child under 16; in 1962 allowances were staggered according to number of children, and in 1973 a supplement for children under three years of age introduced.

1966 (no. 270)
Laki kunnallisesta kodinhoitoavusta (Municipal Home Help Assistance Act): entitled families to home help services during periods of illness or birth.

1973 (no. 36)
Laki lasten päivähoidosta (Children's Day-Care Act): provided framework for organizing and developing municipal day-care services.

1975 (no. 704)
Laki lapsen elatuksesta (Children's Maintenance Act): redefined parents' responsibilities regarding the maintenance of children.

1977 (no. 122)
Laki lapsen elatuksen turvaamisesta (Securing of Children's Maintenance Act): re-organized maintenance for children in cases of divorce and illegitimacy.

1983 (no. 683)
Lastensuojelulaki (Child Welfare Act): replaced the 1936 Act and defined the rights of children.

V Public assistance

Income maintenance

In 1982 public assistance expenditure amounted to about 325 million FM, which corresponded to 0.1% of GDP and 0.6% of social security expenditure.

Table 9
Expenditure on public assistance in 1982, in million FM[a]

	Mill. FM	%
Public assistance	211.0	65.0
Special and other assistance	73.1	22.5
Military allowances	33.1	10.2
Demobilization benefits	7.6	2.3
Total	324.8	100.0

[a] (Source 3, p. 66).

Public assistance is the last means of securing income maintenance. According to the Public Welfare Act the municipality is responsible for the provision of maintenance for those who are unable to maintain themselves. The minimum standards for providing public assistance are determined by the state, but in practice the scheme is administered by municipal welfare boards. In 1981, 163,000 persons received public assistance, the average amount of which was 1,400 FM (Source 3, p. 95). It is tax-free and paid by the state and municipalities. Special and other assistance includes public assistance not given under the Public Assistance Act.

Military allowance is granted in order to maintain the relatives (wife, children, parents) of the draftee, where military service affects their livelihood. The Ministry for Social Affairs and Health issues detailed instructions, and municipal welfare boards actually grant the allowance, which is tax-free and paid by the state. Demobilization benefit is granted to all draftees at the end of their military service; in 1983 it was 200 FM, tax-free and paid by the state.

Core laws

1948 (no. 566)
Sotilasavustuslaki (Military Allowance Act): introduced means-tested allowances for relatives of draftees where livelihood is affected by military service; extended in 1969.

1956 (no. 116)
Huoltoapulaki (Public Assistance Act): abolished 1922 Poor Relief Act and made municipalities responsible for the provision of maintenance and care for those unable to do so themselves; revisions in 1970 (no. 275), 1972 (no. 766), 1977 (no. 123), and 1980 (no. 1).

1977 (no. 910)
Kotiuttamisrahalaki (Demobilization Benefit Act): abolished means-testing of demobilization benefits.

1982 (no. 677/-)
Laki sosiaali- ja terveydenhuollon suunnittelusta ja valtionosuudesta (Social and Health Services Planning Act): introduced five-year plans for social and health services; equalized state aid to social and health services organized by local government bodies.

1982 (no. 710)
Sosiaalihuoltolaki (Public Welfare Act): defined the tasks of the municipalities in social service sector; public assistance renewed, and state aid to public assistance schemes standardized.

VI Education

1. Education system

In 1981, education expenditure amounted to 10,400 million FM, or 4.9% of GDP. All children attend comprehensive school at the age of 7 for nine years. They leave at the age of 16, and have the option to attend a three-year secondary school, a vocational school taking from one to three years, or to start working. Secondary school is the major route to higher education, i.e. to universities, but it is possible to enter higher education via vocational institutes.

Primary, secondary and higher education are provided by public institutions, with very few exceptions. All expenditure as a result of attending comprehensive school is paid by the state and municipalities: instruction, educational materials, health services, school meals, transport and accommodation - if needed - are free to pupils. Secondary educational institutions have, in some cases, nominal fees, and they do not provide quite as extensive free services as the comprehensive schools. Higher education institutions have no tuition fees, but students buy their educational materials, and have their own health service system with state aid.

Adult education is provided by many types of associations, which receive state aid for this purpose. It is, very loosely, integrated into the proper educational system.

2. Study allowances and loans

Allowances and loans may be granted by central government to students in secondary and higher education. In order to qualify, the student must study full-time with average success, and must not have an income exceeding a certain amount.

Study allowances include a basic and a housing allowance. In 1984, 235,000 students received the basic allowance, of which 78,000 received also a housing allowance. Together, this amounted to 580 million FM. Study allowances are granted annually, for a maximum of seven years.

Study loans are available to students at a lower than market rate of interest. Repayment by instalment commences shortly after the completion of studies when the student has taken a job. They are also guaranteed by the state. In 1984 the interest subsidy of the state was estimated at 170 million FM, and altogether 119,000 students received a study loan.

Core laws

1957 (no. 247)
Kansakoululaki (People's School Act): replaced the 1921 People's School Act and extended basic compulsory education to eight years.

1959 (no. 3)
Asetus ammattioppilaitoksista (Vocational School Act): reorganized vocational schooling.

1966 (no. 266)
Laki korkeakoululaitoksen kehittämisestä vuosina 1967-1981 (University Development Act 1967-1981): outlined plan for a considerable quantitative growth of university personnel and resources.

1968 (no. 467)
Laki koulujärjestelmän perusteista (Educational System Act): replaced old parallel school system with the comprehensive system.

1972 (no. 28)
Opintotukilaki (Study Allowance Act): introduced first major scheme for study allowances and loans.

1978 (no. 474)
Laki keskiasteen koulutuksen kehittämisestä (Secondary Education Development Act): remodelled secondary (general and vocational) education in order to improve coordination with comprehensive school system.

VII Housing

Housing and housing environments are planned on a national, regional and municipal level. Detailed plans guide the land use and give instructions concerning the type of dwellings permitted to be built. Municipal authorities control the construction and standards of new dwellings. In addition, housing policy consists of: the regulation of rents, subsidies for the construction and purchase of houses and dwellings, and housing allowances.

1. Regulation of rents

The state regulates conditions for the renting and leasing of houses, and legislation has strengthened the rights of tenants. In 1940 the state legislated against exorbitant rents. Since 1940 rental regulation has been the rule. After World War II, there was an enormous housing deficit, those with large apartments were obliged to take tenants, rents were regulated, and other price controls were imposed. Gradually intervention diminished, and from 1965-68 it ceased altogether. The 1968-69 Promotion of Economic Growth Act reintroduced government powers to supervise and regulate rents.

2. Subsidies and tax credits for housing construction

The post World War II housing shortage was a major social problem. The state therefore promoted housing construction by granting low-interest loans. Since then this policy has continued and expanded. In 1981, 53% of new dwellings were subsidized. These state loans covered 25% (owner-occupied housing) to 55% (rented housing) of the costs of new housing (Source 9, pp. 32, 53). In 1981, the interest subsidy of the state loans amounted to 1,200 million FM (Source 14, p. 28).

State loans can cover from 10% to 60% of construction costs, depending on the type of house and the income of the beneficiary. State loans and the selection of tenants for houses built with such loans, are governed by income limits, approved by the Council of State. The standards, use and transfer of such housing are state-controlled.

The state also supports the purchase of owner-occupied dwellings by allowing the interest on private loans to be deducted from taxable income. At present, the maximum deduction is 25,000 FM. Due to the progressive character of income tax, the actual benefit of deductions increases with income level. In 1978 the total tax rebate for private housing loans amounted to 550 million FM (Source 8, p. 10).

3. Housing allowances

Housing allowances are available for: families living in rented or owner-occupied housing; persons living on old age pensions; young married couples and students. It is scaled according to family size, income, and housing expenses. At the end of 1982, about 101,000 families were in receipt of housing allowances. In 1982, total expenditure on housing allowances amounted to 535 million FM (Source 3, p. 94). These figures do not include housing allowances of the national pension scheme and the study allowance scheme.

Core laws

1949 (no. 224)
Laki asuntolainoista, -takuista ja -avustuksista (Housing Loans, Guarantees and Subsidies Act).

1949 (no. 225)
Laki asutuskeskusten asuntorakennustuotannon edistämisestä (Promotion of Housing Production in Densely Populated Areas Act).

1949 (no. 226)
Laki asutuskeskusten asuntorakennustuotannon tukemisesta valtion varoin (State Support of Housing Production in Densely Populated Areas Act): so-called ARAVA-laws started state support for housing production, previously supported by state funds as part of postwar settlement policies.

1953 (no. 488)·
Asuntotuotantolaki (Housing Production Act): united the three laws of 1949 with some minor changes.

1959 (no. 176)
Laki asuntotuotantolain muuttamisesta (Housing Production Act): enlarged the scope of the law to include housing allowances for families with at least three children.

1961 (no. 585)
Laki eräiden vuokrasuhteiden järjestämisestä huoneenvuokrasäännöstelyn päättyessä (Rented Dwellings Act): improved tenants' rights.

1961 (no. 586)
Laki lapsiperheiden asumistuesta (Housing Allowances Act): introduced housing allowances for families with two children.

1966 (no. 251)
Laki asuntohallituksesta (Housing Production Act): National Housing Board established.

1968 (no. 88)
Asuntotuotantoasetus (Housing Production Act): introduced two forms of support for housing companies formed by house occupants, and for individuals who intend to purchase a dwelling.

1968 (no. 207)
Laki taloudellisen kehityksen turvaamisesta vuosina 1968-69 (Promotion of Economic Growth Act 1968-69): gave the government important economic rights, including that of controlling and regulating housing rents; Act renewed for the years 1970-73, after which it has been amended in various forms.

1971 (no. 921)
Laki lapsiperheiden asumistuesta annetun lain muuttamisesta (Housing Allowance Act): extended housing allowances to one-child families.

1974 (no. 72)
Laki huoneenvuokralain muuttamisesta (Rented Dwellings Act): reorganized system of rent control; final decision on legitimate right to raise rents taken by Council of State subsequent to a rent council hearing.

1975 (no. 408)
Asumistukilaki (Housing Allowances Act): extended housing allowances to families without children.

1978 (no. 591)
Eläkkeensaajien asumistukilaki (Housing Allowances Act): under the national pension scheme; extended eligibility to new groups of national pension recipients.

1979 (no. 34)
Laki asuntojen perusparantamisesta (Improvement and Modernization of Dwellings Act): regulated state loans for improvement and modernization of dwellings.

Sources

(1) *Statistical Yearbook of the Social Insurance Institution 1982.* Social Insurance Institution of Finland, Helsinki, 1983.

(2) *Tilastotietoja valtion eläkkeistä ja valtiokonttorin eläkeosaston toiminnasta vuodelta 1982.* Valtiokonttori, 1983.

(3) Esa Arajärvi. *Social Expenditure in 1981 and Preliminary Data for 1982.* Official Statistics of Finland XXXII: 95. Special Social Studies, Ministry of Social Affairs and Health, Research Department, 1983.

(4) *Työeläkejärjestelmän tilastollinen vuosikirja 1982.* OSA I. Tilastotietoja työeläkkeen saajista. Eläketurvakeskus, Helsinki, 1982.

(5) Figures provided by the National Board of Social Affairs.

(6) Osmo Toivola and Matti Toivola, *Sosiaaliturvan pääpiirteet.* Sosiaaliturvan keskuslitto, Mänttä, 1983.

(7) *Statistics of Income and Property 1978.* Official Statistics of Finland IVB: 44. Central Statistical Office of Finland, Helsinki 1980.

(8) *Current Trends and Policies in the Field of Housing, Building and Planning in Finland.* Ministry of the Interior and National Housing Board, Helsinki, 1980.

(9) *Statistics of the National Housing Board of Finland 1949-1981.* National Housing Board, Helsinki, 1983.

(10) *Kunnallinen eläkelaitos. Tilastovuosi 1982.* Helsinki, 1983.

(11) *Työeläke ja muu sosiaalivakuutus 1983.* Turenki, 1983.

(12) Unpublished data received from Avustuskassojen yhdistys.

(13) *Labour Reports,* Vol. 26, 1983:4. Ministry of Labour, Planning Department, Helsinki, 1983.

(14) Ossi Paukku, *Asumisen tuki 1970-1981.* Asuntoreformiyhdistyksen julkaisuja No. 22. Helsinki, 1983.

(15) *Income Distribution Statistics 1978.* Official Statistics of Finland XLI:2. Central Statistical Office of Finland, Helsinki, 1981.

(16) *Bulletin of Statistics* 1983, No. IV. Central Statistical Office of Finland, Helsinki, 1983.

Notes

[1] We would like to thank Mr. Esa Arajärvi, Mr. Osmo Lampinen, Mr. Martti Lujanen, Mr. Heikki Niemelä, and Ms. Kirsti Suomivuori, who, as experts in the various areas of social policy, have helped us to make this synopsis. Of course, the authors alone are responsible for the text.

[2] In 1982, social expenditure (net) amounted to 55,683.8 million FM, and GDP to 236,705 million FM (Source 3, pp. 28, 67).

[3] The average wage/salary in 1978 was 33,900 FM. By using a wage and salary index we obtained the following estimates for average monthly wage/salary: 4,400 FM in 1982; 4,588 FM in the last quarter of 1982; and 4,863 FM in the third quarter of 1983 (Source 15, p. 83; Source 16, p. 47).

Bibliography

Contents

I General contributions

1.0 Bibliographies

HOLM, Tor W., IMMONEN, Erkki J.: Bibliography of Finnish Sociology 1945-1959.Transactions of the Westermarck Society, Vol. XIII, Helsinki, 1966, 179 p. Bibliography of Finnish sociology for the period 1945-1959. Includes major works in social policy.

LAMMINEN, Hilkka Sisko, in collaboration with TULANDER, Majlis: Bibliography of Finnish Sociology 1960-1969. Transactions of the Westermarck Society, Vol. XIX, Helsinki, 1973, 370 p. Bibliography of Finnish sociology for the period 1960-1969. Includes major works in social policy.

PAAKKANEN, Liisa, ERÄSAARI, Risto: Yhteiskunta-taloudellinen yhteiskuntatutkimus ja sosiaalipolitiikka (Socio-economic Social Research and Social Policy). Sosiaalipoliittisen yhdistyksen julkaisuja, Vol. 10, Helsinki, 1975, 289 p. A selective bibliography of socio-economic research for the period 1870-1945, and of discussions on social policy research in the period 1870-1974.

SOSIAALITURVAN KESKUSLIITTO: Sosiaaliturvan kirjallisuus Suomessa 1972-1976 (Finnish Literature on Social Security, 1972-1976). Helsinki, 1978, 314 p. Bibliography of Finnish literature on social security, 1972-1976.

SOSIAALITURVAN KESKUSLIITTO: Sosiaaliturvan kirjallisuus Suomessa III. Vuodet 1977-1980 (Finnish Literature on Social Security III, 1977-1980). Helsinki, 1982, 352 p. Bibliography of Finnish literature and research on social security, 1977-1980.

VAISTO, Erkki: Sosiaaliturvan kirjallisuus Suomessa 1965-1971 (Finnish Literature on Social Security, 1965-1971), Helsinki, Sosiaaliturvan keskusliitto, 1973, 336 p. Bibliography of Finnish literature and research on social security, 1965-1971.

1.1 General histories of social policy

KUUSI, Eino: Sosiaalipolitiikka I-II (Social Policy I-II). Porvoo, WSOY, 1931, 1071 p. An account of social policy in terms of the German tradition with special emphasis on labour relations.

KUUSI, Eino, KUUSI, Reino: Sosiaalinen kysymys ja sosiaalinen liike kautta aikojen (The 'Social Question' and Social Movement Throughout History), 2nd ed. Helsinki, WSOY, 1948, 509 p. General description of social classes, social movements and the 'social question', the problem of peaceful cooperation between social classes up until the interwar decades.

NIEMINEN, Armas: Mitä on sosiaalipolitiikka? (What is Social Policy?). Porvoo, WSOY, 1955, 228 p. Study of the concept of social policy in terms of the means, motives, agents and ends of social policy.

RUOTSALAINEN, Seppo: Sosiaaliturvapolitiikan vaikuttimet, perustelut ja kehityssuunnat marxilaisen yhteiskuntateorian valossa (Motives, Arguments and Developments of Social Security Policy in the Light of Marxist Theory of Society). Helsingin yliopisto. Sosiaalipolitiikan laitos. Tutkimuksia, No. 7, Helsinki, 1971, 230 p. A study of the development of ideas of social policy starting from Adam Smith's 'question of poverty'.

1.2 Accounts of specific historical periods

ERÄSAARI, Risto: Historiallinen taloustiede - Katederisosialismi - Verein für Sozialpolitik (Historical Political Economy - Cathedersocialism - Association for Social Policy). Helsingin yliopisto. Sosiaalipolitiikan laitos. Tutkimuksia, No. 5, Helsinki, 1976, 266 p. A theoretical study of the major conceptualizations of the ideas of social policy (Schmoller, Wagner, Brentano) in Germany during the last quarter of the nineteenth century.

SALMELA, Alpo: Kansaneläkelaitos 1937-1967 (The Social Insurance Institution, 1937-1967). Helsinki, Kansaneläkelaitos, 1967, 77 p. The history of the Social Insurance Institution from 1937 to 1967. Includes a statistical Appendix.

TUOMINEN, Uuno, PULKKINEN, Anneli (eds): Sosiaaliministeriö 1917-1967 (The Ministry for Social Affairs, 1917-1967). Helsinki, Sosiaaliministeriö, 1967, 279 p. The history of the Finnish Ministry for Social Affairs, 1917-1967.

1.3 Histories of social policy in Finland

ALAPURO, Risto, ALESTALO, Matti: Konkreettinen sosiaalitutkimus (Early Social Research in Finland). *In* ALAPURO, Risto, ALESTALO, Matti, HAAVIOMANNILA, Elina (eds.): Suoma laisen sosiologian juuret. Porvoo-Helsinki, WSOY, 1973, pp. 84-147. An overview of early socioeconomic research and socio-political research in Finland from the 1870s to the 1940s.

ERÄSAARI, Risto, RAHKONEN, Keijo (eds): Työväenkysymyksestä sosiaalipolitiikkaan (From the Labour Question to Social Policy). Tapiola, Gaudeamus, 1975, 315 p. A collection of major papers defining social policy from 1874 to 1948. Includes an introduction on the intellectual background of the Finnish discussions on social policy for this period.

KARISTO, Antti, TAKALA, Pentti, HAAPOLA, Ilkka: Elintaso, elämäntapa, sosiaalipolitiikka (Standard of Living, Way of Life, Social Policy). Helsingin yliopisto. Lahden tutkimus- ja koulutuskeskus. Lahti, 1983, 410 p. A historical account of the standard of living, ways of life and social policy from the nineteenth century to the present.

LAATI, Iisakki, SALOMAA, Niilo: Social Legislation and Work in Finland. Helsinki, Ministry for Social Affairs, 1953, 189 p. An introduction to past and contemporary social legislation and social policy in Finland.

PIIRAINEN, Veikko: Vaivaishoidosta sosiaaliturvaan (From Poor Relief to Social Security). Hämeenlinna, Arvi A. Karisto, 1974, 469 p. A historical introduction to the development of public assistance and public assistance organizations.

SIIPI, Jouko: Ryysyrannasta hyvinvointivaltioon (From Rags to the Welfare State). Helsinki, Tammi, 1967, 261 p. A historical account of the development of living conditions and social policy in Finland.

1.4 Introductions to the system of social policy in Finland

AUVINEN, Riitta: Tämän päivän sosiaalipolitiikka (Modern Social Policy), 5th-6th ed. Helsinki, Kirjayhtymä, 1980, 204 p. An introduction to social policy in Finland.

AUVINEN, Riitta (ed.): Sosiaalipalvelu (Social Service), 2nd ed. Helsinki, Kirjayhtymä, 1977, 179 p. An introduction to social services in Finland.

THE MINISTRY OF SOCIAL AFFAIRS AND HEALTH: Health Services in Finland. Helsinki, 1979, 32 p.; Labour Protection in Finland. Helsinki, 1980, 36 p.; Social Welfare in Finland. Helsinki, 1980, 44 p.; Social Insurance in Finland. Helsinki, 1980, 47 p. Brief official introductions to the welfare state in Finland.

TOIVOLA, Osmo, TOIVOLA, Matti: Sosiaaliturvan pääpiirteet (An Overview of Social Security). Mänttä, Sosiaaliturvan keskusliitto, 1983, 234 p. A standard introduction to present social policy legislation.

WARIS, Heikki: Suomalaisen yhteiskunnan sosiaalipolitiikka (Social Policy ofFinnish Society), 7th ed. Helsinki, WSOY, 1980, 360 p. Major introduction to social policy in Finland.

1.5 Reports by investigating committees or experts

ECONOMIC PLANNING CENTRE: Quality of Life, Social Goals and Measurement. Helsinki, 1973, 68 p. An English summary of the major study on social indicators of health, education, environment, inequality, housing, and working conditions.

KOMITEANMIETINTÖ 1971:A25: Sosiaalihuollon periaatekomitean mietintö I (Parliamentary Committee Report on the Principles of Public Assistance). Helsinki, 1971, 99 p. Major parliamentary statement on the principles underlying the development of the Finnish welfare state.

SOSIAALI- JA TERVEYSMINISTERIÖ: Sosiaali- ja terveyspolitiikan lähtökohtia ja suuntaviivoja (Points of Departure and Directions for Social and Health Policy). Sosiaalinen aikakauskirja, Vol. 76, 1982: 3-4, pp. 8-102. A long-term plan for social policy by the Ministry of Social Affairs and Health.

SOSIAALITURVAN MENOKEHITYSTÄ JA TAVOITTEIDEN TOTEUTUMISMAHDOLLISUUKSIA ARVIOIVA TYÖRYHMÄ (STAT): Sosiaaliturvan menokehitystä ja tavoitteiden toteutumismahdollisuuksia arvioivan työryhmän raportti (Report from the Working Group for the Evaluation of the Development of Social Expenditure and Social Policy Goals). Sosiaalinen aikakauskirja, Vol. 74,1980: 3, pp. 1-80. A forecast of the development of social expenditure up until the year 2000.

1.6 Social science interpretations, evaluations or analyses

ALLARDT, Erik: About Dimensions of Welfare. Research Group for Comparative Sociology, University of Helsinki, Research Reports, No. 1, Helsinki, 1973, 128 p. Report on the first findings from the comparative Scandinavian Welfare Survey.

ALLARDT, Erik: Att ha, att älska, att vara (Having, Loving, Being). Lund, Argos, 1975, 239 p. A comparative study on the dimensions of welfare in Denmark, Finland, Norway and Sweden.

JAAKKOLA, Risto, KARISTO, Antti, ROOS, J.P. (eds): Sosiaalipolitiikka, historiallinen kehitys ja yhteiskunnan muutos (Social Policy, Historical Development and Social Change). Espoo, Weilin & Göös, 1981, 270 p. A *festschrift* for Heikki Waris. Includes 13 articles on historical development of social policy, the current state of social policy, and Heikki Waris' work as a social researcher.

KARVONEN, Lauri: 'Med vårt västra grannland som förebild (Our Western Neighbour as a Model)'. Meddelanden från Stiftelsens för Åbo Akademi Forskningsinstitut, No. 62, Åbo, 1981, 274 p. Study of the diffusion of public and social policy reforms from Sweden to Finland.

KOSKIAHO, Briitta: Elintason osatekijöiden kasautumisesta ja elintasoon vaikuttavista tekijöistä Länsi-Euroopassa (On the Components of the Standard of Living and their Determinants in Western Europe). Acta Universitatis Tamperensis, Ser. A:30, Tampere, 1969, 171 p. Comparative study of the basic dimensions of the standard of living and the effects of industrialization in Western Europe.

KOSKIAHO, Briitta et al.: Sosiaalipolitiikan arvot, tavoitteet ja käytäntö (Values, Goals and Practices in Social Policy). Acta Universitatis Temperensis, Ser. A:49, Tampere, 1973, 194 p. A *festschrift* for Armas Nieminen, with 20 articles on theoretical questions of social policy.

MARTIKAINEN, Tuomo, YRJÖNEN, Risto: Näkökohtia julkisten palvelusten tuotannosta ja organisaatiosta Suomessa (On the Production and Organization of Public Services in Finland). Helsingin yliopiston yleisen valtio-opin laitoksen tutkimuksia, Sarja A, No. 46. Helsinki, 1977, 269 p. An analysis of public welfare services (welfare assistance, the education system, and health services), from the viewpoint of regional differentiation and organization of public household and services.

RAUNIO, Kyösti: Hyvinvointi ja taloudelliset muutokset (Welfare and Economic Changes). Sosiaalipoliittisen yhdistyksen tutkimuksia, Vol. 41, Turku, 1983, 274 p. An analysis of the welfare effects of economic development in Finland in 1950-1977.

ROOS, J.P.: Welfare Theory and Social Policy. A Study on Policy Science. Commentationes Scientiarum Socialium 4, Helsinki, Societas Scientiarum Fennica, 1973, 251 p. A theoretical study on welfare and its relation to social policy.

SIPILÄ, Jorma: Sosiaalipolitiikka (Social Policy), 3rd ed. Helsinki, Tammi, 1974, 133 p. An introduction to the theory of social policy.

SIPILÄ, Jorma: Sosiaalisten ongelmien synty ja lievittäminen (The Rise of Social Problems and their Relief). Helsinki, Tammi, 1979, 199 p. A discussion of social welfare, social services and income maintenance systems from the social theory viewpoint, and the means necessary for the solution of social problems.

TOMPPO-VÄÄNÄNEN, Irma: Työmarkkinajärjestöjen rooli sosiaalipolitiikan kehittämisessä Suomessa vuosina 1956-1979 (The Role of Labour Market Organizations in the Development of

Social Policy in Finland, 1956-1979). Helsingen yliopisto. Sociaalipolitiikan laitos. Tutkimuksia, No. 6. Helsinki, 1981, 219 p. A study of the role of employees' and employers' unions in the development of the Finnish welfare state.

VEPSÄ, Kirsti: Elintason muutos Suomessa v. 1910-1965 (The Change in the Standard of Living in Finland, 1910-1965). Helsinki, WSOY, 1973, 151 p. An analysis of the changes in the standard of living with approximately fifty time series (nutrition, housing, health services, health standards, basiceducation standards, number of pensioners, unemployment, leisure etc.) from 1910-1965.

1.7 Policy proposals and debates

ELINKEINOELÄMÄN VALTUUSKUNTA: Minne menet hyvinvointiyhteiskunta? (Where is the Welfare Society Heading?). Helsinki, 1981, 52 p. A critical report on the expansion of the public sector.

HARVA, Urpo: Ihminen hyvinvointivaltiossa (Man in the Welfare State). Helsinki, Kirjayhtymä, 1964, 183 p. A critical analysis of Pekka Kuusi's book on the social policy of the 1960s and the welfare state.

KUUSI, Pekka: Social Policy for the Sixties. A Plan for Finland. Kuopio, Finnish Social Policy Association, 1964, 295 p. An evaluation of the achievements and shortcomings of social policy in Finland in the 1940s and 1950s, together with a proposal for coordination and planning of social policy in the 1960s.

SOSIAALITURVAN KESKUSLIITTO: Sosiaaliturva 80-luvulla (Social Security in the Eighties). Helsinki, 1980, 181 p. An analysis of the present system of income maintenance, social services and the administration of social security and proposals for their development.

1.8 Opinion polls

ALESTALO, Matti, UUSITALO, Hannu: Suomalaiset ja sosiaaliturva. Sosiaaliturvan kehittämistä koskevat mielipiteet vuosina 1975 ja 1980 (Finns and Social Security. Opinions about the Development of Social Security in 1975 and 1980). Suomen Gallupin julkaisusarja, Julkaisu No. 6, Helsinki, 1981, 25 p. An analysis of the development of opinions concerning social security by population groups in 1975-1980.

HELENIUS, Yrjö: Omavastuu vai yhteisvastuu (Self-reliance or Community Responsibility). Helsinki, WSOY, 1971, 293 p. A study of attitudes to social security in different income groups in one Finnish city in 1964.

TUOMINEN, Eila: Vaëstön mielipiteitä sosiaaliturvasta vuosina 1972 ja 1979 (Attitudes among the Population in Finland towards Social Security in 1972 and 1979). Eläketurvakeskuksen tutkimuksia, 1981:2, Helsinki, 1982, 88 p.A comparison of two survey studies (1972 and 1979) on public attitudes to social security and pension security.

1.9 Sources of statistics or institutional regulations

1.9.1 Official sources

ELÄKETURVAKESKUS: Työeläkejärjestelmän tilastollinen vuosikirja (Statistics on Occupational Pensions). Published annually, Helsinki, 1971-. Major statistical source of private sector occupational pension schemes.

NATIONAL HOUSING BOARD OF FINLAND: Statistics of the National Housing Board of Finland 1949-1981. 1983, 131 p. Includes statistics on the various forms of housing support.

OFFICIAL STATISTICS OF FINLAND XI:1-: Health Services. Published annually, National Board of Health, 1884-. Major statistics on national health, health services and expenditure.

OFFICIAL STATISTICS OF FINLAND XXIA:1-: Social Welfare. Published annually, National Board of Social Welfare, Bureau for Planning and Statistics, 1881-. Major statistics on social welfare, expenditure and personnel.

OFFICIAL STATISTICS OF FINLAND XXIB:1-: Yearbook of Social Welfare. Published annually, National Board of Social Welfare, Bureau for Planning and Statistics, 1957-. A summary of statistics on public assistance.

OFFICIAL STATISTICS OF FINLAND, SPECIAL SOCIAL STUDIES XXXII:56.: The Development of Social Security in Finland from 1950 to 1977. Helsinki, Ministry of Social Affairs and Health, Research Department, 1978.A study of the development of social security in Finland forthe period 1950-1977.

OFFICIAL STATISTICS OF FINLAND, SPECIAL SOCIAL STUDIES XXXII:49,53,57,60, 70,77,88,95: Social Expenditure. Published annually, Ministry of Social Affairs and Health, Research Department, 1974-. Major statisitical source for social expenditure. Earlier statistics on social expenditure published in *SOSIAALINEN AIKAKAUSIKIRJA*, see 1.9.3.

ONIKKI, Erkki (ed.): Sosiaalilainsäädäntö 1977 (Social Legislation 1977). Helsinki, Suomen lakimiesliitto, 1977, 328 p. A collection of laws and acts dealing with social legislation.

SOCIAL SECURITY IN THE NORDIC COUNTRIES: Published every three years, The Nordic Statistical Secretariat, 1954-. Comparative statistics on social security and welfare institutions in Denmark, Finland, Iceland, Norway and Sweden.

STATISTICAL YEARBOOK OF THE SOCIAL INSURANCE INSTITUTION OF FINLAND: Published annually, Helsinki, The Social Insurance Institution, 1965-. Major statistical source of national pensions and national sickness insurance.

1.9.2 Private sources

SEPPÄNEN, Paavo: Suomalainen yhteiskunta (Finnish Society). Helsingin yliopiston sosiologian laitoksen julkaisuja, No. 66, Helsinki, 1971, 115 p. A collection of over time series on social change in Finland from 1911 to the 1960s. Appendix in English; Seppänen, Paavo: Finnish Society (Social Change as Time Series). Institute of Sociology, University of Helsinki. Research Reports, No. 172, Helsinki, 1972, 30 p.

1.9.3 Major periodicals

SOSIAALINEN AIKAKAUSKIRJA (Social Review): Published six times annually, Helsinki, Ministry of Social Affairs and Health, (1907-). Major official journal on social policy. The major statistics on social expenditure have been published in this review.

SOSIAALIPOLITIIKKA (Social Policy): Published annually, (1976-). Yearbook of the Finnish Social Policy Association.

SOSIAALITURVA (Social Security): Helsinki, Huoltaja-säätiö (1912-). Major periodical on social welfare and social welfare work.

SOSIAALIVAKUUTUS (Social Insurance): Published ten times annually, Helsinki, Social Insurance Institution, (1963-). A periodical on the national pension system and general sickness insurance.

TYÖVOIMAKATSAUS (Labour Reports): Published monthly, Helsinki, Ministry of Labour, Planning Division, (1958-). Major official journal on the labour force, employment and unemployment.

II Single programmes or aspects

2.1 Pensions

AARNIO, Margaretha, JANHUNEN, Jouko: Eläketurva eri maissa vuonna 1977 (Pension Security in Various Countries in 1977). Eläketurvakeskuksen tutkimuksia 1977:1, Helsinki, 1977, 207 p. Survey of pension schemes in 20 countries including Scandinavia, Western Europe, Eastern Europe (5 countries), Canada and the U.S.

HALONEN, Ilpo, JOKELAINEN, Matti: Eläkepolitiikka Suomessa (Pension Policy in Finland). Helsinki, Kansankulttuuri, 1979, 94 p. Critical analysis of pension policy in Finland.

JANHUNEN, Jouko: Pohjoismaiden eläkejärjestelmät (Pension Schemes in the Nordic Countries). Eläketurvakeskuksen tutkimuksia 1981:1, Mänttä, 1981, 99 p. Comparative description of current pension schemes in Denmark, Finland, Iceland, Norway and Sweden.

LOUHELAINEN, Pekka: Eduskunta ja eläketurva (Parliament and Pension Security). Helsinki, Eläketurvakeskus, 1972, 333 p. Study of party voting patterns on pension matters in the parliament during the 1960s.

NIEMELÄ, Pauli, RUOTSALAINEN, Seppo: Suomalaisen eläketurvan sosiaalipoliittiset perusteet (Social Policy Principles of Finnish Pension Security). Kansaneläkelaitoksen julkaisuja A 20. Helsinki, 1983, 221 p. An analysis of the values underlying national and occupational pension schemes in Finland.

PULKKINEN, Terho: Eläketurva ja toimeentulo (Pension Security and Income Maintenance). Helsinki, WSOY, 1969, 328 p. Analysis of pension schemes, incomes and consumption patterns of pensioners. Includes a forecast on social security expenditure and proposals for the development of the pension system.

SUOMINEN, Risto, ARAJÄRVI, Esa: Eläkeläistalouksien tulo- ja kulutusrakenne vuonna 1976 (The Structure of Income and Consumption in Pensioner Households in 1976). Official Statistics of Finland, Special Social Studies XXXII:64. Helsinki, Ministry of Social Affairs and Health, Research Department, 1980, 186 p. Detailed study of incomes, consumption, taxes, pensions, social security benefits and transfers, etc. in pensioner households; based on the 1976 household survey.

VAROMA, Pekka: Työeläkekeskustelun rivejä ja välejä vuosikymmenen ajalta ('Lines and Gaps' in the Public Debate on Occupational Pensions). Eläketurvakeskuksen tutkimuksia 1971:1, Helsinki, 1972, 162 p. Descriptive analysis of the creation of occupational pension schemes, together with a content analysis of current discussion of these schemes during the 1960s.

2.2 Health

KALIMO, Esko: Lääkintäpalvelusten käyttöön vaikuttavat tekijät (Determinants of Medical Care Utilization). Kansaneläkelaitoksen julkaisuja, Sarja A:5, Helsinki, 1969, 253 p. Multivariate analysis of behaviour in cases of illness, and of factors affecting it among the adult population prior to the introduction of general sickness insurance.

KALIMO, Esko, NYMAN, Kauko, KLAUKKA, Timo, TUOMIKOSKI, Hannu, SAVOLAINEN, Eero: Terveyspalvelusten tarve, käyttö ja kustannukset 1964-1976 (Need, Use and Expenses of Health Care Services, 1964-1976). Kansaneläkelaitoksen julkaisuja A 18. Helsinki, 1982, 490 p. and Appendix. Major analysis of the distribution of needs, usage and expenditure of health care services as revealed by survey analyses in the period 1964-1976.

KARISTO, Antti: Hyvinvointi ja sairauden ongelma (Welfare and the Problem of Illness). Kansaneläkelaitoksen julkaisuja M. 46. Helsinki, 1984, 239 p. A comparative study of illness differences by population group and of illness as a welfare deficit in Finland and the other Scandinavian countries.

MUSTONEN, Maija, SUOMINEN, Risto, SUONOJA, Kyösti: Imeväiskuolleisuuteen vaikuttavat sosiaaliset ja taloudelliset tekijät Suomessa 1910-1971 (Social and Economic Factors Influencing Infant Mortality in Finland between 1910 and1971). Official Statistics of Finland, Special Social Studies XXXII:46. Helsinki, Ministry of Social Affairs and Health, Research Department, 1976, 148 p. Empirical study on the trends of infant mortality explained with reference to health services, maternity and child care, structural factors, levels of knowledge and standard of living.

OHTONEN, Jukka, KOSKI, Paula, VINNI, Kari: Katsaus Suomen terveydenhuoltojärjestelmän kehitykseen (Survey on the Development of Health Services in Finland). Official Statistics of Finland. Special Social Studies XXXII:96. Helsinki, Ministry of Social Affairs and Health, Research Department, 1983, 244 p. A collection of statistics on various health services in 1955-1980.

PURO, Kari: Terveyspolitiikan perusteet (Principles of Health Policy), 3rd ed. Helsinki, Tammi, 1976, 221 p. General introduction to health policy. Discusses health as the basis for welfare, measurement of health, the major focus of health policies and ways of preventing and dealing with illnesses.

PUROLA, Tapani, KALIMO, Esko, NYMAN, Kauko: Health Services Use and Health Status under National Sickness Insurance. Publications of the Social Insurance Institution, Finland, A:11/1974, Helsinki, 309 p. Empirical analysis of the effects of sickness insurance on the use of health care services and of the health of the population.

VAUHKONEN, Onni, LAURINKARI, Juhani, BÄCKMAN, Guy: Suomalaista terveyspolitiikkaa (Finnish Health Care Policy). Helsinki, WSOY, 1978, 188 p. General introduction to health care policy in Finland. Includes a historical survey on the development of health care and an introduction to the income maintenance system and the organization of health care administration.

2.3 Unemployment

JOKIPERÄ, Timo, HILTUNEN, Timo: Valtion toimenpiteiden välittömät javälilliset työllistävyysvaikutukset (Direct and Indirect Effects of State Policies on Employment). Työvoimaministeriö. Työvoimapoliittisia tutkimuksia, No. 21, Helsinki, 1977, 120 p. Analysis of the effects of state policies on employment in 1976 and 1977.

JYRKÄMÄ, Jyrki (ed.): Työttömänä Suomessa (Unemployed in Finland). Helsinki, Tutkijaliitto, 1981, 196 p. A reader on unemployment in Finland; includes articles on the general background of the problem, labour force policy, life as an unemployed person, and unemployment as an income maintenance problem, etc.

KAUPPINEN, Timo: Labour Relations in Finland. Helsinki, The Committee for Labour Relations, 1983, 36 p. Brief official introduction to labour relations and organizations.

LIND, Jouko: Työvoiman rakennemuutokset (Structural Changes in the Labour Force). Sosiaalipoliittisen yhdistyksen julkaisuja, Vol. 35, Turku, 1980, 357 p. Analysis of labour supply and demand for the period 1962-1978; also describes the structure of the labour force as a function of economic fluctuations.

MIKKOLA, Matti: Työttömyysturvan ehdoista (On Conditions of Unemployment Security). Suomalaisen lakimiesyhdistyksen julkaisuja. A-sarja, No. 141, Helsinki, 1979, 329 p. Legal analysis of the position and legal protection of those applying for unemployment benefits.

VÄHÄTALO, Kari: Työtön ja yhteiskunta (The Unemployed and Society). Helsingin yliopisto. Sosiaalipolitiikan laitos. Tutkimuksia, No. 7. Helsinki, 1983, 199 p. A study of the effects of unemployment on the unemployed and on society.

2.4 Accidents

EKLUND, Kari, SUIKKANEN, Asko: Työväensuojelusta työsuojeluun: työsuojelun ja työolojen kehitys Suomessa 1970-luvulla (From the Protection of Workers to Labour Protection: the Development of Labour Protection and Working Conditions in the 1970s). Helsinki, Tammi, 1982, 225 p. Description of labour protection in the 1970s, of occupational injuries and a comparison of surveys in 1973 and 1980 on working conditions, work satisfaction and labour protection.

LÄHTEINEN, Matti, JUUSELA, Tuulikki, PENTTILÄ, Aino: Työtapaturmat, työntekijän ominaisuudet ja tapaturmien sattumisajankohta (Industrial Accidents, Particularly Relating to Injured Persons, and Times of Accidents). Official Statistics of Finland XXXII:38. Special Social Studies. Helsinki, Ministry of Social Affairs and Health, 1974, 177 p. Study based on the statistics for industrial accidents in 1970 includes survey on industrial accidents in the period 1960-1972.

TYÖSUOJELUHALLITUS: Työsuojelu (Labour Protection). Helsinki, Tammi, 1974, p. A reader on labour protection. Includes descriptions of workers' health and job safety, benefits for labour accidents (industrial accident benefits), and the organization of labour protection.

2.5 Public assistance

LEHTO, Markku: Kuntien sosiaalihuollon menot 1969 (Expenditure of Public Assistance paid by Local Authorities in 1969). Official Statistics of Finland XXXII:29. Special Social Studies. Helsinki, Ministry of Social Affairs and Health. Research Department, 1972, 156 p. Study of expenditure of various forms of public assistance in Finnish municipalities.

RAUHALA, Urpo: Huostaanotto (Taking into Custody). Official Statistics of Finland. Special Social Studies, XXXII:54. Helsinki, 1978, 161 p. Empirical analysis of taking into custody in Finland in the early 1970s.

LO, Reino: Sosiaalihuolto (Public Assistance). Helsinki, WSOY, 1981, 264 p. Introduction to the system of public assistance.

2.6 Family programmes

HALLA, Klaus: Yksinhuoltajien asema ja ongelmat (The Position and Problems of Single Parents). Official Statistics of Finland XXXII:82. Special Social Studies. Helsinki, Ministry of Social Affairs and Health, Research Department, 1982, 168 p. Survey on economic and social problems of single-parent families.

HEIKKILÄ, Matti, KARJALAINEN, Timo, LIHR, Silja, NIINIVAARA, Reijo: Perhekustannusten tasausjärjestelmä Suomessa. Latuma-projektin loppuraportti (The System of Family Policy Transfers in Finland). Sosiaalihallituksen julkaisuja 4:1980. Helsinki, 1980, 70 p. and Appendix. Study on the effects of family policy transfers, subsidies and tax credits on family income.

SUOMINEN, Leena: Lapsiperhe Suomessa (Families with Children in Finland). Kolmikantasarja, Vol. 7. Helsinki,Väestöliitto, 1979, 158 p. Survey on the living conditions, structure, employment patterns, income, education and housing of families with children.

SUOMINEN, Leena: Perhepolitiikan perustelut Suomessa (The Motives of Family Policy in Finland). Väestöntutkimuslaitoksen julkaisuja, Sarja B:36, Helsinki, 1975, 101 p. Content analysis of the family policy proposals of the M.P.s in 1934-1973.

SUOMINEN, Risto, TUISKU, Terho: Lapsiperheiden tulo- ja kulutusrakenne vuonna 1976 (Structure of Income and Consumption of Families with Children). Official Statistics of Finland XXXII: 59. Special Social Studies. Helsinki, Ministry of Social Affairs and Health. Research Department, 1979, 125 p. Study based on the 1971 and (mostly) the 1976 household budget survey on income structure. Special emphasis on income transfers and social support received in cash benefits or at prices below factor costs.

2.7 Housing

HEIKKONEN, Eero: Asuntopalvelukset Suomessa 1860-1965 (Housing in Finland,1860-1965). Suomen Pankin taloustieteelisen tutkimuslaitoksen julkaisuja. Kasvututkimuksia III. Helsinki, 1971, 297 p. Macro-economic and quantitative description of the housing sector in the Finnish economy . Changes in housing are explained by demographic factors and economic growth.

ISOTALO, Seppo: Asunnoista (On Housing). Helsinki, Helsingin sosiaali ja terveystyöntekijäin Sos.Dem. Yhdistys, 1974, 84 p. Comparison of housing policy in Finland and Sweden.

JUNTTO, Anneli: Arava-asukkaiden tulot ja tuen tarve vuonna 1972 (Incomes and Need of Support of Households Living in State Supported Dwellings in 1972). Asuntohallitus. Tutkimus- ja suunnitteluosasto, Sarja A:9,Helsinki, 1976, 303 p. A study on legislation in the field of housing, public support of housing in the postwar period, and the incidence of state support for housing.

KARJALAINEN, Pirkko: Vanhusten asumisolot (Housing Conditions of Old People). Official Statistics of Finland XXXII: 67. Special Social Studies. Helsinki, Ministry of Social Affairs and Health. Research Department, 1980, 104 p. Survey on incomes, housing conditions, housing expenditures, etc. of old people in 1976. Includes a comparison with the situation in 1962/63.

KOSONEN, Mirja, PAUKKU, Ossi: Asumisolot ja asumisen tuki Suomessa (Housing Conditions and Support for Housing in Finland). Asuntoreformiyhdistyksen julkaisuja No. 21, Kotka,

1978, 131 p. A statistical description of housing conditions by population groups and a collection of statistics on the forms of housing support in Finland in 1956-1978.

MÄENPÄÄ, Jorma: Asuntopolitiikkamme ja sen tavoitteet (Housing Policy and its Goals). Helsinki, Tammi, 1968, 229 p. Introduction to housing policy.

MANNINEN, Matti: Asuntopolitiikan perusteista (On the Foundations of Housing Policy). Helsinki, Gaudeamus, 1976, 226 p. Introduction to the housing policy in Finland.

PAUKKU, Ossi: Asuminen tuki 1970-1981 (Support for Housing 1970-1981). Asuntoreformiyhdistyksen julkaisuja No. 22, Helsinki, 1983, 36 p. A collection of statistics on the forms of housing support in Finland in 19701981.

SUVIRANTA, Aulikki, MYNTTINEN, Arto: Nuorten perheiden asunto-olot vuonna 1978 (Housing Conditions of Young Families in 1978). Official Statistics of Finland XXXII: 66. Special Social Studies. Helsinki, Ministry of Social Affairs and Health. Research Department, 1980, 208 p. Repetition of Suviranta's study in 1967. Two groups of couples, married in 1971 and 1977 were surveyed on first and present dwellings, on housing costs and subsidies and on housing goals.

2.8 Education

ISOSAARI, Jussi: Suomen koululaitoksen rakenne ja kehitys (Structure and Development of the Finnish School System), 2nd ed. Helsinki, Otava, 1973, 139 p. Historical introduction to the Finnish educational system.

SARJALA, Jukka: Suomalainen koulutuspolitiikka (Finnish Educational Policy). Helsinki, WSOY, 1981, 166 p. General description of Finnish educational policy. Analyzes the goals of education, history of educational policy and reforms as a part of the general decision-making system in society.

TAKALA, Tuomas: Oppivelvollisuuskoulu ja yhteiskunnalliset intressit (Compulsory Education and Social Interests). Acta Universitatis Tamperensis, Ser. A: 151. Tampere, 1983, 308 p. Theoretical and empirical study on the process leading to the legislation of compulsory education in 1921 and on the comprehensive school in 1968.

2.9 Public household

HEISKANEN, Ilkka: Julkinen, kollektiivinen, markkinaperusteinen (Public, Collective and Market-based). Helsingin yliopiston valtio-opin laitos, Deta, No. 31. Helsinki, 2nd ed., 1977, 477 p. Comprehensive study on administration patterns and public decision-making in the 1960s and 1970s. Includes a large section on public services and the welfare sector.

MARTIKAINEN, Tuomo: Julkisen sektorin kasvu Suomessa (The Growth of the Public Sector in Finland). Helsingin yliopiston yleisen valtio-opin laitoksen tutkimuksia, Deta, No. 15. Helsinki, 1975, 174 p. Analysis of public sector expenditure from 1811 to 1974 with an affluent statistical Appendix including a disaggregation of public sector expenditure.

NIKKILÄ, Juhani: Valtion budjettimenojen kehitys tehtävittäin 1920-1976 (Expenditure by Function in the State Budget, 1920-1976). Tampereen yliopisto. Julkishallinon julkaisusarja, No. 1/1979. Tampere, 1979, 144 p. and Appendix. Theoretical and empirical analysis of the changes in the functions of the state from 1920 to 1976.

PALOHEIMO, Heikki: Politiikka, talous ja yhteiskunnan muutos (Politics, Economy and Change in Society). Turun yliopiston julkaisuja. Ser. C 32. Turku, 1981, 218 p. Discussion on the theories of the state and the development of capitalist societies. Also includes empirical analyses on economic growth, sectoral development, unemployment, political development and state intervention in the OECD-area.

WILLMAN, Alpo: Julkiset menot vuosina 1950-1977 (Public Expenditure in 1950-1977), Suomen Pankki, A:51. Helsinki, 1980, 125 p. Analysis of growth and structure of public expenditures in Finland, 1950-1977.

2.10 Public employment

TALKKARI, Antti: Valtionhallinnon henkilöstön määrällinen ja rakenteellinen muutos itsenäisyyden aikana Suomessa (Growth and Structure of Personnel in State Administration during Independence in Finland). Tampereen yliopisto. Julkishallinon julkaisusarja A:3. Tampere, 1979, 225 p. Study on the growth and structural changes among civil servants from 1910 to 1976. Includes also some analyses on expenditure development.

III The impact of social programmes

3.1 Poverty

HAATANEN, Pekka: Suomen maalaisköyhälistö tutkimusten ja kaunokirjallisuuden valossa (The Rural Proletariat in Finland). Helsinki, WSOY, 1968, 365 p. Historical analysis of rural poverty and the rural proletariat in Finland from the 1690s to 1960s. Employs statistics, studies and excerpts from fiction to describe rural poverty.

HALLA, Klaus, KARJALAINEN, Pirkko: Erityisryhmien olot (The Conditions of Special Groups). Official Statistics of Finland XXXII: 61. Special Social Studies. Helsinki, Ministry of Social Affairs and Health. Research Department, 1980, 122 p. Study on living standards of such groups as families with children, large families, young families, single parent families, old people, war invalids, veterans, visually handicapped, Lapps, gypsies.

HALLA, Klaus, KYRÖ, Matti: Alimman viidenneksen tulo- ja kulutusrakenne vuonna 1976 (Structure of Income and Consumption in the Lowest Quintile in 1976). Official Statistics of Finland XXXII:63. Special Social Studies. Helsinki, Ministry of Social Affairs and Health. Research Department, 1980, 109 p. Study of the poorest 20 per cent of Finnish households in 1976.

RAUNIO, Kyösti: Köyhyys ja taloudelliset muutokset (Poverty and Economic Changes). Turun yliopisto. Sosiaalipolitiikan julkaisuja A:3. Turku, No year of printing, 71 p. Poverty is defined by the share of public assistance beneficiaries and its changes are analyzed in relation to economic growth and unemployment.

VISURI, Elina: Poverty and Children. A Study of Family Planning. Transactions of the Westermark Society, Vol. XVI. Helsinki, 1969, 154 p. Survey on the family planning of couples that received public assistance in Helsinki in 1965.

3.2 Inequality and income distribution

CENTRAL STATISTICAL OFFICE OF FINLAND: Living Conditions 1950-1975. Statistical Surveys No. 58. Helsinki, 1977, 228 p. Collection of statistical data on living conditions. Includes information on economic resources, conditions of work, distribution of income, health, education, social security, housing, environment, leisure use, social participation, etc.

SUOMINEN, Risto: Sosiaalisten tulonsiirtojen kohtaanto (The Incidence of Social Transfers). Official Statistics of Finland. Special Social Studies XXXII:51. Helsinki, Ministry of Social Affairs and Health. Research Department, 1977, 109 p. Study on the vertical and horizontal redistribution effects of income transfers, taxation and social support on the basis of the data from 1966 and 1971 household budget surveys.

SUOMINEN, Risto: Tulojen uudelleenjako Suomessa vuonna 1976 (Redistribution of Income in Finland in 1976). Official Statistics of Finland. Special Social Studies XXXII:58. Helsinki, Ministry of Social Affairs and Health. Research Department, 1979, 168 p. Study on the redistributive effects of income transfers, taxation and social support on the basis of the household budget survey data (1966, 1971 and 1976). In addition, the incidence of tax deductions and the support an average person receives at various stages in his life is analyzed.

UUSITALO, Hannu: Income and Welfare. Research Group for Comparative Sociology. University of Helsinki. Research Reports, No. 8. Helsinki, 1975, 359 p. Comparative analysis of income as a component of welfare in Denmark, Finland, Norway and Sweden based on the survey material of the Scandinavian Welfare Survey.

UUSITALO, Hannu: 'Tulopolitiikka ja tulonjako (Income policy and income distribution)', pp. 51-102. *In*: *Sosiaalipolitiikka* 1982. Helsinki, Sosiaalipoliittinen yhdistys, 1982. Analysis of the periods of income policy and the development of income distribution. Special emphasis on income differences between socio-economic groups from 1966 to 1978. Appendix on major studies on income distribution.

3.3 Economic effects

KOLJONEN, Kalevi, TUOVINEN, Marja: Sosiaaliturva ja sen rahoitus kansantaloudessa (Social Security and its Financing in the Economy). Taloudellinen suunnittelukeskus. Erillisselvitys 2/1979. Helsinki, 1979, 61 p. and Appendix. Analysis on social expenditure development from 1960 to 1977 and exploration of the development of expenditure to the year 2000 with an analysis of their effects on the state expenditure.

UUSITALO, Hannu: The Economic and Social Effects of Income Policy: The Case of Finland, Scandinavian Political Studies. Vol. 1983:1., pp. 1-25. Discussion of the role of income policy (including the effects of social security benefits and taxation) on redistribution in Finland. Offers some comparisons with the other OECD-countries.

Appendix Tables

Contents

Table 1

Gross Domestic Product and Total Public Expenditure

Year	GDP (at market prices, in million FM)						Total public expenditure (in million FM)						Year
	Old SNA			New SNA			A		B		C		
	at current prices	at constant (1975) prices	annual real growth rate	at current prices	at constant (1975) prices	annual real growth rate	at current prices	as % of GDP Old SNA	at current prices	as % of GDP New SNA	at current prices	as % of GDP New SNA	
1948	4 089	26 829											1948
1949	4 391	27 817	3.7										1949
1950	5 424	29 849	7.3				1 417	26.1					1950
1951	7 901	32 630	9.3				1 893	24.0					1951
1952	8 181	33 753	3.4				2 229	27.2					1952
1953	8 074	33 795	0.1				2 470	30.6					1953
1954	8 969	36 855	9.1				2 518	28.1					1954
1955	9 922	39 636	7.5				2 792	28.1					1955
1956	11 031	40 425	2.0				3 310	30.0					1956
1957	12 025	41 039	1.5				3 642	30.3					1957
1958	12 954	41 007	-0.1				4 050	31.3					1958
1959	14 079	43 980	7.3				4 245	30.1					1959
1960	15 824	48 348	9.9	16 038	52 502		4 506	28.5					1960
1961	17 626	52 239	8.0	18 141	56 483	7.6	5 004	28.4					1961
1962	18 856	54 477	4.3	19 392	57 994	2.7	5 629	29.9	5 280	27.2			1962
1963	20 541	55 831	2.5	21 026	59 914	3.3	6 630	32.3	6 088	28.9	6 091	29.0	1963
1964	23 554	59 501	6.6	23 718	63 082	5.3	7 639	32.4	7 188	30.3	7 201	30.4	1964
1965	25 828	62 560	5.1	26 216	66 416	5.3	8 799	34.1	8 142	31.1	8 171	31.2	1965
1966	27 777	64 044	2.4	28 071	67 814	2.1	9 435	34.0	9 085	32.4	9 138	32.6	1966
1967	30 109	65 739	2.6	30 744	69 381	2.3	10 493	34.8	10 219	33.2	10 302	33.5	1967
1968	34 148	67 314	2.4	35 231	71 136	2.5	12 077	35.4	11 737	33.3	11 872	33.7	1968
1969	39 013	74 338	10.4	40 228	77 980	9.6	13 135	33.7	12 803	31.8	13 005	32.3	1969
1970	43 592	80 485	8.3	44 858	84 148	7.9	14 304	32.8	13 954	31.1	14 231	31.7	1970
1971	47 661	82 422	2.4	49 243	85 695	1.8	16 403	34.4	16 071	32.6	16 465	33.4	1971
1972	54 909	88 205	7.0	57 401	92 158	7.5	19 530	35.6	19 049	33.2	19 628	34.2	1972
1973	66 746	93 926	6.5	69 845	98 180	6.5	22 927	34.3	22 189	31.8	22 967	32.9	1973
1974	84 174	97 925	4.3	88 143	101 290	3.2	30 507	36.2	28 894	32.8	29 944	34.0	1974
1975	97 961	97 961	0.0	101 882	101 882	0.6	38 944	39.8	37 294	36.6	38 759	38.0	1975
1976	110 122	97 806	-0.2	115 003	102 141	0.3	45 435	41.3	43 858	38.1	45 962	40.0	1976
1977	121 633	98 130	0.3	127 065	102 512	0.4	51 254	42.1	49 989	39.3	52 866	41.6	1977
1978	130 776	97 995	-0.1	139 918	104 845	2.3			54 590	39.1	58 111	41.5	1978
1979				161 957	112 813	7.6			62 027	38.3	66 048	40.8	1979
1980				186 846	119 627	6.0			70 401	37.7	75 162	40.2	1980
1981				211 964	121 306	1.4							1981

Table 2

Year	Deflators (base 1975) GDP old SNA	GDP new SNA	Public consumption old SNA	Public consumption new SNA	Cost of living index	Total public expenditure (in million FM) A at constant (1975) prices	A annual real growth rate	B at constant (1975) prices	B annual real growth rate	C at constant (1975) prices	C annual real growth rate	Year
1948	15.2		8.7		17.9							1948
1949	15.8		9.3		18.3							1949
1950	18.2		11.9		20.8	11 908						1950
1951	24.2		15.4		24.2	12 292	3.2					1951
1952	24.2		16.4		25.2	13 591	10.6					1952
1953	23.9		16.7		25.5	14 790	8.8					1953
1954	24.3		16.8		25.1	14 988	1.3					1954
1955	25.0		17.7		24.3	15 774	5.2					1955
1956	27.3		20.5		27.1	16 146	2.4					1956
1957	29.3		21.8		30.8	16 706	3.5					1957
1958	31.6		23.2		33.6	17 457	4.5					1958
1959	32.0		24.2		34.1	17 541	0.5					1959
1960	32.7	30.5	25.2	24.1	35.2	17 881	1.9					1960
1961	33.7	32.1	26.5	25.4	35.8	18 883	5.6					1961
1962	34.6	33.4	27.7	26.9	37.4	20 321	7.6	19 599		19 599		1962
1963	36.8	35.1	30.0	29.3	39.2	22 100	8.8	20 750	5.9	20 758	5.9	1963
1964	39.6	37.6	32.8	32.7	43.3	23 290	5.4	21 989	6.0	22 028	6.1	1964
1965	41.3	39.5	35.0	34.9	45.4	25 140	7.9	23 307	6.0	23 394	6.2	1965
1966	43.4	41.4	37.5	37.6	47.1	25 160	0.1	24 165	3.7	24 307	3.9	1966
1967	45.8	44.3	40.7	40.9	49.8	25 781	2.5	24 996	3.4	25 199	3.7	1967
1968	50.7	49.5	45.1	45.4	54.0	26 778	3.9	25 829	3.3	26 130	3.7	1968
1969	52.5	51.6	47.3	47.6	55.2	27 770	3.7	26 871	4.0	27 297	4.5	1969
1970	54.2	53.3	49.8	50.3	56.7	28 723	3.4	27 748	3.3	28 305	3.7	1970
1971	57.8	57.5	54.4	54.8	60.4	30 153	5.0	29 335	5.7	30 049	6.2	1971
1972	62.3	62.3	59.5	59.6	64.7	32 824	8.9	31 948	8.9	32 916	9.5	1972
1973	71.1	71.1	67.5	67.3	72.3	33 966	3.5	32 991	3.3	34 152	3.8	1973
1974	86.0	87.0	82.5	82.1	84.9	36 978	8.9	35 179	6.6	36 472	6.8	1974
1975	100.0	100.0	100.0	100.0	100.0	38 944	5.3	37 294	6.0	38 759	6.3	1975
1976	112.6	112.6	113.3	113.3	114.3	40 102	3.0	38 683	3.7	40 538	4.6	1976
1977	124.0	124.0	123.2	122.5	128.9	41 602	3.7	40 798	5.5	43 139	6.4	1977
1978	133.5	133.5		129.2	138.5			42 240	3.5	44 978	4.3	1978
1979		143.6		141.1	148.6			43 952	4.1	46 828	4.1	1979
1980		156.2		158.0	165.8			44 564	1.4	47 578	1.6	1980
1981		174.7		177.6	185.8							1981

Table 3 Public Expenditure by

Economic Function

Year	Total exp. at curr. pr. mill. Fm	Publ. inv.	Publ. cons.	Trans-fers	Subsid.	Debt ser-vice
1948						
1949						
1950	1 417.4	23.4	44.3	32.3		
1951	1 893.4	21.1	42.6	36.3		
1952	2 228.6	24.6	40.6	34.8		
1953	2 469.6	28.3	40.1	32.1		
1954	2 517.9	25.8	39.4	34.8		
1955	2 792.4	23.9	40.9	35.2		
1956	3 310.1	24.8	41.1	34.2		
1957	3 642.4	25.7	41.3	33.0		
1958	4 049.7	28.1	41.0	30.9		
1959	4 244.7	25.3	43.7	31.0		
1960	4 505.9	23.8	44.3	31.9		
1961	5 003.9	24.1	44.0	31.9		
1962	5 628.8	23.5	44.8	31.6		
1962	5 280	16.4	46.2	25.6	9.3	2.5
1963	6 088	15.8	46.7	24.3	10.6	2.6
1964	7 188	16.8	45.0	23.8	11.4	3.0
1965	8 142	16.9	44.4	24.9	10.1	3.4
1966	9 085	16.0	44.9	25.7	10.2	3.2
1967	10 219	15.4	45.5	26.8	8.9	3.4
1968	11 737	14.7	46.6	26.7	8.6	3.4
1969	12 803	13.8	46.3	26.9	9.5	3.5
1970	13 954	12.3	47.4	27.3	9.7	3.3
1971	16 071	12.2	47.5	28.4	8.9	3.0
1972	19 049	13.1	47.1	28.6	8.5	2.7
1973	22 189	13.1	48.2	28.3	7.9	2.4
1974	28 894	11.9	47.3	28.4	10.3	2.0
1975	37 294	12.1	47.7	27.2	11.1	1.8
1976	43 858	10.7	48.6	27.9	11.1	1.7
1977	49 989	10.5	47.9	29.0	10.5	2.0
1978	54 590	9.8	48.1	29.8	10.1	2.2
1979	62 027	9.4	48.0	28.6	11.5	2.5
1980	70 401	9.7	49.1	27.7	10.8	2.7
1981						

Purpose I

Year	Total exp. at curr. pr. mill. Fm	De-fence	Publ. adm.	Soc. serv.	Health	Educ.	Trans-port & comm.
1948	406.5	13.2	31.7	9.5	14.4	22.6	8.6
1949	470.8	12.4	30.3	9.6	13.8	23.8	10.1
1950	627.9	13.0	29.4	9.2	14.4	25.1	8.9
1951	806.7	12.9	27.6	9.0	15.1	27.3	8.0
1952	904.7	13.0	26.8	9.0	15.0	28.6	7.5
1953	989.4	12.6	25.7	10.0	15.4	28.8	7.4
1954	992.1	11.3	25.9	10.2	15.6	29.9	7.0
1955	1 141.6	11.2	24.6	10.1	16.0	30.7	7.4
1956	1 359.1	11.3	24.9	9.4	16.0	31.2	7.1
1957	1 506.0	11.9	24.8	8.5	15.8	31.6	7.4
1958	1 659.4	11.1	24.8	8.9	16.1	32.2	7.0
1959	1 855.7	11.2	23.8	8.8	17.1	32.1	7.0
1960	1 966.8	11.6	24.3	9.0	17.5	32.3	6.9
1961	2 201.3	12.5	23.3	7.2	17.6	32.5	6.9
1962	2 523.3	12.0	23.0	7.2	17.7	32.6	7.4
1962	2 523.3	12.0	23.0	7.2	17.7	32.6	7.4
1963	2 924.7	13.6	22.8	7.3	18.0	31.3	7.0
1964	3 349.0	12.7	22.8	7.2	19.3	31.3	6.6
1965	3 758.8	11.3	23.9	7.9	19.7	30.6	6.6
1966	4 235.0	11.2	24.3	7.5	20.2	30.5	6.4
1967	4 852.4	10.3	24.5	7.3	20.8	31.0	6.1
1968	5 693.5	10.5	24.3	7.6	21.5	30.7	5.5
1969	6 212.2	9.4	24.0	7.9	22.5	30.6	5.7
1970	6 914.0	9.4	24.0	8.1	22.7	30.2	5.6
1971	7 936.7	9.3	24.2	8.1	22.6	30.4	5.4
1972	9 294.7	9.1	24.2	8.3	22.7	30.1	5.4
1973	11 162.3	9.3	24.3	8.3	23.3	29.8	5.1
1974	14 219.8	8.6	24.1	8.8	22.9	30.3	5.3
1975	18 331.6	8.8	24.1	9.0	22.5	30.5	5.0
1976	21 751.2	8.1	23.7	9.6	22.8	30.9	4.9
1977	24 746.0	8.3	23.4	9.8	22.9	31.1	4.5
1978							
1979							
1980							
1981							

Purpose II

Total exp. at curr. pr. mill. Fm	De-fence	Publ. adm.	Soc. sec.	Health	Hous-ing	Educ.	Econ. serv.	Other	Year
									1948
									1949
									1950
									1951
									1952
									1953
									1954
									1955
									1956
									1957
									1958
									1959
									1960
									1961
									1962
									1962
									1963
									1964
									1965
									1966
									1967
									1968
									1969
									1970
									1971
									1972
									1973
									1974
17 790.4	7.8	17.0	11.3	21.0	3.6	30.0	9.1	0.2	1975
21 295.6	7.0	16.8	11.7	21.1	3.7	30.6	8.9	0.2	1976
23 969.3	7.3	16.8	11.6	21.4	3.6	30.5	8.6	0.3	1977
26 252.3	7.5	16.5	12.1	21.3	3.6	30.4	7.9	0.6	1978
29 755.2	7.5	16.3	12.4	21.5	3.7	30.2	8.0	0.5	1979
34 737.5	7.8	16.4	12.8	21.4	3.5	29.5	8.0	0.5	1980
40 391.5	7.3	16.4	12.8	21.5	3.5	29.9	8.2	0.5	1981

Table 4

Social Expenditure

Year	at current prices (in million FM)							at constant (1975) prices (in million FM)							Year
	Income Maint.	Health	Educ-ation	Social services	Total I	Hous-ing	Total II	Income Maint.	Health	Educ-ation	Social services	Total I	Hous-ing	Total II	
1950	230	68	132	138	568			1 106	571	1 109	1 160	3 946			1950
1951	329	90	185	143	747			1 360	584	1 201	929	4 074			1951
1952	406	107	217	161	891			1 611	652	1 323	982	4 568			1952
1953	440	112	240	259	1 051			1 726	671	1 437	1 557	5 391			1953
1954	449	122	249	230	1 050			1 789	726	1 482	1 375	5 372			1954
1955	478	146	295	227	1 146			1 967	825	1 667	1 283	5 742			1955
1956	549	169	356	233	1 307			2 026	824	1 737	1 137	5 724			1956
1957	707	197	400	255	1 559			2 296	904	1 835	1 170	6 205			1957
1958	768	244	449	275	1 736			2 286	1 052	1 935	1 177	6 450			1958
1959	813	263	500	281	1 857			2 384	1 087	2 066	1 161	6 698			1959
1960	886	288	533	296	2 003	104	2 107	2 517	1 143	2 115	1 175	6 950	319	7 269	1960
1961	1 064	323	600	336	2 323			2 972	1 219	2 264	1 268	7 723			1961
1962	1 210	367	692	347	2 616	124	2 740	3 193	1 330	2 507	1 511	8 541	357	8 898	1962
1963	1 312	428	769	370	2 879			3 347	1 427	2 563	1 233	8 570			1963
1964	1 497	531	879	465	3 372	155	3 527	3 457	1 619	2 680	1 418	9 174	384	9 558	1964
1965	1 732	659	965	527	3 883			3 815	1 883	2 757	1 506	9 961			1965
1966	2 053	764	1 085	725	4 627	222	4 849	4 359	2 037	2 893	1 933	11 222	511	11 733	1966
1967	2 434	931	1 264	719	5 348			4 888	2 288	3 106	1 767	12 049			1967
1968	2 869	1 170	1 467	662	6 168	304	6 472	5 313	2 594	3 253	1 468	12 628	611	13 239	1968
1969	3 146	1 332	1 594	687	6 759			5 699	2 816	3 370	1 452	13 337			1969
1970	3 614	1 497	1 755	831	7 697	507	8 204	6 374	3 006	3 524	1 669	14 573	938	15 511	1970
1971	4 387	1 765	2 028	944	9 124			7 263	3 245	3 728	1 735	15 971			1971
1972	5 371	2 245	2 354	1 054	11 024	844	11 868	8 301	3 773	3 956	1 771	17 801	1 348	19 192	1972
1973	6 370	2 746	2 791	1 361	13 268			8 811	4 068	4 135	2 016	19 030			1973
1974	8 166	3 481	3 619	1 655	16 921	1 474	18 395	9 618	4 219	4 387	2 006	20 230	1 662	21 892	1974
1975	10 387	4 537	4 721	2 206	21 851	1 904	23 755	10 387	4 537	4 721	2 206	21 851	1 904	23 755	1975
1976	13 032	5 514	5 751	3 004	27 301	2 242	29 543	11 402	4 867	5 076	2 651	23 996	2 030	26 026	1976
1977	15 932	6 303	6 429	3 779	32 443	2 546	34 989	12 360	5 145	5 248	3 085	25 838	2 042	27 880	1977
1978	18 109	6 866	6 993	4 479	36 447	2 539	38 986	13 075	5 314	5 413	3 467	27 269	1 921	29 190	1978
1979	19 782	7 688	7 827	5 253	40 550	2 967	43 517	13 312	5 449	5 547	3 723	28 031	2 049	30 080	1979
1980	22 441	8 970	8 880	5 981	46 272	3 040	49 312	13 535	5 677	5 620	3 785	28 617	1 859	30 476	1980
1981	25 983	10 445	10 416	6 884	53 728	3 182	56 910	19 984	5 881	5 865	3 876	29 606	1 753	31 359	1981

Table 5

Social Expenditure I

Year	As % of gross domestic product (old SNA/new SNA) Income maint.	Health	Educ-ation	Social services	Total	As % of public expenditore (A/B) Income maint.	Health	Educ-ation	Social services	As % of public expenditore (C) Income maint.	Health	Educ-ation	Social services	Percent distribution (current prices) Income maint.	Health	Educ-ation	Social services	Year
1950	4.2	1.3	2.4	2.5	10.5	16.2	4.8	9.3	9.7					40.5	12.0	23.2	24.3	1950
1951	4.2	1.1	2.3	1.8	9.5	17.4	4.8	9.8	7.6					44.0	12.1	24.8	19.1	1951
1952	5.0	1.3	2.7	2.0	10.9	18.2	4.8	9.7	7.2					45.6	12.0	24.4	18.1	1952
1953	5.5	1.4	3.0	3.2	13.0	17.8	4.5	9.7	10.5					41.9	10.7	23.8	24.6	1953
1954	5.0	1.4	2.8	2.6	11.7	17.8	4.9	9.9	9.1					42.8	11.6	23.7	21.9	1954
1955	4.8	1.5	3.0	2.3	11.6	17.1	5.2	10.6	8.1					41.7	12.7	25.7	19.8	1955
1956	5.0	1.5	3.2	2.1	11.8	16.6	5.1	10.8	7.0					42.0	12.9	27.2	17.8	1956
1957	5.9	1.6	3.3	2.1	13.0	19.4	5.4	11.0	7.0					45.3	12.6	25.7	16.4	1957
1958	5.9	1.9	3.5	2.1	13.4	19.0	6.0	11.1	6.8					44.2	14.1	25.9	15.8	1958
1959	5.8	1.9	3.6	2.0	13.2	19.2	6.2	11.8	6.6					43.8	14.2	26.9	15.1	1959
1960	5.6	1.8	3.4	1.9	12.7	19.7	6.4	11.8	6.6					44.2	14.4	26.6	14.8	1960
1961	6.0	1.8	3.4	1.9	13.2	21.3	6.5	12.0	6.7					45.8	13.9	25.8	14.5	1961
1962	6.4	2.0	3.7	1.8	13.9	21.5	6.5	12.3	6.2					45.3	14.0	26.5	13.3	1962
1962	6.2	1.9	3.6	1.8	13.5	22.9	7.0	13.1	6.6					45.3	14.0	26.5	13.3	1962
1963	6.2	2.0	3.7	1.8	13.7	21.6	7.0	12.6	6.0	21.5	7.0	12.6	6.1	45.6	14.9	26.7	12.9	1963
1964	6.3	2.2	3.7	2.0	14.2	20.8	7.4	12.2	6.5	20.8	7.4	12.2	6.5	44.4	15.7	26.1	13.8	1964
1965	6.6	2.5	3.7	2.0	14.8	21.3	8.1	11.9	6.5	21.2	8.1	11.8	6.5	44.6	17.0	24.9	13.6	1965
1966	7.3	2.7	3.9	2.6	16.5	22.6	8.4	11.9	8.0	22.5	8.4	11.8	7.9	44.4	16.5	23.5	15.7	1966
1967	7.9	3.0	4.1	2.3	17.4	23.8	9.1	12.4	7.0	23.6	9.0	12.3	7.0	45.5	17.4	23.6	13.4	1967
1968	8.1	3.3	4.2	1.9	17.5	24.4	10.0	12.5	5.6	24.2	9.9	12.4	5.6	46.5	19.0	23.8	10.7	1968
1969	7.8	3.3	4.0	1.7	16.8	24.6	10.4	12.5	5.4	24.2	10.2	12.3	5.3	46.6	19.7	23.6	10.2	1969
1970	8.1	3.3	3.9	1.9	17.2	25.9	10.7	12.6	6.0	25.4	10.5	12.3	5.8	47.0	19.5	22.8	10.8	1970
1971	8.9	3.6	4.1	1.9	18.5	27.3	11.0	12.6	5.9	26.6	10.7	12.3	5.7	48.1	19.3	22.2	10.4	1971
1972	9.4	3.9	4.1	1.8	19.2	28.2	11.8	12.4	5.5	27.4	11.4	12.0	5.4	48.7	20.4	21.4	9.6	1972
1973	9.1	3.9	4.0	2.0	19.0	28.7	12.4	12.6	6.1	27.7	12.0	12.2	5.9	48.0	20.7	21.0	10.3	1973
1974	9.3	4.0	4.1	1.9	19.2	28.3	12.1	12.5	5.7	27.3	11.6	12.1	5.5	48.3	20.6	21.4	9.8	1974
1975	10.2	4.5	4.6	2.2	21.5	27.9	12.2	12.7	5.9	26.8	11.7	12.2	5.7	47.5	20.8	21.6	10.1	1975
1976	11.3	4.8	5.0	2.6	23.7	29.7	12.6	13.1	6.9	28.4	12.0	12.5	6.5	47.7	20.2	21.1	11.0	1976
1977	12.5	5.0	5.1	3.0	25.5	31.9	12.6	12.9	7.6	30.1	11.9	12.2	7.1	49.1	19.4	19.8	11.7	1977
1978	12.9	4.9	5.0	3.2	26.1	33.2	12.6	12.8	8.2	31.2	11.8	12.0	7.7	49.7	18.8	19.2	12.3	1978
1979	12.2	4.8	4.8	3.2	25.0	31.9	12.4	12.6	8.5	30.0	11.6	11.9	8.0	48.8	19.0	19.3	13.0	1979
1980	12.0	4.8	4.8	3.2	24.8	31.9	12.7	12.6	8.5	29.9	11.9	11.8	8.0	48.5	19.4	19.2	12.9	1980
1981	12.3	4.9	4.9	3.2	25.4									48.4	19.4	19.4	12.8	1981

Table 6

Expenditure on Income Maintenance

Year	at current prices (in million FM)										percent distribution									Year
	Total	Pensions	Industr. accid.	Sick- ness	Unempl.	Family allow.	Soc. ass.	Mil. and war vict.	Hous. allow.	Study allow.	Pen- sions	Ind. accid.	Sick- ness	Un- empl.	Fam. all.	Soc. ass.	Mil. and war vict.	Hous. all.	Study all.	
1950	230.0	39.8	20.3		0.2	107.4	8.4	53.9			17.3	8.8		0.1	46.7	3.7	23.4			1950
1951	329.0	67.2	25.7		0.3	165.9	10.2	59.7			20.4	7.8		0.1	50.4	3.1	18.2			1951
1952	405.7	112.0	29.6		0.3	193.6	12.4	57.8			27.6	7.3		0.1	47.7	3.1	14.2			1952
1953	439.8	141.5	30.5		0.4	197.8	14.0	55.6			32.2	6.9		0.1	45.0	3.2	12.6			1953
1954	448.7	145.9	30.2		0.5	200.6	16.2	55.3			32.5	6.7		0.1	44.7	3.6	12.3			1954
1955	478.3	160.9	33.9		0.6	203.1	17.2	62.6			33.6	7.1		0.1	42.5	3.6	13.1			1955
1956	549.2	209.2	38.0		0.7	205.5	19.5	75.8	0.5		38.1	6.9		0.1	37.4	3.6	13.8	0.1		1956
1957	707.0	363.6	42.0		1.2	208.0	18.3	73.4	0.5		51.4	5.9		0.2	29.4	2.6	10.4	0.1		1957
1958	768.2	414.6	43.4		1.1	210.5	25.3	74.5	0.6		54.0	5.7		0.1	27.4	3.3	9.7	0.1		1958
1959	812.9	437.8	54.4		1.3	214.0	28.5	76.2	0.7		53.9	6.7		0.2	26.3	3.5	9.4	0.1		1959
1960	885.9	506.6	54.1		1.9	215.0	29.3	78.1	0.9		57.2	6.1		0.2	24.3	3.3	8.8	0.1		1960
1961	1 063.8	587.6	58.3		4.6	256.4	28.2	127.5	1.2		55.2	5.5		0.4	24.1	2.7	12.0	0.1		1961
1962	1 209.5	686.6	68.0		6.8	296.7	30.5	118.4	2.5		56.8	5.6		0.6	24.5	2.5	9.8	0.2		1962
1963	1 312.2	757.4	73.5		13.6	303.5	37.1	122.7	4.4		57.7	5.6		1.0	23.1	2.8	9.4	0.3		1963
1964	1 497.1	883.1	85.3	9.4	18.4	319.0	41.7	133.2	7.0		59.0	5.7	0.6	1.2	21.3	2.8	8.9	0.5		1964
1965	1 731.8	1 023.3	92.2	67.8	24.2	333.6	43.5	137.7	9.5		59.1	5.3	3.9	1.4	19.3	2.5	8.0	0.6		1965
1966	2 052.9	1 281.7	103.6	84.2	41.1	332.8	46.3	150.4	12.8		62.4	5.1	4.1	2.0	16.2	2.3	7.3	0.6		1966
1967	2 434.3	1 550.0	113.1	120.8	66.4	346.6	56.2	163.9	17.3		63.7	4.7	5.0	2.7	14.2	2.3	6.7	0.7		1967
1968	2 868.8	1 820.8	134.5	131.9	140.5	359.0	71.0	187.5	23.6		63.5	4.7	4.6	4.9	12.5	2.5	6.5	0.8		1968
1969	3 146.2	2 066.0	140.2	141.8	137.7	352.2	70.1	210.7	27.5		65.7	4.5	4.5	4.4	11.2	2.2	6.7	0.9		1969
1970	3 613.9	2 471.0	166.7	183.5	113.2	358.8	61.2	227.9	31.6		68.4	4.6	5.1	3.1	9.9	1.7	6.3	0.9		1970
1971	4 386.6	3 110.8	189.4	223.0	120.1	400.3	60.8	246.0	36.2		70.9	4.3	5.1	2.7	9.1	1.4	5.6	0.8		1971
1972	5 371.3	3 806.2	229.0	284.5	199.4	432.3	65.4	300.2	42.8	11.5	70.9	4.3	5.3	3.7	8.1	1.2	5.6	0.8	0.2	1972
1973	6 370.0	4 690.0	264.2	309.3	173.8	439.4	65.6	346.3	50.9	30.5	73.6	4.2	4.9	2.7	6.9	1.0	5.4	0.8	0.5	1973
1974	8 165.8	6 163.2	313.9	341.8	172.1	618.7	71.4	384.5	58.9	41.3	75.5	3.8	4.2	2.1	7.6	0.9	4.7	0.7	0.5	1974
1975	10 386.6	7 759.2	396.2	376.8	224.3	941.7	79.8	461.9	105.9	49.8	74.7	3.8	3.6	2.2	9.1	0.8	4.5	1.0	0.5	1975
1976	13 031.9	9 711.0	450.7	427.6	470.3	1 117.3	101.0	549.9	148.3	55.8	74.5	3.5	3.3	3.6	8.6	0.8	4.2	1.1	0.4	1976
1977	15 932.4	11 728.8	478.9	406.4	842.8	1 384.5	124.1	622.4	246.2	98.3	73.6	3.0	2.6	5.3	8.7	0.8	3.9	1.6	0.6	1977
1978	18 108.8	13 173.2	567.9	396.6	1 211.0	1 482.3	149.6	666.1	311.9	150.2	72.7	3.1	2.2	6.7	8.2	0.8	3.7	1.7	0.8	1978
1979	19 782.0	14 657.6	608.7	394.7	1 058.6	1 662.6	150.5	723.7	336.4	189.2	74.1	3.1	2.0	5.4	8.4	0.8	3.7	1.7	1.0	1979
1980	22 440.7	17 033.5	712.4	396.1	817.0	1 873.9	156.8	798.3	409.4	243.3	75.9	3.2	1.8	3.6	8.4	0.7	3.6	1.8	1.1	1980
1981	25 983.8	19 811.0	805.6	400.0	963.9	2 148.6	184.8	910.6	459.0	299.8	76.3	3.1	1.5	3.7	8.3	0.7	3.5	1.8	1.2	1981

Table 7

Expenditure on Major Pension Programmes

at current prices (in million FM)

Year	National Pensions							Private Sector Pensions						Public Sector Pensions				Total	Year
	Total	Old age	Invalid.	Sur-vivors'	Un-empl.	Front veter-ans	Hous. allow.	Total	Old age	Invalid.	Sur-vivors'	Un-empl.	Farm clos.	Total	State pensions Old age, invalid., unempl.	State pensions Sur-vivors'	Local gov. pens.		
1950	11.5														29.0				1950
1951	19.5																		1951
1952	46.8																		1952
1953	67.6																		1953
1954	69.7																		1954
1955	76.0													75.0	62.0	10.0	3.0	151.0	1955
1956	100.1																		1956
1957	254.7	182.7	72.0																1957
1958	288.5																		1958
1959	299.6																		1959
1960	340.7	245.1	95.6											148.0	115.2	17.8	15.0	488.7	1960
1961	398.4													175.3	125.2	19.1	31.0	573.7	1961
1962	469.4													197.9	142.6	22.3	33.0	667.3	1962
1963	504.8							2.9	0.9	2.0				226.9	161.8	25.1	40.0	705.6	1963
1964	579.1							12.6	4.7	7.9				268.2	190.0	29.2	49.0	859.9	1964
1965	669.5	498.1	171.4					28.6	11.3	17.3				299.6	210.7	31.9	57.0	997.7	1965
1966	847.4	631.4	216.0					53.0	21.6	31.4				345.7	240.8	35.9	69.0	1 246.1	1966
1967	983.2	722.4	260.8					83.3	35.9	44.8	2.6			442.8	285.5	41.3	116.0	1 509.3	1967
1968	1 097.9	797.3	300.6					134.8	56.0	69.2	9.6			545.4	351.0	52.4	142.0	1 778.1	1968
1969	1 197.0	858.8	329.1	9.1				202.3	88.6	95.0	18.7			626.1	400.6	59.5	166.0	2 025.4	1969
1970	1 372.7	930.1	378.9	63.7			21.6	276.9	124.0	122.8	30.1			739.9	469.2	71.7	199.0	2 389.5	1970
1971	1 684.7	1 121.3	472.7	71.6	0.1	19.0	36.5	393.6	173.3	175.4	44.8	0.1		876.5	552.3	84.2	240.0	2 954.8	1971
1972	1 941.5	1 234.2	543.5	78.6	1.0	84.2	45.3	579.5	246.5	266.9	65.5	0.6		1 080.0	673.7	103.3	303.0	3 601.0	1972
1973	2 366.7	1 505.8	676.7	89.1	2.3	92.8	58.9	778.4	324.8	364.3	87.9	1.3		1 295.0	804.8	121.2	369.0	4 440.1	1973
1974	3 204.2	2 012.4	939.5	119.9	4.9	127.5	104.9	1 049.9	436.0	491.9	119.5	2.3	0.2	1 599.8	976.0	160.8	463.0	5 853.7	1974
1975	3 852.6	2 404.0	1 157.4	140.2	6.4	144.6	133.7	1 478.4	637.2	651.3	172.7	3.2	14.0	2 064.0	1 236.6	220.4	607.0	7 381.0	1975
1976	4 492.6	2 824.5	1 341.9	158.4	7.8	160.0	163.2	2 136.1	921.4	927.3	251.4	5.0	31.0	2 621.6	1 555.7	276.9	789.0	9 219.3	1976
1977	5 082.2	3 233.6	1 475.8	174.2	10.2	188.4	189.8	2 915.5	1 278.0	1 244.4	346.5	9.6	37.0	3 158.5	1 851.9	332.6	974.0	11 119.2	1977
1978	5 557.2	3 542.6	1 544.6	185.8	15.6	268.6	212.9	3 440.2	1 536.2	1 415.6	420.0	20.4	48.0	3 514.1	2 048.8	369.3	1 096.0	12 463.5	1978
1979	5 902.5	3 810.9	1 585.4	193.0	30.8	282.4	240.0	4 083.3	1 871.8	1 583.7	513.1	52.7	62.0	3 907.6	2 260.7	412.9	1 234.0	13 831.4	1979
1980	6 887.2	4 485.8	1 794.0	218.8	75.0	313.6	276.4	4 843.8	2 231.0	1 784.1	618.6	127.1	83.0	4 417.6	2 531.2	474.4	1 412.0	16 065.6	1980
1981	7 930.4	5 122.8	2 005.0	263.3	114.8	424.5	372.3	5 734.4	2 685.1	2 020.9	750.1	168.3	110.0	5 136.8	2 951.6	546.2	1 639.0	18 691.6	1981

Table 8

Expenditure on Major Pension Programmes

at constant (1975) prices (in million FM)

Year	National Pensions: Total	Old age	Invalid.	Survivors'	Unempl.	Front veterans	Hous. allow.	Private Sector Pensions: Total	Old age	Invalid.	Survivors'	Unempl.	Farm clos.	Public Sector Pensions: Total	State pensions: Old age, invalid., unempl.	State pensions: Survivors'	Local gov. pens.	Total Pensions	Year
1950	55.3														139.5				1950
1951	80.5																		1951
1952	185.6																		1952
1953	264.6																		1953
1954	277.3																		1954
1955	313.1													309.0	255.4	41.2	12.4	622.1	1955
1956	369.4																		1956
1957	828.2	594.1	234.1																1957
1958	859.7																		1958
1959	879.6																		1959
1960	968.6	696.8	271.8											420.7	327.5	50.6	42.6	1 389.3	1960
1961	1 112.7													489.6	349.7	53.3	86.6	1 602.3	1961
1962	1 255.2													529.1	381.3	59.6	88.2	1 784.3	1962
1963	1 287.2							7.4	2.3	5.1				578.6	412.6	64.0	102.0	1 873.2	1963
1964	1 337.7							29.1	10.9	18.2				619.6	438.9	67.5	113.2	1 986.4	1964
1965	1 476.2	1 098.3	377.9					63.0	24.9	38.1				660.6	464.6	70.3	125.7	2 199.8	1965
1966	1 797.3	1 339.2	458.1					112.4	45.8	66.6				733.1	510.7	76.1	146.3	2 642.8	1966
1967	1 974.3	1 450.6	523.7					167.3	72.1	90.0	5.2			889.1	573.3	82.9	232.9	3 030.7	1967
1968	2 034.4	1 477.4	557.0					249.8	103.8	128.2	17.8			1 010.6	650.4	97.1	263.1	3 294.8	1968
1969	2 167.8	1 555.3	596.0	16.5				366.4	160.5	172.0	33.9			1 133.9	725.5	107.8	300.6	3 668.1	1969
1970	2 420.1	1 639.8	668.0	112.3			38.1	488.2	218.6	216.5	53.1			1 304.4	827.2	126.4	350.8	4 212.7	1970
1971	2 790.0	1 856.9	782.8	118.6	0.2	31.5	60.4	651.9	287.0	290.5	74.2	0.2		1 451.4	914.6	139.4	397.4	4 893.3	1971
1972	3 001.6	1 908.1	840.3	121.5	1.5	130.2	70.0	895.9	381.1	412.6	101.3	0.9		1 669.6	1 041.5	159.7	468.4	5 567.1	1972
1973	3 273.1	2 082.5	935.9	123.2	3.2	128.3	81.5	1 076.4	449.2	503.8	121.6	1.8		1 790.9	1 113.0	167.6	510.3	6 140.4	1973
1974	3 774.5	2 370.6	1 106.7	141.2	5.8	150.2	123.6	1 236.8	513.6	579.5	140.8	2.7	0.2	1 884.5	1 149.7	189.4	545.4	6 893.6	1974
1975	3 852.6	2 404.0	1 157.4	140.2	6.4	144.6	133.7	1 478.5	637.2	651.3	172.8	3.2	14.0	2 064.0	1 236.6	220.4	607.0	7 381.1	1975
1976	3 931.0	2 471.4	1 174.2	138.6	6.8	140.0	142.8	1 869.1	806.2	811.4	220.0	4.4	27.1	2 293.9	1 361.2	242.3	690.4	8 066.9	1976
1977	3 943.8	2 509.3	1 145.2	135.2	7.9	146.2	147.3	2 262.4	991.7	965.7	268.9	7.4	28.7	2 451.0	1 437.1	258.1	755.8	8 628.5	1977
1978	4 012.3	2 557.8	1 115.2	134.1	11.3	193.9	153.7	2 483.8	1 109.1	1 022.1	303.2	14.7	34.7	2 537.1	1 479.2	266.6	791.3	8 998.5	1978
1979	3 972.4	2 564.7	1 067.0	129.9	20.7	190.1	161.5	2 748.0	1 259.7	1 065.8	345.3	35.5	41.7	2 629.9	1 521.5	277.9	830.5	9 308.6	1979
1980	4 152.9	2 704.9	1 081.8	131.9	45.2	189.1	166.7	2 920.7	1 345.3	1 075.8	373.0	76.6	50.0	2 663.8	1 526.3	286.1	851.4	9 687.4	1980
1981	4 266.7	2 756.1	1 078.7	141.7	61.8	228.4	200.3	3 085.1	1 444.6	1 087.2	403.6	90.5	59.2	2 763.7	1 588.0	293.9	881.8	10 056.3	1981

Table 9

Expenditure on Sickness and Health

Year	at current prices (in million FM)					at constant (1975) prices (in million FM)					Year
	Sickness cash benefits	Refunds of medical costs	Total sickness insurance	Health/ hospital services	Total sickness/ health	Sickness cash benefits	Refunds of medical costs	Total sickness insurance	Health/ hospital services	Total sickness/ health	
1950			4.8	62.9	67.7			23.1	302.5	325.6	1950
1951			6.8	83.3	90.1			28.1	343.8	371.9	1951
1952			7.1	99.4	106.5			28.2	394.2	422.4	1952
1953			7.3	104.8	112.1			28.6	410.2	438.8	1953
1954			7.9	113.8	121.7			31.4	452.8	484.2	1954
1955			8.5	137.0	145.5			35.0	564.4	599.4	1955
1956			9.3	159.9	169.2			34.3	590.0	624.3	1956
1957			10.3	187.1	197.4			33.5	608.4	641.9	1957
1958			11.4	232.5	243.9			34.0	692.9	762.9	1958
1959			12.6	249.9	262.5			37.0	733.7	770.7	1959
1960			14.3	273.8	288.1			40.7	778.4	819.1	1960
1961			15.9	307.2	323.1			44.4	858.0	902.4	1961
1962			17.1	349.6	366.7			45.7	934.8	980.5	1962
1963			17.8	409.9	427.7			45.4	1 045.2	1 090.6	1963
1964	9.4	12.9	50.7	489.7	540.4	21.6	29.8	117.1	1 131.2	1 248.3	1964
1965	67.8	61.5	129.3	597.6	726.9	149.4	135.5	284.9	1 317.7	1 602.6	1965
1966	84.2	74.8	159.0	689.5	848.5	178.6	158.7	337.3	1 462.4	1 799.7	1966
1967	120.8	139.5	260.3	791.8	1 052.1	242.5	280.1	522.6	1 589.9	2 112.5	1967
1968	131.9	174.9	306.8	994.6	1 301.4	244.4	324.1	568.5	1 843.0	2 411.5	1968
1969	141.8	198.4	340.2	1 133.5	1 473.7	256.7	359.3	616.0	2 052.8	2 668.8	1969
1970	183.5	229.1	412.6	1 267.8	1 680.4	323.6	403.8	727.4	2 235.1	2 962.5	1970
1971	223.0	279.7	502.7	1 485.6	1 988.3	369.2	463.2	832.4	2 460.2	3 292.6	1971
1972	284.5	353.2	637.7	1 892.1	2 529.8	439.8	546.1	985.9	2 925.2	3 911.1	1972
1973	309.3	428.6	737.9	2 317.0	3 054.9	427.8	592.7	1 020.5	3 204.4	4 224.9	1973
1974	341.8	551.3	893.1	2 929.9	3 823.0	402.6	649.4	1 052.0	3 451.4	4 503.4	1974
1975	376.8	658.3	1 035.1	3 878.6	4 913.7	376.8	658.3	1 035.1	3 878.6	4 913.7	1975
1976	427.6	826.7	1 254.3	4 686.9	5 941.2	374.2	723.4	1 097.6	4 101.0	5 198.6	1976
1977	406.4	956.5	1 362.9	5 346.2	6 709.1	315.4	742.2	1 057.6	4 148.7	5 206.3	1977
1978	396.6	963.5	1 360.1	5 902.8	7 262.9	286.3	695.6	981.9	4 261.8	5 243.7	1978
1979	394.7	1 053.6	1 448.3	6 634.2	8 082.5	265.7	709.1	974.8	4 464.8	5 439.6	1979
1980	396.1	1 187.5	1 583.6	7 782.0	9 365.6	238.9	716.0	954.9	4 692.5	5 647.4	1980
1981	400.0	1 418.6	1 818.6	9 026.6	10 845.2	215.2	763.2	978.4	4 856.3	5 834.7	1981

Table 10

Expenditure on Children and Families

Year	Child allow.	Special child allow.	Family allow.	Total child/ fam. all.	Maternity allow.	Family serv-ices	Total family	Childr. tax credits	Total child/ fam. all.	Maternity allow.	Family serv-ices	Total family	Childr. tax credits	Year
	at current prices (in million FM)								at constant (1975) prices (in million FM)					
1950	101.6		5.8	107.4		23.4	186.2	17.0	516.5		112.5	895.4	81.8	1950
1951	160.2		5.7	165.9		34.1	236.1	20.0	684.7		140.7	974.4	82.5	1951
1952	187.9		5.7	193.6		40.2	277.8	25.0	767.8		159.4	1 101.8	99.2	1952
1953	191.9		5.9	197.8		44.5	292.9	27.0	774.2		174.2	1 146.4	105.7	1953
1954	194.8		5.8	200.6		46.4	290.2	24.0	798.2		184.6	1 154.7	95.5	1954
1955	197.2		5.9	203.1		53.1	302.2	26.0	836.8		218.8	1 245.1	107.1	1955
1956	199.5		6.0	205.5		66.2	313.6	25.0	758.3		244.3	1 157.1	92.3	1956
1957	202.0		6.0	208.0		73.3	327.2	27.0	676.4		238.4	1 064.0	87.8	1957
1958	203.0		7.5	210.5		77.2	325.0	22.0	627.3		230.1	968.5	65.6	1958
1959	205.3		8.7	214.0		82.4	337.7	24.0	628.3		241.9	991.5	70.5	1959
1960	206.3		8.7	215.0		93.4	355.0	28.0	611.2		265.5	1 009.3	79.6	1960
1961	242.3	5.4	8.7	256.4		96.2	401.6	33.0	716.1		268.7	1 121.7	92.2	1961
1962	275.3	12.7	8.7	296.7		106.6	409.5	90.0	793.4		285.0	1 095.0	240.7	1962
1963	281.6	13.3	8.6	303.5		119.3	430.5	92.0	773.9		304.2	1 097.8	234.6	1963
1964	289.9	15.6	7.8	313.3	5.7	154.9	494.9	99.0	723.7	13.2	357.8	1 143.2	228.7	1964
1965	288.4	14.8	8.6	311.8	21.8	174.5	531.3	105.0	687.5	48.0	384.8	1 171.5	231.5	1965
1966	285.6	14.3	8.1	308.0	24.8	197.4	555.8	114.0	653.3	52.6	418.7	1 178.8	241.8	1966
1967	295.9	14.5	7.1	317.5	29.1	221.8	602.6	122.1	637.6	58.5	445.4	1 210.0	245.2	1967
1968	306.0	16.6	6.5	329.1	29.9	257.7	648.7	131.5	609.8	55.4	477.5	1 202.0	243.7	1968
1969	299.2	14.9	8.7	322.8	29.4	299.9	687.9	141.0	584.6	53.3	543.1	1 245.8	255.4	1969
1970	304.6	12.0	8.4	325.0	33.8	319.2	705.4	154.2	573.0	59.6	562.7	1 243.6	271.9	1970
1971	336.6	5.6	9.9	352.1	48.2	351.6	810.9	164.0	583.1	79.9	582.2	1 342.8	271.6	1971
1972	354.4	12.4	8.1	375.9	56.4	323.8	816.0	171.0	581.1	87.1	500.6	1 261.6	264.4	1972
1973	358.0	14.0	8.1	380.1	59.3	418.1	937.1	154.0	525.7	82.1	578.2	1 296.0	213.0	1973
1974	498.0			498.0	120.7	538.4	1 248.1	103.4	586.6	142.1	634.2	1 470.3	121.8	1974
1975	698.1			698.1	243.6	767.3	1 875.1	333.7	698.1	243.6	767.3	1 875.1	333.7	1975
1976	817.5			817.5	299.8	1 036.3	2 373.9	473.7	715.3	262.3	906.8	2 077.2	414.5	1976
1977	1 061.8			1 061.8	322.7	1 425.6	3 143.5	527.1	824.0	250.4	1 106.3	2 439.4	409.0	1977
1978	1 126.8			1 126.8	355.5	1 614.0	3 586.0	595.3	813.5	256.7	1 165.3	2 589.0	429.8	1978
1979	1 251.6			1 251.6	411.0	1 849.4	4 042.5	640.6	842.3	276.6	1 244.6	2 720.6	431.1	1979
1980	1 435.0			1 435.0	438.9	2 227.5	4 695.1	700.5	865.3	264.7	1 343.2	2 831.1	422.4	1980
1981	1 672.9			1 672.9	475.7	3 108.2	5 459.8	833.2	900.0	255.9	1 672.2	2 937.4	448.3	1981

Table 11 Expenditure on Unemployment

Year	at current prices (in million FM)					at constant (1975) prices (in million FM)					Year
	Unempl. insur./assist.	Public work	Retrain-ing	Empl. services	Total	Unempl. insur./assist.	Public work	Retrain-ing	Empl. services	Total	
1950	0.2	40.5	4.2	0.8	45.7	1.0	194.8	20.2	3.8	219.8	1950
1951	0.3	18.6	4.8	1.0	24.6	1.2	76.7	19.8	4.1	101.5	1951
1952	0.3	23.4	5.1	1.2	30.1	1.2	92.8	20.2	4.8	119.4	1952
1953	0.4	86.0	6.2	1.3	93.9	1.6	336.6	24.3	5.1	367.5	1953
1954	0.5	77.2	5.8	1.4	84.9	2.0	307.2	23.1	5.6	337.8	1954
1955	0.6	56.7	7.3	1.6	66.2	2.5	233.6	30.1	6.6	272.7	1955
1956	0.7	86.0	6.0	2.9	95.6	2.6	317.3	22.1	10.7	352.8	1956
1957	1.2	103.9	7.7	3.8	116.5	3.9	337.9	25.0	12.4	378.9	1957
1958	1.1	107.5	8.9	4.6	122.2	3.3	320.3	26.5	13.7	364.2	1958
1959	1.3	101.5	10.8	5.2	118.8	3.8	298.0	31.7	15.3	348.8	1959
1960	1.9	71.6	6.2	5.5	85.2	5.4	203.6	17.6	15.6	242.2	1960
1961	4.6		8.3	7.4	20.3	12.8		23.2	20.7	56.7	1961
1962	6.8	155.0	7.4	7.8	177.0	18.2	414.5	19.8	20.9	473.3	1962
1963	13.6	180.0	9.7	10.3	213.6	34.7	459.0	24.7	26.3	544.7	1963
1964	18.4	218.0	13.1	12.1	261.6	42.5	503.6	30.3	28.0	604.3	1964
1965	24.2	245.0	14.0	13.8	297.0	53.4	540.2	30.9	30.4	654.9	1965
1966	41.1	264.0	16.8	14.3	236.2	87.2	559.9	35.6	30.3	713.1	1966
1967	66.4	272.0	19.7	19.0	374.6	133.3	546.2	39.6	38.2	752.2	1967
1968	140.5	307.7	18.2	21.3	487.7	260.3	570.2	33.7	39.5	903.7	1968
1969	137.7	112.0	26.1	21.9	297.7	249.4	202.8	47.3	39.7	539.1	1969
1970	113.2	112.4	56.5	25.3	307.4	199.6	198.2	99.6	44.6	541.9	1970
1971	120.1	130.3	82.1	22.0	360.6	198.9	215.8	136.0	36.4	597.2	1971
1972	199.4	196.4	91.5	27.2	520.9	308.3	303.6	141.5	42.1	805.3	1972
1973	173.8	235.7	113.7	34.7	565.8	240.4	326.0	157.2	48.0	782.5	1973
1974	172.1	277.0	125.0	44.8	629.2	202.7	326.3	147.3	52.8	741.2	1974
1975	224.3	319.5	195.8	53.8	808.7	224.3	319.5	195.8	53.8	808.7	1975
1976	470.3	524.6	347.6	62.3	1 421.9	411.5	459.0	304.2	54.5	1 244.2	1976
1977	842.8	527.8	472.6	68.3	1 929.2	654.0	409.6	366.7	53.0	1 497.1	1977
1978	1 211.0	695.1	594.8	78.6	2 599.9	874.3	501.9	429.4	56.7	1 877.1	1978
1979	1 058.6	917.4	693.8	94.3	2 787.6	712.4	617.4	466.9	63.5	1 876.1	1979
1980	817.0	1 020.4	758.3	108.9	2 732.8	492.7	615.3	457.3	65.7	1 647.9	1980
1981	963.9	1 120.6	833.6	126.3	3 080.2	518.6	602.9	448.5	67.9	1 657.1	1981

Table 12

Expenditure on Housing

Year	at current prices (in million FM)						Deflator	at constant (1975) prices (in million FM)						Year
	Housing allow-ances	Interest subvention of state loans	Net expend. on public housing loans	Total	Tax credits for interests on private housing loans	Total incl. tax credits	Building cost index	Housing allow-ances	Interest subvention of state loans	Net expend. on public housing loans	Total	Tax credits for interests on private housing loans	Total	
1950														1950
1951														1951
1952														1952
1953														1953
1954														1954
1955														1955
1956	0.5													1956
1957	0.5													1957
1958	0.6													1958
1959	0.7													1959
1960	0.9	35.7	68.7	105.3	104.8	210.1	31.6	2.6	101.5	217.6	321.7	297.9	619.6	1960
1961	1.2						33.0							1961
1962	2.5	47.8	76.3	126.6	132.6	259.2	34.1	7.0	133.5	223.5	364.0	370.4	734.4	1962
1963	4.4						36.2							1963
1964	7.0	59.7	94.9	161.6	169.1	330.7	38.6	16.2	137.9	245.9	400.0	390.6	790.6	1964
1965	9.5						40.4							1965
1966	14.4	77.5	144.3	236.2	168.0	404.2	41.6	30.5	164.4	346.5	541.4	356.3	897.7	1966
1967							44.1							1967
1968	26.8	72.7	231.1	330.6	194.2	524.8	48.6	49.7	134.7	476.1	660.5	359.9	1 020.4	1968
1969							50.5							1969
1970	54.3	106.8	400.0	561.1	223.9	784.2	53.3	95.7	188.3	749.6	1 033.6	394.7	1 428.3	1970
1971							57.4							1971
1972	90.2	169.7	674.1	934.0	237.2	1 171.2	62.1	139.4	262.4	1 085.3	1 487.1	366.7	1 853.8	1972
1973							72.5							1973
1974	168.9	364.8	1 109.3	1 643.0	785.6	2 428.6	90.0	199.0	429.7	1 232.4	1 861.1	925.4	2 786.5	1974
1975	243.7	444.5	1 459.4	2 147.6	985.0	3 132.6	100.0	243.7	444.5	1 459.4	2 147.6	985.0	3 132.6	1975
1976	317.8	566.7	1 675.0	2 559.5	1 271.6	3 831.1	109.2	278.1	495.9	1 534.3	2 308.3	1 112.6	3 420.9	1976
1977	469.3	617.9	1 928.5	3 015.7	1 455.9	4 471.6	123.5	364.2	479.5	1 562.1	2 405.8	1 129.8	535.6	1977
1978	588.1	628.4	1 910.5	3 127.0	1 485.8	4 610.8	130.2	424.6	453.7	1 467.3	2 345.6	1 072.7	3 418.3	1978
1979	651.0	892.2	2 075.1	3 618.3	1 618.2	5 236.5	143.2	438.1	600.4	1 448.4	2 486.9	1 089.0	3 575.9	1979
1980	790.0	1 087.9	1 952.3	3 830.2	1 847.2	5 677.4	162.4	476.4	656.0	1 202.6	2 335.0	1 113.9	3 448.9	1980
1981	967.3	1 227.6	1 953.9	4 148.8	2 326.9	6 475.7	178.9	520.4	660.4	1 092.3	2 273.1	1 251.9	3 525.0	1981

Table 13

Other Social Expenditure

Year	at current prices (in million FM)					at constant (1975) prices					Year
	Old age welfare	Benefits to war disabled	Occupational insuries insurance	Public assistance	Rehabilitation	Old age welfare	Benefits to war disabled	Occupational injuries insurance	Public assistance	Rehabilitation	
1950	n.d.	53.9	20.3	37.2	4.7	n.d.	259.2	97.6	178.9	22.6	1950
1951	n.d.	59.7	25.7	50.3	5.8	n.d.	246.4	106.1	207.6	23.9	1951
1952	n.d.	57.8	29.6	57.0	6.1	n.d.	229.2	117.4	226.1	24.2	1952
1953	n.d.	55.6	30.5	61.1	6.6	n.d.	217.6	119.4	239.1	25.8	1953
1954	n.d.	55.3	30.2	65.2	6.6	n.d.	220.0	120.2	259.4	26.3	1954
1955	n.d.	62.6	33.9	68.0	7.3	n.d.	257.9	139.7	280.2	30.1	1955
1956	n.d.	75.8	38.0	77.4	9.4	n.d.	279.7	140.2	285.6	34.7	1956
1957	n.d.	73.4	42.0	71.2	10.9	n.d.	238.7	136.6	231.5	35.4	1957
1958	n.d.	74.5	43.4	81.5	11.2	n.d.	222.0	129.3	242.9	33.4	1958
1959	n.d.	76.2	54.4	89.2	12.7	n.d.	223.7	159.7	261.9	37.3	1959
1960	31.3	78.1	54.1	66.4	13.4	89.0	222.0	153.8	188.8	38.1	1960
1961	36.4	127.5	58.3	63.2	13.4	101.7	356.1	162.8	176.5	37.4	1961
1962	46.0	118.4	68.0	59.8	14.8	123.0	316.6	181.8	159.9	39.6	1962
1963	57.1	122.7	73.5	71.5	16.5	145.6	312.9	187.4	182.3	42.1	1963
1964	63.3	133.2	85.3	78.1	20.3	146.2	307.7	197.0	180.4	46.9	1964
1965	69.6	137.7	92.2	92.1	22.4	153.5	303.6	203.3	203.1	49.4	1965
1966	78.8	150.4	103.6	101.8	23.1	167.1	319.0	219.7	215.9	49.0	1966
1967	89.0	163.9	113.1	116.3	26.6	178.7	329.1	227.1	233.5	53.4	1967
1968	113.2	187.5	134.5	126.8	32.0	209.8	347.4	249.2	235.0	59.3	1968
1969	123.4	210.7	140.2	133.4	35.2	223.5	381.6	253.9	241.6	63.7	1969
1970	130.4	227.9	166.7	149.0	40.8	229.9	401.8	293.9	262.7	71.9	1970
1971	191.3	246.0	189.4	136.3	45.7	316.8	407.4	313.6	225.7	75.7	1971
1972	225.7	300.2	229.0	152.3	59.1	348.9	464.1	354.0	235.5	91.4	1972
1973	332.7	346.3	264.2	158.9	74.2	460.1	478.9	365.4	219.8	102.6	1973
1974	375.3	384.5	313.9	186.5	95.3	442.1	452.9	369.8	219.7	112.3	1974
1975	470.6	461.9	396.2	231.4	153.9	470.6	461.9	396.2	231.4	153.9	1975
1976	566.3	549.9	450.7	291.7	177.1	495.5	481.2	394.4	255.2	155.0	1976
1977	710.2	622.4	478.9	346.4	212.6	551.1	483.0	371.6	268.8	165.0	1977
1978	783.9	666.1	567.9	415.8	241.3	566.0	480.9	410.0	300.2	174.1	1978
1979	881.8	723.7	608.7	457.5	273.9	593.5	487.0	410.0	307.9	184.3	1979
1980	1 010.2	798.3	712.4	465.8	325.6	609.2	481.4	429.6	280.9	196.3	1980
1981	1 154.1	910.6	805.6	545.4	400.2	620.9	490.0	433.4	293.4	215.3	1981

Table 14 Financing of Public and Social Security Expenditure

Year	General government receipts, saving and net lending: Total current receipts at current prices	Total current receipts at constant (1975) pr.	Total current receipts as a percentage of GDP	Savings as a percentage of GDP	Net lending as a percentage of GDP	Indirect taxes as % of total receipts	Direct taxes as % of total receipts	Social sec. contrib. as % of total receipts	Social security receipts, Percent distribution: state	municip-alities	employers	insured	Year
1950									46.2	16.1	31.2	6.4	1950
1951									40.5	16.7	35.7	7.1	1951
1952									42.1	17.9	33.7	6.3	1952
1953									48.6	17.1	28.8	5.4	1953
1954									50.0	17.3	27.6	5.1	1954
1955									47.4	17.9	29.5	5.3	1955
1956									45.7	18.5	31.5	4.3	1956
1957									47.5	20.2	27.3	5.1	1957
1958									44.6	20.8	27.7	6.9	1958
1959									42.4	21.2	29.3	7.1	1959
1960	4 808	19 948	30.0	8.2	3.9	44.3	34.1	8.5	37.9	21.1	32.6	8.4	1960
1961	5 242	20 559	28.9	7.3	3.4	44.8	34.4	8.8	40.4	19.1	33.0	7.4	1961
1962	5 845	21 697	30.1	7.4	3.3	43.6	35.2	9.1	37.4	18.7	37.4	6.5	1962
1963	6 201	21 133	29.5	5.1	1.0	42.5	35.8	9.9	33.0	18.8	41.4	7.1	1963
1964	7 391	22 609	31.2	5.9	1.3	39.8	37.3	10.6	31.9	18.1	42.2	7.8	1964
1965	8 417	24 098	32.1	6.3	1.5	39.8	37.4	11.3	30.8	19.2	40.8	9.2	1965
1966	9 365	24 911	33.4	6.2	1.5	39.2	38.6	11.1	35.3	21.6	35.3	7.9	1966
1967	10 846	26 529	35.3	7.2	2.6	39.9	36.9	12.4	31.7	21.4	37.9	9.0	1967
1968	12 496	27 504	35.5	7.0	2.8	40.8	37.0	12.0	36.8	24.1	39.1	9.8	1968
1969	13 865	29 103	34.5	7.0	3.4	40.5	37.5	12.0	32.7	18.9	39.6	8.8	1969
1970	15 647	31 122	34.9	7.6	4.4	38.9	38.4	12.6	30.6	19.0	40.8	9.5	1970
1971	17 985	32 823	36.5	7.9	4.6	38.1	39.2	13.4	24.8	18.6	46.0	10.6	1971
1972	20 827	34 927	36.3	7.5	3.9	38.4	39.7	13.3	27.4	17.3	45.8	9.5	1972
1973	25 786	38 344	36.9	9.3	5.8	36.7	41.0	14.3	24.7	17.2	47.7	10.3	1973
1974	32 372	39 429	36.7	7.9	4.7	35.0	42.1	14.8	24.8	16.4	48.7	10.1	1974
1975	39 475	39 475	38.7	6.6	2.7	33.0	43.2	15.8	25.1	15.4	48.6	11.0	1975
1976	48 624	42 886	42.3	8.2	5.0	31.0	45.7	15.1	25.4	15.1	49.0	10.5	1976
1977	52 869	43 141	41.6	6.4	3.2	33.7	43.1	14.9	26.2	15.1	48.6	10.1	1977
1978	55 302	42 804	39.5	4.3	1.4	36.9	39.6	14.1	29.0	16.1	47.0	7.9	1978
1979	61 550	43 639	38.0	3.3	0.5	38.5	38.6	13.2	30.5	15.4	46.3	7.8	1979
1980	70 536	44 649	37.8	3.6	0.8	38.4	39.7	12.7	31.0	15.3	46.0	7.8	1980
1981									31.2	15.2	45.7	7.9	1981

Table 15

Coverage of Social Insurance Programmes
(insured members in 1,000)

Year	Total pop.	Labour force	Employees	Occupational pension ins.				Occup. injuries ins.		Unemployment ins.			Year
				Private	Public	Total	as % of lab. force	Total	as % of lab. force	Total	as % of employees	unemployed	
1950	4 030				242	242				134			1950
1951	4 065				249	249				134			1951
1952	4 117				257	257				129			1952
1953	4 165				264	264				132			1953
1954	4 211				271	271				172			1954
1955	4 259				278	278				197			1955
1956	4 305				286	286				224			1956
1957	4 343				293	293				216			1957
1958	4 376				300	300				216			1958
1959	4 413	2 080	1 337		307	307	14.8	1 337	64.3	241	18.0	45	1959
1960	4 446	2 128	1 371		315	315	14.8	1 371	64.4	276	20.1	31	1960
1961	4 476	2 147	1 423		321	321	15.0	1 423	66.3	330	23.2	26	1961
1962	4 507	2 160	1 465	538	328	866	40.1	1 465	67.8	384	26.2	28	1962
1963	4 540	2 158	1 471	808	334	1 142	52.9	1 471	68.2	417	28.3	32	1963
1964	4 558	2 186	1 530	907	341	1 248	57.1	1 530	70.0	450	29.4	33	1964
1965	4 570	2 185	1 538	913	348	1 261	57.7	1 538	70.4	474	30.8	30	1965
1966	4 592	2 192	1 557	939	354	1 293	59.0	1 557	71.0	499	32.0	33	1966
1967	4 620	2 177	1 596	970	361	1 331	61.1	1 569	73.3	531	33.3	63	1967
1968	4 633	2 158	1 614	981	368	1 349	62.5	1 614	74.8	573	35.5	85	1968
1969	4 614	2 158	1 630	1 022	374	1 396	64.7	1 630	75.5	657	40.3	61	1969
1970	4 598	2 167	1 667	1 570	381	1 951	90.0	1 667	76.9	796	47.8	41	1970
1971	4 626	2 172	1 688	1 663	397	2 060	94.8	1 688	77.7	907	53.7	49	1971
1972	4 653	2 173	1 727	1 659	413	2 071	95.3	1 727	79.5	1 017	58.9	55	1972
1973	4 679	2 215	1 801	1 684	428	2 112	95.3	1 801	81.3	1 155	64.1	51	1973
1974	4 702	2 268	1 865	1 688	444	2 132	94.0	1 865	82.2	1 214	65.1	39	1974
1975	4 720	2 272	1 897	1 686	460	2 146	94.4	1 897	83.5	1 269	66.9	51	1975
1976	4 731	2 254	1 930	1 648	481	2 129	94.4	1 930	85.6	1 304	67.6	91	1976
1977	4 747	2 248	1 956	1 586	502	2 088	92.9	1 956	87.0	1 342	68.6	137	1977
1978	4 758	2 253	1 976	1 556	522	2 078	92.2	1 976	87.7	1 407	71.2	169	1978
1979	4 771	2 273	1 994	1 603	543	2 146	94.4	1 994	87.7	1 474	73.9	139	1979
1980	4 788	2 315	2 034	1 641	564	2 205	95.2	2 034	87.9	1 528	75.1	112	1980
1981	4 812	2 369	2 090					2 090	88.2	1 561	74.7	125	1981
1982	4 841	2 430	2 148					2 354	96.9	1 593	74.2	150	1982

Table 16

Pensioners
(in 1,000)

Year	National pensioners							Private occup. pensioners					Public occup. pensioners		Year
	old age	inval-idity	surv.	unempl.	old age assistance	inval. assistance	total	old age	inval-idity	surv.	unempl.	total	state	local gov.	
1950	38	55					93						27	n.d.	1950
1951	58	65					123						n.d.	n.d.	1951
1952	78	73			140		291						n.d.	n.d.	1952
1953	96	82			130		310						n.d.	n.d.	1953
1954	115	90			118		323						n.d.	n.d.	1954
1955	131	97			106	24	358						42	n.d.	1955
1956	149	106			94	26	375						n.d.	n.d.	1956
1957	311	114					431						n.d.	n.d.	1957
1958	316	118					440						n.d.	n.d.	1958
1959	325	120					453						n.d.	n.d.	1959
1960	329	122					472						49	n.d.	1960
1961	337	123					483						50	n.d.	1961
1962	344	125					494	0.1	0.1			0.2	52	n.d.	1962
1963	354	128					508	1	2			3	53	n.d.	1963
1964	364	127					518	4	7			11	54	n.d.	1964
1965	373	125					525	10	12			22	56	n.d.	1965
1966	384	130					541	16	20			36	58	n.d.	1966
1967	395	141					563	25	26	3		54	62	25	1967
1968	405	152					585	34	35	7		76	64	28	1968
1969	417	160	54				659	45	45	11		101	69	29	1969
1970	429	172	77				709	61	57	17		135	80	32	1970
1971	444	187	77	0.3			763	82	77	23	0.2	182	89	37	1971
1972	459	208	77	0.5			805	104	102	31	0.5	238	90	40	1972
1973	475	223	74	1			830	126	129	38	1	294	97	44	1973
1974	492	240	72	1			863	150	149	46	1	346	103	48	1974
1975	509	249	71	1			884	174	161	54	1	390	111	52	1975
1976	424	256	70	2			902	197	171	63	2	433	118	55	1976
1977	540	256	68	2			914	220	177	71	2	470	124	59	1977
1978	554	251	67	4			927	243	178	80	5	506	130	64	1978
1979	568	247	64	7			935	264	177	88	8	537	136	66	1979
1980	577	243	62	13			940	283	176	96	14	569	143	71	1980
1981	587	240	60	17			946	304	174	104	18	600	148	74	1981
1982								322	171	112	23	628	152	79	1982

Table 17

Other Welfare Clienteles
(in 1,000)

Year	Occup. injuries (no. of cases)	Sickness cash b.	Maternity allow.	Child allowances		Unemployment ins.		Public assistance			Year
				children	families	total unempl.	beneficaries	home help	incl. family	total incl. other	
1950	98			1 262	592			57 018	108 523	176 709	1950
1951	110			1 286	599			53 521	101 391	173 818	1951
1952	108			1 311	607			55 606	108 125	184 761	1952
1953	106			1 336	616			59 891	126 626	212 627	1953
1954	115			1 335	624			62 761	132 927	224 240	1954
1955	122			1 371	631			56 676		291 096	1955
1956	121			1 390	638			58 985		307 632	1956
1957	120			1 400	643			57 116		316 151	1957
1958	112			1 415	648			69 679		366 074	1958
1959	123			1 427	654			71 746		389 717	1959
1960	143			1 433	657			66 249		373 382	1960
1961	156			1 431	658	26		60 409		335 031	1961
1962	160			1 404	649	28	3.8	60 758		329 057	1962
1963	157			1 381	646	32	8.0	67 127		337 571	1963
1964	163	n.d.	n.d.	1 357	641	33	10.6	69 740		328 105	1964
1965	163	n.d.	n.d.	1 335	638	30	11.7	68 800		319 947	1965
1965								81 200	193 700	269 570	1965
1966	170	n.d.	n.d.	1 310	640	33	14.6	83 600	208 600	267 708	1966
1967	167	n.d.	n.d.	1 294	638	63	24.7	87 900	204 800	269 971	1967
1968	160	298	87	1 276	640	85		97 800	252 700	285 795	1968
1969	179	335	79	1 250	640	61	29.2	95 800	212 200	255 071	1969
1970	206	367	75	1 218	637	41	20.4	91 300	192 200	235 870	1970
1971	220	411	73	1 189	637	49	25.4	98 000	208 900	258 648	1971
1972	231	488	71	1 164	638	55	37.6	100 700	210 300	255 950	1972
1973	242	449	68	1 149	641	51	32.1	97 600	200 600	239 603	1973
1974	258	444	75	1 131	645	39	25.1	90 426	184 006	212 995	1974
1975	241	420	92	1 118	649	51	33.7	85 598	170 117	192 006	1975
1976	232	412	94	1 105	651	91	57.9	86 286	170 289	193 051	1976
1977	208	383	92	1 084	645	137	96.9	90 405	178 168	198 560	1977
1978	197	359	90	1 069	641	169	132.7	90 663	173 345	194 201	1978
1979	205	364	97	1 053	636	139	111.5	87 262	160 590	181 960	1979
1980	220	369	96	1 038	627	112	79.8	82 154	148 299	167 985	1980
1981	217	370	99	1 032	622	125	93.8	79 624	143 841	162 791	1981
1982	210			1 026		150	114.6				1982

Table 18

Indicators of Services

Year	For old people (in 1,000)				For children (in 1,000)				For sick persons (in 1,000)		Housing		Education		Year
	pop. 65+	places in homes	places in service dwellings	home helpers	pop. 0–6	pop. 0–16	places in day nurseries	places in family day care	physicians	beds in public hospitals	dwellings financed by state loans or interest subsidies in 1,000	dwellings financed by state loans or interest subsidies as % of all dwellings	people passed matriculation examination in 1,000	people passed matriculation examination as % of pop. 19	
1950		19.8				1 261			2.0	26.9			4.1	6.4	1950
1951						1 285			2.1	27.4			4.1	6.7	1951
1952						1 309			2.1	28.3			4.1	7.1	1952
1953						1 333			2.2	28.6			4.1	6.8	1953
1954						1 356			2.3	29.3			4.5	7.2	1954
1955		23.0			634	1 371			2.4	31.0			4.7	7.5	1955
1956					621	1 391			2.5	31.9			5.0	7.7	1956
1957					611	1 398			2.6	33.1			5.6	8.1	1957
1958					600	1 413			2.6	34.4			6.2	8.8	1958
1959					590	1 425			2.7	37.1			6.7	11.2	1959
1960	328	24.9			583	1 432			2.8	38.5	12.3	39.1	7.7	9.3	1960
1961	335				574	1 432			3.0	40.2	12.6	33.9	8.4	14.8	1961
1962	341				568	1 402			3.1	41.4	10.0	26.7	9.6	13.8	1962
1963	352				562	1 350			3.3	42.2	10.8	24.4	10.1	13.9	1963
1964	361				557	1 358			3.4	43.1	11.7	33.1	11.6	12.8	1964
1965	370	25.0			553	1 348	20.4		3.6	44.0	11.6	31.7	13.4	13.5	1965
1966	380	25.4			549	1 322	21.7		3.8	45.3	14.3	39.2	14.6	14.6	1966
1967	391	25.6			545	1 303	23.0		4.0	46.2	14.4	37.3	15.8	15.9	1967
1968	401	25.6			537	1 288	23.8		4.2	47.3	16.0	44.5	16.5	17.2	1968
1969	413	25.5			522	1 264	24.4		4.5	48.6	20.3	50.2	17.4	18.8	1969
1970	428	25.7			489	1 232	26.2		4.8	49.1	21.5	43.2	18.3	22.0	1970
1971	442	25.4		3.9	475	1 198	28.8	3.4	5.1	50.9	23.0	45.6	19.9	23.1	1971
1972	458	25.6		4.7	461	1 163	33.5	5.0	5.5	49.6	32.6	54.4	21.4	25.6	1972
1973	475	25.9		5.4	446	1 146	37.0	5.6	5.8	50.2	37.2	59.7	23.2	27.6	1973
1974	492	25.6	10.1	5.8	436	1 133	43.9	13.2	6.2	50.5	35.4	48.5	23.8	28.8	1974
1975	509	26.0	11.3	6.2	431	1 119	50.0	21.8	6.7	51.4	36.6	52.7	24.8	29.9	1975
1976	524	26.0	12.3	6.4	431	1 102	56.2	26.6	7.1	52.7	38.3	66.7	25.4	31.9	1976
1977	541	26.3	13.3	7.0	431	1 082	62.1	30.9	7.6	53.0	33.8	59.3	26.9	35.7	1977
1978	554	26.0	14.1	7.2	433	1 067	66.7	35.5	8.1	54.3	34.2	61.9	26.2	34.0	1978
1979	568	25.9	15.7	7.5	438	1 043	70.8	41.0	8.5	55.4	33.6	66.8	27.2	35.8	1979
1980	577	25.4	16.8	8.0	445	1 038	75.3	48.0	9.0	55.5	29.2	58.8	28.7	37.8	1980
1981	586	25.6	17.4			1 031	79.4	54.9			24.7	52.5			1981
1982															1982

Table 19 Disposable Income of Households by Socio-Economic Group

Socio-economic status of household	1966 in 1,000 FM	1966 as % of all househ.	1971 in 1,000 FM	1971 as % of all househ.	1976 in 1,000 FM	1976 as % of all househ.	1977 in 1,000 FM	1977 as % of all househ.	1978 in 1,000 FM	1978 as % of all househ.	1979 in 1,000 FM	1979 as % of all househ.
All households	11.3	100	16.2	100	34.7	100	38.3	100	42.0	100	45.8	100
Economically active households	12.4	110	18.4	114	39.6	114	44.6	117	49.1	117	54.4	119
Farmers	10.0	89	16.6	103	38.3	110	44.9	117	49.8	119	53.7	117
Employers and self-employed outside agriculture	15.3	135	20.1	124	41.9	121	46.2	121	55.1	131	58.7	128
Managers and upper white collar employees	20.7	183	29.6	183	52.0	150						
White collar workers with graduate university degree					59.4	171	67.7	177	72.9	174	80.3	175
White collar workers with vocational educ.					42.5	123	48.7	127	53.0	126	59.3	130
Lower white collar employees	13.5	120	18.0	111	37.1	107						
Other white collar workers					35.6	103	39.1	102	43.6	104	49.7	109
Workers	10.7	95	16.8	104	37.7	109	41.8	109	45.4	108	50.1	109
Economically inactive households	6.0	53	9.5	59	20.9	60	20.9	55	23.6	56	23.5	51

Table 20 Distribution of Parliamentary Seats by Party Finland

Party	1945	1948	1951	1954	1958	1962	1966	1970	1972	1975	1979	1983
SKDL (Communists)	49	38	43	43	50	47	41	36	37	40	35	26
SDP (Social Democrats)	50	54	53	54	48	38	55	52	55	54	52	57
Other Socialists					3	2	7					
Socialists	99	92	96	97	101	87	103	88	92	94	87	83
KES (Centre Party)	49	56	51	53	48	53	49	36	35	39	36	38
KOK (National Coalition)	28	33	28	24	29	32	26	37	34	35	47	44
Other Bourgeois	24	19	25	26	22	28	22	39	39	32	30	35
Bourgeois	101	108	104	103	99	113	97	112	108	106	113	117
Total	200	200	200	200	200	200	200	200	200	200	200	200

Table 21 Members of Central Interest Organizations (in 1,000)

	Central Organization of Finnish Trade Unions (SAK)	Confederation of Salaried Employees (TVK)	Confederation of Technical Employees' Organizations (STTK)	Central Organization of Professional Associations (AKAVA)	Central Union of Agricultural Producers (MTK)
1950	269	63	8	12	111
1951	261	66	10	14	118
1952	242	64	10	18	121
1953	240	65	10	19	121
1954	249	65	10	18	123
1955	269	78	12	19	129
1956	289	102	12	20	133
1957	239	107	13	21	140
1958	239	110	13	22	144
1959	251	111	12	22	150
1960	282	114	11	23	152
1961	290	119	12	23	155
1962	311	135	12	24	158
1963	325	145	13	26	159
1964	337	148	14	28	162
1965	353	152	16	29	162
1966	367	162	18	31	166
1967	383	166	19	39	167
1968	393	174	21	40	165
1969	566	194	24	41	166
1970	650	211	27	42	166
1971	722	242	37	43	164
1972	794	259	56	55	
1973	847	276	69	63	
1974	885	281	76	72	
1975	921	293	85	104	157
1976	951	280	89	130	154
1977	961	288	91	146	152
1978	981	303	92	150	150
1979	1 004	317	98	157	148
1980	1 032	324	115	171	146
1981	1 039	331	115	184	142

Notes to and sources for appendix tables

Tables 1 and 2

New SNA is based on the UN recommendation System of National Accounts (SNA)' in 1968; total public expenditure A is public expenditure according to old SNA; total public expenditure B is public expenditure according to new SNA; total public expenditure C is total public expenditure B plus private sector occupational pensions (see Table 7). For constant prices, GDP has been deflated by GDP deflator, public expenditure by public consumption deflator; GDP and public consumption deflators have been calculated from the national statistics' sources given in Table 1; public consumption deflator is based on the cost of consumption per fixed consumption unit.

Sources: (1), pp. 6,8; (2), pp. 6,8; (3), pp. 244-245, for old SNA; (4), pp. 12-15; (5), pp. 12-13; (6), for new SNA; (7), p. 89; (8), p. 89 for total public expenditure B; (1), pp. 60-69; (9), pp. 24-25, 51-52 for total public expenditure A; (10), for old age invalidity, unemployment and survivors' pensions of private sector occupational pensions; (11), for change-of-generation and farm closure pensions of private sector occupational pensions; (12), p. 262 for cost of living index.

Table 3

The distribution of public expenditure by economic function for the years 1950-1962 is based on old SNA; for years 1962-1980, on new SNA; public expenditure by purpose includes public consumption expenditure only; purpose I is based on old SNA, purpose II on new SNA.

Sources: (1) pp. 59-60; (9), pp. 24-25, 51-52, for public expenditure by economic function, 1950-1962; (7), p. 89; (8), p. 89, for public expenditure by economic function 1962-1980; (1), p. 61; (9), p. 53, for public consumption expenditure by purpose I; (5), p. 31 for

Table 4

Figures for 1981 are preliminary. In calculating the figures at constant prices, the public consumption deflator (see Table 2) has been used for health, education and social services' expenditure, and the cost of living index (Table 2) for income maintenance expenditure. Expenditure equals the total of all programmes in Table 6; health expenditure (Table 9) includes expenditure on health and hospital services, refunds on medical costs (not sickness cash benefits which are included under income maintenance); education expenditure is our estimate based on national accounts statistics; public consumption expenditure on education according to SNA includes expenditure on research and development and recreation and cultural services; our estimate excludes these forms of expenditure and is arrived at in the following way - data on proper education expenditure for 1975-1979 (National Accounts Statistics, Central Statistical Office of Finland), in 1975 this was 84 percent of total education expenditure (old SNA); data for 1950-1974 was obtained by multiplying old SNA figures by .84, i.e. we assumed that the proportions of education expenditure and research and development expenditure and recreation and cultural expenditure remained the same in the postwar period; study allowances and study loans are not included under education expenditure but under income maintenance; expenditure on social services includes (a) expenditure on family services (Table 10) and central family policy administration and is calculated as total expenditure on children and families (Table 10) minus family, child and maternity allowances and minus housing allowances (included under income maintenance, Table 6); (b) expenditure on public work, training and services for the unemployed (Table 11), and central employment administration, calculated as total unemployment expenditure (Table 11) minus expenditure on unemployment insurance, and assistance included under income maintenance (Table 6); (c) expenditure on public and unspecified assistance (Table 13) minus expenditure on assistance in cash included under income maintenance (Table 6); (d) expenditure on rehabilitation and employment of partially disabled (Table 13) and on welfare for the old (Table 13). Social expenditure I is the sum of income maintenance, health, education and social services.

Social expenditure II includes in addition such housing expenditure as interest subvention on state loans and net expenditure on public housing loans (Table 12).

Sources: see sources to Tables 6, 9-13.

Table 5

In calculating the major components of social expenditure as percentages of GDP, GDP figures (old SNA) have been used for the period 1950-1962 and new SNA data for 1962-1981 (Table 1); social expenditure components as percentages of public expenditure are based on the public expenditure concept A (1950-1962), concept B (1962-1981), and concept C (1963-1981) (Table 1).

Sources: see sources to Tables 1 and 4.

Table 6

Figures for 1981 are preliminary. Pensions: expenditure on major pension schemes (Table 7), administrative costs and some minor schemes (national burial grants, rehabilitation and health care under the national invalidity pension scheme, compulsory employee group life insurance, and invalidity assistance), which account for the difference in totals between Tables 6 and 7.

Sources: 1950-1974; (13), p. 77; to which we have added the following pension types not included in the original time series: war veterans' pensions and supplements, child care allowances and national pension child increments, and from which we have subtracted voluntary additional pensions; (11), pp. 29, 59-60, source (11) does not give figures for 1951-1954 and 1956-1959, which we have estimated by linear interpolation.
1975-1981; (14); to which we have added survivors' pensions, war veterans' pensions and supplements, child care allowances and national pension child increments, and from which we have subtracted voluntary additional pensions, all given in the source and by Mr. Esa Arajärvi, Ministry of Social Affairs and Health.

Industrial accidents: expenditure on compulsory occupational insurance.
Sources: (14); (15).

Sickness: sickness insurance daily allowances.
Source: (11), p. 71.

Unemployment: unemployment insurance and assistance.
Sources: (14); (15).

Family allowances: expenditure on child allowances, special child allowances (1962-1973), family allowances (1950-1973), and maternity allowances.
Sources: (16)-(19); (11), p. 71.

Social assistance: expenditure on home help only, mainly in cash.
Sources: (21); figures for 1971-72 from Ms. Kyllikki Korpi, National Board of Social Affairs; 1981 figures are our own estimates.

Military and war victims: expenditure on relief to military victims and the relatives of war casualties, not including war veterans' pensions and supplements.
Sources: (14); (15).

Housing allowances: expenditure on housing allowances paid under the Housing Allowances Act, i.e. excluding housing allowances under national pension schemes (included under pensions) and housing allowances included under study allowances.
Source: (22).

Study allowances: expenditure on allowances paid under the 1972 Study Allowance Act, not including study loans.
Source: (23).

Tables 7 and 8

National pensions: expenditure on pensions paid by the Social Insurance Institution under the National Pension Act: old age pensions and assistance; invalidity pensions; survivors' pensions

(widows' and orphans' pensions, child allowances and increments); unemployment pensions; and war veterans' pensions; housing allowances are singled out as a special category, although already included under the various pension schemes.
Sources: (11), pp. 59-60; (24), pp. 59-60, 90.

Private sector pensions: expenditure on compulsory occupational pensions paid to former private sector employees, except those paid under the Seamen's Pension Act: old age, invalidity, unemployment and survivors' pensions.
Sources: (10); (11), p. 29.

Public sector pensions: expenditure on public occupational pensions: state pensions for old age, invalidity and unemployment; state pensions for survivors; local government pensions; not including pensions paid under the Evangelical-Lutheran Church Pension Act, and the orthodox church pension scheme, as well as pensions for employees of the Social Insurance Institution, the Post Office Savings Bank, and the Bank of Finland.

Sources: (24), p. 28 for state pensions in 1950 and 1955; unpublished data from State Treasury for state pensions in 1960-1975; (20), p. 5 for state pensions in 1976-1981; (11), p. 29 for local government pensions. All figures at constant prices in Table 8 deflated by the cost of living index (see Table 2).

Table 9

Sickness cash benefits: expenditure on sickness insurance daily allowances.
Source: (11), p. 71.

Refunds of medical costs: refunds for medicines, treatment, and doctors' fees, and some smaller items paid under sickness insurance.
Source: (11), p. 71.

Total sickness insurance: includes sickness insurance by relief funds and private insurance institutions for 1950-1964; for 1965-1981 expenditure on daily allowances and refunds of medical costs; compulsory employers' compensation payments not included as data are only available from 1974 onwards; maternity allowances are included under family allowances.
Sources: (13), p. 76; (11), p. 71.

Health and hospital services: expenditure on in-patient and out-patient medical services, treatment for drug and alcohol addiction, care of mentally retarded, and all administrative costs of sickness insurance and health services.
Sources: (13), p. 76; (14).

All figures at constant prices are deflated by the cost of living index.

Table 10

Expenditure on children and families: cash benefits (general child allowances, special child allowances, family allowances and maternity allowances), and family services (child day care, public child welfare, school meals, and home helps); total expenditure in addition includes expenditure on central family policy administration; tax credits due to children, which are not included under social expenditure, equal the estimated tax revenue loss of the state and from 1962 municipalities (important change in estimation, 1975).

Sources: (16)-(19); (13), p. 79; (14); (11), p. 71. All figures at constant prices are deflated by the cost of living index.

Table 11

Expenditure on unemployment: unemployment insurance and assistance, public work for the unemployed, retraining, and unemployment services; total expenditure in addition includes the costs of central employment administration; figures for 1960 and 1961 are not comparable because expenditure on public work for the unemployed has only been included for part of 1960.
Sources: (14); (15). All figures at constant prices are deflated by the cost of living index.

Table 12

Housing allowances: include housing allowances paid under the Housing Allowance Act and National Pension Act, in addition to student housing allowances.

Interest subvention: on state housing loans is the difference between market interests and interest rates on state housing loans, i.e. an estimate of the state income loss due to this subvention.

Tax credit: to households on interest paid on private housing loans; is an estimate of state income loss on tax revenue.

Net expenditure on public housing loans: is the difference between annual (gross) state expenditure on housing loans and income received by the state on repayment of loans.
Sources: (25), p. 89; (26), p. 28.

Housing allowances, interest subvention, and tax credit have been deflated by the cost of living index; net expenditure of public housing loans by the construction cost index.
Source: (12), p. 262.

Table 13

Old age welfare: old people's homes, home help services (since 1969) and grants to organizations serving old people.
Sources: (14); (15).

Benefits to war disabled: social expenditure on military or war casualties' relatives, except war veterans' pensions and supplements, included under national pensions.
Sources: (14); (15).

Occupational injury insurance.
Sources: (14); (15).

Public assistance: public and unspecified assistance, including central administration costs of public welfare activities.
Sources: (14); (15).

Rehabilitation: rehabilitation and employment of partially disabled.
Sources: (14); (15).

Table 14

General government receipts, saving and net lending.
Sources: (4), pp. 78-79; (8), p. 89.

Social security contributions.
Sources: (13), p. 82; (14), for years 1974-81, but we have made the following changes - tax credits due to children subtracted from state and municipality contributions, as they do not come under our concept of social expenditure; employers' payments in the case of sickness, employers' franchise payments for employee health services, and additional pension protection have been subtracted from employers' contributions, and (where relevant) contributions by the insured, and from financial surplus.

Table 15

Total population.
Sources: (13), p. 83; (28), p. 40; (29), p. 3.

Labour force and employees.
Sources: (30), pp. 10, 31; (31), pp. 28-32.

Number of persons covered by private occupational pension schemes.
Source: (10).

Number of persons covered by public occupational pension schemes is estimated by the number of employees in the public sector, based on a linear interpolation of census data for 1950, 1960, 1970, 1975, 1980.
Source: (32), p. 83.

The coverage of occupational injuries insurance is the number of employees in the labour force, except for 1982, when farmers became insured.
Source: (31), p. 36 (for farmers), based on the number of people employed in agriculture.

Unemployment insurance total: number of members in unemployment funds.
Source: (33).

The number of unemployed.
Sources: (30); (31).

Table 16

National pensioners: total includes old age assistance (since 1957), child care allowance recipients (since 1970), and war veteran pensioners (since 1971), in addition to other pension types distinguished in Table 16.
Sources: (34), pp. 28-29; (11), p. 45.

Private occupational pensioners: invalidity pensions include partial invalidity pensions since 1973.
Source: (35).

State pensioners.
Sources: (20) for 1950, 1955, 1976-82; (36) for 1960-75.

Local government pensioners.
Source: (35).

Table 17

Occupational injuries: includes injuries of state employees in the period 1976-1982, and of farmers in 1982.
Sources: (14); (38).

Sickness cash benefits and maternity allowances.
Source: (11), p. 74.

Child allowances: the number of families in receipt of child allowances.
Source: (17).

The number of children receiving child allowances.
Source: (21); (14) for years 1980-1982.

Unemployment insurance: total number of unemployed and the number of unemployment insurance or assistance recipients.
Sources: (30); (31), pp. 28, 65.

Public assistance: in 1955 and 1965 statistics were renewed and figures are not comparable. Total also includes public assistance recipients in various institutions.
Source: (21).

Table 18

Population aged 65+, 0-6 and 0-16 years.
Sources: (13), p. 83; (39); (17).

Services for old people.
Source: (21).

Services for children, places in public day care nurseries and family day care.
Source: (21).

The number of doctors.
Source: (17).

The number of public hospital beds.
Source: (17).

Education.
Source: (40).

Housing production.
Source: (22), pp. 30, 32.

Table 19

Source: (41).

Table 20

Source: (42).

Table 21

Figures for SAK also include members of SAJ in 1960-68; figures for MTK only include farmer members.
Sources: (27), p. 4; (12), pp. 304-305; (28).

Enumerated sources to appendix tables

(1) *National Accounting in Finland 1948-1964.* Central Statistical Office of Finland, Statistical Surveys, No. 43, Helsinki, 1968.

(2) *National Accounts 1964-1976/I-II.* Central Statistical Office of Finland, Statistical Reports, KT 1976:4, Helsinki, 1976.

(3) *Statistical Yearbook of Finland 1978.* Central Statistical Office of Finland, Helsinki, 1979.

(4) *Revised National Accounts for 1960-1978.* Central Statistical Office of Finland, Statistical Surveys, No. 66, Helsinki, 1981.

(5) *National Accounts 1975-1981.* Central Statistical Office of Finland, Statistical Reports, KT 1982:7, Helsinki, 1982.

(6) Figures for 1981 provided by the Central Statistical Office of Finland.

(7) *National Accounts of OECD Countries, 1962-1979,* Vol. II. OECD, Paris, 1982.

(8) *National Accounts Statistics, 1963-1980,* Vol. II. OECD, Paris, 1982.

(9) *National Accounts 1964-1977.* Central Statistical Office of Finland, Statistical Reports, KT 1978:7, Helsinki, 1978.

(10) Statistics provided by the Central Pension Security Institute for the Ministry of Social Affairs and Health, 1962-1981.

(11) *Statistical Yearbook of the Social Insurance Institution 1981.* Social Insurance Institution, Helsinki, 1982.

(12) *Statistical Yearbook of Finland 1981.* Central Statistical Office of Finland, Helsinki, 1982.

(13) *The Development of Social Security in Finland from 1950 to 1977.* Official Statistics of Finland, Special Social Studies XXXII:56, Ministry of Social Affairs and Health, Research Department, Helsinki, 1978.

(14) Social expenditure of social security in 1974 and preliminary data for 1975, and subsequent publications for 1975-1981. Official Statistics of Finland, *Special Social Studies* XXXII:49,53,57,60,70,77,88, Ministry of Social Affairs and Health, Research Department, Helsinki, various years.

(15) *Sosiaalinen aikakauskirja* 1959:1-2; 1960:1-2; 1963:1-2; 1964:5-6; 1965:5-6; 1969:2; 1970:1; 1971:3; 1972:3; 1973:6; 1974:5; 1975:6.

(16) *The Cost of Social Security 1949-1952* . ILO, Geneva.

(17) *Statistical Yearbook of Finland.* Central Statistical Office of Finland, Helsinki, various years.

(18) *Social Welfare 1979.* Official Statistics of Finland, XXIB:23, Central Statistical Office of Finland, Helsinki, 1980.

(19) *Statistical Report 1981*:1. National Board of Social Affairs, Office for Planning and Statistics, Helsinki, 1981.

(20) *Tilastotietoja valtion eläkkeistä ja valtiokonttorin eläkeosaston toiminnasta vuodelta 1980*; the same report for the years 1981 and 1982, Helsinki, various years.

(21) *Social assistance.* Official Statistics of Finland XXIA:7-13, 30-33, Central Statistical Office of Finland, Helsinki, various years; Social Welfare. Official Statistics of Finland XXIB:1-23, Helsinki, various years.

(22) *Statistical Tables of the National Housing Board of Finland 1949-1978*; and the same publication for 1949-1981. National Housing Board of Finland, Helsinki, 1979 and 1983.

(23) Valtiopäivät. Asiakirjat, 1972 II; 1973 II; 1974 II; 1975:A1; 1976:A2; 1977:A2; 1978:A3; 1979:A1; 1980:A2; 1981:A3.

(24) *Statistical Yearbook of the Social Insurance Institution 1980.* Social Insurance Institution, Helsinki, 1981.

(25) Ossi Paukku, Asuntosektorin tukipolitiikka Suomessa vv. 1956-1975, in *Asumisolot ja asumisen tuki Suomessa Asuntoreformiyhdistyksen julkaisuja*, No. 21, Kotka, 1978, p. 89.

(26) Ossi Paukku, *Asumisen tuki 1970-1981 Asuntoreformiyhdistyksen julkaisuja*, No. 22, Helsinki, 1983, p. 28.

(27) Olavi Borg, *Palkansaajien järjestövoiman kasvu 1945-80* University of Tampere, Institute of Political Science, Research reports, No. 56, Tampere, 1980.

(28) Figures for 1981 have been provided directly by the respective organizations, as have all figures for MTK.

(29) *Bulletin of Statistics*, 1983, No. III. Central Statistical Office of Finland, Helsinki, 1983.

(30) Results of the labour force surveys for the years 1959-1975. *Statistical Surveys*, No. 61, Central Statistical Office of Finland, Helsinki, 1978.

(31) *Labour Reports*, 1983, No. 3. Ministry of Labour, Planning Department, Helsinki, 1983.

(32) Occupation and industry; economically active population, *Population and Housing Census 1980*, Vol. IB. Official Statistics of Finland VIC:106. Central Statistical Office of Finland, Helsinki, 1983.

(33) Unpublished data received from Insurance Department, Ministry of Social Affairs and Health.

(34) *Statistical Yearbook of the National Pension Institute of Finland*, 1965. Helsinki, 1967.

(35) Unpublished data from Central Pension Security Institute; *Tilastotietoja työeläkkeen saajista vuodelta 1979* Helsinki, 1980, p. 25; *Työeläkejärjestelmän tilastollinen vuosikirja 1981*, Vol. I, Helsinki, 1982, p. 24; *Työeläkejärjestelmän tilastollinen vuosikirja 1982*, Vol. I, Helsinki, 1983, p. 24.

(36) Unpublished State Treasury mimeo.

(37) Unpublished data from the local government pension authority for the years 1967-74, and *Kunnallinen eläkelaitos. Tilastovuosi 1982*, Helsinki, 1983, for the years 1975-82 (sources for old scheme); *Kunnallinen eläkelaitoksen toimintakertomus vuodelta 1980* Helsinki, 1981, p. 22 for years 1970-74 and *Kunnallinen eläkelaitos. Tilastovuosi 1980*, p. 12 for years 1975-82 (sources for new scheme).

(38) *The Insurance Companies.* Official Statistics of Finland, XXIIA:56-87, Central Statistical Office of Finland, Helsinki, various years.

(39) *Vital Statistics*, 1951-65. Official Statistics of Finland VI:113-149, various years.

(40) Paavo Seppänen, *Finnish Society*. University of Helsinki, Institute of Sociology, Research Reports, No. 166, 1971, p. LVI for years 1950-54; *General secondary education*, Official Statistics of Finland IX:78,82,84,87,90, Central Statistical Office of Finland, Helsinki, various years; *General education 1980/1981* Official Statistics of Finland XA:103, Central Statistical Office of Finland, Helsinki, 1982.

(41) Hannu Uusitalo, Tulopolitiikka ja tulonjako'. *Sosiaalipolitiikka*, Vammala, 1982, p. 96; Income *distribution statistics 1979*. Official Statistics of Finland. XLI:3. Central Statistical Office of Finland, Helsinki, 1982, p. 22.

(42) Jaakko Nousiainen, *Suomen poliittinen järjestelmä* Juva, 1980, p. 152.

Denmark

Lars Nørby Johansen

Institutional Synopsis

Contents

Glossary of abbreviations

ATP	*Arbejdsmarkedets Tillægspension* (Labour Market Supplementary Pension)
EFG	*Erhvervsfaglige Grunduddannelser* (Basic Vocational Training)
HF	*Højere Forberedelseseksamen* (Higher Preparatory Examination)
KVU	*Kortere Videregående Uddannelser* (Shorter Further Education Courses)
SU	*Statens Uddannelsesstøtte* (State Education Fund)

Introduction

The following synopsis will be described mainly along functional as opposed to institutional lines. This is the case for aggregate figures showing the economic importance of various social security schemes. To a certain extent it also holds true concerning the qualitative description of individual schemes. As a consequence, some benefits and services have been taken out of their proper institutional context. However, cross-references should enable the reader to reconstruct social security schemes in institutional terms. The institutional synopsis including the registration of core laws covers only the period 1945-1980. However, the description of the pension scheme has been updated to 1984 in order to include major changes in the pension system. Concerning other legislative changes from 1980-84, see Section V of the country chapter (Recent developments and policy choices: Adjustment or crisis of the welfare state?).

Administrative structure of the social security system

Since the enactment of the 1970 Social Administration Act (*Lov om styrelse af sociale og visse sundhedsmæssige anliggender*), an administratively unified social security system has been built up.

Municipal Social Welfare Committees (*socialudvalg*) constitute the nucleus of this system and are responsible for providing the bulk of social security benefits and related services: public general pensions, daily cash benefits in cases of sickness, maternity, childbirth etc., family and child allowances, social assistance in the form of both cash benefits and services, including a variety a social institutions, and finally, rent subsidies and housing allowances. An individual must present himself at one administrative unit only, regardless of his specific needs or problems. The Municipal Social Welfare Committee is one of several committees under the Local Council (*kommunalbestyrelsen*). The decisions of the Municipal Social Welfare Committee are executed by the Social Service Department (*socialforvaltningen*). The country is divided into 275 municipalities.

At regional level the County Council (*amtsrådet*), and its Social Welfare and Health Committees (*social og sundhedsudvalg*), are responsible for planning and supervising social security measures in municipalities within their jurisdiction. Counties also run the public health security scheme, hospitals, and a variety of social institutions for the specialized treatment of children, juveniles, and various types of handicapped people. Social centres (*socialcentre*) related to counties provide guidance and expert advice for municipalities. Rehabilitation and pension boards (*Revaliderings- og pensionsnævn*) attached to social centres decide on pre-retirement pensions (as a consequence of the 1984 pre-retirement pension reform) and rehabilitation measures. Boards of appeal (*Ankenævn*), also at the county level, deal with first instances of appeal regarding decisions made by the Municipal Social Welfare Committees. The country is divided into 14 counties (*amter*).

At the central government level, the Ministry of Social Affairs (*Socialministeriet*), and three adjacent special divisions, the National Social Office (*Socialstyrelsen*), the National Social Security Office (*Sikringsstyrelsen*), and the National Social Board of Appeal (*Den sociale Ankestyrelse*), perform the functions of: central administration, planning, financing and final appeal.

The one important exception to this is the administration of unemployment insurance, which is kept outside the unified system of social security. This scheme is operated by self-governing unemployment funds attached to unions, but is regulated and supervised by the Ministry of Labour (*Arbejdsministeriet*). The Ministry of Labour also supervises the work injuries scheme.

Statistical sources used

Three different types of statistical source have been used for the quantitative description in the synopsis. All figures on aggregate social security expenditure are taken from a report on social security expenditure published in *Statistisk tiårsoversigt*, 1981, p. 86 (all aggregate figures refer to 1979). Figures for GDP, total public expenditure, and education expenditure, (not included under social expenditure), are taken from national accounts statistics. More detailed statistics on the individual schemes are drawn from special reports published in *Statistiske Efterretninger*. Expenditure figures in these scheme-specific reports do not always correspond to the aggregate statistics, and some of the figures are for more recent years. Major deviations, however, are explained in the footnotes.

I Pensions

In 1979 expenditure on state pensions amounted to 40,532 million DKR, which corresponded to 11.7 % of GDP, 21.5 % of total public expenditure and 44.4 % of social expenditure. This amount is composed of 29,651 million DKR for cash benefits and related benefits (73 %), and 10,881 million (27 %) for related services.

Income Maintenance

Public pension schemes in 1979 by number of pensions and pension expenditure

	Pensions (thousands)	%	Expenditure Million DKR	%
General old age pensions	677	80	16,127	54
Civil servants' o. a pensions (a)			6,758 (a)	23
Invalidity pensions	152	18	6,262 (b)	21
Survivors' pensions	16	2	504	2
	845	100	29,651	100

(a) Including the Labour Market Supplementary Pension (*Arbejdsmarkedets tillægspension*, ATP), pension funds supervised by the Insurance Council (*Forsikringsrådet*), and severance pay (*efterløn*).
(b) Including cash benefits to families with disabled children or adults.

Coverage

The Danish pension system consists of three types of schemes:

- as of October 1, 1984 one comprehensive scheme (*Lov om social pension*) covers all public pension schemes for all Danish citizens. This scheme is divided into old age pension (*folkepension*) and pre-retirement pension (*førtidspension*). The latter provides for invalidity, survivors' and other kinds of pre-retirement pensions;
- occupational pension schemes consisting of (a) the Labour Market Supplementary Pension (*Arbejdsmarkedets tillægspension*, ATP) which is statutory for all wage earners, (b) a pension scheme for civil servants which covered 200,000 or 8% of the labour force in 1981, (c) various schemes for specific occupational groups, mostly public employees without civil servant status. These schemes are mostly organized through pension funds attached to (professional) unions;
- a great variety of private pension savings schemes with insurance companies and banks. These pension schemes are either provided at the enterprise level as a kind of fringe benefit particularly for white collar workers or by the individuals themselves, mostly self-employed and farmers, but also a great many wage earners.

In 1981 approximately 500,000 persons, or 19 % of the labour force, were covered by occupational pension schemes, and some 777,000, or 29 % of the labour force, had private pension insurance schemes.

Every Danish citizen having completed at least three years of residence in Denmark (between 15 and 67 years of age) is entitled to public pensions. Danish citizenship is not compulsory for citizens from other EC countries and the Nordic countries if certain residence requirements are met.

Every Danish citizen who has met the requirements of citizenship and residence and has reached the age of 67 is entitled to old age pension. A full pension requires 40 years of residence. Any shorter period of residence results in reduced pension according to the number of years of residence.

Every Danish citizen between the age of 18 and 67 who has met the requirements of citizenship and residence is entitled to pre-retirement pension. A full pre-retirement pension requires a period of residence corresponding to 4/5 of the years between 15 years of age and the time when the pension is payable.

A pre-retirement pension consists of (a) highest pre-retirement pension (*højeste førtidspension*), (b) medium pre-retirement pension (*mellemste førtidspension*), (c) increased ordinary pre-retirement pension (*forhøjet almindelig førtidspension*), and (d) ordinary pre-retirement pension (*almindelig førtidspension*). The exact pre-retirement pension is granted according to type of risk and age. The scheme distinguishes between two types of risk: reduced working capacity, and social conditions and other conditions of ill-health. The relationships between type of pre-retirement pension, type of risk and age are shown below:

Pre-retirement Pension

Risk	Reduced working capacity						Social and other circumstances of ill-health	
	Only insignificant working capacity intact		Working capacity reduced by 2/3		Working capacity reduced by at least 1/2			
Age	18-59	60-66	18-59	60-66	18-59	60-66	50-59	60-66
Pre-retirement pension	highest	medium	medium	ordinary	increased ordinary	ordinary	increased ordinary	ordinary

All pre-retirement pensions are replaced by old age pensions from the age of 67.

ATP, enacted in 1964, covers wage earners between 16 and 66 years of age, benefits being payable from the age of 67.

Since 1978 a special scheme, severance pay (*efterløn*), has been effective in order to stimulate voluntary retirement from the labour market for those between 58 and 66 years of age. (Since this scheme is based on rules for unemployment benefits, it will be treated under Section III-Unemployment Insurance.)

Benefits

A public pension consists of four types of benefits (a) old age pension (*folkepension*), (b) pre-retirement pension (*førtidspension*), (c) invalidity allowance (*invaliditetsydelse*), and (d) supplements (*tillæg*).

The old age pension is a basic flat-rate allowance which has been paid to everyone over age 67 since 1970.

The supplement is divided into the pension supplement (*pensionstillægget*), and personal supplements (*personalige tillæg*) which are means-tested supplements granted discretionarily by the local social welfare committee. The former is income-tested, the latter is means-tested. In 1981 about half of all old age pensioners received maximum pension supplement (no reduction according to income-tests), about 1/5 received a reduced pension supplement, and about 1/3 did not receive this supplement at all. The pension supplement (maximum) amounts to approximately 20 percent of the flat-rate old age pension allowance. In 1981 an old age pension plus the pension supplement amounted to 47 percent of the average net earnings of a male industrial worker. The earnings replacement ratio for civil servants is slightly above 2/3.

The four types of pre-retirement pension consist of the following benefits:

Highest pre-retirement pension:
old age pension allowance (the base amount) + pension supplement + invalidity amount (*invaliditetsbeløb*) + working incapacity amount (*erhvervsudygtighedsbeløb*)

Medium pre-retirement pension:
old age pension allowance + pension supplement + invalidity amount

Increased ordinary pre-retirement pension:
old age pension allowance + pension supplement + pre-retirement amount (førtidsbeløb)

Size of annual benefit components and pensions in DKR as of October 1, 1985

Benefit Components	Married	Others
Old age pension allowance	32,688	35,580
Pension supplement	6,708	6,252
Invalidity amount	14,196	16,560
Working incapacity amount	16,620	22,956
Pre-retirement amount	8,280	8,280
Pensions		
Old age pension (including pension supplement)	39,396	41,832
Highest pre-retirement pension	70,212	81,348
Medium pre-retirement pension	53,592	58,392
Increased ordinary pre-retirement pension	47,676	50,112
Ordinary pre-retirement pension	39,396	41,832

Pre-retirement pensioners who need special care may receive special supplements in the form of an assistance supplement (*bistandstillæg*) or care supplement (*plejetillæg*). Disabled persons who are entitled to highest medium pre-retirement pension, but who do not receive the pension because they are gainfully employed are entitled to an invalidity allowance (*invaliditetsydelse*).

The following benefit components of the pre-retirement pension are income-tested: the old age pension allowance and the pension supplements. The following benefit components are not income-tested: the invalidity amount, the pre-retirement amount, the working incapacity amount, the assistance and care supplement and the invalidity allowance.

In 1981 the highest pre-retirement pension amounted to 76 (single) or 88 (married with two children) percent of average net earnings for an industrial worker.

All pensions are indexed, i.e. adjusted to the consumer price index twice yearly, and to wage development by separate acts, normally following bi-annual collective agreements.

ATP benefits are calculated on the basis of seniority of membership, and are not indexed. In 1975, 120.000 persons received 115 million DKR under this scheme.

Financing and administration

All taxpayers pay 3.5 % of taxable income as a special contribution to old age pensions (*Folkepensionsbidrag*). This contribution is paid as a part of the normal personal income tax.

The ATP is financed by contributions from employers (two-thirds), and employees (one-third).

Old age pensions are administered by local authorities. As a main rule, Regional Rehabilitation and Pension Boards decide on pre-retirement pensions, the invalidity allowance plus assistance and care supplements, but on recommendation from the Municipal Social Welfare Committee.

Services

There are three main services for old age and other pensioners: (a) Care or nursing homes for those who are unable to stay in their own homes due to their state of health. Pensioners contribute to the relevant costs by relinquishing their pension for the duration of their stay in the home. They receive a certain amount for personal expenses. In January 1981, 44,514 old age pensioners, or 6.5 % of all old age pensioners, together with 4,112 invalidity pensioners (2.7 % of all invalidity pensioners), were living in nursing homes. In 1980, 41,079 persons were employed in nursing and day-care homes. (b) The following services are available for pensioners living at home: home helps, home nursing, day-care homes and day-care centres. (c) Housing facilities for pensioners consist of: special local authority housing, service housing, sheltered flats, and special housing allowances (see Housing).

Core laws

All dates in the following sections on core laws refer to time of enactment. Numbers refer to the official law number.

Initial situation in 1945:

1933 *Lov om Folkeforsikring* (National Social Insurance Act): old age and invalidity compensation for the elderly and disabled (*Alders- og invaliderente*); entitlement based on membership of sickness insurance funds.

26.6.46 (no. 360) *Lov om Folkeforsikring* (National Social Insurance Act): benefits for old age invalidity pension scheme increased; age limit for old age pensions increased from 60 to 65 for men; if warranted by ill-health or special circumstances, old age pensions may be granted from age of 60.

24.4.50 (no. 167) *Lov om Folkeforsikring* (National Social Insurance Act): concept of disability changed so as to put more emphasis on social factors; special benefits and supplements for those disabled, who despite being handicapped are able to perform a job.

26.9.56 (no. 258) *Lov om Folkeforsikring* (National Social Insurance Act): fundamental reforms of old age and invalidity pension scheme; *Alders- og invaliderente* became people's pension (*folkepension*) and invalidity pension (*invalidepension*), indicating a shift from particularistic to universalistic public pensions; age limit for old age pensions increased from 65 to 67 for men, and from 60 to 62 for single women; if warranted by ill-health or other special circumstances a (means-tested) old age pension may be granted from the age of 60; first step taken towards the full old age pension (*den fulde folkepension*) - a flat-rate minimum pension granted to all those over the age of 67.

5.3.59 (no. 70) *Lov om pension og hjælp til enker* (Survivors' Pension Act): general survivors' pension scheme introduced, including specific provisions for single women having reached the age of 50; benefits income-tested.

24.5.60 (no. 238) *Lov om invalide- og folkepension* (Invalidity and Old Age Pension Act): existing National Insurance Act repealed; new Act on old age and invalidity pensions abolished insurance features; beneficiaries of public assistance, formerly excluded from pension benefits, now included; entitlement based solely on citizenship, residence and age; concept of disablement changed so as to take possibilities of rehabilitation into consideration; disability allowance introduced - applicable to those able to maintain a working income in spite of fact that, according to medical assessment, they are entitled to invalidity pension.

3.3.64 (no. 46) *Lov om ATP* (Labour Market Supplementary Pension Act): enacted as an off-shoot of collective bargaining; financed through contributions paid by employees (one-third) and employers (two-thirds); benefits determined on basis of seniority in scheme membership.

28.5.64 (no. 195) *Lov om invalide- og folkepension* (Invalidity and Old Age Pension Act): introduced plan for a gradual transition to full old age pension until its adoption in 1970; income tests and related rules of income deductions to be gradually abolished; pensioners without substantial income, apart from pension, entitled to special income-related supplements.

31.5.65 (no. 218 and 219) *Lov om Folkepension* (Old Age Pension Act) and *Lov om Invalidepension* (Invalidity Pension Act): old age pension and invalidity pensions brought under two separate acts.

18.6.75 (no. 336) *Lov om Invalidepension* (Invalidity Pension Act): effective from 1976; right to grant invalidity pensions as well as pre-retirement pensions transferred to regional Rehabilitation and Pension Boards composed of representatives from the state, counties, municipalities, associations of disabled, trade unions and employers' associations.

1.6.83 (no. 248) *Lov om førtidspension* (Pre-retirement Pension Act): reform of pre-retirement pension system; those between 18 and 67 years of age entitled to a pre-retirement pension; the reform distinguishes between two major types of risk: (1) reduced working capacity (basically those between 18 and 60 years of age) and (2) social and other special circumstances (basically those between 60 and 67 years of age); Survivors' Pension Act repealed and benefit structure also changed.

16.5.84 (no. 217) *Lov om social pension* (Social Pension Act): all pensions gathered in one Act covering both old age pensions and pre-retirement pensions.

II Sickness insurance/Health services

In 1979 expenditure on sickness and health amounted to 25,273 million DKR, which corresponded to 7.3 % of GDP, 13.4 % of total public expenditure and 27.7 % of social expenditure, excluding education. This amount is composed of 18,181 million DKR (72 %) for hospitals and other health services and 7,092 million DKR (28.0 %) for sickness cash benefits. The latter figure includes an estimate of the cash benefits paid by employers.

Income maintenance

Daily allowances by number of cases and expenditure in 1980

	Number of cases	%	Expenditure (b) Million DKR	%
Sickness				
Compulsory protection first five weeks (a)	482,946	65.8	914.1	18.3
Compulsory protection after five weeks:				
- wage earners	148,680	20.3	2 853.5	57.1
- self-employed	13,933	1.9	305.1	6.1
Voluntary insurance:				
- self-employed	30,673	4.1	79.0	1.6
- domestic	953	0.1	6.3	0.1
Maternity childbirth and adoption:				
- compulsory protection	56,372	7.7	838.2	16.8
- voluntary	9		0.2	
- adoption	648	0.1	4.7	0.1
Total	734,214	100.0	5,001.1	100.0

(a) Including cash benefits to workers paid by insured employers, daily cash benefits to unemployed and reimbursement to employers for the fourth and fifth weeks.

(b) Excluding daily cash benefits paid by employers apart from those cases mentioned in note (a).

Coverage

Since 1973 daily allowances for sickness and maternity form an integral part of the unified social security system, built up during the 1970s. The scheme protects the economically active part of the population against temporary loss of income due to: sickness, injury (including work injuries), maternity, childbirth and adoption. Wage earners are automatically entitled to daily cash benefits from the first day of sickness. In this respect, the regulations instituted in 1972 and 1973 extended rights already enjoyed by civil servants and public employees, to wage earners. The scheme includes compulsory protection for the self-employed and their assisting spouses, in the case of illness lasting more than five weeks. The self-employed are, however, only entitled to daily cash benefits from the first day of a period of illness, if voluntarily insured under the scheme. Employers of casual workers, or smaller employers, may insure against cash benefits payable to their employees during the first five weeks of a period of illness. Domestic workers may insure voluntarily within the scheme. In 1977 voluntary insurance covered: 4,092 domestic workers, 28,431 self-employed, 7,296 (smaller) employers and 3,086 employers of casual workers. Daily cash benefits are paid at a rate of 90 % of previous earnings up to a maximum of 90 % of average industrial earnings (including cost-of-living supplements but excluding other supplements). Sickness cash benefits are payable weekly without a fixed time limit. Maternity and childbirth allowances are equivalent to sickness cash benefits, and are payable for up to 18 weeks, including a four-week period prior to confinement. Adoption allowances are payable at the same rate and for up to 14 weeks after the birth of the child. Recent developments include: the introduction of one waiting day (1982), maximum duration periods, i.e. 91 weeks within last 3 years (1982), temporary suspension of indexation, but also extensions, 4 weeks extension of maternity leave (1980) and a further extension to 14 weeks for both parents (see Section V of the country chapter).

Financing and administration

Sickness cash benefits are paid to wage earners by the employer for the first five weeks of illness. Since 1978 the state has temporarily taken over the costs of the fourth and fifth weeks by means of reimbursement to employers. Daily cash benefits in the case of illness (payable after the fifth week), maternity and childbirth, and adoption payable under voluntary insurance schemes, are paid by the Municipal Social Welfare Offices, which are then reimbursed by the Daily Cash Benefit Fund (*Dagpengefonden*) at a rate of 75 %. Contributions are raised from taxpayers who pay an additional 1 % income tax, voluntary insurance and central government transfers. In 1980 the state financed over 80 % of the total expenditure for cash benefits for sickness etc. If cash benefits paid by employers are excluded, the figure comes to about 98 %.

Services

The system of health security is based on two schemes, one providing in-patient treatment (hospitals) and one providing out-patient treatment (primary health). Both schemes are universal: everyone with permanent residence in Denmark is entitled to free medical treatment in hospitals and free medical care outside hospitals. Dental treatment is only partly covered by the scheme. Medicines are subsidized at rates of 75 % and 50 % according to a classified list drawn up by the central health authorities. Both the hospitals and the health service are administered by the counties. They are financed by means of income and property taxes, levied by the individual county authorities, and by central government grants. There are no sickness funds or similar agencies.

Core laws

1933 *Lov om Folkeforsikringsloven* (National Social Insurance Act): Compulsory and semi-universal sickness insurance. Membership of sickness funds based on income: income ceiling for 'active' membership corresponds to average annual earnings of skilled workers. Persons with higher incomes may insure in non-subsidized sickness benefit societies, and must become 'passive' members in order to qualify for old age pensions; sickness cash benefits require six weeks of 'active' membership, maternity allowances 10 months; benefits vary according to contribution rates between 0.40-6.00 DKR a day; sickness cash benefits paid for a maximum of 26 weeks in 12 consecutive months, after a waiting period of three days; maternity allowances are paid for 14 days after confinement; insurance financed through contributions by passive members (2.40 DKR annually), active members (annual contribution equal to two days' wages of unskilled worker), central government (2 DKR annually for all active members below income limit), and municipalities; active members entitled to free medical care in hospitals and as out-patients; certain important medicines subsidized at rates of 75 % and 50 %; some sickness funds provide additional benefits including, specialist and dental care; sickness funds are run by autonomous member-elected governing bodies, but must be approved by the state and supervised by the Ministry of Social Affairs.

13.4.56 (no. 93) *Lov om forhold mellem fagforeninger og arbejdsgiverorganisationer* (Law on relations between trade unions and employers' associations): as an offshoot of collective agreement on the labour market, a new scheme provided sickness cash benefits considerably higher than in the existing health insurance scheme; new scheme only covered trade union members and those employed by members of the Danish Employers' Association; scheme financed by contributions from employees and employers, and administered by sickness funds.

1.6.60 (no. 239) *Lov om offentlig sygesikring* (National Health Insurance Act): existing National Social Insurance Act repealed and replaced by three different acts covering old age and invalidity pensions (see Pensions), rehabilitation (see Social Assistance), and health insurance; the limited scheme for daily cash benefits in the case of sickness, dating from 1956, also repealed; new scheme for daily allowances in the case of sickness under National Health Insurance Act covers all insured wage-earners; time limits abolished; administered by sickness funds and financed by contributions from employees, employers and central government transfers; daily cash benefits for confinement financed by central government; membership now universal but medical care free only for A-members (those with incomes below a certain limit), constituting the majority of the population; B-members (those with incomes above this limit) pay higher premiums and part of the costs related to medical care; in return for which B-members enjoy some liberties as to the choice of general practitioners and specialists.

28.5.71 (no. 311) *Lov om offentlig sygesikring* (National Health Insurance Act): new National Health Insurance Act effective from 1973; sickness funds dissolved; administration and financing transferred to public authorities; free medical care for all with permanent residence in Denmark.

2.6.72 (no. 262) *Lov om dagpenge ved sygdom og fødsel* (Law on daily cash allowances in the case of sickness and maternity): new scheme for daily cash benefits in the case of sickness and maternity, effective from 1972 and 1973 respectively; uniform regulations for granting daily cash benefits in cases of sickness, injury, childbirth and adoption; benefits increased to 90 % of previous earnings within a maximum limit equal to 90 % of average earnings for an industrial worker; as in the case of unemployment benefits; all economically active covered; system of administration and financing simplified.

III Unemployment insurance/Employment policy

In 1979 expenditure on unemployment insurance and employment measures amounted to 11,163.7 million DKR or 3.2 % of GDP, which corresponded to 5.9 % of total public expenditure and 12.0 % of social security expenditure. This amount is composed of unemployment cash benefits, 10,943.9 million DKR (98 %) and expenditure on various employment and training services, 219.8 million DKR (2 %).

Income maintenance

Coverage

The unemployment insurance scheme covers members of approved unemployment funds. All those who are resident in Denmark, are between 16 and 65 years of age, and have been employed for five weeks, working an average of 30 hours a week, or who have completed an occupational training lasting a minimum of 18 months are eligible. Membership in unemployment funds also covers part-time employees and was extended to cover the permanently self-employed in 1976. In 1980 some 85 % of all wage earners were members of unemployment funds.

Since 1978 a special scheme provides severence pay (efterløn) to those trade union members between 58 and 66 years of age who opt for a voluntary, early retirement.

Unemployment benefits are paid at a rate of 90 % of the claimants previous average earnings with a maximum limit equal to 90 % of the average industrial wage, (including cost-of-living supplements but excluding other supplements). The maximum is adjusted annually. Benefits are payable from the first day of unemployment. In 1980 unemployment benefits covered 83 % of average net earnings for an industrial worker.

The main conditions for payment of unemployment benefits are (a) membership of an unemployment fund for a minimum of six months (self-employed 12 months); (b) that the claimant be capable, willing and registered for employment; (c) that unemployment is not due to voluntary resignation, misconduct, labour dispute, or refusal of suitable offer; and (d) at least 26 weeks' employment during the last three years. This so-called 26 weeks' rule has been temporarily changed in recent years in accordance with changing government policies towards long-term unemployment.

In cases of voluntary retirement, a severance pay is payable based on unemployment benefits. This severance pay is gradually reduced from maximum unemployment benefits to 60 %. The fact that this special scheme is more favourable to claimants than existing provisions for pre-retirement pensions, no doubt explains why so many have opted for it. In 1980, 48,000 were receiving severance pay. In 1983, expenditure on severance pay amounted to 6.650 million DKR, or 7.2 % of all cash transfers to households.

Financing and administration

Unemployment is financed by employees (annual contribution of 2.25 times the daily cash benefit rate), employers (fixed amount of 135 DKR a year per full-time employee insured under the Industrial Injuries Act), and the central government, which covers all expenses exceeding fixed contributions from employees and employers. In 1980 central government financed approximately 95 % of total expenditure on unemployment benefits.

Collection of contributions and payment of benefits is carried out by local branches of unemployment funds. These funds are self-governing, but are regulated and supervised by the Ministry of Labour. Unemployment funds must be approved by the Ministry of Labour before benefit expenditure can be reimbursed by central government.

Services

Services include: (a) employment exchanges run by local offices, (b) training and retraining programmes, including compensation for loss of income while enrolled in these programmes, (c) travel and relocation allowances, rent allowances varying with locality, etc., (d) employment works, and (e) a variety of special programmes for the young and long-term unemployed, e.g. provision of jobs in the public sector and subsidization of employers in the private sector. Despite these measures, expenditure on unemployment services is negligible when compared with that for unemployment benefits (see above). Concerning recent changes in services for the unemployed, e.g. the provision of new job opportunities, see Section V of the country chapter.

Core laws

1933 *Lov om arbejdsanvisning og arbejdsløshedsforsikring* (Employment Exchange and Unemployment Insurance Act): the unemployment insurance scheme covered voluntarily insured members of unemployment funds, (between 18 and 60 years of age); casual workers, the self-employed and persons with property exceeding 8,000-18,000 DKR in value, are not eligible; unemployment benefits vary according to fund; daily cash benefits on limited scale of four-fifths of average earnings for those with dependents (maximum benefit 9.60 DKR), and two-thirds for none (maximum benefit 8.60 DKR); qualifying conditions are a waiting period of 6-15 weeks, 12 months membership of fund and employment for 39 weeks, 26 of which in the 18 months preceding claim for benefit, maximum duration of four years and minimum duration of 90 days, and that unemployment is not due to labour disputes, voluntary resignation, or refusal of suitable employment.

Financing: members contribute between 0.2 % and 0.4 % of earnings, depending on fund; employers pay fixed amount of 15 DKR a year for each employee, and central government contributes annual grant to funds, calculated as a percentage of members' contributions in preceding fiscal year; percentage fixed at 15 % to 90 % in proportion to average annual earnings in occupations and districts.

Administration: carried out by self-governing unemployment funds attached to trade unions; funds supervised by central government (Director of Labour, Ministry of Labour).

16.2.67 (no. 40) *Lov om arbejdsanvisning og arbejdsløshedsforsikring* (Employment Service and Unemployment Insurance Act): unemployment benefits increased and linked to official wage index; benefits for insured, both with and without dependents, administered within same fund; waiting periods abolished; member contributions fixed in accordance with size of daily cash benefit (2.25 times daily cash benefit per year);

costs in excess of fixed employer/employee contributions covered by government reimbursement funds.

10.6.76 (no. 311) *Lov om dagpengeret og arbejdsløshedsforsikring* (Law on entitlement to unemployment benefits): entitled the permanently self-employed to membership in unemployment funds, and consequently to unemployment benefits.

15.11.78 (no. 555) *Lov om efterløn* (Severance Pay Act): introduced pre-retirement remuneration which provided unemployment benefits (for those between 58 and 66) in cases of voluntary retirement.

4.4.79 (no. 145) *Ferielov* (National Holiday Act): extension of obligatory number of holidays to 30 days.

4.6.80 (no. 235) *Arbejdstilbudsordning* (Job Offer Scheme): entitlement to unemployment benefits for those who are long-term unemployed cannot be lost without an offer of a new job.

IV Work injury

In 1979 expenditure on work injuries insurance amounted to 581.2 million DKR, or 0.1 % of GDP, 0.3 % of total public expenditure and 0.5 % of social security expenditure. This amount consists of cash compensations: 476.6 million DKR (82 %); and related services, 104.6 million DKR (18 %).

Income maintenance

The 1978 Work Injuries Act (*Arbejdsskadeloven*) covers all employed persons and protects them against: work accidents, injuries lasting a few days, and occupational diseases, as determined by the National Social Security Office (*Sikringsstyrelsen*).

Benefits

Benefits under the scheme are as follows: medical care, rehabilitation, aids etc; compensation for permanent injury, fixed by the National Social Security Office on the basis of minimum 5 % permanent injury, and granted in the form of flat-rate lump sum payments; compensation for loss of earning capacity, fixed by the National Social Security Office on a discretionary basis and granted only where earning capacity is reduced by at least 15 %; loss of earning capacity by 100 % entitles the claimant to 75 % of prior annual earnings, within a given maximum, which is adjusted annually (in 1978 approximately 90 % of all workers were estimated to have had annual earnings below this maximum); compensation for the loss of a financial supporter, which is fixed in accordance with the extent of previous support together with the survivor's means of subsistence; compensation is granted for a limited period (maximum 10 years) annually and covers 30 % of the deceased's earnings; a transitional allowance payable to all survivors; compensation for dependent children fixed at 10 % of the deceased's earnings.

Financing and administration

The scheme is financed by premiums from employers. Central government covers administrative costs, and subsidizes certain employers in order to reduce premiums (civil servants and conscripts protected by the scheme). Work injury insurance is administered by private insurance companies which are regulated and supervised by the National Social Security Office.

Services

Services mainly consist of government inspection and control of workplaces and working conditions.

Core Laws

1933 *Ulykkesforsikringsloven* (Accident Insurance Act): covered all employed persons, and provided medical care after expiration of sickness fund benefits, compensation for temporary invalidity; 75 % of prior earnings within a given maximum; waiting period of 13 weeks (during which period sickness benefits may be claimed by active members of sickness funds); for permanent injury or disablement: 62 % of previous earnings, within a given maximum, payable for life, or until recovery; for invalidity of compensation normally converted into lump sums for invalidity of less than 50 %; survivors' compensation and funeral benefits; financed by employers liable to insure, and administered by insurance companies approved and supervised by Office of Accident Insurance (*Direktoratet for Ulykkesforsikring*) attached to Ministry for Social Affairs.

20.3.59 (no. 96) *Lov om forsikring mod følger af ulykker* (Accident Insurance Act): scheme extended to cover occupational diseases; compensation for survivors converted from lump sums into running benefits; waiting periods reduced; independent board of appeal established.

6.12.64 (no. 403) *Lov om forsikring mod følger af ulykker* (Accident Insurance Act): indexed benefits.

3.3.78 (no. 79) *Lov om Arbejdsskadeforsikring* (Work Injury Insurance Act): benefit structure altered; work injury compensation based on two components: flat-rate compensation (lump sum) in the case of permanent injury, fixed according to degree of injury over 5 %, and compensation for loss of earning capacity over 15 %, fixed by the National Social Security Office on a discretionary basis; loss of earning capacity maximum considerably increased; equality for widows and widowers; compensation for surviving spouse fixed in accordance with degree of financial dependence on the deceased, and present means of subsistence.

V Families and children

In 1979 expenditure on families and children amounted to 9,678.3 million DKR or 2.8 % of GDP; 5.1 % of total public expenditure and 10.6 % of social security expenditure. This amount is composed of: cash benefits, 4,101.3 million DKR (42.0 %) and related services, 5,577.0 million DKR (58.0 %).

Income maintenance

Number of children receiving child allowances, related allowances and expenditure by type of allowance in 1979

	Number in thousands	% of app. relevant age groups	Expenditure (a) Mill. DKR	%
Child maintenance payments	156	10.5 (b)	678 (e)	20.8
Ordinary child allowance	1,052	95.5 (c)	1,783	54.6
Increased child allowance	110	10.0 (c)	492 (d)	15.1
Special child allowance	62	4.2 (b)	313	9.5
Total			3,266	100.0

(a) Excluding expenditure on youth and daily cash benefits for maternity, childbirth and adoption. These items are included in the 4,101.3 million DKR mentioned above.

(b) Percentage of children between 0-19 (relevant age group 0-18).

(c) Percentage of children between 0-14 (relevant age group 0-15).

(d) Including extra expenditure on child allowances.

(e) Including repayments by those liable, according to civil law (71 %).

Coverage

The 1969 Family Allowance Act (*Familieydelsesloven*) entitled all resident citizens, aliens covered by EEC regulations or reciprocity agreements, and other aliens having been resident in Denmark for at least one year (with one or more children), to benefits. The scheme covers child allowances, youth benefits and child maintenance payments.

Child allowances, like all family allowances, are tax free and payable to the mother. They are divided into: (a) ordinary child allowance (*almindeligt børnetilskud*) payable for any child under 16 years of age; (b) increased child allowance (*forhøjet børnetilskud*), payable upon application for children of single parents and automatically for children of parents receiving old age or invalidity pensions; (c) an extra child allowance (*ekstra børnetilskud*) payable to single parents to supplement the increased child allowance; and (d) special child allowance (*særligt børnetilskud*) payable at three rates, in addition to (a), (b) and (c). Orphans receive the highest rate, followed by children of widows/widowers or single parents without maintenance orders. The lowest rates are received by the children of certain invalidity pension beneficiaries.

Youth benefit (*ungdomsydelse*) is payable for children aged between 16 and 18 for their maintenance and education.

Child maintenance payments (*børnebidrag*) are payable in advance to single parents where such payment has been avoided by the person legally responsible.

Since 1977, ordinary, increased and extra child allowances (but not special child allowances) have been income-tested. The full rate is reduced by 6 % of taxable income in excess of a certain, taxable income limit. Since 1981 the income limit has been fixed in accordance with the Social Income Act (*Lov om socialindkomst*), i.e. income prior to certain deductions (most notably interest on private debts) and with due regard to property and wealth. As a result the actual income limit has been reduced. Youth benefit is both means-tested and income-tested. Tests are carried out by the Municipal Social Welfare Committees. The full rate is reduced where family and youth income exceed certain limits. Since 1981 'Social Income' has also been applied when fixing income limits in the context of youth benefits. Benefits from the family allowance scheme are adjusted twice yearly according to the consumer price index. Income limits are adjusted annually according to the wage index.

Financing and administration

The scheme is operated by the Municipal Social Welfare Committees which are in turn reimbursed by central government at a rate of 100 %.

Services

According to the 1974 Social Assistance Act (*Bistandsloven*), municipalities are obliged to provide day nurseries (*vuggestuer*) for children up to two years of age, nursery schools (*børnehaver*) for children between three and six, age-integrated institutions (*aldersintegrerede institutioner*) for children up to the age of 14, and youth centres (*fritidshjem*) for children between 7 and 14 years of age. Local councils also organize and subsidize private day care (*dagpleje*) and provide a home help service. This service includes permanent home help for the permanently sick or infirm, and temporary home help for short-term illness, confinement and convalescence. Fees for this service are income-tested. Specialized child care institutions are dealt with under Social Assistance.

Public expenditure for child day-care institutions is shared on a 50/50 basis between the central government and local councils. Parental fees are fixed at a percentage of certain current expenditure; 35 % for pre-school children and 25 % for those in secondary and tertiary education. Since 1981 fees have been organized according to a minimum, medium or upper income limit. Parents within the minimum limit pay no fees: those within the medium limit pay reduced fees and those within the upper income bracket pay full fees. The Municipal Social Welfare Committees enjoy some liberties in fixing the parental fees. As a consequence, parental fees vary from municipality to municipality.

Core laws

Initial situation in 1945: at this time there was no coherent scheme providing for families and children, and provision of benefits and services was covered under various different acts and schemes; the 1939 Care of Mothers Act (*Lov om mødrehjælp*) provided advice and guidance for pregnant women and mothers with small children, maternity home care and limited cash benefits; pension schemes provided for orphans, children of old age and invalidity pensioners.

12.4.49 (no. 175) *Lov om husmoderafløsning* (Home Help Act): obliged municipalities to operate a home help service.

31.3.52 (no. 112) *Lov om børnetilskud* (Child Allowance Act): covered residents with one or more child aged up to 16 years; benefits mainly in the form of tax credits, strictly income-tested; means-tested cash benefits only granted to single mothers with small incomes, the unemployed and pensioners; operated by municipalities and reimbursed by central government.

22.3.61 (no. 76) *Lov om udskrivning af indkomst- og formueskatten* (Tax Law): abolished tax credits and replaced them with flat-rate cash benefits.

30.5.67 (no. 236) *Familieydelseslov* (Family Allowance Act): revised in 1969 and effective from 1970; combined various child and family allowances under one act; covers residents with one or more children; distinction made between (a) ordinary child allowance, i.e. a flat-rate and universal cash benefit payable to all children up to 18, (b) increased child allowance to single parents, and (c) special child allowance payable to children of old age and invalidity pensioners and orphans; also provision for advance maintainance payments and flat-rate maternity grant payable as a lump sum on birth of each child, in addition to child allowance; operated by municipal social welfare committees; costs reimbursed by central government at rate of 100 %.

8.6.73 (no. 336) *Familieydelseslov* (Family Allowance Act): restricted entitlement to child allowances for single parents; maternity grant withdrawn.

26.6.75 (no. 310) *Familieydelseslov* (Family Allowance Act): reduced age limit for children entitled to ordinary child allowances to 16; introduced income-tested youth benefit (related to income of both parents and youth) for children aged 16 and 17.

25.8.76 (no. 425) *Familieydelseslov* (Family Allowance Act): abolished flat-rate cash benefits; child allowances became incometested.

1981 reduced income limits for child allowances by the introduction of the concept of Social Income (see Social Assistance).

VI Social assistance

In 1979 expenditure on social assistance amounted to 2,783.9 million DKR, or 0.8 % of GDP, 1.5 % of total public expenditure and 3.0 % of social security expenditure. This amount is composed of expenditure on cash benefits, 2,664.0 million DKR (96.0 %) and expenditure on related services, 119.9 million DKR (4.0 %).

Income maintenance

Number of families receiving cash benefits under the Social Assistance Act (a) and expenditure by main types of benefit in 1979

	Number of families (b)	Expenditure Million DKR	%
Temporary assistance	208,274	1,742.1	61.1
Continuing assistance	8,303	117.7	4.1
Support for education etc.	23,089	378.2	13.3
Support to persons living at home	23,031	278.6	9.8
Support for maintenance of children with physical or mental handicaps living at home	38,153	114.9	4.0
Other cash benefits	66,395	218.3	7.7
Total	271,967 (c) or 10 % of all families	2,849.8 (d)	100.0

(a) Benefits according to sec. 9-11 and par. 58.3 of the Social Assistance Act;

(b) Including cohabiting spouse, all other adults and persons under 18, if married, having or expecting children, orphans/those without supporter or having own residence;

(c) Due to the fact that the same family, as defined above, may receive various forms of benefits this figure is smaller than the sum of the individual categories;

(d) The difference between this figure and the amount of 2,664 million DKR mentioned above may be explained by the fact that the latter figure excludes certain benefits which appear under other schemes.

Coverage

The 1974 Social Assistance Act provides the following three types of tax free cash benefits:

Temporary assistance (*forbigående hjælp*) for those who are temporarily unable to maintain themselves, on condition that normal circumstances have been altered, expenses cannot be otherwise obtained and the claimant has 'utilized his employment opportunities'. The value of the benefit is discretionary, and is fixed at an amount equal to the basic old age pension (see Pensions), plus supplements for each child, equal to special child allowance (see Families and Children), plus coverage of fixed expenses and non-recurrent expenses. There is no fixed time limit, but after a maximum of three months the Municipal Social Welfare Offices decide whether some other form of assistance is more appropriate. In 1980 temporary assistance excluding coverage of fixed expenses covered 32 % (single) and 54 % (married) of average net earnings of an industrial worker.

Secondly, continuing assistance (*varig hjælp*) is available for persons who are unable to maintain themselves for a longer period of time, by means of either temporary or other assistance (e.g. pensions). Benefits should not usually exceed the basic old age pension allowance plus the pension supplement (see Pensions).

Thirdly, assistance may be granted in special cases *(Hjælp i særlige tilfælde)*, for medical and dental treatment etc, and for removal expenses incurred by persons maintaining handicapped children or adults at home.

Since 1981 a benefit ceiling has been introduced to ensure that no one receives cash benefits under the Social Assistance Act in excess of the maximum daily sickness cash benefits.

Financing and administration

Cash benefits are paid by the Municipal Social Welfare Committees, and municipalities are then reimbursed at a rate of 50 % by central government.

Services

Services provided under the Social Assistance Act include advice and guidance, home help services (see Pensions, Families and Children), and various aids. Town councils provide day-care institutions for children (see Families and Children), day-care homes and centres for juveniles needing special care outside the home, nursing homes and special flats for the elderly (see Pensions). The counties provide child and juvenile guidance centres, rehabilitation centres, homes for women before and after confinement, special nursing homes for juveniles and, since 1980 (enacted in 1978), special care institutions for the handicapped. In 1978, 28,897 handicapped people were living in these special institutions, and expenditure amounted to 1,808 million DKR. Section VIII of the Social Assistance Act deals with supportive measures taken without consent, i.e. procedures for taking supportive action with regard to children and young persons, without the consent of their guardians.

Financing

Expenditure for guidance, advice and administration is financed solely by municipalities. For expenditure on day care institutions see Section V - Families and Children. County spending on social institutions is financed by taxes levied by the county plus central government transfers.

Core laws

1933 *Lov om offentlig forsorg* (Public Assistance Act): provided three forms of public assistance: special assistance (*særhjælp*), communal assistance (*kommunehjælp*) and poor relief (*fattighjælp*); recipients of communal assistance and poor relief obliged to repay benefits; poor relief recipients forefeited the right to vote or marry without consent of the Social Welfare Committees.

12.4.49 (no. 177) *Lov om offentlig forsorg* (Public Assistance Act): introduced special treatment and assistance (transferred from communal assistance or poor relief) for TB patients.

12.1.50 (No. 21) *Lov om foranstaltninger for døve og tunghøre* (Law on measures for the deaf and dumb): introduced special provisions for the deaf and partially deaf within the framework for the special care of the handicapped.

31.3.53 (no. 77) *Lov om offentlig forsorg* (Public Assistance Act): introduced special treatment and assistance for polio patients.

26.4.55 (no. 152) *Lov om hjælp til enlige mødre* (Law on assistance to single mothers): introduced special assistance for widows with children and certain other categories of single women.

12.5.59 (no. 192) *Lov om forsorg for åndssvage* (Law on care for the mentally handicapped): reorganized the administration of care for the mentally handicapped; private homes converted into local care centres under a national foundation, supervised by Ministry for Social Affairs.

31.3.60 (no. 170) *Revalideringsloven* (Rehabilitation Act): created a unified framework providing rehabilitation, vocational training, aids, special training centres for handicapped and partially disabled.

16.5.61 (no. 169) *Lov om offentlig forsorg* (New Public Assistance Act): replaced 1933 Act; public assistance no longer resulted in loss of political rights and restrictions on marriage; benefits repayable only in special cases; two types of cash benefit - general assistance (*hjælp ved trang i almindelighed*) discretionally fixed with maximum 85 % of old age pension, together with supplements for children, and special assistance (*udvidet hjælp*) for special groups (e.g. TB patients, polio patients, conscripts and single mothers with children) fixed discretionally at a higher rate designed to former living standards.

28.5.64 (no. 193) *Lov om børne og ungdomsforsorg* (New Care of Children and Juveniles Act): local child and juvenile welfare committees authorized to grant cash benefits to certain families with children, to avoid placing children in the care of the Municipal Social Welfare Offices; new criteria for day-care institutions which stressed social, educational, and therapeutic aspects; municipalities obliged to provide facilities for day-care and other related services.

13.6.74 (no.333) *Bistandsloven* (Social Assistance Act): combined seven existing acts: Public Assistance Act, Child and Juvenile Care Act, Maternity Aid Centres Act, Rehabilitation Act, Care of Disabled and Old Age Pensioners Act, Home Help Service Act, and Supervision of Reception and Work Centre Act; Municipal Social Welfare Committees now responsible for all relevant services and cash benefits; the latter divided into temporary assistance, discretionally fixed at higher rates, continuing assistance dicretionally fixed at lower rates, and assistance in special cases; coordination of provision for cash benefits and services; uniform system of financing introduced; effective from 1976.

31.5.78 (no. 257) *Lov om udlægning af særforsorgen* (Law on decentralization of special care institutions): series of acts covering decentralization of special care for the handicapped; special care for the the handicapped transferred to municipalities and counties from 1980.

16.6.80 (no. 258) *Bistandsloven* (Social Assistance Act): introduced cash benefit ceiling to correspond to maximum daily cash benefits for sickness.

VII Housing

In 1979 expenditure on social housing policies amounted to 1,230.1 million DKR, or 0.4 % of GDP, 0.7 % of total public expenditure and 1.3 % of social security expenditure. Social housing policies may be divided into the three following sections:

- Rent subsidies for tenants, fixed according to household income, rent, number of children and size of dwelling. Groups with particularly low incomes, e.g. pensioners, may apply for a housing allowance (*boligydelse*) fixed roughly in accordance with the criteria applied to rent subsidies, but available at a higher rate. The Municipal Social Welfare Offices may also grant loans for tenants' deposits.
- Tax credits for owner-occupiers. All interest charged on mortgages, maintenance costs and property taxes are deductible. Owing to the system of progressive taxation, tax credits benefit high-income families. In 1979 the value of tax credits to owner-occupiers is estimated to have been about 6,000 million DKR.
- Subsidies for non-profit housing schemes which divide into: (a) provision of non-repayable basic capital; in addition to normal, open-market loans, which finance 74 % of construction costs, non-profit housing is financed by means of non-repayable basic capital by up to 26 % (government loans - 10 %, local authority loans - 6 %, loans from National Building Fund for Non-Profit Housing - 7 %, and tenants deposits - 3 %); (b) central government interest guarantees given in the form of subsidy representing the differential between a basic 6 % rate of interest and the market rate on bond loans during the four years following construction; (c) in 1980 a special subsidy was introduced to help cover operating costs. This is to assist non-profit housing schemes which experience difficulties in attracting tenants willing to pay an 'economic' rent; (d) subsidies for the construction of dwellings for vulnerable groups, e.g. old age pensioners and the disabled.

Financing and administration

Rent subsidies and housing allowances are paid by the Municipal Social Welfare Offices, which are then reimbursed by central government at a rate of 40 %. In 1979 subsidies for the rental sector (excluding tax credits to owner-occupiers) totalled 2,400 million DKR or 1.3 % of total public expenditure. It should be noted that the previously mentioned figure of 1,230 million DKR does not include all subsidies, but only expenditure on rent subsidies, housing allowances, dwellings for pensioners and deficits accruing from public guarantees on loans for tenants' deposits.

Core laws

22.8.45 (no. 400) *Lov om boliganvisning* (Housing Allocation Act): introduced obligatory allocation of vacant housing to ensure that vacant flats are let in the first instance to those with low incomes; tight rent controls established;

30.4.46 (no. 235) *Byggestøtteloven* (Building Subsidy Act): low interest rates made available by central government to support housing construction for the needy; rent supplements introduced for families with smaller incomes.

8.6.51 (no. 251) *Lov om leje* (Rent Act): extended rent control and security of tenure to cover houses built after 1939; certain rent increases permitted.

1.10.54 (no. 304) Central government mortgages to reduce individual housing costs; subject to prevailing market interest rate combined with an annual subsidy based on floor area.

13.4.55 (no. 106) *Lov om leje* (Rent Act): allowed further rent increases in the old housing market, designed to modify rent control and housing allocation.

18.12.58 (no. 355) *Lov om leje* (Rent Act): central government withdrew from mortgage market and set up mortgage credit funds to issue loans on open-market terms; central government continued to subsidize certain forms of rented housing.

21.4.66 (no. 160) *Boligforliget* (Housing Act): fundamental reform intended to free housing market over a transition period of eight years; attempted to level rents for different housing categories (i.e. raise rent in older housing and lower it in newer housing) based on a general rent assessment; reduced tax credits for owner-occupiers by raising rental values of owner-occupied housing; non-profit housing rents lowered by guaranteeing fixed low interest mortgage rates; individual rent subsidies based on tenants' income, composition of household, size of rent and flat; provisions for converting rented dwellings into owner-occupied housing.

14.3.75 (no. 81) *Lov om midlertidig regulering af boligforholdene* (Law on regulation of housing conditions): restructured subsidies to non-profit housing; based on non-repayable basic capital and interest guarantees; cost-based rent introduced; rent control limited to municipalities of over 20,000 inhabitants; tenant conditions improved.

1982 Fixed rent subsidies and housing allowances in accordance with social income (see Families and Children).

VIII Education

Expenditure on public education system by type of education. Absolute and relative contribution in 1978.

	Million DKR	%	% of public expenditure
Administration	417	1.8	0.3
Primary/lower secondary school	11,928	51.2	7.4
Juvenile education (a)	3,570	15.3	2.2
Further education (b)	4,102	17.6	2.5
Voluntary juvenile/adult ed.	1,647	7.0	1.0
Measures of support	412	1.8	0.3
Research	1,237	5.3	0.8
Total	23,313	100.0	14.5
	or 7.5 % of GDP		

(a) Includes academic and vocational education for those between 16 and 19 years of age.

(b) Includes short courses of further education (1-2 years), medium courses (3-4 years) and higher education (over 4 years).

Income maintenance

The State Education Fund (*Statens Uddannelsesstøtte*, SU), is the only general state form of student support. Students over 18, attending an SU approved educational course of a minimum of six months' duration are entitled to SU support. (For support of children aged 16 and 17, see Families and Children.)

Support is in the form of student allowances (*stipendier*) or public guarantee (*statskaution*) for loans with private banks. Allowances for students between 18 and 22 years of age are related to both parental and student income. The maximum rate is payable if parents' income is below a certain income limit. No allowance is payable to students whose parents have incomes above this limit. A student's own income (gross income including the allowance received) may not exceed a certain limit. Allowances are reduced proportionately with incomes exceeding that limit. For students over 22 years of age, allowances are fixed solely in accordance with their own incomes.

Public guarantees on private loans may be obtained by all those entitled to SU support up to an upper limit. Loans and interest are repayable by students.

Education System

The basic component in the Danish educational system is the State School (*Folkeskole*) which provides primary and lower secondary education. Attendance is free and admission is open to all children between the ages of 6-17. Since 1972 education has been compulsory for a basic nine-year period. The *Folkeskolen* are attended by 94 % of all children born in any one year. The remainder attend private schools, which are subsidized by the state at a rate of 85 %. The 1975 Basic Education Act (*Folkeskoleloven*) established a nine-year general basic education with an optional tenth year and pre-school class effective in 1976. In principle, and to a large extent in practice, the *Folkeskolen* are comprehensive. However, in the eighth to tenth forms pupils may choose between a basic and an advanced course. At the end of the ninth form, pupils may enter for the Leaving Examination (*Folkeskolens afgangseksamen*) in one or more subjects. At the end of the tenth form, pupils may enter for either the *Folkeskole* Leaving Examination or, if they have followed an advanced course, the *Folkeskole* Advanced Leaving Examination.

The *Folkeskole* is followed by either, an academic (*studieforberedende uddannelser*) or a vocational education course (*erhvervsforberedende uddannelser*).

Academically oriented courses are designed to prepare students for higher education and include courses run at the *Gymnasia* and those leading to the Higher Preparatory Examination (*Højere Forberedelseseksamen*, HF). The *Gymnasia* provide a three-year course of education comprising two types of study: languages and mathematics, both with options for further specialization. HF provides a two-year course of education. *Gymnasia* courses terminate with the Upper Secondary School Leaving Examination (*studentereksamen*), and HF terminates with HF Leaving Examination, both of which qualify for entry into further education. It is possible to take the *Studentereksamen* after a two-year course run by special Students' Courses (*studenterkurser*). In 1979/80 the number of students attending Gymnasia totalled 56,826, those attending HF totalled 10,494 and those attending Students' Courses totalled 2,152.

Vocationally oriented education covers (a) apprenticeship training (*lærlingeuddannelser*) covering 3-4 years combined practical training under the supervision of a master (employer) and theoretical training at technical schools; (b) since 1977 basic vocational training (*erhvervsfaglige grunduddannelser*, EFG), consists of a 3-4 year vocational training including a one-year basic course at a school followed by alternate theoretical training at the school and practical training at a place of work. EFG courses divide into eight main vocational fields; and (c) other types of vocational training. In 1978 students enrolled in vocational training totalled 109,334, or 29.3 % of those between 15 and 19 years of age.

Further education (*videregående uddannelser*) covers all courses of further and higher education entered after 12 years of basic education, regardless of previous academic or vocational orientation. Further education divides into (a) short courses of further education (*kortere videregående uddannelser*, KVU) comprising 1-2 years of practically-oriented courses, (b) medium to long-term courses of further education (*mellemlange videregående uddannelser*) which last for 3-4 years - typical examples being teacher training courses and courses at engineering colleges; and (c) long courses of further education (*lange videregående uddannelser*) which take four or more years comprising courses run at universities (Denmark has five universities), and institutions of higher education, e.g. technical high schools (*tekniske højskoler*) and business schools. These institutions do not come within the jurisdiction of universities although they provide courses of the same length and at the same level. There is no Danish equivalent of courses leading to a Bachelor's Degree. Students normally specialize from the beginning. In 1978 the figures for stock of students, entrance and examinations were: KVU 27,533, 12,056 and 9,713; medium to long-term courses: 30,050, 10,567 and 8,108; and higher education: 69,208, 14,482 and 7,187.

Formal education is free at all levels. In addition to the formal educational system there are a variety of voluntary courses for youth and adult education. In Denmark, great importance has traditionally been attached to adult education. Hence in 1976/77 603,554 persons or 17.0 % of the population over the age of 19 attended these courses.

Administration and Financing

The *Folkeskolen* are run by town councils which are in turn reimbursed by the central government. The *Gymnasia* and HF are run by counties and reimbursed by central government. Many educational institutions, especially those which are vocationally oriented, are independent, with Boards of Governors consisting of representatives from interest groups, public authorities and educational experts. Universities and other higher education institutions are run by the Ministry of Education which supervises most educational programmes. The Ministry of Labour is involved in most vocationally oriented courses.

Core laws

Initial situation in 1945: seven years compulsory education; lower and upper secondary education based on system of merit according to qualifications and on examinations. The 1937 *Folkeskolelov* (Basic Education Act) provided, however, opportunities for examination-free secondary system (*mellemskole*) as supplement to basic seven years; this secondary system never gained recognition among parents or in business.

20.9.56 (no. 261) *Lov om lærlinge* (Apprenticeship Act): theoretical training introduced at technical schools as part of apprenticeship training.

30.5.58 (no. 163) *Folkeskolereform* (New Reform of Basic Education): examination-free secondary system abolished; basic education of 7-8 years extended to a ninth form; fifth form pupils divide into theoretical (*boglig*) and practical (*almen*) subjects, based on qualifications; parents and local authorities may opt for no streaming at this level; leaving examination in eighth and ninth forms; introduction of a three-year upper secondary course (*realskole*) terminating with upper secondary leaving examination (*realeksamen*); difference in basic education between rural and urban areas to be eliminated.

1.6.66 (No. 236) *Lov om HF* (HF Act): HF introduced for those wishing to re-enter academic education; introduction of two-year courses providing further education qualifications.

7.4.72 (no. 121) *Lov om folkeskolen* (Basic Education Act): extended compulsory basic education from seven to nine years; (seven years compulsory basic education introduced in 1814).

4.4.75 (no. 113) *Lov om statens uddannelsesstøtte* (Educational Allowance Act): state loans to students, with low or no interest charges, replaced by public guarantees for bank loans.

13.6.75 (no. 313) *Folkeskolelov* (New Basic Education Act): effective from 1976; introduced nine-year general, basic education with optional tenth year and pre-school class; comprehensive principle established for basic education.

2.6.77 (no. 289) *Lov om erhvervsfaglig grunduddannelse* (Vocational Training Act): EFG established in the field of vocational training after extensive experimental period. The year also witnessed the introduction of a general numerus clausus system covering higher education.

Bibliography

Contents

I General contributions

1.1 General histories of social policy

DICH, Jørgen S.: Kompendium i socialpolitikkens historie (Compendium on the history of social policy). Århus, Økonomisk Institut, Århus Universitet, 1967. Historical account of social policy up to the 1933 social reform.

DICH, Jørgen S.: 'Socialpolitikkens udviklingstendenser', *Nationaløkonomisk Tidsskrift*, 76: 1, 1938, pp. 4-33. An attempt to construct a typology of social policies and the motives behind them.

DYBDAHL, Vagn: Dansk social historie 5: Det nye samfund på vej 1871-1913 (Danish social history vol. 5: The transition to the new society). København, Gyldendal, 1982. Broad historical account on social relations, living conditions, demographic changes, social policies, etc. covering the period 1871-1913.

HANSEN, Sven Aage, HENRIKSEN, Ingrid: Dansk social historie 6: Sociale brydninger 1914-39 (Danish social history vol. 6: Social cleavages 1914-39). København, Gyldendal, 1980. Broad historical account on social relations, living conditions, demographic changes, social policies, etc. covering the period 1914-39.

HANSEN, Sven Aage, HENRIKSEN, Ingrid: Dansk social historie 7: Velfærdsstaten 1940-1978 (Danish social history vol. 7: The welfare state 1940-1978). København, Gyldendal, 1981. Broad historical account on social relations, living conditions, demographic changes, social policies, etc. covering the period 1940-1978.

OTTE, Helle, SANDVEJ, Henriette, STIGEL, Lars, SØRENSEN, Else Marie: 'Socialpolitik i Danmark, 1891-1977' (Social policy in Denmark, 1891-1977), *Jyske Historiker*, 10, 1977, pp. 5-163. Marxist interpretation of the development of social policy.

PETERSEN, Jørn Henrik: The Development of the Danish Welfare State and its Present Status. Odense, Odense Universitet, Institut for Samfundsvidenskab, 1978. Traces the development of the Danish welfare state since the 1880s. Includes a number of quantitative time-series.

PHILIP, Kjeld: Staten og fattigdommen (The State and Poverty). København, Gjellerup, 2nd ed., 1965. Major historical account of the development of social policy in Denmark up to World War II.

RASMUSSEN, Erik: 'Velfærdsstaten på vej 1913-1939' (The breakthrough of the welfare state, 1913-1939). *In* Politikkens Danmarkshistorie, vol. 13. København, 1965. Broad political history on the breakthrough of state regulation, including social policies, and new patterns of interactions between the state and interest groups. Focusing on the political struggle, parties and parliament.

1.2 Accounts of specific periods

Danmarks Sociale Lovgivning 1891-1941 (Social security legislation in Denmark, 1891-1941), *Socialt Tidsskrift* København, 1941. Important reference work for social security legislation in the period, 1891-1941.

ENGELSTOFT, P., JENSEN, Hans: Bidrag til arbejderklassens og arbejderspørgsmålets historie i Danmark 1864-1900 (Contributions to the history of the working class and the working class question in Denmark, 1864-1900). København, 1931. Major historical account of the early mobilization of the working class and the general debate and policy pertaining to the working class question.

ENGELSTOFT, P., JENSEN, Hans: Sociale studier i dansk historie efter 1857 (Social studies in Danish history after 1857). København, 1930. Historical account of issues in social policy during the formative years after 1857.

JØRGENSEN, Harald: Studier over det offentlige fattigvæsens historiske udvikling i Danmark i det 19. århundrede (Studies on the historical development of public poor relief in Denmark in the 19th century). København, 1947. Major historical account of the early development of public poor relief.

KUHNLE, Stein: 'The growth of social insurance programs in Scandinavia: Outside influences and internal forces'. *In* FLORA, Peter and Arnold J. HEIDENHEIMER (eds): The Development of Welfare States in Europe and America. New Brunswick, N.J., Transaction Inc., 1981, pp. 125-150.

Socialpolitikken i Danmark 1939-1945. Belyst ved udviklingen i de sociale udgifter i finansårene 1939/39 - 1945/46 (Social policy in Denmark, 1939-1945. Illustrated by the development in social welfare expenditure during the fiscal years 1938/39 -1945/46), *Socialt Tidsskrift*, 1947, pp. 251-309.

STEINCKE, K.K.: Fremtidens forsørgelsesvæsen I (The future of the system of public maintenance, vol. I). København, 1920. Historical account of the development of poor relief, with proposals on how to change the system of public maintenance. Written by the 'father' of the 1933 Social Reform, the social democratic Minister of Social Affairs, K.K. Steincke.

Sygekassenævnet: Fra laugssygekasse til folkeforsikring (The Sickness Insurance Board: From guild sickness insurance funds to universal sickness insurance). København, 1942. Traces the development of sickness insurance from the medieval guilds through voluntary sickness insurance funds to a publicly supported social insurance system.

1.3 Introductions into the system of social policies

FRIIS, Henning: 'Issues in social security policies in Denmark'. *In* JENKINS, Shirley (ed.): Social Security in International Perspective. New York, Columbia University Press, 1969.

GECKLER, Søren: Sociale forhold (Social Affairs). København, 1978. Introduction to the system of social security, organized according to individual schemes and programmes.

JOHANSEN, Lars Nørby: The Danish Welfare State, 1945-1980: Institutional Profile and Basic Tables. Odense, Odense Universitet, Institut for Samfundsvidenskab, *Rapporter og Dokumentation*, 12, 1982.

LUNDQVIST, Per: Sociallovgivning (Social Legislation). København, Nyt Nordisk Forlag, 1982. Introduction to social security legislation.

MARCUSSEN, Ernst: Social Welfare in Denmark. København, Det Danske Selskab, 1980. Broad and descriptive introduction to the system of social security.

Sociale love (Social Laws). København, Schultz's lovservice, continuously updated. Basic collection of laws, governmental decrees and circulars, rules, benefit scales, etc. in the field of social security. Organized according to the following entries: daily cash benefits, old age and invalidity pensions, structure and administration, child allowances and health security, accident insurance, social assistance and special care, other pensions and foreigners plus a register-volume.

1.4 Reports by investigating committees or experts

ARBEJDSGRUPPEN OM SOCIALINDKOMST: Socialindkomst (Social Income). København, Direktoratet for Statens Indkøb, 1980. Public report on the concept of 'social income', i.e. a new income measure for income-related social benefits.

SOCIALFORSKNINGSINSTITUTTET (Danish National Institute of Social Research): Socialreformundersøgelserne (Studies for Social Reform), 44, 49 and 53 (English summaries). København, Socialforskningsinstituttet, 1970, 1971 and 1972. Empirical analyses of various aspects of the system of social security. Based on a largescale national survey. Important background material for the Social Reform Commission. Covers the following topics: the citizen and the welfare agencies (Vol. II), the social benefits and services (Vol. III) and social vulnerability and resistance (Vol. IV).

SOCIALREFORMKOMMISSIONEN (Social Reform Commission): Det sociale tryghedssystem. Struktur og dagpenge (The Social Security System: Structure and Daily Cash Benefits), *Betænkning* no. 543, København, 1969. Very important report from the Social Reform Commission leading to thorough reforms of the system of administration, and the system of reimbursement from state to local authorities. Includes a description of both the development of the social security system and the system existing at that time.

SOCIALREFORMKOMMISSIONEN (Social Reform Commission): Det sociale tryghedssystem: Service og bistand (The Social Security System: Services and Assistance), *Betænkning* no. 664, København, 1972. Very important report from the Social Reform Commission leading to the 1976 Social Assistance Act. Includes a description of the development of social assistance and of the relationship between social assistance in cash and in kind.

1.5 Social science interpretations, evaluations, or analyses

ABRAHAMSEN, Peter et al.: Socialpolitik og kapitalisme: en antologi (Social Policy and Capitalism). København, Kurasje, 1978. Essays on the role of social policy in advanced capitalism from a marxist perspective.

ANDERSEN, Bent Rold: Bedre prioritering i socialpolitikken (Better Priorities in Social Policy). København, Det Danske Forlag, 1971. Analytical treatment of how to make priorities in social policy. An example of 'expert advice' that came to play an important role for the introduction of social reforms in the 1970s.

ANDERSEN, Bent Rold: 'A Danish study of the functioning of the system of social security', *Journal of Social Policy*, 1, 1972, pp. 331-344. English summary of the social reform investigations, i.e. the empirical analyses of the working of the social security system prior to the social reforms of the 1970s.

ANDERSEN, Bent Rold: Grundprincipper i socialpolitikken (Basic Principles in Social Policy). København, Det Danske Forlag, 1973. General analysis of fundamental social policy principles, with a host of empirical examples. These principles came to exert influence over actual social policies during the 1970s.

ANDERSEN, Bent Rold: Socialpolitik i velfærdssamfundet (Social Policy in the Welfare State). København, 1966. General discussion of the role of social policy in a welfare society. Includes a wealth of Danish examples and illustrations.

ANDERSEN, Bent Rold: Velfærdsstat og velfærdsteori (Welfare State and Welfare Theory). København, 1961. General analytical treatment of welfare economics and social policy.

DICH, Jørgen S.; Den herskende klasse: En kritisk analyse af social udbytning og midlerne imod den (The Ruling Class: A Critical Analysis of Social Exploitation and Counter Measures). København, Borgen, 1974. Provocative analysis of the producers of social services in the fields of social welfare, health care and education. Shows how this 'class' promotes their own interests to the detriment of workers by means of humanistic ideology and political manoeuvering.

DICH, Jørgen S.: 'Udviklingen af skatte- og tilskudspolitikken siden 1939' (The development of policies of taxation and subsidization since 1939), *Økonomi og Politik*, 39, 1965, pp. 227-260. An attempt to account for the development of policies of taxation and subsidization by focusing on vote maximizing party strategies. Makes the case that the Social Democratic party has not met the interests of its core-voters (workers) to the benefit of floating or marginal voters.

ESPING-ANDERSEN, Gösta: 'Comparative social policy and political conflict in advanced welfare states: Denmark and Sweden', *International Journal of Health Services*, 9: 2, 1979, pp. 269-293.

ESPING-ANDERSEN, Gösta, KORPI, Walter: 'From poor relief to institutional welfare states: The development of Scandinavian social policy'. *In* ERIKSSON, R. et al. (eds): Welfare Research and Welfare Society. New York, M.E. Sharp, forthcoming.

ESPING-ANDERSEN, Gösta: Social Class, Social Democracy, and State Policy: Party Policy and Party Decomposition in Denmark and Sweden. København, Nyt fra Samfundsvidenskaberne, 1980. Comparative analysis of the effects of welfare state policies - especially housing policy, on the electoral support of political parties, especially the Social Democratic party. Includes descriptions of Social Democratic parties and social policies in Denmark and Sweden.

HOFFMEYER, Erik (ed.): Velfærdsteori og velfærdsstat (Welfare Theory and Welfare State). København, Berlingske Forlag, 1962. Essays on welfare economics and the Danish welfare state.

HORNEMANN MØLLER, Iver: Klassekamp og Sociallovgivning 1850-1970 (Class Struggle and Social Legislation, 1850-1970). København, Socialistiske Økonomer, 1981. Analysis, description and interpretation of the development of social policy within a structuralist-marxist theoretical framework.

JENSEN, Mogens Kjær: Sociale problemer og ydelser 1966-1977 (Social problems and benefits, 1966-1977), *Meddelelse*, 30. København, Socialforskningsinstituttet, 1980. Empirical analysis of the relationship between various kinds of risks and problems and social benefits. Based on survey data.

KNUDSEN, Rita: De kontante ydelsers størrelse - 1978 (The size of cash benefits -1978), *Publikation*, 88. København, Socialforskningsinstituttet, 1979. Analysis of various types of compensation ratios for various types of social cash benefits. Updating a previous analysis of the same kind (see below).

KNUDSEN, Rita: Størrelsen af de sociale underholdsydelser (The size of social benefits), *Publikation*, 20. København, Socialforskningsinstituttet, 1965. Analysis of various types of compensation ratios for various types of social benefits. Includes time-series.

LOGUE, John: 'The welfare state: victim of its success', *Daedalus*, 108 (special issue on the state), 1979, pp. 69-87. Discussion of contemporary traits and problems of the Scandinavian welfare states with special emphasis on the Danish welfare state.

PERS, Henrik: Velfærdsstatens gennembrud i Danmark (The Breakthrough of the Welfare State in Denmark). København, Uglen, 1981. Comprehensive analysis of the politics surrounding the introduction of universal, flat-rate public old-age pensions.

PETERSEN, Jørn Henrik: Socialpolitisk teori. Vols I - III (Theories of Social Policy. Vols I - III). Odense, Odense Universitetsforlag, 1972, 1974 and 1978. General theoretical analyses mainly based on welfare economics, public goods and public choice theories, but also including a host of empirical analyses and examples drawn from Danish social policy experiences plus a description of the development of social policy in Denmark.

1.6 Policy proposals and debates

BJERREGAARD, Ritt, LUNDGAARD, Lars: Til venner og fjender af dansk socialpolitik (To Friends and Foes of Danish Social Policy). København, Gyldendal, 1982. Essays on various aspects of social policy written by two prominent social politicians.

CHRISTIANSEN, Terkel: Synspunkter på 1970'ernes socialreform (Viewpoints on the Social Reform of the 1970s). Odense, Odense Universitetsforlag, 1974. Collection of relevant sources, debates, rules, etc., in the context of the social reforms of the 1970s.

HAARDER, Bertel: Institutionernes tyranni (The Tyranny of Institutions). København, Bramsen og Hjort, 1974. Discussion of growth-mechanisms in the public sector focusing on the role of public institutions. Written by a prominent politician from the Agrarian Liberals.

HAMMER, Ole, MALTESEN, Ib (eds): Socialpolitik i klemme: 80'ernes udfordringer! (The Squeeze on Social Policy: Challenges of the 1980s). København, Socialpolitisk Forening, 1980. Critical essays on social policies in the 1980s.

LYKKETOFT, Mogens (ed.): Kravet om lighed. En redegørelse fra den socialdemokratiske folketingsgruppes lighedskommission (The Demand for Equality. A Report from the Social Democratic Commission on Equality). København, Fremad, 1975. Social Democratic essays on equality policy based on a report from a Social Democratic commission.

SOCIALDEMOKRATIET (Social Democratic Party): Redegørelsen fra lighedskommissionen (Report from the Equality Commission). København, 1973. Social Democratic policy statement on equality.

RISHØJ PEDERSEN, Søren (ed.): Fagbevægelsen og socialpolitikken (Trade Union Movement and Social Policy), København, Socialpolitisk Forening, 1976. Critical essays on the trade union movement's attitudes and policies towards social policies and of the relationship between labour market policies and traditional social policies.

1.7 Opinion polls

ANDERSEN, Jørgen Goul: 'Den folkelig tilslutning til socialpolitikken. En krise for velfærdsstaten?' (Popular support of social policy. A crisis of the welfare state?). *In* ANCKAR, Dag, DAMGAARD, Erik, VALEN, Henry (eds): Partier, ideologier og våljare (Parties, Ideologies and Voters). Åbo, Publications of the Research Institute of the Åbo Akademi Foundation, Åbo Akademi, 1982, pp. 175-209. Analysis of popular attitudes towards social policy and social reform across various background variables (party identification, gender, class, age, etc.) in the 1970s, based on survey data.

Danish Data Guide. Update 1982, Dansk Dataarkiv, DDA (Danish Data Archives), Odense, 1982. Updated survey of documented and machine-readable data archives. Includes a variety of data archives on popular opinions towards social policy and the welfare state, public expenses, social security system, social indicators, social problems and relations as well as more specific data archives on unemployment, education, standards of living, environmental effects, etc.

1.8 Sources of statistics or institutional regulations

DANMARKS STATISTIK (The Danish Statistical Bureau): Bistandslovsstatistik (Statistics on Social Assistance). København, published periodically. Detailed statistics on social assistance.

DANMARKS STATISTIK (The Danish Statistical Bureau): Statistisk Årbog (Statistical Yearbook). København, annual publication. Wide coverage of statistics related to public expenditure and revenues, social expenditure, social conditions and social welfare.

DANMARKS STATISTIK (The Danish Statistical Bureau): Statistiske efterretninger (Statistical Reports). København, published periodically. Reorganized from 1983; includes now a special series on social security and law (Social sikring og retsvæsen). More detailed reports on specific aspects of social security, e.g. beneficiaries of social assistance by type of social assistance, old age and invalidity pensioners by type of pension, cash benefits in case of sickness by type and duration, unemployment figures.

DANMARKS STATISTIK (The Danish Statistical Bureau): Statistisk tiårsoversigt (Statistical Ten-Year Survey). København, annual publication. Gives ten years' time-series for key-figures on public expenditure and revenues both by real and functional categories, social expenditure and social conditions.

MOURITZEN, Poul Erik, PETERSEN, Kjeld Juel: Sociale data (Social Data). Århus, Politica, 1979. Key to social data and statistics at the level of local authorities.

NORDISK STATISTISK SKRIFTSERIE (Series of Nordic Statistics): Social trygghet i de nordiske lande (Social Security in the Nordic Countries), published every three years, different locations. The series started in 1954. Gives a comparative outline of social security and welfare institutions and statistics on financing and expenditure in Denmark, Finland, Iceland, Norway, and Sweden.

1.9 Major periodicals

Nationaløkonomisk Tidsskrift (Journal of Economics), København, quarterly publication. General journal in the field of economics, but often including articles on social policy.

Socialt Tidsskrift (Journal of Social Policy), København, published monthly. Discontinued in 1978, but a new periodical with same title is presently under publication. Includes articles on various aspects of social policy plus various types of documentary materials.

Økonomi og politik (Journal of Economics and Politics), Odense, published quarterly. General journal for social science research which frequently publishes analyses relating to welfare state topics.

II Single programmes

2.1 Pensions

Betænkning no. 452, 1967: Betænkning om principperne for en almindelig tillægspensionsordning (Report on Principles for a General Superannuation Scheme). København, 1967. Report from a public commission proposing a number of models for supplementary pensions or superannuation.

Betænkning no. 755, 1975: Rapport om udvidet adgang til førtidig folkepension og fleksibel pensionsalder (Report on Increased Access to Early Old Age Pensions and a Flexible Pension Age). København, 1975. Report from a public commission proposing models for extended access to early retirement schemes.

Betænkning no. 799, 1975: Rapport om principper for en reform af de sociale pensioner (Report on Principles for a Reform of Social Pensions). København, 1975. Major report from a public commission on reforms of various pension schemes.

Betænkning no. 835, 1978: Betænkning om efterløn (Report on Severance Pay). København, 1979. Report from a public commission proposing a scheme on severance pay, which was subsequently translated into law.

FRIIS, Henning, HANSEN, Per Vejrup: Pensions and Retirement Up to the Year 2000. København, The Danish National Institute of Social Research, 1980. Analysis of the development of expenditure for the welfare of the elderly and early retirement from the labour market in the context of changing demographic and economic conditions.

JENSEN, Carsten Vesterø: Det tvedelte pensionssystem i Danmark (The dual pension system in Denmark), unpublished working paper. Florence, European University Institute, 1982. Analysis of the public pension system vis-a-vis private pension and savings schemes. Data on incidence and social distribution of private pension and savings schemes.

SOCIALFORSKNINGSINSTITUTTET (The Danish National Institute of Social Research): Invalidepensionistundersøgelse (Surveys of Disabled Pensioners), *Publikation*, 84, 85, 95, 100 (English summaries). København, Socialforskningsinstituttet, 1978, 1979, 1980. Empirical analyses of various aspects of disabled pensioners based on a large-scale nation-wide survey. Covers: applicants for disability pensions (vol. IV), situation after the first application (vol. IV), living conditions of disabled pensioners (vol. VI), family and occupational background (vol. VII).

SOCIALFORSKNINGSINSTITUTTET (The Danish National Institute of Social Research): Undersøgelser af fysisk handicappede i Danmark (Surveys of Physically Handicapped in Denmark), *Publikation*, 16, 18, 22, 26, 27, (English summaries). København, Socialforskningsinstituttet, 1964, 1965, 1966, 1967. Empirical analyses of various aspects of physically handicapped based on a nation-wide survey. Covers: summary of major results (vol. II), housing conditions and transport problems (vol. III), work and employment (vol. IV), economic and social conditions (vol. V), psychological characteristics (vol. VI).

SOCIALFORSKNINGSINSTITUTTET (The Danish National Institute of Social Research): Undersøgelser af de ældres levevilkår (Surveys of Living Conditions of the Aged), *Publikation*, 17, 23, 28, 29, 33, 40 (English summaries). København, Socialforskningsinstituttet, 1965, 1966, 1967, 1968, 1970. Empirical analyses of the living conditions of the aged based on a large-scale, nation-wide survey. Covers: income (vol. III), household and dwelling (vol. IV), mobility and incapacity for self-care (vol. V) and family contacts (vol. VI).

SOCIALFORSKNINGSINSTITUTTET (The Danish National Institute of Social Research): Undersøgelser af de ældres levevilkår (Surveys of Living Conditions of the Aged), *Publikation*, 74, 79, 105 (English summaries). København, Socialforskningsinstituttet, 1976, 1977, 1981. Surveys of living conditions of the elderly based on panel and cohort analysis. Covers: family contacts in the early stages of old age, retirement from work and income, work and retirement.

ÆLDREKOMMISSIONEN (The Old Age Commission): Sammenhæng i ældrepolitikken (Coherence in Policies towards the Elderly). København, Socialministeriet, 1981. Concluding report from a public commission set up to investigate a number of problems pertaining to old age.

2.2 Health

Betænkning no. 809: Prioritering i sundhedsvæsenet (Priorities in the Health Sector). København, Indenrigsministeriet, 1977. Report from a public commission on priorities in the health care sector. Includes a wealth of statistical data and descriptions of most aspects of the public health care system.

SOCIALFORSKNINGSINSTITUTTET (The Danish National Institute of Social Research): Undersøgelse i den primære sundhedstjeneste (Survey of the Primary Health Service), *Publikation*, 92, 97, 106 (English summaries). København, Socialforskningsinstituttet, 1979, 1980, 1981. Empirical analyses of various aspects of primary health services. Based in part on survey data. Covers: home nurses, organization, functions and co-operation (vol. I), health-visitors, organization, functions and co-operation (vol. II), and co-operation within the primary health care system (vol. IV).

STEENSTRUP, Jens Erik, ØSTERBYE, Kristian Madsen: Sundhedssektoren. Ressourcer og produktion siden 1965 (The Health Care Sector. Production and Resources since 1965). København, Amtskommunernes og kommunernes forskningsinstitut, 1980. Introduction to the institutional structure of the health care sector plus statistics on production, resources, etc. since 1965.

SUNDHEDSSTYRELSEN (The Health Board): Medicinalberetninger, Sygehusstatistik (Health Reports, Statistics on Hospitals). København, published periodically. Important source of statistics on hospitals and health care.

SYGESIKRINGENS FORHANDLINGSUDVALG (The Negotiating Committee of the Health Security System): Sygesikringsstatistik (Statistics on Health Security). København, published periodically. Important source of statistics particularly on the primary health care sector.

2.3 Unemployment

MØLLER, Iver Hornemann: Ungdomsarbejdsløshed (Youth unemployment), *Meddelelse*, 25. København, Socialforskningsinstituttet, 1978.

PEDERSEN, Peder J.: 'Arbejdsstyrke og beskæftigelse 1911-70' (Labour force and employment, 1911-70), *Social Tidsskrift*, 2, 1977. Analysis of labour force and employment development, containing important time-series (also on the development of unionization).

SOCIALFORSKNINGSINSTITUTTET (The Danish National Institute of Social Research): Arbejdsløshedsundersøgelserne (The Unemployment Surveys), *Publikation*, 91, 96, 107, 111 (English summaries). København, Socialforskningsinstituttet, 1979, 1980, 1982. Empirical analyses of unemployment. Based in part on a large-scale, nation-wide survey. Covers: demand and supply of the labour market (vol. I), extent of unemployment and sickness absence (vol. II), market, state policy and consequences on welfare (vol. III) and wage differences, wage policy and employment in the 1970s (vol. IV).

2.4 Accidents

EYBEN, Bo von: Kompensation for personskade I (Compensation in Case of Accident, Vol. I). København, 1982. Major work on accident insurance.

2.5 Social assistance

FRIIS, Henning, WARBURG, Erik: Langvarigt forsorgsunderstøttede (Persons on Long-Term Public Maintenance), *Publikation*, 1. København, Socialforskningsinstituttet, 1960. Empirical analysis of beneficiaries of long-term social benefits and services.

KÖRMENDI, Eszter: Psykisk handicappede (Mentally Handicapped), *Publikation*, 67. København, Socialforskningsinstituttet, 1976. Empirical analysis of standards of living of various groups of mentally retarded and of social services for these groups.

LINDBOE, Ole, THORSEN, Hanne (eds): Bistandsloven. Myte og realitet (Social Assistance Act. Myth and Reality). København, 1978. Critical evaluation of the Social Assistance Act focusing on the effects of changed economic conditions for the functioning of social assistance.

SOCIALFORSKNINGSINSTITUTTET (The Danish National Institute of Social Research): Socialreformundersøgelserne (Surveys of Social Reform), *Publikation*, 112. København, Socialforskningsinstituttet, 1982. First report from a larger project on the effects of the social reforms of the 1970s.

2.6 Family programmes

BØRNEKOMMISSIONEN (The Commission on Children): Børnefamiliernes økonomi og arbejdsforhold. Udvalgsrapport nr. 1 (Economy and Working Conditions of Families with Children, Report no. 1). København, 1980. Report from a public commission focusing on the economy and working conditions of families.

BØRNEKOMMISSIONEN (The Commission on Children): Småbørn, daginstitutioner og dagpleje. Udvalgsrapport nr. 3 (Small Children, Day Care Institutions and Day Care, Report no. 3). København, 1980. Report from a public commission on day care institutions and day care for small children.

BØRNEKOMMISSIONEN (The Commission on Children): Småbørn i bolig og miljø. Udvalgsrapport nr. 2 (Housing and Environmental Conditions of Small Children, Report no. 2). København, 1980. Report from a public commission focusing on housing and environmental conditions for small children.

BØRNEKOMMISSIONEN (The Commission on Children): Småbørn og tidlig indsats. Udvalgsrapport nr. 4 (Small Children and Early Social Services. Report no. 4). København, 1980. Report from a public commission focusing on preventative and other social services for small children.

DUE, Johannes: 'De familiepolitiske kontantydelser 1903-76' (Cash benefits in the field of families and children, 1903-76), *Social Tidsskrift*, 5, 1977. Longitudinal analysis of cash benefits for children and families. Includes aggregate data as well as data on compensation ratios.

2.7 Housing

WENDT, P.: Housing Policy - The Search for Solutions. Berkely, University of California Press, 1962. Somewhat outdated but still a good introduction to Danish housing policy and problems in the construction sector.

WENDT, Peter: Byggeri og boligforhold (Construction and Housing). København, 1975. Introduction to the housing and construction sector including descriptions of public policies in this field.

WILHJELM, Preben: Dansk boligpolitik - forbrydelse eller dumhed? (Danish Housing Policy - Crime or Stupidity?). København, Røde Hane, 1971. Critical evaluation of Danish housing policy.

2.8 Education

HANSEN, Erik Jørgen: De 14-20 åriges uddannelsessituation 1965. Bind I. Social og geografisk rekruttering (The Educational Conditions in 1965 for Those Between 14 and 20 Years of Age. Vol. I: Social and Geographical Recruitment), *Publikation*, 31. København, Socialforskningsinstituttet, 1968.

HANSEN, Erik Jørgen: De 14-30 åriges uddannelsessituation 1965. Bind II. Ungdom og uddannelse (The Educational Conditions in 1965 for Those Between 14 and 20 Years of Age. Vol. II: Youth and Education), *Publikation*, 47. København, Socialforskningsinstituttet, 1971.

2.9 Public household

HANSEN, Finn Kenneth: Forbrugsmuligheder og omfordelinger over den offentlige sektor (Consumption Choices and Redistribution through the Public Sector). København, Lavindkomstkommissionen, 1981. Report from the Low Income Commission focusing on redistribution through the public sector.

HANSEN, Kurt: 'Udviklingen i det offentliges indtægter og udgifter siden 1929' (Development of public expenditure and revenues since 1929), *Økonomi og Politik*, 31, 1957, pp. 167-184. Analysis of the development of public expenditure and revenues since 1929. Contains important data for the period between the World Wars.

NORDSTRAND, Rolf: 'Den offentlige sektor i 80'erne' (The public sector in the 80's), *Nationaløkonomisk Tidsskrift*, 3, 1979, pp. 396-408.

PETERSEN, Jørn Henrik: 'Væksten i den offentlige sektor 1960-75 i internationalt perspektiv' (Growth in the public sector 1960-75 in an international perspective), *Nationaløkonomisk Tidsskrift*, 118: 2, 1980, pp. 184-200. Empirical analysis of the growth of public expenditure in Denmark in an international perspective.

2.10 Public employment

NORDSTRAND, Rolf: Personaleforbrug, produktion og arbejdsproduktivitet i den offentlige sektor i Danmark (Consumption of manpower resources, production and work productivity in the public sector in Denmark), memo no. 105. København, Københavns Universitets Økonomiske Institut, 1981. An attempt to measure and analyse productivity in the public sector.

III Impact of social programmes

3.1 Poverty

FRIIS, Henning: Poverty and Poverty Policy in Denmark. København, The Danish National Institute of Social Research, 1980. In Danish: Nederst ved vordet (At the End of the Table), *Publikation*, 108. København, Socialforskningsinstituttet, 1981. Report on poverty and poverty policy in Denmark prepared for the Commission of the European Communities. Contains a wealth of data on achievements and shortcomings of the Danish welfare state.

3.2 Inequality and income distribution

Betænkning no. 673, 1972: Betænkning vedrørende ligestilling (Report on Equality between the Sexes). København, 1972.

BJERKE, Kjeld, BRODERSEN, Søren: 'Studies of income redistribution in Denmark for 1963 and 1971', *Review of Income and Wealth*, 24, 2, 1978.

GECKLER, Søren, HANSEN, Erik Jørgen: The Development in the Distribution of the Standard of Living in Denmark. København, Socialforskningsinstituttet, 1976.

HANSEN, Bent: Velstand uden velfærd: en kritik af det danske klassesamfund (Wealth without Welfare). København, Fremad, 1976. Description and analysis of various aspects of inequality written by a prominent Social Democrat.

HANSEN, Erik Jørgen: The Distribution of Living Conditions in Denmark, *Publikation*, 110 (English summary of Publikation, 82, see below). København, Socialforskningsinstituttet, 1982.

HANSEN, Erik Jørgen et al.: Fordelingen af levekårene. Bind I-V (The Distribution of Living Conditions. Vol. I-V), *Publikation*, 82. København, Socialforskningsinstituttet, 1978-80. Comprehensive study of various aspects of standards of living based on an extensive nationwide survey.

LAVINDKOMSTKOMMISSIONEN (The Low Income Commission): Lavindkomstkommissionens betænkning (The Low Income Distribution), *Betænkning* no. 946. København, 1982.

Final report issued by the Low Income Commission. Summarizes the findings from a large number of working papers and interim reports from the commission.

LAVINDKOMSTKOMMISSIONEN (The Low Income Commission): Udviklingen i den personlige indkomstfordeling for erhvervsaktive 1970-1976 (Development of Personal Income Distribution among the Economically Active, 1970-1976), Delrapport 1. København, 1979. Report from the Low Income Commission focusing on the distribution of personal income among the economically active, applying various measures of income inequality.

LAVINDKOMSTKOMMISSIONEN (The Low Income Commission): Udviklingen i formuefordelingen 1960-1977 (Development of the Distribution of Property 1960- 1977). København, Lavindkomstkommissionen, 1979.

OLSEN, P. Bjørn, KAMPMANN, Viggo: 'Indkomstudjævningen i Danmark' (Income equalization in Denmark), *Socialt Tidsskrift* 24, 1948, pp. 49-60. Empirical analysis of tendencies towards income equalization.

WORM, Kirsten (ed.): Levevilkår i Danmark: Statistisk oversigt 1980 (Living Conditions in Denmark: A Statistical Survey 1980). København, Socialforskningsinstituttet, 1980. Summary of findings on various aspects of standards of living based on a nationwide survey.

DET ØKONOMISKE RÅDS FORMANDSKAB (The Economic Council): Den personlige indkomstfordeling og indkomstudjævningen over de offentlige finanser (The Personal Income Distribution and Redistribution through the Public Household). København, 1967. Basic analysis of income distribution and redistributive effects of the public sector's activities.

3.3 Economic effects

ANDERSEN, Bent Rold: Socialpolitikkens virkninger: Måling og vurdering (The Effects of Social Policy: Measurement and Evaluation). København, Amtskommunernes og Kommunernes Forskningsprojekt, 1976. Discussion and analysis of how to measure and evaluate the effects of social policy.

ARBEJDSGRUPPEN TIL UNDERSØGELSE AF FINANSIERINGSFORHOLDENE I DEN SOCIALE SEKTOR OG TILGRÆNSEDE OMRÅDER (Working Group on Systems of Financing in the Social and Related Sectors): Rapport om finansiering (Report on Financing). København, Socialministeriet, 1981. Presentation of the existing system of financing social security plus reform proposals.

DICH, Jørgen S.: 'Administration og økonomiske problemer i socialpolitikken' (Administrative and economic problems in social policy), *Socialt Tidsskrift*, 46, 1970, pp. 91-115. Critical evaluation of economic effects stemming from the social security system's administrative structure as proposed by the Social Reform Commission.

JENSEN, J. Børglum: 'Skatte- og tilskudspolitikkens omfordelende virkninger' (Redistributive effects of tax policies and state subsidies), *Nationaløkonomisk Tidsskrift*, 113: 2, 1976, pp. 335-351.

SEIERUP, H.C.: 'Socialreform og socialpolitik i samfundsøkonomisk perspektiv' (Social reform and social policy in a macro-economic perspective), *National økonomisk Tidsskrift*, 109, 1971, pp. 254-265. Discussion by the chairman of the Social Reform Commission on the economic preconditions for and effects of social reforms, with emphasis placed on the social reforms of the 1970s.

Appendix Tables

Contents

Table 1 Gross National Product and Total Public Expenditure

Year	GNP (at market prices, in million DKR)			Deflators (base 1975)				Total Public Expenditure (in million DKR)				Year
	At current prices	At 1975 prices	Annual real growth rate	GDP	Private cons.	Public cons.	Gross cap. form	At current prices	As % of GNP	At 1975 prices	Annual real growth rate	
1950/51	23 132							5 126	22.2			1950/51
1951/52	25 050	91 423		27.4	31.8	15.4	30.2	5 958	23.8	27 759		1951/52
1952/53	26 690	92 997	1.7	28.7	32.5	16.6	32.1	6 597	24.7	29 075	4.7	1952/53
1953/54	28 550	98 448	5.9	29.0	32.9	16.8	31.0	7 087	24.8	31 262	7.5	1953/54
1954/55	29 891	101 670	3.3	29.4	33.4	17.6	31.4	7 458	25.0	32 170	2.9	1954/55
1955/56	31 270	101 526	-0.1	30.8	34.9	18.4	32.1	7 943	25.4	32 785	1.9	1955/56
1956/57	33 403	103 415	1.9	32.3	36.3	19.6	33.9	8 531	25.5	33 224	1.3	1956/57
1957/58	35 542	108 030	4.5	32.9	36.8	20.1	34.9	9 297	26.2	35 096	5.6	1957/58
1958/59	37 132	111 174	2.9	33.4	37.0	21.3	35.3	9 933	26.8	36 092	2.8	1958/59
1959/60	41 101	118 447	6.5	34.7	38.0	21.6	35.7	10 706	26.0	38 313	6.2	1959/60
1960/61	44 430	125 864	6.3	35.3	39.2	22.2	36.3	11 493	25.9	40 005	4.4	1960/61
1961/62	49 375	134 171	6.6	36.8	40.6	25.5	38.0	13 830	28.0	43 699	9.2	1961/62
1962/63	55 686	141 695	5.6	39.3	43.1	27.5	40.0	15 981	28.7	47 434	8.6	1962/63
1963/64	59 185	142 614	0.6	41.5	45.5	28.9	41.5	17 470	29.5	49 291	3.9	1963/64
1964/65	67 696	155 623	9.1	43.5	47.3	31.0	42.8	19 947	29.5	53 413	8.4	1964/65
1965/66	76 065	162 880	4.7	46.7	50.2	35.3	45.2	23 372	30.7	56 807	6.4	1965/66
1966/67	83 710	167 756	3.0	49.9	53.5	38.5	47.5	26 956	32.2	60 853	7.1	1966/67
1966/67	83 710	181 584		46.1	47.5	39.1	46.3	26 956	32.2	62 713		1966/67
1967/68	91 796	187 722	3.4	48.9	50.7	41.6	48.5	31 887	34.7	69 739	11.2	1967/68
1968/69	101 192	193 115	2.9	52.4	54.5	46.2	51.2	37 238	36.8	74 746	7.2	1968/69
1969/70	115 168	205 657	6.5	56.0	57.1	48.9	54.6	42 222	36.7	79 419	6.3	1969/70
1970/71	127 944	211 478	2.8	60.5	61.2	54.5	59.2	51 226	40.0	89 044	12.1	1970/71
1970/71	118 627	196 078		60.5	61.2	54.5	59.2	51 136	43.1	88 799		1970/71
1971/72	131 120	201 104	2.6	65.2	66.2	60.8	63.1	58 250	44.4	92 363	4.0	1971/72
1972/73	150 729	211 996	5.4	71.1	71.6	66.2	67.7	66 662	44.2	97 380	5.4	1972/73
1973/74	172 860	219 924	3.7	78.6	79.4	73.1	75.1	75 530	43.7	99 842	2.5	1973/74
1974/75	193 629	218 297	-0.7	88.7	90.9	86.8	89.5	94 952	49.0	107 115	7.3	1974/75
1975/76	216 256	216 256	-0.9	100.0	100.0	100.0	100.0	108 136	50.0	108 136	1.0	1975/76
1976	251 214	230 472	6.6	109.0	109.8	108.9	107.8	121 364	48.3	111 204	2.8	1976
1977	279 310	235 705	2.3	118.5	120.3	117.4	117.9	138 238	49.5	116 516	4.8	1977
1978	311 376	239 889	3.7	129.8	131.1	126.2	127.2	159 508	51.2	124 278	6.7	1978
1979	346 892	248 668	3.7	139.5	144.8	135.8	136.9	186 485	53.8	133 434	7.4	1979
1980	374 732	248 167	-0.2	151.0	159.5	149.6	150.3	212 376	56.7	137 966	3.4	1980
1981	414 823	248 397	0.1	167.0	178.5	166.5	168.8	246 957	59.5	143 583	4.1	1981
1982	469 779	254 623	2.5	184.5	197.2	184.7	187.5	286 716	61.0	150 441	4.8	1982

Table 2

Public Expenditure by

Year	Economic Function: Percent distribution						Major Purpose: Percent distribution					Government level: Percent distribution				Year
	Gross capit. form.	Public final consumpt.	Of which: salaries	Transfers and subsidies	Of which: to private households	Interest on public debt	Education	Health	Social security	Defense	Others	Central govt.	Counties	Local govt.	Social insur.	
1950/51	24.4	43.0	25.4	27.9	24.6	4.7	8.4	10.6	25.7	6.6	48.7					1950/51
1951/52	23.4	44.1	25.3	28.2	24.7	4.3	8.3	10.3	25.5	8.0	47.9					1951/52
1952/53	22.2	44.9	25.8	28.3	24.6	4.6	8.4	10.2	25.6	8.4	47.3					1952/53
1953/54	22.5	45.7	26.6	26.7	23.9	5.1	8.5	10.2	25.7	11.5	44.1					1953/54
1954/55	22.7	47.5	27.9	24.8	22.9	5.0	9.4	10.6	24.8	11.1	44.1					1954/55
1955/56	22.0	47.0	27.8	25.9	24.4	5.1	11.3	11.0	26.2	11.3	40.3					1955/56
1956/57	22.0	46.7	28.6	26.3	24.7	5.0	11.7	11.2	26.3	10.9	39.9					1956/57
1957/58	21.3	45.5	28.0	28.3	26.9	4.9	11.1	11.0	28.3	9.8	39.8					1957/58
1958/59	21.8	45.3	28.7	28.5	26.8	4.4	11.5	11.3	27.7	9.4	40.1					1958/59
1959/60	21.8	45.6	28.3	28.3	26.6	4.3	12.7	11.5	27.1	8.9	39.8					1959/60
1960/61	22.4	45.3	27.8	28.3	26.2	4.0	13.4	11.4	26.5	9.1	39.6					1960/61
1961/62	22.0	45.2	29.7	29.5	24.7	3.3	14.1	12.0	25.1	8.7	40.1					1961/62
1962/63	21.3	46.3	31.0	29.4	24.6	3.0	14.8	12.2	24.8	9.7	38.6					1962/63
1963/64	21.2	45.9	30.5	29.7	25.2	3.2	14.5	12.4	24.7	9.1	39.2					1963/64
1964/65	22.5	46.2	30.9	28.2	23.9	3.1	14.1	12.2	23.5	9.0	41.2					1964/65
1965/66	22.1	46.4	32.0	28.6	24.8	2.9	14.9	12.6	24.5	8.1	40.0					1965/66
1966/67	21.7	43.3	32.0	32.2	25.5	2.8	15.2	13.6	24.7	7.4	39.2					1966/67
1967/68	21.6	45.3	31.3	30.5	26.1	2.6	15.0	13.2	25.9	7.2	38.7					1967/68
1968/69	21.1	44.7	31.0	31.8	26.8	2.4	15.1	13.3	26.5	6.3	38.8					1968/69
1969/70	20.8	44.7	31.1	31.9	26.9	2.6	16.1	13.8	26.1	5.9	38.2					1969/70
1970/71	14.6	47.0	32.3	34.5	26.3	3.9	16.4	12.7	35.3	5.8	29.7	37.4	8.3	48.9	5.4	1970/71
1971/72	13.4	48.6	33.7	34.4	26.3	3.6	16.9	12.9	35.9	5.7	28.6	37.3	8.3	48.8	5.7	1971/72
1972/73	12.1	49.7	34.0	35.1	26.5	3.1	17.4	12.9	37.0	5.2	27.5	37.2	7.9	48.8	6.1	1972/73
1973/74	10.7	50.4	35.0	35.9	26.2	3.0	16.8	12.4	37.6	5.0	28.2	37.8	10.2	50.7	1.3	1973 74
1974/75	11.2	50.2	34.6	36.0	26.6	2.6	16.5	12.6	38.7	5.1	27.1	36.5	10.3	49.9	3.3	1974/75
1975/76	10.4	50.9	35.8	36.2	28.5	2.5	16.5	12.3	40.3	5.0	25.9	35.6	10.2	49.0	5.1	1975/76
1976	10.5	50.0	35.4	36.7	28.0	2.8	15.7	12.1	39.7	4.9	27.8	35.0	11.6	48.4	5.0	1976
1977	9.8	48.5	34.8	37.9	28.6	3.8	15.0	11.2	39.9	4.6	29.3	35.3	10.7	48.2	5.9	1977
1978	9.4	47.8	34.1	38.5	29.1	4.3	14.5	10.8	40.4	4.4	29.9	34.5	10.8	48.2	6.5	1978
1979	9.1	46.5	33.1	37.9	28.6	6.5	14.3	10.4	40.2	4.0	31.1	35.6	10.9	46.9	6.6	1979
1980	8.1	47.1	32.9	37.9	29.2	6.9	14.2	10.2	40.2	4.4	31.0	36.6	11.4	44.6	7.4	1980
1981	7.6	46.4	32.4	36.9	29.4	8.7	14.0	9.7	40.2	4.4	31.7	34.4	11.6	44.9	9.1	1981
1982	7.1	45.9	32.4	37.3	29.2	9.7	13.5	9.6	39.5	4.3	33.1	36.1	11.1	43.8	9.0	1982

Table 3 Current Social Expenditure

Year	At current prices (in million DKR)							At constant (1975) prices (in million DKR)							Year
	Social security I	Social security II	Health	Education	Housing	Total I	Total II	Social security I	Social security II	Health	Education	Housing	Total I	Total II	
1951/52	1 519		600	497		2 616		4 931		3 896	3 227		12 054		1951/52
1952/53	1 690		671	556		2 917		5 551		4 042	3 349		12 942		1952/53
1953/54	1 825		722	602		3 149		5 945		4 298	3 583		13 826		1953/54
1954/55	1 850		789	699		3 338		5 933		4 483	3 972		14 388		1954/55
1955/56	2 075		876	894		3 845		6 348		4 761	4 859		15 968		1955/56
1956/57	2 244		957	995		4 196		6 576		4 883	5 077		16 536		1956/57
1957/58	2 635		1 022	1 027		4 684		7 656		5 085	5 109		17 850		1957/58
1958/59	2 752		1 126	1 143		5 021		7 831		5 286	5 366		18 483		1958/59
1959/60	2 900		1 233	1 358		5 491		8 047		5 708	6 287		20 042		1959/60
1960/61	3 053		1 304	1 539		5 896		8 338		5 874	6 932		21 144		1960/61
1961/62	3 471		1 663	1 953		7 087		9 046		6 522	7 659		23 227		1961/62
1962/63	3 955		1 953	2 362		8 270		9 652		7 102	8 589		25 343		1962/63
1963/64	4 318		2 172	2 531		9 021		9 990		7 516	8 758		26 264		1963/64
1964/65	4 672		2 440	2 820		9 932		10 369		7 871	9 097		27 337		1964/65
1965/66	5 724		2 936	3 485		12 145		12 027		8 317	9 873		30 217		1965/66
1966/67	6 643		3 670	4 099		14 412		13 111		9 533	10 647		33 291		1966/67
1966/67								14 407		9 386	10 483		34 276		1966/67
1967/68	8 248		4 204	4 798		17 250		16 758		10 106	11 534		38 398		1967/68
1968/69	9 719		4 952	5 621		20 292		19 059		10 719	12 167		41 945		1968/69
1969/70	10 994		5 829	6 815		23 638		19 859		11 681	13 937		45 477		1969/70
1970/71	13 699		6 820	8 380		28 899		23 057		12 541	15 376		50 974		1970/71
1970/71	13 699	14 719	7 253	8 380	446	29 778	30 798	23 057	24 720	13 147	15 376	753	52 333	53 996	1970/71
1971/72	16 851	17 997	8 305	9 862	515	35 533	36 679	25 678	27 409	13 554	16 220	816	56 268	57 999	1971/72
1972/73	19 207	20 497	9 826	11 452	552	41 037	42 327	26 986	28 788	14 691	17 299	815	59 791	61 593	1972/73
1973/74	22 139	23 699	10 586	12 595	603	45 923	47 483	28 647	30 612	14 338	17 230	803	61 018	62 983	1973/74
1974/75	28 408	30 367	13 368	15 444	635	57 855	59 814	31 709	33 864	15 309	17 793	709	65 520	67 675	1974/75
1975/76	34 886	37 151	14 907	17 598	709	68 100	70 365	34 886	37 151	14 907	17 598	709	68 100	70 365	1975/76
1976	38 514	41 016	16 661	18 975	781	74 931	77 433	35 160	37 439	15 284	17 424	724	68 592	70 871	1976
1977	44 392	47 170	17 995	20 857	883	84 127	86 905	37 147	39 456	15 278	18 666	790	71 881	74 190	1977
1978	51 477	54 601	20 644	23 313	903	96 337	99 461	39 711	42 094	16 183	18 473	710	75 077	77 460	1978
1979	57 722	61 138	23 092	26 599	1 236	108 649	112 065	40 627	42 986	16 837	19 587	903	77 954	80 313	1979
1980	65 535	69 464	25 604	30 206	1 493	122 838	126 767	41 871	44 334	16 972	20 191	993	80 027	82 490	1980
1981	77 472	81 990	27 972	34 586	1 732	141 762	146 280	44 279	46 810	16 569	20 772	1 026	82 646	85 177	1981
1982	90 382	95 595	31 927	38 744	1 994	163 047	168 260	46 707	49 351	16 968	20 977	1 063	85 715	88 359	1982

Table 4 Current Social Expenditure by Major Component

Year	As % of gross national product: Social security I	Social security II	Sickness/ health	(Income maint.)	Educa- tion	Hous- ing	Total	As % of public expenditure: Social security I	Social security II	Sickness/ health	(Income maint.)	Educa- tion	Hous ing	Total	As % of social expenditure I: Social security I	Sickness/ health	(Income maint.)	Educa- tion	Hous- ing	Year
1951/52	6.1		2.4		2.0		10.4	25.5		10.1		8.3		43.9	58.1	22.9		19.0		1951/52
1952/53	6.3		2.5		2.1		10.9	25.6		10.2		8.4		44.2	57.9	23.0		19.1		1952/53
1953/54	6.4		2.5		2.1		11.0	25.8		10.2		8.5		44.4	58.0	22.9		19.1		1953/54
1954/55	6.2		2.6		2.3		11.2	24.8		10.6		9.4		44.8	55.4	23.6		20.9		1954/55
1955/56	6.6		2.8		2.9		12.3	26.1		11.0		11.3		48.4	54.0	22.8		23.2		1955/56
1956/57	6.7		2.9		3.0		12.6	26.3		11.2		11.7		49.2	53.5	22.8		23.7		1956/57
1957/58	7.4		2.9		2.9		13.2	28.3		11.0		11.0		50.4	56.3	21.8		21.9		1957/58
1958/59	7.4		3.0		3.1		13.5	27.7		11.3		11.5		50.5	54.8	22.4		22.8		1958/59
1959/60	7.1		3.0		3.3		13.4	27.1		11.5		12.7		51.3	52.8	22.5		24.7		1959/60
1960/61	6.9		2.9		3.5		13.3	26.6		11.3		13.4		51.3	51.8	22.1		26.1		1960/61
1961/62	7.0		3.4		4.0		14.4	25.1		12.0		14.1		51.2	49.0	23.5		27.5		1961/62
1962/63	7.1		3.5		4.2		14.9	24.7		12.2		14.8		51.7	47.8	23.6		28.6		1962/63
1963/64	7.3		3.7		4.3		15.2	24.7		12.4		14.5		51.6	47.9	24.1		28.0		1963/64
1964/65	6.9		3.6		4.2		14.7	23.4		12.2		14.1		49.8	47.0	24.6		28.4		1964/65
1965/66	7.5		3.9		4.6		16.0	24.5		12.6		14.9		52.0	47.1	24.2		28.7		1965/66
1966/67	7.9		4.4		4.9		17.2	24.6		13.6		15.2		53.5	46.1	25.5		28.4		1966/67
1967/68	9.0		4.6		5.2		18.8	25.9		13.2		15.0		54.1	47.8	24.4		27.8		1967/68
1968/69	9.6		4.9		5.6		20.0	26.1		13.3		15.1		54.5	47.9	24.4		27.7		1968/69
1969/70	9.5		5.1		5.9		20.5	26.0		13.8		16.1		56.0	46.5	24.7		28.8		1969/70
1970/71	10.7		5.3		6.5		22.6	26.7		13.3		16.4		56.4	47.4	23.6		29.0		1970/71
1970/71	11.5	12.4	6.1		7.0	0.4	25.1	26.8	28.8	14.2		16.4	0.8	58.2	46.0	24.4		28.1	1.5	1970/71
1971/72	12.9	13.7	6.3		7.5	0.4	27.1	28.9	30.9	14.3		16.9	0.9	61.0	47.4	23.4		27.8	1.4	1971/72
1972/73	12.7	13.6	6.5		7.6	0.4	27.2	28.8	30.7	14.7		17.2	0.8	61.6	46.8	23.9		27.9	1.3	1972/73
1973/74	12.8	13.7	6.1		7.3	0.3	26.6	29.3	31.4	14.0		16.7	0.8	60.8	48.2	23.1		27.4	1.3	1973/74
1974/75	14.7	15.7	6.9		8.0	0.3	29.9	29.9	32.0	14.1		16.3	0.7	60.9	49.1	23.1		26.7	1.1	1974/75
1975/76	16.1	17.2	6.9		8.1	0.3	31.5	32.3	34.4	13.8		16.3	0.7	63.0	51.2	21.9		25.8	1.0	1975/76
1976	15.3	16.3	6.6		7.6	0.3	29.8	31.7	33.8	13.7		15.6	0.6	61.7	51.4	22.2		25.3	1.0	1976
1977	15.9	16.9	6.4		7.5	0.3	30.1	32.1	34.1	13.0		15.1	0.6	60.9	52.8	21.4		24.8	1.0	1977
1978	16.5	17.5	6.6		7.5	0.3	30.9	32.3	34.2	12.9		14.6	0.6	60.4	53.4	21.4		24.2	0.9	1978
1979	16.6	17.6	6.7		7.7	0.4	31.3	31.0	32.8	12.4		14.3	0.7	58.3	53.1	21.3		24.5	1.1	1979
1980	17.5	18.5	6.8		8.1	0.4	32.8	30.9	32.7	12.1		14.2	0.7	57.8	53.4	20.8		24.6	1.2	1980
1981	18.7	19.8	6.7		8.3	0.4	34.2	31.4	33.2	11.3		14.0	0.7	57.4	54.6	19.7		24.4	1.2	1981
1982	19.2	20.3	6.8		8.2	0.4	34.7	31.5	33.3	11.1		13.5	0.7	56.9	55.4	19.6		23.6	1.2	1982

Table 5

Social Security Expenditure

Year	At current prices (in million DKR) Pensions I	II	Unemploy-ment	Fami-lies	Occup. inj.	Social assist.	Ad-min.	Total I	II	At constant (1975) prices (in million DKR) Pensions I	II	Unemploy-ment	Fami-lies	Occup. inj.	Social assist.	Ad-min.	Total I	II	Year
1951/52	682		275	388	58	79	37	1 519		2 164		865	1 234	181	247	240	4 931		1951/52
1952/53	750		334	412	60	93	41	1 690		2 369		1 027	1 435	186	287	247	5 551		1952/53
1953/54	826		307	490	66	93	43	1 825		2 584		932	1 690	199	282	258	5 945		1953/54
1954/55	872		268	507	66	91	46	1 850		2 674		803	1 725	198	272	261	5 933		1954/55
1955/56	964		351	548	69	95	48	2 075		2 832		1 006	1 780	197	272	261	6 348		1955/56
1956/57	1 077		364	579	70	100	54	2 244		3 038		1 003	1 791	193	275	276	6 576		1956/57
1957/58	1 368		426	610	70	103	58	2 635		3 896		1 158	1 854	183	279	286	7 656		1957/58
1958/59	1 558		325	631	75	114	49	2 752		4 324		878	1 888	203	308	230	7 831		1958/59
1959/60	1 725		251	683	91	98	52	2 900		4 678		662	1 969	240	257	241	8 047		1959/60
1960/61	1 878		199	724	109	88	55	3 053		5 030		507	2 050	279	224	248	8 338		1960/61
1961/62	2 128		208	869	118	84	64	3 471		5 422		512	2 362	291	208	251	9 046		1961/62
1962/63	2 432		252	992	119	90	70	3 955		5 804		584	2 525	275	209	255	9 652		1962/63
1963/64	2 764		243	1 018	122	96	75	4 318		6 266		533	2 453	267	211	260	9 990		1963/64
1964/65	3 069		190	1 102	127	100	84	4 372		6 684		402	2 533	268	211	271	10 369		1964/65
1965/66	3 701		257	1 379	175	113	99	5 724		7 709		513	2 952	348	225	280	12 027		1965/66
1966/67	4 412		257	1 504	219	137	114	6 643		8 629		480	3 015	435	256	296	13 111		1966/67
1966/67										9 561		541	3 264	460	239	292	14 407		1966/67
1967/68	5 194		564	1 943	246	167	134	8 248		10 537		1 113	3 972	486	328	322	16 758		1967/68
1968/69	6 188		783	2 262	270	216	157	9 719		12 074		1 437	4 316	496	396	340	19 059		1968/69
1969/70	7 025		727	2 507	301	247	187	10 994		12 777		1 272	4 476	527	432	375	19 859		1969/70
1970/71	9 304	10 324	568	3 126	342	359		13 699	14 719	15 642	17 305	947	5 324	558	586		23 057	24 720	1970/71
1971/72	11 049	12 195	1 101	3 800	408	493		16 851	17 997	16 691	18 422	1 676	5 950	617	744		25 678	27 409	1971/72
1972/73	12 781	14 071	954	4 475	464	533		19 207	20 497	17 775	19 577	1 342	6 476	648	745		26 986	28 788	1972/73
1973/74	15 161	16 721	996	5 079	376	527		22 139	23 699	19 593	21 558	1 264	6 653	473	664		28 647	30 612	1973/74
1974/75	18 117	20 076	3 121	5 945	353	872		28 408	30 367	20 234	22 389	3 439	6 689	388	959		31 709	33 864	1974/75
1975/76	20 975	23 240	5 505	6 668	450	1 288		34 886	37 151	20 975	23 240	5 505	6 668	450	1 288		34 886	37 151	1975/76
1976	22 672	25 174	6 509	7 020	434	1 879		38 514	41 016	20 706	22 985	5 929	6 419	395	1 711		35 160	37 439	1976
1977	25 332	28 110	9 047	7 283	529	2 201		44 392	47 170	21 222	23 531	7 524	6 131	440	1 830		37 147	39 456	1977
1978	29 295	32 419	10 549	8 467	580	2 586		51 477	54 601	22 649	25 082	8 053	6 594	442	1 973		39 711	42 094	1978
1979	33 454	36 870	11 164	9 678	642	2 784		57 722	61 138	23 602	25 961	7 720	6 939	443	1 923		40 627	42 986	1979
1980	36 463	40 392	13 538	11 942	665	3 527		65 535	69 464	23 348	25 811	8 498	7 397	417	2 211		41 871	44 334	1980
1981	40 446	44 964	19 031	12 812	731	4 452		77 472	81 990	23 193	25 724	10 674	7 508	410	2 494		44 279	46 810	1981
1982	46 123	51 336	23 375	14 507	900	5 477		90 382	95 595	23 915	26 559	11 869	7 690	456	2 777		46 702	49 351	1982

Table 6

Expenditure on Income Maintenance

Year	National pensions	Sickness cash ben.	Unemployment benefits	Child allow.	Social assist.	Total	National pensions	Sickness cash ben.	Unemployment benefits	Child allow.	Social assist.	Total	Year
	At current prices (in million DKR)						At constant (1975) prices (in million DKR)						
1952/53	730	218	285		93	1 326	2 247	671	877		287	5 408	1952/53
1959/60	1 657	390	188		98	2 333	4 360	1 026	495		432	6 313	1959/60
1970/71	7 123	802	500	2 048	359	10 832	11 640	1 311	817	3 346	586	17 700	1970/71
1971/72	8 179	785	1 017	2 239	493	12 713	12 355	1 186	1 537	3 383	744	19 205	1971/72
1972/73	9 300	1 333	869	2 489	533	14 524	12 989	1 862	1 214	3 476	745	20 286	1972/73
1973/74	10 574	1 324	906	2 718	527	16 049	13 318	1 668	1 141	3 423	664	20 214	1973/74
1974/75	12 276	1 569	3 013	3 087	872	20 817	13 505	1 716	3 315	3 396	959	22 891	1974/75
1975/76	14 084	1 719	5 381	3 328	1 288	25 800	14 084	1 719	5 381	3 328	1 288	25 800	1975/76
1976	14 952	2 032	6 363	3 579	1 879	28 805	13 617	1 851	5 795	3 260	1 711	26 234	1976
1977	17 315	2 452	8 887	3 533	2 201	35 388	14 393	2 038	7 387	2 937	1 830	28 585	1977
1978	19 856	3 228	10 348	3 889	2 586	39 907	15 170	2 462	7 893	2 966	1 973	30 464	1978
1979	22 573	3 667	10 944	4 101	2 784	44 069	15 589	2 533	7 558	2 832	1 923	30 435	1979
1980	25 015	3 993	13 287	4 440	3 527	50 262	15 683	2 503	8 330	2 784	2 211	31 511	1980
1981	27 360	4 057	18 723	4 641	4 452	59 233	15 333	2 134	10 489	2 601	2 494	33 051	1981
1982	30 808	4 385	22 965	4 800	5 477	68 435	15 623	2 105	11 646	2 434	2 777	34 585	1982

Table 7 Expenditure on Public Pensions and Related Services

Year	At current prices (in million DKR)						At constant (1975) prices (in million DKR)						Year
	Old age pensions	Invalidity pensions	Widows' pensions	Total national pensions	Services for elderly and handicapped	Civil servants' pensions	Old age pensions	Invalidity pensions	Widows' pensions	Total national pensions	Services for elderly and handicapped	Civil servants' pensions	
1951/52	545.9	131.0		676.9	5.5		1 716.7	411.9		2 128.6	35.7		1951/52
1952/53	587.1	143.1		730.2	20.2		1 806.5	440.3		2 246.8	212.7		1952/53
1953/54	644.9	155.9		800.8	25.1		1 960.2	473.9		2 434.1	149.4		1953/54
1954/55	681.2	167.1		848.3	23.8		2 039.5	500.3		2 539.8	133.7		1954/55
1955/56	753.2	183.9		937.1	27.0		2 158.2	526.9		2 685.1	146.7		1955/56
1956/57	835.9	211.4		1 047.3	30.0		2 302.8	582.4		2 885.2	153.1		1956/57
1957/58	1 046.4	242.4		1 288.8	79.1		2 843.5	558.7		3 502.2	393.5		1957/58
1958/59	1 212.4	287.8		1 500.2	57.4		3 276.8	777.8		4 054.6	269.5		1958/59
1959/60	1 309.3	326.6	20.7	1 656.6	68.7		3 445.5	859.5	54.5	4 359.5	318.1		1959/60
1960/61	1 383.5	336.9	34.3	1 754.7	122.9		3 529.3	859.4	87.5	4 476.2	555.6		1960/61
1961/62	1 530.8	426.4	46.6	2 003.8	124.0		3 770.4	1 050.2	114.8	4 935.4	486.3		1961/62
1962/63	1 727.9	514.9	65.2	2 308.0	123.5		4 009.1	1 194.7	151.3	5 355.1	449.1		1962/63
1963/64	1 950.8	585.6	75.4	2 611.8	151.8		4 287.5	1 287.0	165.7	5 740.2	525.3		1963/64
1964/65	2 157.6	652.1	84.6	2 894.3	175.0		4 561.5	1 378.7	178.9	6 119.1	564.5		1964/65
1965/66	2 457.4	725.0	107.6	3 290.0	411.4		4 895.2	1 444.2	204.4	6 543.8	1 165.4		1965/66
1966/67	2 800.5	938.8	116.7	3 856.0	555.7		5 895.8	1 976.4	245.7	8 117.9	1 443.4		1966/67
1966/67							5 234.6	1 754.8	218.1	7 207.5	1 421.2		1966/67
1967/68	3 222.0	1 165.3	131.2	4 518.5	675.7		6 355.0	2 298.4	258.8	8 912.2	1 624.3		1967/68
1968/69	3 317.2	1 405.5	148.0	4 870.7	1 317.4		6 086.6	2 578.9	271.6	8 937.1	3 136.7		1968/69
1969/70	3 685.0	1 667.7	161.9	5 414.6	1 610.7		6 453.6	2 745.5	283.5	9 482.6	3 293.9		1969/70
1970/71	5 065.5	1 866.5	191.3	7 123.3	2 181.4	1 020	8 277.1	3 049.8	312.6	11 639.5	4 002.6	1 663	1970/71
1971/72	5 730.2	2 236.3	212.2	8 178.7	2 870.7	1 146	8 655.9	3 378.1	320.5	12 354.5	4 336.4	1 731	1971/72
1972/73	6 433	2 635	232	9 300	3 481.3	1 290	8 985	3 680	324	12 989	4 762	1 802	1972/73
1973/74	7 330	2 993	251	10 574	4 587	1 560	9 232	3 770	316	13 318	6 275	1 965	1973/74
1974/75	8 494	3 497	285	12 276	5 841	1 959	9 344	3 847	314	13 505	6 729	2 155	1974/75
1975/76	9 749	4 017	318	14 084	6 891	2 265	9 749	4 017	318	14 084	6 891	2 265	1975/76
1976	10 514	4 132	306	14 952	7 720	2 502	9 576	3 763	278	13 617	7 089	2 279	1976
1977	12 170	4 808	337	17 315	8 017	2 778	10 116	3 997	280	14 393	6 829	2 309	1977
1978	14 029	5 459	367	19 856	9 439	3 124	10 701	4 164	305	15 170	7 479	2 383	1978
1979	16 127	6 044	403	22 573	10 881	3 416	11 137	4 174	278	15 589	8 013	2 359	1979
1980	17 940	6 643	431	25 015	11 448	3 929	11 248	4 165	270	15 683	7 665	2 463	1980
1981	19 698	7 215	456	27 360	13 086	4 518	11 035	4 042	256	15 333	7 859	2 531	1981
1982	22 207	8 124	477	30 808	15 315	5 213	11 261	4 120	242	15 623	8 292	2 644	1982

Table 8

Expenditure on Sickness and Health

Year	At current prices (in million DKR)					At constant (1975) prices (in million DKR)					Year
	Hospitals (incl. adm.)	Outpatient care	Sickness cash ben.	Total	Occupational injuries ben.	Hospitals (incl. adm.)	Outpatient care	Sickness cash ben.	Total	Occupational injuries ben.	
1951/52				600	58				3 896	181	1951/52
1952/53				671	60				4 042	186	1952/53
1953/54				722	66				4 298	199	1953/54
1954/55				789	66				4 483	198	1954/55
1955/56				876	69				4 761	197	1955/56
1956/57				957	70				4 883	193	1956/57
1957/58				1 022	70				5 085	183	1957/58
1958/59				1 126	75				5 286	203	1958/59
1959/60				1 233	91				5 708	240	1959/60
1960/61				1 304	109				5 874	279	1960/61
1961/62				1 663	118				6 522	291	1961/62
1962/63				1 953	119				7 102	275	1962/63
1963/64				2 172	122				7 516	267	1963/64
1964/65				2 440	127				7 871	268	1964/65
1965/66				2 936	175				8 317	348	1965/66
1966/67				3 670	219				9 533	409	1966/67
1966/67									9 386	460	1966/67
1967/68				4 204	246				10 106	486	1967/68
1968/69				4 952	270				10 719	490	1968/69
1969/70				5 829	301				11 681	527	1969/70
1970/71				6 820	342				12 514	558	1970/71
1970/71	4 885	1 566	802	7 253		8 963	2 873	1 311	13 147		1970/71
1971/72	5 685	1 835	785	8 305	408	9 350	3 018	1 186	13 554	617	1971/72
1972/73	6 346	2 147	1 333	9 826	464	9 586	3 243	1 862	14 691	648	1972/73
1973/74	7 140	2 122	1 324	10 586	376	9 767	2 903	1 668	14 338	473	1973/74
1974/75	9 089	2 710	1 569	13 368	353	10 471	3 122	1 716	15 309	388	1974/75
1975/76	10 276	2 912	1 719	14 907	450	10 276	2 912	1 719	14 907	450	1975/76
1976	11 585	3 044	2 032	16 661	434	10 638	2 795	1 851	15 284	395	1976
1977	11 958	3 585	2 452	17 995	529	10 186	3 054	2 038	15 278	440	1977
1978	13 400	4 016	3 228	20 644	580	10 539	3 182	2 462	16 183	442	1978
1979	15 059	4 366	3 667	23 092	642	11 089	3 215	2 533	16 837	443	1979
1980	16 667	4 944	3 993	25 604	665	11 180	3 289	2 503	16 972	417	1980
1981	18 562	5 353	4 057	27 972	731	11 217	3 218	2 134	16 569	410	1981
1982	21 516	6 026	4 385	31 927	900	11 562	3 301	2 105	16 968	456	1982

Table 9 Expenditure on Unemployment, Children/Families, and Social Assistance

Year	At current prices (in million DKR)							At constant (1975) prices (in million DKR)							Year
	Unempl. services	Unempl. benefits	Total unempl.	Family services	Child allow.	Total family	Social assist.	Unempl. services	Unempl. benefits	Total unempl.	Family services	Child allow.	Total family	Social assist.	
1951/52			275.2			388.0	78.6			865.4			1 233.6	247	1951/52
1952/53			333.6			411.9	93.1			1 026.5			1 435.2	287	1952/53
1953/54			306.5			490.9	92.9			931.6			1 689.7	282	1953/54
1954/55			268.2			507.0	90.7			803.0			1 724.5	272	1954/55
1955/56			351.1			548.2	95.0			1 006.0			1 779.9	272	1955/56
1956/57			363.9			578.6	99.8			1 002.5			1 791.3	275	1956/57
1957/58			426.0			610.1	102.6			1 157.6			1 854.4	279	1957/58
1958/59			325.0			630.5	114.0			878.4			1 887.7	308	1958/59
1959/60			251.4			683.2	97.8			661.6			1 968.9	257	1959/60
1960/61			198.8			723.6	87.9			507.1			2 049.9	224	1960/61
1961/62			208.0			869.2	84.4			512.3			2 362.0	208	1961/62
1962/63			251.7			992.2	90.1			584.0			2 524.7	209	1962/63
1963/64			242.6			1 018.1	96.2			533.2			2 453.3	211	1963/64
1964/65			190.0			1 101.7	99.7			401.7			2 532.6	211	1964/65
1965/66			257.4			1 378.6	112.9			512.8			2 952.0	225	1965/66
1966/67										540.8			3 014.8	256	1966/67
1966/67										480.2			3 263.5	289	1966/67
1967/68			564.2			1 942.5	166.5			1 112.8			3 972.4	328	1967/68
1968/69			782.9			2 261.8	215.8			1 436.5			4 316.4	390	1968/69
1969/70			726.5			2 506.5	246.9			1 272.3			4 475.9	432	1969/70
1970/71	68	500	568	1 078	2 048	3 126	358.6	125.0	817.0	942.0	1 978.0	3 346.2	5 324.2	586	1970/71
1971/72	84	1 017	1 101	1 561	2 239	3 800	492.5	138.7	1 536.9	1 675.6	2 567.8	3 382.6	5 950.4	744	1971/72
1972/73	85	869	954	1 986	2 489	4 475	533	128.4	1 213.7	1 342.1	3 000.0	3 476.3	6 476.3	745	1972/73
1973/74	90	906	996	2 361	2 718	5 079	527	123.1	1 141.1	1 264.2	3 229.8	3 423.2	6 653.0	664	1973/74
1974/75	108	3 013	3 121	2 858	3 087	5 945	872	124.4	3 314.6	3 439.0	3 292.6	3 396.3	6 688.9	959	1974/75
1975/76	124	5 381	5 505	3 340	3 328	6 668	1 288	124.0	5 381.0	5 505.0	3 340.0	3 328.0	6 668.0	1 288	1975/76
1976	146	6 363	6 509	3 441	3 579	7 020	1 879	134.1	5 795.1	5 929.2	3 159.8	3 259.6	6 419.4	1 711	1976
1977	160	8 887	9 047	3 750	3 533	7 283	2 201	136.3	7 387.4	7 523.7	3 194.2	2 936.8	6 131.0	1 830	1977
1978	201	10 348	10 549	4 578	3 889	8 467	2 586	159.3	7 893.2	8 052.5	3 627.6	2 966.4	6 594.0	1 973	1978
1979	220	10 944	11 164	5 577	4 101	9 678	2 784	162.0	7 558.0	7 720.0	4 106.8	2 832.2	6 939.0	1 923	1979
1980	251	13 287	13 538	6 902	4 440	11 342	3 527	167.8	8 330.4	8 498.2	4 613.6	2 783.7	7 397.3	2 211	1980
1981	308	18 723	19 031	8 171	4 641	12 812	4 452	185.0	10 489.1	10 674.1	4 907.5	2 600.6	7 508.1	2 494	1981
1982	410	22 965	23 375	9 707	4 800	14 507	5 477	222.0	11 645.5	11 868.5	5 255.5	2 434.1	7 689.6		1982

Table 10 Public Revenues, Taxation, Financing of Social Security and Health

Year	Public revenues	Savings	Net lending	Public rev.	Savings	Net lend.	Total taxes	Direct taxes	Ind. tax.	Soc.sec. contrib.	Other	Financing of social security and health: Total	State	Local	Empl.	Insured	Year
	(in million DKR)			(as % of GDP)			(mill. DKR)	(percent distribution)				(mill. DKR)	(percent distribution)				
1950/51	4 089	813		20.3	3.5		4 339	45.2	46.3	7.7	0.8	1 885	57.7	26.5	3.3	12.5	1950/51
1951/52	5 285	722		21.1	2.9		4 965	47.4	45.2	6.7	0.7	2 104	57.9	26.2	3.2	12.6	1951/52
1952/53	5 827	695		21.8	2.6		5 520	49.9	43.2	6.3	0.7	2 328	58.0	26.7	3.0	12.2	1952/53
1953/54	6 687	1 553	476	23.4	5.4	1.7	5 966	50.1	43.2	6.1	0.6	2 569	59.4	25.5	2.9	12.3	1953/54
1954/55	7 088	1 699	313	23.7	5.7	1.1	6 239	51.0	42.5	5.9	0.6	2 679	58.9	25.9	2.8	12.3	1954/55
1955/56	7 706	1 913	492	24.6	6.1	1.6	6 894	49.8	44.2	5.4	0.6	2 915	60.5	25.2	2.7	11.5	1955/56
1956/57	8 282	2 061	498	24.8	6.2	1.5	7 351	50.4	43.8	5.2	0.6	3 194	61.2	25.3	2.5	11.0	1956/57
1957/58	9 003	2 143	528	25.3	6.0	1.5	7 994	50.5	43.6	5.3	0.6	3 591	62.6	24.4	2.2	10.9	1957/58
1958/59	9 679	2 350	594	26.1	6.3	1.6	8 744	49.1	45.1	5.3	0.5	3 868	61.6	25.1	2.3	11.0	1958/59
1959/60	10 857	2 942	1 047	26.4	7.2	2.5	9 722	48.3	45.9	5.2	0.6	4 142	61.2	25.2	2.8	10.8	1959/60
1960/61	11 826	3 331	1 229	26.6	7.5	2.8	10 609	47.2	47.0	5.2	0.6	4 388	62.9	22.9	3.2	11.0	1960/61
1961/62	12 887	2 558	29	26.1	5.2	0.1	11 661	47.4	46.6	5.4	0.6	5 118	67.4	19.0	3.5	10.1	1961/62
1962/63	15 273	3 186	327	27.4	5.7	0.6	14 115	47.4	47.1	5.0	0.5	5 920	68.5	18.6	3.3	9.5	1962/63
1963/64	17 146	3 930	1 005	29.0	6.6	1.7	16 004	47.9	47.0	4.5	0.6	6 481	69.6	18.4	3.1	8.9	1963/64
1964/65	19 509	4 660	1 127	28.8	6.9	1.7	18 198	46.9	46.9	5.7	0.5	7 126	69.4	18.7	3.0	8.9	1964/65
1965/66	22 930	5 391	1 269	30.2	7.1	1.7	21 471	47.7	45.7	5.9	0.6	8 418	71.2	19.6	0.4	8.7	1965/66
1966/67	27 029	6 553	1 770	32.3	7.8	2.1	25 214	47.8	45.9	5.8	0.6	10 773	66.8	13.9	5.2	9.1	1966/67
1967/68	30 215	6 043	297	32.9	6.6	0.3	28 171	48.2	45.6	5.6	0.5	12 824	68.4	18.7	4.7	8.2	1967/68
1968/69	35 947	7 467	1 033	35.5	7.4	1.0	34 169	47.3	47.1	5.1	0.5	15 151	68.5	19.5	4.4	7.7	1968/69
1969/70	41 141	8 828	1 496	35.7	7.7	1.3	38 483	47.0	47.8	4.8	0.4	17 090	68.8	19.7	4.1	7.3	1969/70
1970/71	54 739	10 651		46.1	9.0		48 031	52.8	42.6	4.2	0.4	21 570	73.4	16.3	3.7	6.6	1970/71
1971/72	62 765	11 892	4 515	47.9	9.1	3.4	57 187	55.7	40.1	4.0	0.3	25 590	73.1	17.0	3.6	6.4	1971/72
1972/73	73 402	14 301	6 840	48.7	9.5	4.5	64 774	54.9	40.4	4.2	0.4	29 722	72.1	17.3	3.9	6.6	1972/73
1973/74	85 382	17 310	9 852	49.4	10.0	5.7	73 430	57.8	39.7	2.2	0.4	35 526	69.0	22.2	7.7	1.2	1973/74
1974/75	97 643	12 443	2 691	50.4	6.4	1.4	85 772	62.2	35.9	1.5	0.3	44 653	69.9	23.1	5.9	1.1	1974/75
1975/76	105 387	7 418	- 2 749	48.7	3.4	-1.3	89 637	60.6	37.4	1.6	0.4	53 457	67.3	25.6	6.0	1.1	1975/76
1976	120 723	10 877	- 641	48.1	4.3	-0.3	104 697	58.9	38.9	1.7	0.4	60 364	59.3	33.1	6.5	1.2	1976
1977	136 616	10 219	- 1 622	49.0	3.7	-0.6	117 306	57.1	40.8	1.7	0.4	68 266	58.8	33.3	6.5	1.4	1977
1978	158 396	12 013	- 1 112	50.8	3.9	-0.4	135 341	56.2	41.8	1.6	0.5	78 474	58.8	33.7	6.0	1.5	1978
1979	180 633	9 157	- 5 852	52.2	2.7	-1.7	154 592	55.3	42.5	1.8	0.4						1979
1980	200 224	2 805	-12 152	53.5	0.8	-3.2	170 552	56.6	40.8	2.0	0.6						1980
1981	217 733	-13 030	-29 224	52.5	-3.1	-7.0	185 375	56.7	40.5	2.4	0.4						1981
1982	243 715	-25 983	-43 001	51.9	-5.4	-9.2	207 571	56.7	39.7	3.2	0.5						1982

Table 11

Welfare Clienteles

Year	Total population	Population aged 0–14	Population aged 65+	Labour force	Pensioners: Old age	Pensioners: Invalidity	Pensioners: Widows	Unempl. benef.	Social assistance	Child allow.	Year
	(1,000)	(%)	(%)		(1,000)	(1,000)	(1,000)	(1,000)	(1,000)	(1,000)	
1950	4 252	26.2	9.0	1 929	244	45		55	122		1950
1951	4 285	26.4	9.1		254	46		63	128		1951
1952	4 315	26.4	9.3		265	48		82	137		1952
1953	4 349	26.5	9.4		273	49		61	132		1953
1954	4 389	26.5	9.5		279	49		54	129		1954
1955	4 424	26.6	9.7	2 010	291	51		66	141		1955
1956	4 454	26.5	9.9		300	53		76	142		1956
1957	4 874	26.5	10.0		348	55		71	135		1957
1958	4 501	26.3	10.2		363	60		68	134		1958
1959	4 532	25.9	10.3		359	68	6	44	114		1959
1960	4 565	25.5	10.5	2 064	376	72	8	31	93		1960
1961	4 594	24.9	10.7		373	84	13	25	99		1961
1962	4 630	24.4	10.9		382	90	14	23	88		1962
1963	4 606	24.1	11.0		390	94	15	32	82		1963
1964	4 703	23.9	11.2		399	97	16	19	83		1964
1965	4 741	23.8	11.3	2 233	407	95	16	16	60		1965
1966	4 777	23.8	11.5		419	95	17	18	61		1966
1967	4 818	23.9	11.6		434	100	17	22	63		1967
1968	4 858	23.8	11.8		452	107	17	39	77		1968
1969	4 877	23.6	12.0		475	112	18	31	84		1969
1970	4 907	23.4	12.2	2 310	590	118	17	25	96	1 406	1970
1971	4 951	23.2	12.4	2 409	611	129	18	32	116	1 412	1971
1972	4 976	23.1	12.6	2 424	634	139	18	33	143	1 417	1972
1973	5 008	23.0	12.8	2 446	609	144	18	22	151	1 417	1973
1974	5 030	22.8	13.0	2 479	622	147	18	51	147	1 409	1974
1975	5 054	22.7	13.3	2 486	635	150	18	126	179	1 267	1975
1976	5 065	22.5	13.5	2 531	644	150	17	133	209	1 252	1976
1977	5 080	22.3	13.7	2 579	652	151	17	164	236	1 247	1977
1978	5 097	22.0	14.0	2 645	665	151	17	191	270	1 232	1978
1979	5 112	21.6	14.2	2 627	677	152	16	162	272	1 217	1979
1980	5 122	21.1	14.3		684	152	16	184		1 192	1980
1981	5 124									1 155	1981
1982	5 119									1 120	1982

Table 12

Elections

Distribution of votes by party

Party	1945 Oct.	1947 Oct.	1950 Sep.	1953 Apr.	1953 Sep.	1957 May	1960 Nov.	1964 Sep.	1966 Nov.	1968 Jan.	1971 Sep.	1973 Dec.	1975 Jan.	1977 Feb.	1979 Oct.	1981 Dec.	1984 Jan.
Communist Party	12.5	6.8	4.6	4.8	4.3	3.1	1.1	1.2	0.8	1.0	1.4	3.6	4.2	3.7	1.9	1.1	0.7
Left Socialists	-	-	-	-	-	-	-	-	-	2.0	1.6	1.5	2.1	2.7	3.7	2.7	2.7
Socialist Peoples Party	-	-	-	-	-	-	6.5	5.8	10.9	6.1	9.1	6.0	5.0	3.9	5.9	11.3	11.5
Social Democrats	32.8	40.0	39.6	40.4	41.3	39.4	42.1	41.9	38.2	34.2	37.3	25.6	29.9	37.0	38.3	32.9	31.6
Schleswig Party	-	0.4	0.3	0.4	0.5	0.5	0.4	0.4	-	0.2	0.2	-	-	-	-	-	-
Pensioners' Party	-	-	-	-	-	-	-	-	-	-	-	-	-	0.9	-	-	-
Radical Liberals	8.2	6.9	8.2	8.6	7.8	7.8	5.8	5.9	7.3	15.0	14.4	11.2	7.2	3.6	5.4	5.1	5.5
Danish Union	3.1	1.2	-	0.8	-	-	-	0.4	-	-	-	-	-	-	-	-	-
Liberal Center	-	-	-	-	-	-	-	-	2.5	1.3	-	-	-	-	-	-	-
Justice Party	1.9	4.5	8.2	5.6	3.5	5.3	2.2	1.3	0.7	0.7	1.7	2.9	1.8	3.3	2.6	1.4	1.5
Agrarian Liberals	23.4	27.6	21.3	22.1	23.1	25.1	21.1	20.8	19.3	18.6	15.6	12.3	23.3	12.0	12.5	11.3	12.1
Center Democrats	-	-	-	-	-	-	-	-	-	-	-	7.8	2.2	6.4	3.2	8.3	4.6
Christian Peoples Party	-	-	-	-	-	-	-	-	-	-	2.0	4.0	5.3	3.4	2.6	2.3	2.7
Conservatives	18.2	12.4	17.8	17.3	16.8	16.6	17.9	20.1	18.7	20.4	16.7	9.2	5.5	8.5	12.5	14.5	23.4
Progress Party	-	-	-	-	-	-	-	-	-	-	-	15.9	13.6	14.6	11.0	8.9	3.6
Independents	-	-	-	-	2.7	2.3	3.3	2.5	1.6	0.5	-	-	-	-	-	-	-
Others	0.0	0.2	0.0	0.0	0.0	0.0	0.0	0.0	0.0	0.0	0.0	0.0	0.0	0.0	0.4	0.2	0.1
Total (%)	100.1	100.0	100.0	100.0	100.0	100.0	100.0	100.0	100.0	100.0	100.0	100.0	100.0	100.0	100.0	100.0	100.0
Total vote (in 1000s)	2 055	2 089	2 059	2 077	2 172	2 321	2 439	2 640	2 802	2 864	2 904	3 070	3 068	3 105	3 194	3 124	3 387

Notes to and sources for appendix tables

Tables 1 and 2

Gross national product:
Even though national statistics based on the new System of National Accounts (SNA) have been calculated from 1966 onwards, the year 1970 has been chosen as the general point of data break for all the appendix tables concerned, i.e. all figures before 1970 are based on the old SNA, and all figures from 1970 onwards are based on the new SNA. The problems deriving from the introduction of the new SNA for Danish national accounting practices are thoroughly dealt with in (6) and, in a more condensed form, in (7). The most important difference between the old and the new SNA is that 'repair and maintenance costs' are directly included in GNP in the old system, but transferred to 'consumption of raw and auxiliary materials' under the new SNA.

Total public expenditure:
Up to 1970, national accounts statistics on public expenditure excluded expenditure on gross capital formation, which was reported separately in a special account on investments (*investeringerne*). These figures on gross capital formation have been added to the figures on total current expenditure. Since 1970/71 total public expenditure has been published in a standardized form in accordance with the principles of the new SNA. One should be aware that from 1970 'repair and maintenance costs' have been excluded from public gross capital formation (cf. above). Up to 1970, data on gross capital formation were based on the calendar year whereas data on current public expenditure were based on the fiscal year. No attempt has been made to recalculate these figures on a common basis. Thus, e.g. the calendar year 1945 was simply considered equivalent to the fiscal year 1945/46 (beginning in April 1945), and so forth. From 1970/71 to 1975/76 both gross capital formation expenditure and current expenditure were based on fiscal years. From 1976 onwards the calendar year is the common basis.

By and large, the definition of the public sector has been the same throughout the postwar period. The public sector is defined both in functional and institutional terms. Functionally, the public sector includes the public consumption of goods and services as well as the public transfers (above all to private households), but excludes the goods and services produced by publicly owned enterprises, which are supposed to produce services for private consumption at market prices. Institutionally, the public sector entails the three levels of central government, the counties, and the municipalities. At each level there are three kinds of public institution: a) the integrated public institutions which appear directly on the relevant account (apart from publicly owned enterprises); b) non-integrated public institutions with independent accounts, and c) quasi-public institutions which are formally private but publicly financed and produce public goods and services (included since 1969). The public sector also includes social insurance funds.

Deflators:
GNP-figures have been deflated by the GNP-deflator as provided by the OECD (12). Total public expenditure has been deflated by three separate deflators: public gross capital formation expenditure by the OECD gross capital formation-deflator; public final consumption by the OECD public consumption-deflator; public transfers (including transfers to households, subsidies and interest on public debt) by the OECD private consumption-deflator which has been chosen owing to the lack of a consistent cost-of-living deflator. As the deflators shift basis in 1966, the tables include two sets of deflated figures for 1966/67. This means that the annual real growth rates for 1965/66 to 1966/67 and 1966/67 to 1967/68 have also been calculated on the basis of two different figures for 1966/67.

It has not been possible to construct a full and consistent breakdown of total public expenditure by major purpose, especially before 1970. The breakdown by purpose in Table 2 is based on the expenditure figures for education, health and social security from Table 3 plus defence expenditure. The residual category 'others' has been calculated simply by subtracting these categories from total public expenditure as reported in Table 1.

Sources: Throughout the period GNP-figures are taken from national accounts statistics as produced by the Danish Statistical Bureau (*Danmarks Statistik*): 1947-59: (3), 1960-69: (4), 1970-75: (5) and 1975-82: (10). Figures on public expenditure are drawn from special reports on public finances (*Det offentliges indtægter og udgifter*). 1947/48-1951/52: (2), 1952/53-1959/60: (3), 1960/61-1968/69: (4), 1969/70-1975 (old SNA): (5), 1970/71-1982 (10).

Tables 3 and 4

In Denmark, there is no distinction between 'social expenditure' and 'social security expenditure'. The term 'social expenditure' normally includes 'social security expenditure' as defined in Table 5 plus health expenditure but excludes education expenditure. Current social expenditure excludes gross capital formation expenditure.

The difference between social security expenditure I and II (and hence, between social expenditure I and II) is accounted for by the expenditure on civil servants' pensions which is only included in II (see notes to Table 7).

Health expenditure includes sickness benefits paid by sickness insurance funds (after 1973 paid by municipalities), sickness benefits paid by employers covering the 'employer-period', out-patient care (general practitioners), hospitals, care for mentally retarded, midwives, dental care for children and in schools.

Education expenditure includes expenditure devoted to the various levels in the educational system (see Institutional Synopsis), research and development, educational allowances and certain auxiliary measures like e.g. transportation.

Housing expenditure primarily covers housing allowances, dwellings for pensioners and subsidies to non-profit housing associations.

Deflators: social security: private consumption deflator, health and education: public consumption deflator, housing: gross capitel formation deflator.

Sources: In general, social expenditure and social security expenditure are not reported in national accounts statistics (as are public expenditure figures) but in a special social expenditure account (*Udgifter til sociale formål/ydelser*). Thus, there is no internal consistency between the breakdown of public expenditure by purpose (not even after the introduction of a consolidated statistics in 1970) and the separate social expenditure statistics. Up to 1970, it is impossible to distinguish between expenditure on benefits in cash and benefits in kind. 1945/46-1948/49: (1), 1948/49-1949/50: (8), 1950/51-1957/58: (9), 1958/59-1982 (10).
For education, see sources to Table 2.

Table 5

Social security expenditure consists of total pension expenditure as defined in Table 7, total unemployment expenditure as defined in Table 9, total expenditure on families as defined in Table 9, occupational injuries expenditure as defined in Table 8, expenditure on social assistance as defined in Table 9, and administrative costs (until 1970 a separate category; then included in the individual social programmes).

Deflators: private consumption deflator for all items except administrative costs for which the public consumption deflator has been used (see Table 1).

Sources: see sources to Tables 7, 8 and 9.

Table 6

Due to a lacking distinction between benefits in cash and benefits in kind before 1970, it has been impossible to construct time series on income maintenance covering the entire period. Prior to 1970 some data have been taken from the national accounts statistics on public finances (3) and (4), but one should be careful in comparing the figures before and after 1970. The figures from 1970/71-1982 are taken from (10).

Deflator: private consumption deflator (see Table 1).

Table 7

Up to 1970 expenditure data on old age, invalidity and widows' pensions are drawn from two different standard tables in (8), (9) and (10) and the the category of 'services for elderly and handicapped' is calculated by subtracting the sum of cash benefits (as reported in '*Folke-, invalide- og enkepension'*) from total expenditure on pensions (as reported in '*Udgifter til social formål'*). From 1970 onwards expenditure on benefits in kind to the elderly and the handicapped are taken from the national accounts statistics on public finances - and so are the figures on civil servants' pensions.

Old age pension expenditure includes the (modest) labour market supplementary pensions, and from 1979 severance payments and special housing allowances for the elderly.

Expenditure on services for elderly and handicapped includes special care and care homes for the handicapped, home help and various services for elderly, nursing homes and other homes for elderly.

Deflators: all pension expenditure deflated by the private consumption deflator, expenditure on 'services for elderly and handicapped' by the public consumption deflator (see Table 1).

Table 8

Hospitals, outpatient care and sickness cash benefits:
Sources: 1951/52-1970/71: standard table table '*Udgifter til sociale formål'* in (8), (9) and (10);
1970/71-1982: national accounts statistics on public finances in (10).

Occupational injuries benefits:
Sources: standard table '*Udgifter til sociale formål'* in (8), (9) and (10).

Deflators: public consumption deflator for 'hospitals' and 'outpatient care', private consumption deflator for sickness and occupational injuries benefits.

Table 9

Child allowances include child allowances and youth benefits plus daily cash benefits in case of maternity and adoption. Family services include day care facilities and 'day care mothers'.

Social assistance expenditure covers primarily cash benefits provided by the Social Assistance Act. Services provided by that Act are transferred to other expenditure items, most notable family services.

Services deflated by the public consumption deflator, cash benefits deflated by the private consumption deflator.

Sources: standard table '*Udgifter til sociale formål'* in (8), (9) and (10).

Table 10

Public revenue data are drawn from the same sources as public expenditure data: 1947/48-1951/52: (2), 1952/53-1959/60: (3), 1960/61-1968/69: (4), 1969/70-1975 (old SNA): (5) and 1970/71-1982 (10).

(Gross) saving is defined as current public expenditure minus current public revenues. Net lending is defined as total public revenues (current plus capital revenues) minus total public expenditure (current plus capital formation expenditure).

Figures on public capital revenues in the early fifties are not very reliable, but very small in absolute terms.

The figures on taxes are taken from (13) which gives one consistent and consolidated series from 1947 to 1982. The curious fact that total taxes in 1950 were higher than total public revenues may be explained by the use of different sources and data uncertainty for the early fifties. Otherwise, the difference between total public revenues and total taxes is accounted for by the residual income (*restindkomst*), surplus of public enterprices, property incomes, imputed contributions to social insurance funds, other transfers to the public sector (since 1972/73 most notably from the EC) and capital revenues.

Data on the financing of social security and health are taken from the sources (8), (9) and (10). The fact that the percentages do not add up to 100 is explained by a small residual 'interest revenues/transfers to/from funds', not included in Table 10.

Table 11

Data on demographic and clientele variables are from (8), (9), (10) and (11).

Unemployed are registered unemployed. The number of registered unemployed is approximately 10 percent higher than the number of insured unemployed, but this percentage has been decreasing recently.

Table 12

Source: (4).

Enumerated sources for appendix tables

(1) 'Socialpolitikken i Danmark siden socialreformen belyst ved udviklingen i de sociale udgifter', *Socialt Tidsskrift*, vol. 1954.

(2) *Statistiske Meddelelser, 4. række, 160. bind, 2. hæfte*, Danmarks Statistik, Copenhagen 1954.

(3) *Statistiske Undersøgelser nr. 7*, Danmarks Statistik, Copenhagen 1966.

(4) *Statistiske Efterretninger nr. 79*, Danmarks Statistik, Copenhagen 1972.

(5) *Statistiske Efterretninger A nr. 36*, Danmarks Statistik, Copenhagen 1976.

(6) *Statistiske Undersøgelser nr. 30*, Danmarks Statistik, Copenhagen 1973.

(7) *Statistiske Efterretninger A nr. 20*, Danmarks Statistik, Copenhagen 1978.

(8) *Statistisk Tiårsoversigt 1948-1959*, Danmarks Statistik, Copenhagen 1959.

(9) *Statistisk Tiårsoversigt 1951-1961*, Danmarks Statistik, Copenhagen 1961.

(10) *Statistisk Tiårsoversigt 1962, 1963, 1964, 1965, 1966, 1967, 1968, 1969, 1970, 1971, 1972, 1973, 1974, 1975, 1976, 1977, 1978, 1979, 1980, 1981, 1982, 1983*, Danmarks Statistik, Copenhagen, various years.

(11) *Statistisk Årbog*, various years, Danmarks Statistik.

(12) *National Accounts: Historical Statistics, Main Aggregates* OECD, 1984.

(13) *Statistiske Efterretninger, Nationalregnskab, Offentlige Finanser, Betalingsbalance*, 1983:12, Danmarks Statistik, Copenhagen 1983.

(14) Mogens N. Pedersen, *Denmark: The Breakdown of a 'Working Multiparty System'*, Odense University, 1981.

Germany

Jens Alber

Institutional Synopsis

Contents

Introduction

The following synopsis centres on statutory regulations applying to the entire country. The core of German social legislation consists of social security law. This may be subdivided into four major areas which partly represent different policy approaches: (1) the classical social insurance programmes (*Sozialversicherung*); (2) some special non-contributory security schemes (*Sozialversorgung*); (3) support measures for needy persons (*soziale Fürsorge*); and (4) the promotion programmes to improve individual opportunities (*soziale Förderung*).

Most programmes combine cash benefits providing income maintenance with certain benefits in kind and social services. Whereas statutory regulations specify entitlements to income maintenance with considerable legal formality and precision, the social services are much less closely regulated by legal norms. This is partly a reflection of a central principle of German social policy which states that a state responsibility for support should only arise in cases which are not catered for in any other way. The social services, especially those for the young, the elderly, and persons dependent upon social assistance, are therefore provided by a largely uncoordinated plurality of voluntary organizations together with local authority agencies as the prime public carriers. This 'subsidiary' nature of a state responsibility for individual well-being was formally confirmed by a Federal Constitutional Court decision of 1967. The emphasis of this synopsis is on institutional regulations, and it correspondingly concentrates on legal entitlements to statutory benefits, giving only cursory attention to social services not grounded in federal legislation.

References to laws refer to the day of issue in the official journal as well as to the section and page number. The abbreviation 'WiGBl' stands for the official journal of the unified economic zone preceding the establishment of the Federal Republic (*Gesetzblatt des Vereinigten Wirtschaftsgebietes*); 'BGBl' stands for the official journal of the Federal Republic (*Bundesgesetzblatt*). Quantitative data on programme expenditure refer to 1979 as the most recent date for which detailed official figures were available in January 1984 (Source: *Sozialbericht 1980*). Due to discrepancies in statistical definitions, the total expenditure data for single institutions may deviate from the aggregate statistics in the Appendix Tables which are based on the definitions of the government's 'social budget'. If not stated otherwise, the information on institutional regulations always refers to the situation in 1983.

I Pensions

German pension insurance consists of three schemes which all provide old age, invalidity and survivors' pensions. There is a scheme for manual workers which dates back to 1889 (*Arbeiterversicherung*), a scheme for employees, established in 1911 (*Angestelltenversicherung*), and a special scheme for miners established in 1923 (*Knappschaftliche Rentenversicherung*). Together these three systems are generally referred to as pension insurance (*Rentenversicherung*). In 1938 a special pension scheme for independent artisans was established (*Handwerkerversicherung*). Although providing some special regulations, it was administered as part of the employees' system until 1962, and has since been incorporated into the workers' scheme. In addition, there are four other separate pension schemes covering special social categories. A compulsory pension scheme for independent farmers was established in 1957 (*Altershilfe für Landwirte*). Civil servants draw pensions under the civil service scheme (*Beamtenver-*

sorgung). Other public employees are compulsory members of a special supplementary scheme (*Zusatzversicherung*), introduced in 1967, and designed to augment pensions under the workers' and employees' scheme, in order to provide pensions similar to those of tenured civil servants. Although this scheme is based on collective bargaining agreements, membership is obligatory. There are similar self-governing programmes covering seamen, agricultural and horticultural workers, miners in the Saar and chimney sweepers. These will not be dealt with in any detail here. Finally, members of various professions are covered by self-governing compulsory insurance institutions under legislation made by the single states (*Versorgungswerke*). Private occupational pension schemes are not dealt with in this synopsis; today about two-thirds of all employed persons are covered by such schemes, which complement but do not substitute the public programmes. In 1979, pension expenditure amounted to 160,140 million DM (excluding transfers to other insurance schemes). This corresponded to 36.8% of total social expenditure, 57.9% of social security expenditure, and 11.5% of GDP. In the same year, outlays for the three pension insurance schemes amounted to 120,395 million DM, or 27.7% of social expenditure, 43.5% of total social security expenditure, and 8.6% of GDP. Expenditure was distributed as follows among the various schemes:

Expenditure by scheme in 1979 (million DM)

			Total	%
Pension insurance:			120 395	75.2
- workers	66 418	41.5		
- employees	43 569	27.2		
- miners	10 408	6.5		
Civil servants			32 987	20.6
Public employees (supplementary schemes)			4 128	2.6
Farmers			2 630	1.6
Total			160 140	100.0

In addition, expenditure on schemes for the professions amounted to 732 million DM, and expenditure on the other supplementary schemes (see above) of a self-governing nature, amounted to 133 million DM.

Services

The pension insurance schemes do not provide services for the elderly. This comes within the competence of various voluntary welfare associations and municipalities. In 1981, there were 5,901 homes for the elderly with a total of 422,362 places. This corresponds to 4.4% of the population aged 65 or over. The bulk of these day care institutions is provided by voluntary (55%), or private (27%) carriers. Public agencies run only 18% of all homes with 23% of all places (Source: *Gesellschaftliche Daten 1982:313*). Expenditure on services is only included in our definition of social expenditure to the extent that these services are born by the social assistance scheme, which may carry the cost of nursing as part of its benefits for particular circumstances.

1. Pension insurance

Expenditure in 1979 (million DM)

	Total	%
Pensions:		
- old age	67 483	49.8
- invalidity	13 591	10.0
- survivors'	32 985	24.4
Rehabilitation measures	4 241	3.1
Contributions to sickness insurance	14 058	10.4
Other expenditure	549	0.4
Administration	2 532	1.9
Total	135 439	100.0
Transfers	14 412	
Various reimbursements	632	
Total in social budget	120 395	

Coverage

All dependent workers are compulsorily covered for pension insurance. Since the abolition of the income-limit in 1968, compulsory membership has been extended to all white-collar employees. Workers and employees in the mining sector are covered by the miners' scheme. Self-employed artisans are compulsorily covered under the workers' scheme, irrespective of their level of income. Other self-employed persons are usually not compulsorily covered, but may join the insurance system on a voluntary basis. Recipients of unemployment benefits and some other minor categories are also compulsorily covered. Other persons may join the insurance system on a voluntary basis. In 1980 there were 21.6 million compulsory contributors to pension insurance (12.0 in the workers' scheme, 9.3 in the employees' system, and 0.3 in the miners' scheme). This corresponded to 82% of the labour force. An additional 5.4 million persons had pension insurance entitlements as a result of earlier compulsory or voluntary contributions.

Benefits

The majority of pension insurance benefits consist of pensions for old age, invalidity and survivors. In addition, the insurance system covers expenditure on rehabilitation programmes. Rehabilitation benefits consist of medical care, vocational training and special cash allowances during courses of treatment or training (*Übergangsgeld*). The pension insurance schemes may also finance rehabilitation research and preventive health care activities. Until the cutbacks of 1977 they could also subsidize private housing construction schemes and places in homes for the elderly.

Old age pensions are earnings-related and are designed to maintain the relative standard of living attained by the recipient during his working life. Entitlement to an old age pension presupposes a minimum insurance record of 15 years (as from 1984:5 years) of contributions and attainment of the age limit of 65 years. Women and the long-term unemployed are entitled to a pension from the age of 60. Since the introduction of the flexible age limit in 1972, persons with an insurance record of 35 years may opt for a pension from the age of 63, or 60 if handicapped. The amount of individual pensions is basically a function of the contribution record of the insured person and the level of his earnings. More specifically, the German pension is assessed on the basis of the following four factors: (1) number of contribution years; (2) a general coefficient of augmentation for each contribution year, fixed at 1.5% for workers and employees, and at 2.0% for miners; (3) a 'personal assessment basis' (*persönliche Bemessungsgrundlage*), calculated by dividing individual earnings for each contribution year, by the average earnings of all insured persons for each respective year, and then taking the average percentage for the whole period; (4) the 'general computation basis' (*allgemeine Bemessungsgrundlage*), calculated on average earnings of all insured persons in the first three of the last four employment years. For a worker with a contribution record of forty years and life-time earnings corresponding to the average income of all insured persons, this procedure leads to an old age pension of 60% of recent average earnings, or 15,267 DM in 1983 (1,272 DM per month; calculated as 40 x 1.5 x 100% of the general computation basis which amounted to 25,445 DM; based on legislation prior to the cutbacks of 1977, the general computation basis would have amounted to 29,376 DM, giving a pension of 1,469 DM per month). Pensioners with children receive special supplements for each child which exceed the benefits under the general child allowance scheme. Since 1978, these have been fixed at 152.90 DM for each child. Following the cutbacks of 1984, future pensioners will instead receive the lower rate general child allowance.

The general rules are subject to a variety of specifications. Thus, credit may be given for periods where no contributions were paid, due to military service, political exile, or political imprisonment (substitute periods, *Erzatzzeiten*), or for periods of higher education, illness or unemployment (reckonable periods, *Ausfallzeiten*). The 'personal assessment basis' is taken into account only up to a ceiling of 200%. The basis is raised to 75% if it falls below this limit, provided the applicant has a contribution record of at least 25 years.

Invalidity pensions are calculated on the same basis. Entitlement is subject to a contribution record of at least five years (as from 1984, three years during the five-year period preceding the claim). Pensions are paid in two forms: a higher benefit in cases of total incapacity to pursue any gainful employment (*Erwerbsunfähigkeit*), here referred to as a 'full invalidity pension', and a lower benefit for incapacity to continue the previous occupation (*Berufsunfähigkeit*), here referred to as a 'partial invalidity pension'. The latter presupposes a reduction of at least 50% of the normal capacity required in the particular occupation. In the case of full incapacity the pension formula is the same as for old age pensions. Benefits for less severe occupational invalidity are calculated with a coefficient of augmentation of 1.0% (miners 1.2%). If disability occurs below the age of 55, the pension is calculated as though the applicant had paid contributions up to this age. An invalid with previous average earnings, who joined the insurance scheme at the age of 20, and suffered a severe handicap at or below the age of 55, would thus be entitled to a pension of 52.5% of recent average earnings or 13,354 DM equal to 1,113 DM per month in 1983, i.e. (35 x 1.5 = 52.5 x 100% x 25,445). Child supplements are the same as for old age pensioners.

Survivors' pensions are paid to the widows and orphans of the insured. Widows receive the equivalent of the full invalidity pension to which the deceased would have been entitled, for a period of three months. Thereafter, they receive a pension amounting to 60% of the full invalidity pension (60% of the partial invalidity pension if below age 45 and not economically active or caring for at least one child). In addition they are entitled to child supplements. Widows have an unconditional entitlement to the pension, whereas widowers may only draw benefits if the deceased wife had been the main source of family income. A Supreme Court ruling of March 1975 declared this procedure unconstitutional and demanded a legislative reform until 1984. Orphans are entitled to one tenth of a full invalidity pension (20% for full orphans). All survivors' pensions together must not exceed the amount corresponding to a full invalidity pension. All pensions have been indexed since 1957. The annual adjustments generally correspond to the increases in the 'general computation basis', thus reflecting the development of average employment earnings. Deviations from the routine adjustment procedure occurred in 1958 (no increase) and in the years 1979 to 1981, when the regular indexation formula was replaced by discretionary lower rates of 4.5%, 4.0% and 4.0% respectively. As from 1984, pensions will be increased at the rate of growth of average employment earnings in the previous year. Each annual adjustment requires special legislation.

Financing

Pension insurance schemes are financed by earnings-related contributions which amount to 18.5% of earnings (23.5% in the miners' scheme). Employees and employers each pay one half of this total rate (in miners' scheme employers 15%, employees 8.5%). Earnings above a ceiling (in principle calculated as double the amount of the 'general computation basis'), are exempted from contributions. Independent artisans pay a flat-rate contribution which corresponds to the amount payable for workers with average incomes. The federal government contributes about 20% of aggregate resources (27.1 billion DM in 1979). The state share amounts to 7% for the employees', 20% for workers', and 62% for the miners' scheme. Since 1969 the separate schemes for workers and employees have been financially coordinated. If liquidity reserves fall below a certain limit in one system while remaining above a qualified threshold in the other, resources are transferred. Today the insurance schemes function on a pay-as-you-go basis with a minimum reserve fund of one month's expenditure. Contribution rates must be increased if financial forecasts show that reserves will fall below one month's expenditure in two consecutive years.

Administration

The pension insurance schemes are run by self-governing bodies under state supervision. There are 18 regional insurance corporations for the workers' scheme and two special corporations for railwaymen and seamen. The employees' and miners' schemes each have one central administrative body. The bureaucratic staff of all corporations together amount to more than 70,000 employees. Insured persons and employers each delegate one half of the members of the board of directors and the board of supervisors. Decisions regarding pension claims are subject to legal review by a special branch of the judiciary (Social courts, *Sozialgerichte*).

Core laws

17.6.1949 (WiGBl.:99)
Sozialversicherungsanpassungsgesetz (Social Insurance Adaptation Law): restored pre-Nazi insurance principles; compulsory coverage for all workers and for employees below income-limit; individual pensions composed of flat-rate amount and contribution-

related part; age limit 65; financed by earnings-related contributions shared equally between insured persons and employers (amounting to 10% of earnings up to contribution ceiling); financing in principle based on funding system; (increases of running pensions were legislated in all subsequent years except 1950 and 1952).

23.11.1954 (BGBl.I:345)
Rentenmehrbetragsgesetz (Pension Increase Law): increased pensions applying a new calculation principle; contribution-based benefits no longer based on the nominal value of past contributions, but on the basis of their current 'real' value.

23.2.1957 (BGBl.I:45/88)
Rentenneuregelungsgesetz (Pension Reform Law): basic reform of insurance system: introduced new pension formula (cf. text), designed to maintain the relative standard of living attained during employment; abolished flat-rate component; lowered the age limit for women with a long insurance record to 60; introduced partial invalidity pension to complement former all-or-nothing full invalidity pension; quasi-automatic annual indexation of pensions linked to changes in wages (with time-lag); annual adjustment in all subsequent years except 1958; increased contribution rates from 11% (since 1955) to 14% of earnings; abolished funding system and introduced a pay-as-you-go procedure with limited funding to cover expenditure for one year; equalized provisions under workers' and employees' schemes.

25.6.1960 (BGBl.I:93)
Fremdrenten- und Auslandsrenten-Neuregelungsgesetz (Modification of Foreign Pension Entitlements Law): improved pension entitlements for refugees; those with a pension record in a foreign country dealt with in the same way as permanent contributors to the German system.

9.6.1965 (BGBl.I:476)
Rentenversicherungs-Änderungsgesetz (Härtenovelle) (Pension Insurance Modification Law): modified criteria for the calculation of pensions, e.g. increased credit for periods of non-contribution in specific cases, resulting in sizeable increases in benefits; readjusted income-ceiling for compulsory insurance of employees from 1,250 DM to 1,800 DM per month.

21.12.1967 (BGBl.I:1259)
Finanzänderungsgesetz (Public Finance Modification Law): introduced measures for financial consolidation; drastic cuts of federal subsidies for the period 1968-71, amounting to over 4 billion DM; increased contribution rates for three subsequent years (15% in 1968, 16% in 1969, 17% in 1970); abolished income-limit for compulsory insurance of employees; introduced sickness insurance contribution for pensioners (2% of pension; re-abolished in 1970 with reimbursement of past contributions in 1972); abolished reimbursement of past contributions for women leaving the insurance system in the case of marriage; coefficient of augmentation in the miners' scheme reduced from 2.5% to 2.0%.

28.7.1969 (BGBl.I:956)
Drittes Rentenversicherungs-Änderungsgesetz (Third Pension Insurance Modification Law): introduced measures for financial consolidation: financial unification of workers' and employees' schemes to balance liquidity reserves; minimum reserve fund reduced to equal three month's expenditure (previously 12); contribution rates increased to 18% as from 1973; government obliged to publish annual forecasts for likely expenditure over the following 15 years; (these measures led to a sizeable surplus in subsequent years).

16.10.1972 (BGBl.I:1965)
Rentenreformgesetz (Pension Reform Law): second basic pension insurance reform providing more generous benefits: anticipation of annual pension adjustments by half a year; introduced a minimum pension component raising personal assessment basis to 75% for those in low income groups with a minimum contribution record of 25 years; introduced flexible age limit, lowering pensionable age to 63 years for persons with a minimum contribution record of 35 years (62 if handicapped); introduced voluntary membership for non-insured persons (mostly the self-employed), with the option of making retrospective contributions for past years; several other minor modifications favouring beneficiaries; institutionalized the norm that standard pension (of average earners with contribution record of 40 years), must not fall below 50% of current average gross earnings.

19.12.1974 (BGBl.I:3610)
Gesetz zur Verbesserung der betrieblichen Altersversorgung (Occupational Pension Insurance Improvement Law): established ground rules for occupational pension funds; acquired entitlements to occupational pensions must not expire after leaving a firm and occupational pensions must not be reduced as a result of receipt of benefits under the public insurance system.

12.3.1975
Supreme Court ruling that entitlements to survivors' pensions must be equal for widows and widowers, and that a reform of current provisions be realized by 1984.

14.6.1976 (BGBl.I:1421)
Erstes Ehereformgesetz (First Marriage Reform Law): stated that pension entitlements acquired during marriage must be shared with the economically weaker spouse after divorce.

27.6.1977 (BGBl.I:1040)
Gesetz zur 20. Rentenanpassung und zur Verbesserung der Finanzgrundlagen der gesetzlichen Rentenversicherung (20th Pension Adjustment and Improvement of the Financial Basis of Pension Insurance): financial consolidation with drastic cuts; annual pension adjustments postponed for half a year; new calculation method for the 'general computation basis' leading to lower pension entitlements; abolished child supplements in instances where the child is in receipt of an orphan's pension; child supplements exempted from future indexation; further limitation of earnings compatible with pensions under flexible age limit; unemployment institution to pay contributions for the compulsory coverage of the unemployed; cut in transfers to sickness insurance for the insurance of pensioners; increased minimum contribution for voluntary members; reduced minimum liquidity reserve equivalent to one month's expenditure; introduced various other minor consolidation measures; (total savings up to 1980 estimated at 60 billion DM).

25.7.1978 (BGBl.I:1089)
21. Rentenanpassungsgesetz (21st Pension Adjustment Law): financial consolidation - suspended the regular indexation procedure for three years in favour of lower discretionary increases of 4.5% (1979), and 4.0% (1980 and 1981); raised contribution rates to 18.5% as from 1981.

27.7.1981 (BGBl.I:705)
Künstlersozialversicherungsgesetz (Artists' Social Insurance Law): introduced compulsory insurance for artists below an income-limit; entitlements and contribution rates as under the general insurance scheme for employees; insured persons contribute the standard rate of employees; two-thirds of the remaining half are paid by the agencies marketing the artists' work, and one-third by the federal government.

1.12.1981 (BGBl.I:1205)
Rentenanpassungsgesetz 1982 (Pension Adjustment Law): reintroduced standard procedure of pension adjustments following the development of gross wages; increases of 5.76% for 1982; lowered contribution rates from 18.5 to 18% (in compensation for higher rates of unemployment insurance); introduced individual contributions to pensioners' sickness insurance as from 1983; modified procedures for the calculation of the official target relationship between standard pensions and wages, thus lowering the official target (*Rentenniveausicherungsklausel*); introduced stricter qualifying conditions for some special benefits (anticipated old age pensions in cases of unemployment, participation in rehabilitation cures, etc.).

20.12.1982 (BGBl.I:1857)
Haushaltsbegleitgesetz 1983 (Supplementary Budget Law): postponed annual pension adjustments by half a year (from July to January); increased contribution rates from 18 to 18.5% as from September 1983; set individual contributions to pensioners' sickness insurance at 1% for 1983, 3% for 1984, and 5% for 1985; reduced federal subsidy to pension insurance by 0.9 billion DM; lowered contributions payable for the unemployed and draftees, making 68% rather than full wages the basis for contributions; made sick insurance cash benefits subject to pension insurance contributions (total expenditure cuts estimated at 4 billion DM, reduced receipts estimated at 3.2 billion DM).

22.12.1983 (BGBl.I:1532)
Haushaltsbegleitgesetz 1984 (Supplementary Budget Law): modified methods of pension indexation linking annual adjustments to the increase of wages in the previous year (leading to increases of 3.4% in 1984 instead of 5.1% using the old method); implemented individual sickness insurance contributions by pensioners of 2%; reduced waiting period for regular old age pensions (*Altersruhegeld*) from 15 to 5 years; replaced child supplements by lower general child allowance for all new beneficiaries; introduced stricter qualifying conditions for full invalidity pension (contingent upon three years' compulsory coverage in the five years preceding the claim); subjected previously exempted components of income to compulsory contributions; other minor modifications (total savings for pension insurance officially estimated at 5.45 billion DM).

2. Farmers' pensions

Expenditure in 1979 (million DM)

	Total	%
Pensions:		
- old age (incl. special pensions)	2 337	88.5
- survivors'	19	0.7
Rehabilitation and health measures	198	7.5
Other expenditure	2	0.1
Administration	85	3.2
Total expenditure	2 641	100.0
Transfers to other social insurance schemes	11	
Total according to social budget	2 630	

Coverage

All independent farmers are compulsorily covered regardless of income. Part-time farmers with very small farms are excluded. In 1980, there were 597,395 compulsory contributors.

Benefits

The scheme provides old age, invalidity and survivors' pensions which are designed to supplement other sources of income. A special pension is payable to farmers who cede unprofitable farms. In addition the system covers expenditure for rehabilitation, and subsidizes the acquisition of pension entitlements under the pension insurance system through the payment of retrospective voluntary contributions. Those who have reached the age of 65, have a contribution record of 15 years and have ceded their farm, (to heirs or buyers), are entitled to an old age pension. Widows of deceased farmers are entitled to old age pensions at the age of 60. Benefits are flat-rate and vary with civil status and contribution record. In 1983, the basic pension amounted to 502.80 DM for married recipients and 335.40 DM for single persons (roughly 25% and 17% of average net wages respectively). For each year of contributions exceeding 15 years, these payments are augmented by 3%. In 1980, 465,388 regular old age pensions were paid. Farmers who have reached the age of 60, or are handicapped, are entitled to a higher special pension if they are willing to cede a farm which is unprofitable according to certain criteria (*Landabgaberente*). In 1980, 49,045 persons were in receipt of this pension. In the case of disablement, farmers or their widows are entitled to an anticipated payment of old age pensions, provided that they cede their farm and have a contribution record of at least five years. Some 89,000 anticipated pensions were paid in 1980. Orphans receive a survivors' pension up to age 18 if the deceased had a contribution record of at least five years. Orphans' pensions amount to about 25% of the regular old age pension for single persons. Pensions have been indexed since 1975 (1973 law).

Financing and administration

The system is financed by contributions and subsidies from the federal government. In 1979 federal subsidies covered 80% of total expenditure. Individual contributions are flat-rate, the annual rate being regulated by federal decrees. The insurance system is administered by various self-governing corporations under state supervision. The corporations are united in one central organization which distributes federal subsidies.

Core laws

27.7.1957 (BGBl.I:1063)
Gesetz über eine Altershilfe für Landwirte (Law on Old Age Support for Farmers): established pension system with flat-rate benefits and flat-rate contributions for the insured population.

3.7.1961 (BGBl.I:845)
Neuregelungsgesetz (Modification Law): increased contributions and introduced a federal subsidy.

23.5.1963 (BGBl.I:353)
Zweites Änderungsgesetz (Second Modification Law): increased pensions by two-thirds, and introduced invalidity pensions (anticipated old age pensions).

13.8.1965 (BGBl.I:476)
Drittes Änderungsgesetz (Third Modification Law): increased pensions by 50%; increased contributions; introduced rehabilitation measures; opened up membership to family workers over the age of 50.

29.7.1969 (BGBl.I:1017)
Viertes Änderungsgesetz (Fourth Modification Law): introduced special pensions for the cession of unprofitable farms; increased benefits and contributions (successive increases in subsequent years).

19.12.1973 (BGBl.I:1937)
Siebtes Änderungsgesetz (Seventh Modification Law): linked the indexation of farmers' pensions to the indexation of the general pension insurance scheme; flat-rate benefits augmented by 3% for each additonal contribution year after 15 years of contributions; introduced sizeable pension increases; linked the indexation of federal subsidies to increases in expenditure.

22.12.1981 (BGBl.I:1523)
Zweites Haushaltsstrukturgesetz (Second Budget Structure Law): reduced federal subsidy by 105 million DM limiting subsidies to 2.105 billion DM in 1982 and 1983.

22.12.1983 (BGBl.I:1532)
Haushaltsbegleitgesetz (Supplementary Budget Law): reduced federal subsidies from 79.5 to 75% of expenditure.

3. Civil servants' pensions

Expenditure in 1979 (million DM)

	Total	%
Pensions	30 815	93.4
Other expenditure	200	0.6
Administration and general services	1 972	6.0
Total	32 987	100.0

Coverage

All tenured civil servants are covered (1979: 1.8 million persons).

Benefits

Pensions are payable for old age, invalidity and survivors. Old age pensions are a function of (last) earnings and length of service. Entitlement is based on a minimum of five-years' service, and benefits are usually payable at the age of 65. For up to ten years of service, benefits amount to 35% of gross earnings. For each additional year up to 25 years of service, this percentage is increased by two percentage points, and by one percentage point for each additional year of service over 25 years. Old age pensions must not fall below a specified minimum and cannot exceed 75% of earnings (reached after 35 years of service). Retirement pensions granted as a result of incapacity for further service are calculated in the same way. If incapacity occurs before the age of 55, one-third of the time remaining until attainment of this age is credited for the calculation of pensions. Invalidity pension granted as a result of occupational injuries amounts to at least two-thirds of last reckonable earnings. Widows or widowers are entitled to a survivors' pension which amounts to 60% of the retirement pension to which the deceased would have been entitled at the day of his death. Orphans receive a pension of 12% of this amount (20% for full orphans). All pensions are indexed to changes in the salaries of active civil servants and constitute taxable income.

Financing and administration

Benefits are financed out of general revenues. State bureaucracies deal with the administration of benefits as part of their general tasks.

Core laws

(See Section V)

4. Public employees' supplementary pensions

Expenditure in 1979 (million DM)

	Total	%
Pensions	3 811	92.3
Other expenditure incl. health	18	0.4
Administration	299	7.3
Total	4 128	100.0

Coverage

All public employees and apprentices over the age of 17 are compulsorily covered by the supplementary scheme (in 1979, approximately 1.8 million persons, including the postal service and railways).

Benefits

Benefits are intended to supplement payments made under the pension insurance scheme, and are a function of the recipient's earnings and his contribution record. The aim is to provide old age pensions amounting to 75% of past gross earnings. In some cases this leads to pensions which are higher than previous net earnings. Invalidity pensions amount to 80% of the old age pension. Survivors' pensions are paid to widows and orphans, and in special cases, to widowers. They must amount to at least one half of the survivors' benefits under the pension insurance system. Benefits are indexed and tax-free. In 1979, some 496,000 pensions were paid.

Financing and administration

The system is financed by earnings-related contributions made by public employees, which amounted to 2.5% of earnings (1977). It is administered by a central self-governing body under state supervision.

Core laws

22.12.1966
Statute of the central administrative body based on the collective agreement of 4.11.1966 (effective from 1.1.1967, with several subsequent modifications).

5. Professionals' pensions

Expenditure in 1979 (million DM)

	Total	%
Pensions:		
- old age	243	33.2
- invalidity	39	5.3
- survivors'	232	31.7
Administration	219	29.9
Total	733	100.0
Transfers to other social insurance schemes	1	
Total according to social budget	732	

Coverage

Doctors, veterinarians, pharmacists, lawyers and members of some other professions are compulsorily covered by schemes run by the chambers of their professions, regulated by state (*Länder*) legislation. In 1979 approximately 138,000 persons were compulsory members of such schemes.

Benefits

The schemes provide invalidity, survivors', and in some cases, old age pensions. Schemes without explicit old age pensions usually pay invalidity pensions for which entitlement is not dependent upon incapacity after a certain age. Pensionable age is usually between 68 and 70. Receipt of a pension usually presupposes the cessation of work. Benefits vary from one scheme to another, being flat-rate in some instances and earnings- and/or contribution-related in others.

Financing and administration

The schemes are financed by contributions from insured persons which vary from scheme to scheme. Contributions are earnings-related, and in some cases vary with age. In 1979 the total contributions of all schemes amounted to 1.2 billion DM. The schemes are usually organized as special property funds of the respective professional chambers.

Core laws

Legislation varies from one profession to another, and from state to state.

II Sickness insurance/Health services

The German health system centres on the core institution of public sickness insurance to which 90% of the population are affiliated. The insurance system carries the cost of medical benefits and provides income maintenance. During the first six weeks of illness the employers pay full wage continuation. Civil servants are protected under special regulations for the public sector.

Medical treatment outside hospitals is an autonomous activity controlled by the sickness insurance funds on the one hand and medical doctors on the other. Almost all private doctors are under contract to sickness funds (*Kassenärzte*). Other medical services provided by specialists are regulated to varying degrees by sickness insurance legislation. Hospitals are maintained by public bodies (36% of all 3,300 hospitals in 1979), non-profit organizations (34%), and private carriers (30%). They are financed on a dual basis. The capital expenditure of all hospitals included in the public plans of hospital demand is financed out of general revenues of the federal government and the single states. Their running costs are born by patients' fees which the insurance system pays for its members directly to the carrier organizations. The public health service only carries out minor functions. Its role is limited to the supervision of health conditions, to counselling and the provision of health information.

In 1979, expenditure on health services amounted to 113 billion DM, corresponding to 26.0% of social expenditure, or 8.1% of GDP. These figures do not include all public outlays for hospitals. Public expenditure for hospital investment amounted to 3.4 billion DM in 1979. Total public outlays for hospitals arrived at 20.1 billion DM in the same year, but this figure includes running costs which are reimbursed by the sickness insurance system (where they appear as part of the expenditure on hospital care).

Health expenditure in 1979 (million DM)

	Total	%
Sickness insurance	80 520	71.2
Wage continuation from employers	25 800	22.8
Civil servants' medical benefits	5 401	4.8
Public health	1 388	1.2
Total	113 109	100.0

According to a purely functional classification in the German social budget, total health expenditure amounted to 141.7 billion DM or 10.1% of GDP in 1979 (excluding hospital investment).

1. Sickness insurance

In 1979 total outlays for sickness insurance amounted to 80.520 billion DM (excluding transfers). This corresponded to 18.5% of social expenditure, 29.1% of social security expenditure, and 5.8% of GDP. Of the total amount 6.9 billion DM were spent on cash benefits. Wage continuation paid by employers amounted to another 25.8 billion DM so that altogether 32.7 billion DM (2.3% of GDP) were spent on income maintenance during sickness.

The major part of sickness insurance expenditure (86% or 70 billion DM in 1979) is spent on medical benefits. The insurance funds carry the cost of these benefits, but do not provide services themselves. Self-governing doctors' corporations under state supervision have the legal responsibility to provide adequate medical services throughout the country. The prices of medical goods and services are negotiated by collective bargaining between the umbrella associations of the insurance funds and the corporations of the various supplier groups (doctors, dentists, opticians, hospitals, etc.). Each year the doctors' corporations and the insurance fund associations negotiate an aggregate sum of medical expenditure which the doctors' corporations then distribute among their individual members on a fee-for-service basis. The price of hospital care is negotiated between the insurance funds and the hospital carrier organizations in accordance with legal ground rules (*Bundespflegesatzverordnung*). The negotiated lump sum fee per day must cover all hospital running expenditure (on average, 189 DM per day in 1980). The price of the various medical goods such as dentures is similarly negotiated between the funds and the supplier corporations. The price of drugs is determined by the pharmaceutical industry without participation of the funds. Since 1977, the various interest groups active in the health sector meet twice a year with government representatives in a bargaining body called 'concerted action' (*Konzertierte Aktion*). This body issues recommendations concerning the annual increase of the various components of health expenditure. The general goal is to confine the rise of health outlays to the rate of wage increases.

Sickness insurance expenditure in 1979 (million DM)

	Total	%
Cash benefits (excl. wage continuation):	6 953	8.6
- sickness allowances	5 959	
- birth and death allowances	994	
Benefits in kind:	70 154	86.4
- for doctors, dentists, medical treatment	25 889	
- hospital care	23 259	
- medicine	15 731	
- maternity and other	5 275	
General services administration	3 413	4.2
Transfers	655	0.8
Total (social budget)	81 175	100.0
Net total (excluding transfers)	80 520	
Wage continuation from employers	25 800	
Net total incl. wage continuation	106 320	

Coverage

Compulsory coverage for sickness insurance extends to the following groups: all workers (except part-time workers with small incomes); employees below an income-limit (defined as 75% of the contribution ceiling under pension insurance and thus indexed to wage changes - 3,750 DM per month in 1983); self-employed farmers and foresters; some special groups of self-employed persons if their income remains below the limit for compulsory coverage of employees (e.g. self-employed teachers); the unemployed; students; the handicapped and pensioners. Employees who exceed the income-limit may become voluntary members under certain conditions. The number of compulsory members amounted to 20.6 million in 1980 (excluding pensioners). This corresponded to 75% of the labour force. Including 10.3 million pensioners and 4.4 million voluntary contributors, total active membership of the sickness insurance system amounted to 35.4 million in 1980. If one includes the indirectly insured family members, 90% of the population are covered by the sickness insurance system.

Income maintenance

Expenditure for income maintenance covers about 9% of total spending for sickness insurance. The insurance system pays cash benefits (*Krankengeld*), as from the seventh week of illness. The self-employed, students, pensioners and family members of the insured are not entitled to cash benefits. Benefits are earnings-related, amounting to 80% of lost gross earnings up to the income-limit for compulsory coverage, and must not exceed previous net earnings. Cash benefits are payable for a maximum of 78 weeks for the same illness. They are indexed in the same way as pensions. Insured persons on leave from work in order to care for a sick child, are entitled to draw insurance cash benefits for a maximum of five days per year and child. Sickness insurance also provides some special allowances. Previously employed mothers are entitled to a maternity allowance (*Mutterschaftsgeld*) which is paid regularly for a period of six weeks before and eight weeks after confinement. The allowance is earnings-related and is paid up to a maximum of 750 DM per month. At the end of the regular protection period after confinement previously employed mothers may continue to draw benefits for another four months (*Mutterschaftssurlaubsgeld*, cut to DM 510 as from 1984). If an insured person dies, a lump sum payment (equalling 20 times the daily earnings of the deceased with a minimum of 100 DM) is made by the insurance system in order to cover the cost of burial.

Services

The insurance system covers the cost of medical care for insured persons and their dependent family members. This includes the consultation of doctors, hospital care, and prescriptions. Pregnancy, confinement and legal abortion all constitute part of the risks covered. Medical benefits and hospital care are granted without a time limit. The insured may choose among the practitioners licensed by the insurance system. Practically all independent doctors possess a license.

Insured persons with children below the age of eight are entitled to household assistance (*Haushaltshilfe*), if they are unable to take care of the home due to sickness. In such cases the insurance system either provides personnel or reimburses the costs up to a certain ceiling. Self-employed farmers without employees or family workers are entitled to the services of a substitute (*Betriebshilfe*), who will run the farm for a maximum of three months. Finally, the insurance system provides preventative services such as x-rays, vaccinations or information campaigns, and provides free preventative medical check-ups in specific cases (i.e. children under the age of four, and early diagnosis of cancer for adults over a certain age).

Financing

The system is financed by earnings-related contributions shared equally between employers and employees. The rates vary from one fund to another. On average they amounted to 12.0% in 1983. In addition to their contributions, the insured bear part of the costs of prescriptions (2 DM for each drug prescribed), and of specific items such as spectacles and dentures. The self-employed pay their contributions alone; students pay small flat-rate amounts, and pensioner contributions are paid by the pension insurance system. The cost of wage continuation is born by employers. Small undertakings with less than 20 employees receive reimbursements of 80% which are financed by employers of the respective industrial branch on a cost-sharing basis. The government contributes a lump sum of DM 400 to each maternity allowance and pays part of the students' contributions. In 1979 state contributions amounted to 1.6% of total receipts.

Administration

The insurance system is administered by some 1,300 independent funds. These are classified into seven organizational types with separate umbrella associations. Local funds (*Ortskrankenkassen*) are the basic type of fund to which all compulsorily covered persons are affiliated, in cases where they are not covered by a special fund. There are five types of special funds: firm funds (*Betriebskrankenkassen*), artisans' funds (*Innungskrankenkassen*), and three funds for specific occupational groups (sailors, miners, farmers). Insured persons may also choose to become members of substitute insurance funds (*Ersatzkassen*) which have a special legal standing, but must provide the statutory minimum of benefits. All funds are self-governing bodies under state supervision. Insured persons and employers each delegate one half of the members of the managing boards of the major types of funds. Special regulations apply to the funds of sailors, miners, and farmers. The substitute insurance funds are managed by representatives of insured persons only.

Core laws

17.6.1949 (WiGBl.:99)
Sozialversicherungsanpassungsgesetz (Social Insurance Adaptation Law): restored the pre-Nazi insurance system; income-limit for compulsory coverage of employees fixed at 375 DM per month (about 142% of average gross wage); cash benefits fixed at 50% of lost earnings (together with child supplements) for a maximum of 26 weeks; earnings-related contributions to be born equally by the insured and employers (the insured previously paid two-thirds, average rate in 1950: 6% in workers' funds).

22.2.1951 (BGBl.I:124)
Selbstverwaltungsgesetz (Self-administration Law): re-established self-administration abolished under the Nazi regime; equal representation of the insured and employers in all branches of social insurance, abolishing traditional two-thirds majority by employee representatives in sickness insurance.

17.8.1955 (BGBl.I:513)
Kassenarztgesetz (Law on Doctors under Contract to Sickness Insurance Funds): established regional and federal doctors' associations with the status of self-governing corporations and the responsibility for organizing the provision of medical services; the associations represent doctors' interests in collective bargaining with insurance funds' associations, and distribute fund payments to individual doctors.

17.8.1955 (BGBl.I:524)
Krankenkassenverbandsgesetz (Sickness Fund Organization Law): established ground rules for the organization of insurance funds in self-governing regional and federal associations that function as representatives of the funds in collective bargaining with doctors' corporations.

12.6.1956 (BGBl.I:500)
Rentnerkrankenversicherungsgesetz (Pensioners' Sickness Insurance Law): pension insurance schemes made responsible for the payment of pensioners' sickness insurance contributions.

26.6.1957 (BGBl.I:649)
Verbesserungsgesetz (Improvement Law): increased cash benefits from 50% to 65% of lost gross earnings; obliged employers to increase workers' benefits to 90% of net earnings during the first six weeks; reduced waiting period from three to two days.

12.6.1961 (BGBl.I:913)
Änderungsgesetz (Modification Law): obliged employers to pay full difference between insurance cash benefits and net earnings during the first six weeks of illness; abolished waiting period; extended maximum duration of cash benefits and hospital care from 26 to 78 weeks.

22.12.1967 (BGBl.I:1259)
Finanzänderungsgesetz (Finance Modification Law): raised individual fees for prescriptions to 1 DM (*Rezeptblattgebühr*); reduced maternity allowances; introduced pensioners' contributions to sickness insurance.

27.7.1969 (BGBl.I:946)
Krankenversicherungsänderungsgesetz (Sickness Insurance Modification Law): equalized entitlements to wage continuation for employees and workers; employers required to pay full wage continuation to both groups for up to six weeks.

21.12.1970 (BGBl.I:1770)
Zweites Krankenversicherungsänderungsgesetz (Second Sickness Insurance Modification Law): linked the indexation of the income-limit for compulsory employee coverage to the development of the pension insurance contribution ceiling (75% of the ceiling); extended the criteria for voluntary membership of employees; obliged employers to pay 50% of contributions in the case of voluntary membership; introduced regular preventive medical check-ups for specific groups.

10.8.1972 (BGBl.I:1433)
Krankenversicherungsgesetz der Landwirte (Farmers' Sickness Insurance Law): introduced compulsory insurance for independent farmers, family workers in agriculture, and pensioners under the farmers' pension scheme; medical benefits for all covered groups, cash benefits only for family workers who are under compulsory coverage for pension insurance.

19.12.1973 (BGBl.I:1925)
Leistungsverbesserungsgesetz (Benefit Improvement Law): entitlement to hospital care made legally binding (entitlements already enjoyed in practice); abolished time limit for hospital care; introduced entitlement to household assistance under specific conditions, and entitlement to leave of absence from work and cash benefits in the event of a child's illness.

7.5.1975 (BGBl.I:1061)
Behinderten-Sozialversicherungsgesetz (Social Insurance Law for the Handicapped):

extended compulsory coverage to handicapped persons working in special establishments for the handicapped (medical benefits and cash benefits to replace earnings from work).

24.6.1975 (BGBl.I:1536)
Studenten-Krankenversicherungsgesetz (Students' Sickness Insurance Law): extended compulsory coverage to students (medical benefits only).

28.12.1976 (BGBl.I:3871)
Krankenversicherungs-Weiterentwicklungsgesetz (Sickness Insurance Development Law): empowered doctors' corporations to define regional health requirements and to influence the regional distribution of individual doctors; obliged the corporations to include the insurance funds in the planning procedure, thus weakening the traditionally exclusive responsibility of the corporations for the provision of health services.

27.6.1977 (BGBl.I:1069)
Kostendämpfungsgesetz (Cost Curtailment Law): introduction of corporatist 'concerted action' in the planning and controlling of the development of medical expenditure (representatives of insurance funds, doctors' corporations, employers, unions, and the government); obliged insurance funds and doctors' associations to negotiate a maximum annual amount for pharmaceutical expenditure; laid down rules for collective bargaining; strengthened supervision of prescription practice of individual doctors; limited indirect insurance of family members to persons with earnings below a certain ceiling; minor cuts in various medical benefits; increased private contribution to prescription fees; introduced the balancing of financial burdens between various funds of the same type.

15.12.1979 (BGBl.I:2241)
Mittelverwaltungsgesetz (Financial Administration Law): regulations concerning the property of insurance funds; limited the funds' capacity to build up reserves in order to ensure sufficient liquidity and stabilize contribution rates.

27.7.1981 (BGBl.I:705)
Künstlersozialversicherungsgesetz (Artists' Social Insurance Law): introduced compulsory insurance for independent artists below a certain income-limit; entitlements and contribution rates as under the general insurance scheme; insured persons contribute employee rates under the general system; two-thirds of remaining half paid by agencies marketing artists' work (publishing companies, theatres, etc.), and one-third by the federal government.

22.12.1981 (BGBl.I:1578)
Kostendämpfungs-Ergänzungsgesetz (Cost Curtailment Amendment Law): reduced various medical benefits and increased private fees; raised fees for prescriptions from 1 DM to 1.50 DM per item; reduced covered hospitalization period after confinement from 10 to 6 days; limited payments for dental prosthesis from 80 to 60% of cost; made maximum rather than fixed prices the basis of collective bargaining between funds and suppliers; made 'concerted action' recommendations more binding; issued various guidelines for collective bargaining.

22.12.1981 (BGBl.I:1523)
Zweites Haushaltsstrukturgesetz (Second Budget Structure Law): confined maternity allowances to mothers with an employment record of nine months prior to confinement; limited federal government maternity allowance for mothers not covered by sickness insurance to 400 DM.

20.12.1982 (BGBl.I:1857)
Haushaltsbegleitgesetz 1983 (Supplementary Budget Law): increased private fees for medical benefits; prescription fees raised from 1.50 to 2 DM per item; introduced private fee for hospital care of 5 DM per day during first two weeks; introduced private fee of 10 DM for rehabilitation cures; introduced individual contribution of pensioners to sickness insurance (1% of pensions in 1983, 3% in 1984, 5% in 1985); issued list of drugs no longer paid by the insurance system; introduced fines of 20,000 DM for doctors sanctioning benefit abuse.

22.12.1983 (BGBl.I:1532)
Haushaltsbegleitgesetz 1984 (Supplementary Budget Law): made sickness insurance cash benefit recipients liable to pay contributions to pension and unemployment insurance; one half of contributions to be paid by the insured and other half by his insurance funds; cash benefits thus reduced by 11.55%.

2. Wage continuation

Workers and employees are equally entitled to full wage continuation, payable by employers during the first six weeks of illness without any waiting period. Employees obtained this privilege in the nineteenth century (legally binding since 1930). Workers were put on the same legal footing by legislation passed in 1957, 1961 and 1969 (see Core Laws for Sickness Insurance).

3. Civil servants

There is no special insurance scheme for civil servants. However, the 1.8 million tenured civil servants are entitled to salary continuation during sickness, and receive reimbursements of 50% of the costs of medical benefits from their employing agency (plus additonal 5% for each dependent family member up to a ceiling of 70%). The remainder is usually covered by contracts with private insurance companies. In 1979 reimbursements amounted to 5.4 billion DM, or 1.2% of social expenditure. For Core Laws, see Section V.

4. Public health

The public health service plays a minor role in the German health system. Its main task is to control sanitary conditions, register contagious diseases, and help prevent illness (regular x-rays in educational institutions and information campaigns). It also prepares medical references for public agencies. In 1978 there were 337 public health offices (*Gesundheitsämter*) staffed by 12,600 professional people (i.e.doctors, medical assistants, social workers etc., not including administrative personnel). In 1979 total expenditure amounted to 139 million DM, of which personnel constituted the largest single item of expenditure.

Core laws

Public health and hospitals

27.2.1952 (BGBl.I:121)
Gesetz zur Errichtung eines Bundesgesundheitsamts (Law to establish a Federal Health Office): established a federal health office to carry out research in the public health sector, register disease statistics, and combat drug addiction.

12.5.1969 (BGBl.I:363)
22. Grundgesetzänderungsgesetz (22nd Constitutional Modification Law): constitutional amendment which entitled the federal government to pass legislation affecting the hospital sector.

29.6.1972 (BGBl.I:1009)
Krankenhausfinanzierungesetz (Hospital Financing Law): secured the supply of hospitals and lowered the cost of hospital care; defined the financing of hospital investment as a public responsibility; single states to issue plans for hospital development, and the federal government to bear the cost of hospital investment covered in the plans; rates for hospital care thus based on running costs alone; hospitals to ensure that public subsidies together with insurance fund payments for patients cover total costs.

22.12.1981 (BGBl.I:1568)
Krankenhaus-Kostendämpfungsgesetz (Hospital Cost Curtailment Law): introduced collective bargaining on current cost of hospitals, obliging hospitals to negotiate daily rates with insurance funds (*Pflegesätze*); introduced guidelines for determination of daily rates; improved procedures to plan the demand for hospital facilities; introduced incentives to reduce number of hospitals and beds.

III Accident insurance

In 1979 total expenditure on occupational injuries insurance (in the definition of the social budget, excluding transfers) amounted to 9 billion DM. This corresponded to 2.1% of social expenditure, 3.2% of social security expenditure, and 0.6% of GDP.

Expenditure in 1979 (million DM)

	Total	%
Cash benefits:	6 400	67.7
- pensions	5 728	
- other[a]	672	
Benefits in kind	1 503	15.9
Services and administration	1 068	11.3
- administration	715	
Transfers	479	5.1
Total (social budget)	9 450	100.0
Net total in social budget	8 971	

[a] Cash benefits during rehabilitation, funeral grants

Coverage

Insurance against occupational injuries and accidents is compulsory for practically all employed persons irrespective of income and for several categories of self-employed persons (e.g. self-employed farmers, owners of small industrial undertakings). The total number of insured persons amounted to 27.9 million in 1980. This corresponded to 25.6 million full-time workers or 96% of the labour force. Civil servants are protected under special regulations (*Dienstunfallversorgung*). In addition to economically active persons the insurance system covers some 14.6 million pupils, students, and kindergarten children against accidents. Besides these directly insured persons, all those who have an accident whilst performing certain public functions (e.g. life saving, blood donation, etc.) are automatically covered.

Benefits

The insurance system covers work accidents and occupational diseases in addition to certain accidents which are treated as being the legal equivalents of work accidents (e.g. accidents occuring between home and workplace, accidents involving children, etc.). In the case of injury, the system provides three types of benefit: transitory benefits to promote rehabilitation (in cash or kind), pensions in case of full or partial incapacity to work, and survivors' pensions. The insurance system is also responsible for the prevention of accidents by establishing safety rules governing production activities. Rehabilitation measures have priority over pension payments, and consist of medical treatment and vocational retraining. Those taking part in rehabilitation programmes are also entitled to cash benefits (*Übergangsgeld*) which amount to 80% of lost gross earnings (with previous net earnings as maximum). Persons in need of day care are entitled to special cash benefits (*Pflegegeld*). Entitlement to a pension presupposes a minimum of 20% reduction in earning capacity. The pension varies with past earnings and degree of incapacity. In the case of full disability it amounts to two-thirds of lost gross earnings (up to a given earnings' ceiling). Partially disabled persons receive the percentage of the full pension which corresponds to the reduction of their earning capacity. In the case of minor incapacity they may opt for a lump sum payment instead of a pension. Severely disabled pensioners in receipt of a minimum of 50% of the full pension are also entitled to supplements for children under 18 (10% of the pension). Pensions for pupils and students are calculated as percentages of special assessment bases, which vary with the age of the recipient. This insurance accounts for approximately 3% of total benefit expenditure. In the case of a fatal accident, the deceased's spouse and orphans are entitled to survivors' pensions (widowers only if the wife provided the major part of the family income). Widows' pension amounts to 30% of gross earnings of the deceased (40% if over 45 or caring for a dependent child). During the first three months the pension is augmented to correspond to the full invalidity pension to which the deceased would have been entitled. Survivors' benefits also include a lump sum funeral grant equal to one month of the deceased's earnings. Orphans' pensions amount to 20% of the deceased's earnings (30% for full orphans). All survivors' pensions together must not exceed a ceiling of 80% of the deceased's gross earnings.

Financing

The cost of insurance for the economically active is born entirely by employers. Contribution rates are calculated on the basis of the running costs of the preceding year, and vary widely according to occupation. The average contribution amounts to roughly 1.5% of the payroll. The cost of insurance for children, pupils, students, and persons suffering accidents whilst performing public functions, is financed out of general revenues.

Administration

The insurance system is administered by 35 autonomous occupational associations (*Be-*

rufsgenossenschaften) in industry, 19 agricultural associations, and by special funds established by local authorities, states or the federal government. The occupational associations are self-governing bodies under state supervision, managed by elected representatives of employees and employers. They are united in three central associations for industry, agriculture, and the public sector. In 1975 the industrial and agricultural associations employed some 15,000 persons. They issue rules on occupational safety, carry out factory inspection, and have counselling and supervisory functions. Running parallel to these, the single states maintain a special bureaucracy to supervise the implementation of occupational safety regulations (*Gewerbeaufsicht*).

Core laws

10.8.1949 (WiGBl.:251)
Gesetz über Verbesserungen der gesetzlichen Unfallversicherung (Accident Insurance Improvement Law): abolished special war provisions; increased benefits; established fixed minima and maxima for pensions; introduced full pension entitlement for those suffering accidents occuring between the home and workplace.

22.2.1951 (BGB1.I:124)
Selbstverwaltungsgesetz (Self-administration Law): introduced bipartite administration with employer and employee representatives (administration previously run exclusively by employers).

29.4.1952 (BGB1.I:253)
Unfallversicherungszulagengesetz (Accident Insurance Benefit Supplement Law): increased benefits by 25% and specified new pension minima - full invalidity 90 DM per month, widows' 54 DM, orphans' 40 DM; (decree of 26.7.1952 also increased the number of recognized occupational diseases from 27 to 40).

27.7.1957 (BGB1.I:1071)
Geldleistungs-Neuregelungsgesetz (Reorganization of Cash Benefits Law): linked benefits to rises in prices and wages, with sizeable increases; lowered age-limit for entitlement to higher widow pensions from 60 to 45 years.

29.12.1960 (BGB1.I:1085)
Zweites Geldleistungs-Neuregelungsgesetz (Second Reorganization of Cash Benefits Law): adapted benefits to rises in prices and wages with sizeable increases.

30.4.1963 (BGBl.I:241)
Unfallversicherungsneuregelungsgesetz (Accident Insurance Reform Law): basic reform law; increased accident prevention; obliged employers with more than 20 employees to employ occupational safety specialists; extended insurance to prisoners; inclusion of accidents caused by colleagues; general inclusion of occupational diseases instead of special enumeration of covered diseases; stressed priority of rehabilitation over pensions; increased pensions and indexed them to changes in wages.

18.3.1971 (BGBl.I:237)
Unfallversicherung der Schüler, Studenten und Kinder in Kindergärten (Accident Insurance for Pupils, Students and Kindergarten Children): extended accident insurance to pupils, students and children in kindergartens; organized and financed by states and local authorities; pension entitlements defined as proportions of average earnings of insured economically active persons, the proportions varying with age (from 25% for children under 6 to 60% for children over 18).

25.7.1978 (BGBl.I:1089)
21. Rentenanpassungsgesetz (21st Pension Adjustment Law): introduced new indexation procedure for accident insurance pensions; linked annual adjustments to annual change in wages (with time lag); based future adjustment on decrees rather than parliamentary legislation (increases for 1979 and 1980 were 6.9 and 5.2% respectively, and decreed increases for 1981, 1982 and 1983 were 5.5, 6.5 and 4.8% respectively).

22.12.1983 (BGBl.I:1532)
Haushaltsbegleitgesetz 1984 (Supplementary Budget Law): linked indexation of pensions to wage changes in previous year (thus reducing time lag in adjustment formula); replaced child supplements by lower general child allowances; reduced widows'/widowers' lump sum benefit in cases of remarriage from five times to twice the annual pension.

IV Unemployment insurance/Employment services

German unemployment policy combines two instruments, i.e. social insurance benefits to replace lost earnings and various measures to promote employment. Both tasks are the responsibility of a central employment institution (*Bundesanstalt für Arbeit*), and are financed by the general contributions to the insurance system. In 1979 expenditure for unemployment policy amounted to 15.6 billion DM (excluding 5.1 billion DM transfers to the social insurance schemes). This corresponds to 3.6% of social expenditure, 5.6% of social security expenditure, and 1.1% of GDP.

Expenditure in 1979 (million DM)

	Total	%
Income replacement:	9 659	46.9
- insurance benefits	7 468	
- assistance benefits[a]	1 978	
- bankruptcy benefits	213	
Income supplements:	2 539	12.3
- part-time workers' benefits	334	
- construction industry benefits	2 205	
Vocational education:	2 230	10.8
- promotion of vocational educat.	1 050	
- cash benefits during training	1 180	
Rehabilitation	1 049	5.1
Promotion of employment:	2 339	11.3
- insurance system	1 795	
- federal government	544	
Administration and general services	2 801	13.6
Total	20 616	100.0
Total in social budget	20 673	
Transfers (included under benefits above)	5 111	
Net total in social budget	15 562	

[a] Including 331 million of federal government assistance and 3 million of special federal government benefits to refugees.

Coverage

All employed persons, except civil servants, are compulsorily covered for unemployment insurance regardless of income. Apprentices, part-time workers and some special categories may be exempted from contributions. In 1980 there were 21.4 million compulsory contributors, i.e. 80% of the labour force.

Benefits

Benefits provided by the employment institution consist of: income maintenance for periods of unemployment; income supplements during periods of part-time work; payments to support participation in vocational training courses; subsidies to promote employment; and general services, e.g. labour exchanges and occupational counselling. Today, classical income maintenance payments only account for roughly one half of total expenditure. They are granted in three forms: insurance benefits, assistance benefits, and benefits to compensate for wages lost due to bankruptcies. Insurance benefits (*Arbeitslosengeld*), amount to 68% of lost net earnings (cut to 63% for persons without children as from 1984). Earnings are reckonable up to a certain ceiling (approximately 180% of average earnings). Entitlement is subject to a minimum contribution period of 12 months within the four years preceding the claim. Insurance benefits are paid for a maximum of up to 12 months if the recipient has a contribution record of at least three years. Persons who have exhausted their entitlements to insurance benefits or who do not fulfill the qualifying conditions, are entitled to assistance benefits (*Arbeitslosenhilfe*), which amount to 58% of past earnings (56% for persons without children as from 1984). Since 1974 net wages and social insurance contributions which are overdue after the bankruptcy of an employer, are fully paid by the insurance for a maximum period of three months (*Konkursausfallgeld*). Recipients of unemployment benefits are entitled to child allowance under the general child allowance scheme. In cases of reduced working hours, the employment institution pays income supplements (*Kurzarbeitergeld*), which compensate for 68% of last earnings (63% for persons without children as from 1984). Special supplements compensate for loss of earnings due to seasonal fluctuations in the construction industry. Since 1959, bad weather benefits (*Schlechtwettergeld*), reimburse 68% (63%) of earnings lost during winter months. Since 1972, wages may be augmented by lump sum benefits (*Wintergeld*) for the period from December to March, in order to compensate for the higher cost of winter employment. To maintain winter employment, employers receive subsidies for investments and increased costs. In 1979 the payments for the construction industry together amounted to 11% of total unemployment expenditure. In recent years the measures to promote vocational education have become increasingly important, and their share of total expenditure has risen from 2% in 1965 to 11% in 1979. The employment institution carries part of the cost of occupational training or retraining, and may also subsidize the organization of such courses. Participants in full-time training courses are entitled to special cash benefits (*Unterhaltsgeld*), amounting to 68% (63%) of net earnings if the recipient is unemployed. Costs arising from vocational training measures and born by employers are partly or totally reimbursed. Special benefits are designed to promote the occupational integration of handicapped persons (*berufliche Rehabilitation*). The employment institution carries the costs of their vocational training courses, pays cash benefits during the participation in such courses, and subsidizes programmes for the training of handicapped persons organized by employers. In 1979 expenditure on rehabilitation measures amounted to 5% of total unemployment expenditure. The employment institution also organizes employment promotion programmes. In order to facilitate regional mobility it either pays for, or subsidizes, the costs of removals and journeys between home and workplace, where the employee is unable to meet these costs himself. Employers may receive subsidies or grants for the employment of persons who would otherwise be difficult to place, and for the creation of new jobs in fields considered to be in the public interest. The federal government contributes to special employment programmes on an irregular basis. In 1979, 11% of total expenditure was spent on employment promotion programmes. Finally, the central employment institution acts through its local offices as a labour exchange, which registers vacancies, and provides counselling for persons in search of work. Individual beneficiaries are covered under the other social insurance systems to which the central labour office pays contributions (transfers to other schemes).

Financing

The insurance system is financed by contributions from insured persons, employers, and the federal government. In 1983, employees and employers each paid 2.3% of gross earnings up to a contribution ceiling. The ceiling is indexed and amounted to 5,000 DM per month in 1983 (as compared to average wages of 2,774 DM). Contribution rates are determined by decrees. Lump sum benefits and subsidies for the construction industry in winter months are financed exclusively by employers. The same applies to special benefits in the case of bankruptcies. The federal government carries the cost of assistance benefits and subsidizes the employment institution if its resources are exhausted.

Administration

The system is administered by a central institution (*Bundesanstalt für Arbeit*), which is sub-divided into nine state offices and 146 local offices. It is managed by tripartite boards of representatives of the insured, the employers and the state. The administrations function as autonomous self-governing bodies under state supervision. In 1979, their full time personnel numbered 51,000 persons.

Core laws

17.6.1949 (WiGBl.:99)
Sozialversicherungsanpassungsgesetz (Social Insurance Adaptation Law): restored the pre-Nazi insurance system; established compulsory coverage for dependent workers up to income-limit; benefits degressively related to various wage levels without a fixed legal earnings-replacement ratio (approximately 40% of net earnings for average earners); special supplements for family members; insurance benefits paid up to a maximum of 26 weeks after a waiting period of seven days; earnings-related contributions shared equally between employers and employees (4% of gross earnings; lowered to 3% in 1955, then lowered by steps to 1.3% from 1964 to 1971, then repeatedly increased again).

10.3.1952 (BGBl.I:123)
Gesetz über Errichtung der Bundesanstalt (Law on the Establishment of the Central

Employment Institution): created the central employment institution with tripartite representation of employers, employees and the state, referred to as *Bundesanstalt für Arbeit* since 1969.

24.8.1953 (BGBl.I:1022)
Änderungs- und Ergänzungsgesetz (Modification and Implementation Law): made sizeable increases in benefits from around 40% to 47% of net wages for average earners; increased maximum duration of benefits to one year, conditional on an insurance record of five years; moderated the degressive effect for higher benefits.

23.12.1956 (BGBl.I:1018)
Grosse Novelle (Major Amendment): basic reformulation; higher income-limit for compulsory coverage; higher benefits (about 50% of net wages for average earners) with new moderation of degressive effect; maximum duration of one year conditional on an insurance record of three years; shorter waiting period of three days; lower contributions.

7.12.1959 (BGB.I:705)
Zweites Änderungsgesetz (Second Modification Law): introduced bad weather benefits for the construction industry, together with measures to promote employment during winter months.

10.3.1967 (BGBl.I:266)
Siebtes Änderungsgesetz (Seventh Modification Law): increased insurance benefits to around 62.5% of net earnings; assistance benefits correspondingly raised to 52.5% (formerly 45%); introduced special cash benefits to cover periods of vocational training, amounting to about 75% of net earnings.

21.12.1967 (BFGB1.I:1259)
Finanzänderungsgesetz (Public Finance Modification Law): abolished income-limit for compulsory coverage (implicit consequence of changes in pension insurance coverage).

25.6.1969 (BGBl.I:2630)
Arbeitsförderungsgesetz (Promotion of Employment Law): basic reform which stressed the role of the employment institution as a promoter of employment; creation of systematic labour market research; central employment institution to subsidize private investment in order to create jobs; introduced subsidies to the construction industry for the maintenance of employment during winter; introduced new subsidies for the organization of occupational training courses; expanded occupational counselling services; established individual entitlement to occupational education.

17.7.1974 (BGBl.I:1481)
Drittes Änderungsgesetz (Third Modification Law): introduced special benefits to compensate for wages not paid as a result of bankruptcy (for a maximum of up to three months); financed by special employer contributions on a cost-sharing basis.

21.12.1974 (BGBl.I:3666)
Einführungsgesetz zur Einkommenssteuerreform (Introductory Income Tax Reform Law): increased insurance benefits, part-time workers' benefits and bad weather payments to 68% of net wages; raised assistance benefits to 58% of net earnings; special benefits during vocational training fixed at 90% of net earnings; abolished special family benefits in favour of the inclusion of the unemployed under general child allowance scheme.

18.12.1975 (BGBl.I:3113)
Haushaltsstrukturgesetz (Budget Structure Law): financial consolidation measures; established a stricter definition of 'suitable employment', which unemployed persons are obliged to accept; abolished assistance benefits for unemployed school-leavers and graduates; reduced benefits during vocational training to 80% of net earnings with stricter qualifying conditions; increased contribution rates from 2% to 3% of earnings.

12.12.1977 (BGBl.I:2557)
Viertes Änderungsgesetz (Fourth Modification Law): established stricter controls for beneficiaries; entitlement to benefits subject to repeated re-examination; limited the normal duration of assistance benefits to one year, with subsequent re-examination of the claim.

23.7.1979 (BGBl.I:1189)
Fünftes Änderungsgesetz (Fifth Modification Law): a combination of tightened controls and increased promotion of vocational training; stricter definition of 'suitable employment'; beneficiaries required to report regularly to the local labour office, and obliged to take part in vocational training courses if required to do so; extended access to vocational training and entitlement to benefits during such courses.

22.12.1981 (BGBl.I:1497)
Arbeitsförderungskonsolidierungsgesetz (Employment Promotion and Consolidation Law): introduced higher contributions (from 3 to 4% of wages) and lower benefits; raised qualification period for benefit entitlements (from 6 to 12 months' contributions for 13 weeks' benefit, and from one to two years' contribution in three years preceding claim for benefit with maximum duration of one year); introduced new procedure for calculation of reckonable earnings thus effectively lowering benefits without changing official earnings-replacement ratio (special payments for holidays and Christmas no longer considered part of regular earnings); extended disqualification period from four to eight weeks, and disqualification resulting from non-registration at labour offices from one to two weeks; tied assistance entitlements more closely to previous employment record; reduced educational training allowance from about 80 to 68% (75% for parents); several other minor cuts.

20.12.1982 (BGBl.I:1857)
Haushaltsbegleitgesetz 1983 (Supplementary Budget Law): raised contribution rate from 4 to 4.6% of wages; increased qualification period for six months' benefits from 12 to 18 months, for one year's benefits from two to three years' contributions (now in four years preceding claim); cut benefits during rehabilitation from 75 to 70% of net earnings (from 90 to 80% for parents); made benefits rather than previous earnings the basis for contributions to pension insurance, thus lowering financial obligations of the unemployment insurance scheme and consequently the federal government's liability to cover deficits.

22.12.1983 (BGBl.I:1532)
Haushaltsbegleitgesetz 1984 (Supplementary Budget Law): cut benefits; reduced earnings-replacement ratio of insurance cash benefits for persons without children from 68 to 63% of net earnings; cut assistance benefits for the same group from 58 to 56%; cut educational training allowance to 63% (70% for parents); cut benefits during rehabilitation from 70 to 65% (from 80 to 75% for parents); transformed special payments for educational promotion (*Weiterbildung*) from obligatory to discretionary benefit (granted as loans); subjected additional income to contributions (by including special payments as reckonable earnings).

V Civil servants' benefits

Civil servants are not incorporated into the general social security schemes. They receive benefits under special regulations which are usually more generous than provisions under the general schemes.

Benefits are of three types: pensions, reimbursement of health expenditure, and special family supplements (*erhöhte Ortszuschläge*). All benefits are financed by the public agency for which the recipient works.

In 1979 total expenditure for civil servants' benefits amounted to around 46 billion DM. This corresponded to 10.5% of social expenditure, or 3.3% of GDP.

Expenditure in 1979 (million DM)

	Pensions	Sickness reimbursements	Family supplements	Total
Cash benefits	30 815	15	7 338	38 168
Benefits in kind	200	5 146	-	5 346
General services administration	1 972	240	140	2 352
Total	32 987 (72%)	5 401 (12%)	7 478 (16%)	45 866 (100%)

Core laws

22.8.1949 (WiGBl.:259)
Gesetz über Massnahmen auf besoldungsrechtlichem und versorgungsrechtlichem Gebiet (Law on Civil Service Salaries and Social Benefits): established guidelines for the employment conditions of the new German civil service.

14.7.1953 (BGBl.I:551)
Bundesbeamtengesetz (Federal Civil Servants' Law): regulated employment conditions for federal civil servants; specified entitlements to social benefits (old age and survivors' pensions, occupational injuries benefits).

1.7.1957 (BGBl.I:667)
Beamtenrechtsrahmengesetz (Civil Service Guidelines Law): specified guidelines for the standardization of employment conditions and social security entitlements of civil servants in federal, state and local government.

27.7.1957 (BGBl.I:993)
Bundesbesoldungsgesetz (Civil Service Salary Law): regulated salaries for federal civil servants, judges and soldiers, including entitlements to special child supplements as component of salary.

24.8.1976 (BGBl.I:2485)
Beamtenversorgungsgesetz (Federal Civil Servants' Benefit Law): specified types and

levels of social benefits for civil servants; provided for indexation of benefits to changes in civil servants' salaries.

VI Families and children

Social policy for families and children consists of two major instruments: cash benefits under the general child allowance scheme (*Kindergeld*), and various special services for the young (*Jugendhilfe*). These specific social policy instruments are complemented by a set of legislative regulations under family law and labour law which define the mutual responsibilities of parents and children and establish norms for the protection of mothers or children, especially in the work sphere.

In 1979 expenditure on the general child allowance scheme amounted to around 17 billion DM (excluding transfers). This corresponded to 3.9% of total social expenditure, 6.0% of social security expenditure, or 1.2% of GDP. These figures do not include indirect payments made through tax credits for persons with children, or special family supplements received by civil servants in addition to the standard benefits *(erhöhte Ortszuschläge)*. Supplements under the civil service scheme amounted to around 7.5 billion DM in 1979, i.e. 1.7% of social expenditure, 2.7% social security expenditure, or 0.5% of GDP. Private employees may receive additional payments on the basis of collective bargaining agreements which are not considered here as part of public provisions. Public outlays for youth services amounted to 5.3 billion DM in 1979 (1.2% of total social expenditure, or 0.4% of GDP).

Expenditure in 1979 (million DM)

Total child allowances	24 890
- General child allowances	16 744
- Civil service child supplements	7 478
- Transfers to other social security schemes	668
Total youth welfare services	5 318
- Public measures	3 512
-in residential homes	482
-outside residential homes	3 030
- Subsidies to non-public carriers	1 296
- Administration and other	510
Total	30 208

Coverage

All persons resident in the Federal Republic or West Berlin are entitled to public child allowances. Only the receipt of child supplements under other social transfer schemes precludes benefits under the general system. Since 1979, single parents (with children up to the age of 6) who do not receive maintenance payments from the liable parent are entitled to a public maintenance benefit (*Unterhaltsvorschuss*).

Benefits

Benefits are universal and, in principle, flat-rate. In 1983 benefits amounted to DM 50 per month for the first child, DM 100 for the second child, DM 220 for the third child, and DM 240 for the fourth and subsequent children. Since 1983, parents with two children and annual net earnings above the limit of DM 42,000 (plus DM 7,800 for additional children) receive lower benefits for the second child and additional children (minimum of DM 70 for the second, DM 140 for the third and subsequent children). Direct transfers are complemented by indirect tax subsidies which have been repeatedly modified in recent years. Prior to 1975, the tax deductions (*Kinderfreibeträge*) constituted a major policy tool. In 1975 these were abolished in favour of direct allowances, but in 1979 special deductions for extraordinary family burdens were introduced (*Kinderbetreuungskosten*) which partly re-established the dual system of direct and indirect transfers. In 1983, these special deductions were replaced by a new general tax credit for children (*Kinderfreibetrag*), which amounts to DM 432 to be deducted from the family's taxable income. The special public maintenance benefit for single parents is designed as an advance payment which amounts to the sum payable by fathers of illegitimate children under family law. It is paid for a maximum period of 36 months if the other parent fails to meet his responsibilities. The claim against the liable parent is taken over by the state which advances the payment.

Financing and Administration

General child allowances are entirely financed by the central government out of general revenues. The scheme is administered by the central employment institution (*Bundesanstalt für Arbeit*). Civil servants receive child allowances directly from their public employers. The public maintenance benefit is financed from general revenues. The federal government and the states each pay one half of the expenses not recovered from liable parents.

Services

Under the 1961 Youth Welfare Law the state has the duty to assist parents in the upbringing of children. Where private or voluntary efforts fail, the state has a subsidiary responsibility to promote the development of socially deprived children. Personal services have precedence over benefits in cash and kind. Public services range from counselling and educational assistance in cooperation with parents, to the transference of children to foster parents or public homes. In addition to the measures for deprived children, the state also provides general services for young people and children (kindergartens, leisure facilities, subsidies for youth organizations, etc.).

In 1979, there were a total of 23,900 kindergartens with 1.4 million places corresponding to 77% of all children in the age group 3-5. 28% of all kindergartens are run by public agencies, 70% by voluntary organizations (mostly churches), and 2% are privately owned. In addition to the above, there were another 3,100 homes with 105,000 places catering for school age children (62% public, 35% voluntary, 3% private). A total of 66,500 children, or 0.5% of all minors, lived in residential homes.

Public outlays for these services are financed by general federal government revenues, the states and the local authorities. Youth welfare programmes are administered by 16 state youth offices and some 650 local youth offices.

Core laws

13.11.1954 (BGBl.I:333)
Kindergeldgesetz (Child Allowance Law): introduced flat-rate child allowances for third child and subsequent children of private sector employees; financed and administered by employers' funds (*Familienausgleichskassen*).

23.12.1955 (BGBl.I:841)
Kindergeldergänzungsgesetz (Child Allowance Supplementation Law): extended entitlement to domestic workers, public employees and the economically non-active; the cost of benefits for the last two groups, together with administration costs, are born by the federal government.

27.7.1957 (BGBl.I:1061)
Kindergeldänderungs- und -ergänzungsgesetz (Child Allowance Modification and Supplementation Law): increased benefits from DM 25 to DM 30; small employers under an income-limit exempted from the obligation to pay contributions (*Beitragsfreigrenze*).

16.3.1959 (BGBl.I:153)
Zweites Änderungs- und Ergänzungsgesetz (Second Modification and Supplementation Law): increased benefits from DM 30 to DM 40; increased income-limit for exemption from compulsory contributions.

18.7.1961 (BGBl.I:1001)
Kindergeldkassengesetz (Child Allowance Funds' Law): introduced an allowance for the second child for those with an income below the limit of DM 7,200 per year; benefits amounted to DM 25 per month; financed out of general federal government revenues; administered by special public fund (*Kindergeldkasse*).

11.8.1961 (BGBl.I:1205)
Jugendwohlfahrtsgesetz (Youth Welfare Law): replaced 1922 Youth Welfare Law; strengthened state responsibility for promotion of young people and supervision of upbringing; widened catalogue of services for deprived children; broadened the scope of youth promotion; established rules for cooperation of public and voluntary carrier organizations.

14.4.1964 (BGBl.I 265)
Bundeskindergeldgesetz (Federal Child Allowance Law): basic reorganization; financing entirely shifted to federal government; increased benefits for third child from DM 40 to DM 50; introduced special allowances for fourth child of DM 60, and for fifth child and subsequent children of DM 70; increased income-limit for second child allowance from DM 7,200 to DM 8,400 for families with three or more children; administrative centralization; established unemployment insurance institution as carrier organization for all child allowances.

16.12.1970 (BGBl.I:1725)
Zweites Änderungs- und Ergänzungsgesetz (Second Modification and Supplementation Law): increased allowance for the third child from DM 50 to DM 60; increased income-limit for second child allowance from DM 7,800 to DM 13,200; subsequently increased to DM 15,000 by third modification law (13.12.1971, BGBl.I:1969), to DM 16,800 by fourth modification law (8.11.1973, BGBl.I:1593), and to DM 18,360 by fifth modification law (27.12.1973, BGBl.I:1969).

5.8.1974 (BGBl.I:1769)
Einkommenssteuerreformgesetz (Income Tax Reform Law): basic restructuring of child allowance provisions; abolished general tax credits; abolished income-limit for entitlement to direct allowances; introduced universal flat-rate allowance of 50 DM for first child; increased benefits for second child from 25 DM to 70 DM, for third child and subsequent children from 60 DM to 120 DM (previously DM 70 for fifth and subsequent children).

16.8.1977 (BGBl.I:1586)
Steueränderungsgesetz (Tax Modification Law): increased allowance for second child from 70 DM to 80 DM, and from 120 DM to 150 DM for third and subsequent children.

14.11.1978 (BGBl.I:1757)
Achtes Bundeskindergeldänderungsgesetz (Eighth Federal Child Allowance Modification Law): increased allowance for third child and subsequent children from DM 150 to DM 200.

30.11.1978 (BGBl.I:1849)
Steueränderungsgesetz (Tax Modification Law): increased allowance for second child from DM 80 to DM 100 (effective from July 1979); introduced special tax credit in cases of particular financial burden due to children (*Kinderbetreuungskosten*).

23.7.1979 (BGBl.I.1184)
Unterhaltssicherungsgesetz (Maintenance Security Law): introduced public advance payments for single parents not in receipt of maintenance payments from the liable parent; public benefits payable up to 36 months; private claims against a parent not meeting a maintenance liability taken over by state.

16.8.1980 (BGBl.I:1381)
Steuerentlastungsgesetz 1981 (Tax Relief Law): increased benefits for second child from DM 100 to DM 120, and from DM 200 to DM 240, for third child and subsequent children; effective from 1.2.1981.

22.12.1981 (BGBl.I:1523)
Zweites Haushaltsstrukturgesetz (Second Budget Structure Law): reduced benefits for second child from DM 120 to DM 100, and from DM 240 to DM 220 for third child and subsequent children; effective from 1.1.1982.

20.12.1982 (BGBl.I:1857)
Haushaltsbegleitgesetz 1983 (Supplementary Budget Law): introduced income-limit for entitlement to standard benefits for second and further children; parents with two children and net earnings over DM 42,000 (plus DM 7,800 for every additional child) receive lower allowances (at least DM 70 for the second and DM 140 for each additional child); replaced special tax deduction for particular burdens incurred by children (*Kinderbetreuungskosten*) by new general tax credit for children of DM 432 per child (*Kinderfreibetrag*).

VII Social assistance

In 1979 expenditure for social assistance amounted to 12.5 billion DM. This corresponded to 2.9% of social expenditure, 4.5% of social security expenditure, and 0.9% of GDP.

Expenditure structure in 1979 (million DM)

	Total	%
Regular benefits:	3 921	32.3
- in institutions	608	
- outside institutions	3 313	
of which:		
- regular	2 702	
- special	611	
Particular benefits:	8 208	67.7
- nursing/day care	4 614	
- rehabilitation	2 420	
- sickness	752	
- other purposes	422	
of which:		
- in institutions	6 990	
- outside institutions	1 218	
Total	12 129	100.0
Total in social budget:	12 533	
- cash benefits	4 812	38.4
- benefits in kind	6 416	51.1
- general services and admin.	1 305	10.4

Coverage

Every needy citizen without sufficient means to maintain himself, has a legal entitlement to social assistance. In 1980, 2.1 million persons were in receipt of benefits. This corresponded to 3.5% of the population. One fourth of all recipients were resident in institutions such as homes for the elderly or the blind. Approximately one third of recipients were over 65 years of age, another third were below 21 years, and about one fourth were children under 14.

Benefits

Benefits are given in cash, in kind, or as personal services. Cash benefits are usually granted on a regular basis, but may also be awarded as special lump sum payments to cover particular needs. Benefits in kind consist mostly of medical treatment, and in some cases, clothing or furniture. Services include nursing, help with housework (home help) and counselling. Institutionally, social assistance benefits are subdivided into two classes: regular benefits which cover the running costs of living (*Hilfe zum Lebensunterhalt*), and special benefits for particular circumstances (*Hilfe in besonderen Lebenslagen*). Benefits are officially intended to help recipients to lead a life in keeping with human dignity, including adequate participation in social activities. Benefits vary with the individual situation of the beneficiary, and are granted as subsidiary means when other sources of income or help are not available. Regular assistance benefits represent about one third of total expenditure, and are mostly payable to persons living outside social institutions (in 1979 benefits for these persons accounted for 84% of all regular benefits). In these cases assistance normally consists of cash payments. Benefits cover the difference between the person's private means and his needs. Private means are determined as the resources of the claimant, his spouse, or parents (where the claimant is a minor living at home). Special regulations define to what extent private property may be exempted from an assessment of means. Personal need is defined as a certain standard cash amount (*Regelsatz*), which varies with family size and housing costs. The rates of the standard amount vary from region to region, and are subject to annual revision. In 1983 the standard average rate amounted to 345 DM per month (about 18% of average net wages). Those over 65, pregnant women, and the economically active, are entitled to an increase of 20% of the standard amount. Dependent family members are credited with supplements amounting to 80% of the standard amount for a spouse, and 45-90% for children, depending on their age (45% for children below 7, 90% for those between 16 and 21). In 1983, a married couple over 65 were entitled to regular social assistance benefits if their income fell below DM 745.20 (345 + 276, i.e. 80% for spouse = 621 + 124.20, i.e. 20% for old age) in addition to the cost of housing (e.g. DM 400), together DM 1,145.20. The assistance system then pays the difference between family income and this amount. Persons not entitled to regular benefits may be granted particular payments to cover the costs of special necessities, such as winter clothing, heating or housing. The greater part (two-thirds) of social assistance expenditure consists of special benefits for particular circumstances. They are mostly granted to persons in day care institutions (85% of total expenditure on special benefits). Benefits are mainly payable for the support of elderly or seriously handicapped persons in need of nursing (56%), rehabilitation measures (29%), and medical assistance for sick persons without entitlements to benefits under the sickness insurance scheme (9%). The remaining 6% is distributed for various other purposes such as special aid for persons without shelter, prisoners, or other marginal groups, (support of the blind, treatment of tuberculosis, preventive medical care, family planning etc). Benefits may be given in cash or in kind, and are intended to supplement insufficient private means. Where private means are below a certain income-limit, claimants are entitled to full benefits covering the cost of the contingency. Where private means are above this limit, the assistance system pays the difference between the actual costs and the reckonable means above the limit. The income-limit for benefits in special circumstances varies with the type of contingency, but is always higher than the limit for regular benefits (in most cases twice as high). In 1983 the full benefit for persons in need of day care (*Pflegegeld*), amounted to DM 276 per month. This benefit should generally be revised bi-annually following changes in the general computation basis of the pension insurance system, but has been frozen at a constant level by legislation passed in 1981. In 1980, 1.1 million persons were in receipt of benefits covering particular needs (463,000 were in receipt of day care allowances, and 377,000 in receipt of sickness assistance).

Financing and administration

Approximately 80% of social assistance costs are born by local authorities. The remaining 20% is almost entirely paid by the single states out of general revenues. The federal government only bears the minor costs of some specific benefits such as tuberculosis aid. The system is administered by the local authorities, or by rural districts above the local level. The public carriers cooperate closely with voluntary welfare organizations which have been formed by the churches (Catholic, Protestant, and Jewish), the Red Cross, the labour movement, and by an association of several minor agencies. These six major organizations provide many services for persons in need. Their competences frequently overlap with those of public carriers. In 1967, a supreme court decision confirmed their competence beside public bureaucracies and established that the state must subsidize their activities.

Services

The social assistance scheme provides various services as part of the benefits for particular circumstances described above. Many of the general services which benefit social assistance recipients (special educational institutions, homes for the handicapped or the old) are run by voluntary welfare organizations which provide about 35% of all beds in homes for children, 35% of all hospital beds, and 64% of all places in homes for the elderly. In recent years, several towns and districts have established a new service of social care centres (*Sozialstationen*). These pool the personnel and facilities of public and voluntary carriers in order to provide medical treatment, nursing and personal services for sick or handicapped persons in their own homes. They are subsidized from general revenues. In 1980, there were 1,040 subsidized social care centres.

Core laws

20.8.1953 (BGBl.I:967)
Fürsorgerechts-Änderungsgesetz (Poor Law Modification Law): substantial revision of 1924 assistance decrees; established rules for the coordination of benefits in various local authorities; specified that benefits must cover cost of living; introduced benefit increases of 20% for special groups - elderly, handicapped, economically active mothers; specified private means compatible with receipt of assistance benefits.

24.7.1954
Federal Administrative Court ruling establishing an individual entitlement to social assistance.

27.2.1957 (BGBl.I:147)
Körperbehindertengesetz (Handicapped Persons' Law): introduced assistance for the handicapped and those likely to become handicapped; introduced registration of handicapped persons; medical and vocational rehabilitation programmes; established special medical services for the handicapped.

30.6.1961 (BGBl.I:289)
Bundessozialhilfegesetz (Federal Social Assistance Law): new basic law which replaced traditional legislation dating from 1924; strengthened individual entitlements and extended functions of social assistance; designed to enable every citizen to enjoy a minimum standard of living with minimum income, housing and capacity to participate in social life; stressed subsidiary and individual character of assistance, obliged the recipient to make use of private means and the administration to observe individual needs and preferences; classified benefits into regular assistance and assistance for particular circumstances; stressed the function of benefits in kind and services to strengthen recipient's capacity to help himself; specified income-limits and means compatible with receipt of assistance benefits; standard regular assistance benefit (*Regelsatz*) amounted to DM 197 in 1962.

31.8.1965 (BGBl.I:1027)
Änderungs- und Ergänzungsgesetz (Modification and Supplementation Law):

increased allowances for the blind from DM 200 to DM 240; extended entitlements to blind allowances; increased benefits for special groups from 20% to 30% of standard amount; increased income-limit compatible with receipt of full benefits for particular circumstances.

14.8.1969 (BGBl.I:1153)
Zweites Änderungsgesetz (Second Modification Law): established right of assistance carriers to grant benefits in special cases not explicitly listed by law; developed measures for rehabilitation; extended access to promotion of education by lowering qualifying conditions; increased supplements to family members, and various special benefits such as day care allowances; increased income-limit compatible with receipt of full benefits.

25.3.1974 (BGBl.I:777)
Drittes Änderungsgesetz (Third Modification Law): extended individual entitlements by means of higher income-limits compatible with receipt of benefits and lowered age limits for certain special benefits; child supplements expressed as percentages of standard amounts and thus indexed to their changes; extended rehabilitation measures; exempted grandparents of recipients from potential liability to reimburse expenditure of social assistance carrier.

22.12.1981 (BGBl.I:1523)
Zweites Haushaltsstrukturgesetz (Second Budget Structure Law): limited standard benefit increase to 3% (instead of being adjusted to cost-of-living increases of 5.4%); reduced augmentation of standard amounts for special groups from 30% to 20%; reduced special allowance for the blind from DM 778 to DM 750 DM; froze level of day care allowances for two years (at DM 276); reduced amount of property compatible with receipt of benefits; reduced other special benefits (aggregate cuts estimated at 350 million DM).

20.12.1982 (BGBl.I:1857)
Haushaltsbegleitgesetz 1983 (Supplementary Budget Law): limited standard benefits increase to 2% and postponed date of adjustment by half a year (from January to July, leading to an effective annual increase of 1% in the presence of an inflation rate of 3%).

22.12.1983 (BGBl.I:1532)
Haushaltsbegleitgesetz 1984 (Supplementary Budget Law): weakened individual entitlements in favour of stronger administrative discretion; established increase of cost of living index as the upper limit (rather than the norm) for annual adjustments of standard benefit; limited obligation of assistance carrier to bear the cost of housing to the carrying of 'reasonable' costs.

VIII Housing

German housing policy makes use of three basic instruments: (1) subsidies to increase the private supply of housing; (2) rent allowances to enable tenants to pay market prices; (3) and regulative legislation subjecting the housing market to a certain degree of public control. The direct supply of public housing is of negligible importance in the Federal Republic. Public authorities, however, frequently hold shares in publicinterest building corporations (*gemeinnützige Wohnungsbaugesellschaften*) which play a prominent role in housing construction and which have supplied about onefourth of all dwellings built since 1949. The corporations must conform to certain regulations concerning investment, the calculation of rents, and admissible profits. In return, they receive sizeable tax credits (mostly exemption from corporation tax, property tax, and excise tax). They are usually carried by public authorities (mostly municipalities, but also federal and state governments, post, and railways), trade unions, churches, social insurance carriers, and, to a lesser degree, private business corporations. Corporations carried by public authorities own about 60% of all dwellings held by public-interest building corporations.

Direct public outlays for housing amounted to around 11 billion DM in 1979 (including loans, which are partially repaid in subsequent years). This corresponded to 2.6% of aggregate social expenditure and to 0.8% of GDP. In addition, around 9 billion DM were spent on indirect subsidies for the housing sector.

Expenditure in 1979 (million DM)

	Total	%
Direct payments:		
Housing allowances	2 031	17.8
Promotion of housing construction:	7 415	65.2
- social housing	2 231	
Premiums on savings for housing purposes	1 933	17.0
Total	11 379	100.0
Indirect subsidies[a]:		
Special interest rates for social housing	2 427	26.7
Special interest rates for building activities of public agencies	713	7.8
Tax credits for dwellings	3 850	42.3
Tax credits for real estate property	1 340	14.7
Tax credits for private savings for building	770	8.5
Total	9 100	100.0

[a] Not included here under 'social expenditure'.

1. State subsidization of housing supply

At present, subsidies for housing construction are the major policy tool. Subsidies are given in four forms: (1) sizeable direct subsidies granted in combination with tax credits to promote housing for low-income groups (*sozialer Wohnungsbau*); (2) special tax credits granted in addition to general tax deductions (*steuerbegünstigter Wohnungsbau*); (3) general tax credits for all private builders (*freifinanzierter Wohnungsbau*); (4) public premiums on private savings for construction (*Bausparprämien*).

Under the social housing programme (*sozialer Wohnungsbau*), builders who meet certain public standards concerning the size and cost of the dwelling may receive loans, subsidies to lower the debt burden, and tax credits. The programme is divided into two branches. The first (*1. Förderungsweg*) deals mostly with the supply of apartment housing. Builders must observe public limits on the size and cost of dwellings and must let their apartments to tenants below a certain income-limit at an approved public authority-fixed rent (*Bewilligungsmiete*). In return they are entitled to low-interest public loans, subsidies to reduce the debt burden, and to an exemption from land tax for ten years. Subsidies are designed to bridge the gap between the cost rent and the approved rent. Builders with earnings under the income-limit set for tenants (in 1983 about 44,000 DM for a family of four persons, i.e. about one-third higher than individual average gross earnings) may also receive subsidies if they construct the dwelling for themselves. Subsidies are heavier, however, for tenant housing than for housing constructed for personal use, amounting to 50% and 30% of costs respectively (including tax credits). About two-thirds of all dwellings built under the first branch of the social housing programme were constructed by public-interest building corporations.

The second branch of the programme (*2. Förderungsweg*) is aimed primarily at the promotion of owner-occupied housing (*Eigenheimbau*). The incomelimits are 40% higher than under the first branch, and the size limits are extended by 20%. Builders only receive tax credits and subsidies to lower the interest on debt, but no public loans. The degree of subsidization amounts to about 10-20% of the cost. About three-quarters of all housing built under this branch of the programme is constructed by private owners for their own use.

Approximately 43% of all dwellings built since 1949 were subsidized by the social housing programme. In 1979, social housing subsidies amounted to 4.6 billion DM, consisting of 2.2 billion DM on direct subsidies, and 2.4 billion DM on indirect payments in the form of reduced interest rates for loans. Of the subsidies, 90% went to the first branch of the programme which only covered about 23% of the total of 70,000 subsidized cases. In recent years the second branch has gained in importance.

Private builders not willing to meet the standards of the social housing programme are only subsidized indirectly by tax credits. Builders who remain within certain limits regarding the cost and size of dwellings (20% higher than under the social housing programme) are entitled to an exemption from land tax for ten years and to a public guarantee for mortgages (*steuerbegünstigtes Wohnen*). In addition, they receive general tax credits which are available for all private builders. The special tax credits for the land tax amounted to 1.3 billion DM in 1979.

All private builders including those not willing to observe the above public standards may deduct outlays from their annual taxable income (*Abschreibungen im frei finanzierten Wohnungsbau*). Tax credits for builders of one-family dwellings are lower than those for builders of dwellings for two or more families. Both groups may deduct 5% of the construction costs up to a limit (DM 200,000 for one-family dwellings, DM 250,000 for multiple-family dwellings) from their taxable income for eight years (1.5% in the following 40 years). In addition, the latter group may also deduct interest payments on debt. Builders who do not live in the houses they construct may deduct a certain percentage of the cost under other income tax regulations (3.5% of the cost for 12 years, lower percentages in subsequent years). These tax credits lead to high tax savings especially for higher income groups. They are difficult to quantify, but the 5% deductions alone were estimated to be well over 3 billion DM in 1979.

Finally, the state subsidizes private savings for construction, both directly and indirectly. Savings up to a certain maximum (DM 800 per year for single persons, and DM 1,600 for married couples) are subsidized by public premiums (*Bausparprämien*) of 14% (plus 2% for each dependent child), if the saver's annual taxable earnings are below the income-limit (DM 48,000 for married couples and DM 24,000 for single persons, as compared to average wages of DM 33,293 in 1983 of which about 77% constitutes taxable income). In 1979 public expenditure on premiums amounted to 1.9 billion DM. Persons above the income-limit may deduct savings for construction from their taxable income up to a certain limit. In 1979 these tax credits amounted to 770 million DM.

2. Housing allowances

Tenants and owner-occupiers are entitled to a public housing allowance if their family income remains below a certain limit. This is calculated on the basis of gross earnings minus a general deduction (30% for economically active persons with compulsory contributions to social insurance, 6% as a general minimum), and special deductions which vary with the family size and personal circumstances. Family fathers with average earnings are usually close to the income-limit if other members of the family do not contribute additional earnings.

The allowance is paid in the form of a rent supplement which is designed to cover the difference between the actual cost of the rent (up to a reckonable maximum), and a 'reasonable rent' (*tragbare Miete*). The maximum rent varies according to family size, date of construction, fixtures and fittings, and the size of the town (which influences the market price of rents). The reasonable rent was originally defined as a percentage of family income considered as a bearable burden, but today it is only implicitly contained in tables which show the allowance payable in various circumstances. In 1983 a married worker with average earnings (about DM 2,800 per month), two children, living in a an apartment with standard modern fixtures and fittings, built before 1965, situated in a city of 100,000-500,000 inhabitants, and with a rent of DM 500, would have been entitled to a housing allowance of DM 87 or 17% of the rent. In practice, about 65% of all housing allowance recipients are pensioners, and on average the allowance covers about 30% of rent.

3. Regulative legislation

Up to 1960 public control of the housing market was relatively severe. Today, however, market controls only persist in the form of protective legislation for tenants, which specifies the legal conditions for rent increases and notice. Rents in subsidized dwellings are subject to public regulation. Rents in privately financed apartments may be legally challenged by tenants if they exceed the 'normal rent' (*Vergleichsmiete*) for similar houses in the same area. The federal government has the jurisdiction over legislation regulating tenant protection.

Financing

The social housing programme is funded out of general revenues of the federal government and the single states. Tax credits are regulated by federal legislation, but the reduction of public revenues affects all levels of government. The cost of direct subsidies for private savings is shared equally between the federal government and the single states, as is the cost of housing allowances. The administrative cost of housing allowances is born entirely by the states and local authorities.

Core laws

8.3.1946 (No. 18)
Wohnungsgesetz (Housing Law): implemented by the Allied Control Commission; established a tight administration of housing markets involving allocation of tenants and state fixing of rents.

24.4.1950 (BGBl.I:83)
Wohnungsbaugesetz (Housing Construction Law): eased public control of housing market; abolished administration of newly constructed apartments; promoted private building activities, distinguished three types of construction with varying degrees of public promotion: (1) *Sozialer Wohnungsbau* with public subsidies (loans, special low interest rates) in exchange for public allocation of tenants (who are below the income-limit for compulsory coverage of the pension insurance scheme for employees, with allowances for family members) and public standards regulating the size of dwellings, rents, notice, etc.; (2) *steuerbegünstigter Wohnungsbau* with tax credits on income and land tax in exchange for acceptance of a regulated rent; (3) *frei finanzierter Wohnungsbau* receiving income tax credits only.

17.3.1952 (BGBl.I:139)
Wohnungsbauprämiengesetz (Housing Construction Premiums Law): provided public grants to supplement private savings for housing purposes; entitlement to grants without income ceilings; public premium of 25% on savings (up to maximum of 400 DM per year); housing savings deductable from taxable income.

31.3.1953 (BGBl.I:97)
Wohnraumbewirtschaftungsgesetz (Housing Administration Law): replaced Housing Law passed by the Allied Control Council; confirmed public administration of housing market; extended the cases for exemption from housing market controls.

27.7.1955 (BGBl.I:458)
Erstes Bundesmietengesetz (First Federal Rent Law): loosened public control of rents for dwellings constructed prior to 1950; legalized general rent increases of 10% and further increases for well-equipped apartments.

27.6.1956 (BGBl.I:523)
Zweites Wohnungsbaugesetz (Second Housing Construction Law): defined order of priority for distribution of public grants, established precedence for family houses and other private dwellings over collective dwellings; increased maximum size of dwellings compatible with subsidization; defined minimum standards for apartments meriting subsidization; special no-interest loans for family dwellings.

23.6.1960 (BGBl.I:389)
Gesetz über den Abbau der Wohnungszwangswirtschaft (Reduction of Housing Market Controls Law): far-reaching reform legislation with various sub-laws; re-oriented housing policy with gradual termination of public administration of the market; gradual liberalizing of rent controls; weakened tenant protection thus facilitating notice; introduced rent allowances for tenants in subsidized or old dwellings where rent exceeds bearable burden (ranging from 7% to 20% of income depending on income and family size).

29.7.1963 (BGBl.I:508)
Wohnungsbeihilfengesetz (Housing Assistance Law): introduced various types of housing allowances depending on regional variations in the administration of housing market; entitlement to allowance if annual family income below 9,000 DM (plus addi-

tional 1,800 DM for each family member); allowances to supplement rents covering 35% to 90% of the cost exceeding bearable rent; bearable rent varies from 7% to 24% of income depending on income and family size.

23.3.1965 (BGBl.I:140)
Wohngeldgesetz (Housing Allowance Law): generalized and standardized 1963 housing allowance programme; bearable rent now varying between 5% and 22% of income; allowance rates vary according to income and family size as before; income-limits unchanged.

24.8.1965 (BGBl.I:945)
Wohnungsbauänderungsgesetz (Housing Construction Modification Law): stressed precedence of family houses and private dwellings over collective forms of housing with respect to subsidization; increased loans for family houses; registration of all dwellings built with the aid of public subsidies; income-limits for tenants in social housing 9,000 DM per year plus 2,400 DM per family member.

12.8.1969 (BGBl.I:1211)
Steueränderungsgesetz (Tax Modification Law): introduced special premiums on savings for housing purposes by low-income families; ordinary premiums increased by 30%; income-limit of 12,000 DM per year (6,000 DM for single persons); normal premium remained at 25%. (plus 2% for each dependent child up to a maximum of 35% for large families).

14.12.1970 (BGBl.I:1637)
Zweites Wohngeldgesetz (Second Housing Allowance Law): simplified administration of housing allowances and extended entitlements; income-limit increased to 9,600 DM per year plus 2,400 DM for each family member; increased general deduction on income to determine reckonable income from 15% to 20%; allowance rates listed in tables replacing complicated calculation procedure based on 'bearable rent burdens'.

4.11.1971 (BGBl.I:1745)
Gesetz zur Verbesserung des Mietrechts (Rent Improvement Law): strengthened the position of tenants; notice may be ruled illegal where appropriate substitute accommodation not available; landlords obliged to specify reasons for notice.

25.11.1971 (BGBl.I:1839)
Kündigungsschutzgesetz (Eviction Protection Law): established tenant protection against rent increases and notice; notice only lawful if in the 'justified interest' of the landlord, higher rents not recognized as justified interest; originally planned as temporary legislation up to the end of 1974, made permanent in 1974.

17.12.1971 (BGBl.I:1993)
Wohnungsbauänderungsgesetz (Housing Construction Modification Law): increased income-limit for access to low rent apartments under the social housing programme from 9,000 DM to 12,000 DM per year plus 3,000 DM (instead of 2,400) for each family member; introduced special subsidies to lower the debt burden for builders not surpassing the regular income-limit by more than 40% (*2. Förderungsweg*); (limits increased to 18,000 DM plus 9,000 DM for the second and 4,200 DM for additional family members by legislation of 21.12.1973/BGBl.I:1970).

5.8.1974 (BGBl.I:1769)
Einkommenssteuerreformgesetz (Income Tax Reform Law): financial consolidation legislation; introduced income-limits for grants under the savings programme for housing purposes; limit 24,000 DM of taxable income per year for single persons, and

48,000 DM for married couples (plus 1,800 DM for each child); premium reduced from 25% to 23%; maximum savings for calculation of premiums: 800 DM (1,600 for couples); abolished special additional premiums for low-income groups.

18.12.1974 (BGBl.I:3603)
Zweites Wohnraumkündigungsschutzgesetz (Second Eviction Protection Law): 1971 tenant protection made permanent; notice only lawful where landlord proves justified personal interest in the apartment; rent increases only lawful if not above normal comparable rents in the same area (*ortsübliche Vergleichsmiete*).

18.12.1975 (BGBl.I:3091)
Haushaltsstrukturgesetz (Budget Structure Law): financial consolidation legislation; reduced premiums on savings for housing purposes from 23% to 18%.

23.8.1977 (BGBl.I:1159)
Viertes Änderungsgesetz zum zweiten Wohngeldgesetz (Fourth Modification of Housing Allowance Law): established new tables for housing allowances, adapting them to changes in rents and earnings; increased maximum reckonable rents by about 30%; increased income-limits (from 800 DM to 1,020 DM for single persons); increased allowances (varying with income and family size).

4.8.1980 (BGBl.I:1159)
Fünftes Änderungsgesetz (Fifth Modification Law): increased income-limits for housing allowances; increased maximum reckonable rents; increased allowance rates with overproportionate increases for large families.

22.12.1981 (BGBl.I:1523)
Zweites Haushaltsstrukturgesetz (Second Budget Structure Law): narrowed entitlement to housing allowance by reducing deductions made in calculation of income-limit; reduced public premiums on savings for construction from 18 to 14%.

20.12.1982 (BGBl.I:1857)
Haushaltsbegleitgesetz 1983) (Supplementary Budget Law): restricted entitlement to housing allowance by introducing less favourable method of calculation of income-limit; abolished housing allowance for students; abolished payment of allowances below DM 20; reduced allowance increase for handicapped persons (total savings estimated at 200 million DM per year; every second recipient household expected to be affected; average cut per beneficiary estimated at DM 25 per month with average allowance amounting to DM 105); improved promotion of private building through introduction of new tax deduction for builders of owneroccupied houses (interest payments on debt deductable up to 10,000 DM per year for three years); (during the same month other measures introduced subsidies to reduce the interest rate of builders under the savings programme for construction (*Bausparer*) by 2.5% for credits up to DM 80,000, and abolished the exemption from the land acquisition tax for special groups of builders in favour of a general reduction of this tax from 7 to 2%).

20.12.1982 (BGBl.I:1912)
Gesetz zur Erhöhung des Angebots an Mietwohnungen (Law to Increase the Supply of Apartment Housing): weakened tenant protection; extended rights of landlords to raise rents (increases up to 30% in three years legally acceptable); allowed the introduction of time contracts (*Zeitmietverträge*) and contracts with gradually increasing rents (*Staffelmiete*); modified calculation of admissible rent (*ortsübliche Vergleichsmiete*) in favour of landlords.

IX Education

In 1979 expenditure on education amounted to 66,294 million DM. This corresponded to 15.2% of social expenditure and 4.8% of GDP. Total expenditure was distributed as follows:

Expenditure in 1979 (million DM)

	Total	%
Pre-school level	1 982	3.0
Primary education	18 165	27.4
Secondary education[a]	19 256	29.0
Post-secondary education	16 065	24.2
Education allowances[b]	3 648	5.5
Other[c]	7 178	10.8
Total	66 294	99.9

[a] Including vocational schooling (5,335)

[b] Including promotion of student housing; the figures reported for education allowances in the social budget which exclude subsidies for student housing are lower, i.e. 3,145 million DM.

[c] School administration (3,386), pupils' transport (1,589), youth and adult education outside regular educational institutions (2,212).

In 1979, 67% of total expenditure was spent on personnel, 19% on running materials, and 14% for investment.

1. Education system

Under the German Constitution, the single states (10 Länder and West Berlin), are responsible for education, and maintain education ministries and regional school offices. The federal government has only a limited co-responsibility for educational planning, scientific research, and the financing of the post-secondary sector. In order to maintain a certain degree of national standardization, however, there are various inter-state advisory councils and commissions which issue unifying recommendations.

General education at all levels can also be provided by private organizations, if approved by state authorities. Vocational training is provided under a dual system of apprenticeship in private, or public firms, and education in part-time vocational schools run by public authorities. Education is compulsory from the age of 6 until 18. Nine of the twelve compulsory years are full-time, the remaining three years may be attended either full-time in general schools, or part-time in vocational schools. Children under six years of age may attend kindergartens for pre-primary education on a voluntary basis. About 70% of all kindergartens are privately organized, the remainder being run by local authorities. Primary education in elementary schools (*Grundschule*), covers all children from six to ten years of age. Curricula and funding are the responsibility of the single states. Local authorities share in the administrative expenditure. Private schools are of negligible importance and cover about 0.5% of pupils. Post-primary school pupils must choose between three different types of institutions for secondary stage I (ages 11-16): the five-year ordinary school (*Hauptschule* - six years in some states); the six-year intermediary school (*Realschule*); and the secondary school (*Gymnasium*), which prepares pupils for university. At secondary stage II (ages 16-18) *Hauptschule* pupils enter a job or apprenticeship and continue part-time vocational education up to the age of 18. *Realschule* graduates may either take the same option or continue education in higher technical schools which in some cases qualifies them for entry to post-secondary education institutions. *Gymnasium* students continue their studies for the *Abitur*, or graduation examination, which entitles them to university entrance. Since 1968 a growing number of comprehensive schools (*Gesamtschulen*) have attempted to overcome the rigid selection procedure under the traditional German system of institutionally separate secondary education. About 10% of all secondary school pupils attend private schools.

Post-secondary education institutions consist of some 60 universities or university-type institutions with the right to confer doctoral degrees, several teachers' colleges (*Pädagogische Hochschulen*), colleges of art and music, and over 70 polytechnical colleges (*Fachhochschulen*). With the exception of two recently established smaller institutions, universities and teachers' colleges are public institutions under the responsibility of the single states. In addition there are some 900,000 *Volkshochschulen* for voluntary adult education which are attended by some four million people.

2. Education allowances

Education allowances are paid to post-secondary students if their parents (or in special cases, they themselves) do not have an income above a certain limit. Since the cut-back legislation of 1982 these allowances are granted as loans which are repayable without interest. Secondary pupils in the tenth and higher grades of secondary school also received allowances until 1983, but today are only entitled to benefits in some special cases.

In 1983 the full allowance for students amounted to DM 660 (DM 690 as from 1984) per month with an additional DM 60 where the cost of housing exceeded a certain limit. The allowance is paid for the period corresponding to the (specified) normal duration of the respective academic subject (in most cases five years). The special categories of pupils who are still entitled to benefits receive lower rates. These vary between DM 200 for pupils in ordinary schools and DM 625 for those attending evening classes who have already finished their occupational training.

The full allowance is a maximum amount payable where parental net income (including social transfers) is below a certain limit; this in turn varies with family size and the age of the children. Earnings in excess of the limit lead to reductions of the allowance. The income limit for a family with two children above 15, of which one is the applicant, amounted to DM 1,970 in 1983 (DM 1,450 for the parents plus a credit of DM 520 for the two children). To determine the actual rate of the allowance this limit is compared with the parental income of two years prior to the claim. Any income which exceeds the limit after certain deductions have been made (which again vary with family size) is subtracted from the full allowance, until the payable amount eventually reaches zero. In actual practice this means that students from working class families with two children and earnings corresponding to the average wage of skilled male industrial workers are entitled to almost the full allowance, as the income limit in this standard case amounts to about 95% of reckonable earnings. The payable allowance for claims made in 1983 would reach zero in this standard case, where parental earnings amount to DM 3,170 or about 150% of the average wage of skilled male industrial workers. The average allowance actually paid in 1982 amounted to DM 510 for students and DM 285 for pupils.

Recipients of student allowances must repay loans in monthly instalments beginning five years after the termination of their studies provided that they have earnings above a certain limit (the earnings of employed academics are usually above this limit). All benefits must be repaid within 20 years by means of monthly instalments amounting to at least DM 120. Deductions are made for students finishing among the top 30% of graduates and/or for those ending their studies within the standard time limit.

In addition to education allowances all parents with children in educational institutions are entitled to tax credits which vary with the age and place of residence of the child. In the case of children above 18 who do not live with their parents, the tax credit which is subtracted from the parental taxable income amounts to DM 2,100 as from 1984 (previously DM 4,200). Any earnings which the child has, either from work or social transfer payments, which surpass a certain limit, reduce the credit.

Financing

Education is free of charge in all state institutions, with the exception of some limited administrative fees payable in the post-secondary sector. Expenditure is mostly (75%) carried by the states out of general revenues. Local authorities contribute to the financing of pre-primary and primary education, providing 19% of the costs. The federal government only shares in the funding of post-secondary education and education allowances; it pays 65% of the latter (states 35%). Its contribution to the total cost of the education system amounts to 6%.

Core laws

The single states have legislative competence for most education issues. The following are all federal laws.

25.6.1947 (Dir. no 54)
(Directive no. 54 of the Allied Control Commission): re-built the education system; abolished education fees and reformed the teacher training system.

23.5.1949
Grundgesetz (Constitution of the Federal Republic): established ground rules for the organization of the education system; established cultural autonomy of the states and their responsibility for education policy.

12.5.1969 (BGBl.I:359)
Finanzreformgesetz (Budget Reform Law): modified constitutional articles 74, 75 and 91, thus authorising the federal government to pass legislation concerning education allowances and the post-secondary sector; federal co-responsibility for university planning, scientific research, and financing of the post-secondary sector.

19.9.1969 (BGBl.I:1719)
Ausbildungsförderungsgesetz (Promotion of Education Law): introduced national education allowances for pupils in the secondary sector from the eleventh grade upwards; full allowance 150 DM for secondary school pupils, 300 DM for polytechnical school students (if living with their parents); full allowance only paid if parental income below limit of 700 DM per month, plus 50 DM for applicant and 160 DM for each dependent child under 15 (240 DM if over 15); benefit rates increased by laws of 27.6.1970/BGBl.I:919, and 14.5.1971/BGBl.I:666.

26.8.1971 (BGBl.I:1409)
Bundesausbildungsförderungsgesetz (Federal Promotion of Education Law): introduced general education allowance for secondary and post-secondary students; full allowance amounted to 160 DM for pupils and 420 DM for students; income-limit for full allowance 800 DM plus an additional 130 DM if both parents work, 50 DM for applicant, and 200 DM for other dependent children (270 DM if over 15); financed by federal government (65%) and the states (35%).

2.9.1971 (BGBl.I:1465)
Graduiertenförderungsgesetz (Promotion of Graduate Education Law): introduced special education allowance for promotion of post-graduate education; rates to be determined by decree; normal duration two years; financed by federal government (75%) and by single states (25%); modifying legislation: 22.1.1976/BGBl.I:207, and 28.3.1978/BGBl.I:445.

31.7.1974 (BGBl.I:1649)
Zweites Änderungsgesetz (Second Modification Law): increased full allowance and income-limit for full allowance by around 20%; full allowance increased from 160 DM to 200 DM for pupils, and from 420 DM to 500 DM for students; parental income-limit raised from 800 DM to 960 DM, plus 60 DM for applicant and 240 DM for any additional dependent children below 15,320 DM if above 15; introduced loans as a component of the total allowance; extended entitlements to cover tenth grade pupils not living with their parents; extended entitlements to cover special groups (persons above 35, persons studying abroad).

18.12.1975 (BGBl.I:3091)
Haushaltsstrukturgesetz (Budget Structure Law): raised proportion of loans in student allowances; transformed allowances for postgraduates completely into loans.

26.1.1976 (BGBl.I:185)
Hochschulrahmengesetz (University Guidelines Law): first nationwide law on education institutions; established ground rules for university organization, admission procedures and disciplinary action against students.

26.4.1977 (BGBl.I:653)
Viertes Änderungsgesetz (Fourth Modification Law): increased full allowance for pupils from 200 DM to 235 DM, and from 500 DM to 580 DM for students; increased parental income-limit compatible with full allowance from 960 DM to 1,130 DM.

17.11.1978 (BGBl.I:1794)
Fünftes Änderungsgesetz (Fifth Modification Law): extended entitlement to education allowance to cover all tenth grade pupils in vocational education institutions; devised as incentive to continue education beyond the compulsory age with an additional year of vocational training (*Berufsbildungsjahr*).

16.7.1979 (BGBl.I:1037)
Sechstes Änderungsgesetz (Sixth Modification Law): increased full allowance from 235 DM to 260 DM for pupils, and from 580 DM to 620 DM for students; increased parental income-limit compatible with full allowance from 1,130 DM to 1,220 DM.

13.7.1981 (BGBl.I:625)
Siebtes Änderungsgesetz (Seventh Modification Law): increased full allowance from 260 to 275 DM for pupils and from 620 to 660 DM for students; raised parental income limit compatible with full allowance from 1,220 to 1,400 DM, but also introduced stricter method of calculation; augmented minimum rate of monthly instal-

ments for the repayment of loans from 80 to 120 DM; abolished entitlement to allowances for some special groups already in possession of educational degrees.

18.12.1981 (BGBl.I:1523)
Zweites Haushaltsstrukturgesetz (Second Budget Structure Law): considerably restricted entitlement to allowances by introducing new method of calculating the income limit; announced cut in pupils' allowances for 1983.

20.12.1982 (BGBl.I:1857)
Haushaltsbegleitgesetz 1983 (Supplementary Budget Law): abolished entitlement to allowances for most categories of pupils; cut allowances for pupils living with their parents to 200 DM payable only in exceptional cases; transformed allowances for students completely into loans (without changing the rates); partly adjusted the income limit compatible with full allowance by raising it from 1,400 to 1,450 DM.

Inter-state concordats

1948
Westdeutsche Rektorenkonferenz: established the Conference of University Presidents, which issues recommendations for the coordination of post-secondary education.

1949
Ständige Konferenz der Kultusminister, KMK: established a permanent conference of state ministers of education to coordinate education matters.

22.10.1955
Honnefer Modell: introduced study allowances for talented students.

17.12.1955
Düsseldorfer Abkommen: agreement between the prime ministers of the states to standardize the school system.

5.9.1957
Wissenschaftsrat: agreement between states and federal government to establish a science council as an advisory body for reforms in the post-secondary sector.

28.10.1964
Hamburger Abkommen: agreement between state prime ministers to further standardize the school systems and to introduce a ninth year of compulsory education; last implemented in Bavaria in 1969.

15.7.1965
Deutscher Bildungsrat: agreement between states and federal government to establish an education council for planning in the school sector; abolished in 1976.

25.6.1970
Bund-Länder Kommission für Bildungsplanung: agreement between states and federal government to establish a joint commission for education planning.

1973
Zentralstelle für die Vergabe von Studienplätzen: agreement among states to establish a central admission office for university entrance; access to certain subjects made contingent upon previous performance at school (*numerus clausus*).

1979
Agreement among states to introduce a tenth year of compulsory education.

Bibliography

Contents

I General contributions

1.1 General histories of social policy

BRAUN, Heinrich: Industrialisierung und Sozialpolitik in Deutschland (Industrialization and Social Policy in Germany). Köln, 1956, 125 p. An historian's account of the origins and basic traits of modern social programmes; covering factory legislation, collective bargaining, labour legislation, social insurance, social assistance, and family allowances; appendix with statistical tables, partly as time series.

GLADEN, Albin: Geschichte der Sozialpolitik in Deutschland (History of Social Policy in Germany). Wiesbaden, Steiner, 1974, 207 p. Chronologically ordered history of social policy from the early 19th century to 1972 with the focus on income maintenance and labour legislation; standard work for introductory purposes.

HENTSCHEL, Volker: Geschichte der deutschen Sozialpolitik 1880-1980 (History of German Social Policy 1880-1980). Frankfurt, Suhrkamp, 1983, 318 p. History of social security and labour legislation with rich statistical and institutional data, including a part on social policy in the German Democratic Republic.

INTERNATIONALE VEREINIGUNG FÜR SOZIALE SICHERHEIT: Entwicklung und Tendenzen der sozialen Sicherheit: Bundesrepublik Deutschland (Development and Trends of Social Security: Federal Republic of Germany). Genf, Internationale Vereinigung für soziale Sicherheit, 1959, 286 p. Part of a series on the systems of social security in member countries of the European Communities; covering the four social insurance schemes and family allowances; with historical accounts of the most important legislative steps in the development of the systems and detailed descriptions of their functioning at the end of the 1950s; rich statistical and institutional data.

KÖLLERMAN, Hans Werner: Sozialpolitik in Deutschland - Eine geschichtliche und systematische Einführung (Social Policy in Germany - A Historical and Systematic Introduction). Stuttgart, Kohlhammer, 1971, 64 p. Brief but informative introduction on social policy in Germany with emphasis on income maintenance and factory legislation; centering on the situation in the Federal Republic but containing a very useful tabular synopsis of the most important laws from 1833 to 1970.

PESCHKE, Paul: Geschichte der deutschen Sozialversicherung. Der Kampf der unterdrückten Klassen um soziale Sicherung (History of German Social Insurance. The Struggle of the Suppressed Classes for Social Security). Berlin, Tribüne, 1962, 496 p. Detailed historical account of the development of social insurance systems from the beginning of the 19th century to 1960 in a Marxist perspective; with a concluding chapter comparing the social programmes of East and West Germany.

PETERS, Horst: Die Geschichte der Sozialversicherung (The History of Social Insurance), 3rd ed. Fortbildung und Praxis 39. Sankt Augustin, Asgard, 1978, p. 240. History of social insurance schemes from the middle ages to the present; detailed description of institutional developments in Imperial Germany, the Weimar Republic, the Third Reich, and the Federal Republic; written by a former president of a state social court.

SYRUP, Friedrich: Hundert Jahre staatliche Sozialpolitik 1839-1939 (A Hundred Years of State Social Policy 1839-1939). Aus dem Nachlass bearbeitet von Julius Scheuble und Otto Neuloh. Stuttgart, Kohlhammer, 1957, 603 p. Standard source on the history of German social policy; parts on labour legislation, collective bargaining, social insurance, and social assistance; chronologically divided into three periods (1839-1918, 1919-1932, 1932-1939); Appendix with embracive list of social legislation from 1839 to 1939; the author and one editor were presidents of the central unemployment insurance institution.

TENNSTEDT, Florian: Sozialgeschichte der Sozialversicherung (Social History of Social Insurance). *In* BLOHMKE, Maria, VON FERBER, Christian, KISKER, Karl Peter, SCHAEFER, Hans (eds): Handbuch der Sozialmedizin Band III.Sozialmedizin in der Praxis. Stuttgart, Enke, 1976, pp. 385-492. Detailed account of the institutional development of pension, sickness, and occupational injuries insurance with a focus on the decision making process in the social bureaucracies; covering the period from the establishment of the schemes to 1974; presents useful statistical information.

ZÖLLNER, Detlev: Ein Jahrhundert Sozialversicherung in Deutschland (A Century of Social Insurance in Germany). Schriftenreihe für Internationales und Vergleichendes Sozialrecht Band 6a. Berlin, Duncker & Humblot, 1981, 134 p. Account of the institutional development of social insurance since the establishment of the first public schemes, written by a (former) chief civil servant in the social ministry of the Federal Republic.

1.2 Accounts of specific historical periods

GUILLEBAUD, C.W.: The Social Policy of Nazi Germany. New York, Howard Fertig, 1971, 133 p. Descriptive account with some quantitative information; parts on labour policy and industrial relations, employment policy, state regulation of labour conditions, social insurance, social assistance, population policy, and housing policy; rather cursory, but useful as a first introduction.

MASON, Timothy W.: Sozialpolitik im Dritten Reich. Arbeiterklasse und Volksgemeinschaft (Social Policy in the Third Reich. Working Class and National Community), 2nd ed. Opladen, Westdeutscher Verlag, 1978, 374 p. By now standard account of social policy in Nazi Germany, concentrating on labour market policy and labour legislation; interpretation in terms of class theory.

PRELLER, Ludwig.: Sozialpolitik in der Weimarer Republik (Social Policy in the Weimar Republic), 2nd ed. Kronberg Düsseldorf, Athenaeum Droste, 1978, 570 p. Very detailed standard work on the subject by one of the former social policy experts of the Social Democratic Party; thorough description of legislative developments and their social and political bases in the periods 1914-1918 and 1918-1933; covering labour legislation, social insurance, employment policy, the regulation of industrial conflict, and housing policy.

VOGEL, Walter: Bismarcks Arbeiterversicherung. Ihre Entstehung im Kräftespiel der Zeit (Bismarck's Workers' Insurance. Its Emergence in the Power Relationships of the Time). Braunschweig, Westermann, 1951, 192 p. Qualitative account of the political struggles behind the introduction of the first social insurance schemes in Imperial Germany.

1.3 Histories of social policy in the Federal Republic

BARTHOLOMAEI, Reinhart, BODENBENDER, Wolfgang, HENKEL, Hardo, HÜTTEL, Renate (eds): Sozialpolitik nach 1945. Geschichte und Analysen (Social Policy after 1945. History and Analyses). Bonn, Bad Godesberg, Neue Gesellschaft, 1977, 592 p. Standard source on post-war institutional developments, political conceptions and struggles; with 48 contributions from persons who played an influential role in the development of social policies; articles about pension insurance, health policy, unemployment and labour market policy, work safety, social assistance, family policy, labour legislation, co-determination, property formation, and on the positions of the most important pressure groups in social policy.

BETHUSY-HUC, Viola Gräfin von: Das Sozialleistungssystem der Bundesrepublik Deutschland (The System of Social Benefits in the Federal Republic of Germany). Tübingen, Mohr, 2nd ed. 1976, 346 p. Standard account of institutional regulations, reform plans, proposals and positions of political parties and interest groups with focus on cash benefit schemes (social insurance, assistance, family allowances).

HARTWICH, Hans-Hermann: Sozialstaatspostulat und gesellschaftlicher status quo (The Postulate of the Social State and the Societal Status Quo). Opladen, Westdeutscher Verlag, 3rd ed. 1978, 461 p. Description of the constitutional bases of social policies in the Federal Republic and analysis of the process by which the policy model of 'social capitalism' won precedence over the alternative model of 'democratic socialism'.

HOCKERTS, Hans Günter: Sozialpolitische Entscheidungen im Nachkriegsdeutschland. Alliierte und deutsche Sozialversicherungspolitik 1945 bis 1957 (Social Policy Decisions in Postwar Germany. Allied and German Social Insurance Policy 1945 to 1957). Stuttgart, Klett,

1980, 463 p. Detailed account of political struggles and parliamentary debates about the reconstruction of social insurance after the Second World War up to the pension reform of 1957.

KLEINHENZ, Gerhard, LAMPERT, Heinz: Zwei Jahrzehnte in der BRD. Eine kritische Analyse (Two Decades of Social Policy in the Federal Republic. A Critical Analysis). Ordo Jahrbuch für die Ordnung von Wirtschaft und Gesellschaft 22, 1971: 103-158. Description and evaluation of social policy in the Federal Republic with emphasis on legal developments; useful for its rich institutional information.

STANDFEST, Erich: Sozialpolitik als Reformpolitik. Aspekte der sozialpolitischen Entwicklung in der Bundesrepublik Deutschland (Social Policy as Reform Policy. Aspects of the Development of Social Policy in the Federal Republic). WSI Studie zur Wirtschafts- und Sozialforschung Nr. 39. Köln, Bund Verlag, 1979, 139 p. Useful qualitative summary of the development of social policy since 1945, written by a representative of the research institute of the labour unions; focuses on income maintenance schemes.

ZACHER, Hans.: Sozialpolitik und Verfassung im ersten Jahrzehnt der Bundesrepublik Deutschland (Social Policy and Constitution in the First Decade of the Federal Republic of Germany). Berlin, Schweitzer, 1980, 1219 p. Detailed account of social legislation by one of the outstanding experts in social law.

1.4 Introductions to the system of social policy in the Federal Republic

BÄCKER, Gerhard, BISPINCK, Reinhard, HOFEMANN, Klaus, NÄGELE, Gerhard: Sozialpolitik - Eine problemorientierte Einführung (Social Policy - A Problem-oriented Introduction). Köln, Bund Verlag, 1980, 407 p. Description of social problems and respective policy measures with an evaluation of the effectiveness of the schemes; focusing on five problem dimensions: income maintenance, employment, vocational training, health, old age; written by members of the research institute of the labour unions.

BOEPPLE, Arthur: Sozialpolitik in der BRD. Löcher im Netz der sozialen Sicherung (Social Policy in the Federal Republic. Holes in the Net of Social Security). Frankfurt, Verlag Marxistische Blätter, 1980, 166 p. Description and evaluation of social policies in the Federal Republic seen from the perspective of a representative of the German communist party (DKP); containing a list of core laws in social policy development.

BRAUN, Hans: Soziale Sicherung System und Funktion (Social Security System and Function), 2nd ed. Stuttgart, Berlin, Köln, Mainz, Kohlhammer, 1973, 103 p. Introduction into the system of social security from a sociological perspective; with parts on the concept of social security, determinants of the development of social security,institutional types of social policy, the organization of German social security schemes, and future tasks in social policy.

BRÜCK, Gerhard W: Allgemeine Sozialpolitik. Grundlagen - Zusammenhänge - Leistungen (General Social Policy. Bases - Contexts - Achievements), 2nd ed. Köln, Bund Verlag, 1981, 369 p. Embracive introduction into social policy with parts on social security, family policy, and housing; with historical synopses of the development of each scheme and an analysis of the position of unions; standard account besides Lampert (cf. below).

LAMPERT, Heinz: Sozialpolitik (Social Policy). Berlin Hamburg New York, Springer, 1980, 519 p. Standard introduction into German social policies written by a leading professor in social administration; with a theoretical part on the concept of social policy, an historical part on policy developments since the 19th century, and a systematic part on present programmes (factory legislation, social security, labour market policy, co-determination, housing, family policy, policies for special groups, and property formation); with rich statistical and institutional information.

PRELLER, Ludwig: Praxis und Probleme der Sozialpolitik (Practice and Problems of Social Policy), 2 vols. Tübingen, Mohr, 1970, 754 p. Systematic introduction to the goals and instruments of German social policies by a leading expert in the Social Democratic Party; with parts on social security, labour legislation, housing, and on the relationship between social and economic policy.

1.5 Reports by investigating committees (in chronological order)

BOGS, Walter: Grundfragen des Rechts der sozialen Sicherheit und seiner Reform (Basic Questions of Social Security Law and its Reform). Berlin, Duncker & Humblot, 1955, 144 p. Expertise by request of the social ministry, written by the president of the federal social court; description of prevailing provisions on social security and proposals for reform.

ACHINGER, Hans, HÖFFNER, Joseph, MUTHESIUS, Hans, NEUNDÖRFER, Ludwig: Neuordnung der sozialen Leistungen (Reorganization of Social Benefits), 2 vols. Köln, Greven, 1955, 136 and 50 p. Analysis of the system of social security with proposals for reform; written by request of the Chancellor; also known as 'Rothenfelser Denkschrift' (Rothenfelser memorandum).

BOGS, Walter., ACHINGER, Hans., MEINHOLD, Helmut., NEUNDÖRFER, Ludwig., SCHREIBER, Wilfried.: Sozialenquete. Soziale Sicherung in der Bundesrepublik Deutschland (Social Inquiry. Social Security in the Federal Republic of Germany), 2 vols. Stuttgart, Berlin, Köln, Mainz, Kohlhammer, 1966, 354 and 194 p. Expertise on the system of social security and possibilities of its reform; written by request of the federal government; parts on social conditions in the country, principles of social legislation, economic problems of social security, and on the major single schemes (old age, sickness, family, housing, social assistance); with rich statistical information, partly in the form of time series.

TRANSFER-ENQUETE-KOMMISSION: Das Transfersystem in der Bundesrepublik Deutschland (The Transfer System in the Federal Republic of Germany). Stuttgart/Berlin/Köln/Mainz, Kohlhammer, 1981, 300 p. Standard analysis of the magnitude, structure, and distributional effects of the transfer system written by request of the federal government.

1.6 Social science interpretations

ALBERS, Willi: Möglichkeiten einer stärker final orientierten Sozialpolitik (Possibilities of a More Goal-oriented Social Policy). Schriften der Kommission für wirtschaftlichen und sozialen Wandel 119. Göttingen, Schwartz, 1976, 120 p. Influential analysis of the social security system advocating a re-organization of schemes along functional rather than causal lines.

BADURA, Bernhard, GROSS, Peter: Sozialpolitische Perspektiven. Eine Einführung in Grundlagen und Probleme sozialer Dienstleistungen (Perspectives of Social Policy. An Introduction to Bases and Problems of the Social Services). München, Piper, 1976, 360 p. An influential analysis of the system of social programmes centering on social services; written by two sociologists who elaborate negative side-effects of the bureaucratization of social services for the self-help potential of primary groups and associations.

BANK, Hans-Peter: Sozialpolitik und Wahlpolitik (Social Policy and Electoral Policy). Berichte des Deutschen Industrieinstituts zur Sozialpolitik 2, 1968,Nr. 11. Köln, Deutscher Industrieverlag, 1968, 74 p. Empirical analysis of the timing of social legislation finding a close relationship between the electoral cycle and the legislative output of social laws.

VON FERBER, Christian: Sozialpolitik in der Wohlstandsgesellschaft (Social Policy in the Welfare Society). Hamburg, Wegner, 1967, 171 p. Influential sociological critique of German social policies, pinpointing the predominance of legal and economic criteria in the definition of social problems which lead to a neglect of social and cultural factors.

VON FERBER, Christian, KAUFMANN, Franz-Xaver (eds): Soziologie und Sozialpolitik (Sociology and Social Policy). Kölner Zeitschrift für Soziologie und Sozialpsychologie Sonderheft 19. Opladen, Westdeutscher Verlag, 1977. A reader prepared for an annual meeting of the German Sociological Association, representative for sociological theorizing on the welfare state among German scholars; containing, among others, contributions by Horst Baier on the system of authority in the social state, and by Lenhardt and Offe on the origins and functions of the welfare state in capitalist societies.

GREVEN, Michael Th., PRAETORIUS, Rainer, SCHILLER, Theo: Sozialstaat und Sozialpolitik. Krise und Perspektiven (Social State and Social Policy. Crisis and perspectives). Neuwied Darmstadt, Luchterhand, 1980, 279 p. Contains one article by each author who all represent 'radical' political science. Schiller discusses 'problems of a theory of the social state', Greven deals with 'social problems and political answers - social policy conceptions and conflicts of the seventies', Praetorius writes about 'democracy or dismantling - on the reasons for decentralization in social policy'.

KAUFMANN, Franz-Xaver: Sicherheit als soziologisches und sozialpolitisches Problem (Security as a Problem of Sociology and Social Policy), 2nd ed. Stuttgart, Enke, 1973, 407 p. Analysis of the rise of the normative idea of 'social security' to one of the fundamental values of modern societies, questioning the potential of public social programmes to promote subjective feelings of security.

KLAGES, Helmut: Überlasteter Staat - Verdrossene Bürger? Zu den Dissonanzen der Wohlfahrtsgesellschaft (Overloaded State -Vexed Citizens? On the dissonances of the welfare society). Frankfurt, Campus, 1981, 169 p. Critical account of the explosion of aspirations and entitlements threatening to jeopardize the functioning of the state, written by a sociologist.

LIEFMANN-KEIL, Elisabeth: Ökonomische Theorie der Sozialpolitik (Economic Theory of Social Policy). Berlin, Springer, 1961, 424 p. Description of goals, strategies and instruments of social policy, focusing on social security schemes and labour legislation; written by one of the leading economic experts on social policy.

LUHMANN, Niklas: Politische Theorie im Wohlfahrtsstaat (Political Theory in the Welfare State). München, Olzog, 1981, 158 p. Theoretical analysis of the role of the state, criticizing the idea that the state can successfully shape societal change in complex societies; written by one of the foremost sociological theorists in Germany.

MÜLLER, Wolfgang, NEUSÜSS, Christel: Die Sozialstaatsillusion und der Widerspruch von Lohnarbeit und Kapital (The Illusion of the Social State and the Contradiction Between Capital and Labour). Probleme des Klassenkampfes Sonderheft 1, 1970:7-70. Influential Marxist analysis of the determinants and functions of social policies in capitalist societies, stressing the economic determinants of policies and the limited autonomy of the state.

NARR, Wolf-Dieter, OFFE, Claus (eds): Wohlfahrtsstaat und Massenloyalität (Welfare State and Mass Loyalty). Neue Wissenschaftliche Bibliothek 79 Soziologie. Köln, Kiepenheuer & Witsch, 1975, 383 p. A reader consisting mostly of translations of Anglo-Saxon contributions, but with a theoretical introduction by the editors on late capitalism, welfare state, mass loyalty and pluralism, formulating starting points for a Marxist theory of the welfare state.

STRASSER, Johano: Grenzen des Sozialstaats? Soziale Sicherung in der Wachstumskrise (Limits of the Social State? Social Security in the Economic Crisis). Köln, Frankfurt, Europäische Verlagsanstalt, 1979, 192 p. Theoretical analysis of the arguments of political defenders and critics ofthe welfare state, of new social problems and adequate policy responses; politically influential book by one of the representatives of the intellectual new left criticizing the bureaucratization of social provisions.

WIDMAIER, Hans Peter: Sozialpolitik im Wohlfahrtsstaat (Social Policy in the Welfare State). Reinbek bei Hamburg, Rowohlt, 1976, 184 p. Analysis of social policy from the perspective of political economy, stressing the neglect of unorganized interests and demanding a more active social policy which would be preventive rather than reactive.

1.7 Policy proposals and debates

AUERBACH, Walter, GLEITZE, Bruno, JAHN, E., PRELLER, Ludwig, SCHELLENBERG, Ernst: Sozialplan für Deutschland (Social Plan for Germany). Berlin, Hannover, Dietz, 1957, 208 p. Embracive plan for the reform of social policies, ordered and endorsed by the Social Democratic Party.

BRÜCK, Gerhard W., EICHNER, Harald: Perspektiven der Sozialpolitik (Perspectives of Social Policy). Schriften der Kommission für wirtschaftlichen und sozialen Wandel 41. Göttingen, Schwartz, 1974, 312 p. Description of manifestos of political parties and major interest groups concerning pension and sickness insurance, vocational education, public assistance, youth programmes, public health, co-determination, property formation, family policy, housing, and rehabilitation; combined with brief overview of the most important legislative steps in each field.

CHRISTMANN, Alfred, HESSELBACH, Walter, JAHN, Manfred, MOMMSEN, Ernst Wolf (eds): Sozialpolitik (Social Policy). Köln, Verlag Wissenschaft und Politik, 1974, 589 p. A reader with contributions from politicians, representatives of interest groups (churches, labour unions, employer associations) and of academic social administration, representing the perspectives of almost everyone who counted in German social policies in the early 1970s.

EHRENBERG, Herbert, FUCHS, Anke: Sozialstaat und Freiheit. Von der Zukunft des Sozialstaats (Social State and Freedom. On the Future of the Social State). Frankfurt, Suhrkamp, 1980, 468 p. Assessment of the major problems and achievements of social policy written by the (then) minister of social affairs together with his junior minister; interesting for its rich descriptive information (qualitative and quantitative) and for its definition of major social policy issues from the perspective of leading Social Democrats.

GEISSLER, Hans: Die neue soziale Frage. Analyse und Dokumente (The New Social Question. Analysis and Documents). Freiburg, Herder, 1976, 160 p. A very influential attack on conventional social policies drawing attention to the large number of poor persons who do not receive benefits and have no political representation; written by a leading representative of the Christian Democratic Union.

JUNGBLUT, Michael (ed.): Bundesrepublik ratlos? Den Sozialstaat durch die Krise retten (Federal Republic Helpless? To Save the Social State Through the Crisis). München, Goldmann, 1982, 254 p. A collection of articles on the crisis of the public household and the social security schemes which appeared in the influential weekly 'Die Zeit'; written by journalists, politicians and academic observers giving a good overview of current debates on the welfare state.

KATZER, Hans: Aspekte moderner Sozialpolitik (Aspects of Modern Social Policy). Köln, Kohlhammer, 1969, 108 p. Comments upon social policy by a leading social policy expert of the Christian Democratic Union and former federal minister of social affairs.

KOSLOWSKI, Peter, KREUZER, Philipp, LÖW, Reinhard (eds): Chancen und Grenzen des Sozialstaats (Chances and Limits of the Social State). Tübingen, Mohr, 1983, 265 p. Proceedings of a conference on problems of the welfare state with discussion reports and contributions by leading scholars, social administrators, and politicians; excellent summary of current academic and political debates on social policy.

KUELP, Bernhard, SCHREIBER, Wilfried (eds): Soziale Sicherheit (Social Security). Neue Wissenschaftliche Bibliothek 40 Wirtschaftswissenschaften. Köln Berlin, Kiepenheuer & Witsch, 1971, 463 p. A reader with 25 articles by leading experts of social policy most of whom served as government advisors; parts on the definition, tasks and principles of social policy, on the economic impact of social security systems, on income policy and property formation plans; giving a good summary of policy proposals and academic debates on social administration.

MOLITOR, Bruno: Sozialpolitik auf dem Prüfstand (Social Policy on Trial). Hamburg, Verlag Weltarchiv, 1976, 356 p. A collection of articles written between 1965 and 1975 on the social security systems, the labour market, housing policy, and labour legislation; from a prominent member of a renowned economic research institute.

PFAFF, Martin, VOIGTLÄNDER, Hubert (eds): Sozialpolitik im Wandel. Von der selektiven zur integrierten Sozialpolitik (Social Policy in Transition. From the Selective to an Integrated Social Policy). Bonn, Verlag Neue Gsellschaft, 1978, 308 p. Analysis of current problems of social policy as seen by leading Social Democratic politicians and scholars, with thirteen articles on various topics (e.g. the cost explosion in the health sector, poverty, the financial problems of pension insurance etc.).

RICHTER, Max (ed.): Die Sozialreform. Dokumente und Stellungnahmen. (The Social Reform. Documents and Comments). Bonn, Bad Godesberg, Asgard, 1970 (11 volumes, loose leaf collection). Standard documentation of the politics of social policy from 1953 to 1968, presenting policy statements of the government, white papers, parliamentary debates, manifestos of parties and interest groups.

STANDFEST, Erich: Sozialpolitik und Selbstverwaltung. Zur Demokratisierung des Sozialstaats (Social Policy and Autonomous Administration. On the Democratization of the Social State). WSI Studie zur Wirtschafts- und Sozialforschung Nr. 35. Köln, Bund Verlag, 1977, 277 p. Study sponsored by the research institute of the labour unions to explore the potential for a vitalization of autonomous social insurance bodies as a means for a democratization of the social state; with an interesting overview of various normative models of social policy.

1.8 Opinion polls

BUNDESMINISTER FÜR ARBEIT UND SOZIALORDNUNG (ed.): Bürger und Sozialstaat (Citizen and Social State). Infratest Sozialforschung Forschungsbericht Nr. 22(by Horst Becker and Walter Ruhland). Bonn, Bundesministerium für Arbeit undSozialordnung, 1980, 101 p. Results and analysis of an opinion poll on public attitudes toward the welfare state, carried out by a private research institute on request of the ministry.

BUNDESMINISTER FÜR ARBEIT UND SOZIALORDNUNG (ed.): Herausforderungen der Sozialpolitik (Challenges of Social Policy). Forschungsbericht Nr. 92 (by Harald Bielenski, Bernhard von Rosenbladt and Walter Ruhland on behalf of Infratest Sozialforschung). Bonn, Bundesminister für Arbeit und Sozialordnung, 1983, 133 p. Results and analysis of a 1983 opinion poll, carried out on request of the ministry.

COUGHLIN, Richard M.: Ideology, Public Opinion and Welfare Policy.: Attitudes Toward Taxes and Spending in Industrialized Societies. Monograph No. 42. Berkeley, Institute of International Studies, 1980, 195 p. A comparative analysis of surveys in Germany, Sweden, Denmark, France, United Kingdom, Canada, United States and Australia, covering trends in the post war period.

GROSER, Manfred, VEIDERS, Wolfgang: Die neue soziale Frage (The New Social Question). Forschungsbericht Nr. 2, edited by the Konrad-Adenauer-Stiftung. Melle, Knoth, 1979, 170 p. Results and analysis of a 1977 opinion poll on attitudes towards the welfare state.

KAUFMANN, Franz-Xaver: Reaktionen und Motivationen der Bevölkerung gegenüber sozialpolitischen Umverteilungsmassnahmen (Reactions and Motivations of the Population with Respect to Social Redistribution Measures). Materialien aus der empirischen Sozialforschung Heft 8. Dortmund, Sozialforschungsstelle an der Universität Münster, 1969, 127 p. Results and analysis of a 1963 opinion poll carried out by an academic sociological research institute.

1.9 Sources of statistics or institutional regulations

1.9.1 Official sources

BUNDESMINISTER FÜR ARBEIT UND SOZIALORDNUNG: Arbeits- und Sozialstatistik Hauptergebnisse (Labour and Social Statistics: Main Results). Bonn, Bundesminister für Arbeit und Sozialordnung, yearly series, 1953-. Major statistical publication of the social ministry, with data on demographic, social and economic conditions, on the standard of living and wages, on the national product, and on the social security schemes; most of the data are presented as time series.

BUNDESMINISTER FÜR ARBEIT UND SOZIALORDNUNG: Sozialbericht (Social Report). Bonn, Bundesministerium für Arbeit und Sozialordnung, irregular series, 1968-. Major official statement of developments in social policies with financial forecasts of the years ahead; with rich institutional data and statistics of receipts and expenditure of all social programmes (except education); standard source for financial statistics of welfare schemes, with a host of other social and economic statistics; the first edition in 1968 appeared underthe title 'Sozialbudget'; under the present title since the second edition in 1970, with subsequent editions in 1971, 1972, 1973, 1976, 1978, 1980, and 1983; the 1976 edition was accompanied by a 'Materialband' (Statistical appendix) with time series data for the period 1965 to 1974.

BUNDESMINISTER FÜR ARBEIT UND SOZIALORDNUNG: Statistisches Taschenbuch (Statistical Hand Book). Bonn, Bundesminister für Arbeit und Sozialordnung, yearly series, 1977-. Useful compendium of statistics on social programmes in time-series form extending back to 1950; previous editions were published from 1974 under the title 'Statistiken für Arbeits- und Sozialpolitik'.

BUNDESMINISTERIUM FÜR ARBEIT UND SOZIALORDNUNG: Übersicht über die soziale Sicherung (Overview of Social Security). Bonn, Bundesministerium für Arbeit und Sozialordnung, irregular series, 1956-. Major official source on the instititutional profiles of the various social security schemes with rich statistical time series data; covering the social insurance programmes, social assistance, civil servants, family allowances, rehabilitation, benefits for war victims, equalization of war burdens, housing allowances, and educational allowances; editions appeared in 1956, 1958, 1960, 1962, 1964, 1967 (two editions), 1970, 1974, and 1977.

BUNDESMINISTERIUM FÜR INNERDEUTSCHE BEZIEHUNGEN (ed.): Bundesrepublik Deutschland- DDR Systemvergleich 1. Politik- Wirtschaft- Gesellschaft. Bericht und Materialien zur Lage der Nation 1971 (Federal Republic, German Democratic Republic System Comparison 1. Politics, Economy, Society. Report and Materials on the State of the Nation). Opladen, Westdeutscher Verlag, 1971, 416 p. First in a series of three official reports with information compiled by social scientists upon request of the government; the first volume contains, among information on other topics, parts on education, on social security, and on youth policies, which provide useful summaries of the system of policies in the respective field.

BUNDESMINISTERIUM FÜR INNERDEUTSCHE BEZIEHUNGEN (ed.): Bundesrepublik Deutschland - DDR Systemvergleich 2. Recht. Bericht und Materialien zur Lage der Nation 1972 (Federal Republic, German Democratic Republic System Comparison 2. Law. Report and Materials on the State of the Nation). Opladen, Westdeutscher Verlag, 1972, 361 p. Comparison of the judicial systems in East and West Germany with parts on constitutional principles, family law, and labour legislation.

BUNDESMINISTERIUM FÜR INNERDEUTSCHE BEZIEHUNGEN (ed.): Bundesrepublik Deutschland - DDR Systemvergleich 3. Nation - Staatliche und gesellschaftliche Ordnung - Wirtschaft - Sozialpolitik. Materialien zum Bericht zur Lage der Nation 1974 (Federal Republic, German Democratic Republic System Comparison 3. Nation, State and Social Order, Economy, Social Policy. Materials for the Report on the State of the Nation 1974). Opladen, Westdeutscher Verlag, 1974, 594 p. Third volume in the series with parts on labour relations, social policy, income distribution, and the civil service.

PRESSE-UND INFORMATIONSAMT DER BUNDESREGIERUNG (ed.): Gesellschaftliche Daten (Societal Data). Bonn, Presse- und Informationsamt der Bundesregierung, irregular series, 1973-. Major official source on social indicators, published in 1973, 1977, 1979, and 1983, 356 p.

STATISTISCHES BUNDESAMT: Fachserie 13:Sozialleistungen (Special Series 13: Social Benefits). Stuttgart, Berlin, Köln, Mainz, Kohlhammer, yearly series, 19..-. Major publication of the central statistical office on social benefits; up to 1973 published as 'Fachserie K Sozialleistungen'. The series consists of the following separately published sub-series (all yearly): Reihe 1: Versicherte in der Kranken- und Rentenversicherung (Insured persons in sickness and pension insurance); Reihe 2: Sozialhilfe (Social assistance); Reihe 3: Kriegsopferversorgung (Benefits to war victims); Reihe 4: Wohngeld (Housing allowances); Reihe 5: Behinderte und Rehabilitationsmassnahmen (Handicapped and rehabilitation measures); Reihe 6: Öffentliche Jugendhilfe (Public youth programmes).

STATISTISCHES BUNDESAMT: Bevölkerung und Wirtschaft 1872-1972 (Population and Economy 1872-1972). Stuttgart/Mainz, Kohlhammer, 1972, 278 p. Major time-series publication of the central statistical office, including data on income maintenance programmes, health, housing, and education.

1.9.2 Private sources

BALLERSTEDT, Eike, GLATZER, Wolfgang (eds): Soziologischer Almanach. Handbuch gesellschaftlicher Daten und Indikatoren (Sociological Almanac. Handbook of Social Data and Indicators), 3rd ed. Frankfurt, Campus, 1979, 615 p. Standard reference work with a host of data on social conditions, written by several authors connected to 'SPES', the major social science research project in the Federal Republic; among others parts on housing, education, health, social security, income distribution, the public household.

ERMRICH, Roland: Basisdaten. Zahlen zur ökonomischen Entwicklung der Bundesrepublik Deutschland (Basic Data. Figures on the socio-economic development in the Federal Republic).

Bonn, Bad Godesberg, Verlag Neue Gesellschaft, 1974, 648 p. Data handbook which in some cases is a useful complementation of the 'Soziologischer Almanach'; with parts on education, health, housing, the social budget, and income distribution.

GLATZER, Wolfgang, ZAPF, Wolfgang (eds): Lebensqualität in der Bundesrepublik (Quality of life in the Federal Republic). Frankfurt, Campus, 1984, 443 p. Standard account of subjective welfare and living conditions based on national welfare surveys in 1978 and 1980; parts on private incomes, housing, employment conditions, family life, health, political and social participation, marginal groups, and other topics.

KOPF, Jürgen, KERN, Rainer, SCHMIDT, Gerhard: Volkswirtschafliche Basisdaten (Basic Economic Data). Frankfurt, Campus, 1980, 535 p. Collection of national accounts statistics in time-series form covering the period 1960 to 1978; including data on public receipts and expenditure.

WIEGAND, Erich, ZAPF, Wolfgang (eds): Wandel der Lebensbedingungen in Deutschland (Change of Living Conditions in Germany). Frankfurt, Campus, 1982, 469 p. Standard source on living conditions since the industrialization with rich time series data; parts on working hours, wages and cost of living, budgets of private households, unemployment, health, housing.

ZAPF, Wolfgang (ed.): Lebensbedingungen in der Bundesrepublik 1950-1975 (Living Conditions in the Federal Republic 1950-1975). Frankfurt, Campus, 2nd ed. 1978, 946 p. Standard source on living conditions in Germany; analyses of political goals and policy achievements in selected fields, containing a general introduction by the editor, and ten contributions on demographic developments, social inequality and mobility, the labour market and employment conditions, income distribution, private consumption, public transport and traffic, housing, health, education, and social and political participation.

1.9.3 Major periodicals

BUNDESARBEITSBLATT (Federal Journal of Labour): Bonn, yearly, 1949-. Major official journal on social policy, with yearly list of social laws, and articles on policy by civil servants, politicians, and academics.

SOZIALER FORTSCHRITT (Social Progress): Published annually, 1952-. Major forum for discussion of issues in social policy, with contributions from politicians, civil servants and academics.

II Single programmes or aspects

2.1 Pensions

2.1.1 Descriptions, evaluations, analyses

DÖRING, Dieter: Das System der gesetzlichen Rentenversicherung. Eine sozialpolitische Einführung (The System of Public Pension Insurance. A Social Policy Introduction). Frankfurt, Campus, 1980, 136 p. Useful introduction into the functioning of pension insurance based on official documents, including statistical data and an historical synopsis with a description of the original law of 1889.

KIESAU, Gisela: Die Lebenslage älterer Menschen in der Bundesrepublik Deutschland. Analyse der Mängel und Vorschläge zur Verbesserung (Living Conditions of Old People in the Federal Republic of Germany. Analysis of shortcomings and proposals for improvement), 2nd ed. WSI Studie zur Wirtschafts- und Sozialforschung Nr. 31. Köln, Bund Verlag, 1976, 463 p. Study by the research institute of the labour unions.

LIEFMANN-KEIL, Elisabeth: Gegenwart und Zukunft der sozialen Altersvorsorge (Present and Future of Social Provisions for Old Age). Göttingen, Vandenhoeck & Ruprecht, 1967, 203 p. Study by an outstanding economic expert in social policy of the possibility to substitute public by private provisions; written upon request of the employers' associations.

MIEGEL, Meinhard: Sicherheit im Alter. Plädoyer für die Weiterentwicklung des Rentensystems (Security in Old Age. Plea for a Further Development of the Pension System). Stuttgart, Bonn

Aktuell, 1981, 211 p. Account of the development of the German pension system, comparison with foreign pension schemes (Sweden, Denmark, Switzerland, France, United Kingdom, United States); discussion of shortcomings, and proposals for reform, written by an advisor of the Christian Democratic Party.

SCHMÄHL, Winfried: Systemänderung in der Altersvorsorge: von der einkommensabhängigen Altersrente zur Staatsbürger-Grundrente (System Change in Old Age Pensions: From the Earnings-related Old Age Pension to Flat-rate National Pensions). Opladen, Westdeutscher Verlag, 1974, 294 p. A theoretical and empirical analysis of economic problems which would be related to a change of the pension formula discussing various scenarios.

SCHMÄHL, Winfried: Das Rentenniveau in der Bundesrepublik (The Level of Pensions in the Federal Republic). Frankfurt, Campus, 1975, 126 p. Standard study of benefit levels in the pension scheme by a member of the 'SPES' group, the central social science research project on the Federal Republic.

SOZIALBEIRAT: Langfristige Probleme der Alterssicherung in der Bundesrepublik Deutschland (Long-term Problems of Social Security in Old Age in the Federal Republic of Germany). Bonn, Bundesminister für Arbeit und Sozialordnung, 3 volumes, 1981, 88, 204 and 357 p. Standard analysis of pension insurance developments including forecasts and reform proposals; written by leading scholars affiliated to the official social council on request of the federal government.

2.1.2 Sources

BUNDESMINISTER FÜR ARBEIT UND SOZIALORDNUNG (ed.): Die Rentenversicherung der Arbeiter und Angestellten in der Bundesrepublik Deutschland im Jahre .... STATISTISCHER und finanzieller Bericht (The Pension Insurance of Workers and Employees in the Federal Republic in the Year ....Statistical and financial report). Bonn, Bundesministerium für Arbeit und Sozialordnung, published annually. Official statistics on the major pension schemes on a yearly basis.

BUNDESMINISTER FÜR ARBEIT UND SOZIALORDNUNG (ed.): Die Renten-, Pensions- und Unterstützungsempfänger im Jahre 1962 in der Bundesrepublik Deutschland (The Pension, Annuity, and Assistance Recipients in 1962 in the Federal Republic of Germany). Bonn, Bundesministerium für Arbeit und Sozialordnung, 1965, 23 p. Official analysis of the social conditions of pension recipients based on the microcensus of October 1962.

DEUTSCHER BUNDESTAG: Rentenanpassungsbericht (Report on the Adjustment of Pensions). Bonn, Bundestagsdrucksache, yearly, 1958-. Major source on the German pension systems; yearly report issued by a committee of experts (Sozialbeirat) with legal status; analysis of the situation of the pension scheme and proposal of the new rate of annual augmentation, with a host of statistical and institutional data; from 1959 to 1969 appearing as 'Sozialbericht'.

STATISTISCHES BUNDESAMT (ed.): Die sozialen Verhältnisse der Renten und Unterstützungsempfänger (The Social Conditions of Pension and Assistance Recipients). Statistik der Bundesrepublik Deutschland 137, Stuttgart/Köln, Kohlhammer, 2 volumes, 195 and 154 p. Results of an official inquiry into the social conditions of pension recipients based on a legislative decree of 1953.

STATISTISCHES BUNDESAMT: Die älteren Mitbürger und ihre Lebensverhältnisse (The Older Citizens and their Living Conditions). Stuttgart/Mainz, Kohlhammer, 1971, 72 p. Official report on the living conditions of the elderly presenting statistics on income, health, and housing.

STATISTISCHES BUNDESAMT: Die Lebenverhältnisse älterer Menschen (The Living Conditions of Elderly People). Stuttgart/Mainz, Kohlhammer, 1977, 64 p. Updated version of the report above.

TRANSFER-ENQUETE-KOMMISSION: Zur Einkommenslage der Rentner. Zwischenbericht der Kommission (On the Income Position of Pensioners. Interim Report of the Commission). Stuttgart, Berlin, Köln, Mainz, Kohlhammer, 1979, 215 p. First report of the commission on the public transfer system established by the federal government; inquiry into the number of households living from pensions, the cumulative receipt of various transfer payments, and the economic conditions of pension recipients.

2.2 Health

2.2.1 Descriptions, evaluations, analyses

BAIER, Horst: Medizin im Sozialstaat. Medizinsoziologische und medizinpolitische Aufsätze (Medicine in the Social State. Essays on the Sociology of Medicine and Medical Policy). Stuttgart, Enke, 1978, 180 p. A collection of articles by the author, a renowned sociologist; contributions on 'medicine in the welfare society', 'social system, social structure, and the health system', 'sickness in industrial society', 'the position of medical doctors in society'.

BLOHMKE, Maria, VON FERBER, Christian, KISKER, Karl Peter, SCHAEFER, Hans (eds): Handbuch der Sozialmedizin Band III. Sozialmedizin in der Praxis (Handbook of Social Medicine Vol. III. Social Medicine in Practice). Stuttgart, Enke, 1976, 873 p. Basic account of the German health system in historical perspective, with 31 chapters by specialists on various topics; contains contributions on the sick rate in international perspective, on the system of general medicine (general practitioners), on the history and organization of hospitals, on the administration and financing of sickness insurance; each part contains a useful bibliography.

DEPPE, Hans-Ulrich (ed.): Gesundheitssysteme und Gesundheitspolitik in Westeuropa (Health Systems and Health Policy in Western Europe). Frankfurt, Campus, 1983, 271 p. Comparison of public health in Germany, France, Great Britain, Italy, the Netherlands, Austria, and Sweden, providing useful introductions to the national health systems written by natives of the respective countries.

VON FERBER, Christian: Gesundheit und Gesellschaft. Haben wir eine Gesundheitspolitik? (Health and Society. Do We Have a Health Policy?). Stuttgart, Berlin, Köln, Mainz, Kohlhammer, 1971, 104 p. Sociological analysis of the concept of health and of health policy, with proposals for the planning and organization of preventative as opposed to merely curative medicine.

HELBERGER, Christof: Ziele und Ergebnisse der Gesundheitspolitik in der Bundesrepublik Deutschland (Goals and Results of Health Policy in the Federal Republic). *In* ZAPF, Wolfgang (ed.): Lebensbedingungen in der Bundesrepublik 1950-1975. Frankfurt, Campus, 1978, pp. 677-741. Standard source, with information on health policy and a host of health indicators.

HERDER-DORNEICH, Philipp: Gesundheitsökonomik. Systemsteuerung und Ordnungspolitik im Gesundheitswesen (Health Economics. System Control and Regulatory Policy in the Health Sector). Stuttgart, Enke, 1980, 203 p. Analysis of developments in the health sector from a systems theory perspective.

JAHN, Erwin, JAHN, Hans-Joachim, KRASEMANN, Ernst Otto, MUDRA, Wolfgang, ROSENBERG, Peter, RUDOLPH, Fritz, THIEMEYER, Theo: Die Gesundheitssicherung in der Bundesrepublik Deutschland. Analyse und Vorschläge zur Reform (The Health System in the Federal Republic. Analysis and Reform Proposals). WSI Studie zur Wirtschafts- und Sozialforschung Nr. 20. Köln, Bund Verlag, 1973, 96 p. Study on the German health system, finished in 1971, by a research group of the research institute of the labour unions, focusing on shortcomings of the pervailing system.

NASCHOLD, Frieder: Kassenärzte und Krankenversicherungsreform. Zu einer Theorie der Statuspolitik (Insurance Fund, Doctors and Reform of the Sickness Insurance System. On a theory of status policy). Freiburg, Rombach, 1967, 288 p. Analysis of the aggregation and articulation of interests among medical doctors, and their resistance against modifications of the present system which the author relates to status concerns rather than to economic interests; containing a short historical summary of the changing economic position of doctors.

REINERS, Hartmut, VOLKHOLZ, Volker: Das Gesundheitssystem in der BRD. Eine Einführung (The Health System in the Federal Republic. An Introduction). Hamburg Berlin, VSA, 1977, 171 p. Useful introduction into the German health system with parts on sickness insurance, ambulant and hospital care, and the professions in the health sector; including basic statistical data.

RICHTER, Max, MÜLLER, Albert: Kampf um die Krankenversicherung 1955-1965 (Struggle on Sickness Insurance 1955-1965). Bad Godesberg, Verlag der Ortskrankenkassen, without year, ca. 1965, 116 p. Account of the political debates about sickness insurance reform, and the failure of the intended major reform in the 1960s.

ROSENBERG, Peter: Möglichkeiten der Reform des Gesundheitswesens in der Bundesrepublik Deutschland. Eine Literaturanalyse (Possibilities of a Reform of the Health System in the Federal Republic. An Analysis of the Literature). Kommission für wirtschaftlichen und sozialen Wandel Schriften 48. Göttingen, Schwartz, 1975, 362 p. Reform proposals based on a secondary analysis of the available literature on the health system, including an extensive bibliography.

SAFRAN, William: Veto Group Politics. The Case of Health Insurance Reform in West Germany. San Francisco, Chandler, 1967, 261 p. Analysis of the conflicts between the government and various interest groups in the struggle for the reform of sickness insurance in the early 1960s.

SCHREIBER, Wilfried, ALLEKOTTE, H. (eds): Kostenexplosion in der gesetzlichen Krankenversicherung (Cost Explosion in Public Sickness Insurance). Köln, Wison, 1970, 83 p. A reader with nine contributions analyzing various determinants of the cost explosion.

WIRTSCHAFTS- UND SOZIALWISSENSCHAFTLICHES INSTITUT: Integrierte medizinische Versorgung: Notwendigkeit, Möglichkeit, Grenzen (Integrated Provision of Medicine: Necessity, Possibility, Limits). WSI-Forum am 25. und 26. April 1975. WSI Studie zur Wirtschafts- und Sozialforschung 32. Köln, Bund Verlag, 1975, 228 p. Report of a colloquium held by the labour unions' research institute on the possibility of a national health system in the Federal Republic.

2.2.2 Sources

BUNDESMINISTER FÜR ARBEIT UND SOZIALORDNUNG: Die gesetzliche Krankenversicherung im Jahre....Statistischer und finanzieller Bericht (Public Sickness Insurance in the Year....- Statistical and Financial Report). Bonn, Bundesministerium für Arbeit und Sozialordnung, yearly series, 1949-. Central official source on the statistics of sickness insurance, up to 1962 published under the title: Die soziale Krankenversicherung im Jahre....

BUNDESMINISTER FÜR JUGEND, FAMILIE UND GESUNDHEIT: Das Gesundheitswesen der Bundesrepublik Deutschland im internationalen Vergleich (official English title: Statistical Atlas on Public Health in the Federal Republic of Germany). Bonn, Bundesminister für Jugend, Familie und Gesundheit, irregular series, published in 1963, 1965, 1967, 1970, 1974. Rich compendium of health statistics with international comparisons, published for foreign readers with texts in German, English, and French.

BUNDESMINISTER FÜR JUGEND, FAMILIE UND GESUNDHEIT: Gesundheitsbericht (Health Report). Stuttgart/Berlin/Köln/Mainz, Kohlhammer, 1971, 196 p. Official report of the federal government on the health system in the Federal Republic.

BUNDESMINISTER FÜR JUGEND, FAMILIE UND GESUNDHEIT (ed.): Daten des Gesundheitswesens (Data of the Health System). Bonn, Bundesministerium für Arbeit und Sozialordnung, irregular series, published in 1977, 356 p., 1980, 365 p., 1983, 355 p. Standard source with rich data on administrative and financial aspects of public health, on morbidity and mortality.

STATISTISCHES BUNDESAMT: Fachserie 12: Gesundheitswesens (Special Series 12.: Health System). Stuttgart, Kohlhammer, yearly series, 1959-. Under this title since 1977, previously published as Fachserie A, Bevölkerung und Kultur, Reihe 7. Central official publication on statistics of the health system with six separately published sub-series three of which are of interest here: Reihe 1: Ausgewählte Zahlen für das Gesundheitswesen (Selected figures on the health system); Reihe 5: Berufe des Gesundheitswesens (Vocations in the health sector); Reihe 6: Krankenhäuser (Hospitals).

2.3 Unemployment

2.3.1 Descriptions, evaluations, analyses

BALSEN, Werner, NAKIELSKI, Hans, RÖSSEL, Karl, WINKEL, Rolf: Die neue Armut. Ausgrenzung von Arbeitslosen aus der Arbeitslosenunterstützung (The New Poverty. Exclusion of the unemployed from unemployment compensation). Köln, Bund Verlag, 1984, 171 p. Study of the functioning of unemployment compensation schemes after the curtailment legislation, written from the perspective of beneficiaries; based on research supported by the trade unions.

BIEDENKOPF, Kurt H., MIEGEL Meinhard: Wege aus der Arbeitslosigkeit. Arbeitsmarktpolitik in der sozialen Marktwirtschaft (Ways out of Unemployment. Labour market policy in the social market economy). Stuttgart, Bonn Aktuell, 1978, 112 p. A political analysis of the causes of the unemployment crisis with proposals for reforms in the direction of a liberal growth policy, written by leading representatives of the Christian Democratic Party.

LEIBFRIED, Stephan: Die Institutionalisierung der Arbeitslosenversicherung in Deutschland (The Institutionalization of Unemployment Insurance in Germany). Kritische Justiz 10, 1977: 289-301. Short historical synopsis of the institutional development of unemployment insurance.

LUTZ, Burkhart, SENGENBERGER, Werner: Arbeitsmarktstrukturen und öffentliche Arbeitsmarktpolitik. Eine kritische Analyse von Zielen und Instrumenten (Structures of the Labour Market and Labour Market Policy. A Critical Analysis of Goals and Instruments). Schriften der Kommission für wirtschaftlichen und sozialen Wandel 26. Göttingen, Schwartz, 1974, 154 p.

NIESS, Frank: Geschichte der Arbeitslosigkeit: Ökonomische Ursachen und politsche Kämpfe - ein Kapitel deutscher Sozialschichte (History of Unemployment: Economic Causes and Political Struggles - A Chapter of German Social Policy). Köln, Pahl Rugenstein, 1979, 250 p. Account of the historical development of unemployment and unemployment policy from a Marxist perspective with polemic undertones. Probleme des Klassenkampfes Oktober 1975: Kapitalistische Krise, Arbeitslosigkeit und Krise der Gewerkschaftspolitik in der Bundesrepublik (Capitalist Crisis, Unemployment and Crisis of Labour Union Politics in the Federal Republic). General theme of the triple volume of: Probleme des Klassenkampfes 19-21, 1975. Marxist analysis of unemployment policy in the recession with articles on 'capitalist crisis and unemployment in the Federal Republic', 'the development of employment structure and of unemployment', 'the system of social security for the unemployed'.

SCHMID, Günther: Steuerungssysteme des Arbeitsmarktes. Vergleich von Frankreich, Grossbritannien, Schweden, DDR und Sowjetunion mit der Bundesrepublik Deutschland (Steering Systems of the Labour Market. Comparison of France, Great Britain, Sweden, German Democratic Republic, and Soviet Union with the Federal Republic). Schriften der Kommission für wirtschaftlichen und sozialen Wandel 84. Göttingen, Schwartz, 1975, 355 p.

2.3.2 Sources

BUNDESANSTALT FÜR ARBEIT: Arbeitsstatistik (Yearly Figures). Nürnberg, Bundesanstalt für Arbeit, yearly series, 1950-. Major source of official statistics on unemployment and unemployment policy; originally entitled 'Jahreszahlen zur Arbeitsstatistik', under the present title since 1969.

BUNDESANSTALT FÜR ARBEIT: Amtliche Nachrichten der Bundesanstalt für Arbeit (Official News of the Federal Institution of Labour). Nürnberg, Bundesanstalt für Arbeit, yearly series, 1950-.

2.4 Accidents

BUNDESMINISTER FÜR ARBEIT UND SOZIALORDNUNG: Die gesetzliche Unfallversicherung im Jahre .... in der Bundesrepublik Deutschland (The Statutory Accident Insurance in the Year .... in the Federal Republic). Bonn, Bundesministerium für Arbeit und Sozialordnung, yearly series, 1950-. Major official source on the functioning of the accident insurance scheme.

2.5 Social assistance

2.5.1 Descriptions, evaluations, analyses

ADAMY, Wilhelm, NAEGELE, Gerhard, STEFFEN, Johannes: Sozialstaat oder Armenhaus?

(Welfare State or Poorhouse?). Sozialer Fortschritt 32, 1983: pp. 193-200. Informative account of the development of social assistance during the period of cutback legislation interpreting the generosity of assistance benefits as a function of labour market developments.

FLAMM, Franz: Sozialwesen und Sozialarbeit in der Bundesrepublik Deutschland (Social Services and Social Work in the Federal Republic). Schriften des Deutschen Vereins für öffentliche und private Fürsorge Nr. 250. Frankfurt, Deutscher Verein für öffentliche und private Fürsorge, 3rd ed. 1980, 264 p. Introduction into German social work; an English version under the stated title was published in 1974.

KRITISCHE JUSTIZ 9, 1976. Schwerpunktheft Sozialrecht (Special Issue on Social Law of the periodical Kritische Justiz). Several articles on social assistance from the perspective of 'radical' social science, among them Barabas and Sachsse: Bundessozialhilfegesetz: Sozialstaatliche Versorgung oder Armenpolizei (Federal social assistance law: public provision of benefits or poor police); Leibfried: Armutspotential und Sozialhilfe in der Bundesrepublik. Zum Prozess des Filterns von Ansprüchen auf Sozialhilfe (The potential of poverty in the Federal Republic. On the filtering process of assistance claims); Mückenberger: Thesen zur Funktion und Entwicklung des Sozialrechts (Theses on the function and the development of social law).

LEIBFRIED, Stephan: Public Assistance in the United States and the Federal Republic of Germany. Does social democracy make a difference? Comparative Politics 11, 1978: 59-76. Comparative description and analysis of the development of the German and the American social assistance schemes.

MATTHES, Joachim: Gesellschaftspolitische Konzeptionen im Sozialhilferecht. Zur soziologischen Kritik der neuen deutschen Sozialhilfegesetzgebung (Conceptions of Society in Social Assistance Law. On a Sociological Critique of the German assistance legislation). Stuttgart, Enke, 1964, 134 p. Theoretical analysis of the conceptions underlying the German social assistance legislation and of the structural and functional changes of the assistance scheme, by one of the major representatives of German sociology.

SCHULTE, Bernd, TRENK-HINTERBERGER, Peter: Sozialhilfe. Eine Einführung (Social Assistance. An Introduction). Königstein, Athenäum, 1982, 451 p. Standard introduction into the functioning of the assistance scheme including a useful synopsis of legislative developments.

2.5.2 Sources

STATISTISCHES BUNDESAMT.: Fachserie 13, Reihe 2: Sozialhilfe (Special Series 13, Subseries 2: Social Assistance). Stuttgart/Berlin/Köln/Mainz, Kohlhammer, yearly series, 1963-. Prior to 1975 published under the title Fachserie K, sub-series Öffentliche Fürsorge. Major official source on statistics of the social assistance scheme.

2.6 Family and youth programmes

2.6.1 Descriptions, evaluations, analyses

BÜNGER, Fritz Emil: Familienpolitik in Deutschland (Family Policy in Germany). Berlin, Duncker & Humblot, 1970, 196 p. Discussions of the distributive effects of child allowances and tax credits for children advocating more selective benefits.

KAUFMANN, Franz-Xaver, HERLTH, Alois, STROHMEIER, Klaus Peter, SCHULZE, Hans-Joachim: Sozialpolitik und familiale Sozialisation. Zur Wirkungsweise öffentlicher Sozialleistungen (Social Policy and family Socialization. On the Impact of Public Benefits). Schriftenreihe des Bundesministers für Jugend, Familie und Gesundheit Nr. 76. Stuttgart, Berlin, Köln, Mainz, Kohlhammer, 1980, 452 p. Analysis of family policy by a sociological study group examining the impact of social policy.

LÜSCHER, Kurt (ed.): Sozialpolitik für das Kind (Social Policy for the Child). Stuttgart, Klett-Cotta, 1979, 280 p. A reader with nine articles on various aspects of social policies for children.

WINGEN, Max: Familienpolitik. Ziele, Wege und Wirkungen (Family Policy. Goals, Approaches and Effects). 2nd ed. Paderborn, Bonifacius, 1965, 284 p. Standard account of the goals and instruments of German family policy departing from an analysis of the situation of the family in industrial society.

ZEPPERNICK, Rolf: Untersuchungen zum Familienlastenausgleich (Investigations on Family Allowances). Institut für Wirtschaftspolitik an der Universität zu Köln. Untersuchungen Nr. 30. Köln, Institut für Wirtschaftspolitik, 1974, 263 p. A dissertation trying to evaluate the effectiveness of child allowances.

2.6.2 Sources

BUNDESMINISTER FÜR JUGEND, FAMILIE UND GESUNDHEIT (ed.): Bericht über die Lage der Familie in der Bundesrepublik Deutschland - Familienbericht (Report on the Situation of the Family in the Federal Republic - Family Report). Bonn, Bundestagsdrucksache V/2532, 1968, 256 p. Government report on the situation of the family and family policy; a second report under the same title appeared in 1975 (Zweiter Familienbericht, Bundestagsdrucksache VII/3502), 188 p.; a third report was issued in 1979 (Dritter Familienbericht, Bundestagsdrucksache 8/3121), 218 p.

BUNDESMINISTER FÜR JUGEND, FAMILIE UND GESUNDHEIT (ed.): Jugendbericht (Youth Report). Bonn, Bundestagsdrucksache, irregular series, 1965-. Government report on the situation of the young which according to the law should be issued every four years; the first report appeared as Bundestagsdrucksache IV/3515, 191 p. the sixth and most recent report was published in 1984 as Bundestagsdrucksache 10/1007, 68 p.

BUNDESMINISTER FÜR JUGEND, FAMILIE UND GESUNDHEIT (ed.): Leistungen für die nachwachsende Generation in der Bundesrepublik Deutschland. (Benefits for the Young Generation in the Federal Republic). Schriftenreihe des Bundesministers für Jugend, Familie und Gesundheit Nr. 73. Stuttgart/Berlin/Köln/Mainz, Kohlhammer, 1980, 198 p. An expertise by the scientific council on family questions trying to develop a comprehensive account of all public transfers for families and children in the late 1970s including information on the functioning of voluntary organizations; rich statistical and institutional data.

STATISTISCHES BUNDESAMT: Die Situation der Kinder in der Bundesrepublik Deutschland 1979 (The Situation of Children in the Federal Republic). Stuttgart/ Berlin/Köln/Mainz, Kohlhammer, 1979, 138 p. Statistical report on living conditions and activities of children, presenting time series data for the 1960s and 1970s.

STATISTISCHES BUNDESAMT: Zur Situation der Jugend in der Bundesrepublik Deutschland (On the Situation of Young People in the Federal Republic). Stuttgart, Berlin, Köln, Mainz, 1984. 225 p. Statistical report on living conditions and life styles of young people.

2.7 Housing

2.7.1 Descriptions, evaluations, analyses

BIEDENKOPF, Kurt H., MIEGEL, Meinhard: Wohnungsbau am Wendepunkt. Wohnungspolitik in der sozialen Marktwirtschaft (Housing Construction at the Turning Point. Housing Policy in the Social Market Economy). Stuttgart, Bonn Aktuell, 1978, 150 p. A critical evaluation of housing policy by prominent representatives of the Christian Democratic Party; with reform proposals and a statistical appendix containing time series data.

BLUMENROTH, Ulrich: Deutsche Wohnungspolitik seit der Reichsgründung - Darstellung und kritische Würdigung (German Housing Policy Since the Establishment of the Reich - Description and Critical Evaluation). Beiträge zum Siedlungs- und Wohnungswesen und zur Raumplanung Band 25. Münster, Selbstverlag des Instituts für Siedlungs- und Wohnungswesen der Universität Münster, 1975, 410 p. Standard account of the historical development of housing policy in Germany with some statistical tables.

BRECH, Joachim (ed.): Wohnen zur Miete, Wohnungsversorgung und Wohnungspolitik in der Bundesrepublik (Housing for Rent. Provision of Housing and Housing Policy in the Federal Republic). Weinheim Basel, Beltz, 1981, 306 p. A reader with 17 articles from a 'radical' perspective, including a description of the working of the social construction programme, an overview of the policy proposals of parties and major interest groups; with ample statistical information and useful bibliographies.

BREDE, Helmut, KOHAUPT, Bernhard, KUJATH, Hans-Joachim: Ökonomische und politische Determinanten der Wohnungsversorgung (Economic and Political Determinants of the Provision of Housing). Frankfurt, Suhrkamp, 1975, 114 p. Attempt to analyze the housing market and housing policies with categories of Marxist political economy.

GLATZER, Wolfgang: Ziele, Standards und soziale Indikatoren für die Wohnungsversorgung (Goals, Standards and Social Indicators for the Provision of Housing). *In* ZAPF, Wolfgang (ed.): Lebensbedingungen in der Bundesrepublik 1950-1975. Frankfurt, Campus, 1978, pp. 575-675. Basic summary of official goals in housing policy, policy proposals, and actual output, impact and achievements, with a host of statistical information on construction activities and housing conditions in time series form.

GLATZER, Wolfgang: Wohnungsversorgung im Wohlfahrtsstaat (Housing Provision in the Welfare State). Frankfurt, Campus, 1980, 275 p. Standard account of housing in the Federal Republic with rich time series data; extended version of the article above.

HECHT, Michael: Subventionsformen in der Wohnungswirtschaft (Forms of Subsidization in the Housing Economy). Schriftenreihe Wirtschaftswissenschaftliche Forschung und Entwicklung 20. München, Florenz, 1978, 215 p.

LEVIATHAN 3-4: 1981 issue of a prominent 'radical' journal dedicated predominantly to housing policy with articles on the unpolitical housing policy (Häussermann and Siebel), housing provision and housing shortage (Neef), housing policy and urban structure (Pesch and Selle), theses on the housing situation (Ipsen and Mussel), and the movement of tenants (Nelles and Wanders).

MAIROSE, Ralf, ORGASS, Gerhard: Wohnungs- und Bodenpolitik in der Bundesrepublik. Kostenmiete, Städtebaurecht, Wohnungseigentum durch Mietkauf (Housing and Landed Property Policy in the Federal Republic. Cost Rent, Urban Construction Law, Property by Rent Purchase), 2nd ed. Opladen, Leske & Budrich, 1975, 160 p. Description and critical evaluation of policy instruments in the housing sector, with statistical and institutional information and a documentation of political reform proposals; written by experts in housing policy one of whom is a member of the housing committee of parliament.

MÜNCH, D.: Ziele, Massnahmen und Ergebnisse staatlicher Wohnungspolitik in Europa (Goals, Measures and Results of Public Housing Policy in Europe). Münster, Institut für Siedlungs- und Wohnungswesen der Westfälischen Wilhelms-Universität, Sonderdruck 41, 1967, 405 p. A comparison of housing policy in the Federal Republic, Belgium, France, Sweden, Switzerland, and the United Kingdom.

PETZINGER, Renate, RIEGE, Marlo: Die neue Wohnungsnot. Wohnungswunder Bundesrepublik (The New Housing Shortage. The Housing Miracle in the Federal Republic). Hamburg, VSA, 1981, 146 p. Discussion of the causes of the new shortage of housing with a review of past housing policies and construction activities, and an evaluation of alternative policy proposals; appendix with statistical tables and a list of core laws in housing policy.

WULLKOPF, Uwe: Wohnungsbau und Wohnungspolitik in der Bundesrepublik (Housing Construction and Housing Policy in the Federal Republic). Aus Politik und Zeitgeschichte B10, 1982: pp. 11-25. Concise summary of housing conditions and housing policy including a synopsis of postwar developments.

2.7.2 Sources

BUNDESBAUBLATT. Zeitschrift für Wohnungswesen, Städtebau, Raumordnung, Baurecht und Bauforschung (Federal Construction Journal). Wiesbaden, yearly periodical, 1951-. Basic periodical for information on housing with statistics and analyses by politicians, civil servants, academic experts.

BUNDESMINISTERIUM FÜR RAUMORDNUNG, BAUWESEN UND STÄDTEBAU: Das Wohnen in der Bundesrepublik (Housing in the Federal Republic). Bonn, Bundesministerium für

Raumordnung, Bauwesen und Städtebau, 1975, 126 p. Official report summarizing the results of the 1972 housing survey.

STATISTISCHES BUNDESAMT: Fachserie 5. Bautätigkeit und Wohnen (Special Series 5: Construction Activities and Housing). Stuttgart/Köln/Bonn/Mainz, yearly series, 1961-. Prior to 1977 published as Fachserie E, Bauwirtschaft, Bautätigkeit und Wohnen. Official statistics on housing with three separately published sub-series: Reihe 1: Bautätigkeit (Construction Activity); Reihe 2: Bewilligungen im sozialen Wohnungsbau (Concessions in the Social Construction Programme); Reihe 3: Bestand an Wohnungen (Supply of houses).

STATISTISCHES BUNDESAMT: Fachserie 13: Sozialleistungen, Reihe 4: Wohngeld (Special Series 13: Social Benefits, sub-series 4: Housing allowances). Stuttgart, Köln, Bonn, Mainz, Kohlhammer, 1964-. Prior to 1977 published as Fachserie E (see above), Reihe 7. Official statistics of the housing allowance programme.

STATISTISCHES BUNDESAMT: Das Wohnen in der Bundesrepublik Deutschland. Ausgabe 1981 (Housing in the Federal Republic. Edition 1981). Stuttgart/ Berlin/Köln/Mainz, Kohlhammer, 1981, 120 p. Official report on German housing based on the 1978 housing survey.

2.8 Education

2.8.1 Descriptions, evaluations, analyses

ARNOLD, Rolf, MARZ, Fritz: Einführung in die Bildungspolitik. Grundlagen, Entwicklungen, Probleme (Introduction into educational policy. Bases, development, problems). Stuttgart, Berlin, Köln, Mainz, Kohlhammer, 1979, 182 p. Description of the development of the educational system since 1945, describing policies on the federal, the state and the local level; without quantitative data, but with charts on the distribution of institutional competence, and synopses of the goals of educational policy in the constitutions of the single states.

DAHRENDORF, Ralf: Bildung ist Bürgerrecht. Plädoyer für eine aktive Bildungspolitik (Education is a Right of Citizens. Plea for an Active Educational Policy). Hamburg, Nannen, 1965, 155 p. Sociological interpretation of German educational policy advocating the widening of educational opportunity, written by one of the politically most influential German sociologists.

DEUTSCHER BILDUNGSRAT: Bildungsforschung (Educational Research). Gutachten und Studien der Bildungskommission (Reports and Studies of the Education Commission), vols 50 (part I) and 51 (part II). Stuttgart, Klett, 1975, 413 and 464 p. Various analyses from academic observers, with, among others, an article by Offe on 'the educational system, the employment system, and educational policy'.

FÜHR, Christoph: Das Bildungswesen in der Bundesrepublik Deutschland. Ein Überblick (The Educational System in the Federal Republic. An Overview). Weinheim/Basel, Beltz, 1980, 202 p. Introduction to the German educational system,intended especially for foreigners; with statistical appendix and useful bibliography.

HAUG, Frigga, OHM, Christof, RANG, Adalbert, RANG, Brita, RÜCKRIEM, Georg (eds): 30 Jahre Bildungspolitik in der Bundesrepublik (30 Years of Educational Policy in the Federal Republic). Das Argument. Sonderband AS 38. Berlin, Argument-Verlag, 1979, 216 p. A reader with fourteen contributions from a Marxist perspective with emphasis on the primary, secondary, and vocational sector, excluding the universities; includes articles on the reform of primary education, the development of educational opportunity, and on the educational policy of the Social Democratic Party.

HÜFNER, Klaus (ed.): Bildungswesen: mangelhaft. BRD- Bildungspolitik im OECD-Länderexamen (Educational Sector: Deficient. German Educational Policy in the Country Examination of the OECD). Frankfurt, Diesterweg, 1973, 149 p. German edition of a widely discussed OECD report highlighting the shortcomings of the West German educational system.

MAX PLANCK INSTITUT FÜR BILDUNGSFORSCHUNG PROJEKTGRUPPE BILDUNGSBERICHT (ed.): Bildung in der Bundesrepublik Deutschland. Daten und Analysen (Education in the Federal Republic of Germany. Data and Analyses). Reinbek bei Hamburg, Rowohlt, 1980 (2 volumes, together 1404 p.). Standard account of the educational system in the

Federal Republic in a historical perspective by the central educational research institute. The first volume centers on developments since 1950 with parts on major trends in educational policies, the institutional framework, the development of curricula, and educational opportunity. The second volume centers on current problems such as the linkage between the educational system and the labour market, the shrinking number of students, and the integration of children of foreign workers.

OFFE, Claus: Berufsbildungsreform. Eine Fallstudie über Reformpolitik (Reform of Vocational Education. A Case Study of Reform Policy). Frankfurt, Suhrkamp, 1975, 328 p. Analysis of the reform of vocational education in 1969 based on a structural model of policy-making in capitalist societies; trying to elaborate functions which the state must perform for the economic system.

PEISERT, Hansgert: Soziale Lage und Bildungschancen in Deutschland (Social Position and Educational Opportunities in Germany). München, Piper, 1967, 205 p. Pioneer study of social and regional inequalities in educational opportunities.

PEISERT, Hansgert, FRAMHEIN, Gerhild: Das Hochschulsystem in der Bundesrepublik Deutschland. Funktionsweise und Leistungsfähigkeit (The University System in the Federal Republic. Functioning and Efficiency). Stuttgart, Klett-Cotta, 1980, 215 p. Introduction into the system of post-secondary education with useful institutional information and rich statistics, partly in time-series form for the period 1950-1977.

PICHT, Georg: Die deutsche Bildungskatastrophe (The German Educational Catastrophe). München, dtv, 1965, 153 p. A collection of politically influential articles denouncing the comparative backwardness of German secondary and post-secondary education.

RUGE, Rainer: Bildung (Education). *In* ZAPF, Wolfgang (ed.): Lebensbedingungen in der Bundesrepublik 1950-1975. Frankfurt, Campus, 1978, pp. 743-841. The best and most concise summary of the goals of German educational policy, party programmes, and the structure of the educational system; with ahost of quantitative data on educational participation and the performance of the educational system.

2.8.2 Sources

BUNDESMINISTER FÜR BILDUNG UND WISSENSCHAFT: Bildungsbericht '70. Bericht der Bundesregierung zur Bildungspolitik (Report on Education '70. Report of the Federal Government on Educational Policy). Bonn, Heger, 1970, 156 p. Official report on political goals of the federal government in the educational sector, also published as a parliamentary paper (Bundestagsdrucksache VI/925); with numerous statistical tables, graphical illustrations, and some international comparisons; based on a description and analysis of the development of the educational system since 1945, it develops political reform proposals.

BUNDESMINISTER FÜR BILDUNG UND WISSENSCHAFT: Grund- und Strukturdaten (Basic and Structural Data). Bonn, yearly series, 1974-. Data on students and personnel in schools, universities, and institutions of vocational education; with international comparisons; in 1974 published in two separate volumes entitled 'Grunddaten' and 'Strukturdaten', since 1975 under the current title and in the present form.

BUNDESMINISTER FÜR BILDUNG UND WISSENSCHAFT (ed.): Bericht der Bundesregierung über die strukturellen Probleme des föderativen Bildungssystems (Report ofthe Federal Government on the Structural Problems in the Federal System of Education). Bonn, Bundestagsdrucksache 8/1551, 1978, 195 p. Government report on the functioning of the educational system with useful appendix on inter-state agreements and on party platforms.

STATISTISCHES BUNDESAMT: Bildung im Zahlenspiegel (Education in Figures). Stuttgart, Köln, Bonn, Mainz, Kohlhammer, yearly series, 1974-. Central official summary publication on educational statistics; the editions 1974, 1975, 1977 were published by Bundesminister für Bildung und Wissenschaft; since 1978 published by Statistisches Bundesamt; data are presented by level of education.

STATISTISCHES BUNDESAMT: Fachserie 11: Bildung und Kultur (Special series 11: Education and culture). Stuttgart/Köln/Bonn/Mainz, Kohlhammer, yearly series, 1960-. Central series with detailed official statistics of the educational system with several separately published sub-series; from 1960 to 1973 appearing under the title 'Fachserie A: Bevölkerung und Kultur, Bildungswesen'; the four subseries of interest here are: Reihe 1: Allgemeines Schulwesen (General School System); Reihe 2: Berufliches Schulwesen (Vocational School System); Reihe 3: Berufliche Bildung (Vocational Education); Reihe 4: Hochschulen (Universities).

2.9 Public household and employment

2.9.1 Descriptions, evaluations, analyses

ALBERS, Willi: Ursachen, Wirkungen und Begrenzungsmöglichkeiten einer wachsenden Staatsquote. Die Lage in der Bundesrepublik Deutschland (Causes, Effects, and Limitation Possibilities of a Growing State Share. The Situation in the Federal Republic). In RÜHLE, Hans, VEEN, Hans-Joachim (eds): Wachsende Staatshaushalte. Stuttgart, Bonn Aktuell, 2nd ed. 1978, pp. 19-50. Informative description and analysis of public expenditure developments from 1960 to 1977.

ANDIC, Suphan, VEVERKA, Jindrich: 'The growth of government expenditure in Germany since the unification'. *Finanzarchiv N.F.* 23, 1963/64: 169-278. The central study of the historical development of public expenditure in Germany from 1872 to 1958; with rich statistical tables and empirical analyses.

BIEDENKOPF, Kurt H., MIEGEL, Meinhard: Die programmiert Krise. Alternativen zur staatlichen Schuldenpolitik (The Programmed Crisis. Alternatives to the Policy of Public Debt). Stuttgart, Bonn Aktuell, 1979, 143 p. Description of the development of public debt in the Federal Republic since 1949, combined with a critique of government policies and proposals for reform; written by representatives of the Christian Democratic party.

GRAUHAN, Rolf Richard, HICKEL, Rudolf (eds): Krise des Steuerstaats? Widersprüche, Perspektiven, Ausweichstrategien (Crisis of the Fiscal State? Contradictions, Perspectives, Evasion Strategies). Leviathan Sonderheft 1, 1978. Opladen, Westdeutscher Verlag, 1978, 252 p. Theoretical analysis of the crisis of the fiscal state from a Marxist perspective; with thirteen articles discussing the concept of a crisis of the public household, and evaluating political strategies to cope with the crisis.

INSTITUT FINANZEN UND STEUERN: Der Fiskus als Sozialpolitiker (The Tax System as Social Politician). Schriftenreihe des Instituts Finanzen und Steuern Heft 77. Bonn, Stollfuss, 1965, 296 p. An analysis of the social implications of the tax system by a prominent economic research institute, sponsored by the German Science Foundation.

LANG, Eva, KOCH, W.A.S.: Staatsverschuldung - Staatsbankrott? (Public Debt - State Bankruptcy?). Würzburg Wien, Physica, 1980, 180 p. An introduction to public finance with statistics on the development of public debt, questioning the adverse effects of a public debt at the comparatively modest level of that of the Federal Republic.

LITTMANN, Konrad: Definition und Entwicklung der Staatsquote. Abgrenzung, Aussagekraft und Anwendungsbereiche unterschiedlicher Typen von Staatsquoten (Definition and Development of the State Share. Delimitation, Informative Value and Range of Application of different Types of Public Expenditure Ratios). Schriften der Kommission für wirtschaftlichen und sozialen Wandel 42. Göttingen, Schwartz, 1975, 203 p. Standard account of the development of the state share since 1950 applying various statistical concepts.

MUSGRAVE, Richard A., MUSGRAVE, Peggy B., KULLMER, Lore: Die öffentlichen Finanzen in Theorie und Praxis (Public Finance in Theory and Practice). Tübingen, Mohr, 1978, four volumes with 216, 288, 187, and 330 p. Standard introduction to the German system of public finance with rich institutional and statistical data; based on the American study of public finance by the Musgraves.

RECKTENWALD, Horst Claus: Umfang und Struktur der öffentlichen Ausgaben in säkularer Entwicklung (Size and Structure of Public Expenditure in Secular Development). *In* NEUMARK, Fritz, ANDEL, Norbert, HALLER, Heinz (eds): Handbuch der Finanzwissenschaft. Tübingen, Mohr, 1976, pp. 713-752. Statistical analysis of public expenditure development from 1872 to 1972 discussing various theories of expenditure growth.

2.9.2 Sources

BUNDESMINISTERIUM DER FINANZEN.: Finanzbericht (Financial Report). Bonn, yearly series, 1961-. Central source for official statistics and descriptions of the public household.

BUNDESMINISTERIUM DER FINANZEN: Personalentwicklung bei Bund, Ländern und Gemeinden 1960-1980 (Personnel Development in Federal, State, and Communal Government). Finanznachrichten 34, 1981: 2-7. Description and consistent statistical data on public employment in 1960, 1970, and 1980.

SACHVERSTÄNDIGENRAT ZUR BEGUTACHTUNG DER GESAMTWIRTSCHAFTLICHEN ENTWICKLUNG: Jahresgutachten des Sachverständigenrates (Yearly Expertise of the Council of Economic Advisors). Bonn, Bundestagsdrucksache, yearly series, 1965-. Analysis of economic policy by an expert committee with legal standing; includes analyses of public finance developments with rich time series data in the appendix.

STATISTISCHES BUNDESAMT.: Fachserie 14: Finanzen und Steuern (Special series 14: Finance and taxes). Stuttgart/Köln/Bonn/Mainz, Kohlhammer, yearly series, 1962-. Major series of official statistics on the public household, published in ten separate sub-series; prior to 1977 published as Fachserie L, Finanzen und Steuern; five sub-series are of special interest: Reihe 1: Haushaltsansätze (Budget Plans); Reihe 2: Vierteljahreszahlen zur öffentlichen Finanzwirtschaft (Quarterly Figures on Public Finance); Reihe 3: Rechnungsergebnisse (Accounting Results); Reihe 5: Schulden der öffentlichen Haushalte (Debt of Public Households); Reihe 6: Personal des öffentlichen Dienstes (Personnel of the Civil Service).

STATISTISCHES BUNDESAMT: Lange Reihen zur Wirtschaftsentwicklung (Long Time series on Economic Development). Stuttgart/Köln/Bonn/Mainz Kohlhammer, yearly series, 1973-. Official time series data on economic development extending back to 1950; including data on public receipts and expenditure.

STATISTISCHES BUNDESAMT: Das Personal der öffentlichen Verwaltungen und Betriebe (The Personnel of Public Administration and Public Enterprises). Wirtschaft und Statistik 3, 1951: pp. 482-485. Description and detailed data on public employment in 1950.

III Impact of social programmes

3.1 Poverty

BUJARD, Otker, LANGE, Ulrich: Theorie und Praxis der Sozialhilfe. Zur Situation der einkommensschwachen alten Menschen (Theory and Practice of Social Assistance. On the situation of old persons with low income). Schriftenreihe des Bundesministers für Jugend, Familie und Gesundheit 56. Stuttgart/Berlin/Köln/Mainz, Kohlhammer, 1978, 183 p. Inquiry into the causes of poverty and the determinants of benefit claims in the social assistance scheme, based on survey research.

HARTMANN, Helmut: Sozialhilfebedürftigkeit und 'Dunkelziffer' der Armut (Social Assistance Need and the Ratio of Hidden Poverty). Schriftenreihe des Bundesministers für Jugend, Familie und Gesundheit 98. Stuttgart/ Berlin/Köln/Mainz, Kohlhammer, 1981, 187 p. Empirical analysis of the effectiveness of the assistance scheme and the extent of poverty, based on survey research in 1979/1980.

HAUSER, Richard, CREMER-SCHÄFER, Helga, NOUVERTNÉ, Udo: Armut, Niedrigeinkommen und Unterversorgung in der Bundesrepublik Deutschland (Poverty, Low Income and Deprivation in the Federal Republic). Frankfurt, Campus, 1981, 352 p. Standard analysis of social assistance and poverty in Germany, written as the national poverty report on behalf of the commission of the European Communities.

HAUSER, Richard: Armut im Wohlfahrtsstaat - empirischer Befund und Lösungsansätze (Poverty in the Welfare State - Empirical Findings and Possibilities of a Solution). *In* LAMPERT, Heinz, KÜHLEWIND, Gerhard: Das Sozialsystem der Bundesrepublik Deutschland. Beiträge zur Arbeitsmarkt-und Berufsforschung Nr. 83. Nürnberg, Institut für Arbeitsmarkt und Berufsforschung der Bundesanstalt für Arbeit, 1984, pp. 214-263. Update of the national poverty report by its senior author.

KLANBERG, Franz: Armut und ökonomische Ungleichheit in der Bundesrepublik Deutschland (Poverty and Economic Inequality in the Federal Republic of Germany). Frankfurt, Campus, 1978, 307 p. Standard work on poverty in the Federal Republic; methodological discussion of various concepts of poverty and quantitative indicators of the extent of poverty based on the microcensus and income statistics.

KORTMANN, Klaus: Zur Armutsdiskussion in der Bundesrepublik Deutschland (On the Discussion of Poverty in the Federal Republic of Germany). Nachrichtendienst des Deutschen Vereins für öffentliche und private Fürsorge 56, 1976, Nr.5, pp. 144-149. A critical summary and evaluation of various studies and estimates of the population living in poverty with some new empirical data and fresh calculations; an extended version appeared as SPES Arbeitspapier No 50, Universität Frankfurt (mimeo), 1976, 31 p.

ROTH, Jürgen: Armut in der Bundesrepublik. Über psychische und materielle Verelendung (Poverty in the Federal Republic. On Psychic and Material Pauperization). Frankfurt, Fischer, 1974, 233 p., new ed. Best-selling polemic report on poverty, declaring one fourth of all German households to be living in misery.

STRANG, Heinz: Erscheinungsformen der Sozialhilfebedürftigkeit. Beitrag zur Geschichte, Theorie und empirischen Analyse der Armut (Manifestations of the Need for Assistance. Contribution to the History, Theory and Empirical Analysis of Poverty). Stuttgart, Enke, 1970, 248 p. Historical study of poverty and public assistance in Germany, with statistical data for the period since 1880.

TRANSFER 1: Gleiche Chancen im Sozialstaat (Equality of Opportunity in the Social State?). Opladen, Westdeutscher Verlag, 1975, 158 p. Thirteen articles on a variety of topics; among them, a report on poverty based on an empirical study in the city of Dortmund, an article by Krupp on how to measure income inequality, and a contribution on regional disparities in the provision of public goods.

WIDMAIER, Hans-Peter: Zur neuen sozialen Frage (On the New Social Question). Schriften des Vereins für Socialpolitik N.F. 95, Berlin, Duncker & Humblot, 1978, 249 p. Seven articles by social policy experts on the amount of poverty, and the nexus between poverty and underprivileged positions in the labour market, representing part of the public discussion triggered off by the book of Geissler on the new social question.

3.2 Inequality and income redistribution

ALBERS, Willi (ed.): Öffentliche Finanzwirtschaft und Verteilung (Public Finance and Distribution). Schriften des Vereins für Socialpolitik Nr. 75, 2 vols. Berlin, Duncker & Humblot, 1974, 164 and 144 p. Proceedings of a 1973 conference of the 'Verein für Socialpolitik' including, among others, contributions on income and property distribution (by Hauser), and on redistributive effects of the tax system (by Albers).

DREISSIG, Wilhelmine (ed.): Öffentliche Finanzwirtschaft und Verteilung (Public Finance and Distribution). Schriften des Vereins für Socialpolitik Nr. 75, vols. 3-5, 1975, 82 p. 1976, 150 p. 1977, 202 p. Continues the two volumes above with proceedings of a further conference with several analyses of the distributional effects of various social security schemes.

GLATZER, Wolfgang: Einkommenspolitische Zielsetzungen und Einkommensverteilung (Goals of Income Policy and Income Distribution). *In* ZAPF, Wolfgang (ed.): Lebensbedingungen in der Bundesrepublik 1950-1975. Frankfurt, Campus, 1978, pp. 323-384. Summary of political and academic debates on income policy, with a rich set of indicators of income distribution in a longitudinal perspective.

GRÜSKE, Karl-Dieter: Die personale Budgetinzidenz (The Personal Incidence of the Budget). Göttingen, Vandenhoeck & Ruprecht, 1978, 373 p. Analysis of the incidence of the budget in the period 1963 to 1973 including a part on international comparisons.

HAKE, Wilfried: Umverteilungseffekte des Budgets - Eine Analyse der personalen Inzidenz (Redistributional Effects of the Budget - An Analysis of Personal Incidence). Göttingen, Vandenhoeck & Ruprecht, 1976, 259 p. Empirical analysis of the redistributional effects of taxation, public expenditure, and collective goods, based on 1963 data.

HANUSCH, Horst: Verteilung öffentlicher Leistungen. Eine Studie zur personalen Inzidenz (Distribution of Public Services. A Study on Personal Incidence). Göttingen, Vandenhoeck & Ruprecht, 1976, 259 p. Empirical analysis of the incidence of public services in 1963 and 1969, based on various model assumptions.

HAUSER, Richard, ENGEL, Bernhard (eds): Soziale Sicherung und Einkommensverteilung. Empirische Analyse für die Bundesrepublik Deutschland (Social Security and Income Distribution. Empirical Analysis for the Federal Republic). Frankfurt, Campus, 1984, 360 p. A reader with analyses of redistributive effects of the social security system written by collaborators of the major research project on social policy in Germany.

HEILMANN, Martin: Die Umverteilung der Einkommen durch den Staat 1960-1972 (The Redistribution of Income by the State 1960-1972). Schriften der Kommission für wirtschaftlichen und sozialen Wandel Nr. 71. Göttingen, Schwartz, 1976, 138 p. Analysis of the redistributive effects of public transfers based on national accounts statistics and on surveys of private household incomes held in 1962/63 and 1969.

KRUPP, Hans-Jürgen, GLATZER, Wolfgang (eds): Umverteilung im Sozialstaat. Empirische Einkommensanalysen für die Bundesrepublik (Redistribution in the Social State. Empirical Income Analyses for the Federal Republic of Germany). Frankfurt, Campus, 1978, 350 p. A reader with eight articles and an introduction by the editors, all based on empirical analyses.

KRUPP, Hans-Jürgen: Das monetäre Transfersystem in der Bundesrepublik Deutschland - Elemente einer Gesamtbilanz (The System of Cash Transfers in the Federal Republic of Germany - Elements of an All-inclusive Evaluation). *In* KRUPP, Hans-Jürgen, GLATZER, Wolfgang (eds): *op. cit.*, pp. 21-70. Assessment of the incidence of positive and negative cash transfers in various income groups, based on official microcensus data.

Von LÖFFELHOLZ, Hans Dietrich: Die personale Inzidenz des Sozialhaushalts. Eine theoretische und empirische Studie (The Personal Incidence of the Social Budget. A Theoretical and Empirical Study). Göttingen, Vandenhoeck & Ruprecht, 1979, 373 p. Re-analysis of an official sample survey on income and consumption carried out in 1973.

METZE, Ingolf: Soziale Sicherung und Einkommensverteilung (Social Security and Income Distribution). Berlin, Duncker & Humblot, 1974, 170 p. Analysis of the distributive effects of the financing of schemes.

MIEGEL, Meinhard: Die verkannte Revolution (1) Einkommen und Vermögen der privaten Haushalte (The Ignored Revolution (1) Income and Property of Private Households). Stuttgart, Bonn Aktuell, 1983, 202 p. Investigation into the standard of living pinpointing the 'revolutionary' upgrading of private household resources in the postwar period which in the author's opinion make welfare state schemes largely obsolete.

RECKTENWALD, Horst Claus: Gerechte Einkommens- und Vermögensverteilung (Fair Distribution of Income and Property). *In* LÖWENTHAL, Richard, SCHWARZ, Hans-Peter: Die zweite Republik. 25 Jahre Bundesrepublik Deutschland. Eine Bilanz. Stuttgart, Seewald, 3rd ed. 1979, pp. 762-790. Useful introduction to German income policy with basic statistics in time-series form and more detailed data for 1962/63 and 1969.

SCHMÄHL, Winfried: Einkommensverteilung im Rahmen von Einrichtungen der Sozialen Sicherung (Income Redistribution Under Social Security Schemes). *In* KUELP, Bernhard, HAAS, Heinz-Dieter (eds): Soziale Probleme der modernen Industriegesellschaft. Schriften des Vereins für Socialpolitik N.F. 92/II. Berlin, Duncker & Humblot, 1977, pp. 519-576. Discussion of redistributive effects of social security focusing on conceptual problems and the redistributional potential of given institutional regulations, with special emphasis on pension insurance.

SCHMIDT, Klaus-Dieter, SCHWARZ, Ursula, THIEBACH, Gerhard: Die Umverteilung des Volkseinkommens in der Bundesrepublik Deutschland 1955 und 1960 (The Redistribution of National Product in the Federal Republic 1955 and 1960). Tübingen, Mohr, 1965, 216 p. Estimates of the net effects of taxes and benefits, based on national accounts statistics; in some ways a predecessor of the transfer enquete commission report and as such useful for comparisons over time.

STOLZ, Irene: Einkommenumverteilung in der Bundesrepublik Deutschland (Income Redistribution in the Federal Republic). Frankfurt, Campus, 1983, 348 p. Detailed analysis of the redistributive effects of public transfers based on the official 1969 income and consumption survey.

ZEPPERNICK, Ralph: Staat und Einkommensverteilung (State and Income Distribution). Tübingen, Mohr, 1976, 115 p. Conceptual discussion of the types of state-provided income and their redistributive effects.

Appendix Tables

Contents

Table 1 Gross Domestic Product and Total Public Expenditure

Year	GDP (at market prices, in billion DM) at current prices	at constant (1970) prices	annual real growth rate	Deflators (base 1970) gross domestic product	cost of living	private consumption	public consumption	Total public expenditure (in billion DM) at current prices	as % of GDP	at constant (1970) prices GDP defl.	at constant (1970) prices publ. cons. defl.	annual real growth rate GDP defl.	annual real growth rate publ. cons. defl.	Year
1950	98.05	186.13		52.7	64.3			36.49	37.2	69.27				1950
1951	120.01	205.59	10.5	58.4	69.2	67.7	41.1	44.91	37.2	76.94	109.27	11.1		1951
1952	136.97	223.72	8.8	61.2	70.8	70.0	44.2	51.60	37.7	84.28	116.74	9.5	6.8	1952
1953	147.72	242.27	8.3	61.0	69.4	68.0	45.5	57.22	38.7	93.84	125.76	11.3	7.7	1953
1954	159.06	260.82	7.7	61.0	69.7	68.4	46.1	61.67	38.8	101.12	133.77	7.8	6.4	1954
1955	182.00	292.22	12.0	62.3	70.8	69.5	47.8	67.34	37.0	108.12	140.88	6.9	5.3	1955
1956	200.95	313.20	7.2	64.2	72.6	71.0	50.5	73.75	36.7	114.95	146.04	6.3	3.7	1956
1957	218.89	330.82	5.6	66.2	74.0	72.8	52.3	81.23	37.1	122.77	155.32	6.8	6.4	1957
1958	234.37	342.51	3.5	68.4	75.7	74.6	54.2	88.03	37.6	128.65	162.42	4.8	4.6	1958
1959	255.14	367.89	7.4	69.4	76.4	75.4	54.5	100.09	39.2	144.32	183.65	12.2	13.1	1959
1960	284.77	400.63	8.9	71.1	77.4	76.1	57.4	110.54	38.8	155.51	138.63	7.8	2.7	1960
1960	302.80	428.74		70.6		75.9	58.6	113.97	37.6	161.37	194.49			1960
1961	331.80	450.58	5.1	73.6	79.2	78.5	62.2	128.44	38.7	174.42	206.50	8.1	6.2	1961
1962	360.88	470.46	4.4	76.7	81.6	80.9	65.0	140.93	39.1	183.72	216.82	5.3	5.0	1962
1963	382.47	484.50	3.0	78.9	84.0	83.3	68.4	152.72	39.9	193.46	223.27	5.3	3.0	1963
1964	420.28	517.01	6.7	81.3	86.0	85.4	70.8	165.92	39.5	204.11	234.35	5.5	5.0	1964
1965	459.27	546.12	5.6	84.1	88.8	88.2	75.7	179.82	39.2	213.82	237.54	4.8	1.4	1965
1966	488.34	559.75	2.5	87.2	91.9	91.5	80.1	192.75	39.5	220.94	240.64	3.3	1.3	1966
1967	494.46	558.84	- 0.2	88.5	93.4	93.1	82.0	205.15	41.5	231.86	250.18	4.9	4.0	1967
1968	534.90	593.97	6.3	90.1	94.9	94.8	85.1	218.72	40.9	242.87	257.02	4.7	2.7	1968
1969	596.95	640.46	7.8	93.2	96.8	96.6	91.2	243.37	40.8	261.11	266.85	7.5	3.8	1969
1970	678.75	678.75	6.0	100.0	100.0	100.0	100.0	277.66	40.9	277.66	277.66	6.3	4.0	1970
1971	754.88	700.68	3.2	107.7	105.2	105.4	112.4	319.76	42.4	296.80	284.48	6.9	2.5	1971
1972	825.99	726.28	3.7	113.7	111.1	111.3	119.8	356.18	43.1	313.18	297.31	5.5	4.5	1972
1973	918.60	761.84	4.9	120.6	118.8	119.2	131.4	419.31	45.6	347.75	319.11	11.0	7.3	1973
1974	987.13	765.95	0.5	128.9	127.1	127.5	146.6	462.31	46.8	358.72	315.35	3.2	- 1.2	1974
1975	1 034.03	751.80	- 1.8	137.5	134.7	135.4	155.7	519.70	50.3	377.85	333.78	5.3	5.8	1975
1976	1 122.82	790.59	5.2	142.0	140.4	141.4	161.1	559.94	49.9	394.26	347.57	4.3	4.1	1976
1977	1 200.49	814.58	3.0	147.4	145.6	146.7	168.9	598.20	49.8	405.90	354.17	3.0	1.9	1977
1978	1 286.38	840.84	3.2	153.0	149.6	150.5	174.0	643.22	50.0	420.44	369.67	3.6	4.4	1978
1979*	1 393.94	878.32	4.5	158.7	155.8	156.4	182.6	686.18	49.2	432.36	375.78	2.8	1.7	1979
1980*	1 488.92	895.14	1.9	166.3	164.3	164.8	193.9	742.44	49.9	446.36	382.90	3.2	1.9	1980

Table 2 Public Expenditure by

Year	Economic Function: Total exp. at curr. pr. bill. DM	Per cent distribution: Publ. inv.	Publ. cons.	Trans-fer/ subs.	Cap. trans-fer	Inter. on debt	Purpose: Total exp. at curr. pr. bill. DM	Per cent distribution: De-fence	Publ. adm.	Educ. sc., cult.	Soc. sec. health recreat.	Housing and reg. planning	Econ. serv.	Other	Inter. on debt	Level of Government: Total exp. at curr. pr. bill. DM	Per cent distribution: Centr. gov.	Länder	Loc. gov.	Other	Year
1950	32.10	5.8	47.5	44.9	-	1.7	28.14	15.2	4.0	8.5	30.7	12.6	11.3			28.14	41.4	32.5	18.9	7.1	1950
1951	38.58	6.1	48.8	43.4	-	1.7	37.40	21.1	4.3	8.3	30.1	12.9	10.5	10.6	2.1	37.40	49.1	27.3	17.1	6.4	1951
1952	45.07	6.4	49.3	42.6	-	1.7	41.55	19.0	4.3	8.6	28.0	10.3	10.5			41.55	50.0	27.5	18.2	4.3	1952
1953	48.64	7.1	46.7	44.6	-	1.6	44.31	12.5	4.5	9.5	32.1	10.5	10.2	18.3	2.4	44.31	45.7	29.2	19.6	5.5	1953
1954	52.06	7.1	45.7	44.9	-	2.3	47.68	12.4	4.6	9.7	30.3	11.0	11.4			47.68	43.9	28.8	20.1	7.2	1954
1955	57.05	8.5	45.0	44.3	-	2.2	51.23	11.9	4.5	9.8	30.5	10.3	11.5	18.5	3.0	51.23	43.7	30.3	21.0	5.0	1955
1956	63.04	8.7	43.3	45.8	-	2.2	59.91	12.1	4.2	9.8	29.7	9.7	13.3			59.91	46.0	30.3	19.7	4.0	1956
1957	72.41	8.0	40.6	49.5	-	1.9	66.35	11.3	4.2	9.8	30.1	9.1	13.9	19.1	2.6	66.35	47.8	29.3	19.1	3.9	1957
1958	82.10	7.9	40.2	50.2	-	1.8	71.50	12.2	4.3	10.2	29.6	9.0	13.7	18.4	2.7	71.50	47.3	29.5	18.9	4.3	1958
1959	89.40	9.0	40.5	48.7	-	1.8	76.57	12.4	4.0	10.4	30.1	9.6	13.4	17.4	2.8	76.57	48.0	28.5	19.1	4.4	1959
1960	93.52	9.5	41.2	47.5	-	1.8															1960
1960	98.38	9.9	41.4	46.5	4.8	2.2	(64.56)	13.1	4.0	10.5	27.9	9.6	14.4	17.6	3.0	(64.78)	47.5	29.4	19.8	3.4	1960
1961	111.92	10.2	41.2	46.6	6.3	2.0	95.28	13.8	3.9	11.2	27.2	7.9	13.8	19.4	2.7	95.28	48.0	30.2	19.2	2.6	1961
1962	128.16	11.1	41.5	45.5	7.0	1.9	107.23	15.9	3.7	10.7	26.3	8.3	14.7	17.5	2.8	107.23	46.9	31.1	18.7	3.4	1962
1963	138.51	12.4	43.1	42.6	4.6	1.9	116.77	16.6	3.9	11.1	25.0	7.7	15.7	17.5	2.4	117.14	46.8	31.2	18.9	3.2	1963
1964	151.67	13.8	41.2	43.2	4.9	1.9	128.11	14.8	3.8	11.9	26.2	7.8	15.9	17.1	2.4	128.11	45.7	31.6	19.8	2.8	1964
1965	168.50	12.4	41.6	44.1	4.7	1.9	140.58	13.4	3.8	12.4	26.8	7.3	15.3	18.4	2.5	140.58	46.2	31.7	19.7	2.4	1965
1966	179.79	11.7	42.3	43.6	4.1	2.3	146.72	13.3	3.9	12.9	26.8	6.8	14.6	18.6	3.0	146.72	46.4	32.3	19.7	1.7	1966
1967	190.51	9.9	42.3	45.0	4.1	2.7	155.94	13.5	3.8	12.8	27.0	5.9	14.7	18.7	3.6	155.94	48.9	31.1	18.2	1.8	1967
1968	202.88	10.2	41.2	45.8	3.9	2.7	159.19	11.0	4.0	13.4	27.3	5.8	15.8	19.1	3.6	159.14	47.4	31.4	19.0	2.1	1968
1969	226.44	10.5	41.6	45.2	4.7	2.6	174.72	11.4	4.0	14.0	26.2	5.3	16.2	19.3	3.6	174.72	46.9	31.8	19.5	1.9	1969
1970	257.79	12.0	41.9	43.5	4.8	2.6	196.33	10.1	4.0	15.1	25.8	5.5	16.3	19.7	3.5	196.33	44.5	33.1	20.9	1.6	1970
1971	296.51	11.3	43.6	42.6	5.2	2.5	225.18	9.7	4.1	16.6	25.7	5.6	14.2	20.7	3.4	225.18	43.5	33.1	22.1	1.3	1971
1972	332.22	10.2	43.4	43.9	5.2	2.6	251.27	9.9	4.1	16.9	25.9	5.6	13.4	20.6	3.5	251.27	44.4	32.7	21.7	1.1	1972
1973	376.78	9.3	44.2	43.7	5.0	2.7	277.67	9.8	4.3	17.3	24.7	5.7	12.8	21.6	3.8	277.67	43.8	33.7	21.6	0.8	1973
1974	433.58	9.4	44.7	43.0	5.1	2.8	316.50	9.7	4.4	17.7	26.0	5.8	12.0	20.4	4.0	316.50	42.3	34.8	22.0	0.8	1974
1975	493.35	8.3	43.6	45.2	4.6	2.9	360.51	9.0	4.2	17.5		5.3	10.8		4.1	406.31	39.1	36.0	24.9	-	1975
1976	528.64	7.6	43.0	46.1	5.4	3.3	376.76	8.9	4.3	17.1		5.8	10.0		4.8	423.67	39.0	36.4	24.6	-	1976
1977	564.31	7.1	42.4	46.9	5.4	3.6	395.17	8.7	4.4	17.3		5.4	9.9		5.3	441.64	39.0	36.6	24.4	-	1977
1978	604.59	7.3	42.5	46.6	4.9	3.6	431.83	8.5	4.3	17.0		5.6	10.5		5.1	482.80	39.3	36.6	24.2	-	1978
1979	653.04	7.8	42.7	45.9	4.9	3.7	467.04	8.3	4.3	17.2		6.0	10.9		5.4	523.06	38.9	36.7	24.4	-	1979
1980	705.72	8.3	43.0	44.6	4.8	4.1	505.93	8.1	4.4	17.4		6.2	10.7		5.8	566.73	38.1	36.7	25.2	-	1980

Table 3

Social Expenditure

Year	Total I ILO defin.	Total II German official statistics	Total III German official statistics	Total IV Florence definition	Total V Florence definition	At current prices (in million DM): Social security Income maint.	Social security Services/ Ben. in k.	Health	Housing	Education	At constant (1970) prices (in million DM): Total V	Social security Income maint.	Social security Services/ Ben. in k.	Health	Housing	Education	Year
1950	14 501			18 273	18 783	11 997	1 254	1 760	1 675	2 097	33 575	18 650	1 949	4 706	2 671	5 607	1950
1951	16 492			21 477	22 089	13 571	1 433	2 100	2 406	2 579	36 384	19 600	2 070	5 005	3 563	6 146	1951
1952	19 323			25 041	25 755	15 904	1 679	2 442	2 668	3 062	40 858	22 468	2 372	5 412	3 821	6 786	1952
1953	20 528			27 243	28 059	16 994	1 873	2 739	2 909	3 544	45 003	24 493	2 700	5 897	4 289	7 630	1953
1954	21 596			30 931	31 849	19 049	2 441	3 141	3 348	3 870	50 653	27 345	3 504	6 674	4 908	8 223	1954
1955	25 802			33 704	34 724	21 209	2 648	3 498	3 173	4 196	54 047	29 962	3 741	7 168	4 577	8 598	1955
1956	28 939			37 905	39 321	24 058	2 803	3 948	3 713	4 799	59 202	33 132	3 860	7 658	5 243	9 308	1956
1957	34 834			44 618	46 430	29 613	2 918	4 538	3 960	5 401	68 019	40 008	3 942	8 499	5 454	10 115	1957
1958	39 641			50 070	52 278	33 743	3 230	5 230	4 067	6 008	74 616	44 573	4 267	9 452	5 466	10 858	1958
1959	41 517			53 149	55 753	35 217	3 426	5 774	4 800	5 536	79 084	46 093	4 484	10 378	6 383	11 747	1959
1960	45 424			58 666	61 666	38 428	3 912	6 623	5 291	7 412	85 632	49 656	5 055	11 302	6 971	12 648	1960
1960	46 760	58 171	62 772	64 354	67 354	42 319	4 999	7 333	5 291	7 412	93 277	54 684	6 460	12 514	6 971	12 648	1960
1961	51 704	64 694	69 755	70 385	73 885	47 426	5 448	8 382	4 433	8 196	99 049	59 871	6 878	13 476	5 647	13 177	1961
1962	56 349	70 708	76 289	77 320	81 320	51 762	5 900	9 343	5 129	9 186	105 509	63 433	7 230	14 374	6 340	14 132	1962
1963	60 751	75 411	81 500	83 290	87 290	54 976	6 197	10 296	5 273	10 548	109 639	65 456	7 378	15 053	6 330	15 421	1963
1964	67 788	82 531	89 111	91 749	95 749	59 869	6 509	11 456	5 616	12 299	117 352	69 652	7 573	16 181	6 576	17 371	1964
1965	76 271	93 009	112 679	102 856	107 356	66 770	7 173	13 356	5 774	14 283	126 360	75 222	8 081	17 643	6 546	18 868	1965
1965	76 271	93 009	112 679	102 632	107 132	65 760	7 809	13 506	5 774	14 283	126 137	74 084	8 797	17 841	6 546	18 868	1965
1966	83 838	103 075	124 651	112 258	117 258	71 758	8 435	15 944	5 642	15 479	132 701	78 122	9 183	19 905	6 166	19 325	1966
1967	91 336	111 367	133 376	121 057	125 557	77 176	9 323	17 481	5 261	16 316	139 479	82 631	9 982	21 318	5 651	19 898	1967
1968	97 699	119 129	141 813	128 311	133 311	82 389	9 237	19 360	4 866	17 459	144 904	86 777	9 729	22 750	5 133	20 516	1968
1969	106 404	130 263	153 587	139 800	145 800	89 391	10 132	21 617	4 356	20 304	153 321	92 375	10 470	23 703	4 509	22 263	1969
1970	115 716	149 966	174 736	155 428	167 928	101 567	12 027	24 720	4 830	24 784	167 928	101 567	12 027	24 720	4 830	24 784	1970
1971	131 424	172 800	198 786	179 947	193 447	111 612	14 279	30 490	5 779	31 287	180 117	106 098	13 574	27 126	5 483	27 835	1971
1972	152 726	196 544	223 960	204 839	219 839	124 991	16 297	35 726	7 174	35 651	193 203	112 508	14 669	29 821	6 446	29 759	1972
1973	173 665	223 354	252 634	232 071	250 071	140 835	18 423	42 660	7 726	40 427	203 747	118 528	15 505	32 466	6 482	30 766	1973
1974	201 997	258 388	288 937	273 299	292 869	160 520	22 383	51 306	9 309	49 351	219 859	126 288	17 610	34 997	7 301	33 664	1974
1975	243 416	301 940	330 288	319 974	338 534	189 101	25 812	60 747	9 044	53 830	239 828	140 396	19 164	39 015	6 679	34 573	1975
1976	262 516	324 394	354 947	341 348	361 758	204 011	26 656	66 479	9 691	54 921	246 445	145 256	18 979	41 266	6 854	34 091	1976
1977	279 738	346 442	380 605	362 073	383 543	218 047	29 325	69 875	8 885	57 411	251 263	149 710	20 134	41 371	6 057	33 991	1977
1978		365 591	403 479	384 552	408 662	231 936	30 454	74 807	10 138	61 327	260 394	155 060	20 360	42 993	6 736	35 245	1978
1979		384 874	425 091	409 029	434 829	243 639	33 161	80 356	11 379	66 294	265 299	156 421	21 290	44 007	7 276	36 306	1979
1980		405 730	449 473	435 132	462 282	255 243	36 720	85 130	12 260	72 929	266 628	155 327	22 346	43 904	7 439	37 612	1980

Table 4 Social Expenditure

Year	Total ILO defin.	Total Off. German defin.	As % of gross domestic product: Total Florence defin.	Social Income maint.	sec. Serv.	Health	Hous-ing	Educa-tion	As % of public expenditure: Total Florence defin.	Social Income maint.	sec. Serv.	Health	Hous-ing	Educa-tion	As % of social expenditure: Social Income maint.	sec. Serv.	Health	Hous-ing	Educa-tion	Year
1950	14.8		19.2	12.2	1.3	1.8	1.7	2.1	50.8	32.4	3.4	4.8	4.5	5.7	63.9	6.7	9.4	8.9	11.2	1950
1951	13.7		18.4	11.3	1.2	1.7	2.0	2.1	48.5	29.8	3.1	4.6	5.3	5.7	61.4	6.5	9.5	10.9	11.7	1951
1952	14.1		18.8	11.6	1.2	1.8	1.9	2.2	49.2	30.4	3.2	4.7	5.1	5.9	61.8	6.5	9.5	10.4	11.9	1952
1953	13.9		19.0	11.5	1.3	1.9	2.0	2.4	48.3	29.3	3.2	4.7	5.0	6.1	60.6	6.7	9.8	10.4	12.6	1953
1954	13.6		20.0	12.0	1.5	2.0	2.1	2.4	50.9	30.4	3.9	5.0	5.3	6.2	59.8	7.7	9.9	10.5	12.2	1954
1955	14.2		19.1	11.7	1.5	1.9	1.7	2.3	50.8	31.0	3.9	5.1	4.6	6.1	61.1	7.6	10.1	9.1	12.1	1955
1956	14.4		19.6	12.0	1.4	2.0	1.8	2.4	52.3	32.0	3.7	5.3	4.9	6.4	61.2	7.1	10.0	9.4	12.2	1956
1957	15.9		21.2	13.5	1.3	2.1	1.8	2.5	55.9	35.7	3.5	5.5	4.8	6.5	63.8	6.3	9.8	8.5	11.6	1957
1958	16.9		22.3	14.4	1.4	2.2	1.7	2.6	57.9	37.4	3.6	5.8	4.5	6.7	64.5	6.2	10.0	7.8	11.5	1958
1959	16.3		21.9	13.8	1.3	2.3	1.9	2.6	54.3	34.3	3.3	5.6	4.7	6.4	63.2	6.1	10.4	8.6	11.7	1959
1960	16.0		21.7	13.5	1.4	2.3	1.9	2.6	54.3	33.8	3.4	5.8	4.7	6.5	62.3	6.3	10.7	8.6	12.0	1960
1960	15.4	19.2	22.2	14.0	1.7	2.4	1.7	2.4	57.6	36.2	4.3	6.3	4.5	6.3	62.8	7.4	10.9	7.9	11.0	1960
1961	15.6	19.5	22.3	14.3	1.6	2.5	1.3	2.5	56.0	35.9	4.1	6.4	3.4	6.2	64.2	7.4	11.3	6.0	11.1	1961
1962	15.6	19.6	22.5	14.3	1.6	2.6	1.4	2.5	56.1	35.7	4.1	6.4	3.5	6.3	63.7	7.3	11.5	6.3	11.3	1962
1963	15.9	19.7	22.8	14.4	1.6	2.7	1.4	2.8	55.7	35.1	4.0	6.6	3.4	6.7	63.0	7.1	11.8	6.0	12.1	1963
1964	16.1	19.6	22.8	14.2	1.5	2.7	1.3	2.9	56.3	35.2	3.8	6.7	3.3	7.2	62.5	6.8	12.0	5.9	12.8	1964
1965	16.6	20.3	23.4	14.3	1.6	2.9	1.3	3.1	58.2	36.2	3.9	7.2	3.1	7.7	62.2	6.7	12.4	5.4	13.3	1965
1965	16.6	20.3	23.3	14.5	1.7	2.9	1.3	3.1	58.1	35.7	4.2	7.3	3.1	7.7	61.4	7.3	12.6	5.4	13.3	1965
1966	17.2	21.1	24.0	14.7	1.7	3.3	1.2	3.2	59.3	36.3	4.3	8.1	2.9	7.8	61.2	7.2	13.6	4.8	13.2	1966
1967	18.5	22.5	25.4	15.6	1.9	3.5	1.1	3.3	59.9	36.8	4.4	8.3	2.5	7.8	61.5	7.4	13.9	4.2	13.0	1967
1968	18.3	22.3	24.9	15.4	1.7	3.6	0.9	3.3	59.6	36.8	4.1	8.7	2.2	7.8	61.8	6.9	14.5	3.7	13.1	1968
1969	17.8	21.8	24.4	15.0	1.7	3.6	0.7	3.4	58.5	35.8	4.1	8.7	1.7	8.1	61.3	6.9	14.8	3.0	13.9	1969
1970	17.0	22.1	24.7	15.0	1.8	3.6	0.7	3.7	57.9	35.0	4.1	8.5	1.7	8.5	60.5	7.2	14.7	2.9	14.8	1970
1971	17.4	22.9	25.6	14.8	1.9	4.0	0.8	4.1	58.0	33.5	4.3	9.1	1.7	9.4	57.7	7.4	15.8	3.0	16.2	1971
1972	18.5	23.8	26.6	15.1	2.0	4.3	0.9	4.3	59.2	33.7	4.4	9.6	1.9	9.6	56.9	7.4	16.3	3.3	16.2	1972
1973	18.9	24.3	27.2	15.3	2.0	4.6	0.8	4.4	57.2	32.2	4.2	9.8	1.8	9.2	56.3	7.4	17.0	3.1	16.2	1973
1974	20.5	26.2	29.2	16.3	2.3	5.2	0.9	5.0	60.8	33.3	4.6	10.6	1.9	10.2	54.8	7.6	17.5	3.2	16.9	1974
1975	23.5	29.2	32.7	18.3	2.5	5.9	0.9	5.2	62.9	35.1	4.8	11.3	1.7	10.0	55.9	7.6	17.9	2.7	15.9	1975
1976	23.4	28.9	32.2	18.2	2.4	5.9	0.9	4.9	62.3	35.2	4.6	11.5	1.7	9.5	56.4	7.4	18.4	2.7	15.2	1976
1977	23.3	28.9	31.9	18.2	2.4	5.8	0.7	4.8	61.9	35.2	4.7	11.3	1.4	9.3	56.9	7.6	18.2	2.3	15.0	1977
1978		28.4	31.8	18.0	2.4	5.8	0.8	4.8	61.2	34.8	4.6	11.2	1.5	9.2	56.8	7.5	18.3	2.5	15.0	1978
1979		27.6	31.2	17.5	2.4	5.8	0.8	4.8	61.1	34.2	4.7	11.3	1.6	9.3	56.0	7.6	18.5	2.6	15.2	1979
1980		27.2	31.0	17.1	2.5	5.7	0.8	4.9	60.1	33.2	4.8	11.1	1.6	9.5	55.2	7.9	18.4	2.7	15.8	1980

Table 5

Expenditure on Social Security Programmes

Social security expenditure at current prices (in million DM)

Year	Pensions	Occup. injur.	Sickness insur.b)	Unempl. insur.	Family allow.	Social assist.	War conseq.	Other
1950	5 983	584	1 099	1 470	159	934	2 947	
1951	7 048	657	1 313	1 551	183	904	3 193	
1952	8 767	822	1 523	1 636	231	832	3 502	
1953	9 374	884	1 774	1 601	281	943	3 326	
1954	10 808	982	1 953	2 333	303	1 191	3 727	
1955	12 235	1 040	2 245	1 948	786	1 246	4 151	
1956	14 097	1 129	2 826	1 724	857	1 348	4 653	
1957	18 117	1 470	3 894	1 685	913	1 368	4 850	
1958	21 192	1 654	4 717	1 925	1 022	1 428	4 787	
1959	22 487	1 648	5 237	1 583	1 218	1 463	4 743	
1960	25 128	1 753	6 119	1 153	1 361	1 781	5 045	
1960	25 739	1 753	6 119	1 153	3 084	1 781	7 160	529
1961	28 302	2 055	7 028	978	3 919	1 855	8 131	606
1962	30 728	2 163	7 903	1 219	4 630	1 942	8 400	677
1963	33 350	2 309	8 003	1 722	4 869	2 206	7 955	759
1964	36 388	2 838	7 961	1 419	5 878	2 283	8 664	947
1965	40 454	3 140	8 960	1 439	7 136	2 350	9 192	1 272
1965	40 320	3 091	8 724	1 377	7 114	2 184	9 487	1 272
1966	44 335	3 415	9 638	1 395	7 821	2 418	9 773	1 398
1967	49 090	3 569	8 682	2 807	7 768	2 656	10 531	1 396
1968	52 954	3 759	9 607	2 733	7 843	2 780	10 531	1 369
1969	58 933	4 047	10 908	2 576	8 409	2 984	10 164	1 502
1970	64 594	4 124	15 923	3 593	9 059	3 461	11 033	1 807
1971	71 189	4 437	17 538	4 409	10 006	4 173	11 695	2 364
1972	81 164	4 971	19 506	5 205	10 191	4 979	12 354	2 918
1973	92 070	5 519	22 943	6 043	10 690	5 808	12 964	3 221
1974	106 405	6 214	24 657	8 972	11 259	7 452	14 092	3 852
1975	118 875	6 845	24 015	15 785	21 388	8 612	15 115	4 278
1976	132 234	7 415	25 933	13 954	21 039	9 805	15 639	4 648
1977	146 149	7 967	27 141	13 474	20 720	10 609	16 295	5 017
1978	153 130	8 473	30 193	14 647	22 615	11 497	16 462	5 373
1979	160 140	8 971	32 753	15 562	24 222	12 533	16 782	5 837
1980	158 558	9 460	34 963	17 203	24 541	13 944	16 903	6 391

Income maintenance expenditure at current prices (in million DM)

Pensions	Occup. injur.	Sickness insur.	Unempl. insur.	Family allow.	Social assist.	War conseq.	Other	Year
5 559	431	1 099	1 393	169	621	2 725		1950
6 664	469	1 313	1 471	183	556	2 915		1951
8 224	594	1 523	1 550	231	505	3 277		1952
9 276	613	1 774	1 511	281	546	2 993		1953
10 267	672	1 953	1 791	303	711	3 352		1954
11 649	697	2 245	1 350	771	730	3 767		1955
13 401	735	2 826	1 198	842	802	4 254		1956
17 327	1 051	3 394	1 179	898	806	4 458		1957
20 215	1 182	4 717	1 421	1 005	814	4 388		1958
21 395	1 157	5 237	1 086	1 200	315	4 327		1959
23 712	1 220	6 119	633	1 338	872	4 534		1960
23 848	1 220	6 119	633	3 018	872	6 522	87	1960
26 155	1 457	7 028	482	3 827	886	7 472	119	1961
28 354	1 509	7 903	714	4 516	951	7 692	123	1962
30 776	1 625	8 003	1 215	4 751	1 247	7 233	126	1963
33 810	2 145	7 961	871	5 756	1 215	7 892	219	1964
37 587	2 370	8 960	852	7 015	1 240	8 368	378	1965
37 239	2 357	8 724	851	7 025	834	8 352	378	1965
41 135	2 612	9 638	784	7 730	905	8 558	396	1956
45 607	2 748	8 682	2 125	7 673	974	9 046	321	1967
49 743	2 923	9 507	1 954	7 745	995	9 164	257	1968
55 394	3 124	10 903	1 589	8 302	1 079	8 727	268	1969
60 453	3 050	15 923	2 162	8 943	1 269	9 475	292	1970
66 538	3 263	17 538	2 415	9 879	1 568	9 979	432	1971
75 759	3 631	19 506	3 029	10 061	1 923	10 472	610	1972
85 791	4 046	22 943	3 778	10 549	2 272	10 913	543	1973
98 780	4 411	24 657	6 212	11 104	2 930	11 904	522	1974
110 759	4 888	24 015	11 615	21 263	3 358	12 698	505	1975
123 948	5 348	25 933	10 464	20 908	3 808	13 136	466	1976
136 894	5 725	27 141	9 487	20 592	4 061	13 717	430	1977
144 532	6 079	30 193	9 868	22 475	4 557	13 822	410	1978
151 197	6 400	32 753	9 912	24 082	4 812	14 015	468	1979
158 839	6 734	34 963	10 699	24 399	5 041	13 967	601	1980

Table 6

Expenditure on Income Maintenance Programmes

Year	At constant (1970) prices (in million DM) Pensions	Occup. injur.	Sickness benef.	Unempl. benef.	Family allow.	Social assist.	Benefits to war victims	Other	As % of total expenditure on income maintenance Pensions	Occup. injur.	Sickness benef.	Unempl. benef.	Family allow.	Social assist.	Benefits to war victims	Other	Year
1950	8 642	670	1 708	2 166	263	965	4 236		46.3	3.6	9.2	11.6	1.4	5.2	22.7		1950
1951	9 624	677	1 896	2 124	264	803	4 210		49.1	3.5	9.7	10.8	1.3	4.1	21.5		1951
1952	11 618	839	2 152	2 190	326	713	4 629		51.7	3.7	9.6	9.7	1.5	3.2	20.6		1952
1953	13 369	884	2 557	2 178	405	787	4 314		54.6	3.6	10.4	8.9	1.7	3.2	17.6		1953
1954	14 738	965	2 804	2 571	435	1 021	4 812		53.9	3.5	10.3	9.4	1.6	3.7	17.6		1954
1955	15 457	985	3 172	1 907	1 089	1 031	5 322		54.9	3.3	10.6	6.4	3.6	3.4	17.8		1955
1956	18 456	1 012	3 692	1 650	1 160	1 104	5 859		55.7	3.1	11.7	5.0	3.5	3.3	17.7		1956
1957	23 410	1 420	5 261	1 593	1 213	1 089	6 023		58.5	3.5	13.1	4.0	3.0	2.7	15.1		1957
1958	26 703	1 561	6 231	1 877	1 329	1 075	5 796		59.9	3.5	14.0	4.2	3.0	2.4	13.0		1958
1959	28 002	1 514	6 854	1 421	1 571	1 067	5 663		60.8	3.3	14.9	3.1	3.4	2.3	12.3		1959
1960	30 640	1 576	7 907	818	1 729	1 127	5 859		61.7	3.2	15.9	1.6	3.5	2.3	11.8		1960
1960	30 815	1 576	7 907	818	3 900	1 127	8 428	112	56.4	2.9	14.5	1.5	7.1	2.1	15.4	0.2	1960
1961	33 018	1 839	8 872	608	4 831	1 118	9 433	150	55.1	3.1	14.8	1.0	8.1	1.9	15.8	0.3	1961
1962	34 747	1 849	9 685	875	5 534	1 165	9 426	151	54.8	2.9	15.3	1.4	8.7	1.8	14.9	0.2	1962
1963	36 643	1 935	9 529	1 447	5 657	1 485	8 612	150	56.0	3.0	14.6	2.2	8.6	2.3	13.2	0.2	1963
1964	39 335	2 495	9 262	1 013	6 697	1 414	9 182	255	56.5	3.6	13.3	1.5	9.6	2.0	13.2	0.4	1964
1965	42 345	2 670	10 094	959	7 903	1 397	9 427	426	56.3	3.5	13.4	1.3	10.5	1.9	12.5	0.6	1965
1965	41 953	2 655	9 828	959	7 914	940	9 409	426	56.6	3.6	13.3	1.3	10.7	1.3	12.7	0.6	1965
1966	44 783	2 844	10 493	854	8 416	935	9 317	431	57.3	3.6	13.4	1.1	10.8	1.3	11.9	0.6	1966
1967	48 830	2 942	9 296	2 275	8 215	1 043	9 685	344	59.1	3.6	11.2	2.8	9.9	1.3	11.7	0.4	1967
1968	52 392	3 079	10 119	2 058	8 157	1 049	9 652	271	60.4	3.5	11.7	2.4	9.4	1.2	11.1	0.3	1968
1969	57 243	3 228	11 272	1 642	8 579	1 115	9 018	277	62.0	3.5	12.2	1.8	9.3	1.2	9.8	0.3	1969
1970	60 453	3 050	15 923	2 162	8 943	1 269	9 475	292	59.5	3.0	15.7	2.1	8.8	1.2	9.3	0.3	1970
1971	63 251	3 102	16 672	2 296	9 391	1 491	9 486	411	59.6	2.9	15.7	2.2	8.9	1.4	8.9	0.4	1971
1972	68 193	3 268	17 558	2 726	9 056	1 731	9 426	549	60.6	2.9	15.6	2.4	8.0	1.5	8.4	0.5	1972
1973	72 202	3 405	19 309	3 180	8 878	1 912	9 184	457	60.9	2.9	16.3	2.7	7.5	1.6	7.7	0.4	1973
1974	77 714	3 470	19 399	4 887	8 736	2 305	9 365	411	61.5	2.7	15.4	3.9	6.9	1.8	7.4	0.3	1974
1975	82 232	3 629	17 830	8 623	15 787	2 493	9 428	375	58.6	2.6	12.7	6.1	11.2	1.8	6.7	0.3	1975
1976	88 251	3 808	18 464	7 450	14 886	2 711	9 353	332	60.8	2.6	12.7	5.1	10.2	1.9	6.4	0.2	1976
1977	93 991	3 931	18 635	6 514	14 138	2 788	9 418	295	62.8	2.6	12.4	4.4	9.4	1.9	6.3	0.2	1977
1978	96 626	4 064	20 185	6 597	15 026	3 047	9 241	274	62.3	2.6	13.0	4.3	9.7	2.0	6.0	0.2	1978
1979	97 072	4 109	21 028	6 364	15 461	3 089	8 998	300	62.1	2.6	13.4	4.1	9.9	2.0	5.8	0.2	1979
1980	96 661	4 098	21 277	6 511	14 848	3 068	8 500	366	62.2	2.6	13.7	4.2	9.6	2.0	5.5	0.2	1980

Table 7

Expenditure on Pension Programmes
At current prices (in million DM)

Year	All systems: Total I	Total II	Admin./ Gen. serv.	Benefits in kind	Cash benefits	Social insurance: Total I	Total II	Admin./ Gen. serv.	Benefits in kind	Cash ben. A	Cash ben. B	Old age/ inval.	Inval. only	Surv.	Year
1950	6 169	5 883	113	211	5 559	3 919	3 633	113	211	3 309	3 564				1950
1951	7 449	7 048	120	264	6 664	4 977	4 576	120	264	4 192	4 486				1951
1952	9 258	8 767	255	288	8 224	6 137	5 646	255	288	5 103	5 546				1952
1953	10 390	9 874	291	307	9 276	6 598	6 082	291	307	5 484	5 982				1953
1954	11 363	10 808	199	342	10 267	7 213	6 658	199	342	6 117	6 086				1954
1955	12 843	12 235	232	354	11 649	8 323	7 715	232	354	7 129	7 088	4 985		2 103	1955
1956	14 809	14 097	299	397	13 401	9 925	9 213	299	397	8 517	8 468				1956
1957	19 093	18 117	312	478	17 327	13 928	12 952	311	478	12 163	12 166				1957
1958	23 244	21 192	387	590	20 215	17 363	15 311	382	590	14 339	14 299				1958
1959	24 615	22 487	410	682	21 395	18 567	16 439	404	682	15 353	15 247				1959
1960	27 900	25 739	913	978	23 848	20 596	18 435	470	941	17 024	16 645	11 260		5 385	1960
1961	30 694	28 302	1 028	1 119	26 155	22 547	20 155	533	1 077	18 545	18 028				1961
1962	33 998	30 728	1 102	1 273	28 354	25 059	21 789	556	1 226	20 007	19 496				1962
1963	36 842	33 350	1 201	1 373	30 776	26 972	23 480	602	1 322	21 556	20 999				1963
1964	39 692	36 388	1 273	1 305	33 810	29 099	25 795	631	1 252	23 912	23 281				1964
1965	45 136	40 454	1 463	1 404	37 587	33 463	28 783	761	1 342	26 680	26 060	17 796		8 264	1965
1965	42 838	40 320	1 477	1 604	37 239	31 165	28 649	775	1 542	26 332	26 060	17 796		8 264	1965
1966	47 170	44 335	1 389	1 811	41 135	34 605	31 774	635	1 741	29 398	29 098	18 860		10 238	1966
1967	52 512	49 090	1 494	1 989	45 607	39 095	35 677	685	1 909	33 083	32 745	22 446		10 299	1967
1968	57 022	52 954	1 569	1 642	49 743	42 812	38 749	720	1 549	36 480	36 169	24 864		11 305	1968
1969	63 442	58 933	1 759	1 790	55 394	47 483	42 979	770	1 683	40 526	40 193	27 705	5 649	12 489	1969
1970	70 268	64 594	2 109	2 032	60 453	52 162	46 494	871	1 910	43 713	43 508	30 028		13 480	1970
1971	78 331	71 189	2 290	2 361	66 538	57 474	50 339	1 008	2 210	47 121	46 893	32 387		14 506	1971
1972	89 400	81 164	2 577	2 828	75 759	66 660	58 433	1 188	2 662	54 583	53 024	36 652		16 372	1972
1973	101 888	92 070	2 991	3 298	85 791	76 198	66 391	1 434	3 083	61 874	61 612	42 991	7 730	18 598	1973
1974	117 854	106 405	3 755	3 870	98 780	88 777	77 340	2 017	3 604	71 719	71 274	50 052	8 501	21 222	1974
1975	132 836	118 875	3 976	4 140	110 759	101 072	87 126	2 113	3 783	81 230	80 498	56 702	9 307	23 796	1975
1976	148 515	132 234	4 288	4 058	123 948	114 672	98 406	2 232	3 680	92 494	91 619	64 345	10 508	27 274	1976
1977	161 334	146 149	4 943	4 252	136 894	125 259	110 089	2 817	3 859	103 353	102 564	72 735	11 780	29 829	1977
1978	166 901	153 130	4 559	4 039	144 532	129 256	115 500	2 355	3 652	109 493	108 716	77 149	13 002	31 557	1978
1979	174 569	160 140	4 701	4 242	151 197	134 807	120 395	2 354	3 826	114 215	113 587	80 591	13 591	32 996	1979
1980	183 623	168 558	5 051	4 668	158 839	141 543	126 494	2 560	4 218	119 716	119 544	84 946		34 598	1980

Table 8 Expenditure on Pension Programmes II
At current prices (in million DM)

Occupational Injuries Insurance
At current prices (in million DM)

Year	Farmers' pensions Total I	Total II	Admin./ Gen. serv.	Ben. in kind	Cash ben.	Civil servants' pensions Total	Admin./ Gen. serv.	Ben. in kind	Cash ben.	Civil service supplementary schemes Total I II	Admin./ Gen. serv.	Ben. in kind	Cash ben.	Occupational Injuries Insurance Total I	Total II	Admin./ Gen. serv.	Ben. in kind	Cash ben.	Year
1950						2 250	0	0	2 250					584	584	70	83	431	1950
1951						2 472	0	0	2 472					657	657	85	103	469	1951
1952						3 121	0	0	3 121					822	822	100	128	594	1952
1953						3 792	0	0	3 792					884	884	113	158	613	1953
1954						4 150	0	0	4 150					982	982	128	182	672	1954
1955						4 520	0	0	4 520					1 040	1 040	139	204	697	1955
1956						4 884	0	0	4 884					1 129	1 129	159	235	735	1956
1957	4	4	1	0	3	5 161	0	0	5 161					1 470	1 470	171	248	1 051	1957
1958	160	160	5	0	155	5 721	0	0	5 721					1 654	1 654	184	288	1 182	1958
1959	210	210	6	0	204	5 838	0	0	5 838					1 648	1 648	188	303	1 157	1959
1960	181	181	5	0	176	6 782	407	34	6 341	341	31	3	307	1 754	1 753	206	327	1 220	1960
1961	180	180	6	0	174	7 585	455	38	7 092	382	34	4	344	2 056	2 055	233	365	1 457	1961
1962	183	183	8	0	175	8 336	500	42	7 794	420	38	5	378	2 165	2 163	253	401	1 509	1962
1963	270	270	10	0	260	9 140	548	46	8 546	460	41	5	414	2 336	2 309	275	409	1 625	1963
1964	326	326	11	0	315	9 775	587	48	9 140	492	44	5	443	2 937	2 838	305	388	2 145	1964
1965	489	489	14	0	475	10 648	640	55	9 953	536	48	7	479	3 240	3 140	335	435	2 370	1965
1965	488	487	13	0	474	10 648	640	55	9 953	536	48	7	479	3 258	3 091	290	444	2 357	1965
1966	658	656	19	3	634	11 308	680	60	10 568	599	55	7	535	3 602	3 415	311	492	2 612	1966
1967	701	699	19	9	671	12 018	720	65	11 233	698	70	6	620	3 746	3 569	332	489	2 748	1967
1968	723	721	20	15	686	12 596	750	70	11 776	891	79	8	801	3 961	3 759	368	468	2 923	1968
1969	836	834	23	22	789	14 121	840	75	13 206	1 002	126	10	873	4 260	4 047	423	500	3 124	1969
1970	909	906	26	34	846	15 839	950	80	14 809	1 358	262	8	1 085	4 280	4 124	500	574	3 050	1970
1971	967	963	31	50	882	18 321	1 075	90	17 156	1 569	176	11	1 379	4 610	4 437	516	658	3 263	1971
1972	1 108	1 103	38	60	1 005	19 779	1 180	95	18 504	1 853	171	11	1 667	5 165	4 971	619	721	3 631	1972
1973	1 468	1 461	55	100	1 316	22 086	1 320	105	20 661	2 136	182	10	1 940	5 727	5 519	671	802	4 046	1973
1974	1 658	1 650	48	125	1 477	24 806	1 483	129	23 194	2 613	207	12	2 390	6 440	6 214	767	1 036	4 411	1974
1975	1 878	1 868	47	154	1 667	26 682	1 592	190	24 900	3 204	224	13	2 962	7 185	6 845	830	1 127	4 888	1975
1976	2 080	2 071	52	163	1 856	28 240	1 689	200	26 351	3 523	255	15	3 247	7 816	7 415	866	1 201	5 348	1976
1977	2 291	2 281	57	177	2 047	29 919	1 788	200	27 931	3 865	281	16	3 563	8 397	7 967	955	1 287	5 725	1977
1978	2 505	2 496	57	170	2 269	31 235	1 864	200	29 171	3 905	283	17	3 599	8 916	8 473	1 010	1 384	6 079	1978
1979	2 641	2 630	76	198	2 356	32 987	1 972	200	30 815	4 134	299	18	3 811	9 450	8 971	1 068	1 503	6 400	1979
1980	2 794	2 784	82	220	2 482	34 978	2 090	211	32 677	4 308	319	19	3 964	9 963	9 460	1 132	1 595	6 734	1980

Table 9 Expenditure on Sickness Insurance and Health

At current prices (in million DM)

Year	Income maintenance		Sickness insurance					Civil servants	Public health	Health service	Year
	Total	Wage continuat.	Insurance cash ben.	Insurance Total I	Insurance Total II	Admin./ Gen. serv.	Benefits in kind	Total	Total	Total	
1950	1 099	510	589	2 261	2 261	155	1 517		88	1 760	1950
1951	1 313	612	701	2 713	2 713	193	1 819		88	2 100	1951
1952	1 523	714	809	3 161	3 161	223	2 129		90	2 442	1952
1953	1 774	816	958	3 602	3 601	252	2 391		96	2 739	1953
1954	1 953	918	1 035	4 077	4 074	283	2 756		102	3 141	1954
1955	2 245	1 020	1 225	4 606	4 603	296	3 082		120	3 498	1955
1956	2 826	1 416	1 410	5 226	5 223	367	3 446		135	3 948	1956
1957	3 894	1 812	2 082	6 480	6 475	391	4 002		145	4 538	1957
1958	4 717	2 208	2 509	7 594	7 589	457	4 623		150	5 230	1958
1959	5 237	2 604	2 633	8 254	8 251	470	5 148		156	5 774	1959
1960	6 119	3 000	3 119	9 584	9 582	696	5 767	552	318	7 333	1960
1961	7 028	3 500	3 528	10 755	10 753	771	6 454	793	364	8 382	1961
1962	7 903	4 000	3 903	12 032	12 032	848	7 281	799	415	9 343	1962
1963	8 003	4 000	4 003	12 973	12 972	929	8 040	897	430	10 296	1963
1964	7 961	4 000	3 961	13 938	13 937	982	8 994	1 002	478	11 456	1964
1965	8 960	4 500	4 460	16 100	16 100	1 045	10 595	1 187	529	13 356	1965
1965	8 724	4 500	4 224	16 195	16 014	1 071	10 719	1 187	529	13 506	1965
1966	9 638	5 000	4 638	18 852	18 652	1 167	12 847	1 357	573	15 944	1966
1967	8 682	4 500	4 182	19 762	19 545	1 241	14 121	1 510	609	17 481	1967
1968	9 607	5 000	4 607	21 908	21 691	1 301	15 783	1 627	649	19 360	1968
1969	10 908	6 000	4 908	24 293	24 051	1 415	17 728	1 776	698	21 617	1969
1970	15 923	12 500	3 423	25 650	25 376	1 649	20 304	2 009	758	24 720	1970
1971	17 538	13 500	4 038	31 642	31 337	1 890	25 409	2 286	905	30 490	1971
1972	19 506	15 000	4 506	36 910	36 580	2 171	29 903	2 592	1 060	35 726	1972
1973	22 943	18 000	4 943	43 936	43 568	2 734	35 891	2 926	1 109	42 660	1973
1974	24 657	19 570	5 087	51 902	51 442	2 432	43 923	3 742	1 209	51 306	1974
1975	24 015	18 560	5 455	61 148	60 603	2 727	52 421	4 300	1 299	60 747	1975
1976	25 933	20 410	5 523	66 740	66 131	2 846	57 762	4 566	1 305	66 479	1976
1977	27 141	21 470	5 671	69 932	69 327	3 037	60 619	4 845	1 374	69 875	1977
1978	30 193	24 110	6 083	74 991	74 369	3 254	65 032	5 187	1 334	74 807	1978
1979	32 753	25 800	6 953	81 175	80 520	3 413	70 154	5 401	1 388	80 356	1979
1980	34 963	27 150	7 813	86 536	85 849	3 629	74 406	5 623	1 472	85 130	1980

Table 10

Expenditure on Unemployment

At current prices (in million DM)

Year	Total I	Total II	Admin./ Gen.serv.	Benef. in kind	Cash benefits	Total III	Empl. prom.	Other serv.	Vocation. serv.	train. cash	Income suppl.	Redund. Allow.	Insur. cash ben.	Ass. cash ben. A	Ass. cash ben. B	All cash	Oth. fed.	Total fed.	Year
1950	1 625	1 470	77	0	1 393	880							585		872	1 457	125	997	1950
1951	1 705	1 551	80	0	1 471	1 185							755		1 120	1 875	113	1 233	1951
1952	1 811	1 636	86	0	1 550	1 397							821		1 043	1 864	129	1 172	1952
1953	1 783	1 601	90	0	1 511	1 648							987		1 013	2 000	156	1 169	1953
1954	2 564	2 333	140	402	1 791	1 505							985		900	1 885	124	1 024	1954
1955	2 122	1 948	107	491	1 350	1 406							899		538	1 437	143	681	1955
1956	1 887	1 724	125	401	1 198	1 340							870		387	1 257	82	469	1956
1957	1 829	1 685	87	419	1 179	1 607							1 132		344	1 476	67	411	1957
1958	2 126	1 925	101	403	1 421	1 747							1 208		306	1 514	64	370	1958
1959	1 753	1 583	88	409	1 086	1 249							681		181	862	49	230	1959
1960	1 251	1 153	520	0	633	617							221		59	280	20	79	1960
1961	1 053	978	496	0	482	1 049							367		49	416	20	69	1961
1962	1 316	1 219	505	0	714	1 356					490		362		35	887	12	47	1962
1963	1 872	1 722	507	0	1 215	1 896					904		468		36	1 408	8	44	1963
1964	1 533	1 419	548	0	871	1 571					595		412		36	1 043	7	43	1964
1965	1 547	1 439	587	0	852	1 582	42	506	41		602		391		31	1 024	6	37	1965
1965	1 611	1 377	474	52	851	1 582	42	506	41		602		391		31	1 024	6	37	1965
1966	1 630	1 395	532	88	784	1 557	41	565	45		505		401		27	933	5	32	1966
1967	3 311	2 807	578	104	2 125	3 171	42	627	113	9	628		1 642	110	32	2 421	4	36	1967
1968	3 185	2 733	648	131	1 954	2 987	73	669	149	32	713		1 179	172	46	2 142	7	53	1968
1969	2 985	2 576	751	236	1 589	2 889	111	770	253	98	901		674	82	33	1 788	5	38	1969
1970	3 969	3 593	988	443	2 162	3 907	141	899	478	371	1 315		651	52	19	2 408	1	20	1970
1971	4 987	4 489	1 250	824	2 415	4 928	141	1 160	916	769	1 021		868	53	22	2 733	2	24	1971
1972	5 836	5 205	1 388	788	3 029	5 794	131	1 291	900	1 110	994		1 284	84	29	3 501	2	31	1972
1973	6 784	6 043	1 560	705	3 778	6 807	162	1 513	902	1 233	1 494		1 395	108	36	4 266	5	41	1973
1974	10 285	8 972	1 979	781	6 212	10 352	155	1 745	1 027	1 494	2 086	71	3 552	222	80	7 505	11	91	1974
1975	18 429	15 785	3 091	1 079	11 615	17 836	313	2 094	1 308	1 991	3 327	262	7 765	776	203	14 324	14	217	1975
1976	16 562	13 954	2 867	623	10 464	15 930	443	2 131	1 204	1 427	2 252	268	6 906	1 299	243	12 395	122	365	1976
1977	15 911	13 474	3 290	697	9 487	15 082	963	2 297	1 199	771	1 961	276	6 283	1 332	263	10 886	436	699	1977
1978	18 577	14 647	3 979	800	9 868	17 522	1 396	3 980	1 433	744	2 083	223	6 270	1 393	264	10 977	588	852	1978
1979	20 673	15 562	6 153	1 110	9 912	19 739	1 795	2 801	2 099	1 180	2 539	213	7 468	1 644	331	13 375	546	877	1979
1980	22 655	17 203	5 228	1 275	10 699	21 674	1 751	3 048	3 076	1 498	2 445	206	8 110	1 540	363	14 162	795	1 158	1980

Table 11 Expenditure on Child Allowances and Youth Assistance

At current prices (in million DM)

Year	General child allowances scheme: Total I	Total II	Admin./ Gen. serv.	Cash benefits	Civil servants' child allowances: Total I II	Admin./ Gen. serv.	Cash benefits	Youth assistance: Total I II	Admin./ Gen. serv.	Benefits in kind	Cash benefits	Year
1950					169	0	169					1950
1951					183	0	183					1951
1952					231	0	231					1952
1953					281	0	281					1953
1954					303	0	303					1954
1955	446	446	15	431	340	0	340					1955
1956	478	478	15	463	379	0	379					1956
1957	503	503	15	488	410	0	410					1957
1958	585	585	16	569	437	0	437					1958
1959	792	792	18	774	426	0	426					1959
1960	911	911	23	888	2 173	43	2 130	442			22	1960
1961	1 293	1 293	39	1 254	2 626	53	2 573	479			24	1961
1962	1 612	1 612	54	1 558	3 018	60	2 958	551			28	1962
1963	1 565	1 565	52	1 513	3 304	66	3 238	634			32	1963
1964	1 877	1 877	42	1 835	4 001	80	3 921	702			35	1964
1965	2 800	2 800	40	2 760	4 336	81	4 255	823	443	334	46	1965
1965	2 884	2 778	8	2 770	4 336	81	4 255	823	443	334	46	1965
1966	2 981	2 933	0	2 933	4 888	91	4 797	936	493	396	47	1966
1967	2 694	2 654	0	2 654	5 114	95	5 019	1 009	516	445	48	1967
1968	2 635	2 596	0	2 596	5 247	98	5 149	1 088	563	477	48	1968
1969	2 732	2 675	0	2 675	5 734	107	5 627	1 218	634	534	50	1969
1970	2 891	2 841	0	2 841	6 218	116	6 102	1 492	787	653	52	1970
1971	3 299	3 217	0	3 217	6 789	127	6 662	1 397	987	850	60	1971
1972	3 274	3 194	0	3 194	6 997	130	6 867	2 234	1 164	1 005	65	1972
1973	3 207	3 119	0	3 119	7 571	141	7 430	2 614	1 385	1 057	72	1973
1974	3 247	3 054	0	3 054	8 205	145	8 050	3 254	1 284	1 888	82	1974
1975	14 638	14 338	0	14 338	7 050	125	6 925	3 705	1 483	2 121	101	1975
1976	14 359	14 089	0	14 089	6 950	131	6 819	4 101	1 641	2 364	96	1976
1977	14 070	13 800	0	13 800	6 920	128	6 792	4 520	1 835	2 565	120	1977
1978	15 196	14 994	0	14 994	7 621	130	7 481	4 901	2 045	2 734	122	1978
1979	17 412	16 744	0	16 744	7 478	140	7 338	5 318	2 251	2 926	141	1979
1980	17 605	16 925	0	16 925	7 616	142	7 474	5 876	2 462	3 134	280	1980

Table 12 Expenditure on Social Assistance and Other Compensation Programmes

At current prices (in million DM)

Year	Social Assistance: Total I II	Admin./ Gen. serv.	Benefits in kind	Cash benefits	Total III	of which as % ordinary	of which as % extraord.	of which as % instit.	of which as % out-door	Other Compensation Programmes: Total I II	Admin./ Gen. serv.	Benefits in kind	Cash benefits	Year
1950	934	0	313	621	936			34.7	65.3					1950
1951	904	0	348	556										1951
1952	832	0	327	505	1 005			42.5	57.5					1952
1953	943	0	397	546										1953
1954	1 191	0	480	711	1 189			44.5	55.5					1954
1955	1 246	0	516	730	1 248			44.2	55.8					1955
1956	1 348	0	546	802	1 280			46.0	54.0					1956
1957	1 368	0	562	806										1957
1958	1 428	0	614	814	1 467			46.8	53.2					1958
1959	1 463	0	648	815	1 507			48.4	51.6					1959
1960	1 781	176	733	872	1 199			52.4	47.7	87			65	1960
1961	1 855	184	785	886	1 651			50.5	49.4	127			95	1961
1962	1 942	192	799	951	1 749			50.8	49.8	126			95	1962
1963	2 206	201	758	1 247	1 860	46.1	53.9	48.1	51.9	125			94	1963
1964	2 283	207	861	1 215	1 943	42.3	57.7	48.9	51.1	245			184	1964
1965	2 350	210	900	1 240	2 106	39.6	60.4	50.4	49.6	449	41	76	332	1965
1965	2 185	233	1 117	834	2 106	39.6	60.4	50.4	49.6	449	41	76	332	1965
1966	2 419	260	1 253	905	2 318	39.1	60.9			462	43	70	349	1966
1967	2 657	284	1 398	974	2 550	38.2	61.8	51.3	48.7	387	35	79	273	1967
1968	2 781	295	1 489	996	2 671	37.0	63.0	52.6	47.4	281	26	46	209	1968
1969	2 985	317	1 588	1 079	2 859	36.3	63.7			284	26	40	218	1969
1970	3 462	364	1 828	1 269	3 335	35.4	64.6	52.7	47.3	315	28	47	240	1970
1971	4 175	438	2 167	1 568	4 017	35.7	64.3	54.3	45.7	467	42	53	372	1971
1972	4 981	526	2 530	1 923	4 817	36.6	63.4	54.2	45.8	684	62	77	545	1972
1973	5 810	615	2 921	2 272	5 656	36.7	63.3	54.4	45.6	607	55	81	471	1973
1974	7 452	775	3 747	2 930	7 136	37.1	62.9	54.4	45.6	598	53	105	440	1974
1975	8 612	908	4 346	3 358	8 411	36.0	64.0	56.2	43.8	573	53	116	404	1975
1976	9 805	1 029	4 968	3 808	9 597	36.0	64.0	56.7	43.3	547	50	127	370	1976
1977	10 609	1 114	5 434	4 061	10 452	35.5	64.5	56.6	43.4	497	45	138	310	1977
1978	11 497	1 204	5 736	4 557	11 349	33.6	66.4	61.4	38.6	472	43	132	288	1978
1979	12 533	1 305	6 416	4 812	12 129	32.3	67.7	62.6	37.4	519	46	135	327	1979
1980	13 944	1 393	7 510	5 041	13 266	32.7	67.3	62.5	37.5	515	46	132	321	1980

Table 13

Expenditure on War Consequences

At current prices (in million DM)

Year	War victims' benefits: Total I	Total II	Admin./ Gen. serv.	Benefits in kind	Cash benefits	Equalisation of burdens: Total I	Total II	Admin./ Gen. serv.	Benefits in kind	Cash benefits	Political reparation payments: Total	Admin./ Gen. serv.	Benefits in kind	Cash benefits	Year
1950	2 219	2 156	83	139	1 934	791	791			791					1950
1951	2 769	2 513	138	140	2 235	680	680			680					1951
1952	3 343	2 855	154	171	2 530	747	747			747					1952
1953	2 896	2 617	157	75	2 284	709	709			709					1953
1954	3 129	2 880	170	205	2 505	847	847			847					1954
1955	3 476	3 212	172	212	2 828	939	939			939					1955
1956	4 062	3 595	179	220	3 196	1 058	1 058			1 058					1956
1957	3 853	3 827	189	203	3 435	1 023	1 023			1 023					1957
1958	3 666	3 633	193	206	3 234	1 154	1 154			1 154					1958
1959	3 543	3 508	201	215	3 092	1 235	1 235			1 235					1959
1960	3 725	3 686	212	222	3 252	1 359	1 359	77		1 282	2 115			1 988	1960
1961	4 439	4 393	207	233	3 953	1 420	1 420	80		1 340	2 318			2 179	1961
1962	4 414	4 361	225	246	3 890	1 694	1 694	96		1 598	2 345			2 204	1962
1963	4 178	4 124	231	266	3 627	1 671	1 671	95		1 576	2 160			2 030	1963
1964	5 026	4 969	256	300	4 413	1 815	1 815	103		1 712	1 880			1 767	1964
1965	5 460	5 400	280	330	4 790	2 000	2 000	105		1 895	1 792	103	6	1 683	1965
1965	5 803	5 700	277	514	4 909	2 014	1 995	139	96	1 760	1 792	103	6	1 683	1965
1966	6 040	5 839	377	477	4 985	1 992	1 970	131	100	1 739	1 964	115	15	1 834	1966
1967	6 933	6 753	428	702	5 623	1 838	1 815	119	99	1 597	1 963	119	18	1 826	1967
1968	6 760	6 589	387	667	5 535	1 850	1 827	117	99	1 611	2 165	129	18	2 018	1968
1969	6 730	6 555	407	671	5 477	1 778	1 756	111	118	1 527	1 853	113	17	1 723	1969
1970	7 486	7 316	450	734	6 132	1 782	1 758	109	128	1 521	1 959	118	19	1 822	1970
1971	8 073	7 887	452	866	6 569	1 821	1 796	110	127	1 549	2 012	129	22	1 861	1971
1972	8 577	8 366	506	932	6 928	1 814	1 787	104	137	1 546	2 201	182	21	1 998	1972
1973	9 172	8 945	549	1 053	7 343	1 749	1 720	99	146	1 475	2 299	182	22	2 095	1973
1974	10 129	9 915	633	1 127	8 155	1 793	1 765	101	169	1 495	2 412	137	21	2 254	1974
1975	11 135	10 902	726	1 218	8 928	1 844	1 816	104	179	1 533	2 397	137	23	2 237	1975
1976	11 823	11 577	780	1 288	9 509	1 876	1 846	105	178	1 562	2 216	128	23	2 065	1976
1977	12 450	12 198	789	1 352	10 057	1 893	1 865	107	180	1 578	2 232	127	23	2 082	1977
1978	12 693	12 441	853	1 353	10 235	1 833	1 802	104	180	1 518	2 219	127	23	2 069	1978
1979	13 103	12 837	908	1 429	10 500	1 783	1 754	101	130	1 473	2 191	127	22	2 042	1979
1980	13 400	13 122	1 084	1 433	10 606	1 719	1 689	96	182	1 411	2 092	121	21	1 950	1980

Table 14

Expenditure on Housing and Education

At current prices (in million DM)

Year	Housing: Total	Subs. of housing constr.	Premiums on savings	Hous. allow. total	Hous. allow. cash benef.	Total I	Educ. allow.	Educ. allow. cash benef.	Education: Total II	Pre-school educ. %	Schools %	Post-second. educ. %	Adult educ. %	Educ. promot. % (incl. allow.)	Total III	Pers. expend. %	Running costs %	Invest-ment %	Year
1950	1 675	1 675				2 097													1950
1951	2 406	2 406				2 579													1951
1952	2 668	2 668				3 062													1952
1953	2 909	2 882	27			3 544													1953
1954	3 348	3 282	66			3 870													1954
1955	3 173	3 044	129			4 196													1955
1956	3 713	3 525	188			4 799													1956
1957	3 960	3 735	225			5 401													1957
1958	4 067	3 784	283			6 008													1958
1959	4 800	4 431	369			6 536													1959
1960	3 966	3 559	407	2		5 559	86	77											1960
1961	4 433	3 891	528	14		8 196	118	106											1961
1962	5 129	4 560	544	25		9 186	133	120											1962
1963	5 273	4 643	592	38		10 548	132	119											1963
1964	5 616	4 877	684	55		12 299	149	134											1964
1965	5 774	4 782	814	178	148	14 283	171	155	15 042	4.1	67.9	23.5	1.9	2.6					1965
1966	5 642	4 210	977	455	396	15 479	213	194	16 237	4.0	68.2	22.9	1.8	3.0					1966
1967	5 261	3 703	1 074	484	428	16 316	252	229	17 056	3.8	67.6	23.6	1.8	3.2					1967
1968	4 866	3 207	1 096	563	512	17 459	259	235	18 235	3.7	67.2	24.3	1.8	3.0					1968
1969	4 356	2 506	1 221	629	577	20 304	359	326	21 165	3.6	66.4	25.0	1.7	3.3					1969
1970	4 830	2 541	1 635	654	600	24 784	629	572	26 455	3.4	62.6	26.0	2.2	5.8	23 941	57.7	13.8	28.5	1970
1971	5 779	2 814	2 063	902	835	31 287	1 165	1 059	33 381	3.5	62.1	25.3	2.0	7.2	29 747	57.5	13.5	29.0	1971
1972	7 174	3 381	2 507	1 286	1 202	35 651	1 757	1 597	37 552	3.9	59.9	25.1	2.1	9.0	33 103	58.9	13.9	27.2	1972
1973	7 726	3 581	2 918	1 227	1 139	40 427	1 924	1 749	42 684	4.1	61.2	25.0	2.2	7.6	38 178	60.4	14.6	25.0	1973
1974	9 309	4 643	3 088	1 578	1 468	49 351	2 036	1 851	50 570	4.6	60.7	25.4	2.6	6.7	44 733	60.5	14.3	25.2	1974
1975	9 044	4 082	3 165	1 797	1 655	53 830	2 740	2 627	54 146	4.2	61.0	25.1	1.8	7.9	48 467	61.5	16.3	22.2	1975
1976	9 691	5 687	2 245	1 759	1 620	54 921	2 544	2 439	55 255	4.5	61.2	24.9	2.2	7.2	49 820	63.9	17.0	19.1	1976
1977	8 885	5 410	1 858	1 617	1 470	57 411	2 628	2 520	57 455	4.4	61.4	24.8	2.3	7.1	52 158	65.3	18.2	16.5	1977
1978	10 138	6 296	1 873	1 969	1 790	61 327	2 945	2 824	61 276	4.8	61.2	23.9	2.8	7.1	57 366	63.8	18.5	17.8	1978
1979	11 379	7 415	1 933	2 031	1 846	66 294	3 145	3 015	65 860	5.0	60.5	24.2	3.0	7.3	59 351	67.0	18.6	14.4	1979
1980	12 260	8 225	1 989	2 046	1 860	72 929	3 322	3 185											1980

Table 15 Public Revenues

Year	Revenues (in billion DM)					Deficit as % of public expend.	Revenues by type (percent distribution)					Tax ratios					Year
	Total revenues	Taxes	Social security contrib.	Other receipts	Statistical deficit		Taxes	Social security contrib.	Other	Direct taxes	Indirect taxes	Aggregate tax burden (% of GDP) Revenues	Taxes	Individual tax burden (% of gross earnings) Total	Income tax	Soc.sec.contr.	
1950	32.90	20.98	8.92	3.00	0.72	2.2	63.8	27.1	9.1			33.6	21.4	12.5	4.6	7.9	1950
1951	42.26	28.04	10.60	3.62	3.68	9.5	66.4	25.1	8.6			35.2	23.4	13.9	6.1	7.8	1951
1952	50.30	33.84	12.00	4.46	5.23	11.6	67.3	23.9	8.9			36.7	24.7	14.5	6.8	7.7	1952
1953	(54.94)	(36.80)	13.37	4.77	(6.30)	(13.0)	(67.0)	(24.3)	(8.7)			(37.2)	24.9	14.1	6.2	7.9	1953
1954	58.95	38.96	14.50	5.49	6.89	13.2	66.1	24.6	9.3			37.1	24.5	13.9	6.0	7.8	1954
1955	65.77	42.72	16.65	6.40	8.72	15.3	65.0	25.3	9.7			36.1	23.5	14.1	6.3	7.3	1955
1956	72.80	47.43	18.57	6.80	9.76	15.5	65.2	25.5	9.3			36.2	23.6	14.4	6.7	7.7	1956
1957	80.05	50.37	22.12	7.56	7.64	10.6	62.9	27.6	9.4			36.6	23.0	13.9	5.2	8.7	1957
1958	85.76	52.72	25.00	8.04	3.66	4.5	61.5	29.2	9.4			36.6	22.4	14.9	5.6	9.3	1958
1959	94.56	59.58	26.62	8.36	5.43	6.1	63.0	28.2	8.8			37.1	23.4	14.7	5.3	9.4	1959
1960	108.02	68.90	29.72	9.40	9.50	9.6	63.8	27.5	8.7			37.9	24.2	15.8	6.4	9.4	1960
1960	107.86	69.70	30.37	7.79	9.48	9.6	64.6	28.2	7.2	26.0	38.7	35.6	23.0	15.9	6.4	9.6	1960
1961	121.46	79.91	33.42	8.13	9.54	8.5	65.8	27.5	6.7	27.8	38.0	36.6	24.1	16.6	7.2	9.3	1961
1962	133.43	87.84	36.92	8.67	5.27	4.1	65.8	27.7	6.5	28.4	37.5	37.0	24.3	17.0	7.6	9.4	1962
1963	142.22	93.23	39.72	9.27	3.71	2.7	65.6	27.9	6.5	28.5	37.1	37.2	24.4	17.4	8.0	9.4	1963
1964	154.80	101.91	42.58	10.31	3.13	2.1	65.8	27.5	6.7	28.7	37.1	36.8	24.2	17.8	3.5	9.3	1964
1965	165.92	107.79	47.12	11.01	-2.58	-1.5	65.0	28.4	6.6	27.5	37.5	36.1	23.5	17.2	7.8	9.4	1965
1966	178.97	114.84	53.23	11.90	-0.82	-0.5	64.2	29.2	6.6	27.6	36.6	36.6	23.5	18.3	8.6	9.7	1966
1967	183.58	117.32	53.63	12.63	-6.93	-3.6	63.9	29.2	6.9	26.9	37.0	37.1	23.7	18.6	8.8	9.9	1967
1968	198.37	124.42	59.31	14.64	-4.51	-2.2	62.7	29.9	7.4	27.7	35.1	37.1	23.3	19.7	9.4	10.3	1968
1969	233.20	148.41	68.70	16.09	6.76	3.0	63.6	29.5	6.9	27.4	36.2	39.1	24.9	21.1	10.3	10.7	1969
1970	259.98	160.02	81.53	18.43	2.19	0.8	61.6	31.4	7.1	28.0	33.5	38.3	23.6	22.7	11.8	10.9	1970
1971	295.36	181.33	93.54	20.49	-1.15	-0.4	61.4	31.7	6.9	28.8	32.6	39.1	24.0	24.1	13.3	10.8	1971
1972	328.20	198.63	107.04	22.53	-4.02	-1.2	60.5	32.6	6.9	27.7	32.8	39.7	24.0	24.0	12.8	11.2	1972
1973	387.71	234.21	126.97	26.53	10.93	2.9	60.4	32.7	6.8	29.9	30.5	42.2	25.5	26.5	14.8	11.8	1973
1974	420.02	250.59	140.89	28.54	-13.56	-3.1	59.7	33.5	6.8	30.6	29.1	42.5	25.4	27.6	15.8	11.8	1974
1975	433.56	250.52	153.60	29.44	-59.79	-12.1	57.8	35.4	6.8	28.6	29.2	41.9	24.2	27.5	15.0	12.5	1975
1976	488.49	282.00	172.97	33.52	-40.15	-7.6	57.7	35.4	6.9	29.4	28.3	43.5	25.1	29.2	16.0	13.3	1976
1977	535.09	313.70	185.62	35.77	-29.22	-5.2	58.6	34.7	6.7	30.8	27.9	44.6	26.1	30.0	16.6	13.4	1977
1978	570.13	331.34	198.60	40.19	-34.46	-5.7	58.1	34.8	7.0	29.4	28.7	44.3	25.8	29.3	15.9	13.5	1978
1979	612.09	355.28	213.53	43.28	-40.95	-6.3	58.0	34.9	7.1	28.7	29.4	43.9	25.5	29.1	15.6	13.5	1979
1980	654.90	377.68	230.56	46.05	-51.43	-7.3	57.7	35.2	7.0	.	.	43.9	25.4	29.8	16.3	13.5	1980

Table 16

Revenues of Public Authorities

Year	Total revenues (in billion DM)	Statistical deficit (in billion DM)	Deficit as % of expend.	Revenues by level of government: Total (in bill. DM)	Revenues: Federal (percent distribution)	Revenues: State	Revenues: Local	Taxes by level of government: Total (in bill. DM)	Taxes: Federal (percent distribution)	Taxes: State	Taxes: Local	Taxes by type: Total (in bill. DM)	Direct (percent distribution)	Indirect	Year
1950	26.44	-1.70	-6.0	28.95	40.2	34.8	25.0	18.84	52.3	34.5	13.2	20.93	(43.2)	(56.8)	1950
1951	36.08	-1.32	-3.5	39.44	43.9	34.8	21.3	27.31	59.0	28.9	12.1	29.38			1951
1952	41.45	-0.05	-0.1	45.90	45.0	34.4	20.7	32.22	59.8	28.2	11.9	34.03			1952
1953	44.66	0.35	0.8	48.80	44.7	34.0	21.3	34.39	59.2	28.4	12.4	36.43			1953
1954	48.40	0.73	1.5	52.64	44.9	33.1	21.9	36.99	59.4	28.0	12.6	39.25			1954
1955	53.80	2.57	5.0	58.11	45.3	32.7	22.1	40.86	59.8	28.1	12.1	43.63	(51.0)	(49.0)	1955
1956	58.61	-1.30	-2.2	65.32	43.3	34.7	22.0	45.73	57.8	30.1	12.2	47.91			1956
1957	62.05	-4.30	-6.5	70.10	41.8	35.9	22.4	48.09	56.2	30.8	12.9	50.13			1957
1958	67.56	-3.94	-5.5	75.76	42.0	35.6	22.4	51.65	56.1	30.8	13.1	53.86			1958
1959	74.76	-1.82	-2.4	83.87	42.2	35.7	22.1	58.41	55.7	31.1	13.2	60.64			1959
1960	(65.46)	(0.91)	(1.4)	(74.30)	(41.8)	(35.8)	(22.5)	(51.74)	(54.6)	(32.3)	(13.1)	68.45	53.5	46.5	1960
1961	95.61	0.33	0.3	107.54	41.7	36.5	21.8	76.81	54.3	33.5	12.3	78.53	54.5	45.5	1961
1962	105.37	-1.90	-1.8	119.70	41.8	35.7	22.5	84.56	55.0	33.0	12.0	86.38	55.5	44.5	1962
1963	111.35	-5.42	-4.6	127.35	41.5	35.4	23.0	89.80	55.0	33.2	11.8	91.08	55.8	44.2	1963
1964	121.90	-6.21	-4.8	139.01	41.2	34.9	23.2	98.09	55.6	32.8	11.6	99.39	55.6	44.4	1964
1965	130.31	-10.27	-7.3	148.72	42.7	33.9	23.3	104.50	56.5	32.2	11.3	105.46	54.0	46.0	1965
1966	138.12	-8.60	-5.9	158.16	42.0	34.2	23.8	111.18	56.0	32.6	11.4	112.45	54.4	45.6	1966
1967	142.38	-13.57	-8.7	163.51	41.4	34.5	24.2	113.41	55.7	33.1	11.2	114.63	53.4	46.6	1967
1968	151.81	-7.38	-4.6	174.32	40.8	35.4	23.8	120.44	55.0	34.0	11.1	121.81	55.0	45.0	1968
1969	177.19	2.47	1.4	200.59	41.7	34.3	24.0	144.09	54.5	33.6	11.9	145.29	54.6	45.4	1969
1970	188.31	-8.03	-4.1	213.49	41.5	34.7	23.8	152.27	55.0	34.1	10.9	154.14	53.6	46.4	1970
1971	209.82	-15.36	-6.8	239.27	40.8	34.8	24.4	169.97	52.4	34.5	11.3	172.41	54.3	45.7	1971
1972	237.11	-14.16	-5.6	273.48	39.0	36.2	24.8	194.06	52.4	35.7	11.9	197.00	55.9	44.1	1972
1973	268.66	-9.01	-3.2	312.80	38.3	36.4	25.3	221.45	51.9	35.8	12.3	224.80	58.3	41.7	1973
1974	288.81	-27.70	-8.8	355.96	35.0	35.1	24.9	235.56	50.7	36.8	12.5	239.58	60.2	39.8	1974
1975	296.65	-63.84	-17.7	342.22	36.2	36.9	26.9	235.00	50.7	36.4	12.9	242.07	58.8	41.2	1975
1976	328.70	-48.03	-12.7	375.66	36.4	37.0	26.6	259.71	50.4	36.6	13.0	268.08	59.8	40.2	1976
1977	364.00	-31.18	-7.9	409.55	36.6	37.5	25.9	289.82	49.7	37.2	13.1	299.44	61.9	38.1	1977
1978	392.33	-39.45	-9.1	442.44	36.9	37.1	26.0	309.32	49.8	37.4	12.8	319.10	60.1	39.9	1978
1979	421.37	-45.88	-9.8	477.97	37.1	37.1	25.8	332.49	50.0	37.6	12.4	342.83	58.6	41.4	1979
1980	449.48	-56.40	-11.1	511.65	36.8	36.3	26.9	354.38	49.7	36.9	13.4	364.70	58.6	41.4	1980

Table 17

Public Debt

Year	Volume of debt: Total (million DM)	Volume of debt: Total (% of GDP)	Federal (percent distribution)	State (percent distribution)	Local (percent distribution)	Annual changes of debt (in mill. DM): Total (net)	Federal (gross)	State (gross)	Local (gross)	Interest on debt (in mill.DM): Public sector	Public authorities	Year
1950	20 634	21.0	35.3	62.3	2.4					550		1950
1951	22 365	18.6	36.8	59.4	3.8	1 731	930	450	350	670	765	1951
1952	24 044	17.6	37.0	57.0	5.9	1 679	677	423	580	750		1952
1953	33 901	22.9	49.8	43.3	6.9	9 857	7 829	846	890	800	1 061	1953
1954	38 699	24.3	49.0	41.1	9.9	4 798	1 168	455	1 280	1 190		1954
1955	40 943	22.5	46.9	40.8	12.3	2 244	-26	505	1 070	1 270	1 525	1955
1956	41 892	20.8	45.2	40.4	14.4	949	-254	218	940	1 370		1956
1957	43 614	19.9	48.5	34.3	17.2	1 722	2 109	-1 778	1 400	1 380	1 709	1957
1958	46 122	19.7	46.5	34.1	19.4	2 508	354	745	1 360	1 450	1 962	1958
1959	49 084	19.2	46.1	32.8	21.1	2 962	909	212	1 260	1 650	2 107	1959
1960	52 182	18.3	46.6	30.3	23.1	3 098	1 586	-225	1 539	2 190	1 919	1960
1961	56 564	17.0	49.3	26.4	24.3	4 382	3 369	-792	1 636	2 210	2 615	1961
1962	59 984	16.6	48.9	24.0	27.0	3 420	1 315	-501	2 263	2 410	3 032	1962
1963	66 687	17.4	49.3	21.8	28.9	6 703	2 880	-73	2 618	2 660	2 839	1963
1964	73 107	17.4	46.8	21.4	31.8	6 420	1 202	962	3 578	2 910	3 130	1964
1965	82 981	18.1	43.3	22.8	33.9	9 874	1 679	3 110	4 580	3 240	3 577	1965
1966	92 291	18.9	41.7	23.8	34.5	9 310	2 564	2 927	3 621	4 130	4 459	1966
1967	107 175	21.7	43.6	24.3	32.1	14 884	7 887	3 860	2 521	5 200	5 557	1967
1968	115 870	21.7	43.8	24.5	31.7	8 695	3 724	2 151	2 200	5 400	5 748	1968
1969	116 141	19.5	42.1	23.9	34.0	271	-1 832	-568	2 477	5 860	6 356	1969
1970	125 890	18.5	41.0	24.1	34.9	9 749	1 963	2 015	3 632	6 600	6 864	1970
1971	140 399	18.6	37.6	25.5	36.9	14 509	1 441	5 251	7 632	7 430	7 703	1971
1972	156 063	18.9	34.9	23.4	35.4	15 664	6 535	3 926	8 057	8 480	8 814	1972
1973	167 754	18.3	37.5	24.1	38.5	11 691	6 057	2 499	7 019	10 220	10 556	1973
1974	192 383	19.5	38.8	25.5	35.7	24 629	10 782	7 861	3 372	12 200	12 544	1974
1975	256 389	24.8	43.4	26.8	29.8	64 006	36 364	19 678	8 036	14 230	14 510	1975
1976	296 650	26.4	44.3	28.2	27.5	40 261	19 947	14 804	5 419	17 500	17 810	1976
1977	328 484	27.4	46.5	27.7	25.8	31 834	21 701	7 778	3 515	20 470	20 650	1977
1978	370 811	28.8	48.5	27.9	23.7	42 327	27 368	12 556	3 355	21 520	21 840	1978
1979	413 935	29.7	49.6	28.3	22.1	43 124	25 114	13 761	3 706	24 210	24 690	1979
1980	468 612	31.5	49.9	29.6	20.5	54 677	29 688	21 904	4 802	28 730	29 110	1980

Table 18

Receipts of Social Programmes

Year	Social security schemes (ILO) Total (in million DM)	Insured persons (percent distribution)	Employers	State	Other	Social programmes (official German definition) Total (in million DM)	Insured persons (percent distribution)	Employers	State	Other	Year
1950	15 339	21.5	39.7	38.3	0.5						1950
1951	17 896	22.4	39.2	37.4	1.0						1951
1952	20 510	21.8	40.0	36.7	1.5						1952
1953	22 502	22.5	41.1	34.8	1.6						1953
1954	24 030	22.8	41.2	34.1	1.9						1954
1955	28 596	23.0	42.4	32.3	2.4						1955
1956	31 966	23.3	41.2	32.4	3.1						1956
1957	36 756	24.1	41.6	31.2	3.1						1957
1958	41 122	25.2	42.8	29.2	2.9						1958
1959	43 036	25.6	43.0	28.4	2.9						1959
1960	47 956	26.2	43.4	27.4	3.0						1960
1960	49 298	25.9	44.4	26.5	3.3						1960
1961	56 434	25.2	42.3	29.4	3.1						1961
1962	59 044	26.5	43.9	26.4	3.2						1962
1963	63 311	26.8	44.4	25.7	3.1						1963
1964	70 956	26.0	41.6	29.4	3.0						1964
1965	79 061	26.1	40.3	30.8	2.9	97 189	21.7	42.4	29.9	6.0	1965
1966	86 106	26.4	40.4	30.2	3.0	107 016	21.8	42.2	30.0	6.0	1966
1967	89 340	26.0	38.7	31.7	3.6	110 787	21.8	41.4	30.7	6.1	1967
1968	95 912	27.6	40.5	28.9	3.0	118.749	23.0	42.3	29.1	5.6	1968
1969	106 402	29.3	40.4	27.7	2.7	131 736	24.2	43.3	27.3	5.2	1969
1970	120 467	28.9	42.3	25.9	2.9	156 572	23.5	45.7	25.6	5.2	1970
1971	136 989	29.2	42.9	25.2	2.7	180 295	22.7	45.6	25.9	5.8	1971
1972	158 864	29.1	42.1	24.7	4.2	205 118	23.1	44.9	26.1	5.9	1972
1973	184 964	29.6	42.7	23.2	4.5	237 411	23.6	45.6	24.4	6.4	1973
1974	205 262	29.9	42.1	23.6	4.4	272 431	23.0	43.3	26.7	7.0	1974
1975	240 953	28.2	39.6	28.6	3.6	308 992	22.6	40.6	31.1	5.7	1975
1976	262 283	29.3	40.4	27.1	3.2	335 029	23.6	41.5	29.5	5.4	1976
1977	275 312	29.5	41.1	26.4	3.0	350 953	23.8	41.9	29.0	5.3	1977
1978	312 369	33.3	34.0	28.8	4.0	375 563	23.9	42.5	28.7	4.9	1978
1979	328 684	33.1	34.6	28.8	3.6	394 365	24.1	43.0	28.6	4.3	1979
1980	359 305	33.8	34.1	29.1	3.0	421 987	24.1	42.8	29.0	4.1	1980

Table 19 Welfare State Clienteles (in thousands)

Year	Persons living predominantly from social transfers	Pensioners					Recipients of											Year
		Survivors' pens.	Invalidity pens.	Old age pensions Total	Old age pensions of which: age 65 +	Occup. injur. ins.	Sickn. cash benef.	Unemployment benef. Total	Unemployment benef. Insurance	Unemployment benef. Assistance	Child allow. Families	Child allow. Children	War victims benef.	Social assistance	Housing allow.	Education allow.	
1950		2 547		2 786		636	477	1 455	538	917			3 939	1 633			1950
1951		2 845		2 979		695	491	1 377	478	899			4 089				1951
1952		2 920		3 102		745	499	1 344	504	841			4 378	1 310			1952
1953		3 098		3 463		772	542	1 230	480	750			4 335				1953
1954		3 067		3 566		806	542	1 181	526	655			4 296	1 325			1954
1955		3 285		3 661		830	621	890	454	436			4 165	1 328			1955
1956		3 408		3 736		857	665	717	441	276		(1 033)	4 046	1 285			1956
1957		3 409	1 501	2 402	2 375	874	750	610	411	199		(1 015)	3 813				1957
1958		3 414	1 542	2 647	2 583	891	813	640	466	174		(1 056)	3 634	1 239			1958
1959		3 467	1 612	2 779	2 693	906	815	480	364	116		.	3 449	1 178			1959
1960	7 200	3 447	1 628	2 901	2 776	916	902	226	175	51		.	3 276	1 134			1960
1961	7 222	3 429	1 632	3 035	2 864	967	938	143	119	24		.	3 186	1 058			1961
1962	7 603	3 432	1 640	3 177	2 956	978	.	122	105	17		.	3 038	1 032			1962
1963	7 511	3 463	1 620	3 311	3 047	986	901	142	126	16		.	2 893	1 491			1963
1964	7 813	3 531	1 603	3 478	3 168	999	819	121	106	15	2 014	3 675	2 834	1 418	163		1964
1965	7 799	3 597	1 595	3 645	3 287	1 011	850	109	97	12	2 171	4 827	2 813	1 404	395		1965
1966	7 959	3 664	1 590	3 820	3 416	1 016	879	107	97	10	2 123	4 851	2 771	1 445	606		1966
1967	8 207	3 755	1 594	4 053	3 582	1 017	740	356	320	36	2 051	4 774	2 740	1 531	691		1967
1968	8 411	3 817	1 611	4 223	3 670	1 015	811	245	192	53	2 059	4 872	2 687	1 503	811		1968
1969	8 726	3 886	1 628	4 421	3 782	1 012	848	133	105	28	2 086	4 998	2 647	1 479	851		1969
1970	9 087	3 969	1 657	4 585	3 869	1 018	1 003	113	96	17	2 113	5 176	2 587	1 491	908		1970
1971	9 226	4 020	1 686	4 749	3 964	1 022	976	136	120	15	2 535	5 589	2 533	1 548	1 154	360	1971
1972	9 577	4 086	1 732	4 890	4 034	1 025	1 033	177	157	20	2 585	5 612	2 475	1 645	1 278	439	1972
1973	9 806	4 130	1 724	5 165	4 090	1 026	1 154	176	154	23	2 462	5 443	2 416	1 730	1 302	540	1973
1974	10 245	4 223	1 759	5 475	4 149	1 027	1 067	392	352	40	2 494	5 353	2 352	1 916	1 650	560	1974
1975	10 538	4 314	1 822	5 703	4 151	1 018	1 014	817	707	110	7 253	14 027	2 318	2 049	1 666	665	1975
1976	10 794	4 405	1 883	5 922	4 160	1 014	1 023	780	615	164	7 241	13 715	2 234	2 109	1 585	625	1976
1977	10 752	4 480	1 937	6 091	4 148	1 014	1 050	721	557	163	7 241	13 598	2 178	2 164	1 467	610	1977
1978	10 915	4 541	1 989	6 180	4 097	1 010	1 086	673	516	157	7 153	13 145	2 107	2 120	1 549	689	1978
1979	11 054	4 582	2 046	6 250	4 034	1 009	1 152	582	447	134	7 121	13 017	2 044	2 095	1 518	770	1979
1980	11 195	4 617	2 141	6 349	3 940	1 005	1 176	576	454	122	6 967	12 663	1 981	2 144	1 486	830	1980

Table 20

Data on Housing and Education

in 1,000s

Year	Number of dwellings			Kinder-garten (places)	Primary/ upper pr. schools	Secondary schools		Number of students			Teaching personnel					Year
	Total stock	Annual construction Total	(social housing)			Total	(Gymnasia)	Univ. en-trants	Univers./ teachers' colleges	Total post-secondary	Primary/ upper primary	Secondary Total	(Gym-nasia)	Total post-second.	Total incl. adult education	
1950	9 512	371.9	255.0						135							1950
1951	10 053	425.4	295.6		5 849.4	879.5	643.1			151.9	126.4	36.7	29.5		(173.0)	1951
1952	10 534	460.8	317.5		5 425.1	950.5	684.0	25.9			127.1	39.9	31.5			1952
1953	11 092	539.7	304.2		5 140.7	1 018.4	728.1				127.2	42.1	32.7	(10.5)		1953
1954	11 679	571.5	309.5		4 832.4	1 073.0	763.5				126.9	44.3	34.1			1954
1955	12 260	568.4	289.0		4 636.5	1 098.7	775.3	30.7	160		125.6	46.0	34.8			1955
1956	12 864	591.1	305.7		4 574.2	1 082.0	767.5				124.8	48.5	36.8			1956
1957	13 428	559.6	293.2		5 032.7	1 221.2	854.6				139.1	57.4	43.1			1957
1958	13 943	520.5	269.2		5 031.3	1 217.7	856.4				140.0	58.8	44.2			1958
1959	14 538	588.7	301.2		5 138.2	1 221.4	861.2				140.4	60.2	45.3			1959
1960	16 270	574.4	263.2	817.2	5 290.9	1 222.3	853.4	44.5	238.4	291.1	142.1	61.4	46.0	19.1	229.1	1960
1961	16 762	565.8	241.9	827.9	5 343.0	1 232.9	848.0		259.4		145.0	62.3	46.1			1961
1962	17 228	573.4	242.5	859.0	5 445.0	1 254.0	846.7		276.5		149.6	65.2	48.1			1962
1963	17 661	569.6	228.8	889.4	5 469.3	1 236.0	858.7		289.3		151.9	68.5	49.3			1963
1964	18 137	623.8	248.5	920.8	5 525.2	1 387.6	890.1		298.9		157.7	70.5	50.4			1964
1965	18 550	591.9	228.6	952.9	5 607.4	1 497.1	957.9	48.1	299.7	384.4	161.1	71.8	50.4	36.6	279.7	1965
1966	18 987	604.8	203.5	983.2	5 710.9	1 628.2	1 038.1	46.5	320.8	406.7	167.1	76.7	53.4	37.3		1966
1967	19 383	572.3	192.7	1 027.5	5 755.5	1 888.9	1 194.4	50.4	331.0	418.4	172.6	84.5	57.8	39.7		1967
1968	19 825	519.9	177.7	1 053.8	5 886.8	2 032.0	1 271.0	58.2	352.9	443.6	177.4	90.3	61.3	41.6		1968
1969	20 226	499.7	183.2	1 104.5	6 079.9	2 178.3	1 349.3	70.1	375.9	473.1	180.9	97.8	66.1	45.1		1969
1970	20 608	478.1	137.1	1 160.7	6 347.5	2 233.3	1 379.5	64.3	410.1	510.5	187.7	103.9	69.7	53.2	366.2	1970
1971	21 046	555.0	148.7	1 228.9	6 476.2	2 416.8	1 442.8	68.7	466.2	597.8	196.1	112.2	71.3	64.6		1971
1972	21 587	660.6	153.2	1 319.1	6 509.7	2 631.8	1 567.3	74.1	536.4	661.5	205.0	122.9	75.6	70.4		1972
1973	22 183	714.2	169.3	1 388.1	6 499.6	2 837.2	1 686.3	77.2	591.2	729.0	217.3	133.5	81.1	74.6		1973
1974	22 678	604.4	148.1	1 435.9	6 481.3	3 015.5	1 779.8	78.5	641.8	790.5	227.9	142.9	85.4	78.4		1974
1975	23 014	436.8	126.7	1 478.9	6 425.1	3 176.5	1 863.5	85.1	680.2	840.8	235.0	152.6	89.7	77.9	500.0	1975
1976	23 986	392.4	127.8	1 463.0	6 277.6	3 349.6	1 914.0	84.6	705.0	877.3	239.6	166.3	94.8	78.0		1976
1977	24 369	409.0	139.6	1 441.0	6 019.1	3 486.6	1 971.7	88.9	732.7	913.3	243.7	176.1	98.7	77.7		1977
1978	24 708	368.1	90.2	1 396.9	5 721.9	3 567.3	2 013.4	87.5	756.9	945.9	245.3	185.7	103.8	77.9		1978
1979	25 040	357.8	80.2	1 390.7	5 354.0	3 668.4	2 088.8	96.2	784.2	983.6	246.8	195.0	109.5	79.1		1979
1980	25 406	388.9		1 393.7	5 044.4	3 690.4	2 119.0	96.1	823.9	1 044.2	248.0	203.9	115.8	78.6	573.3	1980

Table 21

Data on Population and Labour Force

in 1,000s

Year	Total population	Selected age groups ('potential clienteles') 60+ (pen-sioners)	0–18 (child allow.)	3–6 (Kinder-garten)	6–19 (all schools)	10–19 (second. schools)	19–22 (univ. entr.)	19–26 (stu-dents)	Total Labour Force I	Unem-ployed I	In de-pendent employ-ment	Vacan-cies	Unem-ployed II	Total Labour Force II	Year
1950	47 696	6 575	13 383						21 577	1 580	13 674	116	1 869	21 577	1950
1951	48 306								21 952	1 432	14 286	116	1 714	21 952	1951
1952	48 709	6 930	13 538		10 048	7 514	1 959	4 873	22 289	1 379	14 754	115	1 652	22 289	1952
1953	49 278	7 092	13 537		10 008	7 513		4 991	22 684	1 259	15 344	123	1 491	22 684	1953
1954	49 736	7 262	13 496		9 937	7 431		5 092	23 216	1 221	15 968	137	1 411	23 216	1954
1955	50 318	7 436	13 471		9 899	7 165	2 497	5 260	23 758	928	16 840	200	1 074	23 758	1955
1956	50 111	7 514	13 225		9 691	6 885		5 331	24 196	761	17 483	219	876	24 196	1956
1957	51 836	7 922	13 620		9 889	6 895	2 644	5 554	24 602	662	17 992	217	754	24 602	1957
1958	52 158	8 042	13 595		9 809	6 790	2 720	5 738	24 807	683	18 188	216	764	24 807	1958
1959	52 778	8 294	13 588		9 628	6 587	2 860	6 106	24 857	476	18 508	280	540	24 857	1959
1960	53 381	8 540	13 704	2 408	9 478	6 428	2 928	6 389	25 027	235	19 005	449	271	25 027	1960
1961	56 175	9 413	.						26 772	181	20 730	552	181	26 722	1961
1962	56 938	9 733	14 465	2 605	9 770	6 614	2 654	6 522	26 845	155	21 032	574	155	26 937	1962
1963	57 587	10 011	14 827	2 695	9 854	6 624	2 474	6 463	26 930	186	21 261	555	186	27 066	1963
1964	58 266	10 303	15 266	2 791	10 074	6 755	2 297	6 253	26 922	169	21 484	609	169	27 148	1964
1965	59 012	10 568	15 640	2 915	10 520	7 025	2 093	5 797	27 034	147	21 757	649	147	27 300	1965
1966	59 638	10 862	15 954	3 003	10 762	7 152	2 040	5 403	26 962	161	21 765	540	161	27 243	1966
1967	59 873	11 101	16 154	3 054	10 970	7 241	2 209	5 243	26 409	459	21 054	302	459	26 410	1967
1968	60 184	11 328	16 327	3 081	11 197	7 348	2 359	5 322	26 291	323	21 183	488	323	26 291	1968
1969	60 848	11 542	16 514	3 081	11 484	7 522	2 484	5 462	26 535	179	21 752	747	179	26 535	1969
1970	(60 651)	(11 679)	(16 451)	3 028	11 511	7 543	2 465	5 149	26 817	149	22 246	795	149	26 817	1970
1971	61 284	11 892	16 562	2 962	12 006	7 926	2 482	5 671	27 002	185	22 606	648	185	26 910	1971
1972	61 672	12 062	16 569	2 842	12 298	8 175	2 480	5 846	26 990	246	22 633	546	246	26 901	1972
1973	61 976	12 230	16 485	2 651	12 540	8 439	2 540	6 019	27 195	273	22 906	572	273	26 986	1973
1974	62 054	12 366	16 326	2 471	12 706	8 680	2 531	6 003	27 147	582	22 640	315	582	26 798	1974
1975	61 829	12 401	16 067	2 259	12 723	8 837	2 557	5 953	26 884	1 074	22 014	236	1 074	26 398	1975
1976	61 531	12 280	15 737	2 075	12 635	8 986	2 605	5 976	26 651	1 060	21 939	235	1 060	26 149	1976
1977	61 400	12 099	15 398	1 908	12 513	9 100	2 685	6 075	26 577	1 030	22 029	231	1 030	26 074	1977
1978	61 326	11 902	15 033	1 806	12 294	9 151	2 779	6 217	26 692	993	22 264	246	993	26 223	1978
1979	61 359	11 801	14 679	1 788	12 013	9 137	2 885	6 429	26 915	876	22 659	304	876	26 449	1979
1980	61 566	11 888	14 368	1 769	11 709	9 013	3 009	6 657	27 191	889	22 986	308	889	26 721	1980

Table 22 Legal regulations listed in the institutional synopsis, core laws, and selection of core laws used for roll-call analysis

Scheme	Number of regulations listed in the institutional synopsis	Number of core laws (in brackets: excluded regulations)	Number of selected core laws (in brackets: included laws)
Pension insurance	17	15 (1949, 1975)	8 (1957, 1967, 1969, 1972, 1974, 1977, 1978, 1983)
Farmers' pensions	8	8	4 (1957, 1961, 1973)
Public employees' pensions	1	- (all)	-
Sickness insurance	22	21 (1949)	10 (1951, 1955, 1955, 1957, 1969, 1970, 1973, 1977, 1981, 1982)
Public Health	4	4	3 (1969, 1972, 1981)
Accident insurance	9	8 (1949)	4 (1951, 1957, 1963, 1971)
Unemployment insurance	16	15 (1949)	9 (1952, 1953, 1956, 1969, 1974, 1975, 1981, 1982, 1983)
Civil servants' benefits	5	- (all)	-
Families and children	16	16	6 (1954, 1961, 1964, 1974, 1979, 1982)
Social Assistance	10	9 (1954)	7 (1953, 1961, 1969, 1974, 1981, 1982, 1983)
Housing	23	22 (1946)	11 (1950, 1956, 1960, 1965, 1965, 1970, 1971, 1971, 1974, 1982, 1982)
Education	15	12 (1947, 1949, 12.5.1969)	6 (1969, 1971, 1971, 1975, 1976, 1982)
Total	146	130	68

Notes to and sources for appendix tables

Table 1

GDP

Sources: (17) p. 44 (1950-60, excluding Saar and Berlin); (11) pp. 258-259 (1960-80, including Saar and Berlin).

Deflators:
GDP: calculated from current and constant figures in sources above.
Cost of living: combination of two series:
Sources: (20) p. 250 (1950-62); (11) p. 328 (1962-80), re-calculated on basis 1970.
Private consumption: calculated from current and constant figures.
Sources: (17) p. 44 and (1) p. 320.
Public consumption: procedure and sources as under private consumption.

Public expenditure:
Most embracive definition of public sector outlays in national accounts statistics including special financial transactions.
Sources: (10) p. 138 (1950-60, excluding Saar und Berlin); (11) p. 277 (1960-80, including Saar and Berlin).

Table 2

Total public expenditure by economic function:
National accounts statistics excluding special financial transactions. Transfers and subsidies including capital transfers.
Sources: (10) p. 139 (1950-60, excluding Saar and Berlin); (11) p. 280 (1960-80, including Saar and Berlin).

Total public expenditure by purpose:
Outlays of public authorities in public finance statistics excluding social insurance; 1960: fiscal year, 9 moths only.

Other expenditure:
Non-specified outlays including payments for war consequences and for measures to stabilise the economy (calculated as difference between total outlays and sum of components; not calculable after 1974).

Social security etc.: Not available after 1974 (because post-1974 data include social insurance outlays which are not included in total expenditure).

Sources for total expenditure: (22) ed. 1973, p. 124 (1950-59); (23) ed. 1981, p. 410 (1960-74); (11) p. 284 (1975-80): 1974 in new definition (consistent with 1975): 318.26;

Sources for components: (23), 1981, p. 409 (1951-74); ed. 1982, p. 413 (1975-80), and (1) p. 486 (for 1950, 52, 54, 56).

Total expenditure for distribution by level of government: Up to 1974 net expenditure excluding transfers between various levels, 1975-1980 gross outlays summing up outlays of various levels; 1974 in new definition (consistent with 1975): 363.94 (and 36.8%, 36.8%, 26.3%).

Other expenditure:
Outlays for ERP programme and equalisation of burdens fund (not available after 1974).
Sources: (22) ed. 1973, pp. 124-125 (1950-61), ed. 1978, pp. 140-141 (1962-74); (11) pp. 284-285 (1975-80).

Table 3

Total I:
Social security spending in the definition of the International Labour Office.
Source: (15) various editions (see also the reproduction of raw data in (13) pp. 497-498.

Total II:
"Direct paymants" in the official social budget (including employers' schemes).

Sources: (3) ed. 1978, p. 107 (1960-65); (4) eds. 1976, pp. 484-500, 1980, pp. 22-34.

Total III:
Total social spending in German social budget including tax credits.
Sources: as for Total II.

Total IV:
Excluding wage continuation from employers, otherwise identical with Total V.

Total V:
Sum of social security, health, housing, and education as defined below.

Social security:
Sum of pension insurance, occupational injuries insurance, sickness insurance/cash benefits, wage continuation, unemployment compensation, child allowances, farmers' pensions, civil service benefits excluding sickness benefits, civil service supplementary pensions, benefits to war victims, equalisation of burdens, political reparation payments, other compensation programmes, social assistance, youth assistance. Income maintenance refers to cash benefits of these schemes. The sources are listed in the notes to the tables for the special schemes. In the standard case the data are from various editions of (3) in the period 1950 to 1965, and from the social budget data in (4) in the period 1965 to 1980. Breaks in statistical definitions occur in 1960 and 1965.

Health:
Sum of sickness insurance excluding cash benefits, civil service sickness benefits, and public health. For sources see Table 9.

Housing:
Sum of subsidies for housing construction, premiums on savings for housing purposes, and housing allowances. For sources see Table 14.

Education:
Sum of outlays for schools and universities, science and research, and cultural affairs in public finance statistics; for sources see Table 14.

Deflators:
For social security: cost of living; for health and education: public consumption; for housing: private consumption.

Table 4

For definitions and sources see notes to Table 3. GDP percentages are based on GDP data in Table 1. Public expenditure percentages are based on public sector outlays in the most embracive definition (see Table 1) plus wage continuation outlays (because wage continuation does not form part of public expenditure in German official statistics). Social expenditure in the official German definition refers to direct payments in the German social budget. Percentages of social expenditure refer to the total in the Florence definition including wage continuation (Total V).

Table 5

Social security expenditure:
Total outlays excluding transfers.

Income maintenance:
Cash benefits of social security schemes.

Pensions:
Sum of pension insurance schemes, farmers' pensions, civil service pensions, civil service supplementary schemes.

Sickness insurance:
Cash benefits plus wage continuation.

War consequences:
Sum of benefits to war victims, equalisation of burdens, and (since 1960) political reparation payments.

Other:
Sum of youth assistance and other compensation programmes. Data for unemployment compensation ("employment promotion" in the terminology of the social budget, i.e. insurance, assistance, and other benefits), occupational injuries insurance, family allowances and social assistance taken from the sources listed for the tables on the various special schemes.

Table 6

Definitions as in Table 5; deflator: cost of living index.

Table 7

All systems:
Sum of three social insurance schemes, farmers', civil servants' and civil service supplementary schemes. Total I gross expenditure including transfers, Total II net expenditure excluding transfers; 1960 break in statistical definitions; Total I in old definition (consistent with 1959): 27, 289.

Social insurance:
Sum of workers', employees', and miners' schemes.

Sources: (3) eds. 1955, p. 88 (1950-53), 1960, p. 104 (1954-59), 1965, p. 96 (1960-64); (4) eds. 1976, pp. 484-500 (1965-1973), 1980, pp. 22-34 (1974-80). Data for 1950 to 1965 are raw sums of the three single insurance schemes including transfers among these schemes, subsequent data are net totals excluding transfers among the various pension insurance programmes.

Cash benefits A:
Cash benefits in the definition of the social budget, consistent with and from same sources as data on total expenditure.

Cash benefits B:
Sum of various cash payments for pensions, consistent with data on special types of pensions in the following columns.

Sources: (7) ed. 1964, p. 73 (1950-53); (3) eds. 1965, p. 129 (1954-59), 1980, p. 113 (1960-78), 1982, p. 107 (1979-80).

Pensions by type:
Sources: (3) eds. 1970, p. 10 (1950-69), 1978, p. 105 (1970-77), 1982, p. 95 (1977-80); sources for invalidity only: (5) eds. 1976, pp. 124-129 (1969-74), 1978, p. 96 (1975-77), 1980, p. 96 (1978-79).

Table 8

Farmers' pensions
Sources: (3) eds. 1960, p. 104 (1957-59), 1965, p. 96 (1960-64); 4, eds. 1976, pp. 484-500 (1965-73), 1980, pp. 22-34 (1974-80); Total I including/Total II excluding transfers as in all subsequent tables on single schemes if not otherwise specified.

Civil servants' pensions:
Data for 1950-59 are estimates based on figures in (15) eds. 1958, p. 65, 1961, p. 77, 1964, p. 93 which give total civil service expenditure for the period 1950-60 and pension expenditure for 1957 and 1960; the percentages of total expenditure were then inter- and extrapolated.

Sources: for subsequent years (3) ed. 1978, p. 107 (1960-64); (4) eds. 1976 and 1980 as under farmers' pensions (as in all following cases where page numbers of these editions are not specified or reference is made to standard sources).

Civil service supplementary schemes:
Sources: (3), ed. 1978, p. 107 (1960-64); 4, eds. 1976 and 1980.

Occupational injuries insurance
Sources: (3) eds. 1955, p. 88 (1950-53), 1960, p. 104 (1954-59), 1965, p. 96 (1960-65); (4) eds. 1976 and 1980.

Table 9

Income maintenance total:
Sum of sickness insurance cash benefits and wage continuation.
Sources: See below

Wage continuation:
Data for 1950-60 are estimates based on interpolations of figures for 1950, 1955, and 1960.
Sources: (3) eds. 1970, p. 102, 1978, p. 107; sources for subsequent years: (3) ed. 1978, p. 107 (1960-65); (4) eds. 1976 and 1980 as in standard case (see farmers' pensions).

Sickness insurance:
Total II (net, excluding transfers) for period 1950-65 calculated as sum of single sickness insurance components, in subsequent years immediate source data.
Sources: (3) eds. 1955, p. 88 (1950-53), 1960, p. 104 (1954-59), 1965, p. 96 (1960-65); (4) eds. 1976 and 1980.

Civil servants:
Sources: (3) and (4) as under wage continuation.

Public health:
Sources: (15) eds. 1958, p. 65, 1961, p. 79, 1964, p. 95 for period 1950-59; 1960 change in sources and statistical definitions; 1960 in old definition (consistent with 1959): 160; for period 1960-80 standard sources (3) and (4) as for wage continuation.

Health services:
Sum of sickness insurance benefits in kind, administration and general services, civil servants' benefits, and public health; 1960 break in statistical definition, in old definition (consistent with 1959): 6 623.

Table 10

Columns 1-5:
Standard definitions following social budget.

Total III:
Outlays of the Federal Employment Office (sum of columns 7-14; prior to 1965 deviating from the sum due to missing data for some components).

Employment promotion:
Sum of two columns in source data, i.e. measures to create jobs and promotion of work (*Förderung der Arbeitsaufnahme*).

Other services:
Administration and general services (equal to difference between total and sum of single other components).

Vocational training services:
Sum of four columns in source data on promotion of vocational training plus vocational rehabilitation measures.

Income supplements:
Sum of five components in sorce data, i.e. short time work benefits plus four types of benefits for the construction industry.

Redundancy allowances:
Immediate source data (*Konkursausfallgeld*).

Insurance cash benefits:
Immediate source data (*Arbeitslosengeld*) including transfers for social insurance contributions.

Assistance cash benefits A:
Unemployment assistance paid by the Federal Employment Office (*Anschluß-Arbeitslosenhilfe*).

Assistance cash benefits B:
Unemployment assistance paid by the federal government.

All cash benefits:
Sum of insurance cash benefits, both types of assistance benefits, vocational training cash benefits, various income supplements, and redundancy allowances.

Total federal outlays:
Sum of unemployment assistance cash benefits B and other federal outlays.
Sources: For columns 1 to 5 (Total I to cash benefits): (3) eds. 1955, p. 88 (1950-53), 1960, p. 104 (1955-59), 1965, p. 96 (1960-65); (4) eds. 1976 and 1980;
For all other columns: (7) ed. 1964, p. 104 (1950-61); (3) eds. 1965, p. 114 (1962-64), 1970, pp. 124-125 (1965-67), 1982, pp. 160-161 (1968-80).

Table 11

General child allowances:
Sources: (3) eds. 1960, p. 104 (1955-59), 1965, p. 96 (1960-65); (4) eds. 1976 and 1980.

Civil servants' child allowances:
Sources: Data for 1950-59 are estimates based on figures in (15) eds. 1958, p. 65, 1961, p. 77, 1964, p. 93 which give total civil service expenditure for the period 1950-60 and child allowance expenditure for 1957 and 1960; the percentages of total expenditure were then inter- and extrapolated; 1960 change in sources and statistical definitions; in old definition (consistent with 1959): 450; for period 1960-80 standard sources (3) ed. 1978, and (4) eds. 1976 and 1980.

Youth assistance:
Sources: Standard sources (3) ed. 1978, and (4) eds. 1976 and 1980.

Table 12

Social assistance:
Columns 1-4 standard definition following social budget.
Sources: (3) eds. 1955, p. 89 (1950-53), 1960, p. 105 (1954-59), 1965, p. 98 (1960-65); (4) eds. 1976 and 1980 (1965-80).

Total III:
From administrative statistics, basis for the percentage distributions in the following four columns.
Sources: For period 1950-1975 (7) eds. 1964, p. 151, 1967, p. 179, 1970, p. 245, 1974, p. 309, 1977, p. 357; for subsequent years: (23), table '*Sozialhilfe*' (various years).

Percentage distribution of ordinary benefits (*Hilfe zum Lebensunterhalt*) and extraordinary benefits (Hilfe in besonderen *Lebenslagen*) calculated from raw data in (23) as above.
Percentage distribution of institutional (*In Anstalten*) and out-door payments (*Außerhalb Anstalten*) calculated from raw data in sources listed for Total III.

Other compensation programmes:
'*Sonstige Entschädigungen*' in social budget.
Sources: (3) ed. 1978, p. 107 (1960-65); (4) eds. 1976 and 1980.

Table 13

War victims and equalisation of burdens:
Sources: (3) eds. 1955, p. 89 (1950-53), 1960, p. 105 (1954-59), 1965, p. 98 (1960-65); (4) eds. 1976 and 1980.

Political reparation payments:
Sources: (3) ed. 1978; (4) eds. 1976 and 1980.

Table 14

Total housing outlays:
Calculated as sum of subsidies for housing construction, premiums on savings, and housing allowances. 1960 fiscal year, 9 months only.

Subsidies:
Special series kindly supplied by the Federal Statistical Office, letter of november 30, 1982.

Premiums on savings:
Special series kindly supplied by the Federal Statistical Office, letter of december 12, 1982.

Housing allowances:
Standard sources (3) ed. 1978; (4) eds. 1976 and 1980.

Education outlays/Total I:
Sum of three columns in public finance statistics on government expenditure, i.e. schools and universities, science and research, cultural affairs.

Sources: (23) ed. 1981, p. 409 and 1982, p. 413 (data for 1950, 1952, 1954, and 1956 are interpolations), 1960 fiscal year, 9 months only.

Total II:
Data in statistical definition of the educational budget excluding general promotion of research; basis for distribution by educational sector in the following five columns. (Percentage distribution by sector calculated from raw data in same source.)
Source: (9) ed. 1980-81, p. 182.

Total III:
Net expenditure calculated as sum of raw data for the following three columns on distribution by purpose.
Distribution by purpose: Calculated from raw data in (9) ed. 1980-81, p. 185.

Table 15

Total revenues:
Revenues of public sector in national accounts statistics, including social insurance, but excluding special financial transactions (corresponding to definition of public expenditure in Table 2 on economic functions).

Revenues by type (columns 2-4):
As defined in national accounts statistics.

Statistical deficit:
Difference between public revenues and public expenditure in Table 2, column 1; positive figures indicate surplus.

Direct/indirect taxes:
Definition of national accounts statistics, sum identical with total taxes (discrepancies due to rounding errors).

Aggregate tax burden:
Columns 1 and 2 as % of GDP in Table 1.

Individual tax burden:
Direct taxes and social insurance contributions paid by dependent workers as % of gross earnings of the dependent labour force; national accounts statistics.

Sources: for columns 1-9: (10) p. 138 (1950-60); (11) p. 280 (1960-80); for direct/indirect taxes: (16) p. 156 (1960-75); (18) p. 111 (1976-79); for aggregate tax burden: same as columns 1-9; for individual tax burden: (4), ed. 1980, p. 229.

Table 16

All data relate to public authorities (excluding social insurance) in the definition of public finance statistics; 1975/75 break in statistical definitions; 1960 fiscal year, 9 months only.

Total revenues and statistical deficit:
government (corresponding to definition of public expenditure in Table 2 on distribution by purpose).

Revenues and taxes by level of government: Gross aggregates summing up data for the various levels of government (including transfers between these levels).

Taxes by type:
In statistical definition of cash keeping data (*Kassenmäßige Steuereinnahmen*); direct taxes: sum of seven items in source data, i.e. income tax (*Einkommen- und Körperschaftssteuer*), property tax, land tax (categories A, plus B/C in source data), trade tax (*Gewerbesteuer*), two types of special taxes (*Ergänzungs- und Sonderabgabe*); indirect taxes calculated as difference between total and direct taxes.

Sources: for columns 1-3: (22) ed. 1973, pp. 124-125 (1950-59); (23) ed. 1981, p. 410 (1960-74); (11) p. 284 (1975-80); 1974 in new definition (consistent with 1975): 290.88;
for columns 4-11 (distribution by level of government): (22) eds. 1973, pp. 124-125 (1950-61), 1978, pp. 140-141 (1962-74); (11) pp. 284-285 1978, pp. 140-141 (1962-74); (11) pp. 284-285 (1974-80); 1974 in new definition (consistent with 1975): 336.07 - 36.8 - 37.2 - 26.0 for total revenues and 235.55 - 50.4 - 37.1 - 12.5 for taxes;
for columns 12-14 (taxes by type): (22) ed. 1973, p. 124 (1950-59); (2) ed. 1981, pp. 226-230 (1960-80); percentages in brackets are based on a different total and taken from the data collection compiled by Kurt Seebohm in (13), p. 305.

Table 17

Total:
Public authorities excluding debt between various levels of government.

Distribution by level of government:
Based on gross total summing up debt of federal, state, and local government.

Annual changes:
Calculated as difference between annual levels of debt; net total for all public authorities deviates from gross figures for various levels of government.

Interest of debt:
For public sector (including social insurance) definition of national accounts statistics, for public authorities (excluding social insurance), definition of public finance statistics.

Sources: for volume and changes of debt: (11) p. 287; for interest of debt/public sector: (10) p. 139 (1950-60, excluding Saar and Berlin); (11) p. 277 (1960-80, including Saar and Berlin); for interest on debt/public authorities: (23) ed. 1981, p. 410 and ed. 1982, p. 414 (1950-74); (11) p. 284 (1975-80); 1974/75 break in statistical definitions; 1974 in new definition (consistent with 1975): 12 440.

Table 18

Social security:
Sources: (15) eds. 1958, 1961, 1964, 1967, 1972, 1976, 1982, 1985 (see also the reproduction of raw data in (13) pp. 499-500).

Social programmes:
Total: excluding transfers; State: sum of special taxes allocated to social security, state participation, and participation of other public authorities; Other: sum of income from capital and other receipts.
Sources: for social programmes: (4) eds. 1976 and 1980 (social budget data on direct payments).

Table 19

Persons living from transfers:
Microcensus data, persons reporting social transfers as their predominant source of living.
Sources: (3) eds. 1971, p. 19 (1960-63), 1975, p. 14 (1963-72), 1982, p. 11 (1973-80).

Pensioners:
Sum of workers', employees', and miners' schemes, each at the end of the stated year.
Sources: (7) eds. 1964, pp. 53-54 and 1967, p. 32 (1950-59); (3) ed. 1982, p. 114 and - for miners - eds. 1970, p. 135 and 1982, p. 115 (1960-80).

Occupational injuries:
Total no. of pensions including survivors' pensions.
Sources: (6) eds. 1981, 8.12, and (for 1980) 1982, 8.13.

Sickness insurance recipients of cash benefits:
Calculated from data on sickness ratio among compulsory members assuming that all sick members are in receipt of cash benefits.
Sources: (3) eds. 1960, pp. 107 and 122 (1950-59), 1970, p. 107 (1960-69), 1975, p. 176 (1970-74), 1982, pp. 138-139 (1975-80).

Unemployment compensation:
Source: (6) ed. 1981, 8.14.

Child allowances:
Sources: (7) ed. 1960, p. 87 (1956-58); (3) ed. 1970, p. 149 (1964-69); (7) ed. 1977, p. 239 (1970-73); (5) eds. 1980, p. 109 (1974-79), 1983, p. 91 (1980).

War victims:
Total number of pension recipients including survivors' pensions.
Source: (6) ed. 1981, 8.14.

Social assistance:
Total number of beneficiaries, since 1963 under new legislation and in a new statistical definition (ordinary and extraordinary benefits).
Sources: (7) ed. 1964, p. 142 (1950-62); (6) ed. 1982, 8.16 (1963-80).

Housing allowances:
Number of households in receipt of allowances.
Sources: (7) ed. 1977, p. 341 (1964-68); (23) table '*Wohngeld*', various years (1969-80).

Education allowances:
Pupils and students in receipt of allowances according to Ministry of Labour statistics presumably referring to monthly averages.
Sources: (5) eds. 1974, p. 104 (1971), 1980, p. 125 (1972-78), 1983, p. 110 (1979-80).

Table 20

Dwellings:
Sources: (14) p. 82 (1950-75, up to 1959 excluding Saar and Berlin); (23) ed. 1981, p. 221 (1976-80); 1960 and 1976 changes in statistical definitions; 1960 in old definition: 15 110, 1976 in old definition: 23 309.

Annual housing construction and social housing:
Sources: (19) ed. 1982, p. 265.

Kindergarten places:
Sources: (12) p. 218 (1960-64); (9) eds. 1978, p. 12 (1965-69), 1981/82, p. 12 (1970-74), 1984/85, p. 12 (1975-80).

Primary and main schools (*Volks- und Hauptschulen*):
Sources: (20) p. 127 (1951-68); (21) ed. 1984, p. 44.

Secondary schools:
Sum of categories *Mittel-/Realschulen, Gesamtschulen, Gymnasien*
Sources: (20) p. 128 (1951-68); (23) table '*Schulen, Schüler und Lehrer im allgemeinen Schulwesen*', various years (1969-80); same sources for *Gymnasien*

University entrants:
Universities and theological seminars, excluding teachers' colleges, Germans only.
Sources: (24) p. 13 (1952 and 1955); (21) ed. 1984, p. 89 (1960-80).

Students in universities and teachers' colleges: Germans and foreigners.
Sources: (8) p. 21 (1950 and 1955); (23) ed. 1970, p. 71 (1960-64); (9) eds. 1978, p. 107 (1965-69), 1981/82, p. 105 (1970-80).

Entire post-secondary sector:
Universities and various colleges (*Fachhochschulen*), Germans and foreigners.
Sources: (24) p. 9 (1952); (9) eds. 1978, p. 107 (1960-69), 1981/82, p. 105 (1970-80).

Teaching personnel of various schools:
Same sources as for pupils in these schools.

Teaching personnel/entire post-secondary sector:
Scientific personnel in universities and various colleges.
Sources: (8) p. 89 (1953, excluding colleges); (9) eds. 1978, p. 132 (1960-70), 1981/82, p. 153 (1970-80).

Total teaching staff:
Sum of teaching personnel in schools (including adult education) and scientific personnel in post-secondary sector.
Sources: (21) ed. 1984, p. 43; for 1951 estimate based on sum of teachers in main and secondary schools and teaching staff in universities reported for 1953, excluding adult education.

Table 21

Total population and age groups 60+, 0-18:
Sources: (23) table '*Wohnbevölkerung nach dem Alter*', various years; 1950-56, excluding Saar and Berlin (1957 in old definition: total 50 817, 60+ 7 791); 1957-60 excluding Berlin.

Other age groups:
Sources: Up to 1964 from source above; 1965-80 from (9) eds. 1978, pp. 165-166 (1965-69), 1981/82, pp. 203-204 (1970-79), 1984/85, pp. 231-233 (1980).

Total labour force:
Sources: (25) p. 262 (1950-60 excluding Saar and Berlin; 1960 in new definition: 26 518).

Unemployed, dependent employment, and vacancies:
Source: As for total labour force (1960 in new definition: 271 - 20,257 - 465).

Unemployed II:
Statistical definition consistent with data on unemployment compensation beneficiaries in Graph 37.
Source: (6) ed. 1981, 2.10.

Total labour force II:
Statistical definition consistent with data on social insurance coverage in Graph 32.
Sources: (25) p. 262 (1950-60); (3) eds. 1970, p. 8 (1961-66), 1975, p. 12 (1967-69), 1982, p. 7 (1970-80).

Table 22

Compiled from list of legal regulations in Institutional Synopsis.

Enumerated sources for appendix tables

(1) E. Ballerstedt, W. Glatzer (eds), *Soziologischer Almanach* Frankfurt, 1979.

(2) Bundesministerium der Finanzen, *Finanzbericht*. Bonn, various years.

(3) Der Bundesminister für Arbeit und Sozialordnung, *Arbeits- und Sozialstatistik Hauptergebnisse*. Bonn, various years.

(4) Der Bundesminister für Arbeit und Sozialordnung, *Materialband zum Sozialbudget*. Bonn, various years.

(5) Der Bundesminister für Arbeit und Sozialordnung. *Sozialbericht*. Bonn, various years.

(6) Der Bundesminister für Arbeit und Sozialordnung. *Statistisches Taschenbuch* Bonn, various years.

(7) Der Bundesminister für Arbeit und Sozialordnung, *Übersicht über die soziale Sicherung.* Bonn, various years.

(8) Der Bundesminister für Bildung und Wissenschaft, *Bildungsbericht '70.* Bonn, 1970.

(9) Der Bundesminister für Bildung und Wissenschaft, *Grund- und Strukturdaten.* Bonn, various years.

(10) Deutscher Bundestag, *Jahresgutachten 1964/65 des Sachverständigenrates zur Begutachtung der gesamtwirtschaftlichen Entwicklung* (Bundestagsdrucksache IV/2890). Bonn, 1964.

(11) Deutscher Bundestag, *Jahresgutachten 1981/82 des Sachverständigenrates zur Begutachtung der gesamtwirtschaftlichen Entwicklung* (Bundestagsdrucksache 9/1061). Bonn, 1981.

(12) R. Ermrich, *Basisdaten. Zahlen zur ökonomischen Entwicklung der Bundesrepublik Deutschland.* Bonn-Bad Godesberg, 1974.

(13) P. Flora et al., *State, Economy, and Society in Western Europe 1815-1975* Vol. I, Frankfurt 1983.

(14) W. Glatzer, *Wohnungsversorgung im Wohlfahrtsstaat* Frankfurt, 1980.

(15) International Labour Office, *The Cost of Social Security.* Geneva, irregular series.

(16) J. Kopf, R. Kern, W. Schmidt (eds), *Volkswirtschaftliche Basisdaten.* Frankfurt, 1980.

(17) OECD, *National Accounts 1950-1978.* Volume I. Paris, 1980.

(18) OECD, *National Accounts 1962-1979.* Volume II. Paris, 1981.

(19) Presse- und Informationsamt der Bundesregierung, *Gesellschaftliche Daten.* Bonn, irregular series.

(20) Statistisches Bundesamt, *Bevölkerung und Wirtschaft 1872-1972.* Stuttgart-Mainz, 1972.

(21) Statistisches Bundesamt, *Bildung im Zahlenspiegel* Stuttgart-Mainz, various years.

(22) Statistisches Bundesamt, *Lange Reihen zur Wirtschaftsentwicklung.* Stuttgart-Mainz, irregular series.

(23) Statistisches Bundesamt, *Statistisches Jahrbuch für die Bundesrepublik Deutschland.* Stuttgart-Mainz, various years.

(24) Wissenschaftsrat, *Empfehlungen zu Umfang und Struktur des Tertiären Bereichs.* Köln.

(25) Deutscher Bundestag, *Jahresgutachten 1984/85 des Sachverständigenrates zur Begutachtung der gesamtwirtschaftlichen Entwicklung* (Bundestagsdrucksache 10/2541). Bonn, 1984.

United Kingdom

Richard Parry

Institutional Synopsis

Contents

Glossary of abbreviations

DES	Department of Education and Science
DHSS	Department of Health and Social Security
DOE	Department of Employment
HMSO	Her Majesty's Stationery Office
HSC	Health and Safety Commission
MSC	Manpower Services Commission
NHS	National Health Service

Introduction

1. Governmental structure

The United Kingdom has two elected tiers of government: central government and local authorities. Central government is organized in functional departments, the most important for social policy being the Department of Health and Social Security (DHSS), the Department of Education and Science (DES), and the Department of the Environment (DOE), which is responsible for housing. For most functions, these departments cover England only. Scotland, Wales and Northern Ireland have their own territorial departments which administer generally comparable policies, though education and housing in Scotland have, for historical reasons, some particularly distinctive features.

Social security is the only large social programme administered by central government and implemented by its staff. Health is administered through health authorities and boards appointed and financed by central government. Education, housing and personal social services (residential care and social worker services) are local government responsibilities though operating in a legislative and financial framework determined from the centre.

Local government consists of two elected tiers: counties, known as regions in Scotland, and districts. Counties are responsible for education and social services, and districts for housing, except in seven English metropolitan authorities (including Greater London), where the second tier authorities have more responsibility, and Northern Ireland, where there are only districts and all important social functions are administered by central government. Local government was extensively reorganized in 1974, when boundaries and distribution of power were altered, and the number of authorities much reduced.

2. Official publications

Government proposals are made in 'White Papers', or properly 'Command Papers' presented to Parliament, and which are cited as 'Cmnd 1234' etc. Proposals or suggestions at an earlier stage of deliberation are published as 'Consultative Documents'. Proceedings and reports of the House of Commons Select Committees (which cover all government departments and conduct investigations), and reports from various public bodies, are published as 'House of Commons Papers', (cited as HC 123 session 1978-79 etc.). Acts of Parliament are usually cited by their short title only e.g. the National Health Services Act 1946, they also have a chapter number (c.1 etc).

The majority of British central government publications, whether parliamentary papers or issued directly by departments, are published by Her Majesty's Stationery Office (HMSO).

3. Summary of income maintenance systems

The British system of income maintenance is not organized into separate schemes in terms of circumstances covered, but into three types of benefit system: National Insurance, non-contributory benefits, and means-tested benefits.

National Insurance provides retirement pensions and unemployment, sickness and disability insurance (largely flat-rate) in return for contributions (initially flat-rate but earnings-related since 1974). The present scheme dates from 1948, replacing earlier, less comprehensive schemes which started in 1912. Legislation is now consolidated in the 1975 Social Security Act. This covers the entire workforce, including the self-employed, but payment of benefit requires the fulfillment of minimum contributions. In 1975 a new earnings-related pension scheme was introduced. This is still being phased in and will pay a second pension. Members of occupational pension schemes are free to contract-out of this scheme and pay a lower contribution rate.

National Insurance is financed on a pay-as-you-go basis by the National Insurance Fund, which receives contributions from employees and employers (collected through the income tax system), and a state subsidy of approximately 20%. In 1980, 'employed earners' (i.e. those with a contract of service) paid 6.75% of their earnings, within the range UKL 23 to UKL 165 a week, whilst employers paid 11.7%. For those contracted-out of the earnings-related pension scheme the rates are 4.25% and 7.2% respectively. The lower and upper earnings limits are revalued annually in line with earnings. Self-employed persons with earnings in excess of UKL 1,250 a year pay a flat-rate contribution of UKL 2.50 a week. In general, entitlement to benefit is dependent upon the payment of contributions throughout the preceding year. Benefits are lower for those with lower contributions.

In 1980 expenditure on National Insurance benefits amounted to UKL 7,14,416 million, which corresponded to 6.4% of GDP and 65% of income maintenance expenditure.

Non-contributory benefits provide pensions for those not covered by National Insurance, benefits for the disabled, and child allowances to all mothers of infant and school-age children. In 1980 expenditure on non-contributory benefits amounted to UKL 5,000 million, which corresponded to 2.2% of GDP and 22.5% of income maintenance expenditure. Non-contributory benefits are financed out of general taxation.

The principal means-tested benefits are a scheme of social assistance payable to those not in full-time employment whose income does not exceed the scale rate of benefit, and Family Income Supplement for the working poor with children. In 1980 expenditure on means-tested benefits amounted to UKL 2,800 million, which corresponded to 1.2% of GDP and 12.5% of income maintenance expenditure. These benefits are financed out of general taxation.

Administration is carried out by central government, through the DHSS. The major pension and child benefit schemes are administered from computerized central offices which cover the entire country. Means-tested schemes are administered through a network of local offices. There are appeal procedures to tribunals and the National Insurance Commissioners to resolve disputes on eligibility and boards to determine medical facts.

Throughout this synopsis, benefits are summarized in the following way. Rates given are weekly payments current from November 1980. Expenditure is for 1980, when total social security expenditure amounted to UKL 22,211 million, and average earnings amounted to UKL 106.30 a week. 'Numbers receiving' refers to the average number of recipients at any one time in late 1979 when population amounted to 55.9 million.

I Pensions

In 1980 expenditure on cash benefits for national pensions amounted to UKL 10,952, which corresponded to 4.9% of GDP and 49.3% of social security expenditure (excluding public sector occupational pensions). In addition, approximately UKL 1,000 million were spent on services for the elderly.

Income maintenance

The National Insurance retirement pension provides a minimum flat-rate pension for all citizens. Starting in 1975, a new earnings-related pension scheme has been gradually introduced which will pay a second pension for those not already covered by an earnings-related occupational pension scheme provided by a public or private employer. Such schemes cover 50% of employees. These pensions are paid in addition and without detriment to the flat-rate National Insurance pension in both the public and private sector. Public sector pensions are index-linked.

Pension benefit expenditure (1980), number of beneficiaries (1980)

	in million UKL	%	in 1,000s	%
Social security pensions:				
Retirement pensions (flat-rate)			9 386	94.7
Earnings-related pensions	10 277	93.8	(298)[a]	(3.0)
Graduated pensions			(4 988)[a]	(50.3)
Non-contributory pensions	40	0.4	56	0.6
Widows' pensions			318	3.2
Widows' allowances	635	5.8	35	0.4
Widowed mothers' allowances)			118	1.2
Total	10 952	100.0	9 913	100.0
Public sector occupational pensions:				
Civil service	1 057[b]		424	
Armed forces	663[b]		284	
National Health Service	622[b]		237	
Teachers' pension scheme	925[b]		212	
Local government	740[b]		352	
Police fire service	289[b]		100	
Nationalized industries	1 362		860	
Total	5 658[b]		2 469	

[a] These also receive flat-rate retirement pensions
[b] 1982-1983
Source: (1), (2), (7); House of Commons Hansard, 19 October, 1982, Vol. 29, cols. 83-84 written answer; Social Security Statistics 1981, Tables 13.45 and 13.47.

1. Retirement pensions

Retirement pensions are payable at 65 for men and 60 for women. However, if the recipient is under the age of 70 (65 for women), and post-retirement earnings exceed UKL 52 per week, the pension is reduced. In 1980 basic retirement pension amounted to UKL 27.15 a week for a single person, and UKL 16.30 for a married woman qualifying on her husband's contributions, i.e. 25.5% and 15.3% of average earnings. The pension is UKL 0.25 higher for those over the age of 80 and increments are paid if retirement is deferred until the age of 70 (65 for women).

A graduated pension scheme was in operation from 1961-1975 through the National Insurance Fund. These pensions required contracting-in and are payable with the flat-rate retirement pension according to contributions paid. In 1980 the average additional amount was UKL 0.58 per week. These pensions were superseded by the new earnings-related pension scheme in 1978. Phasing-in from 1978-98, these pensions are payable when an employer has not contracted-out his employees (see below). The pension pays 1.25% of earnings within the upper and lower limits for National Insurance contributions: in 1980 this amounted to a maximum of up to 20 years at a rate of UKL 23 to UKL 165 a week. The upper earnings limit is set at one and a half times average earnings.

In 1970 non-contributory retirement pensions were instituted for those over the age of 80 qualifying for either no or lower National Insurance pensions. In 1980 married women received UKL 9.30, and others UKL 16.30, which amounted to 8.7% and 15.3% of average net earnings.

2. Widows' pensions

National Insurance widows' benefits were instituted in 1948. Widows' pension is payable to widows over the age of 40. Entitlement is dependent upon husbands' contributions and is payable irrespective of earnings until remarriage or retirement. The rate varies according to the age at which the claimant was widowed or when children grew up, whichever is the later. In 1980 this amounted to UKL 27.15 a week, or 25.5% of average earnings, for those aged 50 and over. For those aged 40-49 the amount is reduced in annual steps to a final level of UKL 8.15. Widows' pension is replaced by retirement pension at the age of 60. Widows with at least one child eligible for child benefit (see page 20) receive widowed mothers' allowance at the rate of UKL 27.15, plus UKL 7.50 for each child per week.

A higher widows' allowance is paid during the first 26 weeks of widowhood when neither partner was over retirement age. In 1980 the rate amounted to UKL 38.00 per week, or 35.7% of average earnings, together with UKL 7.50 for each dependent child.

3. Public sector occupational pensions

In the public sector 74% of employees are in jobs entitling them to an occupational pension. The main exceptions are part-time employees. Central and local government employees receive index-linked pensions, together with a lump sum payment (normally amounting to six months of final salary) which is usually paid on retirement. The flat-rate National Insurance retirement pension is paid in addition, but public sector employees will be contracted-out from the state earningsrelated pension.

The principal civil service pension scheme was instituted in 1974. It replaced previous schemes, is non-contributory and payable at the age of 60. A lump sum is also payable. The rate of payment per week amounts to 1/80 of final wage for each year of service (maximum 40 years). The armed forces pension is also non-contributory, and payable immediately to members of the armed forces leaving after a minimum of 16 years (officers), and 22 years service (other ranks). For those with a minimum of five years service the pension is payable at 60. Weekly payment is made according to rank and length of service. Maximum payment (amounting to around half of final pay) is earned after a period of 34 years and 37 years service for officers and other ranks respectively. A lump sum payment is also made. Pension schemes for the National Health Service (NHS), teachers, local government officers, the police force and firemen are funded and earnings-related with benefits being dependent on final pay and length of service. Each nationalized industry or public corporation has its own funded scheme. These are not index-linked by statute, but are in practice.

The civil service and armed forces schemes are non-contributory, (apart from the component for widows and dependents), and are funded by a general levelling down of wages. Other schemes are funded by earnings-related contributions from employers and employees, though in many cases the income is contributed on a pay-as-you-go basis, and is not actually invested. The administration and financing of these schemes is quite separate from the social security system.

4. Private sector occupational pensions

Many employers provide contributory pension schemes for their employees. In 1975 when the latest comprehensive survey was taken coverage was as follows:

Occupational pensions in 1979

	Private Sector	Public Sector	Total
Number of employees			
- in 1,000s	15 700	7 450	23 150
Members of pension schemes			
- in 1,000s	6 200	5 600	11 800
Percentage of			
- employees covered	39%	75%	51%
Pension payments (in 1,000s)			
- former employees	1 200	1 800	3 000
- widows of dependents	200	500	700
Value of final pension as % of final earnings per service year			
- 1/60 or over	3 180	5 150	8 960
- 1/80 - 1/60	1 560	300	1 860
- less than 1/80	250	70	320

Source: (7).

Approximately 10 million employees are covered by schemes contracted-out of the state earnings-related scheme. This requires approval from the Occupational Pensions Board, a government body. Schemes must offer a 'requisite benefit' and 'guaranteed minimum pension' or GMP which is at least equivalent to the state scheme. Retirement age, increments for deferred retirement and survivors' benefits must also be comparable. Index-linking of that part of an occupational scheme up to GMP level is financed by the state under the same phasing-in provisions (1978-1998). Employers' and employees' contributions are exempt from income tax: in 1981-1982 the cost of this amounted to UKL 1,000 million.

Services

A variety of home and institution based care is available for the elderly through the health and personal social services. Hospital and day care services are free of charge, but residential homes and home helps are charged on the basis of a means-test. Other services include the provision of aids for and adaptations to the home, visits by social workers, health visitors and district nurses.

Health and social services for the elderly 1980-81

	Expenditure in mill. UKL	Persons over 65 in 1,000s
Hospital and community health services	3 636	
Family practitioner services	589	
Personal social services	876	
Total	5 101	8 163

Source: (8) Tables 2.11.7 and 2.12.2

Core Laws

1946 (c.67)
National Insurance Act: introduced National Insurance retirement pensions and widows' benefits and specified qualifying conditions and initial level, but no provision for automatic uprating; entitlement to new pensions was possible through contributions to 1925 scheme, with most of those without sufficient contributions to qualify from 1958; introduction of benefits effective from 5.7.1948.

1959 (c.47)
National Insurance Act: introduced a second graduated pension for contracted-in employees; effective from 1961, with level determined by number of contributions paid.

1970 (c.51)
National Insurance (Old Persons' and Widows' Pensions and Attendance Allowances) Act: covered old persons' and widows' pensions and attendance allowances; introduced noncontributory pensions for those (now over 80) not covered by the 1946 Act.

1971 (c.56)
Pensions (Increase) Act: pensions paid to former central and local government employees; to be index-linked annually in line with prices.

1974 (c.14)
National Insurance Act: introduced annual increases to keep pensions in line with wages and prices, whichever was the greater.

1975 (c.60)
Social Security Pensions Act: enacted the phasing-in of a second earnings-related pen-

sion (1978-98) for employees not contracted-out to an occupational scheme; new pension payable on basis of best 20 contribution years, earnings-related up to one and a half times average earnings, inflation-proofed and payable at 65 (60 for women); 1961 graduated scheme wound up.

1980 (c.30)
Social Security Act: pensions to be up-rated in line with prices only.

1980 (c.39)
Social Security Act: earnings limit (prior to which retirement pension is not lowered for those under 70) frozen at existing cash level of UKL 52 per week.

II Sickness and health

Welfare provision for ill-health consists of two distinct components: Firstly, cash benefits for the sick, disabled and occupationally injured paid under the social security system, with National Insurance benefits dependent on contributions. Secondly, the National Health Service, which is available without any contribution conditions (although part of the National Insurance contribution is notionally allocated to it). In 1980, total health expenditure amounted to UKL 14,254 million or 6.3% of GDP.

Expenditure on sickness and health in 1980 in million UKL

		%	benefit recipients
National Health service:			
Health authority services	8 834[a]	70.0	
Family practitioner services	2 279[ab]	16.0	
Cash benefits			
Sickness benefit	660	4.6	503
Invalidity pension	1 195	8.4	620
Non-contributory invalidity pension	112	0.8	165
Attendance allowance and			304
invalidity care allowance	266	1.9	6
Mobility allowance	135	0.9	140
Death grant	17	0.1	593
(single grants)			
Injury benefit	47	0.3	51
Industrial disablement pension	282	2.0	204
Industrial death benefit	41	0.3	32
War disablement pension			276
War widows' pension	386	2.7	79
War orphans' and other dependents' pension			12
Total	14 254		

[a] 1980-81 financial year
[b] net of charges which yield 9.5% of gross expenditure
Sources: for [a], (4) Table 4.2; for [b] expenditure (1), number (2).

Income maintenance

1. Sickness benefits

National Insurance sickness benefit was instituted in 1948 and carried an earnings-related supplement from 1966 to 1982. Sickness benefit is payable to those previously employed or self-employed, but incapable of work due to sickness or disability, as established by a medical certificate issued by a doctor or hospital, for up to six months (after three waiting days). From 1983 claimants may self-certify their sickness for the first week. Until 1971, when invalidity pension was introduced there was no time limit. In 1980 the rate amounted to UKL 20.65 per week, or 19.4% of average earnings, together with UKL 12.75 for each dependent adult and UKL 1.25 for each dependent child. The earnings-related supplement was about 15% of earnings, up to a maximum of UKL 17.67 per week. In 1983 the responsibility for paying benefit at a simplified flat-rate during the first eight weeks of sickness, was transferred to employers, who deduct the cost from their National Insurance contributions.

2. Invalidity pensions a.o.

National Insurance invalidity pension was introduced in 1971 to replace sickness benefit at a higher rate: in 1980, UKL 26.00 per week, i.e. 24.5% of average earnings, and UKL 15.60 (adult) or UKL 7.50 (children) for each dependent after six months. It is claimable until retirement age. There is an additional invalidity allowance if the claimant becomes sick before the age of 45. Non-contributory invalidity pension (introduced in 1975) is payable to adult claimants incapacitated for at least 28 weeks, incapable of working and ineligible for invalidity pension. In 1980 the weekly rates amounted to UKL 16.30, i.e. 15.3% of average earnings, together with UKL 9.80 or UKL 7.50 for adult and child dependents respectively. Attendance allowances (introduced in 1971), are payable to the severely disabled in need of frequent attention or constant supervision. In 1980 attendance allowance amounted to UKL 21.65 a week if both day and night care is required, and UKL 14.45 for either day *or* night care. Invalidity care allowance (introduced in 1967), is payable to those (with the exception of wives), who are neither employed nor in full-time education, because they have to care for a severely disabled relative at home. Rates for the invalidity care allowance are the same as for a non-contributory invalidity pension. Mobility allowance (introduced in 1976), is payable to disabled persons aged 5-65, who are unable to walk but are capable of using other forms of transport. In 1980 mobility allowance amounted to UKL 14.50 a week. The death grant (introduced in 1948) is payable to the closest survivor on the death of the insured or a near relative. The grant is a contributory National Insurance benefit, and consists of a lump sum payment of UKL 30.00.

3. Occupational injury benefits a.o.

Three types of National Insurance occupational injury benefit were introduced in 1948. Injury benefit is payable for up to six months to claimants incapable of work as a result of industrial injury or disease. In 1980 the weekly rate amounted to UKL 23.40 plus UKL 12.75, or 22% of average earnings, and UKL 1.25 for each adult and child dependent respectively. After six months it is replaced by industrial disablement pension which is payable until retirement age. The amount depends on the extent of disablement as determined by a medical board. In 1980 the weekly rate for 100% disablement amounted to UKL 44.30, or 41.7% of average earnings, reduced to pounds

8.86 for 20% disablement. Supplements are payable for dependents, unemployability, a need for constant attendance, special hardship and exceptionally severe disability. Compensation for disability assessed at less than 20% is paid as a lump sum. Holders of industrial disablement pensions are eligible in addition for invalidity pension. Widows and dependent near relatives of those killed by industrial injury or disease receive industrial death benefit, an alternative to widows' benefits and payable at a similar rate.

4. War pensions a.o.

War pensions are non-contributory. Those disabled due to service in the armed forces receive war disablement pension according to rank and the extent of disability. For those 100% disabled the basic weekly rate (1980) is between UKL 44.30 and UKL 50.29, i.e. 41.7% and 47.3% of average earnings respectively. Supplements are payable as for industrial disablement pension. Widows of severely disabled war pensioners or those whose death was attributable to service in the armed forces receive war widow's pension of between UKL 35.30 and UKL 49.06 per week (1980) according to husband's rank, i.e. between 33.2% and 46.2% of average earnings. War orphans and other dependents are also eligible for pensions according to their age and need.

Services

The NHS consists of hospital services organized under health authorities appointed by central government (all hospital staff, including medical staff, are salaried employees, but most consultant doctors are under contracts which allow them to accept private patients); and family practitioner services (general medical, dental and optical practitioners). These practitioners remain self-employed and are paid fees and allowances for NHS work and are able to give private treatment. Fees (less than the full cost) are payable by patients for drug prescriptions, dental and optical treatment, subject to wide exemptions for those not in employment.

Core Laws

1946 (c. 6)
National Insurance Act: provided for sickness benefit (without time limit after three waiting days) for eligible persons unable to work; effective from 5.7.48.

1946 (c. 81)
National Health Service Act: provided universal free coverage financed out of general taxation and a small specific portion of National Insurance contributions. 'Tripartite' structure: all voluntary and local authority hospitals organized under centrally-appointed hospital boards; general practitioners organized under separate Executive Councils; local authority home-based and preventative services under Medical Officers of Health. Effective from 5.7.48.

1952 (c. 25)
National Health Service Act: imposed charges for drug prescriptions, dental and optical treatment.

1970 (c. 51)
National Insurance (Old Persons' and Widows' Pensions and Attendance Allowance) Act: introduced attendance allowance for those caring for adult relatives.

1970 (c. 44)
Chronically Sick and Disabled Persons Act: required local authorities to identify and make provision for such persons.

1971 (c. 50)
National Insurance Act: introduced invalidity pension to replace sickness benefit at a higher rate after six months.

1973 (c. 32)
National Health Service Reorganization Act: replaced 1948 tripartite structure by integrated Regional and Area Authorities, with members appointed by central government, each supervising a Management Team drawn from the various specializations. The new authorities incorporated the community health services previously operated by local government. A separate structure of Family Practitioner Committees replaced the Executive Councils. (England only; Scotland, Wales and Northern Ireland were reorganized into simpler, single-tier structures at about the same time).

1975 (c. 14)
Social Security Act: introduced mobility allowance and invalid care allowance.

1976 (c. 83)
Health Services Act: began the phasing-out of private beds in NHS hospitals ('pay beds', an inheritance from pre-1948) and established controls on non-NHS hospital building.

1980 (c. 53)
Health Services Act: repealed 1976 pay bed provisions, increased charges and abolished area tier of administration.

1980 (c. 39)
Social Security Act (no. 2): abolished earnings-related addition to sickness benefit (introduced in 1968) and made it liable to income tax (both to be implemented in 1982).

III Unemployment insurance/Employment police

In 1980 total unemployment expenditure amounted to UKL 3,278 million or 1.5% of GDP. Of this sum, more than 60% were spent on unemployment cash benefits.

Total unemployment expenditure in 1980-81 in million UKL

		%
Unemployment benefit	1 329	40.5
Supplementary benefit for the unemployed	649	19.8
Unemployment benefit	1 329	40.5
Supplementary benefit for the unemployed	649	19.8
Labour market services	748 (GB)	22.8
Special employment measures	552 (GB)	16.8
Total	3 278	99.9

Sources: [4] Table 2.4; [6] Table 1.2

Income maintenance

Unemployment benefit is part of the contributory National Insurance, the present scheme having been introduced in 1948. It carried an earnings-related supplement from 1965, but this was abolished in 1982. Benefit is payable after three waiting days, for a period of up to one year to unemployed claimants capable of, and available for, employment (as expressed by registration at an Unemployment Benefit Office). The beneficiary may be disqualified for up to 6 weeks if he refuses a suitable offer of employment, left his previous job as a result of misconduct, or voluntarily without just cause. Weekly payment is the same as for sickness benefit. The many unemployed who do not qualify receive a comparable level of benefit on a means-tested basis from the supplementary benefits scheme (See Section V). In late 1980, 503,000 persons were in receipt of unemployment benefit (200,000 with the earnings-related addition), and 678,000 with supplementary benefit alone. Unemployment benefit is paid from the National Insurance Fund and administered by the DHSS, through a network of local offices on behalf of the Department of Employment (DOE).

Services

Services for the unemployed consist of:
- labour market services, including a network of employment exchanges to place the unemployed in jobs and industrial training schemes;
- a variety of special employment measures to counteract high unemployment by subsidizing or creating jobs.

The coverage of the various special employment measures is as follows:

	Numbers participating (in 1,000s)	
	1980-1981	1984
Temporary short-time working compensation	984.5	12
Job release scheme	59	94
Youth opportunities programme	140	2
Community industry	6.5	7
Special Temporary Employment Programme	13	0
Training opportunities scheme	28	20
Youth Training Scheme	0	242
Community Programme	0	113
Enterprise Allowance Scheme	0	29
Young Workers' Scheme	0	92
Total	1 231	593

Source: Manpower Services Commission Annual Report 1980-81 and 1983-84.

The Temporary Short-Time Working Compensation Scheme (phased out by 1984) paid to employers for up to nine months 50% of the normal wages of staff working less than normal hours ('short-time') and who would otherwise be declared unemployed. The Job Release Scheme is for employees of over 62 years of age, who withdraw from the labour force and are replaced by an unemployed person. The Youth Opportunities Programme offers one year's employment and training to unemployed school-leavers; it is now replaced by the more comprehensive Youth Training Scheme. Community Industry, the Special Temporary Employment Scheme, the Community Programme and the Enterprise Allowance Scheme are all variants of job creation schemes, financing the unemployed to perform socially useful tasks. Training Opportunities include short-term courses (average 20 weeks) at government centres, colleges or employers' premises, for which an allowance is paid to the trainee. The Young Worker's Scheme offers a subsidy to induce employers to hire young workers at low rates of pay.

Financing and administration

Unemployment benefit is paid from the National Insurance Fund; otherexpenditure is financed from general taxation. The employment exchange service, industrial training and the Youth Opportunities Programme (see below) are operated by the Manpower Services Commission (MSC), a body appointed and financed by central government. Other special employment measures are operated and financed by the DOE.

Core Laws

Note: legislation dealing primarily with collective bargaining and industrial relations has been excluded; much industrial training and safety legislation consolidates earlier provisions.

1945 (c. 67)
National Insurance Act: established flat-rate unemployment benefit payable after three waiting days for up to one year for eligible claimants.

1964 (c. 16)
Industrial Training Act: established Industrial Training Boards (ITBs) for most industries financed by government and an employer levy of up to 1% of payroll.

1965 (c. 62)
Redundancy Payments Act: entitled employees with two years service to a lump sum payment according to earnings and length of service in the event of redundancy; partly financed by industry-levied funds.

1966 (c. 6)
National Insurance Act:introduced earnings-related supplement for the first six months of unemployment benefit.

1968 (c. 71)
Race Relations Act: made it unlawful to discriminate on grounds of colour, race, and national or ethnic origin in employment and training.

1970 (c. 41)
Equal Pay Act: specified that women doing the same or equivalent work to men should receive equal pay and conditions of employment.

1973 (c. 50)
Employment and Training Act: established Manpower Services Commission (MSC) to operate public training and employment services; obliged local authorities to provide a Careers Service to advise young people seeking work.

1974 (c. 37)
Health and Safety at Work Act: placed duties on all connected with work activities to prevent accidents and ensure suitable work conditions. Enforced by regulations issued by the Health and Safety Commission (HSC).

1975 (c. 71)
Employment Protection Act: extended notice of dismissal for all employees and maternity rights for the period during and after pregnancy for female employees, and established new rights of appeal to industrial tribunals against unfair dismissal.

1980 (c. 42)
Employment Act: increased qualifying period for right of appeal against unfair dismissal from one to two years.

1980 (c. 39)
Social Security (No. 2) Act: abolished earnings-related addition to unemployment benefit and made it liable to income tax. Both implemented in 1982.

IV Families and children

Provision for families and children is fragmented among a variety of programmes and institutions: income maintenance, education, health, and personal social services.

Principal expenditure on families and children, 1980

	in million UKL	%	beneficiaries (1,000s)
Cash child benefit	2 944	76.2	13 300
Maternity allowance	49	1.3	80
Family Income Supplement and grant	163	4.2	115
Guardians' and special allowances	2		5
Residential care (1979-80)	228[a]	5.9	
School meals and milk	397[b]	10.3	
School health	79[b]	2.1	
Total	3 862	100.0	

[a] England 1979-80
[b] England 1980-81
Source: (1), (2), (4) Table 2.10, (5) p. 105-6.

Income maintenance

The principal income support for children is child benefit, a non-contributory weekly payment of UKL 4.75 paid to 7.4 million families in respect of 13.3 million children

(1980). This succeeded family allowances (paid from 1945) and child income tax allowances in 1977. Child benefit is paid in cash to the mother (or other responsible adult) for each child under 16 (under 19 if remaining in full-time education). An additional single-parent benefit of UKL 3.00 per week (1980), is paid for the first child in a single-parent family.

National Insurance maternity benefits (1948) may be earned on the contributions of either the mother or her husband. A maternity allowance of UKL 20.65 per week (1980) is payable for up to 18 weeks, starting 11 weeks before the birth is due , for weeks in which no paid work is done. A lump sum maternity grant of UKL 25.10 (1980) is paid for each birth.

Family Income Supplement (FIS) is a means-tested benefit for families where the breadwinner is in full-time work and where there is at least one child qualifying for child benefit. The income limitin 1980 amounted to UKL 56.00 per week for a one child family, plus UKL 4.50 for each additional child. The benefit pays 50 % of the difference between the actual income and the income limit, up to a weekly maximum (1980) of UKL 13.50 (with one child) plus UKL 1.00 for each additional child. Awards are for a minimum of one year irrespective of subsequent changes in income.

There are two minor National Insurance benefits, which in 1980 paid UKL 7.50 per week for each child. Guardian's allowance (introduced in 1948) is paid to the guardians of orphans on the basis of the late parent's contributions. Child's special allowance (introduced in 1957) is paid to a divorced mother in the event of the death of an ex-husband previously contributing to the support of the child and is based on his contributions.

Services

The principle services for children consist of preventative health services under the NHS (not all of it separately quantifiable), residential provision for the disabled and homeless, subsidized school meals for most school-children and free milk for those under the age of eight. Children in families receiving supplementary benefit or family income supplement receive free school meals from the local education authority. Other children may also be eligible subject to a parental means-test. Most authorities also provide a general subsidy for the cost of school meals.

Core Laws

1945 (c. 41)
Family Allowances Act: introduced universal cash payment of UKL 0.25 perweek for all children in a family under the age of 15, with the exception of the first child.

1946 (c. 67)
National Insurance Act: introduced maternity grants and allowances. Effective from 1948.

1975 (c. 61)
Child Benefit Act: introduced child benefit which replaced family allowances and income tax allowances for children. Benefits payable in cash to the mother and extended to the first child, but at a lower rate (except for one-parent families); phased-in in three stages from 1977 to 1979.

V Social assistance

In 1980, total expenditure on public assistance, now known as supplementary benefits, amounted to UKL 2,693 million, or 1.2.% of GDP. Public assistance provides the fall-back welfare service for those whose needs exceed their income. In December 1980, there were over 3 million such cases at a single time, distributed as follows:

Breakdown of supplementary benefit recipients, December 1980

	in 1,000s	%
Supplementary pensions	1 694	54.3
Supplementary allowances	1 423	45.6
- unemployed with NI	176	5.6
- unemployed without NI	678	21.7
- sick with NI	57	1.8
- sick without NI	148	4.7
- widows	15	0.5
- other lone parents	316	10.1
- others	34	1.1
Total	3 118	100.0

Source: Social Security Statistics 1981, Table 34.41.

Income maintenance

The supplementary benefits scheme received its present name in 1966, replacing national assistance. It is payable to adult heads of households in full time work whose income is less than their assessed 'needs'. Those with capital of more than UKL 2,500 are not eligible. In 1980 weekly needs were defined as a basic rate of UKL 21.30 (single person) or UKL 34.60 (married couple), i.e. 20.0% or 32.5% of average earnings, (increased to a 'long-term rate' of UKL 27.15 or UKL 43.45 for pensioners or those on supplementary benefits for more than one year, except the unemployed); together with UKL 17.05 for each adult dependent and between UKL 7.30 and UKL 13.10 for each child dependent (according to age). There is an additional heating allowance of UKL 1.40 (UKL 3.40 at the long-term rate) where there are sick, aged or infant persons in the household, together with various other allowances. Until 1982 actual housing costs were included in the calculation of weekly needs. Now, however all housing support, with the exception of that for owner-occupiers, is provided by means of rent allowances and rebates. The amount of supplementary benefit is the difference between actual household income after some disregards (including other income maintenance benefits) and assessed needs. Single lump sum payments are also available for specified essential household expenses.

The scheme is administered by the DHSS, through local offices and based on postal applications, with interviews or home visits in some cases.

Services

Advice to those in need, including information on claiming social assistance cash benefits is available from local authority social services departments.

Core Laws

1948 (c. 29)
National Assistance Act: abolished the Poor Law, and established the National Assistance Board 'to assist persons who are without resources to meet their needs', based on a scale rate according to number of dependents derived from pre-war studies of subsistence needs with the addition of actual housing costs.

1966 (c. 20)
Ministry of Social Security Act: replaced national assistance with supplementary benefits, administered by a Supplementary Benefits Commission appointed and funded by central government; scale rates improved, with a statutory right to benefit for the out-of-work needy, but scheme not changed in essentials.

1980 (c. 30)
Social Security Act: simplified supplementary benefits at no net cost, restricting both eligibility and the use of discretion. Supplementary Benefits Commission abolished, with administration returning directly to the DHSS.

VI Education

1. School system

Total education expenditure, 1980-81

	million UKL	%
Schools	8 108	59.2
Higher and further education	3 653	26.9
Administration/other services	648	4.8
Northern Ireland (total)	459	3.4
Student awards	770[a]	5.7
Total	13 568	100.0

[a] England only
Source: (4) Table 4, 2.

The modern system of public education dates from the 1870 Education Act in England and Wales, (Scotland and Ireland have separate systems). Until the 1944 Education Act the minimum school leaving age was still 14 and universal secondary education (age 11 upwards) in separate schools had not yet been fully implemented. The 1902 Education Act made education, with the exception of universities, the responsibility of top-tier local authorities. Standards are set by central government by means of inspection and advice. There is no national school-leaving examination.

Public education is organized at four levels: Nursery education: up to the age of 5, voluntary, not available in all areas; Primary education: compulsory from the age of 5 to 11 years; Secondary education: from the age of 11 to 18 years, compulsory to the age of 16; the great majority of secondary schools are now comprehensive and cater for all ability groups. Further education: covers universities, polytechnics and a variety of local authority colleges providing teacher training and vocational courses. Universities are self governing but 90% financed by central government through the University Grants Committee (UGC). Local authorities provide mandatory grants to cover tuition fees and maintenance of qualified students. Polytechnics award degrees and are administered by local authorities.

No fees are levied at or below the secondary level. A small minority of pupils attend fee-paying schools, including the so-called 'public schools'. Some public sector schools are managed by religious denominations, but teachers' salaries and the great majority of building costs are met from public funds.

The public education systems in Scotland and Northern Ireland are administered separately, and there are differences in structure, age of transfer between sectors, and the position of denominational schools.

2. Student grants

Student grants (introduced on a uniform national basis in 1962), cover the cost of fees and a maintenance allowance for students on approved courses of higher education. A first degree course is covered automatically. Other courses are supported at the discretion of local education authorities which administer the scheme. If the student is under 25 and has not been in employment for three years a means-tested parental contribution is assumed. The rate of grant is dependent upon the income of the student and that of his parents, type of course, and whether or not the student lives at home. In 1979-80, 166,000 students received the full grant and 269,000 a grant that assumed a parental contribution. In addition, awards at a higher rate covering full fees and maintenance were made to 16,000 post-graduates.

Core Laws

Note: these refer to England and Wales. Legislation for Scotland and Northern Ireland is separate but generally comparable.

1944 (c. 31)
Education Act: raised school-leaving age minimum from 14 to 15 with provision for extension to 16 (not implemented until 1971). Established tripartite division into primary (age 5 to 11), secondary (age 11 to 18) and further (over 18) sectors. Pupils were to be allocated to three types of secondary school (grammar, technical and secondary modern) according to ability and aptitude by examination (the '11-plus'). County colleges of further education were to offer day release and other courses for the post-16 group. Various education welfare duties (including provision of meals) were established for local education authorities.

1962 (c. 12)
Education Act: introduced system of mandatory awards, administered by local authorities, for students entering courses of further and higher education.

1964 (c. 82)
Education Act: allowed the organization of 'middle schools' for the 8 to 13 age range without selective allocation at 11.

1971 (c. 74)
Education (Milk) Act: removed the obligation to provide free daily milk for non-primary pupils.

1976 (c. 81)
Education Act: required the few local authorities who had not yet done so to submit schemes for the comprehensive (non-selective) reorganization of secondary schools, and withdrew public grants from direct grant schools (privately organized but with publicly subsidized fees), leaving them the choice of becoming independent or of joining the state system.

1979 (c. 49)
Education Act: removed the compulsion to secondary reorganization in the 1976 Act.

1980 (c. 20)
Education Act: removed the obligation on education authorities to provide school meals, except for the children of supplementary benefit recipients. Reorganized the governing bodies of schools, and introduced an 'assisted places' scheme to remit the fees of some children at independent schools on the basis of a parental means-test.

VII Housing

British public policy on housing dates from the First World War, notably with the 1919 Housing and Town Planning Act (the Addison Act) which launched major programmes of local authority housebuilding. Since then, policy has had two continuing elements, which are of equal financial importance.

a) Construction of rented housing by local authorities, financed by central government loans, which subsidize interest repayments, thus reducing rents. Except for a few specialized agencies (e.g. new towns), central government does not build, manage or allocate housing itself.

b) Promotion of private housing construction and occupation by fiscal incentives, the most important of which is income tax relief of the interest payments on mortgages advanced by Building Societies (from 1983 an equivalent relief is payable by a direct subsidy to the societies rather than through the income-tax system)

An important development in recent years has been financial support for co-operative Housing Associations building for rent, often for special need groups. Throughout the period, rent levels in private rented accommodation have been subject to varying degrees of regulation. Since 1967 low-income tenants received a means-tested subsidy on their rents. In 1980 there were 1,568,000 tenants in receipt of these allowances.

Total housing expenditure, 1980-81

	million UKL	%
Rent subsidies on public sector houses and rent allowances	2 453	30.9
Subsidies on mortgages for owner-occupiers	2 258[a]	28.4
Capital expenditure on local authority housebuilding	1 995[b]	25.1
Other capital (mainly housing associations)	846	10.7
Administration	147	1.9
Northern Ireland (total)	244	3.1
Total	7 943	100.1

[a] includes UKL 2,030 and tax expenditures
[b] net figure, allowing for UKL 640, from sales repayments
Source: (4) Tables 4.2 and 4.9.

Core Laws

1946 (c. 48)
Housing (Financial and Miscellaneous Provisions) Act: established new subsidy system for local authority rented housing, assuming a standard rent of UKL 0.50 per week, with remaining costs met by the Exchequer (central) and rate fund (local) contributions.

1949 (c. 60)
Housing Act: introduced improvement grants for householders for the installation of basic amenities (available by right since 1959, with a more generous subsidy level since 1969).

1957 (c.25)
Rent Act: removed all private rented property, with the exception of low-value accommodation, from rent controls.

1965 (c. 75)
Rent Act: reversed effect of 1957 Act.

1967 (c. 29)
Housing Subsidies Act: introduced new subsidy system for local authority housing, replacing fixed sums with subsidies related to cost of building and interest rates; tendency for subsidies to increase.

1972 (c. 47)
Housing Finance Act: introduced new subsidy scheme based on 'fair rents'. Local authorities were required gradually to increase rents, and mandatory national rent rebate scheme was introduced, including rent allowances for tenants in private unfurnished accommodation. Legislation for Scotland involved a higher subsidy, reflecting historically lower rent levels.

1974 (c. 51)
Rent Act: extended security of tenure and rent control to private furnished rented accommodation. Previously only unfurnished accommodation was covered.

1974
Housing Act: increased public support for Housing Associations channelled through the Housing Corporation.

1975 (c. 44)
Housing Rents and Subsidies Act: restored local authorities' powers to fix and subsidize rents for their own housing, but not to make a current account profit on such housing.

1976 (c. 80)
Rent (Agriculture) Act: extended security of tenure to agricultural workers in 'tied cottages'.

1977 (c. 48)
Housing (Homeless Persons) Act: obliged local housing authorities to provide secure accommodation for homeless persons (previously dealt with by the social services).

1978 (c. 27)
Home Purchase Assistance and Housing Corporation Guarantee Act: gave help to first-time home buyers.

1980 (c. 51)
Housing Act: gave local authority tenants the right to buy their homes; introduced a 'Tenant's Charter' for local authority tenants; established a new shorthold tenure in the private rented sector, with less restriction; and introduced a new subsidy system from 1981-82 more directly related to need.

Sources

(1) National Income and expenditure, 1981 edition, London, HMSO. Tables 7.3 and 7.6.

(2) Annual Abstract of Statistics, 1981, London, HMSO. Table 3.16.

(3) The Government's Expenditure Plans 1981-82 to 1983-84, Cmnd 8175, 1981. Table 2.12.2 and various tables in *Social Security Statistics 1981*, HMSO; they refer to a single date in late 1979 when a count was taken of the numbers receiving.

(4) *The Government's Expenditure Plans 1982-83 to1984-85*, HMSO,Cmnd 8494 ,1982.

(5) *Public Expenditure on the Social Services*, third Report from the Social Services Committee, House of Commons, 1980-81, note F: Programme Budget Report 1981 (by Department of Health and Social Security, HC 324-II/1980-81).

(6) First *Report* of the Social Security Advisory committee 1981, HMSO, 1982.

(7) *Occupational Pension Schemes 1979: fifth Survey by the Government Actuary*, London: HMSO, 1981.

(8) *The Government's Expenditure Plans* 1983-84 to 1985-86, Cmnd. 8789, 1983.

Data in sources (4), (5) and (6) are given and cited by financial year (1 April-31 March).

Bibliography

Contents

I General contributions

1.1 General histories of social policy

BRUCE, Maurice: The Coming of the Welfare State. London, Batsford, 1961, 374 p. History of social problems and public social policy, concentrating on the historical background and development of policy in the nineteenth and early twentieth century. Summary treatment only of post-1945 policies.

FRASER, Derek: The Evolution of the British Welfare State. London, Macmillan, 1973, 299 p. Social policy and ideology from the 1830s to the 1940s, concentrating on the conflict between laisser-faire and state intervention.

MARSHALL, T.H.: Social Policy in the Twentieth Century. London, Hutchinson, 1975, 240 p. Later edition of a textbook first published in 1965 which analyses the objectives and mechanisms of social policy, particularly since 1945.

THANE, Pat (ed.): The Origins of British Social Policy. London, Croom Helm, 1978, 209 p. Papers on aspects of British social policy from 1870 to 1945, especially social control, eligibility and discretion.

THANE, P.: The Foundations of the Welfare State. London, Longman, 1982, p. 383. Student textbook covering developments from 1870 to 1945.

1.2 Accounts of specific historical periods

ADDISON, Paul: The Road to 1945: British Politics and the Second World War. London, Jonathan Cape, 1975, 334 p. Analysis of British politics from 1939 to 1945, including the evolution of welfare state policies within the coalition government.

GILBERT, Bentley B.: The Evolution of National Insurance in Britain: The Origins of the Welfare State. London, Michael Joseph, 1966, 497 p. History of social policy from 1885 to 1914.

GILBERT, B.B.: British Social Policy 1914-1939. London, Batsford, 1970, 343 p. A continuation of Gilbert's history.

HARRIS, Jose: William Beveridge: A Biography. Oxford, Clarendon Press, 1977, 488 p. Standard biography of the author of the 1942 Beveridge report and a central figure in British administrative history.

MacNICHOL, John: The Movement for Family Allowances 1918-1945. London, Heinemann, 1980, 256 p. Case study of an important cross party policy.

MOMMSEN, W.J. (ed.): The Development of Welfare States in Britain and Germany. London, Croom Helm, 1981. Papers on historical themes, including Poor Law policy in the nineteenth century and the German influence on British social insurance.

TITMUSS, Richard: Problems of Social Policy. London, HMSO and Longman, 1950, 596 p. A volume of the official British history of the Second World War, describing the response of the social services to wartime conditions.

1.3 Postwar histories

COOPER, Michael H. (ed.): Social Policy: a Survey of Recent Developments. Oxford, Basil Blackwell, 1973, 278 p. Survey of developments in each social service in the late 1960s and early 1970s.

DONNISON, David, SOTO, Paul: The Good City: a Study of Urban Development and Policy in Britain. London, Heinemann, 1980, 224 p. Analysis of the pattern of urban development in postwar Britain and of public environmental policies.

EDWARDS, John, BATLEY, Richard: The Politics of Positive Discrimination. London, Tavistock Publications, 1978, 287 p. Evaluation of the Urban Programmes to deal with the problems of inner-city areas, 1967-1977.

FIELD, Frank: Poverty and Politics: the Inside Story of the Child Poverty Action Group's Campaigns in the 1970s. London, Heinemann, 1982, 224 p. Analysis of a pressure group's campaigns with selected documents, 1970 to 1979.

MacGREGOR, Susanne: The Politics of Poverty. London, Longman, 1981, 170 p. An up-to-date textbook on postwar social policy.

WEBB, Adrian, WISTOW, Gerald: Whither State Welfare: Policy and Implementation in the Personal Social Services 1979-80. London, Royal Institute of Public Administration, 1981, 93 p. Study of policy implementation by the 1979 Conservative Government.

YEARBOOK OF SOCIAL POLICY IN BRITAIN: edited by JONES, Kathleen (1971-76); BROWN, Muriel, BURDEN, Sally (1977-79); JONES, Catherine, STEVENSON, June (1980-81, combined edition). London, Routledge and Kegan Paul, 1972-82 annually. Papers on developments in the previous year and further analysis from current research.

1.4 Reports by investigating committees or experts (in chronological order)

BEVERIDGE REPORT: Social Insurance and Allied Services. London, HMSO, Cmnd 6404, 1942, 299 p. The one-man report that laid the foundations of the postwar national insurance system.

ROBBINS REPORT: Higher Education, London, HMSO, Cmnd 2154, 1963, 333 p. Recommended that places in higher education should be made available to all qualified school-leavers and led to an expansion of provision.

PLOWDEN REPORT: Children and their Primary Schools. London, HMSO, 1967. Research-based discussion of changing educational methods.

SEEBOHM REPORT: Local Authority and Allied Personal Social Services. London, HMSO, Cmnd 3703, 1968, 370 p. Proposed the integration of local authority welfare services into integrated social services departments; implemented in 1970.

HALSEY REPORT: Educational Priority. London, HMSO, 1972, Vol. 1 Education Problems and Priorities, 209 p. Summary report of a major research project into the concentration of help in deprived areas through action-research projects. Four other volumes followed by 1974.

FINER REPORT: One-parent Families. London, HMSO, Cmnd 5629, 1974, 519 p. Examined this emerging social problem and recommended a new type of cash benefit.

SOCIAL ASSISTANCE: Review of the Supplementary Benefit Scheme in Great Britain. London, Department of Health and Social Security, 1978, 127 p. Review by a team of officials that produced recommendations for the reform of the social assistance system at nil or low cost.

BARCLAY REPORT: Social Workers: their Role and Tasks. London, Bedford Square Press, 1982, 283 p. Semi-official report on the practice, context and clients of the social work profession.

GRIFFITHS REPORT: NHS Management Inquiry, London, Department of Health and Social Security, 1983, ISBN 0 946539 01 4), 24 p. Report of a study team recommending a Central Management Board for the National Health Service, with general managers in health authorities.

1.5 Social science interpretations, evaluations and analyses

BOSANQUET, Nick: After the New Right. London, Heinemann, 1983. An interpretation of the ideology of the 1979 Conservative government.

BROWN, Muriel, MADGE, Nicola: Despite the Welfare State. London, Heinemann, 1982, 388 p. Report of a major research programme in the 1970s into transmitted deprivation; the extent, form and causes of continuing deprivation in Britain and the implications for policy.

CAWSON, Alan: Corporatism and Welfare. London, Heinemann, 1982, 160 p. The political and economic context of social policy, especially recent neo-Marxist and corporatist theory.

GEORGE, Vic, WILDING, Paul: Ideology and Social Welfare. London, Routledge and Kegan Paul, 1976, 162 p. Marxist oriented analysis of British social thinkers: anti-collectivists, 'reluctant collectivists', Fabian socialists and Marxists.

GOUGH, Ian: The Political Economy of the Welfare State. London, Macmillan, 196 p. Discussion of the operation of welfare state policies in relation to the capitalist economic system.

HALL, Phoebe, LAND, Hilary, PARKER, Ray, WEBB, Adrian: Change, Choice and Conflict in Social Policy. London, Heinemann, 1975, 555 p. Introduction to the actors and processes in British social policy, and case studies of family allowances, the Open University, health centres, detention centres, clean air and national assistance.

HECLO, Hugh: Modern Social Politics in Britain and Sweden. New Haven and London, Yale University Press, 1974, 349 p. Analysis of the development of social insurance in terms of administrative learning in the two countries.

HIRSCH, Fred: Social Limits to Growth. London, Routledge and Kegan Paul, 1977, 208 p. Development of Hirsch's theory of 'positional goods' whose scarcity inhibits growth and prevents the achievement of social equality.

LE GRAND, Julian, ROBINSON, Ray (eds): Privatisation and the Welfare State, London, George Allen and Unwin, 1984, 233 p. Contributions on the ideology and policy of increased private sector provision, and on the record for individual services.

MARSHALL, T.H.: The Right to Welfare and Other Essays. London, Heinemann, 1981, 192 p. Marshall's final statement of his liberal position on welfare.

MISHRA, Ramesh: Society and Social Policy. London, Macmillan, 1977 and 1981 (2nd ed.), 240 p. Textbook about the various theoretical approaches to welfare in relation to social structure.

PARKER, Julia: Social Policy and Citizenship in Londom, Macmillan, 1975,192 p. The alternative approaches to social policy rights in terms of citizenship entitlements.

PINKER, Robert: Social Theory and Social Policy. London, Heinemann, 1971, 240 p. The theoretical roots of British social policy.

PINKER, R.: The Idea of Welfare. London, Heinemann, 1979, 265 p. Social policy in relation to ideology, especially the notion of altruism.

REISEMAN, David, TITMUSS, Richard: Welfare and Society. London, Heinemann, 1977, 192 p. Intellectual biography of the leading theorist of the postwar British welfare state.

ROOM, Graham: The Sociology of Welfare. Oxford, Basil Blackwell and Martin Robertson, 1979, 288 p. Comprehensive analysis of the theoretical basis of British social policy through discussion of the Marxist, liberal and social democratic approaches.

RUNCIMAN, W.G.: Relative Deprivation and Social Justice. London, Routledge and Kegan Paul, 1966, 338 p. Report of a 1962 survey into attitudes to social inequality used as the basis of an influential theory about perceived relative deprivation deriving from social psychology, as the basis of British class attitudes.

TAYLOR-GOOBY, Peter, DALE, Jennifer: Social Theory and Social Welfare. London, Edward Arnold, 1981, 294 p. The Welfare State examined from contemporary Marxist perspectives on the market and the state.

TITMUSS, R.: Essays on 'the Welfare State'. London, George Allen and Unwin, 1963, 232 p. Essays and lectures dealing with sociological and historical themes.

TITMUSS, R.: Commitment to Welfare. London, George Allen and Unwin, 1983, 272 p. Essays, especially on health care and redistribution.

TITMUSS, R.: The Gift Relationship. London, George Allen and Unwin, 1970. Practice on blood donation in various countries used to develop a theory on the nature of reciprocal links in society and social policy.

TITMUSS, R.: Social Policy: an Introduction. London, George Allen and Unwin, 1974, 160 p. An edited version of Titmuss' introductory lectures to the social administration courses at the London School of Economics.

TOWNSEND, Peter: Sociology and Social Policy. Harmondsworth, Penguin, 1973, 371 p. Essays, especially on equality and distribution.

WILDING, P.: Professional Power and Social Welfare. London, Routledge and Kegan Paul, 1982, 169 p. Critique of the basis and extent of professional power in the British welfare state.

1.6 Policy proposals and debates

BOSANQUET, N., TOWNSEND, P. (eds): Labour and Equality: a Fabian Study of Labour in Power 1974-79. London, Heinemann, 1980, 256 p. Appraisals by Labour sympathisers of the philosophy and actions of the 1974-79 Labour government.

CAMERON, Gordon C. (ed.): The Future of the British Conurbations: Policies and Prescriptions for Change. London, Longman, 1980, 323 p. Trends, policy initiatives and prescriptions for change in various aspects of inner-city policy.

FOGARTY, Michael (ed.): Retirement Policy: the Next Fifty Years. London, Heinemann, 1982, 216 p. Analysis and options for demographic and resource issues in the care of the elderly.

GLENNERSTER, Howard (ed.): The Future of the Welfare State, London, Heinemann, 1983, 234 p. Fabian essays on the redefinition of socialist objectives in the light of the Conservative government's policies.

TOWNSEND, P., BOSANQUET, N. (eds): Labour and Inequality. London, Fabian Society, 1972, 304 p. Essays by sympathisers appraising the performance of the 1964-70 Labour government.

WALKER , Alan: Social Planning: A Strategy for Socialist Welfare, Oxford, Basil Blackwell and Martin Robertson, 1984, 276 p. A call for a wider and more concerted approach to social policy, with a critique of the social construction and economic techniques of the present system.

1.7 Opinion polls

BRITISH PUBLIC OPINION: London, Market and Opinion Research International (MORI), monthly. Reports from MORI surveys of political and social issues.

GALLUP POLITICAL INDEX: London, Gallup, published monthly. Results of the monthly survey of political attitudes and voter preferences.

GOLDING, Peter, MIDDLETON, Susan: Images of Welfare: the Mass Media, Public Attitudes and the Welfare State. Oxford, Basil Blackwell and Martin Robertson, 1982, 283 p. Analysis of an opinion survey into beliefs about welfare, poverty and inequality, and a discussion of the role of the mass media.

JOWELL, Roger, AIREY, Colin: British Social Attitudes, the 1984 report. Aldershot, Gower, 1984, 221 p. Reports a major survey taken in March/April 1983, into economic, social and political attitudes, intended to be the first of a series.

OFFICE OF POPULATION CENSUSES AND SURVEYS: General Household Survey. London, HMSO, yearly series (1971). The annual microcensus asking a variable schedule of questions about social and economic circumstances as requested by government departments.

1.8 Sources of statistics and institutional regulations

1.8.1 Official sources

CENTRAL STATISTICAL OFFICE: Annual Abstract of Statistics. London, HMSO, yearly series (1946). The main British statistical yearbook, with data (some not published elsewhere) on all aspects of public (including social) policy.

CENTRAL STATISTICAL OFFICE: Regional Trends (formerly Abstract of Regional Statistics and Regional Statistics). London, HMSO, yearly series (1965). Social and economic data classified by area, especially Scotland, Northern Ireland and the eight regions of England.

CENTRAL STATISTICAL OFFICE: Social Trends. London, HMSO, annual series (1970). Analysis of social developments and social policy, with extensive use of charts and diagrams and some specialized articles.

1.8.2 Private sources

BUTLER, David, SLOMAN, Anne: British Political Facts (5th ed.) London, Macmillan, 1980,

492 p. Compendium of facts related to politics and government with chapters on social policy.

HALSEY, A.H.: Trends in British Society since 1900. London, Macmillan, 1972, 578 p. Data on social developments arranged by function with accompanying commentary.

1.8.3 Periodicals

MONTHLY DIGEST OF STATISTICS: London, HMSO, Central Statistical Office, monthly series (1945). Latest statistics with contents being similar in scope to those of the Annual Abstract but less extensive.

ECONOMIC TRENDS: London, HMSO, Central Statistical Office, monthly series (1953). Latest economic data - including public expenditure data - specialized articles. There is also an annual supplement which gives fuller data and longer time series.

II Single programmes or aspects

2.1 Pensions

2.1.1 Descriptions, evaluations and analyses

DEPARTMENT OF HEALTH AND SOCIAL SECURITY: Better Pensions - Fully Protected Against Inflation: Proposals for a New Pensions Scheme. London, HMSO, Cmnd 5713, 1974. Description of the new state pension scheme that was enacted in 1975.

·GOODMAN, John C.: Social Security in the United Kingdom: Contracting-out of the System. Washington DC, American Enterprise Institute, 1981, 72 p. Analysis of the operation of the 1975 scheme.

SCOTT REPORT: Report into the Value of Pensions. London, HMSO, Cmnd 8147, 1981. Report of government inquiry into the relative value of pensions in the private and public sectors, with an analysis of benefits, costs and coverage.

2.1.2 Sources

DEPARTMENT OF HEALTH AND SOCIAL SECURITY: Social Security Statistics, London, HMSO, yearly series (1972). Data on pension coverage and benefits (and other benefits) under the national insurance scheme.

GOVERNMENT ACTUARY: Occupational Pension Schemes 1979. London, HMSO, 1981. Latest survey of the coverage and benefits of all public and private sector occupational pension schemes.

SOCIAL SECURITY ADVISORY COMMITTEE: Annual Report. London, HMSO, yearly series, (1981). Data and analysis of trends by the government-appointed standing advisory committee.

2.2 Health

2.2.1 Descriptions, evaluations, analyses

ABEL-SMITH, Brian: Value for Money in the Health Services. London, Heinemann, 1976, 240 p. Organization, finance and cost pressures analyzed with cross-national evidence.

BARNARD, Keith, LEE, Kenneth (eds): Conflicts in the National Health Service. London, Croom Helm, 1977, 252 p. Papers on inter-professional tension, especially during periods of reorganization.

BEVAN, Gwyn, COPEMAN, Harold, PERRIN, John, ROSSER, Rachel: Health Care: Priorities and Management. London, Croom Helm, 1980, 294 p. Resource allocation studies based on work done for the 1976-79 Royal Commission on the National Health Service.

BROWN, R.G.S: Reorganising the National Health Service. Oxford, Martin Robertson and Basil Blackwell, 1978, 256 p. Analysis of the 1974 reorganization based on a case study of one health authority.

CULVER, A.J.: Need and the National Health Service. Oxford, Martin Robertson, 1976, 163 p. Analysis of the control and directing of health resources in the economic context of need.

HAM, Christopher: Policy-making in the National Health Service. London, Macmillan, 1981, 240 p. Wider concepts of policy analysis applied to the operation of a Regional Hospital Board.

KLEIN, Rudolf: The Politics of the National Health Service, London, Heinemann,1983, 198 p. Analysis of current political and professional variables, with the historical background to them.

YOUNGHUSBAND, Eileen: Social Work in Britain 1950-1975. London, George Allen and Unwin, 1978, 352 p. (Vol. I) and 311 p. (Vol. II). History of the development of the social work profession.

2.2.2 Sources

DEPARTMENT OF HEALTH AND SOCIAL SECURITY: Health and Personal Social Services Statistics. London, HMSO, yearly series (1969). Referred to as the Digest of Health Statistics until 1971, gives data on finance, manpower, hospitals and treatment.

DEPARTMENT OF HEALTH AND SOCIAL SECURITY: Health Care and its Costs, London, HMSO, 1983, 51 p. Analytical data on the real costs of health care in England during the 1960s and 1970s.

MERRISON REPORT: Royal Commission on the National Health Service Report. London, HMSO, Cmnd 7615, 1979, 491 p. Much organizational and statistical detail was brought together in the report and its associated research papers.

OFFICE OF HEALTH ECONOMICS: Compendium of Health Statistics (3rd ed.) London, OHE, 1979. Privately compiled data on health provision and expenditure.

2.3 Unemployment

2.3.1 Descriptions, evaluations and analyses

SHOWER, Brian, SINFIELD, Adrian: The Workless State: Studies in Unemployment. Oxford, Martin Robertson, 1981, 267 p. An examination of the nature of unemployment and its social impact.

2.3.2 Sources

DEPARTMENT OF EMPLOYMENT: Employment Gazette. London, HMSO, monthly series (1945). Formerly the Ministry of Labour Gazette and Department of Employment Gazette. Statistics and articles on employment and unemployment.

DEPARTMENT OF EMPLOYMENT: British Labour Statistics Yearbook. London, HMSO, yearly series, 1969-76. Comprehensive labour statistics, now published only in the Employment Gazette.

DEPARTMENT OF EMPLOYMENT AND PRODUCTIVITY: British Labour Statistics Historical Abstract 1886-1968. London, HMSO, 1971. Comprehensive collection of historical data on the labour market.

MANPOWER SERVICES COMMISSION: Manpower Review. London, MSC, yearly series (1980). Data, projections and analyses of the labour market.

2.4 Accidents

2.4.2 Sources

DEPARTMENT OF HEALTH AND SOCIAL SECURITY: Social Security Statistics. London,

HMSO, yearly series (1972). Details of claims and compensation paid under industrial injuries insurance.

2.5 Social assistance

2.5.1 Descriptions, evaluations and analyses

ASHLEY, Pauline: The Money Problems of the Poor. London, Heinemann, 1983, 226 p. Review of secondary resources of information on household needs, budgeting and debt.

DEACON, Alan, BRIGGS, Eric: Reserved for the Poor: the Means Test in British Social Policy. Oxford, Martin Robertson, 1983, 224 p. Analysis of the role of the means test from the 1940s to the 1960s.

DONNISON, D.: The Politics of Poverty. Oxford, Martin Robertson, 1982, 239 p. The operation of the supplementary benefits scheme and the politics of social assistance described from personal experience by the former chairman of the Supplementary Benefits Commission.

LYNES, Tony: The Penguin Guide to Supplementary Benefits (4th ed.). Harmondsworth, Penguin, 1981, 319 p. The most detailed and informed guide to the practical workings of the British system.

2.5.2 Sources

DEPARTMENT OF HEALTH AND SOCIAL SECURITY: Social Security Statistics. London, HMSO, yearly series (1972).

SUPPLEMENTARY BENEFITS COMMISSION: Annual Report. London, HMSO, yearly series, 1975-79. Statistical detail and analytical, and sometimes critical, comment on the operation of the system.

2.6 Family programmes

2.6.1 Descriptions, evaluations and analyses

LASLETT, Peter (ed.): Families in Britain. London, Routledge and Kegan Paul, 1982, 350 p. Essays on the structure and social needs of households.

WALKER, Alan (ed.): Community Care: the Family, the State and Social Policy. Oxford, Basil Blackwell and Martin Robertson, 1982, 221 p. Essays on different styles of community care and their policy and resource implications.

WYNN, Margaret: Family Policy. London, Michael Joseph, 1970. Study of the social and economic costs of rearing children, the life-cycle of family needs, and the social and economic implications of an integrated family policy.

2.6.2 Sources

DEPARTMENT OF HEALTH AND SOCIAL SECURITY: Social Security Statistics. London, HMSO, yearly series (1972).

DEPARTMENT OF HEALTH AND SOCIAL SECURITY: Health and Personal Social Service Statistics. London, HMSO, yearly series (1969).

2.7 Housing

2.7.1 Descriptions, evaluations and analyses

BRADSHAW, Jonathan, HARRIS, Toby (eds): Energy and Social Policy. Henley, Routledge and Kegan Paul, 1983, 188 p. Studies of fuel expenditure, cold conditions, debt and disconnections.

BURKE, Gill: Housing and Social Justice. London, Longman, 1981, 227 p. Housing discussed in relation to contemporary social issues, including homelessness, squatting and urban and rural deprivation.

CULLINGWORTH, J.B.: Essays on Housing Policy. London, George Allen and Unwin, 1979, 188 p. Alternative kinds of housing provision examined in terms of their efficiency and equity.

DONNISON, D.: The Government of Housing. Harmondsworth, Penguin, 1967, 397 p. The workings of the housing market, including physical and demographic issues, with cross-national comparisons.

DONNISON, David, UNGERSON, Clare: Housing Policy. Harmondsworth, Penguin, 1982, 314 p. Updated and rewritten version of Donnison's 1967 book, with fuller cross-national data, concentration on public policy and finance and a less specialized approach.

DUCLAUD-WILLIAMS, Roger: The Politics of Housing in Britain and France. London, Heinemann, 1978, 280 p. Cross-national comparison of patterns of state intervention.

DUNLEAVY, Patrick: The Politics of Mass Housing in Britain in 1945-75. Oxford, Clarendon Press, 1981, 447 p. Study of high-rise housing in terms of corporative power and professional influence.

LANSLEY, Stuart: Housing and Public Policy. London, Croom Helm, 1979, 246 p. Textbook about the political economy of housing.

MALPASS, Peter, MURIE, Alan: Housing Policy and Practice, London, Macmillan, 1982, 201 p. Up-to-date study of policy and implementation.

MERRETT, Stephen: State Housing in Britain. London, Routledge and Kegan Paul, 1981, 376 p. Textbook with a long historical perspective.

MERRETT, Stephen, GRAY, Fred: Owner Occupation in Britain. Henley, Routledge and Kegan Paul, 1982, 392 p. Wide-ranging study, with theoretical discussion of the concepts of tenure.

MURIE, Alan: Housing Inequality and Deprivation. London, Heinemann, 1983, 250 p. The relationships between housing conditions and family deprivation.

2.7.2 Sources

DEPARTMENT OF THE ENVIRONMENT: Housing Policy - a Consultation Document. London, HMSO, Cmnd 6845, 1977. Discussion document about trends and policy options in the housing market with much factual detail, especially in the technical volume (Cmnd 6845-II).

DEPARTMENT OF THE ENVIRONMENT: Housing and Construction Statistics. London, HMSO, quarterly series (1972). Data on finance, investment and tenure.

2.8 Education

2.8.1 Descriptions, evaluations and analyses

BENN, Caroline, SIMON, Brian: Half Way There: Report on the British Comprehensive School Reform (2nd ed.). Harmondsworth, Penguin, 1972, 591 p. The progress of comprehensive reorganization using survey evidence.

BERNBAUM, Gerald (ed.): Schooling in Decline. London, Macmillan, 1979, 240 p. Essays on the declining salience of education, professional disillusionment and financial cutbacks.

FENWICK, I.G.K.: The Comprehensive School 1944-70. London, Methuen, 1976, 187 p. The politics of secondary school reorganization.

FENWICK, Keith, McBRIDE, Peter: The Government of Education: the Politics and Administration of Education in Britain. London, Methuen, 1981, 256 p. Textbook on educational government.

KOGAN, Maurice: The Politics of Education. Harmondsworth, Penguin, 1971, 208 p. Interviews with former Ministers of Education, Edward Boyle and Anthony Crosland.

KOGAN, Maurice, BECKER, Tony: Process and Structure in the Higher Education System. London, Heinemann, 1980, 232 p. Evaluation and policy-making functions and values in higher education.

MORTIMORE, Jo, BLACKSTONE, Tessa: Disadvantage and Education. London, Heinemann, 1982, 216 p. The definition and causes of educational disadvantage, and an evaluation of public policies designed to alleviate them.

2.8.2 Sources

DEPARTMENT OF EDUCATION AND SCIENCE: Statistics of Education. London, HMSO, yearly series, 1967-79. Comprehensive statistics for England only, arranged in six volumes: school leavers and examinations; further education; teachers; finance and awards; universities.

DEPARTMENT OF EDUCATION AND SCIENCE: Statistics of Education for the United Kingdom. London, HMSO, yearly series, (1967). Summary statistics for all parts of the UK.

2.9 Public household

2.9.1 Descriptions, evaluations, analyses

BOOTH, Tony A. (ed.): Planning for Welfare: Social Policy and the Expenditure Process. Oxford, Basil Blackwell and Martin Robertson, 1979, 224 p. Papers on the general resource allocation process and expenditure issues for particular services.

GLENNERSTER, Howard: Social Service Budgets and Social Policy. London, George Allen and Unwin, 1974. Study of resource allocation and new budgetary techniques.

HOOD, Christopher, WRIGHT, Maurice: Big Government in Hard Times. Oxford, Martin Robertson, 1981, 230 p. Essays on contemporary issues and the implementation of cutbacks.

JUDGE, Ken (ed.): Pricing the Social Services. London, Macmillan, 1980, 176 p. Essays on the use of market criteria in the allocation of social services.

KLEIN, Rudolf (ed.): Social Policy and Public Expenditure 1975: Inflation and Public Priorities. London, Centre for Studies in Social Policy, 1975, 193 p. Essays on each of the social services discussing mid-1970s issues.

WALKER, A. (ed.): Public Expenditure and Social Policy. London, Heinemann, 1982, 256 p. Essays on expenditure allocation and contemporary issues.

2.9.2 Sources

CENTRAL STATISTICAL OFFICE: National Income and Expenditure. London, HMSO, yearly series, (1946). Contains public expenditure data by calendar years on national accounts definitions.

THE GOVERNMENT'S EXPENDITURE PLANS: London, HMSO, annual white paper (1969). Contains expenditure plans for three years ahead and much detail about services.

DEPARTMENT OF EMPLOYMENT: Family Expenditure Survey. London, HMSO, yearly series (1957). Sample survey of household income and expenditure, including taxation and cash benefits and the use of public services.

2.10 Public employment

2.10.1 Descriptions, evaluations and analyses

PARRY, Richard: United Kingdom Public Employment: Patterns of Change 1951-1976. Glasgow, University of Strathclyde, 1980, 50 p. Data at five-year intervals from 1951 and an analysis of the determinants of change.

2.10.2 Sources

WILKINSON, G., JACKSON, P.M.: Public Sector Employment in the UK. Leicester, Public Sector Economics Research Centre, 1981, 136 p. Comprehensive compilation of available official data 1948-78.

III Impact of social programmes

3.1 Poverty

ATKINSON, A.B.: Poverty in Britain and the Reform of Social Security. Cambridge, Cambridge University Press, 1969, 224 p. Economic study of the adequacy of social security provision for low-income families together with possible reforms.

ABEL-SMITH, B., TOWNSEND, P.: The Poor and the Poorest. London, Bell, 1965, 78 p. Analysis of the increase in poverty in the 1950s.

BECKERMAN, Wilfred, CLARK, Stephen: Poverty and Social Security in Britain since 1961. Oxford, Oxford University Press, 1982, 92 p. Economic analysis of the effectiveness of social security and of gaps in the system

BERTHOUD, Richard, BROWN, Joan C: Poverty and the Development of Anti-poverty Policies in the United Kingdom. London, Heinemann, 1981, 320 p. Comprehensive review and evaluation of anti-poverty policies in all parts of the social policy system, 1950-80; part of a European Community study.

KINCAID, J.C.: Poverty and Equality in Britain. Harmondsworth, Penguin, 1973, 276 p. Marxist-oriented interpretation of income distribution and the role of social security.

TOWNSEND, P.: The Concept of Poverty. London, Heinemann, 1970, 260 p. Essays on the nature of poverty and the means of dealing with it.

TOWNSEND, P.: Poverty in the United Kingdom. Harmondsworth, Penguin, 1979, 1,216 p. Major analysis of a 1969 survey into household needs and resources and of associated aggregate data into the distribution of means.

3.2 Inequality and income distribution

3.2.1 Descriptions, evaluations and analyses

ATKINSON, A.B.: The Economics of Inequality. London, Oxford University Press, 1975, 295 p. Basic approaches from economic theory.

FIELD, F.: Inequality in Britain: Freedom, Welfare and the State. London, Fontana, 1981, 252 p. The total effect of public policy, including taxation and private market mechanisms, together with reform proposals.

LE GRAND, Julian: The Strategy of Equality: Redistribution and the Social Services. London, George Allen and Unwin, 1982, 192 p. Evaluation of the consumption patterns and final income effects of welfare state policies, using household survey data.

SANDFORD, Cedric, POND, Chris, WALKER, Robert (eds): Taxation and Social Policy. London, Heinemann, 1980, 242 p. The distributional consequences of taxation and public expenditure and the interaction of taxation with social policies, with proposals for integrated reform.

WEALE, Albert: Equality and Social Policy. London, Routledge and Kegan Paul, 1978, 149 p. Philosophical analysis of the structural basis of distribution.

WEDDERBURN, Dorothy (ed.): Poverty, Inequality and Class Structure. London, Cambridge University Press, 1974, 247 p. Essays on the measurement of inequality and poverty; case studies of poverty and relative deprivation and poverty and class consciousness.

3.2.2 Sources

ROYAL COMMISSION ON THE DISTRIBUTION OF INCOME AND WEALTH 1974-79: Five Reports on main standing reference and special reports on income from residence, higher income from employment and lower incomes. London, HMSO. Summarized *in* An A to Z of Income and Wealth, London, HMSO, 1980, 32 p.

INLAND REVENUE: Inland Revenue Statistics. London, HMSO, yearly series. Data on tax revenues and the distribution of income and wealth.

3.3 Economic effects

ATKINSON, A.B. (ed.): Wealth, Income and Inequality (2nd ed.). Oxford, Clarendon Press, 1980, 412 p. Readings on economic analysis, especially the personal distribution of income and wealth.

CUYLER, A.J.: The Political Economy of Social Policy. Oxford, Martin Robertson, 1980, 333 p. Analysis of the economic impact of the social services.

JUDGE, Ken: Rationing the Social Services. London, Heinemann, 1978, 208 p. Discussion of the various economic models of rationing and their use in the social services.

SANDFORD, C.: Social Economics. London, Heinemann, 1977, 286 p. Textbook of the application of economic analysis to social policy.

Appendix Tables

Contents

Table 1 Gross Domestic Product and Total Public Expenditure

Year	GDP (at market prices, in million UKL)			Deflators (base 1975)				Total public expenditure (in million UKL)				Year
	at current prices	at constant (1975) prices	annual real growth rate	gross domestic product	capital formation	public consumption	private consumption	at current prices	as % of GDP	at constant (1975) prices	annual real growth rate	
1950	12 970	54 193		23.9	24.4	15.9	26.2	4 522	34.9	22 894		1950
1951	14 473	56 163	3.6	25.8	27.0	17.4	28.7	5 371	37.1	24 790	8.3	1951
1952	15 686	56 044	-0.2	28.0	30.0	18.8	30.3	5 962	38.0	25 766	3.9	1952
1953	16 894	58 625	4.6	28.8	30.3	19.2	31.0	6 172	36.5	26 270	2.0	1953
1954	17 813	60 868	3.8	29.3	30.2	19.7	31.5	6 145	34.5	25 790	-1.8	1954
1955	19 177	62 888	3.3	30.5	31.6	20.6	32.7	6 466	33.7	25 795	0.0	1955
1956	20 733	63 877	1.6	32.5	33.2	22.5	34.2	7 041	34.0	26 137	1.3	1956
1957	21 924	65 120	1.9	33.7	34.3	23.9	35.3	7 633	34.8	26 808	2.6	1957
1958	22 833	65 230	0.2	35.0	35.2	25.0	36.3	7 971	34.9	26 835	0.1	1958
1959	24 042	67 822	4.0	35.4	35.0	26.1	36.6	8 449	35.1	27 766	3.5	1959
1960	25 511	71 370	5.2	35.7	35.2	27.1	37.1	8 832	35.0	28 632	3.1	1960
1961	27 240	73 711	3.3	37.0	36.0	28.3	38.1	9 743	35.8	30 144	5.3	1961
1962	28 518	74 421	1.0	38.3	36.9	29.4	39.6	10 387	36.4	31 025	2.9	1962
1963	30 325	77 343	3.9	39.2	38.2	30.4	40.4	10 970	36.2	31 741	2.3	1963
1964	33 075	81 390	5.2	40.6	39.0	31.9	41.8	12 004	36.3	33 404	5.2	1964
1965	35 528	83 271	2.3	42.7	40.4	34.0	43.8	13 326	37.5	35 200	5.4	1965
1966	37 897	84 960	2.0	44.6	41.6	36.1	45.6	14 448	38.1	36 365	3.3	1966
1967	40 018	87 153	2.6	45.9	41.7	37.7	46.9	16 672	41.7	40 683	11.9	1967
1968	43 351	90 749	4.1	47.8	43.4	39.9	49.2	18 289	42.2	42 380	4.2	1968
1969	46 409	92 086	1.5	50.4	45.3	42.5	51.9	19 008	41.0	41 731	-1.5	1969
1970	50 888	94 121	2.2	54.1	48.7	47.1	55.0	20 896	41.1	42 295	1.4	1970
1971	57 112	96 656	2.7	59.1	53.3	52.1	59.6	23 483	41.1	43 332	2.5	1971
1972	63 196	98 792	2.2	64.0	56.7	57.0	63.5	26 366	41.7	45 044	4.0	1972
1973	72 750	106 185	7.5	68.5	67.2	62.4	69.0	30 553	42.0	46 703	3.7	1973
1974	82 727	104 936	-1.2	78.8	81.8	76.3	80.9	39 119	47.3	49 523	6.0	1974
1975	104 143	104 143	-0.8	100.0	100.0	100.0	100.0	51 653	49.6	51 653	4.3	1975
1976	124 027	108 471	4.2	114.3	114.4	113.6	115.6	58 471	47.1	51 127	-1.0	1976
1977	142 693	109 521	1.0	130.3	128.2	110.9	133.1	61 807	43.3	48 215	-5.7	1977
1978	163 609	113 485	3.6	144.2	142.7	138.0	144.5	71 852	43.9	50 937	5.6	1978
1979	189 280	114 524	0.9	165.3	164.2	157.5	162.1	84 906	44.9	52 926	3.9	1979
1980	225 560	113 793	-0.6	198.2	193.1	198.2	189.4	103 720	46.0	53 718	1.5	1980

Table 2 Public Expenditure by

Year	Purpose: Total exp. at curr. pr. mill. pounds	Per cent distribution: publ. adm.	de-fence	welfare	econ. serv.	other	Economic Function: Total exp. at curr. pr. mill. pounds	Per cent distribution: subs./ transf.	final cons.	inter. on debt	capit. form.	Level of Government: Total exp. at curr. pr. mill. pounds	Per cent distribution: central gov.	local gov.	social insur.	Year
1950	4 522		19.0	42.5	20.3	18.1	4 522	27.0	47.5	12.1	13.3	4 522	67.0	24.4	8.6	1950
1951	5 371		22.0	38.4	20.6	19.1	5 371	23.4	47.0	11.0	18.7	5 371	69.5	23.0	7.6	1951
1952	5 962		26.4	38.8	18.8	16.0	5 962	22.2	50.3	10.9	16.5	5 962	68.7	23.4	8.0	1952
1953	6 172		26.7	40.5	16.5	16.3	6 172	22.1	50.8	11.1	16.1	6 172	66.6	24.9	8.6	1953
1954	6 145		26.4	41.3	16.2	16.0	6 145	23.4	52.3	11.2	13.1	6 145	65.6	25.7	8.7	1954
1955	6 466		24.6	41.5	18.3	15.6	6 466	22.5	50.6	11.9	15.0	6 466	65.2	25.3	9.5	1955
1956	7 041		24.1	41.2	16.8	17.9	7 041	21.9	50.1	11.3	16.6	7 041	64.9	25.6	9.5	1956
1957	7 633		21.1	41.0	19.2	18.6	7 633	21.7	48.2	10.5	19.6	7 633	64.7	26.1	9.2	1957
1958	7 971		19.4	42.6	18.5	19.5	7 971	23.5	47.1	11.2	18.2	7 971	62.7	25.9	11.4	1958
1959	8 449		18.7	43.3	18.6	19.4	8 449	23.8	47.2	10.8	18.2	8 449	62.1	26.2	11.7	1959
1960	8 932		18.2	43.7	19.6	18.5	8 932	24.1	47.3	11.4	17.1	8 932	62.3	26.6	11.1	1960
1961	9 743		17.7	44.0	20.6	17.7	9 743	24.8	46.8	11.3	17.1	9 743	60.7	27.7	11.5	1961
1962	10 387		17.7	44.2	20.1	18.0	10 387	25.1	47.0	10.8	17.1	10 387	59.5	28.8	11.7	1962
1963	10 970		17.2	46.3	19.4	17.0	10 970	25.8	46.8	10.9	16.5	10 970	57.3	29.8	12.9	1963
1964	12 004		16.6	47.2	19.5	16.7	12 004	24.4	45.5	10.3	19.6	12 004	56.2	31.4	12.5	1964
1965	13 326		15.8	48.4	19.3	16.5	13 326	25.1	45.0	10.1	19.8	13 326	54.9	31.8	13.3	1965
1966	14 467		15.2	47.6	15.0	22.1	14 467	24.6	45.1	10.1	20.2	14 467	55.1	31.8	13.1	1966
1967	16 691		14.4	46.4	18.2	21.0	16 691	25.0	43.2	9.4	22.3	16 691	56.2	31.3	12.5	1967
1968	18 311		13.3	46.7	18.8	21.2	18 311	26.0	41.8	9.8	22.4	18 311	56.2	30.9	12.9	1968
1969	19 008		12.1	48.0	18.0	21.9	19 008	26.1	42.1	10.1	21.7	19 008	55.2	32.1	12.8	1969
1970	20 896		11.8	48.7	17.4	22.1	20 896	25.8	43.0	9.7	21.5	20 896	54.5	32.5	13.0	1970
1971	23 483		11.8	47.8	18.6	21.8	23 483	25.2	43.6	8.9	22.2	23 483	55.8	31.8	12.5	1971
1972	26 366		11.6	49.9	16.4	22.1	26 366	27.3	44.3	8.7	19.7	26 366	55.0	31.8	13.2	1972
1973	30 553		11.4	50.7	14.9	23.0	30 566	26.9	43.8	9.0	20.3	30 556	53.0	34.2	12.9	1973
1974	39 199		10.4	52.2	15.3	22.1	39 211	28.6	42.4	9.2	19.8	39 211	54.4	33.0	12.6	1974
1975	51 653		10.0	51.4	17.6	19.4	51 631	27.8	44.6	8.2	19.4	51 631	54.9	32.7	12.4	1975
1976	58 471		10.7	53.6	13.4	22.3	58 481	29.1	45.8	9.2	15.9	58 481	54.0	32.4	13.6	1976
1977	61 807		11.1	55.9	9.5	23.5	61 868	31.5	47.3	10.3	10.9	61 868	53.3	31.8	14.9	1977
1978	71 852		10.5	54.5	11.1	23.9	71 903	32.3	45.9	10.1	11.8	71 903	55.7	29.7	14.6	1978
1979	84 906		10.7	53.3	11.8	24.1	84 944	32.3	45.0	10.5	12.2	84 944	57.3	28.7	14.0	1979
1980	103 720		11.0	53.4	11.3	24.3		31.4	46.6	10.9	11.2		57.7	28.4	13.9	1980

Table 3

Social Expenditure

Year	At current prices (in million UKL)						As % of gross domestic product					As % of public expenditure					As % of social expenditure					Year
	Total	Income maint.	Education	Health	Housing	Soc. serv.	Inc. maint.	Educ.	Health	Hous.	Soc. serv.	Inc. maint.	Educ.	Health	Hous.	Soc. serv.	Inc. maint.	Educ.	Health	Hous.	Soc. serv.	
1950	1 924	674	431	478	341	-	5.2	3.3	3.7	2.6		14.9	9.5	10.6	7.5	-	35.0	22.4	24.8	17.7	-	1950
1951	2 060	707	466	498	368	-	4.9	3.2	3.4	2.5		13.1	8.1	9.3	6.9	-	34.3	22.6	24.2	17.9	-	1951
1952	2 316	825	519	510	440	-	5.3	3.3	3.3	2.8		13.8	8.7	8.6	7.4	-	35.6	22.4	22.0	19.0	-	1952
1953	2 500	914	539	526	493	35	5.4	3.2	3.1	2.9	0.2	14.8	8.7	8.5	8.0	0.6	36.6	21.6	21.0	19.7	1.4	1953
1954	2 540	922	579	543	467	38	5.2	3.3	3.0	2.6	0.2	15.0	9.4	8.8	7.6	0.6	36.3	22.8	21.4	18.4	1.5	1954
1955	2 683	1 016	628	585	422	40	5.3	3.3	3.1	2.2	0.2	15.7	9.7	9.0	6.5	0.6	37.9	23.4	21.8	15.7	1.5	1955
1956	2 905	1 087	725	641	415	43	5.2	3.5	3.1	2.0	0.2	15.4	10.3	9.1	5.9	0.6	37.4	25.0	22.1	14.3	1.5	1956
1957	3 131	1 117	858	685	403	47	5.1	3.9	3.1	1.8	0.2	14.6	11.2	9.0	5.3	0.6	35.7	27.4	21.9	12.9	1.5	1957
1958	3 399	1 345	864	728	412	50	5.9	3.8	3.2	1.8	0.2	16.9	10.8	9.1	5.2	0.6	39.6	25.4	21.5	12.1	1.5	1958
1959	3 655	1 450	930	788	434	53	6.0	3.9	3.3	1.8	0.2	17.2	11.0	9.3	5.1	0.6	39.7	25.4	21.6	11.9	1.5	1959
1960	3 899	1 448	1 002	861	490	58	5.7	3.9	3.4	1.9	0.2	16.2	11.2	9.6	5.5	0.6	37.1	25.7	22.1	12.6	1.5	1960
1961	4 284	1 628	1 105	930	555	66	6.0	4.1	3.4	2.0	0.2	16.7	11.3	9.5	5.7	0.5	38.0	25.8	21.7	13.0	1.5	1961
1962	4 590	1 744	1 271	971	529	75	6.1	4.5	3.4	1.9	0.3	16.8	12.2	9.3	5.1	0.7	38.0	27.7	21.2	11.5	1.6	1962
1963	5 083	1 988	1 386	1 036	591	82	6.6	4.6	3.4	1.9	0.3	18.1	12.6	9.4	5.4	0.7	39.1	27.3	20.4	11.6	1.6	1963
1964	5 671	2 099	1 532	1 132	816	92	6.3	4.6	3.4	2.5	0.3	17.5	12.8	9.4	6.8	0.8	37.0	27.0	20.0	14.4	1.6	1964
1965	6 450	2 408	1 712	1 270	955	105	6.8	4.8	3.6	2.7	0.3	18.1	12.8	9.5	7.2	0.8	37.3	26.5	19.7	14.8	1.6	1965
1966	6 883	2 577	1 841	1 375	979	111	6.8	4.9	3.6	2.6	0.3	17.8	12.7	9.5	6.8	0.8	37.4	26.7	20.0	14.2	1.6	1966
1967	7 738	2 900	2 053	1 524	1 129	132	7.2	5.1	3.8	2.8	0.3	17.4	12.3	9.1	6.8	0.8	37.5	26.5	19.7	14.6	1.7	1967
1968	8 546	3 339	2 247	1 656	1 157	147	7.7	5.2	3.8	2.7	0.3	18.3	12.3	9.1	6.3	0.8	39.0	26.3	19.4	13.5	1.7	1968
1969	9 128	3 571	2 412	1 733	1 208	204	7.7	5.2	3.7	2.6	0.4	18.8	12.7	9.1	6.4	1.1	39.1	26.4	19.0	13.2	2.2	1969
1970	10 179	3 921	2 703	1 979	1 319	257	7.7	5.3	3.9	2.6	0.5	18.8	12.9	9.5	6.3	1.2	38.5	26.6	19.4	13.0	2.5	1970
1971	11 233	4 307	3 058	2 248	1 310	310	7.5	5.3	3.9	2.3	0.5	18.3	13.0	9.6	5.6	1.3	38.3	27.2	20.0	11.7	2.8	1971
1972	13 161	5 120	3 569	2 593	1 509	370	8.1	5.6	4.1	2.4	0.6	19.4	13.5	9.8	5.7	1.4	38.9	27.1	19.7	11.5	2.8	1972
1973	15 477	5 534	4 163	2 942	2 328	510	7.6	5.7	4.0	3.2	0.7	18.1	13.6	9.6	7.6	1.7	35.8	26.9	19.0	15.0	3.3	1973
1974	20 455	6 836	4 875	3 845	4 209	690	8.3	5.9	4.6	5.1	0.8	17.4	12.4	9.8	10.7	1.8	33.4	23.8	18.8	20.6	3.4	1974
1975	26 525	8 905	6 976	5 182	4 461	1 001	8.6	6.7	5.0	4.3	1.0	17.2	13.5	10.0	8.6	1.9	33.5	26.3	19.5	16.8	8.0	1975
1976	31 367	11 236	7 747	6 090	5 114	1 180	9.1	6.2	4.9	4.1	1.0	19.2	13.2	10.4	8.7	2.0	35.8	24.7	19.4	16.3	3.8	1976
1977	34 538	13 220	8 261	6 730	5 083	1 244	9.3	5.8	4.7	3.6	0.9	21.4	13.4	10.9	8.2	2.0	38.3	23.9	19.5	14.7	3.6	1977
1978	39 168	15 799	9 000	7 619	5 278	1 472	9.7	5.5	4.7	3.2	0.9	22.0	12.5	10.6	7.3	2.0	40.3	23.0	19.5	14.6	3.8	1978
1979	45 278	18 497	10 086	8 863	6 099	1 733	9.8	5.3	4.7	3.2	0.9	21.8	11.9	10.4	7.2	2.0	40.1	22.3	19.6	13.5	3.8	1979
1980	55 384	22 211	12 396	11 494	7 156	2 127	9.8	5.5	5.1	3.2	0.9	21.4	12.0	11.1	6.9	2.1	40.1	22.4	20.8	12.9	3.8	1980

Table 4

Social Expenditure

Year	Exp. on Education at current prices			Exp. on Health at current prices			Exp. on Soc. Serv. at current prices			Exp. on Housing at current prices			Exp. on Income Maint. at curr. pr.		Benef.at 1975 pr.	Cons.pr. index (1975)	Expenditure at constant (1975) prices						Year
	Total	Curr.	Cap.	Total	Curr.	Cap.	Total	Curr.	Cap.	Total	Curr.	Cap.	Total	Benef.			Inc. maint.	Educ.	Health	Soc. serv.	Hous.	Total	
1950	431	373	58	478	465	13	-	-	-	341	72	269	674	613	2 342	24.5	2 575	2 582	2 960	-	1 379	9 496	1950
1951	466	396	70	498	484	14	-	-	-	368	75	293	707	641	2 237	26.7	2 467	2 536	2 819	107	1 348	9 277	1951
1952	519	441	78	510	497	13	-	-	-	440	83	357	825	751	2 475	29.2	2 719	2 603	2 668	96	1 465	9 551	1952
1953	539	461	78	526	512	14	35	32	3	493	91	402	914	839	2 710	30.0	2 952	2 662	2 702	177	1 621	10 114	1953
1954	579	499	80	543	527	16	38	34	4	467	100	367	922	844	2 677	30.6	2 925	2 793	2 713	185	1 533	10 149	1954
1955	628	539	89	585	567	18	40	36	4	422	99	323	1 016	934	2 857	32.0	3 108	2 891	2 793	187	1 334	10 313	1955
1956	725	612	113	641	623	18	43	39	4	415	108	307	1 087	999	2 926	33.5	3 184	3 060	2 813	185	1 241	10 483	1956
1957	858	726	132	685	659	26	47	42	5	403	108	295	1 117	1 046	2 962	34.8	3 163	3 427	2 834	191	1 166	10 781	1957
1958	864	722	142	728	699	29	50	45	5	412	110	302	1 345	1 272	3 498	35.8	3 699	3 294	2 876	194	1 161	11 224	1958
1959	930	790	140	788	754	34	53	47	6	434	114	320	1 450	1 367	3 724	36.1	3 950	3 427	2 983	197	1 227	11 784	1959
1960	1 002	861	141	861	824	37	58	51	7	490	120	370	1 448	1 362	3 668	36.4	3 899	3 576	3 141	208	1 374	12 198	1960
1961	1 105	532	173	930	885	45	66	57	9	555	133	422	1 628	1 539	4 026	37.6	4 259	3 779	3 254	227	1 520	13 039	1961
1962	1 271	1 055	216	971	916	55	75	64	11	529	127	402	1 744	1 645	4 140	39.2	4 390	4 177	3 266	248	1 409	13 490	1962
1963	1 386	1 162	224	1 036	976	60	82	69	13	591	126	465	1 988	1 884	4 652	40.1	4 908	4 406	3 363	261	1 529	14 467	1963
1964	1 532	1 269	263	1 132	1 056	76	92	74	18	816	137	679	2 099	1 981	4 725	41.4	5 006	4 660	3 509	278	2 069	15 522	1964
1965	1 712	1 436	276	1 270	1 179	91	105	86	19	955	169	786	2 408	2 290	5 205	43.3	5 473	4 909	3 691	300	2 347	16 720	1965
1966	1 841	1 549	292	1 375	1 273	102	111	92	19	979	180	799	2 577	2 442	5 338	45.0	5 633	4 997	3 774	301	2 283	16 988	1966
1967	2 053	1 714	339	1 524	1 399	125	132	110	22	1 129	196	933	2 900	2 748	5 853	46.1	6 177	5 433	4 011	345	2 655	18 621	1967
1968	2 247	1 868	379	1 656	1 513	143	147	122	25	1 157	230	927	3 339	3 170	6 451	48.3	6 795	5 669	4 159	363	2 602	19 588	1968
1969	2 412	2 039	373	1 733	1 596	137	204	175	29	1 208	275	933	3 571	3 388	6 525	51.0	6 496	5 743	4 091	476	2 588	19 394	1969
1970	2 703	2 300	403	1 979	1 828	151	257	225	32	1 319	325	994	3 921	3 709	6 747	54.2	7 132	5 933	4 237	544	2 634	20 480	1970
1971	3 058	2 590	468	2 248	2 067	181	310	271	39	1 310	348	962	4 307	4 068	6 826	59.3	7 227	6 128	4 358	593	2 390	20 696	1971
1972	3 569	3 022	547	2 593	2 370	223	370	331	39	1 509	401	1 108	5 120	4 833	7 612	63.5	8 064	6 566	4 565	650	2 588	22 433	1972
1973	4 163	3 492	671	2 942	2 665	277	510	428	82	2 328	632	1 696	5 534	5 224	7 575	69.4	8 024	6 998	4 722	808	3 441	23 993	1973
1974	4 875	4 215	660	3 845	3 549	296	690	604	86	4 209	1 053	3 157	6 836	6 450	7 972	80.5	8 449	6 888	4 834	896	5 158	26 225	1974
1975	6 976	6 280	696	5 182	4 816	366	1 001	918	83	4 461	1 413	3 048	8 905	8 353	8 353	100.0	8 905	6 976	5 182	1 001	4 461	26 525	1975
1976	7 747	6 986	761	6 090	5 665	425	1 180	1 084	96	5 114	1 802	3 312	11 236	10 506	9 088	116.5	9 719	7 236	5 276	1 039	4 454	27 724	1976
1977	8 261	7 581	680	6 730	6 336	394	1 244	1 190	54	5 083	2 015	3 068	13 220	12 464	9 373	135.0	9 941	7 067	5 251	993	3 908	27 160	1977
1978	9 000	8 401	599	7 619	7 208	411	1 472	1 396	76	5 278	2 261	3 017	15 799	14 971	10 360	146.2	10 933	7 648	5 359	1 065	3 680	28 685	1978
1979	10 086	9 468	618	8 863	8 353	510	1 733	1 647	86	6 099	2 661	3 438	18 497	17 575	10 844	165.8	11 413	7 093	5 459	1 098	3 736	28 799	1979
1980	12 396	11 649	747	11 494	10 880	614	2 127	2 023	104	7 156	3 353	3 803	22 211	21 047	11 113	195.6	11 727	6 783	5 633	1 075	3 793	29 011	1980

Table 5

Expenditure on Income Maintenance Programmes
(benefits only)

at current prices (in million UKL)

Year	Old age pens.	Surviv. pens.	Sickn. benef.	Inval. pens.	Occup. inj.	Unempl. benef.	Family allow.	Social ass.	Other
1950	253	23	68		14	20	64	60	111
1951	270	24	70		16	15	66	71	109
1952	312	28	74		19	28	80	95	115
1953	343	31	90		24	27	108	104	112
1954	351	32	87		25	20	109	108	112
1955	417	36	98		29	18	111	102	123
1956	452	39	105		33	22	116	109	123
1957	468	43	109		33	27	129	117	120
1958	605	57	131		42	49	129	121	138
1959	661	62	140		45	51	133	141	134
1960	679	67	135		46	35	136	172	92
1961	769	79	154		53	36	140	169	139
1962	816	87	163		56	55	140	187	141
1963	930	98	198		65	82	146	218	147
1964	1 022	108	199		71	53	149	225	154
1965	1 204	133	247		85	55	152	241	173
1966	1 281	144	266		87	65	155	277	167
1967	1 351	150	314		91	127	161	392	162
1968	1 550	159	359		99	134	270	421	178
1969	1 605	161	375		98	131	351	489	178
1970	1 800	174	419		104	152	351	517	192
1971	1 947	189	352	50	102	218	362	634	214
1972	2 335	221	321	170	113	246	347	729	351
1973	2 760	246	324	242	124	160	360	705	303
1974	3 490	302	365	316	145	229	360	871	372
1975	4 477	381	418	438	181	396	499	1 103	460
1976	5 509	435	522	565	213	568	563	1 525	606
1977	6 445	470	608	704	245	635	809	1 735	813
1978	7 377	509	680	857	272	668	1 596	2 064	948
1979	8 555	554	664	996	294	637	2 681	2 172	1 022
1980	10 277	637	660	1 195	329	1 097	2 944	2 693	1 215

at constant (1975) prices (in million UKL)

Old age pens.	Surviv. pens.	Sickn. benef.	Inval. pens.	Occup. inj.	Unempl. benef.	Family allow.	Social ass.	Other	Year
967	88	260		53	76	245	229	424	1950
942	84	244		56	52	230	248	380	1951
1 028	92	244		63	92	264	313	379	1952
1 108	100	291		78	87	349	336	362	1953
1 113	102	276		79	63	346	343	355	1954
1 276	110	300		89	55	340	312	376	1955
1 324	114	308		97	64	340	319	360	1956
1 325	122	309		93	76	365	331	340	1957
1 664	157	360		116	135	355	333	380	1958
1 801	169	381		123	139	362	384	365	1959
1 829	180	364		124	94	366	463	248	1960
2 012	207	403		139	94	366	442	364	1961
2 054	219	410		141	138	352	471	355	1962
2 296	242	489		160	202	360	538	363	1963
2 437	258	475		169	126	355	537	367	1964
2 737	302	561		193	125	345	548	393	1965
2 800	315	581		190	142	339	606	365	1966
2 876	320	669		194	271	343	835	345	1967
3 154	324	731		201	273	549	857	362	1968
3 091	310	722		189	252	676	942	343	1969
3 274	317	762		189	276	638	940	349	1970
3 267	317	591	84	171	366	607	1 064	359	1971
3 678	348	506	268	268	387	546	1 148	553	1972
4 002	357	470	351	180	232	522	1 022	439	1973
4 314	373	451	391	179	283	445	1 077	460	1974
4 477	381	418	438	181	396	499	1 103	460	1975
4 765	376	452	489	184	491	487	1 319	524	1976
4 847	353	457	529	184	478	608	1 305	611	1977
5 105	352	471	593	188	462	1 104	1 428	656	1978
5 278	342	410	615	181	393	1 654	1 340	631	1979
5 426	336	348	631	174	579	1 554	1 422	642	1980

Table 6

Expenditure on Pensions

Year	at current prices (in million UKL)						at constant (1975) prices (in million UKL)						Year
	Retirement pensions	Widows' pensions	Invalidity pensions	War pensions	Civil service	Total	Retirement pensions	Widows' pensions	Invalidity pensions	War pensions	Civil service	Total	
1950	253	23		86		362	967	88		328		1 383	1950
1951	270	24		84		378	942	84		293		1 319	1951
1952	312	28		91		431	1 028	92		300		1 420	1952
1953	343	31				374	1 108	100				1 208	1953
1954	351	32		87		470	1 113	102		276		1 491	1954
1955	417	36		88		541	1 276	110		269		1 655	1955
1956	452	39		89		580	1 324	114		260		1 698	1956
1957	468	43		91		602	1 325	122		258		1 705	1957
1958	605	57		100		762	1 664	157		275		2 096	1958
1959	661	62		99	23	845	1 801	169		270	63	2 303	1959
1960	679	67		96	25	867	1 829	180		259	67	2 335	1960
1961	769	79		104	25	977	2 012	207		273	66	2 558	1961
1962	816	87		102	41	1 046	2 054	219		258	104	2 635	1962
1963	930	98		110	47	1 185	2 296	242		272	116	2 926	1963
1964	1 022	108		110	48	1 288	2 437	258		263	115	3 073	1964
1965	1 204	133		121	52	1 510	2 737	302		276	119	3 434	1965
1966	1 281	144		118	59	1 602	2 800	315		259	229	3 603	1966
1967	1 351	150		121	61	1 683	2 876	320		258	130	3 584	1967
1968	1 550	159		125	70	1 904	3 154	324		254	142	3 874	1968
1969	1 605	161		125	78	1 969	3 091	310		241	150	3 792	1969
1970	1 800	174		128	80	2 182	3 274	317		232	145	3 968	1970
1971	1 947	189	50	137	96	2 419	3 267	317	84	230	161	4 059	1971
1972	2 335	221	170	150	116	2 992	3 678	348	268	236	183	4 713	1972
1973	2 760	246	242	164	121	3 533	4 002	357	351	238	175	5 123	1973
1974	3 490	302	316	204	137	4 449	4 314	373	391	252	169	5 499	1974
1975	4 477	381	438	258	221	5 775	4 477	381	438	258	221	5 775	1975
1976	5 509	435	565	283	276	7 068	4 765	376	489	245	239	6 114	1976
1977	6 445	470	704	310	307	8 236	4 847	353	529	233	231	6 193	1977
1978	7 377	509	857	341	365	9 449	5 105	352	593	236	253	6 539	1978
1979	8 555	554	996	375	451	10 931	5 278	342	615	231	278	6 744	1979
1980	10 277	637	1 195	424	501	13 034	5 426	336	631	224	265	6 882	1980

Table 7 Expenditure on Unemployment and Families

Year	at current prices (in million UKL)									at constant (1975) prices (in million UKL)									Year
	Unempl. benef.	Suppl. benef.	Empl. serv.	Total	Family allow.	Child benef.	Matern. benef.	Fam.inc. suppl.	Total	Unempl. benef.	Suppl. benef.	Empl. serv.	Total	Family allow.	Child benef.	Matern. benef.	Fam.inc. suppl.	Total	
1950	20		20	40	64		9		73	76		126	202	245		34		279	1950
1951	15		19	34	66		9		75	52		109	161	230		31		261	1951
1952	28		19	47	80		9		89	92		101	193	264		30		294	1952
1953	27		19	46	108		9		117	87		99	186	349		29		378	1953
1954	20		19	39	109		13		122	63		96	159	346		41		387	1954
1955	18		20	38	111		13		124	55		97	152	340		40		380	1955
1956	22		20	42	116		15		131	64		89	153	340		44		384	1956
1957	27		21	48	129		16		145	76		88	164	365		45		410	1957
1958	49		28	77	129		20		149	135		112	247	355		55		410	1958
1959	51		29	80	133		20		153	139		111	250	362		54		416	1959
1960	35		31	66	136		21		157	94		114	208	366		57		423	1960
1961	36		31	67	140		24		164	94		110	204	366		63		429	1961
1962	55		32	87	140		26		166	138		109	247	352		65		417	1962
1963	82		34	116	146		28		174	202		112	314	360		69		429	1963
1964	53		37	90	149		31		180	126		116	242	355		74		429	1964
1965	55		45	100	152		36		188	125		132	257	345		82		427	1965
1966	65		71	136	155		36		191	142		197	339	339		79		418	1966
1967	127		95	222	161		35		196	271		252	523	343		75		418	1967
1968	134		115	249	270		39		309	273		288	561	549		79		628	1968
1969	131		116	247	351		39		390	252		273	525	676		75		751	1969
1970	152		128	280	351		42		393	276		272	548	638		76		714	1970
1971	218		177	395	362		43	4	409	366		340	706	607		72	7	686	1971
1972	246		208	454	347		44	10	401	387		365	752	546		69	16	631	1972
1973	160		211	371	360		44	13	417	232		338	570	522		64	19	605	1973
1974	229		264	493	360		47	12	419	283		346	629	445		58	15	518	1974
1975	396		476	872	499		55	12	566	396		476	872	499		55	12	566	1975
1976	568	590	697	1 855	563		77	18	658	491	510	614	1 615	487		67	16	570	1976
1977	635	740	967	2 342		809	93	25	927	478	556	773	1 807		608	70	19	697	1977
1978	668	705	1 133	2 506		1 596	119	24	1 739	462	488	821	1 771		1 104	82	17	1 203	1978
1979	637	765	1 229	2 631		2 681	139	24	2 844	393	472	780	1 645		1 654	86	15	1 755	1979
1980	1 097	1 190	1 668	3 955		2 944	163	27	3 134	597	628	841	2 066		1 554	86	14	1 654	1980
1981	1 763	2 260	2 326	6 349		3 527	179	43	3 749	838	1 074	1 029	2 941		1 676	85	20	1 781	1981
1982	1 590	3 540	2 283	7 966		3 938	163	66	4 167	668	1 487	959	3 114		1 654	68	28	1 750	1982

Table 8 Housing: Expenditure and Completions

Year	Expenditure at current prices (in million UKL)				Expenditure at constant (1975) prices (in million UKL)				Completions			Year
	Housing programme		Housing	Tax	Housing programme		Housing	Tax	Public	Private	Total	
	Curr. exp.	Capit. exp.	benefit	relief	Curr. exp.	Capit. exp.	benefit	relief				
1950	72	269			275	1 104			175.2	30.2	205.4	1950
1951	75	293			262	1 086			176.4	25.5	201.9	1951
1952	83	357			274	1 191			211.7	36.7	248.3	1952
1953	91	402			294	1 327			261.9	64.9	326.8	1953
1954	100	367			317	1 216			261.7	92.4	354.1	1954
1955	99	323			303	1 021			208.3	116.1	324.4	1955
1956	108	307			316	925			181.2	126.4	307.7	1956
1957	108	295			306	860			178.8	128.8	307.6	1957
1958	110	302			303	858			148.4	130.2	278.6	1958
1959	114	320			311	916			128.4	153.2	281.6	1959
1960	120	370			323	1 051			132.9	171.4	304.3	1960
1961	133	422			348	1 172			122.4	180.7	303.2	1961
1962	127	402			320	1 089			135.4	178.2	313.6	1962
1963	126	465			311	1 218			129.9	177.8	307.7	1963
1964	137	679			327	1 742			161.9	221.3	383.2	1964
1965	169	786			384	1 963			174.1	217.2	391.2	1965
1966	180	799			393	1 890			187.4	208.7	396.0	1966
1967	196	933			417	2 238			211.3	204.2	415.5	1967
1968	230	927			468	2 134			199.8	226.1	425.8	1968
1969	275	933			530	2 058			192.4	185.9	378.3	1969
1970	325	994			591	2 043			187.9	174.3	362.2	1970
1971	348	962	88		584	1 806	148		168.2	196.3	364.5	1971
1972	401	1 108	199		632	1 956	313		130.2	200.8	330.9	1972
1973	632	1 696	249		916	2 525	361		113.6	191.1	304.6	1973
1974	1 052	3 157	292		1 300	3 858	361		134.4	145.2	279.6	1974
1975	1 413	3 048	392		1 413	3 048	392		167.4	154.5	321.9	1975
1976	1 802	3 312	457		1 559	2 895	395		169.5	155.2	324.8	1976
1977	2 015	3 068	479		1 515	2 393	360		170.2	143.9	314.1	1977
1978	2 261	3 017	538		1 565	2 115	372		136.4	152.2	288.6	1978
1979	2 661	3 438	655		1 642	2 094	404		107.8	144.1	251.8	1979
1980	3 353	3 803	555	4 360	1 770	2 023	293	2 302	109.8	130.6	240.3	1980
1981	3 230	2 409	1 173	4 830	1 535	1 124	557	2 294	87.7	116.4	204.1	1981
1982	2 981	2 446	2 421	5 150	1 252	1 027	1 017	2 163	54.6	143.0	197.5	1982

Table 9 Financing of Public and Social Security Expenditure

Year	General government revenues (and expenditure) at current prices (in million pounds) Total expenditure	Total revenues I	Total revenues II	Percent distribution direct taxes	indirect taxes	national insurance	other	National insurance receipts Total (at current prices, in million pounds)	Percent distribution contributions by employers/insured	of which: graduated	taxation subsidy	Year
1950	4 522	4 852	4 825	41.5	42.7	9.1	6.7	605	71.2		28.8	1950
1951	5 371	5 217	5 185	40.9	43.7	8.7	6.7	614	70.2		29.8	1951
1952	5 962	5 439	5 517	42.3	41.4	8.6	7.7	595	73.4		26.6	1952
1953	6 172	5 555	5 623	40.6	41.9	9.3	8.2	595	80.7		19.3	1953
1954	6 145	5 822	5 841	39.9	42.7	9.1	8.3	638	80.7		19.3	1954
1955	6 466	6 249	6 270	38.9	42.2	9.5	8.5	656	79.6		20.4	1955
1956	7 041	6 555	6 562	38.6	42.9	9.8	8.7	763	79.9		20.1	1956
1957	7 633	6 989	6 993	39.6	42.3	9.4	8.8	789	79.8		20.2	1957
1958	7 971	7 491	7 489	38.8	40.4	11.5	9.3	801	79.0		21.0	1958
1959	8 449	7 819	7 828	37.9	40.7	11.5	9.9	993	76.2		23.8	1959
1960	8 932	8 084	8 104	35.5	41.7	11.3	10.5	1 019	76.1		23.9	1960
1961	9 743	8 895	8 922	37.4	40.7	12.0	9.9	1 026	75.8		24.2	1961
1962	10 387	9 760	9 794	38.0	39.6	12.2	10.2	1 231	79.0	(11.9)	21.0	1962
1963	10 970	9 982	9 982	37.0	40.3	13.1	9.6	1 278	79.0	(13.4)	21.0	1963
1964	12 004	10 853	10 853	35.9	40.9	13.3	9.9	1 461	80.2	(15.2)	19.8	1964
1965	13 326	12 205	12 205	35.8	40.6	13.8	9.8	1 550	81.7	(17.4)	18.3	1965
1966	14 467	13 436	13 436	36.3	40.4	13.4	9.9	1 924	80.6	(15.3)	19.4	1966
1967	16 691	14 956	14 956	37.5	40.1	12.9	9.6	1 972	81.1	(17.6)	18.9	1967
1968	18 311	16 888	16 888	37.2	40.3	12.8	9.7	2 134	81.5	(19.0)	18.5	1968
1969	19 008	18 991	18 991	37.5	41.0	11.8	9.8	2 354	81.7	(18.2)	18.3	1969
1970	20 896	21 188	21 188	38.1	39.7	12.5	9.7	2 485	82.3	(21.2)	17.7	1970
1971	23 483	22 574	22 576	38.4	38.7	12.5	10.4	2 827	82.7	(27.4)	17.3	1971
1972	26 366	23 962	23 962	37.0	38.6	13.9	10.4	3 223	82.0	(32.4)	18.0	1972
1973	30 556	27 030	27 030	37.1	37.4	14.6	10.9	3 790	82.7	(38.9)	17.3	1973
1974	39 211	33 793	33 893	40.0	34.0	14.9	11.2	4 454	84.0	(42.9)	16.6	1974
1975	51 530	42 982	42 982	40.8	32.8	15.9	10.4	6 006	84.4	(46.7)	15.6	1975
1976	58 447	49 981	49 979	39.5	32.9	16.9	10.7	7 510	82.3		17.7	1976
1977	61 860	56 962	56 950	37.3	35.2	16.7	10.8	9 398	82.2		17.8	1977
1978	71 887	63 215	63 188	37.0	36.3	16.0	10.7	10 484	81.6		18.4	1978
1979	85 209	75 790	75 754	34.5	39.4	15.2	10.8	11 410	78.8		21.2	1979
1980	103 979	93 006	92 972	34.5	39.7	15.0	10.9	13 297	78.3		21.7	1980
1981	116 843	108 256	107 316	34.9	39.9	14.8	10.4	16 009	78.4		21.6	1981
1982			120 027	34.9	39.8	15.0	10.3					1982

Table 10

Welfare Beneficiaries

(in 1,000s)

Year	Retirement pensions	Widows' pensions	War pensions	Invalidity pensions	Ind. disablement pensions	Injury benefit	Sickness benefit	Unemployment benefit	Earnings-rel. income suppl.	Child benefit families	Child benefit children	Social assistance households	Social assistance persons	Year
1950	4 229	453	1 038		60	64	942	344		3 149		1 695		1950
1951	4 223	447	1 005		81	59	942	189		3 219		1 763		1951
1952	4 263	453	984		98	58	885	336		3 270		1 911		1952
1953	4 389	452	959		110	61	970	262		3 310		1 966		1953
1954	4 519	452	934		126	60	957	193		3 344		1 974		1954
1955	4 633	450	907		137	60	957	154		3 382		1 759		1955
1956	4 741	452	879		144	60	949	175		3 472		1 779		1956
1957	4 845	466	846		150	56	981	211		3 504		1 819		1957
1958	5 426	500	817		157	59	937	311		3 562		1 740		1958
1959	5 556	528	781		166	63	980	325		3 591		1 838		1959
1960	5 676	557	724		175	62	927	213		3 659		1 903		1960
1961	5 793	588	724		181	62	964	209		3 712	9 532	1 880		1961
1962	5 935	607	700		188	62	975	281		3 724	9 580	2 037		1962
1963	6 107	613	669		193	65	1 011	390		3 806	9 844	1 994		1963
1964	6 286	612	645		198	67	989	220		3 877	10 074	1 980		1964
1965	6 493	610	626		201	76	1 033	188		3 958	10 292	2 012		1965
1966	6 677	597	595		205	73	1 041	208		4 038	10 500	2 495		1966
1967	6 913	584	577		205	74	1 028	361		4 168	10 741	2 648	3 986	1967
1968	7 122	576	557		207	70	1 081	331		4 257	10 958	2 734	4 154	1968
1969	7 343	568	539		209	72	1 090	309		4 323	11 095	2 787	4 260	1969
1970	7 649	560	519		211	68	1 105	327		4 387	11 204	2 840	4 339	1970
1971	7 816	582	502		212	65	1 011	438	82	4 463	11 327	3 013	4 745	1971
1972	7 966	574	481	415	208	62	612	451	93	4 502	11 339	3 033	4 742	1972
1973	8 112	561	464	436	206	59	628	261	107	4 595	11 532	2 772	4 188	1973
1974	8 249	547	447	444	207	60	620	272	79	4 606	11 430	2 778	4 254	1974
1975	8 422	527	430	557	203	46	585	464	67	4 603	11 282	2 897	4 620	1975
1976	8 595	501	413	584	205	n.a.	n.a.	617	85	4 592	11 105	3 049	4 922	1976
1977	8 715	500	397	621	205	47	498	589	97	7 338	13 561	3 106	4 976	1977
1978	8 854	473	382	709	204	51	621	561	89	7 390	13 408	3 048	4 814	1978
1979	8 996	467	367	765	202	51	623	503	89	7 400	13 250	2 970	4 576	1979
1980	9 164	450	355	772	201	43	615	753	106	7 350	13 092	3 247	5 105	1980
1981	9 342	433	341	783	200	43	657	1 206	15	7 313	13 618	3 873	5 145	1981

Table 11

Social Assistance Beneficiaries (GB only)

Numbers (in 1,000s)

Year	Elderly		Unemployed			Sick		One parent	Others	Total	Year
	sole benefit	supplement to contributory benefit	sole benefit	supplement to contributory benefit	eligibility ratio for unemployment benefit	sole benefit	supplement to unemployment benefit				
1950	175	677	39	38			114		307	1 350	1950
1951	202	767	33	33			121		306	1 462	1951
1952	242	856	43	59			138		329	1 667	1952
1953	256	938	46	48			144		329	1 761	1953
1954	257	1 001	50	30			138		320	1 796	1954
1955	265	888	41	20			113		285	1 612	1955
1956	262	927	43	30			117		277	1 656	1956
1957	259	978	55	41			118		261	1 712	1957
1958	240	894	85	66			107		257	1 649	1958
1959	237	976	96	59			128		270	1 766	1959
1960	232	1 075	85	43			139		283	1 857	1960
1961	220	1 056	86	45	.638		134		303	1 844	1961
1962	209	1 122	113	89			148		326	2 007	1962
1963	195	1 100	123	62	.667		146		311	1 791	1963
1964	188	1 154	93	38	.600		146		488	1 961	1964
1965	181	1 196	78	34	.623		149		359	1 997	1965
1966	187	1 630	102	77	.650	142	156	125	71	2 490	1966
1967	187	1 620	138	86	.694	146	164	142	77	2 560	1967
1968	178	1 680	147	73	.654	150	172	157	83	2 640	1968
1969	167	1 710	157	71	.633	156	170	177	82	2 690	1969
1970	156	1 750	166	73	.627	159	164	191	81	2 740	1970
1971	103	1 820	258	129	.565	159	146	213	82	2 910	1971
1972	102	1 810	305	87	.709	161	137	227	81	2 910	1972
1973	97	1 750	201	48	.496	162	118	228	76	2 680	1973
1974	96	1 710	228	73	.560	165	95	245	68	2 680	1974
1975	94	1 590	406	135	.589	165	77	276	47	2 790	1975
1976	95	1 590	654		n/a	169	74	303	55	2 940	1976
1977	102	1 640	543	128	.479	158	71	309	39	2 990	1977
1978	107	1 630	505	93	.440	156	67	322	50	2 930	1978
1979	97	1 630	486	80	.423	155	52	306	44	2 850	1979
1980	101	1 590	678	76	.480	148	57	316	54	3 120	1980
1981	95	1 640	1 084	234		155	66	369	77	3 720	1981
1982	82	1 700	1 437	285		157	83	415	131	4 270	1982

Table 12

Socio-demographic Data

(in 1,000s)

Year	Population total	Population 0–19	Population 65+	Working population	Employed	Unemployed	Year
1950	n/a	n/a	n/a	23 554	23 257	298	1950
1951	50 290	14 658	5 473	23 809	23 603	207	1951
1952	50 430	14 711	5 570	23 925	23 590	336	1952
1953	50 593	14 818	5 628	24 014	23 703	311	1953
1954	50 765	14 939	5 716	24 293	24 038	254	1954
1955	50 946	15 030	5 765	24 508	24 298	210	1955
1956	51 184	15 158	5 835	24 730	24 514	215	1956
1957	51 430	15 263	5 935	24 820	24 543	276	1957
1958	51 652	15 402	5 984	24 684	24 278	406	1958
1959	51 956	15 572	6 044	24 768	24 348	420	1959
1960	52 372	15 812	6 137	24 509	24 183	326	1960
1961	52 807	16 120	6 207	24 744	24 457	287	1961
1962	53 292	16 408	6 271	25 038	24 632	406	1962
1963	53 625	16 609	6 323	25 157	24 661	496	1963
1964	53 991	16 750	6 451	25 299	24 950	349	1964
1965	54 350	16 927	6 585	25 503	25 204	299	1965
1966	54 643	17 072	6 671	25 636	25 355	281	1966
1967	54 969	17 031	6 826	25 495	24 992	503	1967
1968	55 214	17 080	6 945	25 383	24 841	542	1968
1969	55 461	17 139	7 085	25 375	24 857	518	1969
1970	55 632	17 196	7 207	25 308	24 753	555	1970
1971	55 907	17 253	7 345	25 207	24 511	696	1971
1972	56 079	17 324	7 470	25 267	24 489	778	1972
1973	56 210	17 412	7 654	25 614	25 057	557	1973
1974	56 224	17 342	7 779	25 658	25 130	528	1974
1975	56 215	17 263	7 873	25 878	25 040	838	1975
1976	56 206	17 137	7 989	26 093	24 828	1 265	1976
1977	56 179	16 959	8 092	26 209	24 850	1 359	1977
1978	56 167	16 784	8 203	26 342	24 999	1 343	1978
1979	56 228	16 648	8 308	26 610	25 375	1 235	1979
1980	56 314	16 510	8 410	26 819	25 306	1 513	1980
1981	56 379	16 341	8 475	26 718	24 323	2 395	1981
1982	56 335	16 126	8 472	26 663	23 894	2 770	1982
1983	56 377	15 899	8 417	26 577	23 593	2 984	1983

Table 13

Election Results

Percent distribution of votes and seats by party

	Conservative (a)		Labour		Liberal (b)		Others		Electoral	Total number	Majority
	votes	seats	votes	seats	votes	seats	votes	seats	turnout (%)	of seats	
1945 (5 July)	39.6	32.8	48.0	61.4	9.0	1.9	3.4	3.9	72.8	640	Labour 147
1950 (23 February)	43.4	47.7	46.1	50.4	9.1	1.4	1.4	0.5	83.9	625	Labour 6
1951 (25 October)	48.0	51.3	48.8	47.2	2.6	1.0	0.6	0.5	82.6	625	Conservative 16
1955 (26 May)	49.7	54.8	46.4	44.0	2.7	0.9	1.2	0.3	76.8	630	Conservative 59
1959 (8 October)	49.4	57.9	43.8	41.0	5.9	0.9	0.9	0.2	78.7	630	Conservative 99
1964 (15 October)	43.4	48.3	44.1	50.3	11.2	1.4	1.3	-	77.1	630	Labour 5
1966 (31 March)	41.9	40.1	48.0	57.8	8.6	1.9	1.5	0.2	75.8	630	Labour 97
1970 (18 June)	46.4	52.3	43.1	45.7	7.5	1.0	3.0	1.0	72.0	630	Conservative 31
1974 (28 February)	37.9	46.8	37.2	47.4	19.3	2.2	5.6	3.6	78.8	635	Labour -32 (c)
1974 (10 October)	35.8	43.6	39.2	50.2	18.3	2.1	6.7	4.1	72.8	635	Labour 4
1979 (3 May)	43.9	53.4	36.9	42.4	13.8	1.7	5.4	2.5	76.0	635	Conservative 44
1983 (9 June)	42.4	61.1	27.6	32.2	25.3	3.5	4.6	3.2	72.7	650	Conservative 142

(a) Including Ulster Unionists from 1945 to 1970.
(b) Liberal/Social Democratic Party Alliance in 1983.
(c) Minority government.

Notes to and sources for appendix tables

Table 1

GDP and public expenditure at constantn prices are taken from official sources at a 1975 price base and on National Accounts definitions.

Sources: GDP current prices and GDP constant prices (1), United Kingdom main aggregates, line 16. Deflators (2) 1981 pp. 9 and 14. Public expenditure (2) 1981 p.151.

Table 2

"Economic services" include agriculture, employment, industry and transport. "Social insurance" refers to the National Insurance Fund.

Sources: Distribution by purpose 1950-56 (3) 1957 Table 41, 1957 (3) 1958 Table 53, 1958-65 (3) 1969 Table 50, 1966-67 (3) 1976 Table 9.4, 1968 (3) 1979 Table 9.4, 1969-79 (3) 1980 Table 9.4, 1980 (3) 1981 Table 9.4.

Distribution by economic function (2) 1981 pp. 9, 14, 51.

Distribution by level of government (3) 1981 Tables 7.6 and 8.1.

Table 3

Personal social services were not identified separately until 1953: they were previously included in education and health.

Sources: 1950-56 (3) 1961 Tables 43 and 44, 1957 (3) 1968 Table 53, 1958-65 (3) 1969 Table 50, 1966-67 (3) 1976 Table 9.4, 1968 (3) 1979 Table 9.4, 1969-79 (3) 1980 Table 9.4, 1980 (3) 1981 Table 9.4.

Table 4

Constant price series for social expenditure have been calculated as follows:

Income maintenance - deflated by private consumption. Education and health - current expenditure from 1950-66 is deflated by public consumption, from 1967-80 is a published constant price figure: capital expenditure deflated by capital formation.
Personal social services - current expenditure deflated by public consumption, capital expenditure deflated by capital formation. Housing - current grants and subsidies deflated by private consumption, remainder deflated by capital formation.

The consumer price index (rebased to 1975) is given for reference, but the GDP deflator for private consumption has been used in preference to it in the constant price calculations.

Sources: capital/current breakdown as Table 3. Deflators as Table 1. Education and health current expenditure 1967-80 (3) 1977, 1979 and 1980 Tables 2.6, 9.2, 9.3. Consumer price index (4) Tables 90, 91 and 94, and *Employment Gazette*, London, Department of Employment, June 1982 Table 6.4.

Table 5

Old age pensions are retirement pensions, survivors pensions are widows benefits. Invalidity pensions were paid separately only from 1971: recipients previously qualified for sickness benefit. The cost of administration is not available broken down by benefit and is not included (but is included in the income maintenance total in Table 3). Constant price figures have been deflated by private consumption.

Sources: 1950-56 (3) 1957 Tables 36, 38 and 42, 1957 (3) 1968 Tables 41, 44 and 43, 1958-65 (3) 1969 Tables 38, 41 and 5+, 1966-67 (3) 1976 Tables 7.1, 7.4 and 9.4, 1968 (3) 1979 Tables 7.1, 7.4 and 9.4, 1969-80 (3) 1980 Tables 7.2, 7.6 and 9.2.

Table 6

Civil service pensions are defined as "civil superannuation" in national expenditure data.

Sources: as Table 5, except for civil service which is from the same sources as Table 3.

Table 7

Supplementary benefit is as paid to unemployed persons instead of, or as a supplement to, unemployment benefit: its amount has only been calculated separately since 1976. Family income supplement figures are for financial years, and Great Britain only. Deflation to 1975 prices is by public consumption for employment services, by public consumption for the remainder.

Sources: unemployment benefit, family allowances, child benefit maternity benefits as Table 5. Supplementary benefit for the unemployed 1976-77 (5) 1982 (Cmnd 8494) Table 2.12.1, 1978-79 (5) 1984 (Cmnd 9143) Table 2.12.3, 1980-82 (5) 1986 (Cmnd 9702) Table 2.24. Employment services 1950-57 (3) 1961 Table 44, 1958-65 (3) 1969 Table 50, 1966-72 (3) 1976 Table 9.4, 1973-82 (3) 1984 Table 9.4. Family income supplement 1971-76 (6) 1977 Table 44.01, 1977-78 (6) 1980 Table 44.01, 1979-82 (6) 1984 Table 44.01.

Table 8

Housing benefit and tax relief data are for financial years. Housing benefit is means-tested subsidy of rent, for both public and private sector tenants. Tax relief (not counted as public expenditure) is the sum of income tax relief on mortgage interest payments, and capital gains tax relief on the disposal of a principal residence: its amount has only been estimated since 1980. Housing programme constant price expenditure is as in Table 4: housing benefit and tax relief have been deflated by personal consumption. Completions are in thousands.

Sources: housing programme expenditure as Table 4 (1981-82 from (3) 1984 Table 9.4).
Housing benefit 1972-73 (7) 1981 Table 3.6, 1974-82 (7) 1986 Table 3.6.
Tax relief 1980 (5) 1981 (Cmnd 8175) Table 4.14, 1981 (5) 1982 (Cmnd 8494) Table 4.9, 1982 (5) 1983 (Cmnd 8789) Table 4.7.

Table 9

Because the published statistics comparing expenditure and revenue (I) and those giving a breakdown of sources of revenue (II) are on a slightly different basis, two totals for revenue are given. National Insurance receipts refer to Great Britain only, and include the Industrial Injuries Fund, payments in lieu of contributions, and investment income: financial year data.

Sources: total expenditure and total revenues I (2) 1982 p. 162. Total revenues II and breakdown by type of tax Central Statistical Office data bank (unpublished computer printout).
National Insurance receipts 1950-72 S(6) 1972 Table 44.2, 1973-75 (6) 1980 Table 44.02, 1976-81 (6) 1982 Table 44.02.

Table 10

Earnings-related income supplement is as paid to recipients of unemployment benefit. For social assistance, "households" refer to claiming units (people over 16 and their dependant spouses and children under 16), and numbers include those also receiving other benefits.

Sources: 1950-51 (7) 1956 Table 52, 1952-58 (7) 1960 Table 48, 1959 (7) 1971 Table 43, 1966-76 (7) 1977 Tables 3.16 and 3.25, 1977-81 (7) 1981, 1983 Tables 3.16 and 3.25.

Table 11

To obtain a long time series, data have had to be confined to Great Britain only (unlike Table 10). The eligibility ratio is the proportion of unemployed eligible for unemployment benefit.

Sources: 1950-65 (8) 1965 Appendix III and (9) 1957 Table 52 and 1963 Table 55, 1966-81 (6) 1972, 1977, 1980 and 1982 Table 34.30.

Table 12

The basis of calculating the number of employed persons was changes in 1959, reducing the total by 600,000. The figure for 1959 on the old basis has been used in the table.

Sources: population and age-groups 1950-73 (7) 1981 Tables 2.1 and 2.5. Workforce 1950-81 (2) 1985 p. 99, 1982-83 *Employment Gazette* April 1985

Table 13

Sources: F.W.S. Craig, *British Electoral Facts 1832-1980* (1981) Tables 1.40 and 1.41, and *Britain Votes 3* (1984) (Chichester: Political Reference Publications).

Enumerated sources for appendix tables

(1) OECD, *National Accounts Statistics*, various years, Paris, OECD

(2) Central Statistical Office, *Economic Trends Annual Supplement*, various years, London, HMSO

(3) Central Statistical Office, *National Income and Expenditure* (since 1984 known as United Kingdom *National Accounts*), various years, London HMSO

(4) Department of Employment, *British Labour Statistics Historical Abstract*, London, HMSO, 1971

(5) HM Treasury, *The Governments' Expenditure Plans* various years, London, HMSO

(6) Department of Health and Social Security, *Social Security Statistics*, various years, London, HMSO

(7) Central Statistical Office, *Annual Abstract of Statistics*, various years, London, HMSO

(8) National Assistance Board, *Annual Report*, various years, London, HMSO

(9) Ministry of Pensions and National Insurance, *Annual Report*, various years, London, HMSO.

Ireland

Maria Maguire

Institutional Synopsis

Contents

Introduction

The following synopsis describes the Irish social services according to nine functional categories. The expenditure data given here generally refer to 1980, whilst the institutional information describes the situation in 1982. Since social insurance in Ireland is organized within the framework of a single, unified system, the general features of this system are outlined in the first section of the synopsis. Section I also includes data on expenditure and beneficiary numbers for the income maintenance system as a whole which indicate the relative importance of social insurance and means-tested social assistance. All figures are given in Irish pounds (IRL).

I Social insurance system: an overview

Income maintenance in Ireland is provided through two major systems, social insurance and means-tested social assistance, both comprising a variety of schemes differentiated according to specific risks. It should be noted that child allowances fall into neither of the above categories, being paid for all children regardless of parental income and social insurance status.

With two exceptions (the redundancy payments scheme and intermittent unemployment insurance), all of the social insurance schemes have been organized within a unified structure since 1952. Virtually all employees between the ages of 16 and 66 are compulsorily insured under this system. Prior to 1974, however, white-collar employees whose earnings exceeded a specified ceiling were excluded from insurance. The major exceptions from the system at the present time are the self-employed (approximately 19 percent of total labour force in 1981) and those outside the labour force (i.e. people engaged in domestic duties and students). Voluntary insurance for limited benefits is open to persons under the age of 66 who have ceased to be compulsorily insured (e.g. by becoming self-employed). A total of 1,128,530 persons, some 88 percent of the total labour force, were insured in 1981.

Benefits available under the social insurance system are as follows:

- Unemployment benefit
- Disability benefit
- Maternity benefit
- Invalidity pension
- Contributory widow's pension
- Contributory orphan's allowance
- Deserted wife's benefit
- Retirement pension
- Contributory old age pension
- Death grant
- Treatment benefit
- Occupational injuries benefits

The majority of employees are insured for all of the above benefits; however, permanent civil servants and local authority officers are not covered for unemployment and sickness benefits or for old age or retirement pensions since they are guaranteed security of employment, and are covered for sickness and retirement benefits under special public service schemes.

Most outworkers are not covered for unemployment benefit and outworkers without a contract of service are not covered for occupational injuries. Employed persons over

Expenditure on social insurance and assistance benefits in 1980 (in million Irish pounds)

		%
Total social insurance:	502.4	55.0
- Benefits paid through unified social insurance system	495.7	
- Redundancy/intermittent unemployment benefits	6.7	
Total social assistance:	337.1	36.9
- Cash benefits for specified risks	279.8	
- Supplementary welfare benefit	12.3	
- Misc. payments and services	45.0	
Child allowances	74.5	8.1
Total	914.0	100.0

Source: National Income and Expenditure 1981 (Table A20): Report of the Department of Social Welfare 1979-80 (Table 52C); Statistical Information Relevant to the Health Services 1981 (Table J3).

Beneficiaries of the main social insurance and social assistance schemes in 1980

	Total	%
Social insurance:	330 056	32.0
- Pensions	185 107[a]	
- Unemployment benefit	50 726[b]	
- Disability benefit	66 326[a]	
- Maternity benefit	18 489[c]	
- Occupational injuries benefit	6 535[a]	
- Deserted wife's benefit	2 873[a]	
Social assistance:	265 864	26.0
- Pensions	141 449[a]	
- Unemployment assistance	67 266[d]	
- Disablement/Infectious disease allow.	23 283[a]	
- Supplementary welfare allowance	17 413[a]	
- Other allowances	16 453[a][e]	
Child allowances	427 532	42.0
Total	1 023 452	100.0

Source: Report of the Department of Social Welfare 1979-80. Statistical Information Relevant to the Health Services 1981, (Table D1).

[a] Number in receipt on 31 December. [b] Monthly average of number of claimants during year. [c] Number who received benefit during year. [d] Weekly average number of beneficiaries during year -(including smallholders where the figure given is the average number on the last Friday of each month during the year). [e] These include allowances for deserted wives, unmarried mothers, elderly single women, pensioners' wives and domiciliary care of handicapped children.

the age of 66 or persons whose employment is of a subsidiary nature (e.g. certain part-time employment or employment where either the hours worked or earnings fall below a specified limit), are insured for occupational injuries only.

Details of benefits available under the various schemes are dealt with under the appropriate functional headings. Benefits are not index-linked, increases being granted by legislative intervention at the discretion of the Minister for Social Welfare.

The unified social insurance system has two funds, the Social Insurance Fund, which pays all benefits apart from those related to occupational injuries, and the Occupational Injuries Fund. The Social Insurance Fund is financed by contributions from employers, the insured population and the state, whilst the Occupational Injuries Fund is financed entirely by employers. In 1974 the method of financing was changed from a system of flat-rate contributions to a combined flat-rate and earnings-related contribution designed to cover the cost of introducing an earnings-related supplement to the basic flat-rate unemployment, maternity, and sickness cash benefits (i.e. disability benefit). In 1979 the flat-rate contribution element was abolished and contributions became fully earnings-related. In April 1982 the normal rate of contribution to the Social Insurance Fund amounted to 11.3 percent for employers and 5.5 percent for employees on gross earnings up to IRL 9,500 per annum. The employer pays a further 0.3 percent of earnings under this ceiling to the Occupational Injuries Fund. Contributions are credited for periods during which an insured person is receiving unemployment, disability, invalidity, maternity, occupational injury or retirement benefits. The discrepancy between receipts and expenditure under the Social Insurance Fund is met by the state contribution. The system functions on a 'pay-as-you-go' basis, with no significant accumulation of funds over time.

Public service employees and other employees covered for a limited range of benefits pay contributions at reduced rates. Women in receipt of widows' pension, deserted wives' benefit or allowance, or unmarried mothers' allowance, are exempt from the employee contribution.

If all of the social insurance schemes are considered together (e.g. the unified social insurance system, redundancy insurance and intermittent unemployment insurance), the employers' share in financing in 1980 amounted to 55.8 percent, the employees' share to 20.9 percent and the state share to 23.0 percent. The remaining 0.3 percent came from interest on investments and other miscellaneous sources. If both social insurance and social assistance are considered, the sources of income in 1980 were as follows: state 45.7 percent, employers 39.3 percent, employees 14.7 percent, other 0.3 percent.

The data on the preceding page describe the relative importance of social insurance and social assistance in terms of expenditure in 1980.

Core laws

Social insurance

The number after each law is the identification number used in the official legislative series. In the case of laws enacted prior to 1921, the numbering refers to the British legislative series. Statutory Instruments are designated by the prefix S.I.

1946 (no. 38)
Ministers and Secretaries (Amendment) Act: established separate Department of Social Welfare (from 1947) to assume responsibility for social insurance and assist-

ance schemes previously administered by the Department of Local Government and Public Health (pensions) and the Department of Industry and Commerce (unemployment benefits, child allowances and workmen's compensation).

1952 (no. 11)
Social Welfare Act: major reorganization of social insurance system; separate systems for unemployment insurance, health insurance and widows' and orphans' pensions unified in a single system with a common fund and a single social insurance contribution; earnings ceiling for insurance of white-collar employees raised from IRL 5OO to IRL 600 per annum.

1958 (no. 36)
Social Welfare (Amendment) Act: raised earnings ceiling for insurance of white-collar employees to IRL 800 per annum.

1965 (no. 20)
Social Welfare (Miscellaneous Provisions) Act: raised earnings' ceiling for insurance of white-collar employees to IRL 1,200 per annum.

1973 (no. 2)
Social Welfare (Pay-Related Benefit) Act: introduced earnings-related supplement payable with flat-rate unemployment, disability, maternity and, in certain circumstances, injury benefits for up to 147 days; financed by an earnings-related contribution payable in addition to the existing flat-rate contribution.

1973 (no. 10)
Social Welfare Act: abolished earnings limit for compulsory insurance of white-collar employees; effective from 1.4.1974.

1975 (no. 8)
Social Welfare (Pay-Related Benefit) Act: extended maximum duration of earnings-related supplement from 147 to 303 days.

1976 (no. 6)
Social Welfare Act: extended maximum duration of earnings-related supplement to 381 days.

1978 (no. 25)
Social Welfare (Amendment) Act: introduced fully earnings-related social insurance contributions to replace existing combined flat-rate and earnings-related contributions; contributions payable as a percentage of taxable earnings up to a specified ceiling.

1981 (no. 1)
Social Welfare (Consolidation) Act: consolidated all existing social welfare legislation.

II Pensions

In 1980 pension expenditure (excluding public service pensions), amounted to IRL 417.7 million, and expenditure on services and benefits in kind for the elderly amounted to an estimated IRL 33.3 million [1]. Together, these constituted 5.1 percent of GDP and 17.5 percent of total social expenditure.

Coverage

The pension system consists of: (1) insurance schemes forming part of the unified social insurance system and providing old age, retirement, survivors' and invalidity pensions (contributory pensions); (2) means-tested schemes providing old age, blind persons', and survivors' pensions (non-contributory pensions); (3) public service pension schemes. In 1980 expenditure was distributed among the first two types of schemes as follows:

Expenditure on pensions in 1980 by type of pension and scheme (in million Irish pounds)

	Old age pensions	Retirement pensions	Survivors' pensions	Invalidity pensions	Total	%
Contributory	106.0	47.0	86.9	23.3	263.2	63.0
Non. contrib.	140.3	-	14.2	-	154.5	37.0
Total	246.3	47.0	101.1	23.3	417.7	100.0
%	(59.0)	(11.2)	(24.2)	(5.6)	(100.0)	

Source: National Income and Expenditure 1981 (Table A20) and Report of the Department of Social Welfare 1979-80 (Table 52C).

Number of pensioners in 1980 by type of pension and scheme

	Old age pensions	Retirement pensions	Survivors' pensions	Invalidity pensions	Total	%
Contributory	65 401	31 981	70 857	16 868	185 107	56.7
Non-contrib.	130 077	-	11 372	-	141 449	43.3
Total	195 478	31 981	82 229	16 868	326 556	100.0
%	(59.9)	(9.8)	(25.2)	(52.0)	(100.0)	

Source: Report of the Department of Social Welfare 1979-80.

1. Pension insurance

The first general pension insurance scheme, introduced in 1935, provided widows' and orphans' pensions and covered all manual employees in addition to white-collar employees up to an earnings ceiling. This scheme was incorporated into the unified social insurance system in 1952. Until 1961 the only general old age pension scheme was the one dating from 1908 which provided means-tested pensions. Old age pension insurance was added to the social insurance system only in 1960, and the first pensions under the scheme were paid in 1961. Retirement and invalidity pension schemes were added in 1970. The only difference between the old age pension and the retirement pension is that the latter is payable from the age of 65 provided the claimant retires. The old age pension becomes available at the age of 66 and carries no retirement requirement. Since the earnings' limit for insurance of white-collar employees was removed in 1974 (see Section I) all employees, with the exception of those aged over 66 years or whose employment is of subsidiary status, are now insured for pension purposes. Public service employees are covered by special schemes for retirement, invalidity, and survivors' pensions, in addition to which they are also covered by the general scheme for survivors' pensions. The self-employed and those outside the labour force are not covered by public pension insurance. In 1981, some 944,480 persons (83.6 percent of the insured population) were covered for all four types of pension under the social insurance system; a further 161,570 (14.3 percent of the insured population), were insured for widows' and orphans' pensions only.

Benefits

Old age, retirement and widows' pensions consist of a basic amount, which varies according to the annual average number of insurance contributions paid in a specified period (see below), and flat-rate supplements for dependents, pensioners living alone, and those in need of constant care. Invalidity pension consists of a basic flat-rate amount and similar flat-rate supplements. Pension rates are low, providing little more than a subsistence income. Benefits are not automatically indexed but rates have been increased annually since 1966, and twice-yearly since 1975. Occupational pension schemes provide an additional source of retirement income for an increasing proportion of the labour force. Our estimate for the early 1970s indicated that 31 percent of private sector employees and 45 percent of all employees were covered by an occupational scheme [2]. A survey carried out in 1982 indicated that 75 percent of the labour force was covered by an occupational scheme [3].

The qualifying age for the old age pension is 66 years (reduced from 70 years between 1973 and 1977), and 65 years for the retirement pension. While retirement pensioners must not engage in insurable employment between the ages of 65 and 66, there is no other retirement condition attached to either pension. Invalidity pension is normally paid only after a person has been receiving disability benefit (see Section III) for at least a year.

Certain insurance conditions must be fulfilled for all four types of pension. Claimants of old age and retirement pensions must have become insured before the ages of 56 and 55 respectively (the age limit is higher for persons born prior to 1922). In order to qualify for any of the four pensions, the claimant must have a contribution record of at least 156 weekly insurance contributions. In addition, an average test must be satisfied: for the old age pension, a yearly average of at least 20 weekly contributions since 1953 (or since entering insurance if this is later than 1953) is required; for the retirement pension the required average over the same period is 24; for the invalidity pension a minimum of 48 weekly contributions in the contribution year immediately preceding the onset of incapacity for work is required; for the widow's pension an average of 39 contributions in either the three or the five years prior to the husband's death is required, alternatively an extended average of 24 contributions since becoming insured also satisfies the average test for this pension. In all cases, the average test may be satisfied on either paid or credited contributions.

The above averages give encitlement to the minimum basic rate of pension in the case of old age and retirement pensions, while an average of 48 contributions is required for the maximum rate. With regard to widow's pension, the average of 39 on the basis of the three- or five-year test, gives entitlement to the maximum rate of pension, while an average of 48 is required for the maximum rate on the extended average test.

The maximum basic rate for old age and retirement pensions amounted to IRL 40.25 a week in April 1982, (31.4 percent of the average gross industrial wage), increased to

IRL 43.05 for pensioners over the age of 80. The maximum basic weekly rate for widow's pension was IRL 36.25 (28.3 percent of average gross industrial wage), increased to IRL 36.95 for widows over the age of 66, and to IRL 39.45 for widows over 80. The basic rate for the invalidity pension was IRL 35.50 per week (27.7 percent of average gross industrial wage), increased to IRL 36.20 for pensioners over the age of 66, and reduced to IRL 31.25 (under age 66) or IRL 31.80 (over age 66), for a married woman dependent on her husband. In 1982 the orphan's pension amounted to IRL 22.90 (17.9 percent of average gross industrial wage) per week. Recipients of widows' and invalidity pensions may transfer to the old age pension upon reaching the necessary age provided they satisfy the requisite contribution conditions.

Flat-rate supplements to pensions are as follows: all pensioners aged 66 or over who live alone receive a supplement of IRL 2.70 a week. Incapacitated pensioners aged 66 or over who are receiving full-time care from a relative who resides with them, and who is not otherwise employed, receive an allowance of IRL 19.30 a week (referred to as the prescribed relative allowance; in order to qualify for the allowance the pensioner must be living alone, apart from the presence of the relative, or only with children under 18 or persons over 18 who are mentally or physically incapacitated). Supplements for adult dependents are paid with old age or retirement pensions at the rate of IRL 25.70 a week for a dependent under the age of 66 and IRL 30.05 for a dependent over the age of 66; invalidity pensioners are paid a similar supplement at the rate of IRL 23.05 (under age 66) and IRL 23.50 (over age 66). Supplements for dependent children are paid with all four pensions (for the old age pension these were introduced in 1964). Widows receive IRL 9.75 per week for the first child, IRL 10.65 for the second to fifth child, and IRL 9.25 for the sixth child and subsequent children (rates are IRL 9.95, IRL 10.80, and IRL 9.40 for widows over the age of 66). Old age and retirement pensioners receive IRL 8.30 for the first child, IRL 9.20 for the second child, IRL 7.65 for the third to fifth child, and IRL 6.25 for the sixth child and any subsequent children. Invalidity pensioners over 66, receive the same child allowances as old age and retirement pensioners, whilst the rates for invalidity pensioners under 66 are reduced to IRL 8.15, IRL 9.00, IRL 7.45, and IRL 6.05 respectively. The age limit for child dependents is 18 years, except in the case of the children of widows, who continue to qualify as dependents up to the age of 21 if they are in full-time education.

On the death of an old age, retirement, or invalidity pensioner whose pension included an adult dependent's supplement, or would have included such a supplement had the spouse not been receiving a social welfare payment in his or her own right, payment of the pension is continued for six weeks after death, from which time any other benefit arising out of death becomes payable. Since 1970, a death grant has been payable on the death of an insured person, their spouse, child or survivor, provided certain contribution conditions are fulfilled. The full amount of this grant was IRL 100.00 in 1981, reduced in the case of a child's death or where the contribution average is not sufficiently high to qualify for a full grant.

Financing and administration

See Section I.

2. Means-tested pensions

Means-tested pensions (referred to as non-contributory pensions), are paid under the social assistance system to persons who do not qualify for social insurance pensions. These include old age, blind persons' and survivors' pensions. Entitlement is determined according to criteria of age, residence and means. Pensions consist of a basic flat-rate amount and flat-rate supplements for dependents, pensioners living alone, and care by a prescribed relative.

The qualifying age for the old age pension is 66 years, and for a blind persons' pension 18 years. There is no age requirement attached to the widow's pension. Orphan's pension is payable up to age 18 (21 if the recipient is in full-time education or apprenticeship). Pensioners must reside within the state. The means-limit (means include cash income, value of investments and capital and property excluding the personal dwelling) for the full basic rate of the old age, blind persons', and widows' pensions was IRL 6.00 a week in April 1982; a scale of progressively reduced rates operates up to a means limit of IRL 38.00 a week (IRL 36.00 for widows under age 66), and beyond this limit no pension is payable. These limits are doubled in the case of a married couple and are raised for each dependent child.

In April 1982 pension rates were as follows: the full basic rate for a widow under the age of 66 was IRL 33.80 a week (26.4 percent of average gross industrial wage), for a widow over the age of 66 and for the old age and blind persons' pensions, the rate was IRL 34.45 (26.9 percent of average gross industrial wage). In the case of old age and blind persons' pensions, a double pension is paid if both partners of a married couple qualify for a pension; otherwise a supplement equivalent to approximately half the basic pension is paid for an adult dependent. The supplement for dependent children of old age and blind pensioners was IRL 7.30 a week for the first child, IRL 8.20 for the second, IRL 6.40 for the third to fifth child, and IRL 5.10 for the sixth child and any subsequent children. Widows under the age of 66 received IRL 8.80 for the first child, IRL 9.70 for the second to fifth child, and IRL 8.30 for the sixth child and any subsequent children. The respective rates for a widow over age 66 were IRL 9.00, IRL 9.90, and IRL 8.50. Pensioners over the age of 80 received a supplement of IRL 2.50 a week. The living-alone allowance and prescribed relative allowance are paid to non-contributory pensioners at the same rates and under the same conditions as for contributory pensioners.

The non-contributory old age and blind persons' pensions continue to be paid to a spouse for six weeks after the pensioner's death, in the same way as for contributory pensioners.

Non-contributory pensions are financed from general taxation and are administered by the Department of Social Welfare.

3. Public service pensions

There are four main categories of public service pension schemes, catering respectively for civil servants, local government employees, teachers and employees of state-sponsored bodies [4].

Civil service pensions

There are three pension schemes for the civil service, including superannuation and survivor schemes for tenured staff and a superannuation scheme for non-tenured staff.

The superannuation scheme for tenured civil servants dates from 1834 and provides retirement and invalidity pensions. The scheme is non-contributory and benefits are related to length of service and final salary. Normal retirement age is 65 years, or 60 years on the grounds of ill health. Retirement pension consists of one-eightieth of final salary and allowances for each year's service, subject to a maximum of 50 percent of salary after 40 years' service. A lump sum of three-eightieths of salary for each year's service, subject to a maximum of one and a half year's salary is also paid. In the case of premature retirement due to ill health, the pension and lump sum are calculated in the same way, subject to a minimum of five year's service, but additional years may be added to the actual length of service.

A scheme providing survivors' pensions was introduced in 1969 for tenured civil servants. This was originally confined to male staff but coverage was extended to female staff in 1981. Staff already employed at the time of the scheme's introduction were free to choose between opting in or out of the scheme, while membership is compulsory for staff recruited after this time. Members of the scheme pay a contribution of 1.5 percent of salary together with an additional deduction of 1 percent of final salary made for each year of service without contributions. The spouse's pension is equal to half the pension which would have been payable to the member, while children's pensions vary according to whether or not a spouse's pension is also payable. A death gratuity is also paid.

Non-tenured civil servants who are employed full-time are covered by a separate superannuation and invalidity scheme. Retirement age under the scheme is 66 years and is linked with pensionable age under the general social insurance pension scheme. The pension is calculated in the same way as for tenured civil servants. However, since non-tenured staff are also insurable under the social insurance system, any social insurance pension payable is taken into account in calculating the service pension. A death gratuity is also payable for non-tenured civil servants.

Local government pensions

The 1956 Local Government Superannuation Act made provision for two pension schemes for local government employees, covering white-collar staff and manual workers respectively. The scheme was revised in 1977. There is also a non-statutory widows' and orphans' pension scheme for male employees.

Membership of the superannuation scheme is compulsory for white-collar staff. The normal pensionable age is 65 years with the option of retirement at the age of 60 subject to a minimum of 20 years' service. Retirement benefit is calculated in the same way as for tenured civil servants (see above). In the case of premature retirement due to ill health the pension is calculated in the same way, subject to a minimum of 10 years' service and additional years may be added to actual length of service. Members of the scheme pay contributions at the rate of 5 percent of salary.

Membership of the superannuation scheme for manual workers is optional and such workers are fully insurable under the social insurance system. The scheme is contributory, contributions being paid at the rate of 5 percent of earnings in the case of persons who are not fully insured under the social insurance system. Persons who are fully insured under the system pay a lower contribution equivalent to approximately 2.8 percent of earnings (the rate may vary since it is calculated by reducing the 5 percent rate by twice the amount of the basic old age contributory pension payable under the social insurance scheme). Retirement pension consists of one-eightieth of pensionable pay for each year of service up to a maximum of one-half of pensionable pay after 40 years' service. A lump sum is also payable and is calculated in the same way as for white-collar employees. In the case of premature retirement due to ill health the pension is calculated in the same way, subject to a minimum of 10 years' service. In the case of persons fully insured under the social insurance scheme, the pension is reduced by twice the basic rate of the old age contributory pension.

White-collar male employees are compulsorily covered for widows' and orphans' pensions, and both pensions and contributions are calculated in the same way as under the survivors' pension scheme for civil servants. Manual workers may opt to join the widows' and orphans' scheme.

Teachers' pensions

There are separate pension schemes for the various levels of the educational system. National teachers (i.e. in the primary sector), are covered for retirement, invalidity and survivors' pensions on terms similar to those for tenured civil servants, the major distinction being that the superannuation scheme is contributory. The contribution rate is 5 percent of pensionable salary (salary plus allowances), and the remainder of the cost is met by the Exchequer.

Secondary teachers have an optional superannuation and invalidity scheme to which members contribute 5 percent of total salary. The maximum pension is 50 percent of final salary together with a gratuity of one-thirtieth of salary per year of service. There is also an optional widows' and orphans' pension scheme for secondary teachers to which members contribute 1.5 percent of their total salary. A death gratuity of one-thirtieth of pensionable salary per year of service is payable in addition to benefits paid under the widows' and orphans' scheme. The superannuation scheme operates in the same way as a normal occupational pension scheme, being funded by members and employers. However, in recent years a contribution has been needed from public funds in order to meet costs. The scheme is administered by the Minister for Education.

Optional pension schemes cover most permanent employees of third-level educational institutions. Most of the schemes are non-contributory and provide retirement and invalidity pensions. In most cases the retirement pension is approximately equivalent to two-thirds of the final salary for full service. Arrangements for survivors vary considerably, ranging from a portion of the members' pension entitlement to lump sums. The schemes are usually funded and administered by the individual institutions.

Pensions for employees of state-sponsored bodies

State sponsored bodies fall into two main groups, the one includes those performing a commercial function (e.g. the public transport and electricity supply systems), and the other comprises bodies with an advisory or executive role (e.g. the Industrial Development Authority).

Although there are a large number of pension schemes covering employees of state-sponsored bodies, official policy is to ensure uniformity of pension provisions within the public service. As such, the various schemes tend to conform to the civil service pattern: retirement age is generally 65 years and pensions are normally equivalent to at least 50 percent of final earnings after 40 years' service, (inclusive of any social insurance pension which may be payable). However, benefits for manual workers in some of the commercial bodies are flat-rate and are designed to supplement social insurance pensions rather than to replace a fixed proportion of earnings. Most schemes make provision for premature retirement due to ill health. Provision for survivors varies considerably between schemes, and some schemes make no such provision. Membership is compulsory in approximately 85 percent of the schemes.

The majority of schemes are contributory, the normal contribution rate being 5 percent of earnings in the case of retirement schemes and 1.5 percent for survivors' schemes. Most schemes are funded and administered by the joint management-staff committees of the individual organizations.

4. Services

Expenditure on services for the elderly in 1980 (in million Irish pounds)

Free travel, t.v. licences, telephone rental electricity/gas	24.0
Home help service	4.3
Meals service	1.4
Welfare homes for the aged	3.6
Total	33.3

Source: National Income and Expenditure 1981 (Table A20); Statistical Information Relevant to the Health Services 1981 (Table J3).

Public provision of services for the elderly has developed mainly since the late 1960s, and voluntary activity remains important in this field.

A variety of benefits in kind have been introduced during the past 15 years or so. In 1967 free travel on public transport was introduced for old age, blind, and elderly widowed pensioners and the scheme has since been extended to all residents over the age of 66. Various utilities are provided free of charge to pensioners over the age of 66 who live alone: these include a free electricity and gas allowance since 1967, free television and radio licences since 1968, and free telephone rental since 1978.

Domiciliary services have also been developed in recent years. The local health authorities have operated a home help service since 1971 and this is used mainly by the elderly, although it is also available to other families under stress. The health authorities also provide financial support to voluntary bodies serving the aged: among the most important activities of such agencies is the provision of hot meals, clothing, and fuel for old people. With regard to housing for the elderly, local authorities have in recent years reserved approximately 10 percent of their new dwellings for the elderly. Grants are also made to voluntary bodies providing housing for the elderly on a philanthropic basis.

Institutional care for the aged is provided in public geriatric hospitals and welfare homes and in private institutions. In 1975 there were 46 geriatric hospitals, 23 welfare homes and 108 private institutions.

Core laws

1908 (8 Edw. 7. Ch. 40)
Old Age Pensions Act: first general pension scheme, provided means-tested old age pensions from the age of 70.

1920 (10 11 Geo. 5. Ch. 49)
Blind Persons' Act: provided means-tested pensions for blind persons from the age of 50.

1932 (no. 18)
Old Age Pensions Act: reduced qualifying age for blind persons' pensions from 50 to 30 years.

1935 (no. 29)
Widows' and Orphans' Pensions Act: introduced two pension schemes providing widows' and orphans' pensions from January 1936. An insurance scheme covering manual workers and low-income white-collar employees provided flat-rate pension up to the age of 70, at which age a widow was entitled to the means-tested old age pension at the maximum rate without any restriction as to means; pension rates varied according to whether the late husband was engaged in agricultural or non-agricultural employment; pension included supplements for children. A second scheme provided non-contributory means-tested pensions; confined to survivors of insured persons whose insurance record was not sufficient to qualify for a contributory pension and survivors of smallholders; pension granted to widows under the age of 60 only if they had dependent children - upper age limit of 70 years; rates varied between urban and rural areas and according to means and included allowances for children.

1937 (no. 11)
Widows' and Orphans' Pensions Act: extended non-contributory widows' and orphans' pension to all who satisfied the means-test; qualifying age for childless widows reduced to 55 years.

1948 (no. 17)
Social Welfare Act: reduced qualifying age for non-contributory pensions for childless widows to 48 years; qualifying age for blind persons' pension reduced from 30 to 21 years; all pensions substantially raised by inclusion of emergency supplements in basic rates, payable since 1941; considerable relaxation of means-test for non-contributory pensions.

1960 (no. 25)
Social Welfare (Amendment) Act: introduced contributory old age pension scheme under the social insurance system; scheme effective from January 1961; pensions payable at the age of 70; basic pension rates vary according to contribution records; supplement paid for dependent spouse; abolished maximum age limit of 70 years for receipt of widow's contributory pension.

1964 (no. 28)
Social Welfare (Miscellaneous Provisions) Act: introduced supplement for dependent children up to the age of 16 with contributory and non-contributory old age pensions; abolished minimum age limit of 48 for receipt of non-contributory widow's pension by childless women.

1968 (no. 31)
Social Welfare (Miscellaneous Provisions) Act: introduced 'prescribed relative' supplement to pensions; payable when an incapacitated pensioner receives full-time care from a female relative; payable in the case of widow's pension only when pensioner reaches the age of 70.

1969 (no. 19)
Social Welfare (Miscellaneous Provisions) Act: raised age limit for dependent child in

the case of widows' pensioners from 16 to 21 years where the child remained in full-time education or apprenticeship.

1970 (no. 12)
Social Welfare Act: introduced retirement and invalidity pension schemes under the social insurance system; retirement pension payable at the age of 65; age limit for dependent child supplement raised from 16 to 18 years for all pensioners; introduced means-tested 'old age care' allowance for incapacitated persons aged over 70 years who are receiving full time care from a female relative; provided an allowance similar to the 'prescribed relative' allowance, for persons not receiving public pensions.

1972 (no. 15)
Social Welfare Act: extended 'prescribed relative' allowance to invalidity and retirement pensioners from the age of 70; male relatives now qualify for the allowance; increased supplement to the basic pension for pensioners aged 80 and over.

1973 (no. 10)
Social Welfare Act: reduced age limit for old age pensions to 69 years; non-contributory pensioners now allowed to have a small amount of means and still receive maximum rate of benefit; previously, the maximum rate was only paid to pensioners without means.

1974 (no. 14)
Social Welfare (No. 2) Act: reduced age limit for old age pensions to 68 years; adult dependents allowance introduced for non-contributory old age pension where the pensioner's spouse does not qualify for a pension in her own right; provision for continuation of old age, retirement, and invalidity pension for six weeks after death of beneficiary in cases where benefit included an adult dependent's allowance.

1975 (no. 1)
Social Welfare Act: reduced qualifying age for old age pensions to 67 years.

1977 (no. 3)
Social Welfare Act: reduced qualifying age for old age pensions to 66 years; introduced supplement to pension for pensioners aged 66 or over who live alone.

1979 (no. 8)
Social Welfare Act: discontinued old age care allowance as it had become obsolete due to the raising of the means limit for non-contributory old age pension; removed upper age limit of 66 years for receipt of widow's non-contributory pension; provision for deserted wife's benefit to be replaced automatically by widow's contributory pension on death of husband.

1980 (no. 3)
Social Welfare Act: reduced qualifying age for blind person's pension from 21 to 18; provision for deserted wife's allowance to be replaced automatically by widow's non-contributory pension on death of husband.

III Sickness insurance and assistance

In 1980 expenditure on sickness benefits amounted to IRL 150.5 million, which corresponded to 1.7 percent of GDP, or 5.8 percent of total social expenditure.

Expenditure on sickness benefits in 1980 (in million Irish pounds)

		%
Sickness insurance:	123.4	82.0
- Cash benefits (disability benefit)	117.7	
- Dental, optical, and aural treatment	5.7	
Means-tested payments to sick and disabled	27.1	18.0
Total	150.5	100.0

Source: National Income and Expenditure 1981 (Table A20); Statistical Information Relevant to the Health Services 1981 (Table J3).

1. Sickness insurance

Coverage

The British National Insurance Act of 1911 established a sickness insurance scheme in Ireland. Coverage extended to all manual workers and to white-collar employees up to an earnings ceiling. In 1953 the scheme was incorporated into the unified social insurance system.

Benefits

Sickness benefits provided under the social insurance system include cash payments during periods of incapacity for work (known as disability benefit) and reimbursement of the cost of certain dental, optical and aural treatment. Coverage for these benefits extends to all persons entitled to social insurance except permanent and pensionable public servants, employees aged 66 or over and persons whose employment is of a subsidiary nature.

Disability benefit is paid from the fourth day of incapacity and may continue up to the age of 66 provided at least 156 weekly insurance contributions have been paid. Since the introduction of the invalidity pension in 1970 (see Section II), it is normal for persons judged to be permanently incapable of work to transfer to this pension after drawing disability benefit for a period of 12 months, provided they fulfill the necessary insurance conditions. To qualify for disability benefit the claimant must have paid at least 26 weekly insurance contributions and have paid or been credited with 26 contributions in the contribution year preceding the year in which benefit is claimed. For the maximum rate of benefit, 48 paid or credited contributions in the preceding contribution year are required. Where a minimum of 26 but less than 156 weekly insurance contributions have been paid, disability benefit is limited to 52 weeks, after which time a claimant must undertake whatever number of further weeks of insurable employment are necessary to bring the total insurance record to 156 weeks.

Benefit consists of a basic flat-rate payment, an earnings-related supplement (introduced in 1974) and flat-rate supplements for dependents. The basic amount varies according to the number of insurance contributions registered in the contribution year preceding the year in which benefit is claimed. For the minimum and maximum rates, contributions of 26 and 48 weeks respectively are required. In April 1982 the maximum rate for the basic amount amounted to IRL 31.65 per week (24.7 percent of the average gross industrial wage). This is reduced to IRL 27.80 for persons under 18 without dependents and married women dependent on their husbands.

The earnings-related supplement is normally paid from the beginning of the third week of incapacity and continues for up to 381 days provided the basic benefit continues. Benefit is calculated on the claimant's taxable weekly earnings between specified limits in the tax year preceding the claim (the lower limit corresponds to the maximum basic rate of disability benefit payable on the first Monday in January of the year during which the claim is made, while the upper limit corresponds to the ceiling for social insurance contributions in the year of the claim), these earnings are divided by 50 and the benefit rate is 40 percent of the resulting figure for the first 147 days; 30 percent for the next 78 days; 25 percent for a further 78 days; and 20 percent for the final 78 days. The combined total of flat-rate benefit (including any flat-rate supplements payable) and earnings-related benefit must not exceed the earnings on which the benefit is calculated. Flat-rate supplements are paid for adult dependents (IRL 16.40 per week) and child dependents up to the age of 18 (IRL 6.70 per week each for the first two children, IRL 5.55 for each other child). In 1980 a total of 309,363 claims for disability benefit were paid and 66,326 persons were in receipt of benefit on 31 December 1980.

Financing and administration

See Section I.

2. Sickness assistance

Persons with long-term disabilities which prevent them from working, and who do not qualify for insurance benefits, may apply for a means-tested allowance (the disabled person's maintenance allowance). This is paid at a flat-rate of IRL 32.55 per week (1982) and corresponds to 25.4 percent of the average gross industrial wage. A supplement of IRL 18.50 per week is paid for a dependent spouse, IRL 6.55 for the first child, IRL 5.80 for the third to fifth child, and IRL 4.65 for the sixth child and any subsequent children. Severely handicapped persons between the ages of 16 and 66 who are unable to walk, are entitled to a mobility allowance in order to enable them to make trips away from home.

Persons undergoing treatment for certain infectious diseases may also apply for a means-tested allowance, paid at IRL 32.80 per week in 1981, with a supplement of IRL 21.00 for a dependent spouse, IRL 7.20 for the first child, IRL 8.05 for the second to fifth child, and IRL 6.65 for the sixth child and subsequent children.

Blind persons in need receive an additional allowance along with the normal blind persons' pension or with the disabled person's maintenance allowance.

These allowances are all administered by the local health authorities and are financed from the health services budget. For financing of the health services see Section VIII.

Core laws

1911 (1 and 2 Geo. 5, Ch. 55)
National Insurance Act: established health insurance scheme for employees; white-collar employees excluded beyond a certain earnings' limit; benefits include

cash payments during short-term and long-term illness, the latter being payable at a lower rate.

1933 (no. 13)
National Health Insurance Act: established unified National Health Insurance Society to take over organization of health insurance from a number of separate approved societies which had operated up to that time.

1947 (no. 5)
National Health Insurance Act: changed the financial structure of health insurance system; income formerly allocated to a reserve fund was freed for provision of additional benefits (treatment benefits), including cost of dental, optical and specialist medical treatment, medical and surgical appliances and maintenance, and treatment for up to four weeks in hospitals or convalescent homes which had entered into agreements with the health insurance society; fixed limit set on amount which could be provided in a financial year for these benefits; eligibility determined by contribution conditions.

1947 (no. 28)
Health Act: introduced maintenance allowance for persons suffering from certain infectious diseases.

1947 (S.I. no. 228)
National Health Insurance (Transfer of Ministerial Functions) Regulations: transferred responsibility for health insurance from Ministry of Local Government and Public Health to newly established Ministry for Social Welfare.

1950 (no. 14)
Social Welfare Act: National Health Insurance society dissolved and its functions transferred to Department of Social Welfare from 1.8.1950.

1952 (no. 11)
Social Welfare Act: health insurance scheme incorporated into the new, unified social insurance system from January 1953; separate benefits for short-term and long-term illness replaced by single sickness benefit (known as disability benefit) payable for as long as incapacity for work continues, provided the necessary insurance contributions have been registered; eliminated practice of paying a lower benefit in cases of long-term illness.

1954 (S.I. no. 156)
Social Welfare (Treatment Benefit) Regulations: hospital and convalescent home treatment, medical and surgical appliances and specialist medical treatment to be provided henceforth by local health authorities instead of under the social insurance system; insured persons can continue to use these services subject to the contribution conditions already governing their eligibility under the social insurance system.

1970 (no. 12)
Social Welfare Act: following introduction of invalidity pension under this Act, disability benefit now only normally payable for temporary incapacity.

1973 (no. 2)
Social Welfare (Pay-related Benefit) Act: introduced earnings-related supplement to flat-rate disability benefit; payable after two weeks of sickness for up to 147 days, provided flat-rate benefit continues.

1973 (no. 10)
Social Welfare Act: abolished rule requiring married women to register 26 weekly in-

surance contributions after marriage in order to qualify for disability and treatment benefits.

1975 (no. 8)
Social Welfare (Pay-Related Benefit) Act: extended maximum duration of earnings-related supplement to 225 days.

1975 (S.I. no. 206)
Social Welfare (Extension of Duration of Pay-related Benefit) Order: extended maximum duration of earnings-related supplement to 303 days.

1976 (no. 6)
Social Welfare Act: extended maximum duration of earnings-related supplement to 381 days.

IV Occupational injuries insurance

In 1980 expenditure on occupational injuries' benefits amounted to IRL 10.4 million, equivalent to 0.1 percent of GDP and 0.4 percent of total social expenditure.

Coverage

The 1897 Workmen's Compensation Act obliged employers to provide compensation on fixed scales for the injury or death of a worker arising from employment. The Act was originally limited to employment regarded as hazardous, but the scope of the scheme was extended in 1906 to cover all manual workers and low paid white-collar employees.

This system was replaced in 1966 by a scheme for occupational injuries insurance under the social insurance system. Coverage of this scheme extends to all employees with the exception of members of the security and defence forces and outworkers without a contract of service. The scheme provides cash benefits during temporary and permanent incapacity for work due to occupational accidents or diseases, in addition to survivors' pensions and death benefit. Medical costs arising from injuries are also covered.

Benefits

Injury benefit is paid from the fourth day of incapacity (or from the first day if the incapacity lasts for over twelve days) for a maximum of 26 weeks. If the incapacity continues after this period the person may be entitled to disability benefit under the general social insurance scheme (see Section III). Injury benefit consists of a basic flat-rate amount (IRL 43.55 per week in 1982, equivalent to 34 percent of the average gross industrial wage; IRL 34.45, equivalent to 26.9 percent of average gross industrial wage for a married woman dependent on her husband or a person under the age of 18 without dependents). Additional flat-rate amounts are paid for dependents and in 1982 the rates were as follows: IRL 20.50 per week for an adult dependent; IRL 7.50 for the first dependent child; IRL 8.40 for the second child; IRL 6.95 for the third to fifth child; and IRL 5.55 for the sixth child and subsequent children.

An earnings-related supplement is also payable in cases where the beneficiary would be entitled to receive disability benefit were he or she is not receiving injury benefit. This is paid at the same rates as with disability benefit (see Section III). The combined total of flat-rate and earnings-related benefits may not exceed the earnings on which the benefit was calculated.

Disablement benefit is paid in cases where loss of physical or mental faculty is the result of an occupational accident or disease. The rate depends on the degree of disablement: for up to 19 percent disablement a gratuity is paid; from 20 percent upwards a weekly pension is paid, the rates of which increase according to the severity of the disablement. In 1882 the maximum pension rate, payable in case of 95 percent to 100 percent disablement, amounted to IRL 47.40, (37.0 percent of average gross industrial wage) per week for a person under the age of 66 and IRL 38.70, 30.2 percent of average gross industrial wage for a person over the age of 66; these rates are reduced to IRL 37.50 and IRL 38.30 respectively for a married woman dependent on her husband and a person under the age of 18 without dependents. Recipients of disablement benefit who are unfit for work are also paid disability benefit for both themselves and any dependents under the usual conditions covering eligibility, or an 'unemployability supplement' at the same rate as disability benefit, where the recipient does not qualify for disability benefit. Persons in receipt of a 100 percent disablement pension may also receive a 'constant attendance' allowance if they require attendance due to the disablement. In 1982 this was paid at the rate of IRL 37.90 per week in cases of very severe disablement and at reduced rates in cases of less severe disablement. If a person in receipt of a disablement pension of less than the maximum rate receives approved in-patient hospital treatment for the disability, the pension is then increased to the maximum rate for the duration of the stay in hospital. The cost of medical care arising from occupational injury or disease is borne by the occupational injuries scheme.

Pensions payable to survivors of victims of occupational accidents and diseases include widows' and orphans' pensions, dependent widower's pension or gratuity and dependent parents' pension. In 1982 the rates of these pensions were as follows: widow's pension, IRL 45.95 per week (35.9 percent of average gross industrial wage) with an additional IRL 9.75 for the first dependent child, IRL 10.65 for the second to fifth child, and IRL 9.25 for the sixth child and subsequent children; orphan's pension, IRL 24.20 per week; dependent parents' pension, IRL 66.45 per week (51.9 percent of average gross industrial wage) for the parents of an unmarried worker and IRL 41.00 for the parents of a married worker. The rates for widows' and parents' pensions are higher in the case of persons over 66. The prescribed relative allowance and living-alone allowance are payable with these pensions, under the same conditions applicable to other pensioners (see Section II).

A grant for funeral expenses is paid when death occurs as a result of an occupational accident or disease. In 1982 the maximum grant amounted to IRL 220.

At the end of 1980, 1,378 persons were receiving injury benefit, 4,801 persons were drawing disablement pensions and 356 persons were in receipt of survivors' pensions under the occupational injuries scheme.

Financing and administration

See Section I.

Core laws

1897
Workmen's Compensation Act: placed liability on employers to provide compensation on fixed scales for occupational accidents; scope of scheme limited to employment regarded as particularly hazardous.

1906 (6 Edw. 7. c.58)
Workmen's Compensation Act: scope of legislation extended to cover all manual workers and non-manual employers up to an earnings ceiling; provided compensation for injuries caused by industrial diseases.

1934 (no. 9)
Workmen's Compensation Act: consolidated existing legislation and simplified procedures for obtaining compensation.

1966 (no. 16)
Social Welfare (Occupational Injuries) Act: replaced workmen's compensation scheme by occupational injuries insurance scheme under the general social insurance system.

V Unemployment insurance/Assistance

In 1980 expenditure on income maintenance for the unemployed amounted to IRL 131.3 million, equivalent to 2 percent of GDP and 6.9 percent of total social expenditure. Expenditure was distributed as follows:

Expenditure on unemployment benefits in 1980 (in million Irish pounds)

		%
Unemployment insurance	88.2	49.9
Unemployment assistance	81.7	46.3
Redundancy payments	5.1	2.9
Intermittent unemployment insurance	1.6	0.9
Total	176.6	100.0

Source: National Income and Expenditure 1981 (Table A20); Report of the Department of Social Welfare 1979-80 (Table 49).

Coverage

Income maintenance during unemployment consists of: (1) insurance benefits paid under the social insurance system, known as unemployment benefit; (2) means-tested assistance paid where entitlement to insurance benefits is exhausted, known as unemployment assistance; (3) lump sum payments in the case of redundancy, and (4) payments to workers in certain trades for earnings lost due to bad weather.

1. Unemployment insurance

Unemployment insurance was introduced in 1911 on a limited basis and was extended to cover most employees in 1920. The principal exceptions were workers in the agricultural sector and in private domestic service and white-collar employees whose earnings exceeded a certain limit. The scheme was incorporated into the unified social insurance system in January 1953. At the present time coverage extends to all employees with the exception of public servants and outworkers. Benefits are paid from the fourth day of unemployment for a maximum of 390 days (312 days for a married woman living with her husband or receiving financial support from him; 156 days for a person under 18 years of age).

Benefit is paid at the same rates, (including the flat-rate and earnings-related components) as for disability benefit (see Section III). However, the combined total of benefits and income tax rebate may not exceed 85 percent of the previous average weekly net earnings of the beneficiary. In order to qualify for benefit a minimum of 26 weekly insurance contributions are required, and a minimum of 26 contributions must have been paid or credited in the last complete contribution year prior to the year in which benefit is claimed. For the full rate of basic benefit 48 contributions in the preceding year are required. In 1981 a monthly average of 66,802 persons claimed unemployment insurance benefits.

Benefits are paid from the Social Insurance Fund and the scheme is administered by the Department of Social Welfare.

2. Unemployment assistance

Unemployment assistance was introduced in 1933 and is paid to persons who do not qualify for payments under the insurance scheme or who have exhausted their entitlement. Benefits are means-tested and consist of a basic amount (which varies between urban and rural areas) and supplements for dependents. In 1982 the maximum basic urban rate for a person with no means amounted to IRL 26.25 per week, the rural rate was IRL 24.45, equivalent to 20.5 percent and 19.1 percent respectively of average gross industrial wage. These rates are reduced by the amount of any means the beneficiary may possess. An additional IRL 18.95 (18.50 in rural areas) per week is paid for an adult dependent, a further IRL 6.55 per week for the first dependent child, IRL 7.45 for the second child, IRL 5.80 for the third to fifth child, and IRL 4.65 for the sixth and subsequent children.

A special system of unemployment assistance covers smallholders with uneconomic holdings in congested areas of the country. They can choose to have their means assessed on a notional basis related to the land valuation of their farm, thus enabling them to qualify for assistance on a more favourable basis than other claimants. Smallholders' unemployment assistance is paid at lower rates than normal assistance and the basic rate varies according to the land valuation. In 1982, a monthly average of 56,360 persons received ordinary unemployment assistance and a further 20,893 received smallholders' unemployment assistance.

Unemployment assistance is financed from general taxation and is administered by the Department of Social Welfare.

3. Redundancy payments

A scheme of insurance against redundancy was introduced in 1968. Originally this scheme provided a lump sum and also a weekly payment for redundant workers, payable for a limited period of time. The weekly payment was abolished in 1979. The lump sum is calculated according to claimant's earnings up to a certain ceiling and length of service with the employer. Payment is made by the employer who reclaims the cost from the redundancy fund. The scheme is financed by employers' contributions (0.01 percent of earnings up to IRL 9,500 p.a.) to this fund and is administered by the Department of Labour.

4. Intermittent unemployment insurance

This scheme, introduced in 1942, covers workers in the construction, civil engineering and painting trades for loss of earnings due to bad weather. In 1980, 49,889 workers were insured under the scheme. Benefit is paid at hourly flat-rates which vary according to whether the worker is skilled or unskilled and whether over or under 18 years of age. In 1982 hourly benefit rates were IRL 0.87 for a skilled worker, IRL 0.79 for an unskilled worker, and IRL 0.32 for a worker under the age of 18.

The scheme is financed by flat-rate contributions paid in equal parts by the employer and employee. In 1982 the rates amounted to IRL 1.42 per week for a skilled worker, IRL 1.38 for an unskilled worker, and IRL 0.52 for a worker under the age of 18. Contributions are paid into a special fund. Benefit is paid by the employer who then recovers the cost from the fund. The scheme is administered by the Department of Social Welfare.

Services

The National Manpower Service (NMS), established in 1971 under the control of the Minister of Labour, provides a job replacement service for the unemployed. The NMS also provides information on training opportunities for adult workers. Persons in receipt of unemployment benefit or assistance are required to register with the NMS.

The Industrial Training Authority (AnCO), established in 1967, provides and promotes training for industry and commerce. In addition to its activities in the spheres of apprenticeship and company-based training, AnCO also runs training courses for the unemployed, persons needing to change or update employment skills, and persons wishing to enter the labour market. Priority in allocation of training places is given to persons who have been registered as unemployed for at least six months. Trainees are paid allowances which are related to unemployment benefit rates. In 1982, over 22,000 persons participated in AnCO training courses [5]. AnCO also runs a Community Youth Training Scheme set up in 1975 and designed to enable young people to develop basic industrial skills.

In addition to placement and training services, these have also been efforts to promote employment through payment of premiums to employers. The Employment Premium Programme, initiated in 1975, aimed at encouraging the re-employment in agriculture and manufacturing industries of workers who had lost their jobs due to the recession. In February 1977, this scheme was expanded to become the Employment Incentive Scheme. The new scheme covers the service sector and the construction industry as well as agriculture and manufacturing. The scheme now extends to persons under the age of 20 who have left full-time education for at least four months and are without permanent employment. The premium is paid at a reduced rate for young people. Premiums are paid for up to 24 weeks and the employment must last for at least three months.

Several employment creation schemes for young people have been established since the mid-1970s. These include the Environmental Improvement Scheme (EIS), the Temporary Grants Scheme for Young Unemployed (TGS), and the Work Experience Programme (WEP) [6]. The EIS is administered by the Department of the Environment and enables local authorities to employ young people for periods of up to three months on projects designed to improve community amenities or the environment. The TGS, which is administered by the Department of Education, provides finance to enable voluntary local youth organizations to employ young people on projects for improving community amenities. These projects normally run for about six months. The WEP, which is administered by the National Manpower Service, places young people with employers for six months, during which time the young employee is given various types of work experience, and is paid a fixed allowance by the employer who is then reimbursed by the National Manpower Service. Expenditure on the above three schemes and on the Community Youth Training Scheme operated by AnCO rose from IRL 1.2 million in 1977 to IRL 9.4 million in 1979, but fell to IRL 7.3 million in 1981. Participation in the schemes went from 945 people in 1977 to 9,450 in 1981 [7]. In 1982 a Youth Employment Agency was established with the task of evaluating existing youth employment measures, coordinating programmes and developing new policy initiatives. The Agency is financed by a 1 percent levy on gross earnings of each gainfully occupied person.

Core laws

1911 (1 and 2 Geo. 5, Ch. 55)
National Insurance Act: introduced unemployment insurance on a limited basis.

1920 (10 and 11 Geo. 5, Ch.30)
Unemployment Insurance Act: extended insurance to all employees except agricultural workers, domestic servants and white-collar employees over a certain earnings' limit.

1933 (no. 46)
Unemployment Assistance Act: introduced means-tested unemployment assistance for persons not in receipt of unemployment benefit who are capable of work but unable to obtain it; applicants required to be Irish nationals.

1942 (no. 7)
Insurance (Intermittent Unemployment) Act: introduced insurance for intermittent unemployment.

1946 (no. 38)
Ministers and Secretaries (Amendment) Act: transferred administration of unemployment insurance, unemployment assistance and intermittent unemployment insurance from the Department of Industry and Commerce to the Department of Social Welfare.

1952 (no. 11)
Social Welfare Act: unemployment insurance scheme became part of unified social insurance system; unemployment insurance extended to male agricultural employees; changes in the unemployment assistance scheme included relaxation of means-test, replacement of nationality requirement by residence requirement, and reduction of the waiting period from six to three days.

1960 (no. 28)
Social Welfare (Miscellaneous Provisions) Act: introduced supplement to unemployment assistance for third child and subsequent children; prior to this supplements only

paid for first two children; abolished three-day waiting period for those transferring from unemployment benefit to unemployment assistance.

1962 (no. 17)
Social Welfare (Miscellaneous Provisions) Act: fixed means limit for unemployment assistance replaced by variable limit which takes account of number of dependent children of applicant.

1964 (S.I. no. 202)
Social Welfare (Modifications of Insurance) (Amendment) Regulations: extended unemployment insurance to full-time share fishermen.

1965 (no. 20)
Social Welfare (Miscellaneous Provisions) Act: calculation of means of smallholders in congested areas of the country for purposes of unemployment assistance to be made henceforth on a notional basis related to land valuation rather than on a factual basis as previously; enabled more smallholders to qualify for unemployment assistance and removed disincentive to work land to its full capacity; effective from January 1966.

1966 (no. 24)
Social Welfare (Miscellaneous Provisions) Act: extended unemployment insurance to women in private domestic service and agriculture.

1967 (no. 18)
Social Welfare (Miscellaneous Provisions) Act: extended maximum duration of unemployment benefit from 156 days to 312 days for those aged over 18, with exception of married women dependent on their husbands; introduced rule disqualifying claimant from receipt of unemployment benefit or assistance for a specified period for failure to take up a suitable opportunity to attend an approved training course; amended regulation regarding strikes to permit payment of unemployment benefit or assistance to persons unemployed as a result of a strike but not directly involved in it.

1967 (no. 21)
Redundancy Payments Act: introduced redundancy payments scheme.

1973 (no. 2)
Social Welfare (Pay-related Benefit) Act: introduced earnings-related supplement to flat-rate unemployment benefit; payable after first fortnight of unemployment for 147 days.

1973 (no. 10)
Social Welfare Act: abolished rule disqualifying woman from receipt of unemployment benefit after marriage until 26 weekly insurance contributions had been paid subsequent to marriage.

1975 (no. 8)
Social Welfare (Pay-related Benefit) Act: extended maximum duration of earnings-related supplement to 225 days.

1975 (S.I. no. 206)
Social Welfare (Extension of Duration of Pay-related Benefit) Order: extended maximum duration of earnings-related benefit to 303 days.

1976 (no. 6)
Social Welfare Act: extended maximum duration of unemployment benefits from 312 to 390 days and maximum duration of earnings-related supplement extend to 381 days.

1977 (no. 3)
Social Welfare Act: changed conditions relating to entitlement to unemployment assistance in cases of widows and single women without dependents by reducing required number of weekly social insurance contributions from 52 to 26; removed statutory disqualification for receipt of unemployment assistance by widows entitled to widow's pension.

1978 (no. 5)
Social Welfare Act: entitled single women and widows without dependents to unemployment assistance without previous social insurance contribution record.

VI Families and children

In 1980 IRL 99.6 million were spent on cash transfers for families, and income tax deductions in respect of children cost the exchequer a further IRL 43.0 million, and approximately IRL 4.4 million were spent on services for families and children. Together, these sums amounted to 1.7 percent of GDP and 5.7 percent of total social expenditure.

Expenditure for families and children in 1979 (in million Irish pounds)

Child allowances	74.5	50.7
Maternity benefits	4.9	3.3
Unmarried mothers' allowances	7.7	5.2
Benefits for deserted wives and prisoners' wives	10.3	7.0
Deductions from taxable income for children	43.0	29.3
Parental allowance for handicapped children	2.2	1.5
Services [8]	4.4	3.0
Total	147.0	100.0

Source: National Income and expenditure 1981 (Table A20); Report of the Department of Social Welfare 1979-80 (Table 49); Statistical Information Relevant to the Health Services 1981 (Table J3); Office of the Revenue Commissioners.

Income maintenance

Child allowances were introduced in 1944 for the third and subsequent children in a family. The allowance was extended to the second child in 1952 and since 1963 it has been paid for all children. The allowance consists of a monthly payment for each child up to the age of 16 (age 18 if the child remains in full-time education or apprenticeship or is suffering from a long-term incapacity). In 1982 the allowance amounted to IRL 11.25 per month each (equivalent to a weekly payment of 2.2 percent of average gross industrial wage) for the first to fifth child and IRL 17.50 each for subsequent children. Benefits are normally payable to the mother (since 1974). The scheme is financed out of general taxation and administered by the Department of Social Welfare.

A special allowance is paid to parents caring for severely handicapped children. In 1982 this allowance amounted to IRL 55.00 per month. The allowance is administered by the local health authorities and is financed from the health budget.

Income tax deductions are granted for children up to the age of 16, and over this age if the child is in full-time education or apprenticeship. In the tax year 1981/82 the amount deductible from taxable income was IRL 195 for each child. The amount rises to IRL 500 for an incapacitated child and a widow/widower receives an additional deduction of IRL 650 for each child.

Maternity benefits were first introduced as part of the national health insurance scheme in 1911 (see Section III). The social insurance system provides three types of maternity benefit. Firstly, a new scheme introduced in 1981 provides benefits for women in full-time employment who are on maternity leave. The benefit, paid weekly for 14 weeks, amounts to 80 percent of the woman's earnings in the second last tax year, subject to a minimum payment of IRL 56.55 per week. The claimant is required to have had a minimum of 26 weekly insurance contributions in the 12 months preceding maternity leave, or, alternatively, a minimum of 26 contributions paid and a minimum of 26 in the last complete contribution year prior to the year in which benefit is claimed.

A second scheme provides maternity benefits for a period of 12 weeks for women who do not qualify under the first scheme. In 1982 this was paid at a basic rate of IRL 31.65 a week (24.7 percent of average weekly industrial wage) together with an earnings-related supplement payable at the same rates as the earnings-related supplement to disability benefit (see Section III). In order to qualify the claimant must have paid at least 26 insurance contributions and have the same number of contributions paid or credited in the last complete contribution year before the year in which benefit is claimed.

Thirdly, a maternity grant (IRL 8.00 in 1982) is payable on either the woman's own or her husband's insurance. If both partners satisfy the contribution conditions two grants are paid. These conditions are the same as for the second maternity allowance scheme outlined above.

Finally, the local health authorities pay a means-tested maternity grant to low-income mothers for each child born. The rate for this grant was IRL 8.00 in 1982. The grant is financed from the health services budget.

In 1973 a means-tested allowance was introduced for unmarried mothers maintaining a child. In 1982 this amounted to IRL 34.80 per week, equivalent to 27.2 percent of the average gross weekly industrial wage, for the mother and child. An additional payment of IRL 7.75 a week is made for each additional child. This allowance is financed out of general taxation and administered by the Department of Social Welfare.

A means-tested allowance for deserted wives was introduced in 1970. This is paid at the same rates, with the same supplements and subject to the same means-test as for the non-contributory widow's pension (see Section II). In 1973 a benefit for deserted wives was added to the social insurance system: this is paid at the same rates, with the same supplements and according to the same insurance conditions as for the contributory widow's pension (see Section II). In order to qualify for either the means-tested or the insurance benefit the desertion must have lasted for a minimum of three months, during which time the wife is entitled to supplementary welfare allowance. A minimum age limit of 40 years applies in the case of women without child dependents.

In 1974 a means-tested allowance was introduced for the wives of prisoners serving sentences of more than six months. The rates of benefit and supplements and the means-test are the same as for the non-contributory widow's pension (see Section II). Women without dependent children are subject to a minimum age limit of 40 years.

All of the above means-tested allowances are financed from general taxation and are administered by the Department of Social Welfare. The deserted wife's insurance benefit is financed from the Social Insurance Fund.

At the end of 1980, 427,532 families were receiving child allowances, 5,267 mothers were receiving the unmarried mother's allowance, 5,169 allowances were being paid for handicapped children, 5,793 women were in receipt of deserted wives' benefits or allowances, and 182 in receipt of prisoners wives' allowances. During 1980, 18,489 women received maternity allowances.

Services

In addition to medical services for mothers and children (dealt with in Section VIII), the local health authorities operate several other services for this group. Free milk is made available to expectant and nursing mothers in low-income groups, as well as to children up to the age of five who come from poor homes. Orphaned children and children from unsuitable homes are placed either in fosterage or in residential care at the expense of the health authorities. The local health authorities also employ home helps for families under stress, although this service is made use of mainly by the elderly. A scheme providing free footwear for needy children is operated as part of the Supplementary Welfare Allowances Scheme (see Section VII). Local authorities are also empowered to make provision for school meals in primary schools.

Core laws

1911 (1 and 2 Geo. 5, Ch. 55)
National Insurance Act: introduced maternity benefit under sickness insurance scheme.

1944 (no. 2)
Children's Allowances Act: introduced child allowances for all families with three or more children.

1946 (no. 38)
Ministers and Secretaries (Amendment) Act: transferred administration of child allowance scheme from Department of Industry and Commerce to Department of Social Welfare.

1952 (no. 11)
Social Welfare Act: maternity benefits became part of unified social insurance system following abolition of national health insurance scheme.

1952 (no. 12)
Social Welfare (Children's Allowances) Act: extended child allowance to second child.

1963 (no. 26)
Social Welfare (Miscellaneous Provisions) Act: extended child allowance to first child.

1970 (no. 12)
Social Welfare Act: introduced means-tested allowance for deserted wives.

1973 (no. 2)
Social Welfare (Pay-related Benefit) Act: introduced earnings-related supplement to flat-rate maternity benefit.

1973 (no. 10)
Social Welfare Act: introduced means-tested allowance for unmarried mothers maintaining a child, and added deserted wives' benefit to the social insurance system.

1974 (no. 12)
Social Welfare Act: transferred entitlement to child allowances from fathers to mothers.

1974 (no. 14)
Social Welfare (no. 2) Act: introduced means-tested allowance for wives of prisoners serving sentences of six months or more.

1981 (no. 3)
Social Welfare (Amendment) Act: introduced earnings-related maternity benefit for women on maternity leave from full-time employment.

VII Other social welfare

In 1980 expenditure on other social welfare schemes amounted to IRL 20.2 million, equivalent to 0.3 percent of GDP and 0.8 percent of total social expenditure.

Expenditure on other social welfare schemes, 1980 (million Irish pounds)

		%
Supplementary welfare allowance	12.3	60.9
Single woman's allowance	2.5	12.4
Other	5.4	26.7
Total	20.2	100.0

Source: National Income and Expenditure 1981 (Table A20); Statistical Information Relevant to the Health Services 1981 (Table J3); Report of the Dept. of Social Welfare 1979-80 (Table 49).

The Supplementary Welfare Allowance represents the official safety-net for persons unable to provide adequately for themselves. Until 1977, the home assistance scheme fulfilled this function. This scheme which was a direct descendant of the Poor Law, updated by the 1939 Public Assistance Act, which provided discretionary payments for persons in need. Under legislation introduced in 1975, home assistance was replaced by the supplementary welfare allowance, payable as of right and according to uniform standards regarding both assessment of means and the amount of the allowance. In 1982, the allowance for a single person without any means amounted to IRL 24.45 per week (19.1 percent of the average gross weekly industrial wage), this is reduced by the amount of any means the claimant may possess. The rate is increased by IRL 18.50 for an adult dependent, while supplements for dependent children are paid at the same rates as with unemployment assistance. The scheme is administered by the local health authorities under the general direction of the Minister for Social Welfare and is financed jointly by the health authorities and the Department of Social Welfare. On 31 March 1980, a total of 17,413 persons (with 21,940 dependents) were in receipt of the allowance.

In 1974 a means-tested allowance was introduced for single women between the ages of 58 and 66. For a woman with means not exceeding IRL 1.00 per week, the rate in 1982 amounted to IRL 29.50 per week (23.0 percent of the average gross industrial wage). This is reduced by the amount of any means over IRL 1.00 which the claimant may possess. The allowance is financed out of general taxation and administered by the Department of Social Welfare. At the end of 1980, 3,142 women were in receipt of this allowance.

The regional health authorities and the urban local authorities each operate schemes providing weekly fuel vouchers for recipients of long-term welfare cash benefits between October and April each year. The health authorities also operate schemes providing weekly cash benefits for the blind (payable in addition to a blind pension or a disabled person's maintenance allowance - see Sections II and III) and an annual 'mobility' allowance for severely handicapped adults.

The remainder of expenditure in this category consists of miscellaneous small items ranging from grants made to various voluntary welfare agencies to grants to centenarians.

Core laws

1838 (1 and 2 Vic., Ch. 56)
Poor Relief (Ireland) Act: established a poor relief system for Ireland based on workhouses.

1847 (10 and 11 Vic., Ch. 31)
Poor Relief (Ireland) Act: authorized provision of poor relief outside the workhouse to certain categories of persons.

1923 (no. 9)
Local Government (Temporary Provisions) Act: abolished restrictions on the granting of poor relief outside workhouses; outdoor poor relief renamed home assistance.

1939 (no. 9)
Public Assistance Act: consolidated existing provisions relating to public assistance.

1974 (no. 14)
Social Welfare (no. 2) Act: introduced means-tested allowance for single women between the ages of 58 and 68 who have difficulties in securing employment;

1975 (no. 28)
Social Welfare (Supplementary Welfare Allowances) Act: replaced home assistance, payable at discretionary rates under the 1939 Public Assistance Act, by a supplementary welfare allowance payable as of right and at uniform standards; effective from 1.7.77.

VIII Health services

In 1980 current expenditure on the health services amounted to IRL 685.2 million, 7.7 percent of GDP and 26.6 percent of total social expenditure.

Current expenditure on health services in 1980 (million Irish pounds)[a]

		%
Community protection programme	13.0	1.9
Community health services programme	90.4	13.2
Psychiatric programme	93.5	13.6
Programme for the handicapped	59.7	8.7
General hospitals programme	393.8	57.5
Administration, etc.	34.8	5.1
Total	685.2	100.0

Source: Statistical Information Relevant to the Health Services, 1981.

[a] This does not include expenditure on Community Welfare, such expenditure is allocated to the appropriate functional headings.

Coverage

There are three eligibility categories for health services:

Category I includes persons who are unable to pay for general practitioner services for themselves and their families 'without undue hardship', and who are eligible for all health services free of charge. These persons are issued with medical cards by the regional health boards. The health boards fix income guidelines for deciding on eligibility: in 1982 the pre-tax income limit for a single person was IRL 47.50 a week and for a married couple IRL 68.50 per week (37.1 percent and 53.5 percent respectively of the average gross industrial wage). The income-limit is raised to take account of dependents, household expense and cost of travel to work. In 1982 about 35 percent of the population were included in this eligibility category. Medical card-holders are entitled to free general practitioner services from any doctor who has entered into agreement with the health board to provide such services. Prescribed drugs are also provided without charge. Card holders are also eligible for free out-patient and in-patient care in health board hospitals or other approved public hospitals. A subsidy is paid towards the cost of maintenance in approved private hospitals and homes. Home nursing services are available to card-holders and medical care is provided for expectant mothers and infants up to the age of six weeks. Dental care is also provided, mainly by dentists employed by the health boards, but in practice the service is severely limited by a shortage of such dentists. Ophthalmic services are provided by private practitioners in agreement with the health boards. Aural services are also provided.

Category II includes all persons, together with their dependents, whose annual pre-tax income is above the minimum specified limit for Category I eligibility but below IRL 9,500 (June 1982). Approximately 50 percent of the population are in this category. This group is not eligible for free general practitioner, dental, ophthalmic, aural or pharmaceutical services. However, they are entitled to free hospital in-patient services in public wards, and out-patient services at public clinics as well as maternity and infant care services. In addition, persons in this second group are entitled to a refund of the cost of prescribed medicines over IRL 16 a month and to free drugs for certain long-term illnesses.

Category III includes all persons above the income limit for the second category (15 percent of the population). This group is entitled to free maintenance in public hospital wards and free out-patient services in public clinics, but in both cases they are required to pay consultants' fees. They receive a subsidy towards the cost of maintenance in approved private hospitals and homes in the same way as the other two eligibility groups. Reimbursement is made for the cost of prescribed medicines over a certain limit, as for the second eligibility category, and free drugs are provided for long-term illnesses.

In addition to the above services, the health boards also provide various general services. These include periodic medical examination of children of pre-school and primary school age, immunization against infectious diseases, supervision of food and drugs, care of the handicapped and health education programmes.

A system of voluntary insurance was established in 1957 for persons wishing to supplement their coverage for health services. The system is operated by a board, the Voluntary Health Insurance Board, appointed by the Minister for Health and is non-profit making. It is illegal for any other body to provide health insurance except by licence from the Minister for Health. Such licences are only issued for schemes which do not overlap with the coverage provided by the Voluntary Health Insurance Board. This board at present operates three schemes covering hospital costs, offering various combinations of coverage for treatment in private and public wards and hospitals. There is also a scheme covering general practitioner treatment. Insurance premiums are tax deductible. In early 1980, approximately 25 percent of the population were covered by voluntary health insurance.

Financing

The health services are financed mainly out of general taxation, although a system of earmarked contributions was introduced in 1971. Initially the contribution consisted of a flat-rate payment by all persons except those with Category I eligibility. Since 1979 this system has been replaced by a contribution of 1.0 percent of earnings up to a ceiling of IRL 9,500 for persons with Category II and Category III eligibility. In the case of medical card-holders (Category I) who are insured under the social insurance system, the employer pays the 1 percent contribution. Women in receipt of certain social welfare benefits are exempt from contributions. The other sources of finance are grants from the European Communities and a lottery organized by the voluntary hospitals (the hospital sweepstakes). The proportion of current expenditure financed from each source in 1980 was as follows:

Sources of funds for current expenditure on health services in 1980
(in million Irish pounds)

	%
Exchequer	92.0
Health contributions	6.5
Receipts under EEC regulations	1.3
Hospital sweepstakes	0.2
Total	100.0

Source: Statistical Information Relevant to Health Services 1981.

Administration

The administrative structure of the health services was reformed in 1971. The Department of Health exercises a general supervisory function and carries out long-term planning. The day-to-day administration of the services is the responsibility of eight regional health boards. These boards consist of elected members of local authorities, who are in a majority, representatives of medical, nursing, dental and pharmaceutical interests, and three persons nominated by the Minister for Health.

Services are divided into three broad categories covering community care services, general hospital services and special hospital services. The community care services are administered at local government (county) level while hospital services are administered at regional level. The general practitioner service has, since 1971, been provided by private practitioners by agreement with the health boards. Payments to doctors are on a fee-per-service basis. Prescribed medicines are supplied by retail pharmacists. The General Medical Services (Payments) Board, which is composed of officers of the health boards and of the Department of Health, calculates and makes payments to doctors and pharmacists. The hospital service is provided mainly in public hospitals operated either by the health boards or on a voluntary basis. Approximately 10 percent of hospitals are privately owned.

Core laws

1838 (1 and 2 Vic., C. 56)
Poor Relief (Ireland) Act: provided basis for the development of a public hospital system catering for the poor as an adjunct to the workhouse system.

1851
Poor Relief (Ireland) Act: Poor Law Commissioners charged with providing a dispensary medical service for the sick poor.

1878
Public Health (Ireland) Act: codified law on public hygiene and the control of infectious diseases.

1908 (8 Edw. 7, C.56)
Tuberculosis Prevention (Ireland) Act: empowered county councils to provide sanatoria for treatment of tuberculosis.

1915
Notification of Births (Extension) Act: empowered sanitary authorities to provide care for expectant and nursing mothers and children under five years of age.

1919
Public Health (Medical Treatment of Children, Ireland) Act: county councils required to provide medical inspection and treatment service for children in primary schools.

1945 (no. 19)
Mental Treatment Act: reformed the mental health service; admission to mental hospitals changed from a judicial to medical procedure; provision made for temporary and voluntary admission, administration of service transferred from county councils to 18 mental hospital authorities.

1946 (no. 38)
Ministers and Secretaries (Amendment) Act: established separate Department of

Health to take over health functions of former Department of Local Government and Public Health.

1947 (no. 28)
Health Act: codified health legislation; rationalized administrative structure; public health functions of urban district councils transferred to county/borough councils making the latter the sole local health authorities.

1947 (no. 47)
Health Services (Financial Provisions) Act: changed the system of financing health services; existing system relied mainly on local taxations, whereas under new system the Exchequer bears any increase in costs until such time as its contribution equals that of local authorities, costs to be shared equally thereafter.

1953 (no. 26)
Health Act: abolished legal distinction between the public assistance function of local authorities (including general practitioner and general hospital services as well as assistance in cash and kind) and their health function (maternity and child welfare, school medical service, preventive services); henceforth, both sets of services to be administered by local authorities in their capacity as health authorities.
Eligibility for hospital and specialist services, formerly limited to the low-income group and determined by individual means-test, extended to a wider group and determined according to more general criteria; four categories of persons now eligible for these services: persons insured under social welfare system, persons with family incomes under a fixed limit, farmers with farms valued under a fixed limit and other persons who could demonstrate 'undue hardship'; provision made for imposition of small charge on some of these groups for hospital services; provision for hospital and specialist services under the social insurance system withdrawn.
Limited system of maternity care for poor women replaced by a more comprehensive maternity and infant care service for the four groups with eligibility for hospital and specialist services; services also available to persons outside these groups at nominal charge; health authorities required to provide child health services for children up to the age of six.

1957 (no. 1)
Voluntary Health Insurance Act: established Voluntary Health Insurance Board to provide health insurance schemes.

1960 (no. 9)
Health Authorities Act: administrative rationalization; established unified health authorities in the four major cities of Dublin, Cork, Waterford and Limerick to replace existing complex of health, public assistance and mental hospital authorities.

1970 (no. 1)
Health Act: established eight regional health boards to take over administration of health services from the more numerous county authorities and the four city health authorities established in 1960; Hospitals Council set up to coordinate and develop the hospital service; reorganized general practitioner service for low-income groups: service to be provided by doctor of patient's choice (chosen from list of doctors who agree to participate in the scheme) and at the doctor's surgery rather than, as formerly, in a public dispensary by a health authority doctor; prescribed drugs to be provided by retail pharmacists instead of at public dispensaries (scheme operative from 1972); codified existing regulations concerning eligibility for services; group with full eligibility defined as those 'unable without undue hardship' to arrange

medical services for themselves and their dependents; a 'limited eligibility' group included those to whom eligibility for hospital and specialist services and maternity services was extended under the 1953 legislation (see above).

1971 (no. 21)
Health Contributions Act: introduced system of flat-rate health contributions payable by persons in the limited eligibility group.

1979 (no. 4)
Health Contributions Act: new system of eligibility for health services; persons whose income exceeds the ceiling for Category II eligibility are entitled to some of the services provided for this category; services which continue to be excluded for this group include consultants' fees and maternity and infant care services; change in health contribution system - all income-earners with the exception of those with full eligibility and certain social welfare recipients liable to a contribution of 1 percent of income up to a certain ceiling.

IX Education

In 1980 total public expenditure on education amounted to IRL 566.0 million, 6.4 percent of GDP and 22.0 percent of total social expenditure. Of this total, IRL 501.2 million was current expenditure. (Source: National Income and Expenditure, 1981, Table A24).

Current education expenditure by sector in 1980 (million Irish pounds[a]

		%
Primary	201.9	37.9
Secondary	137.8	25.9
Vocational	88.0	16.5
Residential homes and special schools	2.0	0.4
Higher education:		
- Higher Education Authority	60.4	(11.4)
- Grants scholarships	3.8	(0.7)
- Other	2.3	(0.4)
Total	66.5	12.4
Office of the Minister for Education:		
- Administration	10.6	(2.0)
- School transport service	20.4	(3.8)
- Other	5.1	(1.0)
Total	36.1	6.8
Total	532.2	100.0

Source: Department of Education, Statistical Report 1980-81 (Table 7).

[a] The total for current expenditure given here differs slightly from that given above since the Department of Education figures are based on net voted expenditure for the sectors listed and do not include contributions from local authorities to Vocational Education Committees or monies voted to other Departments for educational purposes.

1. Education system

Compulsory education extends from the age of six to fifteen. Primary education normally lasts six years, while secondary education consists of a three-year junior cycle and a two-year senior cycle, each culminating in a public examination. The education system as a whole is characterized by an intricate combination of state and private involvement with a high degree of clerical participation. The state provides most of the finance while the majority of educational establishments are non-public in terms of ownership and administrative structures. The curriculum is set by the state.

At primary level the dominant type of school is the national school. Such schools are largely state financed but most are owned by the diocesan church authorities or by religious orders. A very small number of national schools known as 'model schools', are under direct public control and are wholly state financed. Otherwise, the state provides 85 percent of the building costs for national schools, while the balance as well as the cost of the building site is met out of local contributions. In the case of schools owned by religious orders, the order bears the non-state costs. Running costs are financed by a state capitation grant which must be matched by a smaller local contribution, which may be raised in whatever way the locality wishes. The bishop of the diocese acts as patron to all the ordinary national schools of his denomination within the diocese. Schools are run by management committees whose membership consists of four representatives of the patron (or of the religious order which owns the school, as appropriate), the principal teacher and two representatives of the parents. National school teachers are public employees but are appointed by the management committee. There are a small number of private schools which do not receive any state support. In 1981 the distribution of the various types of primary school was as follows:

Type	No.	%	%
Ordinary National Schools			
- Religious	526		16.0
- Lay	2 763		84.0
Total	3 289	94.2	100.0
Special National Schools for the handicapped:			
- Religious	35		31.0
- Lay	78		69.0
Total	113	3.2	100.0
Private primary schools	91	2.6	
Total	3 493	100.0	

Source: Department of Education, Statistical Report 1980/81.

There are four types of second-level schools. The longest established and most numerous are the secondary schools. Such schools are privately owned, mainly by Roman Catholic religious orders, and provide an academic education. Until the 1960s, secondary school constituted the sole route to third-level education. The schools are financed by a complex system of state grants and private funds. A state capitation grant is paid to all secondary schools. When free secondary education was introduced in 1967, schools had the choice of opting in or out of the scheme. The majority opted for participation in the scheme and these receive a supplementary state capitation grant in lieu of fees. State grants, however, have not kept pace with running costs and many schools have been obliged to seek contributions from parents. Teachers are employees of the school, which pays them a flat-rate basic salary. The major proportion of their salary, however, consists of an incremental state salary. The state provides up to 80 percent of school building costs, the balance and site being provided by the owners. The state also awards grants towards the cost of equipment.

The next most common type of second-level school is the vocational school. These are public institutions owned and managed by local elected committees under the general control of the Minister for Education. Vocational schools were originally intended to provide technical and continuation education. However, the curriculum has changed considerably since the introduction of free education: pupils in these schools now follow courses leading to the same public examinations taken by secondary school pupils, the Intermediate and Leaving Certificates. The vocational school curriculum now includes a higher academic content, while secondary schools have adopted more practical subjects. As such, the distinction between the two types of school is no longer as rigid as in the past and vocational schools now provide an alternative route to the third-level sector.

During the 1960s two new types of second-level schools were introduced: comprehensive and community schools. Comprehensive schools were intended to redress geographical imbalances in educational opportunity. These are state schools, established in areas inadequately served by private schools. They are denominational in character and are managed jointly by representatives of the Department of Education, the local Vocational Education Committee and the Catholic or Protestant bishop of the area. Comprehensive schools are funded entirely by the state. The schools combine academic and vocational subjects. Fifteen such schools were established between 1966 and 1974 and there are no plans to set up more.

Since 1973 community schools have been established in many areas and all new second-level schools must conform to the community school model. These schools are intended to break down the division between traditional secondary and vocational school education and to remove the inefficient use of resources resulting from the existence of several different second-level schools in many areas. While some community schools are newly established many were formed by amalgamating existing second-level schools. The schools are usually managed by boards consisting of representatives of secondary schools, vocational education committees and parents. All current expenditure on community schools, as well as at least 90 percent of capital expenditure is funded by the state, the remainder being provided by the Vocational Education Committee and the religious orders involved in the school. In 1980/81 the relative numbers of different types of second-level institution were as follows:

Second level schools in 1981

Type	No.	%
Secondary	527	61.1
Vocational	242	28.1
Community	34	4.0
Comprehensive	15	1.7
Other[a]	44	5.1
Total	862	100.0

Source: Department of Education, Statistical Report 1980-81.

[a] Includes miscellaneous private schools and schools aided by Departments other than the Department of Education.

Third level education is dominated by the universities - Trinity College, Dublin and the National University of Ireland (NUI). The NUI has three constituent colleges in different parts of the country. The National Catholic Seminary, St. Patrick's College, is a recognized college of the NUI and also accepts lay students. There is one independent medical college, the Royal College of Surgeons.

In 1972 and 1975 the National Institutes for Higher Education were established in Limerick and Dublin respectively. These colleges offer degree and diploma courses with emphasis on technological subjects. In addition, the Dublin Vocational Education Committee controls two colleges of technology in Dublin. These grant diplomas and professional qualifications. The technological sector was expanded by the establishment of regional technical colleges in the period from 1970 onwards. There are now nine such colleges offering courses in the fields of business, engineering and science. These colleges are administered by the Vocational Education Committees. There are a number of specialist teacher training colleges which prepare primary school teachers. Other third-level institutions include the National College of Art and Design and the National College of Physical Education.

The two major sources of funds for third-level institutions are state grants and student fees. The financing arrangements vary from sector to sector. The universities, the National Institutes for Higher Education and the National College of Art and Design are allocated state funds by a statutory body, the Higher Education Authority. In 1978/79, the state grant represented over 83 percent of total income of institutions funded by the HEA. A further portion of the income of these colleges also comes from the state through fees paid under the student grant system. The colleges of technology and regional technical colleges, as well as the teacher training colleges are funded directly by the state.

2. Student support

No fees are payable for secondary education and free books are provided for low-income students. Grants for third-level education on a means-tested basis were introduced in 1968 for approved degree and diploma courses. There is a special system of grants and loans for trainee primary teachers and trainee teachers of practical subjects. A limited number of scholarships are also awarded for third-level study. The numbers of grants, loans and scholarships current in the academic year 1980/81 were as follows:

Type	No.
Higher education grants under Act of 1968	5 021
Grants to students at Colleges of Education, i. e. teacher training	1 098
Loans to students at Colleges of Education	43
Scholarships, grants, allowances to trainee teachers of practical subjects and physical education	217
Scholarships to university	105
Scholarships awarded by Vocational Education Committees to Regional Technical Colleges and Colleges of Technology	1 762
Post-graduate maintenance allowances	285

Source: Department of Education Statistical Report 1980-81.

Core laws

The legislative basis for the educational system is sparse since developments have tended to occur by agreement between the parties involved in the various sectors, rather than as a result of legislative intervention. As such, the laws listed below give a very incomplete picture of the development of the system.

1882 (55 56 Vic. C42)
Irish Education Act: compulsory school attendance for children between the ages of six and fifteen.

1926 (no. 17)
School Attendance Act: stronger provision for enforcement of compulsory schooling.

1930 (no. 29)
Vocational Education Act: established system of vocational schools providing technical and continuation education at second-level.

1961 (no. 34)
Local Authorities (Education Scholarships, Amendment) Act: extended local authority scholarships scheme for university education.

1967 (no. 19)
School Attendance (Amendment) Act: raised school leaving age to 15 years; effective from 1972.

1968 (no. 24)
Local Authorities (Higher Education Grants) Act: introduced system of means-tested local authority grants for university education.

1971 (no. 22)
Higher Education Authority Act: Higher Education Authority set up in 1968 became a statutory body with responsibility for allocation of state funds to certain third-level institutions, and advisory functions as regards the development of higher education.

1978 (no. 26)
Local Authorities (Higher Education Grants) Act: extended local authority higher education grants to a wider range of third-level institutions and courses.

1979 (no. 30)
National Council for Educational Awards Act: NCEA established as awarding body for qualifications in the technological sphere and with responsibility for coordinating development of technological education.

X Housing

In 1980 public expenditure on housing amounted to IRL 314.8 million, equivalent to 3.5 percent of GDP and 12.2 percent of total social expenditure.

Irish housing policy combines a variety of instruments which may be divided into four distinct categories according to the ends towards which they are directed: (1) loans, grants and subsidies designed to encourage the acquisition and improvement of private housing; (2) public housing for low-income groups; (3) rent control legislation for private housing; (4) provision of special purpose housing. Of these policy tools the first two categories are by far the most important.

Expenditure on housing in 1980 (in million Irish pounds)

		%
Subsidies	74.3	23.6
Current transfer payments	0.2	
Current consumption	21.2	6.7
Capital expenditure:		
- Grants to enterprises	4.7	1.5
- Transfer payments	32.5	10.3
- Loans	72.8	23.1
Gross physical capital formation	109.1	34.7
Total	314.8	99.9

Source: National Income and Expenditure 1981 (Table A24).

It has been estimated that the value of state subsidies to housing in 1975, both explicit and implicit, amounted to IRL 45.3 million for owner-occupiers, IRL 21.0 million for local authority tenants who purchased their dwellings, IRL 26.2 million for local authority tenants, and IRL 3.5 million for tenants in rent-controlled housing [9]. Thus, total state subsidies were IRL 96 million, equivalent to 2.6 percent of GDP, and 5.3 percent of public expenditure.

The stimulation of the acquisition of private housing has been the most preferred of all policy measures and has no doubt helped to bring about the high proportion of owner-occupied housing (69 percent in 1971). The provision of public loans for the purchase of private housing dates back to the 1889 Small Dwellings Acquisition Act which enabled local authorities to advance loans for the purchase of existing houses. Under the various Small Dwellings Acts local authorities provide mortgage-type loans at fixed rates of interest and subject to an income limit and a maximum loan amount. Since 1976 there has been a special low-rise mortgage scheme designed to assist local authority tenants, or persons on the local authority housing lists, to purchase reasonably priced private houses. These loans are made at the same interest rates as applicable to other local authority loans and can cover up to 98 percent of the cost of a house. Mortgage repayments are subsidized on a diminishing scale over a nine-year period by the Exchequer and local authorities.

Grants for the acquisition of private housing were first introduced in 1919 for persons building homes for their own occupation. Until 1977 grants were made for this purpose under the various Housing Acts by the Department of Local Government (now the Department of the Environment). In addition local authority grants were made available to new home builders subject to a means-test. The grants system has been used to stimulate housing construction particularly in rural areas through the provision of special grants to persons constructing houses for their own occupation. In 1977 all the existing grants were abolished and a new IRL 1,000 grant for first-time owner-occupiers of new houses was introduced. Grants are also available for house improvement and essential repairs.

Subsidies to private house owners take various forms. Most local authorities operate house purchase schemes under which tenants of local authority housing may purchase their houses at a discount from the market or replacement value of the house. The most important form of indirect subsidy to purchasers of private houses is income tax relief on mortgage interest repayments. A third form of subsidy which has been applied sporadically since 1973 is the subsidization of building society lending rates by the state in order to hold down the cost of mortgages.

The other major policy instrument used in Ireland has been the provision of public housing for rental to low income groups. This approach dates back to the 1880s and 1890s when the first important legislation concerning the housing of the rural and urban working classes was enacted. Current policy has its origins in the 1931 and 1932 Housing Acts which enabled local authorities to acquire land for housing and introduced a system of state assistance to local authority housing schemes. This assistance takes the form of a subsidy on the loan charges incurred by local authorities in financing housing projects. Housing is let at fixed rather than economic rents, (in the case of older housing), and differential, income-related rents (in the case of all post-1967 housing). These schemes are financed by state and local authority subsidies. In 1971, 15.5 percent of households were accommodated in local authority rented housing.

Rent control of private housing has been very limited in Ireland. Statutory control of rents is limited to, roughly speaking, unfurnished tenancies in dwellings constructed prior to 1941. In 1971 unfurnished private lettings constituted only 9 percent of all dwellings in the state (Census of Population, 1971, Vol. VI), and a proportion of even this 9 percent would have been outside the rent-controlled sector. Since rents in the controlled sector have remained low, the main effect of the system has been to encourage landlords to let their property deteriorate. And since no new controlled tenancies are being created the overall impact of rent control on the cost and availability of housing has been negligible. The bulk of private rented accommodation is not subject to rent controls, and tenants do not receive any subsidies commensurate with those received by private house owners and local authority tenants.

The final way in which the state intervenes in the area of housing is through the National Building Agency, established in 1961. Its main objectives are to ensure that appropriate housing is available for personnel recruited in centres of industrial development and to act as an agent for departments of state in meeting the housing needs of employers. It may undertake the provision of dwellings on behalf of local authorities.

Responsibility for public housing policy rests with the Department of the Environment (formerly the Department of Local Government). Most of the public funds for housing are distributed by this department. It exercises general supervision over local authority housing, and promotes legislation affecting both private and public housing. The local authorities responsible for the provision of housing are county councils, county borough councils and urban district councils - 87 authorities in all.

Core laws

1948 (no. 1)
Housing (Amendment) Act: introduced measures to stimulate housing development; more generous grants for construction of private dwellings, particularly to persons constructing dwellings for their own occupation.

1950 (no. 25)
Housing (Amendment) Act: provided grants for house purchase from central and local authorities; higher house purchase loans; strengthened local authority powers to deal with special housing problems.

1952 (no. 16)
Housing (Amendment) Act: provided grants from state to local authorities for housing construction; increased grants for house improvement; provision for local authority grants to persons outside the lower income groups.

1957 (no. 11)
Small Dwellings Acquisition Act: empowered local authorities to advance the full cost of new houses under the Small Dwellings Acquisition scheme.

1962 (no. 27)
Housing (Loans and Grants) Act: provided grants to individuals or bodies for the construction of low cost prototype housing; special grants scheme for housing of the elderly.

1963 (no. 32)
The National Building Agency Limited Act: established National Building Agency with responsibility for provision of housing for personnel in new or expanding industries.

1966 (no. 21)
Housing Act: repealed previous Housing Acts and codified housing legislation; established central role of Department of Local Government in financing, coordinating and regulating local authority housing activities; introduced strict criteria for allocation of local authority housing; outlined duty of every local authority to ascertain housing needs at five-year intervals.

1977 (S.I. no. 240)
Housing Authorities' (Loans for Acquisition or Construction of Houses) (Amendment) Regulations: introduced a low-rise mortgage scheme to assist local authority tenants or persons on housing lists of local authorities to purchase reasonably priced private houses.

Notes

1 For a breakdown of the services included in this figure see section II.4.

2 Department of Social Welfare, *A National Income-Related Pension Scheme*, Dublin, Stationery Office, 1976.

3 Irish Association of Pension Funds, *Survey of Occupational Pension Schemes*, Dublin, 1982.

4 The following description of public service pensions is based on Department of Social Welfare, *A National Income-Related Pension Scheme*, Dublin, Stationery Office, 1976 and on information supplied by the Department of the Public Service.

5 Department of Finance, *Public Expenditure Programmes*, Dublin, Stationery Office, 1982.

6 For a detailed discussion of these schemes, see Brigid Laffan, *Job Creation Schemes in the Republic of Ireland: a Study of Adaptive Implementation*, paper delivered to the European Consortium for Political Research, Freiburg, March 1983 (mimeo).

7 *Ibid.*

8 Includes free milk for mothers and children and payments for children in foster care.

9 National Economic and Social Council, *Report on Housing Subsidies*, Dublin, Stationery Office, 1977.

Bibliography

Contents

I General contributions

1.1 General histories of social policy

See 1.3

1.2 Accounts of specific historical periods

BEW, Paul, PATERSON, Henry: Sean Lemass and the Making of Modern Ireland. Dublin, Gill and Macmillan, 1982, 224p. Analysis of policies pursued by the Fianna Fail party in the postwar period up to 1966, with particular reference to the role of Sean Lemass, leader of the party and Taoiseach (Prime Minister) from 1959 to 1966. Provides useful insights into the factors influencing social policy in this period.

COUGHLAN, Anthony: 'Public affairs, 1916-1966: the social scene', *Administration*, 14:3, 1966, pp. 204-215. Essay outlining the main developments and trends in the fields of health services and social security in the period 1916-1966.

McCASHIN, Anthony: 'Social policy: 1957-82'. *In* LITTON, Frank (ed.): Unequal Achievement: The Irish Experience 1957-1982. Dublin, Institute of Public Administration, 1982, pp. 203-223. Essay analysing the development of social policy since the late 1950s, with indicators of growth of social programmes, evaluation based on secondary evidence and assessment of future prospects.

WHYTE, J.H.: Church and State in Modern Ireland 1923-1979. Dublin, Gill and Macmillan, 1980 (2nd edition). Definitive account of relations between the Roman Catholic Church and the state, with extensive treatment of social policy issues.

1.3 Introductions into the system of social policies

CURRY, John: The Irish Social Services. Dublin, Institute of Public Administration, 1980, 289p. Comprehensive introduction to Irish social programmes. Sections on income maintenance, housing, education, health services and welfare services, tracing development, describing current provisions and providing some evaluative comment. Also section comparing Irish social services with those of other EEC countries.

FARLEY, D.: Social Insurance and Social Assistance in Ireland. Dublin, Institute of Public Administration, 1964. Review of development of social security schemes and detailed description of system in the early 1960s. The author was Information Officer at the Department of Social Welfare at the time of writing.

KAIM-CAUDLE, P.R.: Social Policy in the Irish Republic. London, Routledge and Kegan Paul, 1967, 120p. Introduction to social policies at the time, with overview of development since the foundation of the state and insights into policy debate at a formative period in the development of the social services.

KAIM-CAUDLE, P.R.: Comparative Social Policy. London, Martin Robertson, 1973, 357p. Irish social security programmes examined from a comparative perspective. Brief history of main schemes with description of and comments on current provisions.

1.4 Reports by investigating committees or experts

The Care of the Aged. Report of an inter-departmental committee. Dublin, Stationery Office, 1968, 146p. Review of social services for the aged by a committee drawn from the Departments of Health, Social Welfare and Local Government. Contains recommendations for reforms aimed at helping the aged to remain in the community.

COURTNEY, D., McCASHIN, A.: Social Welfare: The Implications of Demographic Change. Dublin, National Economic and Social Council, Report No. 72, 1984. Study commissioned by official advisory body. Projections of beneficiary numbers within income maintenance schemes to 1991, with analysis of implications for provision of benefits.

DOWLING, B.: Integrated Approaches to Personal Income Taxes and Transfers. Dublin, National Economic and Social Council, Report No. 37, 1978. Study commissioned by official advisory body. Examination of options for closer integration of direct taxation and transfer systems.

FITZGERALD, Eithne: Universality and Selectivity: Social Services in Ireland. Dublin, National Economic and Social Council, Report No. 38, 1978, 260p. Report commissioned by official advisory body. Detailed description of social services, with particular focus on eligibility criteria, programme utilisation, costs and programme efficacy.

1.5 Social science interpretations, evaluations or analyses

ROTTMAN, David, HANNAN, D.B., O'CONNELL, Philip J.: The Redistributive Effects of Social Expenditure and Taxation in the Republic of Ireland: An evaluation of welfare state policies. Paper presented at conference on 'The Future of the Welfare State', Maastricht, December 19-21, 1984, 24p. Analysis of the development of the Irish welfare state in context of various explanatory hypotheses, comparison of Irish welfare state effort with that of other advanced industrial nations and measurement of impact on households of state taxes and benefits in 1973 and 1980. (This paper has not been cited in the text as it came to the author's attention after the manuscript had been finished.)

ROTTMAN, David, O'CONNELL, Philip J.: 'The changing social structure of Ireland'. *In* LITTON, Frank (ed.): Unequal Achievement: The Irish Experience 1967-1982. Dublin, Institute of Public Administration, 1982, pp. 63-88. Essay on evolution of class structures since the late 1950s, with emphasis on effects of economic and social policies.

WHELAN, B.J., VAUGHAN, R.N.: Economic and Social Circumstances of the Elderly in Ireland. Dublin, Economic and Social Research Institute, 1982. Investigation of the main economic and social characteristics of the elderly, with an assessment of the relative living conditions of this group and of the role of the state. Based mainly on a 1977 random sample survey of the elderly population.

1.6 Policy proposals and debates

Building on Reality 1985-1987. Dublin, Stationery Office, 1984. Government's medium-term economic and social policy plans.

COUNCIL FOR SOCIAL WELFARE: A Statement on Social Policy. Dublin, 1973. General and specific proposals for social policy development by the Roman Cahtolic hierarchy's Council for Social Welfare.

DEPARTMENT OF SOCIAL WELFARE: Social Insurance for the Self-Employed - A discussion paper. Dublin, Stationery Office, 1978. Discussion of options for extending social insurance to the self-employed.

Economic Development. Dublin, Stationery Office, 1958. Influential planning document setting out economic strategy for the period 1959-1963 and proposing, *inter alia*, that further improvements in the social services should be deferred until such time as steady economic growth was well established.

NATIONAL ECONOMIC AND SOCIAL COUNCIL: Economic and Social Policy: Aims and Recommendations, 1980-83 (Report No. 53), 1981 (Report No. 61), 1982 (Report No. 70), 1983 (Report No. 75). Dublin, NESC, 1980, 1981, 1983, 1984. Set of reports by official advisory body, reviewing recent economic and social policy developments and making policy recommendations.

NATIONAL ECONOMIC AND SOCIAL COUNCIL: Irish Social Policies: Priorities for Future Development. Dublin, NESC, Report No. 61, 1981. Council's views on social policy priorities, with critical evaluation of existing programmes and policy recommendations.

NATIONAL ECONOMIC AND SOCIAL COUNCIL: Economic and Social Policy Assessment. Dublin, NESC, Report No. 79, 1985. Critical assessment of government's plan for economic and social development in the period 1985-1987 (Building on Reality 1985-1987).

NEVIN, Donal (ed.): Trade Union Priorities in Social Policy. Dublin, Federated Workers' Union of Ireland, 1981. Papers from a symposium organised by the Federated Workers' Union of Ireland. Contributions by union officials, academics and social service professionals on a range of theoretical and substantive issues.

Second Programme for Economic Expansion, Parts I and II. Dublin, Stationery Office, 1963-64. Government programme for economic policy in the period 1964-1970, including outline proposals for the development of the education system.

The Third Programme: Economic and Social Development 1969-72. Dublin, Stationery Office, 1969. Official planning document on economic and social policy.

1.7 Opinion polls

DAVIS, E.E., GRUBE, Joel W., MORGAN, Mark: Attitudes Towards Poverty and Related Social Issues in Ireland. Dublin, Economic and Social Research Institute, 1984. Analysis of survey data on attitudes towards poverty, beliefs about the causes of poverty and attitudes towards improving social welfare benefits.

IRISH MARKETING SURVEYS LIMITED: Political Opinion Poll Prepared for the Irish Times Limited. June 7-8, 1981. Contains questions tapping attitudes towards political salience of social policy issues.

IRISH MARKETING SURVEYS: 'Public spending: where the axe must fall', *Business and Finance*, November 3, 1983. Results of survey of attitudes of leading figures in the business community towards public expenditure cuts.

MARKET RESEARCH BUREAU OF IRELAND LIMITED: Survey Report on the Reaction of the Electorate to Specific Political Issues. Prepared for the Irish Times, November 19-20, 1982. Contains questions tapping attitudes towards political salience of social policy issues.

SHEEHAN, Margaret: The Meaning of Poverty. Dublin, The Council for Social Welfare, 1974. Analysis of survey of recipients of public assistance and recipients of assistance from a major voluntary charity, with information on social and economic characteristics and living conditions of recipients, and examination of role of statutory and voluntary services.

1.8 Sources of statistics or institutional regulations

CENTRAL STATISTICS OFFICE: Statistical Abstract of Ireland. Dublin, Stationery Office, annual. Statistical overview of economic and social conditions, with selected data on social programmes and public finances.

CENTRAL STATISTICS OFFICE: Census of Population. Dublin, Stationery Office, various years. In addition to basic demographic statistics, the census includes statistics on housing, education, employment and other areas of relevance to social policy.

DEPARTMENT OF SOCIAL WELFARE: Report. Dublin, Stationery Office, 1947-49-, triennial. Description of legislative developments and detailed statistics on coverage, beneficiaries, benefits and financing of income maintenance schemes.

DEPARTMENT OF SOCIAL WELFARE: Statistical Information on Social Welfare Services 1983. Dublin, Stationery Office, 1984. Detailed statistical information on income maintenance schemes, including coverage of the social insurance system and beneficiaries, benefits and financing of schemes. This replaces the statistical data formerly appended to the Report of the Department of Social Welfare.

DEPARTMENT OF SOCIAL WELFARE: Summary of Social Insurance and Social Assistance Services. Dublin, Stationery Office, various years. Details of qualification conditions and rates of benefit.

NATIONAL ECONOMIC AND SOCIAL COUNCIL: Towards a Social Report. Dublin, NESC, Report No. 25, 1977. Compilation of statistical and institutional data on social programmes and related areas by governmental advisory body.

1.9 Major periodicals

Administration. Quarterly, 1953-. General journal for articles on public administration, frequently including contributions on social policy.

Economic and Social Review. Quarterly, 1970-. Journal publishing theoretical and applied papers in all areas of social science.

Social Studies. Quarterly, 1972-. (Formerly *Christus Rex*). Discussion and analysis of social issues.

Statistical and Social Inquiry Society of Ireland, Journal Annual. Contributions on statistical investigation and analysis in all areas of social science.

II Single programmes or aspects

2.1 Pensions

2.1.1 Descriptions, evaluations, analyses

DEPARTMENT OF SOCIAL WELFARE: A National Income-Related Pension Scheme - A discussion paper. Dublin, Stationery Office, 1976. Review of existing pension provisions and discussion of options for establishment of earnings-related scheme.

HUGHES, Gerard: Payroll Tax Incidence, the Direct Tax Burden and the Rate of Return on State Pension Contributions in Ireland. Dublin, Economic and Social Research Institute, 1985. Analyses the incidence of social security taxes and the burden of direct taxation, the determinants of social security benefits and the rate of return on state pension contributions.

NATIONAL COUNCIL FOR THE AGED: Incomes of the Elderly in Ireland: An analysis of the State's contribution. Dublin, National Council for the Aged, 1984. Report commissioned by official advisory body, providing a comprehensive review of income maintenance arrangements for the elderly and making policy recommendations.

WHELAN, C.T., WHELAN, B.J.: 'Adjustment to retirement: economic and social influences'. *In* ECONOMIC AND SOCIAL RESEARCH INSTITUTE: Public Social Expenditure - Value for Money? Papers presented at a conference, 20th November 1984. Dublin, 1984. Includes discussion of the sources of income and financial circumstances of the elderly.

2.1.2 Sources

See Section 1.8.1

2.2 Health

2.2.1 Descriptions, evaluations, analyses

The Child Health Services - Report of a Study Group. Dublin, Stationery Office, 1968. Official review of child welfare clinic service and school health examination service with recommendations for improvements.

COUNCIL FOR SOCIAL WELFARE: Future Directions in Health Policy. Dublin, Council for Social Welfare, 1984. Papers from conference organised by the Roman Chatholic hierarchy's Council for Social Welfare. Contributions by health care professionals, administrators and academics.

HENSEY, Brendan M.: The Health Services of Ireland. Dublin, Institute of Public Administration, 1979 (3rd edition). Standard introduction to the development and current features of the health care system by the then Secretary of the Department of Health.

NATIONAL ECONOMIC AND SOCIAL COUNCIL: Some Major Issues in Health Policy.

Dublin, NESC, Report No. 29, 1977. Study of health care provision, with policy recommendations and analysis of future demands arising from demographic change.

NATIONAL ECONOMIC AND SOCIAL COUNCIL: Health Services: The Implications of Demographic Change. Dublin, NESC, Report No. 73, 1984. Analysis of the implications of projected demographic developments up to 1991 for health service requirements with review of major policy issues for health care provision.

Report of the Working Party on the General Medical Service. Dublin, Stationery Office, 1984. Examination of general practitioner service provided for persons with full eligibility for free health care, conducted by working party established by the Minister for Health.

TUSSING, A. Dale: Irish Medical Care Resources: An Economic Analysis. Dublin, Economic and Social Research Institute, 1985, 353 p. Definitive analysis of the health care system from an economic perspective, incorporating extensive information on medical care utilisation drawn from a major sample survey of households conducted by the author. (This work has not been cited in the text as it appeared after the manuscript had been finished.)

2.2.2 Sources

DEPARTMENT OF HEALTH: Report. Dublin, Stationery Office, 1945-49 to 1957-58. Review of legislative developments, description of existing schemes and statistical data on the operation and financing of the health services.

DEPARTMENT OF HEALTH: Statistical Information Relevant to the Health Services. Dublin, Stationery Office, 1978-, annual. Comprehensive set of statistics relating to coverage, utilisation, levels of provision, expenditure, financing, eligibility criteria and population characteristics.

2.3 Unemployment

2.3.1 Descriptions, evaluations, analyses

CONNIFFE, Denis, KENNEDY Kieran A. (eds): Employment and Unemployment Policy for Ireland. Dublin, Economic and Social Research Institute, 1984. Prescriptive analysis of labour market problems, incorporating detailed policy recommendations for the various sectors of employment.

GEARY, R.C., DEMPSEY, M.: A Study of Schemes for the Relief of Unemployment in Ireland. Dublin, Economic and Social Research Institute, 1977, 150p. Review of experience with employment schemes and policy recommendations for the promotion of employment.

HUGHES, Gerard, WALSH, Brendan M.: 'Unemployment duration, aggregate demand and unemployment insurance: A study of Irish live register survival probabilities', *Economic and Social Review*, 14:2, 1983, pp. 93-118. Econometric analysis of responsiveness of unemployment duration to changes in the maximum period of unemployment benefit and in labour market conditions.

SEXTON, J.J.: 'The changing labour force'. *In* ECONOMIC AND SOCIAL RESEARCH INSTITUTE: The Irish Economy and Society in the 1980s. Dublin, Economic and Social Research Institute, 1981, pp. 42-79. Analysis of recent developments in the labour force, with projections and consideration of the implications for labour market policy.

WALSH, Brendan M.: The Structure of Unemployment in Ireland, 1954-1972. Dublin, Economic and Social Research Institute, 1974. Empirical analysis of unemployment trends, including consideration of how unemployment compensation may have affected labour supply.

WALSH, Brendan M.: 'Unemployment compensation and the rate of unemployment: The Irish experience'. *In* GRUBAL, Hubert G., WALKER, Michael A. (eds): Unemployment Insurance: Global Evidence of its Effects on Unemployment. Vancouver, The Fraser Institute, 1978, pp. 172-201. Assessment of whether changes in rates of unemployment benefit have had an impact on the level of unemployment during the postwar period.

2.3.2 Sources

CENTRAL STATISTICS OFFICE: The Trend of Employment and Unemployment. Dublin, Stationery Office, annual. Statistics on employment, unemployment and the administration of the unemployment compensation system.

CENTRAL STATISTICS OFFICE: Labour Force Survey. Dublin, Stationery Office, 1975-, biennial. Labour force estimates disaggregated by industrial group, sex, age, employment status and broad occupational group, with cross-classifications.

CENTRAL STATISTICS OFFICE: Report of the Interdepartmental Study Group on Unemployment Statistics. Dublin, Stationery Office, 1979. Comparison of various sources of unemployment statistics, with recommendations for improving data collection.

NATIONAL MANPOWER SERVICE: Manpower Information Quarterly. Dublin, Stationery Office, 1979-. Survey results on labour market experience of school leavers; statistics on numbers availing of government-sponsored employment schemes and expenditure thereon.

2.4 Sickness insurance and accidents

2.4.1 Descriptions, evaluation, analyses

HUGHES, Gerard: Social Insurance and Absence from Work in Ireland. Dublin, Economic and Social Research Institute, 1982. Analysis of relationship between social insurance and sickness absence using time-series data for the postwar period.

2.4.2 Sources

See Section 1.8.1

2.5 Social assistance

2.5.1 Descriptions, evaluations, analyses

CLIFFORD, J.D.: 'The public, the client, and the social services', *Social Studies*, 35, 1974, pp. 457-498. Study of reasons for non-uptake of social assistance payments, based on survey conducted in an Irish town.

O'CINNEIDE, S.: A Law for the Poor. Dublin, Institute of Public Administration, 1970. Definitive study of the public assistance system.

2.5.2 Sources

See Section 1.8.1

2.6 Family programmes

2.6.1 Descriptions, evaluations, analyses

FITZGERALD, E.: Alternative Strategies for Family Income Support. Dublin, National Economic and Social Council, Report No. 47, 1980. Analysis of family income support system commissioned by official advisory body, including review of existing structures, examination of alternative options and policy recommendations.

2.6.2 Sources

See Section 1.8.1

2.7 Housing

2.7.1 Descriptions, evaluation, analyses

BAKER, T.J., O'BRIEN, L.M.: The Irish Housing System: A critical overview. Dublin, Economic and Social Research Institute, 1979. A critical analysis of instruments of housing policy, with recommendations for reform.

BLACKWELL, John: Housing Requirements and Population Change 1981-1991. Dublin, National Economic and Social Council, Report No. 69, 1983. Assessment of housing requirements to 1991, based on demographic projections and state of existing stock.

KENNEDY, Finola: 'Public expenditure in Ireland on housing in the post-war period', *Economic and Social Review*, 3:3, 1972, pp. 373-401. Analysis of trends in public expenditure on housing in the period 1947-1970, with discussion of effects on housing provision.

MEGHEN, P.J.: Housing in Ireland. Dublin, Institute of Public Administration, 1964. Review of housing legislation.

NATIONAL ECONOMIC AND SOCIAL COUNCIL: Report on Housing Subsidies. Dublin, NESC, Report No. 23, 1977. Analysis of public subsidies to housing, with estimation of distributional effects and policy recommendations.

2.7.2 Sources

DEPARTMENT OF LOCAL GOVERNMENT (since 1977 DEPARTMENT OF THE ENVIRONMENT): Annual Report. Dublin, Stationery Office. Institutional and statistical data on housing system.

DEPARTMENT OF LOCAL GOVERNMENT: *Quarterly Bulletin of Housing Statistics*. Dublin, Stationery Office. Data on completions, housing costs, housing loans, management of public housing, and housing expenditure.

2.8 Education

2.8.1 Descriptions, evaluation, analyses

AKENSON, D.H.: A Mirror to Kathleen's Face: Education in Independent Ireland, 1922-1970. Montreal and London, McGill - Queen's University, 1975. Analysis of development of the education system from a sociological perspective.

BARLOW, A.C.: The Financing of Third-Level Education. Dublin, Economic and Social Research Institute, 1981. Analysis of social and economic consequences of system of financing third-level education, with assessment of alternative financing systems and projection of future costs.

BREEN, Richard: 'Irish educational policy: past performance and future prospects'. *In* ECONOMIC AND SOCIAL RESEARCH INSTITUTE: Public Social Expenditure - Value for Money?. Papers presented at a conference, 20th November 1984. Dublin, 1984. Assessment of achievements of education system, with discussion of medium-term prospects.

CLANCY, Patrick: Participation in Higher Education. Dublin, Higher Education Authority, 1982. Examination of patterns of participation in higher education, with analysis of implications for educational policy.

COOLAHAN, John: Irish Education: Its History and Structure. Dublin, Institute of Public Administration, 1981. Comprehensive history of the education system since 1800, with analysis of current trends and problems.

MURPHY, Dennis: Education: The Implications of Demographic Change. Dublin, National Economic and Social Council, Report No. 71, 1983. Analysis of the implications of projected demographic developments up to 1991 for provision of education services.

NEVIN, Monica: 'A study of the social background of students in Irish universities', *Journal of the Statistical and Social Inquiry Society of Ireland*, 21:4, 1967, pp. 201-225. Analysis of the social correlates of participation in higher education.

TUSSING, A. Dale: Irish Educational Expenditure - Past, Present and Future. Dublin, Economic and Social Research Institute, 1978. Review of structure of the education system, with particular reference to financing, projections of enrolments and expenditure to 1986, and discussion of policy options for coping with anticipated pressures.

2.8.2 Sources

COMMISSION ON HIGHER EDUCATION: I - Presentation and Summary of Report, II - Report, Vols I and II. Dublin, Stationery Office, 1967. Comprehensive investigation of the third level system, including detailed recommendations for reform and extensive statistics on universities and other third level institutions.

DEPARTMENT OF EDUCATION: Annual Report. Dublin, Stationery Office. Institutional and statistical data on the education system.

DEPARTMENT OF EDUCATION: Statistical Report. Dublin, Stationery Office, 1964-65-, annual. Statistics on enrolments and provision of staff, financing and physical resources. Replaces annual report of the Department of Education.

DEPARTMENT OF EDUCATION: White Paper on Educational Development. Dublin, Stationery Office, 1980. Government's plans for the future development of the education system.

Investment in Education - a report of the survey team. Dublin, Stationery Office, 1966. Comprehensive investigation of the education system conducted under the joint auspices of the Irish government and the OECD. The recommendations for reform included in the report had a major impact on the subsequent course of education policy at first and second level. Report includes detailed statistical annex.

2.9 Public household

2.9.1 Descriptions, evaluations, analyses

BRUTON, Richard: Irish Public Debt. Dublin, Economic and Social Research Institute, 1978. Examination of evolution of public borrowing and public debt in the postwar period, with analysis of purposes and implications of borrowing and brief comparison with debt situation in other OECD countries.

GOULD, Frank: 'The growth of public expenditure in Ireland, 1947-77', *Administration*, 29:2, 1981, pp. 115-135. Growth of public expenditure examined in context of various explanatory hypotheses.

KENNEDY, Finola: Public Social Expenditure in Ireland. Dublin, Economic and Social Research Institute, 1975. Empirical, analytical and evaluative study of the development of social expenditure in the period 1947-1974 set in the context of an appraisal of social policy strategies.

KENNEDY, Finola: 'Social expenditure of public authorities and economic growth 1947-1966', *Economic and Social Review*, 1:3, 1970, pp. 385-392. Analysis of relationship between social expenditure and growth of output, with particular reference to extent to which more rapid economic growth in the 1960s was associated with a displacement of social expenditure.

MAGUIRE, Maria: 'Components of growth of income maintenance expenditure in Ireland 1951-1979', *Economic and Social Review* 15:2, 1984, pp. 75-85. Growth of expenditure on old age pensions, child allowances, unemployment benefits and sickness cash benefits examined in terms of respective influences of demographic change, growth in coverage and improvements in benefits.

MAGUIRE, Maria: 'Social expenditure in Ireland and other European OECD countries: past trends and prospective developments'. *In* ECONOMIC AND SOCIAL RESEARCH INSTITUTE: Public Social Expenditure- Value for Money?. Papers presented at a conference, 20th November, 1984, Dublin, 1984. Examination of factors influencing expenditure growth in period 1960-1981, comparison with experience in other European countries and analysis of medium-term prospects.

O'HAGAN, John W.: 'An analysis of the growth of the public sector in Ireland, 1953-1977',

Journal of the Statistical and Social Inquiry Society of Ireland, 24:2, 1979/80, pp. 69-98. Examination of trends in public expenditure and revenue in context of selected hypotheses of public sector growth.

O'HAGAN, John W.: 'Demonstration, income and displacement effects as determinants of public sector expenditure shares in the Republic of Ireland', *Public Finance/Finances Publiques*, 35:3, 1980, pp. 425-435. Analysis of factors associated with growth of public sector, with particular reference to whether there is evidence of a demonstration effect from the United Kingdom.

O'HAGAN, John W., KELLEY, Morgan: 'Components of growth in current public expenditure on education and health', *Economic and Social Review*, 15:2, 1984, pp. 87-93. Examination of factors influencing growth of expenditure on health and education, including demographic changes, changes in utilisation of the services and cost changes.

WALSH, Brendan M.: 'Income maintenance payments in Ireland 1953-1971. Cyclical variations and long-term growth', *Economic and Social Review*, 5:2, 1974, pp. 213-235. Econometric analysis of factors affecting growth of social security expenditure.

2.9.2 Sources

Budget. Dublin, Stationery Office, annual. Annual statement of the government's budgetary plans.

CENTRAL STATISTICS OFFICE: National Income and Expenditure. Dublin, Stationery Office, 1959-, annual. National account statistics.

COMMISSION ON TAXATION: First Report - Direct Taxation. Dublin, Stationery Office, 1982. Comprehensive report with recommendations for reform by commission established by the Minister for Finance.

DEPARTMENT OF FINANCE: Comprehensive Public Expenditure Programmes. Dublin, Stationery Office, 1983 and 1984. Presentation of expenditure data on a programmatic basis for selected programmes.

KENNEDY, Finola: The Growth and Allocation of Public Social Expenditure in Ireland Since 1947. Unpublished Ph.D. thesis, University College, Dublin, 1871. Only source of social expenditure data presented on a national accounts basis for the period 1947-1963.

2.10 Public employment

HUMPHREYS, Peter C.: Public Service Employment. Dublin, Institute of Public Administration, 1983. Detailed examination of public employment strategies, with extensive data for period since 1970 and comparison with other Western European countries.

ROSE, Richard: Changes in Public Employment: A multi-dimensional comparative analysis. Glasgow, Centre for the Study of Public Policy, Paper No. 61, 1980. Includes data on Ireland for 1950s and 1970s.

III Impact of social programmes

3.1 Poverty

COUNCIL FOR SOCIAL WELFARE: Conference on Poverty 1981. Dublin, The Council for Social Welfare, 1982. Papers from conference on poverty organised by the Roman Catholic Hierarchy's Council for Social Welfare. Contributions by academics, public administrators, social work professionals and representatives of voluntary charities. Includes general papers and contributions on specific aspects of social policy, such as housing, health, income redistribution and social service delivery.

JOYCE, L., McCASHIN, A. (compilers): Poverty and Social Policy. Dublin, Institute of Public Administration, 1982. Report prepared in the context of the EEC European Programme of Pilot Schemes and Studies to Combat Poverty. Assessment of extent of poverty and inequality accompanied by examination of major social programmes.

KENNEDY, Stanislaus (ed.): One Million Poor?. Dublin, Turoe Press, 1981. Collection of papers on various aspects of poverty and policy by academics and social work professionals.

O'CINNEIDE, Seamus: 'The extent of poverty in Ireland', Social Studies, 1:4, 1972, pp. 381-400. Influential paper providing estimates of the extent of poverty, presented at conference on poverty organised by the Roman Catholic hierarchy's Council for Social Welfare.

O'CINNEIDE, Seamus: 'Poverty and inequality in Ireland'. *In* GEORGE, Vic, LAWSON, Roger (eds): Poverty and Inequality in Common Market Countries. London, Routledge and Kegan Paul, 1980, pp. 124-160. Review of events leading up to the 'rediscovery' of poverty in the early 1970s, estimates of extent of poverty in 1975 and examination of trends in income.

ROCHE, John D.: Poverty and Income Maintenance Policies in Ireland 1973-80. Dublin, Institute of Public Administration, 1984. Comparison of extent and dimensions of poverty in 1973 and 1980, with assessment of contribution of income maintenance policies to the amelioration of poverty and policy recommendations.

3.2 Inequality and income distribution

CENTRAL STATISTICS OFFICE: Redistributive Effects of State Taxes and Benefits on Household Incomes in 1973. Dublin, Stationery Office, 1980; CENTRAL STATISTICS OFFICE: Redistributive Effects of State Taxes and Benefits on Household Incomes in 1980. Dublin, Stationery Office, 1983. Analysis based mainly on the household budget survey data. Redistributive effects of individual taxes and benefits examined. Estimates of the distribution of direct, gross and disposable income cross-classified with household composition, livelihood status, social group, geographical location.

GEARY, R.C., O'MUIRCHEARTAIGH, F.S.: Equalisation of Opportunity in Ireland: Statistical Aspects. Dublin, Economic an Social Research Institute, 1974. Review of statistical evidence on equalisation of income and opportunity.

NOLAN, Brian: 'The personal distribution of income in the Republic of Ireland', *Journal of the Statistical and Social Inquiry Society of Ireland,* 23:5, 1977/78, pp. 91-162. Analysis based on 1973 Household Budget Survey, with comparison of trends in urban income distribution from 1965/66 to 1976.

O'CONNELL, Philip J.: 'The distribution and redistribution of income in the Republic of Ireland', *Economic and Social Review* 13:4, 1982, pp. 251-2178. Analysis based on 1973 Household Budget Survey, comparing distribution of direct, disposable and final income and examining redistributive effect of each individual tax and benefit.

ROTTMAN, David B., HANNAN, Damian F.: 'Fiscal welfare and inflation: winners and losers'.*In* ECONOMIC AND SOCIAL RESEARCH INSTITUTE: The Irish Economy and Society in the 1980s. Dublin, 1981, pp. 80-112. Analysis of effects on social class and family cycle relativities of changes in income, direct taxes and state transfers in the period 1973-1978.

ROTTMAN, David B., HANNAN, Damian F. with HARDIMAN, Niamh and WILEY, Mirian M.: The Distribution of Income in the Republic of Ireland: A study in social class and family cycle inequalities. Dublin, Economic and Social Research Institute, 1982. Analysis of extent and nature of income inequality with particular reference to the redistributive consequences of taxation and transfer policies.

3.3 Economic effects

See Sections 2.3 and 2.9

Appendix Tables

Contents

Table 1 Gross Domestic Product and Total Public Expenditure

Year	GDP (at market prices, in million pounds)			Deflators (base 1970)				Total public expenditure (in million pounds)				Year
	at current prices	at constant (1970) prices	annual real growth rate	gross domestic product	capital formation	public consumption	private consumption	at current prices	as % of GDP	at constant (1970) prices	annual real growth rate	
1947	307.6	816.3		37.7	45.0	30.9	42.2	80.8	26.3	224.2		1947
1948	340.5	859.3	5.3	39.6	48.6	31.5	43.3	94.7	27.8	252.9	12.8	1948
1949	366.4	903.4	5.1	40.6	48.2	32.5	43.0	107.3	29.3	275.4	8.9	1949
1950	372.2	913.3	1.1	40.8	48.8	33.8	44.0	112.8	30.3	282.6	2.6	1950
1951	391.9	932.8	2.1	42.0	51.1	37.5	47.5	131.8	33.6	304.0	7.6	1951
1952	450.4	956.7	2.6	47.1	54.3	38.5	51.4	137.3	30.5	301.3	-0.9	1952
1953	495.8	982.5	2.7	50.5	54.5	40.4	53.7	149.3	30.1	314.9	4.5	1953
1954	498.2	992.2	1.0	50.2	54.0	40.3	54.1	151.0	30.3	319.4	1.4	1954
1955	522.1	1 016.9	2.5	51.3	55.4	41.8	55.5	157.1	30.1	321.4	0.6	1955
1956	530.1	1 003.9	-1.3	52.8	58.5	44.0	57.1	166.6	31.4	326.0	1.4	1956
1957	548.9	1 002.7	-0.1	54.7	61.5	44.8	59.5	164.2	29.9	311.9	-4.3	1957
1958	568.4	981.8	-2.1	57.9	62.9	47.0	61.7	164.2	28.9	301.1	-3.5	1958
1959	607.5	1 022.2	4.1	59.4	62.7	48.3	62.0	169.7	27.9	307.0	2.0	1959
1960	642.3	1 079.2	5.6	59.5	64.0	49.9	62.5	182.9	28.5	323.4	5.3	1960
1960	631.3	1 063.2		59.4				n.a.	29.0	n.a.	n.a.	1960
1961	679.7	1 113.6	4.7	61.0	66.8	52.2	64.1	208.2	30.6	353.0	9.2	1961
1962	735.8	1 154.6	3.7	63.7	69.0	55.3	66.7	223.6	30.4	361.9	2.5	1962
1963	791.3	1 210.4	4.8	65.4	70.4	57.8	68.3	249.5	31.5	390.1	7.8	1963
1964	900.6	1 261.0	4.2	71.4	74.0	67.2	73.1	294.9	32.7	417.1	6.9	1964
1965	958.9	1 286.1	2.0	74.6	76.8	70.4	76.6	329.9	34.4	445.5	6.8	1965
1966	1 010.4	1 298.8	1.0	77.8	79.1	73.3	79.4	352.4	34.9	458.5	2.9	1966
1967	1 103.6	1 365.6	5.1	80.8	82.0	74.7	81.9	399.9	36.2	505.4	10.2	1967
1968	1 245.2	1 476.6	8.1	84.3	84.8	80.7	86.2	468.0	37.6	558.1	10.4	1968
1969	1 438.3	1 565.9	6.0	91.9	92.3	88.1	92.5	545.1	37.9	599.9	7.5	1969
1970	1 620.2	1 620.2	3.5	100.0	100.0	100.0	100.0	643.8	39.7	643.8	7.3	1970
1971	1 853.1	1 676.0	3.4	110.6	111.5	109.5	109.5	755.0	40.7	687.4	6.8	1971
1972	2 237.8	1 785.1	6.5	125.4	122.5	123.7	120.0	882.1	39.4	724.0	5.3	1972
1973	2 701.6	1 867.9	4.6	144.6	137.0	142.8	133.9	1 068.8	39.6	775.4	7.1	1973
1974	2 988.3	1 946.7	4.2	153.5	170.0	161.1	154.9	1 304.2	43.6	815.4	5.2	1974
1975	3 728.4	1 986.1	2.0	187.7	203.4	207.9	189.5	1 799.9	48.3	906.2	11.1	1975
1976	4 572.3	2 027.7	2.1	225.5	241.5	241.1	225.2	2 166.2	47.4	928.0	2.4	1976
1977	5 485.6	2 167.9	6.9	253.0	280.4	273.9	253.4	2 538.7	46.3	958.4	3.3	1977
1978	6 421.3	2 295.8	5.8	279.7	312.6	302.9	272.5	3 066.5	47.4	1 060.1	10.6	1978
1979	7 480.2	2 373.9	3.4	315.1	359.8	351.3	312.6	3 793.9	50.8	1 119.0	5.6	1979
1980	8 874.9	2 460.7	3.7	360.7	424.3	427.5	365.9	4 862.6	54.8	1 224.1	9.4	1980

Table 2

Public Expenditure by

Year	Purpose: Total exp. (curr.pric. million pounds)	Purpose: Per cent distribution: general services	defence	social serv.	econ. serv.	nat. debt service	Economic Function: Total exp. (curr.pric. million pounds)	Economic Function: Per cent distribution: current subsidies+ transfers	final cons.	nat. debt service	capital formation	capital transfers	Level of Government: Total exp. (curr.pric. million pounds)	Level of Government: Per cent distribution: central gov.	local gov.	social insur.	Year
1947							80.8	38.4	48.1	6.7	6.1	0.6					1947
1948							94.7	38.8	45.0	6.0	9.7	0.5					1948
1949							107.3	35.2	38.9	5.6	17.3	3.0					1949
1950							112.8	34.1	40.0	5.9	19.1	0.9					1950
1951							131.8	33.8	40.9	5.5	18.4	1.4					1951
1952							137.3	32.4	41.2	6.3	18.1	2.1					1952
1953							149.3	30.2	41.5	6.8	15.5	6.0	154.9	60.0	34.4	5.6	1953
1954							151.0	31.6	41.7	7.6	15.0	4.2	156.1	59.2	35.2	5.6	1954
1955							157.1	31.9	41.2	8.3	14.7	4.0	162.7	58.5	35.8	5.7	1955
1956							166.6	31.6	41.2	8.5	13.9	4.7	172.8	58.4	35.5	6.1	1956
1957							164.2	32.8	41.2	9.4	10.7	6.0	171.1	60.7	32.9	6.4	1957
1958							164.2	32.0	42.9	9.6	10.4	5.1	170.9	60.9	32.7	6.4	1958
1959							169.7	32.2	43.5	9.8	10.4	4.1	177.3	62.0	32.0	6.0	1959
1960							182.9	33.4	43.0	9.9	9.7	4.0	188.4	63.0	30.7	6.3	1960
1961							208.2	35.3	40.6	9.7	10.4	4.0	213.9	62.0	29.7	8.3	1961
1962							223.6	33.5	41.2	9.6	11.3	4.4	229.9	61.8	29.8	8.4	1962
1963	257.0	9.6	4.2	48.1	28.8	9.3	249.5	32.9	40.2	9.5	11.9	5.5	256.2	61.9	29.1	9.0	1963
1964	303.6	9.2	4.4	48.8	28.6	8.9	294.9	32.2	40.7	9.1	12.7	5.3	302.7	61.9	29.6	8.5	1964
1965	339.2	9.5	4.2	48.7	28.3	9.4	329.9	32.1	39.5	9.6	12.9	5.8	338.5	62.2	29.6	8.2	1965
1966	360.9	8.8	3.7	49.1	28.3	10.0	352.4	33.8	38.9	10.2	11.8	5.3	362.4	61.1	29.6	9.3	1966
1967	411.4	8.6	3.5	49.1	28.6	10.2	399.9	34.3	36.9	10.4	11.9	6.5	410.2	62.1	29.1	8.8	1967
1968	483.2	10.2	3.2	48.9	28.0	9.7	468.0	34.2	35.7	10.0	11.1	9.1	479.0	63.3	27.9	8.8	1968
1969	561.8	7.3	3.2	50.3	29.2	10.0	545.1	35.2	35.7	10.3	11.8	7.0	557.3	62.4	28.8	8.8	1969
1970	658.8	8.0	3.4	50.1	28.5	10.0	643.8	35.4	36.9	10.2	11.1	6.5	658.7	62.0	28.6	9.4	1970
1971	771.9	7.9	3.4	51.3	28.1	9.3	755.0	34.7	37.4	9.5	11.2	7.1	772.1	60.8	29.4	9.8	1971
1972	900.2	8.4	3.9	52.6	25.8	9.2	882.1	34.4	38.8	9.4	11.4	5.9	900.2	60.5	29.8	9.7	1972
1973	1 088.9	9.0	3.7	56.0	22.1	9.2	1 068.8	33.7	39.5	9.4	12.7	4.7	1 091.0	58.9	31.3	9.8	1973
1974	1 346.4	9.4	3.7	56.3	21.9	8.7	1 304.2	33.5	39.2	9.0	13.7	4.6	1 329.6	57.2	32.7	10.1	1974
1975	1 848.5	8.9	3.6	56.0	22.3	9.2	1 799.9	35.0	39.4	9.5	12.0	4.1	1 833.8	57.3	31.4	11.3	1975
1976	2 219.6	8.6	3.8	55.5	21.2	10.9	2 166.2	35.6	38.8	11.1	10.1	4.5	2 206.9	58.3	30.0	11.7	1976
1976	2 206.9	7.8	3.8	55.4	22.1	10.9											1976
1977	2 590.6	8.0	3.8	54.7	21.7	11.9	2 538.7	34.2	38.9	12.1	10.3	4.5	2 590.6	58.3	30.2	11.5	1977
1978	3 132.3	8.0	3.7	53.5	22.1	12.7	3 066.5	33.5	38.4	12.9	10.5	4.7	3 132.3	59.2	30.0	10.8	1978
1979	3 880.0	8.4	3.6	52.7	22.6	12.6	3 793.9	32.8	38.1	12.9	11.3	4.9	3 880.0	60.7	29.4	9.9	1979
1980	4 964.5	7.8	3.5	53.3	23.0	12.4	4 862.6	31.9	38.7	12.7	11.3	5.5	4 964.5	59.7	29.7	10.6	1980

Table 3 Social Expenditure

Year	At current prices (in million pounds)					As % of gross domestic product					As % of public expenditure					As % of social expenditure				Year
	Total	Income Maint.	Education	Health	Housing	Total	Inc. Maint.	Educ.	Health	Housing	Total	Inc. Maint.	Educ.	Health	Housing	Inc. Maint.	Educ.	Health	Housing	
1947	31.8	13.9	8.3	6.2	3.4	10.3	4.5	2.7	2.0	1.1	39.4	17.2	10.3	7.7	4.2	43.7	26.1	19.5	10.7	1947
1948	38.7	15.4	8.6	7.7	6.7	11.4	4.5	2.5	2.3	2.0	40.9	16.3	9.1	8.1	7.1	40.6	22.2	19.9	17.3	1948
1949	51.4	17.8	9.1	9.5	15.0	14.0	4.9	2.5	2.6	4.1	47.9	16.6	8.5	8.9	14.0	34.6	17.7	18.5	29.2	1949
1950	54.8	17.7	10.7	10.6	15.8	14.7	4.8	2.9	2.8	4.2	48.6	15.7	9.5	9.4	14.0	32.3	19.5	19.4	28.8	1950
1951	62.5	18.8	12.0	13.0	18.7	15.9	4.8	3.1	3.3	4.8	47.4	14.3	9.1	9.9	14.2	30.1	19.2	20.8	29.9	1951
1952	70.9	26.1	12.6	12.9	19.3	15.7	5.8	2.8	2.9	4.3	51.6	19.0	9.2	9.4	14.1	36.8	17.8	18.2	27.2	1952
1953	78.3	29.1	13.7	16.8	18.7	15.8	5.9	2.8	3.4	3.8	52.4	19.5	9.2	11.3	12.5	37.2	17.5	21.4	23.9	1953
1954	78.8	29.4	14.9	16.1	18.4	15.8	5.9	3.0	3.2	3.7	52.2	19.5	9.9	10.7	12.2	37.3	18.9	21.4	23.4	1954
1955	81.1	30.3	15.1	17.0	18.7	15.5	5.8	2.9	3.3	3.6	51.6	19.3	9.6	10.8	11.9	37.4	18.6	21.0	23.1	1955
1956	84.9	32.2	16.8	18.5	17.4	16.0	6.1	3.2	3.5	3.3	51.0	19.3	10.1	11.1	10.4	37.9	19.8	21.8	20.5	1956
1957	83.2	34.8	17.0	17.3	14.1	15.2	6.3	3.1	3.2	2.6	50.7	21.2	10.4	10.5	8.6	41.8	20.4	20.9	16.9	1957
1958	80.2	34.7	18.0	15.5	12.0	14.1	6.1	3.2	2.7	2.1	48.8	21.1	11.0	9.4	7.3	43.3	22.4	19.3	15.0	1958
1959	85.3	35.1	19.6	17.9	12.7	14.0	5.8	3.2	2.9	2.1	50.3	20.7	11.5	10.5	7.5	41.1	23.0	21.0	14.9	1959
1960	89.7	36.4	20.7	18.8	13.8	14.0	5.7	3.2	2.9	2.1	49.0	19.9	11.3	10.3	7.5	40.6	23.1	20.9	15.4	1960
1960	89.7	36.4	20.7	18.8	13.8	14.2	5.8	3.3	3.0	2.2	49.0	19.9	11.3	10.3	7.5	40.6	23.1	20.9	15.4	1960
1961	97.2	40.2	21.8	20.4	14.8	14.3	5.9	3.2	3.0	2.2	46.7	19.3	10.5	9.8	7.1	41.4	22.4	21.0	15.2	1361
1962	106.7	42.6	25.2	22.4	16.5	14.5	5.8	3.4	3.0	2.2	47.7	19.1	11.3	10.0	7.4	39.9	23.6	21.0	15.5	1952
1963	120.0	49.0	29.3	23.6	18.2	15.2	6.2	3.7	3.0	2.3	48.1	19.6	11.7	9.5	7.3	40.8	24.4	19.6	15.2	1963
1964	143.0	55.0	36.7	29.6	21.7	15.9	6.1	4.1	3.3	2.4	48.5	18.7	12.4	10.0	7.4	38.5	25.7	20.6	15.2	1954
1965	161.3	59.9	41.2	32.2	27.9	16.8	6.2	4.3	3.4	2.9	48.9	18.2	12.5	9.8	8.5	37.1	25.5	20.1	17.3	1965
1966	176.6	68.1	42.3	37.1	29.1	17.6	6.7	4.2	3.7	2.9	50.1	19.3	12.0	10.5	8.3	38.6	24.0	20.9	16.5	1966
1967	198.3	73.6	49.8	40.1	34.8	18.0	6.7	4.5	3.6	3.2	49.6	18.4	12.5	10.0	8.7	37.1	25.2	20.0	17.7	1967
1968	232.2	83.8	61.7	47.9	38.8	18.6	6.7	5.0	3.8	3.1	49.6	17.9	13.2	10.2	8.3	36.1	26.6	20.6	16.7	1968
1969	278.1	100.7	73.1	59.3	45.0	19.3	7.0	5.1	4.1	3.1	51.0	18.5	13.4	10.9	8.3	36.2	26.3	21.3	16.2	1969
1970	320.6	122.5	84.5	73.5	40.0	19.8	7.6	5.2	4.5	2.5	49.8	19.0	13.1	11.4	6.2	38.2	26.4	22.9	12.5	1970
1971	383.0	144.1	96.9	88.4	53.6	20.7	7.8	5.2	4.8	2.9	50.7	19.1	12.8	11.7	7.1	37.6	25.3	23.1	14.0	1971
1972	459.0	164.7	117.5	112.5	64.3	20.5	7.4	5.3	5.0	2.9	52.0	18.7	13.3	12.8	7.3	35.9	25.6	24.5	14.0	1972
1973	596.5	219.7	145.1	144.3	87.6	22.1	8.1	5.4	5.3	3.2	55.8	20.6	13.6	13.5	8.2	36.8	24.3	24.2	14.7	1973
1974	750.7	275.1	170.6	178.3	126.6	25.1	9.2	5.7	6.0	4.2	57.6	21.1	13.1	13.7	9.7	36.6	22.7	24.8	16.9	1974
1975	1 014.1	395.4	225.9	240.5	152.3	27.2	10.6	6.1	6.5	4.1	56.3	22.0	12.6	13.4	8.5	39.0	22.3	23.7	15.0	1975
1976	1 189.3	483.6	272.0	291.3	142.3	26.0	10.6	5.9	6.4	3.1	54.9	22.3	12.6	13.4	6.6	40.7	22.9	24.5	12.0	1976
1977	1 367.8	552.3	321.5	347.1	146.9	24.9	10.1	5.9	6.3	2.7	53.9	21.8	12.7	13.7	5.8	40.4	23.5	25.4	10.7	1977
1978	1 622.3	622.3	382.4	431.7	185.9	25.1	9.6	5.9	6.7	2.9	52.9	20.3	12.5	14.1	6.1	38.4	23.6	26.6	11.5	1978
1979	1 976.3	719.2	467.2	541.9	248.0	26.5	9.6	6.3	7.3	3.3	52.1	19.0	12.3	14.3	6.5	36.4	23.6	27.4	12.5	1979
1980	2 575.7	950.4	566.0	744.4	314.9	29.0	10.7	6.4	8.4	3.5	53.0	19.5	11.6	15.3	6.5	36.9	22.0	28.9	12.2	1980

Table 4

Social Expenditure

Year	Expenditure on Education at current prices			Expenditure on Health at current prices			Expenditure on Housing at current prices			Exp. on Income Maintenance at current prices		Expenditure at constant (1970) prices					Year
	total	current	capital	total	current	capital	total	current	capital	total	transfers	Income Maint.	Educ.	Health	Hous-ing	Total	
1947	8.3	8.0	0.3	6.2	5.9	0.3	3.4	1.8	1.6	13.9	12.0	34.6	25.0	19.8	8.3	87.7	1947
1948	8.6	8.2	0.4	7.7	7.3	0.4	6.7	2.4	4.3	15.4	14.0	37.7	25.3	24.0	12.7	99.7	1948
1949	9.1	8.4	0.7	9.5	8.6	0.9	15.0	3.2	11.8	17.8	16.1	42.7	26.0	28.4	33.1	130.2	1949
1950	10.7	9.8	0.9	10.6	9.5	1.1	15.8	2.8	13.0	17.7	16.0	41.4	29.3	30.4	33.7	134.8	1950
1951	12.0	11.1	0.9	13.0	11.2	1.8	18.7	3.0	15.7	18.8	16.8	40.7	30.0	33.4	37.6	141.7	1951
1952	12.6	11.5	1.1	12.9	10.7	2.2	19.3	4.4	14.9	26.1	23.2	52.7	30.2	31.9	37.0	151.8	1952
1953	13.7	12.1	1.6	16.8	11.9	4.9	18.7	4.8	13.9	29.1	27.3	52.8	31.2	38.4	35.4	157.8	1953
1954	14.9	13.2	1.7	16.1	12.1	4.0	18.4	5.3	13.1	29.4	27.4	55.6	34.0	37.5	35.2	162.3	1954
1955	15.1	13.5	1.6	17.0	14.0	3.0	18.7	5.8	12.9	30.3	28.6	55.6	33.4	38.9	34.9	162.8	1955
1956	16.8	14.6	2.2	18.5	15.7	2.8	17.4	6.0	11.4	32.2	30.4	57.3	35.2	40.4	30.9	163.8	1956
1957	17.0	15.4	1.6	17.3	16.1	1.2	14.1	5.8	8.3	34.8	33.2	59.4	34.8	37.9	24.0	156.2	1957
1958	18.0	16.1	1.9	15.5	14.8	0.7	12.0	5.6	6.4	34.7	32.8	57.2	35.3	32.6	19.4	144.5	1958
1959	19.6	17.5	2.1	17.9	17.2	0.7	12.7	6.0	6.7	35.1	33.1	57.5	37.5	36.7	20.5	152.3	1959
1960	20.7	18.5	2.2	18.8	18.2	0.6	13.8	6.3	7.5	36.4	34.4	59.1	38.5	37.4	21.9	156.9	1960
1961	21.8	19.6	2.2	20.4	19.8	0.6	14.8	6.7	8.1	40.2	38.1	63.5	39.0	38.8	22.7	164.0	1961
1962	25.2	22.1	3.1	22.4	21.9	0.5	16.5	7.1	9.4	42.6	40.4	64.6	42.6	40.3	24.4	171.9	1962
1963	29.3	24.9	4.4	23.6	23.0	0.6	18.2	7.8	10.4	49.0	46.0	72.4	47.6	40.7	26.4	187.0	1963
1964	36.7	31.1	5.6	29.6	28.2	1.4	21.7	8.6	13.1	55.0	51.5	75.6	52.8	43.9	29.6	201.9	1964
1965	41.2	34.4	6.8	32.2	30.9	1.3	27.9	9.5	18.4	59.9	56.6	78.6	56.6	45.6	36.6	217.4	1965
1966	42.3	36.7	5.6	37.1	34.4	2.7	29.1	9.5	19.6	68.1	64.2	86.0	56.0	50.4	36.8	229.2	1966
1967	49.8	40.7	9.1	40.1	37.0	3.1	34.8	10.5	24.3	73.6	69.7	90.2	64.1	53.4	42.5	250.2	1967
1968	61.7	49.5	12.2	47.9	45.1	2.8	38.8	10.6	28.2	83.8	79.4	97.6	74.2	59.3	45.6	276.8	1968
1969	73.1	58.1	15.0	59.3	56.4	2.9	45.0	12.1	32.9	100.7	95.7	109.1	80.9	67.0	48.8	305.8	1969
1970	84.5	70.8	13.7	73.5	70.0	3.5	40.0	13.2	26.8	122.5	116.9	122.5	84.5	73.5	40.0	320.6	1970
1971	96.9	82.7	14.2	88.4	84.6	3.8	53.6	15.7	37.9	144.1	137.3	131.5	88.3	80.6	48.3	348.8	1971
1972	117.5	100.3	17.2	112.5	106.0	6.5	64.3	18.8	45.5	164.7	156.7	137.0	96.2	91.1	52.7	377.0	1972
1973	145.1	122.0	23.1	144.3	136.9	7.4	87.6	23.7	63.8	219.7	209.4	163.5	104.7	101.6	64.3	434.1	1973
1974	170.6	142.3	28.3	178.3	169.9	8.4	126.6	29.6	97.1	275.1	262.9	177.2	106.4	110.6	76.2	470.4	1974
1975	225.9	196.4	29.5	240.5	230.7	9.8	152.3	35.9	116.5	395.4	378.2	207.8	112.8	116.5	76.2	513.3	1975
1976	272.0	242.3	29.7	291.3	276.1	15.2	142.3	47.2	95.1	483.6	462.1	214.1	115.8	121.4	60.0	511.3	1976
1977	321.5	282.7	38.8	347.1	322.3	24.8	146.9	42.1	104.8	552.3	523.8	217.1	120.6	127.0	53.8	518.5	1977
1978	382.4	332.3	50.1	431.7	401.4	30.3	185.9	57.2	128.7	622.3	594.8	227.3	130.8	143.0	61.8	562.9	1978
1979	467.2	411.6	55.6	541.9	503.5	38.4	248.0	74.8	173.2	719.2	684.8	228.9	138.8	155.0	71.5	594.2	1979
1980	566.0	501.3	64.7	744.4	692.2	52.2	314.9	95.8	219.1	950.4	910.2	256.9	140.6	175.5	77.0	650.0	1980

Table 5 Expenditure on Income Maintenance Programmes

Year	at current prices (in thousand pounds)									at constant (1970) prices (in thousand pounds)									Year
	old age pensions	survivor pensions	sickness benefits	inval. pens.	occup. inj.	unempl. benef.	family benef.	public asst.	other	old age pensions	survivor pensions	sick. benef.	inval. pens.	occup. inj.	unempl. benef.	family benef.	public asst.	other	
1947	4 841	900	901			2 326	2 242	578	171	11 469	2 132	2 135			5 511	5 312	1 369	405	1947
1948	5 595	1 386	1 081			2 553	2 228	621	541	12 912	3 199	2 495			5 892	5 142	1 433	1 249	1948
1949	7 079	1 763	1 197			2 341	2 251	684	767	16 465	4 101	2 784			5 445	5 235	1 591	1 258	1949
1950	7 021	1 757	1 615			2 103	2 268	695	515	15 983	4 000	3 676			4 787	5 163	1 582	1 172	1950
1951	7 507	1 784	1 770			2 186	2 291	719	570	15 806	3 756	3 727			4 603	4 824	1 514	1 200	1951
1952	8 766	2 555	2 758			3 366	4 500	724	582	17 062	4 973	5 368			6 552	8 759	1 409	1 133	1952
1953	9 258	2 925	3 478			4 135	5 349	747	1 413	17 230	5 444	6 473			7 696	9 955	1 390	2 630	1953
1954	9 299	2 937	3 463			3 717	5 442	751	1 754	17 199	5 432	6 405			6 875	10 065	1 389	3 244	1954
1955	10 195	3 171	3 260			3 488	5 481	628	2 355	18 370	5 714	5 874			6 285	9 876	1 132	4 243	1955
1956	10 179	3 354	3 692			4 576	5 548	622	2 427	17 819	5 871	6 463			8 010	9 712	1 089	4 249	1956
1957	10 500	3 570	4 272			4 739	7 013	660	2 436	17 653	6 002	7 182			7 967	11 790	1 110	4 095	1957
1958	10 366	3 566	4 211			4 621	7 256	617	2 182	16 788	5 775	6 820			7 484	11 752	999	3 534	1958
1959	10 916	3 664	4 224			4 227	7 268	607	2 182	17 600	5 907	6 810			6 815	11 718	979	3 518	1959
1960	11 873	4 024	4 702			3 804	7 291	591	2 161	19 006	6 441	7 527			6 089	11 671	946	3 459	1960
1961	13 691	5 038	5 384			4 032	7 308	559	2 104	21 357	7 859	8 399			6 290	11 400	872	3 282	1961
1962	14 330	5 373	5 755			4 682	7 363	585	2 268	21 494	8 059	8 632			7 023	11 044	877	3 402	1962
1963	15 513	6 113	7 236			5 504	8 555	605	2 443	22 701	8 945	10 589			8 054	12 519	885	3 575	1963
1964	16 990	6 818	7 983			5 935	10 400	673	2 731	23 251	9 331	10 925			8 122	14 233	921	3 737	1964
1965	19 218	7 471	8 632			6 707	10 540	762	3 255	25 102	9 759	11 275			8 761	13 767	995	4 252	1965
1966	21 379	8 791	10 229			8 711	10 685	850	3 597	26 914	11 067	12 877			10 966	13 451	1 070	4 528	1966
1967	22 595	9 271	10 899		536	10 375	10 765	990	4 299	27 593	11 322	13 310		655	12 670	13 146	1 209	5 250	1967
1968	25 336	10 550	12 337		842	13 185	10 837	1 060	5 283	29 402	12 243	14 317		977	15 301	12 576	1 230	6 131	1968
1969	29 121	12 457	15 117		1 035	15 785	14 380	1 217	6 544	31 469	13 461	16 336		1 118	17 058	15 540	1 315	7 072	1969
1970	34 558	15 575	17 413	1 058	1 326	20 302	17 037	1 367	7 720	34 558	15 575	17 413	1 058	1 326	20 802	17 037	1 367	7 720	1970
1971	40 394	18 710	17 957	4 168	1 578	24 570	17 904	1 416	10 569	36 906	17 094	16 406	3 808	1 442	22 448	16 358	1 294	9 656	1971
1972	47 031	21 565	20 127	3 775	1 993	30 445	18 131	1 628	12 043	39 188	17 969	16 771	3 145	1 661	25 368	15 107	1 357	10 035	1972
1973	63 735	27 106	25 130	3 697	2 686	35 921	34 312	1 927	14 902	47 598	20 243	18 767	2 748	2 006	26 826	25 625	1 439	11 129	1973
1974	78 844	31 159	33 135	4 506	3 253	46 337	42 673	2 236	20 799	50 883	20 109	21 384	2 908	2 099	29 905	27 540	1 443	13 423	1974
1975	111 961	39 878	48 063	6 834	4 300	86 205	49 011	2 599	29 371	59 070	21 039	25 358	3 606	2 269	45 481	25 858	1 371	15 496	1975
1976	137 134	48 173	61 570	8 296	5 584	110 832	50 908	3 014	36 567	60 898	21 392	27 342	3 684	2 480	49 218	22 607	1 338	16 238	1976
1977	158 417	55 565	73 895	9 731	6 630	116 577	54 427	3 300	45 220	62 517	21 928	29 162	3 840	2 616	46 006	21 479	1 302	17 846	1977
1978	188 371	62 99	86 703	12 209	7 060	122 788	57 959	5 645	51 093	69 126	23 116	31 816	4 480	2 591	45 058	21 268	2 071	18 749	1978
1979	217 784	74 756	98 512	16 924	6 992	122 743	71 023	11 730	64 296	69 670	23 915	31 514	5 414	2 237	39 266	22 721	3 752	20 569	1979
1980	293 300	102 132	123 400	23 400	9 567	176 555	86 871	12 305	82 670	79 790	27 784	33 570	6 366	2 603	48 030	23 633	3 363	22 491	1980

Table 6

Financing

Year	Total receipts (in million pounds)	General government receipts, saving and net lending: Total receipts	Saving	Net lending	Direct taxes	Indirect taxes	Soc. sec contrib.	Other	Social security receipts: State	Employers	Insured	Other	Social insurance receipts: State	Employers	Insured	Year
		(as a percentage of GDP)			(as a percentage of total receipts)				(percent distribution)				(percent distribution)			
1950									70.1	22.3	6.2	1.7	30.8	33.8	27.7	1950
1951									69.8	22.6	6.0	1.7	30.9	33.8	27.9	1951
1952									71.2	22.0	5.6	1.5	29.7	33.8	28.4	1952
1953	123.6	24.9	0.9	-5.2	20.2	63.3	4.3	12.2	73.2	20.6	5.2	1.0	38.3	29.8	26.6	1953
1954	127.4	25.6	0.7	-4.7	20.8	62.5	4.2	12.5	73.0	20.4	5.5	1.1	25.3	33.7	30.0	1954
1955	132.9	25.5	0.7	-4.6	21.0	62.4	4.1	12.5	71.3	21.5	5.4	2.0	29.8	33.3	30.9	1955
1956	140.5	26.5	0.6	-4.9	19.3	65.0	4.1	11.6	72.4	21.3	5.1	1.0	37.4	31.3	26.3	1956
1957	146.2	26.7	1.5	-3.3	19.2	65.0	4.0	11.8	73.4	20.6	5.1	0.9	40.9	28.2	25.5	1957
1958	149.8	26.4	1.2	-2.5	18.5	65.2	3.9	12.4	73.7	20.3	4.9	1.1	40.4	29.4	24.8	1958
1959	155.6	25.6	1.0	-2.4	17.5	66.5	4.0	12.0	73.7	20.4	4.9	1.0	37.4	29.9	27.1	1959
1960	161.5	25.6	0.0	-3.4	21.1	62.3	4.3	12.3	72.8	21.2	5.0	1.0	38.5	30.3	26.2	1960
1961	179.7	26.4	-0.3	-4.2	21.6	61.0	5.8	11.6	72.0	21.7	5.3	1.1	36.2	31.0	28.7	1961
1962	190.4	25.9	-0.3	-4.5	23.5	59.1	5.9	11.5	67.5	23.9	7.5	1.0	39.0	29.6	27.6	1962
1963	212.9	26.9	0.3	-4.6	24.2	58.4	6.2	11.2	67.7	24.2	7.3	0.9	38.8	29.7	27.9	1963
1964	249.5	27.7	0.3	-5.0	24.5	59.2	6.0	10.3	66.7	24.3	7.9	1.0	37.5	30.0	28.5	1964
1965	276.2	28.7	0.3	-5.6	25.1	58.5	5.9	10.5	67.7	23.5	7.9	1.1	39.5	30.0	28.1	1965
1966	314.3	31.0	1.5	-3.8	25.2	58.2	6.2	10.4	68.8	22.7	7.7	0.7	40.1	29.5	28.0	1966
1967	350.4	31.7	1.5	-4.5	25.2	57.4	6.7	10.7	68.0	22.3	9.0	0.7	35.6	34.8	27.5	1967
1968	401.4	32.3	1.4	-5.4	25.1	56.7	7.3	10.9	66.8	23.5	8.8	0.7	32.2	36.0	28.3	1968
1969	471.5	32.9	1.3	-5.1	24.6	58.2	7.3	9.9	65.7	22.8	10.6	0.9	31.1	36.1	29.9	1969
1970	556.6	34.3	0.8	-5.4	26.2	56.5	7.5	9.7	67.3	19.8	12.3	0.8	32.6	35.5	29.8	1970
1971	658.2	35.5	1.2	-5.2	28.0	54.4	7.8	9.8	66.0	20.0	13.3	0.9	34.2	34.0	29.4	1971
1972	765.5	34.2	0.6	-5.2	26.9	54.1	8.2	10.8	65.4	19.8	14.0	0.8	31.1	35.9	30.8	1972
1973	911.4	33.7	0.0	-5.8	28.3	53.6	8.8	9.3	67.0	18.5	12.8	1.7	29.6	39.1	29.5	1973
1974	1 029.1	34.4	-2.4	-9.2	28.5	51.0	10.7	9.8	62.0	21.9	13.5	2.4	22.0	46.2	30.4	1974
1975	1 279.1	34.3	-7.2	-14.0	29.5	48.3	12.9	9.2	62.0	22.8	11.9	3.4	22.3	48.1	28.7	1975
1976	1 719.3	37.6	-4.0	-9.8	30.2	48.7	12.5	8.6	61.5	24.7	11.4	2.4	20.4	50.3	28.4	1976
1977	2 036.9	37.2	-3.6	-9.1	30.7	46.2	12.6	10.5	60.8	25.3	11.4	2.5	18.1	52.3	28.8	1977
1978	2 333.7	36.1	-5.3	-11.3	31.0	45.1	12.5	11.4	59.7	26.4	12.5	1.4	19.6	53.8	26.1	1978
1979	2 785.6	37.3	-6.7	-13.5	31.8	42.2	12.6	13.3	59.7	27.1	12.2	1.0	20.6	55.1	24.0	1979
1980	3 571.8	40.2	-7.0	-14.5	32.9	41.2	12.7	13.1	61.0	26.3	11.6	1.1	23.7	54.5	21.5	1980
1981													29.0	51.0	19.4	1981

Table 7 Demography and Insurance Coverage

Year	Total population	Labour force (in 1,000s)	Employees	Age groups 0–14	15–64	65+	0–19	60+	Number of insured persons: Total insured (in 1,000s)	Total insured as a percentage of labour force	Insured for all benefits as a percentage of labour force	Year
1950	2 969			858	1 794	317	1 095	439				1950
1951	2 961	1 262	708	855	1 790	316	1 096	438				1951
1952	2 953	1 254		860	1 772	315	1 100	440				1952
1953	2 949	1 231		866	1 755	314	1 106	443	724	58.8	51.7	1953
1954	2 941	1 228		871	1 737	314	1 110	445	728	59.3	52.0	1954
1955	2 921	1 208		876	1 721	313	1 109	444	726	60.1	52.9	1955
1956	2 898	1 188		882	1 704	312	1 108	444	733	61.7	54.5	1956
1957	2 885	1 162		875	1 700	310	1 110	445	721	62.1	54.9	1957
1958	2 853	1 141		869	1 676	308	1 104	443	702	61.6	56.4	1958
1959	2 864	1 129		866	1 671	309	1 108	445	707	62.6	54.8	1959
1960	2 832	1 118		864	1 660	309	1 110	445	710	63.6	55.9	1960
1961	2 818	1 108	650	877	1 626	315	1 111	446	713	64.3	56.8	1961
1962	2 825	1 114		878	1 631	316	1 120	446	712	63.9	56.9	1962
1963	2 843	1 122		882	1 642	319	1 133	447	719	64.1	57.1	1963
1964	2 863	1 124		888	1 653	322	1 143	448	731	65.0	58.4	1964
1965	2 876	1 120		893	1 665	318	1 152	448	744	66.4	59.9	1965
1966	2 884	1 118	702	900	1 661	323	1 160	447	774	69.2	61.6	1966
1967	2 900	1 116		905	1 670	324	1 166	450	771	69.1	63.7	1967
1968	2 913	1 123		909	1 678	325	1 172	452	781	69.6	63.6	1968
1969	2 926	1 122		913	1 686	326	1 177	455	795	70.9	64.9	1969
1970	2 950	1 118		921	1 700	329	1 187	459	796	71.2	65.3	1970
1971	2 978	1 120	737	931	1 717	330	1 199	464	808	72.2	65.5	1971
1972	3 024	1 121		943	1 748	334	1 216	468	818	73.0	66.0	1972
1973	3 072	1 123		956	1 780	338	1 235	473	816	72.6	66.2	1973
1974	3 123	1 131		969	1 813	342	1 254	478	853	75.5	67.3	1974
1975	3 176	1 146		983	1 849	346	1 275	483	969	84.6	72.6	1975
1976	3 228	1 154		995	1 882	350	1 294	487	971	84.1	71.6	1976
1977	3 272	1 172		1 006	1 912	354	1 310	491	975	83.2	70.1	1977
1978	3 314	1 195		1 016	1 941	357	1 326	494	982	82.2	68.6	1978
1979	3 368	1 233	855	1 030	1 977	361	1 347	499	986	80.0	66.5	1979
1980	3 401	1 247		1 034	2 003	364	1 358	503	1 034	82.9	69.3	1980
1981	3 443	1 272	877	1 044	2 030	369	1 370	508	1 129	88.8	74.2	1981

Table 8 Welfare Clienteles: Pensioners (in 1,000)

Year	Social insurance system					Social assistance			Total	Year
	Old Age	Retirement	Survivors	Invalidity	Disablement	Old Age	Blind	Survivors		
1950			16.6			154.3	5.9	28.0	204.8	1950
1951			17.6			150.7	5.9	27.8	202.8	1951
1952			18.5			154.3	6.0	28.0	206.8	1952
1953			18.7			158.7	6.0	28.4	211.8	1953
1954			19.3			160.7	6.3	28.9	215.2	1954
1955			20.0			159.7	6.4	29.1	215.2	1955
1956			20.6			158.1	7.2	28.3	214.2	1956
1957			21.4			158.2	7.3	27.7	214.6	1957
1958			22.1			156.7	7.3	26.8	212.9	1958
1959			22.7			154.2	7.2	25.8	209.9	1959
1960			23.3			153.3	7.0	24.9	208.5	1960
1961	29.1		33.3			117.9	6.7	24.1	211.1	1961
1962	34.8		35.2			111.7	6.4	23.7	211.9	1962
1963	36.5		36.6			115.9		23.3	212.3	1963
1964	37.9		38.3			114.5		22.8	213.6	1964
1965	39.6		40.7			112.2		22.5	214.9	1965
1966	40.6		42.5			112.6		22.2	217.9	1966
1967	42.0		44.9			112.0		21.0	219.8	1967
1968	43.1		47.7		0.2	112.2		20.0	223.8	1968
1969	44.1		50.4		0.7	113.1		18.9	227.5	1969
1970	45.5		51.3		1.3	112.9		17.4	228.0	1970
1971	46.5	3.5	53.8	11.6	1.9	113.6		17.0	249.0	1971
1972	47.5	4.5	55.7	12.2	2.2	110.0		16.2	248.4	1972
1973	48.4	13.0	57.8	8.2	2.9	106.5		15.9	252.7	1973
1974	52.3	19.7	60.2	9.2	3.6	121.8		13.9	280.7	1974
1975	54.7	21.9	61.6	10.0	5.0	131.5		12.8	297.6	1975
1976	55.2	25.8	63.7	10.2	4.8	129.5		12.8	302.0	1976
1977	59.7	28.1	64.6	10.6	4.7	135.7		10.8	314.2	1977
1978	61.8	29.6	66.4	14.1	4.7	133.7		10.1	320.4	1978
1979	63.4	30.8	68.9	14.3	4.6	132.2		10.6	324.9	1979
1980	65.4	32.0	70.9	16.9	4.8	130.1		11.4	331.4	1980
1981	68.0	31.5	72.7	18.7	5.0	129.3		12.4	337.6	1981
1982	70.0	31.6	74.5	20.4	5.4	129.5		13.4	344.8	1982

Table 9

Other Welfare Clienteles (in 1,000)

Year	Child allowances children	Child allowances families	Deserted wives insur. benef.	Deserted wives assist. benef.	Allowances for unmarried mothers	Allowances for prisoners' wives	Public assist./ supplementary welfare allow.	Unemployment insur. benef.	Unemployment assist. benef.	Unemployment smallholders assist.	Sickness cash benefit	Maternity allow	Occupational injury	Year
1950	342.8	146.3					28.2	16.5	35.5		91.4			1950
1951	345.7	147.3					28.0	18.0	31.5		97.8			1951
1952	563.7	215.6					27.5	30.1	32.7		93.2			1952
1953	572.6	218.5					24.4	36.9	28.4		116.2	2.3		1953
1954	576.3	223.4					24.6	32.9	25.7		116.6	2.4		1954
1955	581.2	226.3					21.9	30.7	22.5		113.8	2.5		1955
1956	586.9	226.7					20.5	39.4	24.4		112.2	2.9		1956
1957	588.4	227.3					21.3	36.5	27.4		122.8	2.8		1957
1958	590.5	227.1					21.1	34.1	26.4		115.1	2.7		1958
1959	601.5	226.9					20.3	31.8	23.5		111.3	2.9		1959
1960	605.4	227.0					19.3	27.1	19.0		128.9	3.1		1960
1961	601.0	225.0					16.6	26.0	16.4		126.7	3.5		1961
1962	603.9	225.7					16.3	27.4	16.6		123.6	3.7		1962
1963	604.2	225.8					15.9	27.2	17.0		123.2	3.9		1963
1964	902.0	302.8					15.1	27.2	16.3		132.4	4.1		1964
1965	927.0	310.1					14.9	28.2	17.8		150.5	4.5		1965
1966	942.3	316.7					15.0	31.5	14.1	7.0	144.3	5.1		1966
1967	950.9	322.4					13.0	31.6	20.5	12.7	147.4	5.8	8.4	1967
1968	965.5	327.5					16.6	35.9	19.2	13.3	166.8	6.5	10.7	1968
1969	969.4	329.3					16.7	34.4	20.1	14.9	190.0	7.0	10.4	1969
1970	979.7	336.2					16.3	38.8	23.5	17.4	177.2	8.4	9.8	1970
1971	990.5	342.0		1.3			16.0	38.8	21.2	17.6	177.3	9.2	10.3	1971
1972	1015.2	353.1		1.7				39.1	28.4	19.9	191.9	10.1	9.8	1972
1973	1012.8	358.7		2.1				33.3	29.4	21.6	199.1	11.1	10.9	1973
1974	1113.1	381.9	1.1	2.6	2.2	0.1	14.4	36.7	30.7	24.2	175.8	10.8	8.5	1974
1975	1144.3	394.1	1.4	2.9	2.8	0.1		59.4	39.0	29.2	235.1	15.6	12.9	1975
1976	1152.6	402.2	1.7	3.1	3.3	0.1	16.4	60.0	47.4	29.2	306.8	17.2	10.4	1976
1977	1181.4	411.4	2.0	3.2	3.8	0.1	14.1	54.9	49.9	26.7	309.5	17.2	11.4	1977
1978	1196.6	420.6	2.2	3.0	4.0	0.1	14.8	48.0	48.7	24.6	341.9	17.3	11.3	1978
1979	1200.5	430.6	2.5	2.9	4.6	0.2	16.9	42.0	46.2	22.4	305.6	16.9	8.8	1979
1980	1179.4	427.5	2.9	2.9	5.3	0.2	17.4	50.7	46.4	20.9	309.4	18.5	12.1	1980
1981	1200.0	436.0	3.1	3.1	6.2	0.1	16.6	67.0	56.4		297.7	20.1	11.3	1981
1982	1190.1	443.8	3.4	3.3	7.6	0.2	17.4	77.5	73.6		281.2	19.9	11.5	1982

Table 10 General Elections

Year	Fianna Fail	Fine Gael	Labour	Other Parties	Independent Candidates	Year
			Percent distribution of votes			
1944	48.9	20.5	8.8	13.5	8.4	1944
1948	41.9	19.8	8.7	21.1	8.5	1948
1951	46.3	25.7	11.4	7.0	9.6	1951
1954	43.4	32.0	12.1	6.9	5.7	1954
1957	48.3	26.6	9.1	9.4	6.6	1957
1961	43.8	32.0	11.6	6.7	5.9	1961
1965	47.7	34.1	15.4	0.7	2.1	1965
1969	45.7	34.1	17.0	-	3.2	1969
1973	46.2	35.1	13.7	2.0	3.0	1973
1977	50.6	30.5	11.6	1.7	5.6	1977
1981	45.3	36.5	9.9	4.2	4.2	1981
1982 (Feb.)	47.3	37.3	9.1	3.3	3.0	1982
1982 (Nov.)	45.2	39.2	9.4	3.3	3.0	1982
			Percent distribution of seats			
1944	54.5	21.6	6.0	11.2	6.7	1944
1948	45.9	21.2	9.6	15.0	8.2	1948
1951	46.6	27.4	11.0	5.5	9.6	1951
1954	44.5	34.2	12.3	5.5	3.4	1954
1957	53.4	27.4	7.5	5.5	6.2	1957
1961	48.9	32.9	10.5	3.5	4.2	1961
1965	50.3	32.9	14.7	0.7	1.4	1965
1969	51.7	35.0	12.6	-	0.7	1969
1973	47.6	37.8	13.3	0.0	1.4	1973
1977	57.1	29.3	10.9	0.0	2.7	1977
1981	47.0	39.2	9.0	1.8	3.0	1981
1982 (Feb.)	48.8	38.0	9.0	1.8	2.4	1982
1982 (Nov.)	45.2	42.2	9.6	1.2	1.8	1982

Notes to and sources for appendix tables

Table 1

In the absence of a continuous time series at constant prices, data for the period 1971-80 have been converted from 1975 prices to 1970 prices by a chaining procedure.

The GDP series is broken in 1960 by the change from the former Standardised System of National Accounting to the new System of National Accounting. Data for 1960 are shown for both systems.

Public expenditure includes final consumption expenditure of public authorities, current subsidies and transfers, national debt interest, gross capital transfers, gross physical capital formation and capital payments to the rest of the world.

Public expenditure has been deflated as follows to obtain a series at constant prices: Final consumption by the implicit deflator for public final consumption expenditure; current subsidies and transfers by the implicit deflator for private consumption expenditure; all capital items by the implicit deflator for gross physical capital formation of public authorities.

Sources: (1), (2), Table A1.5 (data used by kind permission of Mrs. Finola Kennedy).

Table 2

Data on the expenditure of public authorities by purpose are only available for the period since 1963. The series is broken in 1976 due to the introduction of a new accounting system. Data for 1976 are shown according to both the old and new systems. The total for public expenditure in this series differs from that shown in Appendix Table 1 because gross current expenditure of public authorities on goods and services has been included instead of public consumption expenditure. It is not possible to obtain a figure for public consumption expenditure by purpose.

The total for public expenditure shown in the breakdown by level of government differs from that shown in Appendix Table 1 because gross current expenditure of public authorities on goods and services has been included instead of public consumption expenditure.

The total for public expenditure by level of government differs from the total for public expenditure by purpose because the two series were revised at different times in the period up to 1976.

Social insurance includes expenditure from the social insurance fund, the occupational injuries fund, payments under the Intermittent Unemployment Scheme and redundancy payments.

Sources: (2), Table A1.5, (3), (4).

Table 3

Social expenditure includes expenditure on health, education, housing and social security and welfare (mainly income maintenance) as defined in the national accounts.

Sources: (2), Table A1.1, (3).

Table 4

Social expenditure at constant prices has been deflated as follows: current transfers by the implicit deflator for private consumption expenditure; current expenditure on goods and services by the implicit deflator for public final consumption; capital expenditure by the implicit deflator for gross physical capital formation of public authorities.

Sources: as for Table 3.

Table 5

Old age pensions include the contributory and non-contributory old age pensions and the retirement pension.

Survivors pensions include the contributory and non-contributory widows' and orphans' pensions, the death grant and the death benefit paid under the occupational injuries scheme.

Sickness benefits include disability benefit, the portion of earnings-related benefit paid to recipients of disability benefit and medical treatment benefit.

Occupational injury benefits include all benefits paid under the occupational injury scheme except the death benefit.

Unemployment benefits include unemployment insurance, unemployment assistance, redundancy benefits, intermittent unemployment benefit and earnings-related benefit paid to recipients of unemployment benefit.

Family benefits include child allowances, maternity benefits and unmarried mother's allowance.

The category 'other' includes deserted wives' benefits, benefits in kind for pensioners, old age care allowances, rehabilitation of disabled persons, grants to voluntary agencies, domiciliary care for handicapped children and the item 'other social payments' shown in the details of transfer payments in the national accounts. This item includes maintenance of persons suffering from infectious diseases, welfare payments to the blind, payments to foster parents, maternity grants, milk for needy mothers and children, bounties for triplets and centenarians, welfare services, pensions for seamen and veterans of the 1916 Insurrection, funeral grants, pilot schemes to combat poverty, payments in respect of disabilities caused by Thalidomide, courses in child care and grants to voluntary agencies.

Source: (3).

Table 6

General government receipts include taxes on income, expenditure and capital, social security contributions, net trading and investment income, current transfers from the rest of the world, capital transfers from the rest of the world and 'other capital receipts'.

Saving is equivalent to the difference between net current receipts and net current expenditure of public authorities.

Net lending is equivalent to the excess of total receipts over total expenditure of public authorities.

The category 'other' within general government receipts includes net trading and investment income, current and capital transfers from the rest of the world, capital taxes and 'other capital receipts'.

Social security receipts include receipts under the social insurance and social assistance schemes, the child allowance scheme, schemes for public employees and public health services.

Social insurance receipts include receipts under the unified social insurance system, the occupational injuries scheme and the intermittent unemployment scheme.

Sources: (3), (5), (6), p. 506.

Table 7

Sources: (4), (6), pp. 506-507, (7), (8), (9).

Table 8

Old age, invalidity, retirement, disablement and blind pensioners - the numbers of recipients refer to the number on 31 March for the years up to 1973 and the number on 31 December for the years from 1974 onwards; Survivor pensioners - number on 31 December 1950-52, number on 31 March 1953-1973, number on 31 December from 1974 onwards.

Sources: (4), (10).

Table 9

Child allowance - number of recipients on 31 December 1950-52, number on 31 March 1953-1973, number on 31 December from 1974 onwards; Deserted wives' benefits, unmarried mother's allowance, prisoner's wife's allowance, public assistance/supplementary welfare allowance - number of recipients on 31 March up to 1973, number on 31 December from 1974; Unemployment benefits - average weekly number of recipients during year ended 31 December 1950-52, average weekly number of recipients in year ended 31 March 1953/54 to 1973/74, average number of recipients in year ended 31 December 1974-1980, average monthly number of recipients in year ended 31 December 1980-82. Sickness benefit, Maternity allowances - total number of recipients in year ended 31 December 1950-53, total number of recipients in year ended 31 March 1954/55 to 1973/74, total number of recipients 1 April to 31 December 1974, total number of recipients in year ended 31 December 1975 onwards; Occupational injury benefit - number of claims allowed in year ended 31 March 1967/68 to 1973/74, number of claims allowed 1 April 1974 to 31 December 1974, number of claims allowed in year ended 31 December 1975 onwards.

Sources: as for Table 8.

Table 10

Sources: (11), (12).

Enumerated sources for appendix tables

(1) OECD, *National Account Statistics, Vol. 1: Aggregates 1950-1979.* Paris, 1981.

(2) Finola Kennedy, *The Growth and Allocation of Public Social Expenditure in Ireland Since 1947*, unpublished Ph.D. thesis, University College, Dublin, 1971.

(3) Central Statistics Office, *National Income and Expenditure*, various years. Dublin, Stationery Office.

(4) *Report of the Department of Social Welfare*, various years. Dublin, Stationery Office.

(5) International Labour Office, *The Cost of Social Security* 1949-57 to 1978-80. Geneva, ILO, 1961 to 1985 (triennial);

(6) Peter Flora et al., *State, Economy and Society in Western Europe 1815-1975*, Vol. 1. Frankfurt and London, Campus and Macmillan, 1983.

(7) *Census of Population of Ireland*, various years. Dublin, Stationery Office.

(8) Central Statistics Office, *The Trend of Employment and Unemployment*, various years. Dublin, Stationery Office.

(9) OECD, *Labour Force Statistics*, various years. Paris.

(10) Central Statistics Office, *Statistical Abstract of Ireland*, various years. Dublin, Stationery Office.

(11) Cornelius O'Leary, *Irish Elections 1918-1977.* Dublin, Gill and Macmillan, 1979.

(12) Michael Gallagher, *Political Parties in the Republic of Ireland.* Manchester, Manchester University Press, 1985.

Italy

Maurizio Ferrera

Institutional Synopsis

Contents

Glossary of abbreviations

CCML *Commissione Centrale per la Mobilità del Lavoro* (Central Commission for Labour Mobility)
CER *Comitato per l'Edilizia Residenziale* (Residential Housing Committee)
CIGA *Cassa per l'Integrazione dei Salari dei Dipendenti* Agricultural Workers)
CIGI *Cassa Integrazione Guadagni per l'Industria* (Earnings Replacement Fund for the Industrial Sector)
ECA *Enti Communali di Assistenza* (Local Authority Assistance Agencies)
ENAOLI *Ente Nazionale per l'Assistenza agli Orfani dei Lavoratori Italiani* (National Institute for the Assistance of the Orphans of Italian Workers)
FNAO *Fondo Nazionale per l'Assistenza Ospedaliers* (National Fund for Hospital Assistance)
FRRI *Fondo per la Ristrutturazione e Riconversione Industriale* (Fund for Industrial Reconstruction and conversion)
GesCaL *Gestione Case per i Lavoratori* (Management of Workers' Housing)
INA *Istituto Nazionale delle Assicurazioni* (National Insurance Institute)
INAIL *Istituto Nazionale per l'Assicurazione contro gli Infortuni sul Lavoro* (National Institute for Insurance against Work Accidents)
INAM *Istituto Nazionale per l'Assicurazione contro le Malattie* (National Institute for Sickness Insurance)
INPS *Istituto Nazionale della Previdenza Sociale* (National Institute for Social Security)
IPAB *Istituzioni Pubbliche di Assistenza e Beneficienza* (Public Institutions for Assistance and Charity)
ONPI *Opera Nazionale per i Pensionati* (National Institute for Italian Pensioners)
SSN *Servizio Sanitario Nazionale* (National Health Service)

Introduction

The following synopsis describes the structure and regulations of the main schemes, programmes and policies of the Italian welfare state. The presentation tries to follow the existing institutional dimensions as closely as possible, and is subdivided into eight sections: pensions, health insurance and the National Health Service, occupational injuries, unemployment insurance, family allowances, social services and public assistance, housing and education.

The quantitative information contained in the expenditure tables does not coincide with data used in the country chapter and reported elsewhere in this appendix for occupational injuries, unemployment insurance, social services and public assistance, and education. A different source has in fact been used in order to offer more detailed break-downs.

I Pensions

In 1979 total pension expenditure amounted to 29,131 billion lire or approximately 10.8% of GDP. The following table gives the expenditure structure by type of pension.

Pension expenditure in 1979 by type of pension (billion lire)

	Total	%
INPS schemes:		
- Old age pensions	9 803	33.6
- Invalidity pensions	8 057	27.7
- Survivors' pensions	3 402	11.7
- Social Pensions	609	2.1
Other Schemes:		
- All pensions	706	2.4
Government employees:		
- All pensions	6 554	22.5
Total	29 131	100.0

Coverage

The Italian pension system provides for old age, disablement and survivors' benefits. The system is divided into a number of occupational schemes, the majority of which are public (only the banking sector has a few private schemes); other private schemes only provide additional benefits. There are four types of public scheme:

(1) a general scheme for dependent workers (blue-collar since 1919 and white-collar since 1939);
(2) schemes for the self-employed (small farmers, sharecroppers and tenant farmers since 1957; artisans since 1959 and small traders since 1966);
(3) schemes for civil servants, most of which date back to the nineteenth century;
(4) schemes for special occupational categories such as the telephone service, electricity board, air crews, miners, the professions etc.; some of these schemes complement the general scheme.

The economically active (dependent and self-employed) are covered by one or more schemes, and the unemployed in receipt of insurance benefits are also eligible for pension rights. In 1963 a special voluntary scheme was introduced to provide benefits for housewives, and in 1969 another special scheme was introduced to provide a social pension (*pensione sociale*) for old people with low incomes who are not eligible for benefits under any other scheme.

In 1979 the insured population amounted to around 22,549,000 i.e. some 40% of total population, of which 12,300,000 were covered by the general scheme for dependent workers, 5,552,000 by the various schemes for the self-employed, 3,340,000 by civil servants' schemes and 1,357,000 by other special schemes.

Benefits

The pension system has two aims: to maintain a sizeable proportion of the pensioner's previous earnings and to provide all old people with at least some sort of subsistence income. The first aim is attained by means of earnings-related pensions, and the second by means of pensions minima and social pensions.

The benefit structure and level vary a great deal from scheme to scheme. For old age pensions, dependent workers insured under the general scheme receive a pension which amounts to 80% of previous earnings up to a certain ceiling, after 40 years of contributions (or at the age of 55 for women and 60 for men). The self-employed are not entitled to earnings-related pensions. Instead, their pensions are based on the actuarial revaluation of their contributions. No pension, however, can be lower than a certain minimum. The age requirement is 65 for men and 60 for women, and the minimum contribution period is 15 years.

Civil servants enjoy earnings-related pensions, with a replacement rate of 80% after 40 years of service; this rate may reach 100% for certain categories. Civil servants must retire at 65, but a pension may be claimed, regardless of age, after 20 years service, and in some cases after only 15 years service.

For disablement, all schemes provide an earnings-related pension equal to 2% of previous earnings multiplied by the number of contribution years (minimum contribution period is five years). No pension can be lower than a given legal minimum.

Survivors' pensions are granted to widows, invalid widowers, children up to the age of 18, (26 if students) and siblings. Their level ranges from 60% to 100% (depending on the number and type of survivors) of the pension to which the deceased member would have been entitled (minimum contribution period is five years). Legal minima also govern survivors' pensions.

All pensions have been indexed to the cost of living since 1969, and have been linked to the minimum contractual industrial wage since 1976.

Financing

The general scheme is financed through earnings-related contributions paid by employers (two-thirds), and employees (one-third). Together these amount to approximately 24% of earnings.

The self-employed pay a flat-rate annual contribution, whereas civil servants pay an earnings-related contribution of around 7% (the employer, in this case the state, does not pay any contribution). Financing conditions are more varied for the special schemes. The state covers any deficit with special contributions which are particularly heavy in the case of schemes for the self-employed.

Since 1969, the funding system for the general scheme has been replaced by the pay-as-you-go system.

Administration

The main administrative agency of the Italian pension insurance system is the National Institute for Social Security (*Istituto Nazionale della Previdenza Sociale*, INPS), which pays more than 90% of all pensions (excluding civil servants). This agency is governed by a board which includes eighteen representatives of the workers' trade unions, nine employers' representatives, nine representatives of the self-employed and three state officials; the board is renewed every fourth year. Since 1969 the administration of INPS has been gradually decentralized. The Institute is subdivided into 18 separate funds and administrations, corresponding to the various schemes (not all for pensions). In addition to INPS, there are a number of smaller agencies which administer special schemes.

Core laws

18.1.1945 (no. 39)
Introduced survivors' pensions within the INPS general scheme, based on previous contributions and insurance years.

1.3.1945 (no. 177)
Established a Social Insurance Supplementation Fund (*Fondo d'Integrazione delle Assicurazioni Sociali*) within INPS, in order to pay supplements to lower pensions; financed by special pay-as-you-go contributions from employers and employees.

29.7.1947 (no. 689)
Established Fund for Social Solidarity (*Fondo di Solidarieta Sociale*) within INPS, in order to pay graduated supplementary allowances to all pensions, compensating for inflation; same financing regulations as above (law no. 177/1945).

28.7.1950 (no. 633)
Extended compulsory pension insurance to employees earning over Lit. 1,500 per month or approximately 6% of the average gross industrial wage for 1950; formerly, social insurance was compulsory only for employees earning less than this amount.

4.4.1952 (no. 218)
First postwar reorganization of pension system, with a thorough redefinition of contributions and benefits; contributions are two-tiered and consist of a basic flat-rate contribution for broad earnings brackets and supplementary earnings-related contribution of 9% with no income ceiling; benefits composed of contribution-based pension together with a supplement which compensates for inflation, takes family dependents into account, and eventually raises the total pension to a legally established (and eventually ad hoc adjusted) minimum.

26.10.1957 (no. 1047)
Extended compulsory pension insurance to small farmers, sharecroppers and tenant farmers; flat-rate annual contributions subject to ad hoc increases; benefits based on revalued contributions, but upgraded, if necessary, to a minimum amount (approx. 50-65% of the minimum for the general scheme); insurance administered by special fund within INPS; minimum contribution required set at 15 years for old age and five years for disablement and survivors' benefits; however, as a result of a special state contribution, the fund started to grant benefits to those meeting the age requirement (65 for men and 60 for women) one year after its establishment, thus blanketing-in the first generation of pensioners.

15.2.1958 (no. 46)
Regulations covering civil servants' pensions; pension age set at 65; minimum period of 15 years service required for a pension; earnings-replacement rate 35% after 15 years of service, plus 1.8% for each additional year up to maximum of 20 years.

13.3.1958 (no. 250)
Extended pension insurance to fishermen.

17.5.1959 (no. 324)
Introduced special additional indemnity (*indennità integrativa speciale*) for retired civil servants; a monthly supplement, indexed to cost of living.

4.7.1959 (no. 463)
Extended pension insurance to artisans, with same regulations applying for farmers but with higher flat-rate contributions.

12.8.1962 (no. 1338)
Introduced supplementary pension payment (*tredicesima mensilità*), equal to one-twelfth of annual amount of pension minima, payable in December; introduced child supplements for pensioners; established commission to draft reform plan of pension system.

5.3.1963 (no. 389)
Introduced voluntary insurance scheme for housewives.

21.7.1965 (no. 903)
New pension provisions under general scheme, in anticipation of a broader reform of entire pension system;
- legal minima raised;
- all current pensions revalued;
- introduction of seniority pensions (*pensioni d'anzianità*); after 35 years of contributions workers can retire even before attaining pensionable age;
- establishment, within INPS, of a Social Fund (*Fondo Sociale*), paying all INPS pensioners a basic uniform pension largely financed by state, the social pension (not to be confused with the later social pension introduced in 1968).

22.7.1966 (no. 613)
Extended pension insurance to small traders, with same regulations as for artisans (cf. law no. 463/1959).

18.3.1968 (no. 238) and 27.4.1968 (no. 488)
Introduced principle of earnings-related pensions within the general scheme; pension formula to equal 1.626% of average earnings in the last three work years multiplied by the number of contribution years (maximum pension: 65% of previous earnings) up to 40.

30.4.1969 (no. 153)
Broad provisions covering pensions under the general scheme;
- multiplying coefficient raised to 1.85%, applied to average earnings of the best three years in last five years of work (maximum pension, after 40 years of contribution: 74% of previous earnings); government to subsequently raise coefficient to 2% by 1975;
- introduction of social pension (*pensione sociale*) for people over 65 with low incomes and not eligible for any type of pension, financed by the state through the Social Fund of INPS;
- introduction of cost of living indexing for all pensions (excluding social pensions), effective from 1971;
- funding system for general scheme replaced by pay-as-you-go system;
- government committed to link pensions to industrial wage by 1975.

30.6.1973 (no. 267)
Cost of living indexing extended to social pension; effective from 1.1.1973.

29.12.1973 (no. 1092)
Regulations covering civil servants' pensions grouped under a single, coherent piece of legislation.

2.3.1974 (no. 30)
Legal minimum for pensions increased to 27.75% of average industrial wage for 1973.

3.6.1975 (no. 160)
Enactment of benefit improvements promised by government in 1969:

- multiplying coefficient raised to 2% and applied to average earnings of the best three years in the last ten years of work;
- automatic annual adjustment of minimum pensions to increase of the minimum contractual wage in the industrial sector (smaller adjustment made for pensions higher than minima);
- government committed to gradual equalizing of minima across schemes.

31.8.1975 (no. 364)
Special additional indemnity for civil servants (see law no. 324/1959) indexed to the cost of living twice yearly instead of once a year; effective from 1976.

29.4.1976 (no. 177)
Pension linkage to the industrial wage extended to civil servants; rate of earnings-related contributions raised.

23.11.1977 (no. 942)
Pension linkage to the industrial wage extended to all other pension schemes not administered by INPS.

21.12.1978 (no. 843)
introduced minor restrictions on cost of living indexing; indexation not applicable where the beneficiary is still active; in cases involving more than one pension, only one is indexed.

29.2.1980 (no. 33)
Pensions indexed to the cost of living twice yearly instead of once a year.

30.3.1981 (no. 119)
Pensions indexed to the cost of living three times a year instead of twice a year.

26.2.1982 (no. 54)
Substantial increases of contributions for the self-employed.

29.5.1982 (no. 297)
Pensions indexed four times a year (same as for wages) instead of three times. Improvement of the pension formula: pensionable earnings raised to one-fifth of the total amount of earnings in the last 260 weeks of work, revalued according to the cost of living index. Indexation of pension ceiling.

25.3.1983
Restriction of special rights for female public employees: pension payments begin at the completion of 20 years' service, even where entitlement would have originally been prior to this.

10.1.1983 (no. 638)
Restriction of minimum pension regulations: where beneficiaries' income equals three times the minimum benefit, pensions lower than the minimum not raised automatically.

II Health insurance and national health service

In 1979 total expenditure on health assistance (in kind and in services) amounted to 16,800 billion lire or 6.2% of GDP, and was structured as follows:

Health expenditure in 1979 (billion lire)

	Total	%
Hospital assistance	7 585	45.1
Pharmaceutical assistance	1 860	11.1
Medical assistance	1 975	11.7
Prevention sanitation	505	3.0
Other services	1 563	9.3
Administration	993	5.9
Other	2 319	13.8
Total	16 800	100.0

Coverage

The health insurance/public health system covers the risks of sickness and maternity, providing both cash benefits and direct medical and hospital assistance.

Until 1979, there were three main types of scheme:

(1) a general scheme insuring all dependent workers in the private sector and their dependents (since 1943);

(2) a number of special schemes for public employees, for the self-employed and for special occupational categories (e.g. journalists, actors, business executives etc.) and their dependents (mostly founded between the wars);

(3) a special scheme insuring against tuberculosis (since 1927).

These schemes provided cash benefits and direct assistance by means of contracts with doctors, hospitals, pharmacies etc. In 1980 the National Health Service (*Servizio Sanitario Nazionale*, SSN) was introduced, with a single general scheme covering all citizens, and replacing all previous schemes (except for the tuberculosis scheme). The SSN provides all benefits in kind; cash benefits (sickness and maternity cash benefits) are now paid by INPS for all workers with the exception of public employees, who are paid directly by the state. In 1977 the insured population amounted to 52,935,000, or approximately 93% of the resident population. Since 1980 the system covers, by definition, the entire population.

Benefits

Until 1979 the various schemes provided benefits in cash and kind according to a variety of regulations. The general scheme provided:

(1) cash benefits (*prestazioni economiche*) including a daily sickness indemnity (*indennità giornaliera di malattia*) equal to 50% of earnings for the first 20 days and 66.66% thereafter, with a waiting period of four days; in practice, contractual regulations granted and still grant wage continuation, paid directly by employers, to all dependent workers in the case of sickness with no waiting period; a maternity indemnity (*indennità di maternità*), equal to 80% of earnings for five months; and a funeral allowance (*assegno funerario*), equal to a flat-rate sum.

(2) health benefits (*prestazioni sanitarie*) including general and specialized medical assistance, provided by doctors under contract to the insurance scheme; medicine, provided free of charge by pharmacies and reimbursed by the scheme; hospital assistance, provided by public hospitals or clinics, under contract to the insurance scheme; and special assistance, including rehabilitation measures, appliances etc.

Since 1980 the SSN has taken over the provision of all benefits in kind offered free of charge (or with a small fee) to all citizens. All special regulations covering the various schemes have been abolished. Cash benefits (*prestazioni economiche*) are paid directly by the employer and subsequently reimbursed by INPS.

Financing

Until 1979 the various insurance schemes raised funds by contributions from employers and employees. Contribution rates varied across industrial sectors and occupational categories, ranging from a flat-rate sum for agriculture, to some 14% of earnings in the industrial sector (0.3% of which were paid by employees). Other funds were contributed by the state and by INPS (these being transfers from the tuberculosis fund).

The establishment of the SSN has substantially modified the system of financing. On the one hand, employers and employees still pay contributions; with the liquidation of older schemes and funds, all contributions are now collected by INPS, at least provisionally. On the other hand, a special National Health Fund (*Fondo Sanitario Nazionale*, FSN) has been set up within the Ministry of Health, centralizing all resources for direct health care (benefits in kind). The FSN then allocates these resources to the various regions. Financial resources come from older liquidated funds, the state, surpluses from public hospitals or the TB insurance scheme; INPS also transfer some funds to the FSN.

Although the financial regulations under the new system are still mixed and fluid, they are evolving towards a dual system of financing through general revenues (for benefits in kind) and contributions (for benefits in cash).

Administration

Until 1979 administration was fragmented, being dispersed among a number of separate funds and agencies. The largest and most important of these was the National Institute for Sickness Insurance (*Istituto Nazionale per l'Assicurazione contro le Malattie*, INAM), which operated the general scheme for dependent workers and their dependents. INAM was governed by a board composed of employer and employee representatives, state officials, doctors and representatives of other social security agencies.

Since 1980 all funds and agencies, including INAM, have been liquidated. Cash benefits are now administered by INPS, and benefits in kind are administered by the SSN.

The administrative structure of the SSN is decentralized. At the central level, it is coordinated by the Ministry of Health, in collaboration with a National Health Council (*Consiglio Sanitario Nazionale*) comprising representatives from the regions, various ministries, a number of experts and the Higher Institute for Health (*Istituto Superiore della Sanità*), a technical research centre. The Ministry lays down the guidelines of the National Health Plan (*Piano Sanitario Nazionale*) which must be presented to Parliament every third year.

The regions have extensive powers for organizing their own health services. They develop their own regional health plans. Local governments take care of the basic administration of health services through special units called Local Health Units (*Unità Sanitarie Locali*) which provide all services (there must be one unit for every 50,000-200,000 inhabitants). The local health units are run by an executive board nominated by the general assembly of the respective local government.

Core laws

9.1.1946 (no. 212)
Reorganized health insurance system for agricultural workers, tenant farmers and sharecroppers; flat-rate contributions for tenant farmers and sharecroppers; earnings-related contributions for agricultural workers, shared equally between employers and workers; cash benefits: flat-rate daily indemnity of Lit. 28 for women and Lit. 60 for men (i.e. 3% and 7% of average gross industrial wage for 1947) for a maximum of 180 days a year; free medical and hospital assistance through INAM.

19.4.1946 (no. 213)
Reorganized health insurance system for industrial employees; earnings-related contributions amounted to 5% for blue-collar and 3% for white-collar workers, shared equally between employers and employees; introduced daily sickness indemnity equal to 50% of earnings, for a maximum of 180 days a year; flat-rate maternity indemnity equal to a lump sum of Lit. 1,000 for 120 days (1% of average gross for industrial wage in 1947); funeral allowance; free medical, hospital and pharmaceutical assistance through INAM.

31.10.1947 (no. 1304)
Reorganized health insurance system for service sector employees (commerce, banking, insurance etc.); earnings-related contributions of 4.5%, shared equally between employers and employees; introduced daily sickness indemnity equal to 50% of earnings for a maximum of 180 days a year; flat-rate maternity payment; funeral allowance; free medical, hospital and pharmaceutical assistance through INAM.

12.2.1948 (no. 147)
Reorganized health insurance system for state employees; earnings-related contributions of 2%, shared equally between employees and state; introduced daily sickness indemnity equal to 50% of earnings for a maximum of 180 days; and free medical, hospital and pharmaceutical assistance.

26.8.1950 (no. 860)
Regulations covering maternity insurance for all female employees:
- job security, throughout the period of pregnancy and until child is one year old;
- exemption from heavy, unhealthy or dangerous work;
- period of leave, starting three months (industry), eight weeks (agriculture), six weeks (others) prior to confinement and ending eight weeks after it;
- daily indemnity during the period of leave equal to 80% of earnings (for agriculture: flat-rate sum ranging from Lit. 12,000 to Lit. 25,000, i.e. 15%-32% of average gross industrial wage for 1950); contributions set at 0.53% of earnings for industry, 0.20 to 0.31% for service sector and 0.45% for agriculture.

30.10.1953 (no. 841)
Extended health insurance to retired public employees; contributions set at 4.5% of pensions (1% paid by pensioners, 0.5% by active public employees, 3% by state); benefits in kind only i.e. free medical, hospital and pharmaceutical assistance; daily sickness indemnity for state employees raised to 80% of earnings for the first 30 days (50% for the subsequent 150 days).

22.11.1954 (no. 1136)
Extended health insurance to self-employed small farmers; special Mutual Aid Fund (*Cassa Mutua*) set up, with sections in every local authority (*comune*) and province; flat-rate contributions by members and state (for each member); benefits in kind only i.e. free medical, hospital and pharmaceutical assistance.

4.8.1955 (no. 692)
Extended health insurance to all pensioners; financed by supplementary earnings-related contribution introduced for pension insurance; revenue transferred from INPS to INAM; contribution rate raised for active members; benefits in kind only i.e. free medical, hospital and pharmaceutical assistance.

29.12.1956 (no. 1533)
Extended health insurance to artisans; same regulations as for self-employed farmers; (see law no. 1136/1954).

13.3.1958 (no. 250)
Extended health insurance to fishermen; flat-rate contributions plus state contribution; benefits in kind only.

13.3.1958 (no. 296)
Established the Ministry of Health (*Ministero della Sanità*).

27.11.1960 (no. 1397)
Extended health insurance to self-employed traders; established special mutual aid fund as for farmers and artisans (see law no. 1135/1954); flat-rate contributions for three broad earnings brackets plus state contribution for each member, but only up to a certain total amount; benefits in kind, as for farmers and artisans.

26.2.1963 (no. 329)
Improved benefits for agricultural workers; flat-rate sickness indemnity replaced by earnings-related indemnity equal to 50% of minimum contractual pay (in each province) for a maximum of 180 days; introduced free pharmaceutical assistance.

26.2.1963 (no. 260)
Extended health insurance to retired artisans; flat-rate supplementary contributions from active members of insurance scheme plus state contribution for each member; benefits in kind only.

22.7.1966 (no. 613)
Extended health insurance to retired traders, with same rules as for retired artisans (see law no. 260/1963).

29.5.1967 (no. 369)
Extended compulsory health insurance to retired farmers, tenant farmers and share-croppers; flat-rate supplementary contributions from active members plus transfers from INPS (TB fund); benefits in kind only; extended health insurance to the unemployed in receipt of unemployment benefits; financed through transfers from INPS (TB scheme) to INAM; benefits in kind only.

12.2.1968 (no. 132)
New provisions covering public hospitals:
- change in legal status of public hospitals, from Public Institutions for Assistance and Charity (*Istituzioni Pubbliche di Assistenza e Beneficienza*, IPAB) to Hospital Agencies (*Enti Ospedalieri*), namely public bodies subject to strict state regulation and control;
- standardized and detailed regulations on the administrative and organizational structure of public hospitals;
- introduction of law on hospital planning and a national hospital plan to be periodically drafted;
- establishment of a national committee for hospital planning within the Ministry of Health;
- introduction of new financing regulations: hospitals must charge all patients a hos-

pital fee (*retta di degenza*), equal to the total operating costs divided by the number of beds;
- establishment of state-financed National Hospital Fund (*Fondo Nazionale Ospedaliero*) within the Ministry of Health, to cover hospital deficits and promote hospital modernization.

30.12.1971 (no. 1204)
New regulations covering protection of female workers and maternity insurance:
- duration of maternity leave extended: two months prior to, and three months after confinement for all employees;
- all female workers entitled to earnings-related indemnity, equal to 80% of earnings (including agricultural workers and tenant farmers);
- entitlement to voluntary extra period of leave for six months during the first year of life of the child, with job security and an indemnity equal to 30% of earnings; effective from 1973;
- entitlement to paid absences due to the child's sickness during the first three years of the child's life;
- introduction of special natality allowance (*assegno di natalità*) for self-employed women in the agricultural, artisan and commercial sectors, financed through supplementary contribution from active members of the respective sickness insurance schemes together with special state contribution.

14.1.1972 (no. 4)
Transferred administration of health and hospital assistance to the regions.

11.8.1972 (no. 485)
Extended health insurance to citizens over 65 receiving a social pension, financed by the state.

17.8.1974 (no. 386)
Provisions for hospital assistance, in anticipation of a broader reform of the health sector:
- given their forthcoming liquidation, all health insurance funds obliged to discharge their debts vis-a-vis hospitals;
- 'freezing' of hospital services and personnel, insurance agency personnel, and contracts with doctors and pharmacies;
- all functions of the various insurance agencies transferred to regions; effective from 1.1.1975;
- extension of hospital assistance to all those not previously covered by any scheme; financed by flat-rate contribution from new members, equal to average per capita annual expenditure of INAM;
- establishment within the Ministry of Health of a National Fund for Hospital Assistance (*Fondo Nazionale per l'Assistenza Ospedaliera*, FNAO) which centralizes all resources for hospital assistance derived from the various health insurance funds, INPS, and the state, which are then allocated to the regions;
- regions to control all public hospitals within their territory hospitals and to be financed by the FNAO (the 1968 system of financing having been abolished).

29.6.1977 (no. 349)
Abolished all existing funds and schemes; transitional regulations for the transfer of jurisdiction to regions, given the forthcoming reform of the health sector.

23.11.1978 (no. 833)
Established the National Health Service (*Servizio Sanitario Nazionale* SSN, with transitional regulations for the complete liquidation of the old system.

5.8.1978 (no. 484)
Introduction of prescription fees.

25.3.1982 (no. 98)
Full cost of dental, optical and aural services/treatment to be born by parents.

26.4.1982 (no. 181)
Introduction of medical test fee; restriction of medicines available on prescription.

12.10.1982 (no. 754)
Increase of prescription fees.

10.11.1983 (no. 638)
Increase of prescription and medical test fees; introduction of additional fixed prescription fee; restriction of medicines available free of charge.

27.12.1983 (no. 730)
Introduction of controls of doctors' medical standards and minor restriction of benefits.

III Occupational injuries

In 1979 total expenditure for occupational injuries and professional diseases amounted to 1,330 billion lire or 0.5% of GDP. the following table gives the structure of this type of expenditure.

Expenditure on occupational injuries and professional diseases in 1979 (billion lire)

	Total	%
Cash benefits:	1 199	89.6
- pensions/rents	869	64.9
- daily allowances	304	22.7
- subsidies	3	0.1
- lump payments	24	1.9
Benefits in kind:	74	5.5
- pharmaceuticals	5	0.4
- physicians	39	2.9
- others	30	2.2
Services	57	4.9
Total	1 330	100.0

Coverage

Insurance against occupational injuries and diseases covers the following risks: permanent and temporary (full or partial) disability due to work accidents; and occupational diseases.

One main insurance scheme covers dependent workers in the industrial sector and dependent and self-employed workers in the agricultural sector. In 1977 the insured population amounted to 6,425,616 (excluding agriculture) i.e. some 29.1% of the labour force.

Benefits

The insurance provides benefits in cash and in kind. The former include:

- a daily allowance for full temporary disablement (*indennità giornaliera per invalidità temporanea assoluta*), an earnings-related benefit of 60% for industrial workers or a flat-rate sum for agricultural workers;
- a pension for permanent disablement (*rendità per invalidità permanente*), a pension related to the degree of disablement and previous earnings in the industrial sector or a conventional wage in the agricultural sector;
- a daily allowance (*assegno giornaliero*), for workers with occupational diseases;
- transitional pension (*rendità di passaggio*), a flat-rate sum for workers with occupational diseases, who are forced to change work;
- survivors' pension (*rendità ai superstiti*), an earnings-related pension with minima and indexation.

Benefits in kind include medical assistance for the disabled and those affected by occupational diseases, in addition to rehabilitation programmes.

Financing

The main insurance scheme derives its funds from: (1) insurance premiums, computed on the basis of risk intensities and average earnings for broad industrial sectors; (2) earnings-related contributions of 3% for agricultural workers (paid by the employers); (3) flat-rate contributions for small farmers, sharecroppers and tenant farmers. The state covers any deficit.

Administration

The insurance is administered by the National Institute for Insurance against Work Accidents (*Istituto Nazionale per l'Assicurazione contro gli Infortuni sul Lavoro*, INAIL), a large public welfare agency similar to INPS, which is governed by a board including representatives form the unions, employers and the state.

Core laws

15.11.1952 (no. 1697)
Increased the number of occupational diseases for which insurance benefits are payable.

21.3.1959 (no. 471)
Extended insurance against occupational diseases to agricultural workers (for seven diseases).

19.1.1963 (no. 15)
Extended the insurance against occupational diseases to artisans; general improvement

of cash benefits: all pensions (*rendite*) adjusted every third year to the minimum contractual wage in the respective industrial sector; earnings-replacement rates raised to correspond to contractual disability rates.

30.6.1965 (no. 1124)
Coordinated various schemes and regulations under a single piece of legislation with more precise definitions of coverage, simplified administrative procedures, stricter controls and minor improvement of benefits.

9.6.1975 (no. 482)
Increased the number of eligible occupational diseases; extended the duration of benefits.

27.12.1975 (no. 780)
Introduced ad hoc upgrading of cash benefits for certain diseases and of all flat-rate allowances.

16.2.1977 (no. 37)
Introduced ad hoc upgrading of cash benefits for agricultural sector.

IV Unemployment insurance

In 1979 total expenditure for unemployment amounted to 1,338 billion lire or approximately 0.5% of GDP. The following table gives the structure of this type of expenditure.

Unemployment expenditure by type of benefit in 1979 (billion lire)

	Total	%
Cash benefits:	1 239	92.6
- benefits for full unemployment	633	
- benefits for partial/temporary unemployment	601	
- subsidies	5	
Services	99	7.4
Total	1 338	100.0

Coverage

The system of unemployment insurance covers the risks of both full and temporary or partial unemployment. A single scheme provides (since 1919) insurance benefits for full unemployment to all dependent workers (except journalists who have their own insurance). Two other schemes provide benefits for temporary and partial unemployment, one for industrial workers (since 1941) and one for agricultural workers (since 1972).

In 1979 a total of 10,430,000 workers were insured with the first scheme (approximately 47% of the labour force). In addition to the insurance system, there have been a number of active labour policies (see Core Laws below) which have recently gained greater emphasis, especially in the fields of labour mobility, professional requalification and youth unemployment.

Benefits

The insurance scheme against full unemployment provides three types of benefits:

(1) benefit for full unemployment (*indennità di disoccupazione*), a flat-rate daily allowance of Lit. 800 (3.4% of the average gross industrial earnings per day in 1978) for a maximum of 180 days per year;

(2) special unemployment benefits (*sussidi straordinari di disoccupazione*) paid under exceptional circumstances by Ministerial decree (level determined ad hoc);

(3) special benefits for full unemployment (*trattamenti speciali/integrativi di disoccupazione*), earnings-related benefits in the industrial sector (80% for 180 days) and standard benefits in the agricultural sector (66.66% of average provincial contractual pay for 90 days for part-time workers).

The insurance scheme against temporary and partial unemployment in the industrial sector provides two types of benefit:

(1) ordinary earnings replacement benefits (*integrazioni salariali ordinarie*) for employment crises limited to single enterprises;

(2) special earnings replacement benefits (*integrazioni salariali straordinarie*) for sectoral crises, industrial reorganization, restructuring, and conversions.

The two types of benefits originally had different replacement rates and duration (see Core Laws below). The replacement rate is set for both benefits at 80% of previous earnings (for a maximum of 40 hours a week); ordinary benefits are payable for three months and are renewable up to a maximum of nine months in a two year period; in principle special benefits last for a period of six months, but can in fact be renewed for the length of the crisis. It should, however, be noted that higher replacement rates and longer periods of payment may be bargained for by the unions in certain cases.

The insurance scheme against temporary and partial unemployment in agriculture provides earnings replacement benefits (*integrazioni salariali*) equal to 80% of the previous daily pay for 90 days.

Financing

The unemployment insurance schemes are financed through contributions paid by employers and calculated on the basis of the worker's pay, in a proportion which varies from one sector to another, and according to the size of the firm (minimum 0.2% to 0.5%, maximum 3% to 5%). The state covers any deficit of the three schemes with special contributions.

Administration

The three schemes for unemployment insurance are administered with separate funds and managements within INPS: Insurance against Involuntary Unemployment (*Assicurazione contro la Disoccupazione Involontaria*); Earnings Replacement Fund for the Industrial Sector (*Cassa Integrazione Guadagni per l'Industria*, CIGI) and Earnings Replacement Fund for Agricultural Workers (*Cassa per l'Integrazione dei Salari dei dipendenti da Imprese Agricole*, CIGA).

Core laws

9.11.1945 (no. 788)
Institutionalized the Earnings Replacement Fund for the Industrial Sector (CIGI); jurisdiction of CIGI formally codified with special provisions for Northern provinces.

12.8.1947 (no. 869)
Grouped all regulations governing earnings replacement benefits under a single piece of legislation; unified the administrative structure of CIGI; extended earnings replacement benefits to cover temporary unemployment; compensation formula for all earnings replacement benefits equalled two-thirds of hourly payments for a maximum of 16 hours a week and 90 days a year.

29.4.1949 (no. 264)
Introduced new provisions for unemployment insurance and labour policy:
- establishment of a Central Commission for Work Training and Assistance for the Unemployed (*Commissione Centrale per l'Avviamento al Lavoro e per l'Assistenza ai Disoccupati*), with the task of monitoring the state of the labour market and the conditions of the unemployed;
- regulations concerning the replacement of the unemployed into the labour market (*Collocamento*);
- establishment of Provincial Offices for Labour and Full Employment (*Uffici Provinciali del Lavoro e della Massima Occupazione*), with local sections, which organize waiting lists, training courses, the allocation of available jobs etc.;
- unemployment indemnity (*indennità di disoccupazione*) raised to Lit. 200 per day or approximately 17% of average gross industrial wage for 1949, and its duration is extended from 120 to 180 days;
- extension of unemployment insurance to agricultural workers, with earnings-related contributions;
- introduction of special unemployment benefit (*sussidio straordinario di disoccupazione*), paid under exceptional circumstances; flat-rate benefit with ad hoc determined level for 90 to 180 days;
- introduction of vocational training and professional requalification programmes for the unemployed;
- establishment of a Fund for Professional Training of Workers (*Fondo per l'Addestramento Professionale dei Lavoratori*) with resources from INPS and the state.

3.2.1957 (no. 818)
Raised daily benefit for full unemployment to Lit. 230 or approximately 13.8% of average gross industrial daily wage for 1957.

20.10.1960 (no. 1237)
Raised daily benefit for full unemployment to Lit. 300 or approximately 16% of average gross industrial daily wage for 1960.

3.2.1963 (no. 77)
Established a special fund for earnings replacement benefits within CIGI for the construction industry; compensation formula: 80% of earnings for a maximum of 40 hours a week for 90 days.

29.3.1966 (no. 129)
Raised daily benefit for full unemployment to Lit. 400 or approximately 12.7% of average gross industrial daily wage for 1966.

5.11.1968 (no. 1115)
Introduced special benefit for full unemployment (*trattamento integrativo di disoccupazione*) for workers in the industrial sector, in cases of total or partial closing down of enterprises or large-scale dismissals, equalling two-thirds of previous monthly earnings for 180 days; extended earnings replacement benefits to cases of sectoral crises

or industrial restructuring with a new special compensation formula equalling 80% of previous earnings for three months (nine months in exceptional circumstances); family allowances paid to those in receipt of unemployment benefits; reorganization of retraining courses for the unemployed.

2.2.1970 (no. 14)
Extended earnings replacement benefits to artisan undertakings in the construction industry.

2.2.1970 (no. 12)
Introduced special benefits for full unemployment (*trattamento speciale di disoccupazione*) for workers in the construction industry, equal to 50% of earnings for 180 days.

6.12.1971 (no. 1058)
Extended earnings replacement benefits to mining undertakings, with the same procedures as for the construction industry (see law no. 77/1963).

8.8.1972 (no. 457)
Established the Fund for Earnings Replacement Benefits for Agricultural Workers (CIGA), within INPS; formula equalled two-thirds of previous earnings for 90 days; introduced special benefits for full unemployment (*trattamento speciale integrativo di disoccupazione*) for agricultural part-time workers, equal to 60% of the average provincial earnings for 90 days.

8.8.1972 (no. 464)
Extended the duration of earnings replacement benefits with no predetermined time limit; earnings replacement benefits extended to cases of industrial reconversions and to white-collar workers; health care and pension rights extended to workers in receipt of earnings replacement benefits; contributions paid by CIGI or CIGA.

16.4.1974 (no. 114)
Improved daily benefits for full unemployment from Lit. 400 to Lit. 800 or approximately 8.6% of gross average industrial earnings for 1974.

20.5.1975 (no. 164)
Standardized the replacement rate for partial or temporary unemployment benefits for all sectors at 80% of previous earnings; contributions raised according to sector and size of enterprise; introduced compulsory consultations between employers and unions in employment crises.

6.8.1975 (no. 427)
Raised special benefit for full unemployment in the construction industry to 66.66% of earnings for 90 days.

16.2.1977 (no. 37)
Raised special benefit for full unemployment for agricultural workers to 66.66% of earnings for 90 days; introduced an additional special benefit for agricultural part-time workers, equal to 40% of earnings for 90 days.

1.6.1977 (no. 285)
Introduced special provisions for youth unemployment; regions and local government required to set up special employment programmes for young people in search of first job.

12.8.1977 (no. 675)
Introduced new provisions for overall coordination of industrial policy and labour market policy:

- established a special Fund for Industrial Restructuring and Conversion (*Fondo per la ristrutturazione e riconversione industriale*, FRRI) within the Ministry of Industry, financed by the state, to promote programmes for industrial restructuring and conversion together with labour retraining.
- established a Central Commission for Labour Mobility (*Commissione Centrale per la mobilità del lavoro*, CCML) together with regional commissions to implement its directives;
- established a Fund for Labour Mobility (*Fondo per la mobilità della Manodopera*), providing financial support for workers willing to move in cases of occupational crises; financed 50% by the FRRI and 50% by CIGI.

21.12.1978 (no. 845)
Legislative guidelines covering professional training; regions required to organize programmes for vocational youth training and labour retraining; special Rotation Fund (*Fondo di rotazione*) established within the Ministry of Labour to finance regions.

11.12.1979 (no. 624)
Introduced new provisions for unemployment benefits; restricted the duration of ordinary and special earnings replacement benefits to a maximum of nine and eighteen months respectively during a two-year period; established a ceiling (indexed) of Lit. 500.000 per month, or approximately 95% of average industrial wage for 1979, for any earnings-replacement benefit; employees allowed to retire at 55 (men) and 50 (women) with full pension, in instances of occupational crises (missing contributions paid by CIGI); special benefits for full unemployment upgraded to 80% of previous earnings for 180 days.

V Families and children

In 1979 total family expenditure amounted to 2,898 billion lire or approximately 1.8% of GDP. The following table gives the structure of this type of expenditure.

Family expenditure by type of benefits in 1979 (billion lire)

	Total	%
Cash benefits:	2 504	86.4
- family allowances	2 418	
- subsidies	72	
- lump payments	14	
Benefits in kind	131	4.5
Services	263	10.1
Total	2 898	100.0

Coverage

Both tax credits and family allowances are provided for family dependents. A general scheme provides family allowances for dependent workers in the private sector (since

1940), the unemployed in receipt of unemployment benefits, pensioners and the self-employed in agriculture. State employees receive family allowances from state funds. In addition to the above, various ad hoc subsidies in cash and kind are provided for needy families. Finally, a number of family services, such as kindergartens, recreation and counselling facilities have been introduced in recent years.

In 1979 the insured population, excluding state employees, numbered approximately 10,254,000 or 18% of total population.

Benefits

The size of tax credits for family dependents, which take the form of income-tax deductions, is very low and varies according to the number and type of dependent (children, spouse, parents etc.), and ranges from Lit. 7,000 for one child to Lit. 150,000 for eight children or more (for 1979 ff.). Family allowances are referred to as (*assegni familiari*) under the general scheme and *aggiunte di famiglia* for state employees. Both consist of a monthly flat-rate sum. Until 1977 there were a number of separate regulations for various occupational categories. Thereafter, benefits have been gradually standardized to correspond to those of industrial workers (in 1980 Lit. 19,760 a month for child and spouse, or approximately 3.5% of average gross industrial wage for 1979; and slightly less for other dependents).

Financing

Family allowances are financed by employer contributions. The rate of contribution varies depending on the sector being equal to 7.5% of earnings in the respective industrial sector. The state covers any deficit the fund might have.

Administration

The general scheme is administered by a special fund within INPS, the Single Fund for Family Allowances (*Cassa Unica per gli Assegni Familiari*). Benefits for state employees are administered directly by the state (Ministry of the Treasury).

Core laws

8.7.1952 (no. 212)
Introduced *aggiunte di famiglia*: a monthly flat-rate sum for all categories of state employees.

30.5.1955 (no. 797)
Grouped all regulations covering *assegni familiari* under a single piece of legislation.

17.10.1961 (no. 1038)
Introduced a single accounting system within the Single Fund for Family Allowances of INPS, replacing the separate accounts for various sectors; ad hoc increase of family allowances for all sectors.

14.7.1967 (no. 587)
Extended family allowances to self-employed farmers, sharecroppers and tenant farmers, financed by the state.

5.11.1968 (no. 1115)
Extended family allowances to the unemployed in receipt of unemployment benefits, financed by the Insurance against Involuntary Unemployment Fund (*Assicurazione contro la Disoccupazione Involontari*) of INPS together with state contribution.

16.4.1974 (no. 114)
Extended family allowances to INPS pensioners, in lieu of child supplements (see law no. 1138/1962).

26.5.1975 (no. 161)
Started a gradual equalization of benefits across sectors and categories.

16.2.1977 (no. 37)
Extended family allowances to agricultural part-time workers; financed by the Single Fund for Family Allowances without contributions.

14.7.1980 (no. 440)
Introduced ad hoc increase and full equalization of family allowances for all sectors.

25.3.1983 (no. 79)
Introduction of special family supplements for lower-income employees and pensioners.

27.12.1983 (no. 730)
Abolition of family allowances for higher-income beneficiaries: families of 28-34 million per year (i.e. 150-190 percent of the average household income) lose one or more allowances according to the number of chidlren; families earning above 34 million lose all entitlement.

VI Social services and public assistance

In 1979 total expenditure for social services and public assistance amounted to some 3,043 billion lire. The following table gives the structure of expenditure by type of benefit and level of government.

Expenditure for Social Services and Public Assistance, 1979 (billion lire)[a]

	Social Security Funds	Central Government	Local Government	Total	%
Cash benefits	755	1 499	199	2 453	80.6
Benefits in kind	99	8	68	175	5.7
Services		211	204	415	13.7
Total	854	1 718	471	3 043	100.0
%	28.0	56.4	15.6	100.0	

A wide variety of social services is provided by the Italian state to people with special needs. (Orphans, the handicapped, the disabled, single parents and, in general, the 'poor'). To the more traditional types of services (e.g. homes for the elderly, the handicapped etc., kindergartens, holiday centres etc.), a number of new services have recently been introduced, often in an experimental form: 'open' structures for permanent, temporary, daily accommodation and recreation, professional training for the handicapped, leisure initiatives, specialized home help etc.

Financing

The activities of the local authorities are financed by the central government and, to a very small extent, by the regions. Separate assistance agencies are financed through state and social security contributions. Public charity institutions have mixed financial regulations and receive subsidies from the state.

Administration

Until the early 1970s, the sector of social services and public assistance were extremely fragmented, being divided among a variety of public charity institutions, a few social security agencies and local governments. Numerous reforms have, however, thoroughly transformed this sector during the last decade (see below). Today, the basic unit for the provision of social services and assistance benefits is the local authority, which operates according to a legislative framework established by central government and the regions. The local authority has wide organizational and administrative autonomy and normally coordinates the provision of social services with that of health services, through the local units of the National Health Service.

Core laws

23.3.1948 (no. 327)
Established the National Institute for Assistance of the Orphans of Italian Workers (*Ente Nazionale per l'Assistenza agli Orfani dei Lavoratori Italiani*, ENAOLI), financed through social security contributions and by the state.

23.3.1948 (no. 361)
Established the National Institute for Italian Pensioners (*Opera Nazionale per i Pensionati d'Italia*, ONPI); provides benefits and services for needy pensioners; financed through social security contributions from pensioners and state contributions.

6.12.1971 (no. 1044)
State funds made available for the construction of a kindergarten in every local authority.

15.1.1972 (no. 9)
Transferred some of the responsibilities for public assistance and social services to the regions.

23.12.1975 (no. 698)
Abolished the National Institute for Maternity and Childhood (*Opera Nazionale Maternità e Infanzia*, ONMI), created in 1934; transferred its functions to local authorities (*comuni*).

24.7.1977 (no. 616)
Local councils given full responsibility for social services and public assistance; liquidated a great number of separate local authority assistance agencies (*Enti Comunali di Assistenza*, ECA).

VII Housing

In 1979, total housing expenditure amounted to some 60 billion lire or approximately 10.002% of GDP. The following table gives the structure of housing expenditure by level of government.

Housing expenditure by level of government in 1979 (billion lire)

	Total	%
Central government	21	35.0
Local government[a]	38	63.3
Other agencies	1	1.7
Total	60	100.0

[a] Expenditure of regions is missing

There are three basic forms of housing policy:

(1) Regulations: the state strictly controls rents through general rules for rent levels and terms of leases under the Fair Rents Law (*regime dell'equo canone*); it also regulates the purchase and expropriation of land and construction by means of the Land Use Law (*regime sull'uso dei suoli*).

(2) Public housing (*edilizia sovvenzionata*) or subsidized housing: the state provides housing for low income families built by special construction firms, the Autonomous Institutions for Economic Housing (*Istituti Autonomi Case Popolari*).

(3) Subsidized private housing: the state grants special low interest loans to private builders willing to meet certain size and rent standards (*edilizia agevolata* or aided housing) or tax credits and direct subsidies to private builders committed to large economic housing programmes (*edilizia convenzionata*, contracted housing).

The state does not, however, provide any direct transfers to households.

Financing

A special fund within the Ministry of Finance collects and allocates the resources, which are mainly derived from the state budget, together with contributions from employers (approximately 0.7% of wages), and employees (approximately 0.35% of wages).

Administration

Housing policies are coordinated by the Residential Housing Committee (*Comitato per l'Edilizia Residenziale*) within the Ministry of Public Works, in close connection with the Interdepartmental Committee for Economic Policy (*Comitato Interministeriale per la Politica Economica*). Both the regions and local government however, have sizeable responsibilities in this sector.

Core laws

27.2.1947 (no. 39) and 23.12.1947 (no. 1461)
First post-war regulation of rents; all rents of economic/popular housing frozen and subject to state control; with minor changes, regulations were effective until the 1978 Fair Rent Law (see law no. 382/1978).

28.2.1949 (no. 43)
Seven-year plan for popular housing launched to increase the stock of economic housing by means of construction or purchase of economic accommodation; established special housing fund (*INA-Casa*) within the National Institute for Insurance (*Istituto Nazionale delle Assicurazioni*, INA) to collect contributions from employers (1.2% of wages), employees (0.6%), and the state.

2.7.1949 (no. 408)
Introduced broad tax exemptions and increased state subsidies for the construction of economic housing.

10.8.1950 (no. 175)
Established fund for the increase of housing stock (*Fondo per l'Incremento Edilizio*) which grants cheap loans to private builders.

9.8.1954 (no. 640)
Investment plan for public construction of economic housing.

18.4.1962 (no. 167)
Introduced broad provisions covering building areas; local government obliged to provide plans of areas suitable for economic housing; introduced strict price controls for building areas to prevent speculation.

14.2.1963 (no. 60)
Abolished special housing fund and established a new agency called the Workers' Housing Fund (*Gestione Case per i Lavoratori*, GesCaL), with a ten-year plan for the overall coordination of economic housing; funds raised through contributions from employers (0.7% of wages), employees (0.35%) and the state.

6.8.1967 (no. 765)
Legge Ponte (Bridge Law): introduced urgent housing provisions as part of an envisaged reform of the entire sector.
- severe constraints on the market of building areas; effective from 1968;
- burden of infrastructure i.e. roads, electricity, sewerage etc., transferred from local government to builders;
- introduction of minimum standards for housing and environment.

22.10.1971 (no. 865)
Riforma della Casa (Housing Reform): introduced broad provisions on housing including the liquidation of GesCaL and all other housing agencies/funds; established a Residential Housing Committee (*Comitato per l'Edilizia Residenziale*, CER) for overall coordination of housing programmes; decentralized planning (regions) and basic administration and coordination (local government); centralized all housing funds within the Ministries of the Treasury and Public Works (which allocate funds to the regions); introduced new tax and incentives regulations; new criteria for land expropriations; and provisions for urban renewals.

28.1.1977 (no. 10)
Regime sull'uso dei suoli (Land Use Law): introduced severe constraints on construction: any modification of a given area must be authorized by local government; new

criteria for land expropriations; complete privatization of infrastructure costs; and introduction of new planning procedures.

27.7.1978 (no. 382)
Regime dell'equo canone (Fair Rent Law): completed state control of rents with general rules for rent levels and terms of leases.

5.8.1978 (no. 457)
Introduced ten-year housing plan, coordinated centrally by CER and the regions; the state makes new funds available to regions for public housing and subsidies for private housing.

15.2.1980 (no. 25)
Introduced urgent housing provisions which included: the freezing of all eviction procedure, special assistance grants for low income families without adequate housing, distribution of special funds to local government for the urgent purchase or construction of economic housing, special provisions favouring the purchase of a first house.

VIII Education

In 1979 total expenditure for education amounted to 11,117 billion lire or approximately 4.1% of GDP. The following table gives the structure of this type of expenditure.

Education expenditure by level of education in 1979 (billion lire)

	Total	%
Primary education	2 936	26.4
Secondary education:		
- lower middle	2 578	23.2
- upper middle	2 378	21.4
Higher education	1 305	11.7
General expenditure	1 920	17.3
Total	11 117	100.0

The Italian educational system comprises general education, vocational training and adult education. School education is compulsory until the age of 14 and is divided into four levels:

(1) voluntary pre-school education (*istruzione pre-scholastica*) for children aged three to five;
(2) primary education (*istruzione primaria*), from the age of six, lasting for five years.
(3) secondary education (*istruzione secondaria*), organized at two sub-levels: lower middle school (*scuola media inferiore*), lasting for three years, with a single unified curriculum, and higher middle school (*scuola media superiore*), lasting for five years, or four years in some cases, with six basic curricula: classical,

scientific, pedagogic, technical, professional, and artistic; these all lead to a compulsory comprehensive examination, which confer a diploma of *maturità*, giving access to higher education;

(4) higher education (*istruzione superiore*) at universities, university institutes and politechnical institutes, with a variety of curricula and lasting from four to six years.

School education is largely provided by state institutions. The relative share of private institutions (many of which are catholic) varies according to the level: approximately 60% at the pre-school level, 6% at the primary level, 1% at the lower secondary level and 30% at the higher secondary level. Most of these private institutions receive state subsidies and must abide by the general principles and curricula followed by state institutions. At the level of higher education, there are a number of 'free' universities, which enjoy special autonomy.

The extra-school sector has been developed more recently and consists of two groups of educational activities: vocational training and adult education. Adult education is mostly provided by public institutions.

Compulsory education is free, and special assistance is given to pupils from poor families. Enrollment fees are minimal for higher secondary education and relatively modest for higher education. A very limited number of scholarships are available for university students and a small allowance or *pre-salario* is granted annually to university students with incomes below a given level.

Financing

The central government is completely responsible for the financing of public institutions and subsidizes those which are private. Regional and local governments have financial competence for educational activities within their respective areas.

Administration

The Ministry of Public Education is responsible for the education system. Regional and local governments are in charge of school assistance, vocational training, and extra-school activities. The school sector is decentralized, and based on collective school councils (*organi collegiali*) consisting of teachers, other school staff, students, parents, representatives of unions and various professional and cultural associations. These councils have wide organizational responsibilities and are elected periodically by students and parents.

Core laws

31.12.1962 (no. 1859)
Extended compulsory education to the age of 14; introduced a single unified curriculum (*scuola media unificata*) lasting for a three-year period after primary education.

14.12.1963 (no. 80)
Introduced annual allowance for university students with income below a given level.

10.3.1968 (no. 44)
Introduced voluntary public pre-elementary education for children aged three to five years.

11.12.1969 (no. 910)
Extended access to higher education to all students holding a higher secondary school diploma; formerly limited to students coming from classical (and in some cases, scientific) curricula.

14.1.1972 (no. 3)
Transferred responsibility for school assistance to the regions.

15.1.1972 (no. 10)
Transferred responsibility for vocational training to the regions.

31.5.1974 (no. 416)
Reorganized administration of school system by the setting up of collective school councils.

24.7.1977 (no. 616)
Local councils made responsible for school assistance and vocational training.

11.7.1980 (no. 382)
Reorganized higher education; introduced university departments and curricula for doctoral research.

Bibliography

Contents

I General contributions

1.1 General studies and interpretations

ARDIGÒ, A., DONATI, P. (eds): Politica sociale e perdita del centro (Social Policy and Loss of Centre). Milan, Franco Angeli, 1982. A collection of articles on the relationship between social policies and the social system, highlighting the disruptive effects of the former on individual and communal *Lebenswelten*.

ASCOLI, U. (ed.): Welfare State all'italiana (The Italian Type of Welfare State). Bari, Laterza, 1984. An anthology presenting general interpretations of the characteristics of the Italian welfare state in a comparative perspective and more detailed analyses on the institutional developments of the various welfare policies.

BARCELLONA, P.: Oltre lo stato sociale (Beyond the Social State). Bari, De Donato, 1981. A neo-Marxist interpretation of the crisis of the welfare state in general and a discussion of possible alternatives.

CENTRO RICERCHE ECONOMICA APPLICATA - CREA: La crisi dello stato assistenziale (The Crisis of the Welfare State). Rome, CREA, 1984. A collection of articles analysing the crisis of the welfare state with a 'public choice' approach. Advocates substantial re-privatization of welfare.

CENTRO STUDI E INVESTIMENTI SOCIALI - CENSIS: Spesa pubblica e politica sociale (Public Expenditure and Social Policy). Milan, Franco Angeli, 1983. A thorough analysis of the development of Italian social policies in recent years and in a comparative perspective, largely based on empirical data. Tries to identify the emerging trends of social policy and speculates as toits future.

DONATI, P.P. (ed.): Pubblico e privato: fine di un'alternativa? (Public and Private: The End of an Alternative?). Bologna, Cappelli, 1978. A collection of articles on social needs and the welfare state and on the changing boundaries between public and private; advances the idea of a new 'social private' sphere, based on voluntary provision of services and self-management.

DONATI, P.P., ROSSI, G. (eds): Welfare state: problemi e alternative (Welfare State: Problems and Alternatives). Milan, Franco Angeli, 1982. An anthology including: general theoretical interpretations on the welfare crisis; short surveys of some foreign experiences; articles on the development of Italian social policies in historical perspective; articles on the future of the welfare state.

FONDAZIONE EINAUDI: Il welfare state possibile (The Possible Welfare State). Florence, Le Monnier, 1984. An anthology of articles on the crisis of the welfare state written by neo-liberal economists and social scientists.

1.2 Historical studies

CENTORRINO, M. (ed.): Consumi sociali e sviluppo economico in Italia (Social Consumption and Economic Development in Italy). Rome, Coines, 1976. A reconstruction of the debate on social services and planning during the 1960s, reporting the contributions of the main participants to that debate.

CHERUBINI, A.: Storia della previdenza sociale (History of Social Insurance). Rome, Editori Riuniti, 1977. A detailed historical reconstruction of Italian social insurance from the unification to the 1960s, with a discussion of all the main laws and proposals on the subject.

CONTI, L.: L'assistenza e previdenza sociale (Social Assistance and Insurance). Milan, Feltrinelli, 1958. A historical survey of the main institutional steps of the Italian system of welfare; focusses extensively on social assistance.

FARGION, V.: 'L'assistenza pubblica in Italia dall'unità al fascismo (Public assistance in Italy from the unification to fascism)'. *Rivista Trimestrale di Scienza dell'Amministrazione*, 1984. A structural functional analysis of the various institutional phases in the development of public assistance.

JOCTEAU, G.C.: 'Le origini della legislazione sociale in Italia. Problemi e prospettive di ricerca

(The origins of social legislation in Italy. Problems and research perspectives)'. *Movimento Operaio e Socialista*, No. 2, 1982, pp. 289-303. A survey of the historical literature on the emergence of social legislation in Italy in the second half of the twentieth century.

MANIN CARABBA, G.: Un ventennio di programmazione (Two Decades of Planning). Bari, Laterza, 1977. A thorough reconstruction of the *programmazione* (planning) debate, from its outset in the late 1950s to the early 1970s, including an illustration of the main social reforms passed during this period.

MARUCCO, D.: Mutualismo e sistema politico (Mutual Aid and the Political System). Milan, Franco Angeli, 1982. A history of Italian friendly societies from the unification until the early twentieth century, and of stateattempts to regulate and control them.

STEFANELLI, R.: 'Il sistema previdenziale. Storia e prospettive (The social insurance system. History and perspectives)'. *Proposte*, No. 51/52, 1977, pp. 3-36. A short survey of Italian social insurance since the unification. Contains a discussion of the problems of the mid-1970s.

1.3 Economic and financial aspects of welfare

CAVAZZUTI, C.: Il nodo della finanza pubblica (The Public Finance Knot). Milano, Feltrinelli, 1978. A short discussion on the main problems of public expenditure and its institutional management in the 1970s.

FAUSTO, D.: Il sistema Italiano di sicurezza sociale (The Italian System of Social Security). Bologna, Il Mulino, 1979. A descriptive account of the various social security sectors, based mainly on mid-1970s financial data.

GERELLI, E., MAJOCCHI, A. (eds): Il deficit pubblico: origini e problemi (Public Deficit: Origins and Problems). Milan, Franco Angeli, 1984. A collection of articles tracing the functional origins of public deficits. Contains detailed chapters on the financing of the welfare state.

GERELLI, E., REVIGLIO. F. (eds): Per una politica della spesa pubblica in Italia (Towards a Public Expenditure Policy in Italy). Milan, Franco Angeli, 1978. A collection of articles on the quantitative development of various expenditure components, including health, education, pensions.

PEDONE, A.: Evasori e tartassati (Evaders and the Harassed). Bologna, Il Mulino, 1979. A reconstruction of the quantitative growth of public revenues in the postwar period in a comparative perspective. Discusses the most controversial issues of Italian fiscal policy.

REVIGLIO, F.: Spesa pubblica a stagnazione dell'economia italiana (Public Expenditure and the Stagnation of the Italian Economy). Bologna, Il Mulino, 1977. An analysis of the various components of public expenditure and of their development over time, with an overall assessment of the impact of public expenditure on economic performance.

RIVISTA DI POLITICA ECONOMICA: Lo stato e i soldi degli Italiani (The State and Italians' Money). Special Issue, No. 1, 1983. Presents the proceedings of a conference on public expenditure and the welfare state organized in 1981; non-specialist, but very informative contributions.

1.4 Social and political aspects of welfare

AMATO, G.: Economia, politica e istituzioni in Italia (Economy, Politics and Institutions in Italy). Bologna, Il Mulino, 1976. An investigation into the politics of public sector growth from the mid-1950s to the mid-1970s. Although not focussing directly on welfare institutions, it offers a picture of the broader political context of the Italian welfare state.

CASSESE, S.: Il sistema amministrativo italiano (The Italian Administrative System). Bologna, Il Mulino, 1983. A comprehensive account of Italian public administration in historical perspective. It includes a detailed analysis of the structures and functioning of welfare institutions.

CAZZOLA, F. (ed.): Anatomia del potere DC (The Anatomy of DC Power). Bari, De Donato, 1979. An analysis of the DC hegemony over the state apparatus in the postwar period. Includes a chapter on political parties and social security funds.

ERGAS, Y.: 'Allargamento della cittadinanza e governo del conflitto: le politiche sociali negli anni settanta in Italia (Citizenship extension and conflict management: social policies in the 1970s in Italy)'.*Stato e Mercato*, No. 2, 1983, pp. 429-464. An analysis of social movements and social policies during the 1970s and the impact of institutional reforms on social mobilization.

FERRERA, M.: 'Sviluppo e crisi del welfare state in Italia, 1945-1980 (Growth and crisis of the Italian welfare state, 1945-1980)'.*In* FERRERA, M. (ed.): Lo stato del benessere: una crisi senza uscita? (The Welfare State: a crisis with no way out?) Florence, Le Monnier, 1981, pp. 123-182. A reconstruction of the development of Italian social policy, presenting some quantative data and illustrating the various phases of institutional expansion.

PACI, M.: 'Il sistema di welfare italiano tra tradizione clientelare e prospettive di riforma (The Italian welfare system between clientelistic traditions and reform prospects)'. *In* ASCOLI, U. (ed.): *op. cit.*, pp. 297-327. An interpretation of the historical development of the Italian welfare state, putting forward the idea of a 'clientelistic-particularistic' type of welfare. Proposes a return to selectivity.

SALVATI, M.: Alle origini dell'inflazione italiana (At the Roots of Italian Inflation). Bologna, Il Mulino, 1978. Although mainly focussing on inflation, contains an analysis of the political economy of welfare growth, especially pensions and health.

SANTAGATA, W.: 'Ciclo politico-economico: il caso italiano, 1953-1979 (Political-economic cycle: the Italian case)'. *Stato e Mercato*, No. 2, 1982, pp. 257-299. An empirical analysis of some political determinants (mainly electoral competition) of the growth of economic output and public/social expenditure.

SERRANI, D.: Il potere per enti: enti pubblici e sistema politico in Italia (Power Through Agencies: Public Agencies and the Political System in Italy). Bologna, Il Mulino, 1978. A discussion of the clientelistic use made by political parties of the various public agencies operating in the field of growth promotion and welfare in the postwar period.

1.5 Reports by investigating committees or experts

CAMERA DEI DEPUTATI: Stato e prospettive dell'assistenza pubblica e privata in Italia (Situation and Prospects of Public and Private Assistance in Italy). Rome, 1972. An investigation of the institutional framework regulating the social assistance sector at the beginning of the 1970s, and a survey of the main reform proposals, in the light of the forthcoming decentralization.

CENTRO STUDI INVESTIMENTI SOCIALI - CENSIS: Rapporto sulla situazione sociale del paese (Report on the Social Situation of the Country). Rome, various years. An annual survey on the qualitative and quantitative development of social policies and industrial relations at both national and local level.

COMITATO DI STUDIO PER LA SICUREZZA SOCIALE (CSSS): Per un sistema di sicurezza sociale (Towards a System of Social Security). Bologna, Il Mulino, 1965.A collection of articles by academics and experts on the institutional development of the Italian welfare state (especially income maintenance, health and social assistance), containing proposals for rationalization and universalization.

CONSIGLIO NAZIONALE DELL'ECONOMIA E DEL LAVORO (CNEL): Osservazioni e proposte sulla riforma della previdenza sociale (Remarks and Proposals on the Reform of Social Insurance). Rome, Istituto poligrafico dello Stato, 1963. An authoritative critical survey of social insurance regulations, supporting proposals for a flat-rate basic pension and the universalization of hospital assistance.

CONSIGLIO NAZIONALE DELL'ECONOMIA E DEL LAVORO (CNEL): Osservazioni e proposte sullo stato di attuazione della riforma sanitaria (Remarks and Proposals on the Implementation of the Health Reform). Rome, 1982. A detailed analysis of the situation of the health sector after the health reform, based on institutional and quantitative indicators. Contains interesting data on the financing of health and on the private sector.

MINISTERO DEL LAVORO E DELLA PREVIDENZA SOCIALE (Commissione Nazionale per i Problemi della Famiglia): Famiglia e reddito. La redistribuzione monetaria del reddito in funzione della situazione familiare (Family and Income. Monetary Income Redistribution according to Family Situation). Rome, 1982. An evaluation of the system of family transfers and its redistributive impact. Puts forward the proposal of a 'social allowance' weighed against family size and income, gradually substituting family allowances and tax credits.

MINISTERO DEL LAVORO E DELLA PREVIDENZA SOCIALE (Commissione per la Riforma della Previdenza Sociale): Relazione sui lavori della Commissione (Report on the Work of the Commission). Rome, 1948. A critical analysis of the institutional framework of welfare provisions inherited from the period of fascism, proposing a thorough rationalization and universalization of the system.

MINISTERO DEL TESORO: La spesa previdenziale e i suoi effetti sulla finanza pubblica (Social Insurance Expenditure and its Effect on Public Finances). Rome, Istituto poligrafico dello Stato, 1981. A detailed, mainly quantitative analysis of the pension system 1960-1980, with time series data on expenditure, contributions, the insured and beneficiaries. Contains proposals for institutional reform.

II Single Programmes

2.1 Pensions

CASTELLINO, O.: Il labirinto delle pensioni (The Pension Labyrinth). Bologna, Il Mulino, 1975. A detailed institutional analysis of the various pension schemes, showing the privileged position of self-employed and government employees, and highlighting some 'perverse' redistributive effects of the pension system. Contains proposals for rationalization and simplification.

FORNI, A.: Il pianeta previdenza (The Social Insurance Planet). Bari, De Donato, 1979. A short but informative pamphlet-type analysis of the institutional, financial and political problems of INPS, written by a trade union leader andformer president of INPS.

MORCALDO, G.: 'Analisi della struttura dei trattamenti pensionistici e della sua evoluzione (An analysis of the structure of pension benefits and their development). *Contributi alla Ricerca Economica*, Banca d'Italia, No. 7, 1977, pp. 77-162. A presentation of time series data on pension expenditure and beneficiaries from the late 1940s to 1976, with an analysis of the demographic and institutional factors underlying their growth.

REGINI, M., REGONINI, G.: 'La politica delle pensioni in Italia: il ruolo del movimento sindacale (Pension policy in Italy: the role of the trade union movement)'. *Giornale di Diritto del Lavoro e di Relazioni Industriali*, No. 10, 1981, pp. 217-242. A reconstruction of the main steps of postwar institutional development of the pension system, identifying the main political actors and their 'interests' with special emphasis on trade unions.

REGONINI, G.: 'Stato e sindacati nella formazione della politica della sicurezza sociale. Il caso delle pensioni (State and trade unions in the making of social security policy: the case of pensions)'. *Quaderni della Fondazione Feltrinelli*, No. 10, 1980, pp. 89-113. An annotated chronology of the main provisions regarding pensions since World War II with a discussion of the underlying political rationale. Contains an accurate reconstruction of some key policy decisions.

REGONINI, G.: 'Il sistema pensionistico: risorse e vincoli (The pension system: resources and constraints)'. *In* ASCOLI, U. (ed.): *op. cit.*, pp. 87116.Contains a survey of quantitative expansion; a theoretical discussion of the paradox of social security and its application in the Italian case; a synthesis of the redistributive effects of pension benefits, and a reconstruction of the political context and actors of Italian pension policy in the postwar period, with special reference to the 1970s.

2.2 Health

BERLINGUER, G.: Una riforma per la salute (A Reform for Health). Bari, De Donato, 1979. A collection of essays on health policy written during the 1970s by the PCI leader responsible for this sector. Contains some useful information on the background discussions leading to the health reform.

BRENNA, A. (ed.): Il governo della spesa sanitaria (The Management of Health Expenditure). Rome, Servizio Italiano Pubblicazioni Internazionali, 1984.A collection of articles analysing the evolution of health expenditure after the reform, its geographical distribution and the problems related to its international control. Contains an analysis of the demand for health and its geographical patterns.

CAVAZZUTI, F., GIANNINI, S.: La riforma malata (The Sick Reform). Bologna, Il Mulino, 1982. A detailed analysis of health expenditure after the reform, with special emphasis on geographical distribution and the institutional setting regulating the flows of financial resources in the sector.

DELOGU, S.: Sanità pubblica, sicurezza sociale e programmazione economica (Public Health, Social Security and Economic Planning). Turin, Einaudi, 1967. A history of health policy through the mid-1960s with a survey of the standpoint of the main political actors in the reform debate during the Centre-left coalition.

GRANAGLIA, E.: Per un nuovo intervento pubblico in sanità (Towards a New Form of Public Intervention in Health). Milan, Franco Angeli, 1981. A comparison of the British and Italian national health services from a public finance perspective. Contains detailed proposals to modify the incentive structures of the Italian health service vis a vis both consumers and producers in order to make the system more efficient.

ISTITUTO DI STUDI SULLA POLITICA ECONOMICA (ISPE): La spesa sanitaria in Italia dal 1964 al 1977 (Health Expenditure in Italy from 1964 to 1977). Rome, ISPE, 1978. A thorough reconstruction of time series data on health expenditure, with institutional, functional and geographical breakdowns.

MORCALDO, G., SALVEMINI, G.: 'Struttura ed evoluzione della spesa sanitaria (Structure and evolution of health expenditure)'. *Rivista di Politica Economica*, No. 12, 1978, pp. 1584-1604. A detailed reconstruction of the quantitative development of the health sector, with an analysis of its demographic and institutional causes, similar to that carried out by Morcaldo on pensions.

PIPERNO, A.: 'La politica sanitaria (Health Policy)'. *In* ASCOLI, U. (ed.): *op. cit.*, pp. 153-184. A historical reconstruction of health policy since the unification, trying to identify the changing boundaries between the private and public sectors.

2.3 Unemployment and labour policy

BECCHI COLLIDÀ, A.: Politiche del lavoro e garanzia del reddito (Labour Policy and Income Security). Bologna, Il Mulino, 1979. A discussion of the dualistic character of the Italian social security system, based on an analysis of the geographical and sectoral distribution of transfer payments and their relationship to the labour market and household incomes. Focusses especially on North/South redistribution.

CINELLI, M.: La tutela del lavoratore contro la disoccupazione (Workers' Protection against Unemployment). Milan, Franco Angeli, 1982.A detailed illustration of the norms and procedures governing unemployment in Italy.

DELL'ARRINGA, C.: L'agenzia per la mobilità della manodopera (The Agency for Labour Mobility). Milan, Vita e Pensiero, 1981. Proposes the establishment of a new agency for labour mobility, with the task of an overall coordination of the labour market.

GAROFALO, M.G., LAGALA, C. (eds): Mercato del lavoro, formazione professionale e collocamento (Labour Market, Professional Training and the Placement of Workers). Bari, De Donato, 1982. Focusses on labour policies aimed at linking demand and supply, and on the institutional framework which has regulated this link since the late 1940s.

ICHINO, P.: Il collocamento impossibile (The Impossible Placement). Bari, De Donato, 1982. A discussion of the shortcomings of the institution of *collocamento* (placement of workers), i.e. the regulations governing the placement of registered unemployed. Contains reform proposals.

REGALIA, I.: 'Le politiche del lavoro (Labour policies)'. *In* ASCOLI, U. (ed.): *op. cit*, pp. 53-86. A historical reconstruction of labour policies in Italy since World War II and of the political actors and context of these policies. Attempts to draw a structural profile of the Italian model of unemployment insurance.

SCAMUZZI, S. (ed.): Riforma del collocamento e mercato del lavoro (The Reform of the Placement System and the Labour Market). Milan, Franco Angeli, 1981. A collection of articles on the malfunctioning of the *Collocamento*, putting forward new proposals for a thorough reorganization of state policy on unemployment.

2.4 Families and children

BALBO, L.: Stato di famiglia (The Family State). Milan, Etas, 1976. An analysis of state policies on the family, offering a typology of Italian families according to the status of members in the labour market and the income maintenance system.

DONATI, P.: Famiglia e politiche sociali (The Family and Social Policy). Milan, Franco Angeli, 1982. A sociological investigation of the changing role and needs of the Italian family in relation to the expansion of state policies, especially in the field of social services.

GORRIERI, E., GUERZONI, L.: Il salario sociale. Famiglia e reddito nella crisi dello stato assistenziale (The Social Wage. Family and Income in the Crisis of the Social State). Rome, Edizioni Lavoro, 1982. An analysis of family transfers and their impact on household incomes, highlighting the inadequacy of the current system: advances the proposal of a guaranteed minimum social wage which is graduated according to household size and income.

ROSSI, G.: La famiglia assistita (The Assisted Family). Milan, Franco Angeli, 1982. An updated description and evaluation of public policies towards the family, with special reference to the conditions of housewives and women in general.

2.5 Housing

BORTOLOTTI, L.: Storia della politica edilizia italiana (A History of Italian Housing Policy). Rome, Editori Riuniti, 1978. A survey of the main phases of institutional development in housing policy during this century, with a specially detailed analysis of the fascist period.

FERRACUTI, G., MARCELLONI, M.: La casa. Mercato e programmazione (Housing. Market and Planning). Turin, Einaudi, 1982. A descriptive reconstruction of the growth of public intervention in the housing sector, with emphasis on both legislative provisions and their implementation.

GINATEMPO, N.: La casa in Italia (Housing in Italy). Milan, Mazzotta, 1975. A descriptive reconstruction of the growth of public intervention in the analysis of the political aspects of housing policy and on its redistributive effects; focusses especially on the situation in the late 1960s and early 1970s.

MAGNANI, I., MURARO, G.: Edilizia e sviluppo urbano (Housing Construction and Urban Development). Bologna, Il Mulino, 1978. An analysis of postwar institutional developments, with some data on public expenditure and on the number of constructions. Contains an analysis of the fiscal regulations on housing and their economic effects.

TOSI, A.: 'La politica della casa (Housing policy)'. *In* ASCOLI, U. (ed.): *op. cit.*, pp. 239-263. A short description of the Italian 'model' of housing policy, its historical evolution, its structural limits and its current political strains.

2.6 Education

DEI, M., ROSSI, M.: Sociologia della scuola italiana (Sociology of Italian Education). Bologna, Il Mulino, 1978. A structural/functional analysis of the educational system in historical perspective, with a discussion of the social conflicts emerging around it during the 1970s.

PEDRAZZI, L.: La politica scolastica del centro sinistra (The Educational Policy of the Centre-left). Bologna, Il Mulino, 1973. A detailed reconstruction of the 1960s' education debate, with a description and evaluation of the various reforms of that decade.

TRIVELLATO, P.: 'La politica della scuola (Educational policy)'. *In* ASCOLI, U. (ed.): *op. cit.*, pp. 207-237. A short synopsis of institutional and quantitative developments, with a discussion of the outcomes of educational policy on school achievements and of reform prospects.

2.7 Social services and assistance

BASSANINI, M., LUCIONI, C., PIETROBONI, P., RANCI-ORTIGOSA, E.: I servizi sociali, realtà e riforma (Social Services, Reality and Reform). Bologna, Il Mulino, 1977. A description of the institutional innovations in the sector during the 1970s and an evaluation of some initial experiences and some proposals for a greater level of efficiency.

DAVID, P.: 'Il sistema assistenziale in Italia (Social assistance in Italy)'. *In* ASCOLI, U. (ed.): *op. cit.*, pp. 185-205. A short survey of the historical development of public assistance since the unification. A more detailed analysis of the situation in the 1970s, based on institutional information and a discussion of future perspectives.

GIANOLIO, R., GUERZONI, L., STORCHI, G.P. (eds): Assistenza e beneficienza tra 'pubblico' e 'privato' (Assistance and Charity between Public and Private). Milan, Franco Angeli, 1980. A very detailed discussion of the new institutional framework from the 1970s, and of the current plans for reform.

LA ROSA, M., MINARDI, E., MONTANARI, A.: I servizi sociali tra programmazione e partecipazione (Social Services between Planning and Participation). Milan, Franco Angeli, 1978. The first part discusses in general the relationship between needs and the welfare state. The second part examines some specific cases of service provision in the field of health assistance for the old, maternity assistance and counselling, etc.

TERRANOVA, F.: Il potere assistenziale (The Power of Assistance). Rome, Editori Riuniti, 1975. An analysis of the relationship between the social assistance sector and the political system in historical perspective; views assistance agencies as instruments of social and political control.

TREVISAN, C.: Per una politica locale dei servizi sociali (Towards a Local Social Services Policy). Bologna, Il Mulino, 1978. Analyzes the first experiences of social service provision at the local level of the first half of the 1970s and discusses the administrative and organizational problems involved in the process of decentralization.

III The impact of social programmes

3.1 Poverty

BRAGHIN, P.: Inchiesta sulla miseria in Italia (1951-1952) (An Investigation on Destitution in Italy, 1951-1952). Turin, Einaudi, 1978. A historical reconstruction of the parliamentary inquiry of the early 1950s, containing a summary of the most interesting findings and of their impact.

CENTRO STUDI INVESTIMENTI SOCIALI - CENSIS: Indagine sulla povertà (An Inquiry on Poverty). Rome, 1979. A short empirical survey on the conditions of underprivileged groups; special emphasis is given to the emergence of the 'new poverty'.

D'APICE, C.: 'La povertà in Italia: note introduttive a una ricerca (Poverty in Italy: introductory remarks on the research)'. *Economia e Lavoro*, No. 2, 1975, pp. 221-238, and No. 4, 1975, pp. 503-522. The first empirical research on poverty after the 1951 parliamentary inquiry; based on the notion of absolute poverty, it offers interesting quantitative estimates.

SARPELLON, G. (ed.): La povertà in Italia (Poverty in Italy). Milan, Franco Angeli, 1982. Presents the Italian section of the EEC project on poverty. In addition to a summary report by the editor, it includes a number of excellent articles on the effects of social policies (income maintenance, health, housing, education, social assistance).

3.2 Inequality and income distribution

BARBAGLI, M.: Disoccupazione intellettuale e sistema scolastico in Italia (Intellectual Unemployment and the Italian School System). Bologna, Il Mulino, 1973. An old, but important research on the relationship between the school system and the labour market. Discusses in depth the role of higher education as an absorber of unemployment.

BRAGHIN, M.: Le diseguaglianze sociali. Analisi empirica sulla situazione della diseguaglianza in Italia (Social Inequality. Empirical Analysis of the State of Inequality in Italy). Milan, Sapere, 1973. The first part deals with the notion of inequality in contemporary sociological debate. The second part gives some statistical evidence of social and economic inequality (income distribution, access to social services, etc.) in Italy in the period 1950-70.

GORRIERI, E.: La giunglia retributiva (The Earnings' Jungle). Bologna, Il Mulino, 1972. A very influential study on the structure of earnings, showing the perverse effect of existing welfare benefit legislation and the privileged position of government employees.

GORRIERI, E.: La giungla dei bilanci familiari (The Household Budget Jungle). Bologna, Il Mulino, 1982. A short comparative empirical study of the income of Italian households and evaluations of the efficacy of the system of family transfers and tax credits. Contains reform proposals.

LIVRAGHI, R., ROBERTI, P., DI FILIPPO, E.: Distribuzione personale dei redditi e spesa sociale (The Distribution of Personal Income and Social Expenditure). Milan, Franco Angeli, 1982. A collection of the most important academic contributions to the empirical analysis of income distribution and the impact of social policies on income distribution.

LONGOBARDI, E.: 'La politica fiscale (Fiscal policy)'. *In* ASCOLI, U. (ed.): *op. cit.*, pp. 119-151. An overview of the fiscal side of the welfare state, containing some quantitative data, a discussion of the redistributive impact of the tax system and a synthesis of the current debate for its reform.

PADOA SCHIOPPA, F.: Scuola e classi sociali in Italia (The School System and Social Class in Italy). Bologna, Il Mulino, 1974. A detailed empirical analysis of the efficacy of educational policies in equalizing school achievement and in redistributing economic resources.

PINNARÒ, G.: Lavoro e redditi in Italia 1978-1979 (Work and Incomes in Italy, 1978-1979). Rome, Editori Riuniti, 1981, pp. 215-243. Gives a picture of earnings' differentials and the distribution of household incomes at the end of the 1970s. Contains a methodological discussion on the reliability of the Bank of Italy surveys on household income.

3.3 Social policy and the South

BECCHI COLLIDÀ, A.: Sussidi, lavoro, mezzogiorno (Subsidies, Employment and the South). Milan, Franco Angeli, 1978. A collection of articles on the situation of the labour market in the South, the role of transfer payments and their geographical distribution. Based on a large collection of statistical data.

BOCCELLI, N.: Il mezzogiorno sussidaito (The Subsidized South). Milan, Franco Angeli, 1982. A thorough analysis of the geographical distribution of transfer payments and other state subsidies. Discusses the efficacy of state policy in promoting the economic development of backward areas in the South.

FORTE, F. (ed.): La redistribuzione assistenziale (The Subsidizing Redistribution). Milan, Etas, 1978. Draws up a balance sheet of inflows and outflows of financial resources in the various regions by means of a detailed analysis of national accounts statistics.

Appendix Tables

Contents

Table 1

Gross Domestic Product and Total Public Expenditure

Year	GDP (at market prices, in billion lire)			Deflators (base)				Total public expenditure (in billion lire) OECD		ISTAT			Year
	at current prices	at constant (1970) prices	annual real growth rate	gross domestic product	capital formation	public consumption	private consumption	at current prices	as % of GDP	at current prices	as % of GDP	at constant (1970) prices	
1951	10 732	20 717		51.80	58.75	33.57	54.67			2 662	24.8	6 278	1951
1952	11 570	21 635	7.0	53.48	60.10	36.60	57.13			3 184	27.5	6 957	1952
1953	12 795	23 258	7.5	55.01	59.64	37.56	58.45			3 560	27.8	7 518	1953
1954	13 634	24 106	3.6	56.56	59.03	40.05	59.85			3 921	28.8	7 955	1954
1955	15 032	25 716	6.7	58.45	59.42	42.39	61.60			4 368	29.1	8 455	1955
1956	16 360	26 918	4.7	60.78	60.75	44.85	64.51			4 826	29.5	8 881	1956
1957	17 565	28 345	5.3	61.97	62.94	46.80	65.57			5 186	29.5	9 236	1957
1958	18 862	29 719	4.8	63.47	62.61	48.65	67.01			5 606	29.7	9 729	1958
1959	20 029	31 658	6.5	63.27	62.02	49.86	66.56			6 129	30.6	10 526	1959
1960	21 632	33 807	6.8	63.99	63.40	51.87	67.65			7 040	32.5	11 178	1960
1960	23 207	36 268									30.3		1960
1961	25 810	39 141	7.9	65.94	65.10	54.70	69.13	7 734	30.0	7 651	29.6	12 539	1961
1962	28 998	41 478	6.0	69.91	68.26	59.44	73.85	8 933	30.8	8 811	30.4	13 471	1962
1963	33 215	43 805	5.6	75.82	73.43	69.45	79.06	10 557	31.8	10 278	30.9	14 281	1963
1964	36 360	45 030	2.8	80.75	78.94	75.28	82.95	11 866	32.7	11 520	31.7	15 053	1964
1965	39 124	46 502	3.3	84.13	80.48	82.16	85.91	13 621	34.8	13 374	34.2	16 268	1965
1966	42 391	49 285	6.0	86.01	81.51	84.19	88.42	14 816	34.0	14 498	34.2	17 246	1966
1967	46 695	52 823	7.2	88.40	83.36	86.10	91.21	15 875	34.0	15 646	33.5	17 988	1967
1968	50 614	56 280	6.5	89.93	84.92	89.22	92.54	17 942	35.4	17 535	34.6	19 908	1968
1969	55 876	59 712	6.1	93.58	90.14	94.08	95.22	19 457	34.8	19 002	34.0	20 638	1969
1970	62 883	62 883	5.3	100.00	100.00	100.00	100.00	21 759	34.6	21 326	33.9	21 759	1970
1971	68 510	63 916	1.6	107.19	107.28	115.88	105.54	25 932	37.8	24 817	36.2	23 624	1971
1972	75 124	65 963	3.2	113.89	113.13	124.54	112.31	29 837	39.7	28 465	37.9	25 477	1972
1973	89 746	70 601	7.0	127.12	131.96	140.84	126.36	34 632	38.6	32 960	36.7	26 192	1973
1974	110 719	73 525	4.1	150.59	169.61	164.65	152.79	42 521	38.4	40 612	36.7	26 865	1974
1975	125 378	70 851	-3.6	176.96	202.24	184.77	179.76	52 496	41.9	54 458	43.4	28 523	1975
1976	156 657	75 011	5.9	208.84	240.69	216.03	212.30	65 186	41.6	66 923	42.7	30 509	1976
1977	190 083	76 435	1.9	248.69	286.22	263.36	250.94	79 391	41.7	81 870	43.1	30 716	1977
1978	222 254	78 488	2.7	283.17	319.55	313.09	283.29	100 872	45.4	104 546	47.0	34 094	1978
1979	269 657	82 308	4.9	327.62	378.07	379.36	326.05	119 106	44.2	123 001	45.6	34 285	1979
1980	337 402	85 569	4.0	394.30	446.23	466.64	392.31	149 385	44.3	154 380	45.7	35 509	1980

Table 2 Total Public Expenditure by Economic Function / Level of Government — Central Government Expenditure by Purpose

Year	Economic Function: Total public exp. at curr. pr. bill. lire	Per cent distribution: subs/ transf.	final cons.	interests on debt	public invest.	Level of Government: Total public exp. at curr. pr. bill. lire	Per cent distribution: local gov.	soc. sec. funds	central gov. and others	Central Government by Purpose: Total public exp. at curr. pr. bill. lire	Per cent distribution: security	const. order	welfare	growth promot	interests	other	Year
1951	2 662	37.4	46.7	6.6	9.3	2 662	22.6			1 894	29.5	5.2	19.4	27.7	5.4	12.8	1951
1952	3 184	38.9	44.4	6.6	10.0	3 184	22.7										1952
1953	3 560	40.9	41.6	6.4	11.2	3 560	23.8			2 310	29.8	5.3	21.3	23.5	6.3	12.9	1953
1954	3 921	38.3	42.0	7.6	12.1	3 921	22.3										1954
1955	4 368	40.3	40.6	7.5	11.6	4 368	22.1			2 619	25.5	5.5	25.0	23.0	7.4	14.3	1955
1956	4 826	41.8	40.2	7.6	10.3	4 826	21.4	25.7	52.9								1956
1957	5 186	42.7	39.7	7.1	10.4	5 186	22.7	25.1	52.2	3 198	22.7	8.7	28.4	20.3	6.9	12.8	1957
1958	5 606	42.8	40.3	6.4	10.5	5 606	22.4	28.5	49.1								1958
1959	6 129	43.4	39.4	7.3	9.9	6 129	23.6	29.4	47.0	3 621	21.5	8.4	30.2	19.5	6.8	13.6	1959
1960	7 040	41.3	37.3	6.8	9.7	7 040	23.5	27.9	48.6								1960
1961	7 734	41.8	42.3	4.8	11.1	7 651	26.4	28.4	45.3	4 682	19.7	8.0	30.1	21.6	5.8	14.9	1961
1962	8 933	42.9	42.4	4.5	10.2	8 811	28.8	31.5	39.8								1962
1963	10 557	42.8	43.7	3.9	9.5	10 278	28.1	32.6	39.2	6 106	18.5	8.0	31.7	23.7	4.4	13.7	1963
1964	11 866	42.8	43.9	3.6	9.8	11 520	27.1	31.3	41.6								1964
1965	13 621	44.9	43.4	3.5	8.1	13 374	26.3	33.6	40.1	8 217	18.4	6.7	35.0	24.3	3.1	12.5	1965
1966	14 816	45.4	42.5	4.1	8.0	14 498	25.7	34.7	39.6								1966
1967	15 875	45.7	42.4	4.7	7.3	15 646	27.2	35.0	37.8	9 914	16.8	6.6	35.0	26.0	2.9	12.7	1967
1968	17 942	46.8	40.9	4.5	8.1	17 535	26.8	35.1	38.0								1968
1969	19 457	46.9	40.8	4.8	7.4	19 002	28.7	37.8	33.4	13 267	14.0	7.9	35.4	25.7	2.3	12.9	1969
1970	21 759	46.8	39.8	5.0	8.4	21 326	28.0	38.1	33.8								1970
1971	25 932	46.5	40.9	5.2	7.4	24 817	28.9	41.4	30.0	16 623	16.2	6.4	37.8	26.6	1.9	11.6	1971
1972	29 837	46.9	40.5	5.5	7.1	28 465	32.1	41.4	26.5								1972
1973	34 632	47.0	40.2	6.2	6.7	32 960	35.2	41.9	22.9	22 930	16.3	6.1	33.0	27.6	2.4	14.7	1973
1974	42 521	45.9	39.3	7.3	7.5	40 612	34.8	46.6	18.6								1974
1975	52 496	44.6	36.9	9.5	8.5	54 458	35.6	40.8	23.6	38 469	11.1	4.1	34.2	22.3	5.0	23.6	1975
1976	65 186	45.8	35.5	10.9	8.6	66 923	35.8	41.3	22.9								1976
1977	79 391	44.0	36.1	11.6	7.9	81 870	32.3	40.1	27.6	62 157	10.6	3.6	37.7	24.5	8.1	16.5	1977
1978	100 872	44.0	34.8	13.0	8.2	104 546	29.5	37.8	32.7								1978
1979	119 106	43.5	36.4	13.1	7.0	123 001	34.8	28.5	36.7	103 886	9.3	4.5	35.4	18.1	10.6	22.0	1979
1980	149 385	42.4	36.4	13.9	7.2	154 380	35.6	31.2	33.2								1980

Table 3 Social Expenditure

Year	At current prices (in billion lire)						Consumer prices deflator (base 1970)	At constant (1970) prices (in billion lire)						Year
	Total	Income maint.	Education & culture	Health	Housing	Public assistance		Total	Income maint.	Education & culture	Health	Housing	Public assistance	
1951			230				371.61			685				1951
1952			264	128			306.75			721	350			1952
1953			295	145	112		265.04			785	386	188		1953
1954	1 830	905	331	159	105	330	235.74	3 531	1 561	826	397	178	569	1954
1955	2 006	990	383	178	97	358	199.60	3 747	1 660	903	420	163	601	1955
1956	2 247	1 090	461	227	89	380	171.29	4 029	1 742	1 028	506	147	607	1956
1957	2 591	1 187	544	335	111	414	146.20	4 564	1 861	1 162	716	176	649	1957
1958	3 055	1 497	598	365	160	435	122.40	5 125	2 239	1 229	750	256	651	1958
1959	3 474	1 657	687	419	254	457	110.90	5 803	2 489	1 378	840	410	687	1959
1960	3 828	1 793	830	507	211	487	105.00	6 242	2 624	1 600	977	333	713	1960
1961	4 234	1 971	1 012	580	163	508	100.00	6 685	2 802	1 850	1 060	250	722	1961
1962	5 041	2 460	1 215	679	117	570	95.17	7 456	3 327	1 044	1 142	171	771	1962
1963	5 948	2 871	1 506	840	88	643	92.57	7 919	3 612	2 169	1 210	120	809	1963
1964	6 503	3 104	1 680	922	104	693	91.40	8 098	3 686	2 232	1 225	132	823	1964
1965	7 826	3 856	1 917	1 178	157	718	89.61	9 169	4 389	2 333	1 434	195	817	1965
1966	8 557	4 198	2 095	1 349	161	754	87.85	9 814	4 685	2 488	1 602	197	841	1966
1967	9 602	4 499	2 501	1 618	177	807	84.19	10 802	4 923	2 905	1 879	212	883	1967
1968	10 694	5 001	2 767	1 775	208	943	79.48	11 757	5 402	3 101	1 990	245	1 019	1968
1969	11 985	5 741	3 067	2 039	184	954	73.92	12 666	6 033	3 260	2 167	204	1 002	1969
1970	13 339	6 276	3 333	2 497	145	1 148	70.33	13 399	6 276	3 333	2 497	145	1 148	1970
1971	15 619	7 038	3 913	3 184	131	1 353	68.34	14 239	6 703	3 377	2 748	122	1 289	1971
1972	17 863	8 343	4 210	3 666	132	1 512	66.57	15 327	7 523	3 380	2 944	117	1 363	1972
1973	20 259	9 617	4 919	3 872	144 (195)	1 656	66.85	15 600	7 857	3 493	2 749	109 (148)	1 353	1973
1974	26 825	13 016	5 632	6 120	161 (356)	1 701	63.79	17 414	8 903	3 421	3 717	95 (210)	1 163	1974
1975	33 829	17 280	6 745	7 384	40 (516)	1 904	62.58	18 101	10 088	3 650	3 996	20 (255)	1 112	1975
1976	41 243	20 481	8 646	9 069	32 (690)	2 357	59.62	19 929	10 261	4 002	4 198	13 (287)	1 181	1976
1977	50 406	24 378	11 350	10 908	61 (937)	2 833	57.99	20 322	10 341	4 310	4 142	21 (327)	1 202	1977
1978	60 629	30 177	13 555	13 021	64 (601)	3 275	56.47	21 298	11 386	4 329	4 159	20 (188)	1 236	1978
1979	73 267	35 994	15 660	16 800	- (1036)	3 777	55.39	21 795	11 734	4 128	4 428	- (274)	1 231	1979
1980	91 179	46 148	29 047	19 604	- (1073)	4 307	53.13	22 314	12 418	4 296	4 201	- (240)	1 159	1980

Table 4

Social Expenditure

Year	As % of gross domestic product						As % of total public expenditure						As % of social expenditure					Year
	Total	Income maint.	Education & culture	Health	Housing	Public assistance	Total	Income maint.	Education & culture	Health	Housing	Public assistance	Income maint.	Education & culture	Health	Housing	Public assistance	
1951			2.1						8.6									1951
1952			2.3	1.1					8.3	4.0								1952
1953			2.3	1.1	0.9				8.3	4.1	3.1							1953
1954	13.4	6.6	2.4	1.2	0.8	2.4	46.7	23.1	8.4	4.1	2.7	8.4	49.4	18.3	8.8	5.8	18.2	1954
1955	13.3	6.6	2.5	1.2	0.6	2.4	45.9	22.7	8.8	4.1	2.2	8.2	49.3	19.3	9.0	4.9	18.0	1955
1956	13.7	6.7	2.8	1.4	0.5	2.3	46.6	22.6	9.6	4.7	1.8	7.9	48.5	20.7	10.2	4.0	17.0	1956
1957	14.7	6.8	3.1	1.9	0.6	2.4	50.0	22.9	10.5	6.5	2.1	8.0	45.8	21.1	13.0	4.3	16.1	1957
1958	16.2	7.9	3.2	1.9	0.8	2.3	54.5	26.7	10.7	6.5	2.9	7.8	49.0	19.7	12.0	5.3	14.3	1958
1959	17.4	8.3	3.4	2.1	1.3	2.3	56.7	27.0	11.2	6.8	4.1	7.5	47.7	19.9	12.1	7.3	13.2	1959
1960	15.5	7.7	3.6	2.2	0.9	2.1	54.5	25.5	11.8	7.2	3.0	6.9	46.8	21.7	13.3	5.5	12.8	1960
1961	16.4	7.6	3.9	2.2	0.6	2.0	55.4	25.8	13.2	7.6	2.1	6.6	46.6	24.0	13.7	3.9	12.0	1961
1962	17.4	8.5	4.2	2.3	0.4	2.0	57.2	27.9	13.8	7.7	1.3	6.5	48.8	24.1	13.5	2.3	11.3	1962
1963	17.9	8.6	4.5	2.5	0.3	1.9	57.9	27.9	14.7	8.2	0.9	6.3	48.3	25.4	14.1	1.5	10.8	1963
1964	17.9	8.5	4.6	2.5	0.3	1.9	56.4	26.9	14.6	8.0	0.9	6.0	47.7	25.9	14.2	1.6	10.7	1964
1965	20.0	9.8	4.9	3.0	0.4	1.8	58.4	28.8	14.3	8.8	1.2	5.4	49.3	24.5	15.1	2.0	9.2	1965
1966	20.6	9.9	4.9	3.2	0.4	1.8	60.3	28.9	14.5	9.3	1.1	5.2	49.1	24.5	15.8	1.9	8.8	1966
1967	20.5	9.6	5.4	3.5	0.4	1.7	61.3	28.7	16.0	10.3	1.1	5.2	46.8	26.1	16.9	1.8	8.4	1967
1968	21.1	9.9	5.5	3.5	0.4	1.9	60.9	28.5	15.8	10.1	1.2	5.4	46.7	25.9	16.6	1.9	8.8	1968
1969	21.4	10.3	5.5	3.6	0.3	1.7	63.1	30.2	16.1	10.7	1.0	5.0	47.9	25.6	17.0	1.5	8.0	1969
1970	21.3	10.0	5.3	4.0	0.2	1.8	62.8	29.4	15.6	11.7	0.7	5.4	46.8	24.9	18.6	1.1	8.6	1970
1971	22.8	10.3	5.7	4.6	0.2	2.0	62.9	28.4	15.8	12.8	0.5	5.4	45.1	25.1	20.4	0.8	8.7	1971
1972	23.8	11.1	5.6	4.9	0.2	2.0	62.8	29.3	14.8	12.9	0.5	5.3	46.7	23.6	20.5	0.7	8.5	1972
1973	22.6	10.7	5.5	4.3	0.2 (0.2)	1.8	61.5	29.2	14.9	11.7	0.4 (0.6)	5.0	47.5	24.3	19.1	1.0	8.2	1973
1974	24.2	11.8	5.1	5.5	0.1 (0.3)	1.5	66.1	32.0	13.9	15.1	0.4 (0.9)	4.2	48.5	21.0	22.8	1.3	6.3	1974
1975	27.0	13.8	5.4	5.9	0.0 (0.4)	1.5	62.1	31.7	12.4	13.6	0.1 (0.9)	3.5	51.1	19.9	21.8	1.5	5.6	1975
1976	26.3	13.1	5.5	5.8	0.0 (0.4)	1.5	61.1	30.6	12.9	13.6	0.0 (1.0)	3.5	49.7	21.0	22.0	1.7	5.7	1976
1977	26.5	12.8	6.0	5.7	0.0 (0.5)	1.5	61.6	29.8	13.9	13.3	0.1 (1.1)	3.5	48.4	22.5	21.6	1.9	5.6	1977
1978	27.3	13.6	6.1	5.9	0.0 (0.3)	1.5	58.0	28.9	13.0	12.5	0.1 (0.6)	3.1	49.8	22.4	21.5	1.0	5.4	1978
1979	27.2	13.3	5.8	6.2	- (0.4)	1.4	59.6	29.4	12.7	13.7	- (0.8)	3.0	48.6	21.5	23.1	1.4	5.2	1979
1980	27.0	13.7	5.9	5.8	- (0.3)	1.3	59.1	29.9	13.0	12.7	- (0.7)	2.8	50.6	22.0	21.5	1.2	4.7	1980

Table 5

E x p e n d i t u r e o n I n c o m e M a i n t e n a n c e P r o g r a m m e s

At current prices (in billion lire)

Year	Pensions							Family Allowances			Unemployment	Work injuries	Sickness & maternity	Year
	Total	Old age	Invalidity	Survivors	Social	Government employees	Others	Total	Private employees	Government employees				
1951	228	71	26	8		123			157		24			1951
1952	344	120	43	15		166			209		25		24	1952
1953	386	139	49	18		180			273		24		27	1953
1954	440	156	57	22		205		387	304	83	22	27	29	1954
1955	496	178	66	25		227		409	324	85	25	28	32	1955
1956	550	196	75	30		249		438	352	86	37	29	36	1956
1957	609	214	84	33		278		465	378	87	36	32	45	1957
1958	886	357	142	61		326		486	399	87	42	38	45	1958
1959	991	386	160	74		371		530	420	110	41	46	49	1959
1960	1 082	415	179	81		396	11	568	450	118	43	51	50	1960
1961	1 179	439	199	89		433	19	612	486	126	60	59	61	1961
1962	1 553	612	284	156		475	26	689	544	145	67	77	73	1962
1963	1 816	700	326	170		588	32	784	562	222	64	108	99	1963
1964	1 962	732	362	181		648	39	809	568	241	82	114	137	1964
1965	2 546	965	532	263		739	47	897	653	244	125	143	145	1965
1966	2 806	1 040	595	276		838	57	966	712	254	106	175	145	1966
1967	3 055	1 126	672	297		892	68	1 003	747	256	88	196	157	1967
1968	3 469	1 253	806	344		986	80	1 037	783	254	98	228	169	1968
1969	4 170	1 492	1 027	413	72	1 068	98	1 018	755	263	108	261	185	1969
1970	4 578	1 581	1 155	450	118	1 160	114	1 069	802	267	113	287	229	1970
1971	5 045	1 751	1 300	500	127	1 236	131	1 114	830	284	251	339	288	1971
1972	6 237	2 075	1 679	617	187	1 514	165	1 095	818	277	226	411	375	1972
1973	7 303	2 464	1 932	778	199	1 713	217	1 109	820	289	305	417	483	1973
1974	9 380	3 183	2 720	992	273	1 923	289	2 001	1 690	311	460	544	630	1974
1975	12 702	4 117	4 037	1 303	411	2 465	369	2 419	2 072	347	652	645	862	1975
1976	15 617	5 020	5 077	1 603	494	2 937	436	2 428	2 064	364	732	721	983	1976
1977	19 234	5 961	6 008	2 052	554	4 127	532	2 021	1 661	360	939	991	1 193	1977
1978	24 019	7 792	7 153	2 603	648	5 199	624	2 379	1 831	548	1 161	1 303	1 315	1978
1979	28 495	9 803	8 057	3 402	609	6 554	706	2 399	1 818	581	1 304	1 388	1 772	1979
1980	37 508	11 918	11 395	4 024	933	8 423	815	3 360	2 523	837	1 371	1 876	2 033	1980

Table 6 Expenditure on Income Maintenance Programmes

At constant (1970) prices (in billion lire)

Year	Pensions						Family Allowances			Unemployment	Work injuries	Sickness & maternity	Year
	Total	Old age	Invalidity	Survivors	Social	Government employees	Others	Total	Private employees	Government employees				
1951	429	134	49	15		231			295		45			1951
1952	621	217	78	27		300			377		45		43	1952
1953	684	246	87	32		319			483		42		48	1953
1954	759	269	98	38		354		667	524	143	38	46	51	1954
1955	832	299	111	42		381		686	543	143	42	46	53	1955
1956	879	313	120	48		398		700	562	137	59	47	57	1956
1957	955	335	132	52		436		729	593	136	56	50	71	1957
1958	1 325	534	212	91		488		727	597	130	63	57	67	1958
1959	1 489	580	240	111		557		796	631	165	62	69	73	1959
1960	1 583	607	262	119		579	16	831	658	173	63	74	73	1960
1961	1 676	624	283	127		616	27	870	691	179	85	83	87	1961
1962	2 101	828	384	211		643	35	932	736	196	91	105	99	1962
1963	2 285	881	410	214		740	40	986	707	279	81	136	125	1963
1964	2 330	869	430	215		770	46	961	675	286	97	135	162	1964
1965	2 898	1 098	606	299		841	54	1 021	743	278	142	162	165	1965
1966	3 131	1 151	664	308		935	64	1 078	795	283	118	195	162	1966
1967	3 342	1 232	735	325		976	74	1 097	817	280	96	215	172	1967
1968	3 748	1 354	871	372		1 065	86	1 120	846	274	106	246	183	1968
1969	4 382	1 568	1 079	434	76	1 122	103	1 070	793	276	113	274	194	1969
1970	4 578	1 581	1 155	450	118	1 160	114	1 069	802	267	113	287	229	1970
1971	4 805	1 668	1 238	476	121	1 177	125	1 061	790	270	239	323	275	1971
1972	5 624	1 871	1 514	556	169	1 365	149	987	738	250	204	370	338	1972
1973	5 967	2 013	1 578	636	163	1 400	177	906	670	236	249	341	395	1973
1974	6 416	2 177	1 860	679	187	1 315	198	1 369	1 156	213	315	372	431	1974
1975	7 415	2 404	2 357	761	240	1 439	215	1 412	1 210	203	381	377	503	1975
1976	7 824	2 515	2 544	803	247	1 496	218	1 216	1 034	182	367	361	492	1976
1977	8 159	2 529	2 549	870	235	1 751	226	857	705	153	398	420	506	1977
1978	9 062	2 940	2 699	982	244	1 962	235	898	691	207	438	491	496	1978
1979	9 437	3 196	2 627	1 109	198	2 137	230	782	593	189	425	452	578	1979
1980	10 094	3 207	3 067	1 083	251	2 267	219	904	679	225	369	505	547	1980

Table 7 Total public revenues and social security receipts

Year	Total public revenues (in billion lire): at current prices	as % of GDP	percent distribution: dir. taxes	indir. taxes	soc. sec. contr.	other	Saving: at current prices (bill. lire)	as % of GDP	Net lending: at current prices (bill. lire)	as % of GDP	Social security receipts (in billion lire): total at current prices	by income of receipt (%): insured	employers	state	other	Year
1951	2 697	25.1	15.1	41.5	19.5	23.9	35	0.3	-222	-2.1	921	4.4	69.2	23.3	3.1	1951
1952	3 018	26.1	16.6	41.7	21.7	20.0	14	0.1	-371	-3.2	1 137	5.2	66.6	24.9	3.3	1952
1953	3 748	29.3	15.6	38.7	20.1	25.6	188	1.5	-344	-2.7	1 338	6.0	65.6	24.6	3.8	1953
1954	4 158	30.5	15.6	39.7	22.7	22.0	237	1.7	-294	-2.2	1 564	5.8	66.9	23.6	3.7	1954
1955	4 607	30.6	15.3	39.3	22.6	22.8	239	1.6	-365	-2.4	1 634	8.6	65.6	21.7	4.1	1955
1956	5 230	32.0	15.6	39.7	23.8	20.9	404	2.5	-194	-1.2	1 808	9.3	67.3	18.9	4.5	1956
1957	5 717	32.5	15.9	38.7	23.1	22.3	531	3.0	-222	-1.3	1 960	9.6	68.0	17.7	4.7	1957
1958	6 050	32.1	16.7	37.9	24.6	20.8	444	2.3	-251	-1.3	2 216	10.6	65.2	17.0	7.2	1958
1959	6 571	32.1	16.8	37.5	25.6	20.1	442	2.2	-293	-1.4	2 364	12.0	66.1	16.8	5.1	1959
1960	6 674	28.8	18.6	42.1	28.9	10.4	632	2.7	-192	-0.8	2 934	12.1	60.0	23.3	4.6	1960
1961	7 263	28.1	17.9	42.6	29.4	10.1	751	2.9	-175	-0.7	2 973	13.7	63.0	17.7	5.6	1961
1962	8 409	29.0	19.3	40.9	30.5	9.3	799	2.8	-254	-0.9	3 541	13.9	64.4	16.5	5.2	1962
1963	9 806	29.5	18.3	38.9	33.3	9.5	656	2.0	-394	-1.2	4 344	15.0	63.4	16.3	5.3	1963
1964	11 122	30.6	19.4	37.9	32.0	10.7	883	2.4	-299	-0.8	5 036	14.2	65.1	15.4	5.3	1964
1965	11 744	30.0	20.4	38.3	32.2	9.1	-214	-0.5	-1 500	-3.8	5 811	13.7	56.1	24.5	5.7	1965
1966	12 757	30.1	20.0	37.9	31.1	11.0	-274	-0.5	-1 603	-3.8	6 074	14.6	60.2	20.1	5.1	1966
1967	14 498	31.0	19.0	38.6	32.5	9.9	472	1.0	-1 044	-2.2	6 353	15.4	64.5	15.2	4.9	1967
1968	15 980	31.5	20.1	37.2	33.6	9.1	289	0.6	-1 409	-2.8	7 462	14.5	62.4	16.8	6.3	1968
1969	17 151	30.7	20.3	37.3	32.3	10.1	68	0.1	-1 742	-3.1	8 570	13.5	59.0	22.3	5.2	1969
1970	19 109	30.4	18.0	36.8	35.1	10.1	116	0.2	-2 215	-3.5	9 756	14.2	61.5	19.6	4.7	1970
1971	21 291	31.1	18.3	34.5	35.9	11.3	-1 381	-2.0	-3 533	-5.2	12 110	14.4	61.7	18.8	5.1	1971
1972	23 181	30.9	20.3	32.9	36.1	10.7	-3 113	-3.9	-5 604	-6.2	13 741	12.3	59.5	21.1	7.1	1972
1973	27 327	30.4	19.7	32.1	37.4	10.8	-3 544	-3.9	-6 275	-7.0	15 748	13.4	62.4	18.4	5.8	1973
1974	33 876	30.6	19.6	32.1	38.3	10.0	-4 211	-3.8	-7 786	-7.0	20 957	13.1	59.8	21.9	5.2	1974
1975	39 166	31.2	21.4	28.0	41.4	9.2	-8 862	-7.1	-14 635	-11.7	22 871	12.3	66.6	17.0	4.1	1975
1976	51 566	32.9	23.3	29.1	38.6	9.0	-8 007	-5.1	-14 089	-9.0	28 510	12.2	65.4	18.5	3.9	1976
1977	65 161	34.3	25.0	29.9	36.4	8.7	-8 115	-4.3	-15 115	-7.9	36.034	13.4	61.2	21.2	4.2	1977
1978	80 114	36.0	27.8	27.9	34.7	9.6	-12 621	-5.7	-21 654	-9.7						1978
1979	96 386	35.7	27.3	26.4	36.3	10.0	-14 635	-5.3	-25 464	-9.1						1979
1980	126 642	37.5	29.7	26.9	33.7	9.7	-11 959	-3.5	-26 181	-7.7						1980

Table 8 Population and Labour Force

Year	Total population in 1,000	Pop. aged 60+ in 1,000	Pop. aged 60+ as % of tot. pop.	Total labour in 1,000	Total labour as % of tot. pop.	Total employed in 1,000	Employed in agric. (percent distribution)	Employed in industry (percent distribution)	Employed in other (percent distribution)	Total unemployed in 1,000	Total unemployed as % of labour force	Year
1951	47 159	5 772	12.2	20 268	43.0							1951
1952	47 339	5 841	12.3	19 358	40.1	18 072	41.5	31.0	27.5	1 451	7.5	1952
1953	47 519	5 911	12.4	n.a.	44.5							1953
1954	47 699	5 980	12.5	11 208	44.5							1954
1955	47 880	6 050	12.6	20 117	42.0							1955
1956	48 060	6 119	12.7	20 092	41.8							1956
1957	48 239	6 189	12.8	20 787	43.1							1957
1958	48 418	6 258	12.9	21 361	44.1							1958
1959	48 604	6 330	13.0	21 879	45.0	20 349	33.8	32.7	33.5	1 530	7.0	1959
1960	48 967	6 550	13.4	21 545	44.0	20 330	32.5	33.7	33.7	1 215	5.6	1960
1961	49 156	6 701	13.6	21 535	43.8	20 427	30.7	34.9	34.3	1 108	5.1	1961
1962	49 444	6 886	13.9	21 306	43.1	20 337	29.1	36.1	34.8	969	4.5	1962
1963	49 949	7 022	14.0	20 852	41.7	20 045	27.1	37.4	35.4	807	3.9	1963
1964	50 730	7 257	14.3	20 870	41.1	19 996	25.7	37.5	36.8	904	4.3	1964
1965	51 380	7 487	14.6	20 612	40.1	19 502	26.2	37.0	37.0	1 110	5.4	1965
1966	51 927	7 922	15.2	20 367	39.2	19 175	25.1	36.8	38.1	1 192	5.9	1966
1967	52 409	7 928	15.1	20 507	39.1	19 401	24.3	37.1	38.6	1 106	5.4	1967
1968	52 778	8 162	15.5	20 555	38.9	19 383	22.3	37.6	39.6	1 172	5.7	1968
1969	53 101	8 205	15.4	20 369	38.4	19 209	21.9	38.7	39.4	1 160	5.7	1969
1970	53 486	8 440	15.8	20 436	38.2	19 325	20.1	39.3	40.6	1 111	5.4	1970
1971	53 517	8 660	16.2	20 404	38.1	19 295	20.1	39.5	40.4	1 109	5.4	1971
1972	53 548	8 880	16.6	20 293	37.9	18 996	18.9	39.4	41.7	1 297	6.4	1972
1973	53 981	9 094	16.8	20 490	38.0	19 185	18.2	38.9	42.3	1 305	6.4	1973
1974	54 541	9 275	17.0	20 714	38.0	19 601	17.4	39.0	43.8	1 113	5.4	1974
1975	54 967	9 370	17.0	20 946	38.1	19 716	16.6	38.9	44.3	1 230	5.9	1975
1976	55 325	9 307	16.8	21 285	38.5	19 859	16.3	38.1	45.6	1 426	6.7	1976
1977	55 576	9 186	16.5	21 607	38.9	20 062	15.7	38.6	45.6	1 545	7.2	1977
1978	55 806	9 062	16.2	21 730	38.9	20 159	15.7	38.0	47.0	1 571	7.2	1978
1979	55 016	9 047	16.4	22 075	40.1	20 377	14.8	38.1	47.7	1 698	7.7	1979
1980	56 121	9 439	16.8	22 372	39.9	20 675	14.1	37.6	48.2	1 698	7.6	1980

Table 9

Membership of Social Insurance Programmes

(in 1,000 and as a % of the labour force)

Year	Pensions total		Pensions private sec.		Pensions public sector		family allowances		unemployment		occupational injuries		health care		sickness cash benefits		Year
1951									3 751	18.5	11 886	58.6	9 514	46.9			1951
1952									3 751	19.4			10 087	52.1			1952
1953									3 925				10 744				1953
1954			8 312	39.2					5 250	24.7			10 967	51.7			1954
1955			8 316	41.3					5 750	28.6	11 368	56.5	13 496	67.1	10 945	54.4	1955
1956			9 543	47.5					7 080	35.2	11 551	57.5	14 155	70.4			1956
1957			15 394	74.1					7 932	38.2	12 317	59.2	14 873	71.5	11 188	53.8	1957
1958			16 333	76.5					8 702	38.4	12 716	59.5	15 131	70.8	11 412	53.4	1958
1959			17 381	79.4					8 202	37.5	12 853	58.7	15 494	70.8	11 792	59.9	1959
1960	20 634	95.8	18 932	87.9	1 702	7.9	5 924	27.5	8 203	38.1	13 364	62.0	16 074	74.6	12 255	56.9	1960
1961	21 454	99.6	19 657	91.3	1 797	8.3	7 716	35.8	8 200	38.1	13 323	61.9	17 066	79.2	12 645	58.7	1961
1962	21 667	101.5	19 762	92.7	1 875	8.8	7 635	35.8	8 700	40.8	13 308	62.5	n.a.	n.a.	13 061	61.3	1962
1963	21 750	104.3	19 792	94.9	1 958	9.4	7 727	37.1	8 700	41.7	13 730	65.8	17 967	86.2	13 111	62.9	1963
1964	19 403	53.0	17 366	83.2	2 037	9.8	7 776	37.3	8 700	41.7	13 006	62.3	17 069	81.8	13 006	62.3	1964
1965	20 558	101.6	18 868	91.5	2 090	10.1	7 517	36.5	9 524	46.2	12 339	59.9	16 668	80.9	12 424	60.3	1965
1966	22 172	108.8	19 985	98.1	2 187	10.7	7 050	34.6	9 493	46.6	12 603	61.9	16 668	81.8	12 379	60.8	1966
1967	22 479	109.6	20 266	98.8	2 213	10.8	7 255	35.4	9 584	46.7	13 647	66.5	17 182	83.8	12 601	61.5	1967
1968	22 151	107.7	19 902	96.8	2 249	10.9	7 694	37.4	9 527	46.3	13 332	64.9	17 100	83.2	12 820	62.4	1968
1969	22 175	108.8	19 883	97.6	2 292	11.2	7 404	36.3	9 497	46.6	12 884	63.2	17 153	84.2	13 070	64.2	1969
1970	21 745	106.4	19 356	94.7	2 393	11.7	7 786	38.1	9 473	46.3	11 182	54.7	17 871	87.4	13 356	65.3	1970
1971	21 952	107.8	19 423	95.2	2 579	12.6	7 584	37.2	9 435	46.2	11 006	53.9	17 454	85.5	13 231	64.8	1971
1972	21 953	106.5	18 947	93.4	2 644	13.1	7 857	38.7	9 700	47.8	9 500	46.8	17 833	87.9	13 369	65.9	1972
1973	21 876	106.8	19 109	93.3	2 767	13.5	8 385	40.9	9 401	45.9	10 047	49.0	17 980	87.7	13 722	67.0	1973
1974	21 624	104.3	18 754	90.5	2 870	13.8	8 030	38.8	9 475	45.7	9 607	46.4	18 577	89.7	14 257	68.8	1974
1975	21 712	103.6	18 710	89.3	3 002	14.3	8 672	41.4	10 290	49.1	9 499	45.3	18 064	86.2	14 323	68.4	1975
1976	21 811	102.4	18 712	87.9	3 099	14.5	8 669	40.7	10 305	48.4	9 575	45.0	18 215	85.6	14 325	67.3	1976
1977	22 333	103.3	19 081	88.3	3 252	15.0	8 330	38.6	10 370	48.0	9 494	43.7	18 468	85.5	14 381	66.6	1977
1978	22 289	102.6	18 994	87.4	3 295	15.2	8 313	38.2	10 300	47.4	9 507	43.7	18 483	85.1	14 381	66.2	1978
1979	22 549	102.0	19 202	86.9	3 340	15.1			10 430	47.2							1979
1980	22 643	101.2	19 275	86.2	3 368	15.0			10 430	46.6							1980

Table 10

Clienteles of Social Insurance Programmes

(number of beneficiaries or benefits in 1,000)

Year	total	Pensions old age	invalidity	survivors	social	government employees	others	family allowances	unemployment benefits	occup. injuries	sickness benefits	public assistance	Year
1951	2 483	1 324	501	172		486			841	251	1 875		1951
1952	2 623	1 418	526	197		482			889	285	2 014	2 803	1952
1953	2 878	1 574	573	243		488			923	320	2 314	2 627	1953
1954	3 188	1 741	654	289		504			921	354	2 191	2 486	1954
1955	3 539	1 951	732	330		526			883	391	2 253	2 695	1955
1956	3 833	2 084	817	390		542			1 259	433	2 604	2 911	1956
1957	4 065	2 182	892	441		550			1 326	467	3 315	2 639	1957
1958	5 042	2 857	976	622		587			1 427	499	2 799	2 617	1958
1959	5 521	3 041	1 092	763		625			1 422	526	2 778	2 557	1959
1960	5 996	3 249	1 224	851		655	17		1 458	554	2 944	2 508	1960
1961	6 306	3 327	1 361	911		679	28		1 565	597	2 881	2 377	1961
1962	6 539	3 364	1 483	968		690	34		1 665	625	3 405	2 331	1962
1963	6 838	3 382	1 656	1 036		719	45		1 608	639	3 795	2 190	1963
1964	7 202	3 431	1 873	1 102		746	50		1 689	647	3 597	2 110	1964
1965	7 675	3 532	2 145	1 187		754	57		1 934	700	3 631	2 034	1965
1966	8 085	3 590	2 405	1 253		774	63		1 921	739	3 235.	1 939	1966
1967	8 669	3 764	2 695	1 335		803	72	6 400	1 734	776	3 867	1 838	1967
1968	9 034	3 785	2 955	1 374		842	78	6 538	1 655	815	3 953	1 721	1968
1969	9 821	3 832	3 146	1 414	471	872	86	6 204	1 577	862	4 199	1 700	1969
1970	10 593	3 868	3 415	1 550	766	902	92	5 548	1 558	895	4 282	1 618	1970
1971	11 121	3 932	3 698	1 648	820	922	101	5 753	1 678	919	4 658	1 532	1971
1972	11 675	4 006	4 030	1 780	805	941	113	5 497	1 812	965	5 149	1 529	1972
1973	12 074	4 033	4 282	1 860	810	962	122	5 585	1 777	1 008	5 777	1 385	1973
1974	12 674	4 163	4 602	1 961	820	1 000	128	8 110	1 661	1 057	6 433	1 215	1974
1975	13 101	4 175	4 959	1 967	824	1 035	141	8 177	1 791	1 055	6 802	1 185	1975
1976	13 413	4 099	5 189	2 055	827	1 105	145	8 254	2 085	1 133	6 750	1 083	1976
1977	13 907	4 157	5 272	2 265	818	1 242	153	7 425	2 099	1 167	6 707	919	1977
1978	13 797	3 955	5 355	2 222	801	1 306	158	7 853	2 069	1 207	n.a.	n.a.	1978
1979	13 944	4 128	5 231	2 305	704	1 398	178	7 762	n.a.	1 238	n.a.	n.a.	1979
1980	14 178	4 165	5 314	2 394	708	1 413	184	7 485	n.a.	1 275	n.a.	n.a.	1980

Notes to and sources for appendix tables

Tables 1 and 2

Gross domestic product:
Data refer to Gross Domestic Product at market prices. The series unites two different series: an older series covering the period 1951-1960 and a more recent series covering the period 1960-1980, which contains an estimate of the non-institutional' (black) sector of the economy. For the year 1960, two figures are given. Data in both current and constant (1970) prices have been drawn from the original sources.
Sources: (1) 1981 and 1982 editions, (2) 1971.

Deflators:
Deflators have been derived by dividing the figures in current prices by the figures in constant prices for the corresponding National Accounts categories given in (1) (implicit deflators).

Total public expenditure:
Data refer to the consolidated public sector. Table 1 presents two distinct series: an OECD series, for the period 1961-1980, and an ISTAT series for the period 1951-1980. There is a difference of definition between OECD and ISTAT: the former does not include capital transfers in its definition of total public expenditure whereas the latter does. The difference in definition should in principle produce higher figures for the ISTAT series, but this only occurs after 1974 (where the discrepancy is due to the inclusion by ISTAT of capital transfers). For earlier years, in spite of its more comprehensive definition, the ISTAT series gives lower figures than the OECD, because data for final consumption are somewhat lower.

The figures at constant prices have been obtained by separately deflating the economic categories of public expenditure and then adding them up. Transfers and subsidies have been deflated using the private consumption deflator; final consumption has been deflated using the public consumption deflator; interests on debt have been deflated using the GDP deflator; and public investment has been deflated using the capital formation deflator. In the disaggregation by economic function, a single series has been used, uniting the ISTAT figures for 1951-1960 (only these are available), and the OECD figures for 1961-1980 (which provide more reliable figures for final consumption).

The disaggregation by level of government is based on the ISTAT series for the whole period. For local government and social security funds it refers to consolidated expenditure. Central government and other' expenditure has been derived residually, by simply subtracting local government and social serucity funds' expenditure from the total: besides central government, it includes expenditure of autonomous state enterprises (*aziende autonome*), such as public railways, telephones, post and telecommunications etc.
Sources: (1), (3) 1973 and 1977 editions (total expenditure and disaggregation by economic function), (4) (disaggregation by level of government).

Central government expenditure:
The totals reported in Table 2 are gross figures including transfers to local government and social security funds and are therefore not comparable with the figures reported in the disaggregation of total public expenditure by economic function or level of government. The disaggregation by purpose has been derived by re-combining similar disaggregations found in the sources. Expenditure on security includes national defence (*difesa nazionale*), foreign relations (*relazioni internazionali*), and war burdens (*oneri in dipendenza della guerra*). Expenditure on constitutional order includes general administration of the state (*amministrazione generale dello stato*) and justice and public order (*giustizia e ordine pubblico*). Expenditure on welfare includes education and culture (*istruzione e cultura*), social burdens (*oneri di carattere sociale*), and housing intervention (*interventi nel campo abitativo*). Expenditure on economic burdens and intervention (?) (*oneri e interventi in campo economica*). Expenditure on interests 138 udes interests on state debts (*interessi su debiti contratti dello stato*).
Source: (4).

Tables 3 and 4

Total social expenditure:
The total figure has not been drawn from original sources, but is simply the sum of the various items listed next to it. The figure in constant prices has been obtained by separately deflating the single items and then adding them up. Income maintenance and public assistance have been deflated using the consumer prices deflator; education and health using the public consumption deflator; and housing using the capital formation deflator.

Income maintenance:
The total figure is the sum of the various items listed in Table 4.

Education and culture:
The figures have been derived by adding central and local government expenditure on education and culture (as found in the sources). Even though not drawn from a consolidated account, the amounts given should not (in principle at least), contain transfers across levels.
Source: (4)

Health:
For the period 1952-1974, the figures have been obtained by adding the following items: central and regional government expenditure on public health and sanitation (*igiene e sanità*), and social security funds' expenditure on benefits in kind (*prestazioni in natura*) for hospital, medical and pharmaceutical assistance. All sickness, maternity and disability schemes are included. For the period 1975-1980, the figures have been drawn directly from the source, under the heading of total health expenditure (*spesa sanitarie totale*). The figures for the latter period are more reliable than those for the former (unfortunately, they are only available after 1975, i.e. after the hospital reform). The two series may not be fully comparable both in functional and institutional terms. Given the major institutional changes in this field, full comparability over time is very difficult to achieve.
Source: (4)

Housing:
For the period 1953-1978 the figures refer to amounts for housing works (*importi per lavori eseguiti nel campo delle abitazioni*), i.e. to actual payments made by central and local government and housing funds for housing construction (grants to private firms are included). Starting from 1974, these figures become quite unreliable (see discussion in text). Thus, a second series is given in parentheses for the years 1973-1980, which refers to engaged investments (*impegni d'investimento*). This difference in definition renders the two series incomparable. For the computation of total social expenditure, the second series has been used for 1973-1980.
Sources: (5), (6).

Public assistance:
For the period 1954-1974, the figures have been obtained by adding the following items: central government expenditure on direct social assistance (*assistenza sociale diretta*), and on war pensions (*pensioni di guerra*); local government expenditure on social and public assistance (*assistenza sociale/pubblica*); expenditure by separate local agencies (ECA, *patronati*) operating in the fields of social assistance; expenditure by compulsory social assistance funds. For the period 1975-1980 the figures have been drawn directly from the source, under the heading assistance expenditure (*spese per l'assistenza*) - see health for problems of comparability.
Source: (4)

Consumer price index:
Source: (3)

Tables 5 and 6

Pensions:
The figures for old age, invalidity and survivors' pensions only refer to INPS schemes (*pensioni di vecchiaia, invalidità e superstiti*). Social pensions refer to social pensions (*pensioni sociali*) under the INPS general scheme. The figures given for government employees refer to the whole public sector and to all types of pensions (the sources do not give breakdowns by type). 'Others' includes all types of pensions under the non-INPS public schemes.

Sources: (4), (7) (old age, invalidity, survivors' and others), (8) (social pensions and government employees).

Family allowances:
The figures for private employees refer to all family allowances (*assegni famigliari*) paid by INPS (includes allowances for the self-employed in agriculture). The figures for government employees refer to family supplements (*aggiunte di famiglie*).
Source: (4)

Unemployment:
The figures refer only to cash benefits, i.e. benefits for full unemployment (*prestazioni di disoccupazione*), and benefits for partial or temporary unemployment (*integrazioni salariali*) paid by INPS.
Source: (4)

Work injuries:
The figures refer to all cash benefits (*prestazioni economiche*) for work injuries paid ty INATL and other public schemes.
Source: (4)

Sickness and maternity (Tables 5 and 6):
The figures refer to all cash benefits (*prestazioni economiche*) for sickness and maternity. For the period 1952-1960, only the INAM general scheme and the INPS tuberculosis scheme are included; for 1961-1977, special schemes are also included. For the years 1978-1980 (when all INAM and special schemes were liquidated), the figures have been taken directly from the source, under the heading sickness and maternity (*malattia e materrità*).
Source: (4)

Table 7

Total public revenues:
The figures have been drawn form the ISTAT series for 1951-1959 and from the OECD series for 1960-1980 (OECD figures are not available for the former period). These two series are not wholly comperable - in fact, the OECD series does not include capital receipts in its total (which thus corresponds to the total of current receipts). The difference in definition explains the change in the percent distribution of revenues by type between 1959 and 1960 (ISTAT includes capital receipts under 'other'). Saving is the balance between current disbursements and current receipts. Net lending is the most inclusive balance of the transactions of general government and is equal to total disbursements (current disbursements, capital transfers paid, gross capital formation, purchases of land and intangible assets), minus total receipts (capital transfers received, consumption of fixed capital). Since the definition is the same in the case of saving and net lending, there is no difference between the ISTAT figures given for 1951-1959 and the OECD figures for 1960-1980.
Sources: (1) 1978 and 1981 editions (1960-1980), (2) 1977 edition (1951-1959).

Social security receipts:
The figures refer to the financing of: social insurance schemes; family allowances; benefits for public employees and war victims; public health; and public assistance.
Sources: (9) p. 513 (1951-1974), (10).

Table 8

Population:
Data refer to the present population. They have been drawn from the census for 1951, from ISTAT estimates for 1952-1958, and from ISTAT labour force annual surveys for 1959-1980.
Soures: (3) (1951-1958 and 1979-1980), (11) (1959-1978).

Labour force:
Data are drawn from ISTAT labour force annual survey; the series is only reliable and comparable starting from 1959.
Sources: as for population.

Table 9

Members of pension insurance:
Data refer to active contributors and do not include pensioners; some double counting is likely, but not extensive.
Sources: (4) (private sector), (8) (public sector).

Members of family allowance insurance:
Data refer to the INPS scheme, thus excluding the public sector. The insured include active workers contributing to the scheme (both single workers not receiving benefits and heads of households receiving them); it excludes pensioners and dependents.
Source: (4).

Members of unemployment insurance:
Data refer to the INPS scheme against full unemployment. In principle, recipients should not be included.
Source: (4).

Members of occupational injury insurance:
Data refer to INAIL and other minor schemes against occupational injuries and diseases. Recipients of long-term benefits are not in principle included among the insured, while recipients of short-term benefits are in principle included.
Soure: (4).

Members of health insurance:
Data refer to all those eligible for medical and hospital assistance as active members of insurance schemes (pensioners and dependents are excluded).
Sources: (4) (1976-1980), (9), p. 515 (1951-1975).

Members of sickness insurance:
Data refer to contributory employees eligible for sickness and maternity cash benefits in both private and public sectors. It should be noted that the insurance scheme for the self-employed (not dealt with here) provides some cash benefit for maternity in the form of a lump sum.
Source: (4).

Table 10

Benefits (beneficiaries) of pension insurance:
Data refer to pension benefits. Since the Italian pension system allows a single recipient to draw more than one benefit at a time, the number of benefits is normally larger than the number of beneficiaries. The breakdown is the same as that used in Table 6.
Sources: (4), (7), (8) (public sector).

Beneficiaries of familiy allowance insurance:
Data refer to heads of households receiving benefits under the INPS scheme. Statistics are only available starting from 1967. The public sector is not included.
Source: (4).

Benefits of unemployment insurance:
Data refer to the number of cases which have been compensated with full unemployment benefits or with full unemployment special benefits (see the Institutional Synopsis) within the year. The figures conceal a considerable amount of double counting. No meaningful data on beneficiaries or benefits can be provided for the insurance scheme against temporary or partial unemployment.
Source: same as for family allowance beneficiaries.

Benefits of work injuries' insurance:
Data refer to the INAIL scheme and include both invalidity and survivors' benefits.
Source: (4).

Benefits of sickness insurance:
Data refer to the number of cases compensated with sickness cash benefits within the year. As in

the case of unemployment, these data conceal multiple counting. Data only refer to the private sector (INAM general scheme).
Source: (4).

Beneficiaries of public assistance:
Data only refer to the recipients of benefits in cash and in kind provided by the *Enti comunali di Assistenza* (see the Institutional Synopsis).
Source: (4).

Enumerated sources for appendix tables

(1) OECD, *National Accounts Statistics*. Paris, various years.

(2) ISTAT, *Annuario di Contabilità Nazionale*. Rome, 1971, various years.

(3) ISTAT, *Annuario Statistico Italiano*. Rome, various years.

(4) Ministero del Bilancio and Ministero del Tesoro, *Relazione Generale sulla Situazione Economica del Paese*. Rome, various years.

(5) ISTAT, *Annuario Statistico dell'Attività Edilizia e delle Opere Pubbliche*. Rome, various years.

(6) Banca d'Italia, *Assemblea Annuale*. Rome, various years.

(7) ISTAT, *Annuario Statistico dell'Assistenza e della Previdenze Sociale*. Rome, various years.

(8) Ministero del Tesoro, *La Spesa Previdenziale e i suoi Effetti sulla Finanza Pubblica*. Rome, 1981.

(9) P. Flora, J. Alber, R. Eichenberg, J. Kohl, F. Kraus, W. Pfenning, K. Seebohm, *State, Economy and Society in Western Europe, 1815-1975*, Vol. I. London and Frankfurt, Macmillan and Campus, 1983.

(10) ILO, *The Cost of Social Security*. Geneva, 1977 edition.

(11) ISTAT, *Note e Relazioni*

Austria

Wolfgang Weigel and Anton Amann

Institutional Synopsis

Contents

Introduction

Analytically, we may distinguish five organizational subsectors in Austrian social policies:

- self-administered social insurance institutions;
- central government benefits in kind and services;
- central government transfers to private households and various institutions (provinces, social insurance etc.);
- provincial and local services;
- private services (religious, voluntary).

Almost nothing can be said about private and charitable services due to a lack of research in this field. Unfortunately, this is also true for the provincial and local authorities, due to a lack of uniform organization of data; these authorities play an important constitutionally defined role in the provision of social services. However, emphasis is only laid on statistical material gathered at central government level.

Social insurance is by far the most important of all organizational sectors. The various social insurance institutions follow occupational/professional distinctions and combine to different degrees pension, health and accident insurance (see following table). They are linked together in the Federation of Austrian Social Insurance Institutes, established in 1955, which operates as a coordinating institution, representing its members in international matters, and acting on their behalf in the negotiation of contracts with doctors, hospitals etc. For the different treatment of civil servants and dependent workers with government contracts, see Section I.
In the following analysis, institutional aspects predominate; where functional aspects are of importance, this is explicitly indicated.

A system of mutual financial compensation operates among a subset of institutions described below. This is given some consideration in cases where it is necessary for an understanding of the institution in question. The tables may include transfer payments among insurance institutes. However, these are not analysed in detail.

In 1981 total expenditure on social insurance amounted to 159,276 million Austrian schillings (AS) or approximately 14.7% of GDP. Of this sum, 108,742 million AS or 69% were spent on pension insurance, 43,488 million AS or 27% on health insurance, and 7,046 million AS or 4% on accident insurance.

Total social insurance expenditure in 1981

	million AS	%	% distribution				
			cash	kind	adm.	other	
Pension Insurance:							
- dependent workers[a]	90 266	56.6	86.7	9.0	2.7	1.6	100.0
- self-employed	18 523	11.6	88.4	6.8	3.4	1.4	100.0
Sickness insurance:							
- dependent workers	38 670	24.3	12.7	78.5	3.9	4.9	100.0
- self-employed	4 838	3.0	2.9	87.2	7.8	2.1	100.0
Accident insurance	7 077	4.5	48.1	27.8	5.0	19.1	100.0
Total	159 374	100.0	2.7	8.8	3.3	5.2	100.0

[a] Note on following page.

Federation of Austrian Social Insurance Institutes
(*Hauptverband der österreichischen Sozialversicherungsträger*)

Pension Insurance	Health Insurance	Accident Insurance
Workers' Pension Insurance Institute (Pensionsversicherungsanstalt für Arbeiter)	9 regional health funds	
Employees' Pension Insurance Institute (Pensionsversicherungsanstalt für Angestellte)	10 enterprise health funds	
		General Accident Insurance Institute (*Allgemeine Unfallversicherungsanstalt*)
Austrian Mining Insurance Institute (*Versicherungsanstalt des österreichischen Bergbaus*)		
Social Insurance Institute for Trade and Commerce (*Sozialversicherungsanstalt der gewerblichen Wirtschaft*)		
Austrian Railways' Insurance Institute (*Versicherungsanstalt der österreichischen Eisenbahnen*)		
Farmers' Social Insurance Institute (*Sozialversicherungsanstalt der Bauern*)		
	Civil Servants' Insurance Institute (*Versicherungsanstalt der öffentlich Bediensteten*)	

Note to table on preceding page:

[a] 'Dependent workers' include blue-collar workers and white-collar employees both here and in the following. Source: *Handbuch der österreichischen Sozialversicherung* 1981, Vol. II.

Social insurance in general is compulsory. It becomes automatically effective with employment or any other automatically insurable activity. Coverage varies with profession and social status, e.g. pupils and students are insured against sickness and accidents, pensioners are only health insured etc. Voluntary insurance is possible in all three branches. Persons are insured either directly or indirectly as relatives of insured persons. The percentage of the Austrian population covered by social insurance is consequently very high (99.1%).

Social insurance is mainly financed by earnings-related contributions shared between the insured and employers, and to a smaller and varying degree, by central government subsidies. It should be noted that there are certain ceilings with regard to earnings which serve as calculation bases for contributions. The maximum calculation base (*Höchstbeitragsgrundlage*) is adjusted annually.

Insurance schemes	Contributions as % of gross earnings in 1983	
	Employers	Insured
Health Insurance:		
- Employees	2.50	2.50
- Workers	3.15	3.15
- Dependent workers without entitlement to sick-leave payments from employers	3.75	3.75
Accident Insurance	1.5	-
Pension Insurance	10.75	9.75

The schemes for the self-employed and farmers receive state subsidies which are substantially higher than those of dependent workers, especially as regards pension insurance. Miners and civil servants are covered by special regulations. In accident insurance, employers pay the contributions for dependent workers, whereas farmers pay their own contributions. From 1965-1973 the federal government contributed a fixed percentage of expenditure, but since 1973 it has been obliged to cover any social insurance deficit.

Total social insurance revenue in 1981

	in million AS	% distribution insurance contrib.	state subsidies	other
Pension Insurance:				
- dependent workers	90 766	71.4	7.9	20.7
- self-employed	18 598	24.6	56.6	18.8
Sickness Insurance:				
- dependent workers	38 904	87.7	-	12.3
- self-employed	4 687	75.3	13.1	11.6
Accident Insurance	7 125	91.1	2.8	6.1
Total	160 081	70.9	11.6	17.5

Source: *Handbuch der österreichischen Sozialversicherung*, 1981, vol. II.

The social insurance institutions are largely autonomous, although their statutes are subject to control by the central government authorities. They are administered by boards of representatives of the insured and the employers who are elected for a period of five years. However, it is worth noting that institutional decisions regarding insurance contributions, are regulated by amendments to the General Social Insurance Act (*Allgemeines Sozialversicherungsgesetz*).

I Pension system

There are two major pension schemes for dependent workers: one covering blue-collar workers (*Pensionsversicherung der Arbeiter*, established in 1935), and the other covering white-collar employees (*Pensionsversicherung der Angestellten*, introduced in 1906). In addition, there are two separate schemes which cover federal railway employees (*Pensionsversicherung der österreichischen Eisenbahnen*, established in 1920), and miners (*Pensionsversicherung des österreichischen Bergbaus*, established in 1933), respectively. In 1957 compulsory pension insurance was extended to the self-employed in trade and commerce (*Pensionsversicherung der gewerblichen Wirtschaft*), and in 1970 another scheme was introduced covering farmers (*Pensionsversicherung der Bauern*). In 1981, expenditure on the above pension schemes amounted to 108,742 million AS or 8.4% of GDP. Of this sum 87.4% were spent on cash benefits.

Pension insurance expenditure in 1981, in million AS

Pension Scheme	Benefits								
	pension benefits	supplement.	health care/ rehab.	contrib. health insur.	other benefits	admin	other exp.	total	%
Workers	43 395	3 093	750	3 189	570	1 262	637	52 896	48.6
Employees	28 666	189	418	2 195	589	1 056	372	33 485	30.8
Railways	810	26	11	77	52	47	11	1 034	1.0
Miners	2 358	54	33	278	10	61	20	2 814	2.6
Dependent workers	75 229	3 362	1 212	5 739	1 221	2 426	1 040	90 229	83.0
%	83.4	3.7	1.3	6.4	1.4	2.7	1.1	100.0	
Trade Commerce	7 780	856	70	595	5	274	93	9 673	8.9
Farmers	6 090	1 616	164	441	11	364	77	8 763	8.1
Self-employed	13 942	2 472	234	1 036	17	641	171	18 513	17.0
%	75.3	13.4	1.3	5.6	0.1	3.5	0.9	100.8	
Total[a]	89 171	5 834	1 446	6 775	1 238	3 067	1 211	108 742	100.0
%	82.0	5.4	1.3	6.2	1.1	2.8	1.1	99.9	

[a] Including pension scheme for notaries

Pension regulations for war victims (*Kriegsopferfürsorge*), armed forces welfare (*Heeresversorgung*), crime victims (*Opferfürsorge*) and 'minimal pension recipients' (*Kleinrentner*), are dealt with under Section VI.

Pension regulations for civil servants differ from those of private and public employees; the latter are insured under the general pension schemes for dependent workers. Pension payments for retired civil servants and their relatives are part of the work contract. Consequently, pension payments are included under personnel expenditure in the public budgets. Legal regulations are made according to occupational grouping (e.g. judges, teachers etc.). The calculation base is 80% of the last gross monthly salary. Minimum pension is 50% of the calculation base after a minimum of ten years' service. For each additional year of service the pension increases by 2%. A maximum of 100% of the calculation base is reached after 35 years' service. The civil servants' pension scheme was introduced under the 1965 Pension Act (*Pensionsgesetz*), and is in many ways similar to the Pension Insurance Acts. However, civil servants pay much smaller contributions than their privately employed colleagues and the pension is thought to form part of their statutes; this explains why civil servants' pension insurance could not be integrated into the General Pension Insurance Acts.

In 1981 the number of pensioners totalled 177,109 (as compared with 289,062 active civil servants). In addition there are a number of occupational groups for which the federal government refunds payments, e.g. provincial teachers (19,633 persons in 1981). In 1981 the amount paid for federal civil servants totalled 26,213.3 million AS.

Occupational pensions (*Betriebsrenten*) are not integrated into the pension insurance scheme. They may be paid under conditions specified in private contracts. A sample survey conducted by the Chamber of Commerce shows that voluntary occupational pensions amount to 1.18% of total labour cost in industry. In 1960 they amounted to 0.48%.

Income maintenance

Coverage

This section only deals with pension schemes under pension insurance acts. All gainfully employed persons are compulsorily insured under the pension system, and family members are indirectly insured under the same system. The various pension schemes cover old age, survivors', and invalidity pensions. Invalidity pensions, however, are also paid under accident insurance for dependent workers (cf. Section III). Civil servants have their own pension scheme (see above).

Entitlement to pension benefits is dependent upon payment of a certain number of contributions. Entitlement to old age pensions is dependent upon a record of 180 monthly payments, referred to as 'waiting time' (*Wartezeit*). The necessary respective contribution record for survivors' and invalidity pensions is 60 monthly contributions in each case, referred to as 'short waiting time' (*kurze Wartezeit*). In addition, entitlement to benefits is conditional on payment of 12 monthly contributions within the last 36 months. This condition is called 'one-third coverage' (*Dritteldeckung*).

Under the following circumstances, periods where no insurance contributions were made may be treated as 'substitute periods' (*Ersatzzeiten*): military service; war imprisonment; childbirth (until 12 months after confinement); and whilst in receipt of sickness, maternity or unemployment benefits.

Number of pensions paid in 1981

Pension Scheme	Total no. of pensions	%	Percent distribution by pension type			
			Old age[a]	Invalid.	Widowers	Orphans
Workers	816 048	54.1	40.7	23.1	30.6	5.6
Employees'	335 133	22.2	55.3	12.7	28.3	3.5
Railwaymen	15 825	1.0	31.5	15.2	49.7	3.5
Miners	30 322	2.0	29.8	26.5	39.6	4.1
Self-employed	135 730	9.0	52.5	12.1	31.2	4.1
Farmers'	174 368	11.6	43.7	25.7	25.0	5.5
Total[b]	1 507 751	99.9	45.1	20.1	29.9	4.9

[a] Including unemployment and early retirement pensions.
[b] Including notaries and civil servants.

Persons satisfying the contribution requirements are entitled to draw old age pensions from the age of 65 (men) or 60 (women). However, there are two important exceptions: unemployment pensions (*vorzeitige Alterspensionen aufgrund von Arbeitslosigkeit*), and early retirement pensions (*vorzeitige Alterspensionen aufgrund langer Versicherungsdauer*). Unemployment pensions may be paid to unemployed persons from the age of 60 (men) or 55 (women), on condition that they have been in receipt of unemployment benefits for the preceding 52 weeks. Early retirement pensions are payable from the age of 60 (men) or 55 (women). The necessary insurance period is 420 months, and the insured must have paid 24 monthly contributions within the last 36 months.

The 1981 Night-shift/Heavy Manual Work Act (*Nachtschichtschwerarbeitergesetz*) should be mentioned here. It introduced preventive health care and a special early retirement pension (*Sonderruhegeld*) for heavy manual workers who, after fulfillment of certain 'waiting time conditions' (see above), are allowed to retire at the age of 57 (men) or 52 (women) respectively.

Entitlement to invalidity pensions stems from temporary or permanent inability to work. In the latter case they are converted into old age pensions after the claimant has reached pensionable age. (Medical, social, preventive and rehabilitative measures may be taken in order to protect persons from becoming unable to work). Vocational and social services, and cost-of-living subsidies for both the insured and his family members, are equal to those granted under accident insurance (see Section III). From the age of 65/60 costs are covered by the appropriate pension institute.

Old age pensions for civil servants are payable from the age of 65 (permanent retirement), or as a result of temporary or permanent incapacity to work. Survivors' pensions are paid to the widows and orphans of pensioners, or former wives of civil servants.

Benefits

In all social insurance schemes old age pension benefits are calculated in the following way:

In general, the 'calculation base' (*Bemessungsgrundlage*) under the General Social Insurance Act corresponds to the average 'contribution base' (*Beitragsgrundlage*), i.e. average gross earnings over the last five years preceding the first year when the pension was received. The flat-rate pension amounts to 30% of the calculation base; starting from this, the entire pension is calculated according to the following scheme:

- for the first 120 months of insurance the rate of increase (*Steigerungssatz*) amounts to 0.05% per month of the calculation base;
- for the next 120 months of insurance, increase rate amounts to 0.075% per month;
- for the next 120 months of insurance, increase rate amounts to 0.1% per month;
- for the next 120 months of insurance, increase rate amounts to 0.125% per month;
- for an additional 60 months of insurance, increase rate amounts to 0.125% per month.

Thus, for an unlikely maximum period of 600 monthly contributions, old age pension amounts to 79.5% of the calculation base. Due to the various bonuses from pension insurance, and additional voluntary contributions and occupational pension benefits on behalf of employers, actual pensions may be higher than pensions calculated on the basis of the insurance period alone.

There are two important exceptions from the general pension formula:

- If the old age pension is below 50% of the calculation base, social insurance administration may decide to pay additional benefits up to a maximum of 10% of the calculation base.
- If the old age pension (together with income from other sources), is below a legally fixed minimum, the difference is paid in the form of supplementary benefits (*Ausgleichszulage*), and financed out of general revenues. Although Austrian social security policy does not recognize the concept of a minimum pension, this regulation effectively implies entitlement to a 'minimum pension' for all insured persons with the required contribution record. In 1980, the minimum amounted to 3,703 AS for single persons, and 5,316 for couples. The minimum (*Richtsatz*), is fixed annually on the basis of a wage index. It may be corrected by a 'factor of adaptation' (*Anpassungsfaktor*), which takes consumer prices into account and is recommended to the Minister of Social Affairs by a board of experts.

Invalidity and survivors' pensions are calculated in the same way as old age pensions. Widows' pension amounts to 60% of the pension of the directly insured; orphans' pension amounts to 12% for partial, and 30% for full orphans.

For the calculation of civil servants' pensions see above. It should be noted that civil servants in high income brackets may be better off since they are not affected by the contribution ceiling (*Höchstbeitragsgrundlage*, see general introduction above).

Financing

Pension schemes are financed on a pay-as-you-go basis, i.e. there is a temporal income redistribution between generations and a certain amount of vertical redistribution with respect to supplementary and other benefits within the pension scheme. The average ratio between contributors and beneficiaries is 1000 to 531 (1981), with a maximum ratio of 1000 to 1.999 in the miners' pension scheme.

Sources of revenue include insurance contributions, central government subsidies (designed to substitute employers' contributions in the case of the self-employed), compensation fund contributions according to a scheme decided by the Ministry of Social Affairs, and other sources. The compensation fund was established in 1978. Revenues stem from a surcharge on pension insurance contributions and transfers from the Unemployment Insurance Institute, which is part of the inter-institutional compensation scheme.

Pension insurance revenue in 1981, in million AS

Scheme	Insurance contrib.	Compensation fund transfers	Federal subsidies	Other [a]	Total	%
Workers	30 266	12 400	9 981	484	53 131	48.6
Railways	651	277	97	14	1 039	1.0
Employees	33 132	-	270	249	33 651	30.8
Miners	717	1 441	643	26	2 827	2.6
Dependent Workers	64 766	14 118	10 991	773	90 648	83.0
%	71.4	15.6	12.1	0.9	100.0	-
Trade Commerce	2 716	-	6 890	109	9 715	8.9
Farmers	1 786	-	6 667	343	8 797	8.1
Self-employed	4 573	-	13 558	457	18 588	17.0
%	24.6	-	72.9	2.5	100.0	-
Total[b]	69 339	14 118	24 549	1 230	109 236	-
%	63.5	12.9	22.5	1.1	-	100.0

[a] Including: federal transfers to cover deficits, and federal subsidies to finance supplementary benefits (*Ersätze für Ausgleichszulagen*), and housing supplements (*Ersätze für Wohnungsbeihilfen*, see Section VIII).
[b] Including notaries pension scheme.

Administration

With the exception of civil servants, the pension system is operated by pension insurance institutes through a central office and provincial offices. These offices have a board consisting of two delegates from the insured employees and two from employers, and one institute staff member. Case decisions are taken unanimously or, where no agreement is reached, by the administration.

Services

Pension insurance institutes operate a number of rehabilitation centres where both board and travel are provided free of charge, in particular for the treatment of rheumatic, heart and lung diseases, and TB.

Core laws

Bracketed figures refer to the number of the law, which is published in the Legislative Bulletin (*Bundesgesetzblatt*, BGBl.) in the respective year. Note that in the course of political changes since 1848 different terms were in use periodically (RGBl, *Reichsgesetzblatt* refers to the time prior to 1918, and StGBl, *Staatsgesetzblatt* refers to 1918-1920).

1906 (RGBl. no. 1/1907)
Pensionversicherungsgesetz für Angestellte (Employees' Pension Insurance Act): white-collar employees in a large number of industries compulsorily insured; central pension insurance institute and provincial institutes established; financed by employer and employee contributions.

1914 (RGBl. no. 138)
Novelle zum 1906 Gesetz (Amendment to the 1906 Act): extended and increased minimal pensions; famous for its definition of employees as 'mainly intellectual workers'.

1927 (no. 127)
Gesetz betreffend die Kranken-, Unfall-, und Invalidenversicherung der Arbeiter (Workers' Sickness, Accident and Invalidity Insurance Act): section 10 provides old age assistance benefits (*Altersfürsorge*) for workers aged 60+, excluding miners and some other groups.

1927 (no. 388)
Verordnung aufgrund des Gesetzes vom 23.11.1927 (Decree on the Law of 23.11.1927): introduced old age assistance benefits for old people and invalid miners.

1928 (no. 235)
Landarbeiterversicherungsgesetz (Agricultural Workers' Insurance Act): included an old age assistance scheme - originally intended as a relief measure but became permanent.

1933 (no. 326)
Verordnung über die Auflösung der bergmännischen Bruderladen (Decree on the Dissolution of Miners' Cooperative Funds): cooperative funds dissolved due to inflation and redundancies; second decree introduced compulsory pension insurance.

1935 (no. 107)
Bundesgesetz betreffend die Gewerbliche Sozialversicherung (Federal Act on Social Insurance in Trade and Industry): system of social security completely reorganized as a consequence of the economic recession; old age pensions and welfare schemes for all gainfully employed with the exception of farm workers, civil servants and public railways' employees.

1946 (no. 142)
Sozialversicherungs-Überleitungsgesetz (Social Insurance Transition Act): dissolved the still existing structure of social insurance institutes after the German occupation; obliged government to provide financial support for pension insurance schemes.

1948 (no. 80)
Act reducing retirement age for employed women to 60.

1949 (no. 115)
Act on pension increases.

1951 (no. 189)
Act on the increase of low pensions; the last in a series of acts dealing with low pensions (since the 1955 ASVG Act, pensions are increased at intervals by amendments to the 1955 Act).

1953 (no. 115)
Gesetz über die Altersunterstützung der Kammern der Gewerblichen Wirtschaft (Chamber of Commerce Old Age Support Act): introduced small flat-rate benefits for retired self-employed; financed by contributions.

1955 (no 189)
Allgemeines Sozialversicherungsgesetz, ASVG (General Social Insurance Act): final reorganization of the postwar social insurance system; pension insurance for most gainfully employed, both white- and blue-collar workers, miners and workers in the mining industries.

1957 (no. 294)
Dritte Novelle zum ASVG (Third ASVG Amendment): introduced early retirement in cases of unemployment.

1957 (no. 292)
Gewerbliche Selbständigen Pensionsversicherung (Pension Insurance Act for the Self-employed in Trade and Industry): attempted to overcome the problems caused by the small subsidies introduced under the 1953 Act; introduced federal subsidy to finance the scheme, thus substituting employers' contributions corresponding to the employers' scheme; also covers solicitors, dentists and journalists.

1957 (no. 293)
Landwirtschaftliches Zuschussrentenversicherungsgesetz (Agricultural Supplementary Pension Insurance Act): covers agricultural workers and their relatives; benefits intended as subsidies for retired farmers and not as pensions; basic flat-rate benefit.

1958 (no. 157)
Künstler-Sozialversicherung (Artists' Social Insurance Act): pension scheme for the self-employed in the fine arts; first in a series of pension insurance acts for the self-employed; in 1964 a pension scheme for veterinary surgeons, doctors, lawyers and other social groups was adopted, and in 1978 managing associates of limited liability companies were included in this scheme.

1960 (no. 294)
10. Novelle zum ASVG (10th ASVG Amendment): introduced compensation fund among institutes, and early retirement pensions in cases of a longer contribution period.

1965 (no. 96)
Pensionsanpassungsgesetz (Pension Adjustment Act): old age pensions automatically indexed to average earnings and derived from the cost of living index.

1970 (no. 28)
Bauern-Pensionsversicherungsgesetz (Farmers' Pension Insurance Act): replaced the 1957 Act; adapted the farmers' pension scheme to those for artists and the self-employed; financed by contributions based on standardized value of agricultural products and a state subsidy.

1977 (no. 192)
Sozialversicherungsänderungsgesetz (Social Insurance Modification Act): established compensation fund for transfers among pension insurance institutes; financed by surcharges on pension insurance contributions.

1978 (no. 684)
Sozialrechtsänderungsgesetz (Social Rights' Modification Act): stipulated the continuation of, or voluntary pension insurance for the time of maternity leave, etc.

1978 (no. 559)
Bauern-Sozialversicherungsgesetz (Farmers' Social Insurance Act): integrated farmers' pensions and sickness insurance.

1978 (no. 624)
Bundesgesetz über die Sozialversicherung freiberuflich selbständig Erwerbstätiger (Fed-

eral Act on Social Insurance for the Professions): opened pension insurance scheme for the self-employed in trade and industry to self-employed groups such as doctors, lawyers upon application by the appropriate legal representative body.

1981 (no 282)
36. Novelle zum ASVG (36th ASVG Amendment): adapted pension schemes to changes in the families' loads equalization scheme; introduced a widowers' pension equivalent to widows' pensions.

II Sickness insurence/Health services

In 1980 expenditure on public health services amounted to 70.1 billion AS, or 7% of GDP. A large proportion of this is spent by the provinces and communities. Contrary to pension outlays, an overview of total expenditure can only be given on highly aggregated levels of administration.

Expenditure on health in 1980, in billion AS

		%
Federal budget	2.6	3.7
Provinces	12.8	18.3
Communities	14.4	20.5
Sickness insurance	40.3	57.5
Total	70.1	100.0

Private households have been estimated to spend another 30.2 billion AS (3% of GDP) on health services (inclusive of private insurance but exclusive of prescription and nursing fees). The high share of expenditure taken by the provinces and communities is spent on the construction of hospitals and operating costs not reimbursed by sickness insurance institutes. Since comparable data on these activities are not readily available, the remainder of this section only deals with sickness insurance.

With respect to medical care, sickness insurance covers practically the entire population. All gainfully employed persons and the self-employed are compulsorily insured. In addition, pensioners, pupils and students are covered, and dependent relatives of insured persons are indirectly insured with minor exceptions, (e.g. under the Social Insurance Act for Trade, only children are automatically covered as relatives of the insured). Thus, in 1981, 7,486,000 persons or 99.1% of the population were protected by the Social Sickness Insurance (*Soziale Krankenversicherung*), 64.3% of whom were directly insured, and 35.6% being indirectly insured family members. Despite this extended coverage, private sickness insurance plays an important role, insofar as hospitals running at a considerable deficit shift part of the costs to privately insured patients, who are in turn reimbursed by their insurance companies.

Cash benefits may be obtained under the Sickness Insurance Act and the Wage Continuation Act. Both are dealt with below.

Sickness insurance institutions' expenditure in 1981, mill. AS[a]

Expenditure	Regional inst.	Enterprise	Miners	Railways	Civil servants	Self-empl.	Farmers	Total
Doctors' visits	7 584 (23.9)	163 (27.7)	93 (19.5)	625 (29.5)	1 221 (32.3)	772 (29.8)	431 (19.1)	10 892 (25.0)
Drugs and Remedies	4 685 (14.8)	115 (17.4)	85 (17.8)	457 (21.6)	628 (16.6)	429 (16.5)	421 (18.7)	6 721 (15.4)
Dental treatment	2 518 (7.9)	62 (9.4)	20 (4.2)	186 (8.8)	412 (10.9)	234 (9.0)	133 (5.9)	3 566 (8.2)
Hospital care	7 437 (23.5)	170 (25.7)	142 (29.8)	542 (25.6)	777 (20.6)	753 (29.0)	616 (27.4)	10 441 (24.0)
Sickness benefits	2 463 (7.8)	46 (6.97)	20 (4.2)	47 (2.2)	- -	28 (1.1)	- -	2 605 (6.0)
Maternity benefits	2 194 (6.9)	9 (1.4)	3 (0.6)	19 (0.9)	87 (2.3)	9 (0.3)	31 (1.4)	2 354 (5.4)
Other	4 970 (15.7)	136 (20.6)	113 (23.7)	241 (0.6)	649 (17.2)	367 (14.1)	613 (27.3)	6.92 (15.9)
Total[b]	31 640 (100)	660 (100)	476 (100)	2 117 (100)	3 774 (100)	2 592 (100)	2 245 (100)	43 508 (100)

[a] Bracketed figures are percentages
[b] Including home nursing.

Income maintenance

Coverage

Compulsory insurance provides sickness cash benefits for dependent workers, the self-employed, and farmers, together with maternity benefits for dependent workers. The self-employed are only entitled to maternity benefits under voluntary or private insurance schemes. As yet, there is no equivalent regulation covering farmers.

The 1974 Wage Continuation Act (*Entgeltfortzahlungsgesetz*), ensures that workers receive payments on behalf of the employer in the case of illness or accident, similar to those enjoyed by employees under the Employees' Act (*Angestelltengesetz*). For details of this, see below. Note that a number of professions are not covered by this law, and instead have their own regulations, e.g. journalists, farm-workers, actors etc.

Benefits

Sickness insurance provides sickness cash benefits, maternity and funeral allowances. Sickness cash benefits (*Krankengeld*), are payable from the fourth day of illness for a maximum of 78 weeks for each case. Benefits are calculated on the basis of the insured's last gross earnings. The amount ranges from 50% to 75%, depending upon the length of illness or incapacity to work, and the number of dependents entitling the claimant to special supplements. Reduced benefits are payable for periods when the insured is receiving hospital care, and amount to 50% of the respective sickness cash benefits for single persons, and two-thirds for employees with dependents.

Entitlement is suspended if wage continuation payments (*Entgeltfortzahlung*) are made by the employer under the Wage Continuation Act. Dependent workers covered by the Wage Continuation Act and Employees' Act are entitled to regular sick-leave payments amounting to last earnings. The duration is dependent upon the length of service prior to illness, the minimum for workers being four weeks' wage continuation after two weeks' service, and the maximum being ten weeks after twenty-five years' service. The figures for employees are eight weeks for up to 13 years' service, and 12 weeks for over 15 years' service.

Maternity allowances are flat-rate benefits. In 1981, maternity allowance amounted to 3,000 AS. A lump sum payment is made on the death of a sick person to cover funeral expenses.

Financing and administration

The main sources of revenue vary from one institute to another. Generally they consist of contributions from the insured, central government transfers, various compensation fund transfers, reimbursements from pension insurance institutes as well as from accident insurance, interest on capital and various other items such as prescription fees.

Sickness insurance institutes' revenues in 1981, in mill. AS[a]

Insurance schemes	Contributions	Federal subsid.	Comp. Fund transfers	Interest on capital	Reimbursements	Other	Total
Regional inst.	27 492 (87.6)	-	347 (1.1)	488 (1.5)	2 205 (7.0)	787 (2.5)	31 364 (100)
Enterprise inst.	616 (89.1)	-	-	31 (4.4)	25 (3.6)	18 (2.6)	691 (100)
Miners	464 (93.7)	-	2 (0.4)	2 (0.4)	14 (2.8)	13 (2.6)	495 (100)
Railways	1 929 (90.0)	-	-	46 (2.1)	40 (1.8)	12 (5.6)	2 143 (100)
Public servants	3 604 (85.5)	-	-	252 (6.0)	42 (1.0)	313 (7.4)	4 212 (100)
Trade Commerce	2 273 (89.2)	-	21 (0.8)	39 (1.5)	22 (0.8)	182 (7.1)	2 547 (100)
Farmers	1 258 (58.8)	615 (28.7)		81 (3.8)	19 (0.9)	165 (7.7)	2 140 (100)
Total	37 637 (86.3)	615 (1.4)	370 (0.8)	939 (2.1)	2 367 (5.4)	1 599 (3.6)	43 591 (100)

[a] Bracketed figures are percentages.

Under the Wage Continuation Act employers pay contributions on behalf of their workers and are in turn reimbursed by the regional funds (*Erstattungsfonds*).

Different amounts of reimbursement are paid according to the size of the firm, small employers being entitled to a lump sum compensation to cover the costs arising from the absence from work of an employee due to illness. In order to compensate for the difference in regional fund expenditure, a special 'compensation fund' (*Ausgleichsfonds*), has been established with the Federation of Austrian Social Insurance Institutes.

Administration

Sickness insurance institutes are organized along similar lines to joint stock companies. They consist of a general assembly, a directory and a supervisory board. Provincial boards have been established with the larger institutes, which may in turn have regional offices.

Information is partly provided for the insured by travelling representatives of the larger institutes.

Sickness cash benefits as well as reimbursements to the insured can only be claimed upon application.

Services

Sickness insurance covers treatment by doctors, medicines and medical aids, hospital care, and some other special services. Treatment by a doctor is free of charge if he is under contract to the Sickness Insurance Institute (*Krankenversicherungsanstalt*); otherwise the patient pays a fee and is partially reimbursed by the insurance institute. Dental treatment is provided under the same conditions. Prescribed medicines are available at all pharmacies on payment of a prescription fee, which amounted to 18 AS in 1983. However, this fee may be waived for needy persons.

Hospital care is in principle provided free of charge for all insured persons. There are, however, two types of treatment available: general class treatment (*Allgemeine Verpflegsklasse*), and special class (*Sonderklasse*), which offers a choice of doctors, menus and private hospital accommodation in addition to the normal services. Only general class treatment is covered by social insurance, whereas special class treatment requires additional payments, which may be covered by private sickness insurance.

Health insurance also covers compulsory check-ups for young employed people between the ages of 15 and 19, school children and university students; free vaccination services for primary schools; preventive examinations to detect particular diseases such as cancer and diabetes; and services for the handicapped.

Although the General Social Insurance Act does not deal with retentions (*Selbstbehalt*), there are some special laws which do, especially for relatives of the insured. Civil servants pay retentions on all services. In general they amount to 20% of the scheduled cost of treatment.

Core laws

1888 (RGBl. no. 33)
Arbeiter Krankenversicherungsgesetz (Workers' Sickness Insurance Act): compulsory health care insurance for all workers except miners and workers in agriculture and forestry; financed by contributions, partly by employers.

1913 (RGBl. no. 24)
Gesetz betreffend die Ausdehnung der Krankenversicherung auf die Betriebe der Seefahrt und Seefischerei (Act on the Extension of Health Insurance to Shipping and Fishing Enterprises): the first act of its kind - introduced compulsory health insurance for small undertakings and for entrepreneurs; partly financed by state subsidies.

1920 (StGBl. no. 311)
Krankenversicherungsgesetz der Staatsbediensteten (Civil Servants' Health Insurance Act): introduced wage continuation replacing low sickness cash benefits; established health insurance institute for civil servants.

1921 (no. 292)
Angestelltengesetz (Employees Act): introduced wage continuation for private employees; a series of consecutive parliamentary acts and amendments introduced protection of female employees in cases of maternity, etc.

1926 (no. 388)
Angestelltenversicherungsgesetz (Employees' Insurance Act): combined health, accident, and old age insurance for private employees and their relatives; financed by employer and employee contributions; introduced benefits for disablement; established the Employees' Insurance Institute.

1927 (no. 125)
Arbeiterversicherungsgesetz (Workers' Insurance Act): combined health, accident, and invalidity insurance for workers; financed mainly by employer and employee contributions; established a central insurance institute: supplementary acts and amendments mainly dealt with the problems of financing benefit schemes.

1928 (no. 235)
Landarbeiterversicherungsgesetz (Agricultural Workers' Insurance Act): this act only became possible once the competence for agricultural legislation had shifted from the provinces to the federal government; materially this law is a supplement to the insurance laws for employees and workers.

1935 (no. 547)
Meisterkrankenversicherungsgesetz (Masters Sickness Insurance Act): introduced compulsory insurance for members of cooperatives and their relatives; also covered the reorganization of health insurance funds.

1935 (no. 107)
Bundesgesetz betreffend die Gewerbliche Sozialversicherung (Federal Act on Social Insurance in Trade and Industry): outlined the general rules for health, invalidity, old age, and accident insurance for dependent workers in all sectors with the exception of agricultural workers, civil servants, notaries and public railway employees.

1947 (no. 142)
Sozialversicherungs-Überleitungsgesetz (Social Insurance Transition Act): re-established pre-war organization of social insurance institutes; adaptation of benefits after currency reform.

1952 (no. 86)
1. Sozialversicherungs-Neuregelungsgesetz (First Social Insurance Replacement Act): final replacement of German law introduced in the period 1938-1945.

1955 (no. 189)
Allgemeines Sozialversicherungsgesetz (General Social Insurance Act): final reshuffling of the postwar social insurance system (see Introduction); part two (par.

116-172) of no. 189 contains all relevant regulations concerning health insurance, income maintenance and benefits. Up to 1982 there were 38 amendments to this Act. More important ones are cited subsequently.

1958 (no. 293)
Vierte Novelle zum ASVG (Fourth ASVG Amendment): introduced fees on medical cards, required for doctors' consultations.

1960 (no. 87)
Sechste Novelle zum ASVG (Sixth ASVG Amendment): abolished fees introduced in 1958.

1960 (no. 294)
Achte Novelle zum ASVG (Eighth ASVG Amendment): introduced compensation funds for transfers between health insurance institutes.

1965 (no. 219)
Bauern-Krankenversicherungsgesetz (Farmers' Sickness Insurance Act): differs from other regulations with respect to decentralized administration, emphasis on benefits instead of income maintenance, etc.

1966 (no. 168)
18. Novelle zum ASVG (18th ASVG Amendment): abolished maximum period of hospital care.

1966 (no. 167)
Gewerbliches Selbständigen Krankenversicherungsgesetz (Sickness Insurance Act for the Self-employed in Trade and Industry): extended coverage with the goal of doubling membership; introduced compulsory insurance subject to ballot among members of industrial groups.

1967 (no. 200)
Beamten-Kranken- und Unfallversicherungsgesetz (Civil Servants' Sickness and Accident Insurance Act): brought civil servants' health insurance regulations into line with those of the General Social Insurance Act (and associated amendments); established the Civil Servants' Insurance Institute.

1969 (no. 17)
23. Novelle zum ASVG (23rd ASVG Amendment): equalized entitlement of voluntarily insured; for further amendments see below.

1971 (no. 287)
Gewerbliches Selbständigen Krankenversicherungsgesetz (Sickness Insurance Act for the Self-employed in Trade and Industry): unification of health and old age insurance institutes, implemented in 1974.

1974 (no. 399)
Entgeltfortzahlungsgesetz (Wage Continuation Act): introduced wage continuation for workers in private enterprises in case of sickness.

1976 (no. 703)
(Fifth Amendment to the Sickness Insurance Act for the Self-employed): established compulsory insurance without group voting as a result of preceding failures.

1977 (no. 192)
Sozialversicherungs-Änderungsgesetz (Social Insurance Modification Act): amendments to all existing social insurance acts, basically dealing with problems of financing.

1978 (no. 580)
Gewerbliches Sozialversicherungsgesetz (Social Insurance Act for the Industrial Self-employed): combined regulations for health and old age insurance.

1978 (no. 624)
Sozialversicherung freiberuflich selbständig Erwerbstätiger (Social Insurance Act for Professions): compulsory sickness insurance for all groups of professions covered by pension insurance.

1978 (no. 559)
Bauern-Sozialversicherungsgesetz (Farmers' Social Insurance Act): united health and old age insurance; organization and benefits corresponding to those for the self-employed.

1978 (no. 684)
Sozialrechts-Änderungsgesetz (Social Rights Modification Act): combined amendment no. 33 of the General Social Insurance Act, and amendment no. 1 to the Insurance Act for the Self-employed, and the Insurance Act for Farmers; dealt mainly with the standardization and financial problems of health insurance.

1982 (no. 359)
Bundesgesetz über die Gewährung der Leistung der Betriebshilfe (des Wochengeldes) an selbständig erwerbstätige Mütter (Law on Maternity Benefits for Self-Employed Women): provides maternity benefits for self-employed women in industry, agriculture and forestry corresponding to the benefits for employed women.

1982 (no. 588)
37. Novelle zum ASVG (37th ASVG Amendment): increased maximum contribution base for health insurance; increased fees for prescriptions, cost-sharing for remedies, etc.; there are also minor adjustments concerning beneficiaries from various schemes; consequently there are amendments to other core laws (farmers, self-employed), inasmuch as schemes are standardized, so as to make all insured persons equally well-off under various schemes.

III Accident insurance

Excluding wage continuation payments due to accidents (see Section II), and invalidity pensions under pension insurance schemes (see Section I), total expenditure on accident insurance in 1981 amounted to ,077 million AS, 4.4% of total social insurance expenditure, and 0.7% of GDP (see table on following page).

Income maintenance

Coverage

The General Accident Insurance Institut (*Allgemeine Unfallversicherungsanstalt*), covers blue-collar workers, white-collar employees, workers in the mining industry and the self-employed, and includes three sections for accident insurance within the social insurance institutions for farmers, railway employees, and civil servants. Accident insurance covers: accidents occurring in that gainful activity which forms the basis of compulsory insurance; accidents on the way to the workplace; and accidents sustained during vocational, school or university education. In addition, people

Accident insurance expenditure in 1981, in million AS[a]

Expenditure items	General insurance institute	Farmers' insurance	Railways' insurance	Public servants	Total
Accident pensions	2 734.9 (46.2)	390.3 (49.6)	152.6 (70.2)	106.3 (68.4)	3 384.2 (47.8)
Therapy	1 484.1 (25.1)	121.8 (15.4)	31.8 (14.6)	25.2 (16.2)	1 663.0 (23.5)
Other services	292.2 (4.9)	50.9 (6.5)	10.1 (4.6)	7.5 (4.8)	360.7 (5.2)
Various expenditure[b]	971.2 (16.4)	115.7 (14.7)	4.0 (1.8)	2.8 (1.8)	1 093.7 (15.4)
Total	5 917.3 (100.0)	786.7 (100.0)	217.3 (100.0)	155.4 (100.0)	7 076 (100.0)

[a] Bracketed figures are percentages.
[b] Exclusive of outlays on administration, outlays compensated by other insurance institutes, and reserve fund.

carrying out life-saving activities or working with volunteer ambulances or fire brigades are also insured.

The General Accident Insurance Scheme is almost entirely financed by employers' contributions; in 1981 they amounted to 99.3% of total accident insurance revenue.

Benefits

Accident insurance provides benefits in the case of accidents and occupational diseases. Short-term benefits are associated with the duration of medical treatment after an accident (see below). Long-term benefits consist of accident pensions (*Versehrtenrenten*), survivor's pension (*Hinterbliebenenleistungen*), and widow's compensation (*Witwenbeihilfe*). Funeral benefits (*Bestattungskostenbeitrag*) are also granted.

Various calculation bases are used according to benefits. It should be noted that some of the benefits go beyond the original scope of accident insurance, especially where the insured has to care for a dependent relative, in which case additional benefits are payable.

In the *short-term*, family and daily allowances (*Familien- und Taggeld*) are paid to compensate income losses during periods of medical treatment and rehabilitation, amounting to one-twelfth of the calculation base, i.e. average income in the year preceding the accident. Subsidies, up to 1.6%, are paid for the first dependent, and 0.4% is paid for each additional dependent up to a maximum of 2.8%. Special subsidies (*besondere Unterstützung*) are payable for long periods of recovery. Transition benefits (*Übergangsgeld*) amount to 60% of the monthly calculation base in cases where vocational training is necessary after recovery (up to 100% for dependent relatives). A supplement (*Zuschuss*) is granted where wages are temporarily lower than regular wages as a result of on-the-job training. Temporary invalid's benefit (*Versehrtengeld*) is paid upon request; this benefit corresponds to sick-leave payments, and is payable by sickness insurance upon request by the accident insurance institutes.

Permanent benefit levels are determined by the following:
- the extent to which a person's capacity to earn is reduced, the minimum being 20% in the case of accidents and 50% in the case of occupational diseases;
- the calculation base; generally, this equals the income of the insured prior to the accident/disease; maximum calculation bases in accordance with the General Social Insurance Act (ASVG) are used; there are separate annually adjusted calculation bases for the self-employed in trade and commerce, and farming; persons under 30 years of age are covered by special regulations.

Pensions may be either full or partial. Accident insurance institutes may provide voluntary supplements (*Zusatzrente*) amounting to 20% of the calculation base, and child allowances (*Kinderzuschuss*), which amount to 10% of the permanent benefits granted. In cases of total dependence, special allowances (*Hilflosenzuschuss*) or nursing benefits (*Pflegegeld*) are payable.

Survivors' pensions are paid up to a maximum of 80% of the calculation base. Reductions are made where orphans, parents or siblings are entitled to pensions in excess of the maximum calculation base. Widow's compensation is the exception to the rule, as it amounts to a lump-sum payment of 40% of the calculation base in the event of the death of a seriously disabled spouse, where death is not a direct consequence of the long-term effects of an accident. In this instance there is no entitlement to a survivor's pension.

Rehabilitation allowances (*Rehabilitationsleistungen*) are paid to persons undergoing vocational training as a part of their rehabilitation. In general they amount to 60% of prior gross earnings.

Financing

The main source of revenues are employers' contributions. A federal subsidy is paid for farmers which amounts to one-third of total contributions. In addition there are various revenues resulting from financial agreements between the insurance institutes and the government.

Revenues of accident insurance institutes in 1981, in million AS[a]

	Insurance contrib.	Federal subsidy	Other	Total
General accident insurance	5 543	-	382	5 925
	(93.6)		(6.4)	(100.0)
Farmers	595	200	38	833
	(71.4)	(24.0)	(4.6)	(100.0)
Railways	214	-	6	220
	(97.3)		(2.7)	(100.0)
Public servants	138	-	9	147
	(93.9)		(6.1)	(100.0)
Total	6 490	200	435	7 125
	(91.1)	(2.8)	(6.1)	(100.0)

[a] Bracketed figures are percentages.

Administration

The accident insurance system is administered in the same way as the pension system through a series of institutes (see Section I). Special committees are established to take decisions on pensions and rehabilitation allowances. In addition to the institutes there is a fairly large apparatus for the administration of hospitals, rehabilitation centres and the promotion of accident prevention programmes.

Services

Services include the provision of first aid, medical treatment for accident victims and rehabilitation. In addition, much emphasis is currently being placed on the prevention of industrial accidents and occupational diseases. The General Accident Insurance Institute operates a number of ambulance stations with a total capacity of 1,029 beds, and rehabilitation centres with a capacity of 492 beds.

Core laws

1880 (RGBl. no. 1)
Gesetz betreffend die Unfallversicherung der Arbeiter (Workers' Accident Insurance Law): comprehensive regulation concerning compulsory insurance; financed by employers; excluding mining, transportation, small enterprises and agriculture.

1889 (RGBl. no. 127)
Bruderladengesetz (Mining Sector Community Funds Act): attempted to equalize accident insurance in the mining industries with that provided by the General Insurance Act.

1919 (StGBl. no. 399)
Vierte Novelle zum Unfallversicherungsgesetz (Fourth Amendment of Workers' Accident Insurance Act): insurance institutes entitled to carry out medical treatment, leading to the establishment of special accident hospitals.

1919 (StGBl. no. 579)
Gesetz über die Durchführung der Unfallversicherung für Bergarbeiter (Accident Insurance Implementation Act for Miners): established regional accident insurance institutes for miners (community funds abolished by 1915).

1926 (no. 388)
Angestelltenversicherungsgesetz (Employees' Insurance Act): one of a series of laws attempting to unify all branches of social insurance with respect to professional grouping.

1927 (no. 125)
Arbeiterversicherungsgesetz (Workers' Insurance Act): the same as the 1926 Employees' Insurance Act.

1928 (no. 50)
17. Novelle zum Unfallversicherungsgesetz (17th Amendment of Workers' Accident Insurance Act): some occupational diseases dealt with in the same way as factory accidents.

1928 (no. 235)
Landarbeiterversicherungsgesetz (Agricultural Workers' Insurance Act): tenants and owners covered by compulsory accident insurance scheme.

1929 (no. 150)
Unfallversicherungsgesetz (Accident Insurance Act): original Act reissued inclusive of all amendments.

1935 (no. 107)
Gesetz betreffend die Gewerbliche Sozialversicherung (Industrial Social Insurance Act): introduced accident insurance for all gainfully employed in trade, industry, mining and banking.

1955 (no. 189)
Allgemeines Sozialversicherungsgesetz (General Social Insurance Act): par. 172-220 deal with the range and amount of accident insurance benefits (see Introduction).

1967 (no. 200)
Beamten Kranken- und Unfallversicherungsgesetz (Civil Servants' Sickness and Accident Insurance Act): introduced accident insurance for civil servants.

1973 (no. 31)
29. Novelle zum ASVG (29th ASVG Amendment): reorganized accident insurance institutes for farmers and workers.

1976 (no. 704)
32. Novelle zum ASVG (32nd ASVG Amendment): accident insurance for pupils and students.

1978 (no. 624)
Gesetz über die Sozialversicherung freischaffend selbständig Erwerbstätiger (Social Insurance Act for Professions): compulsory accident insurance upon application by the professional representative body.

1979 (no. 530)
34. Novelle sum ASVG (34th ASVG Amendment): accident insurance extended to work-related activities.

1980 (no. 563)
Abgabenänderungsgesetz (Tariff Modification Act): contributions for pupils and students' accident insurance payable by the Families' Loads Equalization Fund (*Familienlastenausgleichsfonds*).

IV Unemployment insurance/Employment services

In 1981 expenditure on unemployment benefits and employment services amounted to 9,677 million AS, or 0.9% of GDP. This sum includes 2,474 million AS for maternity benefits which are an integral part of unemployment protection (see table on following page).

Income maintenance

This section covers benefits under the Unemployment Insurance Act (*Arbeitslosenversicherungsgesetz*) and related laws only. Cash benefits may also be granted as a result of labour market activities, and are dealt with under 'Services'. There is no clear-cut

Expenditure on unemployment in 1981, in million AS

		%	%
Unemployment insurance benefits	3 537	70.1	
Unemployment assistance benefits	488	9.8	
Special and transition subsidies	437	8.6	
Transfers to compensation funds of old age pension institutes[a]	583	11.5	
- Total unemployment benefits	5 045	100.0	71.0
General labour market administration	807	37.4	
Promotion of labour market mobility	305	14.1	
Job creation programmes	305	14.1	
Vocational training/retraining	138	6.5	
Programmes for the handicapped	107	4.9	
Foreign workers	2	0.1	
Bad weather compensation	454	21.0	
Investment subsidies for schools, flats, kindergartens	40	1.8	
- Total labour market policies	2 158	100.0	29.0
Total	7 203		100.0
Maternity benefits	2 474		
Total (incl. maternity benefits)	9 677		

[a] See Section I, Financing.

distinction between cash and other benefits. The present form of unemployment insurance was introduced in 1977. It has not been incorporated into the largely autonomous Federation of Austrian Social Insurance Institutes, but forms instead a part of the Federal Ministry of Social Administration (*Bundesministerium für Soziale Verwaltung*). The various forms of unemployment protection are legally based upon a series of laws which have never been coherently integrated. A particular feature of this social administration is its provision of maternity allowances and maternity assistance (see Section V).

Coverage

All dependent workers and employees are protected against loss of income in the event of either short or long-term unemployment, seasonal unemployment in the construction industry, structural unemployment under special circumstances, and unemployment as a result of bankruptcy. In order to be entitled to unemployment benefits for the first time, the insured must have a minimum record (*Anwartschaft*) of 52 insurance weeks during the two years preceding dismissal. The insured must in addition have registered as unemployed, and be willing to work. A record of 20 weeks is sufficient in order to claim unemployment benefits in cases of repeated dismissal. The duration of unemployment insurance coincides with that of health insurance. Civil servants, persons under 15 years of age, and the occasionally employed, are not covered by unemployment insurance.

Benefits

Unemployment insurance benefits (*Arbeitslosengeld*), are paid for a minimum of 12 and a maximum of 30 weeks. The period for which benefits are payable is dependent upon the beneficiary satisfying certain qualifying conditions. The amount of benefit is dependent upon the beneficiary's income during the last four weeks prior to dismissal, and consists of a flat-rate (*Grundbetrag*) of 58% of income for those in low-income brackets, decreasing to 40% for those in higher-income brackets. Family supplements (*Familienzuschlag*), are granted on application. Inclusive of these, unemployment benefits may reach a maximum of 80% of last income earned. Where entitlement claims to unemployment benefits have been exhausted, and no other support is available, the insured is eligible to unemployment assistance (*Notstandshilfe*), which amounts to 75% to 100% of unemployment benefit. Unemployment assistance is payable for a maximum of 26 weeks.

Special unemployment benefits (*Sonderunterstützung*) are provided under the 1973 Special Support Act (*Sonderunterstützungsgesetz*), for dependent workers who have been made redundant owing to structural changes in Austrian industry under the impact of European economic integration. It is calculated in the same way as unemployment benefit. In 1967 a similar law was passed protecting miners in the event of mine closure.

Additionally, the 1957 Bad Weather Compensation Act (*Bauarbeiter-Schlechtwetterentschädigungsgesetz*) entitled workers in the construction industry to full compensation of average earnings for a maximum of 192 work hours in cases of unemployment due to bad weather. Finally, compensation is provided under the 1979 Bankruptcy Wage Continuation Act (*Insolvenz-Entgeltsicherungsgesetz*), for dependent workers made redundant as a result of bankruptcy.

The 1979 Amendment to the 1973 Special Support Act, provides support for employees over the age of 59 (men), or 54 (women), where the firm closes down and there is no possibility of finding appropriate future employment. These unemployment pensions (see Section I), are designed to encourage early retirement in cases where the insured has made the necessary number of insurance contributions. In addition, advance pension payments (*Überbrückungshilfe*) are made where pension insurance benefits are awaiting settlement.

Financing and administration

Unemployment insurance is mainly financed by contributions, the rate being 2.5% of the calculation base for health insurance contributions. Central government subsidies finance unemployment assistance (*Notstandshilfe*), maternity allowances are subsidized by the Families' Loads Equalization Scheme. In addition there is a reserve fund to cover eventual deficits. All decisions regarding unemployment registration and contributions are taken by the health insurance institutes, whilst decisions on benefit amounts are taken by the labour authorities.

Services

Employment policies are based on the 1969 Labour Market Promotion Act (*Arbeitsmarktförderungsgesetz*) and implemented by the Federal Ministry of Social Administration, by means of the provincial labour authorities (*Landesarbeitsämter*) and local labour authorities (*Arbeitsämter*). In addition there are provincial authorities for invalids (*Landesinvalidenämter*) together with a work-place inspectorate (*Arbeitsinspektorate*). Labour market promotion is basically financed through the central government budget, but some of its outlays are financed by unemployment insurance receipts.

Labour market services include the following:
- Promotion of mobility, covering paid vocational training, promotion of geographical mobility, and subsidies for removal expenses.
- Location of labour demand, including assistance to firms obliged to lay-off workers owing to economic recessions; assistance for employers of seasonal labour as regards employment and lay-offs; and long-term increases in unemployment.
- Promotion of handicapped employees, including promotion of mobility, job creation, and vocational training.
- Improvement of conditions for foreign workers, covering the promotion of regional mobility, job creation, vocational training subsidies and facilities;
- Infrastructure promotion covering subsidies for residential facilities, and kindergartens for employees' children.

Core laws

1892 (RGBl. 202)
Hilfskassengesetz (Subsidiary Funds Act): allowed funds to provide subsidies to members in cases of unemployment, and travel expenses associated with search for employment. This act is closely linked to the Association Act (*Vereinsgesetz*) which allowed the free association of workers.

1918 (StGBl. 20)
Vollzugsanweisung über die Arbeitslosenfürsorge (Decree on Implementation of Unemployment Assistance Programme): unemployment assistance from government funds (mainly for World War I veterans).

1920 (StGBl. 153)
Arbeitslosenversicherungsgesetz (Unemployment Insurance Act): introduced welfare schemes for the unemployed; entitlement dependent upon a minimum employment record; maximum period of entitlement of 30 weeks.

1922 (no. 534)
Fünfte Novelle zum Gesetz über die Arbeitslosenversicherung (Fifth Amendment to Unemployment Insurance Act): provided subsidies to provinces and communities for employment creation, thus reducing the burden on unemployment insurance funds.

1922 (no. 924)
Gesetz über die Notstandsaushilfe (Emergency Welfare Act): special welfare programme for persons unemployed for more than 30 weeks.

1935 (no. 107)
Gesetz betreffend die Gewerbliche Sozialversicherung (Industrial Social Insurance Act): incorporated unemployment insurance under Section 5 of this law.

1946 (no. 97)
Arbeitslosenfürsorgegesetz (Unemployment Assistance Act): provided legal basis for postwar unemployment assistance programmes.

1949 (no. 184)
Arbeitslosenversicherungsgesetz (Unemployment Insurance Act): brought all aspects

of unemployment insurance (welfare, organization, etc.) up to date; 11 amendments corrected minor shortcomings and made the law compatible with the general Social Insurance Act and its amendments.

1957 (no. 129)
Bauarbeiterschlechtwetterentschädigungsgesetz (Construction Workers' Bad Weather Compensation Act): established compensation for the risks of unemployment due to bad weather conditions and seasonal changes in demand.

1958 (no. 199)
Arbeitslosenversicherungsgesetz (Unemployment Insurance Act): new edition of the 1949 Act inclusive of all amendments and several changes which made it compatible with the 1956 Employment Protection Act, the 1957 Mothers' Protection Act, and the 1957 Construction Workers' Bad Weather Compensation Act.

Several supplementary acts which regulated entitlements, the range of benefits and financing.

1969 (no. 31)
Arbeitsmarktförderungsgesetz (Labour Market Promotion Act): regulations concerning labour market administration, professional counselling, arbitration and subsidies payable to employees and employers.

1973 (no. 642)
Sonderunterstützungsgesetz (Special Subsidies Act): subsidies to those made redundant as a result of structural changes.

1975 (no. 218)
Ausländerbeschäftigungsgesetz (Foreign Workers' Employment Act): required written job offers for foreign workers; entitled government to set an upper limit to the number of foreign workers for economic or social reasons.

1977 (no. 609)
Arbeitslosenversicherungsgesetz (Unemployment Insurance Act): re-edition of the 1958 Act, including supplementary acts.

1979 (no. 107)
Insolvenz Entgeltsicherungsgesetz (Bankruptcy Wage Continuation Act): claims against bankrupt firms paid from a special fund.

V Families and children

In this chapter, a functional approach dominates since regulations and measures concerning the family simultaneously fall into the sections of pension insurance, sickness insurance,unemployment insurance, social assistance etc.

Besides maternity benefits dealt with below, there are a number of protective regulations for women in employment, laid down in the Mothers' Protection Act (*Mutterschaftsgesetz*). Under this Act employers are obliged to grant maternity leave starting eight weeks prior to childbirth and lasting until eight weeks after childbirth. If birth is premature, thereby reducing the eight week period prior to childbirth, the amount of time lost is added to the post-childbirth period (maximum of 12 weeks). Employers do not pay wages during this 16 week period, as the health insurance institutes pay a weekly amount (*Wochengeld*), calculated (as already mentioned) on the basis of the average net income during the 13 weeks prior to the eight week pre-childbirth period.

In addition there are a number of other important regulations for women in employment: female workers may not be dismissed during pregnancy, the first four months after childbirth, during the period of maternity leave or the first four weeks after it; maternity leave may be granted for periods of up to one year following childbirth; various forms of strenuous employment are prohibited during pregnancy, and the number of hours worked is limited in certain occupations after the fifth month of pregnancy. In 1976, the regulations for mothers' protection were extended to adoptive mothers.

Employers are forbidden to terminate an unlimited work contract from the beginning of pregnancy until the end of the fourth month; but the employee is obliged to inform her employer of the pregnancy. Women can apply for maternity leave (*Karenzurlaub*) from the eighth/twelfth week after childbirth until the child's first birthday. Prohibitive regulations also cover dismissals during the period of maternity leave. Maternity leave regulations also apply to adoptive mothers. There are also various tax concessions for family support under the Income Tax Act (*Einkommenssteuergesetz*).

Prior to 1945, legislation had already been passed which regulated working hours for women, introduced family insurance and provided special protection for mothers before and after childbirth (*Mutterschaftsgesetz*). After 1945 a number of laws were passed which provided coverage for families and children: the 1957 regulation covering employed women; the 1969 Act prohibiting night work for women; and the 1976 Act enabling people to undertake the care of close relatives who are ill. Family subsidies of different kinds have been in existence in Austria since 1921.

Income maintenance

The major income maintenance programmes for families are: the Families' Loads Equalization Scheme (*Familienlastenausgleich*, FLA), which covers all Austrians regardless of social or occupational status, and the Maternity Leave Benefits (*Karenzurlaubsgeld*) for women in employment.

Coverage

The FLA provides family allowances (*Familienbeihilfe*) including additional allowances for handicapped children, travel allowances (*Schulfreifahrt*) and a school travel subsidy (*Schulfahrtbeihilfe*), free school books (*unentgeltliche Schulbücher*), and a lump-sum birth payment (*Geburtenbeihilfe*).

FLA expenditure in 1981, in million AS

		%
Family allowances	24 600	78.5
Birth payments	1 300	4.2
Travel subidies and allowances	2 520	8.0
Free school books	995	3.2
Other	1 923	6.1
Total	31 338	100.0

Family allowances amount to 1,000 AS per month for each child under the age of 10, and 1,200 AS from the age of 10 (from 1982).

A lump sum childbirth payment of 2,000 AS is provided for every female Austrian citizen who gives birth to a child. The payment rises to 8,000 AS if the mother has four medical examinations during pregnancy and the child is examined once during its first week of life. An additional payment of 8,000 AS is payable if the child has four medical examinations at regular intervals during the first year of life (this is controlled in the 'mother-child pass'). The state advances alimony payments for children in certain cases, e.g. when the person or parent responsible does not fulfill his or her duties. Marriage benefits (*Heiratsgeld*) are paid to couples marrying for the first time, and amount to 12,000 AS. Travel allowances are provided for school children and students under the age of 27, and entitle them to travel concessions on all forms of public transport. Students not living at home are entitled to travel allowances for the journey home for school holidays. School travel subsidies differ in total amount according to distance, and are paid monthly. School books free of charge are available to all pupils attending compulsory school as well as medium and higher grade schools.

Under unemployment insurance and the Mothers' Protection Act (*Mutterschutzgesetz*), maternity benefits are payable to all women who are gainfully employed and give birth to a child (for eight weeks before and after childbirth). They are calculated on the basis of the net wage during the last three months of employment. Maternity leave expenditure is carried by unemployment insurance (75%) and social insurance (25%); average monthly benefit amounted to 4,233 AS in 1981; there have been no major changes since 1981.

Services

There are 150 counselling offices providing family and partner counselling, in particular family planning and pregnancy advice. They are staffed by doctors, social workers, psychologists and lawyers, and are paid by the state, the federal provinces and local authorities. These services are available to everyone free of charge.

Under the Youth Protection Act (*Jugendwohlfahrtsgesetz*), the federal provinces are obliged to establish counselling offices for pregnant women and young mothers (*Mütterberatungsstellen*). Their most important function is mothers' counselling (*Mütterberatung*). The Youth Protection Act deals with the control of parental and private child care, institutional child care, and adoption (*behördliche Aufsicht über die Übernahme von Kindern in fremde Pflege, Pflegeaufsicht, Erziehungshilfe, Erziehungsaufsicht, Fürsorgeerziehung, und behördliche Überwachung von Adoption*).

Financing and administration

As the financing and administration of the many different benefits and services are organized by the respective schemes for pension insurance, health insurance, unemployment insurance, social assistance, etc., only the FLA will be described in detail.

The FLA is divided into two sections. In section A expenditure is financed by employers' contributions and covers family allowances for gainfully employed persons. Section B expenditure is financed by income taxes (*Einkommens- und Körperschaftssteuer*), contributions from agricultural enterprises (*land- und forstwirtschaftliche Betriebe*), transfers from the provinces (*Länder*), refunds on advanced alimony payments (*rückgezahlte Unterhaltsvorschüsse*), and from the surplus in Section A (*Überschüsse*). Section B covers expenditure for family allowances for the self-employed, birth subsidies, travel allowances, school travel subsidies, free school books, contributions for maternity leave subsidies, the mother-child pass and other family policy measures.

FLA financing in 1981, in million AS

		%
Contributions from employers/enterprises	18 500	59.0
State contributions	9 651	30.8
Other	100	0.3
Surplus in Section A	3 087	9.9
Total	31 338	100.0

In 1981 FLA expenditure increased by 8.3% as compared to that of 1980. This can be accounted for by increases in family allowances and the considerable rise in free school transport expenditure. In 1981, 1.9 million children received benefits under the FLA.

Core laws

1921 (no. 716)
Kinderzuschussgesetz (Child Supplement Act): first act providing child supplements (*Kinderzuschuss*) to employed persons with children under 14 years of age; paid by employers as part of the wage.

1948 (no. 217)
Ernährungsbeihilfegesetz (Food Allowance Act): allowances for children under 18 to employed persons (financed by employers and refunded by central government), and those living on social security benefits.

1950 (no. 31)
Kinderbeihilfengesetz (Child Allowances Act): increased benefits for children under 21; benefits differentiated according to number of children; allowances paid by employers and refunded from a central government fund (Ministry of Finance); several amendments increased benefits according to living standards.

1955 (no. 18)
1. Familienlastenausgleichsgesetz (First Families' Loads Equalization Act): child allowances extended to self-employed for children under 18 (referred to as *Familienbeihilfen*); second fund (see 1950 Act) established financed from general tax revenues, contributions from agricultural enterprises, and provincial contributions; 1950 programme for employed persons (*Kinderbeihilfen*) continued, but both programmes now providing benefits according to number of children.

1956 (no. 52)
Geburtenbeihilfengesetz (Birth Allowances Act): introduced allowances payable for each birth, upon application from the sixth month of pregnancy.

1957 (no. 76)
Mutterschutzgesetz (Mothers' Protection Act): mainly comprised the regulations from International Agreements on mothers' protection; International Agreement No. 703 was ratified in Austria in 1969 (BGBl. 31/1970); three amendments of the 1957 Act brought about important changes: extension of maternity leave until the child reaches the age of one (previously six months); Under the same Act mothers were for the first time entitled to maternity leave benefits (*Karenzurlaubsgeld*) financed by unemployment insurance; in 1974, the work prohibiting periods before and after birth were extended up to eight weeks; in 1976, the regulations were extended to adoptive mothers.

1960 (no. 239)
Mütterbeihilfengesetz (Mothers' Allowance Act): allowances payable to families with three or more children (two or more children from 1962); abolished by 1967 Act.

1960 (no. 240)
Amendment to 1957 Act: extended maternity leave (*Karenzurlaub*) from 6 to 12 months; introduced maternity benefits under unemployment insurance (*Karenzurlaubsgeld*).

1967 (no. 376)
Familienlastenausgleichsgesetz (Families' Loads Equalization Act): basic act incorporating all previous regulations; universal allowance for children under 18 (under 27 for those in full-time education), now called *Familienbeihilfe*; universal birth allowance (*Geburtenbeihilfe*).

1969 (no. 31)
Arbeitsmarktförderungsgesetz (Labour Market Promotion Act): introduced protective labour market measures comprising regulations affecting, either directly or indirectly, the (economic) situation of families.
From 1967 until 1983 there were no fundamental changes, but several amendments to the 1967 Act were made (benefit levels were increased and a number of special benefits, e.g. travel allowances for pupils/students, free school books, supplements for handicapped children, etc. were introduced).

VI Social assistance

By constitutional law, general social assistance comes within the competence of the provinces (*Bundesländer*), and only matters of principle are dealt with by federal legislation. Thus, the provinces have their own Social Assistance Acts (*Sozialhilfegesetze*), passed between 1971 and 1978, which replaced older legislation. These laws represent comprehensive bodies of regulations in accordance with a modern understanding of social assistance and care, but have also created considerable differences in scope and practice of social assistance among the provinces. At least the following principles, however, are common to all social assistance laws:

- benefits are provided only if all other possibilities have been exhausted (*Subsidiaritätsprinzip*);
- benefits are granted on the grounds of individual needs alone (*Prinzip der individuellen Hilfe*);
- benefits are intended to maintain existing family relationships and to strengthen the ability for self-help (*Prinzip der familiengerechten Hilfe*).

Special social assistance for specific groups is mainly based on federal legislation (assistance for the victims of war, political persecution or crimes, and for the members of the armed forces), with the exception of assistance for the handicapped and blind, which falls within the competence of the provinces.

The following description gives a clarification of the various competences. Social assistance (*Sozialhilfe*), has developed from the old forms of community help (*Armenfürsorge der Gemeinden*), and comes within the competence of the provinces who provide help for those in need, enabling them to have a 'decent' standard of living. In addition to this, there are federal responsibilities established by federal laws, e.g. assistance for the victims of war and political persecution, and members of armed forces, etc.

1. Social assistance by the provinces

In 1981 provincial expenditure on social assistance amounted to 7,981 million AS or approximately 0.8% of GDP.

Provincial social assistance in 1981

	No. of recipients or cases	Expenditure mill. AS	%
Permanently supported persons	39 016	890	12.5
Persons in institutions and homes	40 579	3 039	42.9
Blind and handicapped persons	62 714	1 925	27.1
Non-recurring support (cases)	1 068 2191 23917.5		
Total		7 092	100.0

Source: *Statistisches Handbuch der Republik Österreich*, 1982.

With respect to social assistance for persons in institutions, the most important categories are: homes for the elderly without nursing units (10,318 persons and 432 million AS expenditure in 1981), nursing homes and units (9,988 persons and 645 million AS), homes for children and young people (9,063 persons and 611 million AS), homes for the unsheltered (2,314 persons and 27 million AS). There are no data giving a more detailed breakdown of expenses in non-recurring support.

In general, provincial social assistance benefits may be grouped into three types:

(1) Assistance to secure basic needs (*Beihilfe zum Lebensbedarf*): this goes far beyond the traditional concept of poor relief; it not only guarantees a minimum level of subsistence but also covers general care, health care, help to enable people to earn their own living, and the maintenance of cultural and social contacts. This is the only benefit under social assistance legislation to which people are entitled as a right.

(2) Special assistance (*Hilfe in besonderen Lebenslagen*): this covers people in difficult situations due to personal, family, or economic conditions, or exceptional events (catastrophes), and goes beyond the provision of basic needs.

(3) Social services (*Soziale Dienste*): family assistance, i.e. looking after a family when parents are temporarily unable to do so; household assistance, e.g. home help service, meals on wheels; general and special services, e.g. family, marriage, old age and social counselling; services to improve social contacts, e.g. clubs for the elderly, reductions for theatres, museums, and public transport; recreation schemes for the incapacitated and elderly; homes for the incapacitated or disabled and the elderly.

With the exception of special groups, (e.g. war veterans), social assistance for the handicapped also comes within the competence of the provinces. In some provinces it is incorporated into the social assistance laws, in others special laws for the handicapped (*Behindertengesetze*) were passed between 1964 and 1974.

2. Social assistance by central government

Central government social assistance in 1981

	No. of recipients	Expend. in mill. AS Pensions	Services
War victims	179 801	5 471	
Armed forces welfare	951	34	77
Victims of political persecution	5 002	231	
Victims of crimes	3 721	4	
Total		5 740	

As shown in the table above, there are a number of regulations with respect to the reimbursement of war victims, members of the armed forces, victims of political persecution and of crimes, and special welfare programmes, e.g. for civil servants.

War victims are entitled to medical treatment, vocational and social assistance. Survivors of victims are entitled to compensation payments and survivors' pensions. The latter generally consist of a basic amount plus a supplement. The basic amount is dependent on the degree of invalidity, and the supplement is payable if the victim's income is below a certain minimum. This scheme is not as elaborate as the compensation allowance (*Ausgleichszulage*) under the pension scheme. The second phase of the amendment to the 1957 War Victims' Welfare Act (*Kriegsopferversorgungsgesetz*) was begun in 1981. It increased the basic pension for those handicapped by more than 40%, and introduced an entitlement for a widower's pension subsequent to the death of his wife. Approximately 16,000 male war victims and 78,000 widows benefited from the improved support.

Maintenance programmes for the armed forces were established in 1964 to provide coverage for Austrians whose health has been damaged during service with the armed forces, to dependents of Austrians who died while in military service, and to civilians who died as a result of military action. Entitlements are similar to those for war victims. In 1981 a total of 893 persons received benefits under these maintenance programmes, i.e. 827 disabled, and 124 widows, orphans etc. The cost amounted to 31.7 million AS in 1981. Expenditure on therapeutic facilities and orthopaedic support for war victims and armed forces' welfare amounted to 76.5 million AS.

Victims of crimes are entitled to benefits for the loss of earnings, social and vocational rehabilitation, and medical treatment. Survivors receive benefits which partially cover loss of maintenance. Children receive assistance until the age of 18 (or 26 if they are in full-time education).

The Act for the Assistance of Victims of Political Persecution (*Opferfürsorgegesetz*) was established in 1947. It is meant to support all the victims of the political struggle and persecution in favour of a free and democratic Austria between 6 March 1933 and 9 May 1945: benefits are given in cash and kind.

Financing and administration

Applications for social assistance benefits can be brought to the local community administration. Although social assistance is within the competence of the provinces, the administration is carried out by the district authorities and provincial governments. The financing is guaranteed by the provinces and communities. With the exception of crime victims' maintenance, all services are organized and financed by federal administration. Legislation regulating benefits for the blind and handicapped are dealt with by the federal provinces, except those matters which are already covered in social security legislation; a federal act (*Kriegsopferversorgungsgesetz*) regulates the entitlements of war victims.

Core laws

For laws prior to 1929, see Core Laws under Section I.

1929 (no. 1/1930)
Österreichisches Bundesverfassungsgesetz (Austrian Constitutional Law): established a general competence to legislate on poor relief with respect to protection of vital needs only (*Kompetenztatbestand*); to be implemented by the provinces through special Social Assistance Acts.

1947 (no. 183)
Opferfürsorgegesetz (Assistance Act for the Victims of Political Persecution): introduced support for those who had been victims of political persecution in the period from 6.3.1933 to 9.5.1945, or to their survivors; provides regular or lump sum payments, or benefits in kind.

1957 (no. 27)
Kriegsopferversorgungsgesetz (War Victims' Act): introduced protection for Austrian soldiers and civilians who suffered health damage during the war; provides compensation payments, rehabilitative programmes and medical treatment.

1964 (no. 27)
Heeresversorgungsgesetz (Armed Forces' Maintenance Programme Act): introduced protection for members of the armed forces who suffer health damage while in military service, or their survivors, and also for civilians who suffer health damage as a result of military action, or their survivors.

1969 (no. 22/1970)
Invalideneinstellungsgesetz (Invalids' Employment Act): dealt in particular with the conditions for the employment of war victims (invalids).

1972 (no. 288)
Verbrechensopfergesetz (Crime Victims' Act): established the principle of compensa-

tion for health damages caused, directly or indirectly by crimes punishable by more than six months' imprisonment.

Provincial Acts

1964-1974
Behindertengesetze (Assistance for the Handicapped Acts): unless otherwise stated in the Constitutional Law (Art. 10-12), these acts are the competence of the provinces; assistance for the handicapped is regulated by Social Assistance Acts in some provinces, and by special Acts for the Handicapped in others; acts are published in the provincial legislative bulletin (*Landesgesetzblätter*).

1971-1978
Sozialhilfegesetze (Social Assistance Acts): provincial Social Assistance Acts which deal with the establishment of a comprehensive system of regulations on social assistance.

VII Education

1. Educational system

In 1975 (see note [a] to the following table), public expenditure on education amounted to 37,558 million AS or 5.72% of GDP (see table on following page).

The education system is partly the competence of the federal provinces and partly that of the state e.g. universities. Education in state schools and universities is free of charge, and there are no admission restrictions for Austrian citizens. Private education is of minor importance.

At the pre-primary level there is a highly developed system of *Krippen*, *Horte*, and *Kindergarten* for children aged 2 to 6. In 1981/82 there were a total of 2,534 kindergartens catering for 159,186 children.

The Austrian school system is horizontally and vertically structured. The general primary school (*Volksschule*) provides elementary education for a period of four years and is followed by either lower secondary school (*Sekundärbereich I*) or higher secondary education (*Sekundärbereich II*), both of which offer general education from the fifth grade.

The *Hauptschule* is the main lower secondary school and runs from the fifth to the eighth grade. It concludes compulsory education and pupils subsequently take up employment or enter a lower vocational school of one to three years' duration. Another option is the voluntary ninth grade or polytechnical course (*polytechnischer Lehrgang*) within the *Hauptschule*. There are also special schools for the physically and mentally handicapped (*Sonderschule*).

The eight-year general higher schools (*allgemeinbildende höhere Schulen*) in principle prepare for entry to university. They also start from the fifth grade, and in the first two years a transition from the *Hauptschule* is relatively easy. There are several types of higher secondary school: the *Gymnasium* with a classical, modern language, or natural science orientation, and the *Realgymnasium* with a natural science/mathematics orientation, or as a special higher secondary school for girls.

Education: expenditure and number of pupils

	Expenditure in 1975(a)				No. of pupils and students in 1979/80
	Total mill. AS	%	% distribution central	provincial local	
Kindergarten	1 252	3.3	-	100.0	162.502
General compulsory schools	15 632	41.6	56.4	43.6	867.782
General secondary schools	3 666	9.8	98.5	1.5	182.027
Vocational compulsory schools	1 243	3.3	26.2	73.8	198.509
Medium and higher vocational schools	3 021	8.0	91.5	8.5	102.296[b] 70.602[c]
Agricultural and forestry schools	713	1.9	43.9	56.1	
Teacher training	443	1.2	98.7	1.3	13.898
Universities	5 488	14.6	99.0	1.0	23.463
Adult education	161	0.4	-	100.0	
Study and pupils' allowances	693	1.8	96.8	3.2	
Travel allow. and free books	2 358	6.3	100.0	-	
Other including not classifiable	2 888	7.7	32.7	67.3	
Total	37 558	100.0	65.8	34.2	

[a] After 1975 comparable statistics are not available; see source, note 1 on page 113.
[b] Medium vocational schools.
[c] Higher vocational schools.
Source: *Sozialstatistische Daten 1980*, Vienna 1981, p. 113.

Higher vocational schools (*berufsbildende höhere Schulen*) last from four to five years, and entry may take place after completion of the eighth grade of a higher secondary school or after passing an examination, coming from the *Hauptschule*. There are various types of higher vocational school, the two most important being the higher technical school (*höhere technisch-gewerbliche Lehranstalt*) and the trade school (*Handelsakademie*). The completion of higher vocational school gives access to certain areas of university education. There are in addition, special regulations (*Gesetz über die Berufsreifeprüfung*) which enable those who have not completed higher secondary education to enter university upon passing an examination.

There are a number of institutions devoted to adult education: denominational associations (*Arbeitsgemeinschaft Katholischer Bildungswerke Österreichs, Arbeitsgemein-*

schaft Evangelischer Bildungswerke Österreichs), institutes of Austrian trade unions, etc. These vary considerably in respect of organization, financing and orientation.

Higher adult education (*Volkshochschulen*) was set up by the Social Democratic and workers' movement, and has developed considerably during the last few years. In 1979/80 they offered a total of 22,829 courses, 6,916 events with a total of 348,742 participants and 642,784 visitors.

A system of educational (*Bildungsberatung*) and vocational (*Berufsberatung*) counselling helps to allocate pupils and students and to provide careers' advice. Educational counselling is offered by the psychological school service (*Schulpsychologischer Dienst*) and school counselling (*Schülerberatung*). It provides information about the labour market, apprenticeships, etc.

2. Income maintenance

The educational support system may be divided into direct and indirect support. Direct benefits include: pupil allowances (*Schülerbeihilfen*); study allowances (*Studienbeihilfen*); and educational allowances for those in apprenticeships (*Ausbildungsbeihilfen*). Indirect benefits include: family allowances (*Familienbeihilfe*) and tax deductions for the family breadwinner (*Alleinverdienerabsetzbetrag*); tax deductions according to income tax legislation; benefits already mentioned under the FLA; and subventions for private educational measures (students' homes, etc.).

Study allowances were first introduced in 1963. In 1969 the Student Support Act (*Studienförderungsgesetz*) and subsequent amendments increased the amount of allowances and extended coverage. Under this act study allowances are calculated on a basic annual amount of 25.000 AS for single students and 30.000 for married students. Under certain conditions (e.g. the death of either one or both parents, or partner etc.) the basic amount is augmented by 13.000 AS. Severely handicapped students receive an extra 15.000 AS. Correspondingly, the basic rate is reduced in cases of high parental or student income. The success of the student is also taken into consideration in an assessment of the allowance. In 1976, expenditure on study allowances amounted to 340 million AS.

In 1971, pupils became entitled to allowances. Pupil allowances (*Schülerbeihilfen*) are paid from the tenth grade and special allowances for pupils in homes (*Heimbeihilfen*) from the ninth grade. Benefits are designed to provide partial compensation to parents for the financial burden caused by children continuing into further education after the end of compulsory schooling.

Core laws

1774

Allgemeine Schulordnung für die deutschen Normal-, Haupt- und Trivialschulen in sämtlichen Kaiserlich-königlichen Erbländern (General Act on 'German' Primary and Lower Secondary Schools within the Territory of the Monarchy): introduced general compulsory education; 'german' refers to schools where Latin is not taught.

1849

Entwurf der Organisation der Gymnasien und Realschulen in Österreich (Proposal for the Organization of Upper Secondary Schools in Austria): extended *Gymnasium* to eight years; introduced the principle of 'classical general education'.

1855
Konkordat (Concordat): gave the Catholic Church full control over educational affairs.

1868 (RGBl. no. 48)
Schule-Kirche-Gesetz (School-Church Act): the Catholic Church lost its monopoly over educational affairs; schools became open for everybody regardless of religion, etc.

1869 (RGBl. no. 62)
Reichsvolksschulgesetz (Imperial Primary School Act): schools made inter-denominational and state controlled - even regarding the teaching of religion; compulsory education fixed at eight years' duration; established four-year teacher training schools (*Lehrerbildungsanstalten*).
The Acts of 1849 and 1869 established the basic structural framework - still partially valid today - of the Austrian school system.

1917
Lehrerdienstpragmatik (Teachers' Act): established the rights and obligations of teachers as civil servants; still essentially valid today.

1927
Verfassungsgesetz zur Hauptschule und zur Mittelschule (Secondary Education Act): established the following types of secondary schools for pupils from the age of ten: *Gymnasium*, *Realgymnasium*, *Realschule*, and the *Frauenoberschule* for girls; in addition the four- to five-year's *Aufbauschule* following the eight-years' compulsory school for children from rural areas, and the *Arbeitermittelschule*, a four-year evening school for workers.

1949 (no. 190)
Religionsunterrichtsgesetz (Religious Education Act): regulated the employment of religion teachers and defined the contents of religious teaching.

1962 (no. 240-245)
Various acts, the most important being the *Schulorganisationsgesetz* (School Organization Act, no. 243) which regulated the objectives, educational methods, and organization of the school system as it exists today; abolished the *Aufbauschule* and the *Arbeitermittelschule* created in 1927; regulated the various school types within a horizontally and vertically segmented structure.

1971 (no. 234), 1975 (no. 323)
Schulorganisationsgesetznovellen (Amendments to the School Organization Act): specified the conditions for the implementation of experimental schools and models of education.

1974 (no. 139)
Schulunterrichtsgesetz (School Instruction Act): regulated entry to different school grades, and conditions for progress from one grade to another, increasing the possibilities of transition.

VIII Housing

In 1980, total public expenditure on housing amounted to 16.8 billion AS, or 1.6% of GDP. Of this sum, three-quarters was federal expenditure, one-sixth provincial expenditure, and the rest municipal expenditure.

Public expenditure on housing by level of government and major programmes in 1980, in million AS

		%
Central government	12 584	74.8
- WFG programme	11 772	70.0
- WVG programme	220	1.3
- Other programmes	592	3.5
Provinces	2 900	17.3
- WFG programme	1 002	6.0
- Other programmes	1 892	11.3
Municipalities	1 334	7.9
- Vienna	735	4.4
- municipalities	599	3.5
Total	16 818	100.0

Source: *Die Wohnbaufinanzierung des Bundes, der Bundesländer und Gemeinden.* Verbindungsstelle der Bundesländer beim Amt der Niederösterreichischen Landesregierung, Vienna, 1982.

Central government has the prime responsibility for housing in that it passes basic legislation and finances the major programmes. The provinces (*Länder*) are responsible for the implementation of federal housing laws, the organization of their own supplementary programmes, and for urban planning, land regulation, etc. There are four main areas of housing policy: the promotion of housing construction; improvement of the housing stock; housing allowances; and rent legislation.

In 1977, housing stock consisted of approximately 2.9 million dwellings, of which 2.6 million were occupied. Of these, around 50% were owner-occupied (41% houses, 9% apartments), and around 50% were rented. Average annual housing production in the period 1971-1980 amounted to about 51,000 dwellings. Of these, 8% were constructed by or on behalf of public authorities, 34% by building associations (*gemeinnützige Bauvereinigungen*), 49% by individuals, and 9% by other bodies or institutions.

Non-profit building associations play an important role in the construction and administration of housing. Their origins lie in the association movement (*Genossenschaftsbewegung*), and were first put on a legislative basis in 1940. In 1979, there were a total of 252 membership organizations with a total of 2,623 members, administrating almost half a million dwellings. They held 51% of all subsidized dwellings constructed between 1968 and 1978 (333,673).

The 1968 Housing Construction Promotion Act (*Wohnbauförderungsgesetz*, WFG) promotes the construction of small- and middle-sized dwellings for low-income groups and large families. The construction of housing under the WFG is financed in the following ways:

- by long-term (ca. 50 years) public loans (*Darlehen*) with a 0.5% interest rate covering 45% of total costs; since 1981 provincial funds may provide additional loans covering up to 70% of total costs;

- by private savings covering 10% of total costs, or 5% where construction is carried out by a building association; these savings may be replaced by 20-year interest-free public loans (*Eigenmittelersatzdarlehen*) for young families, families with three or more children, and families in very difficult economic circumstances;
- by private loans covering the remainder of total costs; subject to certain conditions regarding duration and interest rates, interest payments may be subsidized for a period of the first fifteen years (*Annuitätenzuschuss*).

The improvement and restoration of existing housing stock is supported under the 1967 Housing Improvment Act (*Wohnbauverbesserungsgesetz*, WVG). The Act provides for a 40% subvention of interest payments on private loans, public guarantees for such loans, and, since 1975, the extension of housing supplements (*Wohnbeihilfe*) to cover costs of housing improvements. The modernization of housing stock may be supported by up to 25% of total (estimated) costs. Since 1975, more extensive improvements may be subsidized under the terms of an amendment to the WFG, which provides up to 80% of total costs. Under the WFG and WVG a total of 342,237 improvements were carried out in the period 1970-1980. Of these, 122,468 dealt with sanitation and 82,547 dealt with heating, at a total cost of 13.9 billion AS. In addition to the WFG and WVG there are Provincial Housing Construction Acts (*Landeswohnbaufondsgesetze*).

The current monthly payments for WFG and WVG loans and the rent for WFG-constructed housing may be furthermore subsidized by housing supplements. These are payable under certain conditions, and are based on the difference between actual and 'acceptable' rent. 'Acceptable' rent is defined by the provinces as a percentage of family income, differentiated by family size and income level. Since 1976, families with three or more children have been granted these supplements on particularly favourable terms.

There are no general housing allowances. However, a housing rent supplement (*Mietzinsbeihilfe*) is payable in cases where rent increases are excessive and likely to cause economic hardship to the tenant. These supplements are regulated in the Income Tax Act and Housing Rent Act.

Financing and administration

The WFG and WVG together mark a considerable change in the administration and financing, as well as the objectives and instruments, of Austrian housing policy. This is even visible from the official statistical categories which only partially allow the construction of time-series on expenditure.

The WFG is financed through the two central housing funds (*Bundes-, Wohn- und Siedlungsfonds* and *Wohnhauswiederaufbaufonds*) from state contributions, loan repayments and interest on unused supportive capital. The central and provincial government contributions to the two housing funds are in turn financed out of income and corporation tax (11.45%), and from a contribution from the gainfully employed (*Wohnbauförderungsbeitrag*).

Expenditure on the WVG is financed, again via the housing funds, by the federal budget (one-third), the provinces (one-third), and the housing funds themselves (one-third). In 1982, revenues available for housing purposes amounted to 17,779 million AS. Of this sum, 13,275 came from the federal government, 1,873 from the provinces, and the rest from other sources.

Core laws

1921 (no. 252)
Bundes-, Wohn- und Siedlungsfondsgesetz (Federal Housing and Settlement Funds Act): changed and extended older regulations of a State Housing Assistance Fund (*Staatlicher Wohnungsfürsorgefonds*).

1940 (RGBl. no. I/438)
Wohnungsgemeinnützigkeitsgesetz (Non-profit Building Associations Act): established the conditions for state-subsidized construction of housing by building associations.

1948 (no. 130)
Wohnhaus-Wiederaufbaugesetz (Housing Reconstruction Act): first postwar act to accelerate the reconstruction and replacement of housing stock; created the Housing Reconstruction Fund (*Wohnhaus-Wiederaufbaufond*, WWF).

1954 (no. 153)
Wohnbauförderungsgesetz (Housing Construction Promotion Act): promoted the construction of small- and middle-sized housing and apartments.

1967 (no. 426)
Wohnbauverbesserungsgesetz, WVG (Housing Improvement Act): dealt with the improvement and restoration of small- and middle-sized houses and apartments.

1967 (no. 280)
Wohnbauförderungsgesetz, WFG (Housing Construction Promotion Act): first general act unifying the regulations of the 1921, 1948 and 1954 Acts; effective from 1968.

1974 (no. 288)
Bodenbeschaffungsgesetz (Land Purchase Act): dealt with the purchase of land for housing construction.

1974 (no. 287)
Stadterneuerungsgesetz (Town Renovation Act): dealt with the renovation of residential town areas.

1975 (no. 417)
Wohnungseigentumsgesetz (Housing Property Act): established the property rights of house- and flat-owners.

Bibliography

Contents

I General and historical contributions to welfare

ADLER, V.: Über Arbeiterschutz und Sozialreform (On Labourer Protection and Social Reform), Vol. IV. Vienna, 1935.

ARMENPFLEGE UND WOHLTÄTIGKEIT IN ÖSTERREICH: Österreichs Wohlfahrtseinrichtungen, 1848-1898 (Poor Relief and Charity in Austria - Austria's Welfare Institutions, 1848-1898), Vol. I. Vienna, 1899. An overview of the organizational status, goals and functions of different 'welfare' institutions in Austria in the period 1848-1898.

BEIDTEL, I.: Geschichte der Österreichischen Staatsverwaltung, 1740-1792 (A History of State Administration in Austria, 1740-1792). Frankfurt, Sauer & Auvermann Kg, 1968 (Innsbruck, 1896). An in-depth history of state activities and policy in the period 1740-1792, with detailed information on education, social assistance, health care, poor relief, etc.

BRUCKMÜLLER, E., SANDGRUBER, R., STEKL, H.: 'Soziale Sicherheit im Nachziehverfahren (The latecomers to social security)'. *Forschungen in Geschichte und Sozialkunde*, Vol. 3. Salzburg, 1978, p. 240. A critical historical analysis of the development of social security for farmers, farmworkers, the self-employed in small-scale trade and industry, and mothers' helps for mothers with children. Gives an overview of the integration of suchschemes into the social security system.

BRÜGEL, L.: Soziale Gesetzgebung in Österreich, 1848-1918 (Social Policy Legislation in Austria, 1848-1918). Vienna, Leipzig, 1919.

BRUSATTI, A.: Österreichs Wirtschaftspolitik vom Josephinismus zum Ständestaat (Austrian Economic Policy from Emperor Joseph II to the Corporate State), 3rd ed. Vienna, 1963.

DURDICK, C., FELDBAUER, P.: 'Vor- und Frühformen sozialer Sicherung (Precursors and early forms of social security)', *Beiträge zur historischen Sozialkunde*, Vol. 8, 1978.

FEDERAL PRESS SERVICE (ed.): Social Security in Austria. Vienna, 1980. A brief summary of the organization, legislation and main benefits of Austrian social security.

FELDBAUER, P.: Kinderelend in Wien; von der Armenpflege zur Jugendfürsorge (Child Poverty in Vienna; from Charity to Youth Welfare Programmes). Vienna, 1980. An analysis of the causes and consequences of the first attempts to organize education and welfare programmes for orphans in the eighteenth century. Also covers subsequent developments up to the second half of the nineteenth century.

HOFMEISTER, H.: Ein Jahrhundert Sozialversicherung in Österreich (A Century of Social Security in Austria), Berlin, 1981, p. 285. A complete history of insurance for health, old age pensions, accidents and unemployment with emphasis on legislation. Gives a summary of the economic and political background to legislative changes from the nineteenth century until the passing of the General Social Insurance Act in 1955.

INSTITUT FÜR HÖHERE STUDIEN: Sozialversicherung zwischen Staat und Verbänden (Social Insurance between the State and Associations), 3 Vols. Vienna, 1976.

KLEZL, F.: Die Sozialpolitik in Österreich (Social Policy in Austria). Vienna, 1930. A review and analysis of problems regarding work safety regulations and social security; with particular reference to current controversies in this area.

KLOSE, A.: Österreich als Sozialstaat (Austria as a Social State). Vienna, 1963.

KNOPF, M.: Die Wohlfahrtspolitik des österreichischen Herrscherhauses in Vormärz (The Welfare Policy of the Austrian Monarchy before March 1848). Unpublished dissertation, Vienna, 1966. Overview of the measures, legislation and objectives of early welfare policy under the Habsburg Monarchy.

MAYER-MALY, T.: 'Sozialversicherungspolitik (Social insurance policy)'. *In* TAUTSCHER, A. (ed.): Handbuch der österreichischen Wirtschaftspolitik, Vienna, 1961, p. 479 passim.

MAYRHOFER, E.: Handbuch für den politischen Verwaltungsdienst (Handbook of Political Administration), 5th ed., Vol. V., Vienna, 1901, pp. 213-314; 2nd supplementary volume, Vienna 1913, pp. 909-975. Re-edited by PACE, Graf Anton. Two articles containing interesting information on the organization of policy measures in the nineteenth century.

REITHOFER, H.: 'Gesellschaftspolitik und Reformperspektiven der Sozialversicherung (Society and the perspectives for social security reform)'. *Wirtschaftspolitische Blätter*, Vol. 30, 1983, p. 75 passim.

STEKL, H.: 'Soziale Sicherung und soziale Kontrolle. Zur österreichischen Armengesetzgebung des 18. und 19. Jahrhunderts (Social security and social control. Austria's poverty legislation in the eighteenth and nineteenth centuries)'. *Bericht über den 14. österreichischen Historikertag in Wien* (Report on the 14th Congress of Historians in Vienna). Vienna, Verband österreichischer Geschichtsvereine, 1979, pp. 136-151. Short and informative analysis of poverty legislation and its objectives.

TALOS, E.: Staatliche Sozialpolitik in Österreich. Rekonstruktion und Analyse (State Social Policy in Austria. Reconstruction and Analysis). Vienna, 1981, p. 465. A comprehensive historical description and evaluation of the roots and consequences of social policy today.

TESAREK, A. (ed.): Reden und Schriften von Victor Adler (Speeches and Publications of Victor Adler). Vienna, Verlag Wiener Volksbuchhandlung, 1947. Selections from the writings, speeches and publications of the founder of the Austrian Social Democratic Party with descriptions and analyses of the relationship between the writers' movement, state policy and political parties; gives an overview of the workers' fight for liberation.

II Specific programmes or aspects

BERGER, E. (ed.): Krank. Zur Krise der Medizin (Ill. On the Crisis in Medicine). Vienna, 1977.

BOLZ, W.: Probleme der Fürsorge und Sozialhilfe im Wohlfahrtsstaat (Problems of Social Care and Assistance in the Welfare State). Vienna, Braumüller, 1974. Viennese contributions on social and labour law.

BUNDESKAMMER DER GEWERBLICHEN WIRTSCHAFT (ed.): Die Arbeitskosten in der Industrie Österreichs (The Cost of Labour in Austrian Industry). Vienna, 1972 (1st ed.), 1981 (2nd ed.). Includes figures on enterprises' voluntary social benefits to employees, disaggregated by industries, blue-collar workers, and white-collar workers. The 1981 edition allows for a comparative study of the development of these benefits.

BUSCH, G.M.: Sozialpolitik, Wohlfahrt, Gesundheit (Social Policy, Welfare, Health). *In* ABELE, H., et al (eds): Handbuch der österreichischen Wirtschaftspolitik. Vienna, 1982, p. 296 passim. A brief review of the development and main issues in Austrian policy on social insurance, welfare programmes and health care.

CLEMENT, W.: Arbeitsmarktpolitik (Labour Market Policy). *In* ABELE, H., et al (eds): Handbuch der österreichischen Wirtschaftspolitik. Vienna, 1982, p. 277 passim. A brief review of the institutional and social conditions which have generated and shaped labour market policies from the 1960s to the present day. Written by an outstanding labour market economist.

CLEMENT, W. (ed.): 'Finanzwirtschaftliche Probleme des öffentlichen Bildungswesens in Österreich (Financial problems of the Austrian educational system)'. *Schriftenreihe des Bundesministeriums für Unterricht und Kunst*, Vol. 10. Vienna, 1973.

DRAGASCHNIG, A.: 'Notwendigkeit und Chancen einer Reform der Krankenversicherung in Rahmen des ASVG (The need for and chances of a reform of sickness insurance under the ASVG)'. *Wirtschaftspolitische Blätter*, Vol. 30, 1983, p. 39 passim.

INSTITUT FÜR HÖHERE STUDIEN: Systemanalyse des Gesundeitswesens in Österreich (System Analysis of the Austrian Health System). Vienna, 1976.

INSTITUT FÜR SOZIALPOLITIK UND SOZIALREFORM - SOCIAL INSURANCE WORKSHOP.: 'Vorschläge für eine Reform der österr Sozialversicherung (Proposals for a reform of Austrian social insurance)'. *Gesellschaft und Politik*, No. 20, No. 1, 1984.

KODEX DES ÖSTERREICHISCHEN RECHTS.: Sozialversicherung (Social Insurance). Vienna, 1981. The index of federal laws; updated for major changes to laws.

KREJCI, H.: Das Sozialversicherungsverhältnis (The Relation between the Insurer and the Insured). Vienna, 1977.

MAYR, M.: 'Institutionelle Probleme der Sozialversicherung (Institutional problems of social insurance)'. *Wirtschaftspolitische Blätter*, Vol. 30, 1983, p. 66 passim. A critical investigation of the effectiveness of self-administered social insurance institutions.

MINISTRY OF SOCIAL AFFAIRS AND THE FEDERATION OF SOCIAL SECURITY INSTITUTES (eds): 25 Jahre Hauptverband der österreichischen Sozialversicherungsträger (25 Years of the Federation of Austrian Social Insurance Institutes). Vienna, 1973.

OBERHUBER, G.: Vorstands- und Geschäftsführerverträge in Österreich (Contracts of Managers and Directors in Austria). Vienna, Dr. Helmut Neumann, Management Beratung, 1983. An investigation into the size and composition of benefits for directors and managers in middle-sized and large private enterprises.

REIGER, H.: 'Probleme der gewerblichen Sozialversicherung (Problems of social insurance for the self-employed)'. *Wirtschaftspolitische Blätter*, Vol. 30, 1983, p. 45 passim.

RUDDHA, J.: 'Probleme der Arbeitslosenversicherung (Problems of unemployment insurance)'. *Wirtschaftspolitische Blätter*, Vol. 30, 1983, p. 52 passim.

SCHNELL, H.: Die österreichische Schule in Umbruch (The Austrian School System Under Change). Vienna, Jugend und Volk, 1974.

STEINBACH, F.: 'Die gesetzliche Unfallversicherung in Österreich (Legal accident insurance in Austria)'. *Schriftenreihe des Forschungsinstitutes für soziale Sicherheit beim Hauptverband der österreichischen Sozialversicherungsträger*. Vienna, 1979. A historical review from the eighteenth century to 1976.

TOMANDL, T.: Finanzierungsprobleme der österreichischen Sozialversicherung (Problems of Financing Social Insurance). Vienna, Institut für angewandte Sozial- und Wirtschaftsforschung, 1979, p. 197. A review of the development of services, benefits and costs (mainly health, pension and accident insurance); contains reform proposals.

TOMANDL, T.: Grundriss des österreichischen Sozialrechts (An Outline of Austrian Social Law), 2nd ed. Vienna, 1980. A comprehensive study of the principles of social security legislation.

TOMANDL, T. (ed.): System des österreichischen Sozialversicherungsrechts (The System of Austrian Social Insurance Law). Vienna, 1978.

WEIGEL, W., et al.: 'Stand der familienpolitischen Diskussion (State of the discussion on family politics)'. *Gesellschaft und Politik*, Vol. 18, No. 1, 1982.

III Theoretical contributions and empirical evidence

AMANN, A.: Lebenslage und Sozialarbeit (Living Conditions and Social Work). Berlin, Duncker & Humblot, 1983.

BEIRAT FÜR WIRTSCHAFTS- UND SOZIALFRAGEN (Council for Economic and Social Matters): Untersuchung ausgewählter Ausgabenbereiche des Bundeshaushalts (Analysis of Selected Items of Federal Budget Expenditure). Vienna, 1982. Part three gives an overview of federal expenditure on social security for the period 1970-1981, including unemployment insurance and subsidies to insurance institutes.

BÖS, D., HOLZMANN, R.: Simulationsanalysen zur österreichischen Pensionsdynamik (Simulation Analysis of Pension Dynamics). An investigation of the feasibility of income indexing for pensions.

BUNDESMINISTERIUM FÜR SOZIALE VERWALTUNG (ed.): Social Structure of Austria Today. Vienna, 1982. Includes an analysis of the causes of occupational diseases in various industries, an examination of seasonal unemployment, and the effects of labour-saving technology on employment and employment policy; English summaries given for each chapter.

BUSCH, G.M.: 'Die Sozialpolitik in der ökonomischen Theorie (Social policy in economic theory)'. *Wirtschaftspolitische Blätter*, Vol. 30, 1983, p. 11 passim. Written by a research officer in the Austrian Institute for Economic Research.

BUSCH, G.: 'Österreichs Sozialausgaben im internationalen Vergleich (Austrian social security expenditure - an international comparison)'. *Monatsberichte des österreichischen Instituts für Wirtschaftsforschung*, No. 8, 1979, p. 379 passim.

DALLINGER, R.: 'Notwendigkeit und Chancen einer Reform der Pensionsversicherung im Rahmen des ASVG (The need for and chances of a reform of pension insurance under the ASVG)'

DETTER, T.: 'Möglichkeiten der privaten Krankenversicherung (The potential of private health insurance)'. *Wirtschaftspolitische Blätter*, Vol. 30, 1983, p. 39 passim.

FAMILIENBERICHT 1973.: Bericht über die Situation der Familie in Österreich (Report on the Situation of Families in Austria). Vienna, 1979. Comprehensive and detailed government report on families; presents empirical data and a review of legislative changes and their consequences.

FISCHER-KOWALSKY, M., BUCEK, J. (eds): Lebensverhältnisse in Österreich (Living Conditions in Austria). Frankfurt and New York, 1980. Gives a summary of the results of an extensive empirical study carried out by the Institute for Advanced Studies in Vienna. The topics include inequality in education, health, cultural activities, income distribution and political participation.

FISCHER-KOWALSKY, M., BUCEK, J. (eds): Sozialbericht über Ungleichheit in Österreich (Social Report on Inequality in Austria), 3 Vols. Vienna, Institut für Höhere Studien, 1978. Detailed study on inequality structures.

GENSER, B., HOLZMANN, R.: 'Die Sozialen Wohlfahrtsaufgaben der öffentlichen Haushalte: Eine empirisch-institutionelle Analyse für Österreich (Social welfare programmes in public budgets: an empirical/institutional analysis for Austria)'. *Der öffentliche Sektor*, Vol. 7, 1981, p. 2 passim. A quantitative analysis for the period 1968-78 which concentrates on social insurance, the FLA, labour market administration, welfare programmes and price subsidization. Includes provincial and municipal activities.

HÖLLER, M., STRASSER, H., MITTER, P., PREGLAN, M. (eds): Strukturen der Sozialen Ungleichheit in Österreich (The Structures of Social Inequality in Austria), 3 Vols. and summary. Vienna, Institut für Höhere Studien, 1978. Detailed study of inequality structures with emphasis on class analysis, its theory and empirical manifestations; applies class analysis models to Austria.

HOLZMANN, R.: Quantitative Sozialpolitik, Finanzsysteme und Pensionsversicherung (Quantitative Social Policy, Financing and Pension Insurance). Vienna, Verlag der Österreichischen Akademie der Wissenschaften, 1979, p. 254. A description of the prevailing objectives and performance of Austrian pension insurance. Examines reform strategies by means of a simulation model.

INSTITUT FÜR EMPIRISCHE SOZIALFORSCHUNG: Die Gesellschaftliche Reintegration älterer Menschen (The Social Reintegration of the Elderly). Vienna, 1975. National study on social, economic and cultural conditions of integration/reintegration of the elderly in Austria, with special analyses of social assistance and housing questions.

INSTITUT FÜR VERSICHERUNGSMATHEMATIK DER TECHNISCHEN HOCHSCHULE WIEN: 'Demographische Entwicklung der Versicherungsstände bis 1990 (Demographic development of the insured up to 1990)'. *Schriftenreihe des Forschungsinstituts für soziale Sicherheit beim Hauptverband der Österreichischen Sozialversicherungsträger*. Vienna.

KORBER, W.: 'Pensionsrückstellungen (Old age pension reserves)'. *Schriftenreihe der Bundeswirtschaftskammer*, 48. Vienna, 1983, p. 109. Discusses the financing of old age benefits by private enterprises.

KUMMER, K. (ed.): 'Pensionsdynamik - Lösungen und Aufgaben (Pension dynamics - solutions and functions)'. *Gesellschaft und Politik*, Vol. 1, New Series No. 4, 1965.

OZMEC, R.: 'Möglichkeiten der privaten Pensionsversicherung (The potential of private pension insurance)'. *Wirtschaftspolitische Blätter*, Vol. 30, 1983, p. 25 passim.

RUPPE, H.G. (ed.): Sozialpolitik und Umverteilung (Social Policy and Redistribution). Vienna, Institut für Angewandte Sozial- und Wirtschaftsforschung. Contains contributions on theoretical foundations, problems of measurement and the state of federal law on social justice; includes income maintenance on an aggregate level.

VERBINDUNGSSTELLE DER BUNDESLÄNDER BEIM AMT DER NIEDERÖSTER-

REICHISCHEN LANDESREGIERUNG (ed.): Die Wohnbaufinanzierung des Bundes, der Bundesländer und der Gemeinden 1979 und 1980 (The Financing of Housing Construction and Improvement by Federal, Provincial and Municipal Authorities in 1979 and 1980). Vienna, 1982. Statistical report published by the Provincial Government Coordinating Office.

WÖSENDORFER, J.: Arbeitsmarktpolitik (Labour Market Policy). Vienna, 1981.

IV Austrian journals dealing with social services and social welfare

ARBEIT UND WIRTSCHAFT (Labour and Economics): Österreichischer Arbeiterkammertag. Published monthly.

BEITRÄGE ZUR ÖSTERREICHISCHEN STATISTIK (Articles on Austrian Statistics): No. 613, 2nd ed. Vienna, Österreichisches Statistisches Zentralamt, 1981. This revised edition of a volume which was first published in 1977. The data compiled include data from annual reports of various federal institutions as well as from occasional sample analyses by the Federal Statistical Office. Covers statistical data on: health care; education; labour force; social security; welfare for young people, women, the old and disabled; and housing. No economic data are included.

BEITRÄGE ZUR ÖSTERREICHISCHEN STATISTIK, INDIKATOREN ZUR GESELLSCHAFTLICHEN ENTWICKLUNG (Contributions to Austrian Statistics, Indicators of Social Development): No. 523, 2nd ed. Vienna, Österreichisches Statistisches Zentralamt, 1978.

BERICHT ÜBER DAS GESUNDHEITSWESEN IN ÖSTERREICH (Health System Report): Vienna, Bundesministerium für Gesundheit und Umweltschutz, annually.

BERICHT ÜBER DIE SOZIALE LAGE, 'SOZIALBERICHT' (Report on the Social State).: Vienna, Bundesministerium für soziale Verwaltung, current years (1980). The annual report of the federal Ministry of Social Affairs. Gives comments on social policies by main institutionalized interest groups in an addendum.

FINANZNACHRICHTEN (Financial News): edited by H. Knapp. Published weekly.

MONATSBERICHTE DES ÖSTERREICHISCHEN INSTITUTS FÜR WIRTSCHAFTSFORSCHUNG (Monthly Report of the Austrian Institute of Economic Research): Vienna, Österreichisches Institut für Wirtschaftsforschung. Published monthly. Issue No. 5 of each volume contains a review of the development of social security for the previous year.

ÖSTERREICHISCHE MONATSHEFTE - ZEITSCHRIFT FÜR POLITIK (Austrian Monthly Series - Journal of Politics): Bundesparteiorganisation der Österreichischen Volkspartei. Published monthly.

ÖSTERREICHISCHE SOZIALVERSICHERUNG IM JAHRE 19.. (Austrian Social Insurance in 19..): Federation of Austrian Social Insurance Institutes. Published in two volumes, annually. Volume one contains reviews of: recent changes in law and international negotiations; economic and political developments; changes and innovations in organization, etc. Volume two published regularly (but some time after Volume one). and contains figures on services, expenditure and receipts of all institutes within the federation.

ÖSTERREICHISCHER VOLKSWIRT (The Austrian Economist): Vienna, Volkswirtschaftliche Verlagsgesellschaft. Published twice monthly.

PROGRAMM-BUDGET DER ARBEITSMARKTVERWALTUNG (Programme-Budget of the Labour Market Administration): Vienna, Bundesministerium für soziale Verwaltung. Published annually (1973). An institution-oriented systematic review of all activities proposed in the field of unemployment insurance and employment policies.

QUARTALSHEFTE DER GIROZENTRALE (Giro Centre Quarterly): Girozentrale und Bank der österreichischen Sparkassen. Published quarterly. Volume 17 (No. 3, 1982) contains several contributions on the state and tendencies towards reform of the Austrian social insurance system.

SOZIALE SICHERHEIT (Social Security): Vienna, Hauptverband der Sozialversicherungsträger. Published monthly.

STATISTISCHES HANDBUCH FÜR DIE REPUBLIK ÖSTERREICH (Statistical Handbook for the Austrian Republic): Vienna, Österreichisches Statistisches Zentralamt, current years. A compilation of data including demographic development, health care, social insurance, the labour market, occupational safety conditions, welfare programmes and aggregated data on public budgets.

VERSICHERUNGSRUNDSCHAU (The Insurance Review): Vienna, Gesellschaft für Versicherungsfachwissen. Published monthly.

WIRTSCHAFTS- UND SOZIALSTATISTISCHES HANDBUCH (Economic and Social Statistics Handbook): Vienna, Kammer für Arbeiter und Angestellte für Wien, current years. Published annually. Presents data from the Federation of Social Insurance Institutes, the Federal Statistical Office and other sources, together with the Chamber's own data.

WIRTSCHAFT UND GESELLSCHAFT (Economy and Society): Vienna, Kammer für Arbeiter und Angestellte. Published quarterly.

ZUKUNFT - SOZIALISTISCHE ZEITSCHRIFT FÜR POLITIK, WIRTSCHAFT UND KULTUR (Future - Socialist Journal of Politics, Economics and Culture): Vienna, Sozialistische Partei Österreichs. Published monthly.

Appendix Tables

Contents

Table 1 Gross Domestic Product and Total Public Expenditure

Year	GDP (at market prices, in million AS)			Deflators (1970 = 100)					Total public expenditure (in million AS)				Year
	at current prices	at constant (1970) prices	annual growth	cost of living ind.	public consumption	gross investment	overall production vol.	GDP	at current prices	as % of GDP	at constant (1970) prices	annual real growth rate	
1950	51 900	132 154		42.55	21.21	41.01	39.91	39.28					1950
1951				54.38	27.70	49.94	48.53	47.96					1951
1952	80 000	141 218		63.62	34.19	58.87	57.16	56.65					1952
1953	82 520	144 417	2.3	60.20	35.48	61.86	57.94	57.14					1953
1954	93 590	162 398	12.5	62.41	36.78	64.86	58.73	57.63					1954
1955	107 150	180 418	11.1	62.89	39.19	65.15	60.60	59.39	37 243	34.8	62 709		1955
1956	119 190	192 770	6.8	65.09	43.61	68.97	62.63	61.83	43 859	36.8	70 935	13.1	1956
1957	131 950	204 574	6.1	66.53	48.55	70.42	65.68	64.50	50 969	38.6	79 022	11.4	1957
1958	137 420	212 101	3.7	68.05	48.39	72.03	65.41	64.79	58 312	42.4	90 002	13.9	1958
1959	146 320	218 160	2.9	69.16	49.18	72.73	67.33	67.07	60 839	41.6	90 710	0.8	1959
1960	163 250	236 149	8.2	70.16	51.57	74.52	69.13	69.13	64 100	39.3	92 724	3.0	1960
1961	180 760	249 187	5.5	72.39	54.99	77.05	72.21	72.54	71 327	39.5	98 328	6.0	1961
1962	192 350	255 581	2.6	75.91	58.41	78.52	75.00	75.26	79 302	41.2	105 371	7.2	1962
1963	207 320	266 273	4.2	78.07	62.44	82.57	77.47	77.86	87 160	42.0	111 945	6.2	1963
1964	226 730	282 213		81.06	65.25	83.73	79.75	80.34	97 281	42.9	121 087	8.2	1964
1965	246 491	290 434	2.9	85.37	70.69	89.56	84.07	84.87	107 670	43.7	126 865	4.8	1965
1966	268 532	307 034	5.7	86.98	75.21	91.24	86.53	87.46	117 204	43.6	134 009	5.6	1966
1967	285 593	315 956	2.9	90.45	81.99	92.76	89.70	90.39	130 484	45.5	144 357	7.7	1967
1968	306 833	330 034	4.5	92.95	86.56	93.53	91.99	92.97	141 962	46.3	152 697	5.8	1968
1969	335 000	350 932	6.3	95.81	94.41	94.90	95.25	95.46	155 204	46.3	162 586	6.5	1969
1970	375 885	375 885	7.1	100.00	100.00	100.00	100.00	100.00	169 085	45.0	169 085	4.0	1970
1971	419 624	395 015	5.1	104.70	108.81	105.64	106.43	106.23	190 487	45.4	179 316	6.1	1971
1972	479 544	419 475	6.2	111.36	118.13	116.83	118.08	114.32	218 748	45.6	191 347	6.3	1972
1973	543 458	440 404	5.0	119.74	134.11	124.37	122.18	123.40	248 814	45.8	201 632	5.4	1973
1974	618 563	457 720	3.9	131.15	150.88	135.72	136.09	135.14	298 447	48.2	220 843	8.7	1974
1975	656 116	456 080	-0.4	142.22	168.21	142.12	144.63	143.86	344 271	52.5	239 310	8.4	1975
1976	724 747	476 933	4.6	152.63	182.50	147.68	153.08	151.96	387 904	53.5	255 267	6.7	1976
1977	796 191	497 744	4.4	160.99	191.19	158.26	161.27	159.96	416 968	52.4	260 670	2.1	1977
1978	842 332	500 138	0.5	166.75	204.57	166.49	169.19	168.42	475 265	56.4	282 191	8.3	1978
1979	918 537	524 339	4.8	172.93	213.50	172.51	176.41	175.18	513 554	55.9	293 158	3.9	1979
1980	996 974	539 780	2.9	183.87	225.01	183.93	188.38	184.70	553 660	55.5	299 762	2.3	1980
1981	1 058 848	541 223	0.3	196.39	241.39	197.79	202.82	195.64	609 336	57.5	311 458	3.9	1981

Table 2

Public Expenditure by

Year	Total expend. at current prices in million AS	Public consumption	Transfers/ subsidies	Capital formation	Interest on debt	Total expend. at current prices in million AS	Central govt	Regional govt	Local govt	Social insurance	Year
	Economic Category					Level of Government					
			percent distribution					percent distribution			
1950											1950
1951											1951
1952											1952
1953											1953
1954											1954
1955	32 748	39.0	48.3	11.6	1.1						1955
1956	38 353	39.8	47.9	10.9	1.4						1956
1957	44 160	41.1	47.3	10.3	1.4	55 131	53.1	9.2	19.7	18.0	1957
1958	48 745	39.6	47.7	11.0	1.6	59 734	51.8	9.8	20.1	18.2	1958
1959	51 294	39.5	46.6	11.7	2.1	62 030	50.3	9.5	20.6	19.6	1959
1960	54 906	39.3	44.7	13.6	2.4	67 348	50.3	9.3	20.4	20.0	1960
1961	60 619	38.3	45.5	13.7	2.5	76 369	48.5	9.5	20.8	21.1	1961
1962	69 073	37.1	47.0	13.5	2.3	84 816	47.3	9.8	20.8	22.1	1962
1963	76 593	37.0	47.5	13.2	2.3	92 350	47.0	9.8	20.7	22.6	1963
1964	85 050	37.4	46.7	13.7	2.2	103 571	47.0	10.2	20.3	22.5	1964
1965	92 309	37.5	46.4	13.8	2.2	114 279	45.9	10.4	20.9	22.9	1965
1966	102 306	37.9	46.3	13.7	2.2	125 976	44.8	10.6	21.2	23.3	1966
1967	114 197	38.2	45.6	14.1	2.1	139 801	44.6	10.9	21.1	23.4	1967
1968	124 078	38.6	45.6	13.4	2.5	158 668	46.0	10.7	20.3	23.1	1968
1969	135 101	39.3	45.1	13.0	2.6	175 839	45.7	11.1	20.1	23.1	1969
1970	146 940	39.6	44.3	13.4	2.8	197 465	46.5	11.1	19.9	22.5	1970
1971	166 084	39.1	44.5	13.7	2.6	227 035	47.0	10.8	20.0	22.2	1971
1972	190 087	38.8	44.2	14.5	2.5	250 523	47.9	11.9	17.6	22.6	1972
1973	215 769	40.0	43.8	13.7	2.5	300 147	44.2	14.2	20.5	21.1	1973
1974	254 313	39.9	44.1	13.5	2.5	363 972	44.9	14.2	20.2	20.7	1974
1975	302 500	39.4	45.2	12.6	2.8	434 171	48.1	12.9	18.8	20.1	1975
1976	328 019	40.6	47.1	8.6	3.7	473 641	46.8	13.2	18.3	21.6	1976
1977	371 346	39.2	45.7	11.1	4.0	510 538	45.9	13.2	19.1	21.8	1977
1978	418 645	38.7	46.4	10.4	4.5	529 662	42.3	14.3	20.2	23.2	1978
1979	449 650	38.7	46.6	9.9	4.7	571 925	42.5	14.2	19.8	23.5	1979
1980	488 309	38.4	47.1	9.4	5.0	615 010	41.9	14.3	19.9	23.9	1980
1981	536 669	38.3	47.3	9.0	5.5	671 131	42.6	14.2	19.4	23.7	1981

Table 3

Central Government Expenditure

at current prices, in million AS

Year	Education	Science	Culture	Health	Welfare	Housing	Transp.	Defence	Justice	Gen.Admin.a.o.	Total	Year
1950												1950
1951												1951
1952												1952
1953												1953
1954												1954
1955												1955
1956												1956
1957	2 981			85	6 909	339	4 335	1 714	1 578	11 319	29 260	1957
1958	3 125			137	7 862	632	5 451	1 986	1 611	10 146	30 950	1958
1959	3 383			167	8 434	265	5 149	1 989	1 660	10 153	31 200	1959
1960	3 767			196	8 881	433	5 061	1 893	1 763	11 866	33 860	1960
1961	3 868			269	10 850	292	4 659	1 890	1 865	13 357	37 050	1961
1962	4 302			258	12 740	318	5 639	2 076	2 009	12 758	40 100	1962
1963	4 788			292	14 520	222	5 954	2 608	2 194	12 792	43 370	1963
1964	5 605			287	15 770	276	6 930	3 408	2 382	14 052	48 710	1964
1965	6 300			362	16 700	312	6 843	2 956	2 621	16 346	52 440	1965
1966	7 142			384	18 430	308	7 377	3 474	2 898	16 457	56 470	1966
1967	6 075	1 832	744	331	19 600	388	9 119	3 661	3 066	17 544	62 360	1967
1968	6 712	2 043	803	344	22 010	404	10 042	3 775	3 286	23 521	72 940	1968
1969	7 512	2 292	786	384	22 780	425	10 744	4 006	3 524	27 877	80 330	1969
1970	8 471	2 632	892	439	24 700	480	11 486	4 135	3 770	34 725	91 730	1970
1971	9 848	2 933	1 178	477	27 750	426	14 618	4 165	4 062	41 243	106 700	1971
1972	11 700	3 607	1 463	563	31 250	868	16 463	4 712	4 444	45 030	120 100	1972
1973	13 180	4 173	1 558	1 299	34 360	848	18 075	5 130	5 314	48 763	132 700	1973
1974	15 090	5 325	1 958	1 469	41 160	1 018	22 136	6 276	6 051	62 917	163 400	1974
1975	18 050	6 640	2 150	1 747	49 750	1 208	28 531	7 567	6 960	86 297	208 900	1975
1976	20 360	7 340	2 390	1 583	54 630	1 174	28 989	8 274	7 880	89 280	221 900	1976
1977	21 904	7 321	2 433	1 821	59 765	1 214	29 862	9 032	8 358	92 841	234 551	1977
1978	24 386	7 947	2 634	2 301	65 856	1 117	32 742	10 153	9 225	67 599	223 960	1978
1979	26 200	8 660	2 949	2 455	69 757	1 225	34 185	11 187	9 710	76 755	243 083	1979
1980	28 166	9 264	3 114	2 620	67 283	1 242	38 636	11 642	10 270	85 440	257 677	1980
1981	30 663	9 958	3 217	2 648	74 613	1 401	41 516	12 308	11 358	98 420	286 102	1981

Table 4 Regional and Local Government Expenditure

Year	Provinces excl. Vienna						Local government incl. Vienna						Year
	Education	Welfare	Housing	Health	Other	Total	Education	Welfare	Housing	Health	Other	Total	
1950													1950
1951													1951
1952													1952
1953													1953
1954													1954
1955	133	351	942	554	2 078	4 058							1955
1956	133	311	1 050	626	2 430	4 550							1956
1957	158	351	1 237	670	2 663	5 080	785	1 331	2 173	995	5 560	10 844	1957
1958	162	373	1 518	755	3 048	5 856	837	1 351	2 239	1 082	6 524	12 033	1958
1959	173	395	1 590	860	2 886	5 905	1 032	1 380	2 520	1 135	6 722	12 788	1959
1960	193	430	1 676	948	3 024	6 272	1 134	1 499	2 752	1 284	7 064	13 732	1960
1961	234	473	1 897	1 084	3 591	7 278	1 253	1 658	2 875	1 415	8 700	15 901	1961
1962	278	523	2 181	1 265	4 080	8 327	1 419	1 811	3 267	1 571	9 567	17 635	1962
1963	322	546	2 494	1 340	4 324	9 026	1 612	1 934	3 694	1 787	10 082	19 110	1963
1964	410	621	2 878	1 556	5 060	10 525	1 898	2 120	4 178	1 948	10 840	20 984	1964
1965	532	757	3 195	1 808	5 567	11 859	2 233	2 334	4 690	2 134	12 464	23 856	1965
1966	718	818	3 687	2 071	6 078	13 372	2 983	2 299	5 152	2 406	13 885	26 725	1966
1967	1 008	926	4 211	2 348	6 697	15 190	3 481	2 474	5 560	2 785	15 252	29 552	1967
1968	1 120	926	5 064	2 701	7 199	17 010	3 737	2 688	6 099	3 128	16 491	32 143	1968
1969	1 265	960	6 102	3 068	8 126	19 521	4 051	2 870	7 425	3 527	17 461	35 334	1969
1970	1 424	1 075	7 162	3 292	9 050	22 003	4 583	3 061	8 121	3 917	19 682	39 364	1970
1971	1 583	1 174	7 618	3 731	10 521	24 627	5 267	3 363	9 474	4 545	22 745	45 394	1971
1972	1 792	1 365	9 859	4 406	12 367	29 789	6 136	3 728	10 734	5 332	18 104	44 034	1972
1973	8 420	1 669	11 316	5 465	15 888	42 758	7 864	4 175	11 811	6 363	31 273	61 486	1973
1974	9 916	2 330	14 253	6 792	18 544	51 835	9 432	4 326	13 544	7 599	38 482	73 384	1974
1975	11 441	3 115	15 228	7 925	18 371	56 080	10 661	4 754	15 769	8 939	41 607	81 730	1975
1976	14 562	3 421	9 116	8 432	27 164	62 695	13 445	3 137	6 391	8 753	55 048	86 774	1976
1977	15 924	3 961	9 352	9 441	28 798	67 476	14 329	3 582	5 848	9 832	63 838	97 429	1977
1978	17 757	4 377	10 524	10 906	32 209	75 773	15 189	5 671	5 015	11 298	69 644	106 817	1978
1979	19 190	4 733	12 001	11 567	33 757	81 248	15 908	6 195	5 096	12 440	73 632	113 271	1979
1980	20 587	5 179	12 440	12 770	37 077	88 053	16 977	7 206	7 200	14 421	76 332	122 136	1980
1981	22 069	7 948	12 036	14 346	38 863	95 262	17 733	5 591	8 424	16 390	82 258	130 396	1981

Table 5

Social Expenditure

Year	At current prices (in million AS)							At constant (1970) prices (in million AS)							Year
	Income maint.	Education	Health	Other	Total I	Housing	Total II	Income maint.	Education	Health	Other	Total I	Housing	Total II	
1950															1950
1951															1951
1952															1952
1953															1953
1954															1954
1955															1955
1956															1956
1957	14 980	3 924	1 750	3 272	23 926			22 517	8 082	3 605	6 739	40 943			1957
1958	15 102	4 124	1 974	3 445	24 645			22 191	8 523	4 079	7 119	41 912			1958
1959	17 016	4 588	2 162	3 893	27 659			24 604	9 329	4 396	7 916	46 245			1959
1960	17 925	5 094	2 428	4 382	29 829	3 484	33 313	25 548	9 878	4 708	8 497	48 631	4 675	53 306	1960
1961	20 701	5 355	2 768	4 963	33 787	1 733	35 520	28 596	9 739	5 034	9 025	52 394	2 249	54 643	1961
1962	23 099	5 999	3 094	5 523	37 715	1 896	39 611	30 429	10 270	5 297	9 456	55 452	2 415	57 867	1962
1963	25 063	6 722	3 419	5 933	41 137	2 101	43 238	32 103	10 766	5 476	9 502	57 847	2 545	60 392	1963
1964	27 175	7 913	3 791	6 832	45 711	2 391	48 102	33 524	12 127	5 810	10 470	61 931	2 856	64 787	1964
1965	29 913	9 065	4 304	7 709	50 991	3 899	54 890	35 040	12 824	6 089	10 905	64 858	4 354	69 212	1965
1966	33 119	10 843	4 861	8 068	56 891	4 015	60 906	38 076	14 417	6 463	10 727	69 683	4 40C	74 083	1966
1967	36 638	10 564	5 464	8 649	61 315	4 758	66 073	40 505	12 884	6 664	10 549	70 602	5 129	75 131	1967
1968	45 298	11 569	6 173	9 515	72 555	5 203	77 758	48 735	13 365	7 131	10 992	80 223	5 563	85 786	1968
1969	51 574	12 828	6 979	10 262	81 643	5 711	87 354	53 828	13 588	7 392	10 870	85 678	6 018	91 696	1969
1970	55 275	14 478	7 648	11 030	88 431	4 740	93 171	55 275	14 478	7 648	11 030	88 431	4 740	93 171	1970
1971	61 671	16 698	8 753	12 789	99 911	4 967	104 878	58 902	15 347	8 044	11 754	94 047	4 702	98 749	1971
1972	67 422	19 769	10 301	14 609	112 101	6 587	118 688	60 543	16 742	8 720	12 367	98 372	5 638	104 010	1972
1973	76 452	30 471	13 127	16 337	136 387	6 914	143 301	63 847	22 811	9 788	12 182	108 628	5 559	114 187	1973
1974	89 506	35 994	15 860	19 984	161 344	9 052	170 396	68 247	24 010	10 512	13 245	116 014	6 670	122 684	1974
1975	105 043	42 115	18 611	23 490	189 259	9 776	199 035	73 862	25 251	11 064	13 965	124 142	6 879	131 021	1975
1976	118 967	50 725	18 768	25 684	214 144	9 681	223 825	77 945	28 047	10 284	14 073	130 349	6 555	136 904	1976
1977	130 784	54 674	21 094	26 452	233 004	9 700	242 704	81 238	28 844	11 033	13 835	134 950	6 129	141 079	1977
1978	152 024	60 152	24 505	30 927	267 608	10 649	278 257	91 169	29 717	11 979	15 118	147 983	6 396	154 379	1978
1979	165 606	64 263	26 462	33 574	289 905	11 926	301 831	95 766	30 426	12 394	15 726	154 312	6 913	161 225	1979
1980	177 836	68 830	29 811	36 359	312 836	12 256	325 092	96 718	30 898	13 249	16 159	157 024	6 663	163 687	1980
1981	193 466	74 200	33 384	38 594	339 644	14 204	353 848	98 525	31 093	13 830	15 988	159 436	7 181	166 617	1981

Table 6

Social Expenditure

Year	As % of gross domestic product: Income maint.	Educa-tion	Health	Other	Total I	Hous-ing	Total II	As % of public expenditure: Income maint.	Educa-tion	Health	Other	Total I	Hous-ing	Total II	As % of social expenditure: Income maint.	Educa-tion	Health	Other	Hous-ing	Year
1950																				1950
1951																				1951
1952																				1952
1953																				1953
1954																				1954
1955																				1955
1956																				1956
1957	11.4	3.0	1.3	2.5	18.1			29.4	7.7	3.4	6.4	46.9			62.6	16.4	7.3	13.7		1957
1958	11.0	3.0	1.4	2.5	17.9			25.9	7.1	3.4	5.9	42.3			61.3	16.7	8.0	14.0		1958
1959	11.6	3.1	1.5	2.7	18.9			28.0	7.5	3.6	6.4	45.5			61.5	16.6	7.8	14.1		1959
1960	11.0	3.1	1.5	2.7	18.3	2.1	20.4	28.0	7.9	3.8	6.8	46.5	5.4	52.0	53.8	15.3	7.3	13.2	10.5	1960
1961	11.5	3.0	1.5	2.7	18.7	1.0	19.7	29.0	7.5	3.9	7.0	47.4	2.4	49.8	58.3	15.1	7.8	14.0	4.9	1961
1962	12.0	3.1	1.6	2.9	19.6	1.0	20.6	29.1	7.6	3.9	7.0	47.6	2.4	49.9	58.3	15.1	7.8	13.9	4.8	1962
1963	12.1	3.2	1.6	2.9	19.8	1.0	20.9	28.8	7.7	3.9	6.8	47.2	2.4	49.6	58.0	15.5	7.9	13.7	4.9	1963
1964	12.0	3.5	1.7	3.0	20.2	1.1	21.2	27.9	8.1	3.9	7.0	47.0	2.5	49.4	56.5	16.5	7.9	14.2	5.0	1964
1965	12.1	3.7	1.7	3.1	20.7	1.6	22.3	27.8	8.4	4.0	7.2	47.4	3.6	51.0	54.5	16.5	7.8	14.0	7.1	1965
1966	12.3	4.0	1.8	3.0	21.2	1.5	22.7	28.3	9.3	4.1	6.9	48.5	3.4	52.0	54.4	17.8	8.0	13.2	6.6	1966
1967	12.8	3.7	1.9	3.0	21.5	1.7	23.1	28.1	8.1	4.2	6.6	47.0	3.6	50.6	55.5	16.0	8.3	13.1	7.2	1967
1968	14.8	3.8	2.0	3.1	23.6	1.7	25.3	31.9	8.1	4.3	6.7	51.1	3.7	54.8	58.3	14.9	7.9	12.2	6.7	1968
1969	15.4	3.8	2.1	3.1	24.4	1.7	26.1	33.2	8.3	4.5	6.6	52.6	3.7	56.3	59.0	14.7	8.0	11.7	6.5	1969
1970	14.7	3.9	2.0	2.9	23.5	1.3	24.8	32.7	8.6	4.5	6.5	52.3	2.8	55.1	59.3	15.5	8.2	11.8	5.1	1970
1971	14.7	4.0	2.1	3.0	23.8	1.2	25.0	32.4	8.8	4.6	6.7	52.5	2.6	55.1	58.8	15.9	8.3	12.2	4.7	1971
1972	14.1	4.1	2.1	3.0	23.4	1.4	24.8	30.8	9.0	4.7	6.7	51.2	3.0	54.3	56.8	16.7	8.7	12.3	5.5	1972
1973	14.1	5.6	2.4	3.0	25.1	1.3	26.4	30.7	12.2	5.3	6.6	54.8	2.8	57.6	53.4	21.3	9.2	11.4	4.8	1973
1974	14.5	5.8	2.6	3.2	26.1	1.5	27.5	30.0	12.1	5.3	6.7	54.1	3.0	57.1	52.5	21.1	9.3	11.7	5.3	1974
1975	16.0	6.4	2.8	3.6	28.8	1.5	30.3	30.5	12.2	5.4	6.8	55.0	2.8	57.8	52.8	21.2	9.4	11.8	4.9	1975
1976	16.4	7.0	2.6	3.5	29.5	1.3	30.9	30.7	13.1	4.8	6.6	55.2	2.5	57.7	53.2	22.7	8.4	11.5	4.3	1976
1977	16.4	6.9	2.6	3.3	29.3	1.2	30.5	31.4	13.1	5.1	6.3	55.9	2.3	58.2	53.9	22.5	8.7	10.9	4.0	1977
1978	18.0	7.1	2.9	3.7	31.8	1.3	33.0	32.0	12.7	5.2	6.5	56.3	2.2	58.5	54.6	21.6	8.8	11.1	3.8	1978
1979	18.0	7.0	2.9	3.7	31.6	1.3	32.9	32.2	12.5	5.2	6.5	56.5	2.3	58.8	54.9	21.3	8.8	11.1	4.0	1979
1980	17.8	6.9	3.0	3.6	31.4	1.2	32.6	32.1	12.4	5.4	6.6	56.5	2.2	58.7	54.7	21.2	9.2	11.2	3.8	1980
1981	18.3	7.0	3.2	3.6	32.1	1.3	33.4	31.8	12.2	5.5	6.3	55.7	2.3	58.1	54.7	21.0	9.4	10.9	4.0	1981

Table 7

Expenditure on Income Maintenance

At current prices (in million AS)

Year	Old age pensions	Survivors' pensions	Invalidity pensions	Survivors' pensions	Federal pensions	Other public pensions	Unemployment benefits	Sickness benefits	Family benefits	Other	Total	Year
1950					605	1 131	381	314		913		1950
1951					904	1 697	621	402		1 116		1951
1952					1 147	2 116	1 005	456		1 244		1952
1953					1 258	2 229	1 206	450		1 377		1953
1954					1 407	2 401	1 079	476		1 351		1954
1955					1 573	2 717	821	606	260	1 308		1955
1956					1 918	3 217	873	760	572	1 619		1956
1957	3 490	1 131	247	85	2 223	3 738	934	888	698	1 546	14 980	1957
1958	4 000	1 251	258	86	1 176	3 753	1 068	857	841	1 812	15 102	1958
1959	4 571	1 332	269	94	2 209	3 843	1 039	874	1 027	1 758	17 016	1959
1960	5 021	1 471	283	98	2 312	4 044	976	988	942	1 790	17 925	1960
1961	6 023	2 036	397	131	2 365	4 209	1 379	1 139	1 119	1 903	20 701	1961
1962	7 378	2 347	397	136	2 527	4 490	1 098	1 316	1 340	2 070	23 099	1962
1963	8 439	2 638	411	140	2 696	4 721	1 128	1 362	1 484	2 044	25 063	1963
1964	9 589	2 878	440	153	2 854	4 948	1 161	1 365	1 581	2 206	27 175	1964
1965	10 871	3 155	499	175	3 015	5 338	1 416	1 495	1 601	2 348	29 913	1965
1966	12 615	3 571	563	200	3 263	5 909	1 404	1 579	1 629	2 386	33 119	1966
1967	14 245	3 988	615	222	3 628	6 635	1 508	1 623	1 737	2 437	36 638	1967
1968	15 875	4 440	664	244	3 861	7 140	1 791	1 849	6 758	2 676	45 298	1968
1969	17 613	4 916	747	277	5 933	7 972	1 886	2 114	6 996	3 120	51 574	1969
1970	19 240	5 546	796	299	6 425	8 785	1 865	2 171	7 118	3 030	55 275	1970
1971	21 381	6 569	847	330	7 070	9 711	2 112	2 447	7 956	3 248	61 671	1971
1972	23 788	7 566	918	365	7 622	10 693	2 206	2 636	8 380	3 248	67 422	1972
1973	26 453	8 485	1 020	410	8 012	13 761	2 472	3 084	9 141	3 614	76 452	1973
1974	30 901	9 973	1 160	470	11 214	15 740	3 180	3 215	9 766	3 887	89 506	1974
1975	36 038	11 784	1 325	536	13 096	18 084	4 495	2 905	12 064	4 716	105 043	1975
1976	41 641	13 683	1 507	606	14 816	20 493	4 847	3 211	12 954	5 209	118 967	1976
1977	46 144	15 255	1 663	663	16 302	22 174	4 816	3 595	14 858	5 314	130 784	1977
1978	50 779	16 915	1 807	716	18 162	24 900	6 181	4 071	22 696	5 797	152 024	1978
1979	55 816	18 503	1 995	787	19 608	26 429	7 388	4 588	24 324	6 168	165 606	1979
1980	61 579	19 996	2 219	876	20 891	28 322	7 997	5 149	24 416	6 391	177 836	1980
1981	67 746	21 439	2 426	957	22 620	30 802	9 539	5 579	25 688	6 670	193 466	1981

Table 8

Expenditure on Income Maintenance

At constant (1970) prices (in million AS)

Year	Old age pensions	Survivors' pensions	Invalidity pensions	Survivors' pensions	Federal pensions	Other public pensions	Unemployment benefits	Sickness benefits	Family benefits	Other	Total	Year
1950					1 422	2 658	895	738		2 146		1950
1951					1 662	3 121	1 142	739		2 052		1951
1952					1 803	3 326	1 580	717		1 955		1952
1953					2 090	3 703	2 003	748		2 287		1953
1954					2 254	3 847	1 729	763		2 165		1954
1955					2 501	4 320	1 305	964	413	2 080		1955
1956					2 947	4 942	1 341	1 168	879	2 487		1956
1957	5 246	1 700	371	128	3 341	5 619	1 404	1 335	1 049	2 324	22 517	1957
1958	5 878	1 838	379	126	1 728	5 515	1 569	1 259	1 236	2 663	22 191	1958
1959	6 609	1 926	389	136	3 194	5 557	1 502	1 264	1 485	2 542	24 604	1959
1960	7 156	2 097	403	140	3 295	5 764	1 391	1 408	1 343	2 551	25 548	1960
1961	8 320	2 813	548	181	3 267	5 814	1 905	1 573	1 546	2 629	28 596	1961
1962	9 719	3 092	523	179	3 329	5 915	1 446	1 734	1 765	2 727	30 429	1962
1963	10 810	3 379	526	179	3 453	6 047	1 445	1 745	1 901	2 618	32 103	1963
1964	11 830	3 550	543	189	3 521	6 104	1 432	1 684	1 950	2 721	33 524	1964
1965	12 734	3 696	585	205	3 532	6 253	1 659	1 751	1 875	2 750	35 040	1965
1966	14 503	4 106	647	230	3 751	6 794	1 614	1 815	1 873	2 743	38 076	1966
1967	15 749	4 409	680	245	4 011	7 336	1 667	1 794	1 920	2 694	40 505	1967
1968	17 079	4 777	714	263	4 154	7 682	1 927	1 989	7 271	2 879	78 735	1968
1969	18 383	5 131	780	289	6 192	8 321	1 968	2 206	7 302	3 256	53 828	1969
1970	19 240	5 546	796	299	6 425	8 785	1 865	2 171	7 118	3 030	55 275	1970
1971	20 421	6 274	809	315	6 753	9 275	2 017	2 337	7 599	3 102	58 902	1971
1972	21 361	6 794	824	328	6 844	9 602	1 981	2 367	7 525	2 917	60 543	1972
1973	22 092	7 086	852	342	6 691	11 492	2 064	2 576	7 634	3 018	63 847	1973
1974	23 562	7 604	884	358	8 551	12 002	2 425	2 451	7 446	2 964	68 247	1974
1975	25 340	8 286	932	377	9 208	12 716	3 161	2 043	8 483	3 316	73 862	1975
1976	27 282	8 965	987	397	9 707	13 427	3 176	2 104	8 487	3 413	77 945	1976
1977	28 663	9 476	1 033	412	10 126	13 774	2 991	2 233	9 229	3 301	81 238	1977
1978	30 452	10 144	1 084	429	10 892	14 933	3 707	2 441	13 611	3 476	91 169	1978
1979	32 277	10 700	1 154	455	11 339	15 283	4 272	2 653	14 066	3 567	95 766	1979
1980	33 491	10 875	1 207	476	11 362	15 403	4 349	2 800	13 279	3 476	96 718	1980
1981	34 501	10 918	1 235	487	11 520	15 686	4 858	2 841	13 082	3 397	98 525	1981

Table 9 Social Insurance: Expenditure by Scheme

At current prices (in million AS)

Year	Old age pension insurance schemes							Accident insurance schemes					Sickness insurance schemes						Total	Year
	Workers	Employees	Miners	Railways	Agric. workers	Self-employed	Total	General	Farmers	Railways	Publ. serv.	Total	Regional ins.inst.	Public empl.	Self-empl.	Agric. workers	Other	Total	Social Insurance	
1950							1 695					198	851	91	n.a.	81	136	1 159	3 052	1950
1951							2 419					251	1 169	126	n.a.	108	178	1 581	4 251	1951
1952							3 232					308	1 440	153	n.a.	138	224	1 955	5 495	1952
1953							3 428					325	1 523	172	n.a.	155	243	2 093	5 846	1953
1954							3 990					345	1 646	188	n.a.	166	256	2 256	6 591	1954
1955							4 443					440	1 919	209	n.a.	183	305	2 616	7 499	1955
1956							5 020					518	2 206	236	n.a.	211	346	2 999	8 537	1956
1957	3 579	1 389	185	71	580	3	5 807	400	125	36		561	2 526	278	146	236	393	3 579	9 947	1957
1958	3 933	1 542	203	76	608	219	6 581	403	129	37		569	2 633	311	142	246	413	3 745	10 895	1958
1959	4 224	1 672	202	86	755	705	7 644	432	130	38		600	2 710	320	170	254	439	3 893	12 137	1959
1960	4 554	1 960	236	97	791	872	8 510	498	142	40		680	3 045	342	175	267	465	4 294	13 484	1960
1961	5 673	2 413	288	123	960	971	10 428	621	180	52		853	3 495	375	189	301	499	4 859	16 140	1961
1962	6 687	2 998	370	159	1 120	1 086	12 420	629	187	51		867	3 954	414	211	322	566	5 467	18 754	1962
1963	7 490	3 432	390	170	1 230	1 278	13 990	674	195	53		922	4 346	429	226	346	585	5 932	20 844	1963
1964	8 385	3 880	432	196	1 388	1 456	15 737	1 010	204	57		1 271	4 641	476	244	365	618	6 344	23 352	1964
1965	9 510	4 352	497	218	1 602	1 600	17 779	1 141	218	62		1 421	5 083	518	278	387	658	6 924	26 124	1965
1966	10 598	5 390	696	244	1 391	1 871	20 190	1 173	230	70		1 473	5 510	563	598	359	716	7 746	29 409	1966
1967	11 827	6 120	773	271	1 510	2 144	22 645	1 074	250	73	2	1 399	6 014	649	849	366	777	8 655	32 699	1967
1968	12 949	6 923	839	295	1 652	2 459	25 117	1 405	263	80	16	1 764	6 740	716	991	400	847	9 694	36 575	1968
1969	14 338	7 794	909	315	1 776	2 701	27 833	1 476	326	86	28	1 916	7 558	866	1 073	437	971	10 905	40 654	1969
1970	15 557	8 405	981	359	1 896	3 224	30 422	1 587	354	90	33	2 064	8 198	979	1 194	458	1 053	11 882	44 368	1970
1971	17 413	9 476	1 079	434	2 096	4 390	34 888	1 719	373	97	36	2 225	9 239	1 006	1 264	492	1 200	13 201	50 314	1971
1972	19 317	10 706	1 189	457	2 308	5 491	39 468	1 881	407	104	41	2 433	10 257	1 182	1 466	530	1 264	14 699	56 600	1972
1973	21 429	11 827	1 307	475	2 507	6 340	43 885	2 216	450	115	51	2 832	11 615	1 320	1 600	577	1 374	16 486	63 203	1973
1974	27 559	14 256	1 507	552		7 792	51 666	2 721	376	129	58	3 284	15 121	1 665	1 921		1 696	20 403	75 353	1974
1975	31 795	16 904	1 714	607		9 227	60 247	3 180	428	145	70	3 823	17 126	2 056	2 293		1 916	23 391	87 461	1975
1976	35 950	21 821	1 942	695		10 716	71 124	3 383	493	163	81	4 120	19 680	2 398	2 751		2 199	27 028	102 272	1976
1977	38 957	22 644	2 115	758		12 609	77 083	3 743	534	172	96	4 545	21 274	2 567	3 236		2 377	29 454	111 082	1977
1978	42 090	25 501	2 338	818		14 245	84 992	4 171	564	180	106	5 021	23 854	2 943	3 712		2 590	33 099	123 112	1978
1979	45 577	27 931	2 498	884		15 798	92 688	4 869	599	193	118	5 779	26 208	3 174	3 690		2 784	35 856	134 323	1979
1980	49 046	30 620	2 654	957		17 165	100 442	5 301	738	206	134	6 379	29 276	3 465	4 571		3 011	40 323	147 144	1980
1981	52 927	33 473	2 825	1 041		18 523	108 789	5 917	786	217	155	7 075	31 642	3 774	4 837		3 254	43 507	159 371	1981

Table 10

Social Insurance: Expenditure by Scheme

At constant (1970) prices (in million AS)

Year	Old age pension insurance schemes							Accident insurance schemes					Sickness insurance schemes						Total	Year
	Workers	Employees	Miners	Railways	Agric. workers	Self-employed	Total	General	Farmers	Railways	Publ. serv.	Total	Regional ins.inst.	Public empl.	Self-empl.	Agric. workers	Other	Total	Social Insurance	
1950							4 785					652	3 400	420		330	572	4 722	10 159	1950
1951							5 305					639	3 635	447		344	570	4 996	10 940	1951
1952							5 955					650	3 709	439		358	595	5 101	11 706	1952
1953							6 487					690	3 875	477		391	636	5 379	12 556	1953
1954							7 285					707	4 047	503		408	645	5 603	13 595	1954
1955							7 919					869	4 422	524		425	722	6 093	14 881	1955
1956							8 472					952	4 589	532		444	737	6 302	15 726	1956
1957	5 787	2 230	309	116	944	5	9 391	699	213	59		971	4 798	565	298	453	764	6 878	17 240	1957
1958	6 256	2 436	334	120	976	342	10 464	693	217	59		969	5 024	635	292	471	807	7 229	18 662	1958
1959	6 700	2 604	331	134	1 199	1 109	12 077	732	214	61		1 007	5 091	642	343	481	847	7 404	20 488	1959
1960	7 048	3 009	374	152	1 241	1 344	13 168	831	230	64		1 125	5 483	656	337	487	857	7 820	22 113	1960
1961	8 394	3 535	433	185	1 445	1 450	15 442	964	278	77		1 319	5 937	676	341	519	865	8 338	25 099	1961
1962	9 371	4 162	522	225	1 599	1 545	17 424	927	276	72		1 275	6 330	702	359	524	927	8 842	27 541	1962
1963	10 084	4 581	529	230	1 681	1 750	18 855	952	275	72		1 299	6 587	682	360	532	903	9 064	29 218	1963
1964	10 853	4 979	562	257	1 824	1 916	20 391	1 420	277	75		1 772	6 764	724	372	539	913	9 312	31 475	1964
1965	11 611	5 279	610	268	1 991	1 980	21 739	1 493	277	76		1 846	6 876	728	391	530	905	9 430	33 015	1965
1966	12 560	6 348	820	294	1 675	2 238	23 935	1 457	280	84		1 821	7 083	745	790	467	931	10 016	35 772	1966
1967	13 338	6 868	868	309	1 723	2 433	25 539	1 239	287	83	2	1 611	7 176	789	1 031	440	936	10 372	37 522	1967
1968	14 127	7 533	913	324	1 817	2 691	27 405	1 569	289	88	18	1 964	7 660	825	1 142	458	970	11 055	40 424	1968
1969	15 008	8 153	950	330	1 861	2 829	29 131	1 553	342	91	29	2 015	7 977	917	1 136	461	1 028	11 519	42 665	1969
1970	15 557	8 405	981	359	1 896	3 224	30 422	1 587	354	90	33	2 064	8 198	979	1 194	458	1 053	11 882	44 368	1970
1971	16 511	9 002	1 024	409	1 978	4 148	33 072	1 610	352	92	34	2 088	8 568	925	1 164	455	1 109	12 221	47 381	1971
1972	17 155	9 532	1 058	403	2 034	4 844	35 026	1 640	358	92	35	2 125	8 801	1 003	1 244	453	1 079	12 580	49 731	1972
1973	17 526	9 723	1 072	385	2 021	5 124	35 851	1 743	361	93	41	2 238	8 904	989	1 199	437	1 040	12 569	50 658	1973
1974	20 439	10 648	1 123	405		5 705	38 320	1 932	270	95	43	2 340	10 314	1 108	1 281		1 142	13 845	54 505	1974
1975	21 639	11 599	1 172	412		6 191	41 013	2 051	280	98	47	2 476	10 469	1 229	1 373		1 151	14 222	57 711	1975
1976	22 786	13 748	1 236	438		6 695	44 903	2 033	299	101	50	2 483	11 094	1 321	1 519		1 220	15 154	62 540	1976
1977	23 451	13 664	1 279	454		7 495	46 343	2 138	309	102	56	2 605	11 443	1 350	1 707		1 258	15 758	64 706	1977
1978	24 347	14 750	1 358	469		8 126	49 050	2 262	311	102	60	2 735	12 067	1 448	1 830		1 284	16 629	68 414	1978
1979	25 402	15 597	1 399	489		8 692	51 579	2 524	317	105	64	3 010	12 734	1 497	1 743		1 324	17 298	71 887	1979
1980	25 781	16 165	1 400	499		8 906	52 751	2 604	365	106	69	3 144	13 477	1 551	2 047		1 359	18 434	74 329	1980
1981	26 052	16 588	1 394	508		8 997	53 539	2711	363	104	75	3 253	13 591	1 574	2 019		1 369	18 553	75 345	1981

Table 11 Old Age Pension Insurance: Expenditure by Type

Year	At current prices (in million AS)				Percent distribution				At constant (1970) prices (in million AS)				Year
	Old age pensions	Survivors' pensions	Benefits in kind/ services	Other incl. adm.	Old age pensions	Survivors' pensions	Benefits in kind/ services	Other incl. adm.	Old age pensions	Survivors' pensions	Benefits in kind/ services	Other incl. adm.	
1950													1950
1951													1951
1952													1952
1953													1953
1954													1954
1955													1955
1956													1956
1957	3 490	1 131	748	438	60.1	19.5	12.9	7.6	5 246	1 700	1 541	902	1957
1958	4 000	1 251	854	476	60.8	19.0	13.0	7.2	5 878	1 838	1 765	984	1958
1959	4 571	1 332	1 227	514	59.8	17.4	16.0	6.7	6 609	1 926	2 495	1 045	1959
1960	5 021	1 471	1 427	591	59.0	17.3	16.8	6.9	7 156	2 097	2 767	1 146	1960
1961	6 023	2 036	1 716	653	57.8	19.5	16.5	6.3	8 320	2 813	3 121	1 187	1961
1962	7 378	2 347	2 010	685	59.4	18.9	16.2	5.5	9 719	3 092	3 441	1 173	1962
1963	8 439	2 638	2 166	747	60.3	18.9	15.5	5.3	10 810	3 379	3 469	1 196	1963
1964	9 589	2 878	2 471	799	60.9	18.3	15.7	5.1	11 830	3 550	3 787	1 225	1964
1965	10 871	3 155	2 660	1 093	61.2	17.8	15.0	6.2	12 734	3 696	3 763	1 546	1965
1966	12 615	3 571	2 955	1 049	62.5	17.7	14.6	5.2	14 503	4 106	3 929	1 395	1966
1967	14 245	3 988	3 343	1 069	62.8	17.6	14.7	4.7	15 749	4 409	4 077	1 304	1967
1968	15 875	4 440	3 663	1 139	63.2	17.7	14.6	4.5	17 079	4 777	4 232	1 316	1968
1969	17 613	4 916	4 090	1 214	63.3	17.7	14.7	4.4	18 383	5 131	4 332	1 286	1969
1970	19 240	5 546	4 299	1 337	63.2	18.2	14.1	4.4	19 240	5 546	4 299	1 337	1970
1971	21 381	6 569	5 427	1 511	61.3	18.8	15.6	4.3	20 421	6 274	4 988	1 389	1971
1972	23 788	7 566	6 419	1 695	60.3	19.2	16.3	4.3	21 361	6 794	5 434	1 435	1972
1973	26 453	8 485	6 955	1 992	60.1	19.3	15.8	4.5	22 092	7 092	5 186	1 485	1973
1974	30 901	9 973	8 130	2 662	59.8	19.3	15.7	5.2	23 562	7 604	5 388	1 764	1974
1975	36 038	11 784	9 347	3 078	59.8	19.6	15.5	5.1	25 340	8 286	5 557	1 830	1975
1976	41 641	13 683	10 514	5 286	58.5	19.2	14.8	7.4	27 282	8 965	5 761	2 896	1976
1977	46 144	15 255	11 558	4 126	59.9	19.8	15.0	5.4	28 663	9 476	6 045	2 158	1977
1978	50 779	16 915	12 461	4 837	59.7	19.9	14.7	5.7	30 452	10 144	6 091	2 364	1978
1979	55 816	18 503	13 588	4 781	60.2	20.0	14.7	5.2	32 277	10 700	6 364	2 239	1979
1980	61 579	19 996	14 405	4 462	61.3	19.9	14.3	4.4	33 491	10 875	6 402	1 983	1980
1981	67 746	21 439	15 372	4 232	62.3	19.7	14.1	3.9	34 501	10 917	6 368	1 753	1981

Table 12 Old Age Pension Insurance: Expenditure by Scheme and Type

at current prices (in million AS)

Year	Workers					Employees					Miners					Year
	old age pensions	surviv. pens.	ben.in kind/serv. incl.subsidies to minimum pensions	other incl. admin.	total	old age pensions	surviv. pens.	benef. in kind/serv.	other incl. admin.	total	old age pensions	surviv. pens.	benef. in kind/serv.	other incl. admin.	total	
1950																1950
1951																1951
1952																1952
1953																1953
1954																1954
1955																1955
1956																1956
1957	2 185	663	467	264	3 578	801	333	152	103	1 389	94	35	39	17	185	1957
1958	2 420	714	527	272	3 933	896	361	177	108	1 542	107	36	42	18	203	1958
1959	2 494	721	725	284	4 223	991	365	207	109	1 672	103	34	46	19	202	1959
1960	2 689	782	779	304	4 554	1 125	416	283	136	1 960	126	39	50	21	236	1960
1961	3 203	1 197	913	360	5 673	1 440	511	321	141	2 413	159	49	59	21	288	1961
1962	3 950	1 312	1 051	374	6 688	1 823	637	392	146	2 998	217	67	64	22	371	1962
1963	4 484	1 478	1 124	404	7 490	2 146	709	419	158	3 432	228	69	68	25	390	1963
1964	5 078	1 604	1 263	440	8 385	2 468	770	473	169	3 881	260	74	72	26	433	1964
1965	5 806	1 766	1 373	565	9 511	2 778	830	499	245	4 351	298	84	77	38	496	1965
1966	6 617	1 895	1 519	567	10 598	3 530	1 022	572	266	5 391	443	145	79	29	696	1966
1967	7 419	2 103	1 723	582	11 826	4 078	1 148	647	247	6 119	492	161	88	32	773	1967
1968	8 168	2 316	1 851	614	12 949	4 595	1 274	784	270	6 924	534	177	94	34	840	1968
1969	9 016	2 554	2 114	654	14 338	5 196	1 425	877	296	7 795	573	194	108	34	910	1969
1970	9 759	2 863	2 230	705	15 559	5 635	1 574	870	326	8 405	605	218	121	37	981	1970
1971	10 678	3 386	2 558	791	17 413	6 261	1 857	986	372	9 475	647	260	132	40	1 080	1971
1972	11 699	3 885	2 873	860	19 318	6 970	2 132	1 169	435	10 706	701	298	145	45	1 189	1972
1973	12 947	4 342	3 137	1 003	21 429	7 699	2 398	1 224	506	11 827	765	331	161	50	1 308	1973
1974	16 344	5 455	4 372	1 388	27 559	9 179	2 846	1 499	732	14 256	861	382	195	69	1 508	1974
1975	18 800	6 393	4 994	1 608	31 795	10 867	3 397	1 787	853	16 905	967	443	227	77	1 714	1975
1976	21 406	7 391	5 532	1 621	35 951	12 762	3 945	2 095	3 019	21 821	1 094	512	256	80	1 942	1976
1977	23 183	8 161	6 007	1 606	38 957	14 220	4 333	2 279	1 812	22 644	1 194	558	283	80	2 116	1977
1978	25 054	8 971	6 367	1 698	42 091	15 860	4 751	2 496	2 394	25 501	1 320	619	319	80	2 337	1978
1979	27 140	9 769	6 880	1 788	45 577	17 725	5 158	2 840	2 208	27 931	1 409	667	348	74	2 498	1979
1980	29 529	10 528	7 218	1 771	49 046	20 132	5 584	3 112	1 792	30 620	1 506	708	359	81	2 655	1980
1981	32 157	11 267	7 625	1 878	52 927	22 662	5 991	3 424	1 396	33 474	1 611	746	386	82	2 825	1981

Table 13 Old Age Pension Insurance: Expenditure by Scheme and Type

at current prices (in million AS)

Year	Railways					Agricultural workers					Self-employed					Year
	old age pensions	surviv. pens.	benef. in kind/serv.	other incl. admin.	total	old age pensions	surviv. pens.	ben.in kind/serv. incl.subsidies to minimum pensions	other incl. admin.	total	old age pensions	surviv. pens.	benef. in kind/serv.	other incl. admin.	total	
1950																1950
1951																1951
1952																1952
1953																1953
1954																1954
1955																1955
1956																1956
1957	29	27	10	5	71	380	71	80	49	581	1	2			4	1957
1958	33	28	10	5	76	396	74	90	48	608	148	38	8	25	219	1958
1959	40	28	12	6	85	490	83	132	50	756	453	101	105	46	705	1959
1960	44	28	19	6	97	484	85	160	62	791	553	121	136	62	872	1960
1961	56	32	29	6	123	580	108	210	62	960	585	139	184	63	971	1961
1962	76	42	31	10	160	675	132	248	65	1 121	637	157	224	68	1 086	1962
1963	88	46	25	11	169	752	149	263	66	1 230	741	187	267	83	1 277	1963
1964	98	50	37	11	197	845	166	307	70	1 387	840	214	319	83	1 457	1964
1965	111	53	42	12	219	951	184	323	144	1 602	927	238	346	89	1 599	1965
1966	111	60	59	14	244	810	164	342	75	1 392	1 104	285	384	98	1 871	1966
1967	128	64	64	15	271	862	180	387	81	1 510	1 266	332	434	112	2 144	1967
1968	140	72	65	18	295	958	196	412	86	1 652	1 480	405	457	117	2 458	1968
1969	152	77	67	19	315	1 030	213	442	91	1 776	1 646	453	482	120	2 702	1969
1970	162	84	92	21	360	1 088	237	474	97	1 896	1 991	570	512	151	3 224	1970
1971	177	99	135	23	435	1 153	277	565	101	2 096	2 465	690	1 051	184	4 389	1971
1972	197	111	123	26	457	1 238	315	645	110	2 309	2 983	825	1 464	219	5 491	1972
1973	217	122	108	28	475	1 337	347	696	127	2 508	3 488	945	1 629	278	6 340	1973
1974	251	144	124	33	552						4 266	1 146	1 940	440	7 791	1974
1975	297	169	102	39	608						5 107	1 382	2 237	501	9 227	1975
1976	338	192	127	38	696						6 041	1 643	2 504	528	10 717	1976
1977	370	209	130	49	757						7 177	1 994	2 859	579	12 609	1977
1978	403	229	136	50	819						8 142	2 345	3 143	615	14 245	1978
1979	440	246	145	53	884						9 102	2 663	3 375	658	15 798	1979
1980	480	265	158	54	957						9 932	2 911	3 558	764	17 165	1980
1981	529	281	173	58	1 041						10 787	3 154	3 764	818	18 523	1981

Table 14

Accident Insurance: Expenditure by Type

Year	At current prices (in million AS)				Percent distribution				At constant (1970) prices (in million AS)				Year
	Invalidity pensions	Survivors' pensions	Benefits in kind/ services	Other incl. adm.	Invalidity pensions	Survivors' pensions	Benefits in kind/ services	Other incl. adm.	Invalidity pensions	Survivors' pensions	Benefits in kind/ services	Other incl. adm.	
1950													1950
1951													1951
1952													1952
1953													1953
1954													1954
1955													1955
1956													1956
1957	247	85	125	104	44.0	15.2	22.3	18.5	371	128	257	214	1957
1958	258	86	132	93	45.3	15.1	23.2	16.3	379	126	273	192	1958
1959	269	94	163	74	44.7	15.6	27.1	12.3	389	136	331	150	1959
1960	283	98	196	103	41.5	14.4	28.7	15.1	403	140	380	200	1960
1961	397	131	223	102	46.5	15.4	26.1	12.0	548	181	406	185	1961
1962	397	136	238	96	45.7	15.7	27.4	11.1	523	179	407	164	1962
1963	411	140	261	110	44.5	15.2	28.3	11.9	526	179	418	176	1963
1964	440	153	329	349	34.6	12.0	25.9	27.4	543	189	504	535	1964
1965	499	175	400	347	35.1	12.3	28.2	24.4	585	205	566	491	1965
1966	563	200	325	385	38.2	13.6	22.1	26.1	647	230	432	512	1966
1967	615	222	360	202	44.0	15.9	25.8	14.5	680	245	439	246	1967
1968	664	244	433	423	37.7	13.8	24.6	24.0	714	263	500	489	1968
1969	747	277	459	433	39.0	14.5	23.9	22.6	780	289	486	459	1969
1970	796	299	501	468	38.5	14.5	24.3	22.7	796	299	501	468	1970
1971	847	330	633	415	38.1	14.8	28.4	18.6	809	315	582	381	1971
1972	918	365	656	494	37.7	15.0	27.0	20.3	824	328	555	418	1972
1973	1 020	410	878	524	36.0	14.5	31.0	18.5	853	343	655	391	1973
1974	1 160	470	980	674	35.3	14.3	29.8	20.5	884	358	650	447	1974
1975	1 325	536	1 117	845	34.7	14.0	29.2	22.1	932	377	664	502	1975
1976	1 507	606	1 253	754	36.6	14.7	30.4	18.3	987	397	687	413	1976
1977	1 663	663	1 395	824	36.6	14.6	30.7	18.1	1 033	412	730	431	1977
1978	1 807	716	1 584	914	36.0	14.3	31.5	18.2	1 084	429	774	447	1978
1979	1 995	787	1 717	1 280	34.5	13.6	29.7	22.2	1 154	455	804	600	1979
1980	2 219	876	1 853	1 431	34.8	13.7	29.1	22.4	1 207	476	824	636	1980
1981	2 426	957	2 024	1 668	34.3	13.5	28.6	23.6	1 235	487	838	691	1981

Table 15 Accident Insurance: Expenditure by Scheme and Type

at current prices (in million AS)

Year	General scheme					Farmers					Railways					Public service					Year
	inval. pens.	surv. pens.	serv./b. in kind	other (adm.)	total	inval. pens.	surv. pens.	serv./b. in kind	other (adm.)	total	inval. pens.	surv. pens.	serv./b. in kind	other (adm.)	total	inval. pens.	surv. pens.	serv./b. in kind	other (adm.)	total	
1950																					1950
1951																					1951
1952																					1952
1953																					1953
1954																					1954
1955																					1955
1956																					1956
1957	162	62	94	82	401	68	12	29	16	124	17	11	2	6	36						1957
1958	172	62	96	73	408	69	13	33	14	129	17	11	3	6	36						1958
1959	181	69	125	57	432	71	14	34	11	132	17	11	4	6	38						1959
1960	190	73	154	81	499	75	14	37	16	143	18	11	5	6	40						1960
1961	278	99	169	75	621	93	17	49	21	180	26	15	5	6	52						1961
1962	277	103	180	69	629	95	18	53	21	187	25	15	5	6	52						1962
1963	289	107	196	82	675	96	19	58	22	195	26	14	7	6	54						1963
1964	312	118	261	319	1 010	101	20	60	23	205	27	15	8	7	57						1964
1965	361	136	329	315	1 140	108	22	63	25	218	30	17	8	7	63						1965
1966	410	156	257	350	1 173	119	25	59	27	231	34	19	9	8	69						1966
1967	450	173	289	162	1 074	129	29	61	31	249	36	20	9	8	73	0	0	1	1	2	1967
1968	481	190	356	378	1 404	137	31	61	34	263	38	21	12	9	81	8	2	4	2	15	1968
1969	517	209	368	382	1 476	176	41	72	37	327	41	23	12	10	86	13	4	7	4	28	1969
1970	552	225	398	412	1 588	186	45	82	41	354	43	24	13	10	90	15	5	8	5	34	1970
1971	589	247	525	358	1 719	197	50	84	42	373	45	26	15	11	98	16	7	9	4	36	1971
1972	641	275	537	428	1 881	210	54	93	50	408	48	28	16	12	104	19	8	10	4	41	1972
1973	715	308	742	451	2 215	228	61	106	55	451	53	31	18	13	114	24	10	12	5	50	1973
1974	907	380	869	565	2 721	167	43	77	89	375	59	35	21	14	130	27	12	13	6	59	1974
1975	1 034	436	985	725	3 181	191	48	95	94	428	67	38	22	18	145	33	14	15	8	70	1975
1976	1 178	493	1 089	623	3 384	216	54	120	103	494	75	43	26	19	163	38	16	18	9	81	1976
1977	1 304	541	1 215	683	3 743	236	59	128	111	534	80	45	29	18	173	43	18	23	12	97	1977
1978	1 420	585	1 401	765	4 172	253	63	129	119	565	84	47	30	19	181	50	21	24	11	105	1978
1979	1 577	644	1 510	1 138	4 869	274	69	144	112	599	88	50	35	20	193	56	24	28	10	118	1979
1980	1 768	723	1 624	1 186	5 300	293	73	161	211	738	93	53	39	21	206	65	27	29	13	134	1980
1981	1 942	793	1 776	1 406	5 917	312	78	173	223	787	97	55	42	23	217	75	31	33	16	155	1981

Table 16

Sickness Insurance: Expenditure by Type

Year	At current prices (in million AS)						Percent distribution					At constant (1975) prices (in million AS)						Year
	Insured		Relatives				Insured		Relatives			Insured		Relatives				
	benefits in kind	benefits in cash	benefits in kind	benefits in cash	other	total	benefits in kind	benefits in cash	benefits in kind	benefits in cash	other	benefits in kind	benefits in cash	benefits in kind	benefits in cash	other	total	
1950	589	283	124	31	132	1 157	50.9	24.5	10.7	2.7	11.4	2 777	665	585	73	622	4 722	1950
1951	821	369	169	33	189	1 581	51.9	23.3	10.7	2.1	12.0	2 964	679	610	61	682	4 996	1951
1952	1 064	417	222	39	213	1 954	54.5	21.3	11.4	2.0	10.9	3 112	655	649	61	623	5 100	1952
1953	1 184	408	243	42	216	2 092	56.6	19.5	11.6	2.0	10.3	3 337	678	685	70	609	5 379	1953
1954	1 287	432	263	44	230	2 257	57.0	19.1	11.7	2.0	10.2	3 499	692	715	71	625	5 602	1954
1955	1 453	556	290	50	267	2 615	55.6	21.3	11.1	1.9	10.2	3 708	884	740	80	681	6 093	1955
1956	1 381	669	622	91	236	2 999	46.1	22.3	20.7	3.0	7.9	3 167	1 028	1 426	140	541	6 302	1956
1957	1 686	789	705	99	300	3 579	47.3	22.1	19.8	2.8	8.4	3 473	1 186	1 452	149	618	6 878	1957
1958	1 815	758	775	99	298	3 746	48.5	20.2	20.7	2.6	8.0	3 751	1 114	1 602	146	616	7 229	1958
1959	1 901	772	815	102	303	3 890	48.9	19.9	21.0	2.6	7.8	3 865	1 116	1 657	148	616	7 402	1959
1960	2 096	880	878	108	332	4 296	48.8	20.5	20.4	2.5	7.7	4 064	1 254	1 703	154	644	7 819	1960
1961	2 367	1 022	992	117	361	4 860	48.7	21.0	20.4	2.4	7.4	4 304	1 412	1 804	162	657	8 339	1961
1962	2 647	1 190	1 106	126	398	5 465	48.4	21.8	20.2	2.3	7.3	4 532	1 568	1 894	166	681	8 841	1962
1963	2 925	1 234	1 215	128	430	5 931	49.3	20.8	20.5	2.2	7.3	4 684	1 581	1 946	164	689	9 064	1963
1964	3 174	1 233	1 333	132	472	6 344	50.1	19.5	21.0	2.1	7.5	4 864	1 521	2 043	163	723	9 314	1964
1965	3 468	1 360	1 443	135	518	6 924	50.1	19.7	20.8	2.0	7.5	4 906	1 593	2 041	158	733	9 431	1965
1966	4 023	1 441	1 582	138	562	7 746	52.1	18.7	20.5	1.8	7.3	5 349	1 657	2 103	159	747	10 015	1966
1967	4 634	1 478	1 763	145	655	8 655	53.5	17.1	20.4	1.7	7.3	5 652	1 634	2 150	160	774	10 370	1967
1968	5 204	1 686	1 965	163	676	9 694	53.8	17.4	20.3	1.7	7.0	6 012	1 814	2 270	175	781	11 052	1968
1969	5 890	1 930	2 206	184	695	10 906	54.0	17.7	20.2	1.7	6.4	6 239	2 014	2 337	192	736	11 538	1969
1970	6 488	1 989	2 433	182	790	11 880	54.6	16.7	20.5	1.5	6.7	6 488	1 989	2 433	182	790	11 882	1970
1971	7 185	2 255	2 670	195	899	13 201	54.5	17.1	20.2	1.5	6.8	6 603	2 151	2 454	186	826	12 220	1971
1972	8 178	2 435	2 977	201	908	14 698	55.6	16.6	20.2	1.4	6.2	6 923	2 187	2 520	181	769	12 580	1972
1973	9 080	2 863	3 300	221	1 022	16 488	55.1	17.4	20.0	1.3	6.2	6 771	2 393	2 461	185	762	12 572	1973
1974	11 202	2 970	4 124	245	1 862	20 403	55.0	14.6	20.3	1.2	9.2	7 424	2 265	2 733	187	1 234	13 843	1974
1975	13 242	2 639	4 893	266	2 351	23 393	56.6	11.3	21.0	1.1	10.1	7 872	1 856	2 909	187	1 398	14 222	1975
1976	15 616	2 904	5 629	307	2 572	27 028	57.8	10.7	20.8	1.1	9.5	8 557	1 903	3 084	201	1 409	15 154	1976
1977	17 525	3 260	6 033	335	2 481	29 613	59.2	11.0	20.4	1.1	8.3	9 166	2 025	3 156	208	1 298	15 853	1977
1978	19 709	3 703	6 652	368	2 667	33 099	59.5	11.2	20.1	1.1	8.1	9 634	2 221	3 252	221	1 304	16 632	1978
1979	21 269	4 203	7 002	385	2 997	35 856	59.3	11.6	19.5	1.1	8.4	9 962	2 430	3 280	223	1 404	17 299	1979
1980	23 895	4 731	7 603	418	3 676	40 324	59.3	11.7	18.9	1.0	9.1	10 620	2 573	3 379	227	1 634	18 433	1980
1981	26 139	5 130	8 006	449	3 783	43 508	60.1	11.8	18.4	1.0	8.7	10 829	2 612	3 317	229	1 567	18 554	1981

Table 17 Sickness Insurance: Expenditure by Scheme and Type

at current prices (in million AS)

Year	Regional insurance institutes: Insured benef. in kind/serv.	Insured cash benev.	Relatives benef. in kind/serv.	Relatives cash benef.	Other incl. admin.	Total	Public employees: Insured benef. in kind/serv.	Insured cash benef.	Relatives benef. in kind/serv.	Relatives cash benef.	Other incl. admin.	Total	Year
1950	414	237	72	22	106	850	57	3	22	1	8	90	1950
1951	586	308	102	22	151	1 169	83	2	26	3	12	126	1951
1952	765	346	136	25	168	1 439	99	3	30	4	17	153	1952
1953	851	334	148	27	163	1 523	113	3	35	4	17	171	1953
1954	926	356	160	27	177	1 646	126	3	38	5	16	189	1954
1955	1 046	464	174	30	205	1 919	139	4	42	6	18	208	1955
1956	1 017	562	392	59	176	2 206	116	3	87	8	22	236	1956
1957	1 153	663	440	64	206	2 526	135	4	102	10	27	278	1957
1958	1 249	635	482	64	203	2 633	153	4	116	10	28	312	1958
1959	1 281	648	504	66	211	2 711	161	4	122	10	23	321	1959
1960	1 446	748	556	71	224	3 046	168	4	127	10	33	342	1960
1961	1 656	879	639	78	243	3 497	185	4	140	11	35	375	1961
1962	1 852	1 030	710	87	275	3 953	207	5	156	11	35	413	1962
1963	2 080	1 075	796	89	306	4 346	217	5	164	11	32	429	1963
1964	2 265	1 072	878	92	334	4 641	237	5	179	12	43	477	1964
1965	2 474	1 196	951	96	366	5 083	259	5	196	12	46	518	1965
1966	2 719	1 255	1 073	99	364	5 510	283	6	214	13	47	564	1966
1967	3 008	1 290	1 202	104	410	6 015	329	7	248	16	49	649	1967
1968	3 351	1 477	1 345	118	449	6 739	363	9	274	18	52	716	1968
1969	3 770	1 700	1 512	132	444	7 559	469	11	304	22	60	866	1969
1970	4 137	1 752	1 667	129	513	8 198	530	12	347	23	67	978	1970
1971	4 675	1 988	1 857	140	579	9 239	543	12	358	24	69	1 005	1971
1972	5 289	2 166	2 066	144	592	10 258	639	13	425	26	79	1 182	1972
1973	5 920	2 561	2 303	163	668	11 615	713	13	476	27	91	1 321	1973
1974	7 775	2 734	3 033	187	1 392	15 121	866	16	584	33	166	1 665	1974
1975	9 125	2 446	3 569	201	1 785	17 127	1 069	19	721	40	207	2 057	1975
1976	10 755	2 666	4 101	231	1 927	19 680	1 246	22	844	49	237	2 398	1976
1977	11 904	2 966	4 401	254	1 749	21 274	1 333	24	893	53	264	2 567	1977
1978	13 496	3 394	4 822	273	1 869	23 854	1 527	28	1 042	64	282	2 943	1978
1979	14 856	3 884	5 029	287	2 152	26 209	1 680	28	1 145	67	254	3 175	1979
1980	16 610	4 376	5 473	309	2 508	29 276	1 841	31	1 249	77	267	3 465	1980
1981	18 168	4 750	5 716	329	2 679	31 642	2 019	35	1 359	85	276	3 774	1981

Table 18

Sickness Insurance: Expenditure by Scheme and Type

at current prices (in million AS)

Year	Self-employed				Farmers						Other insurance schemes						Year
					Insured		Relatives				Insured		Relatives				
	benef. in kind/serv.	cash benef.	Other incl. admin.	Total	benef. in kind/serv.	cash benef.	benef. in kind/serv.	cash benef.	Other incl. admin.	Total	benef. in kind/serv.	cash benef.	benef. in kind/serv.	cash benef.	Other incl. admin.	Total	
1950					41	19	6	3	12	80	77	24	24	5	6	137	1950
1951					55	24	9	2	18	109	97	35	32	6	8	177	1951
1952					71	31	12	3	21	137	129	37	44	7	7	225	1952
1953					81	35	14	4	21	154	139	36	46	7	15	244	1953
1954					87	35	16	5	23	166	148	38	49	7	14	256	1954
1955					96	39	18	5	25	184	172	49	56	9	19	304	1955
1956					94	46	40	8	23	211	154	58	103	16	15	346	1956
1957	120	4	22	146	102	52	47	8	27	236	176	66	116	17	18	393	1957
1958	115	4	23	142	110	52	50	9	25	247	188	63	127	16	19	412	1958
1959	142	5	23	170	114	52	52	9	27	254	203	63	137	17	19	439	1959
1960	146	5	24	176	119	52	57	9	30	266	217	71	138	18	21	466	1960
1961	157	6	26	188	133	55	71	9	33	301	236	78	142	19	24	499	1961
1962	178	6	27	211	144	61	73	9	35	321	266	88	167	19	26	567	1962
1963	191	6	29	226	156	62	81	9	38	346	281	86	174	19	25	584	1963
1964	208	6	30	245	167	59	90	9	40	365	297	91	186	19	25	618	1964
1965	234	10	34	278	177	61	96	9	44	387	324	88	200	18	28	658	1965
1966	497	27	74	589	172	57	79	7	44	360	352	96	216	19	33	716	1966
1967	717	43	89	850	182	56	76	7	45	366	398	82	237	18	42	777	1967
1968	854	48	89	991	203	60	83	7	47	401	433	92	263	20	39	846	1968
1969	926	49	98	1 073	225	65	91	8	48	437	500	105	299	22	45	971	1969
1970	1 038	50	106	1 194	241	63	95	7	52	460	542	112	324	23	52	1 053	1970
1971	1 098	51	115	1 264	261	66	102	7	56	492	608	135	353	24	80	1 200	1971
1972	1 298	55	113	1 466	288	69	107	7	59	529	664	132	379	24	65	1 266	1972
1973	1 407	66	127	1 600	318	76	111	7	65	578	722	147	410	24	71	1 374	1973
1974	1 668	75	178	1 873							893	145	507	25	126	1 696	1974
1975	2 002	91	200	2 293							1 046	83	603	25	159	1 916	1975
1976	2 405	109	237	2 752							1 210	107	684	27	171	2 198	1976
1977	2 971	148	297	3 236							1 317	122	739	28	171	2 377	1977
1978	3 237	142	333	3 712							1 449	139	788	31	183	2 590	1978
1979	3 153	139	398	3 690							1 580	152	828	31	193	2 785	1979
1980	3 735	153	683	4 572							1 709	171	881	32	218	3 011	1980
1981	4 054	164	619	4 838							1 898	181	931	35	209	3 254	1981

Table 19

Other Social Expenditure

Year	Ministry of Social Affairs: Transfers to social insurance	Ministry of Social Affairs: Labour market adm. I	Ministry of Social Affairs: Labour market adm. II	Ministry of Social Affairs: Other	Ministry of Social Affairs: Total	Family Load Equalization Scheme: Family allowances	Family Load Equalization Scheme: Maternity benef.	Family Load Equalization Scheme: Subsidies for pupils	Family Load Equalization Scheme: Other	Family Load Equalization Scheme: Total	Price subsidies	Regional and local welfare	Voluntary enterprise benefits	Year
1950	441	381		913	1 735				395	395				1950
1951	642	621		1 116	2 379				772	772	90			1951
1952	1 074	1 005		1 244	3 323				1 124	1 124	514			1952
1953	1 037	1 206		1 377	3 620				1 195	1 195	462			1953
1954	1 251	1 079		1 351	3 681				1 242	1 242	432			1954
1955	1 163	820	1	1 308	3 292	260			1 815	2 075	439		2 403	1955
1956	616	856	17	1 619	3 108	460	112		2 118	2 690	765		2 728	1956
1957	1 075	901	33	1 546	3 555	637	61		2 353	3 051	836	1 682	3 030	1957
1958	1 243	1 034	34	1 812	4 123	779	62		6 829	7 670	858	1 724	3 156	1958
1959	1 926	999	40	1 758	4 723	964	63		2 876	3 903	920	1 775	3 365	1959
1960	1 973	926	50	1 790	4 739	880	62		3 145	4 087	858	1 929	3 696	1960
1961	3 434	1 345	34	1 903	6 716	997	122		3 900	5 019	1 186	2 131	4 140	1961
1962	3 940	1 019	79	2 070	7 108	1 203	137		4 584	5 924	1 318	2 334	4 541	1962
1963	4 592	1 018	110	2 044	7 764	1 274	210		5 158	6 642	1 758	2 480	4 911	1963
1964	5 292	1 088	73	2 206	8 659	1 366	215		3 281	4 862	1 823	2 741	4 948	1964
1965	5 687	1 280	136	2 348	9 451	1 391	210		3 465	5 066	1 946	3 091	5 988	1965
1966	7 012	1 282	122	2 386	10 802	1 427	202		3 695	5 324	2 205	3 117	6 605	1966
1967	7 975	1 381	127	2 437	11 920	1 535	202		4 347	6 084	1 809	3 400	7 151	1967
1968	9 089	1 673	118	2 676	13 556	6 512	246		1	6 759	2 089	3 614	7 580	1968
1969	8 951	1 757	129	3 120	13 957	6 792	204		0	6 996	2 435	3 830	8 128	1969
1970	10 917	1 718	147	3 030	15 812	6 931	187		0	7 118	2 339	4 136	8 861	1970
1971	11 642	1 970	142	3 248	17 002	7 744	212		1 142	9 098	2 221	4 537	10 232	1971
1972	13 309	2 027	179	3 248	18 753	8 178	202	141	1 872	10 393	2 268	5 093	11 613	1972
1973	13 883	2 294	178	3 614	19 969	8 951	190	1 007	1 958	12 106	2 409	5 844	13 329	1973
1974	15 228	2 977	203	3 887	22 295	9 429	337	1 556	2 951	14 273	2 606	6 656	15 247	1974
1975	22 152	3 958	537	4 716	31 363	10 794	1 270	1 963	1 824	15 851	2 722	7 869	16 760	1975
1976	24 473	4 362	485	5 209	34 529	11 631	1 323	2 358	1 997	17 309	2 974	6 558	18 110	1976
1977	27 544	4 545	271	5 314	37 674	13 549	1 309	2 517	1 914	19 289	2 802	7 463	19 631	1977
1978	24 098	5 861	320	5 797	36 076	21 411	1 285	2 820	995	26 511	3 520	10 048	21 069	1978
1979	25 569	6 913	475	6 168	39 125	23 033	1 291	2 965	1 032	28 321	2 888	10 928	21 946	1979
1980	23 338	7 497	500	6 391	37 726	23 081	1 335	3 100	1 678	29 194	2 473	12 385	23 126	1980
1981	24 850	9 058	481	6 670	41 059	24 281	1 407	3 735	1 915	31 338	2 420	13 539	24 384	1981

Table 20

Central Government Revenues

(in million AS)

Year	Total revenues	Transfers to provinces/ local communities	Transfers to housing constr. of provinces	Transfers to family load equal.	Total net revenues	Main ear-marked revenues: unempl. contrib.	Main ear-marked revenues: family load equalization total	Main ear-marked revenues: family load equalization employers' contrib.	Main ear-marked revenues: family load equalization income tax share	Main ear-marked revenues: compens. for tax credits	Main ear-marked revenues: price subsidies	Main ear-marked revenues: construction subsidies	Year
1950	11 205	3 078			9 655								1950
1951	16 565	3 949			12 997								1951
1952	19 781	4 838			14 714						55		1952
1953	21 917	5 550			16 873						28		1953
1954	24 528	5 711			19 199						97		1954
1955	27 592	5 889	105	93	22 262						58	155	1955
1956	30 014	6 481	214	136	23 257						33	612	1956
1957	34 452	7 421	280	180	26 088						61	719	1957
1958	35 437	8 047	317	189	26 357						68	743	1958
1959	37 861	7 508	322	199	28 591						101	779	1959
1960	42 156	8 269	341	218	31 812						116	834	1960
1961	49 009	9 719	430	273	36 982						198	957	1961
1962	52 410	11 086	512	309	38 797						259	1 045	1962
1963	54 948	12 009	531	325	40 645						356	1 080	1963
1964	57 865	13 539	595	369	41 351						442	1 230	1964
1965	62 730	14 917	634	426	44 438	1 164	4 989	4 369	(619)		333	1 365	1965
1966	68 538	16 752	705	483	48 200	1 212	5 641	4 964	(623)		344	1 404	1966
1967	72 292	18 227	753	501	49 622	1 265	6 394	5 701	501		436	1 447	1967
1968	77 727	18 755	1 342	493	54 785	1 437	6 731	6 046	493		394	(3 715)	1968
1969	86 025	20 594	2 720	531	60 662	1 589	7 292	6 568	531		417	(4 065)	1969
1970	94 366	23 281	3 402	694	65 620	1 690	7 916	7 104	620		479	(4 639)	1970
1971	104 824	26 743	3 992	718	71 777	1 982	9 098	8 187	718		475	(5 359)	1971
1972	120 209	31 286	4 576	850	81 665	2 152	10 393	9 351	850		514	(6 238)	1972
1973	120 315	35 225	5 136	936	76 935	2 325	12 106	10 978	936		495	1 320	1973
1974	148 598	42 298	6 398	1 178	96 140	2 907	14 273	12 902	1 178		462	1 491	1974
1975	159 533	44 568	6 764	1 175	104 359	3 239	15 751	14 382	1 175		475	1 702	1975
1976	177 904	48 783	7 080	1 258	117 849	3 471	17 309	15 857	1 258		646	1 892	1976
1977	194 781	51 998	8 404	1 488	129 927	4 331	19 289	17 623	1 441		688	2 215	1977
1978	214 872	57 526	9 127	1 606	135 722	5 182	26 511	16 904	1 606	6 780	892	2 542	1978
1979	237 620	59 982	10 033	1 727	153 609	5 739	28 321	17 857	1 727	7 232	838	2 782	1979
1980	259 028	66 084	10 957	1 940	167 122	6 123	29 194	19 229	1 940	7 232	942	2 991	1980
1981	260 118	71 916	12 395	2 188	160 185	7 902	31 618	18 737	2 188	7 232	1 142	3 187	1981

Table 21 Financing of Pension Insurance

Year	Workers and employees				Self-employed				All pension schemes		Year
	total revenues	insur. contrib.	federal subsid.	other rev.	total revenues	insur. contrib.	federal subsid.	other rev.	total revenues	federal subsid.	
	(mill. AS)	percent distribution			(mill. AS)	percent distribution			(in mill. AS)		
1957	5 847	80.9	9.6	9.5					5 847	557	1957
1958	6 452	76.6	13.9	9.4	674	90.6	7.4	2.0	7 126	950	1958
1959	6 913	75.1	13.7	11.2	866	67.5	18.0	14.4	7 779	1 104	1959
1960	7 466	75.7	12.4	11.9	861	53.9	28.2	17.3	8 327	1 172	1960
1961											1961
1962	11 320	71.0	18.4	10.6	1 126	51.6	26.7	21.7	12 446	2 386	1962
1963	12 563	69.7	20.7	9.6	1 219	52.8	24.1	23.1	13 782	2 891	1963
1964	14 538	68.2	21.2	10.6	1 461	50.8	26.5	22.7	15 998	3 475	1964
1965	17 600	67.1	19.4	13.5	1 588	53.7	24.6	21.7	19 188	3 812	1965
1966											1966
1967	21 478	68.9	23.6	7.5	2 116	36.2	43.9	19.9	23 594	5 994	1967
1968	23 375	67.8	24.1	8.1	2 497	34.2	48.6	17.2	25 872	6 842	1968
1969	25 369	68.6	23.4	8.0	2 700	33.6	49.7	16.7	28 069	7 279	1969
1970	27 460	71.0	21.3	7.7	3 427	35.4	50.7	13.9	36 886	7 578	1970
1971	30 930	72.6	20.0	7.4	4 443	32.8	45.3	21.9	35 373	8 195	1971
1972	34 546	74.6	18.0	7.4	5 557	28.0	49.0	23.0	40 104	8 925	1972
1973	39 275	76.5	16.5	7.0	6 417	29.2	49.0	21.8	45 692	9 605	1973
1974	45 526	75.9	17.5	6.6	7 854	26.6	53.3	20.1	53 380	12 155	1974
1975	52 792	72.6	20.4	7.0	9 300	25.1	55.5	19.4	62 092	15 933	1975
1976	62 296	68.0	19.0	13.0	11 048	23.4	57.2	19.4	73 344	18 171	1976
1977	66 264	72.7	20.3	7.0	12 752	23.4	60.1	16.5	79 016	21 145	1977
1978											1978
1979	78 283	81.7	11.7	6.6	15 878	26.7	57.7	15.6	94 161	18 368	1979
1980	84 187	72.0	8.3	19.7	17 237	27.1	52.2	20.7	101 424	15 997	1980
1981	90 766	71.4	7.9	20.7	18 598	24.6	56.6	18.8	109 364	17 676	1981

Table 22 Financing of Social Insurance

Year	Sickness insurance total revenues	insur. contrib.	federal subsid.	other rev.	Accident insurance total revenues	insur. contrib.	federal subsid.	other rev.	Reimbursements to social insurance acc. ins. pupils	matern. benef.	medical control	housing subsidy	poor comp. subsidy	Year
	(mill. AS)	percent distribution			(mill. AS)	percent distribution			(in mill. AS)					
1957	3 511	92.9	0.1	7.0	616	95.2		4.8				194	259	1957
1958	3 680	93.4	0.0	6.6	658	94.1		5.9		40		209	293	1958
1959	3 956	91.4		8.6	707	91.7		8.3		46		216	528	1959
1960	4 518	90.6		9.4	758	91.6		8.4		108		232	660	1960
1961										77		254	361	1961
1962	5 581	91.1		8.9	1 117	91.3		8.7		94		279	982	1962
1963	5 953	90.8		9.2	1 222	88.1		11.9		105		285	1 018	1963
1964	6 472	91.1		8.9	1 355	90.3		9.7		117		291	1 199	1964
1965	7 137	91.4		8.6	1 457	91.4		8.6		129		237	1 229	1965
1966										144		245	1 375	1966
1967	8 628	88.4	2.8	8.8	1 667	91.2		8.8		161		252	1 572	1967
1968	9 792	87.6	2.6	9.8	1 753	91.1		8.9		176		257	1 632	1968
1969	11 089	87.9	2.3	9.8	1 934	89.3	2.9	7.8		189		262	1 732	1969
1970	11 899	88.1	2.2	9.7	2 111	89.9	2.8	7.3		191		265	1 852	1970
1971	13 799	88.0	2.1	9.9	2 336	90.2	2.7	7.1		208		267	2 594	1971
1972	14 962	89.0	2.0	9.0	2 663	90.2	3.3	6.5		223		269	3 150	1972
1973	17 457	89.5	1.8	8.7	3 047	90.0	3.3	6.7		247		271	3 430	1973
1974	20 496	88.9	1.6	9.5	3 404	90.3	3.2	6.5		363		275	3 801	1974
1975	22 833	87.1	1.5	11.4	3 674	90.6	2.7	6.7		652	15	277	4 265	1975
1976	25 643	88.3	1.5	10.2	4 017	91.4	2.7	5.9		584	20	278	4 658	1976
1977	29 885	88.0	1.8	10.2	4 878	91.5	2.9	5.6	30	665	26	278	4 947	1977
1978									30	824	18	277	5 268	1978
1979	37 251	87.2	1.5	11.3	6 130	91.8	2.8	5.4	30	866	21	279	5 482	1979
1980	40 473	86.1	1.5	12.4	6 610	91.4	2.7	5.9	30	983	21	281	5 620	1980
1981	43 591	86.3	1.4	12.3	7 125	91.1	2.8	6.1	30	1 116	20	281	5 841	1981

Table 23

Social Insurance Coverage and Beneficiaries

(in 1,000s)

Year	Sickness insurance contrib-utors	Sickness insurance insured relatives	Pension insurance in-sured	Pension insurance benefi-ciaries	Accident insurance in-sured	Accident insurance inval. pens.	Accident insurance total benef.	Unemployment ins. in-sured	Unemployment ins. benefi-ciaries	Social assistance benef. poverty compens.	Social assistance benef. perma-nent	Social assistance benef. matern. allow.	Year
1950									95.8				1950
1951									90.0				1951
1952									124.3				1952
1953									148.3				1953
1954									129.5				1954
1955	3 211.6		1 939.9	692.1	3 521.5	71.1	89.5	1 528.3	92.8				1955
1956	3 269.4		2 019.3	700.6	3 632.0	73.0	92.1	1 592.3	92.5	80.2			1956
1957	3 324.6		2 057.9	713.2	3 582.2	75.6	95.2	1 733.5	87.8	166.3			1957
1958	3 555.0		2 072.6	776.2	3 592.2	78.3	98.4	1 779.2	97.2	167.6			1958
1959	3 619.6	1 793.0	2 643.4	875.4	3 521.2	80.3	101.0	1 804.7	89.9	250.3			1959
1960	3 651.2	1 809.0	2 660.3	924.5	3 564.0	82.5	103.5	1 849.2	70.3	304.9			1960
1961	3 690.6	1 830.0	2 671.0	965.1	3 604.2	84.8	106.3	1 880.4	53.7	294.3		10.7	1961
1962	3 735.8	1 854.0	2 674.1	1 002.2	3 173.8	86.6	108.5	1 883.9	50.7	309.4		22.4	1962
1963	3 774.1	1 873.0	2 651.3	1 042.2	3 171.4	87.9	110.5	1 881.0	55.0	294.9		27.1	1963
1964	3 823.7	1 899.0	2 656.8	1 083.9	3 090.2	89.9	113.0	1 891.0	51.1	291.9		28.4	1964
1965	4 185.6	2 462.0	2 644.0	1 122.9	3 058.3	90.5	113.7	1 904.0	51.0	288.8		29.4	1965
1966	4 232.4	2 473.0	2 632.1	1 165.0	3 016.4	91.5	115.2	1 920.4	46.8	300.2	40.4	29.3	1966
1967	4 249.3	2 394.0	2 596.8	1 191.9	3 117.0	91.7	115.8	1 931.3	48.9	319.3	39.8	30.0	1967
1968	4 308.0	2 395.0	2 569.4	1 225.4	3 143.1	92.8	117.6	1 918.7	54.5	307.1	39.7	31.8	1968
1969	4 343.6	2 398.0	2 572.2	1 245.5	3 033.8	93.1	118.4	1 915.7	52.5	305.6	39.4	31.6	1969
1970	4 374.9	2 407.0	2 597.0	1 276.2	3 048.6	94.2	119.9	1 937.3	46.0	302.9	39.0	29.4	1970
1971	4 435.0	2 422.0	2 629.7	1 295.5	3 076.6	94.3	120.4	2 003.1	41.1	370.6	37.7	28.8	1971
1972	4 422.6	2 523.0	2 659.9	1 326.0	3 109.4	94.4	121.1	2 059.7	39.0	378.7	36.6	29.1	1972
1973	4 520.6	2 643.0	2 736.1	1 343.9	3 197.8	95.1	122.4	2 180.6	37.8	380.0	36.6	27.8	1973
1974	4 589.3	2 670.0	2 755.3	1 368.0	3 204.7	96.0	123.6	2 186.9	34.8	372.7	38.8	30.4	1974
1975	4 600.3	2 684.0	2 736.9	1 395.5	3 121.8	97.0	124.8	2 157.3	40.2	367.4	41.5	33.9	1975
1976	4 623.9	2 669.0	2 750.2	1 412.7	3 145.2	97.5	125.3	2 185.2	40.3	354.4	42.6	31.3	1976
1977	4 724.0	2 689.0	2 781.1	1 430.1	4 965.0	98.4	126.0	2 225.3	38.9	344.0	42.6	30.8	1977
1978	4 751.5	2 687.0	2 783.8	1 442.9	4 993.0	99.2	126.9		44.8	335.7	41.5	31.4	1978
1979	4 775.4	2 675.0	2 786.5	1 460.2	4 985.4	99.8	127.3	2 242.5	44.5	324.2	40.9	32.9	1979
1980	4 779.3	2 660.0	2 811.1	1 484.6	4 975.3	100.0	127.1	2 252.4	41.3	315.8	39.1	37.9	1980
1981	4 820.0	2 666.0	2 813.9	1 507.8	4 950.1	98.6	125.3	2 258.0	49.9	309.8	39.0	37.9	1981

Table 24

Population and Labour Force

Year	Population (in 1,000s)							Labour force (in 1,000s)				Year
	Total	under 15	15–60	60 and above	birth rate	death rate	growth rate	Potential lab. force	dependent empl.	self-employed	unempl. rate (%)	
1950	6 935	1 579	4 283	1 074	15.6	12.4					6.8	1950
1951	6 935	1 589	4 261	1 086	14.8	12.7			1 984	1 126	5.5	1951
1952	6 928	1 596	4 228	1 104	14.9	12.0			1 939	1 101	7.5	1952
1953	6 932	1 603	4 207	1 122	14.8	12.0	0.72		1 919	1 067	8.7	1953
1954	6 940	1 588	4 212	1 141	15.0	12.2	1.15		1 975	1 040	7.7	1954
1955	6 947	1 552	4 234	1 161	15.6	12.2	0.86		2 074	1 018	5.5	1955
1956	6 952	1 524	4 246	1 182	16.7	12.5	0.86		2 137	999	5.3	1956
1957	6 966	1 517	4 245	1 204	17.0	12.8	1.87		2 185	981	4.9	1957
1958	6 987	1 521	4 239	1 228	17.1	12.3	3.16		2 203	974	5.3	1958
1959	7 014	1 528	4 232	1 254	17.7	12.5	3.86		2 236	955	4.8	1959
1960	7 048	1 554	4 213	1 281	17.9	12.7	4.70	2 369	2 282	936	3.7	1960
1961	7 086	1 589	4 187	1 310	18.6	12.1	5.53	2 391	2 322	922	2.9	1961
1962	7 130	1 616	4 176	1 338	18.7	12.7	6.06	2 405	2 340	892	2.7	1962
1963	7 176	1 639	4 173	1 364	18.8	12.8	6.45	2 413	2 342	872	2.9	1963
1964	7 224	1 667	4 167	1 390	18.5	12.3	6.69	2 430	2 364	847	2.7	1964
1965	7 271	1 698	4 160	1 413	17.9	13.0	6.50	2 447	2 381	809	2.7	1965
1966	7 322	1 729	4 158	1 435	17.6	12.5	7.15	2 448	2 387	773	2.5	1966
1967	7 377	1 760	4 160	1 456	17.3	12.9	7.37	2 424	2 360	746	2.7	1967
1968	7 415	1 787	4 156	1 473	17.0	12.9	5.28	2 410	2 339	727	2.9	1968
1969	7 441	1 807	4 147	1 487	16.3	13.3	3.50	2 425	2 358	706	2.8	1969
1970	7 467	1 819	4 148	1 500	15.0	13.2	3.49	2 448	2 389	686	2.4	1970
1971	7 500	1 824	4 164	1 512	14.5	13.0	4.42	2 507	2 455	656	2.1	1971
1972	7 544	1 823	4 196	1 525	13.8	12.6	5.86	2 562	2 513	621	1.9	1972
1973	7 586	1 813	4 234	1 539	12.9	12.2	5.56	2 650	2 608	579	1.6	1973
1974	7 599	1 793	4 259	1 548	12.8	12.4	1.71	2 698	2 657	660	1.5	1974
1975	7 579	1 761	4 276	1 542	12.4	12.7	-2.76	2 712	2 656	546	2.0	1975
1976	7 566	1 721	4 325	1 520	11.6	12.6	-1.71	2 741	2 686	535	2.0	1976
1977	7 568	1 678	4 399	1 491	11.3	12.2	0.39	2 788	2 737	513	1.8	1977
1978	7 562	1 631	4 470	1 462	11.3	12.5	-0.53	2 816	2 758	501	2.1	1978
1979	7 549	1 582	4 524	1 443	11.4	12.2	-1.72	2 830	2 774	491	2.0	1979
1980	7 549	1 541	4 564	1 444	12.0	12.2	0.00	2 842	2 779	484	1.9	1980
1981	7 565	1 510	4 599	1 456	12.4	12.3	1.98	2 868	2 799	477	2.4	1981

Notes to and sources for appendix tables

Table 1

Gross domestic product:
From 1964 figures according to the 1968 System of National Accounts (SNA); therefore, data before and after 1964 not completely comparable.
Source: (1)

Deflators:
Source: (1)

Total public expenditure:
Consolidated figures of the expenditure of central, regional and local government and of social insurance, i.e. excluding intergovernmental transfers; public expenditure deflated by the GDP deflator.
Source: (12)

Table 2

Public expenditure by economic category is calculated according to the system of national accounts (SNA) which treats public utilities to a large extent as 'private firms'. Total public expenditure of the SNA therefore is lower than the total in Table 1 which is based on financial statistics.
Source: (1)

Table 3

Functional classification according to the central government budget. All categories refer to gross expenditure (i.e. depreciation is not taken into account) and 'effective' expenditure (i.e. including intergovernmental transfers). For an interpretation of these expenditure figures, one should be aware that a variety of services are provided by autonomous funds or state-owned stock companies.

General administration and other:
Farming and forestry, industries, services (such as the promotion of tourism), public utilities, general administration strictu senso, interests on public debt, repayments, civil servants old age pensions, and transfers according to fiscal equalisation scheme.

Source: (1)

Table 4

From 1976, the functional classification follows a modified system of accounting (*Vereinbarung über Form und Gliederung der Voranschläge und Rechnungsabschlüsse der Länder, der Gemeinden und von Gemeindeverbänden)*, published by Verbindungsstelle der Bundesländer. 'Education' includes sports and science, 'Health' includes environment protection.
Source: (1)

Table 5

Social expenditure at current prices:
Income maintenance:
Sum of expenditure items in Table 7.
Health:
Central gov. (Table 3, col. 4), regional and local gov. (Table 4, cols 4 and 10) expenditure on health; sickness insurance: benefits in kind (Table 16, cols 1 and 3); accident insurance: benefits in kind/services (Table 14, col. 3).

Education:
Central gov. (Table 3, col. 1) regional and local gov. (Table 4, cols 1 and 7) expenditure on education; subsidies (Table 19, col. 8).
'Other':
Regional and local welfare expenditure (see Table 19, col. 12); old age pension insurance: benefits in kind/services (Table 11, col. 3); administration (Table 11, col. 4); sickness insurance: administration (Table 16, col. 5); accident insurance:
administration (Table 14, col. 4).
Total I:
Sum of cols 1-4.
Housing:
Consolidated figures, i.e. excluding intergovernmental transfers; figures therefore lower than the sum of central, regional and local government expenditure on housing (see Tables 3 and 4).
Total II:
Sum of cols 5 and 6.

Social expenditure at constant prices:
Income maintenance deflated by the cost-of-living index, health, education, 'other'and housing by the public consumption deflator (see Table 1).

Sources: housing: (1) (2) (9); for the sources of the other expenditure categories, see the respective tables.

Table 6

Percentage based on figures at current prices in Table 5; for GDP and total public expenditure, see Table 1.

Table 7

Old age pensions:
See Table 11, col. 1; including cases of early retirement due to either special labour market programs or long insurance time.
Survivors' pensions:
Old age pension insurance schemes (see Table 11, col. 2).
Invalidity pensions:
See Table 14, col. 1.
Survivors' pensions:
Accident insurance schemes (see Table 14, col. 2).
Federal pensions:
Pensions paid by central government.
Other public pensions:
Pensions of regional and local government, public enterprises and chambers (of commerce etc.).
Unemployment benefits:
Public enterprises and the chambers (of commerce etc.) benefits as well as labour market administration I and II (see Table 19, cols 2 and 3) which include more than cash benefits.
Sickness cash benefits:
See Table 16, cols 2 and 4.
Family benefits:
Family allowances and maternity benefits (see Table 19, cols 6 and 7).
'Other':
Mainly expenditure on social assistance, war victims, but also including some administrative costs (see Table 19, col. 4).

Sources: federal and other public pensions: (15); 'other' benefits: (1) and own calculations; for the other sources, see the respective tables.

Table 8

Figures at current prices from Table 7 deflated by the cost-of-living index (see Table 1).

Table 9

Old age pension insurance schemes:
Cols 1-6: totals from Tables 12 and 13; col. 7: missing data 1950-56: comprehensive statistics are available only after implementation of the General Social Insurance Act 1955.

Accident insurance schemes:
Cols 8-11: totals from Table 15; col. 12: see under old age pensions.

Sickness insurance schemes:
Cols 13-17: totals from Table 17 and 18; col. 18: sum of cols 13-17.

Source: (3)

Table 10

Old age insurance schemes:
Cols 1-6: aggregates of single expenditure items at current prices in Tables 12 and 13, expenditure on old age pensions and survivors' pensions deflated by the cost of living index (see Table 1), expenditure on benefits in kind/services and 'other, incl. administration' deflated by the public consumption deflator (see Table 1).
Col. 7: 1950-1956: total from Table 9 deflated under the assumption that 80 percent of the expenditure are cash benefits (cost of living index) and 20 percent services and benefit in kinds (public consumption deflator); 1957-1981: sum of cols 1-6.

Accident insurance schemes:
Cols 8-11: aggregates of single expenditure items at current prices in Table 15, expenditure on invalidity pensions and survivors' pensions deflated by the cost of living index, expenditure on services/benefits in kind and 'other (adm.)' deflated by the public consumption deflator.
Col. 12: 1950-1956: totals from Table 9 deflated under the assumption that 60 percent of the expenditure are cash benefits (cost of living index) and 40 percent services and benefits in kind (public consumption deflator); 1957-1981: sum of cols 8-11.

Sickness insurance schemes:
Cols 13-17: aggregates of single expenditure items at current prices in Tables 17 and 18, cash benefits deflated by the cost of living index, benefits in kind/services and 'other, incl. administration' deflated by the public consumption deflator.
Col. 18: sum of cols 13-17.
Col. 19: sum of cols 7, 12 and 18.

Sources: see sources to Table 9, for deflators see Table 1.

Table 11

At current prices:
Aggregates of the respective expenditure items of the six pension insurance schemes given in Tables 12 and 13.

At constant prices:
Expenditure on old age pensions and survivors' pensions deflated by the cost of living index, on benefits in kind/services and 'other incl. adm.' deflated by the public consumption deflator (see Table 1).

Sources: see sources to Tables 12 and 13.

Table 12

Old age pensions comprise cases of early retirement due to special labour market relief programs or long insurance time. For self-employed, the old age pensions include payments because of work disability (*Erwerbsunfähigkeitspensionen*). Old age pensions payable due to voluntary higher insurance contributions are also included. Invalidy pensioners are transferred to old age pension schemes after retirement age. Survivors' pensions comprise widows' (widowers') pensions, orphans' pensions, indemnities. Services etc comprise health care and pensioners sickness insurance.

Col. 3: Including health care and sickness insurance, but also minimum pension subsidies (*Ausgleichszulagen*), financed from the federal budget.
Col. 4: Including housing subsidies and carrier charges.

Table 13

See supra, table 12.

Cols 6-10: From 1974 Col. 11: 1957: notaries only.

Table 14

At current prices:
Aggregates of the respective expenditure items of the four accident insurance schemes given in Table 15.

At constant prices:
Expenditure on invalidity pensions and survivors' pensions deflated by the cost of living index, on services/benefits in kind and 'other (adm.)' by the public consumption deflator (see Table 1).

Sources: see sources to Table 15.

Table 15

Invalidity pensions:
Payments vary according to the degree of disability.

Survivors' pensions:
Widows' (widowers') and orphans' pensions.

Services (administration):
Services are almost entirely medical treatment after accidents.

Other:
Including housing assistance and transfers to other social insurance institutes.

1979: Exact figures available only for the sum of the expenditure on invalidity and survivors' pensions; separate figures have been estimated on the basis of assumed percentages for the expenditure on invalidity pensions: 71% in the general scheme, 80% in the farmers' scheme, 64% in the railways' scheme, and 71% in the public service scheme.

Table 16

At current prices:
Aggregates of the respective expenditure items of the various sickness insurance schemes given in Table 17 and 18.

At constant prices:
Expenditure on cash benefits deflated by the cost of living index, on benefits in kind and 'other' by the public consumption deflator (see Table 1).

Sources: see sources to Tables 17 and 18.

Table 17

Benefits in kind/services:
Medical, dental and hospital treatment, drugs and remedies; 1950-1955 including medical treatment of relatives.

Cash benefits:
Mainly sickness cash benefits and birth allowance, but also some expenditure on services which could not be subtracted; for relatives birth allowances only.

Other incl. admin.:
Regional insurance institutes: 1950-55 including death grants/funeral subsidies; public employees: 1950-55 including medical treatment of relatives.

Table 18

For an explanation of the expenditure items, see Table 17.

Farmers:
Since 1974 united with regional health insurance institutes (see Table 17).

Other insurance schemes:
Including enterprise institutes, railwaymen and miners.

Table 19

Expenditure classified by institution; note, however, that the family load equalization scheme is administered by the Ministry of Social Affairs.

Ministry of Social Affairs:
Tansfers to social insurance; mainly subsidies to insurance institutes and reimbursements for housing subsidies.
Labour market administration I: from 1950 to 1964 only unemployment insurance, from 1965 also including labour market promotion.
Labour market administration II: mainly bad weather compensation.
'Other': social assistance, war victims, crime victims and administration.
Total: sum of cols 1-5.

Family Load Equalization Scheme:
Family allowances (prior to 1955 only child allowances).
Maternity benefits.
Subsidies for pupils: transporation subsidies, free school travel, books.
'Other': 1950-1967 including tax allowances for children, 1971-1977 including surplus to reserve funds.
Total: sum of cols 6-9.
Prices subsidies: subsidies for milk, bread etc.
Regional and local welfare: mainly expenditure on youth care and welfare aid (*Jugendhilfe und Wohlfahrtseinrichtungen*), but including district social assistance bodies (*Bezirksfürsorgeverbände*).
Voluntary enterprise benefits: estimated using six-annual investigations by the chamber of commerce on labour costs in industries.

Table 20

Total:
Total revenues include balances of public enterprises.

Transfers to provinces/local communities:
Including taxes on trade and industry.

Transfers to housing construction of provinces:
Excluding transfers to housing construction funds.

Total net revenues:
Total revenues minus intergovernmental transfers (col. 2).

Unemployment contributions:
Prior to 1966 included in joint entry 'revenues of the Ministry of Social Affairs'.

Compensation for tax credits:
Payable since the 1977 reform of the family load equalization which introduces tax credits instead of flat rate benefits.

Price subsidies:
Including subsidies to enterprises for the utilization of oversupplies, mainly to farmers.

Construction subsidies:
Figures in brackets include income tax credits; net subsidies for housing construction not available.

Source: (2).

Table 21
Source: (3).

Table 22
Source: (3).

Table 23
Sources: (3) for cols 1-8, (2) for cols 9-11, (1) for col. 12.

Table 24
Population:
Source: (15); own calculation of population growth rate.

Labour force:
Figures on potential labour force available from 1960 only.
Source: (2).

Enumerated sources for appendix tables

(1) *Statistisches Handbuch für die Republik Österreich* (Statistical Handbook for the Republic of Austria), Austrian Central Statistical Office (ed.), current years.

(2) *Wirtschafts- und sozialstatistisches Handbuch* (Handbook of Economic and Social Statistics), Chamber for Dependent Employed (ed.), current years.

(3) *Statistisches Handbuch der österreichischen Sozialversicherung* (Statistical Handbook of Austrian Social Insurance), Joint Committee of Austrian Social Insurance Institutions (ed.), current years.

(4) *Handbuch der österreichischen Sozialversischerung* (Handbook of Austrian Social Insurance), Joint Committee of Austrian Social Insurance Institutions (ed.), current years.

(5) *Erläuterungen zum Bundesfinanzgesetz* (Comments to the Federal Finances Act), Austrian State Printing Office (ed.), current years.

(6) *Bericht über die soziale Lage* (Report on the State of Social Affairs), Ministery of Social Affairs (ed.), current years (first 1979).

(7) *Programmbudget der Arbeitsmarktverwaltung* (Program Budget of the Labour Market Administration), Ministery of Social Affairs (ed.), current years (first 1978).

(8) *Statistisches Jahrbuch der Stadt Wien* (Statistical Yearbook of the City of Vienna), Magistrate of the City of Vienna (ed.), current years.

(9) *Die Wohnbaufinanzierung des Bundes, der Bundesländer und Gemeinden 1981 und 1982*, Liaison Office of Federal Provinces at the Office of the Government of Lower Austria (ed.), 1984.

(10) *Österreichs Volkseinkommen 1983 mit Langzeitreihen 1954-1983* (Austria's National Income 1983 including Time-series 1954-1983), Austrian Central Statistical Office (ed.), Vienna 1985.

(11) Economic Database, Austrian Institute for Empirical Economic Research, updated occasionally.

(12) Ch. Smekal and M. Gantner, *Die längerfristige Entwicklung der öffentlichen Finanzwirtschaft in Österreich im Zeitraum 1950-1983* (The Long-term Development of Public Finances in Austria in the Period of 1950-1983), Wilhelm Braumüller Publishers, Vienna 1985.

(13) *Forschungsberichte aus Sozial- und Arbeitsmarktpolitik* (Research Reports on Social and Labour Market Policies), Ministery of Social Affairs (ed.), current issues.

(14) *Veröffentlichungen des österreichischen Instituts für Arbeitsmarktpolitik* (Publications of the Austrian Institute on Labour Market Policy), current issues.

(15) *Demographisches Jahrbuch Österreichs 1984* (Demographic Yearbook for Austria 1984), Austrian Central Statistical Office (ed.), Vienna 1986.

(16) H. Abele et al (eds) *Handbuch der österreichischen Wirtschaftspolitik* (Handbook of Austrian Economic Policy), 2nd ed. Vienna 1984.

Switzerland

Peter Gross and Helmut Puttner

Institutional Synopsis

Contents

Glossary of abbreviations

AHV	*Alters- und Hinterlassenenversicherung* (Helvetian Old Age and Survivors' Insurance)
ALVG	*Arbeitslosenversicherungsgesetz* (Unemployment Insurance Law)
BSV	*Bundesamt für Sozialversicherung* (Federal Office of Social Insurance)
EO	*Erwerbsersatzordnung* (Income Compensation)
IV	*Invalidenversicherung* (Invalidity Insurance)
KUVG	*Kranken- und Unfallversicherungsgesetz* (Sickness and Accident Insurance Law)
MV	*Militärversicherung* (Military Insurance)
SUV	*Staatliche obligatorische Unfallversicherung* (Federal Compulsory Accident Insurance)
SUVA	*Schweizerische Unfallversicherungsanstalt* (Swiss Accident Insurance Institute)
WEG	*Wohn- und Eigentumsförderungsgesetz* (Promotion of Housing Construction and Property Law)

Introduction

Swiss welfare state institutions reflect an essential principle of Swiss political structure: that of federalism. The development of the welfare state has always been closely connected with this principle which appears in different ways in a variety of institutional sectors: in the pension system, for example, there are national as well as cantonal regulations; responsibility for family allowances, is divided between central government and the cantons, according to the clientele; sickness insurance legislation covering minimum benefits is made by the state whereas the question of compulsory insurance is dealt with by the cantons; social assistance is partly regulated by the central state, but is in effect operated by means of cantonal or even communal laws. With the exception of vocational training, education is administered by the cantons; public health is likewise the responsibility of the cantons; and housing is regulated by federal laws. The Swiss social security system also contains various private schemes. The majority of sickness funds are organized as private associations, and in addition to the Helvetian pension system there is a private occupational pension system. Consequently the term 'private social security' is often used in discussions of the Swiss welfare state. In the following table, the item Social Security II includes these 'private regulations' which are not a real part of the welfare state.

Total expenditure 1979 in million Swiss Francs (FRS)

		%	
Social Security			
- Federal AHV	10 103	56.8	
- Supplementary benefits to AHV	330	1.9	
- Federal IV	2 010	11.3	
- Supplementary benefits to IV	70	0.4	
- Cantonal AHV/IV	55	0.3	
- Subsidies to approved sickness funds	1 191	6.7	
- Injury insurance (SUVA)	1 416	8.0	
- Military Insurance	167	0.9	
- Regulation for loss of income (EO)	509	2.8	
- Unemployment insurance	210	1.2	
- Family allowances (state)	60	0.3	
- Family allowances (cantonal)	362	2.0	
- Social Assistance	1 318	7.4	
Total Social Security I	17 801	100.0	56.3
Health	4 848		15.3
Education	8 721		27.6
Housing	258		0.8
Total social expenditure	31 628		100.0
% of total public expenditure	19.7		
% of GDP	55.7		
Total Social Security I	17 801		
Approved sickness funds (excl. public subsidies)	4 070		
Occupational pensions	3 098		
Total Social Security II	24 968		

I Pensions

The basis of the Swiss pension system is the so-called three-pillar concept (public pensions, compulsory occupational pensions, voluntary private pensions) first introduced into the constitution in 1972. Public pensions are designed to guarantee an adequate minimum income for the individual and his family, whereas occupational insurance and voluntary private provision are designed to enable the individual to maintain an accustomed standard of living. Social insurance is compulsory whereas the second pillar of the pension system, occupational insurance, is still voluntary and the third pillar, voluntary private pensions, has yet to be implemented.

Pension expenditure in 1979 in million SFR

		%
Federal AHV	10 103.3	80.4
Additional benefits to AHV	329.6	2.6
Federal IV	2 010.0	16.0
Additional benefits to IV	69.9	0.6
Cantonal AHV/IV	55.2	0.4
Total public pension system	12 568.0	100.0
% of total social security I	70.6	
% of GDP	7.8	
% of total social expenditure	39.7	
Public Pension System	12 568.0	80.2
Occupational Pension System	3 098.0	19.8
Total pension system	15 666.0	100.0

1. Public pensions

Coverage

The Swiss pension system provides old age, survivors' and invalidity pensions for all Swiss citizens and foreign residents under certain conditions. Membership of both the Helvetian Old Age and Survivors' Insurance (*Alters- und Hinterlassenenversicherung*, AHV) and Invalidity Insurance (*Invalidenversicherung*, IV), is compulsory. Some cantons still operate cantonal insurance funds, but these are of little importance. Furthermore, AHV and IV supplementary benefits (in accordance with the 1965 law covering supplementary benefits) form an integral part of the pension system but are not insurance based. The state makes contributions to the non-profit carriers, Pro Senectute, Pro Infirmis and Pro Juventute, which are responsible for the distribution supplementary services.

Benefits

The following benefit amounts were established under the ninth AHV-revision, effective from 1 January 1979. AHV pensions are payable as benefits to single persons, married couples, widows, orphans (where either one or both parents are deceased) and, under certain circumstances, to dependents. Men are entitled to claim retirement pensions at the age of 65 and women at the age of 62. Benefits are calculated as a percentage, taking a single person's pension as a base of 100%. Additional allowances amount to 35% for a spouse and 40% for each child. A married couple's pension is payable when both partners have reached pensionable age, and amounts to 150% of a single person's pension. A widow's pension amounts to 80%, an orphan's pension amounts to 80% where both parents are deceased and 40% where one parent is deceased. The size of the pension depends on the beneficiary's period of contribution and former income. Entitlement to an ordinary pension (*ordentliche Rente*) requires a contribution period of more than one year (foreigners: 10 years). Otherwise, extraordinary (*ausserordentliche Renten*) are payable, but only to Swiss citizens. Furthermore, a distinction is made between full pensions (*Vollrenten*) and part-pensions (*Teilrenten*). A full pension is payable to a person whose contribution period equals the average contribution period for his age group. The amount is calculated on an individual basis according to the so-called pension formula. The amount varies between a so-called minimum pension (525 SFR a month) and a maximum pension (1,050 SFR a month), and consists of a fixed amount (80% of the minimum pension or 420 SFR), payable to all those with entitlement to a full pension, and an earnings-related increment. Pensions are adjusted every two years according to a mixed index reflecting price and wage increases. Since the ninth AHV revision, responsibility for indexation lies with the government (*Bundesrat*) rather than parliament, as was previously the case. In addition to retirement pensions, AHV makes so-called social assistance payments (*Hilflosenentschädigung*) for special categories, which amount to 80% of the minimum pension or 420 SFR a month.

The structure and size of invalidity (IV) pensions are similar to those of the AHV. The single invalidity pension corresponds to the single retirement pension, and other pension payments are calculated on the basis of 100%. In order to qualify for IV pensions, which are payable for a reduced working capacity of 50%, the beneficiary must have completed a contribution period of at least one year. Entitlement to a retirement pension disqualifies the insured from invalidity pension payments. A reduced working capacity of 66% entitles the insured to a full IV pension, and a reduced working capacity of 50% entitles him to a half pension. In cases of hardship, a smaller IV pension is payable for a reduced working capacity of 33%. The size of minimum and maximum pensions are fixed according to the AHV schemes. The size of the IV not only depends on the degree of invalidity, but also the last annual income (cf. AHV scheme). Early disablement entitles the insured to a 5% to 15% supplement. In addition, the IV scheme awards so-called disablement payments (*Hilflosenentschädigung)* for seriously disabled beneficiaries which amount to 20-80% of the minimum pension (80% = 420 SFR). Invalidity pensions and supplementary benefits are adjusted according to AHV schemes. The IV also awards benefits in the form of medical aid, medicine, training and re-training courses for which daily allowances are paid. The amount is based on the federal law of 3 October 1975 which covers compensation for loss of earnings for those engaged in compulsory military service and civil defence, and in 1982 rates ranged from 30 SFR to 90 SFR a day.

Financing

AHV is financed on a cost-sharing basis. Revenue comes from employees' and employers' contributions, public subsidies (state and cantons) and income on interest from the Central Compensation Fund (*Zentraler Ausgleichsfonds*), which constitutes the federal institution for all compensation funds. Individual contributions are calculated as a percentage of gross earnings (4.2% per employee and employer) without income limits. The self-employed with an annual income of more than 25,200 SFR pay contributions at a rate of 7.8%; this rate decreases to 4.2% for an income between 25,200 and 4,200 SFR, and below this level a fixed annual amount of 168 SFR is paid. The economically non-active of employable age pay contributions ranging from 168 SFR to 8,400 SFR a year depending on their financial situation. Public subsidies amount to 9% in the case of the central state and 5% for the cantons, and are based on the estimated total AHV expenditure.

The IV is also financed on a cost-sharing basis. Revenue comes from employees' and employers' contributions, income on interest from the Central Compensation Fund and from public subsidies. Employees contribute 1% of gross earnings, half of which is payable by the employer. The self-employed generally contribute 1% of their income. The non-employed pay between 20 SFR and 1,000 SFR a year depending on their financial situation. Public subsidies amount to 50% of annual expenditure, of which 3/4 is paid by the central state and 1/4 by the cantons. The IV is the social institution subsidized to the greatest extent by public money (apart from the supplementary benefit scheme which is less important and the allowances for the families of agricultural workers).

Administration

Both the AHV and the IV are administrated by compensation funds (*Ausgleichskassen*), public institutions set up by the state, the cantons and, on a voluntary basis by employers' associations and the self-employed. These funds are decentralized and for some 100 compensation funds there are approximately 3,000 branches. In addition to compensation funds there are special institutions (*Regionalstellen*) covering IV social and medical services. The definition of entitlements is decided by cantonal IV commissions.

2. Occupational pensions

The state is obliged by law to provide for occupational insurance, which together with the AHV/IV benefits should enable the beneficiary to maintain a reasonable standard of living. This second pillar of the Swiss pension system has been implemented by the Occupational Pension Law of 25 June 1982, which made occupational pension insurance compulsory for employees with an annual income of more than 14,880 SFR, effective from 1 January 1985.

Core laws

Dates given refer to either the date when a federal law was passed in parliament, or the date of a referendum.

6.12.1925
Artikel 34 quater der Bundesverfassung (Art. 34/4 of the Federal Constitution): state empowered to introduce compulsory old age and survivors' insurance in addition to invalidity insurance; implementation to be carried out in co-operation with cantons, professional associations and other private or public organizations.

20.12.1946
Bundesgesetz über die AHV (Federal AHV Law): established coverage for all citizens; effective from 1.1.1948.

19.6.1959
Bundesgesetz über die IV (Federal IV Law): established coverage for all citizens; effective from 1.1.1960.

19.3.1965
Ergänzungsleistungsgesetz (Federal Supplementary Benefits Law): established legal entitlement to supplementary AHV and IV benefits for people with very small pensions; effective from 1.1.1966.

3.12.1972
Änderung des Artikels 34 quater der Bundesverfassung (Amendment to Art. 34/4 of the Federal Constitution): formulation of three-pillar concept for pensions (public, occupational and private pensions).

1951-1979
Nine revisions of AHV/IV benefit structure and financing: the ninth AHV/IV revision, effective from 1.1.1979, empowered the *Bundesrat* to bring benefits in line with general wage and price increases.

1981
Tenth AHV/IV revision: effective from 1.1.1982.

25.6.1982
Bundesgesetz über die berufliche Alters-, Hinterlassenen- und Invalidenvorsorge (Federal Law on Occupational Old Age, Survivors' and Invalidity Provision): introduced compulsory occupational pension insurance for employees with an annual income below a certain ceiling.

II Sickness insurance

Total expenditure of approved sickness funds in 1979 in million SFR

		%
Cash benefits	480.0	9.1
Medical care	3 742.8	71.1
Tuberculosis	13.6	0.3
Maternity	161.1	3.1
Reserve	88.3	1.7
Reinsurance premium	195.0	3.7
Administration	398.8	7.6
Other	181.4	3.4
Total expenditure	5 261.0	100.0
% of total social security II	21.1	
% of GDP	3.3	

Coverage

Sickness insurance includes benefits in the case of illness, and takes the form of outpatient and in-patient treatment (medical care), sickness cash benefits, maternity and tuberculosis benefits. There are separate funds for medical care and cash benefits. Of total sickness insurance fund membership, 44% are entitled to medical care, 9% to cash benefit and 47% are entitled to both. Sickness insurance is not compulsory by federal law, but cantons and local communes may introduce compulsory insurance for all or certain sections of the population. The introduction of compulsory sickness insurance for the entire Swiss population by federal law was rejected in a 1974 referendum. The majority of cantons have made sickness insurance compulsory for particular social groups so that approximately 25% of the Swiss population has compulsory coverage. In practice, however, 96% of the population is covered. Sickness insurance is technically individual insurance, i.e. there is no family insurance. Membership of the cash sickness benefit scheme is open to all persons over the age of 15.

Benefits

The Sickness and Accident Insurance Law (*Kranken- und Unfallversicherungsgesetz*, KUVG) obliges the sickness funds to provide minimum benefits, consisting of medical care (out-patient and in-patient treatment) and cash benefits. The insured may opt for either one or both of the schemes, provided he is not compulsorily insured.

Benefits are provided by the medical insurance scheme. Out-patient treatment consists of medical care, prescribed medicines from an approved pharmaceutical list, laboratory services and officially approved therapy carried out by auxiliary medical staff and treatment by a chiropractitioner.

In-patient benefits consist of those provided for under contract with the individual sickness funds, comprising a minimum of medical treatment and therapy, medicine and laboratory services where rates are based on general ward costs and a minimum daily contribution towards the remaining cost of hospital care. The cost of hospitalization is not automatically covered. It may be covered by complementary insurance (*Spitalpflegezusatzversicherung*), including board and lodging. Medical care may be awarded for one or more cases of illness for a minimum of 720 consecutive days. The KUVG does not provide benefits for normal dental treatment. Maternity care takes the form of ordinary sickness benefits, whereas increased benefits are provided for those suffering from tuberculosis. Benefits in the case of accident are discretionary depending upon the statute of the particular sickness fund.

Regarding cash benefits, the KUVG prescribes a legal minimum benefit of 2 SFR a day where the insured person is unable to undertake any kind of employment (but this is of no practical relevance). Higher benefit rates may be negotiated by means of collective insurance agreements between funds and employers. Cash benefits usually amount to 50% or more of salary and are payable after three days over a minimum period of 720 days.

Financing

Sickness insurance is financed on a pay-as-you-go basis (*Umlageverfahren*). Insurance funds must guarantee reserve capital through a security fund, which must amount to between 15% and 120% of annual expenditure depending on the number of members. Sickness funds benefits are financed through members' contributions (amounting to around 75% of total revenue in 1979), public subsidies (around 20%), voluntary employers' contributions (around 1%), and income on interest from the security fund.

In accordance with the principle of individual insurance, members' contributions are assessed on an individual basis (risk-related contributions). Personal health is taken into account by the sickness funds when assessing members' contributions, consequently women's contributions may be up to 10% higher than men's.

In the case of families with children, contributions for the latter are usually lower. Ultimately, each sickness fund determines each individual member's contribution. The insured person's direct share of the cost in the case of illness amounts to 10% of the cost of out-patient medical care (the patient's share), but at least 30 SFR per case while for higher income groups this amounts to at least 50 SFR per case. There is no fee for medical care in hospitals. State subsidies to sickness funds amount to 10% for men, 35% for women and 30% for children up to the age of 15, and are calculated on the basis of the average cost of medical care in the previous year. The federal government pays a contribution of 2 SFR per fund member for cash sickness benefits and 40% of maternity benefits payable for each confinement and calculated on the basis of the previous year's figures.

Administration

In 1965 there were 984 state approved sickness funds, but by 1978 the number had fallen to 512. The majority of these funds are private organizations (in 1978 approx. 80%), with a relatively small membership. Of total sickness funds, 30% have fewer than 500 members, and a further 50% have fewer than 1,000 members. Small sickness funds combine in so-called reinsurance associations to cover risks. In addition to these there are a few large centralized sickness funds with a membership of several thousand. The organizational framework of sickness funds is extremely decentralized, as small and large sickness funds own sections at communal level. In fact, approximately 3,000 communes in Switzerland have 10,000 sections. These sections are administered to a large extent, on an honorary basis. Final authority in the approved sickness funds is exercised in members' meetings. All fund members have the right to vote and to choose the committee, president, treasurer, and 'inspector' (*Krankenbesucher*) in annual elections.

Core laws

26.10.1890

Artikel 34 bis der Bundesverfassung über die Kranken- und Unfallversicherung (Art. 34/2 of the Federal Constitution): state empowered to introduce sickness and accident insurance by legislation.

13.6.1911

Kranken- und Unfallversicherungsgesetz, KUVG (Federal Sickness and Accident Insurance Law): regulated minimum benefits of approved and subsidized sickness funds.

13.3.1964

Bundesgesetz über die Änderung des ersten Titels (Krankenversicherung) des KUVG (Amendment to Federal KUVG Sickness Insurance): partial revision; legal minimum benefits (cash and medical care) improved, membership conditions for sickness funds relaxed; cost-sharing by patients increased, automatic adjustment of federal contributions to rising costs of medical care; inclusion of chiropractic treatment; introduction of the *tier garant* whereby the patient is billed for treatment, and subsequently reimbursed by the sickness fund; effective from 1.1.1965.

III Accident insurance

Total expenditure on Accident Insurance in 1979 in million SFR

		%
Medical treatment	230.1	16.2
Cash benefits and pensions	798.6	56.4
Administration	104.5	7.4
Reserve	248.6	17.6
Other (i.e. accident prevention)	34.5	2.4
Total expenditure	1 416.3	100.0
% of total social security I	8.0	
% of total social expenditure	4.5	
% of GDP	0.9	

Coverage

The Federal Compulsory Accident Insurance (*staatliche obligatorische Unfallversicherung*, SUV) provides benefits in the case of both occupational and non-occupational accidents and occupational diseases. However, its coverage is limited, and it is in fact only partly compulsory. Accident insurance is pure employee insurance. Persons employed in industry, trade and navigation (approx. two-thirds of all Swiss employees) are covered by federal law, whereas non-family members employed in agriculture are covered by cantonal law. Furthermore, the cantons of Ticino and Geneva provide an accident insurance scheme covering all employees. In addition, four other cantons (Appenzell AR, Appenzell IR, Thurgau and St. Gallen) have introduced compulsory coverage for poorly paid employees and two cantons (Freiburg and Geneva) provide compulsory accident insurance for school pupils and young people. Since 1 January 1983 all employees have been compulsorily covered.

Benefits

Federal compulsory accident insurance scheme benefits are provided on the same level for both occupational and non-occupational accidents and occupational diseases. Cash benefits are earnings-related up to a maximum annual income limit of 46,800 SFR The following benefits are granted under the scheme: medical care covering out-patient treatment, medicines, and travel expenses; sickness cash benefits, amounting to 80% of total earnings up to a limit of 120 SFR a day); and invalidity pensions, which in the case of total disablement amount to 70% of income during the year previous to the accident. SUV invalidity pensions may be combined with IV invalidity pensions (see above) but together they must not exceed the former salary. Survivors' pensions for dependants amount to 15% for orphans who have lost one parent, 25% for full orphans and 30% for the surviving spouse, calculated on the basis of the deceased's most recent salary. Finally, the funeral grant amounts to a lump sum payment of 500 SFR.

Financing

Federal compulsory accident insurance pensions are financed on a capital accumulation basis, whereas medical services and lump sum cash benefits are financed on a pay-as-you-go basis. The insured person pays the whole cost of insurance in the case of non-occupational accidents, which amounts to 12‰ and 8‰ of total earnings for men and women respectively up to the above-mentioned maximum. In the case of occupational accidents the employer pays the whole cost of insurance. Contribution rates vary with the degree of risk involved in the undertaking. Altogether there are 126 categories of risk covering all occupations. The federal compulsory accident insurance scheme is not subsidized.

Administration

The federal compulsory accident insurance scheme is administered by the Swiss Accident Insurance Institute (*Schweizerische Unfallversicherungsanstalt*, SUVA). It is an autonomous public institution operating under the general supervision of the *Bundesrat.*

Core laws

26.10.1890
Artikel 34 bis der Bundesverfassung (Art. 34/2 of the Federal Constitution): state empowered to introduce sickness and accident insurance.

13.6.1911
Kranken- und Unfallversicherungsgesetz, KUVG (Federal Sickness and Accident Insurance Law): established compulsory coverage for employees in industry and trade; effective from 1.1.1918 in the case of accident insurance.

3.10.1951
Bundesgesetz über die Förderung der Landwirtschaft und die Erhaltung des Bauernstandes (Federal Law on the Support of Agriculture and Maintenance of Agricultural Employment Levels): established compulsory coverage for employees, excluding family workers in agriculture; organization by cantons; effective from 1.1.1955.

27.9.1973
Änderung des Bundesgesetzes über die Kranken- und Unfallversicherung (Amendment to 1911 Sickness and Accident Insurance Law): income ceiling for contributions and benefits raised; effective from 1.1.1974.

20.3.1981
Unfallversicherungsgesetz, UVG (Federal Accident Insurance Law): compulsory coverage extended to all employees; voluntary coverage available for the self-employed; effective from 1.1.1983.

IV Unemployment insurance

Due to the low number of unemployed, unemployment insurance is not of major importance in Switzerland. However, foreign seasonal employees and frontier commuters are not taken into consideration, and cannot be found in unemployment statistics.

Total expenditure on Unemployment in 1979 in million SFR

		%
Cash benefits	188.8	90.1
Administration costs	20.7	9.8
Total expenditure	209.5	100.0
% of total social security I	1.2	
% of total social expenditure	0.7	
% of GDP	0.1	

Coverage

Unemployment insurance is controlled by the state in accordance with article 34 novies of the federal constitution which provides for compulsory coverage on national level for all employees. The self-employed may insure themselves in certain circumstances. Previously, only cantons were empowered to introduce compulsory coverage for certain income and professional groups. However, since 25 June 1982, the [federal] government decides matters of compulsory coverage.

Benefits

Unemployment benefits are payable on a daily basis. Since 1 January 1984, single persons have received 70% of their most recent gross income, and persons with maintenance obligations have received 80%, payable for up to 250 days in a calendar year. The upper limit of calculable income amounts to 3,900 SFR. The qualifying condition for benefit is six months of employment with insurance contributions during the last two years.

Financing

Employees and employers pay contributions of 0.5% of the employees' gross earnings up to a maximum of 5,800 SFR a month. Further sources of revenue are interests from central compensation funds and in extraordinary cases federal and cantonal low-interest loans.

Administration

Payment of unemployment benefit is made through unemployment funds administered by trade unions, cantons, communes, individual firms or employer associations. Since 1945 unemployment funds have lost their legal and financial independence, and the collection of contributions is supervised by the Federal Office of Social Insurance (*Bundesamt für Sozialversicherung*, BSV) and implemented by the AHV compensation funds. All contributions are channelled into a central compensation fund supervised by the Federal Office on Industry, Trade and Labour (*Bundesanstalt für Industrie, Gewerbe und Arbeit*).

Core laws

17.10.1924
Bundesgesetz über die Beitragsleistungen an die Arbeitslosenversicherung (Federal Law on Subsidies to Unemployment Insurance): subsidies to autonomous unemployment funds.

6.7.1947
Artikel 34 der Bundesverfassung (Art. 34 of the Federal Constitution): state empowered to introduce unemployment insurance and unemployment assistance.

22.6.1951
Arbeitslosenversicherungsgesetz ALVG (Unemployment Insurance Law): cantons empowered to make unemployment insurance compulsory; effective from 1.1.1952.

13.6.1976
Annahme des neuen Verfassungsartikels 34 novies der Bundesverfassung (New Art. 34/9 of the Federal Constitution): state empowered to make unemployment insurance compulsory at federal level.

1.4.1977
Arbeitslosenunterstützung (Unemployment Provision): transitional unemployment provision until the new unemployment insurance law (*Arbeitslosenversicherungsgesetz*, ALVG) comes into force and will establish compulsory insurance and abolish the legal and financial independence of unemployment funds.

25.6.1982
Bundesgesetz über die obligatorische Arbeitslosenversicherung und die Insolvenzentschädigung (Federal Law on Compulsory Unemployment Insurance): introduced compulsory insurance for all employees; effective from 1.1.1984.

V Families and children

Total expenditure 1979 in million SFR

		%
Federal family allowances:	60.2	14.3
- agricultural workers	11.6	
- small farmers	46.9	
- administration	1.7	
Cantonal family allowances	361.8	85.7
Total family allowances	422.0	100.0
% of total social security I	2.4	
% of total social expenditure	1.3	
% of GDP	0.3	

Coverage

The state is empowered to legislate in the field of family compensation funds and may make membership compulsory for all, or for individual sections of the population.

However, these federal powers have only been used with regard to agricultural workers. Non-agricultural employees and the self-employed in non-agricultural professions below a certain income ceiling are covered by cantonal regulations. There are special arrangements for public employees (for federal employees and partly for cantonal and communal employees). Child allowances are payable for children up to the age of 16, and up to the age of 20 where children are incapable of gainful employment due to illness or invalidity. Children in full-time education receive children's allowances up to the age of 25. Small self-employed farmers with a maximum income of 22,000 SFR, plus a further 3,000 SFR for each child, qualify for benefits as above. Some cantons (Bern, Freiburg, Neuenburg, St. Gallen, Tessin, Waadt and Wallis) pay child allowances to agricultural employees and small farmers which are higher than the respective federal minimum. In general, the children of foreigners have the same rights as Swiss citizens.

Benefits

Agricultural employees and small self-employed farmers are entitled to household (for married couples) and child allowances, independent of income. According to the last revision of Federal law from 14.12.1979, household allowances amount to 100 SFR a month, child allowances to 60 SFR a month (in mountainous areas: 70 SFR) with a higher rate for the third and any subsequent children (70 SFR and 80 SFR respectively).

Cantonal regulations

Payment of family allowances to non-agricultural employees and self-employed below a certain income ceiling was introduced in all cantons at the beginning of 1966. Benefits consist of child allowances and in some cantons birth grants (Geneva, Freiburg, Schwyz and Waadt), and study allowances (Geneva, Freiburg, Neuenburg, Waadt and Wallis). Child allowances vary between 60 SFR and 90 SFR per child per month according to canton. Some cantons offer higher rates depending on the number of children. The age limit according to canton is 15-18 years, and children incapable of gainful employment in addition to those in education, receive children's allowances up to the age of 20. The birth grant consists of a lump-sum payment and ranges from 500 SFR in Geneva to 200 SFR in Schwyz or Waadt. Study allowances (*Ausbildungszulagen*) are awarded between the ages of 15-25 according to canton, and range from 80 SFR to 120 SFR per month per child (for study grants, see under Education).

Financing

The federal programme is financed through agricultural employer's contributions (2% of remuneration in cash and kind). If costs cannot be covered, the federal (two-thirds) and cantonal (one-third) governments share the residual cost. Communes may also be called upon to contribute. The cantonal programmes are financed through employee's contributions (usually 1-3% of payroll).

Administration

The AHV compensation funds administer and pay the federal family allowances. Cantonal family allowances are administered and paid by cantonal family compensation funds (*Familienausgleichskassen*) which consist of private and public funds. There are some 800 approved private family compensations funds.

Core laws

25.11.1945
Artikel 34 quinquies der Bundesverfassung (Art. 34 quinques of the Federal Constitution): state empowered to legislate on family compensation funds.

20.6.1952
Familienzulagen für die Landwirtschaft (Federal Law on Family Allowances for Agricultural Workers and Mountain Farmers): implementation of 1945 law. Payment of child and household allowances to agricultural workers, small farmers and fishermen. Effective from 1.1.1953.

Since 1966 cantonal laws have been implemented in all cantons for family allowances to non-agricultural employees.

VI Income compensation/Military insurance

Total expenditure on Income Compensation 1979 in million SFR

		%
Compensation	507.3	99.7
Administration	1.3	0.3
Total expenditure	508.6	100.0
% of total social security I	2.9	
% of total social expenditure	1.6	
% of GDP	0.3	

Total expenditure on Military Insurance in million SFR

		%
Invalidity and survivors' pensions	100.3	60.2
Cash benefits and medical care	57.1	34.3
Administration	9.2	5.5
Total expenditure	166.6	100.0
% of total social security I	0.9	
% of total social expenditure	0.5	
% of GDP	0.1	

Coverage

Income Compensation (*Erwerbsersatzordnung*, EO) and Military Insurance (*Militärversicherung*, MV) are brànches of social insurance and related to the specific structure of the Swiss army. All Swiss male citizens are liable to military service between the ages of 20 and 60. The EO compensates loss of income for all those doing military service and civil defence. The MV consists of public provisions for sickness and accidents of persons serving the military (and for their dependents).

Benefits

EO benefits consist of income compensation for married couples (25-75% of previous earned income with an upper and lower limit), compensation for single persons (12-35%) and the non-employed such as child and assistance allowances (*Unterstützungszulagen*). EO benefits are calculated as a percentage of previous income, up to a maximum daily amount of 120 SFR (1 January 1982). For a married couple this percentage amounts to 75% (but at least 25% and not more than 75% of the maximum daily amount); for a single person 35% of previous income (but at least 12% and not more than 35% of the daily maximum); non-employed persons receive the minimum EO benefit for employed; child allowances amount to 9% of the maximum amount, dependants' allowances to 18%.

MV benefits are equal to those of the KUVG. They consist of sickness cash benefits, medical care, invalidity pensions, funeral grants, and survivors' pensions.

Financing

The EO scheme is financed through employees' and employers' contributions. Both pay 0.3% of gross earnings to AHV funds. The self-employed pay 0.6% when they earn 25,200 SFR or more a year. Below this level there is a descending contribution scale. The non-employed pay between 6 SFR and 600 SFR a year depending on assets. There are no public subsidies.

The MV scheme is financed entirely out of general revenues, and has no reserve fund.

Administration

The EO is administered by the AHV compensation funds in collaboration with the pay sergeant of the military units or civil defence organizations. The administrative organization is supervised by the *Bundesrat* and a committee responsible for the EO. The MV is administered by a department of the Helvetian Ministry of Defence.

Core laws

Income compensation:

6.7.1947
Artikel 34 ter der Bundesverfassung (Art. 34/3 of the Federal Constitution): state empowered to provide adequate compensation for loss of earnings as a result of military service.

25.9.1952
Bundesgesetz für die Erwerbsausfallentschädigung an Wehrpflichtige (Federal Law on

Compensation of Loss of Earnings for Compulsory Military Service): effective from 1953.

24.5.1959
Artikel 22 bis der Bundesverfassung (Art. 22/2 of the Federal Constitution): income compensation extended to civil defence; improvement of benefits.

3.10.1975
Bundesgesetz über die Erwerbsersatzordnung für Wehr- und Zivilschutzpflichtige, EOG (Federal Law on Compensation for Loss of Earnings for Compulsory Military Service and Civil Defence): implementation of Art. 22/2 of the federal constitution of 24.5.1959; income compensation extended to civil defence; effective from 1.1.1976.

Military insurance:

1874
Artikel 18 Abs. 2 der Bundesverfassung (Art. 18, Section 2 of the Federal Constitution): compulsory military service and compulsory federal assistance in the case of illness, accident or death for the conscript and his survivors.

28.6.1901
Bundesgesetz betreffend die Versicherung von Militärpersonen gegen Unfall und Krankheit (Federal Law on Insurance of Military Personnel against Accident and Sickness): provision for accident and sickness insurance for military personnel; effective from 1.1.1902.

20.9.1949
Bundesgesetz über die Militärversicherung (Federal Military Insurance Law): improved benefits for sickness and accident insurance for military personnel; effective from 1.1.1950.

Since 1950 various smaller amendments.

VII Social security for civil servants

There are no special regulations covering civil servants in Switzerland, with the exception of family allowances where civil servants receive higher rates. The special occupational funds for civil servants (e.g. pension funds for teachers, Swiss railway or postal service employees) are equivalent to the occupational pension funds in the private sector.

VIII Social assistance and services

Total expenditure in 1979 in million SFR

	State	Cantons	Communes	Total
Social Assistance	4.2	616.4	697.3	1 317.9
Percentages	0.3	46.8	52.9	100.0
% of total social security				7.4
% of total social expenditure				4.2
% of GDP				0.8

Coverage

Social assistance (*Soziale Fürsorge*) is mainly the responsibility of communes, and is covered by cantonal law. Federal regulations only cover special areas (e.g. welfare for Swiss citizens working abroad). Responsibility for welfare benefits has gradually shifted from the home commune to the commune of residence as embodied in a 1960 concordat, agreed upon by all cantons. Responsibility for social assistance has now been regulated by a 1977 federal law which institutionalized the residence principle. However, this law does not affect cantonal competency for social assistance. Social assistance is asubsidiary matter, and claims against a social insurance carrier and close relatives must have been exhausted before social assistance may be applied for. The introduction and expansion of social insurance has reduced the importance of social assistance, and special social welfare institutions (e.g. invalidity, alcoholism, drug addiction) have replaced general social assistance to a large extent.

Benefits

Social assistance aims to ensure a reasonable standard of living and is closely linked to both guardianship (*Vormundschaft*) and public health. Social assistance covers unemployment assistance and finances programmes for the prevention of alcoholism, various institutions such as children's homes, and the care and burial of the poor. A legal right to benefit exists only in principle and is not a right to a specific benefit. Some cantonal laws even reject the notion of a legal right. Benefits are in cash and kind (e.g. emergency accommodation for the homeless or the care of neglected children).

Financing and administration

Social assistance benefits are mainly financed through tax revenue raised by cantons and communes. The communes administer social assistance.

Core laws

29.5.1874
Artikel 48 der Bundesverfassung (Art. 48 of the Federal Constitution): social assistance based on place of residence.

22.6.1875
Bundesgesetz über die Verpflegung Kranker anderer Kantone (Federal Law on Social Assistance for the Sick): regulation of food for the sick and the burial of the poor from other cantons.

26.11.1914
Oltener Vereinbarung (Oltener Agreement): agreement concerning general assistance in the case of hardship according to place of residence during the European War; social assistance during the war, where upon the canton of residence and home canton share the costs for assistance (not all cantons are members of this agreement).

27.11.1916
Erstes Konkordat über die Fürsorge nach dem Wohnortprinzip (First Concordat on Social Assistance by Place of Residence): implementation of place of residence principle (not all cantons are members).

15.6.1923
Zweites Konkordat über die Verpflegung Kranker anderer Kantone (Second Concordat on Social Assistance by Place of Residence): canton of residence partially freed from obligation to cover cost of social assistance (not all cantons part of concordat).

6.6.1937
Drittes Konkordat über die Verpflegung Kranker anderer Kantone (Third Concordat on Social Assistance by Place of Residence): canton of residence increasingly freed from obligation to cover cost of social assistance.

16.12.1960
Viertes Konkordat über die Verpflegung Kranker anderer Kantone (Fourth Concordat on Social Assistance by Place of Residence): administrative simplification of third concordat; in 1966 all cantons members of the concordat; effective from 1.7.1961.

7.12.1975
New Art. 48 of the Federal Constitution: social assistance based on place of residence principle.

24.6.1977
Bundesgesetz über die Zuständigkeit für die Unterstützung Bedürftiger (Federal Law on Legal Responsibility for Support of the Needy): law implementing Art. 48; effective from 1.1.1978.

IX Health

Total expenditure 1979 in million SFR

		%
Federal government	33.9	0.7
Cantons	3 394.9	70.0
Communes	1 419.5	29.3
Total expenditure	4 848.3	100.0
% of GDP	3.0	
% of total social expenditure	15.3	

The Public Health system provides the following services: hospitals, medical and non-medical home care, infant care, the treatment and prevention of drug and alcohol addiction, and food hygiene. Public or cantonal health officers are responsible for carrying out measures against infectious diseases. In larger cantons these measures are co-ordinated by Public Health Offices.

Hospitals are generally run by cantons and communes (approx. 60% of beds), associations, foundations and private companies in the form of joint-stock companies. The aim of home medical care, home care and infant care is to avoid or shorten hospitalization. Obstetrics, child and maternity welfare constitute special areas. Home nurses, communal and baby nurses are employed in these areas supported by the Swiss Red Cross. Home care is usually the responsibility of private non-profit organizations, and to a smaller degree that of public organizations such as reformist, catholic and parity parishes in addition to political communes.

Capital expenditure on cantonal and communal hospitals is financed by the federal government, the cantons, and the communes, cantons contributing the largest share. Hospital running costs are financed by sickness insurance (approx. 54%) and deficits are mainly covered by cantons and communes (approx. 40%). Home care is financed by cantonal and communal subsidies (approx. 50%), voluntary insurance payments (approx. 25%), and by patient fees (approx. 25%).

Core laws

Almost exclusively cantonal legislation.

Federal Laws:

19.12.1877
(Federal Law on Mobility of Medical Personnel in Switzerland): national recognition of the medical diploma.

8.12.1905
Bundesgesetz betreffend den Verkehr mit Lebensmitteln und Gebrauchsgegenständen (Federal Law on Handling of Food and Articles of Daily Use).

13.6.1928
Bundesgesetz betreffend Massnahmen gegen die Tuberkolose (Federal Tuberculosis Prevention Law).

3.10.1951
Bundesgesetz über die Betäubungsmittel (Federal Narcotics Law).

18.12.1970
Bundesgesetz betreffend Massnahmen gegen gemeingefährliche Epidemien (Federal Law on Prevention of Infections Diseases).

8.10.1971
Bundesgesetz betreffend Massnahmen gegen die Verunreinigung von Gewässern (Federal Water Pollution Law).

X Education

Total Education expenditure in 1979 in million SFR
(consolidated figures)

	State	Cantons	Communes	Total	%
Primary schools	52.8	2 010.6	2 453.3	4 516.7	51.8
Vocational training	234.5	588.9	240.9	1 064.3	12.2
Middle schools	50.3	982.8	61.4	1 094.5	12.6
Universities	768.4	646.6	3.8	1 418.8	16.3
Research	405.6	4.3	0.1	410.0	4.7
Other	6.7	161.8	48.2	216.7	2.4
Total expenditure	1 518.3	4 395.0	2 807.7	8 721.0	100.0
Percentages	17.4	50.4	32.2		100.0

1. Constitutional framework and organizational structure

The concept of federalism is strongest in the field of education. With the exception of vocational training, education is a cantonal and communal matter. In the 1848 constitution the cantons were given responsibility for education and the state was only empowered to found a university and a polytechnic (*Eidgenössische Technische Hochschule Zürich* ETH, *Erste Polytechnische Universität Lausanne* Epul). Even after the total revision of the federal constitution in 1874 the cantons remained responsible for education. Cantonal autonomy in education has since been somewhat restricted by a series of constitutional provisions and subsequent federal legislation (e.g. the regulation covering a standardized final examination (*Maturität*). Federal intervention, however, is mainly in the financial field. Vocational training is mainly organized on a federal basis and comes under federal jurisdiction. However, cantons do not function solely as executive organs. They organize the more comprehensive vocational training programmes and schools. This decentralization has led to a great diversity between cantons in essential elements such as the duration and form of compulsory education, type and duration of educational courses, qualifications etc. As a result of growing internal migration, cantons were forced to seek a greater degree of coordination by means of concordats, (e.g. the concordat on school coordination of 29 October 1970, the inter-cantonal centre for educational aids in Luzern or in the field of vocational training (*Deutschschweiz, Westschweiz/Tessin*). Within the framework of cantonal autonomy in educational matters some organizational responsibility is delegated to the communes, but this is normally restricted to primary schooling and is at the discretion of the canton.

2. Schooltypes and school system

On account of the variety of cantonal regulations this section can only deal with those aspects of schooling which the different cantons have in common. A systematic approach to the organization of Swiss schools can be made according to institutional criteria as well as length of schooling.

- Nursery School (*Kindergarten*) duration from one to two years, not compulsory, cantons have no legal obligation to provide nursery schooling.
- Primary school (*Primarschule*) the responsibility of the cantons. It lasts from the first to the fourth, fifth or sixth schoolyear according to canton.
- The secondary stage I includes *Abschlussklassen, Real- and Sekundarschulen* and occasionally *Pro-Gymnasien*. They are also the responsibility of the canton. Duration is from the fifth or sixth to the eighth or ninth schoolyear.
- *Gymnasien* and other *Höhere Mittelschulen* like *Lehrerseminarien, Verkehrs- und Höhere Handelsschulen* and vocational training last from the tenth schoolyear to final examination (*Maturität, Patent, Diplom, Lehrabschlusszeugnis*).
- Tertiary stage vocational training (matura or diploma required), and vocational continuation courses.
- University education.

Financing

Education is financed by cantonal subsidies to the communes and communal contributions towards the financing of cantonal institutions. Vocational training is financed by federal subsidies, which are only granted when the canton makes an adequate contribution. Furthermore, the state lends financial support to cantonal universities. Those cantons without universities pay contributions to those that have.

3. Grants

Grants are awarded by the cantons, the federal government, and private organizations; each canton has its own grant system, whereby federal contributions towards cantonal grant costs are provided for. Depending on the financial situation of the canton concerned, the state subsidizes grants awarded by the cantons, communes or private organizations by 30%, 40% or 50%. In 1975 the cantons awarded approx. 137 million SFR (incl. 37 million SFR in federal contributions) for grants while 17 million SFR were paid in the form of loans. In 1975 grants and loans amounted to approximately 4.5% of total education expenditure. In 1979 the average grant amounted to 4,679 SFR per year, and approximately 25% of Swiss students received a grant. Direct federal grants are only awarded to students at the federal technical universities (ETH Zürich and Epul Lausanne) and to foreign students in Switzerland.

Core laws

1848
Art. 22 of the Federal Constitution: education falls within the jurisdiction of the cantons; in the field of higher education the state is empowered to introduce at least one university and one polytechnic (ETH Zürich, Epul Lausanne).

29.5.1874
Art. 27 of the Federal Constitution: regulation of competences between the state and the cantons regarding education.

23.11.1902
Art. 27/2 of the Federal Constitution: state primary school subsidies for the cantons.

25.6.1903
Bundesgesetz über Subventionen im Primarschulbereich (Federal Law on Public Primary School Subsidies): implementation law to Art. 27/2.

8.12.1963
Art. 27/4 of the Federal Constitution: constitutional regulation on study-grants.

19.3.1965
Bundesgesetz über die Gewährung von Beiträgen an die Aufwendungen der Kantone für Stipendien (Federal Law on State Subsidies to Cantonal Study-Grants): revision 23.12.1971; provided federal subsidies to cantonal grants, and grants made by private organizations; implementation law to Art. 27/4.

Vocational training:

1908
Artikel 34 ter Abs. 1 litt. g Bundesverfassung (Art. 34/3 Section 1 litt. g. of the Federal Constitution): Federal government empowered to provide for vocational training.

20.3.1963, 5.10.1967, 9.3.1972
Various federal laws on vocational training: detailed the division of competences between state and cantons.

19.4.1978
Berufsbildungsgesetz (Vocational Training Law): greater provision for state career guidance and vocational training in industry, trade commerce, agriculture and domestic services; effective from 1.1.1980.

XI Housing

Total Housing expenditure 1979 in million SFR
(consolidated figures)

	State	Canton	Communes	Total
Public subsidies for housing construction	49.3	114.0	95.0	258.3
Percentages	19.1	44.1	36.8	100.0
% of GDP		0.2		
% of total social expenditure		0.8		

Housing legislation is constitutionally a federal matter. The federal constitution determines the responsibility for publicly subsidized housing construction and Art. 34 septies par. 2 covers the legal protection of tenants. Public subsidies for housing construction are regulated by the 1974 Promotion of Housing Construction and Property Law (*Wohnbau- und Eigentumsförderungsgesetz*). Provisions within the WEG include subsidies for development, whereby the state mediates and guarantees loans for land development and housing construction (up to 100% of the subsidized cost of installation); in addition, the state awards applicants contributions towards payment on the interest for development loans.

The state provides low-priced housing and has a carefully directed housing policy for low income groups. The state provides financial support by mediating and guaranteeing mortgages of up to 90% of approved installation costs and by repayable loans to tenants and owners (primary reduction) as well as a (*fonds perdu*) contribution towards additional reduction in housing costs (additional reduction).

The state extends security, in the form of loans and capital, to community housing projects. It additionally acquires land, carries out research on housing demand and finances building projects.

A special area of publicly assisted housing construction is provided for by a federal law for the improvement of housing in mountain regions. In particular, this law sets out to aid the restoration of housing which has been condemned on health grounds by the surveyor's office. Under certain circumstances this law may also be applied to new housing projects.

Tenant's rights are safeguarded by rent tribunals where tenants and landlords are equally represented. In particular, the federal resolution (*Bundesbeschluss*), of 7.7.1977 benefits the tenant with regard to extra costs, improved protection against unwarranted notice to quit and, under certain circumstances, the right to have rents reduced.

Financing

These areas are financed by federal subsidies in the form of contributions a *fonds perdu* of up to 25% of approved building costs and in difficult cases of up to 37.5% where there is an absolute maximum level. Federal subsidies presuppose cantonal participation to at least the same degree and cantons may require communes to share the cost of these subsidies. There are no housing allowances.

Core laws

20.3.1970
Federal Law on the Improvement of Housing Conditions in Mountain Areas.

5.3.1972
Art. 34/6, part 1: state undertakes to provide especially economic housing and housing property.

5.3.1972
Art. 34/7, part 2: tenant's rights protected and regulated by the state.

4.10.1974
Wohnbau- und Eigentumsförderungsgesetz (Law on Housing Construction and Private Housing): financial subsidies by the state, in particular, towards loans and guaranteeing credit.

7.7.1977
Federal Resolution on the Abuse of Tenant's Rights, and Protection against Unwarranted Notice to Quit.

Bibliography

Contents

I General contributions

1.1 History of social policy

HAUSER, Albert: Schweizerische Wirtschafts- und Sozialgeschichte (Swiss Economic and Social History). Zürich and Stuttgart, 1961, 400 p. Historical description of social and economic aspects of Swiss history since the formation of the 'Eidgenossenschaft'.

HEINSER, Felix: Die Entstehung des Verfassungsartikels 34 bis. Ein Beitrag zur Geschichte der Sozialversicherung in der Schweiz (The Emergence of the Article 34 bis of the Swiss Constitution. A Contribution to the History of Social Insurance in Switzerland). Zürich, 1976,160 p. Description and analysis of the first step towards a welfare state, the constitutional regulation on sickness and accident insurance.

KÖHLER, P.A., ZACHER, H.F., HESSE, P.H.: Un siècle de sécurité sociale (A Century of Social Security). Lausanne, 1984, 648 p. A comparative reference for the development of social security in Europe: Federal Republic of Germany, France, Great Britain, Austria, Switzerland.

MAURER, Albert: Geschichte des schweizerischen Sozialversicherungsrechts (The History of Swiss Social Insurance Law). Berlin, 1981, 103 p. Description of the development of social insurance law from an institutional viewpoint.

SOMMER, Jürg H.: Das Ringen um die soziale Sicherheit in der Schweiz (The Battle over Social Security in Switzerland). Diessenhofen, 1978, 766 p. Historical analysis of Swiss social insurance from a political decision making perspective.

TSCHUDI, Hans-Peter: '100 Jahre Sozialversicherungen (100 Years of social insurance)'. *Gewerkschaftliche Rundschau*, No. 10, 1981, pp. 281-289. Description of the main steps of the development of social insurance.

1.2 Social science interpretations, evaluations and analyses (see also 1.3)

ACKERMANN, Walter: Soziale Sicherung in der Industriegesellschaft - Tendenzen und Konsequenzen (Social Security in Industrial Society - Tendencies and Consequences). Bern, 1980, 309 p.

BINSWANGER, Peter: 'Staatliche und private Sozialversicherung (State and private social insurance)'. *In* FAGANINI, Hans-Peter, WILI, Hans (eds): Wohlfahrtsstaat, Anspruch und Wirklichkeit (Welfare State, Claims and Reality). Olten and Freiburg, 1978, pp. 148-159. Analyzes the terms 'public/private social insurance' and presents proposals for an integrated system.

BORNER, Silvio: 'Die soziale Sicherheit in der Schweiz, Konzeptionelle Probleme und Alternativen aus volkswirtschaftlicher Sicht (Social security in Switzerland. Conceptional problems and alternatives from the economic perspective)'. *Wirtschaft und Recht*, No. 3, 1979, pp. 165-177. Description of the problems of the social security system from an economic perspective. Proposes alternative ways of achieving increased security and equality with less expenditure.

BUNDESAMT FÜR SOZIALVERSICHERUNG: Bericht über versicherungstechnische, finanzielle und volkswirtschaftliche Aspekte der Sozialen Sicherheit in der Schweiz (Report on the Technical, Financial and Economic Aspects of Swiss Social Security). Bern, 1982, 199 p. Description of the development of social security, and the financial factors determing its growth, together with some comments on the future development of social insurance policy.

FAGANINI, Hans-Peter, WILI, Hans (eds): Wohlfahrtsstaat, Anspruch und Wirklichkeit (Welfare State, Claims and Reality). Olten and Freiburg, 1978, 310 p. A welfare state reader. Includes old and new dimensions of the welfare state, overdependence on the welfare state, and changes in state ideology and perspectives.

GIROD, Roger, DE LAUBIER, Patrick (eds): La politique sociale dans les pays occidentaux, 1945-1980 (The Social Policy of the Western Countries). Lausanne, 1982, 134 p. Comparative analysis of the primacies of social activities in Belgium, Italy, Sweden, USA and Switzerland.

HARTMANN, Karl: Subsidiarität und Föderalismus in der schweizerischen Sozialpolitik (Subsidiarity and Federalism in Swiss Social Policy). Unpublished dissertation, Winterthur, 1971, 193 p. Historical analysis of old age provisions and sickness insurance.

PUTTNER, Helmut: Wohlfahrtsstaat und Föderalismus in der Schweiz (Welfare State and Federalism in Switzerland). Unpublished dissertation, Bamberg, 1983, 210 p. Historical analysis of the distribution of social welfare competences between state and cantons from the beginning of the Swiss welfare state.

REY, Jean-Noel: Trop d'état? (Too Much State?) Lausanne, 1983, 144 p. Pamphlet on the crisis of social welfare and the question of *Too much state?* in social security.

TSCHUDI, H-P.: 'Tendenzen und Zielsetzungen der schweizerischen Sozialpolitik (Tendencies and aims of Swiss social policy)'. *Gewerkschaftliche Rundschau*, No. 10, 1978, pp. 262-273. Discusses how Swiss welfare state has grown out of the Constitution. Describes some characteristics of the Swiss model and makes important points regarding the future of social insurance.

WITTMANN, Walter: 'Möglichkeiten und Grenzen des Sozialstaats (The potential and limits of the social state)'. *Schweizerische Zeitschrift für Gemeinnützigkeit*, No. 5, 1977, pp. 173-180.

WITTMANN, W.: Bundesfinanzen und Sozialstaat (State Finance and the Welfare State). Diessenhofen, 1978, 138 p. Contributions on the the fiscal and social policy of the state.

1.3 Institutional surveys

BANDI, Till: Soziale Sicherung in der Schweiz - institutionelle Grundlagen, volkswirtschaftliche Probleme (Social Security in Switzerland - Institutional Basis, Economic Problems). Diessenhofen, 1982, 353 p. Institutional and economic analysis of the Swiss welfare state with a discussion of alternatives and their consequences.

PAETZOLD, Veronika: Die Sozialversicherung in der Schweiz (Social Insurance in Switzerland). Zürich, 1978, 65 p. An institutional synopsis of Swiss social security.

SAXER, Arnold: Die soziale Sicherheit in der Schweiz (Social Security in Switzerland), 4th ed. Bern, 1977, 285 p. Description of the emergence, structure and present position of all branches of social security.

STÖCKLI, Jakob.: Sozialpaket Schweiz (Switzerland's Social Package). Bern and Stuttgart, 1982, 120 p. A guide to Swiss social security and social insurance.

1.4 Social insurance law and social law

BIGLER-EGGENBERGER, Margrith: Soziale Sicherung der Frau (Women's Social Security). Bern, 1979, 248 p. Legal description and evaluation of women's social security with suggestions for reform.

GREBER, Pierre-Yves: Droit suisse de la sécurité sociale (Swiss Social Security Law). Lausanne, 1982, 572 p. Analysis of the term 'social security' and a description of the institutional structure of Swiss social security schemes.

DE LAUBIER, Patrick, FRAGNIÈRE, Jean-Pierre (eds): Droit et politique sociale (Law and Social Policy). Lausanne, 1982, 116 p. Reader offering analyses of the legal basis of social policy with emphasis on social insurance.

MAURER, A.: Schweizerisches Sozialversicherungsrecht (Swiss Social Insurance Law), Vol. I. Bern, 1979, 540 p. This first volume contains an examination of the fundamental elements of social insurance law, together with a legal analysis ofthe social security system.

MAURER, A.: Schweizerisches Sozialversicherungsrecht (Swiss Social Insurance Law), Vol. II. Bern, 1981, 698 p. The specialized volume contains an institutional description of all branches of the social security system.

SCHWEINGRUBER, Edwin: Sozialgesetzgebung in der Schweiz (Social Law in Switzerland), 2nd ed. Zürich, 1977, 312 p. Deals with basic social policy questions, i.e. labour law, etc.

SCHWEIZERISCHE GESELLSCHAFT FÜR VERSICHERUNGSRECHT: Bericht und Entwurf zu einem Allgemeinen Teil der Sozialversicherung (Report and Suggestions on a General Part of Social Insurance). Bern, 1984. Suggestions for a better co-ordination in social insurance.

TSCHUDI, H-P.: 'Die verfassungsrechtlichen Grundlagen der Sozialversicherung (The constitutional basis of social insurance)'. *Schweizerische Zeitschrift für Sozialversicherung*, No. 2, 1979, pp. 81-104. An analysis of the different social insurance regulations in the Swiss Constitution.

1.5 Sources of statistics or institutional regulations

BUNDESAMT FÜR SOZIALVERSICHERUNG: Statistik über die Krankenversicherung (Sickness Insurance Statistics). Bern, published annually. Data on administration, contributions, benefits, subsidies and clienteles.

BUNDESAMT FÜR SOZIALVERSICHERUNG: Statistik über die Krankenversicherung. Vom Bund anerkannte Versicherungsträger 1966-1976 (Sickness Insurance Statistics. By State Approved Carriers, 1966-1976). Bern, 1978. Data on sickness funds in ten-year time series.

BUNDESAMT FÜR SOZIALVERSICHERUNG: Zahlenspiegel der sozialen Sicherheit in der Schweiz (Swiss Social Security in Figures). Bern, 1983. Provides time series data on social insurance, administration, benefits, financing and clienteles (28 tables).

EIDGENÖSSISCHES STATISTISCHES AMT: Statistisches Jahrbuch der Schweiz (Statistical Yearbook of Switzerland). Bern, published annually. Official data collection containing, among other things, data on the welfare state.

EIDGENÖSSISCHES STATISTISCHES AMT: Öffentliche Finanzen der Schweiz (Public Finances of Switzerland). Bern, published annually. Official data collection on the public household.

EIDGENÖSSISCHES STATISTISCHES AMT: Revidierte Reihen der Nationalen Buchhaltung 1948-1976 (Revised Series of National Accounting 1948-1976). Bern, 1977, 97 p. Time series on public finances since the end of World War II.

1.6 Annual bibliographies

'Bibliographie der schweizerischen Sozialversicherung (Bibliography of Swiss social insurance)'. *Swiss Journal of Social Insurance*. Published annually. Collection of new books and essays on social policy.

BUNDESAMT FÜR SOZIALVERSICHERUNG: Sozialversicherung der Schweiz (Social Insurance in Switzerland). A short overview about data on social insurance.

II Single programmes or aspects

2.1 Pensions (see also 1.3)

BERICHT DER KOMMISSION FÜR ALTERSFRAGEN: Die Altersfragen in der Schweiz (Old Age Problems in Switzerland) Bern, 1979, 434 p. Proposals for a new Swiss pension-policy.

BORNER, Silvio., SOMMER, Jürg H.: Die AHV als Spielball von Experten und Interessen: Fallstudien zu den AHV-Revisionen 1948-1976 (Old Age and Survivors' Insurance as a Play-thing of Experts and Interests: Case Studies of AHV Revisions). St. Gallen, 59 p. Analysis of the different AHV revisions, and the determining role played by experts and interest groups in the changing of the law.

GILLIAND, Pierre: Rentiers AVS. Lausanne, 1983, 472 p. Report on the situation of old age pensioners in Switzerland; cf. the report of W. Schweizer.

GILLIAND, Pierre (ed.): Vieillir aujourd'hui et demain. (Growing Old Today and Tomorrow). Lausanne, 1982, 568 p. Considerations on the various aspects of old age.

HALLER, Mathias (ed.): Zur Verwirklichung der 2. Säule. Auftrag, Probleme, Perspektiven (Towards a Realization of the Second Pillar. Objectives, Problems, Perspectives). St. Gallen, 1981, 277 p. Reader on the occupational pension system.

JANSSEN, Martin C., MÜLLER, Heinz H.: Social Security in Switzerland. Provisions for Old Age and Survivors. Zürich, 1981, 30 p. Economic analysis of the Swiss pension system - redistributional effects and economic consequences of the three pillar system.

MÜLLER, Stefan: Die Entstehung und Entwicklung der AHV von 1945-1978 (The Emergence and Development of the AHV, 1945-1978). Freiburg (Schweiz), 1978, 184 p. Historical analysis of the AHV, particularly from the economic viewpoint.

SCHWEIZER, Wily: Die wirtschaftliche Lage der Rentner in der Schweiz (The Economic Situation of Pensioners in Switzerland). Bern and Stuttgart, 1980, 351 p. (Vol. I) and 298 p. (Vol. II -Statistics). Empirical study on the income and property situation of pensioners, their consumption and saving patterns, and problems of social integration, etc.

2.2 Health (see also 1.3)

AEBI, Hugo, FREY, Ulrich (eds): Schweizerische Gesundheitspolitik heute und morgen (Swiss Health Policy Today and Tomorrow). Bern, 1977, 99 p. Reader on health policy. Discusses the health system and cooperative federalism regarding health policy and education policy.

BOMBACH, Gottfried, KLEINEWEFERS, Henner, WEBER, Luc: Volkswirtschaftliche Probleme der Krankenversicherung (Economic Problems of Sickness Insurance). Zürich, 1979, 120 p.

ERNI, Toni: Die Entwicklung des schweizerischen Kranken- und Unfallversicherungswesens (The Development of Swiss Sickness and Accident Insurance). Freiburg (Schweiz), 1980, 212 p. Historical analysis of the institutional development of sickness and accident insurance.

FRAGNIÈRE, Jean-Pierre, GILLIAND, Pierre (eds): Santé et politique sociale (Health and Social Policy). Lausanne, 1982, 132 p. Analysis of the causes of increasing health system costs in Switzerland; contains reform proposals.

GYGI, Peter, HENNY, Heiner: Das schweizerische Gesundheitswesen (Swiss Health System), 2nd ed. Bern, 1977, 164 p. Institutional description of the Swiss health system.

HÄUSELMANN, Erich, PETERS, Matthias: Die Gesundheitsligen in der Schweiz (Health Societies in Switzerland). Schweizerisches Krankenhausinstitut, Aarau, 1984, 336 p. A presentation of societies and organizations operating between health insurance and self-help groups.

HAUSER, Heinz (ed.): Mehr Wettbewerb in der Krankenversicherung. (More Competition in Health Insurance). SGGP, Horgen, 1984, 103 p. Explanations of the reform proposals in Swiss health insurance.

JAHRBUCH DER NEUEN HELVETISCHEN GESELLSCHAFT: Patient: Gesundheitswesen? (Patient: health system?) Bern, 1980, 127 p. Contributions concerning the major problems of Swiss health policy.

KOCHER, Gerhard (ed.): Zukunftsaspekte unseres Gesundheitswesens (Future Aspects of our Health System). Zürich, 1973, 87 p. Reader on different aspects of the Swiss health system, e.g. future costs and needs, self-provision, etc.

KOCHER, G: Die Solidaritätsleistungen der schweizerischen Krankenkassen (The Solidarity Benefits of Swiss Sickness Funds). Zürich, 1979, 32 p.

LUTZ, Liselotte: Optimale Krankenversicherung. Möglichkeiten der Ausgestaltung und Realisierbarkeit in der Schweiz (Optimal Sickness Insurance. Chances of Realization in Switzerland). Unpublished dissertation, Zürich, 1978, 182 p. Presentation of a model for sickness insurance and discussion of its realization in Switzerland.

2.3 Unemployment (see also 1.3)

BOIS, Phillipe, GREBER, Pierre-Yves: Emploi et politique sociale (Employment and Social Policy). Lausanne, 1982, 272 p. Contributions dealing with employment and social policy in Switzerland.

BUNDESAMT FÜR KONJUNKTURFRAGEN: Die Arbeitsbeschaffungsprogramme 1975/76 (Employment Programmes 1975/76). Studie No. 3, Bern, 1980, 91 p. Study of the effectiveness of labour market programmes.

GREBER, Pierre-Yves, BOIS, Philippe (eds): Emploi et politique sociale (Employment and

Social Policy). Lausanne, 1982, 272 p. A reader which analyses labour market problems, and presents reform proposals.

2.4 Accidents (see also 1.3)

SCHWEIZERISCHE UNFALLVERSICHERUNGSANSTALT: Führer durch die obligatorische Unfallversicherung (Guide to Compulsory Accident Insurance). Zürich, 1979, last edition before the new KUVG became effective (1.1.1984).

2.5 Social assistance

THOMET, Werner: Das Konkordat über die wohnörtliche Unterstützung (The Residential Support Concordat). Bern, 1961, 115 p. Historical analysis with a description of the different concordats on social assistance.

THOMET, W.: Bundesgesetz vom 24. Juni 1977 über die Zuständigkeit für die Unterstützung Bedürftiger (Federal Law on the Responsibility for Support for the Needy). Bern, 1979, 175 p. Comment on the different articles of the federal law.

SCHWEIZERISCHE KONFERENZ FÜR ÖFFENTLICHE FÜRSORGE: Zeitschrift für öffentliche Fürsorge (Journal for Public Assistance). Zürich, published monthly. Contains essays on social assistance.

2.6 Family programmes

BUNDESAMT FÜR SOZIALVERSICHERUNG: Bericht über die Lage der Familie in der Schweiz (Report on the Situation of the Family in Switzerland). Bern, 1979, 202 p. Report giving an orientation on the structural, sociological and economic situation of the family and the different programmes for family benefits.

EIDGENÖSSISCHES DEPARTEMENT DES INNEREN: Familienpolitik in der Schweiz (Family Policy in Switzerland). Bern, 1982, 176 p. Report on the different aspects of family policy and possible new areas of state competence.

EIDGENÖSSISCHER VERBAND PRO FAMILIA (ed.): 50 Jahre Familienpolitik in der Schweiz (50 Years of Family Policy in Switzerland). Luzern, 1982, 33 p. Two essays on family policy with reference to the historical development and actual tasks of policy.

GILLIAND, Pierre (ed.): Familles en rupture. Pensions alimentaires et politique sociale (Broken Families. Alimony and Social Policy). Lausanne, 1984, 244 p. Analysis of the problems of families today in Switzerland, the political, economic and cultural context and possible solutions.

HELD, T., LEVY, R.: Die Stellung der Frau in Familie und Gesellschaft. Eine soziologische Untersuchung am Beispiel der Schweiz (Woman's Position in Family and Society. A Sociological study on the Example of Switzerland). Frauenfeld, Stuttgart, 1974, 378 p. An empir study of the status of women in the family and society.

LÜSCHER, K.K., RITTER, V., GROSS, P.: Early Child Care in Switzerland. New York, Paris, 1973, 122 p. A comprehe for pre-school children in Switzerland.

RIEDI, V.: Die Entwicklung einer schweizerischen Familienschutzpolitik dargestellt am Beispiel des Eidgenössischen Verbandes Pro Familia (Development of Family Care Policy - Example of Pro Familia). Luzern, 1971, 225 p. Unpublished dissertation providing an historical summary of family policy.

2.7 Housing

ANGELINI, Terenzio, GURTNER, Peter: Wohnungsmarkt und Wohnungsmarktpolitik in der Schweiz (Housing Market and Housing Market Policy in Switzerland). Bern, 1978, 170 p. Historical description of housing policy.

BUNDESAMT FÜR WOHNUNGSWESEN: Siedlungswesen in der Schweiz (Settlement in Switzerland). Bern, 1978, 99 p. Analysis of settlement in Switzerland from the political planning perspective.

RAMEL, Lilia, WILLA, Claude, GILLIAND, Pierre: Soins à domicile (Care at Home). Lausanne, 1982, 304 p. Report and evaluation on different possibilities of hospitilization, especially the advantages of care at home.

2.8 Education

EGGER, Eugen, BLANC, Emile, ROHRER, Ursula: Das Schulwesen in der Schweiz (The Education System in Switzerland). Genf, 1976, 52 p. Institutional description of the education system.

PLOTKE, Herbert: Schweizerisches Schulrecht (Swiss Education Law). Bern and Stuttgart, 1979, 540 p. Survey of legal, institutional and financial aspects of the Swiss education system.

2.9 Public household

JAEGER, Franz, SCHIPS, Bernd: Zur ökonomischen Analyse einer Staatsverschuldung. Ergänzt durch eine beispielhafte Untersuchung der Verhältnisse in der Schweiz (The Economic Analysis of Public Debt by Means of an Exemplary Analysis of the Swiss Situation). Diessenhofen, 1982, 100 p. An analysis of the different aspects of the 'public debt' phenomenon using the Swiss situation as a model.

WITTMANN, W.: Bundesfinanzen und Sozialstaat (State Finances and the Social State). Diessenhofen, 1978, 138 p. Collection of essays on public expenditure, revenues, debts, household and financial planning; seeks to rationalize the Swiss welfare state from an economic perspective.

III Social policy and redistribution

BURGISSER-PETERS, Petra: Verteilungswirkungen der staatlichen Altersvorsorge in der Schweiz (Distribution Effects of Public Old Age Provisions). Zürich, 1982, 182 p.

LEPERMEIER, Dirk: Soziale Sicherung und Parafiskalität: Zur Einkommensumverteilungsproblematik im Bereich der Sozialversicherung (Social Security and Parafiscality: Income Redistribution Problems in Social Insurance). Bern and Frankfurt, 1979, 276 p.

Appendix Tables

Contents

Table 1 Gross Domestic Product and Total Public Expenditure

Year	GDP (at market prices, in million SFR)			Deflators (base 1970)		Total public expenditure (in million SFR)				Incl. sickness ins.		Year
	at current prices	at constant (1970) prices	annual real growth rate	gross domestic product	consumer price index	at current prices	as % of GDP	at constant (1970) prices	annual real growth rate	at current prices	as % of GDP	
1948	18 820	33 443		53.1	64.0							1948
1949	18 580	34 092	2.0	54.5	63.6							1949
1950	19 580	36 394	6.8	53.8	62.5	4 067	20.8	7 559		4 199	21.4	1950
1951	21 460	39 376	8.3	54.5	65.5							1951
1952	22 675	39 711	0.8	57.1	67.2							1952
1953	23 800	41 105	3.5	57.9	66.7							1953
1954	25 220	43 408	5.6	58.1	67.2							1954
1955	27 205	46 346	6.8	58.7	67.8	5 214	19.2	8 882		5 419	19.9	1955
1956	29 250	49 409	6.5	59.2	68.8							1956
1957	31 115	51 345	3.8	60.6	70.2							1957
1958	31 990	50 220	-2.2	63.7	71.4							1958
1959	33 975	53 420	6.5	63.6	71.0							1959
1960	37 370	57 141	7.1	65.4	72.0	7 519	20.1	11 497		8 006	21.4	1960
1961	42 040	61 824	8.3	68.0	73.3	9 117	21.7	13 407	16.6	9 625	22.9	1961
1962	46 620	64 750	4.7	72.0	76.5	10 193	21.9	14 157	5.6	10 777	23.1	1962
1963	51 265	67 901	5.0	75.5	79.1	11 499	22.4	15 230	7.6	12 164	23.7	1963
1964	56 825	71 478	5.3	79.5	81.6	13 551	23.8	17 045	11.9	14 227	25.0	1964
1965	60 860	73 770	3.2	82.5	84.4	14 619	24.0	17 220	1.0	15 409	25.3	1965
1966	65 355	75 555	2.3	86.5	88.4	16 357	25.0	18 910	9.8	17 338	26.5	1966
1967	70 350	77 907	3.2	90.3	91.9	17 553	25.0	19 439	2.8	18 644	26.5	1967
1968	75 120	80 687	3.5	93.1	94.2	19 260	25.6	20 687	6.4	20 458	27.2	1968
1969	81 395	85 230	5.6	95.5	96.5	21 742	26.7	22 766	10.1	23 063	28.3	1969
1970	90 665	90 665	6.5	100.0	100.0	24 172	26.7	24 172	6.2	25 659	28.3	1970
1971	102 995	94 318	4.1	109.2	106.0	28 644	27.8	26 231	8.5	30 355	29.5	1971
1972	116 710	97 339	3.2	119.9	113.7	32 702	28.0	27 274	4.0	34 759	29.8	1972
1973	130 060	100 355	3.2	129.6	123.6	39 740	30.6	30 664	12.4	42 057	32.3	1973
1974	141 100	101 804	1.4	138.6	135.7	44 439	31.5	32 063	4.6	47 152	33.4	1974
1975	139 920	94 222	-7.3	148.5	144.8	48 436	34.6	32 617	1.7	51 553	36.8	1975
1976	140 710	92 269	-2.2	152.5	147.3	52 630	37.4	34 511	5.8	56 029	39.8	1976
1977	146 206	95 310	3.2	153.4	149.2	53 384	36.5	34 801	0.8	56 917	38.9	1977
1978	151 693	95 645	0.5	158.6	150.7	54 395	35.9	34 297	-1.4	58 202	38.4	1978
1979	160 432	97 765	2.3	164.1	156.2	56 756	35.4	34 586	0.8	60 826	37.9	1979
1980	170 024	100 785	3.2	168.7		59 705	35.1	35 391	2.3	64 164	37.7	1980
1981						62 755				67 766		1981
1982						68 817				74 363		1982
1983						72 596				78 707		1983

Table 2

Public Expenditure by

Year	Level of Government (percent distribution)			Total (in million SFR)	Major Purpose (percent distribution)						Year
	Central govt	Cantons	Local govt		Admin./ law/order	Defense	Welfare services	Economic services	Interests on debt	Other	
1950	42.3	28.8	29.0	3 898	15.3	14.9	40.0	15.2	12.4	2.2	1950
1951	42.9	28.8	28.4	4 161							1951
1952	47.2	26.1	26.7	4 606							1952
1953	42.3	30.1	27.6	4 487							1953
1954	43.4	29.3	27.3	4 541							1954
1955	41.4	31.2	27.4	4 727	16.3	15.6	38.8	18.1	8.6	2.6	1955
1956	40.2	32.7	27.1	4 922							1956
1957	40.9	32.6	26.5	5 500							1957
1958	43.4	31.4	25.2	6 113							1958
1959	40.0	33.5	26.5	6 224							1959
1960	40.4	33.5	26.1	6 478	14.0	15.5	39.7	19.7	8.2	2.9	1960
1961	42.9	32.0	25.0	7 653							1961
1962	42.5	31.6	25.9	8 710							1962
1963	41.1	32.5	26.4	9 959							1963
1964	42.6	31.6	25.9	11 435							1964
1965	39.9	33.7	26.5	12 374	13.3	13.3	38.0	26.1	5.5	3.8	1965
1966	40.7	32.3	26.9	14 021							1966
1967	39.7	32.9	27.4	14 869							1967
1968	39.5	32.9	27.6	16 399							1968
1969	39.4	33.6	27.0	18 074							1969
1970	38.5	33.3	28.1	20 285	12.2	10.9	41.8	21.1	7.0	7.0	1970
1971	37.2	33.8	29.0	24 230							1971
1972	37.5	33.6	28.9	27 796							1972
1973	36.7	34.4	28.9	31 955							1973
1974	36.7	33.6	29.7	35 900							1974
1975	35.8	34.9	29.3	38 066	11.8	8.2	46.6	18.4	7.8	7.2	1975
1976	38.4	34.0	27.6	41 531							1976
1977	37.3	34.4	28.3	41 821							1977
1978	37.2	34.3	28.5	42 732							1978
1979	37.3	33.8	28.9	44 770							1979
1980	37.0	33.9	29.1	47 240	11.8	8.1	47.8	18.7	7.0	6.6	1980
1981	35.1	35.3	29.7	49 956							1981
1982	35.4	34.8	29.8	54 384							1982
1983	35.3	35.0	29.7	57 443							1983
1984	36.2	34.6	29.2	59 779	11.9	8.2	48.9	18.0	6.3	6.7	1984

Table 3

Social Expenditure

Year	At current prices (in million SFR)						At constant (1970) prices (in million SFR)						Year
	Income maint.	Education	Health	Housing	Other	Total	Income maint.	Education	Health	Housing	Other	Total	
1950	(475)	631	269		(65)	(1 440)	(760)	1 173	500		(121)	(2 554)	1950
1955	(810)	756	359		(108)	(2 033)	(1 195)	1 288	612		(184)	(3 279)	1955
1960	1 350	1 159	528		258	3 295	1 875	1 172	807		395		1960
1961	1 601				548		2 184				806		1961
1962	1 855				354		2 425				492		1962
1963	2 010				724		2 541				959		1963
1964	2 710				460		3 321				577		1964
1965	2 921	2 100	1 019		478	6 518	3 461	2 546	1 235		579	7 821	1965
1966	3 189	2 388	1 148	74	464	7 263	3 608	2 761	1 327	86	536	8 317	1966
1967	3 581	2 622	1 240	94	553	8 090	3 897	2 904	1 373	104	612	8 890	1967
1968	3 645	2 912	1 389	132	601	8 679	3 869	3 128	1 492	142	646	9 277	1968
1969	4 760	3 239	1 513	104	682	10 298	4 933	3 392	1 584	109	714	10 732	1969
1970	5 041	3 756	1 630	137	762	11 326	5 041	3 756	1 630	137	762	11 326	1970
1971	5 827	4 599	2 008	152	883	13 469	5 497	4 212	1 839	139	809	12 495	1971
1972	6 524	5 450	2 352	208	981	15 515	5 738	4 546	1 962	174	818	13 237	1972
1973	9 335	6 522	2 852	301	1 429	20 439	7 553	5 032	2 201	232	1 103	16 121	1973
1974	10 820	7 421	3 376	339	1 395	23 351	7 974	5 354	2 436	245	1 007	17 015	1974
1975	12 793	7 784	3 860	330	1 505	26 272	8 835	5 242	2 599	222	1 014	17 912	1975
1976	13 824	8 192	4 229	303	1 670	28 218	9 385	5 372	2 773	199	1 095	18 824	1976
1977	14 292	8 296	4 157	286	1 627	28 658	9 579	5 408	2 710	186	1 061	18 944	1977
1978	14 712	8 398	4 376	236	1 612	29 334	9 762	5 295	2 759	149	1 014	18 982	1978
1979	15 154	8 721	4 848	258	1 575	30 556	9 702	5 314	2 954	157	960	19 087	1979
1980	16 626	9 300	5 281	261	2 067	33 535	10 231	5 513	3 130	155	1 225	20 255	1980
1981	16 366	9 872	5 878	274	1 936	34 326							1981
1982	18 834	10 657	6 395	302	2 064	38 252							1982
1983		11 286	6 559	290									1983
1984		11 707	6 796	313									1984

Table 4

Social Expenditure

Year	As % of gross domestic product						As % of total public expenditure						Percent distribution					Year
	Income maint.	Educa-tion	Health	Hous-ing	Other	Total	Income maint.	Educa-tion	Health	Hous-ing	Other	Total	Income maint.	Educa-tion	Health	Hous-ing	Other	
1950	2.4	3.2	1.4		0.3	7.4							33.0	43.8	18.7		4.5	1950
1955	3.0	2.8	1.3		0.4	7.5							39.8	37.2	17.7		5.3	1955
1960	3.6	3.1	1.4		0.7	8.8	18.0	15.4	7.0		3.4	43.8	41.0	35.2	16.0		7.8	1960
1961	3.8				1.4		17.6				6.0							1961
1962	4.0				0.8		18.2				3.5							1962
1963	3.9				1.4		17.5				6.3							1963
1964	4.8				0.8		20.0				3.4							1964
1965	4.8	3.5	1.7		0.8	10.7	20.0	14.4	7.0		3.3	44.6	44.8	32.2	15.6		7.3	1965
1966	4.9	3.7	1.8	0.1	0.7	11.1	19.5	14.6	7.0	0.5	2.8	44.4	43.9	32.9	15.8	1.0	6.4	1966
1967	5.1	3.7	1.8	0.1	0.8	11.5	20.4	14.9	7.1	0.5	3.2	46.1	44.3	32.4	15.3	1.2	6.8	1967
1968	4.9	3.9	1.9	0.2	0.8	11.6	18.9	15.1	7.2	0.7	3.1	45.1	42.0	33.6	16.0	1.5	6.9	1968
1969	5.9	4.0	1.9	0.1	0.8	12.7	21.9	14.9	7.0	0.5	3.1	47.4	46.2	31.5	14.7	1.0	6.6	1969
1970	5.6	4.1	1.8	0.2	0.8	12.5	20.9	15.5	6.7	0.6	3.2	46.9	44.5	33.2	14.4	1.2	6.7	1970
1971	5.7	4.5	2.0	0.2	0.9	13.1	20.3	16.1	7.0	0.5	3.1	47.0	43.3	34.1	14.9	1.1	6.6	1971
1972	5.6	4.7	2.0	0.2	0.8	13.3	20.0	16.7	7.2	0.6	3.0	47.4	42.0	35.1	15.2	1.3	6.3	1972
1973	7.2	5.0	2.2	0.2	1.1	15.7	23.5	16.4	7.2	0.8	3.6	51.4	45.7	31.9	14.0	1.5	7.0	1973
1974	7.7	5.3	2.4	0.2	1.0	16.6	24.4	16.7	7.6	0.8	3.1	52.6	46.3	31.8	14.5	1.5	6.0	1974
1975	9.1	5.6	2.8	0.2	1.1	18.8	26.3	16.1	8.0	0.7	3.1	54.2	48.7	29.6	14.7	1.3	5.7	1975
1976	9.8	5.8	3.0	0.2	1.2	20.1	26.3	15.6	8.0	0.6	3.2	53.6	49.0	29.0	15.0	1.1	5.9	1976
1977	9.8	5.7	2.8	0.2	1.1	19.6	26.8	15.5	7.8	0.5	3.1	53.7	49.9	28.9	14.5	1.0	5.7	1977
1978	9.7	5.5	2.9	0.2	1.1	19.3	27.1	15.4	8.0	0.4	3.0	53.9	50.2	28.6	14.9	0.8	5.5	1978
1979	9.5	5.4	3.0	0.2	1.0	19.1	26.7	15.4	8.5	0.5	2.8	53.8	49.6	28.5	15.9	0.8	5.2	1979
1980	9.8	5.5	3.1	0.2	1.2	19.7	27.9	15.6	8.9	0.4	3.5	56.2	49.6	27.7	15.7	0.8	6.2	1980
1981							26.1	15.7	9.4	0.4	3.1	54.7	47.7	28.8	17.1	0.8	5.6	1981
1982							27.4	15.5	9.3	0.4	3.0	55.6	49.2	27.9	16.7	0.8	5.4	1982
1983								15.6	9.0	0.4								1983

Table 5

Expenditure on Income Maintenance

(at current prices, in million SFR)

Year	Old age/ survivors pensions (incl. suppl.	Invalidity pensions benef.)	Ind. acc. cash ben.	Military insur. pensions	Income compensation	Unempl. insur. cash benef.	Agricult. fam. allow.	Cantonal fam. allow.	Social ass.	Total	Sickness, maternity benef.	Total	Year
1948	121.9												1948
1950	164.5		86.1	16.5	—	—	—	—	(208)	(475)			1950
1955	373.1		118.7	20.0	—	—	—	—	(260)	(810)			1955
1960	721.1	27.7	166.7	25.6	63.6	8.6	16.9	19.9	(300)	(1 350)			1960
1961	848.4	59.7	186.1	26.0	71.5	4.8	16.3	22.9	(365)	(1 601)			1961
1962	987.5	97.7	207.5	27.2	84.9	4.4	18.9	33.2	(394)	(1 855)			1962
1963	1 031.3	106.5	234.6	27.8	88.3	6.2	32.1	41.9	441	2 010			1963
1964	1 599.5	148.9	253.8	37.8	126.2	1.8	30.3	52.7	459	2 710			1964
1965	1 670.6	158.8	276.4	41.2	137.2	1.9	28.8	63.8	542	2 921			1965
1966	1 855.8	224.3	295.9	42.5	137.6	1.6	41.2	70.0	520	3 189	298.0	3 487	1966
1967	2 205.0	249.5	325.0	43.0	138.1	1.8	47.1	81.3	490	3 581			1967
1968	2 249.0	253.0	349.5	47.8	147.5	2.5	42.3	87.9	465	3 645			1968
1969	3 066.5	340.6	368.0	47.7	214.0	1.7	41.0	105.4	575	4 760			1969
1970	3 169.6	365.6	407.4	58.2	221.1	1.1	50.1	121.8	646	5 041	368.8	5 410	1970
1971	3 705.3	453.2	461.4	62.9	230.2	0.9	55.9	137.0	720	5 827	391.6	6 218	1971
1972	4 148.7	503.5	521.6	67.8	226.3	0.8	50.5	167.7	837	6 524	424.5	6 948	1972
1973	6 695.0	722.5	584.0	76.8	230.5	0.7	49.6	194.1	992	9 335	477.0	9 812	1973
1974	7 490.0	848.1	669.4	84.7	315.8	2.3	60.2	227.2	1 122	10 820	524.7	11 344	1974
1975	8 819.7	981.8	707.7	93.4	333.6	234.1	81.9	255.8	1 285	12 793	541.4	13 334	1975
1976	9 209.1	1 003.3	713.0	99.3	462.2	563.8	68.1	263.8	1 441	13 824	568.6	14 392	1976
1977	9 950.7	1 146.3	723.9	100.2	483.9	115.9	69.2	269.9	1 432	14 292	582.5	14 875	1977
1978	10 198.9	1 159.1	765.8	100.5	465.9	186.5	60.8	293.1	1 481	14 712	622.0	15 334	1978
1979	10 383.9	1 262.6	798.6	100.3	507.3	188.8	58.5	353.4	1 501	15 154	641.0	15 795	1979
1980	11 019.9	1 016.4	871.5	108.2	481.1	103.9	66.9	387.4	1 571	15 626	680.3	16 307	1980
1981	11 194.9	1 290.9	932.2	109.8	532.4	124.6	79.1	413.4	1 770	16 366	742.6	17 109	1981
1982	12 788.6	1 463.1	1 009.2	121.5	567.7	396.4	74.4	454.5	1 959	18 834	783.9	19 618	1982
1983	13 006.7	1 505.1	1 078.2	121.3	635.1	754.3	73.0	476.1			824.5		1983
1984	14 679.3	1 717.9			655.0		83.0				824.1		1984

Table 6

Expenditure on Social Security

(at current prices, in million SFR)

Year	Old age/ survivors ins. (AHV)	Inval. insur. (IV)	Suppl. to AHV and IV	Industr. accid. (SUVA)	Military insur. (MV)	Income comp. (EO)	Unem- ploym. insur.	Agric. family allow.	Cantonal family allow.	Social security I	Sick- ness insur.	Social security II	Year
1948	126.8												1948
1950	170.3			125.5	36.0					331.8	246.3	578.1	1950
1955	383.2			174.1	40.7	—	—	—	—	(658)	374.0	(1 032)	1955
1960	733.4	53.5		356.6	48.2	63.9	15.5	17.4	19.9	1 308.4	561.3	1 869.7	1960
1961	861.1	156.3		339.2	47.5	71.8	11.7	16.8	22.9	1 783.5	604.5	2 388.0	1961
1962	998.3	168.3		448.7	51.5	85.0	10.9	19.4	33.2	1 815.3	673.5	2 488.8	1962
1963	1 043.4	187.9		488.4	54.2	88.5	12.8	32.6	41.9	1 938.7	758.2	2 696.9	1963
1964	1 611.5	251.8		561.9	66.5	126.4	9.0	30.9	52.7	2 710.7	846.0	3 556.7	1964
1965	1 683.5	275.6		585.9	72.6	137.5	8.7	29.8	63.8	2 857.0	1 003.4	3 860.4	1965
1966	1 742.1	309.2	152.7	596.6	73.8	137.9	8.0	42.1	70.0	3 132.7	1 234.8	4 367.5	1966
1967	1 991.9	358.5	281.9	655.9	74.7	138.4	9.6	48.0	84.7	3 643.5	1 404.9	5 048.4	1967
1968	2 067.1	405.9	243.7	689.2	81.7	147.9	9.8	43.5	91.3	3 780.4	1 560.9	5 341.3	1968
1969	2 896.6	532.9	236.6	741.6	84.4	214.5	9.0	42.2	109.2	4 867.0	1 730.3	6 597.3	1969
1970	2 999.9	592.7	234.9	823.1	99.1	221.5	8.0	51.2	126.0	5 156.9	1 954.7	7 111.6	1970
1971	3 403.6	681.5	389.3	973.3	106.8	230.6	6.0	57.0	141.6	5 989.7	2 255.4	8 245.1	1971
1972	3 805.8	758.2	439.9	1 088.0	118.2	226.7	6.1	51.9	172.8	6 667.9	2 689.8	9 357.7	1972
1973	6 480.3	1 180.5	295.2	1 189.3	133.9	231.2	11.2	51.1	199.4	9 772.5	3 068.6	12 841.1	1973
1974	7 262.7	1 398.7	318.0	1 347.0	145.0	316.7	9.4	61.8	233.7	11 093.0	3 577.9	14 670.9	1974
1975	8 612.1	1 621.7	299.1	1 390.9	159.1	334.6	249.9	83.4	262.7	13 013.4	4 053.9	17 067.3	1975
1976	8 992.0	1 798.2	313.8	1 354.0	167.0	463.6	623.8	69.8	271.2	14 053.0	4 467.1	18 520.1	1976
1977	9 686.7	1 919.4	374.0	1 364.8	166.3	485.4	141.3	71.1	277.9	14 487.2	4 675.3	19 162.5	1977
1978	9 921.0	1 950.2	388.7	1 377.9	164.8	467.3	209.0	62.6	301.0	14 842.5	4 961.5	19 804.0	1978
1979	10 103.2	2 010.0	392.4	1 416.3	166.6	508.6	209.6	60.2	361.8	15 228.8	5 261.0	20 489.8	1979
1980	10 725.6	2 134.5	414.7	1 572.2	173.5	482.5	153.3	68.7	397.2	16 122.2	5 676.7	21 798.9	1980
1981	10 894.9	2 173.0	425.4	1 666.7	178.0	533.8	155.2	80.9	424.2	16 532.1	6 203.4	22 735.5	1981
1982	12 385.0	2 444.6	543.7	1 823.3	194.2	569.1	428.1	76.3	466.2	18 939.5	6 789.7	25 729.2	1982
1983	12 578.9	2 524.0	581.4	1 904.4	201.2	636.5	799.9	74.9	488.3	19 789.6	7 363.8	27 153.4	1983
1984	14 176.9	2 851.4	675.8			657.7		84.9					1984

Table 7

Old Age and Survivors Pension Insurance

Expenditure at current prices, in million SFR

Year	Ordinary pensions					Extra-ordinary pensions					All schemes			Year
	single	married couple	supple-ments	survi-vors	total	single	married couple	supple-ments	survi-vors	total	benefits	admin-istration	Total	
1948						77.0	26.6		19.3	122.8	121.9	4.9	126.8	1948
1950	19.2	16.3		6.9	42.4	76.5	26.4		18.3	121.2	164.5	5.8	170.3	1950
1955	98.8	87.8		36.5	223.1	97.3	30.1		18.4	145.9	373.1	10.1	383.2	1955
1960	254.1	211.9		78.3	544.3	127.3	26.6		15.6	169.5	721.1	12.3	733.4	1960
1961	333.4	292.0		100.6	726.1	149.6	28.6		17.6	195.7	848.4	12.7	861.1	1961
1962	371.7	331.5		109.1	812.3	142.7	23.4		15.8	181.9	987.5	10.8	998.3	1962
1963	397.5	352.4		112.1	862.0	130.4	18.8		13.6	162.9	1 031.3	12.1	1 043.4	1963
1964	644.3	542.1	30.9	148.9	1 366.2	178.7	21.2	0.4	14.5	214.8	1 599.5	12.0	1 611.5	1964
1965	687.5	574.3	36.8	152.9	1 451.6	166.7	17.1	0.5	12.6	196.9	1 670.6	12.9	1 683.5	1965
1966	733.7	607.0	39.7	156.9	1 537.3	153.6	13.6	0.6	11.0	178.8	1 729.3	12.8	1 742.1	1966
1967	849.0	696.2	45.3	174.5	1 765.0	151.1	11.2	0.6	10.4	173.4	1 978.6	13.2	1 991.9	1967
1968	907.5	741.8	48.6	181.0	1 878.9	141.8	9.1	0.6	9.4	161.0	2 052.2	14.9	2 067.1	1968
1969	1 290.2	1 036.3	66.1	244.1	2 636.7	187.0	10.3	0.9	12.0	210.1	2 878.3	18.3	2 896.6	1969
1970											2 983.0	16.9	2 999.9	1970
1971											3 386.5	17.1	3 403.6	1971
1972											3 786.9	18.9	3 805.8	1972
1973											6 454.8	25.5	6 480.3	1973
1974											7 229.1	33.6	7 262.7	1974
1975	4 244.4	3 211.2	171.6	686.4	8 313.6	278.4	7.2	1.2	21.6	309.6	8 574.8	37.3	8 612.1	1975
1976	4 364.4	3 298.8	176.4	686.4	8 526.0	248.4	6.0	1.2	20.4	276.0	8 951.8	39.8	8 992.0	1976
1977	4 666.8	4 718.4	186.0	712.8	9 084.0	235.2	7.2	1.2	20.4	264.0	9 642.7	44.0	9 686.7	1977
1978	4 784.4	3 612.0	189.6	720.0	9 306.0	211.2	6.0	1.2	19.2	337.6	9 878.5	42.5	9 921.0	1978
1979	4 935.6	3 702.0	202.8	753.6	9 594.0	193.2	7.2	1.2	19.2	220.8	10 058.9	44.4	10 103.2	1979
1980	5 338.8	3 831.6	234.0	792.0	10 196.4	183.6	7.2	1.2	20.4	212.4	10 677.2	48.4	10 725.6	1980
1981	5 508.0	3 765.6	253.2	804.0	10 330.8	169.2	6.0	1.2	20.4	196.8	10 843.6	51.3	10 894.9	1981
1982	6 316.8	4 304.4	262.8	906.0	11 790.0	180.0	8.4	1.2	21.6	211.2	12 337.6	47.4	12 385.0	1982
1983	6 434.4	4 375.2	252.0	906.0	11 967.6	169.2	8.4	1.2	21.6	200.4	12 527.6	51.3	12 578.9	1983
1984	7 287.6	4 970.4	271.2	997.2	13 526.4	178.8	9.6	1.2	22.8	212.4	14 126.6	50.3	14 176.9	1984

Table 8

Invalidity Pension Insurance

Expenditure at current prices, in million SFR

Year	Ordinary pensions				Extra-ordinary pensions				All schemes				Year
	single	married couple	supple-ments	total	single	married couple	supple-ments	total	benefits	admin-istration	other	Total	
1960	20.2	3.5	4.0	27.7					49.3	0.2	4.0	53.5	1960
1961	38.2	7.4	7.7	53.3	5.4	0.1	0.8	6.4	150.8	0.8	4.7	156.3	1961
1962	57.6	14.5	14.5	86.6	9.5	0.2	1.4	11.1	161.8	0.9	5.6	168.3	1962
1963	61.6	16.1	16.7	94.4	10.3	0.2	1.6	12.1	179.4	1.2	7.3	187.9	1963
1964	86.9	22.8	23.4	133.1	13.4	0.3	2.1	15.8	241.5	1.4	8.9	251.8	1964
1965	91.8	25.1	25.3	142.2	14.2	0.3	2.1	16.6	262.2	2.5	10.9	275.6	1965
1966	95.8	27.0	27.3	150.1	14.9	0.3	2.1	17.3	294.2	2.7	12.3	309.2	1966
1967	110.3	31.5	32.9	174.7	16.9	0.3	2.1	19.3	340.9	2.9	14.7	358.5	1967
1968	115.8	34.1	35.5	185.4	18.3	0.3	2.1	20.7	391.2	3.6	11.1	405.9	1968
1969	162.9	48.3	49.9	261.1	27.8	0.4	2.9	31.1	514.8	5.4	12.7	532.9	1969
1970									574.1	4.2	14.4	592.7	1970
1971									659.9	4.7	16.9	681.5	1971
1972									733.4	5.7	19.1	758.2	1972
1973									1 150.8	7.0	22.7	1 180.5	1973
1974									1 363.8	9.1	25.8	1 398.7	1974
1975	517.2	122.4	178.8	818.4	102.0	1.2	6.0	109.2	1 580.8	11.3	29.6	1 621.7	1975
1976	525.6	133.2	178.8	837.6	103.2	1.2	4.8	109.2	1 755.7	12.9	29.6	1 798.2	1976
1977	591.6	168.0	199.2	958.8	114.0	1.2	6.0	121.2	1 874.1	13.5	31.8	1 919.4	1977
1978	600.0	165.6	202.8	968.4	116.4	1.2	4.8	122.4	1 900.0	13.4	36.8	1 950.2	1978
1979	668.4	174.0	230.4	1 072.8	123.6	1.2	4.8	122.4	1 955.0	12.9	42.1	2 010.0	1979
1980	681.6	142.8	223.2	807.6	130.8	1.2	4.8	136.8	2 075.1	13.5	45.9	2 134.5	1980
1981	712.8	129.6	231.6	1 074.0	136.8	1.2	4.8	142.8	2 105.5	18.1	49.4	2 173.0	1981
1982	810.0	148.8	246.0	1 204.8	159.6	1.2	4.8	165.6	2 373.9	16.3	54.4	2 444.6	1982
1983	825.6	157.2	247.2	1 230.0	166.8	1.2	4.8	172.8	2 447.1	17.7	59.2	2 524.0	1983
1984	934.8	183.6	274.8	1 393.2	194.4	1.2	6.0	201.6	2 769.5	16.4	65.5	2 851.4	1984

Table 9 Supplementary Pension Benefits and Occupational Pensions

(at current prices, in million SFR)

Year	Supplementary benefits to old age and survivors' pensions			Supplementary benefits to invalidity pensions			Occupational pensions				Year
	Expenditure by			Expenditure by			Total expend-iture	Total reve-nues	Of which:		
	federal govt	cantons	total	federal govt	cantons	total			insur. contrib	capital interests	
1960							730.9	1 484.9	1 484.9		1960
1961							805.5	1 563.2	1 563.2		1961
1962							883.4	1 825.3	1 825.3		1962
1963							994.6	2 109.2	2 109.2		1963
1964							1 077.7	2 350.4	2 350.4		1964
1965							1 185.0	2 505.0	2 505.0		1965
1966	59.6	66.9	126.5	13.3	12.9	26.2	1 340.0	2 743.0	2 743.0		1966
1967	102.3	124.1	226.4	26.1	29.4	55.5	1 356.0	2 920.0	2 920.0		1967
1968	89.2	107.6	196.8	22.3	24.6	46.9	1 325.0	2 909.0	2 909.0		1968
1969	85.7	102.5	188.2	23.2	25.2	48.4	1 460.2	4 490.0	3 301.0	1 189.0	1969
1970	89.3	97.3	186.6	24.1	24.2	48.3	1 677.8	5 272.7	3 455.0	1 817.7	1970
1971	151.0	167.8	318.8	35.1	35.4	70.5	1 783.9	5 529.4	4 011.4	1 518.0	1971
1972	171.0	190.8	361.8	38.7	39.4	78.1	1 655.7	6 307.1	4 551.1	1 756.0	1972
1973	113.4	126.8	240.2	27.1	27.9	55.0	1 879.0	6 746.7	4 802.5	1 944.2	1973
1974	123.1	137.8	260.9	28.0	29.1	57.1	2 107.8	7 914.5	5 732.4	2 182.1	1974
1975	125.6	119.3	244.9	28.9	25.3	54.2	2 305.7	8 850.4	6 273.4	2 577.0	1975
1976	132.1	125.2	257.3	29.9	26.6	56.5	2 611.4	9 089.8	6 223.5	2 866.3	1976
1977	158.0	150.0	308.0	35.0	31.3	66.3	2 762.8	9 265.9	6 311.2	2 954.7	1977
1978	164.6	155.8	320.4	35.6	32.7	68.3	2 969.5	9 998.1	6 831.0	3 167.1	1978
1979	165.8	159.2	325.0	34.8	32.6	67.4	3 193.0	11 120.0	7 936.0	3 184.0	1979
1980	177.5	165.2	342.7	37.6	34.4	72.0	3 458.0	13 231.0	9 674.0	3 557.0	1980
1981	182.2	169.1	351.3	38.5	35.6	74.1	3 743.0	14 588.0	10 434.0	4 154.0	1981
1982	231.5	219.5	451.0	47.4	45.3	92.7	4 112.0	15 928.0	11 116.0	4 812.0	1982
1983	247.3	231.8	479.1	52.5	49.8	102.3	4 507.0	17 167.0	11 900.0	5 267.0	1983
1984	286.5	266.2	552.7	63.4	59.7	123.1					1984

Table 10

Expenditure on

(at current prices, in million SFR)

Year	Industrial Accident Insurance					Sickness Insurance							Year
	health care	cash benef.	ad-min.	reserve a.o.	total	health care	sickness cash b.	matern-ity b.	total benef.	ad-min.	reserve a.o.	total	
1950	23.3	86.1	14.4	1.7	125.5				209.3	24.6	12.4	169.7	1950
1955	34.8	118.7	18.7	1.9	174.1				310.2	35.5	28.3	256.4	1955
1960	49.4	166.7	24.9	115.6	356.6				475.4	54.2	28.4	341.9	1960
1961	55.9	186.1	26.2	131.0	339.2				501.4	60.1	39.1	393.9	1961
1962	62.6	207.5	29.7	148.9	448.7				566.6	67.8	34.2	428.4	1962
1963	68.0	234.6	32.3	153.5	488.4				636.6	76.1	41.6	451.3	1963
1964	71.5	253.8	38.2	198.4	561.9				696.8	89.1	60.1	511.1	1964
1965	75.5	276.4	41.1	192.5	585.9				840.0	101.9	61.5	553.3	1965
1966	79.8	295.9	42.0	179.1	596.6	747.4	231.9	66.1	1 045.4	118.0	71.4	546.2	1966
1967	84.5	325.0	44.9	201.5	655.9				1 195.3	129.8	79.8	544.8	1967
1968	92.3	349.5	48.1	199.6	689.2				1 315.5	144.6	100.8	620.9	1968
1969	100.3	368.0	53.1	220.2	741.6				1 486.5	157.4	86.3	707.6	1969
1970	118.8	407.4	56.4	240.9	823.1	1 319.5	280.8	88.0	1 688.3	173.9	92.5	792.5	1970
1971	131.2	461.4	65.9	314.8	973.3	1 545.5	297.6	93.9	1 937.0	199.2	119.2	858.1	1971
1972	152.1	521.6	75.1	339.5	1 088.0	1 821.5	323.8	100.7	2 246.0	226.6	217.2	904.7	1972
1973	166.5	584.0	90.1	349.1	1 189.3	2 125.4	367.7	109.3	2 602.4	271.3	194.8	994.0	1973
1974	188.6	669.4	99.0	390.0	1 347.0	2 522.6	405.6	119.1	3 047.3	312.8	217.8	1 073.0	1974
1975	205.2	707.7	103.4	374.5	1 390.9	2 942.1	412.6	128.8	3 483.5	333.9	236.5	1 154.3	1975
1976	211.2	713.0	103.7	326.1	1 354.0	3 244.2	431.7	136.9	3 812.8	355.8	298.5	1 298.0	1976
1977	215.7	723.9	100.8	324.7	1 364.8	3 404.3	438.3	144.2	3 986.8	356.4	332.1	1 546.1	1977
1978	220.4	765.8	101.8	289.9	1 377.9	3 626.0	470.6	151.4	4 248.0	374.0	339.5	1 769.1	1978
1979	230.1	798.6	104.5	283.1	1 416.3	3 897.1	480.0	161.1	4 538.2	398.8	324.0	1 904.1	1979
1980	248.5	871.5	111.8	340.4	1 572.2	4 213.4	502.5	177.8	4 893.7	430.9	352.1	1 930.6	1980
1981	268.4	932.2	120.5	345.6	1 666.7	4 674.3	545.6	197.1	5 417.0	462.3	324.1	1 890.6	1981
1982	285.8	1 009.2	140.9	396.4	1 823.3	5 103.7	566.0	217.9	5 887.6	498.2	403.9	1 831.4	1982
1983	297.6	1 078.2	148.7	379.9	1 904.4	5 564.7	591.8	232.7	6 389.2	524.2	450.4	1 864.2	1983
1984						5 850.9	582.4	241.7					1984

Table 11

Expenditure on
(at current prices, in million SFR)

Year	Unemployment Insurance				Income Compensation			Military Insurance				Year
	cash benefits	ad-min.	other	total	cash benef.	ad-min.	total	pen-sions	other benef.	ad-min.	total	
1950	—	—	—	—	—	—	—	16.5	17.4	2.1	36.0	1950
1955								20.0	18.3	2.4	40.7	1955
1960	8.6	5.1	1.8	15.5	63.6	0.3	63.9	25.6	19.4	3.2	48.2	1960
1961	4.8	5.1	1.8	11.7	71.5	0.3	71.8	26.0	18.3	3.2	47.5	1961
1962	4.4	5.1	1.4	10.9	84.9	0.1	85.0	27.2	20.8	3.4	51.5	1962
1963	6.2	5.0	1.6	12.8	88.3	0.2	88.5	27.8	22.7	3.7	54.2	1963
1964	1.8	5.1	2.1	9.0	126.2	0.2	126.4	37.8	24.4	4.3	66.5	1964
1965	1.9	5.0	1.8	8.7	137.2	0.3	137.5	41.2	26.9	4.5	72.6	1965
1966	1.6	4.8	1.6	8.0	137.6	0.3	137.9	42.5	26.7	4.6	73.8	1966
1967	1.8	4.6	3.2	9.6	138.1	0.3	138.4	43.0	27.0	4.7	74.7	1967
1968	2.5	4.5	2.8	9.8	147.5	0.4	147.9	47.8	28.9	5.0	81.7	1968
1969	1.7	4.4	2.9	9.0	214.0	0.5	214.5	47.7	31.3	5.4	84.4	1969
1970	1.1	4.3	2.6	8.0	221.1	0.4	221.5	58.2	35.2	5.7	99.1	1970
1971	0.9	4.5	0.6	6.0	230.2	0.4	230.6	62.9	37.6	6.3	106.8	1971
1972	0.8	4.6	0.7	6.1	226.3	0.4	226.7	67.8	43.3	7.1	118.2	1972
1973	0.7	5.1	5.4	11.2	230.5	0.7	231.2	76.8	49.3	7.7	133.9	1973
1974	2.3	5.4	1.7	9.4	315.8	0.9	316.7	84.7	51.7	8.7	145.0	1974
1975	234.1	13.2	2.6	249.9	333.6	1.0	334.6	93.4	56.4	9.3	159.1	1975
1976	563.8	34.7	25.3	623.8	462.2	1.4	463.6	99.3	58.6	9.1	167.0	1976
1977	115.9	23.1	2.3	141.3	483.9	1.5	485.4	100.2	57.1	9.0	166.3	1977
1978	186.5	22.4	0.1	209.0	465.9	1.4	467.3	100.5	55.3	9.0	164.8	1978
1979	188.8	20.7	0.1	209.6	507.3	1.3	508.6	100.3	57.1	9.2	166.6	1979
1980	103.9	19.8	29.6	153.3	481.1	1.4	482.5	108.2	55.5	9.8	173.5	1980
1981	124.6	18.9	11.7	155.2	532.4	1.4	533.8	109.8	57.9	10.3	178.0	1981
1982	396.4	26.6	5.1	428.1	567.7	1.4	569.1	121.5	61.6	11.1	194.2	1982
1983	754.3	41.6	4.0	799.9	635.1	1.4	636.5	121.3	68.4	11.5	201.2	1983
1984					655.0	1.7	656.7					1984

Table 12 Expenditure on Family Allowances and Social Assistance

Year	Agricultural family allowances			Cantonal family allowances			Social assistance			Year
	benefits	admin.	total	benefits	admin.	total	local	cantonal	total	
1950							(125)	83	(208)	1950
1955	—	—	—	—	—	—	(156)	104	(260)	1955
1960	16.9	0.5	17.4	19.9		19.9	(240)	160	(300)	1960
1961	16.3	0.5	16.8	22.9		22.9	(239)	126	(365)	1961
1962	18.9	0.5	19.4	33.2		33.2	(258)	136	(394)	1962
1963	32.1	0.5	32.6	41.9		41.9	293	148	441	1963
1964	30.3	0.6	30.9	52.7		52.7	296	163	459	1964
1965	28.8	1.0	29.8	63.8		63.8	326	216	542	1965
1966	41.2	1.0	42.1	70.0		70.0	364	194	520	1966
1967	47.1	0.9	48.0	81.3	3.4	84.7	275	215	490	1967
1968	42.3	1.2	43.5	87.9	3.4	91.3	242	223	465	1968
1969	41.0	1.2	42.2	105.4	3.8	109.2	319	256	575	1969
1970	50.1	1.2	51.2	121.8	4.2	126.0	373	273	646	1970
1971	55.9	1.1	57.0	137.0	4.6	141.6	422	298	720	1971
1972	50.5	1.4	51.9	167.7	5.1	172.8	485	352	837	1972
1973	49.6	1.5	51.1	194.1	5.3	199.4	580	412	992	1973
1974	60.2	1.6	61.8	227.2	6.5	233.7	621	501	1 122	1974
1975	81.9	1.5	83.4	255.8	6.9	262.7	707	578	1 285	1975
1976	68.1	1.7	69.8	263.8	7.4	271.2	761	680	1 441	1976
1977	69.2	1.9	71.1	269.9	8.0	277.9	772	660	1 432	1977
1978	60.8	1.8	62.6	293.1	7.9	301.0	783	698	1 481	1978
1979	58.5	1.7	60.2	353.4	8.4	361.8	823	678	1 501	1979
1980	66.9	1.8	68.7	387.4	9.8	397.2	923	684	1 571	1980
1981	79.1	1.8	80.9	413.4	10.8	424.2	1 024	746	1 770	1981
1982	74.4	1.9	76.3	454.5	11.7	466.2	1 189	770	1 959	1982
1983	73.0	1.9	74.9	476.1	12.2	488.3				1983
1984	83.0	1.8	84.9							1984

Table 13

Total Public Revenues

(at current prices, in million SFR)

Year	Public revenues	Public expend-iture	Surplus	Social security revenues	Total public revenues	Direct taxes	Indirect taxes	Social sec. contrib.	Other	Year
						percent distribution				
1950	4 226	3 897	329							1950
1951		4 161								1951
1952	4 410	4 603	- 193							1952
1953	4 619	4 482	137							1953
1954	5 000	4 536	464							1954
1955	5 140	4 731	409							1955
1956	5 575	4 917	658							1956
1957	5 636	5 500	136							1957
1958	6 136	6 113	23							1958
1959	6 392	6 224	168							1959
1960	7 356	6 478	878	1 521	8 877	39.7	24.6	14.5	21.2	1960
1961	8 067	7 652	415	1 721	9 788					1961
1962	9 145	8 710	435	1 911	11 056					1962
1963	10 004	9 920	84	2 114	12 118					1963
1964	11 380	11 435	- 55	2 338	13 718					1964
1965	11 828	12 374	- 546	2 535	14 363	41.5	25.2	15.2	18.1	1965
1966	13 239	14 021	- 782	2 682	15 921					1966
1967	14 192	14 869	- 677	2 933	17 125					1967
1968	15 993	16 399	- 406	3 134	19 127					1968
1969	17 589	18 074	- 485	3 887	21 476					1969
1970	19 840	20 285	- 445	4 328	24 168	44.6	22.6	15.8	17.0	1970
1971	22 232	24 230	-1 998	4 979	27 211	44.5	21.8	16.2	17.5	1971
1972	25 491	27 796	-2 305	5 569	31 060	45.2	22.3	15.9	16.6	1972
1973	29 895	31 955	-2 060	8 158	38 053	44.3	19.5	19.7	16.5	1973
1974	33 485	35 900	-2 415	9 365	42 850	45.3	17.8	20.1	16.8	1974
1975	35 797	38 066	-2 269	10 163	45 960	46.2	16.8	20.2	16.8	1975
1976	38 922	41 531	-2 609	10 878	49 800	46.2	16.1	19.7	18.0	1976
1977	40 343	41 821	-1 478	11 181	51 524	45.3	16.5	20.1	18.1	1977
1978	42 323	42 732	- 409	11 684	54 007	44.0	16.8	20.2	19.0	1978
1979	43 464	44 770	-1 306	12 266	55 730	43.3	16.8	20.7	19.2	1979
1980	46 464	47 240	- 776	13 098	59 562	43.1	16.9	20.6	19.4	1980
1981	49 560	49 956	- 396	14 105	63 665	43.8	16.6	20.8	18.8	1981
1982	52 942	54 384	-1 442	15 122	68 064	44.4	16.4	20.7	18.5	1982
1983	55 537	57 443	-1 906	15 776	71 313	44.6	16.5	20.8	18.1	1983
1984	59 124	59 779	- 655							1984

Table 14

Financing of Social Security

(at current prices, in million SFR)

Year	Old age/survivors' insurance					Invalidity insurance					Sickness insurance					Year
	contributions	state subsidies central	state subsidies cantonal	interests a.o.	total	contributions	state subsidies central	state subsidies cantonal	interests a.o.	total	contributions	state subsidies central	state subsidies cant./local	interests a.o.	total	
1948	417.8	106.7	53.3	4.9	582.7											1948
1950	458.5	106.7	53.3	18.9	637.4						210.8	24.5	13.3	12.6	261.2	1950
1955	600.4	106.7	53.3	92.7	853.1						319.3	31.0	20.0	17.1	387.4	1955
1960	798.2	106.7	53.3	160.9	1 119.1	75.4	17.7	8.9	0.5	102.5	486.7	47.7	26.5	24.3	585.2	1960
1961	906.5	106.7	53.3	177.1	1 243.6	89.4	52.2	26.1	1.5	169.2	536.7	56.8	39.9	22.6	656.0	1961
1962	1 004.8	106.7	53.3	187.9	1 352.7	100.5	56.1	28.0	1.0	185.6	595.1	58.8	30.2	25.7	709.8	1962
1963	1 120.6	106.7	53.3	208.5	1 489.1	112.1	62.6	31.3	0.8	206.8	661.2	61.6	31.5	31.1	785.4	1963
1964	1 235.1	262.5	87.5	207.6	1 792.7	123.5	94.4	31.5	0.5	249.9	734.4	129.6	41.3	22.6	927.9	1964
1965	1 354.5	262.5	87.5	222.8	1 927.3	135.5	103.3	34.5	2.2	275.5	813.7	161.4	51.8	26.9	1 053.8	1965
1966	1 445.9	262.6	87.5	235.2	2 031.1	144.6	115.9	38.6	2.3	301.4	952.6	192.9	61.0	30.5	1 237.0	1966
1967	1 574.2	262.5	87.5	249.8	2 174.0	157.4	134.4	44.8	1.6	338.2	1 059.3	238.8	74.7	33.7	1 406.5	1967
1968	1 669.9	262.5	87.5	258.0	2 277.9	204.6	152.2	50.8	1.3	408.9	1 234.5	280.4	83.0	36.3	1 634.2	1968
1969	2 271.7	429.0	143.0	268.9	3 112.6	267.1	199.8	66.6	0.6	534.1	1 381.6	310.9	98.3	39.8	1 830.6	1969
1970	2 550.0	443.3	147.7	293.0	3 434.0	299.0	222.2	74.1	0.5	595.8	1 507.5	357.2	110.7	59.1	2 034.5	1970
1971	2 946.6	513.8	171.2	317.0	3 948.6	344.6	255.5	85.2	-0.1	685.2	1 719.1	414.4	129.9	66.8	2 330.2	1971
1972	3 307.9	582.0	194.0	340.4	4 424.3	386.4	284.3	94.8	0.0	765.5	1 970.7	478.3	153.6	142.1	2 744.7	1972
1973	5 449.3	988.5	329.5	371.3	7 138.6	570.5	443.0	147.7	-0.9	1 160.3	2 339.4	564.9	186.8	74.1	3 165.2	1973
1974	6 284.9	1 020.0	340.0	419.8	8 064.7	654.9	504.6	168.2	-3.6	1 324.1	2 706.7	647.7	217.1	89.4	3 660.9	1974
1975	6 800.0	780.0	426.5	436.9	8 443.4	766.2	611.5	203.9	-9.0	1 572.6	3 103.5	691.6	244.6	117.6	4 157.2	1975
1976	7 098.5	819.3	439.6	423.4	8 780.8	858.0	678.4	226.1	-10.7	1 751.8	3 452.6	795.3	272.9	119.6	4 640.4	1976
1977	7 286.2	871.8	479.0	407.4	9 044.4	881.9	725.1	241.7	-14.2	1 834.5	3 714.6	856.0	286.4	125.1	4 982.1	1977
1978	7 541.9	1 091.3	496.1	357.9	9 487.2	911.2	736.3	245.4	-13.2	1 879.7	3 937.7	877.9	276.2	139.7	5 231.5	1978
1979	7 965.6	1 111.3	505.2	328.1	9 910.2	955.9	759.4	253.1	-15.0	1 953.4	4 086.5	895.0	296.3	146.7	5 424.5	1979
1980	8 629.4	1 394.3	536.3	335.5	10 895.5	1 035.2	806.9	269.0	-16.9	2 094.2	4 321.5	912.8	304.8	184.1	5 723.2	1980
1981	9 308.2	1 416.3	544.8	377.2	11 640.5	1 116.4	821.8	273.9	-17.5	2 194.6	4 704.6	873.8	317.5	190.6	6 086.5	1981
1982	10 063.8	1 857.7	619.3	406.9	12 947.7	1 206.8	923.6	307.9	-16.4	2 421.9	5 244.1	886.3	348.5	196.4	6 674.7	1982
1983	10 514.6	1 886.8	628.9	438.9	13 469.2	1 261.1	953.5	317.9	-11.9	2 520.6	5 948.7	882.2	370.8	170.3	7 372.0	1983
1984	10 978.1	2 126.5	708.9	445.1	14 258.6	1 316.8	1 077.0	358.9	-8.7	2 744.0						1984

Table 15

Financing of Social Security

(at current prices, in million SFR)

Year	Industrial accident insurance: contributions insured	Industrial accident insurance: contributions employers	Industrial accident insurance: central subsidies	Industrial accident insurance: interests a.o.	Industrial accident insurance: total	Income compensation: contributions	Income compensation: interests	Income compensation: total	Unemployment insurance: contributions	Unemployment insurance: state subs.	Unemployment insurance: interests a.o.	Unemployment insurance: total	Year
1945	24.2	62.0	1.0	17.4	104.6								1945
1950	45.2	97.7	2.5	25.1	170.5								1950
1955	71.1	140.4	2.9	35.5	249.9	—	—	—	—	—	—	—	1955
1960	103.5	185.1	14.7	58.5	361.8	74.9	2.8	77.7	25.0	2.7	8.6	36.3	1960
1961	116.1	205.6	16.7	66.0	404.2	88.7	3.3	92.0	24.3	1.1	9.2	34.6	1961
1962	130.4	230.0	18.6	75.5	454.5	99.9	3.9	103.8	22.8	1.0	9.7	33.5	1962
1963	140.8	246.7	20.0	85.9	493.4	111.5	4.9	116.4	21.2	1.7	10.6	33.5	1963
1964	165.1	286.0	23.5	98.4	573.0	122.0	5.2	128.0	20.7	0.2	11.3	32.2	1964
1965	172.5	290.3	24.5	109.2	596.5	134.8	5.4	140.2	19.1	0.2	12.8	32.1	1965
1966	179.9	284.9	25.6	123.4	613.9	143.8	5.8	149.6	18.4	0.2	13.6	32.2	1966
1967	207.1	314.5	29.5	141.6	693.0	156.7	6.4	163.1	15.2	0.1	15.7	31.0	1967
1968	218.8	324.4		152.5	695.7	166.2	7.3	173.5	12.7	0.3	18.0	31.0	1968
1969	233.5	335.0		170.0	738.6	179.9	7.8	187.7	12.0	0.1	20.0	32.1	1969
1970	254.2	360.1		190.8	805.1	199.8	7.0	206.8	11.8	0.1	21.5	33.4	1970
1971	309.9	417.6		210.9	938.4	228.9	7.1	236.0	10.8	0.0	22.6	33.4	1971
1972	346.7	464.1		242.9	1 053.7	256.6	7.9	264.5	10.1	0.0	24.1	34.2	1972
1973	452.2	494.4		256.1	1 202.7	290.5	9.6	300.1	10.2	0.0	29.5	39.7	1973
1974	522.8	537.7		301.7	1 362.2	327.7	12.6	340.3	10.8	0.0	29.5	40.3	1974
1975	511.0	486.4		361.7	1 358.9	415.0	14.1	429.1	19.7	85.4	84.1	189.2	1975
1976	494.0	454.1		382.7	1 330.8	512.5	17.9	530.4	105.9	245.9	252.9	604.7	1976
1977	504.5	459.1		400.3	1 363.9	526.9	20.0	546.9	399.5		7.8	407.3	1977
1978	521.4	476.8		387.5	1 385.7	544.4	22.2	566.6	580.0		19.3	599.3	1978
1979	540.1	531.8		360.4	1 432.3	571.4	24.4	595.8	598.6		27.5	626.1	1979
1980	576.6	577.7		397.8	1 579.1	618.6	29.4	648.0	428.5		45.2	473.7	1980
1981	610.3	618.6		417.9	1 646.8	667.3	37.8	705.1	427.5		70.6	498.1	1981
1982	636.3	654.7		497.2	1 788.2	721.4	45.5	766.9	283.0		81.8	364.8	1982
1983	729.6	715.6		398.8	1 907.0	753.8	51.6	805.4	307.4		59.3	366.7	1983
1984						787.2	58.5	845.7					1984

Table 16

Financing of Social Security
(at current prices, in million SFR)

Year	Agricultural family allowances				Cantonal family allowances				Total social security				Year
	contrib- utions	state subsidies central	state subsidies cantonal	total	contrib- utions	cant. subs.	inter- ests	total	contrib- utions	state subs.	interest a.o.	total	
1950	—	—	—	—	—	—	—	—					1950
1955													1955
1960	2.1	10.2	5.1	17.4	25.9			25.9	1 776.8	341.7	255.6	2 374.1	1960
1961	2.1	9.8	4.9	16.8	31.5			31.5	2 000.9	415.0	279.7	2 695.6	1961
1962	2.0	11.6	5.8	19.4	43.0			43.0	2 228.5	421.6	303.7	2 953.8	1962
1963	2.5	20.1	10.0	32.6	47.8			47.8	2 464.4	453.0	341.8	3 259.2	1963
1964	2.7	18.8	9.4	30.9	60.0			60.0	2 749.5	765.2	345.6	3 860.3	1964
1965	2.6	18.1	9.1	29.8	72.4		1.3	73.7	2 895.4	825.5	380.6	4 101.5	1965
1966	2.6	26.3	13.2	42.1	78.7		2.4	81.1	3 251.4	1 050.3	413.2	4 714.9	1966
1967	2.8	30.1	15.1	48.0	87.9	0.0	2.5	90.4	3 575.1	1 273.1	451.3	5 299.5	1967
1968	2.9	27.1	13.5	43.5	94.6	0.0	2.8	97.4	3 928.6	1 282.7	476.2	5 687.5	1968
1969	2.7	26.3	13.2	42.2	114.5	0.1	3.1	117.7	4 798.0	1 608.3	510.2	6 916.5	1969
1970	2.8	32.3	16.1	51.2	133.3	0.1	3.8	137.2	5 318.5	1 737.4	575.7	7 631.6	1970
1971	3.0	36.0	18.0	57.0	156.1	0.1	4.4	160.6	6 136.6	2 120.2	628.7	8 885.5	1971
1972	2.8	32.7	16.4	51.9	192.2	0.1	5.2	197.4	6 919.5	2 394.3	762.6	10 076.4	1972
1973	3.2	31.9	16.0	51.1	216.2	0.1	6.0	222.3	9 825.9	2 738.8	745.7	13 310.4	1973
1974	3.6	38.8	19.4	61.8	255.5	0.1	7.3	262.9	11 304.6	3 418.9	856.7	15 580.2	1974
1975	5.1	52.2	26.1	83.4	262.2	0.1	9.5	271.8	12 369.1	3 580.1	1 014.9	16 964.1	1975
1976	5.6	42.8	21.4	69.8	273.3	0.0	10.2	283.5	13 254.5	4 022.5	1 196.0	18 473.0	1976
1977	5.4	43.8	21.9	71.1	286.0		9.9	195.9	14 064.1	4 066.3	956.3	19 086.7	1977
1978	5.7	37.9	19.0	62.6	319.3		9.6	328.9	14 838.4	4 333.6	923.0	20 095.0	1978
1979	5.7	36.3	18.2	60.2	363.2		8.7	371.9	15 618.8	4 433.8	880.8	20 933.4	1979
1980	6.4	41.5	20.8	68.7	424.0		10.4	434.4	16 617.9	4 874.6	985.5	22 478.0	1980
1981	6.8	49.4	24.7	80.9	456.7		12.8	469.5	17 916.4	4 925.6	1 083.4	23 925.4	1981
1982	7.3	46.0	23.0	76.3	518.2		17.3	535.5	19 335.6	5 750.2	1 226.7	26 312.5	1982
1983	7.8	44.7	22.4	74.9	530.6		18.6	549.2	20 769.2	5 889.9	1 125.6	27 784.7	1983
1984	8.6	50.8	25.4	84.9									1984

Table 17

Old Age and Survivors Pensioners

Number of

Year	Ordinary pensions				Extra-ordinary pensions				Suppl. benefits		Pensioners			Year
	single	married couple	supple-ments	survi-vors	single	married couple	supple-ments	survi-vors	old age	survi-vors	old age	survi-vors	total	
1948					147 269	35 028		65 000						1948
1950	34 004	16 388		19 438	144 070	33 997		58 472			278 844	77 910	356 754	1950
1955	125 058	62 474		67 555	149 684	30 901		44 539			461 492	112 094	573 586	1955
1960	250 922	112 109		69 195	167 055	21 691		33 573			685 577	102 768	788 345	1960
1961	243 055	109 387		87 187	138 476	16 554		25 018			633 413	112 205	756 618	1961
1962	290 468	133 123		103 906	146 180	15 139		26 083			733 172	129 992	863 164	1962
1963	306 116	138 666		105 682	134 736	12 403		22 495			742 990	128 177	871 167	1963
1964	340 368	145 186	35 362	103 426	131 406	9 914	731	18 030			781 974	121 456	903 430	1964
1965	360 412	152 924	44 005	106 076	123 917	8 091	1 183	15 991			806 359	122 067	928 426	1965
1966	379 569	160 189	46 991	107 811	114 379	6 506	1 325	14 162	100 015	6 734	827 338	121 973	949 311	1966
1967	395 694	166 035	48 791	109 789	102 764	4 911	1 389	12 667	140 641	6 277	840 350	122 456	962 806	1967
1968	416 975	175 133	51 330	111 933	96 447	4 028	1 407	11 365	139 488	6 571	871 744	123 298	995 042	1968
1969	432 445	181 244	52 017	112 964	87 704	3 102	1 437	10 284	129 807	5 843	888 841	123 248	1 012 089	1969
1970									127 725	5 560				1970
1971									146 187	6 250				1971
1972									147 666	6 127				1972
1973									109 591	4 839				1973
1974									104 547	4 280				1974
1975	493 432	209 639	47 601	116 195	46 979	901	715	7 826	91 796	3 693	961 491	124 021	1 085 512	1975
1976	502 660	214 091	48 761	115 620	41 787	766	699	7 528	91 217	3 614	974 161	123 148	1 097 309	1976
1977	509 884	217 205	49 101	115 878	37 682	725	683	7 372	92 976	3 755	983 426	123 250	1 106 676	1977
1978	519 833	222 658	50 545	117 124	33 894	703	609	7 085	94 355	3 372	1 000 449	124 209	1 124 658	1978
1979	534 087	228 469	54 831	124 301	31 066	744	561	7 378	93 672	2 996	1 023 579	131 679	1 155 258	1979
1980	548 910	225 718	63 215	125 039	28 185	736	539	7 200	93 061	3 045	1 030 003	132 239	1 162 242	1980
1981	563 633	221 804	70 003	127 623	25 991	738	529	7 121	94 240	3 210	1 034 708	134 744	1 169 452	1981
1982	572 800	225 091	69 062	128 974	24 463	776	530	6 935	96 686	3 175	1 048 997	135 909	1 184 906	1982
1983	583 034	228 892	66 549	129 725	23 163	787	486	6 851	98 366	3 144	1 065 555	136 576	1 202 131	1983
1984	592 885	233 672	64 221	128 970	21 950	778	498	6 711	100 573	3 041	1 083 735	135 681	1 219 416	1984

Table 18

Invalidity Pensioners

Year	Number of: Ordinary pensions: single	Ordinary pensions: married couple	Ordinary pensions: supplements	Extra-ordinary pensions: single	Extra-ordinary pensions: married couple	Extra-ordinary pensions: supplements	Supplementary benefits	Pensioners	Year
1960	21 807	1 901	9 674						1960
1961	32 943	2 672	13 717	5 425	65	2 186		43 392	1961
1962	51 372	6 151	28 911	10 319	159	4 479		74 311	1962
1963	54 479	6 808	32 695	11 223	164	4 903		79 646	1963
1964	55 878	6 979	34 526	10 554	132	4 855		80 654	1964
1965	58 370	7 750	36 601	11 222	133	4 932		85 358	1965
1966	60 512	8 324	39 111	11 716	124	4 832	17 294	89 124	1966
1967	64 017	8 937	43 799	12 246	123	4 688	25 640	94 383	1967
1968	64 917	9 319	45 515	12 933	129	4 378	26 401	96 746	1968
1969	66 541	9 910	48 489	13 595	134	4 352	25 466	100 224	1969
1970							24 745		1970
1971							26 199		1971
1972							25 734		1972
1973							21 495		1973
1974							20 037		1974
1975	73 744	8 300	63 792	15 755	74	3 216	17 788	106 247	1975
1976	73 847	8 876	63 535	15 641	82	2 918	17 928	107 404	1976
1977	78 658	10 657	67 375	16 287	91	2 808	18 206	116 441	1977
1978	80 195	10 517	69 365	16 512	88	2 615	18 652	117 917	1978
1979	89 608	10 947	79 922	17 553	96	2 696	18 020	129 247	1979
1980	88 210	8 672	77 303	17 602	83	2 403	18 891	123 322	1980
1981	93 506	7 883	82 785	18 216	85	2 430	18 950	127 658	1981
1982	95 488	8 110	83 599	18 639	82	2 298	19 798	130 511	1982
1983	98 662	8 667	85 450	19 338	96	2 303	20 934	135 526	1983
1984	101 760	9 269	87 072	20 097	104	2 310	22 363	140 603	1984

Table 19

Members of Sickness and Unemployment Insurance

Year	Approved sickness insurance funds						Unemployment insurance funds			Year
	No. of funds	Number of members (in 1,000s)				Of which: residents	No. of funds	Members (in 1,000s)	Beneficiaries (in 1,000)	
		men	women	children	total					
1945	1 151	1 016	986	486	2 488	2 119				1945
1950	1 154	1 254	1 166	618	3 038	2 568				1950
1955	1 135	1 465	1 357	836	3 658	3 147				1955
1960	1 088	1 756	1 608	1 049	4 413	3 872	184	625	27	1960
1961	1 086	1 864	1 675	1 077	4 616	4 051	184	615	17	1961
1962	1 069	1 961	1 753	1 115	4 829	4 247	185	603	16	1962
1963	1 046	2 050	1 818	1 154	5 022	4 435	185	592	17	1963
1964	1 019	2 146	1 898	1 193	5 237	4 643	185	577	6	1964
1965	984	2 170	1 964	1 251	5 385	4 877	182	562	6	1965
1966	898	2 226	2 024	1 301	5 551	5 046	179	550	5	1966
1967	875	2 273	2 082	1 346	5 701	5 192	172	548	4	1967
1968	857	2 304	2 138	1 382	5 824	5 320	165	551	5	1968
1969	840	2 349	2 188	1 416	5 953	5 448	157	544	3	1969
1970	815	2 401	2 243	1 437	6 081	5 569	153	533	2	1970
1971	793	2 469	2 305	1 455	6 229	5 698	153	519	2	1971
1972	763	2 542	2 386	1 468	6 396	5 831	153	512	1	1972
1973	735	2 598	2 463	1 474	6 535	5 949	148	526	1	1973
1974	707	2 636	2 522	1 472	6 630	6 030	139	545	2	1974
1975	662	2 618	2 558	1 446	6 622	6 018	130	1 061	194	1975
1976	634	2 606	2 570	1 409	6 585	5 990	114	1 436	288	1976
1977	615	2 615	2 601	1 379	6 595	6 000	114	2 700	75	1977
1978	598	2 670	2 640	1 350	6 660	6 042	98	2 700	113	1978
1979	577	2 731	2 685	1 319	6 735	6 070	96	2 700	103	1979
1980	555	2 791	2 730	1 291	6 812	6 164	93	2 700	52	1980
1981	537	2 853	2 787	1 270	6 910	6 239	91	2 700	71	1981
1982	514	2 907	2 829	1 247	6 983	6 297	88	2 700	182	1982
1983	492	2 934	2 863	1 225	7 022	6 334	86	2 700		1983

Table 20

Population and Labour Force

Year	Population (1,000s)			Labour force I (1,000s)			Labour force II (1,000s)				Year
	total	0–19	65+	self-employed	employ-ees	total	male	female	total	foreigners	
1950	4 668	1 431	440	392	1 755	2 147					1950
1951	4 717	1 445	451								1951
1952	4 779	1 466	458								1952
1953	4 844	1 489	468								1953
1954	4 907	1 511	477								1954
1955	4 970	1 535	486								1955
1956	5 034	1 558	493								1956
1957	5 097	1 585	503								1957
1958	5 163	1 616	513								1958
1959	5 230	1 645	526								1959
1960	5 296	2 071	538	369	2 302	2 671	1 790	927	2 717	445	1960
1961	5 360	1 704	551				1 880	964	2 844	546	1961
1962	5 508	1 780	567				1 959	995	2 954	641	1962
1963	5 639	1 838	579				1 990	1 009	2 999	698	1963
1964	5 749	1 878	592				2 027	1 019	3 046	732	1964
1965	5 829	1 896	609				2 017	1 008	3 025	714	1965
1966	5 884	1 902	624				2 006	1 008	3 014	702	1966
1967	5 952	1 910	641				2 019	1 011	3 030	714	1967
1968	6 031	1 938	630				2 031	1 017	3 048	732	1968
1969	6 104	1 921	676				2 060	1 039	3 099	763	1969
1970	6 169	1 919	693	300	2 691	2 991	2 075	1 067	3 142	787	1970
1971	6 193	1 921	711				2 112	1 086	3 198	809	1971
1972	6 234	1 475	728				2 141	1 102	3 243	830	1972
1973	6 288	1 925	748				2 152	1 125	3 277	835	1973
1974	6 327	1 919	725				2 143	1 131	3 274	810	1974
1975	6 356	1 906	743				2 035	1 082	3 117	731	1975
1976	6 321	1 871	806				1 969	1 055	3 024	646	1976
1977	6 284	1 832	822				1 967	1 069	3 036	622	1977
1978	6 278	1 804	841				1 978	1 088	3 066	628	1978
1979	6 285	1 781	856				1 991	1 109	3 100	637	1979
1980	6 304	1 760	871	299	2 768	3 067	2 026	1 144	3 170	659	1980
1981											1981
1982											1982
1983											1983
1984											1984

Table 21

Election Results

Distribution of votes by party

Party	1947	1951	1955	1959	1963	1967	1971	1975	1979
FDP	23.0	24.0	23.3	23.7	24.0	23.2	21.9	22.2	24.1
CVP	21.2	22.5	23.2	23.3	23.4	22.1	20.6	21.1	21.5
SPS	26.2	26.0	27.0	26.4	26.6	23.5	22.9	24.9	24.4
SVP	12.1	12.6	12.1	11.6	11.4	11.0	10.2	9.9	11.6
LDU	4.4	5.1	5.5	5.5	5.0	9.1	7.6	6.1	4.1
LPS	3.2	2.6	2.2	2.3	2.2	2.3	2.2	2.4	2.8
EVP	0.9	1.0	1.1	1.4	1.6	1.6	2.1	2.0	2.2
NA						0.6	3.2	2.5	1.3
PDA	5.1	2.7	2.6	2.7	2.2	2.9	2.9	2.4	2.1
POCH							0.1	1.0	1.7
RML								0.4	0.4
Other	3.9	3.5	3.0	3.1	3.6	3.7	2.8	2.1	3.1
Electoral participation	72.4	71.2	70.1	68.5	66.1	65.7	56.9	52.4	48.0

FDP	Freisinnig-demokratische Partei der Schweiz
CVP	Christlichdemokratische Volkspartei der Schweiz
SPS	Sozialdemokratische Partei der Schweiz
SVP	Schweizerische Volkspartei
LDU	Landesring der Unabhängigen
LPS	Liberale Partei der Schweiz
EVP	Evangelische Volkspartei
NA	Nationale Aktion für Volk und Heimat
PDA	Partei der Arbeit der Schweiz
POCH	Progressive Organisationen der Schweiz
RML	Revolutionäre Marxistische Liga

Notes to and sources for appendix tables

Table 1

GDP and deflators:
Source: (1), various years.

Total public expenditure:
Sum of the consolidated expenditure of the central government, the cantons and the local communities given in source (16) plus the total expenditure on social security (excluding sickness insurance) given in Table 6 minus the public subsidies to social security given in Table 17 (excluding sickness insurance). Figures at constant prices have been deflated by the GDP deflator.

Table 2

Consolidated public expenditure by central, cantonal and local government; in consolidating figures, public expenditure is officially counted at the level of government where it comes from and not where it is finally spent.
Sources: (16), (21).

Table 3

At current prices:

Income maintenance:
Total expenditure on income maintenance (see Table 5, col. 10)

Education:
Total expenditure on education and research.
Source: (16).

Health:
Total public expenditure on health, mainly hospital; not including sickness insurance (see Table 6).
Source: (16).

Housing:
Public expenditure on housing construction.
Source: (16)

Other:
Total expenditure on social security (see Table 6, col. 10) minus total expenditure on income maintenance (see Table 5, col. 10) plus expenditure on social assistance (see Table. 5, col. 9).

Total:
Sum of cols 1-5.

At constant prices:
Income maintenance deflated by the consumer price index (see Table 1), health, education, housing and 'other' by the GDP deflator (see Table 1); total = sum of cols 6-9.

Table 4

Social expenditure by major category at current prices (see Table 3) as percentage of GDP (see Table 1, col. 1), as percentage of total public expenditure (see Table 1, col. 6) and as percent distribution.

Table 5

Old age and survivors' pensions:
Sum of benefits of all schemes (Table 7, col. 11) and supplementary benefits (Table 9, col. 3).
The benefits of all schemes include a small amount of non-pension benefits (see notes to Table 7).

Invalidity pensions:
Sum of ordinary and extra-ordinary pensions and supplementary benefits (Table 9, col. 6). For the years 1960-69 and 1975-84 figures on pensions are the sum of cols 4 and 8 in Table 8 (see notes to Table 8). For the years 1970-74 figures on pensions have been estimated at 58% of the benefits of all schemes (Table 8, col. 9).

Industrial accident cash benefits:
Includes sickness cash benefits and pensions (Table 10, col. 2).

Military insurance pensions:
Includes invalidity and survivors' pensions (Table 11, col. 8).

Income compensation:
Compensations for conscripts (Table 11, col. 5).

Unemployment cash benefits:
Table 11, col. 1.

Agricultural family allowances:
Table 12, col. 1.

Cantonal family allowances:
Table 12, col. 4.

Social assistance:
Table 12, col. 9.

Total I:
Sum of cols 1-9.

Sickness, maternity benefits:
Sum of cols 7 and 8 in Table 10.

Total II:
Sum of cols 10 and 11.

Table 6

Old age and survivors' insurance (AHV):
Total expenditure on all schemes (Table 7, col. 13).

Invalidity insurance (IV):
Total expenditure on all schemes (Table 8, col. 12).

Supplementary pension benefits to AHV and IV:
Sum of cols 3 and 6 in Table 9.

Industrial accident insurance (SUVA):
Total expenditure (Table 10, col. 5).

Military insurance (MV):
Total expenditure (Table 11, col. 11).

Income compensation (EO):
Total expenditure (Table 11, col. 7).

Unemployment insurance (AV):
Total expenditure (Table 11, col. 4).

Agricultural family allowances:
Total expenditure (Table 12, col. 3).

Cantonal family allowances:
Total expenditure (Table 12, col. 6).

Social security I:
Sum of cols 1-9.

Sickness insurance:
Total expenditure (Table 10, col. 12).

Social security II:
Sum of cols 10 and 11.

Tables 7 and 8

Ordinary and extra-ordinary pensions differ in the required contribution period entitling for benefits. Married couple's pensions are paid for spouses and children. Survivors' pensions include widows' and orphans' pensions. For the years 1970-74 data are not available for single pension categories because of a change in statistics from an annual to a monthly basis. Official figures in source (2) for 1975 refer to January, and from 1976 to March; they have been multiplied by twelve and are not completely comparable to the figures prior to 1970.

All schemes (old age and survivors' pensions):
Expenditure on 'benefits' differs slightly from the sum of ordinary and extra-ordinary pensions, because it also includes expenditure on individual provisions (*individuelle Maßnahmen*) and transfers to welfare institutions; administrative costs include the costs of implementation (*Durchführungskosten*).

All schemes (invalidity pensions):
Expenditure on 'benefits' differs substantially from the sum of ordinary and extra-ordinary pensions, because it also includes expenditure on other cash benefits, on individual medical care, other individual provisions and on transfers to welfare institutions. (According to source (9) p. 71, in 1982, 65.9% of total expenditure was on pensions and other cash benefits, 6.4% on medical care, 10.1% on other individual provisions, and 14.0% on transfers.) 'Other' expenditure includes the costs of implementation.

Sources: (2), Table 2-7; (17) *Erläuterungen*, pp. III-XII.

Table 9

Supplementary benefits to old age and survivors' insurance and to invalidity insurance were introduced in 1966 and are paid by the federal government and the cantons. Six cantons pay additional supplementary benefits, a small and declining amount, not included in the figures.
Source: (2), Table 13.

Occupational pension insurance was made compulsory in 1985. Figures on total expenditure are estimates and refer to benefits only, administrative costs and other expenditure being unknown. Total revenues include the contributions by employees and employers and from 1966 capital interests for which no figures are available prior to 1966.
Source: (2), Table 16.

Table 10

Industrial accident insurance:
Figures on 'reserve' not available prior to 1960.
Source: (2), Table 21.

Sickness insurance:
Figures on the breakdown of total benefits by cash benefits (sickness cash benefits and maternity benefits) and health care (ordinary insurance, invalidity, tubercolosis and benefits of other insurances) not available for all years (source 18).
Sources: (2), Table 18; (18).

Table 11

Sources: (2), Tables 22, 23 and 25; (20), military insurance 1950 and 1955.

Table 12

Family allowances:
Source: (2), Tables 27 and 28.

Social assistance:
Excluding central govt expenditure which is negligible; local govt expenditure has been estimated at 150 percent of cantonal expenditure for 1950-60 and at 190 percent for 1961-62; cantonal expenditure excludes the social assistance for old people and invalids in the years 1961-64 and 1966.
Source: (1)

Table 13

Figures on public revenues, public expenditure, surplus, direct and indirect taxes are from source (16); social security revenues and social security contributions without state subsidies and excluding sickness insurance (see Tables 14-16); total public revenues = sum of public revenues (of central, cantonal and local government) and social revenues.

Tables 14-16

Contributions to sickness insurance include various kinds of direct charges. In the industrial accident insurance date on reserve expenditure are not available prior to 1960. The financing of total social security includes in addition to the schemes in Table 15-17 also the supplementary benefits to AHV and TV (see Table 9) and the military insurance (see Table 11) both of which are completely financed by the state.
Source: (2), Tables 4, 7, 18, 21, 23, 25, 27, 28.

Tables 17 and 18

Pensions and supplementary benefits:
See notes to Tables 7-9.

Pensioners:
Number of old age pensioners = number of single ordinary and extra-ordinary pensions + number of married couple ordinary and extra-ordinary pensions multipled by 2 because these pensions are paid to couples where both spouses have reached pensionable age;
number of survivors' pensioners = number of ordinary and extra-ordinary survivors' pensions;
number of invalidity pensioners = number of single ordinary and extra-ordinary pensions + number of married couple pensions multiplied by 2.
Source: (2), Tables 5, 6, 12.

Table 19

Source: (2), Tables 17 and 24.

Table 20

Population:
Resident population; annual figures provided by the *Bundesamt für Statistik*.

Labour force I:
Population census statistics.

Labour force II:
Figures are official estimates on the basis of several indicators and census results.
Source: (10).

Table 21

Source: (7).

Enumerated sources to appendix tables

(1) *Statistisches Jahrbuch der Schweiz 1986*, Bundesamt für Statistik (ed.), Basel 1986.

(2) *Zahlenspiegel der sozialen Sicherheit in der Schweiz Ausgabe 1985*, Bundesamt für Sozialversicherung (ed.), Sektion Statistik, Bern 1985.

(3) *Statistik der Ergänzungsleistungen zu den AHV/IV-Renten in den Kantonen Bern und St. Gallen*, Bundesamt für Sozialversicherung (ed.), Sektion Statistik, Bern 1985.

(4) Ulrich Klöti (ed.), *Handbuch Politisches System der Schweiz*, Vol. 2, Strukturen und Prozesse, Bern and Stuttgart 1984.

(5) *Öffentliche Finanzen der Schweiz 1983*, in: Statistische Quellenwerke der Schweiz, Heft 785, Bundesamt für Statistik (ed.), Bern 1985.

(6) *Schülerstatistik 1985/86*, Statistische Resultate Nr. 15 (Bildung und Wissenschaft), Bundesamt für Statistik (ed.), Bern 1986 (Amtliche Statistik der Schweiz, Nr. 15).

(7) *Nationalratswahlen 1979*, Statistische Quellenwerke der Schweiz, Heft 654, Bundesamt für Statistik (ed.), Bern 1980.

(8) *Bildungsstatistik*, Statistik aktuell Nr. 4, Nov. 1986, Bundesamt für Statistik (ed.), Bern 1986.

(9) P. Gygi and A. Frey, *Das Schweizerische Gesundheitswesen*, Zahlenspiegel, Anbieter von Gesundheitsgütern, Preisbildung, Organisationsstrukturen, Basel 1984.

(10) *Info à la carte*, Statistik der Erwerbstätigen, Mai 1986, Bundesamt für Statistik (ed.), Bern 1985.

(11) BIGA-Sozialstatistik, Bern various years.

(12) *Die Wohnbautätigkeit im Jahre 1984*, in: Die Volkswirtschaft, Juni 1985, Bundesamt für Industrie, Gewerbe und Arbeit (BIGA).

(13) *Bildungsstatistik Nr. 4* (Nov. 1986), Statistik aktuell, Bundesamt für Statistik (ed.), Bern 1986.

(14) *Almanach der Schweiz.* Daten und Kommentare zu Bevölkerung, Gesellschaft und Politik. Soziologisches Institut der Universität Zürich (ed.), Bern, Frankfurt am Main, Las Vegas 1976.

(15) *Volkszählung 1980*, Statistische Quellenwerke der Schweiz, Heft 708, Bundesamt für Statistik (ed.), Bern 1983.

(16) *Öffentliche Finanzen der Schweiz.* Statistische Quellenwerke der Schweiz, verschiedene Jahrgänge, Bundesamt für Statistik (ed.), Bern various years.

(17) *Die AHV- und IV-Renten im Lichte der Statistik*, Bundesamt für Sozialversicherung (ed.), Erläuterungen. Bern 1981/82.

(18) *Die Entwicklung der Krankenpflegekosten, der Einnahmen und Ausgaben sowie des Vermögens seit 1966.* Bundesamt für Sozialversicherung. Bern 1986.

(19) *Statistik über die Krankenversicherung.* Vom Bunde anerkannte Versicherungsträger 1984. Bundesamt für Sozialversicherung. Bern 1986.

(20) *Statistik Militärversicherung 1985.* Hrsg. Bundesamt für Militärversicherung. Bern 1987.

(21) *Die Finanzen von Bund, Kantonen und Gemeinden 1938-1971.* Eidgenössisches Statistisches Amt. Bern 1974.

Netherlands

Joop Roebroek and Theo Berben

The institutional synopsis, bibliography and appendix tables are based on earlier versions, prepared by Rinus van Schendelen and his collaborators, which have been extended and thoroughly rivised by the authors.

Institutional Synopsis

Contents

Glossary of abbreviations

AAW	*Algemene Arbeidsongeschiktheidswet* (General Disablement Benefits Act)
ABP	*Algemeen Burgerlijk Pensioenfonds* (Public Servants' Superannuation Fund)
ABW	*Algemene Bijstandswet* (National Assistance Act)
AKW	*Algemene Kinderbijslagwet* (General Family Allowances Act)
AOW	*Algemene Ouderdomswet* (General Old Age Pensions Act)
AWBZ	*Algemene Wet Bijzondere Ziektekosten* (Exceptional Medical Expenses Act)
AWW	*Algemene Weduwen en Wezenwet* (General Widows' and Orphans' Benefits Act)
BKR	*Beeldende Kunstenaars Regeling* (Scheme for State Aid to Artists)
GAB	*Gewestelijk Arbeidsbureau* (Regional Employment Offices)
IW	*Invaliditeitswet* (Invalidity Act)
KKZ	*Kinderbijslagwet Zelfstandigen* (Self-Employed Persons Family Allowances Act)
KTO	*Kindertoeslagregling voor Overheidspersoneel* (Public Service Employees Family Allowances Scheme)
KWL	*Kinderbijslagwet Loontrekkers* (Wage-Earners Family Allowances Act)
RWW	*Rijksgroepsregeling Werkloze Werknemers*
VUT	*Vervroegd Uittreden* (Early Retirement pensions)
WAO	*Wet op de Arbeidsongschikthheidsverzekering* (Disablement Insurance Act)
WRO	*Wachtgeldregeling Overheidspersoneel* (Public Servants Redundancy Pay Scheme)
WSW	*Wet Sociale Werkvooziening* (Sheltered Employment Act)
WW	*Werkloosheidswet* (Unemployment Insurance Act)
WWV	*Wet Werkloosheidsvoorziening* (Unemployment Provisions Act)
ZFW	*Ziekenfondswet* (Health Insurance Act)
ZW	*Ziektewet* (Sickness Benefits Act)

Introduction

The Dutch social security system is highly complex. It consists of a great variety of social insurance schemes for the total or the employed population, a number of general or special welfare provisions, and various private occupational pension schemes.

National insurance schemes (Volksverzekeringen)

Contributions are remitted to the Government Tax Department. This system applies to the: General Disablement Benefits Act (AAW), Exceptional Medical Expenses Act (AWBZ), General Old Age Pensions Act (AOW), General Widows' and Orphans' Benefits Act (AWW), and the General Family Allowances Act (AKW) with (until 1980) its related acts for self-employed persons (KKZ) and wage-earners (KWL). The AWBZ occupies a special position, its administrative structure is limited to the reimbursement of medical expenses and it has no other effect on income maintenance. The National Insurance Schemes, with the exception of the AAW and the AWBZ, are implemented by the Social Insurance Bank (*Sociale Verzekeringsbank*), which is an autonomous administrative body, in which employers and employees are equally represented and make decisions under the chairmanship of a government representative. Policy is executed through the 22 regional Labour Councils (*Raden van Arbeid*), which are controlled by the Social Insurance Bank. The AWBZ and the ZFW programmes (an employed persons' insurance scheme), are implemented by the approximately 60 Health Insurance Funds (*Ziekenfondsen*), and the many private insurance corporations (*Ziektekostenverzekeraars*), controlled by the Health Insurance Funds Council (*Ziekenfondsraad*). Finally, the AAW programme is implemented by Industrial Insurance Boards (*Bedrijfsverenigingen*), which also play a major role in the second type of Insurance Schemes.

Employed persons insurance schemes (Werknemersverzekeringen)

Contributions are remitted to industrial insurance boards. This system applies to the: Unemployment Insurance Act (WW), Sickness Benefits Act (ZW), Disablement Insurance Act (WAO) and, only for reimbursement, the Compulsory Health Insurance Act (ZFW). The first three welfare programmes are implemented by 26 Industrial Insurance Boards (*Bedrijfsverenigingen*), each of which deals with a branch of industry, in which employers and employees cooperate. The WAO programme is partly implemented through the Joint Medical Office (*Gemeenschappelijke Medische Dienst*), which gives medical advice to the Industrial Insurance Boards. The same framework (Joint Medical Office, Industrial Insurance Boards) is used to implement the national insurance scheme (AAW), and is controlled by the Social Insurance Council (*Sociale Verzekeringsraad*), which represents employees, employers, and government, and which ultimately authorizes the Social Insurance Bank.

General welfare provisions

These schemes are financed by government, as opposed to the insured's contributions. This applies to the different schemes: Public Assistance Act (ABW), Sheltered Employment Act (WSW), and Unemployment Provisions Act (WWV), Government Unemployment Assistance Regulations (RWW), and the Scheme for State Aid to Artists (BKR). While the Ministry of Social Affairs and Employment is responsible for supervising the administration of these schemes, application in individual cases is entrusted to the authorities in the municipality, the Social Offices (*Sociale Diensten*).

In addition, there are a variety of private pension programmes, agreed upon by employers and employees within a (branch of) industry. Most of these agreements are implemented through private pension corporations. The pensions for public servants and other publicly employed personnel are administered by the General Public Pension Fund (*Algemeen Burgerlijk Pensioenfonds*), an autonomous administrative body.

I Pensions

Under the Dutch pension system we have included not only old age, survivors' and invalidity pensions, but also sickness cash benefits which, since 1967, have formed an integrated scheme with invalidity pensions. In 1983, total pension expenditure amounted to 68,584 million HFL, i.e. 61.7% of total public expenditure on social security or 17.9% of GDP.

Pension expenditure in 1983 in million HFL

		%
General old age pensions (AOW)	21 831	31.8
Early retirement pensions (VUT)[a]	715	1.0
Public servants superannuation	6 426	9.4
Other public servants pensions[b]	1 763	2.6
Occupational pensions	7 570	11.0
General widows/orphans pensions (AWW)	2 692	3.9
Invalidity insurance benefits	165	0.2
General invalidity pensions (AAW)	9 386	13.7
Employees' invalidity pensions (WAO)	7 599	11.1
Sickness benefits (ZW)	6 772	9.9
Public servants' sickness benefits	3 665	5.4
Total	68 584	100.0

[a] Inclusive of government early retirement regulations.
[b] Military pensions, pensions for ex-Indonesian public servants, and pensions for railwaymen.

Source: Ministry of Social Affairs and Employment,

1. Old age and survivors' pensions

Income maintenance

The pension system consists of basic pensions covering all residents, special pension schemes for public servants, and a variety of occupational pension schemes for private employees (and to some extent also for self-employed). In 1983, on the base of the AOW and the AWW, 1,393,000 and 175,000 people respectively were entitled to benefits, amounting together to 24,523 million HFL, i.e. 22.1% of the total expenditure on social expenditure, or 6.4% of GDP. In 1983 total public expenditure on old age and survivors' pensions amounted to 33,427 million HFL, i.e. 30.1% of total public expenditure on social security, or 8.7 of GDP.

Public pension expenditure in 1983 in million HFL

		%
General old age pensions (AOW)	21 831	65.3
Early retirement pensions (VUT)[a]	715	2.1
Public servants' superannuation	6 426	19.2
Other public servants' pensions[b]	1 763	5.3
General widows' and orphans' pensions (AWW)	2 692	8.1
Total	33 427	100.0

[a] Inclusive of government early retirement regulations.
[b] Military pensions, pensions for ex-Indonesian public servants, and pensions for railwaymen.

Source: Ministry of Social Affairs and Employment, *Financiele nota sociale zekerheid 1985*, The Hague, 1984, pp. 97, 98, 101.

Coverage

General pensions are based on the 1957 General Old Age Pensions Act (*Algemene Ouderdomswet*, AOW) and the 1959 General Widows' and Orphans' Benefits Act (*Algemene Weduwen en Wezenwet*, AWW). They replaced the non-contributory and means-tested pension scheme of 1947, established under the Old Age Pensions (Emergency Provision) Act (*Noodwet Ouderdomsvoorziening*). As from 1957 all residents have received a flat-rate pension at the age of 65 which is supposed to provide a basic social minimum. Until 1983 married women did not have an individual entitlement to an old age pension. Since 1977 a number of early retirement schemes (*Vervroegd Uittreden*, VUT) have been introduced on the initiative of the government in collaboration with employers' and employees' organizations. From 1962, widows between the ages of 40 and 64 who are unfit to work, or have one or more children under the age of 18, have been entitled to a pension. In the case of pregnancy a widow is entitled to a pension from the date of the husband's death. Widows not qualifying for a pension under these conditions receive temporary benefits. An orphan's pension is granted to full orphans up to 16 years of age. In certain cases (e.g. if the child is disabled) an orphan's pension is payable up to the age of 18 or, if the child is studying, up to the age of 27.

In addition to the general provisions, there are various private sector supplementary pension schemes, organized either on an enterprise (*Ondernemingspensioenfondsen*) or an industry-wide basis (*Bedryfspensioenfondsen*). Separate funds exist for doctors, medical specialists, etc. The industry-wide Pensions Funds Act of 1949 (*Wet op de verplichte deelneming aan een bedryfspensioenfonds*), empowered the Minister of Social Affairs to make membership of such schemes compulsory, if requested to do so by employer and employee representatives. In 1980 there were 83 industry-wide funds in existence, 62 of which had compulsory membership. Pension schemes organized on an enterprise basis are also subject to some statutory control, under the 1952 Pensions and Savings Fund Law (*Pensioen- en spaarfondsen wet*), which covers the organization and administration of pension and savings funds. In 1980 there were about 1,000 enterprise pension funds in existence, in addition to which there were more than 20,000 pension contracts made on a collective basis with an insurance company. Approximately 85% to 90% of all private sector employees are members of one of the occupational pension schemes. Occupational pension funds bear risks either on their own, or by means of reinsurance with a life insurance company. However, no exact data are available concerning this reinsurance.

Occupational pension expenditure in 1983 in million HFL

		%
Enterprise pensions[a]	2 110	27.9
Industry-wide pensions[b]	1 744	23.0
Collective insurance pensions	3 500	46.2
Other occupational pensions	216	2.9
Total	7 570	100.0

[a] *Ondernemingspensionenfondsen.*
[b] *Bedrijfspensioenfondsen.*

Source: Ministry of Social Affairs and Employment, *Financiele nota sociale zekerheid 1985*, The Hague, 1984, p. 101.

Benefits

General pensions provide universal flat-rate benefits. The net old age pension for a married couple today equals the net minimum wage which is linked to a special wage index (*index van Regelingslonen*). On 1 January 1984, this pension amounted to 1,083.38 HFL a month for single persons (with 63.34 HFL holiday allowance), and 1,554.05 a month for married couples (with 90.48 HFL holiday allowance). Widows with a child under the age of 18 are provided with a full pension. Other widows receive the same amount as single pensioners, i.e. 70% of the full pension. In 1970, a provision was introduced in the General Old Age Pensions Act under which a holiday allowance is paid. Since 1977 this allowance has amounted to 7% of the pension over the preceding 12 months.

Entitlement to a full pension is dependent upon a 50-year insurance period, but this principle is of little significance in practice. 'Blanketing-in' was very simple in 1957, and since contributions to the pension scheme are levied in conjunction with the general income tax system, non-payment is a very rare occurrence.

Public servants receive an old age pension amounting to 1.75% for every year of service, times their average wage in the last two years of service. Public servants receive a special old age pension which is coordinated with their AOW benefits. The pension's amount is calculated in two steps: firstly, 1.75% of the average wage in the last two years is multiplied by the number of years of service; secondly, the resulting sum is then reduced by 2% for every year of service, up to a maximum of 80% of this sum. Thus, in the case of public servants, flat-rate AOW benefits are supplemented by a wage-and-service-years related pension. These ABP benefits are comparable with occupational pension schemes for private sector employees. A public servant's widow's pension, in general, amounts to five-sevenths of the husbands' old age pension. A public servant's orphan's pension amounts to one-seventh for 'half' orphans and two-sevenths for 'full' orphans. However, these pensions are also reduced, as public servants' widows and orphans are in receipt of AWW benefits.

Occupational pension schemes are also supplementary to AOW benefits. They differ from one industry or enterprise to another, but in general, the pension amounts to 0.5%-1.75% of average earnings for either the entire period, or the last years of employment, times the number of years of employment.

Financing

Pensions are financed on a pay-as-you-go basis. Flat-rate benefits are financed mainly by contributions from the insured (employees and self-employed persons are obliged to contribute, to the Old Age Pensions Fund, whereas employers are not), together with a small central government subsidy. Contributions are earnings-related, with a maximum income ceiling. In 1984 contribution rates were 11.65% for the old age pension scheme and 1.45% for the widows' and orphans' pension scheme. The maximum income above which no additional contributions were required was 62,850 HFL a year. The combination of earnings-related contributions and flat-rate benefits results in a significant degree of income redistribution, albeit limited by the existence of a contribution ceiling. Public servants' pensions are financed by government which pays contributions to the Public Servants' Pensions Fund (*Algemeen Burgerlijk Pensioenfonds*), which then passes part of these costs on to public servants' wages. In 1984, public servants paid 11.7% of their wages, after a franchise (amounting to 19,008 HFL in 1984) had been subtracted from their taxable income.

Occupational pension schemes are financed either by employers, or by both employers and employees.

Administration

The state pension scheme is administered by 22 regional Labour Councils (*Raden van Arbeid*), which consist of a chairman appointed by the Crown, and six members appointed by the Minister of Social Affairs and Employment (*Minister van Sociale Zaken en Werkgelegenheid*), of whom three represent the employers and three the employees. They are supervised by the Social Insurance Bank in Amsterdam (*Sociale Verzerkeringsbank*), composed of a chairman, appointed by the Minister, and 15 members, equally representing employers, employees, and government. The Social Insurance Bank is controlled by the Social Insurance Council (*Sociale Verzekeringsraad*).

Public servants' pensions are administered by the Board of the Public Servants' Pensions Fund which is controlled by a Supervisory Body (*Raad van Toezicht*).

Under the Pensions and Saving Funds Law, occupational pension schemes are legally required to have sufficient funds to cover risks. The law also contains regulations covering the constitution of the funds, their investments etc. Each fund is required to present an annual report to the Insurance Chamber (*Verzekeringskamer*).

Services

No services are financed under the AOW and AWW. On 1 January 1981, 133,715 old people were living in 1,510 old age homes, i.e. 8% of the total population over 65 years of age. Elderly people living at home are entitled to home service nursing, household assistance, etc., (all paid for under the National Assistance Act). In 1983, home services were provided in a total of 214,208 cases, of which more than 70% were for the elderly.

Core laws

Laws are cited with their *Staatsblad* or statute book number, indicated by the abbreviation Stb. Laws may be either Bills passed by parliament, or decrees passed by governmental bodies empowered by parliament.

5.6.1913 (Stb. 205)
Invaliditeitswet (Invalidity Insurance Act): established the first insurance scheme covering old age, survivors' and disability pensions; old age pensions based on value of contributions; membership limited to manual and white-collar workers below a certain income limit; effective from 3.12.1919.

4.11.1919 (Stb. 628)
Ouderdomswet (Old Age Pensions Act): introduced voluntary old age insurance for the self-employed; supplementary to the 1913 Invalidity Insurance Act; pensions guaranteed by the state.

5.5.1922 (Stb. 204)
Pensioenwet (Pensions Act): provided pensions for public servants, their widows and orphans.

21.4.1933 (Stb. 181)
Mijnarbeiders, Invaliditeits- en Ouderdomswet (Miners' Invalidity and Old Age Act): insurance for miners against the financial risks of invalidity and old age.

24.5.1947 (Stb. H155)
Noodwet Ouderdomsvoorziening (Old Age Pensions Emergency Provisions Act): provided means-tested pensions for all persons over 65 irrespective of previous employment record.

17.3.1949 (Stb. J121)
Wet betreffende verplichtesplitdeelneming in een bedryfspensioenfonds (Occupational Pensions Funds Act): membership of industry-wide pension funds made compulsory.

15.5.1952 (Stb. 275)
Pensioen en spaarfondsenwet (Pensions and Savings Funds Act): established regulations concerning the organization and administration of savings and pension funds.

31.5.1956 (Stb. 218)
Algemene Ouderdomswet (General Old Age Pensions Act): replaced 1947 scheme; introduced universal flat-rate old age pensions for all residents as a right and with no retirement condition at the age of 65; financed by earnings-related contributions of all income receivers; indexation of benefits according to a wage-index; effective from 1.1.1957.

9.4.1959 (Stb. 139)
Algemene Weduwen en Wezenwet (General Widows' and Orphans' Benefits Act): provided pensions for widows with one or more children at home, disabled widows, and widows over the age of 50; orphans eligible for pensions if under the age of 16 (or 27 if still studying); financed by earnings-related contributions from all income receivers; benefits linked to AOW benefits.

25.5.1962 (Stb 205)
Pensions for widows who have already reached the age of 40 and those with one or more children no longer at home; under certain conditions divorced women are also entitled to widows' pensions.

10.12.1964 (Stb. 486)
Introduction of a 'social minimum': pension for a married couple set at 70% of the minimum guaranteed gross income for an industrial worker; pension for a single person set at 70% of a couple's pension.

30.7.1965 (Stb. 347)
Pensions for orphans between 16 and 27, caring for a younger sister/brother already entitled to an orphans' pension.

6.1.1966 (Stb. 6)
Algemene Burgelyke Pensioenwet (Public Servants' Superannuation Act): introduction of new regulations covering pensions of public servants and their relatives.

9.7.1970 (Stb. 350)
Structural increase of AOW and AWW benefits as a step towards an envisaged full net pension amounting to 100% of net minimum wage (gross pension being 85% of gross minimum wage); introduction of the right to holiday allowances of 6% (previously 3%) for the AOW and AWW.

24.12.1970 (Stb. 648)
Structural increase of AOW and AWW benefits by 2% as from 1.1.1971.

26.1.1972 (Stb. 65)
Structural increase of AOW and AWW benefits by 4% from 1.1.1972.

23.12.1972 (Stb. 703)
Structural increase of AOW and AWW benefits by 4% as from 1.1.1973.

24.3.1976 (Stb. 236)
State contribution for AOW raised from 250.8 to 864.3 million HFL. In 1975, however, the contribution was 520 million.

12.5.1977 (Stb. 328)
AOW and AWW holiday allowances raised from 6% to 7%.

14.12.1977 (Stb. 670)
Introduction of measures against improper use.

29.12.1978 (Stb. 750)
State contributions for 1978, 1979, 1980 diminished.

3.12.1979 (Stb. 752)
Besluit vervroegd uittreden burgerlyk rykspersoneel (Voluntary Retirement Regulation for Public Servants): entitled public servants who retire early (at the age of 63, or, in some cases, earlier), to 80% of the last earned wage until the age of 65.

20.12.1979 (Stb. 711)
Net pension benefits equal to net minimum wage.

24.12.1980 (Stb. 765)
Revision of the state contributions to the Old Age Pensions Fund.

2. Invalidity pensions/Sickness cash benefits

Sickness and invalidity pension expenditure in 1983 in million HFL

		%
Sickness benefits (ZW)	6 772	24.5
Public servants' sickness benefits (DSO)[a]	3 665	13.3
Invalidity pensions (IW)	165	0.6
General invalidity pensions (AAW)	9 386	34.0
Employees' invalidity pensions (WAO)	7 599	27.6
Total	27 587	100.0

[a] *Doorbetaling Salaris Overheidspersoneel*.

Source: Ministry of Social Affairs and Employment, *Financiele nota sociale zekerheid 1985*, The Hague, 1984, p. 97.

Income maintenance

The regulations covering sickness and permanent disablement are today based on the complete reorganization of the schemes in 1967. Since that time no distinction has been made between persons unfit for work owing to physical or mental illness and those whose incapacity is due to an accident or industrial disease. Both receive the same benefit irrespective of the cause of illness or accident. Sickness cash benefits are provided for a maximum period of one year, after which time general invalidity pensions, which may be supplemented by special invalidity pensions for employees, are payable. In 1983, on the base of the ZW, the WAO (and IW) and the AAW, 230,000, 551,000 and 186,000 people respectively were entitled to benefits, together amounting to 27,587 million HFL, i.e. of the total expenditure on social security, or 7.2% of GDP.

Sickness cash benefits

Coverage

Since the introduction of the 1967 Sickness Benefits Act (*Ziektewet*, ZW), all employees (with the exception of public servants who have their own scheme) are covered by sickness insurance. They are entitled to sickness cash benefits when incapacitated by illness, accident or confinement. Benefits are paid after a statutory period of two days, but large groups of insured people receive non-statutory benefits from the first day from the industrial insurance boards which administer sickness insurance schemes. Sickness benefits are paid up to a maximum period of 52 weeks (after which time the invalidity schemes come into effect), and operate up to the age of 65. Public servants' salary is continued for a maximum period of 18 months, in the case of temporary unfitness to work, after which period, he receives 80% of his gross wage.

Benefits

Sickness cash benefits are earnings-related up to a certain maximum wage ceiling. In 1984, insured persons received 80% of the daily wage (the maximum daily wage amounted to 262.28 HFL). For large groups of insured persons statutory benefits of 80% are supplied by non-statutory regulations. Maternity allowances amount to 100% of the daily wage and are paid six weeks before and after the date of confinement.

Financing

National sickness benefit insurance contributions are paid by employers and employees. On average, employers pay 4.8% of the wage and the employees 1%. Employees' contributions are generally higher in industries where the insurance also covers the first two days of sickness.

Administration

Since the 1952 Organization of Social Insurance Act (*Organisatiewet Sociale Verzekeringen*), sickness benefit insurance has been administered by obligatory Industrial Insurance Boards (*Bedrijfsverenigingen*) of employers and employees. The 26 boards for the different branches of industry are controlled by the Social Insurance Council.

Core laws

5.6.1913 (Stb. 204)
Ziektewet (Sickness Benefits Act): insured employees with wages below a certain maxi-

mum, against financial consequences of illness not caused by accidents; effective from 1.2.1930; in 1935 insurance extended to home-workers and commercial travellers on a commission basis, and in 1942 to domestic personnel.

8.8.1947 (Stb. 284)
Sickness benefits now payable up to a maximum of 52 weeks instead of the previous 26; introduction of two-day waiting period.

12.6.1952 (Stb. 344)
Organisatiewet Sociale Verzekeringen (Organization of Social Insurance Act): made the formation of Industrial Insurance Boards (*Bedrijfsverenigingen*) compulsory; these administer the Sickness Benefits Act, replacing the Labour Councils, (see scheme 1); effective from 1.1.1953.

18.2.1966 (Stb. 85)
As a consequence of the abolition of the Industrial Injuries Insurance Acts, people incapacitated by work injuries were entitled to claim an allowance under the Sickness Benefits Act; coordination with new Disablement Insurance Act necessitated the abolition of the former wage limit which existed under the Sickness Benefits Act; effective from 15.7.1967.

20.4.1967 (Stb. 213)
Supplementary regulations for administrative coordination of the Sickness Benefits Act and new Disablement Insurance Act; effective from 1.5.1967.

25.9.1967 (Stb. 473)
Sickness Benefits Act reinsured due to the extent of alterations regarding accidents, occupational injuries, and coverage of employees with higher incomes.

14.9.1970 (Stb. 420)
Introduction of pension for survivors in the case of death of an employee receiving sickness benefits at the time of death.

14.12.1977 (Stb. 670)
Measures against improper use enacted; this measure makes it possible to reclaim unjustly paid benefits.

20.12.1979 (Stb. 710)
Introduction of age limit: at the age of 65 sickness benefits are no longer payable; prior to this change, persons could receive pensions and sickness benefits for up to one year without returning to work.

Invalidity pensions

Income maintenance

Coverage

The current system of invalidity pensions is based on two acts: the 1967 Disablement Insurance Act (*Wet op de Arbeidsongeschiktheidsverzekering*, WAO), and the 1976 General Disablement Insurance Act (*Algemene Arbeidsongeschiktsheidswet*, AAW). Both schemes insure against the financial consequences of lasting illness, disablement or occupational injuries, and provide pensions after a waiting period of 52 weeks during which period insured persons are entitled to claim sickness cash benefits. The General Disablement Insurance Scheme pays basic pensions to all citizens over 18, and with a certain income prior to disablement. In January 1983, the minimum annual income amounted to 4,446.78 HFL. The Disablement Insurance Scheme pays supplementary pensions to all employees, except public servants and railway employees, who are covered by their own schemes. The pension is provided by the Public Servants' Superannuation Fund according to the Public Servants' Superannuation Act.

Benefits

WAO invalidity benefits correspond to the degree of the claimant's incapacity and his previous earnings (up to a certain ceiling which amounted to a daily amount of 262.28 HFL on 1 January 1984). Starting with a 15% incapacity, there are seven benefit grades (10%, 20%, 30%, 40%, 50%, 65%, and 80% of the daily wage up to the maximum) corresponding to different degrees of disablement (15-25%, 25-35%, 35-45%, 45-55%, 55-65%, 65-80%, 80% and more). Where the beneficiary is totally disabled and requires regular attendance and nursing, the pension is increased to 100% of the daily wage. In addition, all beneficiaries are paid holiday allowance.

AAW invalidity benefits are calculated in the same way as WAO benefits, corresponding to a scale of invalidity consisting of six benefit grades (except for the first degree, 15-25% invalidity, which does not exist here). Benefits are flat-rate and not related to former earnings. In 1984, the standard daily amount was 80.33 HFL for single persons and 114.02 for married couples. Since the implementation of the AAW in 1976, the WAO benefits have become supplementary. The WAO scheme defines maximum benefits to which a beneficiary may be entitled, and provides the difference between AAW benefits and these maximum benefits.

Invalidity pensions for public servants under the Public Servants Pensions Act, vary with age. Below 65 years, the pension amounts to 1.75% times the number of service years (as under the old age regulation). If this amount is less than a given percentage (which varies with the degree of invalidity) of the last earned wage, then the pension is fixed to this percentage, up to the age of 65. From 65 onwards, the pension is calculated in the same way, except that the years in which the public servant has been either fully or partially disabled, are counted as service years.

Financing

The WAO scheme is financed through employees' contributions, 17.6% (no contribution is payable for the first 91 HFL earned per day), and employers' contributions, 1.5% (again, no contribution is payable for the first 91 HFL earned per day) which are paid to the Disablement Fund (*Arbeidsongeschiktheidsfonds*). The AAW is financed by the employers, who pay 6.5% of wages (up to an annual wage of 62,850 HFL) to the General Tax Department. For the financing of the public servants' regulations, see under old age and survivors' pensions.

Administration

See under sickness benefits. For public servants, see under old age and survivors' pensions.

Core laws

Industrial Injuries Insurance:

2.1.1901 (Stb. 1)
Ongevallenwet (Industrial Injuries Insurance Act): insured employees against the financial consequences of accidents; only for most dangerous branches of industry.

8.5.1915 (Stb. 214)
Zeeongevallen Wet (Maritime Industrial Injuries Insurance Act): accident insurance for maritime people.

28.6.1921 (Stb. 700)
Ongevallenwet (Industrial Injuries Insurance Act): extended Industrial Injuries Insurance Act to cover all branches of industry (except branches covered by their own Acts) for work accidents and other accidents; extended to cover occupational diseases in 1928.

20.5.1922 (Stb. 365)
Land- en tuinbouw Ongevallen Wet (Agricultural and Horticultural Industrial Injuries Insurance Act): accident insurance for agricultural and horticultural people.

7.6.1950 (Stb. Kl91)
Wetten tot aanvulling van ongevallenrenten (Supplementary Law to Industrial Injuries Insurance Acts): complemented the three Industrial Injuries Insurance Acts of 1919/22; introduced an indexation of benefits.

The three accident insurance acts covered wage-earners in almost all branches of industry with the exception of public servants who had their own regulations. They provided for medical treatment, cash benefits amounting to 80% of the daily wage of the insured and 60% for his survivors in case of his death. Contributions were paid entirely by employers, whereas supplementary benefits were paid by the state. In the early 1950s benefits were raised by supplementary laws.

Invalidity insurance:

5.6.1913 (Stb. 205)
Invaliditeitswet (Invalidity Act): made employer-financed insurance compulsory for employees with incomes below a certain limit, between 14 and 65 years of age; effective from 3.12.1919.

21.4.1933 (Stb. 181)
Mijnwerkersinvaliditeitswet (Miners' Invalidity Act): insured miners against the financial consequences of invalidity and old age.

15.7.1948 (Stb. I303)
Wet tot aanvulling van renten krachtens de invaliditeitswet (Supplementary Law to Invalidity Insurance Act): as there were no automatic adjustments for inflation under the Invalidity Insurance Act, this law introduced supplementary benefits; benefits were further increased in 1962 and 1964.

19.12.1963 (Stb. 534)
Interimwet Invaliditeitsrentetrekkers (Interim Invalidity Pensioners Act): insurance scheme contributions to be paid entirely by employers; benefits financed by state and employer contributions, based on the wage of an unskilled worker, and index-linked.

14.7.1966 (Stb. 336)
Starting on 1.7.1966, four benefit grades were established (previously three) corresponding to degrees of invalidity: invalidity of 80% or over entitles the beneficiary to a pension of 5,628 HFL, i.e. 114.9% of the wage for an unskilled worker; invalidity between 67% and 80% = pension of 4,578 HFL or 93.4%; invalidity between 55% and 66% = pension of 3,522 HFL or 71.9%; invalidity between 45% and 55% = pension of 2,814 HFL or 57.4%. (Figures of 1 January 1967).

Disablement insurance:

18.2.1966 (Stb. 84)
Wet op de Arbeidsongeschiktheidsverzekering (Disablement Insurance Act): replaced Industrial Injuries Insurance and Invalidity Insurance Acts; scheme covered all employees except public servants and railway employees; pensions paid after a waiting period of 52 weeks (see sickness benefits) in compensation for total or partial incapacity; benefits related to degree of incapacity and previous earnings, and linked to wage index; contributions by employees (1/4) and employers (3/4).

30.6.1967 (Stb. 367)
Introduction of holiday allowances.

29.12.1975 (Stb. 674)
Algemene Arbeidsongeschiktsheidswet. (General Disablement Benefits Act): provided basic benefits for all citizens (aged 18-65) and provided facilities for rehabilitation and other improvements of living conditions. These benefits form the base of the WAO payments; where the WAO payment is higher than the basic AAW benefit, it is financed through the WAO scheme.

20.12.1979 (Stb. 708)
Introduction of equal right to benefits for men and women; married women entitled to claim invalidity pension based on minimum wage.

20.12.1979 (Stb. 711)
Net benefits equal to net minimum wage (as for old age and survivors' pensions).

II Unemployment

Income maintenance

Income maintenance for unemployed people is based on three acts: the 1952 Unemployment Insurance Act (*Werkloosheidswet*, WW), providing short-term benefits, the 1965 Unemployment Provision Act (*Wet Werkloosheidsvoorziening*, WWV) providing long-term benefits, and the social assistance regulations, the Government Unemployment Assistance Regulations (*Rijksgroepsregeling Werkloze Werknemers*, RWW), the Scheme for State Aid to Artists (*Beeldende Kunstenaars Regeling*, BKR) and the Sheltered Employment Act (*Wet Sociale Werkvoorziening*, WSW). Public servants have their own regulations: Public Servants Redundancy Pay Scheme (*Wachtgeldregeling Overheidspersoneel*, WRO). In 1983 unemployment expenditure amounted to 18,533 million HFL, i.e. 16.7% of total public expenditure on social security or 4.9% of GDP. A total of 120,000 unemployed were paid under the WW scheme; 244,000 people were covered by unemployment provision benefits and 312,000 received unemployment assistance (RWW and BKR). In addition to the unemployed 79,000 people were placed under the Sheltered Employment Act (WSW).

Unemployment expenditure in 1983 in million HFL

		%
Unemployment insurance (WW)[a]	4 047	21.8
Unemployment provisions (WWV)	7 166	38.7
Unemployment assistance (RWW)	4 360	23.5
Unemployment assistance (BKR)	114	0.6
Unemployment assistance (WSW)	1 992	10.7
Public servants scheme (WRO)	854	4.7
Total	18 533	100.0

[a] Inclusive of the Risk Fund (for delays caused by bad weather); this amounted to 140 million HFL in 1983.

Source: Ministry of Social Affairs and Employment, *financiele nota sociale zekerheid 1985*, The Hague, 1984, pp. 97, 98, 101.

Coverage

Unemployment insurance covers all employees under the age of 65 and some self-employed with a similar status. Under the WW scheme, any insured person who has been working for at least 130 days in the same branch of industry or trade during the 12 months preceding unemployment is entitled to interim benefits from the industrial insurance boards of that industry for eight weeks. If he continues to be unemployed beyond this period he is entitled to unemployment benefit for a further 18 weeks.

In the event of bankruptcy or suspension of payment by the employer, the Act entitles the employee to claim any insurance board back-pay and holiday allowance due to him, from the industrial insurance board for a certain period if the employer is not in a position to pay it.

After a 26 week period, insured employees are entitled to benefits under the Unemployment Provision Act up to a maximum period of two years. A married woman who is not a breadwinner (as defined by the Unemployment Provisions Act) is not entitled to benefit. In order to be entitled to benefit under the Unemployment Provisions Act, young people under the age of 23 must have been in employment for at least 130 days in the 12 months preceding their unemployment, and must also have fulfilled a period of employment of a non-incidental nature for at least 130 weeks during the three years preceding their unemployment. Benefit is paid for a maximum of one year and not two. Additionally, unemployed persons not qualifying for benefits under the Unemployment Insurance Act, may claim under the Unemployment Provision Act. People unemployed for more than two and a half years (WW and WWV) receive unemployment assistance under the Government Unemployment Assistance Regulations (RWW), a scheme also for groups without sufficient employment record. Benefits are paid until the age of 65.

Benefits of the Reduced Pay Scheme for Public Servants (WRO) are provided in the event of involuntary unemployment of public servants, e.g. due to administrative reorganization. Those not eligible for the WRO, for example public servants with temporary contracts, receive benefits under the 1966 Allowance Regulation.

Benefits

With the exception of unemployment assistance, all benefits are wage-related, and linked to a special wage index. The relevant daily wage is that earned during the three months preceding unemployment. The interim unemployment benefits (first eight weeks) and unemployment insurance benefits (next 18 weeks), which together form the WW, amount to 80% of the daily gross wage (with a daily wage of 262.28 HFL in 1984, and a minimum daily wage of 123.24 HFL for breadwinners). They are supplemented by a holiday allowance payable as a lump sum. Unemployment provision benefits amount to 75% of the daily wage (with the same maximum wage as above, and a minimum wage for breadwinners of 131.52 HFL in 1984). Unemployment assistance benefits are calculated on the basis of personal circumstances and are means-tested. Breadwinners are entitled to receive benefits amounting to the net minimum wage. In 1984 this amounted to approximately 1,446.90 HFL a month. Unmarried persons are entitled to benefits of 70% of the net minimum wage. Unemployed school leavers or those still living with their parents, receive lower benefits.

Public servants' WRO benefits are earnings-related and amount to 100% of the last gross wage during the first three months, 90% in the next nine months, 80% in the next four years, and 70% thereafter. Benefits under the 1966 Allowance Regulation amount to 100% of the last earned wage in the first two months, 90% in the next two months, 80% in the next eight months, and 75% thereafter, up to a maximum period of one-sixth of the time of service, with a maximum of two years. For those with a period of service of less than three years, 80% benefits are provided during a 130 days period.

Financing

Unemployment benefits are financed by contributions from employers, employees and the state. Unemployment insurance contributions on average amount to 3.57% of the earned wage (maximum 262 HFL per day); 0.56% paid by the employer and 3.01 paid by the employee.

- Unemployment Insurance Act (WW): Interim Benefits Regulation (*Wachtgeldregeling*). The proportion of contribution varies, depending on the rate of unemployment in the sector in question. They are paid on a fifty-fifty basis by employers and employees. Unemployment insurance contributions amount to 1.5% of the earned wage (maximum 243 HFL a day), one-quarter paid by the employer, one-quarter paid by the employee and a half paid by the state. The average contribution of employers and employees within the division amounts to 0.775% each.
- Unemployment Provisions Act (WWV): This law is administered by the municipalities, who are financed out of central government revenues.
- Government Unemployment Assistance Regulations (RWW): This regulation is part of the Social Assistance Act, and is consequently paid out of general revenues (90% central government, 10% other government).

Administration

The WW is administered by 26 industrial insurance boards (*Bedrijfsverenigingen*), in which employers and employees participate. The Social Insurance Council, in which state, employers and employees are represented, controls the implementation of the WW by these industrial insurance boards. The WWV and RWW are implemented by local government i.e. Municipal Social Offices (*Gemeentelijke Sociale Dienst*), and are ultimately controlled by the Ministries of Social Affairs and Cultural Affairs respectively.

Services

The Regional Employment Offices (*Gewestelijke Arbeidsbureaus*, GAB), register both the unemployed and work vacancies offered. Where necessary, they organize re-training programmes and in a few cases they have started their own enterprises. The unemployed can take part in social case work provision schemes, organized by public corporations, or start up an enterprise on their own, with the continuation of their unemployment allowance for a limited period. Central government provides subsidies for experiments with part-time jobs and for the creation of employment programmes within the public sector. Due to the decentralized and discretionary character of employment policies, national data on expenditure and beneficiaries are not available.

Core laws

2.12.1916 (Stb. 522)
Werkloosheidsbesluit 1917 (1917 Unemployment Decree): introduced state contributions to voluntary unemployment funds, raised in branches of industry.

3.8.1922 (Stb. 479)
Introduction of the WRO for public servants

4.3.1935 (Stb. 76)
Foundation of an unemployment fund to improve the division of the burdens between central and local government.

22.8.1944 (Stb. E79)
Buitengewoon Besluit Werklozenzorg (Social Provisions for the Unemployed): introduced state reimbursement of municipal unemployment payments, providing basic needs.

9.9.1949 (Stb. J423)
Werkloosheidswet (Unemployment Insurance Act): introduced obligatory insurance of wage-earners below a maximum wage ceiling; effective from 1.7.1952; continuous upgrading of maximum wage ceiling until 1964.

10.12.1964 (Stb. 484)
Maximum wage abolished; mandatory insurance extended to all wage-earners; benefits amount to 80% of the former daily wage.

10.12.1964 (Stb. 485)
Wet Werkloosheidsvoorziening (Unemployment Provisions Act): provision of benefits by municipalities, during a maximum period of two years, amounting to 75% of the former wage, for those no longer eligible under the Unemployment Insurance Act (WW).

21.12.1964 (Stb. 553)
Rijksgroepsregeling Werkloze Werknemers (Government Unemployment Assistance Regulations): provided social assistance for those with insufficient living income due to unemployment, and who are not eligible for benefits under other unemployment schemes.

20.7.1967 (Stb. 396)
Insurance extended from wage-earners to all employed persons (incl. domestic personnel and the occasionally employed); insurance benefits for a maximum period of 26 weeks (five-day working weeks): interim benefits for first eight weeks and insurance benefits for next 18 weeks, both at 80% of former daily wage.

10.7.1968 (Stb. 375)
Obliged industrial insurance boards to assume the responsibilities including the full payment of wage where applicable.

17.9.1968 (Stb. 502)
Structural changes in the determination of RWW benefits; minimum wage becomes the base.

8.9.1970 (Stb. 420)
Allowances for survivors of unemployed wage-earners.

22.2.1974 (Stb. 66)
Supplementary benefits available for the unemployed who accept lower paid work; those over 45 receive supplements amounting to 100% of their former wage during the first six months, 95% in the next six months, and 85% during the second, third and fourth year; those under 45 receive supplements amounting to 90% during six months, 85% during the next two years.

26.6.1976 (Stb. 368)
Enabled employees of 60 years of age, two years after first date of receipt of benefits (WWV scheme), to continue receiving them until 65; intended to improve financial circumstances of older employees who are unemployed for a long time.

14.12.1977 (Sbt. 670)
Introduction of various articles against improper use of the law.

20.12.1979 (Stb. 711)
Net benefits of the WW and WWV made equal to net minimum wage, in the case of full unemployment (as old age, survivors, and invalidity pensions).

26.3.1981 (Stb. 132)
Workers within the WSW taken into the WW.

26.3.1981 (Stb. 133)
Qualification period for entitlement to unemployment benefit extended from 65 to 130 days during the twelve months preceding unemployment.

29.12.1982
Changes in the minimum daily wage regulations; this minimum no longer applies to 'non-breadwinners'.

III Families and children

Income maintenance

Since 1980 there has been a radical simplification of the legislation and administration of family allowances. The existing schemes (KWL, KKZ, AKW and KTO) were converted into a single new General Family Allowances Act (*Algemene Kinderbijslagwet*), under which all residents of the Netherlands became entitled to allowances for the first child and subsequent children. From 1 January 1980 child allowances have been dependent on the age of the child. In 1983, 7,561 million HFL were paid under the AKW, (i.e. 6.8% of total public expenditure on social security or 2% of GDP) in respect of 237,000 children.

Expenditure on family allowances in 1979 in million HFL

		%
General family allowances (AKW)	2 310	36.5
Family allowances for the self-employed (KKZ)	42	0.7
Family allowances for wage-earners (KWL)	3 178	50.3
Family allowances for public servants (KTO)	790	12.5
	6 320	100.0

Coverage

As a basic and general rule, allowances are payable to an insured person in respect of his own children, stepchildren and adopted children:

- under 16 and members of the insured's household;
- under 16, not household members, but who are maintained largely at the expense of the insured;
- aged 16-27, spending at least half their available working hours in education or vocational training, and being maintained to a significant extent at the expense of the insured;
- aged 16-18 who are unemployed and not receiving benefit under an unemployment regulation, if they are being maintained to a significant extent at the expense of the insured.
- aged 18-21 who have completed their studies or vocational training and are unemployed, or are unemployed after settling in, or returning to the Netherlands, if they are being maintained to a significant extent at the expense of the insured;
- aged 16-18 who, as a consequence of sickness or disability, are not deemed capable of earning 55% of the wage of a physically and mentally healthy child of the same age in similar circumstances, provided that they are maintained to a significant extent at the expense of the insured;
- finally, under certain conditions the insured is entitled to an allowance for one of his children aged 16-27 if that child runs the household and is maintained to a significant extent at his expense.

Benefits

Under certain conditions one child may be counted as two children: if not living at home.

- children under 16 who do not belong to the insured person's household or to any other household because of invalidity;
- children between 16 and 17 who are studying away from home, or do not live at home because of invalidity;
- children between 18 and 27 who are studying (whether at home or not).

However, compensation for higher costs is only provided if children are more than 50% maintained at the expense of the insured. A child aged between 18 and 27 who is studying and is not a member of his parent's household may even be counted as three children, if maintained at least 90% by his parents.

The size of the allowance is dependent upon the age of the child; for families with up to eight children on 1 January 1984 the rates were as follows (in HFL per quarter):

Children aged		0-5		6-11	12-17	18-26
	60%	70%	90%	100%	115%	101%
Families with:						
1 child	174.19	203.22	261.28	290.31	333.86	293.78
2 children		266.54	342.70	380.77	437.89	385.32
3 children		285.41	366.96	407.73	468.89	412.60
4 children		311.75	400.83	445.36	512.17	450.68
5 children		327.55	421.14	467.93	538.12	498.42
6 children		344.78	443.28	492.54	566.42	498.42
7 children		357.08	459.11	510.12	586.64	516.21
8 children		371.78	478.01	531.12	610.79	537.46

In the table three different percentages are given in respect of children aged 0-5 years inclusive, namely:

- 60% if there is only one child in the family and that child is under the age of three years;
- 70% (a) for children born after 31 December 1982 (except in the case of the first child, where the figure drops to 60%); (b) for the eldest child, if under three years of age and in family with at least two children; (c) for a child which has reached the age of three years after 1 January 1983, if there are no other older children in the family;
- 90% for all other children aged 0-5 years inclusive.

Financing

The contributions of those not in employment are levied by the Tax Department in the form of an assessment. In the case of insured persons whose wages or salaries are taxed or a similar deduction is made at source, the employee's contribution is paid to the Tax Department by the employer. That is 3.95% from 1 January 1984 (paid up to a maximum of 62,850 HFL per annum).

Administration

The General Family Allowances Act is administered by the Labour Councils.

Services

See sections on Education and Housing.

Core laws

23.12.1939 (Stb. 806)
Kinderbijslagwet (Family Allowances Act): introduced an employees' allowance for the third and any subsequent child under the age of 15; effective from 1.1.1941.

21.12.1946 (Stb. G373)
Temporary measures entitling wage-earners to an allowance for first and second child under 18 years.

15.7.1948 (Stb. I309)
Kinderbijslagwet Rentetrekkers (Pensioners' Family Allowances Act): introduced family allowance for those in receipt of old age, invalidity or survivors' benefits according to the Invalidity Insurance Act 1919; abolished in 1963.

21.8.1950 (Stb. K369)
Monthly (previously annual) fixing of the number of children for whom allowances are claimable. Established equal rights for illegitimate children; allowance for disabled children between 16 and 20 years of age.

9.11.1950 (Stb. K501)
Kindertoelagewet voor Gepensioneerden (Retired Persons' Family Allowances Act): introduced a special allowance for pensioned public servants with children; abolished in 1963.

15.6.1951 (Stb. 212)
Noodwet Kinderbijslagwet voor kleine Zelfstandigen (Temporary Family Allowances Act for the Self-employed): entitled self-employed persons with low income to family allowance for first and second child; abolished in 1963.

3.2.1952 (Stb. 68)
Allowance for studying and for disabled children until the age of 27. (Introduction of allowances for children in full-time education, and for disabled children until the age of 27 in both cases).

12.6.1952 (Stb. 342)
Administration delegated to industrial insurance boards (same as for sickness benefits).

26.4.1962 (Stb. 160)
Algemene Kinderbijslagwet (General Family Allowances Act): reorganization of the family allowances acts; there are three regulations dating from 1.1.1963.

Algemene Kinderbijslagwet (General Family Allowances Act, AKW): entitled every resident to an allowance for the third child and subsequent children.

Kinderbijslagwet Loontrekkers (Wage-Earners Family Allowances Act, KWL): entitled employees to an allowance for the first and second child.

Kinderbijslagwet Zelfstandigen (Self-Employed Persons Family Allowances Act, KKZ): entitled the self-employed with an income of less than 14,000 HFL a year to an allowance for the first and second child. The Act abolished the Retired Persons' Family Allowances Act (*Kindertoeslagenwet voor Gepensioneerden*), and the Temporary Family Allowances Act for the Self-Employed (*Noodwet Kinderbijslagwet Kleine Zelfstandigen*, NKKZ).

14.5.1963 (Stb. 219)
Introduced the Public Service Employees' Family Allowances Scheme (*Kindertoeslag-regeling voor Overheidspersoneel*) according to the KWL.

13.12.1963 (Stb. 555)
Maximum income ceiling of 14,000 HFL abolished, except for self-employed.

10.12.1964 (Stb. 486)
Benefits linked to wage index; maximum income ceiling for self-employed raised as an initial step in a series of further increases.

24.4.1968 (Stb. 226)
Allowances revised when the wage index increased by at least 3%.

13.12.1972 (Stb. 702)
Benefits no longer automatically wage index linked. Effective from 1 January 1973.

14.9.1978 (Stb. 465)
Part of tax-deductions changed to direct payments.

20.12.1979 (Stb. 709)
Algemene Kinderbijslagwet (General Family Allowances Act): extended allowances to first and second child; replaced the Family Allowances Acts for wage-earners and self-employed persons, as well as the regulation for public servants.

29.12.1982 (Stb. 746)
Age-dependent child allowances introduced from 1.1.1983 onwards.

29.12.1982 (Stb. 750)
Unemployed children aged 16 and 17 entitled to a child allowance (instead of an RWW benefit).

IV Social assistance

Income maintenance

Social assistance in the broader sense of 'general welfare provisions' also includes unemployment programmes (WWV, RWW, BKR and WSW). Social assistance expenditure, in the narrower sense, amounted to 8,355 million HFL, i.e. 7.5 % of total public expenditure on social security or 2.2% or GDP. In 1983, 285,000 people received assistance under one of the existing schemes (excluding those for unemployment).

Expenditure [a] on social assistance in 1983 in million HFL

		%
National assistance (ABW)[b]	6 131	73.4
Special war schemes	818	9.8
Lump sum benefits	192	2.3
Family care and family help	1 214	14.5
Total	8 355	100.0

[a] Benefits in cash and kind.
[b] Excluding unemployment assistance (RWW).

Source: Ministry of Social Affairs and Employment *Financiele nota sociale zekerheid 1985*, The Hague, 1984, p. 99.

Coverage

The Public Assistance Act (*Algemene Bijstandswet*, ABW) gives financial assistance to everyone living in the Netherlands who is unable to provide for his own maintenance. Foreigners, living in the Netherlands, are entitled to the benefits under the Act where there is a mutual treaty between the Netherlands and the foreign state. The ABW provides a minimum benefit ensuring a basic standard of living. The extent of the benefit depends on the circumstances of the beneficiary (and his family), and varies accordingly. There is no maximum income above which one cannot apply for an allowance. In principle anyone can make application under the ABW, especially if his or her income is below that necessary to provide certain basic requirements. If benefits are received from other social provisions or social insurance schemes, ABW payments become supplementary. The ABW also includes specific regulations regarding social groups needing special attention.

One of these regulations is the Government Unemployment Assistance Regulations (*Rijksgroepsregeling voor Werkloze Werknemers*, RWW), which is dealt with in the section on unemployment. Other Special Government Schemes (*Rijksgroepsregelingen*) are: for war victims, repatriated persons, the Ambionese, retirement savings, the self-employed and older self-employed persons.

Benefits

Since 1981 a lump sum benefit has been paid annually to the recipients of a minimum benefit in the national assistance schemes. This amount is fixed annually without any clear definition. Public Assistance benefits are dependent upon personal circumstances and distinguish between those living at home and those living in institutions. For the first group the basic living requirements and the extent of benefits, amount to the net minimum wage (333.90 HFL a week as from 1 January 1984). Benefits for incomplete families or single people amount to 90% and 70% of the net minimum wage respectively, i.e. 300.50 and 233.75 HFL a week (with 63.34 HFL as holiday allowance). The amount is lower for recipients under the age of 23.

For the second group the costs of staying in an institution are reimbursed where the beneficiary is unable to pay the full cost, together with a personal allowance. Those covered by Special Government Schemes receive benefits which vary with the scheme. Other forms of assistance are provided under the ABW, for example, a credit to buy capital goods, thus enabling people to continue a private enterprise, or a credit in the form of a mortgage on one's own house.

Financing

Public Assistance is financed out of general taxation, and is administered under three different systems, as follows:

1. by central government;
2. by municipal government, on account of the central government;
3. by municipal government, on their own account.

Administration

While the Minister for Social Affairs and Employment is responsible for supervising the administration of the ABW, application in individual cases is entrusted to the authorities in the municipalities, the Municipal Social Offices (*Gemeentelijke Sociale Dienst*).

Core laws

28.6.1854 (Stb. 100)
Armenwet 1854 (1854 Poor Law): established benefits for the poor in cases of complete 'inevitability' (the 'inevitability principle'); state action only allowed where family, charitable and private organizations had failed ('subsidiary principle').

27.4.1912 (Stb. 165)
Armenwet (Poor Law): provided an allowance for those living on an income below the minimum required for a basic standard of living; organized totally at municipal level.

29.9.1955 (Stb. 456)
(Assistance Regulation for the Homeless): benefits paid by municipalities.

13.3.1963 (Stb. 284)
Algemene Bijstandswet (General Public Assistance Act): introduced system of financial support in the form of supplementary allowances for those with insufficient earnings.

21.12.1964 (Stb. 553)
Rijksgroepsregeling Werkloze Werknemers (State Group Regulation for the Unemployed): introduced a special regulation for those who are unable to meet the cost of living, due to unemployment and non-eligibility for other employment schemes.

10.9.1970 (Stb. 447)
Reintroduction of mortgage loans.

22.11.1972 (Stb. 675)
Transferred certain administrative powers from municipalities to central government; those in receipt of allowances under ABW may be buried at the state's expense.

17.1.1973 (Stb. 32)
Centralization of finance for assistance; municipalities receive at least 90%, as opposed to 80% of real expenditure.

3.7.1974 (Stb. 418)
Besluit Landelijk Normering (National Standardization Decree): introduced general rules for the determination of assistance; net benefits according to the ABW fixed at 100% of the net minimum wage for a married worker aged 23 or over.

16.2.1978 (Stb. 127)
Extended the circumstances under which temporary allowances, in the form of loans, can be granted to self-employed persons whose income is not known at the moment of benefit payment.

20.12.1979 (Stb. 711)
The ABW benefit became legally linked to the net minimum wage.

23.9.1981
Wet Eenmalige Uitkering (Incidental Payment Act): introduced a lump sum benefit to increase the buying power of those with only a minimum income; also paid in 1982, 1983 and 1984.

V Health

Health insurance

The public health system is mainly financed by the health insurance schemes and direct public expenditure.

Direct public expenditure on health in 1983 in million HFL

		%
Hospitals	615	74.6
Ambulatory mental health care[a]	69	8.4
School medical services	140	17.0
Total	824	100.0

[a] Excluding the part paid by the AWBZ (319 million HFL).

Source: Central Bureau for Statistics (CBS).

In 1983 health insurance expenditure amounted to 23,765 million HFL, i.e. 21.4% of total public expenditure on social security or 6.2% of GDP.

Health insurance expenditure in 1983 in million HFL

		%
Health Insurance Scheme (ZFW)	14 372	60.5
- compulsory scheme	8 393	35.3
- old people's scheme	3 655	15.4
- voluntary scheme	2 253	9.5
- supplementary scheme	71	0.3
Public servants' schemes	1 118	4.7
Exceptional Medical Expenses Scheme	8 275	34.8
Total	23 765	100.0

Source: Ministry of Social Affairs and Employment, *Financiele nota sociale zekerheid 1985*, The Hague, 1984, p. 97.

There are two major health insurance schemes:

- a scheme based on the 1964 Health Insurance Act (*Ziekenfondswet*, ZFW), providing ordinary medical benefits, including in-patient and out-patent treatment, dental care and medicines; this scheme contains four sub-schemes - the compulsory scheme, the old people's scheme, the voluntary scheme and the supplementary scheme. Responsibility for the administration of the Health Insurance Act lies with the health insurance funds (*Zieken fondsen*), which are non-profit organizations.
- a scheme providing special medical benefits, in particular, long-term treatment in institutions, based on the 1967 Exceptional Medical Expenses Act (*Algemene Wet*

Bijzondere Ziektekosten, AWBZ). This scheme is also administered by the health insurance funds.

Under the first Act all private employees and beneficiaries of social transfer payments, below a certain income ceiling (i.e. an annual income of not more than 47,850 HFL on 1 January 1984), are compulsorily insured. Family members without income are automatically covered (without an additional contribution). Old age pensioners who had been compulsorily insured prior to retirement remain members of the scheme. Persons not compulsorily insured (mainly public servants), may become voluntary members of the public insurance system, if their family income does not exceed the specified income ceiling (see above). Some groups of public servants, railway employees, and members of the armed forces have their own, comparable schemes. In all other cases one has to insure through an insurance corporation with private or public legal status.

The Health Insurance Act provides compulsory or voluntary members with so-called third-class free medical benefits. Additional insurance contributions entitle the beneficiary to a higher class of benefits, but the difference between the classes is relatively insignificant.

The Health Insurance Scheme is mainly financed by employer and employee contributions, together with a small state subsidy which is fixed annually. Employers and employees contribute 4.85% of the wage, up to a maximum of 156 HFL per day (1 January 1984). The voluntarily insured normally pay a higher contribution, with the exception of old age pensioners below a certain income ceiling (this amounted to 23,834.40 HFL per annum in 1984).

The Exceptional Medical Expenses Act (AWBZ) covers all residents. The scheme reimburses exceptional medical care costs, in particular for long-term and special in-patient treatment. The most important benefits are: hospital treatment for periods exceeding one year (including sanatoria and hospitals for mentally ill), nursing homes, centres for the deaf and blind, homes for the handicapped a.o.; and full-time homecare in special cases. Since 1980, the services of the non-profit organizations (*kruisverenigingen*) have been paid mainly by this scheme, which is financed through a 3.95% income tax allocated for the purpose (up to a certain annual ceiling which amounted to 62,850 HFL in 1984).

Services

There are many facilities in the field of public health care. Some are provided by several non-profit organizations (*Kruisverenigingen*), which provide nursing services, district nursing, maternity care, old age care, family help and information services. Since 1980 these organizations have mainly been financed through the ABWZ and for a lesser part by contributions from their members. Other facilities are ambulatory mental health care, which the state tries to accommodate under the AWBZ, and school medical services. The cost of these services are born by the municipalities and the central government.

Core laws

1.8.1941 (Stb. S804)
Ziekenfondsbesluit (Health Insurance Funds Decree): introduced compulsory health insurance for those insured under the Sickness Benefits Act, including their families; and the option of voluntary insurance.

24.4.1947 (Stb. H135)
Creation of the Health Insurance Funds Council (*Ziekenfondsraad*) as national agency for the organization and implementation of the sickness fund.

30.11.1950 (Stb. K535)
Compulsory health insurance extended to cover other groups e.g. old age and invalidity pensioners.

19.12.1956 (Stb. 634)
Introduced health insurance with special low contributions for old aged pensioners below a certain income ceiling.

15.10.1964 (Stb. 392)
Ziekenfondswet (Health Insurance Act): made insurance compulsory for all private employees and social transfer beneficiaries with income below a certain ceiling; provided basic medical benefits; and introduced the option of voluntary insurance. Effective from January 1966.

14.12.1967 (Stb. 655)
Algemene Wet Bijzondere Ziektekosten (Exceptional Medical Expenses Act): introduced national insurance against exceptionally high costs of long-term sickness and special forms of disablement.

12.2.1969 (Stb. 70)
Income ceiling for compulsory health insurance raised, especially for those aged 65 or over.

29.3.1973 (Stb. 223)
Introduction of annual adjustment of state contribution.

22.12.1976 (Stb. 758)
Raised the annual state contribution to the AWBZ to 1,089 million HFL, and required an incidental payment of 338.9 million HFL.

14.12.1977 (Stb. 670)
Measures to discourage improper use of the Health Insurance Act (*Ziekenfondswet*).

24.12.1980 (Stb. 765)
Revision of the adjustment mechanism for the wage-boundary for compulsory health insurance and the state contribution to the AWBZ.

25.3.1981 (Stb. 290)
Raised the annual state contribution to the AWBZ to 1,706.4 million HFL; effective from 1.1.1980 in connection with the financing of the *Kruisverenigingen* by the central government.

VI Education

1. Education structure

In the Netherlands, education is mainly organized on a private basis, although it is totally government financed. In 1978, 72% of total public education expenditure was spent on private education (mainly on a denominational basis), and only 18% on municipal or state schools.

Public expenditure on education in 1981 in million HFL

		%
Current expenditure		
- personnel	17 985	66.9
- material	4 793	17.8
- interest	1 107	4.1
Capital expenditure	1 818	6.8
Transfers to students	1 189	4.4
Total	26 892	100.0

Source: CBS, *Statistical Yearbook of the Netherlands*.

Nursery education is available, but not compulsory, for children aged from 3-6. Education is compulsory from 6 (primary) to 18 years of age, and full-time from 6-15. School students aged 15-18 may opt for 'partial obligatory education' which allows them to combine education and a job.

Primary school normally lasts for a period of six years, starting from the age of six. At the secondary level, there is a choice between various types of school, the main two being vocational and general. Normally there is a standardized first year which enables school students to shift from the one system to the other. Junior vocational training lasts for 4 years, and is followed by voluntary senior training, which lasts two to five years. This is followed by university education which lasts three to six years. General secondary schools have three, four or five grades. Grammar school has six grades and is the normal route to university education. Adult education is organized in the same way, but may be commercially based. Almost all types of secondary and tertiary (university) education may be attended on a part-time basis.

The government pays all direct study costs for primary education, and the first years of secondary education. These include personnel, materials, capital investments, etc. In the secondary grades, pupils' parents pay a fee, with a maximum of 746 HFL a year (1983/1984), the amount depending on income. Private schools may demand additional payments. At university level both a fee and a subscription are obligatory, amounting to 1,038 HFL in 1983/84.

2. Education allowances

- Allowances for secondary school pupils between the ages of 16 and 17, dependent on parental income. They replace the non-income related family allowance (these children are no longer counted twice, since 1979; cf. family allowance).
- Allowances for university students in the form of scholarships and interest free loans (State Study Allowances). The maximum amount was 6,980 HFL a year in 1983/84, for students living at home, and 10,740 HFL for those living elsewhere. The amount is given to students, whose parents have a taxable income up to 27,000 HFL (in 1984); this ceiling is higher for parents with more children. The allowance is correspondingly reduced when parental income exceeds the ceiling. The first 1,680 HFL are an interest-free loan, and of the remainder, 70% is granted as a free scholarship and 30% as an interest-free loan. If the students do not perform well, the allowance can be stopped.

- Low interest bank loan guaranteed by the state for students not receiving an allowance and amounting to a maximum of 50% of the maximum State Study Allowance.
- Local and central government financed allowances for all other types of education.

As mentioned in the section on family allowances, studying children can be counted twice or three times for the Family Allowances System and tax deductions. In the case of a State Study Allowance the counting is lower.

Between 1959 and 1978 the Ministry of Education, and since 1978 the Ministry of Housing, Physical Planning and Environment, have provided about 38,000 student housing units, with subsidized rents, for students up to the age of 30. Part of these units are for married or 'living together' students.

Administration/Financing

Nursery and primary schooling are mainly administered by private organizations and municipalities, whilst secondary and further education are mainly administered by private organizations and central government (under the constitution private organizations may set up a school). Provided that quality-criteria are met, the school is entitled to be totally financed by central government. In 1978, 94% of total public expenditure on education was financed by central government, and the other 6% by local government. Private schools may have additional sources of income. Government is able to co-administer schools by the imposition of certain quality-criteria. The majority of schools are private and denominational, and are attended by about 70% of the school-age population, although this figure is decreasing slightly.

Public expenditure on education by level and expenditure category in 1981 in million HFL

		%
Primary schools and nursery schools	8 214	32.4
Secondary schools	5 016	19.8
Vocational schools	4 025	15.9
Universities and colleges	6 512	25.7
Other[a]	1 578	6.2
Total	25 345	100.0

[a] Other education expenditure not allocatable by level and administration expenditure.

Source: CBS, *Statistical Yearbook of the Netherlands*.

Services

Private nursery schools and child day care institutions receive a state subsidy for all children within their care. Primary school children are provided with subsidized milk. Disabled children attend special state subsidized schools.

Core laws

The laws on educational allowances are not mentioned here, as they are subject to frequent changes by the Ministry of Education.

7.7.1900 (Stb. 111)
Introduction of compulsory schooling for all children.

9.10.1920 (Stb. 778)
(Primary Education Act): regulated primary education for children and established six one-year classes, where a minimum number of topics must be studied.

8.12.1955 (Stb. 558)
(Nursery Education Act): introduced the option of kindergarten for children from the age of 4 upwards. Established regulations for nursery-school teachers.

22.12.1960 (Stb. 559)
(University Education Act): established the length of university education at four to eleven years.

14.2.1964 (Stb. 40)
(Secondary Education Act): regulated all types of secondary education. Since 1964 new types of school have been introduced: senior vocational training and vocational colleges.

12.5.1966 (Stb. 215)
(Apprenticeship System Act): introduced compulsory partial education scheme up to the age of 17.

2.2.1967 (Stb. 38)
(Special Education Order): regulated education in denominational schools, and schools for the handicapped and mentally disturbed.

30.5.1968 (Stb. 303)
(Compulsory Education Law Amendment): established a ten-year period (or until the age of 16), of compulsory schooling from the age of seven; [cf. text - gives age six] this alteration is merely technical, as children had long since been attending school for a ten-year period.

7.10.1974 (Stb. 565)
(Primary Education Act): retained the system of six one-year classes, but heads of school now have more freedom as regards the programming of curriculum.

14.3.1981 (Stb. 177)
(New University Act): ruled that a period of study must not exceed four years. Students needing specialist training e.g. doctors, teachers and scientists, may attend an extra year after having passed the final examination.

VIII Housing

Housing is provided by:

- private housebuilders, who sell or rent houses; usually not financially supported by the state;

- housing corporations on an association basis; their aim is to provide cheap houses for their members; there are about 1,000 such corporations now; those which are officially recognized by the state on the basis of the Housing Act (*Woningwet*) can receive state contributions; the members of the corporation have formal influence on its policies;
- municipalities produce houses on their own or provide financial support to the housing corporations; the central government can force the municipalities to increase their production or financial support.

in the field of housing the main government functions are:

Control

1. Control of the quality of housing. This is achieved through the Housing Act. The government can give many prescriptions and requirements, which have to be met. If not, the building can be forbidden, terminated, or have to be reconstructed. The policy instrument is the building permission (*bouw-vergunning*). Environmental planning is also covered by this instrument.
2. Control of rents. Through the Rental Act (*Huurwet*) the government fixes the maximum allowable annual increase of the rent of houses. By this Act also the rights of tenants are protected. Termination of tenancy by the landlord is, except in a few cases, not allowed.

Planning and financing

1. General town and country planning. Through the Environmental Planning Act (*Wet op de Ruimtelijk Ordening*) the government regulates the planning of houses to be built, both their locations and their physical forms.
2. Socio-economic planning. Through 'building programmes' the government fixes the amounts of money to be spent on the different types of house in order to ensure that there is a well-balanced supply of houses for different social categories and income groups. This instrument is also used to control the distribution of houses to be built among the different provinces and municipalities.
3. Financial planning: finances for house-building are provided by private house builders, investment funds, pension funds and the government. The government gives the following different types of financial support:
   - Money loans to municipalities and housing corporations for the construction of Housing Act Dwellings (*Woningwetwoningen*), reserved for lower income groups.
   - Financial guarantees to private persons who wish to construct or buy a house. A full 100% guarantee (100% mortgage) can be given to cover rent payments.
   - Lump sum payments to private owners for house improvements, or the demolition of slum housing, and to tenants for renovation or demolition of their houses.
   - Building subsidies to municipalities and housing corporations to help cover the cost of construction and [exploitation], in order to keep rents or selling prices low for low income groups (so-called 'premium buying houses' (*premie-koopwoningen*).
   - Rent subsidies to lower income tenants (so called 'individual rent subsidy', *individuele huursubsidie*); in 1984 approximately 635,000 people received such a subsidy (in 1970 only 31,000), receiving in total 1,130 million HFL, on average 1,1780 HFL a year each net. In addition there is a rent habituation subsidy

(*huur-gewenningsbijdrage*) for tenants who are suddenly confronted with a sharp rent increase, for example people who have to move from a slum district to a new suburb. The number of tenants who received such a subsidy increased from 3,523 in 1976 to 27,113 in 1977/78, and decreased to 12,000 in 1983.

- Energy investment subsidies as part of a national energy saving programme. In 1976 the National Insulation Programme was started. Its objective was to subsidize the insulation of 2.5 million houses in twelve and a half years (up to 1990). In 1984 more than one million houses had been insulated in this way.

Housing statistics

The different types of government financial support are subdivided as follows:

Government subsidies on housing in 1984

Form of subsidy	benefits mill. HFL	% GDP
Rent subsidies to individuals		
Individual rent subsidies	1 130	23.5
Rent habituation subsidies	90	1.9
Subsidies on constructed houses		
to lower rent (premium renting houses)	1 400	29.2
to lower price (premium buying houses)	900	18.8
Subsidy on thermal insulation		
and city renovation	1 279	26.6
Total	4 799	100.0

Source: Ministry for Housing, Physical Planning and Environment.

Core laws

22.6.1901 (Stb. 158)
Woningwet (Housing Act): enabled government to improve bad housing conditions. Municipalities obliged to set standards for housing construction. Government/municipalities empowered to force landlords to improve their dwellings, and to close down dwellings unfit for habitation. Introduced financial support for the construction and improvement of housing.

14.6.1934 (Stb. 316)
Abolished Health Commissions, with the task of locating housing unfit for habitation, occupied by too many people, or in need of improvement or demolition; introduced an Institution of Inspectors of Popular Health, who could be instructed by the municipal authorities.

16.6.1950 (Stb. K 236)
Wederopbouwwet (Reconstruction Act): supplemented the Housing Act and introduced housing construction programmes.

28.9.1950 (Stb. K 415)
Wet voorlopige regeling inzake het nationaal plan en de streekplannen (Regional and Town Planning Act):

13.10.1950 (Stb. K 452)
Huurwet (Implementation of Rent Act): rents and rent increases fixed by Decree.

31.3.1960 (Stb. 116)
(Liberalization of Rent Act): allowed certain municipalities to operate outside of the 'fixed rent', leaving the market price of rents free from restrictions.

5.7.1962 (Stb. 286)
Wet op de Ruimtelijke Ordening (Environmental Planning Act): environmental planning recognized as a government concern. Location and type of building construction to be subject to government planning.

12.7.1962 (Stb. 222)
(New Housing Act): instituted a series of minor changes to the 1901 Housing Act; extended regulations covering building construction; increased government support of housing construction; and introduced articles covering subsidies for the construction of privately owned housing.

15.12.1966 (Stb. 565)
Tenant protection extended to family members of deceased tenant.

18.10.1967 (Stb.537)
Restricted tenant protection in areas 'liberalized' by the 1969 Act.

25.4.1968 (Stb. 202)
Introduced maximum annual rent increase to replace the fixed rent.

24.12.1968 (Stb. 703)
Tasks of Rent Advice Tribunals restricted; no longer decide on housing conditions; only task that of legally establishing rent prices.

18.12.1969 (Stb. 557)
Introduced an annual maximum rent increase of 6% (7% in 1971).

6.5.1971 (Stb. 309)
Brought the rents of social housing into alignment with one another; introduced an article covering the provision of finance for aligning the rents of newly-built and old housing - referred to as 'harmonization'; permitted the raising of the fixed percentage for rent increases in non-liberalized areas; Minister empowered to oblige the parties to a tenancy to abide by this rent increase where they are unable to reach an agreement.

26.3.1975 (Stb. 128)
Fixed rent increase raised to 8%.

26.6.1976 (Stb. 384)
New regulation covering Housing Associations introduced in order to clarify and organize the position of these Associations.

5.3.1977 (Stb. 114)
Fixed rent increase stabilized at 7%.

11.3.1978 (Stb. 143)
Regulation introduced detailing instructions for the improvement of housing conditions; landlords obliged to ensure that dwellings meet certain standards.

Bibliography

Contents

I General Contributions

1.1 General histories of social policy

ANDRIESSEN, J.E. et al.: De sociaal-economische besturing van Nederland (The Socio-economic Management of the Netherlands). Groningen, 1976. An introduction to the socio-economic functioning and relations in the Netherlands.

COMMISSIE VAN RHIJN: Sociale zekerheid (Social Security). Four parts. The Hague, 1945-1946. Proposals to reform the social security system and the organization of the health service by a Royal Commission.

GEMENGDE COMMISSIE VAN RHIJN: Rapport Gemengde Commissie van Rhijn (Report from the Mixed Commission van Rhijn). The Hague, 1948. Revised version of the Report of the Commission van Rhijn - an account of the political and social discussions.

SCHOUTEN, D.B.J., VELDKAMP, G.M.J.: De sociale verzekering in de volkshuishouding (Social Insurance in the Economic System). Amsterdam, 1952. A description of the development of social insurance in the Netherlands.

STICHTING VAN DE ARBEID: De toekomstige organisatie der sociale verzekering (The Organization of Social Insurance in the Future). The Hague, 1945-1946. The response of the Labour Council (Stichting van de Arbeid) to the proposals of the van Rhijn Commission.

TELDERSTICHTING, B.M.: Ontwikkeling van de sociale verzekering (The Development of the Social Insurance System). The Hague, 1965. A discussion on aspects of social security.

VEN, F.J.H.M. van der: Sociale grondrechten (Basic Social Rights). Utrecht, 1957. A description of basic social rights and how they can be realized.

1.2 Accounts of specific historical periods

SOCIALE VERZEKERINGSBANK (The Social Insurance Bank): Vijfenzeventig jaar sociale verzekering (Seventy-five Years of Social Insurance). Amsterdam, 1976. A collection of essays on various aspects of the development of the welfare state in the last seventy-five years.

VELDKAMP, G.M.J.: De crisis in de Nederlandse sociale zekerheid anno 1976, obstructie, destructie, constructie (The Crisis in the Dutch Social Security System in 1976). Amsterdam, 1976. An investigation into the current problems of the social security system.

1.3 Histories of social policy

VELDKAMP, G.M.J.: Individualistische karaktertrekken in de Nederlandse sociale arbeidsverzekering (Individualistic Characteristics of the Dutch Social Labour Insurance). Alphen aan den Rijn, 1949. Describes and analyses the first initiatives towards, and earlier legislation on, social security.

VELDKAMP, G.M.J.: Inleiding tot de sociale zekerheid en de toepassing ervan in Nederland en België (An Introduction to the Social Security System and its Application in the Netherlands and Belgium). Deventer, 1978. Basic handbook on the Dutch social security system.

1.4 Introductions to the system of social policies

GUASCO, R.A.F. de et al.: Het sociaal verzekeringsrecht in Nederland (Social Insurance Law in the Netherlands). Alphen aan den Rijn, Samsom, 1979. A description of laws and of jurisprudence in the field of social insurance in the Netherlands.

HEUVEL, F. van den: 'Het Nederlands stelsel van sociale zekerheid, een overzicht (The Dutch social security system, an overview)'. *Intermediair* (published weekly) 17, No. 33. A comprehensive description of the social security system in the Netherlands.

MINISTERIE VAN SOCIAL ZAKEN EN WERKGELEGENHEID (Ministry of Social Affairs and Employment): Social Security in the Netherlands. The Hague, 1982, 140 p. An overview of the current Dutch social security system.

STAATSUITGEVERIJ (State Publishing House): Over sociale verzekering gesproken (Talking about Social Insurance). The Hague, 1978. Practical introduction to the functioning of social insurance systems.

VERENIGING VAN RADEN VAN ARBEID (Labour Council Association): De Kleine Gids voor de Nederlandse sociale zekerheid (The Small Guidebook to the Dutch Social Security System). Published annually, Amsterdam. Detailed description of the current Dutch social security schemes.

1.5 Reports by investigating committees or experts

HAZEU, C.A.: De groei van de collectieve sector in Nederland, achtergronden en verlaringen (The Growth of the Public Sector in the Netherlands; the background and expectations). Rotterdam, Fiskaal Economisch Instituut, Erasmus Universiteit, 1979, 154 p.

SOCIAAL-ECONOMISCH RAAD (The Social Economic Council): Advies inzake het Sociaal-Economische Beleid op middellange termijn (Report: Average Long-term Advice on Social and Economic Policy). The Hague, 1981.

SOCIAAL-ECONOMISCHE RAAD: Advies over de beperking van de groei van de uitgaven voor sociale zekerheid (Advice on the Reduction of the Growth of Social Security Expenditure). The Hague, 1980, p. 112.

SOCIAAL-ECONOMISCHE RAAD: Advies inzake de omvang en de groei van de collectieve sector (Advice on the Size and Growth of the Public Sector). The Hague, 1978.

SOCIAAL EN CULTUREEL PLANBUREAU (Social and Cultural Planning Office): Profijt van de overheid in 1977 (Government Profits in 1977). The Hague, 1981.

STAATSCOMMISSIE (VELDKAMP) VEREENVOUDIGING EN CODIFICATIE VAN DE SOCIALE ZEKERHEIDSWETGEVING (State Commission on the Simplification and Codification of Social Security Laws): Financieringswet sociale zekerheid (Report on Social Security Financing Laws). The Hague, 1980, 440 p.

WETENSCHAPPELIJKE RAAD VOOR HET REGERINGSBELEID (Academic Council for Government Policy): De verdeling en de waardering van arbeid (The Distribution and Valuation of Labour). The Hague, 1976, 112 p. A statistical and descriptive study of inequality in the labour system.

WETENSCHAPPELIJKE RAAD VOOR HET REGERINGSBELEID: Maken wij er werk van? (Shall we do Something about Employment?). The Hague, 1977. Report on the relation between the active and unemployed population.

1.6 Social science interpretations, evaluations and analyses

BAKHOVEN, A.F., YPMA, Y.M: 'Kwantitatieve en instrumentele betekenis van de sociale zekerheid (Quantitative and instrumental importance of social insurance)'. *In*: Preadvies van de vereniging voor de Staathuiskunde 1974 (Pre-recommendations of the Association of Political Economy). The Hague, 1974. Study of the economic implications of the social security system and the causes of growth of social expenditure.

BERBEN, T., JANSSEN, G.: De vakbeweging en de sociale zekerheid in Nederland na 1945 (The Labour Unions and Social Security in the Netherlands after 1945). Nijmegen, 1982. An analysis of the influence of the labour unions on the social security after 1945.

BERBEN, L., PUSTJENS, J.: Uit de tijd van Methusalem (Out of the Time of Methusalem). Nijmegen, 1982. An pursued with regard to the position of women in the social security system in the last decennia.

BLANC, B.: Op weg naar een economische theorie van de sociale zekerheid (On Economic Thought about Social Security). Deventer, Kluwer, 1978. An economic theory of the developments in social security.

DOORN, J.A.A. van, SCHUYT, C.J.M. (eds): De stagnerende verzorgingsstaat (The Stagnating Welfare State). Amsterdam, 1978. Essays on the problems of the Welfare State from different points of view: economy, political science, ideology and law.

HEUVEL, F.G. van, (ed): Onzekere Zekerheid (Insecure Security). The Hague 1983. Essays on different aspects of the social security system in the light of the actual problems.

JUFFERMANS, P.: Overheidsbeleid en ziekenfondsen (Public Policy and Sickness Funds). Nijmegen, 1977. An analysis of the policy of the state with regard to health insurance and health provisions.

PALLADA, F.W.M.: De druk van de collectieve lasten en de omvang van de collectieve sector (On the Contributions to and the Size of the Public Sector). The Hague, Centraal Planbureau, 1982, 57 p. Discussion of some conceptual problems related to the size of the public sector.

SINNINGHE DAMSTĚ, W.E.: Sociale verzekering; de wetten de uitvoering en de reorganisatie (Social Insurance; Laws, Implementation and Reorganization). Scheveningen, 1981, 79 p. (Stichting Maatschappij en onderneming). Study of the reorganization and simplification of social insurance.

SOCIAAL EN CULTUREEL PLANBUREAU (Social and Cultural Planning Office): Sociaal en cultureel rapport 1980. Published every two years (1974), The Hague, 1980, 410 p. Periodical report discussing a wide range of aspects of the Dutch welfare state and including analyses of statistical information.

VELDKAMP, G.M.J.: Sociale zekerheid in een periode van economische overgang (Social Security in a Period of Economic Transition). Deventer, Kluwer, 1978, 99 p. Critical study of the maintenance of the social security system.

1.7 Policy proposals and debates

ANCIPATIERAAD: Sociale zekerheid en emancipatie (Social Security and Emancipation). The Hague, 1984. Advice of the Council for Emancipation with regard to the revision of the system of social security.

FEDERATIE NEDERLANDSE VAKBEWEGING (Federation Dutch Labour Unions): Diskussienota over stelselwijziging (Discussion note on the reform of the system of social security). Amsterdam, 1983. Points of view of the biggest Trade Union Movement on the reform of the social security system.

ORGANISATIE VAN DE BEHEERSING VAN DE SOCIALE ZEKERHEID (Organization of the Control of the Social Security System): Interim Report. Tweede Kamer (Lower chamber of parliament), session 1978-1979, 15594, Nos. 1-2. Report made by official project group and experts on organizational aspects of the social security system.

PARTIJ VAN DE ARBEID (Labour Party): Contouren voor stelselwijziging sociale zekerheid (Outline for Revision of the Social Security System). The Hague, 1984.

STAATSSECRETARIS VAN SOCIALE ZAKEN EN WERKGELEGENHEID: Herziening van het stelsel van sociale zekerheid (Revision of the System of Social Security). The Hague, 1983. Proposals for institutional reforms and retrenchments by the Undersecretary of Social Affairs and Employment.

TELDERSTICHTING, B.M.: Grenzen aan de sociale zekerheid (Limits to Social Security). The Hague, 1984. The liberal vision on the future development of the system of social security by The Research Office of the Liberal Party, VVD.

VERENIGING VAN NEDERLANDSE WERKGEVERS, NEDERLANDS CHRISTELIJKE WERKGEVERS (Employers' Organizations): Voorstellen voor nieuw stelsel van sociale zekerheid (Proposals for a New System of Social Security). The Hague, 1983. Vision of the two biggest employers' organizations on the reforms and retrenchments in the system of social security.

VERENIGING VOOR DE STAATHUISHOUDKUNDE: Overlevingskansen van de verzorgingsstaat (The Welfare State's Chances of Survival). Leiden and Antwerp, 1981, p. 164. Report on the current and future problems of the welfare state; suggests alternatives.

WETENSCHAPPELIJK INSTITUUT VOOR HET CDA: Vernieuwing om behoud (Renovation for Maintenance). The Hague, 1984. The Christian Democratic vision on the future development of the system of social security by the Research Office of the Christian-Democratic Party, CDA.

1.8 Sources of statistics or institutional regulations

1.8.1 Official sources

CENTRAAL BUREAU VOOR DE STATISTIEK (Central Office of Statistics): Nationale Rekeningen, 1950 (National Accounts since 1950). The Hague, Staatsuitgeverij.

CENTRAAL BUREAU VOOR DE STATISTIEK: Sociale verzekering, pensioenverzekering, levensverzekering (Social Insurance, Pension Insurance, Life Insurance). The Hague, several years (Published irregularly). Statistical overview and changes in laws and regulations.

CENTRAAL BUREAU VOOR DE STATISTIEK: Statistisch Jaarbock der Nederlandes, 1980 (Statistical Yearbook of the Netherlands 1980). Several years (Published irregularly), The Hague, Staatsuitgeverij, 1981, 432 p. Statistical overview of a wide range of subjects.

CENTRAAL BUREAU VOOR DE STATISTIEK: 1899-1979 tachtig jaar statistiek in tijdreeksen (1899-1979, Eighty Years of Statistics in Time Series). The Hague, 1979, 229 p. Five-yearly report covering eighty years on a wide range of subjects.

CENTRAAL BUREAU VOOR DE STATISTIEK: Woningbehoeftenonderzoek 1977/78, Vol. 1,1. Feitelijke en gewenste huisvestingstabellen Nederland (Statistics on Actual and Desired Housing Situation in the Netherlands). The Hague, 1980, 187 p. Statistical study on aspects of housing.

JAARVERSLAG OVER HET JAAR 1983 (Annual Report for 1983). Published since 1950, Amsterdam, 1983.

MINISTERIE VAN SOCIALE ZAKEN EN WERKGELEGENHEID : Financiele nota sociale zekerheid (Financial Note on Social Security). The Hague, 1984. Yearly Financial Report on social security including latest data on expenditure and The Ministry of Social Affairs and Employment.

SOCIALE VERZEKERINGSRAAD (Social Insurance Council): Sociale Zekerheid in Nederland 1948-1950 (Social Security in the Netherlands). The Hague, 1961. Historical overview of the social security regulations for the period 1948-1959; statistical information on expenditure and administrative costs of social security schemes.

1.8.2 Private sources

BLAAS, F., CORNEL, J., STAAL, R.H.: Praktische behandeling van sociale verzekeringswetten (Practical Treatment of Social Insurance Laws). Delwel and Wassenaar, 1981. Description of the current Dutch social security schemes.

FORTUYN, W.S.P.: Kerncijfers 1945-1983 van de sociaal-ekonomische ontwikkeling in Nederland (Key Figures on the Social-Economic Development in the Netherlands between 1945-1983). Deventer, 1983.

KLUWERS SOCIAAL ZAKBOEK (Kluwer's Social vade-mecum...): Deventer, Kluwer, ... Description of social security laws.

NEDERLANDSE STAATSWETTEN (The Laws of the Netherlands): edited by Schuurman & Jordans, various volumes. Tjeenk Willink, Zwolle. Series on the laws of the Netherlands.

SOCIALE VERZEKERINGSWETTEN-BIBLIOTHEEK (The Library of Social Insurance Laws): Ijmuiden, Vermande zonen. Description of social security laws, historical developments, legal changes and jurisprudence.

SOCIALE VERZEKERINGSWETTEN (Social Insurance Laws): Deventer, Kluwer. Extensive treatment of Dutch social security laws, including historical development, legal changes, and jurisprudence. National insurance schemes (Part I, Books 1-3); Employed persons' insurance schemes (Part II, Books 4-9).

1.8.3 Major periodicals

BELEID EN MAATSCHAPPIJ (Policy and Society): Meppel, Boom. Analyses of trends and developments in Dutch policy fields from various social science perspectives; mainly sociology, political science, law and economics.

CBS SOCIALE MAANDSTATSTIEK: (CBS Monthly Social Statistics). The Hague, Centraal Bureau voor de Statistiek. Up to date statistical information from the Central Statistics Office.

OPENBARE UITGAVEN (Public Expenditure): Deventer, Kluwer. Journal providing analyses of actual trends and developments in Dutch public expenditure, by using mainly economic methods and techniques.

PUBLICATIEBLAD, UITGAVE VAN DE SOCIALE VERZEKERINGSRAAD (Social Insurance Council Bulletin): Zoetermeer, ... Publication of recent developments in social insurance/security legislation.

SOCIAAL MAANDBLAD ARBEID (Monthly Social Bulletin on Labour): Alphen aan den Rijn, Samsom. Proposals, discussions and comments on aspects of labour, labour insurance, and pensions.

II Single programmes or aspects

2.1 Pensions

BESSELING, P.J., SCHEEPERS, H.M.J.: Pensionregelingen in Nederland; een vergelijkend onderzoek van 45 pensionenregelingen in Nederland (Old Age Pension Schemes in the Netherlands). The Hague, 1981, 164 p. comparative study of 45 occupational pension schemes in the Netherlands.

GINNEKEN, P.J. van: VUT (Development of the Voluntary Retirement Regulation). The Hague, 1981, 51 p. Describes the recent results of the Voluntary Retirement Regulation.

KOHL, L.J.M.L., VANMEULEBROUCK, H.W.M.: Pensioenen en uitkeringen bij arbeidsongeschiktheid, ouderdom en overlijden (Pensions and Benefits for Invalidity, Old Age and Death). Deventer, Zwolle, 1980.

STEVENS, L.G.M., YPEREN, P. van: Kernpunten van pension (Crucial Points about Pensions). Deventer, Kluwer, 1978, 139 p. Comprehensive treatment of the character of the Dutch pension system.

YPEREN, P. van: De pensioenbreuk in de Nederlandse pensioenregelingen (The Pension-break in the Dutch Pension Regulations). Scheveningen, 1982. Treatise on the problems of transferability of pension rights in the case of alteration of work.

2.2 Health

COMPENDIUM GEZONDHEIDSSTATISTIEK NEDERLAND 1979 (Compendium of Health Statistics): The Hague, Centraal Bureau voor de Statistiek, 1980. Report by the Central Office of Statistics, giving an overview of data on health

HANDBOEK GEZINSVERZORGING (Handbook of Family Health Care): The Hague, Vuga. Description and practical treatment of laws and regulations, organizations and the way in which they function, in the field of health care and family care.

LEENEN, H.J.J.: Struktuur en funktioneren van de gezondheidszorg (The Structure and Functioning of Health Care), 2nd ed. Alphen aan den Rijn and Brussels, 1981, 117 p. Comprehensive description of health care in the Netherlands.

PUTTEN, M. van et al.: Ziekteverzuimbeleid in de praktijk (Policy with Regard to Sickness Absenteeism in Practice). Amsterdam, 1982.

ROSCAM ABBING, E.W.: Bouw en werking van de gezondheidszorg in Nederland (The Development and Functioning of Health Care in the Netherlands). Utrecht, 1979, 417 p. Extensive description of health care.

SANTEMA, S.: Georganiseerde maatschappelijke gezondheidszorg: structuur, werkzaamheden, raakvlakken (Organized Social Health Care: Structure, Activities and Points of Contact). 6th ed. Assen, 1981, 246 p.

SCHRIJVERS, G.: Regionalisatie en financiering van de Engelse, Zweedse en Nederlandse gezonheidszorg (Regionalization and Financing of English, Swedish and Dutch Health Care). Lochem, 1980, 198 p. Comparative study of organization and financing.

WERKBOEK GECOÖRDINEERD BEJAARDENWERK (Handbook of Coordinated Care for the Elderly): The Hague. Description and practical treatment of laws and regulations, organizations and the way in which they function.

2.3 Unemployment

BOUMAN, A.H., HEIJKE, J. de Koning: Ontwikkeling en oorzaken van jeugdwekloosheid (Development and Causes of Youth Unemployment). Ministerie van Sociale Zaken, 1979. Report on youth employment by the Ministry of Social Affairs.

HEERTJE, A., WOLK, W. van der: Werkloosheid, verwording en verwachting; de economische crisis en haar slachtoffers (Unemployment, Deterrioration and Expectations; the Economic Crisis and its Victims). Amsterdam, 1982, p. 263. Essays on unemployment; comment and evaluations from employer, employee, governmental and academic points of view.

OVESEN, E.E.: Werkloosheid, Een inzicht in Psychische en maatschappelijke gevolgen van werkloosheid (Unemployment, an Insight into its Psychological and Social Consequences). Rotterdam, 1979.

WEZEL, J.A.M. van: Herintreding in het arbeidsproces; een onderzoek onder werklozen (Re-entry into the Labour Process; a Study of the Unemployed). Tilburg, 1972. An evaluation of the chances and problems of re-entering the labour market.

2.4 Accident and work disability

BOSCH, J.A.F. van den, PETERSEN, C.: Aspecten van ziekte en arbeidsongeschiktheid in het stelsel van sociale zekerheid (Aspects of Sickness and Work Disability in the System of Social Security). Leiden, 1983.

BOSCH, J.A.F. van den, PETERSEN, C. (eds): Economie en arbeidsongeschiktheid, analyse en beleid (Economy and Work Disability, Analysis and Policy). Deventer, 1983.

DIJCK, J. van., KORGT, T. van der: Gemeentelijke Sociale Dienstverlening in Ontwikkeling (The Development of Municipal Social Assistance). The Hague, VNG, 1977. Report on the developments in social assistance by the Association of Dutch Municipalities.

GROSFIELD, J.A.M.: Arbeidsongeschiktheid in Nederland: omvang van het probleem en inventarisatie van onderzoek vanuit de gedragswetenschappen (Work Disability in the Netherlands: Problems and Inventory of Social Research). Nijmegen, 1982.

KESSEL, J.G.F.M. van: Arbeidsongschiktheid van militairen, ambtenaren en werknemers (Work Disability among Military Personnel, Public Servants and Employees). Antwerp and Amsterdam, 1981. Study of the causes and developments of unfitness for work/inability to work in these groups.

SPRENGER, W.: De Algemene bijstandswet, Rechten en Plichten van burger en overheid (The Public Assistance Act: Rights and Obligations of Citizens and Government). The Hague, Staatsuitgeverij, 1976, 119 p.

VRIES, J. de.: De Algemene Bijstandswet (The Public Assistance Act). Alphen aan den Rijn, Samsom and The Hague, Vuga, 1979. Description of historical development and functioning of the Public Assistance Act, including jurisprudence.

2.5 Social assistance

GEERS, C.M., KOOIMAN, J.: De bijstand op de tweesprong: bestuurlijke scenario's voor de toekomst van de Algemene Bijstandswet in de relatie tot de sociale zekerheid en het specifieke welzijn (Social Assistance at the Crossroads: Administration-Scenarios for the Future of the Social Assistance Law in Relation to Social Security and Specific Welfare). Leiden, 1981.

2.6 Family programmes

MELSEN, D.C. van: De algemene kinderbijslagwet, kinderbijslagwet voor loontrekkenden, kinderbijslagwet en kleine zelfstandigen (The General Family Allowance Act, Family Allowance Act for Employees, Family Allowance Act and Self-Employed). Alphen aan de Rijn, 1962.

SOCIAAL-ECONOMISCHE RAAD (SOCIAL-ECONOMIC COUNCIL): Advies met betrekkiing tot de derde fase van de herstructurering van de kinderbijslag en kinderaftrek (Advice with Regard to the Third Stage of the Reorganization of the Family Allowance and Tax Relief for Children). The Hague, 1979.

2.7 Housing

ADRIAANSENS, C.A., FORTGENS, A.Ch.: Volkshuisvestingsrecht (Public Housing Law). Deventer, Kluwer, 1978. Description of legislation and the current system.

CONIJN, J.S.B.: 'Achtergronden van de stijging van de woonsubsidies (The background to the increase in housing subsidies)'. *Economisch Statistische Berichten*, Dec. 1980. Study on the development of housing subsidies.

CONIJN, J.S.B.: Woonlasten en hun verdeling over de private en collectieve sector: Een onderzoek programma in hoofdlijnen voor de VRA (Housing Costs and their Distribution between the Private and Public Sector: a Research Programme for the VRA). OGO, 1981. Study of the financing of housing in the Netherlands.

DIJHUIZEN, W.C., GERRICHHAUZEN, L.G., GIESSEN, M. van (eds): Documentatie woningcorporaties (Documentation Housing Corporations). The Hague, 1984.

DRIEL, A. van., VLIET, J. van: Wetgeving ruimtelijke ordening en volkshuisvesting (Legislation on Environmental Planning and Housing). Alphen aan den Rijn, Samsom and The Hague, Vuga, 1979. Description of the historical development of legislation and the current system.

INSTITUUT VOOR ONDERZOEK VAN OVERHEIDSUITGAVEN (Institute for Research on Government Expenditure): Kopen of huren (Buying or Renting). The Hague, Staatsuitgeverij, 1979, Vol. 1, 162 p. A comparative study of the choice between buying and renting.

PRIEMUS, H.: Volkshuisvesting in de verdrukking; kritische notities over het Nederlandse woonbeleid (Housing under Hatches: Critical Notes on the Dutch Housing Policy). Alphen aan den Rijn, 1980. Collection of articles published in 'NRC-Handelsblad'.

PRIEMUS, H., LUCASSEN, C.T.J.: Individuele huursubsidie (evaluatie van een instrument van volkshuisvestingsbeleid) (Individual Rent Subsidies). The Hague, Staatsuitgeverij, 1977, 209 p. An evaluation of the functioning of rent subsidies.

2.8 Education

KEMENADE, J.A. van (ed.): Ouderwijs: Bestel en beleid (Education: Polity and Policy). Groningen, Wolters Noordhoff, 1981. Extensive description and evaluation of the development and functioning of the Dutch education system.

VERSLAG VAN DE STAAT VAN HET ONDERWIJS IN NEDERLAND OVER HET JAAR 1981 (Report on the State of Education in the Netherlands, 1981): The Hague, 1982, 272 p. Official report on the development of education in the Netherlands.

VLEUTEN, C.E. van: De vrijheid van onderwijs en de volwasseneducatie (Freedom of Education and Adult Education). Amersfoort, 1977. Notes for recommendations in the field of educational networks.

WETENSCHAPPELIJKE RAAD VOOR HET REGERINGSBELEID (Academic Council for Government Policy): Kansen op onderwijs (Educational Opportunities). The Hague, 1976, 85 p. Study of the literature on inequality in the Dutch education system.

2.9 Public household

FRANCKENA, W.D., GERRITSE, R.: Verdeling in verandering (Distribution in Periods of Change). The Hague, Staatsuitgeverij, 1981, 479 p. Study of the financial relationship between the state and the provinces.

GERRITSE, R.: De publieke sector: ontwikkeling en waardevorming (The Public Sector: Development and Valuation) (a preliminary study). The Hague, 1979, 79 p. Study of the volume and growth of the public sector.

KOOPMANS, L., WELLINK, A.H.E.M.: Overheidsfinanciën (Public Finance). Leiden and Antwerp, Stenfert Kroese, 1978, p. 201. Examination of how to improve the most important official annual publications in the Netherlands.

KOOPMANS, L.: Beheersing van de overheidsuitgaven (The Control of Government Expenditure). Deventer, 1973. Professsorial oration.

WOLFSON, D.J.: Naar een beheersbare collectieve sector (Towards a Controllable Public Sector). Deventer, 1981, 236 p. Study of the public sector in the light of current economic developments.

2.10 Public employment

MINISTERIE VAN SOCIALE ZAKEN EN WERKGELEGENHEID EN MINISTERIE VAN ECONOMISCHE ZAKEN (Ministry of Social Affairs and Employment and Ministry of Economic Affairs): De Werkgelegenheidsnota 1983-1984 (Note on Employment 1983-1984). The Hague, 1983.

PARTIJBESTUUR EN COMMISSIE WERKGELEGENHEID (Labour Party Board and Commission on Employment): Interimrapport over het werkgelegenheidsbeleid (Interim Report on Employment Policy). Amsterdam, 1984. Main features of an alternative employment policy.

III Impact of social programmes

3.1 Poverty

SOCIAAL EN CULTUREEL PLANBUREAU (Social and Cultural Planning Office): Inkomen en rondkomen (Income and How to Make Both Ends Meet). The Hague, 1981, 155 p. Report on the financial position of Dutch households, including recent statistical information.

3.2 Inequality and income distribution

ALBEDA, W., GALAN, C. de: Inkomens, vorming, verdeling en beleid (Income Creation, Distribution and Policy). Groningen, 1970. Analysis of Dutch incomes' policy.

HARTOG, J., VEENBERGEN, J.G.: 'Dutch treat, long-run changes in personal income distribution'. *The Economist* 126, No. 4, 1978. Historical overview of personal income distribution.

NIEKERK, N.C.M. (ed.): Tertiaire inkomensverdeling (Tertiary Income Distribution). Deventer, Kluwer, 1979. Essays on the redistribution of personal income.

PEN, J.: Income Distribution; facts, theories, policies. Translated from Dutch by PRESTON, T.S., New York, Preager, 1971, 424 p. Analytical study on income distribution.

TINBERGEN, J.: Income Distribution; Analysis and Policies. Amsterdam, Oxford and New York. 1975, 170 p. Study which formulates a new quantitative supply-demand theory of income distribution by integrating the notion of human capital with the ideas of the education planning school.

WIARDI BECKMAN STICHTING (The Research Office of the Labour Party): Inkomensverdeling (Income Distribution). Amsterdam, 1969, 72 p. Discussion on labour and income distribution.

3.3 Economic effects

CENTRAAL PLANBUREAU (Central Planning Office): Centraal economisch plan 1982 (Central Economic Plan, 1982). The Hague, 1982, 394 p. Annual report on the state of the Dutch economy on an average long-term.

CENTRAAL PLANBUREAU: Macro Economische Verkenning (Macro-Economic Outlook). Published annually. The Hague, 1982, 95 p. Short-term outlook for the Dutch economy.

DOUBEN, N.H.: Sociale Zekerheid, een economische benadering (Social Security, an Economic Approach). Leiden and Antwerp, 1979, 81 p. Dissertation on the economic consequences of social security.

HALBERSTADT, V.: De economie van de sociale zekerheid (The Economic Aspects of Social Security). Deventer, 1974. Study on social security and the economy.

INSTITUUT ONDERZOEK OVERHEIDSUITGAVEN (Institute Research on Governmental Expenditure): Sociale zekerheid en recessie (Social Security and Recession). The Hague, 1982.

STEVERS, Th. A.: Openbare financiën en economie (Public Finance and Economics). Leiden, Stenfert Kroese, 1971, 330 p. Discussion of public finance as an instrument of economic policy.

VELDKAMP, G.M.J.: De economie en het sociale zekerheidsbeleid (The Economy and Social Security Policy). Deventer, 1980, 232 p. Discussion of aspects of social security and the economy.

VELDKAMP, G.M.J. (ed.): Ombuigen de sociale zekerheid; een paradox voor de ekonomie van de jaren 80 (Retrenchments in Social Security: a Paradox for the Economy of the Eighties). Deventer, 1983.

Appendix Tables

Contents

Table 1 Gross Domestic Product and Total Public Expenditure

Year	GDP (at market prices, in million guilders)			Deflators (1975)					Total public expenditure (in million guilders)				Year
	at current prices	at constant (1975) prices	annual real growth rate	GDP	public final cons.	public investment	composed index	consumer pr. index	at current prices	as % of GDP	at constant (1975) prices	annual real growth rate	
1948	14 784	62 380		23.7	12	20		27					1948
1949	16 579	66 580	6.7	24.9	12	20	21.0	29	5 047	30.4	24 033		1949
1950	18 542	69 540	4.4	26.7	14	22	23.1	32	5 328	28.7	23 065	-4.0	1950
1951	21 173	70 760	1.8	29.9	16	25	25.8	36	6 118	28.9	23 713	2.8	1951
1952	22 103	72 140	2.0	30.6	16	26	25.7	36	6 497	29.4	25 280	6.6	1952
1953	23 516	78 080	8.2	30.1	16	26	25.1	36	7 325	31.1	29 183	15.4	1953
1954	26 279	83 310	6.7	31.5	17	28	26.2	37	8 122	30.9	31 000	6.2	1954
1955	29 385	89 150	7.0	33.0	19	29	28.0	38	9 377	31.9	33 489	8.0	1955
1956	31 886	93 110	4.4	34.2	20	31	28.7	39	10 153	31.8	35 376	5.6	1956
1957	34 718	95 900	3.0	36.2	22	34	31.4	41	11 746	33.8	37 408	5.7	1957
1958	35 007	94 950	-1.0	36.9	22	34	32.4	42	12 251	35.0	37 812	1.1	1958
1959	37 370	99 420	4.7	37.6	23	34	32.9	42	12 408	33.2	37 714	-0.3	1959
1960	41 840	108 390	9.0	38.6	24	35	34.5	44	13 838	33.1	40 110	6.4	1960
1961	44 173	111 710	3.1	39.5	25	36	35.2	44	15 361	34.8	43 639	8.8	1961
1962	47 554	116 150	4.0	40.9	27	37	36.3	45	16 589	34.9	45 700	4.7	1962
1963	51 592	120 360	3.6	42.9	29	39	38.4	47	19 159	37.1	49 893	9.2	1963
1964	60 708	130 320	8.3	46.6	33	42	41.8	49.9	22 681	37.4	54 261	8.8	1964
1965	67 802	137 160	5.2	49.4	36	45	44.6	51.9	25 934	38.2	58 148	7.2	1965
1966	73 829	140 920	2.7	52.4	40	48	48.1	54.9	29 579	40.1	61 495	5.8	1966
1967	80 997	148 360	5.3	54.6	44	49	50.9	56.8	33 975	41.9	66 749	8.5	1967
1968	89 811	157 880	6.4	56.9	46	51	53.1	58.9	38 164	42.5	71 872	7.7	1968
1969	101 715	168 030	6.4	60.5	51	55	57.7	63.3	43 673	42.9	75 690	5.3	1969
1970	114 573	179 290	6.7	63.9	55	59	61.2	66.1	50 912	44.4	83 190	9.9	1970
1971	129 650	186 950	4.3	69.4	62	66	67.2	71.1	60 050	46.3	89 360	7.4	1971
1972	146 730	193 340	3.4	75.9	68	73	73.2	76.5	68 860	46.9	94 071	5.3	1972
1973	168 110	204 370	5.7	82.3	76	81	80.3	82.8	79 930	47.5	99 539	5.8	1973
1974	190 290	211 600	3.5	89.9	88	91	89.7	90.7	93 840	49.3	104 615	5.1	1974
1975	209 420	209 420	-1.0	100.0	100	100	100.0	100.0	113 490	54.2	113 490	8.5	1975
1976	240 170	220 560	5.3	108.9	109	109	108.9	108.8	130 680	54.4	120 000	5.7	1976
1977	261 410	226 730	2.8	115.3	116	115	115.8	115.8	141 870	54.3	122 513	2.1	1977
1978	282 404	231 480	2.1	122.0	123	122	121.5	120.5	157 350	55.7	129 506	5.7	1978
1979	300 422	236 970	2.4	126.8	130	131	127.3	125.6	173 520	57.8	136 308	5.3	1979
1980	320 180	239 010	0.9	134.0	136	141	134.8	133.6	190 460	59.5	141 291	3.7	1980
1981	335 907	237 620	-0.6	141.4	139	152	141.9	142.8	205 450	61.2	144 785	2.5	1981
1982	349 323	233 050	-1.9	149.9	145	156	149.5	151.3	222 730	63.8	148 983	2.9	1982

Table 2 Total Public Expenditure by Economic Category and Level of Govt and Central Govt Expenditure by Major Purpose

Year	Economic Category: final consump.	transfers/ subsidies	interests on debt	invest- ment	Level of Govt: central govt	other govt	social insurance	Central Govt Expenditure by Major Purpose: general adm./ public order	defence	economic services	interests on debt	welfare	Year
	percent distribution				percent distribution			percent distribution					
1949	42.0	48.6		9.4	55.6	31.5	12.9						1949
1950	44.3	46.5		9.2	56.5	30.6	12.9						1950
1951	45.5	44.7		9.8	56.1	30.3	13.6						1951
1952	47.1	44.1		8.8	53.3	33.3	13.4						1952
1953	45.5	32.8	8.6	13.1	54.9	32.9	12.2						1953
1954	46.8	34.1	8.6	10.5	54.7	32.6	12.7						1954
1955	45.9	37.1	7.4	9.6	52.5	35.6	11.9	22.7	23.5	14.3	11.7	27.8	1955
1956	47.8	34.1	7.7	10.4	45.8	34.7	19.5						1956
1957	44.8	37.3	7.3	10.6	43.1	35.8	21.1						1957
1958	41.9	40.4	8.1	9.6	39.2	38.4	22.4						1958
1959	41.4	39.9	8.0	10.7	38.8	38.1	23.1						1959
1960	40.6	40.8	8.2	10.4	41.3	36.8	21.9	14.3	18.3	16.3	11.2	39.9	1960
1961	40.2	41.7	7.6	10.5	37.5	38.7	23.8						1961
1962	41.7	40.4	7.2	10.7	34.4	38.5	27.1						1962
1963	41.4	41.2	6.6	10.8	34.1	38.9	27.0						1963
1964	41.6	40.9	6.3	11.2	32.8	38.2	29.0						1964
1965	40.5	42.7	6.3	10.5	31.5	38.3	30.2	13.3	16.3	21.0	5.7	43.7	1965
1966	39.6	43.8	6.4	10.2	31.6	38.3	30.1						1966
1967	38.7	44.6	6.6	10.1	31.9	37.7	30.4						1967
1968	37.4	45.2	6.7	10.7	30.5	37.7	31.8						1968
1969	37.2	46.4	6.7	9.7	29.1	36.6	34.3						1969
1970	36.7	47.2	6.9	9.2	29.0	36.2	34.8	12.5	13.6	22.3	5.5	46.1	1970
1971	36.1	48.2	6.5	9.2	27.8	36.1	36.1	14.0	12.6	21.2	5.3	46.9	1971
1972	35.5	50.5	6.1	7.9	28.2	35.7	36.1	13.4	12.1	20.4	5.0	49.1	1972
1973	34.3	52.9	6.1	6.7	27.1	36.0	36.9	12.8	11.5	19.6	4.7	51.4	1973
1974	34.6	52.8	6.4	6.2	27.7	35.7	36.6	12.9	12.3	17.7	4.7	52.4	1974
1975	33.7	54.5	5.8	6.0	28.3	35.3	36.4	13.3	11.7	17.0	4.2	53.3	1975
1976	33.2	55.6	5.4	5.8	27.2	34.9	37.9	10.8	10.3	18.6	4.1	56.2	1976
1977	33.6	55.9	5.5	5.0	28.0	33.8	38.2	11.2	11.4	18.8	4.6	54.0	1977
1978	33.1	56.3	5.8	4.8	29.1	32.7	38.2	11.6	10.4	18.2	4.9	54.9	1978
1979	32.7	57.1	5.8	4.4	30.0	31.9	38.1	10.6	11.0	19.5	5.1	53.8	1979
1980	31.4	57.7	6.5	4.4	30.3	32.0	37.7	11.4	10.5	16.6	6.6	54.9	1980
1981	30.3	58.1	7.5	4.1	30.6	32.2	37.2	11.1	10.3	17.4	7.5	53.7	1981
1982	29.0	58.9	8.4	3.7	31.7	32.4	35.9	10.9	10.2	16.4	8.9	53.6	1982

Table 3

Social Expenditure

Year	At current prices (in million guilders)						At constant (1975) prices						Year
	Total	Income maint.	Education	Health	Housing	Other	Total	Income maint.	Education	Health	Housing	Other	
1948	1 967	1 175	437	267	11	77	10 917	4 350	3 641	2 225	55	645	1948
1949	2 170	1 276	486	307	20	81	11 782	4 398	4 050	2 558	100	675	1949
1950	2 468	1 421	557	355	38	97	11 817	4 442	3 979	2 532	173	692	1950
1951	2 700	1 511	620	406	58	105	11 495	4 198	3 875	2 536	232	654	1951
1952	2 990	1 643	684	437	112	114	12 714	4 563	4 275	2 733	431	712	1952
1953	3 344	1 796	801	490	130	128	14 355	4 987	5 006	3 061	500	800	1953
1954	3 866	2 044	934	547	188	152	15 804	5 525	5 494	3 220	671	893	1954
1955	4 448	2 233	1 126	636	223	231	17 130	5 876	5 926	3 346	769	1 213	1955
1956	4 884	2 413	1 300	686	246	240	18 109	6 186	6 500	3 430	794	1 200	1956
1957	5 993	3 166	1 511	767	272	277	20 134	7 722	6 868	3 484	800	1 260	1957
1958	6 723	3 658	1 596	843	317	309	22 135	8 709	7 255	3 833	932	1 406	1958
1959	7 126	3 746	1 772	920	364	324	23 102	8 919	7 704	3 999	1 071	1 409	1959
1960	7 892	4 179	1 995	1 017	393	307	24 452	9 498	8 313	4 237	1 123	1 281	1960
1961	8 510	4 488	2 315	1 115	297	295	25 924	10 200	9 260	4 458	825	1 182	1961
1962	9 400	4 978	2 637	1 243	227	315	27 211	11 062	9 767	4 604	614	1 165	1962
1963	11 273	6 352	2 985	1 398	196	343	30 313	13 515	10 293	4 820	503	1 182	1963
1964	13 562	7 455	3 764	1 703	200	441	33 317	14 939	11 406	5 159	476	1 336	1964
1965	15 972	9 010	4 320	1 972	205	469	36 588	17 351	12 000	5 479	456	1 303	1965
1966	18 442	10 460	4 940	2 349	203	507	38 935	19 023	12 350	5 873	423	1 266	1966
1967	21 155	11 932	5 653	2 776	201	593	41 922	21 008	12 848	6 308	410	1 348	1967
1968	24 089	13 111	6 358	3 751	183	686	46 086	22 259	13 822	8 154	359	1 492	1968
1969	28 302	15 281	7 378	4 647	199	797	49 643	24 141	14 467	9 111	362	1 563	1969
1970	32 886	17 580	8 541	5 627	270	869	54 392	26 595	15 529	10 230	458	1 579	1970
1971	39 204	20 921	9 936	6 834	350	1 163	58 880	29 424	16 026	11 023	530	1 877	1971
1972	45 962	24 532	11 199	8 367	460	1 404	63 536	32 068	16 469	12 304	630	2 065	1972
1973	53 718	29 153	12 802	9 328	600	1 835	67 482	35 209	16 845	12 273	741	2 415	1973
1974	63 945	35 226	14 909	10 675	800	2 336	71 443	38 838	16 942	12 130	879	2 654	1974
1975	77 574	43 297	17 694	12 474	1 150	2 959	77 574	43 297	17 694	12 474	1 150	2 959	1975
1976	89 905	50 591	19 916	14 146	1 340	3 912	82 567	46 499	18 272	12 978	1 229	3 589	1976
1977	100 138	57 256	21 526	15 820	1 590	3 945	86 423	49 444	18 557	13 638	1 383	3 401	1977
1978	110 715	63 704	23 272	17 556	1 780	4 402	91 098	52 866	18 920	14 273	1 459	3 579	1978
1979	120 295	70 024	24 683	19 131	1 810	4 647	94 411	55 752	18 987	14 716	1 382	3 575	1979
1980	128 828	75 258	25 802	20 744	2 020	5 005	95 584	56 246	18 972	15 253	1 433	3 680	1980
1981	138 278	82 197	26 628	22 350	1 970	5 133	97 786	57 561	19 157	16 079	1 296	3 693	1981
1982	150 266	91 242	27 499	24 150	1 890	5 486	100 920	60 305	18 965	16 655	1 212	3 783	1982

Table 4

Social Expenditure

Year	As percent of GDP						As percent of public expenditure						Percent distribution					Year
	Total	Income maint.	Educ-ation	Health	Hous-ing	Other	Total	Income maint.	Educ-ation	Health	Hous-ing	Other	Income maint.	Educ-ation	Health	Hous-ing	Other	
1948	13.3	7.9	3.0	1.8	0.1	0.5							59.7	22.2	13.6	0.6	3.9	1948
1949	13.1	7.7	2.9	1.9	0.1	0.5	43.0	25.3	9.6	6.1	0.4	1.6	58.8	22.4	14.2	0.9	3.7	1949
1950	13.3	7.7	3.0	1.9	0.2	0.5	46.3	26.7	10.5	6.7	0.7	1.8	57.6	22.6	14.4	1.5	3.9	1950
1951	12.8	7.1	2.9	1.9	0.3	0.5	44.1	24.7	10.1	6.6	0.9	1.7	56.0	23.0	15.0	2.1	3.9	1951
1952	13.5	7.4	3.1	2.0	0.5	0.5	46.0	25.3	10.5	6.7	1.7	1.8	54.9	22.9	14.6	3.7	3.8	1952
1953	14.2	7.6	3.4	2.1	0.6	0.5	45.7	24.5	10.9	6.7	1.8	1.7	53.7	24.0	14.6	3.9	3.8	1953
1954	14.7	7.8	3.6	2.1	0.7	0.6	47.6	25.2	11.5	6.7	2.3	1.9	52.9	24.2	14.2	4.9	3.9	1954
1955	15.1	7.6	3.8	2.2	0.8	0.8	47.4	23.8	12.0	6.8	2.4	2.5	50.2	25.3	14.3	5.0	5.2	1955
1956	15.3	7.6	4.1	2.2	0.8	0.8	48.1	23.8	12.8	6.8	2.4	2.4	49.4	26.6	14.0	5.0	4.9	1956
1957	17.3	9.1	4.4	2.2	0.8	0.8	51.0	27.0	12.9	6.5	2.3	2.4	52.8	25.2	12.8	4.5	4.6	1957
1958	19.2	10.4	4.6	2.4	0.9	0.9	54.9	29.9	13.0	6.9	2.6	2.5	54.4	23.7	12.5	4.7	4.6	1958
1959	19.1	10.0	4.7	2.5	1.0	0.9	57.4	30.2	14.3	7.4	2.9	2.6	52.6	24.9	12.9	5.1	4.5	1959
1960	18.9	10.0	4.8	2.4	0.9	0.7	57.0	30.2	14.4	7.3	2.8	2.2	53.0	25.3	12.9	5.0	3.9	1960
1961	19.3	10.2	5.2	2.5	0.7	0.7	55.4	29.2	15.1	7.3	1.9	1.9	52.7	27.2	13.1	3.5	3.5	1961
1962	19.8	10.5	5.5	2.6	0.5	0.7	56.7	30.0	15.9	7.5	1.4	1.9	53.0	28.1	13.2	2.4	3.3	1962
1963	21.9	12.3	5.8	2.7	0.4	0.7	58.8	33.2	15.6	7.3	1.0	1.8	56.3	26.5	12.4	1.7	3.0	1963
1964	22.3	12.3	6.2	2.8	0.3	0.7	59.8	32.9	16.6	7.5	0.9	1.9	55.0	27.8	12.6	1.5	3.3	1964
1965	23.6	13.3	6.4	2.9	0.3	0.7	61.6	34.7	16.7	7.6	0.8	1.8	56.4	27.0	12.3	1.3	2.9	1965
1966	25.0	14.1	6.7	3.2	0.3	0.7	62.3	35.3	16.7	7.9	0.7	1.7	56.6	26.8	12.7	1.1	2.7	1966
1967	26.1	14.7	7.0	3.4	0.2	0.7	62.3	35.1	16.6	8.2	0.6	1.7	56.4	26.7	13.1	1.0	2.8	1967
1968	26.8	14.6	7.1	4.2	0.2	0.8	63.1	34.4	16.7	9.8	0.5	1.8	54.4	26.4	15.6	0.8	2.8	1968
1969	27.8	15.0	7.3	4.6	0.2	0.8	64.8	35.0	16.9	10.6	0.5	1.8	54.0	26.1	16.4	0.7	2.8	1969
1970	28.7	15.3	7.5	4.9	0.2	0.8	64.6	34.5	16.8	11.1	0.5	1.7	53.5	26.0	17.1	0.8	2.6	1970
1971	30.2	16.1	7.7	5.3	0.3	0.9	65.3	34.8	16.5	11.4	0.6	1.9	53.4	25.3	17.4	0.9	3.0	1971
1972	31.3	16.7	7.6	5.7	0.3	1.0	66.7	35.6	16.3	12.2	0.7	2.0	53.4	24.4	18.2	1.0	3.1	1972
1973	32.0	17.3	7.6	5.5	0.4	1.1	67.2	36.5	16.0	11.7	0.8	2.3	54.3	23.8	17.4	1.1	3.4	1973
1974	33.6	18.5	7.8	5.6	0.4	1.2	68.1	37.5	15.9	11.4	0.9	2.5	55.1	23.3	16.7	1.3	3.7	1974
1975	37.0	20.7	8.4	6.0	0.5	1.4	68.4	38.2	15.6	11.0	1.0	2.6	55.8	22.8	16.1	1.5	3.8	1975
1976	37.4	21.1	8.3	5.9	0.6	1.6	68.8	38.7	15.2	10.8	1.0	3.0	56.3	22.2	15.7	1.5	4.4	1976
1977	38.3	21.9	8.2	6.1	0.6	1.5	70.6	40.4	15.2	11.2	1.1	2.8	57.2	21.5	15.8	1.6	3.9	1977
1978	39.2	22.6	8.2	6.2	0.6	1.6	70.4	40.5	14.8	11.2	1.1	2.8	57.5	21.0	15.9	1.6	4.0	1978
1979	40.0	23.3	8.2	6.4	0.6	1.5	69.3	40.4	14.2	11.0	1.0	2.7	58.2	20.5	15.9	1.5	3.9	1979
1980	40.2	23.5	8.1	6.5	0.6	1.6	67.6	39.5	13.5	10.9	1.1	2.6	58.4	20.0	16.1	1.6	3.9	1980
1981	41.2	24.5	7.9	6.7	0.6	1.5	67.3	40.0	13.0	10.9	1.0	2.5	59.4	19.3	16.2	1.4	3.7	1981
1982	43.0	26.1	7.9	6.9	0.5	1.6	67.5	41.0	12.3	10.8	0.8	2.5	60.7	18.3	16.1	1.3	3.7	1982

Table 5

Social Insurance Expenditure

Year	At current prices (in million guilders) Total	Pen- sions	Inval- idity	Sick- ness	Unem- ploym.	Family allow.	Health ins.	At constant (1975) prices Total	Pen- sions	Inval- idity	Sick- ness	Unem- ploym.	Family allow.	Health ins.	Year
1948	778	132	140	123		195	188	2 466	489	613	515		61	788	1948
1949	885	148	154	141		223	219	2 652	510	635	566		86	856	1949
1950	973	160	164	146		247	257	2 614	500	606	530		84	894	1950
1951	1 111	181	182	160		291	297	2 625	503	602	508		98	914	1951
1952	1 213	195	187	161	57	301	313	2 925	542	613	507	198	104	960	1952
1953	1 374	216	193	173	132	311	350	3 383	600	639	542	441	98	1 064	1953
1954	1 555	263	219	195	141	347	391	3 722	711	706	608	455	91	1 152	1954
1955	1 723	277	232	225	151	374	464	3 989	729	711	680	466	95	1 307	1955
1956	1 820	294	250	258	125	392	501	4 094	754	744	744	384	95	1 374	1956
1957	2 550	856	259	339	96	436	564	3 563	97	724	908	285	93	1 455	1957
1958	2 870	925	275	349	212	485	625	4 002	89	754	915	569	103	1 572	1958
1959	3 036	1 024	284	381	174	504	670	4 198	192	769	988	467	107	1 674	1959
1960	3 504	1 312	317	430	129	578	738	4 644	534	818	1 066	343	125	1 758	1960
1961	3 719	1 398	345	458	101	613	805	4 865	556	875	1 129	271	128	1 907	1961
1962	4 275	1 657	368	530	164	649	907	5 416	630	902	1 262	404	128	2 090	1962
1963	5 568	1 969	637	625	337	966	1 034	8 646	672	1 451	1 415	756	2 078	2 274	1963
1964	6 605	2 376	789	760	202	1 217	1 261	9 546	754	1 691	1 603	437	2 466	2 595	1964
1965	8 205	3 347	910	910	223	1 363	1 453	10 546	917	1 826	1 831	457	2 652	2 864	1965
1966	9 475	3 790	978	1 034	322	1 599	1 753	11 554	973	1 828	1 952	611	2 939	3 252	1966
1967	10 804	4 199	1 120	1 198	406	1 781	2 099	12 863	1 047	2 008	2 163	740	3 161	3 744	1967
1968	12 757	4 521	1 341	1 606	384	1 903	3 003	15 254	1 074	2 319	2 782	675	3 255	5 150	1968
1969	15 075	5 307	1 640	1 963	384	2 113	3 668	16 764	1 150	2 631	3 152	627	3 359	5 845	1969
1970	17 475	6 039	1 909	2 279	498	2 333	4 417	18 703	1 236	2 921	3 495	772	3 549	6 730	1970
1971	20 919	7 136	2 441	2 633	541	2 662	5 506	20 857	1 342	3 459	3 740	776	3 759	7 782	1971
1972	24 737	8 088	2 880	3 011	866	2 976	6 918	23 293	1 409	3 786	3 969	1 147	3 903	9 078	1972
1973	28 774	9 593	3 573	3 469	788	3 271	8 081	24 784	1 526	4 333	4 214	963	3 960	9 787	1973
1974	34 443	11 312	4 532	4 176	1 128	3 673	9 623	27 146	1 609	5 003	4 613	1 248	4 054	10 620	1974
1975	41 200	13 288	5 729	4 808	1 724	4 058	11 594	29 604	1 692	5 729	4 808	1 724	4 058	11 594	1975
1976	47 666	15 468	7 396	5 382	1 752	4 421	13 187	31 330	1 794	6 797	4 946	1 610	4 063	12 120	1976
1977	53 478	17 173	9 542	5 850	1 470	4 654	14 790	33 212	1 863	8 239	5 051	1 269	4 019	12 772	1977
1978	60 314	18 992	11 671	6 532	1 552	5 210	16 358	36 218	1 955	9 676	5 414	1 285	4 321	13 567	1978
1979	66 450	20 342	13 023	6 980	2 613	5 644	17 849	38 668	2 010	10 352	5 545	2 074	4 490	14 197	1979
1980	72 879	22 091	14 251	7 287	2 346	7 122	19 782	40 030	2 098	10 643	5 440	1 750	5 321	14 778	1980
1981	77 858	23 210	15 180	7 059	3 782	7 185	21 442	40 426	2 110	10 644	4 954	2 655	5 035	15 028	1981
1982	82 949	24 696	16 221	6 950	4 281	7 454	23 347	40 731	2 153	10 744	4 610	2 841	4 932	15 453	1982

Table 6

Expenditure on Income Maintenance

Year	At current prices (in million guilders)									At constant (1975) prices									Year
	Pen-sions	Inval-idity	Sick-ness	Unem-ploym.	Family allow.	Social assist.	Educ. allow.	Hous. allow.	Total	Pen-sions	Inval-idity	Sick-ness	Unem. ploym.	Family allow.	Social assist.	Educ. allow.	Hous. allow.	Total	
1948	403	119	153	8	287	204			1 175	1 493	441	567	30	1 064	756			4 350	1948
1949	425	133	170	12	316	220			1 276	1 466	457	585	41	1 091	759			4 398	1949
1950	469	140	175	12	338	283	5		1 421	1 466	438	545	38	1 056	884	15		4 442	1950
1951	491	154	199	10	401	251	5		1 511	1 364	428	553	28	1 114	697	14		4 198	1951
1952	510	159	203	53	419	294	5		1 643	1 417	442	563	148	1 163	817	13		4 563	1952
1953	538	163	220	121	439	309	6		1 796	1 494	452	612	336	1 220	858	15		4 987	1953
1954	633	183	246	125	493	358	7		2 044	1 711	494	665	338	1 331	968	20		5 525	1954
1955	691	193	280	132	536	389	12		2 233	1 818	509	736	347	1 410	1 024	32		5 876	1955
1956	731	209	323	108	569	448	25		2 413	1 874	535	828	276	1 460	1 149	64		6 186	1956
1957	1 336	216	406	85	625	473	25		3 166	3 260	527	989	207	1 524	1 154	62		7 722	1957
1958	1 480	229	422	199	679	618	32		3 658	3 524	545	1 005	474	1 616	1 471	75		8 709	1958
1959	1 556	236	463	165	699	590	37		3 746	3 706	563	1 102	393	1 663	1 405	88		8 919	1959
1960	1 853	266	513	120	792	594	41		4 179	4 212	604	1 166	272	1 801	1 350	94		9 498	1960
1961	2 037	292	534	96	840	643	47		4 488	4 630	663	1 213	217	1 910	1 461	107		10 200	1961
1962	2 275	312	625	160	851	699	56		4 978	5 054	694	1 389	356	1 892	1 553	124		11 062	1962
1963	2 680	566	779	334	1 134	790	69		6 352	5 702	1 204	1 658	711	2 413	1 681	146		13 515	1963
1964	3 273	683	973	202	1 408	831	86		7 455	6 559	1 368	1 949	404	2 821	1 665	173		14 939	1964
1965	4 276	824	1 162	247	1 571	818	107	5	9 010	8 239	1 588	2 239	475	3 028	1 576	206	10	17 361	1965
1966	4 894	908	1 307	373	1 818	1 023	120	16	10 460	8 914	1 655	2 380	679	3 312	1 863	219	29	19 052	1966
1967	5 440	1 051	1 504	551	2 012	1 245	111	20	11 932	9 577	1 850	2 648	970	3 542	2 192	195	35	21 008	1967
1968	5 904	1 253	1 977	647	2 153	1 010	150	18	13 111	10 023	2 127	3 356	1 099	3 655	1 715	254	31	22 259	1968
1969	6 897	1 537	2 427	656	2 378	1 183	169	34	15 281	10 896	2 429	3 833	1 037	3 757	1 869	266	54	24 141	1969
1970	7 797	1 800	2 847	776	2 624	1 461	206	69	17 580	11 796	2 723	4 307	1 174	3 969	2 210	312	104	26 595	1970
1971	9 230	2 321	3 393	871	2 971	1 766	250	120	20 921	12 981	3 265	4 772	1 225	4 179	2 484	351	169	29 424	1971
1972	10 491	2 745	3 944	1 440	3 305	2 097	320	190	24 532	13 713	3 589	5 156	1 882	4 320	2 741	419	248	32 068	1972
1973	12 405	3 412	4 566	1 611	3 611	2 932	356	260	29 153	14 982	4 120	5 515	1 946	4 361	3 541	430	314	35 209	1973
1974	14 651	4 337	5 515	2 188	4 024	3 782	389	340	35 226	16 153	4 782	6 080	2 413	4 437	4 170	429	375	38 838	1974
1975	17 269	5 488	6 423	3 567	4 444	5 094	493	520	43 297	17 269	5 488	6 423	3 567	4 444	5 094	493	520	43 297	1975
1976	19 978	6 915	7 351	4 344	4 841	5 682	599	880	50 591	18 362	6 356	6 757	3 993	4 450	5 222	551	809	46 499	1976
1977	22 152	9 108	8 805	4 429	5 171	5 829	691	1 070	57 256	19 130	7 866	7 604	3 825	4 465	5 034	597	924	49 444	1977
1978	24 356	11 157	9 537	4 759	5 832	6 023	771	1 270	63 704	20 212	9 259	7 914	3 949	4 840	4 998	640	1 054	52 866	1978
1979	26 127	12 424	10 280	6 057	6 337	6 581	858	1 360	70 024	20 801	9 892	8 185	4 823	5 046	5 240	683	1 083	55 752	1979
1980	28 257	13 395	10 671	6 086	6 950	7 250	1 028	1 420	75 258	21 119	10 161	7 975	4 549	5 194	5 419	768	1 061	56 246	1980
1981	29 745	14 464	10 333	9 120	7 005	8 098	1 802	1 630	82 197	20 830	10 129	7 236	6 387	4 906	5 671	1 262	1 142	57 561	1981
1982	32 060	15 441	10 233	13 081	7 270	8 889	2 227	2 040	91 242	21 190	10 206	6 763	8 646	4 805	5 875	1 472	1 348	60 305	1982

Table 7

Expenditure on Old Age and Survivors' Pensions
(at current prices, in million guilders)

Year	General old age pensions (AOW)		General widows' orphans' pens. (AWW)		Civil servants' pensions General (ABP)		Civil servants' pensions Other		Volontary early retirement pensions (VUT) Non-government		Volontary early retirement pensions (VUT) Government	Total		Year
	benefits	admin.	benefits	admin.	benefits	admin.	benefits	admin.	benefits	admin.	benefits	benefits	admin.	
1948	132				152	2	119	1				403	3	1948
1949	148				156	2	121	1				425	3	1949
1950	160				173	2	136	1				469	3	1950
1951	181				191	2	119	1				491	3	1951
1952	195				205	2	110	1				510	3	1952
1953	216				210	2	112	1				538	3	1953
1954	263				243	3	127	1				633	4	1954
1955	277				276	3	138	1				691	4	1955
1956	294				285	4	152	1				731	5	1956
1957	834.4	21.3			320	5	182	2				1 336.4	28.3	1957
1958	905.2	19.5			348	5	227	2				1 480.2	26.5	1958
1959	960.9	19.6	41.4	1.9	354	5	200	2				1 556.3	28.5	1959
1960	1 095.3	17.0	194.8	5.0	372	6	191	2				1 853.1	30.0	1960
1961	1 169.9	17.7	205.2	4.7	433	6	229	2				2 037.1	30.4	1961
1962	1 393.3	17.5	233.2	12.8	436	7	212	2				2 274.5	39.3	1962
1963	1 669.2	15.5	273.6	10.6	497	8	240	2				2 679.8	36.1	1963
1964	2 015.4	19.0	328.3	12.8	642	10	287	2				3 272.7	43.8	1964
1965	2 887.4	22.7	421.7	14.8	666	11	301	3				4 276.1	51.5	1965
1966	3 271.1	24.9	477.7	16.1	797	15	348	4				4 893.8	60.0	1966
1967	3 620.2	32.9	523.3	22.3	901	19	395	4				5 439.5	78.2	1967
1968	3 905.3	36.9	556.2	22.8	1 021	23	421	6				5 903.5	88.7	1968
1969	4 594.7	40.7	648.5	23.5	1 185	30	469	7				6 897.2	101.2	1969
1970	5 235.7	44.6	733.5	25.0	1 304	34	524	7				7 797.2	110.6	1970
1971	6 193.6	51.3	861.9	29.0	1 591	39	583	8				9 229.5	127.3	1971
1972	7 021.1	58.5	974.6	33.5	1 828	45	667	9				10 490.7	146.0	1972
1973	8 338.9	65.0	1 147.4	41.9	2 163	60	756	10				12 405.3	176.9	1973
1974	9 856.3	73.2	1 335.3	47.0	2 568	73	891	11				14 650.6	204.2	1974
1975	11 596.2	84.0	1 553.3	54.2	3 075	83	1 044	13				17 268.5	234.2	1975
1976	13 516.1	98.3	1 793.1	60.4	3 510	98	1 159	14				19 978.2	270.7	1976
1977	15 015.9	99.0	1 972.6	61.5	3 886	110	1 255	14	22.9	1.0		22 152.4	285.5	1977
1978	16 633.0	101.1	2 139.8	59.7	4 175	115	1 351	14	57.0	1.0		24 355.8	290.8	1978
1979	17 810.8	109.8	2 247.8	63.2	4 490	124	1 426	14	106.0	3.7	46	26 126.6	315.0	1979
1980	19 281.0	117.0	2 393.3	69.0	4 684	143	1 489	14	224.0	7.0	186	28 257.0	350.0	1980
1981	20 202.0	124.0	2 478.0	71.0	4 996	150	1 560	15	325.0	10.0	184	29 745.0	370.0	1981
1982	21 448.0	128.0	2 592.0	73.0	5 808	166	1 684	15	442.0	13.0	86	32 060.0	395.0	1982

Table 8

Expenditure on Invalidity Pensions

(at current prices, in million guilders)

Year	Old Acts		Interim Act		Disablement Act		General Disabl. Act		Ind. Injur. Acts		Total Invalidity			Year
	benef.	admin.	benef.	admin.	benefits	admin.	benefits	admin.	benef.	admin.	benefits	admin.	services	
1948	70.6	8.3							48.5	12.3	119.1	20.6		1948
1949	82.3	8.4							50.3	12.9	132.6	21.3		1949
1950	84.9	9.2							55.4	14.3	140.3	23.5		1950
1951	90.1	10.9							63.8	17.0	153.9	27.9		1951
1952	93.1	10.9							66.0	16.5	159.1	27.4		1952
1953	94.2	11.7							68.6	18.1	162.8	29.8		1953
1954	98.7	12.9							84.0	23.2	182.7	36.1		1954
1955	104.3	14.0							89.1	24.4	193.4	38.4		1955
1956	108.9	15.0							99.6	26.8	208.5	41.8		1956
1957	115.3	16.5							100.8	26.8	216.1	43.3		1957
1958	122.8	17.9							105.9	28.1	228.7	46.0		1958
1959	128.0	17.5							108.4	30.0	236.4	47.5		1959
1960	145.6	19.4							120.3	31.9	265.9	51.3		1960
1961	159.8	18.9							131.7	34.1	291.5	53.0		1961
1962	169.2	21.0							143.0	35.1	312.3	56.1		1962
1963	114.1	18.8	286.7	11.2					165.0	41.6	565.8	71.6		1963
1964	109.8	21.4	393.3	11.6					179.4	73.8	682.5	106.8		1964
1965	117.2	21.6	506.9	15.1					199.9	49.0	824.0	85.7		1965
1966	120.6	19.1	647.1	17.5					140.7	32.5	908.4	69.1		1966
1967	119.2	17.5	423.9	15.0	507.6	37.2					1 050.7	69.7		1967
1968	110.0	17.2	23.4	4.3	1 119.3	67.0					1 252.7	88.5	2.4	1968
1969	116.8	20.5	6.5	3.4	1 414.1	79.0					1 537.4	102.9	5.6	1969
1970	120.0	18.9	2.9	1.1	1 677.1	88.8					1 800.0	108.8	3.2	1970
1971	122.3	18.7	1.5	0.6	2 197.3	101.0					2 321.1	120.3	12.4	1971
1972	124.3	18.7	0.8	0.3	2 620.2	115.4					2 745.3	134.4	21.2	1972
1973	127.1	19.5	0.4	0.1	3 284.1	142.0					3 411.6	161.6	34.9	1973
1974	129.6	21.8			4 207.2	173.4					4 336.8	195.2	51.7	1974
1975	131.9	22.2			5 356.1	219.0					5 488.0	241.2	75.5	1975
1976	128.2	18.5			6 544.5	243.0	242.7	109.4			6 915.4	370.9	95.7	1976
1977	120.5	19.0			7 144.0	192.3	1 843.9	222.7			9 108.4	434.0	203.3	1977
1978	113.0	19.9			7 590.2	194.0	3 454.1	300.3			11 157.3	514.2	332.5	1978
1979	105.4	18.3			7 748.5	224.8	4 570.0	354.4			12 423.9	597.5	420.5	1979
1980	98.0	17.0			7 719.0	239.0	5 778.4	400.0			13 595.4	656.0	439.6	1980
1981	91.0	17.0			7 604.0	258.0	6 769.4	441.0			14 464.0	716.0	478.0	1981
1982	84.0	18.0			7 665.0	271.0	7 692.4	491.0			15 441.4	780.0	522.6	1982

Table 9

Expenditure on

(at current prices, in million guilders)

Year	Sickness Cash Benefits: General Scheme benefits	General Scheme admin.	Miners ben.	Miners adm.	Publ. Serv. benef.	Total benefits	Total admin.	Unemployment Cash Benefits: Insurance benefits	Insurance admin.	Seasonal ben.	Seasonal adm.	Provision benef.	Assist. benef.	Publ.Serv. ben.	Total benefits	Total admin.	Year
1948	102.8	12.6	6.4	0.7	44	153.2	13.3							8	8.0		1948
1949	118.1	15.5	6.5	0.8	45	169.6	16.3							12	12.0		1949
1950	121.3	17.5	6.2	0.9	47	174.5	18.4							12	12.0		1950
1951	133.3	17.6	7.8	1.0	58	199.1	18.6							10	10.0		1951
1952	133.5	16.5	9.3	1.2	60	202.8	17.7	45.3	11.6					8	53.3	11.6	1952
1953	143.7	16.4	11.5	1.3	65	220.2	17.7	81.8	20.1	29.1	1.1			10	120.9	21.2	1953
1954	157.1	24.3	11.8	1.5	77	245.9	25.8	82.7	22.3	34.2	1.3			8	124.9	23.6	1954
1955	178.0	31.5	13.6	1.9	88	279.6	33.4	74.5	24.9	49.3	1.8			8	131.8	26.7	1955
1956	209.3	32.1	14.7	1.8	99	323.0	33.9	68.0	23.9	31.7	1.8			8	107.7	25.7	1956
1957	282.3	37.2	17.2	1.9	106	405.5	39.1	61.3	23.1	10.4	1.2			13	84.7	24.3	1957
1958	293.3	37.0	16.6	2.0	112	421.9	39.0	151.5	27.8	31.4	1.6			16	198.9	29.4	1958
1959	321.5	39.6	17.3	2.1	124	462.8	41.7	109.8	25.3	37.2	1.7			18	165.0	27.0	1959
1960	366.9	44.1	17.0	2.2	129	512.9	46.3	72.0	24.5	30.7	1.8			17	119.7	26.3	1960
1961	389.2	48.8	17.3	2.4	127	533.5	51.2	56.7	22.6	19.9	1.6			19	95.6	24.2	1961
1962	448.2	55.2	23.7	2.5	153	624.9	57.7	69.7	23.8	68.6	2.2			22	160.3	26.0	1962
1963	530.4	62.6	28.8	2.7	220	779.2	65.3	115.2	25.7	192.9	3.3			26	334.1	29.0	1963
1964	651.3	75.2	30.4	3.0	291	972.7	78.2	79.2	28.2	91.6	3.0			31	201.8	31.2	1964
1965	788.5	86.9	31.6	3.2	342	1 162.1	90.1	114.1	30.3	75.6	2.7	19	2	36	246.7	33.0	1965
1966	901.7	98.5	30.0	3.3	375	1 306.7	101.8	163.9	34.2	120.0	3.5	36	5	48	372.9	37.7	1966
1967	1 075.9	104.3	16.0	1.7	412	1 503.9	106.0	335.3	44.7	23.4	3.0	114	14	64	550.7	47.7	1967
1968	1 490.6	115.6			486	1 976.6	115.6	285.3	46.1	49.1	3.0	195	27	91	647.4	49.1	1968
1969	1 826.5	136.1			600	2 426.5	136.1	240.5	49.7	89.9	3.8	183	39	104	656.4	53.5	1969
1970	2 125.1	154.2			722	2 847.1	154.2	279.8	55.1	156.9	5.9	170	42	127	775.7	61.0	1970
1971	2 452.8	179.7			940	3 392.8	179.7	384.1	67.9	84.7	4.6	213	57	132	870.8	72.5	1971
1972	2 804.3	206.3			1 140	3 944.3	206.3	702.3	91.4	67.2	4.9	408	92	170	1 439.5	96.3	1972
1973	3 236.1	232.6			1 330	4 566.1	232.6	651.0	106.6	25.4	4.5	596	139	200	1 611.4	111.1	1973
1974	3 904.8	270.7			1 610	5 514.8	270.7	948.2	129.2	44.1	6.1	755	221	220	2 188.3	135.3	1974
1975	4 492.7	315.1			1 930	6 422.7	315.1	1 551.6	158.9	7.3	6.1	1 257	421	330	3 566.9	165.0	1975
1976	5 041.1	340.5			2 310	7 351.1	340.5	1 401.9	175.1	168.1	7.1	1 814	600	360	4 344.0	182.2	1976
1977	5 485.1	364.7			3 320	8 805.1	364.7	1 231.4	184.3	45.7	8.2	1 891	751	510	4 429.1	192.5	1977
1978	6 126.8	405.1			3 410	9 536.8	405.1	1 205.8	198.0	139.8	8.8	1 906	937	570	4 758.6	206.8	1978
1979	6 529.9	449.9			3 750	10 279.9	449.9	1 499.8	224.5	877.5	10.7	1 961	1 079	640	6 057.3	235.2	1979
1980	6 791.0	496.0			3 880	10 671.0	496.0	1 898.0	265.0	172.0	11.0	2 116	1 240	660	6 086.0	276.0	1980
1981	6 521.0	538.0			3 812	10 333.0	538.0	3 093.0	327.0	350.0	12.0	3 329	1 668	680	9 120.0	339.0	1981
1982	6 392.0	558.0			3 841	10 233.0	558.0	3 492.0	370.0	407.0	12.0	5 806	2 616	760	13 081.0	382.0	1982

Table 10

Expenditure on Family Allowances

(at current prices, in million guilders)

Year	General		Pensioners		Wage earners		General		Self-empl. benef.		Public	Total		Year
	benef.	admin.	benef.	admin.	benef.	admin.	benef.	admin.	(A)	(B)	benef.	benef.	admin.	
1948	186.5	5.8	2.8	0.3							98	287.3	6.1	1948
1949	206.0	5.3	11.3	0.3							99	316.3	5.6	1949
1950	227.7	5.7	13.1	0.3							97	337.8	6.0	1950
1951	266.5	8.4	15.6	0.3					2		117	401.1	8.7	1951
1952	275.1	9.1	16.6	0.2					4		123	418.7	9.3	1952
1953	286.0	8.4	16.1	0.1					5		132	439.1	8.5	1953
1954	322.5	7.4	17.1	0.2					6		147	492.6	7.6	1954
1955	346.7	8.3	19.1	0.2					6		164	535.8	8.5	1955
1956	363.4	8.5	19.9	0.2					5		181	569.3	8.7	1956
1957	406.2	9.1	20.7	0.3						4	194	624.9	9.4	1957
1958	449.7	8.8	25.9	0.3						5	198	678.6	9.1	1958
1959	466.5	9.0	28.0	0.3						4	200	698.5	9.3	1959
1960	531.8	10.3	35.5	0.4						4	221	792.3	10.7	1960
1961	565.0	10.6	37.2	0.3						4	234	840.2	10.9	1961
1962	598.7	11.1	38.6	0.3						4	210	851.3	11.4	1962
1963					519.9	10.0	427.3	8.3		5	182	1 134.2	18.3	1963
1964					627.7	13.7	563.0	12.5		10	207	1 407.7	26.2	1964
1965					697.4	15.5	633.9	15.7		10	230	1 571.3	31.2	1965
1966					799.0	18.6	762.4	19.4		10	247	1 818.4	38.0	1966
1967					878.7	22.7	853.0	26.5		12	268	2 011.7	49.2	1967
1968					954.5	24.6	895.5	27.9		15	288	2 153.0	52.5	1968
1969					1 079.6	27.2	976.6	29.3		15	307	2 378.2	56.5	1969
1970					1 215.8	29.9	1 056.7	31.0		17	344	2 623.5	60.9	1970
1971					1 408.2	35.6	1 182.7	35.8		20	360	2 970.9	71.4	1971
1972					1 590.3	38.9	1 304.6	42.1		20	390	3 304.9	81.0	1972
1973					1 738.2	41.6	1 442.5	48.4		20	410	3 610.7	90.0	1973
1974					1 910.4	49.6	1 658.5	54.7		25	430	4 023.9	104.3	1974
1975					2 079.7	59.1	1 856.3	62.7		28	480	4 444.0	121.8	1975
1976					2 238.0	66.8	2 049.3	67.0		34	520	4 841.3	133.8	1976
1977					2 358.0	71.5	2 155.9	68.5		37	620	5 170.9	140.0	1977
1978					2 779.7	77.9	2 284.3	67.7		38	730	5 832.0	145.6	1978
1979					3 181.7	83.0	2 309.6	70.1		16	830	6 337.3	153.1	1979
1980							6 950.0	172.0				6 950.0	172.0	1980
1981							7 005.0	180.0				7 005.0	180.0	1981
1982							7 270.0	184.0				7 270.0	184.0	1982

Table 11 Social Assistance and other Social Provisions

(in million guilders)

Year	General social assist.	Victims of persecution	Special pensions	General (war) disabl.	War prisoners	Colonial pensions	Pension replacement b.	National serv. allow.	Lump-sum benef.	Sheltered employment	Local govt empl. provision	Aid to artists	Total cash benef.	Labour market regul.	Home help	Year
1948	134		9					44		17			204	15		1948
1949	140		12					43		25			220	14		1949
1950	160		10			8		55		28	22		283	23		1950
1951	146		13			14		10		43	25		251	21		1951
1952	144		12			20		7		81	30		294	19		1952
1953	202		14			21		9		38	25		309	19	2	1953
1954	243		15	5		29		12		28	26		358	22	3	1954
1955	265		19	7		36		13		32	17		389	82	5	1955
1956	289		26	7		60		18		37	10	1	448	82	6	1956
1957	297		21	8		65		18		54	9	1	473	89	6	1957
1958	330		25	7		144		25		62	24	1	618	114	6	1958
1959	322		28	6		106	4	25		73	25	1	590	121	9	1959
1960	322		33	8		100	5	28		83	14	1	594	90	10	1960
1961	363		33	8		107	6	28		89	8	1	643	68	13	1961
1962	420		33	7		99	8	32		90	9	1	699	63	11	1962
1963	477		37	9		124	6	27		98	11	1	790	55	12	1963
1964	451		38	11		136	5	25		153	10	2	831	73	16	1964
1965	413		44	10		140	6	26		177		2	818	82	20	1965
1966	576		48	10		142	6	39		199		3	1 023	88	25	1966
1967	729		57	12		149	9	44		242		3	1 245	117	31	1967
1968	416		65	13		147	12	46		306		5	1 010	140	41	1968
1969	519		71	13		151	14	50		359		6	1 183	151	57	1969
1970	729		75	15		152	18	41		421		10	1 461	130	77	1970
1971	933		90	16		170		40		507		10	1 766	154	245	1971
1972	1 128		110	17		170		40		620		12	2 097	191	312	1972
1973	1 801		140	17		180		40		739		15	2 932	382	391	1973
1974	2 359	50	200	18		180		40		914		21	3 782	539	532	1974
1975	3 173	189	233	19		189		56		1 204		31	5 094	774	679	1975
1976	3 504	197	254	19		193		47		1 430		38	5 682	1 139	875	1976
1977	3 558	234	306	19		194		45		1 414		59	5 829	890	1 001	1977
1978	3 685	285	359	19		193		35		1 380		67	6 023	1 012	1 022	1978
1979	4 078	294	360	19		188		30		1 525		87	6 581	928	1 023	1979
1980	4 518	316	384	19		197		21		1 677		118	7 250	886	1 129	1980
1981	5 179	315	384	17	28	171		5	55	1 830		114	8 098	553	1 291	1981
1982	5 675	342	377	17	192	169		5	131	1 848		133	8 889	602	1 306	1982

Table 12

Expenditure on Public Health and Health Insurance

(at current prices, in million guilders)

Year	Public health				Compulsory ins.		Voluntary ins.		Old people's ins.		Other schemes		Except.med.exp.		Total insurance		Year
	central	prov.	local	total	benef.	adm.	benef.	adm.	benef.	adm.	benef.	adm.	benef.	adm.	benefits	admin.	
1948				98	105.5	13.7	53.5	5.0			10.0	0.7			169.0	19.4	1948
1949				109	121.2	14.8	64.6	5.2			12.2	0.8			198.0	20.8	1949
1950				121	146.2	16.6	73.8	5.5			13.5	0.9			233.5	23.0	1950
1951				134	190.6	19.6	64.9	4.7			16.2	1.2			271.7	25.5	1951
1952				150	201.0	20.1	67.6	4.6			18.7	1.2			287.3	25.9	1952
1953	74	12	81	167	226.2	20.7	75.2	4.5			21.4	1.6			322.8	26.8	1953
1954				186	255.2	23.1	82.2	5.0			24.0	1.6			361.4	29.7	1954
1955				204	310.7	25.7	97.8	5.2			23.2	1.6			431.7	32.5	1955
1956				222	334.6	28.8	103.8	6.3			25.6	1.7			464.0	36.8	1956
1957				240	320.8	27.0	107.0	6.3	58.4	2.6	40.3	1.8			526.5	37.7	1957
1958	132	19	107	258	356.9	28.2	116.0	6.4	68.3	2.9	44.1	1.8			585.3	39.3	1958
1959				290	382.2	28.3	121.5	6.5	74.8	3.0	51.2	2.3			629.7	40.1	1959
1960				322	419.4	30.2	132.7	6.9	82.2	3.2	60.6	2.5			694.9	42.8	1960
1961				354	459.1	31.7	141.6	7.0	93.2	3.3	66.6	2.7			760.5	44.7	1961
1962				386	511.8	35.3	157.9	7.7	112.2	3.7	75.3	3.3			857.2	50.0	1962
1963	206	15	198	419	604.4	40.5	180.3	8.6	129.9	4.1	64.3	2.3			978.9	55.5	1963
1964				507	743.3	48.0	217.9	10.0	162.3	4.9	72.1	2.7			1 195.6	65.6	1964
1965				595	850.7	55.5	248.7	11.4	192.7	5.6	85.2	3.1			1 377.3	75.6	1965
1966				683	1 021.0	63.6	293.1	13.0	237.6	6.4	114.3	3.9			1 666.0	86.9	1966
1967				771	1 228.8	68.9	349.8	14.0	284.6	7.1	141.5	4.5			2 004.7	94.5	1967
1968	697	14	146	857	1 424.8	75.4	395.8	15.0	332.8	7.8	159.4	4.7	581.2	5.7	2 894.0	108.6	1968
1969				1 112	1 643.6	86.5	451.7	16.6	389.2	9.1	186.0	5.3	864.1	15.6	3 534.6	133.1	1969
1970	1 159	17	192	1 368	1 957.7	99.4	471.2	17.1	509.7	11.7	232.7	6.6	1 087.3	23.1	4 258.6	157.9	1970
1971				1 509	2 390.0	113.4	544.6	18.6	636.1	13.7	269.5	6.8	1 485.1	28.3	5 325.3	180.8	1971
1972	1 429	15	221	1 665	2 848.8	133.2	640.8	21.5	798.4	16.7	340.0	9.5	2 073.8	34.9	6 701.8	215.8	1972
1973				1 502	3 272.9	155.4	730.7	25.0	940.5	20.1	395.8	11.2	2 485.7	43.6	7 825.6	255.3	1973
1974				1 355	3 836.2	186.7	857.3	30.0	1 125.6	24.7	465.4	13.0	3 035.0	48.9	9 319.5	303.3	1974
1975	912	13	308	1 233	4 478.0	214.8	1 023.4	34.8	1 428.9	28.9	559.5	15.8	3 750.8	59.0	11 240.6	353.3	1975
1976	1 002	17	334	1 353	5 011.3	237.0	1 160.2	38.9	1 692.7	32.9	647.8	20.3	4 280.6	65.6	12 792.6	394.7	1976
1977	1 081	20	364	1 465	5 547.7	267.7	1 293.7	44.1	1 937.9	37.7	718.8	21.4	4 857.2	64.0	14 355.3	434.9	1977
1978	1 245	22	405	1 672	6 015.1	296.1	1 440.8	49.1	2 245.1	42.2	804.9	22.7	5 378.2	64.1	15 884.1	474.2	1978
1979	1 333	23	449	1 805	6 496.8	327.9	1 568.0	54.4	2 509.2	47.1	892.8	25.0	5 859.0	68.8	17 325.8	523.2	1979
1980	1 197	14	351	1 562	6 976.0	374.0	1 742.0	63.0	2 713.0	54.0	964.0	27.0	6 787.0	82.0	19 182.0	600.0	1980
1981	1 214	17	345	1 576	7 472.0	423.0	1 919.0	72.0	3 031.0	61.0	1 035.0	28.0	7 317.0	84.0	20 774.0	668.0	1981
1982	1 191	18	350	1 559	8 022.0	472.0	2 115.0	80.0	3 332.0	68.0	1 121.0	32.0	8 001.0	104.0	22 591.0	756.0	1982

Table 13

Expenditure on Education and Housing

(at current prices, in million guilders)

Year	Transfers to students	Total expend. on education	Central govt percent distribution	Local govt percent distribution	Total expend. on housing	Rent subsidies	Capital subsidies	Temporary subsidies	Rent allow.	Year
1948		437	72	28	11	11				1948
1949		486	69	31	20	20				1949
1950	4.8	557	66	34	38	37	1			1950
1951	5.2	620	66	34	58	44	14			1951
1952	4.8	684	66	34	112	58	54			1952
1953	5.5	801	64	36	130	66	64			1953
1954	7.2	934	64	36	188	99	89			1954
1955	12.2	1 126	64	36	223	120	103			1955
1956	25.0	1 300	67	33	246	125	121			1956
1957	25.4	1 511	68	32	272	117	155			1957
1958	31.5	1 596	69	31	317	120	197			1958
1959	36.9	1 772	71	29	364	121	243			1959
1960	41.4	1 995	76	24	393	147	246			1960
1961	46.9	2 315	90	10	297	142	155			1961
1962	55.6	2 637	91	9	227	143	84			1962
1963	68.7	2 985	91	9	196	145	51			1963
1964	86.4	3 764	91	9	200	146	54			1964
1965	106.9	4 320	91	9	210	151	54	5		1965
1966	120.4	4 940	91	9	219	160	43	16		1966
1967	110.8	5 653	91	9	221	158	43	19	1	1967
1968	149.5	6 358	92	8	201	151	32	16	2	1968
1969	168.5	7 378	92	8	233	181	18	14	20	1969
1970	206.0	8 541	94	6	339	256	14	6	63	1970
1971	249.5	9 936	94	6	470	340	10	10	110	1971
1972	320.2	11 199	94	6	650	440	20	20	170	1972
1973	355.7	12 802	92	8	860	580	20	10	250	1973
1974	389.1	14 909	93	7	1 140	780	20	40	300	1974
1975	493.2	17 694	93	7	1 670	960	190	60	460	1975
1976	599.1	19 916	94	6	2 220	1 230	110	40	840	1976
1977	691.1	21 526	96	4	2 660	1 500	90	70	1 000	1977
1978	770.6	23 272	94	6	3 050	1 620	160	70	1 200	1978
1979	858.2	24 683	93	7	3 170	1 610	200	60	1 300	1979
1980	1 028.1	25 802	90	10	3 440	1 720	300	40	1 380	1980
1981	1 802.1	26 628	90	10	3 600	1 670	300	50	1 580	1981
1982	2 227.2	27 499	89	11	3 930	1 750	140	60	1 980	1982

Table 14 Public Revenues and Deficits

Year	Public revenues (in million guilders)					Percent distribution				Govt deficit		As percentage of GDP					Year
	Total revenues	Direct taxes	Indirect taxes	Other revenues	Soc.sec. contrib.	Direct taxes	Indir. taxes	Other rev.	Soc. sec.	Statist. (million guilders)	Total (million guilders)	Total rev.	Total taxes	Soc. sec.	Stat. deficit	Total deficit	
1948		2 258	1 891		666						26 637		28.1	4.5		180.2	1948
1949		2 496	2 052		725						28 623		27.4	4.4		172.6	1949
1950		2 569	2 349		804						27 809		26.5	4.3		150.0	1950
1951		2 938	2 770		903					-596	27 384		27.0	4.3	-2.8	129.3	1951
1952		3 654	2 621		1 009					-392	25 771		28.4	4.6	-1.8	116.6	1952
1953	8 186	3 321	2 769	965	1 131	40.6	33.8	8.0	13.8	112	26 054	34.8	25.9	4.8	0.5	110.8	1953
1954	8 605	3 223	3 121	1 007	1 254	37.5	36.3	11.9	14.6	655	25 445	32.7	24.1	4.8	2.5	96.8	1954
1955	8 999	3 385	3 258	971	1 385	37.6	36.2	8.0	15.4	1 291	25 707	30.6	22.6	4.7	4.4	87.5	1955
1956	10 243	4 325	3 440	941	1 537	42.2	33.6	6.8	15.0	1 177	26 089	32.1	24.4	4.8	3.7	81.8	1956
1957	12 070	4 686	3 534	1 070	2 780	38.8	29.3	4.1	23.0	1 249	27 483	34.8	23.7	8.0	3.6	79.2	1957
1958	11 910	4 406	3 442	1 178	2 884	37.0	28.9	3.7	24.2	1 743	28 646	34.0	22.4	8.2	5.0	81.8	1958
1959	12 778	4 713	3 727	1 298	3 040	36.9	29.2	3.5	23.8	677	29 904	34.2	22.6	8.1	1.8	80.0	1959
1960	14 436	5 389	4 143	1 466	3 438	37.3	28.7	4.3	23.8	388	30 402	34.5	22.8	8.2	0.9	72.7	1960
1961	15 754	6 039	4 461	1 527	3 727	38.3	28.3	3.3	23.7	867	31 706	35.7	23.8	8.4	2.0	71.8	1961
1962	16 736	6 362	4 730	1 632	4 012	38.0	28.3	2.1	24.0	1 574	33 038	35.2	23.3	8.4	3.3	69.5	1962
1963	19 484	6 606	5 718	1 985	5 175	33.9	29.3	3.4	26.6	1 722	34 670	37.8	23.9	10.0	3.3	67.2	1963
1964	22 942	7 936	6 690	2 066	6 250	34.6	29.2	2.4	27.2	2 937	37 760	37.8	24.1	10.3	4.8	62.2	1964
1965	26 697	9 074	7 505	2 384	7 734	34.0	28.1	3.9	29.0	3 077	41 171	39.4	24.5	11.4	4.5	60.7	1965
1966	30 176	10 273	8 304	2 575	9 024	34.0	27.5	2.0	29.9	3 377	44 664	40.9	25.2	12.2	4.6	60.5	1966
1967	34 169	11 667	9 228	2 916	10 358	34.1	27.0	3.6	30.3	3 829	48 512	42.2	25.8	12.8	4.7	59.9	1967
1968	38 654	12 416	10 640	3 304	12 294	32.1	27.5	2.3	31.8	4 104	53 201	43.0	25.7	13.7	4.6	59.2	1968
1969	44 412	14 743	11 119	4 075	14 475	33.2	25.0	2.9	32.6	4 107	57 199	43.7	25.4	14.2	4.0	56.2	1969
1970	51 173	16 089	13 468	4 852	16 764	31.4	26.3	1.9	32.8	3 948	61 369	44.7	25.8	14.6	3.4	53.6	1970
1971	60 831	19 348	15 468	6 080	19 935	31.8	25.4	3.2	32.8	4 524	66 477	46.9	26.9	15.4	3.5	51.3	1971
1972	70 260	22 612	17 886	6 970	22 792	32.2	25.5	3.0	32.4	2 391	69 286	47.9	27.6	15.5	1.6	47.2	1972
1973	83 254	26 253	20 069	8 600	28 332	31.5	24.1	4.6	34.0	2 218	70 550	49.5	27.6	16.9	1.3	42.0	1973
1974	95 026	30 334	21 415	9 310	33 967	31.9	22.5	2.5	35.7	4 944	75 702	49.9	27.2	17.9	2.6	39.8	1974
1975	109 392	34 752	24 026	12 080	38 534	31.8	22.0	2.3	35.2	10 020	85 014	52.2	28.1	18.4	4.8	40.6	1975
1976	127 917	38 675	29 465	16 700	43 077	30.2	23.0	3.1	33.7	10 744	95 655	53.3	28.4	17.9	4.5	39.8	1976
1977	141 453	41 931	34 132	18 530	46 860	29.6	24.1	2.2	33.1	9 243	103 193	54.1	29.1	17.9	3.5	39.5	1977
1978	158 337	48 542	38 919	19 463	51 413	30.7	24.6	2.7	32.5	10 852	115 991	56.1	31.0	18.2	3.8	41.4	1978
1979	165 486	48 496	38 176	22 502	56 312	29.3	23.1	2.9	34.0	14 531	132 218	55.1	28.9	18.7	4.8	44.0	1979
1980	181 262	53 508	40 887	25 650	61 217	29.5	22.6	2.2	33.8	21 484	150 959	56.6	29.5	19.1	6.7	47.1	1980
1981	190 421	53 052	41 456	29 741	66 172	27.9	21.8	2.1	34.8	25 373	173 476	56.7	28.1	19.7	7.6	51.6	1981
1982	200 563	53 888	42 402	31 777	72 496	26.9	21.1	2.1	36.1	30 727	199 594	57.4	27.6	20.8	8.8	57.1	1982

Table 15

Taxes and Social Security Receipts

Year	Total taxes (in million guilders	Percent distribution by level of government: central	prov.	local	other	Social security receipts (in million guilders): Total receipts	Employers' contrib.	Households' contrib.	Govt transfers	Inter-ests	Percent distribution: Empl.	House-holds	Govt	Inter-ests	Year
1948	6 198	88.6	0.7	10.2	0.5	727	507	159	26	35	69.7	21.9	3.6	4.8	1948
1949	5 112	83.2	1.0	15.2	0.6	808	550	175	48	35	68.1	21.7	5.9	4.3	1949
1950	5 014	82.7	1.0	15.5	0.7	903	605	199	60	39	67.0	22.0	6.6	4.3	1950
1951	5 789	82.8	1.0	15.6	0.6	1 020	676	227	74	43	66.3	22.3	7.3	4.2	1951
1952	6 361	84.5	1.1	13.8	0.6	1 162	716	293	103	50	61.6	25.2	8.9	4.3	1952
1953	6 179	83.8	1.0	14.8	0.7	1 316	775	356	137	48	58.9	27.1	10.4	3.6	1953
1954	6 418	81.8	1.1	16.4	0.7	1 459	865	389	150	55	59.3	26.7	10.3	3.8	1954
1955	6 667	80.9	1.1	17.3	0.7	1 610	960	425	166	59	59.6	26.4	10.3	3.7	1955
1956	7 790	82.2	1.0	16.1	0.6	1 789	1 068	468	186	67	59.7	26.2	10.4	3.7	1956
1957	8 218	82.1	1.0	16.2	0.7	3 037	1 197	1 583	175	82	39.4	52.1	5.8	2.7	1957
1958	7 851	82.0	1.1	16.2	0.8	3 148	1 228	1 656	168	96	39.0	52.6	5.3	3.0	1958
1959	8 441	82.0	1.1	16.2	0.7	3 318	1 279	1 761	169	109	38.5	53.1	5.1	3.3	1959
1960	9 535	83.0	1.0	15.3	0.7	3 757	1 478	1 960	199	120	39.3	52.2	5.3	3.2	1960
1961	10 500	85.4	1.0	12.9	0.6	4 071	1 608	2 119	213	131	39.5	52.1	5.2	3.2	1961
1962	11 092	84.0	1.0	14.3	0.7	4 383	1 674	2 338	229	142	38.2	53.3	5.2	3.2	1962
1963	12 324	84.7	1.0	13.7	0.7	5 574	2 212	2 963	259	140	39.7	53.2	4.6	2.5	1963
1964	14 628	84.7	1.0	13.7	0.6	6 689	2 716	3 534	286	153	40.6	52.8	4.3	2.3	1964
1965	16 579	84.6	1.0	13.8	0.6	8 372	3 021	4 713	476	162	36.1	56.3	5.7	1.9	1965
1966	18 577	84.3	1.0	14.1	0.6	9 678	3 806	5 218	490	164	39.3	53.9	5.1	1.7	1966
1967	20 895	83.9	1.0	14.4	0.6	11 052	4 336	6 022	533	161	39.2	54.5	4.8	1.5	1967
1968	23 056	84.0	1.0	14.4	0.6	13 440	5 338	6 956	969	177	39.7	51.8	7.2	1.3	1968
1969	25 862	84.2	1.0	14.2	0.7	15 847	6 466	8 009	1 141	231	40.8	50.5	7.2	1.5	1969
1970	29 557	83.1	0.9	15.3	0.6	18 203	7 530	9 234	1 145	294	41.4	50.7	6.3	1.6	1970
1971	34 816	83.7	0.9	14.8	0.6	21 622	8 939	10 996	1 358	329	41.3	50.9	6.3	1.5	1971
1972	40 498	83.2	0.8	15.4	0.6	24 595	9 924	12 868	1 490	313	40.3	52.3	6.1	1.3	1972
1973	46 322	85.1	0.8	13.4	0.7	30 515	12 720	15 612	1 805	378	41.7	51.2	5.9	1.2	1973
1974	51 749	85.8	0.7	11.8	0.7	36 556	15 245	18 722	1 992	597	41.7	51.2	5.4	1.6	1974
1975	58 778	85.6	0.9	12.7	0.8	42 995	16 947	21 587	3 834	627	39.4	50.2	8.9	1.5	1975
1976	68 140	83.8	1.0	14.3	0.9	49 660	18 905	24 172	5 855	728	38.1	48.7	11.8	1.5	1976
1977	76 063	83.2	0.9	14.9	0.9	53 352	20 620	26 240	5 754	738	38.6	49.2	10.8	1.4	1977
1978	87 461	78.3	0.9	14.2	0.9	61 071	22 357	29 056	8 864	794	36.6	47.6	14.5	1.3	1978
1979	86 672	84.0	0.9	14.1	1.0	67 323	24 688	31 624	10 060	951	36.7	47.0	14.9	1.4	1979
1980	94 395	84.3	0.9	13.7	1.0	73 873	27 470	33 747	11 678	978	37.2	45.7	15.8	1.3	1980
1981	94 508	83.2	1.1	14.5	1.2	77 172	28 455	37 717	10 057	943	36.9	48.9	13.0	1.2	1981
1982	96 290	80.5	1.4	16.8	1.3	81 265	29 419	43 077	8 003	766	36.2	53.0	9.8	0.9	1982

Table 16

Welfare State Clienteles I

(in 1,000s)

Year	Total major clienteles	Pensioners old age	Pensioners survivors	Pensioners invalidity	Pensioners disabl.	disabl.	Sickness benef.	(Un-)Employment total benef.	(Un-)Employment sheltered progr.	Aid to artists	Social assist. benef.	Year
1948	469	297		114			58					1948
1949	481	300		116			65					1949
1950	491	309		121			61					1950
1951	504	318		124			62					1951
1952	564	332		128			60	44				1952
1953	563	343		129			50	41				1953
1954	600	360		132			61	37	10			1954
1955	617	369		136			68	32	12			1955
1956	619	369		138			73	27	12			1956
1957	1 000	739		141			84	21	15			1957
1958	1 061	765		146			80	51	19			1958
1959	1 191	788	106	152			88	35	22			1959
1960	1 229	814	116	161			93	22	23			1960
1961	1 244	830	115	167			93	16	23			1961
1962	1 299	850	130	174			103	19	23			1962
1963	1 350	873	134	183			109	28	23			1963
1964	1 395	901	137	203			113	18	23			1964
1965	1 681	926	142	221			122	27	24		219	1965
1966	1 757	952	145	240			127	36	26		231	1966
1967	1 854	979	147	92	137		136	79	30	1	253	1967
1968	1 936	1 005	150	89	163		165	79	35	1	249	1968
1969	2 037	1 035	153	84	194		185	65	44	1	276	1969
1970	2 109	1 061	155	79	215		204	59	44	1	291	1970
1971	2 185	1 088	159	75	237		204	70	44	1	307	1971
1972	2 306	1 116	163	71	261		212	113	46	1	323	1972
1973	2 373	1 141	167	66	287		223	112	49	1	327	1973
1974	2 488	1 171	166	61	313		239	139	52	1	346	1974
1975	2 661	1 197	168	57	349		244	212	56	2	376	1975
1976	2 764	1 221	171	52	374	90	250	222	61	2	321	1976
1977	2 825	1 252	172	47	404	116	253	218	66	2	295	1977
1978	2 904	1 280	173	43	435	134	264	219	69	2	285	1978
1979	2 979	1 309	173	39	461	147	268	226	72	3	281	1979
1980	3 072	1 333	174	35	486	159	268	256	74	3	284	1980
1981	3 230	1 356	175	31	499	171	253	374	76	3	292	1981
1982	3 430	1 376	176	28	513	179	240	535	78	3	302	1982

Table 17

Welfare State Clienteles II

(in 1,000s)

Year	Unemployment benef. insur-ance	Unemployment benef. provi-sions	Unemployment benef. govt assist.	Child allow. (families)	Special health services	Home help benef.	War victims pens.	Colonial service pens.	National service allow.	Social assist. (lump-sum)	Rent subs. benef.	Temporal subs. benef.	Student allow. benef.	Year
1948				672										1948
1949				706										1949
1950				728									3	1950
1951				752									3	1951
1952	44			766									2	1952
1953	41			782									3	1953
1954	37			805									4	1954
1955	32			825									5	1955
1956	27			838									6	1956
1957	21			862									7	1957
1958	51			875									9	1958
1959	35			899									11	1959
1960	22			928				18	10				12	1960
1961	16			964				18	9				13	1961
1962	19			1 002				17	11				15	1962
1963	28			1 333				18	10				17	1963
1964	18			1 410				17	9				22	1964
1965	21	4	2	1 442			8	18	7				24	1965
1966	27	7	2	1 486			8	18	8				23	1966
1967	53	20	6	1 508			8	20	9				25	1967
1968	41	31	7	1 537	49		8	19	9				25	1968
1969	31	26	8	1 585	63	133	8	19	8				53	1969
1970	31	20	8	1 614	67	147	8	18	8		31		55	1970
1971	37	22	11	1 650	74	163	8	17	7		58		61	1971
1972	60	37	16	1 685	85	166	8	17	7		76		76	1972
1973	48	45	19	1 701	87	177	8	16	6		98		76	1973
1974	61	48	30	1 743	89	189	9	16	6		129		87	1974
1975	89	70	53	1 753	91	206	36	15	5		348		91	1975
1976	73	89	60	1 770	101	208	37	14	4		357	28	97	1976
1977	60	88	70	1 766	103	206	38	14	1		384	27	104	1977
1978	55	83	81	1 763	105	209	38	13	1		395	23	105	1978
1979	64	80	82	1 751	107	204	39	13	1		418	27	105	1979
1980	68	87	101	2 174	108	221	40	12			456	12	107	1980
1981	110	139	125	2 189	109	264	40	12		313	530	13	119	1981
1982	123	219	193	2 180	110	254	40	12		468	629	12	130	1982

Table 18

Indicators of Health Care

Year	Physicians	Family doctors	Dentists	Pharmacists	Midwives	Hospitals: no.	beds (1,000)	patients (1,000)	days (1,000)	average stay	Year
1948	8 000		1 400	795		263	40.4	579	12 945	22.4	1948
1949						261	40.8	605	13 328	22.0	1949
1950		3 482				261	41.9	551	12 139	22.0	1950
1951			1 591	750		253	45.1	660	14 105	21.4	1951
1952	9 000		1 668	750	1 000	256	46.8	690	14 117	20.5	1952
1953			1 860			264	48.2	741	14 946	20.2	1953
1954	10 993		1 879	834	1 241	266	49.8	758	15 212	20.1	1954
1955	10 500		2 000	798		268	51.0	784	15 759	20.1	1955
1956	10 763	4 527	2 302	843	910	268	51.9	784	16 274	20.8	1956
1957	11 675	4 215	2 403	847	880	269	53.4	821	16 683	20.3	1957
1958	12 526	4 320	2 489	862	891	270	54.7	859	17 495	20.4	1958
1959	12 629	4 343	2 573	851	899	276	56.2	912	18 203	20.0	1959
1960	12 809	4 405	2 492	856	788	276	58.0	916	18 448	20.1	1960
1961	13 027	4 649	2 592	856	784	274	58.9	939	18 786	20.0	1961
1962	13 238	4 581	2 605	856	790	267	59.5	962	19 166	19.9	1962
1963	13 642	4 587	2 722	845	787	265	60.4	990	19 618	19.8	1963
1964	13 904	4 416	2 837	947	752	260	61.5	1 031	20 043	19.4	1964
1965	14 362	4 452	2 955	974	778	268	65.3	1 054	21 459	20.4	1965
1966	14 550	4 477	3 034	999	785	272	68.2	1 088	22 440	20.6	1966
1967	14 774	4 506	3 133	1 008	775	273	69.8	1 135	22 851	20.1	1967
1968	15 128	4 472	3 243	1 008	781	262	70.1	1 181	23 320	19.7	1968
1969	15 644	4 492	3 205	1 019	775	265	72.0	1 236	23 825	19.3	1969
1970	16 292	4 470	3 364	1 057	836	256	72.4	1 264	23 714	18.8	1970
1971	17 381	4 504	3 468	1 084	883	258	73.8	1 317	23 979	18.2	1971
1972	18 142	4 559	3 654	1 114	829	261	75.5	1 362	24 115	17.7	1972
1973	19 328	4 702	3 889	1 138	879	255	75.5	1 393	23 762	17.1	1973
1974	20 200	4 809	4 110	1 166	862	254	75.1	1 422	23 549	16.6	1974
1975	21 892	4 937	4 462	1 197	850	256	74.5	1 443	23 182	16.1	1975
1976	22 913	4 926	4 608	1 257	830	244	74.2	1 488	22 969	15.4	1976
1977	23 769	5 188	4 817	1 309	788	242	74.3	1 503	22 875	15.2	1977
1978	24 878	5 339	5 052	1 382	874	239	74.0	1 542	22 853	14.8	1978
1979	25 947	5 468	5 346	1 463	898	233	73.7	1 561	22 548	14.4	1979
1980	26 987	5 556	5 688	1 529	914	231	73.1	1 588	22 295	14.0	1980
1981	28 037	5 492	5 970	1 601	947	231	72.7	1 605	21 919	13.7	1981
1982	28 807	5 634	6 271	1 672	974	227	69.8	1 622	21 624	13.3	1982

Table 19

Pupils and Students

(in 1,000s and as percentage of respective age groups)

Year	Kindergarten		Primary education		Special primary		Secondary education		Higher education		Vocational education		Year
	in 1,000	as % of age 4–6	in 1,000	as % of age 6–13	in 1,000	as % of age 6–13	in 1,000	as % of age 12–18	in 1,000	as % of age 18–25	old def. in 1,000s	new def. in 1,000s	
1948	289.7	50.0	1 154.2	86.2	23.9	1.2	216.4	19.1	27.0	2.1	282.6		1948
1949	315.7	53.2	1 167.2	84.9	26.6	1.3	214.1	19.0	28.6	2.2	304.3		1949
1950	341.5	51.2	1 215.8	85.6	32.9	1.5	216.4	19.1	29.7	2.3	333.1		1950
1951	364.6	50.8	1 239.7	85.5	35.3	1.5	221.4	19.5	29.9	2.3	343.4		1951
1952	369.9	48.7	1 288.6	83.5	37.4	1.6	231.6	20.2	28.7	2.2	347.3		1952
1953	368.2	51.3	1 356.7	83.6	39.1	1.6	245.2	21.3	28.0	2.2	356.4		1953
1954	371.4	54.3	1 413.4	84.0	41.2	1.7	262.6	22.4	28.8	2.3	378.3		1954
1955	370.2	55.6	1 452.2	83.6	43.5	1.7	285.3	23.7	29.6	2.3	409.1		1955
1956	349.1	52.8	1 469.6	82.6	45.7	1.8	312.0	25.1	30.9	2.4	433.5		1956
1957	361.9	54.8	1 479.1	82.1	47.0	1.8	339.3	26.8	32.6	2.6	460.9		1957
1958	372.8	55.8	1 475.5	80.5	49.6	1.9	376.7	27.7	35.1	2.7	502.9		1958
1959	384.2	57.7	1 448.1	77.7	52.5	1.9	416.4	28.9	37.7	2.9	534.0	614.3	1959
1960	397.8	59.3	1 415.7	77.8	54.6	2.0	445.5	29.6	40.7	3.1		645.1	1960
1961	411.7	60.8	1 397.8	78.1	56.1	2.0	462.6	29.7	43.9	3.3		662.1	1961
1962	422.4	61.5	1 395.0	78.3	57.7	2.1	472.0	29.7	47.9	3.4		677.4	1962
1963	435.5	62.4	1 395.4	78.3	59.2	2.2	481.2	30.0	52.4	3.7		678.7	1963
1964	446.8	63.6	1 397.8	77.9	60.8	2.2	489.9	29.8	58.4	3.8		702.0	1964
1965	457.1	64.0	1 409.0	77.7	62.8	2.3	498.4	31.1	64.4	4.0		718.6	1965
1966	469.0	65.3	1 418.7	77.7	64.9	2.4	504.5	32.1	71.3	4.3		728.4	1966
1967	481.2	66.0	1 428.0	77.3	67.6	2.4	520.0	33.4	77.9	4.5		743.9	1967
1968	488.8	66.7	1 438.8	77.1	70.5	2.5	542.6	34.8	84.8	4.8		758.1	1968
1969	493.1	67.3	1 450.6	76.8	72.3	2.6	561.7	35.8	93.6	5.2		760.1	1969
1970	491.7	67.9	1 462.4	76.5	74.1	2.6	591.3	37.4	103.4	5.6		788.3	1970
1971	491.5	68.8	1 464.5	76.0	76.3	2.7	626.4	39.2	112.9	6.0		806.4	1971
1972	495.1	69.9	1 461.5	75.5	78.1	2.7	662.1	41.0				843.1	1972
1973	506.0	70.4	1 455.0	75.1	80.2	2.8	706.6	43.1				850.9	1973
1974	513.6	71.1	1 448.2	74.5	81.4	2.8	740.3	44.5	113.7	6.3		845.1	1974
1975	518.9	72.4	1 453.5	74.3	83.4	2.9	766.4	45.3	120.1	6.6		875.5	1975
1976	498.8	72.9	1 448.1	74.1	84.9	2.9	794.7	46.4	129.2	7.0		893.8	1976
1977	466.0	72.6	1 434.7	74.1	86.3	3.0	812.0	47.1	137.4	7.4		915.8	1977
1978	438.2	72.7	1 413.3	74.1	87.3	3.1	820.6	47.5	143.2	7.6		911.8	1978
1979	418.5	73.6	1 379.9	74.0	90.2	3.3	823.6	47.4	151.8	7.5		936.8	1979
1980	409.6	74.3	1 333.3	73.2	92.4	3.5	823.7	47.4	152.9	7.9		954.3	1980
1981	399.8	74.5	1 269.9	72.0	94.3	3.6	828.7	50.9	152.1	7.7		984.3	1981
1982	398.8	74.9	1 201.5	70.5	95.7	3.8	836.2	48.2	155.0	7.8		1 011.9	1982

Table 20

Data on Housing

Year	Housing units (1,000s)				Newly built houses (1,00s)					Newly built houses (percent distributions)					Year
	Total stock	Newly built	Loss	Net increase	Social housing	Subsidized	Non-subsidized	For rent	Not for rent	Social housing	Subsidized	Non-subsidized	For rent	Not for rent	
1948		36.4													1948
1949		42.8													1949
1950		47.3			45.6 *		1.7			96.4 *		3.6			1950
1951		58.7			54.6 *		4.1			93.0 *		7.0			1951
1952		54.6			52.0 *		2.6			95.2 *		4.8			1952
1953		59.6			57.9 *		1.7			97.1 *		2.9			1953
1954		68.5			38.3	28.7	1.5			55.9	41.9	2.2			1954
1955		60.8			28.6	29.7	2.5			47.0	48.8	4.1			1955
1956	2 546	68.3			32.1	32.4	3.8			47.0	47.4	5.6			1956
1957		88.4			43.9	39.4	5.1			49.7	44.6	5.8			1957
1958		89.0			49.1	36.9	3.0			55.2	41.5	3.4			1958
1959		83.6			45.5	35.9	2.2			54.4	42.9	2.6			1959
1960	2 824	83.8	11.1	72.7	38.9	37.3	7.6	55.3	28.5	46.4	44.5	9.1	66.0	34.0	1960
1961		82.7	12.8	69.9	32.3	30.6	19.9	51.2	31.5	39.1	37.0	24.1	61.9	38.1	1961
1962		78.4	13.1	65.3	27.4	25.0	26.0	46.2	32.2	34.9	31.9	33.2	58.9	41.1	1962
1963		79.5	13.3	66.2	29.6	21.9	28.0	50.4	29.1	37.2	27.5	35.2	63.4	36.6	1963
1964	3 111	101.0	13.9	87.1	38.3	27.9	34.8	65.1	35.9	37.9	27.6	34.5	64.5	35.5	1964
1965		115.0	14.4	100.6	50.0	28.3	38.7	77.1	37.9	43.5	24.6	33.7	67.0	33.0	1965
1966		121.7	16.9	104.8	60.0	27.0	34.7	83.5	38.2	49.3	22.2	28.5	68.6	31.4	1966
1967	3 450	127.4	16.9	110.5	69.4	26.5	31.5	88.8	38.6	54.5	20.8	24.7	69.7	30.3	1967
1968		122.8	18.3	104.5	62.1	39.5	21.2	86.3	36.5	50.6	32.2	17.3	70.3	29.7	1968
1969		123.1	18.3	104.8	50.9	53.6	18.6	80.5	42.6	41.3	43.5	15.1	65.4	34.6	1969
1970		117.3	18.5	98.8	45.3	51.8	20.2	74.3	43.0	38.6	44.2	17.2	63.3	36.7	1970
1971	3 729	136.6	18.6	118.0	50.0	64.3	22.3	85.3	51.3	36.6	47.1	16.3	62.4	37.6	1971
1972		152.3	18.6	133.7	53.5	72.3	26.5	97.3	55.0	35.1	47.5	17.4	63.9	36.1	1972
1973		155.4	15.3	140.1	55.8	68.6	31.1	95.6	59.8	35.9	44.1	20.0	61.5	38.5	1973
1974		146.2	17.1	129.1	48.3	62.2	35.7	82.0	64.2	33.0	42.5	24.4	56.1	43.9	1974
1975	4 281	120.8	14.6	106.2	40.1	54.5	26.2	64.4	56.4	33.2	45.1	21.7	53.3	46.7	1975
1976	4 388	106.8	14.7	92.1	36.4	49.5	20.9	54.4	52.4	34.1	46.3	19.6	50.9	49.1	1976
1977	4 480	111.0	14.7	96.3	36.0	47.8	27.2	51.2	59.8	32.4	43.1	24.5	46.1	53.9	1977
1978	4 578	105.8	13.5	92.3	31.1	44.1	30.6	42.1	63.7	29.4	41.7	28.9	39.8	60.2	1978
1979	4 672	87.5	14.0	73.5	25.8	32.8	28.9	31.7	55.8	29.5	37.5	33.0	36.2	63.8	1979
1980	4 850	113.7	15.0	98.7	40.4	44.3	29.0	49.9	63.8	35.5	39.0	25.5	43.9	56.1	1980
1981	4 957	117.7	14.2	103.5	55.1	44.5	18.1	70.8	46.9	46.8	37.8	15.4	60.2	39.8	1981
1982	5 072	123.3	12.6	110.7	65.6	48.6	9.1	89.2	34.1	53.2	39.4	7.4	72.3	27.7	1982

* For 1950–1953 a brace spans "Social housing" and "Subsidized": one combined value is printed for both columns.

Table 21

Population and Labour Force

(in 1,000s)

Year	Total population	Age groups 0–19	Age groups 20–64	Age groups 65+	Age groups (%) 0–19	Age groups (%) 20–64	Age groups (%) 65+	Labour force persons	Labour force men years	Vacancies	Unemployed	Unempl. rate (%)	Year
1948	9 801	3 649	5 413	739	37.2	55.2	7.5		3 700		29.9		1948
1949	9 955	3 712	5 482	761	37.3	55.1	7.6		3 751		42.9		1949
1950	10 114	3 774	5 557	783	37.3	54.9	7.7		3 773		58.8		1950
1951	10 265	3 830	5 628	807	37.3	54.8	7.9		3 787		68.4		1951
1952	10 382	3 874	5 677	831	37.3	54.7	8.0		3 771		105.7	3.8	1952
1953	10 493	3 920	5 718	855	37.4	54.5	8.1		3 840		76.2	2.7	1953
1954	10 615	3 973	5 764	878	37.4	54.3	8.3		3 944		51.8	1.7	1954
1955	10 750	4 032	5 817	901	37.5	54.1	8.4		4 016		32.9	1.1	1955
1956	10 889	4 094	5 871	924	37.6	53.9	8.5		4 078		23.5	0.8	1956
1957	11 026	4 156	5 922	948	37.7	53.7	8.6		4 100		33.1	1.0	1957
1958	11 187	4 229	5 982	976	37.8	53.5	8.7	3 900	4 062		69.0	2.2	1958
1959	11 348	4 301	6 042	1 005	37.9	53.2	8.9		4 104		48.5	1.5	1959
1960	11 487	4 359	6 094	1 034	37.9	53.1	9.0		4 182		28.8	0.9	1960
1961	11 638	4 424	6 150	1 064	38.0	52.8	9.1		4 243		21.2	0.6	1961
1962	11 806	4 497	6 215	1 094	38.1	52.6	9.3		4 328		21.2	0.6	1962
1963	11 966	4 558	6 288	1 120	38.1	52.5	9.4	4 222	4 378		23.5	0.7	1963
1964	12 128	4 608	6 372	1 148	38.0	52.5	9.5		4 464		20.7	0.6	1964
1965	12 296	4 658	6 460	1 178	37.9	52.5	9.6	4 551	4 502	129.2	25.2	0.7	1965
1966	12 456	4 673	6 579	1 204	37.5	52.8	9.7	4 582	4 537	114.9	35.6	1.0	1966
1967	12 598	4 650	6 713	1 235	36.9	53.3	9.8	4 609	4 523	68.2	74.8	2.0	1967
1968	12 730	4 639	6 824	1 267	36.4	53.6	10.0	4 649	4 565	77.3	68.2	1.8	1968
1969	12 878	4 648	6 934	1 296	36.1	53.8	10.1	4 707	4 657	106.3	49.4	1.3	1969
1970	13 038	4 668	7 045	1 325	35.8	54.0	10.2	4 749	4 709	127.1	44.5	1.1	1970
1971	13 195	4 687	7 154	1 354	35.5	54.2	10.3	4 835	4 732	106.7	62.0	1.6	1971
1972	13 329	4 693	7 254	1 382	35.2	54.4	10.4	4 885	4 690	63.3	108.0	2.8	1972
1973	13 439	4 681	7 347	1 411	34.8	54.7	10.5	4 906	4 693	67.0	109.9	2.8	1973
1974	13 546	4 659	7 444	1 443	34.4	55.0	10.7	4 943	4 701	69.2	134.9	3.5	1974
1975	13 666	4 635	7 556	1 475	33.9	55.3	10.8	4 991	4 670	47.2	195.2	5.0	1975
1976	13 774	4 602	7 670	1 502	33.4	55.7	10.9	5 036	4 669	47.0	210.8	5.3	1976
1977	13 857	4 554	7 771	1 532	32.9	56.1	11.1	5 090	4 680	55.4	203.6	5.1	1977
1978	13 942	4 504	7 873	1 565	32.3	56.5	11.2	5 152	4 713	63.3	205.6	5.0	1978
1979	14 038	4 456	7 984	1 598	31.7	56.9	11.4	5 233	4 773	68.1	210.0	5.1	1979
1980	14 150	4 414	8 107	1 629	31.2	57.3	11.5	5 416	4 807	53.9	247.9	5.9	1980
1981	14 247	4 363	8 229	1 655	30.6	57.8	11.6	5 575	4 736	20.9	385.3	9.0	1981
1982	14 313	4 292	8 343	1 678	30.0	58.3	11.7	5 694	4 619	11.3	541.7	12.5	1982

Table 22

Results of Elections

(% of votes and number of seats)

	1948		1952		1956		1959		1963		1967		1971		1972		1977		1981		1982	
	%	n	%	n	%	n	%	n	%	n	%	n	%	n	%	n	%	n	%	n	%	n
Political Reformed Party	2.4	2	2.4	2	2.3	3	2.2	3	2.3	3	2.0	3	2.3	3	2.2	3	2.1	3	2.0	3	1.9	3
Reformed Political Union			0.7		0.6		0.7		0.7	1	0.9	1	1.6	2	1.8	2	1.0	1	0.8	1	0.8	1
Reformatoric Political Party																			1.2	2	1.5	2
Evangelist People's Party																			0.5		0.7	1
Anti-Revolutionary Party	13.2	13	11.3	12	9.9	15	9.4	14	8.7	13	9.9	15	8.6	13	8.8	14	Christian Democratic Appeal					
Christian Historical Union	9.2	9	8.9	9	8.4	13	8.1	12	8.6	13	8.1	12	6.3	10	4.6	7	31.9	49	30.8	48	29.3	45
Catholic People's Party	31.0	32	28.7	30	31.7	49	31.6	49	31.9	50	26.5	42	21.8	35	17.7	27						
Catholic National Party	1.3	1	2.7	2																		
Roman Catholic Party													0.4		0.9	1	0.4					
Radical Political Party													1.8	2	4.8	7	1.7	3	2.0	3	1.6	2
Labour Party	25.6	27	29.0	30	32.7	50	30.4	48	28.0	43	23.6	37	24.6	39	27.3	43	33.8	53	28.2	44	30.4	47
Communist Party	7.7	8	6.2	6	4.7	7	2.4	3	2.8	4	3.6	5	3.9	6	4.5	7	1.7	2	2.1	3	1.8	3
Pacifist Socialist Party							1.8	2	3.0	4	2.9	4	1.4	2	1.5	2	0.9	1	2.1	3	2.2	3
Democratic Socialists '70													5.3	8	4.1	6	0.7	1	0.6			
Liberal Party	7.9	8	8.8	9	8.8	13	12.2	19	10.3	16	10.7	17	10.3	16	14.4	22	17.9	28	17.3	26	23.1	36
Farmers Party									2.1	3	4.8	7	1.1	1	1.9	3	0.8	1	0.2			
Democrats '66											4.5	7	6.8	11	4.2	6	5.4	8	11.0	17	4.3	6
Middle Class Party													1.5	2	0.4							
Centre Party																			0.1		0.8	1
Others	1.7		1.3		0.9		1.2		1.6		2.5		2.3		0.9		1.7		1.1		1.6	
		100		100		150		150		150		150		150		150		150		150		150

Notes to and sources for appendix tables

Table 1

Gross domestic product:
Figures at current prices are based on the 1969 (SNA) definition. The 1950-59 figures had to be recalculated by the author according to the 1969 definition; that recalculation is based on the average difference between comparable figures for 1960-69; the same holds for the 1978-82 figures; that recalculation is based on the differences between comparable figures for 1977. Figures at constant (1975) prices have been deflated by the GDP-deflator.
Sources: (1) 1958, p. 102 (1948-49); (2) p. 56-57 (1950-77); (3) p. 54-55; (1978-82).

GDP Deflator:
Sources: 1948-49: based on figures for 1948-50 in: (1) 1959, p. 70; and the 1950 figure in: (2) p. 56; 1950-77 figures have been based on the GDP-figures in current and constant prices in: (2) p. 56-57; 1978-82 figures on the GDP-figures in current and constant prices in: (3) p. 54-55.

Public final consumption and investment deflators:
Sources: (1) 1959, p. 70 (1948-53); 1965, p. 70 (1954-62); 1974, p. 98 (1963-67); 1980, p. 153 (1968-80); 1982, p. 142 (1981-82).

Consumer price index:
Sources: (1) 1959, p. 70 (1948-53); 1965, p. 70 (1954-62); 1974, p. 98 (1963); (4) various years (1964-82).

Composed index deflator:
Based on the percent distribution of total government expenditure by economic function in Table 2, the respective percentages being deflated by different deflators and then aggregated: thus, the percentage of public final consumption deflator, transfers and subsidies by the consumer price index, interests on public debt by the GDP-deflator, and public investments by the public investment deflator (e.g. 1980: 31.4 x 136 + 57.7 x 133.8 + 6.5 x 134 + 4.5 x 141 = 133.8).

Total public expenditure:
Expenditure by central government, other public corporations (provinces, municipalities, and polder boards), and social security funds. Total public expenditure at constant prices has been deflated by the composed index.
Source: (5) various years.

Table 2

Total public expenditure by economic category and level of government:
For absolute figures, see Table 1; i.e. figures are consolidated, exclude transfers between central government and social insurance.
Source: (5), various years.

Central government expenditure by major purpose:
Sources: (6) for 1955, 1960 and 1965; (4), various years, for 1970-82.

Table 3

Social expenditure at current prices:

Total:
Sum of cols 2-6; totals in part contain estimates on public health expenditure (see notes to Table 12).

Income maintenance:
Total expenditure on income maintenance (see Table 6, col. 9).

Education:
Total expenditure on education (see Table 13, col. 2).

Health:
Sum of
(a) total public health expenditure (see Table 12, col. 4); official data are not available for the years 1948-52, 1954-57, 1957-62, 1964-67, 1969, 1971, 1973-74; for these years figures have been interpolated on the assumption of equal growth rates (see notes to Table 12);
(b) total expenditure on health insurance: expenditure on services and benefits in kind (see Table 12, col. 15).

Subsidies to lower rent of houses (Table 13, col. 7) and capital costs (Table 13, col. 8).

Other:
Other social expenditure includes the administrative costs of
(a) pension insurance (Table 7, col. 13);
(b) invalidity pensions (Table 8, col. 12);
(c) sickness insurance (Table 9, col. 7);
(d) unemployment insurance (Table 9, col. 16);
(e) family and child allowances (Table 10, col. 13);
(f) health insurance (Table 12, col. 16).
It also includes the expenditure on services:
(a) invalidity pensions (Table 8, col. 13);
(b) labour market regulations (Table 11, col. 14);
(c) home help and family care (Table 11, col. 15).

Social expenditure at constant prices:

Expenditure on income maintenance has been deflated by the consumer price index, expenditure on housing by the public investment deflator and all other social expenditure items by the public final consumption deflator (for deflators see Table 1).

Table 4

Social expenditure categories (see Table 3) as percent of GDP and total public expenditure (see Table 1) and as percent distribution.

Table 5

Social insurance expenditure at current prices:

Total:
Sum of cols 2-6.

Pensions:
Expenditure on pensions (including administrative costs) according to the Old Age Pensions (Emergency Provisions) Act from 1948-1956 and the General Old Age Pensions Act (AOW) from 1957 (see Table 7, cols 1-2), according to the General Widows and Orphans Benefits Act (AWW) (see Table 7, cols 3-4) and the Industrial Early Retirement Schemes (VUT) (see Table 7, cols 9-10).

Invalidity:
Total expenditure on invalidity pensions (including administrative costs) (see Table 8, cols 11-12).

Sickness:
Expenditure on sickness cash benefits (including administrative costs) according to the General Scheme (ZW) (see Table 9, cols 1-2) and the Miners Sickness Fund (see Table 9, cols 3-4).

Unemployment:
Expenditure on benefits (including administrative costs) according to the Unemployment Insurance Act (WW) (see Table 9, cols 8-9) and the special schemes for seasonal unemployment benefits (see Table 9, cols 10-11).

Family allowances:
Total expenditure on family allowances (including administrative costs) (see Table 10, cols

12-13) but excluding family allowances for public servants (see Table 10, col. 11) and self-employed persons (see Table 10, cols 9-10).

Health insurance:
Total expenditure on health insurance, including benefits and administrative costs (see Table 12, cols 15-16).

Social insurance expenditure at constant prices:
Expenditure on cash benefits has been deflated by the consumer price index, expenditure on benefits in kind, services and administrative costs by the public final consumption deflator (see Table 1).

Table 6

Expenditure at current prices:

Pensions:
Total expenditure on old age and survivors' pensions (see Table 7, col. 12).

Invalidity:
Total expenditure on invalidity and disablement pensions (see Table 8, col. 11).

Sickness:
Total expenditure on sickness cash benefits (see Table 9, col. 6).

Unemployment:
Total expenditure on unemployment cash benefits (see Table 9, col. 15).

Family allowances:
Total expenditure on family and child allowances (see Table 10, col. 12).

Social assistance:
Total expenditure on cash benefits (see Table 11, col. 13).

Education allowances:
Transfers to students (see Table 13, col. 1).

Housing allowances:
Temporary subsidies and housing allowances (see Table 13, cols 8-9).

Total:
Sum of preceding columns.

Expenditure at constant prices:

Expenditure at current prices deflated by the consumer price index (see Table 1).

Table 7

General old age pensions:
Pensions according to the Old Age Pensions (Emergency Provisions Act (1948-1956) and the General Old Age Pensions (AOW).
Sources: (7) p. 58 (1948-1956); (8) p. 24 (1957-62); (9) p. 27 (1963-71); (10) p. 26 (1972-75); (11) p. 29 (1976-79); (12) p. 35 (1980-82).

General widows' and orphans' pensions:
Pensions according to the General Widows' and Orphans' Benefits Act (AWW).
Sources: (8) p. 26 (1957-62); (9) p. 29 (1963-71); (10) p. 28 (1972-75); (11) p. 31 (1976-79); (12) p. 37 (1980-82).

General public servants' pensions:
Pensions according to the Public Servants' Superannuation Fund (ABP); including extra allowances.
Sources: (7) p. 44 (1948-54); (8) p. 56 (1955-62); (9) p. 38 (1963-71); (19) p. 37 (1972-75); (11) p. 42 (1976-79); (12) p. 49 (1980-82).

Other public servants' pensions:
Military pensions, pensions for ex-Indonesian public servants, and pensions for railwaymen; including extra allowances.
Sources: (7) pp. 46-49 (1948-54); (8) pp. 57-58 and (13) p. 98 (1955-62); (9) pp. 39-40 (1963-71); (10) pp. 38-40 (1972-75); (11) pp. 43-45 (1976-79); (12) pp. 49-51 (1980-82).

Non-government:
(Industrial) early retirements schemes.
Sources: (11) p. 38 (1977-79); (12) p. 44 (1980-82).

Government:
Early retirements schemes for public servants.
Source: (13) p. 101 (1979-82).

Total expenditure on pension benefits:
Sum of cols 1, 3, 5, 7, 9 and 11.

Total expenditure on pension administration:
Sum of cols 2, 4, 6, 8 and 10.

Table 8

Old Acts:
Invalidity Act, Old Age Pensions Act, and the Supplementary Law to Invalidity Act; benefits include (inclusive redemption payments).
Sources: (7) p. 22 (1948-54); (8) p. 16 (1955-62); (9) p. 16 (1963-71); (10) p. 13 (1972-75); (11) p. 15 (1976-79); (12) p. 22 (1980-82).

Interim Act:
Interim Invalidity Pensioners Act.
Sources: (9) p. 16 (1963-71); (10) p. 14 (1972-73).

Disablement Act:
Disablement Insurance Act (WAO); from 1968-1976 excluding expenditure on services (see note to Total Invalidity: services). The official Dutch statistics provide only figures which include these services.
Sources: (9) p. 17 (1967-71); (10) p. 17 (1972-75); (11) p. 19 (1976-79); (12) p. 25 (1980-82).

General Disablement Benefits Act:
For the period 1977-1982 excluding the services by the General Disablement Benefits Act (AAW), earlier paid by the Disablement Insurance Act (WAO). The official Dutch statistics offer figures which include these services (see note to Total Invalidity: services).
Sources: (11) p. 17 (1976-79); (12) p. 24 (1980-82).

Industrial Injuries Acts:
Industrial Injuries Insurance Act, Maritime Industrial Injuries Insurance Act, and the Agricultural and Horticultural Industrial Injuries Insurance Act.
Sources: (7) pp. 18-21 (1948-54); (8) p. 16 (1955-62); (9) p. 15 (1963-67).

Total expenditure on invalidity benefits:
Sum of cols 1, 3, 5, 7 and 9.

Total expenditure on invalidity administration:
Sum of cols 2, 4, 6, 8 and 10.

Total expenditure on invalidity services:
Services according the Disablement Insurance Act (1968-1976) and the General Disablement Benefits Act (1977-1982).
Source: figures provided by the Central Bureau of Statistics.

Table 9

Sickness cash benefits:

General schemes:
Sickness Benefits Act (ZW).
Sources: (7) p. 31 (1948-54); (8) p. 29 (1955-62); (9) p. 19 (1963-71); (10) p. 18 (1972-75); (11) p. 20 (1976-79); (12) p. 25 (1980-82).

Miners:
Miners' Sickness Fund, including the Sea-Risk Fund for the the period 1948-1959.
Sources: (7) pp. 31-32 (1948-54/59); (8) p. 30 (1955-62); (9) p. 18 (1963-67).

Public servants:
Public Servants' Sickness Fund (DSO).
Sources: (7) p. 57 (1948-49); (13) p. 101 (1950-82).

Total expenditure on sickness cash benefits:
Sum of cols 1, 3 and 5.

Total expenditure on sickness benefits administration:
Sum of cols 2 and 4.

Unemployment cash benefits:

Insurance:
Unemployment Insurance Act (WW).
Sources: (7) p. 28 (1948-54); (8) p. 42 (1955-62); (9) p. 21 (1963-71); (10) p. 20 (1972-75); (11) p. 23 (1976-79); (12) p. 38 (1980-82).

Seasonal:
Special schemes for seasonal unemployment benefits.
Sources: (7) p. 29 (1948-54); (8) p. 43 (1955-62); (9) p. 21 (1963-71); (10) p. 20 (1972-75); (11) p. 23 (1976-79); (12) p. 39 (1980-82).

Provision:
Unemployment Provisions Act (WWV).
Source: (13) p. 99 (1965-82).

Assistance:
Government Unemployment Assistance Regulations (RWW).
Source: (13) p. 99 (1965-82).

Public servants:
Public Servants Redundancy Pay Scheme (WRO).
Source: (7) p. 58; (13) p. 101 (1950-82).

Total expenditure on unemployment benefits:
Sum of cols 1, 3, 5-7.

Total expenditure on unemployment benefits administration:
Sum of cols 2 and 4.

Table 10

General:
Family Allowance Act (KW).
Sources: (7) p. 39 (1948-54); (8) p. 44 (1955-62).

Pensioners:
Pensioners Family Allowances Act.
Sources: (7) p. 40 (1948-54); (8) p. 45 (1955-62).

Wage-earners:
Wage Earners Family Allowances Act (KWL).
Sources: (9) p. 34 (1963-71); (10) p. 33 (1972-75); (11) p. 37 (1976-79).

General:
General Family Allowances Act (AKW).
Sources: (9) p. 34 (1963-71); (10) p. 33 (1972-75); (11) p. 37 (1976-79); (12) p. 43 (1980-82).

Self-employed:
(A) Temporary Family Allowances Act for Self-employed.
Source: (13) p. 99 (1951-56).
(B) Self-Employed Persons Family Allowances Act.
Source: (13) p. 91 (1957-79).

Public:
Public Service Employees Family Allowances Scheme.
Sources: (7) p. 40 and p. 57 (1948-49); (13) p. 101 (1950-82).

Total Expenditure on family allowances:
Sum of cols 1, 3, 5, 7, 9-11.

Total expenditure on family allowances administration:
Sum of cols 2, 4, 6 and 8.

Table 11

General social assistance:
Benefits according to the National Assistance Act (ABW) excluding the benefits according to the Government Unemployment Assistance Regulations (RWW).
Sources: (7) p. 58 (1948-49); (13) p. 99 (1950-82).

Victims of persecution:
Benefits for the victims of persecution 1940-1945.
Source: (13) p. 99 (1974-82).

Special pensions:
Benefits according to the Special Pensions Act 1940-45 (WBP) for persons disabled as a result of their participation in the resistance.
Sources: (7) p. 58 (1948-49); (13) p. 99 (1950-82).

General (war) disablement benefits:
Sources: (13) p. 99 (1954-82).

War prisoners:
Benefits for Indonesian war prisoners.
Source: (13) p. 99 (1981-82).

Colonial pensions:
Pensions for former civil servants in overseas areas.
Sources: (7) p. 58 (1948-49); (13) p. 101 (1950-82).

Pension replacement benefits:
Pensions for Ambonese members of the Dutch Colonial Army during the Indonesian War of Independence, without Dutch citizenship.
Source: (13) p. 99 (1959-1970).

National service allowance:
Allowances for the wife (and children) of a breadwinner recruited to the military service.
Sources: (7) p. 58 (1948-49); (13) p. 101 (1950-82).

Lump-sum benefits:
(Partial) inflation compensation for people with minimal social security or social assistance benefits.
Source: (13) p. 99 (1981-82).

Sheltered employment:
Employment offered by local governments to socially and/or physically handicapped persons.
Sources: (7) p. 58 (1948-49); (13) p. 99 (1950-82).

Local government employment provisions:
Local government projects to provide work for unemployed persons.
Source: (13) p. 99 (1956-82).

State aid to artists:
Source: (13) p. 99 (1956-82).

Total cash benefits:
Sum of preceding columns.

Labour market regulations:
Expenditure on labour market regulations.
Sources: Figures provided by the Ministry of Social Affairs and Employment (1948-80); (14) Appendix 1, tables 4, 5, and 6 (1981-82).

Home help:
Expenditure on home help and family care.
Sources: (13) p. 99 (1953-82).

Table 12

Public health:
Public health expenditure by central, regional and local government (mainly municipal health services, preventive health care, medical research, training, subsidies for services), supplementing health insurance as the major source of financing health expenditure. For earlier years, the Central Bureau of Statistics carried out only some enquetes (1953, 1958, 1963, 1968, 1970, and 1972); figures on total expenditure for 1954-57, 1959-62, 1964-67, 1971, 1973-74 have been interpolated on the assumption of equal growth rates; figures for 1948-52 have been estimated on the basis of the average growth rate 1953-58.
Sources: (15) p. 48 (1953-72); (4) various years (1975-82).

Compulsory insurance:
Health Insurance Act (compulsory scheme).
Sources: (7) p. 34 (1948-54); (8) p. 33 (1955-62); (9) p. 21 (1963-71); (10) p. 20 (1972-75); (11) p. 22 (1976-79); (12) p. 28 (1980-82).

Voluntary insurance:
Health Insurance Act (voluntary scheme).
Sources: (7) p. 34 (1948-54); (8) p. 34 (1955-62); (9) p. 21 (1963-71); (10) p. 20 (1972-75); (11) p. 23 (1976-79); (12) p. 29 (1980-82).

Old people's insurance:
Health Insurance Act (old people's scheme).
Sources: (8) p. 35 (1957-62); (9) p. 22 (1963-71); (10) p. 21 (1972-75); (11) p. 24 (1976-79); (12) p. 30 (1980-82).

Other schemes:
Included are the Supplementary Health Insurance Scheme, the General Miners Health Insurance Scheme, the Scheme for Mine Employees, the Service Health Care for Police, and some minor public servants schemes.
Sources: (7) pp. 36-37 (1948-54); (8) pp. 35-38 (1955-62); (9) pp. 22-24 (1963-71); (10) pp. 21-23 (1972-75); (11) pp. 24-25 (1976-79); (12) pp. 30-31 (1980-82).

Exceptional medical expenses:
Sources: (9) p. 25 (1968-71); (10) p. 23 (1972-75); (11) p. 26 (1976-79); (12) p. 32 (1980-82).

Total insurance:
Benefits: Sum of cols 5, 7, 9, 11 and 13.
Administrative costs: Sum of cols 6, 8, 10, 12 and 14.

Table 13

Transfers to students:
Including education allowances for pupils in secondary education, scholarships and interest-free loans for students, and allowances for all other types of education financed by local and central government.
Source: figures provided by the Central Bureau of Statistics (1950-80); (16) p. 107 (1981-82).

Total expenditure on education:
Expenditure on education by central and local government, in million guilders and as percent distribution
Source: (4) various years (1948-82).

Total expenditure on housing:
Sum of cols 6-9.

Rent subsidies:
Subsidies to lower rent of houses:
Sources: (1) 1959, p. 85 (1948-52); 1964, p. 83 (1953-62); 1970, p. 90 (1963-68); 1976, p. 111 (1969-74); 1980, p. 167 (1975-78); 1982, p. 170 (1979-80); 1985, p. 167 (1981-82).

Capital subsidies:
Subsidies for capital costs (e.g. therminal isolation).
Sources: (1) 1959, p. 86 (1950-52); 1964, p. 84 (1953-62); 1970, p. 91 (1963-68); 1976, p. 112 (1969-74); 1980, p. 168 (1975-78); 1982, p. 171 (1979-80); 1985, p. 168 (1981-82).

Temporal subsidies:
Subsidies for moving to higher rent house.
Sources: (1) 1970, p. 34 (1965-68); 1976, p. 109 (1969-74); 1980, p. 165 (1975-78); 1982, p. 168 (1979-80); 1985, p. 164 (1981-82).

Rent allowances:
Individual subsidies (for a longer period) and promotion of own tenure of houses.
Sources: (1) 1970, p. 34 (1967-68); 1976, p. 109 (1969-74); 1980, p. 165 (1975-78); 1982, p. 168 (1979-80); 1985, p. 164 (1981-82).

Table 14

Total public revenues:
Sum of cols 2-5.

Direct and indirect taxes:
Source: (17) p. 175.

Other revenues:
Source: (1) various years.

Social security contributions:
Contributions by employers and households.
Source: (17) p. 206.

Statistical government deficit:
Budget deficit of central and local government.
Source: (19) various years.

Total government deficit:
Accumulated national debt.
Source: (18) p. 176.

Total 15

Total taxes:
Including some special taxes for 1948-60. In million guilders and as percent distribution by level of government.
Source: (18) p. 175.

Social security receipts:
Total receipts = sum of social security contributions by employers and households, government transfers and receipts from interests.
Source: (19) p. 206.

Table 16

Total major clienteles:
People living predominantly from social transfers: recipients of old age pensions, widows' and orphans' pensions, invalidity and disablement pensions, sickness benefits, unemployment benefits, sheltered employment benefits, benefits for artists, and social assistance benefits.

Pensioners:

Old age:
Old Age Pensions (Emergency Provisions) Act and General Old Age Pensions Act.

Survivors:
General Widows and Orphans Benefits Act.

Invalidity:
Invalidity Act, Interim Invalidity Pensioners Act, Old Age Pensions Act, Industrial Injuries Insurance Act, Maritime Industrial Injuries Insurance Act, and the Agricultural and Horticultural Industrial Injuries Insurance Act.
Sources: (17) p. 204 (1948-64); (13) pp. 103-105 (1965-82).

Disablement:
Disablement Insurance Act. General Disablement Benefits Act.
Source: (13) pp. 103-105 (1976-82).

(Un-)Employment:

Total beneficiaries:
Sum of cols 1-3 in Table 17.

Sheltered programmes:
Beneficiaries of sheltered employment provisions.
Sources: (4) various years (1954-64); (13) pp. 106-108 (1965-82).

Aid to artists:
Beneficiaries of the state aid scheme to artists.
Source: (13) pp. 106-108 (1965-82).

Social assistance beneficiaries:
Benefits according to the National Assistance Act (ABW) excluding the benefits according to the Government Unemployment Assistance Regulations (RWW). Including all beneficiaries of various kind with a periodical assistance benefit.
Source: (13) pp. 106-108 (1965-82).

Table 17

Unemployment beneficiaries:

Insurance:
Beneficiaries according to the Unemployment Insurance Act and special schemes for seasonal unemployment benefits.
Sources: (17) p. 204 (1948-64); (13) pp. 103-105 (1965-82).

Provisions:
Beneficiaries according to the Unemployment Provisions Act.
Source: (13) pp. 106-108 (1965-82).

Government assistance:
Beneficiaries according to the Government Unemployment Assistance Regulations.
Source: (13) pp. 106-108 (1965-82).

Child allowances:
Number of families receiving child allowances according to the Family Allowance Act, the Pensioners' Family Allowances Act, the Wage-earners Family Allowances Act, and the General Family Allowances Act.
Source: (17) p. 204 (1948-82).

Special health services:
Beneficiaries of special health services (nursing) according to the Exceptional Medical Expenses Act.
Source: (13) pp. 103-105 (1968-82).

Home help beneficiaries:
Beneficiaries of home help and family care.
Source: (13) pp. 106-108 (1965-82).

War victims pensioners:
Beneficiaries of pensions according to the Victims of Persecution (1940-45) Act, the Special Pension Act, the General (War) Disablement Benefits Scheme, and the Indonesian War Prisoners Benefits Act.
Sources: (12) 1983, p. 15; (13) pp. 106-108 (1965-82).

Colonial service pensioners:
Beneficiaries of pensions for former civil servants in overseas areas. Breadwinners' and income allowances for national servicemen.
Source: The Foundation Administration Indonesian Pensions. The Ministry of Defence.

National service allowances:
Beneficiaries of breadwinners' income allowances for national servicemen.
Source: Ministry of Defence.

Social assistance:
Beneficiaries of lump-sum benefits.
Source: (12) 1983, p. 15.

Rent subsidy beneficaries:
Source: Figures provided by the Ministry for Housing, Physical Planning and Environment.

Student allowances' beneficaries:
Source: Figures provided by the Central Bureau of Statistics.

Table 18

Source: (17) pp. 40-41.

Table 19

Special primary education comprises schools for children with behavioural or mental problems. Vocational education includes technical, agricultural and horticultural, and social-pedagogical education as well as the teacher training for kindergartens, primary education and part of secondary education.
Source: (17) pp. 52-53.

Table 20

Social housing comprises houses built by housing associations and subsidized by the state and houses built by municipalities, all for rent. Subsidized housing comprises privately built houses subsidized by the state.
Sources: (17) pp. 44-45; (4) 1983, p. 89.

Table 21

Total population and age groups:
Source: (17) p. 25.

Labour force (persons):
Sources: (17) p. 79 (1947); (4) various years (1958, 1960, 1963, 1965-70); (17) p. 79 (1971-78); (4) various years (1979-82).

Labour force (men years):
Sources: (20) p. 68 (1947-69); (4) various years (1969-82).

Vacancies:
Source: (4) various years.

Unemployment:
Source: (17) p. 79.

Table 22

Source: (21).

Enumerated sources for appendix tables

(1) Centraal Bureau voor de Statistiek, *Nationale Rekeningen* The Hague.

(2) OECD, *National Accounts 1950-1978*, Volume 1, Paris 1980.

(3) OECD, *National Accounts 1960-1984*, Volume 1, Paris 1986.

(4) Centraal Bureau voor de Statistiek, *Statistical Yearbook of the Netherlands*, The Hague.

(5) *Nota over de toestand van 's rijksfinanciën (Miljoenennota)*, Tweede Kamer, The Hague.

(6) Gerritse, R., *De publieke sector: ontwikkeling en waardevorming*, The Hague 1979.

(7) Sociale Verzekeringsraad, *Sociale Zekerheid in Nederland 1948-1959*, The Hague 1961.

(8) Centraal Bureau voor de Statistiek, *Sociale Verzekering, pensioenverzekering, levensverzekering 1955-1964*, The Hague 1966.

(9) Centraal Bureau voor de Statistiek, *Sociale Verzekering, pensioenverzekering, levensverzekering 1963-1972*, The Hague 1974.

(10) Centraal Bureau voor de Statistiek, *Sociale Verzekering, pensioenverzekering, levensverzekering 1972-1976*, The Hague 1977.

(11) Centraal Bureau voor de Statistiek, *Sociale Verzekering, pensioenverzekering, levensverzekering 1976-1980*, The Hague 1981.

(12) Centraal Bureau voor de Statistiek, *Sociale Verzekering, pensioenverzekering, levensverzekering 1979-1983*, The Hague 1984.

(13) Ministerie van Sociale Zaken en Werkgelegenheid, *Financiële Nota Sociale Zekerheid 1985*, The Hague 1984.

(14) Ministerie van Sociale Zaken en Werkgelegenheid, *Jaarverslag Arbeidsmarktvoorziening 1983*, The Hague 1984.

(15) Centraal Bureau voor de Statistiek, *Kosten en Financiering van de gezondheidszorg 1972*, The Hague 1977.

(16) Centraal Bureau voor de Statistiek, *Statistisch Zakboek 1985*, The Hague 1985.

(17) Centraal Bureau voor de Statistiek, *Vijfentachtig jaren statistiek in tijdreeksen*, The Hague 1984.

(18) Centraal Bureau voor de Statistiek, *Statistische en Econometrische Onderzoekingen*, The Hague 1958.

(19) De Nederlandsche Bank NV, *Jaarverslag*, Amsterdam.

(20) Centraal Bureau voor de Statistiek, *Tachtig jaren statistiek in tijdreeksen*, The Hague 1979.

(21) Flora, Peter et al., *State, Economy and Society in Western Europe*, Vol. I. Frankfurt, London, Chicago 1983.

Belgium

Jos Berghman, Jan Peeters and Jan Vranken

Institutional Synopsis

Contents

Glossary of abbreviations

ASLK *Caisse génerale d'épargne et de retraite, Algemene Spaar en Lijfrentekas* (General Savings and Annuity Bank)
BH *Administration du logement, Bestuur voor de Huisvesting* (Housing Directorate)
BP *Prépensions, Brugpensioenen* (Transitional Pension Schemes)
BTK *Cadre spécial temporaire, Bijzonder Tijdelijk Kader* (Special Temporary Employment Scheme)
COO *Commission d'assistance publique, Commissie van Openbare Onderstand* (Public Assistance Committee)
CSHMV *Commissie voor Sociaal Hulpbetoon aan Minder-Validen* (Social Assistance Committee)
DAC *Troisième Circuit de Travail, Derde Arbeidscircuit* (Third Employment Scheme)
FB *Fonds des maladies professionnelles, Fonds voor Beroepsziekten* (Occupational Diseases Funds)
GIB *Revenue garanti aux personnes agées, Gewaarborgd inkomen voor Bejaarden* (Guaranteed Income for the Elderly)
GKB *Allocations familiales garanties, Gewaarborgde Kinder Byslag* (Guaranteed Family Allowance Scheme)
HKWU *Caisse auxiliaire de paiement des allocations de chômage, Hulpkas voor Werkloosheidsuitkeringen* (Subsidiary Fund for Payment of Unemployment Benefits)
HRMW *Hoge Raad voor Minder-Validen* (High Commission for the Disabled)
LLM *Union nationale des mutualités libérales, Landsbond van Liberale Mutualiteiten* (National Federation of Liberal Mutual Aid Societies)
LNM *Union nationale des mutualités neutres, Landsbond van Neutrale Mutualiteiten* (National Federation of Neutral Mutual Aid Societies)
LPM *Union nationale des mutualités professionnelles, Landsbond van Professionele Mutualiteiten* (National Federation of Occupational Mutual Aid Societies)
LSM *Union nationale des mutualités socialistes, Landsbond van Socialistische Mutualiteiten* (National Federation of Socialist Mutual Aid Societies)
NFH *Fonds national du logement, Nationaal Fonds voor de Huisvesting* (National Housing Fund)
NH *Caisse auxiliaire nationale, Nationale Hulpkas* (National Auxiliary Fund)
NIH *Institut national du logement, Nationaal Instituut voor de Huisvesting* (National Housing Institute)
NLM *Société nationale terrienne, Nationale Landmaatschappij* (National Land Society)
NMH *Société nationale du logement, Nationale Maatschappij voor de Huisvesting* (National Housing Society)
NVCM *Alliance nationale des mutualités chrétiennes Nationaal Verbond van Christelijke Mutaliteiten* (National Federation of Christian Mutual Aid Societies)
OCMW *Centres publiques d'aide sociale, Openbare Centra voor Maatschappelik Welzijn* (Public Social Welfare Centres)
RBM *Droit à un minimum de moyens d'existence, Recht op het Bestansminimum* (Right to a Subsistence Minimum)
RKW *Office national d'allocations familiales pour travailleurs salariés, Rijksdienst voor Kinderbijslag voor Werknemers* (National Family Allowance Office for Wage-earners)
RIZIV *Institut national d'assurance maladie-invalidité, Rijksdienst voor Ziekte en Invaliditeitsverzekering* (National Institute for Sickness and Invalidity Insurance)
RROP *Caisse nationale des pensions de retraite et de survie, Rijkskas voor Rust en Overlevingspensioenen (National Office for Payment of Old Age and Survivors' Pensions)*
RSZ *Office national de sécurité sociale, Rijksdienst voor Sociale Zekerheid* (National Social Security Office)

RSVZ *Institut national d'assurances sociales des travailleurs indépendants, Rijksinstituut voor de Sociale Verzekeringen der Zelfstandigen* (National Social Insurance Office for the Self-employed)
RVA *Office national de l'emploi, Rijksdienst voor Arbeidsvooziening* (National Employment Office)
RWP *Office national des pensions pour ouvriers, Rijksdienst voor Werknemerspensioenen* (National Pension Office for Wage-earners)
SSZ *Le statut social des travailleurs indépendants, Sociaal Statuut voor Zelfstandigen* (Social Security System for the Self-employed)
SVK *Caisse d'assurances sociales, Sociaal Verzekeringskas* (Social Insurance Fund)
VSO *Enseignement Secondaire Renové, Vernieuwd Secundair Onderwijs* (Renewed Secondary Education)
WF-BKGB *Fonds du logement de la ligue des familles nombreuses de Belgique, Woningsfonds van de Bond voor Kroostrijke Gezinnen van België* (The Belgian League for Large Families' Housing Fund)

Introduction

In this institutional synopsis Belgian welfare provisions are presented along functional lines in nine sections. Within these sections, however, an institutional approach has been used. The first six sections deal with the various social security schemes, the major function of which is income maintenance. The following three sections deal with major public policies in the fields of health, education and housing.

In the field of social security there are different schemes for employees and for the self-employed. The various categories of established civil servants have their own statutory schemes, with the exception of health care insurance where they are covered by the general scheme for employees (only railwaymen have their own health care scheme). The various insurance or statutory based schemes are supplemented by social assistance and various minimum benefit schemes which are means-tested.

The previous insurance schemes for blue-collar and white-collar workers, and for miners and seamen, have become increasingly, though to a varying degree, integrated into general employees' schemes. These schemes are administratively and financially subdivided into six sectors (see Table below) and are financed to various degrees by employees' and employers' contributions and by state subsidies.

There is some coordination between schemes, especially with respect to financing. All contributions (employers' and employees') are transferred by the employer to the National Social Security Office (*Office national de sécurité sociale, Rijksdienst voor Sociale Zekerheid*, RSZ) which then distributes them among the national offices of the various schemes according to fixed contribution rates.

As a rule all national social security offices are managed by boards of representatives of trade unions and employers' associations (Act of 25 March 1963 on parity administration), and supervised by the Ministry of Finance and, according to the sector, by the Ministry of Social Security, Employment or Health.

The social security system for the self-employed (*Le statut social des travailleurs indépendants, Sociaal Statuut voor Zelfstandigen*, SSZ) was set up in 1967, combining previously existing schemes for pensions, family allowances and health care insurance. In 1971 a scheme for sickness/invalidity cash benefits was added. The schemes are financed by contributions from the self-employed, on the basis of degressive contribution rates, and by very substantial state subsidies.

The financing of social security schemes for employees

Sector	Contribution rates as % of gross earnings (1.1.1984)[a]			Financing in 1981			
	Blue- and White-collar[b]			Total	% Shares		
	employ-ees	employ-ers	total	mill. BFR	employ-ees	employ-ers	state
Pensions	7.50	8.86	16.36	200.404	34.6	46.3	19.1
Family allowances	-	7.00	7.00	85.167	-	100.0	-
Unemploy-ment	0.87	1.23	2.10	150.394	9.9	8.9	81.2
Health:				214.666	18.8	34.7	46.5
-cash benefits	1.15	2.20	3.35				
-medical care	2.55	3.80	6.35				
Industrial accidents	-	0.30	0.30	22.834	-	100.0	-
Occupat. diseases	-	0.65	0.65	14.712	-	47.6	52.4
Total	12.07	24.04	36.11	688.177	18.1	43.0	38.9

[a] Under the pressure of the economic crisis some additional measures were taken in the early 1980s, on the one side to lighten the contribution burden for blue-collar workers in export industries (in 1984, by way of a quarterly flat-rate deduction of the contribution by 1,250 BFR for each blue-collar worker as a general rule or by 4,250 BFR for small firms and enterprises accepting a collective labour agreement on the reduction of working hours and compensating recruitment), on the other side to find additional financial resources by: the diminution of the monthly family allowance by 375 BFR for each beneficiary - an equivalent contribution of 675 BFR a month was imposed on single persons and couples without children; the introduction of 'a special and unique contribution for social security' at the amount of 25% of the income between 3 and 5 million BFR and of 10% of income above 5 million BFR; the introduction of a contribution of 1.8% chargeable on all pensions above 27,963 BFR a month (without family burden) or 33,139 BFR a month (with family burden), this contribution will be transferred to the medical care scheme; the introduction of a contribution on the double holiday allowance (for employees this was a deduction of the allowance by 12.07% and for employers a quarterly contribution of 1.6% on gross earnings of the employee). All figures refer to 1 January 1984.

[b] In 1982 all income ceilings for the calculation of contributions were abolished, and the contribution rates for blue- and white-collar workers were equalized. Until then, blue-collar contribution rates were higher.

Source: Ministerie van Sociale Voorzorg, *Statistisch Jaarboek van de Sociale Zekerheid 1981*, Brussels, 1983, p. 25.

The financing of social security schemes for the self-employed[a]

	Contribution rates (1.1.1984) as % of annual income of (BFR)		Financing in 1981		
			Total	% Shares	
	up to 1 020 010	1 020 010-1 569 246	mill. BFR	Self-empl.	State
Pensions			38 916	54.3	45.7
	12.0	7.47			
Family allow.			12 922	65.9	34.1
Sickness and invalidity[b]			15 087	53.3	46.7
Medical care	3.3	3.3			
Total	15.3	10.77	66 925	56.3	43.7

[a] Some measures were also taken to find additional sources for the self-employed: the diminution of the monthly family allowance by 375 BFR for each beneficiary, and an equivalent contribution of 675 BFR a month for single persons and couples without children; the 'special and unique contribution for social security', see the employees scheme in previous table; a pensions contribution, see the employees scheme in previous table; the introduction of an annually fixed 'social solidarity contribution' (maximum of 3% of annual revenues in 1982); all figures refer to 1 January 1984.

[b] Cash benefits.

Source: Ministerie van Sociale Voorzorg, *Statistisch Jaarboek van de Sociale Zekerheid 1981*, Brussels, 1983, p. 106.

The self-employed pay contributions to one of the 17 recognized Social Insurance Funds (*Caisse d'assurances sociales, Sociale Verzekeringskas*, SVK). Contributions are transferred to the National Social Insurance Office for the Self-Employed (*Institut national d'assurances sociales des travailleurs indépendants, Rijksinstituut voor de Sociale Verzekeringen der Zelfstandigen*, RSVZ). The self-employed who are not members of a recognized social insurance fund are obliged to pay contributions to the National Auxiliary Fund (*Caisse auxiliaire nationale, Nationale Hulpkas*, NH) which is affiliated to the RSVZ.

The RSVZ is managed by a board which mainly represents the organizations of the self-employed. It administers pension and family allowance schemes whilst the health sector (sickness/invalidity cash benefits and medical care) is run by the National Institute for Sickness and Invalidity Insurance (*Institut national d'assurance maladie-invalidité, Rijksdienst voor Ziekte- en Invaliditeitsverzekering*, RIZIV) which is also responsible for the health insurance schemes (both cash benefits and medical care) covering all employees and for the civil servants' medical care insurance. Non-established public employees, i.e. employed either temporarily or before statutory appointment, are covered by the general employees' schemes. However, social security for established civil servants is provided by statute. There are several different statutes covering the various government or semi-government employing bodies. As a rule the protection provided covers invalidity, retirement and survivors' pensions, family allowances, medical care, industrial accidents and occupational diseases. Schemes are financed entirely by the employing body with the exceptions of survivors' pensions where civil servants contribute 7.5% of gross salary, and medical care insurance where contribution rates are 1.8% and 3.75% of gross earnings for employees and employers respectively. These rates are the same as in the general scheme for employees.

Estimation of social security financing for civil servants in 1980
in million BFR

		%
Pensions[a]		
- national adm. bodies	82 426.2	
- provinces	1 490.6	
- communes	12 646.5	
	96 563.3	77.49
Family allowances		
- national adm. bodies[b]	6 140.6	
- prov. and communes[c]	4 021.0	
	10 161.6	8.16
Medical care[d]		
- civil servants	16 712.4	
- retired civil servants	1 172.6	
	17 885.0	14.35
Total in BFR	124 609.9	100.00
as % of GDP	3.75	

[a] Based on expenditure figures (Source: Ministerie van Sociale Voorzorg, *Statistisch Jaarboek van de Sociale Zekerheid 1980*, Brussels, 1982, p. 140).
[b] Based on expenditure figures for 1980 (Source: see [a] p. 129).
[c] Based on expenditure figures (Source: see [a] p. 141).
[d] Based on contributions received by RIZIV (Source: RIZIV, *Algemeen Verslag - 2de deel: Financieel Verslag 1980*, Brussels, s.d., pp. 102-103).

Up to the late 1960s these insurance or statutory schemes were supplemented only by a long-established, locally run social assistance system providing means-tested benefits. Since the late 1960s, means-tested national minimum benefit schemes have been introduced which are to a large extent integrated with the national social security schemes. Minimum benefits for the elderly (Guaranteed Income for the Elderly) are dealt with in Section I on Pensions, minimum benefits for children (Guaranteed Child Allowances) in Section V on Family Allowances, and minimum benefits for the handicapped (Allowances for the disabled) in Section II on Sickness and Invalidity.

In contrast to the other national minimum benefits, the Right to a Subsistence Minimum scheme (*Droit à un minimum de moyens d'existence, Recht op het bestaansminimum*, RBM) was not affiliated to the social security system but was integrated into the locally organized social assistance system and is therefore dealt with in Section VI on Social Assistance. The social assistance system is administered locally by the multifunctional Public Centres for Social Welfare (*Centres publiques d'aide sociale, Openbare Centra voor Maatschappelijk Welzijn*, OCMW) which provide financial assistance (see Section VI on Social Assistance) and can also play a part in the organization of health services (see Section VII on Sickness Insurance and Health Services).

Social security benefits are revalued in two ways. Firstly, all benefits are automatically linked to the consumer price index. The price index-linking systems which were introduced in the various social security sectors from 1954 onwards were coordinated under the Act of 2 August 1971: a uniform method replaced the various methods of consumer price indexing introduced since 1954. Secondly, all benefits (with the exception of child allowances), are 'welfare related', i.e. their amount is adjusted annually in accordance with the level of national prosperity (increase in GDP) under the Act of 16 July 1974. Since 1976, however, the originally proportional increases have been replaced by flat-rate welfare adjustments.

Social security benefit expenditure in 1981, in million BFR

Sector	Employees	Self-empl.	Civil servants	Minimum benefit	Total Mill. BFR	%	% GDP
Pensions	208 868	36 509	107 606[a]	4 463	357 446	41.83	9.88
Family allowances	79 194	11 578	11 035	45	101 852	11.92	2.82
Unemployment	146 691	-	-	-	146 691	17.17	4.06
Health:							
-cash benefits	65 331	2 764	-	10 693[c]	78 788	9.22	2.18
-medical care	138 326	10 138	[b]		148 464	17.37	4.11
Industr. accidents	6 766	-	-		6 766	0.79	0.19
Occupat. diseases	14 527	-	-		14 527	1.70	0.40
Total	659 703	60 989	118 641	15 210	854 534	100.00	23.64
%	77.20	7.14	13.88	1.78	100.00		
% GDP	18.25	1.69	3.28	0.42	23.64		

[a] Estimate: some communes did not provide any information.
[b] Included in medical care scheme for employees.
[c] Allowances for the disabled.

Source: Ministerie van Sociale Voorzorg, *Statistisch Jaarboek van de Sociale Zekerheid 1981*, Brussels, 1983, pp. 78-85, 124-125, 133, 144-145, 165.

In order to understand the Belgian welfare state, its structure and evolution, one should be aware of the structural subdivision of Belgian society along ideological lines into pillars (*piliers, zuilen*): the Christian-Democrat, Socialist and Liberal pillars. Each of these pillars became an organizationally loose but politically cohesive conglomeration of organizations involved in different policy areas but of the same ideological/political stance. Pillarization helps to explain why these organizations continue to play an important role in the policy making and daily administration of the welfare state.

One should also be aware of the shift towards devolution. So far the consequences for the Welfare State have been that national responsibilities for important aspects of social housing policy, health policy and personal social services have been transferred either to the regions (Flanders, Wallonia and Brussels) or to the communities (Flemish and French).

I Pensions

Income maintenance

Coverage

The Belgian pension system consists of four schemes: a general scheme for employees which in its unified form dates from 1967; a special scheme for the self-employed initiated in the mid-1950s; a minimum pension scheme called Guaranteed Income for the Elderly (*Revenue garanti aux personnes agées; Gewaarborgd Inkomen voor Bejaarden*, GIB) introduced in 1969; and various schemes for civil servants.

All schemes provide old age and survivors' pensions with the exception of the GIB which only provides old age pensions. No invalidity pensions are provided. In 1981, expenditure on pensions amounted to 357,177 million BFR or approximately 9.9% of GDP.

Expenditure on pensions in 1981, in million BFR

Type of pension	Pension scheme					
	Employees	Self-empl.	GIB	Civil servants	Total	%
Old age pension	127 616.9	24 165.2		69 378.8	221 160.9	61.92
Widows' pension	65 009.1	11 976.2		22 739.6	99 724.9	27.92
Welfare adjustments	1 007.5				1 007.5	0.28
Widows' benefits	678.9	99.6			778.4	0.22
Holiday allowances	12 712.5				12 712.5	3.56
Other benefits	1 843.2				1 843.2	0.52
Unspecified			4 462.9	15 478.1[a]	19 950.0	5.58
Total	208 868.0	36 241.0	4 462.9	107 605.5	357 177.4	
%	58.48	10.14	1.25	30.13		100.00

Source: Ministerie van Sociale Voorzorg, *Statistisch Jaarboek van de Sociale Zekerheid 1981*, Brussels, 1983, pp. 82, 125, 144, 161.

On 1 January 1982 the number of pensions paid was as follows: 1,428,882 employee pensions, 488,558 pensions for the self-employed, 69,115 guaranteed income pensions, and 301,153 civil servants' pensions. As a person may be in receipt of more than one pension, the number of pensions paid does not correspond to the number of pensioners.

Number of pensions paid and of pensioners on 1 January 1984 (except civil servants' schemes)

	Wage earners	Self-employed	GIB	Correction for overlap	Number of pensioners
Pensions:					
Men:					
retirement pens. married couple's rate	232 209	92 519	6 526	-62 924	268 330
single person's rate	272 600	88 422	9 129	-66 958	303 193
total	504 809	180 941	15 655	-129 882	571 523
Women:					
retirement pens.	489 830	127 950	55 093	-97 039	575 836
survivor's pens.	467 734	149 693	-	-82 359	533 068
total	957 564	275 643	55 093	-179 396	1 108 904
Pensions:					
total number of pensions	1 462 373	456 854	70 748	-309 278	1 680 427
correction for overlap	-193 081	-23 995	-	-24 421	-241 497
non-distributed cases	11	4	3	-1	17
Pensioners:					
total number of pensioners	1 269 303	432 593	70 751	-333 700	1 438 947

Source: RROP, *Jaarlijkse Statistiek van de pensioengerechtigden*, 1984, pp. 20-21.

Pensions are automatically price indexed and in addition a 1973 Act states that pensions should be adjusted annually in accordance with the level of national prosperity. Since 1976, however, the originally proportional increases have been replaced by flat-rate welfare adjustments.

1. General pension scheme

The general scheme was established in 1967 by integrating the older special schemes for seamen (1844) and miners (1911) with newer and more general schemes for manual workers and white-collar employees. The latter had originally been introduced in

1924 and 1925 respectively, as compulsory insurance schemes, and had provided earnings-related pensions from 1930 and 1925 respectively. As inflation rendered these funded pension schemes increasingly inadequate, a new system was introduced in 1945, providing mainly minimum flat-rate pensions. Earnings-related pension schemes were re-introduced in 1955 for manual workers and in 1957 for white-collar employees.

Since the earnings-related pension scheme will not be fully effective until 2002, and since benefits are calculated on earnings up to a certain ceiling only, some private occupational pension schemes have been set up. They are mainly organized for high income white-collar workers in the more prosperous industries and are mainly based on collective labour agreements within the firm.

Benefits

In principle, entitlement to a full old age pension requires a period of employment of 45 years for men and 40 years for women. In practice, however, this qualifying condition will not be effective prior to 1991, as all persons who can prove that they have been employed since 1946 and have paid contributions since the establishment of the respective earnings-related schemes (1955 for manual workers, 1956 for seamen, 1957 for white-collar employees, and 1968 for miners) are entitled to a full pension. Periods when the individual was not in employment due to ill-health, involuntary unemployment or similar reasons, are regarded as equivalent. Missing years after 1946 may furthermore be substituted by years prior to 1946 for which a person can prove that he was employed. For any missing year, the actual pension is reduced by 1/45 for men and 1/40 for women.

A full old age pension amounts to 75% (married couple) or 60% (single) of the employee's average annual earnings in the relevant period. For the years before the introduction of earnings-related pension schemes, flat-rate earnings, and for periods considered as equivalent to employment, ficticious earnings are taken into account. All earnings are revalued in line with the consumer price index.

In 1962 the minimum pensions (full career), introduced in 1945, were abolished for all persons not yet retired. In April 1983, the minimum pension for a married couple was 23,603 BFR for manual workers and 29,505 for white-collar employees or 54.3% and 67.9% respectively of average monthly earnings for male manual workers in industry.

Until 1984 only men were entitled to a married couple's pension, and only women were awarded a survivor's pension. Then, the Mainil Act ended all female discrimination and also introduced a widowers' pension. If both the husband and wife are entitled to an old age pension, they can choose either to both receive their own pension at the single rate (60%), or to receive only one pension at the married couple's rate (75%). The surviving partner is entitled to a survivor's pension which is equal to the single person's rate of the old age pension for the deceased partner. Unless the surviving partner is caring for a child or is 66% disabled, he/she must be 45 years of age in order to qualify for a full survivors' pension. Otherwise he/she is only entitled to a minimun survivors' benefit consisting of a lump sum payment equal to one annual amount of the deceased's annual pension (single rate). When the surviving partner is entitled to both a survivor's pension and an old age pension, he/she may combine both benefits up to 110% of the higher pension. Pensioners are also entitled to ordinary and supplementary holiday allowances. In 1983, these amounted to 4,285 and

12,516 BFR for married couples and 2,571 and 10,872 BFR respectively for other pensioners, i.e. 10%, 29%, 6% and 25% of average monthly earnings for a male manual worker in industry.

Financing and administration

The general scheme is financed on a pay-as-you-go basis and has three main sources of finance: employers' contributions (46.3% of total revenue in 1981), employees' contributions (34.6%), and state subsidies (19.1%). In 1984, the contribution rate on the employee's total earnings was 8.86% for employers and 7.50% for employees.

Contributions are transferred by the employer to the National Social Security Office (RSZ), which operates as the central social security contribution collector. Pension applications must be made to the municipal administration. Pension benefits are determined by the National Pension Office for Wage Earners (*Office national des pensions pour ouvriers; Rijksdienst voor Werknemerspensioenen*, RWP). Pensions are paid by the National Office for Payment of Old Age and Survivors' Pensions (*Caisse national des pensions de retraite et de survie; Rijkskas voor Rust- en Overlevingspensioenen*, RROP).

2. Pension scheme for the self-employed

A statutory scheme for the self-employed was established in 1956. Unlike the general scheme, it provides only relatively low flat-rate pensions, payable to men from the age of 65 and to women from the age of 60. A full flat-rate pension requires that a person has been self-employed since 1946 and has contributed regularly since 1957; for any shorter period, the pension is correspondingly reduced. In 1983, full flat-rate benefit for a married couple amounted to 14,645 BFR, or 34% of the average monthly earnings of manual worker in industry. Single persons' and widows' pensions amount to 80% of married couple's pensions.

Since 1960 the scheme has been financed on a pay-as-you-go basis by contributions from the insured (54.3% of total revenue in 1981) and state subsidies (45.7%). In 1984, the overall contribution rate for pensions, family allowances and invalidity benefits was 12% up to an annual income of 1,020,000 BFR and 7.47% for annual incomes between 1,020,010 and 1,569,246 BFR. Since 1981, 68.46% of these contributions are used for the pension scheme. The self-employed pay contributions to their social insurance fund (SVK), which transfers payments to the National Social Insurance Office for the Self-employed (*Institut National d'assurances sociales des travailleurs indépendents, Rijksinstituut voor de Sociale Verzekeringen der Zelfstandigen*, RSVZ). The administration for pension applications and payments is the same for the self-employed and employees. Pensions are determined by the RSVZ.

3. Pension schemes for civil servants

There are various schemes for civil servants (magistrates, clergy, military, the teaching profession, etc.), the first being set up in 1844. Non-established public employees are covered by the general scheme.

Number of civil servants' pensions in payment on 1 January 1984

	Old age	Survivors'	Total
Govt. adm. and equivalent	38 129	37 343	122 663
Subsidized schools	39 343		
Clergy	1 553		
Regies	6 295		
Ex-colonial officials	5 742	2 244	7 986
Semi-governmental adm.	2 610	1 283	3 893
Army and national police	35 286	20 900	56 186
Railways	31 975	28 247	60 222
Water Supplies Board	271	163	434
Communes	-	-	44 585[a]
Provinces	-	-	5 202
Total			301 153

[a] Estimate: some communes did not provide any information.

Source: Ministerie van Sociale Voorzorg, *Statistisch Jaarboek van de sociale zekerheid 1981*, Brussels, 1983, p. 140.

As a general rule, public servants qualify for a pension at the age of 65, assuming that they have completed 20 years of service. For each year of service 1/60 of average earnings over the last 5 years is granted. However, there are many exceptions. Thus, military pensions are calculated on the earnings of the last year of service, and primary school teachers are granted 1/50 for each year of service. Old age pensions for civil servants are financed entirely by the Exchequer and no differentiation is made between a married couple's rate and that of a single person.

Civil servants pay a compulsory contribution of 7.5% of their earnings for survivors' pensions. A survivors' pension requires that the deceased must have been in the civil service for at least one year. When the marriage takes place after the civil servant's retirement, a survivor's pension is only paid if the retired has served for 20 years. Since the Mainil Act a full survivor's pension amounts to 60% of average earnings for the last five years of service, with a maximum of 50% of the last year's earnings. Incomplete survivors' pensions are proportional to the deceased's period of employment in public service.

4. Guaranteed income for the elderly (minimum pensions)

This scheme was introduced in 1969, and replaced the 1893 subsidized voluntary pension insurance scheme. It acts as a general safety net for all citizens over normal pensionable age who are either not covered at all or who are inadequately covered by other pension schemes. Benefits are flat-rate and means-tested. The initial benefit level was very low, equivalent to 24% and 16% for a couple and single person respectively of gross average earnings of adult males in industry. In 1983 the pension amounted to 16,806 BFR for a married couple and 12,100 BFR for a single person, i.e. 39% and 28% of average monthly earnings for a male manual worker in industry. When income from other sources exceeds a certain level, the minimum pension is reduced accordingly.

The scheme is financed by general state revenues, and is administered together with the general pension scheme for employees.

Core laws

Note: in Belgium, legislation enacted in parliament (*Chambre des Représentants, Kamer van Volksvertegenwoordigers*, and *Sénat, Senaat*), is called an Act (*Loi, Wet*). If it is commissioned to do so, the government can further elaborate and specify an Act. This is done by Royal Decrees (*Arrêté Royal, Koninklijk Besluit*).

After World War II when the King was temporarily replaced by a Regent, the government issued Regent's Decrees (*Arrêté du Régent, Regentsbesluit*) instead of Royal Decrees (e.g. Regent's Decree 26.5.1945 on unemployment insurance).

In exceptional periods the government may ask parliament for special powers on specific issues in a Special Empowering Act (*Loi de pouvoirs spéciaux, Wet op bijzondere machten*). Any Royal Decrees passed on this basis are numbered and have the status of an Act (e.g. Royal Decree no. 50 of 24.10.1967 on pensions).

During and immediately after World War II the government had full powers to legislate on most issues by an Extraordinary Empowering Act (*Loi de pouvoirs extraordinaires, Wet op de buitengewone machten*). On the basis of this Act the government issued Decrees (*Arrêté-Loi, Besluitwet*) with the status of Acts (e.g. Decree 28.12.1944 on social security for wage earners).

General Scheme:

Decree 28.12.1944
Arrêté - Loi concernant la sécurité sociale des travailleurs, Besluitwet betreffende de Maatschappelyke Zekerheid der Arbeiders (Decree on Social Security for Wage Earners): increased pension benefits and contribution rates; contributions to be paid to newly organized National Social Security Office (RSZ).

Decrees 10.1.1945 and 7.2.1945
Introduced pension schemes for miners and seamen on similar lines to the 28.12.1944 Decree for wage-earners.

Act 30.12.1952
Abolition of pension contribution ceiling for blue-collar workers.

Act 29.12.1953
Introduced wage-related pension formula for blue-collar workers; contribution rates increased.

Act 28.6.1954
Suspension of wage-related pension formula for blue-collar workers; increased minimum pension and introduced index linking for pension benefits.

Act 26.5.1955
Reintroduced wage-related pension formula for blue-collar workers; payments conditional on retirement.

Act 12.7.1957
Introduction of wage-related pension formula for white-collar workers; planned increases of contribution ceiling and introduction of old age and survivors' pensions, the payment of which would be partly unconditional upon retirement.

Act 22.2.1960
Slowed down increases of contribution ceiling for white-collar workers and reinforced 1957 system of unconditional old age and survivors' pensions.

Act 3.4.1962
Strengthened wage-relation, abolished system of minimum pensions for future pensioners, improved survivors' pension formula and allowed pensioners to work part-time.

Royal Decree no. 50, 24.10.1967
Royal Decree on Retirement and Survivors' Pension for Wage Earners: fused existing pension schemes for blue-collar and white-collar workers, miners and seamen; increased contribution rates and pension benefits (espec. survivors' pensions) and introduced holiday allowances.

Act 1.4.1969
Revenu garanti aux personnes agées, Gewaarborgd Inkomen voor Bejaarden (Guaranteed Income for the Elderly): income-tested scheme introduced.

Act 28.3.1973
Introduced annual adjustment of pensions to level of economic prosperity.

Act 22.12.1977
Introduced special transitional pension measures for the elderly unemployed and elderly disabled.

Act 8.8.1980
Introduced a solidarity contribution on the higher pensions in favour of the medical care scheme.

Dhoore Act 29.6.1981
Loi établissant les principes généraux de la sécurité sociale des travailleurs salariés, Algemene beginselenwet inzake de sociale zekerheid voor werknemers (Act on general social security principles for employees): introduced, in principle, a widowers' pension; increased the contribution ceiling for white-collar workers; reorganized state subsidies for pension schemes.

Act 10.2.1981 and Royal Decree no. 21, 23.3.1982.
Increased contribution rates, mainly for employees.

Royal Decree no. 32, 30.3.1982
Replaced widows' benefit (lump sum payment) by a survivors' pension awarded for one year.

Royal Decree no. 96, 28.9.1982
Abolished the contribution ceiling for white-collar workers.

Mainil Act 15.5.1984
Partially standardized the three pension schemes for employees, the self-employed and civil servants without integrating them; standardized male and female rights; administrative simplification.

Self-employed:

Act 11.3.1954
Made membership of existing voluntary pension insurance scheme compulsory for the self-employed.

Act 30.6.1956
Introduced compulsory pension scheme for the self-employed.

Act 28.3.1960
Introduced pay-as-you-go financing, partly replacing the existing funding financing.

Royal Decree no. 38, 27.7.1967
Introduced Social Security System for the Self-employed (SSZ) by fusing pension, family allowances and health care allowances schemes.

Royal Decree no. 72, 10.11.1967
Increased pension benefits, liberalized income test and increased state subsidies.

Act 9.6.1970
Plan to increase contribution rates and pension amounts, to liberalize entitlement conditions and to abolish income test.

Act 6.2.1976
Abolished remainder of funding financing.

Royal Decree no. 34, 30.3.1982
Replaced the widows' benefit (lump sum payment) by a survivors' pension awarded for one year.

II Sickness and invalidity

The Act of 9 August 1963 divided general health insurance into two sectors: medical care insurance covering virtually the entire population (see Section VII), and cash benefits limited to private employees and non-established civil servants, i.e. sickness cash benefits for the first year of work incapacity and invalidity cash benefits from the second year onwards. In addition to these benefits there is a wage continuation scheme guaranteeing a monthly wage for white-collar workers and a weekly wage for blue-collar workers in the case of work incapacity. Permanently disabled persons with either no or insufficient coverage under these schemes are entitled to separate allowances. Insurance against industrial accidents and occupational diseases is separately organized and will be dealt with in Section III.

Income maintenance

Income maintenance in the case of sickness or invalidity is guaranteed to a different degree for white-collar workers, blue-collar workers, civil servants and the self-employed. Different schemes are applicable according to the duration of the sickness or disablement, (wage continuation, sickness cash benefits, invalidity benefits).

A key notion is that of 'disability to work'. A person is considered to be disabled if he stops working and his earning capacity is reduced to one-third or less of what is considered as 'normal', which results in a 66% disability. A wage earner whose disability is below 50% is allowed to resume professional activities compatible with his state of health.

Revenue and expenditure of sickness and invalidity insurance schemes[a]

	Revenues					Expenditure		
	Contributions		State subsidies		Total	Benefits		Total
	absolute	%	absolute	%		absolute	%	
General scheme:								
Total	30 551	47.6	31 635	49.3	64 149	61 071	92.8	65 781
Sickness cash						25 269		
Invalidity						34 742		
Funeral expenses						1 060		
Self-empl.:								
Total	1 277	41.0	1 753	58.8	2 981	2 781	92.8	2 996
Sickness cash						431		
Invalidity						2 350		

[a] Figures are for 1981 and in million BFR.

Source: 'Herziening begrotingsvooruitzichten voor de uitkeringsverzekering (dienstjaar 1981)', in *RIVIZ, Algemeen Verslag 1981*, deel 5: Dienst voor Uitkeringen, Brussels, s.d., p. 93.

1. Wage continuation

In the case of work incapacity due to sickness or accident (other than industrial accidents or occupational diseases), white-collar workers receive a guaranteed monthly wage paid by the employer. Blue-collar workers receive a guaranteed weekly wage, after which period they fall back on sickness cash benefits. However, a large proportion of blue-collar workers are covered by national collective agreements guaranteeing a supplement to these benefits during the remainder of the first month. After these periods all wage earners fall back on sickness benefits only (see below). Civil servants are entitled to a sickness leave, which may amount to 30 days per year in service. The self-employed cannot rely on an income continuation scheme; the majority subscribe to a voluntary insurance scheme with a mutual aid society.

2. Sickness cash benefits

A wage-earner considered unable to return to normal professional activity (by both his own and a controlling doctor) receives a sickness cash benefit during the first year, the so-called 'primary incapacity period' (*incapacité primaire, primaire arbeidsongeschiktheid*). Benefits amount to 60% of the former gross wage, from a minimum of 18,121 BFR in 1983 to a ceiling of 42,034 BFR. In the case of pregnancy leave, benefits amount to 79.5%.

A civil servant still unable to return to work after sickness leave is 'placed at disposal', a situation which can theoretically last for an indefinite period. During this period the civil servant receives 60% of his full former wage.

The self-employed are entitled to flat-rate cash benefits after a period of three months. The only differentiation is made on the basis of dependents. Monthly benefits amounted to 10,899 BFR for a single self-employed person, and 13,419 for a self-employed person with dependents, i.e. to 25.07% and 30.87% of average wage (all figures for April 1983).

3. Invalidity benefits

After one year of sickness leave the claimant is entitled to invalidity benefits. These amount to 65% of lost wage for wage-earners with dependents and 43.5% for single persons up to a certain ceiling. For wage-earners who have been regularly employed, this invalidity benefit may not fall below a threshold which corresponds to the full minimum retirement pension for blue-collar workers. Funeral expense benefits are paid in the case of death.

Civil servants 'placed at disposal' are entitled to apply for early retirement where there is no possibility of their health improving, in which case the civil servant is covered by his retirement pension scheme (see above).

After one year of work incapacity, the self-employed receives an invalidity benefit when obliged to cease all professional activity. The flat-rate benefit received in the case of invalidity is somewhat higher than the previous sickness cash benefits. It amounts to 11,722 BFR for single persons, and 14,639 BFR for self-employed persons with dependents, i.e. to 26.96% and 33.67% of average monthly wage (1 April 1984).

Financing

Sickness and invalidity insurance for wage-earners is mainly financed in two ways:

- by contributions from wage-earners (1.15% and 2.20%) of wages respectively;
- by state subsidies for invalidity benefits and funeral expense benefits.

The National Institute for Sickness and Invalidity Insurance (RIZIV), reimburses the cost of sickness, invalidity and funeral expense benefits already paid by mutual aid societies. The scheme for civil servants is financed out of general revenues, whilst that for the self-employed is financed by contributions (41% of total revenue in 1981), and state subsidies (59%).

Administration

For the wage-earners' scheme see the general introduction. Since sickness and invalidity provisions for the civil servants are regulated by their statute, no separate administration is necessary. The self-employed scheme is administered by a separate board with a majority of representatives from the major organizations of the self-employed.

4. Disabled persons' allowances

The Act of 27 June 1969 and the Royal Decrees of 17 November 1969 and 24 December 1974, introduced five types of allowances.

The Ordinary Allowance (*Allocation aux handicapés, Tegemoetkoming aan Minder-Validen*), to which all persons of Belgian nationality (and some foreigners) above the age of 14, who are permanently disabled (physically or motorically) to a level of at least 30% and whose annual income falls below a given ceiling, are entitled. On

1 April 1983 this ceiling amounted to 97,351 BFR for a single person, and 112,457 BFR for a married person; labour income up to 250,000 BFR a year is exempted from this means-test. Disabled persons not entitled to the Ordinary Allowance (mainly mentally disabled), may apply for the Special Allowance (*Allocation spéciale pour handicapés, Bijzondere Tegemoetkoming aan Minder-Validen*), under similar conditions. Applicants must be at least 25 years old and have a permanent disability of at least 65%.

Both the Ordinary and the Special Allowance consist of:

- a basic amount equal to the Subsistence Minimum (see Section VI).
- a variable amount, which depends on the degree of disability (between 116,833 BFR for a 100% disability and 11,682 BFR for a 30% disability in 1983).

Once either the disabled person or their spouse/partner reaches normal pensionable age or becomes entitled to a pension, both the Ordinary and Special Allowances are converted into a Supplementary Allowance (*Allocation complémentaire, Aanvullende Tegemoetkoming*), which is means-tested and fixed in the same way as the above allowances, but with an exemption being made for income from labour.

The aged who are entitled to benefits under the GIB and who become disabled to a degree of 65%, receive a special supplement amounting to 43,328 BFR on 1 April 1983.

In special cases an Allowance for Assistance (*Allocation pour assistance, Tegemoetkoming voor Hulp van Derde*) is paid for the help of a person not belonging to the household. On 1 April 1983 the amount varied between a minimum of 32,894 BFR and a maximum of 65,792 BFR.

All allowances are related to the price index; in addition the Ordinary Allowance, Special Allowance and Allowance for Assistance are 'welfare-related'. As these allowances are means-tested, cumulation is excluded.

Financing and administration

These allowances are financed by the state out of general revenue. In 1981 this amounted to 10,693 million BFR for 93,086 beneficiaries, i.e. an average benefit of 114,872 BFR. Various public authorities are concerned with the administration of these schemes, and a series of advisory councils look after the application of existing laws and regulations, such as the Commission for Social Assistance for the Disabled (*Commissie voor Sociaal Hulpbetoon aan Minder-Validen*), and the High Council for the Disabled (*Hoge Raad voor Minder-Validen*).

Core laws

See Section VII

III Industrial accidents/Occupational diseases

1. Industrial accident insurance

Coverage

The Act of 10 April 1971 coordinated the existing legislation and introduced compulsory insurance against industrial accidents for all wage-earners who are members of the general system, miners and seamen; plus a number of persons not covered by social security (e.g. students in temporary employment). Civil servants are covered by their own statute (Act of 3 June 1967).

Coverage is not restricted to the workplace but also applies to the journey to and from the workplace.

Benefits

Benefits consist of general and special allowances. Special allowances are of relatively minor importance, with the exception of allowances compensating for the absence of annuity indexation. General allowances cover loss of earnings, medical care and funeral expenses. Benefits are determined according to the degree of disability with a maximum ceiling of 689,160 BFR on 1 April 1983. In the case of 100% disability, the allowance amounts to 418,596 BFR. Psychological damage is not covered. In more detail, benefits cover:

- funeral expenses equalling 30 times the average daily wage;
- survivors' pensions, the amount of which depends on the degree of kinship with the deceased;
- temporary disability to work: the injured worker receives a guaranteed wage during the first week or month and thereafter a benefit which amounts to 90% of average daily wage up to a ceiling;
- permanent disability to work; the wage earner receives, during a period of three years, an annual benefit based on his annual earnings during the preceding year on the degree of his work disability, ranging from 10% to 150%. After these three years the disability is assessed definitively, and the annual benefit is replaced by an annuity based on the insured capital provided by the insurance company.

Medical care is virtually free of charge.

Financing and administration

Employers pay insurance premiums to approved insurance companies which can adapt premiums to the nature and extent of risks. For workers not insured by their employers in this way, and for particular groups in general, a public Fund for Industrial Accidents (*Fonds des accidents du travail, Fonds voor Arbeidsongevallen*) has been set up, which is administered by representatives of trade unions and employers' associations. This Fund is financed out of a contribution of 0.30% on total wage. In 1981 contributions amounted to 4,340 million BFR (for 2,132,269 contributors and 108,791 entitled persons, which means an average contribution of 1,903 BFR and an average benefit of 39,893 BFR).

2. Occupational diseases

Coverage

All members of the general scheme for wage-earners are covered by the Occupational Diseases Insurance (*Assurance maladie professionnelle, Beroepsziekteverzekering*), together with a number of other groups, such as apprentices. Labour contract and apprenticeship are considered equivalent to the extent that they both lead to the same type of risk. Employers in industrial sectors with a recognized risk are obliged to insure with the Occupational Diseases Fund (*Fonds des maladies professionnelles,*

Fonds voor de Beroepsziekten). Persons not covered can insure against occupational diseases with the Fund on a voluntary basis. Civil servants have a separate scheme established by the Act of 3 June 1967.

Benefits

The following may be compensated: death of the entitled person and subsequent funeral expenses; complete/partial, temporary/permanent disability to work; medical, surgical, pharmaceutical and nursing expenses.

As far as possible, benefit criteria and benefit levels for the Occupational Diseases Scheme, have been made congruent with those of the Industrial Accidents Scheme, although the former scheme remains somewhat more generous. However, the clearly preventative character of the occupational diseases scheme is unique when compared with the other social security schemes.

Financing and administration

The Occupational Diseases Scheme is financed by:

- contributions by employers in industrial sectors with a high risk of occupational disease, amounting to 0.65% of payroll;
- state subsidy covering 60% of all silicosis compensation expenses;
- contributions by the voluntarily insured;

The Occupational Diseases Fund is the only insurance institution and is also responsible for all other preventative tasks. It is administered according to the principles of the 25 March 1963 Act on parity administration in Social Security.

In 1981, total revenue stood at 14,712 million BFR as against 14,527 million BFR expenditure. State subsidies constituted 52.4% of total revenue, contributions 47.6% (for 2,132,090 contributors, i.e. 3,117 BFR per person). A total of 81,286 persons were entitled to benefits i.e. an average benefit of 178,715 BFR.

Core laws

Act 24.12.1903
Introduced the principle of 'professional risk' for industrial accidents.

Act 24.7.1927
Introduced compensation for occupational diseases.

Act 24.12.1963
Occupational Diseases Act: promoted preventative action and extended the list of occupation and enlarged the list of occupational diseases. Contributions collected by National Office for Social Security, introduction of parity administration.

Royal Decree 28.3.1969
Codified list of occupational diseases.

Royal Decree 9.12.1969
Brought coverage for industrial accident coverage in line with that for the general sickness and disability scheme for wage-earners.

Royal Decree 3.6.1970
Coordinated existing occupational injury legislation.

Act 10.4.1971
Coordinated existing legislation and introduced compulsory insurance against industrial accidents paid for by employers.

IV Unemployment insurance/Employment policy

In 1981, expenditure on unemployment amounted to 146,687 million BFR or 4.1% of GDP. When compared with 1969, these figures reflect the higher level of unemployment, in addition to a change in expenditure distribution. (Source: Ministerie van Sociale Voorzorg, *Statistisch Jaarboek van de Sociale Zekerheid 1970*, Brussels, 1972, p. 187, and *idem*. 1981, Brussels, 1983, p. 81).

Benefit expenditure on unemployment in 1969 and 1981 in million BFR

	1969		1981	
		%		%
Unemployment benefits	7 193	90.1	95 959	65.4
Unemployment pensions	-	-	23 718	16.2
Employment programmes:	449	5.6	23 788	16.2
- Public authority employment programme	(449)	(5.6)	(12 319)	(8.4)
- Special temporary employment scheme			(11 469)	(7.8)
Retraining programmes	344	4.3	3 221	2.2
Total	7 986	100.0	146 687	100.0
as % of GDP	0.7		4.1	

A relatively high percentage of the registered unemployed are covered either by unemployment insurance or by employment programmes.
Unemployment insurance was first established by local trade unions, and this system remained in operation until the Second World War. However, the inadequacy of collected funds induced government to heavily subsidize these initiatives and to establish special social assistance schemes for the unemployed. Immediately after the Second World War unemployment insurance providing flat-rate, universal benefits was made compulsory for wage-earners. In 1971 wage-related benefits were introduced. In recent years transitional pension schemes have been added.

Coverage

All wage-earners (including non-established civil servants and miners, but excluding seamen who have special, but similar schemes), under normal pensionable age who are compulsorily insured under the general social security scheme are members of the unemployment insurance scheme. Actual entitlement to benefits is dependent upon a minimum work record, which varies with the age of the unemployed person. The beneficiary must not be in receipt of any regular income, nor be voluntarily unemployed. He must be prepared to accept any suitable offer of employment and has to present himself daily at the municipal unemployment control.

Some Transitional Pension Schemes (*Prépensions, Brugpensioenen*, BP), were established during the mid-1970s. Under specified conditions wage-earners aged five years below normal pensionable age may either apply for or be compelled to take, a transitional pension until normal pensionable age.

Number of unemployed (monthly averages for 1983)

	Males	Females	Total
Fully unemployed entitled to unemployment benefit	234 955	270 007	504 962
- others	33 818	64 031	97 849
Partially unemployed	n. a.	n. a.	78 024
Transitional pensions	97 717	22 017	119 734
Total			800 569

Source: Rijksdienst voor Arbeidsvoorziening, *De werkloosheid in 1983*, Brussels, 1984.

Benefits

Since 1971 unemployment benefits represent 60% of last gross earnings during the first year of unemployment. For the second year of unemployment, the rate is reduced to 40 for unemployed persons without dependents. However, for an increasing number of categories measures have been taken during the last years that testify to a shift from earnings-related to flat-rate benefits. Indeed, from the third year onwards unemployment benefits become flat-rate: single persons receive an amount equalling 50% of the national minimum wage, and persons living with another income earner receive an amount equalling the Right to a Subsistence Minimum (see Section VI). Second year rates are extended, however, by 78 days for each year of previous employment. Wage-earners who have either been employed for at least 20 years, or who have a disability of at least 33%, continue to receive the 40% (of last gross earnings) benefit rate whilst they are unemployed.

A special category are young graduates. After a waiting period, graduates who are head of a family are entitled to minimal unemployment benefits; graduates without dependents receive a so-called 'waiting allowance' which is much lower, namely at the amount of the Right to a Subsistence Minimum. These 'waiting allowances' are further reduced for graduates under the age of 21 years.

In addition, all unemployment benefits and waiting allowances for persons living with another income earner are reduced by 6%, except for households with replacement incomes only.

Benefits vary between a minimum and maximum level; in April 1983 these amounted to 21,136 BFR and and 25,414 BFR a month for the head of a family, corresponding to 48% and 58% of average monthly earnings for a male manual worker in industry.

In the transitional pension schemes benefits consist of unemployment benefit for the first year to which the transitional pensioner would have been entitled and a supplement equalling half the difference between unemployment benefit and last net earnings.

Services

From 1935 onwards the National Unemployment Assistance Fund and its successor, the National Employment Office (RVA), have been responsible for organizing labour exchanges. During the 1950s and 1960s much emphasis was placed on training and retraining facilities. In recent years some special employment programmes have either been activated or developed, especially for the young unemployed.

Persons in employment programmes in 1983 (monthly averages)

	Males	Females	Total
Public authority employ. programmes	16 466	12 184	28 650
Young people on probation			
- full-time	13 526	11 133	24 659
- part-time	3 806	5 953	9 759
Special temporary employ. scheme	5 775	8 065	13 840
Third employment scheme	3 278	4 288	7 566
Total	42 851	41 623	84 474

Source: Rijksdienst voor Arbeidsvoorziening, *De Werkloosheid in 1983*, Brussels, 1984.

In the first programme the employing public authority pays out a normal wage through the unemployment insurance administration and is partially reimbursed by unemployment insurance funds. In the second programme, enterprises and public administration with at least 50 employees, have been compelled to give temporary employment to young people on probation (*Stagiaires, Stage voor Jongeren*). They constitute at least 3% of total staff and receive at least 90% of the normal wage. The third programme, the so-called Special Temporary Employment Scheme (*Cadre spécial temporaire, Bijzonder Tijdelijk Kader*, BTK), allows central, local and semi-government bodies, foundations and cultural and social welfare organizations to employ registered unemployed for special projects. Wages are covered totally by the state budget during the first year and thereafter partially also by the respective administration/organization. The last programme, the so-called Third Employment Scheme (*Troisième Circuit de Travail, Derde Arbeidscircuit*, DAC) allows a wide range of governmental bodies and non-commercial organizations to employ registered longterm unemployed on projects concerning public projects. Wages are covered totally by the state budget.

Financing and administration

Unemployment benefits and employment services are financed by contributions from employees and employers (in 1984 0.87% and 1.23% of earnings) and state subsidies.

Contributions are paid to the National Social Security Office (RSZ), which in turn transfers contributions to the National Employment Office (*Office National de l'emploi; Rijksdienst voor Arbeidsvoorziening*, RVA). In 1981 the state subsidy which is designed to cover the deficit, amounted to 122,118 million BFR or 81.2% of total revenue.

The sector is administered by the RVA which has 30 regional offices each of which is made up of an unemployment bureau and an employment service. The former adjudicates on unemployment benefits, the latter is responsible for most of the employment programmes and services. Unemployment benefits are paid out by the approved trade unions and by the Subsidiary Fund for Payment of Unemployment Benefits (*Caisse auxiliaire de paiement des allocations de chômage, Hulpkas voor Werkloosheidsuitkeringen*, HKWU).

Unemployment sector financing 1969 and 1981 in million BFR

	1969		1981	
		%		%
Personal contribution	3 127	36.0	14 842	9.9
Employer's contribution	3 079	35.5	13 434	8.9
Total contribution	6 206	71.5	28 276	18.8
State subsidies	2 475	28.5	122 118	81.2
Total	8 681	100.0	150 394	100.0
- as % GDP	0.7		4.2	

Source: Ministerie van Sociale Voorzorg, *Statistisch Jaarboek van de Sociale Zekerheid 1970*, Brussels, 1972, p. 72 and *idem*. 1981, Brussels, 1983, p. 25.

Core laws

Regent's Decree 28.12.1944
Introduced compulsory unemployment insurance.

Regent's Decree 26.5.1945
Organized post-war unemployment insurance system.

Royal Decree 20.12.1963
Coordinated and codified existing legislation on unemployment insurance and employment services.

Royal Decree 11.9.1964
Abolished existing diversification of unemployment benefits by category of municipality.

Royal Decree 3.10.1968
Extended entitlement to unemployment benefits to school-leavers.

Act 1.7.1969
Central government made responsible for financing the deficit of unemployment benefits scheme.

Royal Decree 1.11.1971
Replaced existing flat-rate benefits system by wage-related benefits.

Royal Decree 27.6.1973
Abolished remainder of flat-rate benefits and introduced minimum benefits.

Royal Decree 20.12.1975
Related benefits to increase of GDP ('welfare-related' benefits).

Royal Decree 16.1.1975
Act 30.3.1976
Act 22.12.1977
} Introduced transitional pension schemes

Act 30.3.1976
Introduced compulsory employment programme for 'young people on probation'.

Act 22.12.1977
Introduction of Special Temporary Employment Scheme (BTK).

Royal Decree 24.12.1980
Divided the unemployed without dependents into two categories: single persons, and the unemployed living with another income-earner; reduced benefits for the latter; doubled the 'waiting period' for graduates over the age of 21.

Royal Decree no. 25, 24.3.1982
Introduced the Third Employment Scheme (DAC).

Royal Decree 30.3.1982
Replaced unemployment benefits for young graduates without dependents by 'waiting allowances'; admitted graduates from first degree vocational and technical schools to the waiting period; reduced all unemployment benefits and waiting allowances for the unemployed living with another income-earner by 6%; fixed daily allowance at one-twenty-sixth instead of one-twenty-fifth of average monthly earnings.

V Families and children

In 1981, expenditure on family allowances amounted to 101,852 million BFR or 2.8% of GDP. Of this sum 79,194 million BFR were spent on the the employees' scheme, 11,578 million BFR on the self-employed scheme, 11,035 million BFR on civil servants' and 45 million BFR on guaranteed child allowance scheme. The number of child allowances paid in 1981 was 2,320,178 of which 1,828,328 were paid under the employees scheme, 190,112 under the self-employed scheme, 299,890 under the civil servants' scheme, and 1,848 under the guaranteed child allowance scheme.

Coverage

Belgium was one of the pioneering countries for family allowances. As early as 1921 some employers organized the first compensation fund for family allowances (*Caisse de compensation, Compensatiekas*). A compulsory child allowance scheme was introduced for wage earners in 1930 and for the self-employed in 1937. Civil servants had their own similar schemes.

In all three schemes entitlement to family allowances was restricted to employed persons. In more recent years, however, entitlement has been extended to cover pensioners, handicapped persons, the unemployed, prisoners, deserted wives and students.

Expenditure on and number of family allowances in 1981 (schemes for employees and self-employed)

	Expenditure in mill. BFR		Number of benefits	
	Employees	Self-employed	Employees	Self-employed
Total	79 193.9	11 578.3	1 920 904	379 946
	% distribution			
Child allowances	80.2	86.1	95.2	97.6
- ordinary	68.6	76.1	86.4	91.8
- orphans	5.4	8.2	3.1	4.2
- handicapped parent	6.2	1.8	5.7	1.6
Supplements	17.8	12.7		
- handicapped child	3.9	5.0		
- holiday allowance	7.0	-		
- study allowance	6.9	7.7		
Maternity allowance	2.0	1.2	4.8	2.4
	100.0	100.0	100.0	100.0

Source: Ministerie van Sociale Voorzorg, *Statistisch Jaarboek van de Sociale Zekerheid 1981*, Brussels, 1983, pp. 69, 71, 82, 121, 123, 125.

In 1971 a Guaranteed Family Allowance Scheme (*Allocations familiales garanties, Gewaarborgde Kinderbijslag*, GKB) was introduced for families not entitled to benefits under one of the three previous schemes. It provides minimal coverage and is means-tested.

Child allowances in general are paid up to the age of 14, but entitlement is extended to: the age of 16 for children with low incomes; the age of 21 for children in apprenticeship; and the age of 25 for full-time students, children running households and severely handicapped children.

Benefits

There are three types of family allowance:

- child allowance (ordinary, for orphans and for children of handicapped parents);
- supplements (age supplements, supplements for handicapped children, holiday and study allowances);
- maternity grants.

Ordinary child allowances are the same under all the schemes, varying with the number of children (the only exception being the allowance for the first child in the case of the self-employed and of the GKB schemes). Special child allowances for orphans and children whose parents are unable to work for a certain period, were introduced in 1946 and 1947. On 1 April 1983 the respective monthly rates were as follows:

Ordinary child allowance:	1st child	1 972[a]
	2nd child	3 648
	3rd child	4 995
	4th child	5 094
	5th child etc.	5 132
Orphans' allowance:		7 135
Child allowances for children of the handicapped:	1st and 2nd child	3 815
	3rd child	4 995
	4th child	5 094
	5th child, etc.	5 132

[a] Self-employed and Guaranteed Child Allowances Scheme 574 BFR.

The basic allowance is increased by an age supplement which in 1983 amounted to 369 BFR for children aged 6-10; 650 BFR for those aged 10-14; and 1,053 BFR for children over the age of 14. These supplements are the same in all schemes. However, the age supplement for the first child is not granted under the self-employed and GKB schemes. All severely handicapped children (at least 65%) receive a flat-rate supplement (introduced in 1969) up to the age of 25. In 1983, this amounted to 8,356 BFR. In addition the employees' and civil servants' schemes both grant holiday allowances (introduced in 1962), in May and September respectively. They equal the child allowances, including the age supplement. The scheme for the self-employed covers only study allowances.

In recent years crisis measures have been taken in the family allowance schemes. In 1982, the monthly family allowance was cut by 500 BFR for each beneficiary. In 1983, this cut was reduced to 375 BFR. In 1983 the holiday and study allowances for the first child were abolished (except when the beneficiary is unemployed, a pensioner or disabled, and when the first child is disabled or an orphan). The holiday and study allowances for the second child and subsequent children were incorporated in the basic allowances. In 1984 the age-limits for receipt of age supplements were raised from 10 to 12, and from 14 to 16 years respectively.

Maternity grants are the same in all schemes. They take the form of a lump sum payment, the amount of which varies with the number of births (in 1983 this amounted to 25,672 BFR for the first child; 17,356 BFR for the second; 9,336 BFR for the third and any additional children, i.e. 59%, 40%, and 21% of monthly average earnings for a male manual worker in industry).

Allowances have been linked to the consumer price index since 1957. In the employees' and GKB schemes, benefits are normally paid to the mother, in the scheme for the self-employed they are paid to the father. Civil servants receive allowances together with their salary.

Financing and administration

The employees' scheme is financed almost entirely by employers' contributions. In 1984 the contribution rate amounted to 7% of total gross earnings. All employers are obliged to join one of the 50 approved compensation funds which pay family allowances to employees. The employers' contributions are paid to the National Social Security Office (RSZ), which transfers them to the National Family Allowances Office for Wage Earners (*Office national d'allocations familiales pour travailleurs salariés, Rijksdienst voor Kinderbijslag voor Werknemers*, RKW), which in turn distributes them among the compensation funds.

In contrast, the scheme for the self-employed is considerably subsidized by the state (34% in 1981). The remainder is provided by contributions from the self-employed which account for 22.6% of their overall social security contributions. Family allowances for civil servants and benefits under the GKB scheme are financed out of general revenues.

Core laws

Royal Decree 22.12.1938
Coordinated legislation on child allowances for the self-employed.

Royal Decree 19.12.1939
Coordinated legislation on child allowances for wage-earners.

Regent's Decree 29.12.1944
Introduced maternity grants.

Regent's Decree 27.8.1946
Introduced orphans' allowances.

Regent's Decree 28.2.1947
Introduced special child allowance rates for children of the handicapped.

Act 27.3.1951
Entitled students and children running households to allowances up to the age of 21.

Royal Decree 10.4.1957
Introduced age supplements and linked allowances to consumer price index.

Act 25.7.1962
Introduced holiday allowances.

Act 9.3.1964
Entitled students to allowances up to the age of 25.

Act 4.7.1969
Introduced supplements for severely handicapped children.

Act 14.5.1971
Entitled children running households to allowances up to the age of 25.

Act 20.7.1971
Introduced guaranteed child allowances.

Act 28.12.1973
Introduced central government financing of allowances for the unemployed.

Act 16.7.1974
Allowances became 'welfare-related'.

Act 28.3.1975
Introduced study allowances.

Act 29.3.1976, Royal Decrees 8.4 and 27.4.1976
Coordinated legislation covering family allowances for the self-employed.

Royal Decree no. 35, 1.4.1982
Reduced allowances by a flat-rate 500 BFR a month for each beneficiary.

Royal Decree no. 131, 30.12.1982
Abolished holiday and study allowances for the first child; incorporated them into the basic allowances for the second child and subsequent children.

Royal Decree no. 228, 9.12.1983
Reduced the monthly flat-rate reduction to 375 BFR.

VI Social assistance

Under the 1925 Act a Public Assistance Committee (*Commission d'assistance publique, Commissie van Openbare Onderstand*, COO), was set up in each commune to provide financial assistance for the needy, take measures to prevent destitution and provide help for medical care (see Health). The members of these local committees were nominated by the communal board and had complete discretionary power to decide whether or not a person or family was in need and the type and amount of assistance to be awarded. Consequently, assistance benefits varied widely from one commune to another.

In the mid-1970s three important acts were adopted: the 1974 Act which introduced a 'Right to a Subsistence Minimum' (*Droit à un minimum de moyens d'existence, Recht op het Bestaansminimum*, RBM); the 1975 Act which fused the 2,359 existing Belgian communes, creating 596 larger ones, and the 1976 Act which transformed the public assistance committees into Public Centres for Social Welfare (*Centres publiques d'aide sociale, Openbare Centra voor Maatschappelijk Welzijn*, OCMW).

All residents are entitled to the 'Right to a Subsistence Minimum' (RBM), if they are either Belgian citizens, citizens from a member EEC country, displaced persons, or political refugees who have been living in Belgium for the last five years. Benefits are income-tested. In 1983 the income limit amounted to 12,500 BFR a year for a couple, 10,000 BFR for single persons and persons living together and having unmarried dependent children under 21, and 6,250 BFR for other persons. Where income exceeds these limits, benefits are reduced accordingly.

The basic amounts are set at the same level as for the Guaranteed Income for the Elderly (GIB). In 1983 this meant that married couples could receive 16,805 BFR a month, and single persons 12,099 BFR a month. Contrary to the GIB scheme, claimants living together with persons other than unmarried dependent children receive only half the rate for married couples. Thus, they could receive 8,403 BFR a month in 1983.

Applications are made to the local Public Centres for Social Welfare (*Centres publiques d'aide sociale, Openbare Centra voor Maatschappelijk Welzijn*, OCMW), which carry out income-tests, assess and pay out benefits. The scheme is financed by the OCMW; half of the amount is reimbursed by central government (Department of Public Health). In 1982 expenditure amounted to 2.7 billion BFR.

Number of RBM-recipients by rate of benefit and category (Aug. 1979)

Rate/category	A. F.	%
Full benefit rate:		
I married couples	744	3.79
II single persons	7 180	36.58
III living together	4 314	21.98
Subtotal	12 238	62.35
Partial benefit rate:		
I married couples	657	3.35
II single persons	5 145	26.21
III living together	1 589	8.09
Subtotal	7 391	37.65
Total	19 629	100.00

Source: Department of Public Health

The fusion of 2,359, frequently small, Belgian communes into larger ones resulted in the more efficient staffing and organization of these committees. Even prior to 1 January 1977, when the new communes and public assistance committees became operational, the latter had been transformed by the Act of 8 July 1976, into Public Centres for Social Welfare (OCMW). This act established a legal right to social aid, which obliged the OCMW to provide material and other assistance necessary to provide a decent living 'worthy of a human being', appeal against their decisions being possible with special appeal courts.

Apart from this, the Act did not drastically change the organization of financial assistance. A majority of OCMW continue to provide assistance benefits that are somewhat higher than those guaranteed under the 'Right to a Subsistence Minimum' (RBM) and the Guaranteed Income for the Elderly (GIB), above all by providing special allowances for rent, heating and food.

In 1977 all OCMW together spent a total of 5,754.5 million BFR on assistance which represented 20.2% of their total current expenditure. They are subsidized by a national assistance fund and by the communes which cover any deficit.

Core laws

Act 10.3.1925
Established a Social Assistance Committee within each commune.

Act 7.8.1974
Introduced the Right to a Subsistence Minimum.

Act 30.12.1975
Fused existing communes, creating larger ones.

Royal Decree 28.1.1976
Extended the Right to a Subsistence Minimum to citizens of member EEC countries, displaced persons and political refugees.

Act 8.7.1976
Transformed social assistance committees into Public Centres for Social Welfare.

VII Medical care insurance/Health services

The Belgian health system has a strong private character but is financed mainly out of public resources. The patient is free to choose the medical service but is only reimbursed for amounts agreed upon in the fee schedule. Public authorities have a number of responsibilities, which frequently interfere with policy making: they operate some of the health care services themselves, subsidize virtually the entire sector, and issue health care regulations.

Estimation of the costs of health care (1 July 1980) in million BFR

	National sickness and invalidity insurance	Central gov.	Prov- inces	Munic- ipal- ities	Semi-public/ private sector	Total
Curative health care	156 893	25 485	1 427	11 553	62 757	258 115
General, preventive, and occupational health care		21 566	1 383	4 609	231 453	259 012
Environmental hygiene		12 955	3 940	83 108	97 444	147 447
Special medical and social assistance	62 460	9 280	3 900	20 669		96 310
Education, research and miscellaneous		17 881	342		3 549	21 771
Total	219 353	87 167	10 992	69 939	395 203	782 655

Source: Ministerie van Volksgezondheid en van het Gezin, *Statistisch Jaarboek van Volksgezondheid*, Brussels, 1981, p. 393.

1. Medical care insurance

Coverage

Coverage by medical care insurance is virtually universal, approximately 98% of the Belgian population are covered by the health insurance system today, either on a compulsory or voluntary basis.

Two categories of insured persons are distinguishable:

- primary entitled persons (*titulaires indemnisables primaires, primaire uitkeringsgerechtigden*), i.e. wage-earners and all other persons for whom insurance is compulsory, e.g. the self-employed, the disabled, the unemployed, retired persons and their widows;
- dependent persons, mainly children and housewives.

Although medical care insurance is universal, not all persons are covered to the same extent. Unlike wage-earners and civil servants, the self-employed (and their dependents) are compulsorily covered only for the most expensive health care items (e.g. hospital care, operations, and the so-called 'social diseases' such as cancer and TB).

Benefits

A (large) number of medical services (curative and preventative care, general and specialized care) are covered by medical care insurance. For these services the patient has all or a part of his expenses reimbursed by his mutual aid society. For a number of particularly expensive medical services (hospital and operation costs), the so-called system of the 'third payer' (*tiers payant, derde betaler*) has been introduced, whereby the costs are paid directly by the insurance fund.

Number of persons entitled to medical care (30 June 1981)[a]

	Entitled persons	Wives and husbands	Dependent Persons	
			Ascendents	Descendents
Primary entitled persons and equivalent persons	4 045 140[b]	1 252 099	26 491	2 600 929
Pensioners	976 753	342 807	1 430	49 713
Widows and orphans	408 387	2 416	451	48 611
Disabled persons	9 313	772	71	1 053
Non-protected persons	69 127	8 819	102	20 467
Total	5 508 720	1 606 913	28 545	2 720 773
%	55.8	16.3	0.3	27.6

[a] General scheme and scheme for the self-employed (main occupation). Not included are railwaymen, seamen, conscripts, and the regular military stationed abroad.

[b] Under the general scheme this covers the employed, sick and unemployed, blue-collar workers (1,654,402), white-collar workers (1,124,599) and miners (26,998), the disabled (167,383), professional cyclists, students and main entitled civil servants (total 543,113). Under the self-employed scheme it includes members of religious orders, and excludes those for whom self-employment is an additional occupation.

Source: Ministerie van Sociale Voorzorg, *Statistisch Jaarboek van de Sociale Zekerheid 1981*, Brussels, 1983, pp. 46, 112.

Services that are reimbursed are indicated on a nomenclature, a national fee schedule established after agreement between the medical profession and mutual aid societies. Reimbursement for the cost of drugs differs according to whether the drug is made up by a pharmacist or prepared by a manufacturer, in which case the patient pays a higher share of the cost. Hospitalization in a general ward, whether in public or in private hospitals, used to be fully supported by the insurance programme and the Department of Public Health. In recent years, however, patients have been charged a share of the cost.

Full reimbursement of expenses of a number of medical care items is the exception enjoyed by only some population groups, such as the disabled, widows, orphans and pensioners whose income does not exceed a given ceiling. The standard situation is that the patient pays a so-called moderating ticket (*ticket modérateur; remgeld*), the amount of which has been increased substantially for all patients in recent years in order to check consumption of medical services.

Financing

Medical care insurance is financed as follows:

- contributions by wage-earners and employers amounting to 2.55% and 3.80% of total wage; for civil servants the employers contribution is paid by the state.
- personal contributions by some groups such as the self-employed (3.30% of incomes up to 1,569,246 BFR a year on 1 January 1984);
- state subsidies covering 80% of the medical care expenses for the disabled, widows, orphans, pensioners and their dependents.

Administration

Contributions are paid to the National Social Security Office (RSZ) and the National Social Insurance Office for the Self-employed (RSVZ). Both offices transfer money to the National Institute for Sickness and Invalidity Insurance (RIZIV) which is controlled by a board of directors, representing the national federations of mutual aid societies, wage-earners, employees, self-employed, the hospitals, physicians and allied medical professions, and which negotiates with the medical professions on fees, regulates the general policies of the national federations and provides various services for its members. RIZIV transmits its part of the money to the six national federations.

Five of the six national federations of mutual aid societies are non-governmental unions or alliances of regional federations of mutual aid societies: the National Federation of Christian Mutual Aid Societies (*Alliance national des mutualités chrétiennes; Nationaal Verbond van Christelijke Mutualiteiten*), with nearly half of total membership; the National Federation of Socialist Mutual Aid Societies (*Union nationale des mutualités socialistes; Landsbond van Socialistische Mutualiteiten*); the National Federation of Neutral Mutual Aid Societies (*Union nationale des mutualités neutres; Landsbond van Neutrale Mutualiteiten*); the National Federation of Occupational Mutual Aid Societies (*Union nationale des mutualités professionnelles; Landsbond van Professionele Mutualiteiten*) and the National Federation of Liberal Mutual Aid Societies (*Union nationale des mutualités libérales; Landsbond van Liberale Mutualiteiten*). (The sixth is the Auxilary Fund of Sickness and Disability Insurance, organized by the government for those persons who are not satisfied with any of the long-established funds of the ideological type.)

These federations are based on some 2,000 local mutual aid societies which receive claims and refund medical care expenses to their members, or make certain payments directly to health care providers. People are free to enter the mutual aid society of their choice. Notwithstanding their local basis, mutual aid societies are very much ruled from the top, democratic control by members being almost non-existent.

Among the organizations of the medical professions the following play a decisive role in national health policy making:

- the Order of Physicians (*Ordre des médecins, Orde der Geneesheren*), the official body concerned with medical ethics has almost absolute power in this field.

- 'medical syndicates' which represent physicians in negotiations on fee schedules, but which in fact have a much larger scope of interest.

2. Curative health care

General curative health care is provided by general practitioners, home care and pharmacies. General practitioners, who numbered 12,998 in 1982, (i.e. one per 758 inhabitants), are normally engaged in private individual practice; private group practices are rare. The family doctor can be chosen freely by the patient, even the 'socially insured' are not obliged to register with a practitioner. Home care is still underdeveloped, probably due to the abundance of hospital beds. It is organized by the Public Centres for Social Welfare (OCMW), and private organizations such as the Yellow and White Cross, whose services are financed to a large degree by payments from mutual aid societies. Belgium is well covered with private pharmacies which numbered 5,543 in 1982 (i.e. one per 1,778 inhabitants).

Specialized curative health care is provided by specialists, hospitals and other services. In 1982 there were 10,777 specialists in Belgium. Nearly all of them combine a private office with a staff appointment in hospitals. Dental care also is covered by the Belgian health insurance programme. As is the case for general practitioners and dentists, the patient can go directly to the specialist of his choice.

Hospitals are run either by public authorities (the state, provinces, local municipalities or inter-municipal associations, social welfare centres) or private bodies (religious orders, mutual aid societies and insurance societies). The former represent 37% of a total of 94,037 hospital beds (i.e. one bed per 105 inhabitants in 1982). Hospitals may be general, specialized, geriatic, psychiatric or sanatoriums. Each hospital must be approved by the Department of Public Health and the Family.

Other curative health care is provided by geriatric and rehabilitation services (R-services), services for those suffering from chronic diseases, old people's homes, day and night centres, and social help centres.

3. Preventive health care

This is organized in the same heterogeneous way as the rest of Belgian health care. The most important provisions are concerned with children's welfare (National Programme for Children's Welfare); medical school examination, mental health care, early cancer detection, occupational health care, marriage and family care and congenital metabolic handicaps.

Financing

The general rule is that the national, regional and local authorities subsidize the construction and equipment of health care institutions, even when these are run by private bodies. State subsidies usually amount to 60% of the building costs (75% for public hospitals); provincial and municipal administration can grant additional subsidies. The remaining 40% is met through state guaranteed loans from private companies.

Current expenditure for preventive health care is normally carried by the state, with the exception of occupational medical care and mental health care services. Curative health care is financed by medical care insurance, by the patients themselves, the state, the Public Centres for Social Welfare (for the poor living within their administrative area) and a number of other organizations.

Administration

The Belgian health care system is administered at the national, regional, provincial and municipal level.

Responsibilities on the national level are shared among several Departments, the most important being the Department of Public Health and the Family, followed by the Department of Social Security (for sickness and invalidity insurance), the Department of Labour and Employment (occupational medical care), the Department of Economic Affairs (supervision of prices of drugs) and the Department of Education (training of medical personnel).

The main functions of the Department of Public Health and the Family are: the preparation, implementation and supervision of legislation and regulations on public health in general and the administration of grants and subsidies to lower public administrations and private bodies.

As a consequence of devolution, important responsibilities in the matter of health policy, are now being delegated to the regions, such as the implementation of laws on environmental sanitation, home care, homes for the aged, mental health care, preventive health care, health information and education and the entire hospital sector. On the regional level responsibilities are also scattered over a number of departments.

There is no uniform and organized structure for health care on the provincial level. The Provincial Health Officer (usually engaged in a private practice) is appointed by the King as a provincial representative of the National Department of Health in the field of 'public hygiene'. A small public health department is responsible for health inspection, grants, subsidies, and the occasional setting up of new health care centres.

On the local level the mayor, aldermen and town council are responsible for health care covering food regulations, contagious diseases, labour protection, in addition to more general preventative health services and the preventative health services for school children. Public hospitals are mostly administered by the Public Centres for Social Welfare, which frequently provide additional services for family care, the aged etc.

Core laws

1849
Established the principle of partial state funding to cover the costs of mutual aid societies.

3.4.1851
Exempted government-approved mutual aid societies from certain charges.

25.6.1894
Enabled mutual aid societies to set up common services.

18.3.1898
Introduced state subsidies for government-approved mutual aid societies.

5.5.1912
State subsidies made compulsory for mutual aid societies with a disability fund.

28.12.1944
Introduced the principle of compulsory insurance.

Organic Decree 21.3.1945
Introduced compulsory sickness and invalidity insurance for all public sector wage-earners.

Royal Decree 31.12.1952
Introduced changes in the nomenclature of medical services reimbursable by mutual aid funds.

Royal Decree 14.12.1954
Created a system of medical control for cases of work incapacity, a national service for professional re-education and a National Invalidity Fund.

Royal Decree 22.9.1955
Reorganized Sickness and Disability Insurance.

Act 14.2.1961
The so-called *Loi Unique, Eenheidswet*, which contained a number of important regulations such as a stricter control over the provision of medical services and provided a legal framework for agreements with the medical professions.

Act 9.8.1963
Introduced a number of new principles: the financing from general funds such as the direct linkage of reimbursement to medical fees, the organization of the compulsory system of sickness and invalidity into two sectors; Act implemented by Royal Decree of 4.11.1963.

Act 23.12.1963
The Hospital Act provided a legal basis for planning in the hospital sector.

Royal Decree 30.7.1964
Extended the 1963 Act to cover the self-employed for large risks and social diseases.

Royal Decree 22.3.1965
Introduced compulsory medical care for civil servants.

Act 27.6.1969 and Royal Decree 24.12.1974
Introduced the new scheme for disabled persons' allowances with five types of allowance.

Royal Decree 28.6.1969
Introduction of a medical care scheme for persons 'not yet covered'.

Royal Decree 20.1.1971
Introduced sickness cash and disability benefits for the self-employed.

Dhoore Act 29.6.1981
Reorganized the state subsidies for the National Institute for Sickness and Invalidity Insurance (RIVIZ).

VIII Education

In Belgium education is provided by central government, private bodies (i.e. mainly Catholic organizations), by each of the nine provinces, and municipalities. The relationship between the different 'school networks' has been a major political issue in Belgian history. The 'school-war', (1953-1958) was brought to an end by the 'school-pact', a gentleman's agreement between the three main political parties (Christian

Democrats, Socialists, and Liberals) in 1958. This agreement became law the following year on 29 May 1959. It introduced an obligatory and equitable distribution of state grants for education among all kinds of approved schools. It recognized the right of every authority (state, private organization, province and municipality) to control its own system of schools and to draft its own curricula in accordance with requirements laid down by the Ministry of Education. It leaves each authority absolutely free to decide on its teaching methods. Parents are completely free to choose between the state school system and the private system. The state has the prime responsibility of ensuring that parents throughout the country, have sufficient schools of all kinds within reasonable travelling distance for their children.

Estimates of the number of students (1981-1982)

	State	Provinces	Municipal.	Private	Total
Nursery	50 066	395	113 959	223 244	387 664
Primary	125 710	2 777	264 794	441 430	834 711
Secondary	205 303	48 702	72 710	522 188	848 903
- Traditional	15 847	16 092	33 004	351 589	416 532
- Comprehens.	189 456	32 610	39 706	170 599	432 371
Higher educ.	49 545	13 405	10 727	127 569	201 246
- Non-univ.					
- Shorter	15 458	11 263	7 756	45 397	79 874
- Longer	6 774	2 142	2 971	14 239	26 126
- University (1980-1981)	27 313	-	-	67 933	95 246
Total	430 624	65 279	462 190	1 314 431	2 272 524

Source: Nationaal Instituut voor de Statistiek, *Statistisch Jaarboek van België*, boekdeel 102, 1982, pp. 158-185.

Education used to be compulsory throughout Belgium for nine school-years starting from the age of six. Only in 1983 was education made compulsory for children up to the age of 18 years. It is composed of the following four levels: nursery school (three years); primary education (six years); secondary education (six years); and higher education. In addition, there are special programmes organized for working and unemployed people. On completion of the primary school at the age of twelve, a pupil passes into secondary education. At this level there are various options as Belgium has two different and parallel curricula for secondary education: the traditional system and the comprehensive system.

The traditional secondary education system (two times three years), is characterized by parallel, yet socially stratified and hierarchical options (grammar, technical and vocational school). In this system both stratification and institutional diversification takes places after six years of primary education. Though it is possible to enter higher education after technical training, the general rule is entrance after grammar school.

In 1979 a comprehensive secondary education system (Renewed Secondary Education, *Enseignement Secondaire Renové, Vernieuwd Secundair Onderwijs*, VSO), was set up which runs parallel with the traditional system. All options available under the traditional system, with the exception of vocational school, were inserted into this system. In 1981-82 some 51% of secondary level pupils attended comprehensive secondary schools.

Since 1971 Higher Education has been composed of:

- university education which is divided into a bachelors degree (taken after two years), and the final degree examination (*licentiaat*), taken after another two years (with the exception of some subjects like medicine which requires five years).
- non-university higher education, which can be a) of a longer duration, i.e. four years of study, divided into a bachelor's and a *licentiaat's* degree, or b) of a shorter duration, i.e. two or three years of study.

The successful completion of full secondary education of any type entitles a student to attend the higher courses of his choice.

- No fees are payable for primary and secondary education, and in higher education minimal fees are payable.
- Free travel is provided for 'state school' pupils.
- Allowances are granted by central government to students in secondary and higher education. In order to qualify the student must be registered as a full-time student, have passed the previous year with success, and must be dependent on parental or family income not exceeding a certain amount. The allowances are rather low for secondary students but can rise to substantial amounts for students in higher education.
- University social expenditure (social services, student accommodation, health services) are partly subsidized by the state.

Financing

The abolition of fees in all schools in both the public and private (mainly Catholic) sectors, has made it imperative to ensure that current expenditure (including teachers' wages) in both sectors are born by the state. The only differentiation allowed, indeed, concerns the provision of school buildings. The state is fully responsible for the maintenance of its own schools. Provinces and municipalities are entitled to a 60% subsidy for building projects and to low-interest loans for the remaining 40%. The private sector is only entitled to low-interest loans.

Administration

The main executives at the national level are the Ministries of Education (one for the Dutch and one for the French speaking community). The Ministries prepare acts and are responsible for the adjudication and payment of grants to the different educational sectors and for teachers' wages. All important decisions on educational policy however are discussed in the political National School Pact Commission. Every political party of some importance is a member of this commission. In addition, all bills are discussed first by the Permanent Executive School Pact Commission. Every 'school network' has its own executive and coordinating organism. State and local government school networks are mainly coordinated by the Permanent Commission of Official Neutral Education (*Commission Permanente pour l'Enseignement Officiel Neutral, Permanente Commissie voor het officieel neutraal onderwijs*). The Catholic school network is coordinated by the National Secretariat of Catholic Education (*Secrétariat*

National de l'Enseignement Catholique, Nationaal Secretariaat van het Katholiek Onderwijs, NSKO)

Current expenditure for education: approximations of disaggregationable items for budget year 1979 in million BFR

	State	Provinces and Municipal.	Private	Correction	Total
Nursery/primary	10 284	16 146	26 063	+64	52 557
Secondary	31 398	11 418	48 504	-	91 320
Higher non-univ.	3 102	1 739	5 993	-799	10 035
Subtotal in BFR	44 784	29 303	80 560	-735	153 912
in %	29.10	19.04	52.34	-0.48	100.0
University	n. a.		n. a.		22 455
Total					176 367

Core laws

Acts 29.5.1959, 11.7.1973
School Pact Acts: organized the relationship between different school networks into a type of 'subcontracting' where the state covers the expenditure of all networks and the networks accept some legal obligations.

Act 2.8.1960
University Act: increased the state subsidies to universities (*Universitaire Expansie*).

Act 7.7.1970
Higher Education Act: restructured higher education with a focus on a more comprehensive system.

Act 19.7.1971
Secondary School Act: introduced a comprehensive secondary school system.

Acts 19.3.1954, 19.7.1971
Allowance Acts: introduced study allowances.

Acts 20.8.1957, 14.7.1975
Organization of primary education.

Act 29.6.1983
Prolonged compulsory education to the age of 18.

IX Housing

In Belgium, housing policy is oriented towards private ownership of middle-sized dwellings, especially for moderate and low income households. In 1981 some 60.5% of all dwellings were owner-occupied. The two most important instruments of this policy of 'social housing' (*logement social, sociale huisvesting*), are:

- subsidized housing construction by semi-public housing societies;
- subsidized private housing construction and acquisition.

Since World War II on average half of all new building has been directly subsidized (51.3% in 1960, 32.5% in 1982). In 1982, 33% of these new subsidized houses were built on private initiative, the rest by the social housing companies. Since approximately one-third of new building by the social housing companies is directed towards private ownership, more than two-thirds of total new building in the social housing sector is acquired by private persons. The rest is directed towards the social rent sector which in 1977 covered 14% of all rented dwellings.

Housing policies used to be devised and implemented by the Housing Directorate (*Administration du logement, Bestuur voor de Huisvesting*, BH) of the Department for Public Works, in close cooperation with the two national housing societies and with the National Housing Institute (*Institut nationale du logement; Nationaal Instituut voor de Huisvesting, NIH*) which is engaged in the study of housing problems. Housing expenditure is centralized in the National Housing Fund (*Fonds nationale du logement; Nationaal Fonds voor de Huisvesting*, NFH) which is part of the Department for Public Works but supervised by the Department of Finance.

Subsequent to the 1974 and 1980 Devolution Acts, financial and administrative responsibilities in housing policy have been transferred to the regional authorities, thus giving Belgium three regional housing policies.

Social housing expenditure, in million BFR

	1962		1978	
		%		%
Private property subsidies	1 208.4	58.7	7 098.5	48.2
Social rent sector	712.9	34.6	6 939.0	47.1
Improvement of housing stock	137.2	6.7	686.0	4.7
Total	2 058.5	100.0	14 723.5	100.0
% of GDP		0.3		0.5

1. Subsidized housing construction by national societies

There are two semi-public national societies involved in the subsidized construction of lower cost housing. The National Housing Society (*Société nationale du logement, Nationale Maatschappij voor de Huisvesting*, NMH) mainly constructs, but also buys houses and land. It is also concerned with the improvement of housing stock. Dwellings are built by approved local companies which are relatively autonomous (284 companies covering 507 out of the 589 Belgian communes in 1983) in collaboration with private building contractors. Dwellings are either let or sold to lower income households. The National Land Society (*Société nationale terrienne, Nationale Landmaatschappij*, NLM) concentrates on improving the housing conditions of low income families in rural areas. The Society's 53 (in 1982) companies construct housing which the Society then sells and does not let.

These national societies raise loans for the construction of lower cost houses on the private capital market. The state subsidizes the interest rates. As a rule, public works accompanying the construction of these houses (roads etc.) are directly covered by central government.

Renting and buying of such houses is subject to certain conditions. In 1984, those with an annual taxable income below 666,000 BFR (increased by 32,500 BFR for each dependent child) were entitled to rent a house. The renting societies are legally compelled to give priority to candidates with an annual taxable income below 518,000 BFR. Those with an annual income below 866,000 BFR (increased by 44,000 BFR for each dependent child) were entitled to buy a house.

2. Subsidized private housing construction

The 1948 De Taeye Act introduced two kinds of subsidies for promoting broad social ownership (*propriété sociale du logement, sociale eigendomsverwerving*). Since World War II, 75% of all subsidized housing has been built with the help of the provisions given in this Act.

Premiums are granted in the form either of building premiums (when the private person builds his own dwelling) or of purchase premiums (when the private person acquires a dwelling built by a social housing society).

Credit facilities are granted in the form of mortgage loans either at a so-called 'low' interest rate (for inhabitants of rural districts, large families, miners), or at a so-called 'social' rate of interest which is somewhat less favourable than the former. There are two important institutions which provide loans at lower interest rates: the General Savings and Annuity Bank (*Caisse générale d'épargne et de retraite, Algemene Spaar- en Lijfrentekas*, ASLK) and the Belgian League for Large Families Housing Fund (*Fonds du logement de la ligue des familles nombreuses de Belgique, Woningfonds van de Bond voor Kroostrijke Gezinnen van België*, WF-BKGB), the loans of which are confined to large families.

Since 1983, and only in Flanders, beneficiaries of a building premium are insured against loss of income. This insurance covers, for a limited period and a limited amount, the loss of income due to unemployment or inability to work.

Fiscal and other advantages are available in the form of deductions in registration fees, property taxes and in notarial charges; fiscal rebates are allowed in the case of all new building and property ownership.

These two provisions are only available under certain ceilings depending on the type of dwelling (size, price of construction or purchase), maximum taxable income, amount of loan, rate of interest, a.o. The ceilings are higher for lower income levels, larger families and recently married couples. They are linked to the consumer price index.

3. Rent legislation

General legislation on renting comes under civil law. Since 1973 legislation has strengthened tenants' rights, and since 1975 public authorities have regulated renting conditions by controlling rent increases.

4. Housing modernization

Owners in both the public and private sector are encouraged to improve the quality of their housing stock. The first measures were passed in 1954, but for a period of nearly twenty years they remained limited. Since the early 1970s, however, more attention has been paid by public authorities to measures to stimulate the sanitation of insalubrious but restorable dwellings and improved equipping of functionally unadapted dwellings.

There are a number of allowances, subsidies and premiums to encourage the improvement of the existing housing stock (e.g. premiums on removal, installation, sanitation and renting). They are paid directly to the individual or to the social housing society. In 1981, expenditure on installation and sanitation premiums amounted to 905 million BFR, this being nearly 4% of all housing expenditure.

Core laws

Act 25.5.1948
De Taeye Act: organized premiums, credit facilities and fiscal rebates for social dwellings built either on private or public initiative.

Act 15.4.1949
Brunfaut Act: organized the financing of the two National Housing Societies; shifted the financial burden of infrastructural works to the state; established a central budgeting organization for governmental social housing policy (NFH).

Act 7.12.1953
Dealt with slum clearance by approved housing societies, municipalities and private persons.

Royal Decree 10/11.2.1955
Introduced allowances to cover demolition and rehousing.

Royal Decree 10.1.1966
Introduced rent and installation allowances for families living in inhabitable dwellings.

Royal Decree 10.8.1967
Introduced sanitation premiums for inhabitable but adaptable dwellings.

Royal Decree 10.7.1970
Introduced special moving, renting, and installation allowances for families living in inhabitable dwellings.

The 1953 Act and subsequent Decrees are continually adapted and have become increasingly divergent between the regions since devolution.

Act 9.7.1971
Breyne Act: Fixed responsibilities of builders/future owners and those of the building contractor before and during construction of the dwelling.

Act 7.11.1973
Strengthened tenants' rights.

Act 10.4.1975
Organized the index linking of rents.

Bibliography

The authors thank Erik de Ridder for his help with the bibliography.

I General contributions

1.1 History of social policy

BARNICH, G.: La législation et l'organisation ouvrière en Belgique (Legislation and Labour Movement in Belgium). Bruxelles, 1911, 669 p.

CHLEPNER, B.: Cent ans d'histoire sociale en Belgique (One Hundred Years of Social History in Belgium). Paris, U.L.B., Institut de Sociologie, 1972, 447 p.

DE VOLDER, N.: Sociale geschiedenis van België 1830-1945, burgerlijk paternalisme en ongeorganiseerd proletariaat, socialisme en christelijke arbeidersbeweging (The Social History of Belgium 1830-1945, Bourgeois Paternalism and Unorganized Proletariat, Socialism and Christian Labour Movement). Mechelen, Sint Franciscus, 1965, 517 p.

DUERINCK, M.: 'De staatsuitgaven in België als maatstaf van de sociale politiek van de staat (1918-1940) (Public expenditure in Belgium as an indicator of the social policy of the state 1918-1940)'. *De Gids op Maatschappelijk Gebied,* 37 (1946), 7-8. Outline of the social policy of the central government on the basis of social expenditure. Includes extensive statistical material.

FUSS, H., GOLDSCHMIDT, P. et.al.: 'Het onstaan van het ontwerp van sociale solidariteit in België (The origin of the draft agreement on social solidarity in Belgium)'. *Arbeidsblad,* 59 (1958), 7-8, pp. 847-882. Text of this agreement on social solidarity in Belgium including social security, principles and methods of parity administration, working hours and wages, commented on by one of the authors of the draft, and a review of the activities of the committee which worked out the agreement.

LEHOUCK, F.: 'Guerre et sécurité sociale (War and social security)'. *Revue du Travail Belge,* (1980), pp. 643-691. Study of the relationship between war and social security. Chapters on the immediate prehistory of social security, on social security and World War II (living conditions of the working class and the social movements) and on the institutionalization of social security in 1944.

LOCCUFIER, S.: Het sociaal budget voor België (The Belgian Social Budget). N.O.S.W., Brussel, 1981. Chapters on the social security policy in Belgium (with a description of the administrative organization and the financing for each social security scheme) and on the share of the social expenditure in the total budget of central government.

MALDAGUE, R.: Balans en toekomst van het sociaal beleid (State of Affairs and Future of Social Policy). Brussel, Planbureau, 1981, 569 p. Chapters on social policy and the economic crisis, on the population structure and social expenditure, and on the efficiency of the social security system in Belgium; attempts to depict the state of affairs of Belgian social policy.

MINISTERIE VAN FINANCIEN: 'De evolutie der uitgaven van de centrale overheid sinds 1950 volgens de functionele en de economische hergroeperingsoptiek (The evolution of public expenditure since 1950 according to the functional and economic re-grouping technique)'. *Documentatieblad,* (1978), 1, pp. 25-301, and (1982), 1-2, pp.95-236. Detailed statistical elucidation of the expenditure of the central government for the period 1950-1975. Includes statistics on public expenditure on welfare facilities, health care, housing and town and country planning.

NAYER, A.: Les inspections sociales en Belgique (The Belgian Social Inspection System). Bruxelles, Eds Vie Ouvrière, 1980. Includes chapters on the evolution of the social inspection system in Belgium, a review and analysis of its present organizational and administrative statute, competences and procedures.

VANDENDRIESSCHE, S.: Evolutie van de Belgische centrale overheidsuitgaven sinds 1919. Onderzoek naar de determinerende factoren (The Evolution of Public Expenditure since 1919. Inquiry into the Determining Factors). Brussel, Ministerie van Financiën, 1978, 730 p. Review of the main political, economic, financial and social events since 1919 with special attention to budget and public debt and an analysis of the evolution of central government expenditure based on and referring to the events reviewed in Part I.

1.2 Introduction to the system of social policies in Belgium

AKKERMANS, T. and NOBELEN, P.: Corporatisme en verzorgingsstaat (Corporatism and Welfare State). Leiden/Antwerpen, 1983. Includes a study on the relationship between the corporate state and welfare state in Belgium ('Towards a Dutch situation').

DE BROECK, G.: 'De sociaal-economische overlegorganen in België (The socio-economic consultative bodies in Belgium)'. *De Gids op Maatschappelijk Gebied,* (1973), 5, pp. 394-411. Review of the socio-economic consultative bodies in Belgium. Includes an inventory of these consultative bodies according to their structure and competences and an analysis with general remarks.

DEKEERSMAEKER, J.F. and VAN STEENBERGHE, J.: Bibliografie van het Belgisch Sociaal Recht (Bibliography on Belgian Social Law). Bibliography of Belgian labour and social security law, based on textbooks, monographs and about 100 periodicals.

DELHUVENNE, M.: 'Veertig jaar sociale zekerheid (1935-1975): een veranderd maatschappijbeeld (Forty years of social security (1935-1975): a changed image of society)'. *Belgisch Tijdschrift voor Sociale Zekerheid,* (1979), 10-11-12, pp. 705-730. Analysis of the evolution of social security between 1935 and 1975 and of the consequences of this evolution on the contents and the functioning of the social security offices.

DETHEE, M.: 'Impact van de demografische evolutie op de sociale uitgaven (Impact of the demographical evolution on social expenditure)'. *GERV-berichten,* (1982), pp. 133-261. Discussion of the consequences of the changing population structure on the volume of social expenditure.

ELST, R.: 'De paritaire beheersorganen op het stuk van de sociale zekerheid (The parity administration of social security)'. *Belgisch Tijdschrift voor Sociale Zekerheid,* 12 (1970), 5-6, pp. 709-722. Discussion of the Act of 25 April 1983.

HUYSE, L. and BERTING, J.: Als in een spiegel? Een sociologische kaart van België en Nederland (As in a Mirror? A Sociological Map of Belgium and the Netherlands). Leuven, 1983, 271 p. A comparison of Belgium and the Netherlands with respect to labour relations, education and educational policies, health care and health policies, public housing and environmental planning. Empirical data and sociological analyses.

LEUS, I.: Sociaal zekerheidsstelsel bedreigd? (Is the Social Security System Threatened?). *Leiding,* 1978. Review of the financing of the social security system for employees and for self-employed (on the basis of employees' and employers' contributions and state subsidies) with emphasis on the necessity of the preservation of the system as it exists.

LEUS, I.: 'Wie ontvangt gelden uit het sociale zekerheidsstelsel? (Who benefits from the social security system?)'. *Belgisch Tijdschrift voor Sociale Zekerheid,* 22 (1980), 9, pp. 710-766. Is the social security system really threatened by the increase in the number of beneficiaries and/or by the level of benefits? Available figures on beneficiaries and benefits are analysed; the latter are compared with poverty-lines in order to evaluate their efficiency.

MINISTERIE VAN SOCIALE VOORZORG: 'De kosten van de sociale zekerheid in België, 1968-1978 (The costs of social security in Belgium, 1968-1978)'. *Belgisch Tijdschrift voor Sociale Zekerheid,* 21 (1979), mei, speciaal nummer. An extensive analysis of the costs of social security in Belgium for the period 1968-1978, with the financial and demographic data and the average contribution and performance for each scheme.

THIRY, J.: Het sociaal beleid in een aanhoudende crisissituatie (Social Policy in a Lasting Crisis Situation). N.O.S.W., 1981.

VAN DAMME, D.: Welzijnswerk en kapitalisme, inleiding op de Marxistische theorie en geschiedenis van het welzijnswerk in België (Welfare Work and Capitalism, Introduction to Marxist Theory and the History of Welfare Work in Belgium). Gent, Masereelfonds, 1981, 223 p. The main part is concerned with the establishment of a Marxist framework for the analysis of social and cultural work, which is then applied to the development of early adult education (until 1914).

VAN LANGENDONCK,: Crisiswetgeving en de sociale zekerheid (Crisis Legislation and Social Security). Antwerpen, Kluwer, 1980. Collection of reports, comments and discussions presented at a congress on 'Crisis Legislation and Social Security' (period 1976-1979) at the University of Leuven (5 October 1979).

WERKGROEP EKONOMISCHE DEMOCRATIE: 'Democratie op het vlak van het sociaal-economisch bestel (Democracy in the socio-economic system)'. *De Nieuwe Maand*, 14 (1971), 7, pp. 382-411. In the first part, the union's views on the socio-economic system are presented and compared; the second part contains a review of existing consultative bodies.

1.3 Reports by investigating committees or experts (in chronological order)

FUSS, H. and LEEN, W.: (rijkscommissarissen voor de maatschappelijke zekerheid), Verslag over de hervorming van de Maatschappelijke Zekerheid (Report on the reform of the social security system). Brussel, Ministerie van Arbeid en Sociale Voorzorg, 1951, 338 p. A description of the social security system as it existed in 1951 and a review of the proposals of the Commissioners for Social Security for the reform of the social security system.

WERKGROEP BELAST MET DE STUDIE VAN HET SOCIAAL STATUUT DER ZELFSTANDIGEN: Verslag voorgelegd aan de regering (Report submitted to the government). Brussel, 1964. Report concerning the social security scheme for the self-employed.

PETIT, J.: Verslag over de ziekteverzekering (Report on the Sickness Insurance Scheme). Brussel, Kamer van Volksvertegenwoordigers, 1976, 535 p. Report of the Royal Commissioner on the reorganization of the sickness insurance scheme aiming at better functioning and lower expenses. Besides chapters on the history, the actual administrative structure, the financing and the earlier reforms of the sickness insurance scheme, the report presents a number of new reform proposals.

CALIFICE, A.: Plan ter hervorming van de sociale zekerheid (Plan to reform social security). Brussel, Ministerie van Sociale Voorzorg, 1979. Plan to reform the social security system in Belgium, with an emphasis on the redressment of the budgetary balance of the most threatened social security schemes.

Rapport met betrekking tot de wet houdende algemene beginselen van de sociale zekerheid voor werknemers (Report concerning the general principles of social security for employees). Brussel, Senaat, 1980. Discussion (general and by clause) of a proposal to embody in an Act the general principles of social security (definitions, principles, regulations and financing).

MINISTERIE VAN SOCIALE ZAKEN EN INSTITUTIONELE HERVORMINGEN: Voorstellen van de Minister van Sociale Zaken tot hervorming van de Sociale Zekerheid (Proposals of the Minister of Social Affairs to reform Social Security). Brussel, 1983, 246 p. Analysis of the evolution (1965-1982) and of the financial perspectives (1984-1990) of social security. Contains also a review of the proposals of the Minister of Social Affairs for the reform of social security (a greater selectivity towards families, harmonization of the different social security schemes, etc.).

BIJZONDERE COMMISSIE VOOR DE PENSIOENEN: Verslag m.b.t. ontwerp van wet houdende maatregelen tot harmonisering in de pensioenregelingen (Report on the bill concerning measures for the harmonization of the pension schemes). Brussel, Senaat, 1984. Besides a description of the different existing schemes, the report contains a discussion (general and by clause) of the proposals concerning the harmonization of the pension schemes.

KONINKLIJKE COMMISSIE BELAST MET DE CODIFICERING, DE HARMONISERING EN DE VEREENVOUDIGING VAN DE WETGEVING BETREFFENDE SOCIALE ZEKERHEID IN HET KADER VAN DE ALGEMENE HERVORMING VAN DIE WETGEVING: Voorontwerp van wetboek van sociale zekerheid en memorie van toelichting. Brussel, 15 maart 1985. Preliminary design of a social security code designed by the 'Royal Commission for the codification, harmonization and simplification of Social Security law'.

1.4 Social science interpretations, evaluations or analyses

BILLIET, J.: Secularisering en verzuiling in het onderwijs (Secularization and Pillarization in the Educational System). Leuven, Universitaire Pers, 1977, 243 p.

BILLIET, J.: 'Verzuiling, conflictregeling en politieke besluitvorming in België (Pillarization, Conflict Settlement and Political Decision-Making in Belgium)'. *Sociologische Gids* 30 (1983), 6, pp. 440-441. Analysis of the relationship between structural pillarization, conflict settlement and political decision-making in Belgium from the point of view that the internal integration of the pillars is a necessary condition for the settlement of conflicts.

DE BEYS, X., et.al.: 'La sécurité sociale (Social Security)'. *La Revue Nouvelle*, 36 (1980), 11, pp. 409-489. Dossier with reports on the results of the Third Employment Scheme experiment, the financing of social security, social security in figures, etc.

DE CLERCQ, J.B.: De slechte staat van de verzorgingsstaat (The bad state of the welfare state). *Kultuurleven*, 49 (1982), 8, pp. 25-e.v.. Analysis of the bad condition the welfare state is in, according to the author, and a review of possible solutions.

DELEECK, H., BERGMAN, J., et.al.: De sociale zekerheid tussen droom en daad (Social Security between Dream and Deed). Antwerpen, Van Loghum Slaterus, 1980. The results of an extensive survey on the effects of social security on living conditions are analysed within the framework of a general theory of social policy and of the historical development of Belgiyn social security.

DE SWERT, G.: De onwillige verzorgingsstaat (The unwilling welfare state). *De Gids op Maatschappelijk Gebied*, 75 (1984), 2, pp. 95-122. Plea for a redistributing system based on national solidarity.

DOBBELAERE, K. and BILLIET, J.: De katholieke zuil nu: desintegratie en integratie (The Catholic pillar: disintegration and integration)'. *Belgisch Tijdschrift voor Nieuwste Geschiedenis*, 13 (1982), 1, pp. 119-160. Discussion of the development of the Catholic 'pillar' in the last decade.

DOBBELAERE, K. and BILLIET, J.: 'Les changements internes au pillier catholique en Flandres: d'une catholicisme de l'église à une chrétienté socio-culturelle (The internal changes in the Catholic pillar in Flanders: from a Catholicism of the Church to a socio-cultural Christianity)'. *Recherches Sociologiques*, 14 (1983), pp. 141-181. Why doesn't the continual decline of religious practice in Flanders result in the disintegration of the Catholic pillar? Is it because of a new sort of solidarity (Gemeinschaftlichkeit)?

HUYSE, L.: Passiviteit, pacificatie en verzuiling in de Belgische politiek (Passivity, Pacification and Pillarization in Belgian Politics). Antwerpen, Standaard Uitgeverij, 1970, 267 p. What is the relationship between political passivity and the whole of the institutional conditions in which the political regime in Belgium functions?

HUYSE, L.: 'Pillarisation reconsidered'. *Acta Politica*, 19 (1984), 1, pp. 145-158. How did the Catholic pillar survive the secularization of the 1970's. Shouldn't the 'pillars' be looked at as complex organizations tout-court, which follow their own course and develop their own logic?

HUYSE, L.: 'De Belgische ziekte (The Belgian disease)'. *De Nieuwe Maand*, 24 (1981), 5, pp. 321-331. Study on the decision-making bodies (parliament, leaders of the major political parties and the advisory bodies) in Belgium and their role as a brake on Belgian political life.

HUYSE, L.: De gewapende vrede. De Belgische politiek na 1945 (The Armed Peace. Belgian Politics after 1945). Leuven, 1980, 93 p. Review of the main developments and events in Belgian political life after World War II from the perspective of the so-called 'pacification' theory.

JACOBS, D. and ROEBROECK, H.: Nieuwe sociale bewegingen in Vlaanderen en Nederland (New Social Movements in Flanders and the Netherlands). Antwerpen, Uitgeverij Leon Lesoil, 1983, 117 p. Study on the development of a number of new social movements in Flanders and the Netherlands (action groups, protest movements, basis initiatives) and their political perspectives.

VRANKEN, J. and HENDERICKX, E. (eds): 'Zorgen om de verzorgingsstaat, een sociologische analyse (Did care kill the welfare state? A sociological analysis)'. *Tijdschrift voor Sociologie*, 5 (1981), 1-2, pp. 1-359 (speciaal nummer). Sociological analysis of the welfare state with chapters on the main trends and problems of the Belgian welfare state: public expenditure and social inequality, welfare state and pillarization, etc.

1.5 Policy proposals and debates

BERGMAN, J.: Theorie van de sociale zekerheid. Bijdrage tot de sociaal-politieke theorie van de sociale zekerheid met een toepassing op de pensioensector (Theory of Social Security. Contribution to a Social Policy Theory of Social Security, Applied to the Pension Scheme). Wilrijk, 1981. With an emphasis on Belgium, this doctoral dissertation synthesizes the historical evolution of social security and the contribution of the social sciences in elucidating it. Hypotheses to enrich the traditional social policy approach with a more explanatory sociological analysis are formulated and tested on the evolution of the Belgian pension schemes.

BOELAERT, R.: 'Alternatieve financieringswijzen voor de sociale zekerheid: een analyse van verschillende voorstellen (Alternative ways of financing social security: an analysis of various proposals)'. *Belgisch Tijdschrift voor Sociale Zekerheid*, 21 (1971), 2, pp. 123-139. A review of a number of proposals aiming at the substitution of the current system of social security financing in Belgium with a new one, based either on total wages (effective since 1983), added value or total imposable income.

DELEECK, H., DE DECKER, M., HUYBRECHS, J.: 'Financiering van de sociale zekerheid door bijdragen berekend op de toegevoegde waarde der Belgische ondernemingen in plaats van op het loon (Financing of social security by contributions calculated on the added value of Belgian enterprises instead of on wages)'. *Cahiers Economiques de Bruxelles*, 72 (1976) and 73 (1977). Contains an inventory of alternative ways of financing social security. Simulates the effects of a transition to an alternative way of financing based on the added value of enterprises.

SCHOONBRODT-CLOTUCHE, G.: 'Financiering van de sociale zekerheid, evaluatie der trends en toekomstplannen (Financing of social security, evaluation of trends and plans for the future)'. *Belgisch Tijdschrift voor Sociale Zekerheid*, 21 (1979), 7-8, pp. 534-554. Analysis and evaluation of a number of proposals on alternative ways of financing social security: adaptation of the current financing structure, (partial or total) fiscalization, choice of a new basis (i.e. added value).

SPITAELS, G., et.al.: Le salaire indirect et la couverture des besoins sociaux (The Indirect Salary and the Covering of Social Needs). Bruxelles, Institut de Sociologie, U.L.B., 1968-1971 (3 dln). A first volume (Le Dossier) gives a socio-economic description of the evolution of the Belgian social security schemes for wage-earners from World War II up to 1966), the second volume (L'enquête) analyses the results of a survey on social security policies with representatives of labour unions and employers, a third volume (La Comparaison) gives an outline of the evolution of the major social security schemes in France, Germany, Italy and the Netherlands from World War II to 1966.

VAN LANGENDONCK, J., et.al.: Recente ontwikkelingen van de sociale zekerheid 1975-1981 (Recent Developments of Social Security 1975-1981). Antwerpen, Kluwer, Rechtswetenschappen, 1981. A review of recent developments in the social security system in Belgium (1975-1981). Includes the different proposals for the reform of social security as well as the points of view of the major political parties.

1.6 Statistical sources or institutional regulations

1.6.1 Official sources

MINISTERIE VAN SOCIALE VOORZORG: Statistisch Jaarboek van de Sociale Zekerheid (Statistical Year-Book of Social Security). Brussel, annual. Statistics on the evolution of the (active) population, of the number of contributors and beneficiaries, of expenditure (for employees, self-employed and public servants).

MINISTERIE VAN VOLKSGEZONDHEID: Statistisch Jaarboek van Volksgezondheid (Statistical Year-Book of Public Health). Brussel, annual. Includes statistics on demographic indicators, morbidity, medical equipment, medical corps, paramedical, technical and other personnel, education, expenditure on public health, etc.

NATIONAAL INSTITUUT VOOR DE STATISTIEK: Statistisch Jaarboek van België (Statistical Year-Book of Belgium). Brussel, annual. Statistics concerning population structure, health care, housing, education, employment, transport, etc.

NATIONAAL INSTITUUT VOOR DE STATISTIEK: Sociale Statistieken (Social Statistics). Brussel, irregular publication.

RIJKSKAS VOOR RUST- EN OVERLEVINGSPENSIOENEN: Jaarlijkse Statistiek van de Pensioengerechtigden (Annual Statistics on Old Age and Survivors' Pension). Brussel, annual.

1.6.2 Private sources

KLUWER, TRENDS: Ekonomisch zakboekje (Economic Pocket-book). Practical information on economic matters (national accounts, population and employment, investments, production of goods and services, money and credit, prices, wages and welfare, etc.).

KLUWER, TRENDS: Financieel zakboekje (Financial Pocket-book). Practical information on financial matters (the Belgian money and capital market, the monetary policy, public finances, the financial situation of Belgian companies and of the Belgian households).

KLUWER, TRENDS: Fiscaal zakboekje (Fiscal Pocket-book).

KLUWER, TRENDS: Politiek zakboekje (Political Pocket-book). Practical information on political matters (national, regional, provincial and municipal institutions, political parties, etc.).

KLUWER, TRENDS: Sociaal zakboekje (Social Pocket-book). Practical information on social matters (collective labour law, individual labour law, social security law, etc).

1.6.3 Major periodicals

MINISTERIE VAN SOCIALE VOORZORG: Algemeen Verslag over de Sociale Zekerheid (General Report on Social Security). Brussel, annual. Comments on the legal, economic and financial evolution of social security. Includes the accounts (general as well as for each scheme) of income and expenditure on social security (for employees, self-employed and for residual measures) as well as an estimate of income and expenditure for the next year.

MINISTERIE VAN SOCIALE VOORZORG: Beknopt overzicht van de sociale zekerheid in België (Brief Review of Social Security in Belgium). Brussel, irregular publication, last publication 1981, 322 p. General review of the social security system. Includes a summary of the social security system for the self-employed.

RIJKSDIENST VOOR ARBEIDSVOORZIENING: Jaarverslag (Annual Report of the National Employment Office). Brussel, annual.

RIJKSDIENST VOOR KINDERBIJSLAG VOOR WERKNEMERS: Jaarverslag (Annual Report of the National Family Allowances Office for Wage-Earners). Brussel, annual.

RIJKSINSTITUUT VOOR DE SOCIALE VERZEKERING DER ZELFSTANDIGEN: Jaarverslag (Annual Report of the National Social Insurance Office for the Self-Employed). Brussel, annual.

RIJKSINSTITUUT VOOR ZIEKTE- EN INVALIDITEITSVERZEKERING: Algemeen Verslag (General Report of the National Institute for Sickness and Invalidity Insurance). Brussel, annual.

DE COCK, J.: De sociale zekerheid in .... Een documentair overzicht (Social security in .... A documentary review). Antwerpen, Kluwer, 1980, 1981. Gives an annual review of the social security system and analyses, per scheme, the evolution which has taken place in that year.

DE COCK, J.: Sociaal Jaarboek ... (Social Year-book ...). Kalmthout, Biblo, 1981, 1982, 1983, 1984. Continuation of 'De sociale zekerheid in ...'.

II Single programmes or aspects

2.1 Pensions

BERGHMAN, J.: Theorie van de sociale zekerheid. Bijdrage tot de sociaal-politieke theorie van de sociale zekerheid met een toepassing op de pensioensector (Theory of Social Security. Contribution to a Social Policy Theory of Social Security, Applied to the Pension Scheme). Wilrijk, 1981. See Section 1.5.

MASYN, R.: 'De pensioenen voor werknemers (The pension scheme for wage-earners)'. *De Ontwikkeling van de Belgische wetgeving van sociale zekerheid 1970-1976*, Brussel, F. Larcier, 1977, pp. 123-140. Gives the most important tendencies in the evolution of the employees' pension scheme in the period 1970-1976 (horizontal broadening, tendency towards the introduction of special reglementations for assistance to professional groups, tendency towards the lowering of the pension age, etc.).

MASYN, R.: 'Het K.B. nr. 50 over de pensioenen voor werknemers (The Royal Degree nr. 50 on the pension scheme for employees)'. *De ontwikkeling van de Belgische wetgeving van sociale zekerheid 1965-1970*, Leuven, Instituut voor Sociale Zekerheid, 1971, pp. 147-158. Most important tendencies in the pension scheme (period 1965-1970) with the emphasis on the Royal Decree nr. 50 concerning the unification of the pension scheme for wage earners.

ROMANS, J. and KERKHOFS, J.: 'De pensioenstelsels in België (The pension schemes in Belgium)'. *CEPESS-documenten*, 1973, 4, pp. 1-139. Chapters on the general pension schemes for wage-earners, self-employed and civil servants, guaranteed income pensions, the social effectiveness of the pension schemes and a comparison of the different pension schemes.

VERGAUWEN, L.: 'De pensioenen voor zelfstandigen (The pension scheme for the self-employed)'. *De ontwikkeling van de Belgische wetgeving van sociale zekerheid*, Leuven, Instituut voor Sociale Zekerheid, 1971, pp. 159-168. Short review of the pension scheme for the self-employed with an emphasis on the basic principles of this pension scheme.

VERGAUWEN, L.: 'De pensioenen voor zelfstandigen (The pension scheme for the self-employed)'. *De ontwikkeling van de Belgische wetgeving van sociale zekerheid 1970-1976*, Brussel, F. Larcier, 1977, pp. 337-352. Review of the evolution of the pension scheme for the self-employed (period 1970-1976), including the changes by the act of 6 February, 1976.

DENAEYER, J.: 'Het gewaarborgd inkomen voor bejaarden in de residuele sociale zekerheid (The guaranteed income for the elderly in the residual social security)'. *Belgisch Tijdschrift voor Sociale Zekerheid*, 1983, pp. 391-487. Inquiry into the statistical and financial components of the Guaranteed Income for the Elderly, especially into the distribution of the amounts payed and the classification of the beneficiaries into categories.

2.2 Health

CARLIER, M.: 'La génèse de l'assurance maladie-invalidité obligatoire en Belgique (The origin of the compulsory sickness and invalidity insurance in Belgium)'. *Courrier hebdomadaire* CRISP, 1980, 872, pp. 1-47. Historical analysis of the national sickness and invalidity insurance scheme in Belgium.

CARRIN, G. and VAN DAEL, J.: 'An empirical model of the demand for health care in Belgium'. *Applied Economics*, 1984, 3, pp. 317-334.

DEHAENE, J. L.: 'Het medisch en paramedisch aanbod in België (The medical and parmedical supply in Belgium)'. *Belgisch Tijdschrift voor Sociale Zekerheid*, (1984), 1-2, pp. 3-157. Figures up to 1981/1982.

FOETS, M. and NUYENS, Y.: Focus op de Belgische gezondheidszorg: feiten, tendensen, ontwikkelingen (Focus on Belgian Health Care: Facts, Tendencies, Developments). Leuven, S.O.I., 1980, 359 p. Critical analysis of Belgian health care at the level of public assistance (role of the government, the professional organizations, the sickness funds, etc.), the level of the means (financial and manpower) and the level of the policy making.

LEROY, X.: L'accès aux soins médicaux, évolution 1974-1976 (The Access to Medical Care, Evolution 1974-1976). Bruxelles, SESA-UCL, 1982, 197 p.

LEROY, X.: 'De toegang tot de geneeskundige verzorging (The Access to Medical Care)'. *Belgisch Tijdschrift voor Sociale Zekerheid* (1982), pp. 903-1054, and (1983), pp. 3-180. Study of the supply and consumption of medical care and the access to medical care.

LEUS, I.: 'Medische consumptie (Medical consumption)'. *De Gids op Maatschappelijk Gebied,* (1976), 6-7, pp. 621-632. Results of a study confirming the theory that expenditure on medical examinations increases proportionally with income.

MINISTERIE VAN VOLKSGEZONDHEID: Eerste en voornaamste uitkomsten van de enquête in de verzorginsinstellingen, toestand per 1 januari 1982 (First and Most Important Results of the Inquiry into the Health Care Institutions, Situation on 1 January 1982). Brussel, 1982.

NUYENS, Y.: De eerste lijn is krom: gezondheidszorg tussen onderzoek en beleid (First-Line Health Care between Research and Policy). Deventer, Van Loghum Slaterus, 1980, 270 p. Presents the results of a research programme on first-line health care in Belgium.

PRIMS, A., QUAETHOVEN, P. AND CARPREAU-COLLA, A.: 'Consumptie van ziekenhuiszorgen (Consumption of hospital care)'. *Belgisch Tijdschrift voor Sociale Zekerheid,* (1978), 11-12, pp. 817-885, (1980), 1, pp. 3-78, and (1980), 11-12, pp. 939-1064. Presents the results of extensive research (9,500 patients) on the consumption of hospital care, analysed with respect to a number of personal, social and institutional variables.

PRIMS, A.: 'De organisatie van de gezondheidszorg in België. Een schematisch overzicht (The organization of health care in Belgium. A schematic review)'. *Belgisch Tijdschrift voor Sociale Zekerheid,* (1979), 4-5, pp. 249-301. Description of the organization of health care in Belgium: its administrative structure, curative health care, preventive health care, financing.

SCHUTYSER, K.: 'Overzicht van betalingssystemen (Review of payment systems)'. *Acta Hospitalia,* 6 (1976), pp. 7-19. Study in which the author tries to provide a survey of payment systems where physicians in Belgian hospitals are concerned.

WERKGROEP ALTERNATIEVE EKONOMIE: Dure Geneeskunde. Ekonomische aspecten van de gezondheidszorg in België (Expensive Health Care. Economic Aspects of Health Care in Belgium). Leuven, 1975, 112 p. Analysis of the economic aspects of health care in Belgium (supply and demand, price formation and financing of health care).

2.3 Unemployment

H.I.V.A.: 'Dossier werkloosheid (Niemand heeft ons aangeworven) (Report on unemployment (Nobody has hired us))'. *Kultuurleven,* 49 (1982), 10, pp. 843-928. General description of the unemployment problem with an emphasis on the experience and perception of the situation.

LAMBERT, M.: 'De werkloosheidscijfers anders bekeken (Unemployment statistics looked at in another way)'. *De Gids op Maatschappelijk Gebied,* 69 (1978), 12, pp. 889-903. Critical analysis of the unemployment problem: who is affected, female and youth unemployment, sanctions, etc.

LUX, B.: 'Une approche dynamique du chômage: les flux mensuels de sortie et une estimation pour la Belgique (A dynamic approach to unemployment: the monthly flows in unemployment and an estimation for Belgium)'. *Population et Famille,* 1 (1980), 49, pp. 1-22. An econometrical approach to unemployment: analysis of labour turn over, unemployment duration, mobility of the unemployed, selectivity and dynamics of unemployment.

LUX, B.: 'Les facteurs déterminant de la durée individuelle du chômage (The determinant factors of individual unemployment duration)'. *Cahiers Economiques de Bruxelles,* (1982), 94, 245 e.v. Analysis of the determinant factors of unemployment duration in two Walloon regions.

ROSSEEL, E.: 'Werkloosheidsbeleving: bevindingen van en bemerkingen bij een onderzoek van een representatieve steekproef van Belgische werklozen (The perception of unemployment: results of and remarks regarding a survey based on a representative sample of the Belgian unemployed)'. *Tijdschrift voor Sociologie* (1982), 2, pp. 117-137. Analysis of a survey by the National Employment Office concerning the application behaviour, the readiness to make sacrifices and the perception of unemployment of a representative sample of the Belgian unemployed.

SPINNEWIJN, F.: 'De doorstroming in de werkloosheid in België in 1971-1982 (Unemployment turn over in Belgium in 1971-1982)'. *Maandschrift Economie*, 47 (1983), 2, pp. 115-121. A dynamic analysis of unemployment statistics: how employment opportunities are distributed over the unemployed.

VAN RAEMDONCK, C.: 'Loopbanen van ongeschoolden en laaggeschoolden (Careers of the unskilled and low skilled)'. *Economisch en Sociaal Tijdschrift*, (1980), 1, pp. 43-51. Inquiry into the effects of the interaction between unemployment and marginal employment on the one hand and career and employment possibilities on the other.

2.4 Accidents

PUTTENEERS, A. and VAN DE RYCK, J.: Arbeidsongevallen (Industrial Accidents). Antwerpen, De Verzekeringswereld, 1980, 192 p. Discussion of the so-called 'adjustment of average' in relation to the Industrial Accidents Act of 10 April 1971 (with comments on parliamentary activities, *advices* from the Council of State, etc.).

VAN DE VELDEN, A. and SCHAMP, H.: Arbeidsongevallen privé-sector (Industrial Accidents - Private Sector). Antwerpen, Kluwer, 1981. Textbook dealing with the industrial accidents insurance in the private sector (Act of 10 April 1971). Includes a systematic legal analysis of the basic principles of this Act.

VAN LAETHEM, J.: 'Arbeidsongevallen (Industrial Accidents)', in VAN LANGENDONCK, J. (ed.), Recente ontwikkelingen in de sociale zekerheid 1975-1981 (Recent Developments in Social Security 1975-1981). Antwerpen, Kluwer, 1981, pp. 371-451. Short review of the industrial accidents scheme (concepts, adjustment of average, disability, medical care, basic wage, third party liability, insurance institutions, etc.); situation before 1975 and recent developments since 1975.

2.5 Social assistance

BERGER, J.-M.: Le défi des Centres Publics d'Aide Sociale (The Challenge of the Public Social Welfare Centres). Brussel, Labor, 1978, 206 p. Contains chapters on the place and the essential characteristics of the Poor Law Administration in the Belgian welfare state and gives a description of the aims of this Poor Law Administration.

BREDA, J.: Innovatie en organisatie. Een onderzoek naar innovatie in de sociale hulpverlening (Innovation and Organization. An Inquiry into Innovations in Social Assistance). Wilrijk, 1981. The introduction of new social services is no longer determined by internal organizational characteristics, but by the place the institutions take in the network of welfare work. The dynamics of innovation (seven innovations were analysed) are based on the interorganizational innovation processes.

ELCHARDUS, M.: 'De Stille netwerken en de luidruchtige dienstverleners (The silent networks and the noisy professionals)'. *Bevolking en Gezin*, (1981), 3, pp. 367-392. Gives an account of the current practices for children in Flanders.

FRET, L.: 'Welzijnswerk: van zacht engagement tot politieke strategie (Welfare work: from soft engagement to political strategy)'. *De Nieuwe Maand*, 25 (1982), 6, pp. 404-412. Plea for the fusion of welfare work organizations and for the elaboration of an own political strategy in order to avoid further pillarization.

LAMMERTIJN, F., et.al., Meer kansen voor kansarmen. Een sociologisch onderzoek naar de welzijnszorg in Vlaanderen (More Opportunities for the Poor. A Sociological Inquiry into Welfare Work in Flanders). Zele, D.A.P., Reynaert-uitgaven, 1979. Description of the structure and the functioning of all kinds of welfare work organisations, of the ambulant social provisions, of the financial provisions, etc.

MAES, A.: Gids van het nieuwe (Guide to What's New). Nazareth, Echnaton, 1981, 269 p. A review of a number of new organizations and groups working in the field of well-being in the largest sense of the word.

RENIER, R. and VAN ONSEM, L.: Cliënteel en hulpverlening van het O.C.M.W. anno 1981 (Clients and Help by Public Social Welfare Centres in 1981). Brussel, Koning Boudewijnstichting, 1983. Results of an inquiry into the profile of the clients and the nature of the assistance of Public Social Welfare Centres.

SAMOY, E. and WATERPLAS, L.: 'Nieuwe accenten in het welzijnswerk (New emphases in welfare work)'. *De Gids op Maatschappelijk Gebied*, 74 (1983), 12, pp. 941-952. The authors plead for professional support for the informal means of assistance.

VAN OUTRIVE, L.: 'Op zoek naar de identiteit van het welzijnswerk (In search of the identity of welfare work)'. *Tijdschrift voor Sociaal Welzijn*, (1982), 3, pp. 14-25. Search for the contents and the meaning of welfare work. Must (can) welfare work be differentiated from other forms of social work or health care.

2.6 Family programmes

LESTHAEGHE, R.: 'Demographic Change, Social Security and Economic Growth: Interferences from the Belgian Example'. *Schweizerische Zeitschrift für Volkswirtschaft und Statistik*, (1981), 3, pp. 225-255. Discussion of the demographic effects on those sectors of the social security system which are based on the principle of intergenerational solidarity and which affect the demographic balance between the active and the non-active population; also of the macro-economic effects of alternative demographic trends.

LESTHAEGHE, R. and WILLEMS, P.: 'Gezinsvorming en -uitbouw in België: onderzoek naar de culturele en economische achtergronden van transformatie (Family formation and development in Belgium: Inquiry into the cultural and economic background of transformation)'. *Bevolking en Gezin*, (1983), pp. 191-226. Inquiry into the regional differentiation of fertility decrease, based on the hypothesis that this decrease is caused by the decline of income and employment possibilities for the younger generation.

VAN HOUTTE, J. and BREDA, J.: Behoeftige bejaarden en onderhoudsplichtige kinderen (Elderly Persons in Need and Children Obliged to Care Them). Deventer, Van Loghum Slaterus, 1976. An empirical analysis of the obligation of children towards needy parents; analysis in light of alimentation reports and legal decisions concerning alimentation.

WILLEMS, P., WIJEWICREMA, S. and LESTHAEGHE, R.: 'De evolutie van de vruchtbaarheid in België 1950-1980 (The evolution of fertility in Belgium 1950-1980)'. *Bevolking en Gezin*, (1981), 3, pp. 257-292. Study on the evolution of fertility in Belgium. Includes (comparative) statistics.

2.7 Housing

DEMAL-DUREZ, M.: De Begunstigden van het sociaal huisvestingsbeleid (The Beneficiaries of Social Housing Policy). Brussel, Nationaal Instituut voor de Huisvesting, 1982, 184 p. plus attachments. Study on the distribution of different housing allowances to different population groups.

DESCHAMPS, L.: De bewoners van een woning van de Nationale Maatschappij voor de Huisvesting (The Occupants of a Dwelling of the National Housing Society). Brussel, C.B.G.S., 1985. Inquiry into the housing behaviour of the occupants of social housing estates in Flanders.

DETHE, M.: 'De planning van de sociale investeringen (The planning of social investments)'. GERV-berichten, (1978), 19-e.v. The planning of social investments with social housing as one of the planning instruments.

GOOSSENS, L.: Het sociaal huisvestingsbeleid in België. Een historisch-sociologische analyse van de maatschappelijke probleembehandeling inzake wonen (Social Housing Policy in Belgium. A Historical-Sociological Analysis of the Social Problem Treatment Concerning Housing). Leuven, 1982.

GOOSSENS, L.: 'La politique du logement social en Belgique (Social Housing policy in Belgium)'. *Recherches Sociologiques*, (1983), 2, pp. 203-228. Summary of doctoral dissertation (see above).

GOOSSENS, L. and KNOPS, G.: Sociaal woonbeleid (Social Housing Policy). Brussel, Koning Boudewijnstichting, 1983, 120 p. Study on the functioning of the social housing sector in Flanders.

KETELS, D.: 'Het huisvestingsbeleid in budgettair perspectief (Social housing policy from a budgetary perspective)'. *Documentatieblad Ministerie van Financiën*, (1982), 1-2, pp. 17-51.

NATIONAAL INSTITUUT VOOR DE HUISVESTING: Peilingsenquête 1982-1983 - Vlaams gewest (Housing Inquiry 1982-1983 - Flanders). Brussel, N.I.H., 1984, 3 dln. Inquiry into the housing quality in Flanders.

NATIONAAL INSTITUUT VOOR DE HUISVESTING: Woon beter (Better Housing). Brussel, N.I.H., 1984, 86 p. Legislation and regulations concerning social housing in Flanders.

SCHOONBRODT, R.: Sociologie de l'habitat social. Comportement des habitants et architecture des cités (Sociology of Social Housing. Behaviour of Occupants and Architecture of Cities). Bruxelles, Ed. des Archives d'Architecture Moderne, 1979. Inquiry into the living culture of the occupants of social housing estates in Brussels and Wallonia.

SMETS, M.: De ontwikkeling van de tuinwijkgedachte in België. Een overzicht van de Belgische volkswoningbouw van 1830 tot 1930. (The Development of the Idea of Social Housing Estates in Belgium. A Review of Social Housing in Belgium from 1830 to 1930). Brussel/Luik, Pierre Mardaga, 1977.

SPELTINCK, H.-J.: Historique de la législation Belge relative au logement social (History of Belgian Legislation Concerning Social Housing). Bruxelles, Institut National du Logement, 1980.

VERMEERSCH, C.: Sociale stadsvernieuwing en structuurplanning (Social City Improvement and Structure Planning). Gent, Snoeck-Ducaju en zoon, 1981. New tendencies in city-improvement and structure planning and their influence on social housing in Flanders.

VLAEMINCK, S.: Sociale stadsvernieuwing concreet. Middelen, moeilijkheden, mogelijkheden (Social City-Improvement. Means, Difficulties, Possibilities). Gent, Snoeck-Ducaju en zoon, 1981. Study of some concrete city-improvement projects in Flanders.

WERKGROEP ALTERNATIEVE EKONOMIE: Ongezond verbeterbaar. Ekonomische en sociale aspecten van het wonen in België (Unhealthy Improvable. Economic and Social Aspects of Housing in Belgium). Leuven, Kritak, 1977. Study of the economic and social dimensions of housing in Belgium: housing policy, quality of dwellings and unequal distribution of this quality.

2.8 Education

BONTE, A.: 'Vijfduizend diploma's. Balans van twaalf jaar universitaire expansie in Vlaanderen (Five thousand diplomas. An account of 12 years of university expansion in Flanders)'. *Wetenschappelijke Tijdingen*, (1979), 1, pp. 2-18. Statistical analysis of 12 years of university expansion (during 1965-1977 the number of new university graduates tripled) in Flanders and the consequences of this expansion (academic unemployment and under-employment).

BUSEYNE, C., et. al.: 'Het sociaal hoger onderwijs van het korte type in Vlaanderen (The social higher education of the short type in Flanders)'. *De Gids op Maatschappelijk Gebied*, (1982), 6-7, pp. 525-585. Reports on the institutions and departments, the number of students, the personnel and the number of university graduates in the social higher education of the short type, including statistical data.

CANTILLON, B.: 'Studietoelagen en democratisering van hoger onderwijs (Study allowances and the democratization of higher education)'. *De Nieuwe Maand*, (1982), 9, pp. 669-677. Have study allowances stimulated the democratization of higher education? On the basis of data, mostly on university education, the author comes to the conclusion that study allowances have been an attendant circumstance, but haven't been the propelling force. This results from the fact that insufficient amounts have been given to too many households.

CANTILLON, B. and REYNAERT, R.: 'De sociale afkomst van de studenten in het Hoger Onderwijs Buiten de Universiteit (The social background of students in the Higher Education Outside the University)'. *De Gids op Maatschappelijk Gebied*, (1983), 2, pp. 123-132. Although the Higher Education Outside University gets less attention from the government than

University Education, it seems as if Higher Education Outside University has a greater democratizing force. On the basis of an inquiry into the situation of students in the Higher Education Outside University, the socio-economic profile of those students is compared with the profile of university students.

DELEECK, H., et. al.: 'De democratisering van het hoger onderwijs: feiten, en middelen (The democratization of higher education: facts and means)'. *De Gids op Maatschappelijk Gebied*, (1981), 6-7, pp. 507-533. Analysis of the state of affairs of the democratization of education. This democratization has taken place in favour of the middle classes and not in favour of the lowest social classes. The problem of the democratization of education is not so much a matter of money as of structures and pedagogics.

DEVRIES, R.: 'Onderwijsvernieuwing in Vlaanderen: een terugblik (Education innovation in Flanders: a retrospective review)'. *De Nieuwe Maand*, (1978), 5, pp. 186-204. Comment on some trends in education during the period 1960-1975 (democratization, non-institutional alternatives, anti-authoritative experiments, Renewed Secondary Education, etc.)

MINISTERIE VAN NATIONALE OPVOEDING: Statistisch jaarboek van het onderwijs (Statistical Year-book on Education). Brussel, annual. Statistics concerning school population, diplomas, certificates, etc.

2.9 Special groups

BOLLEN, R: and MOULAERT, F.: Racisten hebben ongelijk (Racists are Wrong). Leuven, Kritak, 1982. Do migrant workers really live at the expense of social security? Analysis of existing prejudices and their refutation on the basis of laws, regulations and statistics on unemployment, family allowances and pensions.

DUMON, W.: Het profiel van de vreemdelingen in België (The Profile of the Migrants in Belgium). Leuven, Davidsfonds, 1982, 144 p. Elucidation of the problems concerning migrants in Belgium (number, characteristics, economic activity, housing, culture, etc.)

MARTENS, A.: 25 jaar wegwerparbeiders: het Belgische immigratiebeleid na 1945 (25 Years of Cast-Away Workers: Belgian Immigration Policy after 1945). Leuven, S.O.I., 1973, 322 p. Analysis of the Belgian immigration policy: description of the situation at the eve of World War II and of the postwar immigration.

2.10 Public household

MOESEN, W. and VAN ROMPUY, V.: Inleiding tot de openbare financiën (Introduction to Public Finance). Leuven, Acco, 1977, 270 p.

N.: Le budget de l'état Belge (Belgian Public Expenditure). Bruxelles, Centre Internationale de Recherches et d'Information sur l'Economie, A.S.L.K., 1979. Consists of 4 reports: public expenditure in general, the fiscal receipts, the budgetary balance and the financing of the budgetary deficits.

N.: 'Les finances publiques belges.' *Revue française de finances publiques*, 1984, no. 4, pp. 1-164. Articles on: public finance in Belgium from 1955 to 1983, budgetary policy, public debt, taxing, monetary policy, social security, the effects of regionalization and on the budgetary procedure.

SIXIEME CONGRES DES ECONOMISTES BELGES DE LANGUE FRANCAISE: Les finances publiques Belges (Belgian Public Expenditure). Bruxelles, CIFoP, 1984, 3 dln. Three reports: statistical information on public finance in Belgium (concepts, techniques, sources and recent data), a macro-economic approach to public finance and the contribution of public finance to the support of economic activity.

SPREUTELS, M.: Openbare financiën (Public Finance). Gent, Story, 1969, 572 p.

REGAL, R. (ed.): The Budget Today. Brugge, De Tempel, 1968.

VANDENDRIESSCHE, S.: Evolutie van de Belgische centrale overheidsuitgaven sinds 1919. Onderzoek naar determinerende factoren. (The Evolution of Public Expenditure since 1919. Inquiry into the Determinant Factors.) Brussel, Ministerie von Financiën, 1978, 730 p.

VERENIGING VOOR ECONOMIE: De overheid in de gemengde economie (The Government in a Mixed Economy). 11de V.W.E.C., 1973. Collection of papers presented at the 11th Congress of Flemish Economists on the role of government in a mixed economy.

2.11 Public employment

GRAULICH, B. and NEVE, M.: Les droits et obligations du chômeur (The Rights and Duties of the Unemployed.) Brussel, Labor, 1980, 363 p. Analysis of the problems concerning legislation on full employment with chapters on specific regulations such as part-time work, transitional pension schemes, the Special Temporary Employment Scheme, Public Authority Employment Programmes, etc.

III Impact of social programmes

3.1 Poverty

BERGHMAN, J., et al.: Bestaansminimum (Subsistence Minimum). Antwerpen, Kluwer, 1980. Collection of papers assessing various aspects of the Right to a Subsistence Minimum, five years after its introduction.

BERGHMAN, J.: Poverty and Inequality in Belgium, in GEORGE, V. and LAWSON, R. (eds): Poverty and Inequality in Common Market Countries. London, Routledge and Kegan Paul, 1980, pp. 61-91. Review of poverty policies in Belgium since World War II, of Belgian poverty lines and analyses based on them, and of studies on income inequality and on other forms of deprivation.

COMMISSION OF THE EUROPEAN COMMUNITIES: Final Report to the Council on the Programme of Pilot Schemes and Studies to Combat Poverty. Brussels, 1981.

DELEECK, H., BERGMAN, J., et. al.: De sociale zekerheid tussen droom en daad (Social Security between Dream and Deed). Antwerpen, Van Loghum Slaterus, 1980. The results of an extensive survey on the effects of social security on living conditions are analysed within the framework of a general theory of social policy and of the historical development of Belgian social security.

JANSSENS, P. and VRANKEN, J.: Armoede in België. Een rapport in opdracht van de Europese Commissie (Poverty in Belgium. A Report for the European Commission). Antwerpen, 1980. A review of empirical data which are available on the Belgian poverty situation, described in terms of differential participation at the production process, national income, consumption, education and housing. Contains also a short review of direct and indirect poverty policies. (Partly translated into French and English.)

SENAEVE, P.: De bestrijding van de armoede in België (Combatting Poverty in Belgium). Leuven, ACCO, 1977. Analysis and evaluation of the set of legal instruments available to combat poverty in Belgium. Much attention is paid to their history and the decision-making process involved.

VEREYCKEN, L. and VRANKEN, J.: 'Differentiële participatie en een nadere analyse van de levensomstandigheden van de laagste inkomenscategorieën in België en van hun aantal (Differential participation and a further analysis of living conditions of the lowest income categories in Belgium and of their number)'. *Inkomens-en Vermogensverdeling,* Referaten van het 14de Vlaams Wetenschappelijk Economisch Congres, Brussel, 1979. Analysis of the living conditions of the lowest income groups in Belgium in terms of differential participation and an estimation of their number (using several poverty measures).

VRANKEN, J.: 'Armoede in de Welvaartsstaat: problematiek en enkele krachtlijnen voor een analyse (Poverty in the welfare state: the problem and proposals for an analysis)'. *Economisch en Sociaal Tijdschrift,* 33 (1979), 3, pp. 327-340. The main scientific approaches to poverty (poverty-lines, culture of poverty and social class) are analysed with respect to their dichotomizing characteristics (separation of the population into poor and non-poor).

VRANKEN, J.: 'Anti-poverty Policy in Belgium', in BROWN, J.C. (ed.): Anti-poverty Policy in the European Community. London, P.S.I., 1984, pp. 72-92. Discusses the nature of the policy, influences on the policy, characteristics of anti-poverty measures (with respect to fiscal policy, social security, collective goods), the preventive character of the programmes, temporary and long-term poverty and the barriers to a successful anti-poverty policy.

VRANKEN, J.: 'Non-income dimensions of poverty. An analysis of the Nine National Reports on Poverty', in SARPELLON, G. (ed.): Understanding Poverty. Milano, Franco Angeli, 1984. Based on a background paper for the European Commission's Final Report to the Council (see above).

WERKGROEP ALTERNATIEVE EKONOMIE ed. by VRANKEN, J.: Armoede in België (Poverty in Belgium). Antwerpen, De Nederlandsche Boekhandel, 1972. The first estimation of the number of poor in Belgium (14.5% of the population) which uses an elaborate poverty line (based upon a minimal household budget) and takes into account all population groups.

3.2 Inequality and income distribution

DELEECK, H.: Opstellen over inkomensverdeling, sociale zekerheid en sociaal beleid (Papers on income distribution, social security and social policy). Antwerpen, De Nederlandsche Boekhandel, 1972, p. Collection of articles on income distribution, redistribution policies, social security, inequality and social policy.

DELEECK, H.: Ongelijkheden in de welvaartsstaat (Inequality in the Welfare State). Antwerpen, De Nederlandsche Boekhandel, 1977, 320 p. Collection of articles on aspects of inequality in the Belgian welfare state, in particular on the unequal distribution of income and public goods.

DELEECK, H.: 'L'effet Mathieu: de la répartition inégale des biens collectifs (The Mathew-effect: the unequal distribution of public goods)'. *Recherches Sociologiques*, (1978), 3, pp. 301-326. Description of the process by which higher social classes tend to benefit proportionally more from public expenditure than lower social classes.

DELEECK, H., BERGMAN, J., et al.: De sociale zekerheid tussen droom en daad (Social Security between Dream and Deed). Antwerpen, Van Loghum Slaterus, 1980. The results of an extensive survey on the effects of social security on living conditions are analysed within the framework of a general theory of social policy and of the historical development of Belgian social security.

DELEECK, H., HUYBRECHS, J. and CANTILLON, B.: Het Mathëuseffect. De ongelijke verdeling van de sociale overheidsuitgaven (The Mathew-effect. The Unequal Distribution of Social Expenditure). Antwerpen, Kluwer, 1983. Analysis of the results of a large sample survey on the unequal consumption of public goods. The hypothesis that the higher the income level/socio-professional level of the household, the higher the consumption of public goods, is largely confirmed.

MORISSENS, L.: 'De l'inégalité des revenus à l'inégalité des satisfactions (From the inequality of income to the inequality of satisfactions)'. *Cahiers Economiques de Bruxelles* (1980), 88, pp. 235-259. Analysis of household budgets at different levels for the period 1973-1974.

VLAAMS WETENSCHAPPELIJK ECONOMISCH CONGRES: Inkomens- en Vermogensverdeling (Distribution of income and wealth). Referaten van het 14de V.W.E.C., Brussel, 1979. Collection of papers presented at the 14th Congress of Flemish Economists on the distribution of income and wealth in Belgium.

CLAEYS, U.: Sportbeoefening in Vlaanderen. Sociologisch profiel (Sports Practice in Flanders. Sociological Profile). Brussel, BLOSO, 1979, 199 p. Inquiry into social differences with respect to sports activities in Flanders.

VAN MECHELEN, F. and VALVEKENS, S.: De vrijetijds- en cultuurconsumptie (Leisure and Culture Consumption). Leuven, S.O.I., 1968. Inquiry into the differential leisure and culture consumption of the Flemish population based on an household budget inquiry.

3.3 Economic effects

CARRIN, G. and VAN BROEKHOVEN, E.: 'De invloed van het publieke pensioenstelsel op de gezinsbesparingen: enkele empirische resultaten voor België (The influence of the public pension scheme on household savings: some empirical results for Belgium)'. *Economisch en Sociaal Tijdschrift*, (1981), 3, pp. 397-410.

CARRIN, G.: 'Economic evaluation of health care interventions: a review of alternative methods'. *Social Science and Medicine* (1984), 10, pp. 1015-1030.

VAN ROMPUY, V. and VERTOGHEN, R.: Sociaal-economische kosten- en baten-analyse. Evaluatie van investeringsprojecten in de publieke sector (Social-Economic Costs and Benefits Analysis. Evaluation of Investment Projects in the Public Sector). Leuven, ACCO, 1982. Introduction to the theoretical basis, the methods used and the practical use of the social-economic assets and liabilities analysis concerning investment projects in the public sector.

Appendix Tables

Contents

Table

Table 1 Gross Domestic Product and Total Public Expenditure

Year	GDP (at market prices, in million BFR)			Deflators (base 1970)				Total public expenditure (in million BFR)						Year
	At current prices	At constant (1970) prices	Annual real growth rate	Gross domestic product	Public consumption	Private consumption	Cost of living index	At current prices	As % of GDP	At constant (1970) prices GDP defl.	At constant (1970) prices publ. cons.	Annual real growth rate GDP defl.	Annual real growth rate publ.cons. defl.	
1950								89 625						1950
1951														1951
1952														1952
1953	407 473	636 310		0.640	0.617	0.692								1953
1954	424 306	660 432	3.8	0.642	0.620	0.700	0.682							1954
1955	451 144	690 882	4.7	0.653	0.625	0.693	0.682	123 525	27.3	189 165	197 640			1955
1956	479 553	709 163	2.6	0.676	0.645	0.708	0.702							1956
1957	508 709	723 486	2.0	0.703	0.671	0.735	0.722							1957
1958	512 800	722 740	-0.1	0.709	0.677	0.735	0.729							1958
1959	531 145	746 312	3.2	0.711	0.692	0.757	0.740							1959
1960	563 951	784 399	5.0	0.718	0.700	0.755	0.742	188 096	33.3	261 972	268 709			1960
1961	600 210	825 769	5.3	0.726	0.701	0.772	0.750	190 217	31.8	262 007	271 351	-0.1	1.1	1961
1962	642 669	874 094	5.9	0.735	0.710	0.781	0.761	210 324	32.7	286 155	296 231	9.2	9.2	1962
1963	691 091	912 102	4.4	0.757	0.722	0.807	0.777	228 872	33.0	302 341	316 997	5.6	7.1	1963
1964	773 379	975 695	7.1	0.792	0.749	0.836	0.809	261 213	33.9	329 814	348 749	9.2	10.1	1964
1965	842 133	1 011 907	3.8	0.831	0.790	0.871	0.842	300 339	35.7	361 419	380 176	9.5	8.9	1965
1966	906 112	1 044 113	3.2	0.868	0.832	0.908	0.877	337 175	37.2	388 450	405 258	7.4	6.5	1966
1967	970 612	1 084 950	3.8	0.894	0.865	0.932	0.903	373 988	38.4	418 331	432 356	7.7	6.8	1967
1968	1 038 383	1 131 111	4.4	0.918	0.900	0.952	0.927	409 280	39.3	445 839	454 756	6.5	5.3	1968
1969	1 151 309	1 204 500	6.5	0.956	0.940	0.975	0.962	468 396	40.8	489 954	498 294	9.8	9.5	1969
1970	1 280 924	1 280 924	6.2	1.000	1.000	1.000	1.000	525.696	41.1	525 696	525 696	7.4	5.6	1970
1971	1 402 333	1 330 954	3.8	1.053	1.088	1.049	1.043	604 676	43.2	574 241	555 768	9.2	5.6	1971
1972	1 566 041	1 400 354	5.3	1.118	1.184	1.096	1.100	672 282	42.9	601 326	567 806	4.7	2.3	1972
1973	1 780 747	1 488 526	6.2	1.196	1.282	1.165	1.176	761 968	42.9	637 097	594 359	5.9	4.7	1973
1974	2 092 636	1 558 805	4.7	1.342	1.485	1.307	1.326	889 464	42.6	662 790	598 966	4.1	0.8	1974
1975	2 312 982	1 528 881	-1.9	1.512	1.727	1.455	1.494	1 118 555	48.3	379 785	647 687	11.6	8.0	1975
1976	2 626 288	1 612 278	5.6	1.628	1.883	1.574	1.631	1 273 417	48.6	782 197	676 270	5.6	4.4	1976
1977	2 843 648	1 629 979	1.1	1.745	2.032	1.677	1.748	1 428 343	50.1	818 535	702 925	4.7	3.8	1977
1978	3 057 084	1 683 231	3.2	1.816	2.132	1.751	1.828	1 592 162	52.2	876 741	746 793	7.1	6.2	1978
1979	3 261 132	1 722 530	2.3	1.893	2.192	1.818	1.908	1 732 215	53.1	915 063	790 244	4.4	5.9	1979
1980	3 483 202	1 763 197	2.3	1.976	2.415	1.941	2.036	1 934 944	55.5	979 223	801 219	7.1	1.4	1980
1981	3 615 400	1 742 261	-1.3	2.074	2.610	2.114	2.188							1981
1982	3 893 042	1 737 034	-0.4	2.242										1982

Table 2 Public Expenditure by

Year	Major Purpose: Total exp. at current prices, in million BFR	publ. adm.	de-fence	soc./envi-ronmental services	econ-omic serv.	publ. debt	Economic Category: Total exp. at current prices, in million BFR	Subs./trans-fers	final cons.	inter. on debt	capit. form-ation	Level of Government: Total exp. at current prices, in million BFR	central govt.	local govt.	social insur.	Year
1950	89 625	17.1	12.6	49.9	10.6	9.8										1950
1951																1951
1952																1952
1953																1953
1954																1954
1955	123 525	13.8	15.5	50.8	8.7	11.2										1955
1956																1956
1957																1957
1958																1958
1959																1959
1960	188 096	12.1	12.4	52.3	11.6	11.6										1960
1961	190 217	11.9	11.6	53.3	10.1	13.0										1961
1962	210 324	10.6	11.7	52.1	11.5	14.2										1962
1963	228 872	9.6	12.0	53.7	13.1	11.5	217 554	40.4	42.2	9.4	8.1	200 032	53.7	10.7	35.6	1963
1964	261 213	9.1	11.3	52.9	13.6	13.0	238 356	39.4	41.5	9.4	9.7	215 285	53.3	10.9	35.8	1964
1965	300 339	9.2	10.4	54.4	12.9	13.1	271 762	42.7	40.5	8.9	7.8	250 606	51.5	10.2	38.4	1965
1966	337 175	8.5	9.8	53.5	15.2	13.0	302 756	42.9	40.0	8.7	8.4	277 221	51.1	10.2	38.7	1966
1967	373 988	8.3	9.2	52.8	15.4	14.3	334 567	42.4	39.9	8.7	9.0	304 311	51.2	10.4	38.4	1967
1968	409 280	8.1	9.0	52.6	17.4	12.9	376 885	43.9	38.2	8.4	9.5	341 143	50.4	10.1	39.5	1968
1969	468 396	8.0	8.6	50.2	16.9	16.2	415 941	43.6	38.4	9.0	9.0	378 587	50.9	10.2	39.0	1969
1970	525 696	8.1	8.1	52.0	16.6	15.2	467 493	43.8	37.5	9.2	9.5	423 202	50.4	10.1	39.5	1970
1971	604 676	8.4	8.1	51.7	16.9	15.0	533 086	42.8	37.9	8.7	10.6	476 772	50.5	10.3	39.2	1971
1972	672 282	8.6	8.2	54.3	17.2	11.7	609 238	43.1	38.2	8.5	10.2	546 902	49.6	10.2	40.2	1972
1973	761 968	9.0	7.9	56.8	15.6	10.8	698 252	45.1	37.9	8.5	8.5	638 132	49.7	10.1	40.1	1973
1974	889 464	8.1	7.6	58.7	14.5	11.2	824 780	45.2	38.1	8.9	7.8	760 359	48.5	10.4	41.1	1974
1975	1 118 555	8.1	7.6	59.6	13.3	11.4	1 028 342	46.8	37.8	8.0	7.4	952 058	47.3	10.2	42.5	1975
1976	1 273 417	7.8	7.5	60.2	14.0	10.4	1 183 349	47.1	37.3	8.3	7.4	1 095 955	46.2	10.2	43.6	1976
1977	1 438 343	8.0	7.3	60.3	13.9	10.6	1 325 375	47.2	37.1	8.8	6.9	1 233 867	46.2	10.5	43.3	1977
1978	1 592 162	8.5	7.3	57.7	14.5	12.0	1 464 066	46.8	37.4	9.4	6.5	1 369 496	46.5	10.8	42.7	1978
1979	1 732 215	7.7	7.3	57.5	14.6	13.0	1 612 801	46.6	36.6	10.3	6.5	1 507 947	46.7	11.0	42.3	1979
1980	1 934 944	7.1	6.8	57.4	14.3	14.4	1 799 438	45.3	35.9	11.9	6.8	1 677 194	47.4	11.3	41.3	1980
1981							2 029 398	45.1	34.6	14.2	6.0	1 906 635	48.3	11.2	40.6	1981

Table 3

Social Expenditure

Year	at current prices (in million BFR)						at constant (1970) prices (in million BFR)						Year
	Income Maint.	Educa-tion	Health	Hous-ing	Other	Total	Income Maint.	Educa-tion	Health	Hous-ing	Other	Total	
1950	30 843	7 627	4 621	1 694	209	44 994							1950
1955	47 837	11 642	6 529	1 448	459	67 915	70 142	18 627	10 446	2 317	734	102 267	1955
1960	65 815	25 175	9 872	2 530	548	103 913	88 699	35 964	14 103	3 614	783	143 164	1960
1960	71 573	25 175	9 872	2 530	1 807	110 957	96 460	35 964	14 103	3 614	2 581	152 723	1960
1961	73 740	26 789	10 210	2 417	1 552	114 708	98 320	38 215	14 565	3 448	2 214	156 762	1961
1962	81 826	29 145	11 079	2 746	1 899	126 695	107 524	41 049	15 604	3 868	2 674	170 720	1962
1963	84 890	33 872	12 012	3 007	2 160	135 941	109 253	46 914	16 637	4 165	2 992	179 961	1963
1964	92 955	36 786	16 247	2 642	2 497	151 127	114 901	49 114	21 691	3 527	3 334	192 568	1964
1965	105 525	43 627	23 638	3 591	2 472	178 853	125 326	55 224	29 921	4 546	3 129	218 146	1965
1966	115 135	49 536	28 995	2 921	1 753	198 340	131 283	59 539	34 850	3 511	2 107	231 289	1966
1967	124 215	53 507	31 636	3 802	2 235	214 795	137 558	61 858	36 573	4 395	2 584	242 968	1967
1968	138 946	57 601	35 998	3 646	3 584	240 187	149 888	64 001	39 998	4 051	3 982	261 920	1968
1969	148 887	64 050	38 320	4 229	3 192	260 733	154 768	68 138	40 766	4 499	3 396	271 567	1969
1970	169 775	73 037	48 058	4 660	4 135	299 665	169 775	73 037	48 058	4 660	4 135	299 665	1970
1971	191 382	84 888	56 909	5 344	3 775	342 298	183 492	78 022	52 306	4 912	3 470	322 202	1971
1972	223 399	99 662	67 771	6 392	3 917	401 141	203 090	84 174	57 239	5 398	3 308	353 210	1972
1973	267 671	113 362	79 616	7 883	3 387	471 919	227 611	88 426	62 103	6 149	2 642	386 932	1973
1974	321 305	142 563	96 052	9 520	3 671	573 111	242 311	96 002	64 681	6 411	2 472	411 878	1974
1975	411 165	174 912	122 408	11 877	5 090	725 452	275 211	101 281	70 879	6 877	2 947	457 195	1975
1976	476 678	198 512	138 491	13 370	26 669	853 720	292 261	105 423	73 548	7 100	14 163	492 496	1976
1977	540 083	219 076	159 745	14 760	25 683	959 347	308 972	107 813	78 615	7 264	12 639	515 303	1977
1977	534 404	219 076	159 745	14 760	25 683	954 928	305 723	107 813	78 615	7 264	12 639	512 054	1977
1978	577 582	236 051	169 939	17 371	31 477	1 033 719	315 964	110 718	79 709	8 148	14 764	529 303	1978
1979	640 060	253 602	181 497	20 950	29 957	1 126 066	335 461	115 694	82 800	9 557	13 666	557 179	1979
1980	714 734	274 446	198 874	33 587	27 293	1 248 928	351 048	113 642	82 349	13 908	11 301	572 248	1980

Table 4 Social Expenditure

Year	As % of gross domestic product: Income Maint.	Educa-tion	Health	Hous-ing	Other	Total	As % of public expenditure: Income Maint.	Educa-tion	Health	Hous-ing	Other	Total	Percent distribution: Income Maint.	Educa-tion	Health	Hous-ing	Other	Year
1950							34.5	8.4	5.1	1.8	0.3	50.1	68.4	17.1	10.2	3.9	0.6	1950
1951																		1951
1952																		1952
1953																		1953
1954																		1954
1955	10.5	2.7	1.5	0.3	0.0	15.0	38.7	9.3	5.4	1.2	0.3	54.9	70.5	17.1	9.6	2.1	0.6	1955
1956																		1956
1957																		1957
1958																		1958
1959																		1959
1960	11.7	4.5	1.8	0.3	0.0	18.3	35.1	13.5	5.1	1.2	0.3	55.2	63.3	24.3	9.6	2.4	0.6	1960
1960	12.6	4.5	1.8	0.3	0.3	19.8	38.1	13.5	5.1	1.2	0.9	59.1	64.5	22.8	9.0	2.4	1.5	1960
1961	12.3	4.5	1.8	0.3	0.3	19.2	38.7	14.1	5.4	1.2	0.9	60.3	64.2	23.4	9.0	2.1	1.5	1961
1962	12.6	4.5	1.8	0.3	0.3	19.8	39.0	13.8	5.4	1.2	0.9	60.3	64.5	23.1	8.7	2.1	1.5	1962
1963	12.3	4.8	1.8	0.3	0.3	19.8	37.2	14.7	5.1	1.2	0.9	59.4	62.4	24.9	8.7	2.1	1.5	1963
1964	12.0	4.8	2.1	0.3	0.3	19.5	35.7	14.1	6.3	0.9	0.9	57.9	61.5	24.3	10.8	1.8	1.8	1964
1965	12.6	5.1	2.7	0.3	0.3	21.3	35.1	14.4	7.8	1.2	0.9	59.7	59.1	24.3	13.2	2.1	1.5	1965
1966	12.6	5.4	3.3	0.3	0.3	21.9	34.2	14.7	8.7	0.9	0.6	58.8	57.9	24.9	14.7	1.5	0.9	1966
1967	12.9	5.4	3.3	0.3	0.3	22.2	33.3	14.4	8.4	0.9	0.6	57.3	57.9	24.9	14.7	1.8	0.9	1967
1968	13.5	5.4	3.6	0.3	0.3	23.1	33.9	14.1	8.7	0.9	0.9	58.8	57.9	24.0	15.0	1.5	1.5	1968
1969	12.9	5.7	3.3	0.3	0.3	22.5	31.8	13.8	8.1	0.9	0.6	55.8	57.0	24.6	14.7	1.5	1.2	1969
1970	13.2	5.7	3.9	0.3	0.3	23.4	32.4	13.8	9.0	0.9	0.9	57.0	56.7	24.3	15.9	1.5	1.5	1970
1971	13.5	6.0	4.2	0.3	0.3	24.3	31.8	14.1	9.3	0.9	0.6	56.7	55.8	24.9	16.5	1.5	1.2	1971
1972	14.4	6.3	4.2	0.3	0.3	25.5	33.3	14.7	10.2	0.9	0.6	59.7	55.8	24.9	16.8	1.5	0.9	1972
1973	15.0	6.3	4.5	0.3	0.3	26.4	35.1	15.0	10.5	0.9	0.3	61.8	56.7	24.0	16.8	1.8	0.6	1973
1974	15.3	6.9	4.5	0.6	0.3	27.3	36.0	15.9	10.8	1.2	0.3	64.5	56.1	24.9	16.8	1.8	0.6	1974
1975	17.7	7.5	5.4	0.6	0.3	31.5	36.9	15.6	10.8	1.2	0.6	64.8	56.7	24.0	16.8	1.5	0.6	1975
1976	18.3	7.5	5.4	0.6	0.9	32.4	37.5	15.6	10.8	0.9	2.1	66.9	55.8	23.4	16.2	1.5	3.0	1976
1977	18.9	7.8	5.7	0.6	0.9	33.6	37.8	15.3	11.1	0.9	1.8	67.2	56.4	22.8	16.8	1.5	2.7	1977
1977	18.9	7.8	5.7	0.6	0.9	33.6	37.5	15.3	11.1	0.9	1.8	66.9	56.1	22.8	16.8	1.5	2.7	1977
1978	18.9	7.8	5.7	0.6	0.9	33.9	36.3	14.7	10.8	1.2	2.1	64.8	55.8	22.8	16.5	1.8	3.0	1978
1979	19.5	7.8	5.7	0.6	0.9	34.5	36.9	14.7	10.5	1.2	1.8	65.1	56.7	22.5	16.2	1.8	2.7	1979
1980	20.4	7.8	5.7	0.9	0.9	36.0	36.9	14.1	10.2	1.8	1.5	64.5	57.3	21.9	15.9	2.7	2.1	1980

Table 5

Expenditure on Income Maintenance

Year	at current prices (in million BFR)							at constant (1970) prices (in million BFR)							Year
	Old age survivor pensions	Industr. accid./ occ. disease	Sickness Invalid.	Unempl. benefit	Family allowance	Social welfare	Total	Old age survivor pensions	Industr. accid./ occ. disease	Sickness Invalid.	Unempl. benefit	Family allowance	Social welfare	Total	
1950	13 361	1 409	1 973		6 177	7 923	30 843								1950
1951		1 736	2 406		6 963										1951
1952		2 597	2 887		7 557										1952
1953		2 721	2 921		7 778										1953
1954		2 808	2 972		8 203				4 117	4 358		12 028			1954
1955	24 518	3 102	3 266		8 443	8 508	47 837	35 950	4 548	4 789		12 380	12 475	79 142	1955
1956		3 524	3 519		8 738				5 020	5 013		12 447			1956
1957		3 561	3 725		10 118				4 932	5 159		14 014			1957
1958		3 669	4 036		11 326				5 033	5 536		15 536			1958
1959		3 625	4 605		11 582				4 899	6 223		15 651			1959
1960	31 976	3 733	5 404	—	12 498	12 204	65 788	43 094	5 031	7 283	—	16 844	16 447	88 663	1960
1960	31 976	3 733	5 404	5 758	12 498	12 204	71 573	43 094	5 031	7 283	7 760	16 844	16 447	96 460	1960
1961	34 556	4 088	5 612	4 581	13 976	10 927	73 740	46 075	5 451	7 483	6 108	18 635	14 569	98 320	1961
1962	39 039	4 331	6 048	3 992	16 547	11 869	81 826	51 300	5 691	7 947	5 246	21 744	15 597	107 524	1962
1963	39 723	4 817	5 866	4 593	18 181	11 710	84 890	51 124	6 199	7 549	5 911	23 399	15 071	109 253	1963
1964	42 705	5 591	9 346	3 507	21 100	10 706	92 955	52 787	6 911	11 552	4 335	26 082	13 234	114 901	1964
1965	48 627	6 821	8 147	4 365	25 513	12 052	105 525	57 752	8 101	9 676	5 184	30 301	14 314	125 326	1965
1966	53 204	7 021	10 031	4 771	27 405	12 703	115 135	60 666	8 006	11 438	5 440	31 249	14 485	131 283	1966
1967	56 072	8 197	10 641	6 671	29 228	13 406	123 615	62 095	9 077	11 784	7 387	32 368	14 846	136 894	1967
1968	65 220	9 428	11 557	7 583	32 044	13 526	139 358	70 356	10 170	12 467	8 180	34 567	14 591	150 332	1968
1969	71 093	11 101	13 612	6 830	34 595	13 711	150 942	73 901	11 539	14 150	7 100	35 962	14 253	156 904	1969
1970	84 824	12 326	13 612	6 238	38 531	14 244	169 775	84 824	12 326	13 612	6 238	38 531	14 244	169 775	1970
1971	95 354	14 327	16 551	7 239	42 039	15 872	191 382	91 423	13 736	15 868	6 940	40 306	15 217	183 492	1971
1972	110 360	17 940	19 849	11 117	46 168	17 965	223 399	100 327	16 309	18 044	10 106	41 971	16 332	203 090	1972
1973	140 420	21 893	22 701	12 672	50 362	19 623	267 671	119 405	18 616	19 303	10 775	42 825	16 686	227 611	1973
1974	168 993	24 960	27 947	17 194	59 031	23 180	321 305	127 446	18 823	21 076	12 967	44 518	17 481	242 311	1974
1975	210 637	27 966	37 623	37 344	67 678	29 917	411 165	140 989	18 719	25 183	24 996	45 300	20 025	275 211	1975
1976	239 844	32 018	47 581	47 820	76 651	32 764	476 678	147 053	19 631	29 173	29 319	46 996	20 088	292 261	1976
1977	265 800	37 591	53 952	63 390	83 541	36 709	540 983	152 059	21 505	30 865	36 264	47 792	21 001	309 487	1977
1977	265 800	37 591	53 952	63 390	83 541	31 030	535 664	152 059	21 505	30 865	36 264	47 792	17 752	306 444	1977
1978	282 448	37 272	57 249	78 285	90 474	33 153	578 881	154 512	20 389	31 318	42 826	49 493	18 136	316 675	1978
1979	313 147	39 951	59 645	95 464	95 148	36 699	640 054	164 123	20 939	31 261	50 033	49 868	19 234	335 458	1979
1980	349 100	42 092	65 718	111 472	103 974	42 372	714 728	171 464	20 674	32 278	54 751	51 068	20 811	351 045	1980
1981		44 416	70 875	141 690	102 878				20 300	32 392	64 758	47 019			1981
1982		45 148	79 431	156 536	104 112										1982

Table 6

Expenditure on Old Age and Survivors Pensions

Year	At current prices (in million BFR)					At constant (1970) prices (in million BFR)					Year
	Total	Private employees	Self-employed	Public sector	Guaranteed pensions	Total	Private employees	Self-employed	Public sector	Guaranteed pensions	
1950	13 361	6 100		6 722	539						1950
1951											1951
1952											1952
1953											1953
1954											1954
1955	24 518	9 924		12 161	2 433	35 950	14 551		17 831	3 567	1955
1956											1956
1957											1957
1958											1958
1959											1959
1960	31 976	15 267	2 149	13 968	592	43 094	20 575	2 896	18 825	798	1960
1961	34 556	16 209	2 358	14 751	738	46 075	21 612	3 811	19 668	984	1960
1962	39 039	20 520	2 656	15 041	822	51 300	26 965	3 490	19 765	1 080	1961
1963	39 723	20 478	2 687	15 763	795	51 124	26 355	3 458	20 287	1 023	1963
1964	42 705	21 773	3 234	16 929	769	52 787	26 914	3 997	20 926	951	1964
1965	48 627	24 231	3 680	19 779	937	57 752	28 778	4 370	23 491	1 113	1965
1966	53 204	27 695	3 548	20 973	988	60 666	31 579	4 045	23 914	1 126	1966
1967	56 072	29 330	3 477	22 271	994	62 095	32 481	3 850	24 663	1 101	1967
1968	65 220	36 766	4 129	23 358	967	70 356	39 661	4 454	25 197	1 043	1968
1969	71 093	40 982	4 272	24 850	989	73 901	42 601	4 441	25 831	1 028	1969
1970	84 824	46 945	6 561	30 114	1 204	84 824	46 945	6 561	30 114	1 204	1970
1971	95 354	52 401	8 092	33 607	1 254	91 423	50 241	7 758	32 221	1 202	1971
1972	110 360	61 283	9 648	38 088	1 341	100 327	55 712	8 771	34 625	1 219	1972
1973	140 420	73 044	13 774	52 103	1 499	119 405	62 112	11 713	44 305	1 275	1973
1974	168 993	88 659	17 957	60 320	2 057	127 446	66 862	13 542	45 490	1 551	1974
1975	210 637	109 642	22 928	75 431	2 636	140 989	73 388	15 347	50 489	1 764	1975
1976	239 844	126 908	26 205	83 553	3 178	147 053	77 810	16 067	51 228	1 948	1976
1977	265 800	139 348	29 394	93 515	3 543	152 059	79 718	16 816	53 498	2 027	1977
1978	282 448	151 833	30 717	96 235	3 663	154 512	83 059	16 804	52 645	2 004	1978
1979	313 147	171 398	32 173	105 936	3 590	164 123	89 831	16 862	55 548	1 882	1979
1980	349 106	188 618	34 119	122 254	4 115	171 467	92 641	16 758	60 046	2 021	1980
1981		208 868	36 509		4 463		95 461	16 686		2 040	1981

Table 7

Expenditure on Invalidity and Sickness

Year	At current prices (in million BFR)								At constant (1970) prices (in million BFR)								Year
	Industrial accidents			Occupational diseases	Sickness/invalidity				Industrial accidents			Occupational diseases	Sickness/invalidity				
					Employees		Self-employed						Employees		Self-employed		
	cash	kind	total	cash	cash	refunds	cash	refunds	cash	kind	total	cash	cash	refunds	cash	refunds	
1950			1 608	10	1 973	3 740											1950
1951			1 983	11	2 406	4 160											1951
1952			2 969	14	2 887	4 433											1952
1953			3 106	19	2 921	4 369								7 081			1953
1954			3 201	23	2 972	4 714					4 755	34	4 358	7 603			1954
1955			3 533	28	3 266	5 031					5 242	41	4 789	8 050			1955
1956			4 013	33	3 519	5 336					5 782	47	5 013	8 273			1956
1957			4 050	37	3 725	5 790					5 665	51	5 159	8 629			1957
1958			4 162	48	4 036	6 919					5 766	66	5 536	10 220			1958
1959			4 103	55	4 605	7 682					5 595	74	6 223	11 101			1959
1960			4 213	68	5 404	8 143					5 722	91	7 283	11 633			1960
1961	4 018	610	4 628	70	5 612	8 839			5 357	870	6 228	93	7 483	12 609			1961
1962	4 261	649	4 910	70	6 048	9 739			5 559	914	6 513	92	7 947	13 717			1962
1963	4 721	724	5 445	96	5 866	10 640			6 076	1 003	7 079	124	7 549	14 737			1963
1964	5 208	800	6 008	383	9 346	14 268		314	6 438	1 068	7 506	473	11 552	19 049		419	1964
1965	6 377	831	7 208	444	8 147	20 069		1 250	7 574	1 052	8 625	527	9 676	25 404		1 582	1965
1966	6 349	868	7 217	672	10 031	24 717		1 442	7 240	1 043	8 283	766	11 438	29 708		1 773	1966
1967	6 800	1 189	7 989	1 397	10 641	26 256		1 361	7 531	1 375	8 905	1 547	11 784	30 354		1 573	1967
1968	7 556	1 065	8 621	1 872	11 145	28 383		1 453	8 151	1 183	9 334	2 019	12 023	31 537		1 614	1968
1969	7 607	1 167	8 774	3 494	11 557	30 880		1 738	7 907	1 241	9 149	3 632	12 013	32 851		1 849	1969
1970	8 331	1 271	9 602	3 995	13 612	37 471		1 992	8 331	1 271	9 602	3 995	13 612	37 471		1 992	1970
1971	8 947	1 393	10 340	5 380	16 541	44 641	10	2 729	8 578	1 280	9 859	5 158	15 859	41 030	10	2 508	1971
1972	11 864	906	12 770	6 076	19 337	52 521	512	3 418	10 786	765	11 551	5 524	17 579	44 359	466	2 887	1972
1973	15 395	1 237	16 632	6 498	21 896	59 949	805	4 605	13 091	965	14 056	5 526	18 619	46 762	685	3 592	1973
1974	16 993	1 394	18 387	7 967	26 734	72 230	1 213	5 314	12 815	939	13 754	6 008	20 161	48 640	915	3 578	1974
1975	18 166	1 569	19 735	9 800	36 019	93 585	1 604	7 242	12 159	908	13 068	6 559	24 109	54 189	1 074	4 193	1975
1976	20 847	1 687	22 534	11 171	45 713	105 157	1 868	8 594	12 782	896	13 678	6 849	28 027	55 846	1 145	4 564	1976
1977	25 383	1 805	27 188	12 208	50 918	119 731	2 134	9 379	14 521	888	15 410	6 984	29 129	58 923	1 221	4 615	1977
1978	24 276	1 876	26 152	12 996	53 696	126 906	2 254	9 655	13 280	880	14 160	7 109	29 374	59 524	1 233	4 528	1978
1979	26 258	2 003	28 261	13 699	57 148	132 972	2 497	10 415	13 762	914	14 676	7 180	29 952	60 662	1 309	4 751	1979
1980	27 579	2 184	29 763	14 513	63 102	145 244	2 616	10 971	13 546	904	14 450	7 128	30 993	60 142	1 285	4 543	1980
1981	29 306	2 174	31 480	15 110	67 768	158 165	3 107	12 495	13 394	833	14 227	6 906	30 973	60 600	1 420	4 787	1981
1982	29 029	2 287	31 316	16 119	76 102	174 940	3 329	13 823									1982

Table 8

Expenditure on Unemployment

Year	At current prices (in million BFR)							At constant (1970) prices (in million BFR)							Year
	Total	Unempl. benefits	Unempl. pensions	Employment programmes	Retrain-ing	Admin. costs	Other	Total	Unempl. benefits	Unempl. pensions	Employment programmes	Retrain-ing	Admin. costs	Other	
1960	7 017	5 118		607	33	554	705	9 559	6 898		818	44	791	1 007	1960
1961	5 523	4 208		331	42	587	355	7 452	5 611		441	56	837	506	1961
1962	5 242	3 805		65	122	581	669	7 006	5 000		85	160	818	942	1962
1963	6 029	4 275		82	230	628	815	7 902	5 502		106	296	870	1 129	1963
1964	5 204	3 091		77	339	850	847	6 601	3 821		95	419	1 135	1 131	1964
1965	6 006	3 940		85	340	733	908	7 261	4 679		101	404	928	1 149	1965
1966	5 656	4 288		96	387	777	108	6 504	4 889		109	441	934	130	1966
1967	7 717	6 329		47	395	887	58	8 591	7 009		52	437	1 025	67	1967
1968	10 102	7 053		65	465	888	1 631	10 979	7 608		70	502	987	1 812	1968
1969	8 855	6 418		82	330	909	1 115	9 253	6 671		85	343	967	1 186	1969
1970	9 102	5 691		100	447	1 060	1 804	9 102	5 691		100	447	1 060	1 804	1970
1971	9 621	6 565		109	565	1 152	1 231	9 130	6 294		104	542	1 059	1 131	1971
1972	14 128	9 780		621	716	1 390	1 621	12 649	8 891		565	651	1 174	1 369	1972
1973	14 822	11 138		720	814	1 648	502	12 452	9 471		612	692	1 285	391	1973
1974	19 471	15 297		746	1 151	1 882	395	14 500	11 536		563	868	1 267	266	1974
1975	40 865	34 440		1 301	1 603	2 490	1 033	27 036	23 052		871	1 073	1 442	598	1975
1976	72 802	44 274	268	2 230	1 048	3 647	21 335	42 587	27 145	164	1 367	643	1 937	11 330	1976
1977	87 268	52 773	6 137	3 219	1 261	4 467	19 412	48 016	30 190	3 511	1 841	721	2 198	9 553	1977
1978	107 886	57 951	10 632	8 281	1 421	5 143	24 457	56 709	31 702	5 816	4 530	777	2 412	11 471	1978
1979	123 418	63 867	14 203	15 756	1 638	5 705	22 249	62 786	33 473	7 444	8 258	859	2 602	10 150	1979
1980	136 581	72 193	18 535	18 827	1 917	6 609	18 500	65 148	35 458	9 103	9 247	942	2 737	7 660	1980
1981	181 452	97 597	23 718	19 090	1 285	7 736	32 027	79 993	44 605	10 840	8 725	587	2 964	12 271	1981
1982	193 445	106 096	30 636	18 655	1 149	8 543	28 365								1982

Table 9

Expenditure on Family Allowances

Year	At current prices (in million BFR)				At constant (1970) prices (in million BFR)				Year
	Total	Family allow. employees	Family allow. self-employed	Guaranteed family allow.	Total	Family allow. employees	Family allow. self-employed	Guaranteed family allow.	
1950	6 177	5 540	637						1950
1951	6 963	6 254	709						1951
1952	7 557	6 716	841						1952
1953	7 778	6 847	1 031						1953
1954	8 203	6 961	1 242		12 028	10 207	1 821		1954
1955	8 443	7 223	1 220		12 380	10 591	1 789		1955
1956	8 738	7 528	1 210		12 447	10 723	1 723		1956
1957	10 118	8 922	1 196		14 014	12 357	1 657		1957
1958	11 326	10 062	1 264		15 536	13 802	1 734		1958
1959	11 582	10 290	1 292		15 651	13 905	1 746		1959
1960	12 498	11 232	1 266		16 844	15 137	1 706		1960
1961	13 976	12 465	1 511		18 635	16 620	2 015		1961
1962	16 547	14 797	1 750		21 744	19 444	2 299		1962
1963	18 181	16 065	2 116		23 399	20 676	2 723		1963
1964	21 100	18 987	2 113		26 082	23 470	2 612		1964
1965	25 513	23 103	2 410		30 301	27 438	2 862		1965
1966	27 405	24 537	2 868		31 249	27 978	3 270		1966
1967	29 228	26 118	3 110		32 368	28 924	3 444		1967
1968	32 044	28 503	3 541		34 567	30 748	3 820		1968
1969	34 595	31 119	3 476		35 962	32 348	3 613		1969
1970	38 531	34 249	4 282		38 531	34 249	4 282		1970
1971	42 039	37 469	4 570		40 306	35 924	4 381		1971
1972	46 168	40 804	5 364		41 971	37 094	4 876		1972
1973	50 362	44 370	5 992		42 825	37 729	5 095		1973
1974	59 031	51 499	7 532		44 518	38 838	5 680		1974
1975	67 678	58 284	9 387	7	45 300	39 012	6 283	5	1975
1976	76 651	66 330	10 311	10	46 996	40 668	6 322	6	1976
1977	83 541	72 436	11 092	13	47 792	41 439	6 346	8	1977
1978	90 474	79 148	11 309	17	49 493	43 297	6 187	9	1978
1979	95 148	83 394	11 730	24	49 868	43 708	6 148	13	1979
1980	103 974	91 955	11 987	32	51 068	45 164	5 887	16	1980
1981	102 878	89 855	12 978	45	47 019	41 067	5 931	21	1981
1982	104 112	91 130	12 890	92					1982

Table 10

O t h e r   S o c i a l   W e l f a r e   E x p e n d i t u r e

Year	At current prices (in million BFR)								At constant (1970) prices (in million BFR)								Year
	General social assistance					General social aid			General social assistance					General social aid			
	Central govt	Local govt	Prov. govt	Total	of which: guaranteed min. income	Central govt	of which: war pensions	Local govt	Central govt	Local govt	Prov. govt	Total	of which: guaranteed min. income	Central govt	of which: war pensions	Local govt	
1950	1 677	927		2 604		5 319											1950
1951		981															1951
1952		959															1952
1953		1 027															1953
1954		1 101								1 614							1954
1955	1 889	1 108		2 997		5 511			2 770	1 624		4 394		8 080			1955
1956		1 181								1 682							1956
1957		1 406								1 947							1957
1958		1 439								1 974							1958
1959		1 513								2 044							1959
1960	2 216	1 729		3 945		8 259			2 986	2 330		5 317		11 131			1960
1961	2 232	1 844		4 076		6 851			2 976	2 459		5 435		9 135			1961
1962	2 374	1 879		4 253		7 616			3 120	2 469		5 589		10 008			1962
1963	2 483	2 094		4 577		7 133			3 196	2 695		5 890		9 180			1963
1964	933	2 132		3 065		7 641			1 153	2 635		3 789		9 445			1964
1965	1 230	2 379		3 609		8 443			1 461	2 825		4 286		10 027			1965
1966	1 536	2 364		3 900		8 803	4 727		1 751	2 695		4 447		10 038	5 390		1966
1967	1 453	2 494		3 947		9 459	5 193		1 609	2 762		4 371		10 475	5 751		1967
1968	1 342	2 607		3 949		9 577	5 171		1 448	2 812		4 260		10 331	5 578		1968
1969	1 137	2 438		3 575		10 136	5 698	364	1 182	2 534		3 716		10 536	5 923	378	1969
1970	1 346	2 590		3 936		10 308	5 579	418	1 346	2 590		3 936		10 308	5 579	418	1970
1971	1 428	2 736		4 164		11 708	5 907	505	1 369	2 623		3 992		11 225	5 663	484	1971
1972	1 658	2 896		4 554		13 411	6 192	675	1 507	2 633		4 140		12 192	5 629	613	1972
1973	2 467	2 981		5 448		14 175	6 782	867	2 098	2 535		4 633		12 054	5 767	737	1973
1974	3 199	3 317		6 516		16 664	7 531	1 064	2 413	2 501		4 914		12 567	5 680	802	1974
1975	5 991	3 984	222	10 197	119	19 720	8 506	1 381	4 010	2 667	148	6 825	80	13 199	5 693	924	1975
1976	5 359	4 564	288	10 211	202	22 553	9 632	1 663	3 286	2 798	177	6 261	124	13 828	5 905	1 020	1976
1977	5 201	5 679	318	11 198	414	25 511	10 592	1 975	2 975	3 249	182	6 406	237	14 594	6 059	1 130	1977
1978	6 626		395		533	26 132	10 807		3 625		216		292	14 295	5 912		1978
1979	8 937		484		654	27 278	11 146		4 684		254		343	14 296	5 842		1979
1980	10 315		546		801	31 511	13 667		5 066		268		393	15 477	6 713		1980
1981			664		1 070		13 520				304		489		6 179		1981
1982					1 493		15 029										1982

Table 11

Financing of Public and Social Security Expenditure

Year	Current receipts at current prices (in 1,000 billion BFR): Central government total	Central government transfers to local govt and social security	Local govt	Social security	General govt total receipts	as % of GDP	Savings	General govt financing: Indirect taxes	Direct taxes	Social sec. contrib.	Social security financing: Insured	State	Employers	Year
								percent distribution			percent distribution			
1950														1950
1951														1951
1952														1952
1953	71.8	15.3	12.1	34.0	103.0	25.3	-1.0	39.5	32.2	23.2				1953
1954	70.0	16.3	13.3	36.4	103.4	24.4	-1.4	40.3	30.0	24.5				1954
1955	75.8	15.6	15.0	37.6	112.8	25.0	0.6	41.0	29.	24.8				1955
1956	82.8	16.9	15.0	42.3	123.2	25.7	1.1	41.2	28.9	24.9				1956
1957	90.6	17.0	16.0	46.4	136.0	26.7	2.3	39.9	29.3	25.6				1957
1958	88.1	22.2	17.2	53.3	136.4	26.6	-0.1	40.5	27.8	27.2				1958
1959	94.4	25.5	18.3	55.6	142.8	26.9	-0.4	41.9	28.6	25.5				1959
1960	101.2	24.7	19.2	59.1	154.8	27.4	-0.3	41.9	27.7	26.0	21.3	23.8	54.9	1960
1961	112.1	23.3	19.7	62.2	170.7	28.4	0.8	42.9	27.2	26.1	23.6	22.0	54.4	1961
1962	124.1	25.1	21.0	67.5	187.5	29.2	1.0	42.0	28.9	25.8	23.0	22.4	54.5	1962
1963	131.0	26.4	22.6	75.7	202.9	29.4	0.4	41.6	28.4	27.4	22.6	21.8	55.7	1963
1964	147.6	30.4	23.4	91.2	231.8	30.0	2.2	40.6	27.5	28.9	21.3	20.9	57.7	1964
1965	161.6	34.3	26.0	105.0	258.3	30.7	0.9	39.5	28.4	30.0	22.6	21.0	56.4	1965
1966	184.2	38.5	30.5	116.1	292.3	32.3	1.8	40.8	28.4	29.3	22.5	19.8	57.7	1966
1967	204.3	44.1	34.8	126.6	321.6	33.1	1.8	40.5	28.9	28.4	21.8	21.6	56.6	1967
1968	220.3	48.9	38.2	138.2	347.8	33.5	0.9	39.6	30.2	28.4	22.4	22.6	55.1	1968
1969	250.6	51.2	42.3	150.1	391.7	34.0	1.4	38.9	31.4	28.1	22.1	20.5	57.4	1969
1970	282.5	58.8	50.2	177.3	451.2	35.2	2.2	36.6	31.4	29.2	22.5	19.2	58.3	1970
1971	310.0	65.8	54.8	201.7	500.7	35.7	1.7	35.4	32.7	30.0	21.7	20.1	58.2	1971
1972	339.7	80.5	63.3	234.9	557.5	35.6	0.7	33.3	34.9	31.0	21.2	21.6	57.1	1972
1973	397.2	91.4	69.1	273.8	648.8	36.4	0.6	31.8	36.6	31.2	21.5	21.7	56.9	1973
1974	487.5	112.9	82.7	331.3	788.8	37.7	1.4	30.5	38.0	30.5	20.9	22.2	56.9	1974
1975	575.1	163.1	98.7	424.4	935.2	40.4	-0.7	27.9	40.0	31.1	20.4	26.5	53.2	1975
1976	654.5	200.5	113.4	490.2	1 057.9	40.3	-1.4	29.1	39.3	31.0	20.0	28.9	51.0	1976
1977	740.3	236.4	130.4	550.7	1 184.9	41.7	-1.7	28.3	40.7	30.5	19.1	31.5	49.5	1977
1978	827.6	268.5	149.7	589.8	1 298.6	42.5	-2.3	28.1	42.6	29.1	19.0	32.2	48.8	1978
1979	906.5	289.2	165.4	629.3	1 412.1	43.3	-3.0	27.5	43.1	28.7	18.8	32.5	48.7	1979
1980	968.8	307.9	168.5	679.1	1 508.0	43.3	-4.9	27.4	41.7	29.0	18.8	32.5	48.6	1980
1981	1 012.7	381.2	184.2	774.3	1 590.1	44.0	-8.8	27.6	40.9	29.2	19.3	35.2	45.4	1981

Table 12

Social Insurance Coverage

(insured members)

Year	Social security: Employees (private and public)	Social security: Self-employed main occup.	Social security: Self-employed addit. occup.	Pension insurance: Employees (private sector)	Pension insurance: Self-employed	Unemployment insurance: Blue collar	Unemployment insurance: White collar	Unemployment insurance: Total	Unemployment insurance: As % of employees	Year
1950										1950
1951										1951
1952										1952
1953										1953
1954						1 643 263	409 195	2 052 458		1954
1955						1 634 471	417 190	2 051 661	79.41	1955
1956						1 641 287	430 680	2 071 967		1956
1957						1 657 737	449 561	2 107 298	79.82	1957
1958						1 655 677	469 979	2 125 656		1958
1959						1 608 561	474 367	2 082 928		1959
1960						1 619 734	490 786	2 110 520	79.13	1960
1961						1 621 898	501 745	2 123 643	79.37	1961
1962						1 631 064	531 098	2 162 162	79.31	1962
1963						1 639 905	550 491	2 190 396	79.20	1963
1964	2 100 371					1 675 774	578 121	2 253 895	79.57	1964
1965						1 671 133	607 989	2 279 122	79.49	1965
1966					677 956	1 664 355	632 384	2 296 739	79.25	1966
1967	2 599 940				682 956	1 644 930	650 459	2 295 389	78.65	1967
1968	2 624 909	590 031	69 685		689 605	1 638 543	670 033	2 308 576	78.88	1968
1969	2 632 867	579 022	70 496		690 104	1 655 314	719 988	2 375 302	79.72	1969
1970	2 664 434	465 898	78 761		682 231	1 674 306	805 695	2 480 001	81.42	1970
1971	2 844 140	559 796	80 042		664 419	1 671 273	853 331	2 524 604	81.35	1971
1972	2 885 677	548 175	80 428		651 394	1 659 770	880 421	2 540 191	81.05	1972
1973	2 939 625	538 511	81 137		642 188	1 665 460	929 510	2 594 970	81.34	1973
1974	2 995 204	519 371	79 273		631 762	1 671 095	971 110	2 642 205	81.11	1974
1975	3 020 996	520 212	70 818		618 241	1 656 786	1 008 152	2 664 938	81.01	1975
1976	3 095 099	525 148	63 601	2 390 468	612 468	1 660 255	1 024 492	2 684 747	80.70	1976
1977	3 136 708	510 429	63 186	2 372 494	613 824	1 635 523	1 063 910	2 699 433	80.38	1977
1978	3 177 604	500 117	62 324	2 361 599	614 895	1 626 362	1 085 522	2 711 884	80.24	1978
1979	3 232 165	501 159	58 023	2 382 095	615 215	1 629 314	1 118 399	2 747 713	80.09	1979
1980	3 273 686	504 095	55 489	2 366 903	612 480	1 614 394	1 139 624	2 754 018	79.86	1980
1981	3 311 272	496 534	56 279	2 275 588	612 843	1 591 859	1 153 572	2 745 431	79.52	1981

Table 13

Social Insurance Coverage

(insured members)

Year	Industrial accidents insurance				Occupational diseases insurance				Sickness and invalidity insurance				Year
	Blue collar	White collar	Total	As % of labour force	Blue collar	White collar	Total	As % of labour force	Employees + dependents	Self-employed + dependents	Total	As % of total pop.	
1950	1 230 143	351 646	1 581 789	43.13									1950
1951	1 292 236	362 578	1 654 814										1951
1952	1 261 668	387 878	1 649 546										1952
1953	1 264 555	395 428	1 659 983										1953
1954	1 271 359	396 589	1 667 948										1954
1955	1 315 584	402 626	1 718 210	46.49									1955
1956													1956
1957													1957
1958													1958
1959	1 189 866	458 246	1 648 112										1959
1960	1 204 249	470 705	1 674 954	45.58									1960
1961	1 227 011	485 582	1 712 593	46.65									1961
1962	1 274 628	503 728	1 778 356	47.86									1962
1963	1 342 719	564 883	1 907 602	51.19									1963
1964	1 302 918	568 189	1 871 107	49.67					5 720 655				1964
1965									6 889 246	1 663 010	8 552 256	90.03	1965
1966									7 116 173	1 798 855	8 915 028	93.29	1966
1967	1 163 291	571 265	1 734 556	45.49					7 253 051	1 845 650	9 098 702	94.72	1967
1968	1 273 227	650 250	1 923 477	50.27					7 336 901	1 832 366	9 169 268	95.20	1968
1969	1 313 310	671 524	1 984 834	51.34					7 456 042	1 825 818	9 281 860	96.08	1969
1970	1 264 346	702 900	1 967 246	50.21					7 733 823	1 833 741	9 567 564	99.14	1970
1971	1 385 770	731 013	2 116 783	53.50					7 854 291	1 806 385	9 660 676	99.64	1971
1972	1 162 763	730 627	1 893 390	47.71					7 991 109	1 799 111	9 790 220	100.65	1972
1973	1 290 943	772 319	2 063 262	52.55					8 100 441	1 754 785	9 855 226	101.01	1973
1974	1 165 502	788 831	1 954 333	49.04	1 292 421	799 397	2 091 818	52.49	8 027 375	1 749 631	9 777 006	99.89	1974
1975	1 076 460	798 467	1 874 927	46.84	1 424 259	812 571	2 236 830	55.88	8 340 740	1 751 309	10 092 050	102.84	1975
1976	1 136 504	834 343	1 970 847	48.89	1 396 684	815 788	2 212 472	54.88	8 422 906	1 715 988	10 138 894	103.21	1976
1977	1 368 745	864 472	2 233 217	55.06	1 353 572	846 126	2 199 698	54.23	8 474 464	1 690 471	10 164 936	103.33	1977
1978	1 331 155	889 659	2 220 814	54.44	1 316 633	861 274	2 177 907	53.39	8 533 812	1 661 125	10 194 938	103.59	1978
1979	1 324 723	913 980	2 283 703	55.20	1 324 545	913 980	2 238 525	54.10	8 545 178	1 643 471	10 188 650	103.84	1979
1980	1 296 871	918 278	2 215 149	53.35	1 296 696	918 278	2 214 974	53.35	8 477 501	1 596 602	10 074 103	102.22	1980
1981	1 216 630	915 639	2 132 269	51.24	1 216 451	915 639	2 132 090	51.24					1981

Table 14 Labour Force, Population, Pensioners

Year	Labour force			Population		Beneficiaries of pensions for						Year
	Total	employees	self-employed	Total	Aged 65+	Employees	Self-employed	Public servants	Guaranteed pensions	War pens.	Transitional unempl. p.	
1950	3 667 498	2 489 688	1 093 810	8 653 654	960 664							1950
1951				8 703 120	973 265							1951
1952				8 757 692	990 435							1952
1953				8 798 056	1 002 430							1953
1954				8 840 704	1 016 979							1954
1955	3 696 293	2 583 583	992 674	8 896 246	1 028 491							1955
1956				8 951 444	1 043 112	402 488						1956
1957	3 711 232	2 640 081	958 766	9 026 778	1 057 460	440 469						1957
1958				9 078 636	1 070 840	489 444						1958
1959				9 128 824	1 091 374	510 365						1959
1960	3 674 573	2 667 054	901 892	9 178 154	1 099 479	548 961						1960
1961	3 671 248	2 675 649	886 708	9 189 742	1 123 144	583 012						1961
1962	3 715 976	2 726 142	878 616	9 251 414	1 143 454	618 314	157 043					1962
1963	3 726 545	2 765 597	854 391	9 328 126	1 159 362	642 990	181 064					1963
1964	3 767 479	2 832 529	827 268	9 428 100	1 184 305	682 556	192 177					1964
1965	3 786 193	2 867 350	805 141	9 499 234	1 207 277	635 886	197 104	203 077	61 505			1965
1966	3 804 819	2 898 241	797 364	9 556 380	1 232 149	678 713	210 929	204 477	73 424	422 264		1966
1967	3 812 777	2 918 655	794 908	9 605 602	1 256 918	709 431	220 814	205 956	81 524	415 918		1967
1968	3 826 369	2 926 527	791 569	9 631 910	1 272 108	742 340	232 238	207 447	86 879	440 644		1968
1969	3 866 221	2 979 370	786 678	9 660 154	1 288 936	841 755	244 340	207 770	90 837	463 217		1969
1970	3 918 109	3 045 921	773 771	9 650 944	1 295 708	878 843	255 754	209 056	89 575	461 219		1970
1971	3 956 281	3 103 509	756 505	9 695 380	1 311 141	918 973	259 226	210 026	85 510	489 922		1971
1972	3 968 842	3 134 065	651 412	9 726 850	1 328 542	957 369	279 392	211 080	86 172	487 126		1972
1973	3 926 440	3 190 098	642 053	9 756 590	1 346 489	990 905	292 634	213 634	81 177	477 543		1973
1974	3 985 078	3 257 470	634 346	9 788 248	1 359 551	1 027 665	325 796	215 940	76 271	468 993		1974
1975	4 003 134	3 289 472	630 151	9 813 152	1 370 738	1 063 775	353 046	218 664	71 875	462 036		1975
1976	4 031 483	3 326 716	623 162	9 823 302	1 377 619	1 102 986	372 908	228 563	69 585	465 411		1976
1977	4 055 949	3 358 354	620 548	9 837 414	1 385 389	1 130 017	388 439	262 891	68 784	457 271	33 763	1977
1978	4 079 430	3 379 835	620 822	9 841 654	1 400 142	1 151 401	400 843	269 361	66 855	457 564	48 466	1978
1979	4 137 547	3 430 820	626 122	9 855 110	1 410 115	1 175 036	409 167	274 834	64 382	455 440	59 638	1979
1980	4 152 183	3 448 356	623 484	9 848 647		1 207 637	417 254	292 835	62 757	456 891	71 821	1980
1981	4 161 328	3 452 325	622 214	9 863 374	1 415 323	1 229 675	422 054	300 006	62 463	471 063	87 665	1981
1982	4 180 313			9 858 017		1 245 866	425 042		69 115	462 860	105 384	1982
1983				9 853 023		1 259 040	430 342		71 382	459 270		1983
1984						1 269 292	432 589		70 748			1984

Table 15 Beneficiaries of Unemployment Benefits and Employment Programmes

Year	Total unem-ployed	Beneficiaries full unempl.	Beneficiaries temporary unempl.	Non-beneficiaries voluntary registration	Non-beneficiaries compulsory registration	Transitional unempl. pensions	Retrain-ing progr.	Special tempo-rary empl. scheme	Employed by public authorities	Young people on probation full time	Young people on probation part time	Third empl. scheme	Year
1950		169 972	53 565										1950
1951		153 452	53 068										1951
1952		173 570	72 968										1952
1953		183 606	62 193										1953
1954		166 926	57 826										1954
1955		116 489	55 909										1955
1956		91 034	53 742										1956
1957		77 860	38 950										1957
1958		109 747	71 146										1958
1959		124 975	74 234										1959
1960	166 162	98 451	48 045	2 493	1 970		879		14 324				1960
1961	130 403	75 792	40 331	2 282	2 048		780		9 170				1961
1962	115 416	61 625	38 451	2 181	4 279		685		8 195				1962
1963	101 508	47 617	39 205	2 069	4 278		677		7 662				1963
1964	84 711	45 203	26 727	2 233	2 334		458		7 756				1964
1965	105 718	49 112	36 807	3 652	7 945		625		7 577				1965
1966	112 856	60 251	35 729	4 334	4 190		601		7 751				1966
1967	141 236	81 353	45 870	4 666	2 091		773		6 483				1967
1968	147 384	89 137	42 808	4 977	1 862		857		7 748				1968
1969	120 537	69 717	37 717	3 224	2 025		685		7 169				1969
1970	107 947	60 376	33 712	3 024	3 235		639		6 934				1970
1971	128 921	74 538	39 622	3 075	3 317		1 026		7 343				1971
1972	134 791	79 269	36 580	3 887	5 382		1 477		8 169				1972
1973	141 404	87 656	34 285	3 429	5 575		1 764		8 695				1973
1974	220 886	160 600	41 950	2 562	5 198		1 622		8 954				1974
1975	325 900	215 191	82 541	4 456	10 298		2 181		11 233				1975
1976	330 810	228 537	58 495	6 388	13 708		3 635		16 798	9 586			1976
1977	433 297	264 679	68 977	7 357	15 772	33 763	3 919		21 998	16 832			1977
1978	512 600	276 298	69 418	9 736	20 866	48 466	4 716	22 199	29 949	31 471			1978
1979		294 870	69 407	18 839	38 529	59 638		27 426	34 222	30 778			1979
1980		321 895	66 124	19 555	40 903	71 821		26 984	36 591	29 600			1980
1981		391 785	93 588	22 638	57 138	87 665		24 107	35 138	27 539			1981
1982		456 577	82 184	27 272	75 970	105 384		20 500	32 267	28 647	3 012	1 131	1982
1983		504 962				119 734		13 840	28 650	24 659	9 759	10 766	1983

Table 16

Other Welfare Clienteles

Year	Recipients of cash benefits for								Recipients of child allowances for								Year
	Indust. accid.	Occup. diseases	Sickness employees	Sickness self-empl.	Inval. employees	Invalidity self-empl.	Disable-ment	Right to subsistance min.	Employees children	Employees families	Self-employed childr.	Self-employed fam.	Publ. servants childr.	Publ. servants fam.	Guaranteed all. childr.	Guaranteed all. fam.	
1950							40 622		1 131 097	634 314							1950
1951							45 148		1 205 644	665 792	484 049	241 887					1951
1952							48 526		1 238 778	676 300	476 918	237 856					1952
1953							49 500		1 266 944	686 010	483 550	243 344					1953
1954							49 290		1 313 460	704 519	485 124	243 749					1954
1955		969					51 511		1 356 308	720 445	484 941	243 790					1955
1956		1 001					51 858		1 364 088	731 365	483 872	243 013					1956
1957		1 219					52 365		1 369 055	741 095	486 215	244 012					1957
1958		1 344					51 340		1 367 943	708 414	487 095	245 096					1958
1959		1 439					51 879		1 419 959	727 386	489 055	245 068					1959
1960		1 549					54 777		1 465 813	745 031	486 409	242 166					1960
1961		1 625					55 439		1 511 060	762 636	486 605	241 460					1961
1962		1 801					58 251		1 558 328	775 823	489 764	242 107					1962
1963		2 065					63 183		1 616 394	707 725	494 514	243 033					1963
1964		2 078	2 156 214		65 852		65 238		1 664 911	813 217	485 104	237 312					1964
1965	145 458	3 237	2 216 151		71 188		66 656		1 700 617	828 871	493 236	238 392					1965
1966	145 988	6 377	2 232 833		76 871		69 668		1 716 837	835 527	497 723	238 612					1966
1967	147 005	15 043	2 253 751		80 548		71 739		1 732 046	843 447	502 363	239 808					1967
1968	146 732	27 190	2 242 771		81 456		73 148		1 748 573	852 771	471 321	221 286					1968
1969	145 981	32 584	2 266 583		85 313		73 833		1 770 282	868 288	486 629	228 425	280 700	145 972			1969
1970	144 212	40 195	2 338 828		89 568		80 714		1 784 102	880 596	492 562	231 441	277 977	139 429			1970
1971	142 366	52 057	2 411 521	546 942	94 814		87 951		1 815 933	901 992	476 868	224 502	277 621	140 390			1971
1972	140 307	62 384	2 450 949	536 483	100 261		91 727		1 818 663	911 701	464 971	219 554	281 445	145 262			1972
1973	138 249	62 063	2 497 405	521 592	106 661	9 204	93 574		1 850 691	938 252	463 851	220 091	282 172	146 935			1973
1974	136 117	62 518	2 556 684	522 663	114 136	11 028	95 453		1 833 379	944 852	453 322	216 008	282 760	149 354			1974
1975	134 025	67 299	2 615 855	527 661	118 492	12 622	96 004		1 847 487	962 471	443 477	213 195	284 925	152 669	429	219	1975
1976	132 121	69 436	2 643 944	513 031	127 521	14 575	94 480		1 844 508	974 912	427 698	207 195	284 594	154 459	426	217	1976
1977	130 112	71 594	2 675 366	502 460	132 103	16 030	96 181		1 839 596	983 483	417 259	204 280	284 001	156 623	577	301	1977
1978	128 625	73 694	2 726 201	504 085	138 243	16 731	96 120		1 841 308	993 075	406 804	201 106	285 360	159 251	625	336	1978
1979	120 643	75 328	2 760 615	507 123	144 761	17 243	98 536	19 629	1 830 292	998 401	402 364	202 351	290 926	165 580	963	529	1979
1980	114 873	78 037	2 796 553	499 514	147 556	17 913	98 345	20 880	1 820 362	1 000 473	391 839	198 263	293 899	172 323	1 232	684	1980
1981	108 791	81 286					93 086	22 131	1 840 558	1 021 416	370 701	190 112	299 890	176 868	1 847	995	1981
1982								31 159	1 832 378	1 020 678							1982

Table 17

Indicators of Services

Year	Old age		Health				Education			Housing					Year
	home places	home helpers	hospital beds	physicians	pharmacists	dentists	students	as % of pop. 15–25	study allow. benef.	BGJG-Woningsfonds loans	dwellings let by NMH	dwellings built by NMH	beneficiaries of premiums for building	beneficiaries of premiums for purchase	
1950				8 385	4 062	486				1 690			23 582	1 917	1950
1951			31 862	8 685	4 234	553				975			14 068	1 320	1951
1952				8 935	4 334	585				1 372			15 113	1 410	1952
1953			35 815	9 271	4 552	656				1 872			18 932	1 943	1953
1954				9 598	4 691	701	35 377	2.95		2 125			18 410	2 595	1954
1955			36 053	9 937	4 804	767	36 984	3.14		1 152			12 104	5 490	1955
1956			36 851	10 358	4 927	825	38 956	3.41	10 057	1 610			10 788	2 613	1956
1957				10 793	5 116	905	40 329	3.61	12 593	831			11 796	3 105	1957
1958			39 343	11 013	5 218	964	42 956	3.86	15 685	1 160			11 931	2 450	1958
1959				11 380	5 266	1 041	45 831	4.12	22 253	1 503			26 356	2 303	1959
1960	41 589		40 925	11 703	5 383	1 092	47 755	4.26	32 475	1 377		4 655	21 797	2 667	1960
1961	43 624			12 326	5 622	1 207	50 620	4.38	41 946	1 600		5 103	20 285	2 549	1961
1962	45 867		40 164	12 888	5 714	1 304	55 094	4.64	47 501	1 555		5 981	17 691	3 162	1962
1963	46 683			13 236	5 844	1 356	62 068	5.03	55 052	1 548		6 690	16 126	2 571	1963
1964	48 385			13 473	5 968	1 474	67 412	5.38	60 086	1 699		6 435	18 998	3 863	1964
1965	50 883		42 510	13 993	6 078	1 596	73 987	5.73	66 740	1 903		8 584	15 768	4 157	1965
1966				14 176	6 171	1 671	82 411	6.15	76 325	1 878		7 106	13 044	3 387	1966
1967			43 445	14 517	6 249	1 840	89 823	6.50	82 716	1 867		5 801	13 995	4 142	1967
1968				14 922	6 533	2 194	98 218	6.97		1 959		10 085	13 819	4 188	1968
1969			44 437	14 991	6 735	1 758	110 283	7.69		2 013	126 804	8 718	18 577	5 092	1969
1970	55 087	1 476					117 262	8.08		1 912	132 024	7 710	15 200	3 487	1970
1971		2 058	45 828	14 887			124 857	8.53		2 205	138 528	9 712	14 527	3 236	1971
1972		2 483		15 888		2 087	131 783	8.92		2 226	146 645	12 926	18 146	4 202	1972
1973	58 575	2 839	48 167	16 478			141 002	9.44		2 160	155 204	12 167	27 638	5 456	1973
1974		2 839		17 272	6 614	2 646	150 286	9.88		1 642	161 370	7 109	21 372	5 439	1974
1975		3 361	50 417	18 506	7 688	2 454	159 385	10.35		2 470	167 149	13 031	15 960	4 909	1975
1976	63 980	3 532	50 706	19 872	7 519	2 667	159 434	10.23		2 708	173 993	11 787	17 726	4 709	1976
1977	64 895	3 763	51 267	20 725	8 850	2 967	165 891	10.56		3 954	181 922	11 197	16 775	5 784	1977
1978	65 951	4 297	52 338	22 143	9 187	3 183	174 402	11.05		3 076	189 228	12 169	18 744	5 652	1978
1979	69 049	4 394	52 827	23 415	9 389	3 675	180 154	11.34		3 018	196 642	12 750	17 730	5 520	1979
1980		4 454	53 477	24 536	9 682	4 100	188 232			3 317		10 246	14 041	5 099	1980
1981	71 314	4 337	53 889	25 629	9 942	4 413	196 153	12 37		3 031		9 961	14 928	3 981	1981
1982	73 086	4 270	54 749	26 593	10 177	4 879	201 882			4 429		4 479	10 000		1982

Table 18

Distribution of Parliamentary Seats by Party

	1946	1949	1950	1954	1958	1961	1965	1968	1971	1974	1977	1978	1981
Social Democrats	69	66	77	86	84	84	64	59	61	59	62	58	61
Communists	23	12	7	4	2	5	6	5	5	4	2	4	2
Christian Democrats	92	105	108	95	104	96	77	69	67	72	80	82	62
Liberals	17	29	20	25	21	20	48	47	34	30	33	37	52
Nationalists													
– Flemish				1	1	5	12	20	21	22	20	15	21
– Francophones							5	12	24	25	15	15	8
Others	1			1		2						1	7(a)
Total	202	212	212	212	212	212	212	212	212	212	212	212	212

(a) of which 4 ecologists.

Notes to and sources for appendix tables

Table 1

Gross domestic product:
'GDP at market prices, statistically corrected total'.
Sources: (1) for 1953-70: edition 1970, pp. 666-667, table 2 (current prices), pp. 672-673, table 3 (constant prices, recalculated on basis 1970); (2) for 1970-82: p. 573, table I-4 (current prices), and p. 579, table I-6 (constant prices, recalculated on basis 1970).

Deflators:
GDP: calculated from current and constant figures in sources above.
Public consumption: source (1) various editions, part 'National accounts', tables 'Spending of the national product' at current and at constant prices; calculated from current and constant figures, re-calculated on basis 1970.
Private consumption: procedure and sources as under public consumption.
Cost of living: calculated on the basis of the index figures of consumption prices (basis 1970).
Source: (1) for 1953-66: edition 1970, p. 555; for 1960-82: edition 1985, p. 534.

Total public expenditure:
Sum of the total public expenditure of central government (as given in the 'functional classification of government expenditure'), and the social security receipts from payroll contribution. The total includes the transfers from central to provincial and local government, but excludes the other, relatively small, provincial and local government expenditure, because consolidated figures (i.e. figures excluding intergovernmental transfers) are not available.
Sources: (3) 1982, no 1-2, pp. 128-129; 1983, no 11, p. 20; 'functional classification of government expenditure'; since 1975 budget figures instead of expenditure; debt payments included; (1) for 1953-70: edition 1970, pp. 704-705, table 8 = 'social security contributions employers, employees and self-employed'; (2) for 1970-82: p. 616, table 2 = idem.

Table 2

Public expenditure by major purpose:
Since 1975 budget figures instead of expenditure.
Total: as in table 1.
Public administration: includes general administration, foreign affairs, development aid, and not allocated expenditure.
Defence: includes national defence, and law and order. Economic services: includes traffic, trade and industry and agriculture.
Social/environmental services: includes education, culture and recreation, health care and social services, social insurance, housing policy.
Debt: public debt payments, source (3), budget entry 01.
Sources: (1) for the period 1953-70: edition 1970, part 'national accounts', table 8, pp. 704-705; (2) for the period 1970-82: p. 616, table 2; (3) 1982, no 1-2, pp. 128-129; 1983, no 11, p. 20.

Public expenditure by economic category:
Total: general government expenditure, but excluding the expenditure which cannot be allocated to the categories 'subsidies/transfers', 'final consumption', 'interest on debt' and 'capital formation'.
Sources: (4) p. 73 and (5) p. 142.

Public expenditure by level of government:
Total: as for public expenditure by economic category, but excluding capital formation which cannot be allocated to levels of government.
Central government expenditure: excluding transfers to other sub-sectors of general government.
Sources: (4) pp. 73-75 and (5) pp. 142-145.

Table 3

Income maintenance:
See total of table 5.

Education:
Includes education, culture and recreation, according to the 'functional classification of government expenditure', budget entry 7.
Source: (3) 1982, no 1-2, pp. 128-129; 1983, no 11, p. 20.

Health:
Includes health expenditure as given in the functional classification of government expenditure, and the estimated total expenditure for health care in the sickness and invalidity insurance scheme. The latter is calculated on the basis of the share of health care refunds for employees and self-employed in the total sickness and invalidity insurance benefits (see Table 7, cols 6 and 8).
Sources: (3) 1982, no 1-2, pp. 146-147; 1983, no 11, p. 29, entrees 87, 802 and 812; (6) appendix A, 2 (tables 1A and 1B) and B, 2 (table 1), various years. *Algemene rekening van ontvangsten en uitgaven* for employees and self-employed.

Housing:
Source: (3) 1982, no 1-2, pp. 128-129; 1983, no 11 p. 20, entry 9.

Other:
Includes benefits in kind for industrial accident victims (see Table 7, col. 2; for the years 1950, 1955 and 1960 estimated at 13% of total expenditure; see notes to Table 7) and administration and other costs of the employment scheme (see Table 8, cols 6 and 7).

Total:
Sum of cols 1-5.

Social expenditure at constant prices:
Income maintenance and housing deflated by the cost-of-living index, education, health and 'other' by the public consumption deflator.

Table 4

For definitions and sources see notes to Table 3, for GDP and total public expenditure Table 1.

Table 5

Old age and survivor pensions:
Sum of pensions for private employees, self-employed, public servants and beneficiaries of the means-tested guaranteed pensions (total of Table 6).

Industrial accidents/occupational diseases:
The figures for industrial accidents in source (6) include some medical services which have been excluded here. The cash benefits for industrial accidents 1950-60 have been estimated on the basis of their share in total industrial accidents expenditure for the period 1961-70 (87%).
Source: (6) appendix A, 1, various years: *Algemene rekening van ontvangsten en uitgaven* for employees (total with scheme transfers included).

Sickness and invalidity:
Only cash benefits, not the refunds for health care services included under 'health ' in Table 3 (see notes to Table 3).
Source: (6) appendix A, 2 (tables 1A and 1B) and B, 2 (table 1), various years (total with scheme transfers included).

Unemployment:
Sum of unemployment benefits, unemployment pensions (*brugpensioen*), special unemployment programmes, and retraining allowances.
Source: (6) appendix A, 2 (table 2); various years.

Family allowances:
Sum of benefits for employees, self-employed and guaranteed family allowances.
Sources: (6) appendix A, 1 and B, 1, various years. Total with scheme transfers included; since 1976 'collective services' and 'family allowances funds - *compensatiekassen*' included, also family holiday allowances included; (7) for the guaranteed family allowances: part 4, 'voluntary insurance and social assistance' chapter 2 C, various years since 1975.

Social welfare:
Sum of 'general social assistance' and 'general social aid' in Table 10; for procedures and sources, see notes to Table 10.

All expenditure items deflated by the cost of living-index (see Table 1).

Table 6

Total:
Sum of cols 2, 3 and 5 and the part of public sector pensions given in source (7) and the central government transfer to the public employees' pensions scheme, not given in the social security statistics in source (7), but in the functional classification of public expenditure in source (3).
Sources: (3) 1982, no 1-2, pp. 146-147; 1983, no 11, p. 29, entry 821. Since this figure gives the total transfer of central government to all pension schemes, we have distracted from this total the subsidies to the employees and self-employed schemes already included in cols 2-3; (7) part 3 'public services', chapter 2, C, various years, sum of totals A + B + C = old age and survivors' pensions and local government pensions.

Private employees:
Source: (7) part 1 'employees', chapter 2, C; various years.

Self-employed:
Source: (7) part 2 'self-employed', chapter 2, C, various years.

Guaranteed pensions:
Source: (7) part 4 'voluntary insurances and social assistance', chapter 2, C; various years since 1975.

Public sector:
Total minus cols 2, 3 and 5.

All expenditure items deflated by the cost of living index (see Table 1)

Table 7

Industrial accidents:
Prior to 1961 data are not available separately for cash benefits and for benefits in kind or medical services for the victims of industrial accidents. For the expenditure on income maintenance (see Table 5) it has been assumed that from 1950-1960 87% of total expenditure was on cash benefits (the average percentage from 1961-1970).
Source: (6) appendix A, IV, and A, I (table 5), various years.

Occupational diseases:
Source: (6) appendix A, 1, various years.

Sickness/invalidity:
For earlier years, administrative costs have been allocated to 'cash benefits' and 'refunds' in correspondance with their respective shares. For the earlier years for which only aggregate figures are available for the sickness insurance of miners and seeman, these have been disaggregated in correspondence with the scheme for employees.
Source: (6) appendix A, 2 (tables 1A and 1B), B, 2 (table 1), various years.

Cash benefits deflated by the cost of living index, benefits in kind and refunds by the public consumption deflator (see Table 1); total expenditure on industrial accidents for 1954-1960 has been deflated assuming a 87% share of cash benefits.

Table 8

Total:
Including scheme transfers.

Unemployment benefits:
Includes *uitkeringen voor werkloosheid en bestaanszekerheid* and *werkloosheidsuitkeringen, oninvorderbaar en ten onrechte uitbetaald* (since 1970)

Unemployment pensions:
Brugpensioenen, since 1970.

Employment programmes:
Includes *tewerkstelling van werklozen door openbare besturen assignatiekosten van tewerkgestelde werklozen*, tenlasteneming van *de lasten van de werkgevers*, BTK, DAC, and ten onrechte *uitbetaalde sociale prestaties in deze rubrieken*

Other:
Difference between 'total' and the sum of cols 2-5, mainly including financial costs.

Source: (6), various years, appendix A,1 for 'total', Appendix A, 2, table 2 for cols 2-5.

Expenditure on unemployment benefits and pensions, employment programmes and retraining deflated by the cost-of-living index, administrative costs and other expenditure by the public consumption deflator.

Table 9

Total:
Sum of cols 2-4.

Family allowances for employees:
Includes scheme transfers; since 1976 including 'collective services' and 'family allowances - *compensatiekassen*'.
Source: (6) appendix A, 1, various years.

Family allowances for self-employed:
Source: (6) appendix A, 1, various years.

Guaranteed family allowances:
Source: (7) part 4 'voluntary insurance and social assistance', chapter 2, C, various years.

All expenditure items deflated by the cost-of-living index.

Table 10

General social assistance, central government:
Source: (3) 1982, no 1-2, pp. 146-147, 1983, no 11, p. 29, budget entry 83.

General social assistance, local government:
Figures include transfers from central government for the financing of the guaranteed minimum income, amounting to half of this expenditure item (see col. 5); these transfers have been subtracted from central government general social assistance in col. 1.
Source: (1) part 'Public finance', finances of the *COO* and *OCMW*, uitgaven voor onderstand, various years.

General social assistance, provincial government:
Includes mainly special programmes for orphans, for disabled and for elderly persons.
Source: (1) part 'Public finance', finances of the provinces, *uitgaven voor sociale bijstand*, various years, only available since 1975.

Total:
Sum of cols 1-3.

Guaranteed minimum income:
Source: Parliamentary question no 34 on 16-1-1985 by Senator St. Declerq.

General social aid, central government:
Source: (3) 1982, no 1-2, pp. 146-147, 1983, no. 11, p. 29, budget entry 84.

War pensions:
Source: (8), p. 83.

General social aid, local government:
Source: (9), p. 78 *sociale hulp en gezinsvoorzieningen*

All expenditure items have been deflated by the cost-of-living index.

Table 11

Current receipts and general govt financing:
General govt total receipts (col. 5) includes total receipts, corrected for payments on public debt (items 2.8) which are subtracted in the national accounts. It is identical with the current receipts of central govt (col. 1), local govt (col.3) and social security (col.4) minus the central govt transfers to local govt and social security. Items in sources (1) and (2): savings (2.6), indirect taxes (2.9), direct taxes (2.10 and 2.12), social security contributions (2.11).
Sources: (1) for 1953-70, edition 1970, pp. 704-708; (2) for 1970-81, pp. 616-618.

Social security financing:
Includes sickness and invalidity insurance, unemployment, pensions, family allowances, industrial accidents, occupational diseases, holiday allowances, additional occupational benefits funds and study leaves; only schemes for private employees and self-employed.
Source: (7), various years; part 1 'employees', chapter 1, D; part 2 'self-employed', chapter 1, C.

Table 12

Social security:
Insured members. Additional occupation refers to regular employees or civil servants with an additional occupation as self-employed, who are insured both in the employees' scheme and the self-employed scheme (as 'additional occupation' beneficiary).
Source: (7), various years; chapter 1, A, part 1, 'employees', part 3, 'public services', part 2, 'self-employed'.

Pension insurance:
Insured members.
Source: (7), various years, part 1, 'employees', chapter 1, A; part 2, 'self-employed', chapter 1, A.

Unemployment insurance coverage:
Insured members, absolute number and as % of total employees (Table 14, col. 2).
Source: (11), various years; appendix, part statistical tables, table II.

Table 13

Industrial accident and occupational diseases insurance:
Insured members; absolute number and as % of the labour force (Table 14, col. 1).
Source: (7), various years; part 1, 'employees', chapter 1, A.

Sickness and invalidity insurance:
Insured members; employees and dependents: private and public sector; self-employed: both in main and additional occupation; absolute number and as % of total population (Table 14, col. 4).
Sources: (13), pp. 29-30 (employees 1964-79); pp. 85-86 (self-employed 1965-79); (10), ed. 1980, pp. 75-76, 207.

Table 14

Labour force:
Total: employees, self-employed, cross-border workers and conscripts.
Employees: private and public sector employees, employees of international organisations working abroad, unemployed, apprentices and professional military forces.

Self-employed: self-employed and family workers.
Source: (7), various years; part 'introduction'.

Population:
Source: (1); for total population: ed. 1970, p. 29 (1945-70) and ed. 1983, p. 13 (1970-83); for population aged 65 years and over: various years.

Beneficiaries of pensions:
Employees, self-employed, guaranteed pensions:
Source: (12), ed. 1975, p. 9 (1966-71); ed. 1980, pp. 9-11 (1972-80); ed. 1984, pp. 22-24.

Public servants:
Source: (7), various years, part 3, 'public services', chapter 2, B.

War pensions:
Source: (8), p. 80.

Transitional unemployment pensions:
Includes both conventional and legal unemployment pensions (*brugpensioenen*).
Source: (11), various years, appendix, statistical tables.

Table 15

Figures for temporary unemployment are daily averages, all other figures are monthly averages. Voluntary registered non-beneficiaries include only non-working persons. Total unemployed = sum of all following columns in Table 15.
Source: (11), various years; part 1, B and appendix, various tables.

Table 16

Recipients of cash benefits for:

Industrial accidents and occupational diseases:
Figures for industrial accident beneficiaries include all funds involved (*Maatschappijen en Gemengde Kassen*, Vrijgestelden, ASLK *FWO-Waarborgfonds*, Dienst voor Zeevisserij, Koopvaardij).
Source: (7), various years; part 1, 'employees', chapter 2, B.

Sickness and invalidity cash beneficiaries:
Sources: (13), pp. 31-34 (1964-79), p. 87 (1971-79); (10), ed. 1980, p. 172 (1976-80), pp. 180-82, 193, 195 (1975-80).

Disablement:
Source: (7) part 4 'voluntary insurance and social assistance', chapter 2, B.

Right to subsistence minimum:
Source: Parliamentary question no. 34 of December 10, 1985 by Senator St. Declerq.

Child allowances:

Employees:
Source: (15) various years, appendix.

Self-employed:
Sum of ordinary allowances, and allowances for orphans and for children of handicapped parents.
Source: (7) part 2 'self-employed', chapter 2, B; various years.

Public servants:
Sum of ministries, semi-governmental agencies, provincial and local governments.
Source: (7) part 3 'public services', chapter 2, B; various years.

Guaranteed allowances:
Source: (7) part 4, 'voluntary insurance and social assistance', chapter 2, B; various years.

Table 17

Places in old age homes:
Including the number of beds (both authorized and non-authorized) in private and public nursing homes for the elderly.
Source: (14) ed. 1980, p. 237; ed. 1983, p. 290; various eds for the earliest years.

Home helpers:
Number of geriatric assistants.
Source: (14) ed. 1980, p. 254; ed. 1983, p. 304.

Hospital beds:
Total number of beds for acute care in general purpose hospitals (private and public sector).
Source: (14), various eds, part V 'medical infrastructure'.

Physicians, pharmacists, dentists:
Physicians include general practitioners, specialists and candidate specialist.
Source: (14), various eds, part V 'medical personnel'.

Students:
University and higher non-university education.
Source: (1), various ed., part 'education and culture'.

Study allowances' beneficiaries:
Number of beneficiaries in secondary and higher education.
Source: Dienst van Studietoelagen, Ministerie van de Vlaamse Gemeenschap; not published.

Housing:

BGJG - Woningfonds loans:
Source: (16)

NMH-dwellings:
Source: (17), various editions.

Beneficiaries of premiums:
Source: (1) part 'dwellings and buildings'; various editions.

Table 18

Source: (18).

Enumerated sources to appendix tables

(1) Nationaal Instituut voor de Statistiek. *Statistisch Jaarboek voor België*. Brussel, various years.

(2) Nationaal Instituut voor de Statistiek. De nationale rekeningen van België 1971-1982, *Statistisch Tijdschrift* no. 7-8. Brussel, 1983.

(3) Ministerie van Financiën. *Documentatieblad*, Brussel.

(4) OECD, *National Accounts, 1963-1980*, volume II, Detailed tables. Paris, 1986.

(5) OECD, *National Accounts 1972-1984*, volume II, Detailed tables. Paris, 1986.

(6) Ministerie van Sociale Voorzorg. *Algemeen Verslag over de Sociale Zekerheid*. Brussel, various years.

(7) Ministerie van Sociale Voorzorg. *Statistisch Jaarboek van de Sociale Zekerheid*. Brussel, various years.

(8) Ministerie van Financiën. *Nationale Kas voor Oorlogspensioenen*. Verslag 1985. Brussel, 1986.

(9) R. Goossens, L. Reulens, M. van Bossuyt. *De Sociale Uitgaven in België*. In: Nationaal Onderzoeksprogramma in *de sociale wetenschappen*, part 8C annex. Brussel, 1981.

(10) Rijksinstituut voor ziekte- en Invaliditeitsverzekering. *Algemeen Verslag, 3e deel*: statistisch verslag. Brussel, various years.

(11) Rijksdienst voor Arbeidsvoorziening. *Jaarverslag*. Brussel, various years.

(12) Rijkskas voor Rust- en Overlevingspensioenen. *Jaarlijkse Statistiek van de pensioengerechtigden*. Brussel, various years.

(13) RIZIV. *Voornaamste Financiële en Statistische Resultaten van de verplichte verzekering tegen ziekte en invaliditeit* (1964-1979). Brussel, 1981.

(14) Ministerie van Volksgezondheid en van het gezin. *Statistisch Jaarboek van Volksgezondheid*. Brussel, various years.

(15) Rijksdienst van Kinderbijslag voor Werknemers. *Verslag over het Dienstjaar*. Brussel, various years.

(16) De Ridder, V.A., *Economische en sociologische aspecten van de activiteiten van het Woningfonds 1929-1978*, Woningfonds van de BGJG, Brussel, 1979.

(17) Nationaal Instituut voor de Statistiek. *Statistieken over bouwnijverheid en hisvesting*. Brussel, various years.

(18) Politiek Zakboekje 1985. Kluwer. Antwerpen, 1985, p. 265.

Growth to Limits

The Western European Welfare States
Since World War II

A Series under the Editorship of

Peter Flora

Volume 1:
Sweden, Norway, Finland, Denmark

Volume 2:
Germany, United Kingdom, Ireland, Italy

Volume 3:
Austria, Switzerland, Netherlands, Belgium

Volume 4:
Appendix, (Synopses, Bibliographies, Tables)

Volume 5:
Unity and Diversity — A Comparison